HISTORY OF ZIONISM
A HANDBOOK AND DICTIONARY

HERSHEL EDELHEIT
ABRAHAM J. EDELHEIT

HISTORY OF ZIONISM
A HANDBOOK AND DICTIONARY

HERSHEL EDELHEIT
ABFAHAM J. EDELHEIT

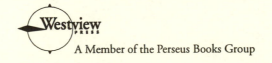
A Member of the Perseus Books Group

This book is dedicated
with love
to the three most important women
in my life:

My Mother, Ann D. Edelheit
My Mother-in-Law, Ethel Stein
and
My Wife, Carol Ann Stein Edelheit

Copyright © 2000 by Westview Press, A Division of HarperCollins Publishers, Inc.
Published in 2000 in the United States of America by Westview Press, 5500 Central Avenue, Boulder, Colorado 80301–2877, and in the United Kingdom by Westview Press, 12 Hid's Copse Road, Cumnor Hill, Oxford OX2 9JJ

Library of Congress Cataloging-in-Publication Data
Edelheit, Abraham J.
   History of Zionism : a handbook and dictionary / Abraham J. Edelheit, Hershel Edelheit.
      p.   cm.
   Includes bibliographical references and index.
   ISBN 0-8133-2981-7 (alk. paper)
   1. Zionism—History.   2. Zionism—Historiography.   3. Zionism Dictionaries.   I. Edelheit, Hershel.   II. Title.

DS149.E25   1999
320.54'095694—dc21   99-25978
                                                                                CIP

10   9   8   7   6   5   4   3   2   1

CONTENTS

Part 2
Dictionary of Zionist Terms

Table of Major Entries

ILLUSTRATIONS

Tables

Graphs

Maps

Illustrations

ABBREVIATIONS

Am	=	Aramaic
Ar	=	Arabic
BCE	=	Before Common Era
BT	=	Babylonian Talmud
CE	=	Common Era
G	=	German
Gr	=	Greek
GN	=	Geographic Name
H	=	Hebrew
Ha-Zach	=	Histadrut ha-Zionit ha-Hadasha
Ha-Zohar	=	Hitahdut ha-Zionim ha-Revisionistiim
HT	=	Historical Term
I	=	Italian
JA	=	Jewish Agency
JAE	=	Jewish Agency Executive
L	=	Latin
Mapai	=	Mifleget Poalei Eretz Israel
P	=	Polish
PN	=	Personal Name
R	=	Russian
T	=	Turkish
UN	=	United Nations
USSR	=	Union of Soviet Socialist Republics
WZO	=	World Zionist Organization
Y	=	Yiddish

PREFACE

Zionism — the Jewish movement for national rebirth — was arguably one of the most successful and, at the same time, one of the least understood examples of modern nationalism. Born in the last third of the nineteenth century, its meaning, goals, and very essence continue to be debated by scholars, politicians, and laypersons from all walks of life. Yet, at its core, Zionism was based on a paradox: an effort to revolutionize Jewry by, in essence, making Jews "like all the nations," Zionism proposed a modern solution to the "Jewish Problem" by restoring Jews to their ancestral homeland. Although tapping into millennia-old traditions of restoration and rebirth, most Zionist thinkers rejected — or at least redefined — all elements of the Jewish tradition that did not specifically relate to restoration, notably religious ritual. Zionism was thus, again, paradoxically, an effort to return the Jew to history thorugh national rebirth while rebelling against Jewish history; an attempt to restore Jewish tradition while recasting that tradition; an effort to make Jews like all the nations while highlighting the unique elements in Jewish culture, tradition, and history.

The paradoxes inherent in Zionism derived in part from the unique nature of Jewish nationalism in the premodern era and also from the specific political, social, and economic conditions under which European Jewry (which then represented the bulk of the world Jewish population) lived a century ago. Specifically, the inner tension over the status of Jewish tradition within the national movement (particularly over religion but also regarding language and culture) resulted from the fact that many of the earliest ideologues who created the Zionist movement, derived their ideology from an assimilationist and not a traditionalist orientation toward Judaism. Put another way, many of its fathers saw Zionism as a means to reformulate the Judaism from which they had tried (unsuccessfully) to escape. Their position was a reflection of the sea changes wrought in Western European Jewry by emancipation, the disappointment felt by Eastern European Jewry over the failure of emancipation to take root, the subsequent decline in religious life concomitant with increasing Jewish secularization, and fears for the future (in both Western and Eastern Europe) created by the rise of modern antisemitism.

It would be wrong, therefore, to emphasize only external factors in the rise of Zionism. Although antisemitism played an important role in the origin of some nationalist schemes for the restoration of Jewish sovereignty, the external catalyst could (and in fact did) drive Jews away from Zionism and toward other ideologies that offered — or seemed to offer — a solution for the "Jewish Problem." In particular, revolutionary socialism, whether in Jewish garb (as Bundism) or not (communism) attracted many Jews with the siren song of freedom, equality, and justice. Then too modern Jewish nationalism did not necessarily have to identify with the land of Israel: Autonomism and territorialism also sought restoration of Jewish national identity (the latter calling for Jewish sovereignty in a diaspora territory) while jettisoning entirely (or almost entirely) the centrality of *Eretz Israel*. Zionism must thus be viewed as deriving in part from an external catalyst (antisemitism) but representing developments of an inner dynamic within the Jewish people at the end of the nineteenth century.

The rise of Zionism coincided with the increasing importance of nationalism in Europe and the Middle East. Simultaneous with the Jewish national rebirth came a similar nationalist rebirth in the Arab world. Tragically, the two Semitic nationalisms came into early conflict, a conflict that became more virulent as decades passed. After five wars and numerous violent clashes — both before and after the establishment of the State of Israel — the first, tentative steps at true reconciliation appear to have been taken. Thus, despite the signing of peace treaties with Egypt (1979) and the Hashemite Kingdom of Jordan (1994) and the continuing Oslo process between Israel and the nascent Palestinian entity, the ease with which Arab leaders have returned to in some cases vile anti-Israel propaganda and further acts of terrorism and violence seem to prove that for all the changes that have occurred since 1993, much has yet to be done to bring true peace to the Middle East.

Jewish and Arab nationalism must both be viewed in a global context. Diplomacy was central to Zionist thought and practice. This was true in Herzl's era — a period of whirlwind (but ultimately abortive) diplomacy — and remained true through two world wars. It is virtually impossible to study Zionism without studying Zionist diplomacy, which at one time or another encompassed virtually every major and minor power on every continent. Of course, diplomacy has its own language, its own codes, and its own etiquette. For example, sensitivity must be used in citing names, places, or terms, lest they fall into the wrong hands and result in embarrassment on all sides. Zionism had an extensive vocabulary of code terms: David Ben-Gurion, the fiery Jewish Agency Executive (JAE) chairman who became Israel's first prime minister, used (or was referred to by) no less than a dozen code names between assuming the JAE chairmanship in 1935 and becoming prime minister in 1948.

The same holds true for the Jewish underground movements in *Eretz Israel*. As revolutionaries they had to mask their activities and identities; anything less would result in failure and death. The plethora of different underground movements existing within the *Yishuv* prior to 1948 was, more than anything else, a reflection of the intense fragmentation within the Zionist movement — Zionism's institutional life also had a language all its own. Considerable effort is often needed to disentangle the history of organizations and parties that arose, split, united, split again, and, in some cases, collapsed entirely.

The purpose of this handbook and dictionary is threefold: To provide the reader with a general overview of Zionist history and historiography, to tabulate all data on Zionism that can possibly be reduced to tabular or graphic form, and to gather in one source as many terms dealing directly or indirectly with Zionism as possible. To that end, we have organized this book into two sections. Part 1 offers an overview of Zionist history, from its intellectual origins in Jewish religious tradition to the establishment of the State of Israel. While concentrating on the political and diplomatic fortunes of the Zionist movement, the text also seeks to elucidate some of the key ideologues and parties active in promoting the re-creation of a Jewish national home. Part 1 is based primarily on a careful reading of published primary and secondary sources and seeks a synthesis of the work of previous generations of historians. Still, it must be emphasized that the writing of anything approaching a definitive history of the Zionism is still many years in the future.

Part 2 defines terms related to Zionism and Jewish nationalism as viewed from the perspective of participants, opponents, and eyewitnesses. This section includes longer entries that not only define but also quantify a subject and relate pertinent information on that subject in tabular, graphic, or illustrative form. Here too we must note the incomplete nature of much of the data. For instance, the extensive lists of organizations included in the entries *"Organizations, Zionist"* and *"Yishuv"* are but a sampling of the numerous organizations and institutions that were established to promote the Zionist idea. It can be safely said that for every organization on which specific data was found, at least two other organizations exist for which no specific data could be found. In the latter case, we did not include an organization's name unless we could add at least some general data about its history.

Although the present work is complete in and of itself, it is organically linked to our previous work, *History of the Holocaust: A Handbook and Dictionary*. This is especially true in terms of certain overlapping entries, of which the following are taken largely, if not entirely from the previous work: *Aliya Bet; Boycott, Anti-Nazi; Briha; Cyprus, Detention Camps; Displaced Persons, Jewish; Ha'apala; Ha'avara; Kibbutz Galuyot; Mechutonim; Palestine Express; Paratroopers, Palestinian; Parrout présent et faire face; Protokolle der Weissen von Zion; Shaliach/shelichim; She'erit ha-Pleta; She'erit ha-Tikva; Tiyul; Tragt ihn mit Stolz, den Gelben Fleck!*; and *Yetziat Eropa*. A number of other entries share titles and some data with parallel entries in the previous book but with the substantial addition of further information. However, since these will be immediately obvious to even the most casual reader, they have not been listed here. Finally, entries marked with the abbreviation (CASE) were written, or substantially contributed to, by Mrs. Carol Ann Stein Edelheit.

This book was originally conceived in the autumn of 1994 with the intention of completing the manuscript in time for Israel's fiftieth anniversary. The untimely illness and passing five years ago today of my coauthor, mentor, and best friend — Hershel Edelheit (1926-1995) forced a delay in publication, but did not substantially change the nature of the work. My father's death has also forced a change in institutional frameworks: whereas the previous handbook was completed under the auspices of the Edelheit Research Institute for Comtemporary History (ERICH), the present one has been completed under the imprint of the Moreshet Zvi Institute for Jewish Communal Studies (Hershel Edelheit Memorial Research Institute), an entity designed to carry on research into the history and ideology of Jewish communal life, with particular focus on the modern era of Jewish history. More handbooks are presently anticipated in this series (covering antisemitism, totalitarianism, and the State of Israel), as are a number of other monographic and synthetic works. Authors interested in pursuing publication of a handbook on a topic not included in the above are encouraged to contact me through the publisher.

Last, but by no means least, it is my great pleasure to acknowledge the assistance received from the following individuals and institutions for their help in completing this book. Although the following individuals and institutions greatly assisted me, I alone bear full responsibility for any errors in the text: Howard L. Adelson; Cindy Adelstein; Seth Bowman; Miriam Cohen; Lee Moses; Abraham J. Peck; William D. Rubinstein; Tammy Schwartz; Chaim Weiner; Yoram Mayorek and the staff of the Central Zionist Archives, Jerusalem; Norman Gechlik and the staff of the New York Public Library Jewish Division; Zachary Baker, and the staff of the YIVO Institute, New York; Tuvia Friling and the staff of the Ben-Gurion Research Center, Kiryat Sde Boker; Adaire Klein and the staff of the Simon Wiesenthal Center; Yerucham Meshel and the staff of the Lavon Institute/Histadrut Archive, Tel Aviv; Amira Stern and the staff of the Jabotinsky Institute Archive, Tel Aviv; and the staff of the Hagana History Archive in Tel Aviv. Thanks as well to Rob Williams and the staff at Westview Press for their professionalism in preparing a difficult manuscript for publication. Special thanks go to Rabbi and Mrs. Amos Edelheit, to David and Phyllis Edelheit, to my mother Mrs. Ann D. Edelheit, and finally to my wife, Carol Ann Stein Edelheit — my favorite environmental engineer and, coincidentally, one of the best proofreaders I've ever met.

Abraham J. Edelheit
February 16, 2000

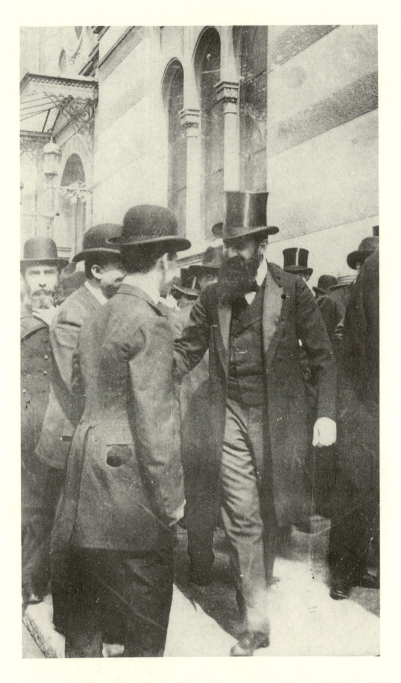

Dr. Theodor Herzl Leaving a Basel Synagogue After a Visit in 1903.
Coutresy of the Central Zionist Archive, Jerusalem

I
Land and State in Jewish Tradition

Biblical Background

Two monumental events have fundamentally transformed the Jewish people in this century: the Holocaust and the establishment of the State of Israel.[1] Although both events were largely *sui generis*, the pattern of destruction and rebirth resonates in prior Jewish history. Thus, while the rebirth of Israel was the culmination of half a century of political Zionism, any attempt to understand the ideological background of the re-creation of Jewish sovereignty must also consider the deeper cultural, religious, and intellectual origins of the Zionist idea. Whereas Zionism is, at its root, a secular nationalist movement framed as a modern revolution against elements of the Jewish past, from its inception Zionism also harked back to a two-millennial tradition of hope for the restoration of Jewry to its ancestral homeland.[2] Therefore, examining the Jewish understanding of concepts of land, statehood, nationalism, and national sovereignty will, therefore, provide key data for understanding Zionism's appeal and its meaning.[3]

At the outset, a few basic premises must be understood. First, the Jewish religious tradition does not distinguish clearly between religious, national, racial, or ethnic identities.[4] Second, nonetheless, a strong sense of bondedness exists throughout the Jewish tradition and is expressed in terms of peoplehood or, in modern terminology, as a concept of nationality (עַם, *Am*). Third, that from the very beginning this sense of peoplehood was identified with the Land of Israel, or (to use the traditional Jewish term) *Eretz Israel*. The fact that *Eretz Israel* was not seen as just a homeland, but also as a land of destiny, was intimately related to this sense of peoplehood and meant that *Eretz Israel* was always seen as central to Jewish life, in theory if not in practice. Finally, throughout the long years of exile Jews always hoped for some form of redemption and return to their ancestral homeland, with a small settlement existing almost continuously.

Regarding national identity, it is important to note that membership in the Jewish people (to use a modern term, citizenship) implied ipso facto adherence to Judaism, while adherence to Judaism, the manifestation of a religious covenant, was viewed as coterminous with membership in Jewry, the manifestation of a national covenant.[5] The member group, *Klal Israel* (כלל ישראל, the Community of Israel), also called the *Edah* (עדה) in traditional terminology, was linked both vertically (with the Divine) and horizontally (with other members in the group, past, present, and future) in a way that combined religious and political elements.

In turn, the religious and national elements of Jewish identity were intimately connected with Eretz Israel. This rootedness with the land may be traced back to the covenants with the forefathers of the Jewish people that derive from

3

the promise to Abraham that "I will give unto thee, and to thy seed after thee . . . all the land of Canaan for an everlasting possession."[6] The covenantal promise was repeated to Isaac (confirmed as Abraham's sole heir in Genesis 21:12) and to Jacob (Genesis 28:13–15). The covenant was formalized with "all the Children of Israel" during the revelation of the Ten Commandments at Mount Sinai (Exodus 20:1–14), in a unifying act that created a single Israelite nation while also promising (in the Fifth Commandment) longevity in the Promised Land if the covenant's terms were upheld.

The divine promise was supplemented by Abraham's purchase of the Machpelah cave and the surrounding field as a burial plot (with a clear contractual provision of the inalienable right of his heir to inherit the land) and by Isaac's insistence that any treaty between himself and Abimelech, king of the Philistines, must be based on the latter's recognition of Isaac's exclusive right to possess the region around Be'er Sheva.[7]

Nonetheless, Israel's possession of the land was conditioned on fealty to the terms of the Sinaitic covenant.[8] The national covenant, was based on the Ten Commandments and came to include all previous and further divine decrees to form what was known as *Torat Moshe* (the Mosaic law). The covenant remained in force throughout the First and Second Jewish Commonwealths, being periodically reconfirmed, and is still considered to be in force among Orthodox circles today.[9]

In the biblical view all land belongs to the divine. For example, in the land regulations included in the so-called Priestly Code, we read, "The land shall not be sold for ever, for the land is Mine and you are [only] strangers and sojourners with me."[10] God apportions the land, in his own inscrutable fashion, to each of the nations. That which he gives, however, may be taken back if the inhabitants do not use their inheritance properly. Thus the Israelites were expected to adhere to specific standards of behavior; they were specifically enjoined from copying

the customs of surrounding nations and were held accountable for creating a just society. "Zion shall be redeemed in justice," cried the prophet Isaiah, "and they shall return to her in righteousness."[11]

The biblical view of religion, nationalism, and statehood had two further implications. First, the land of Israel is — for Jews — more than a national home: It is also, perhaps primarily, Israel's land of destiny. Second, Israel is not "merely" one among nations but is unique in its possession of a divinely inspired mission to become "a kingdom of priests and a holy nation."[12] Moreover, the mission could only be fulfilled in its entirety (in the biblical view) in the land of Israel (even after the Israelites' original twelve tribes were reduced to two and the people became known as Jews).[13]

The last point cannot be underestimated. Many of the *mitzvot* (the 613 commandments that tradition holds incumbent upon all Jews) are directly or indirectly connected with Israel; a large number of them can be fulfilled in *Eretz Israel* only. Among the latter are the various tithes, the seventh year of rest (*Shemittah*), the Jubilee, the ritual of firstfruits, and the cities of refuge.[14] Even those *mitzvot* whose fulfillment is not limited to *Eretz Israel* were framed to emphasize the connection to the land. Thus, the fifth commandment (to honor parents) was devised around a promise that compliance would ensure "that you may long endure on the land that the Lord your God is giving you."[15] The *mitzvot* of *mezuza* and *tefilin* (phylacteries) were similarly framed: These *mitzvot* can be performed anywhere that a Jewish male and his family reside, but they are formulated with a clear connection of *Eretz Israel*. This may be seen clearly in the passage of Deuteronomy 11, which links the two *mitzvot*, as well as the education of youth, with the promise of an enduring residence in the Promised Land.[16]

To be sure, the Israelites did not always live up to the ideals contained in biblical injunctions. Periods of national apostasy and of willful abandonment of much of the Torah's social and religious legislation led to severe criticism by prophets who warned that sin corrupted the land and that apostasy represented a repudiation of the covenant which would lead to divine retribution, including destruction and exile. The oft-repeated prophetic metaphor of the land polluted by sin vomiting out the sinful nation is one reflection of this idea, and once again harks back to the concept of *Eretz Israel* as a land of destiny rather than merely a national home. The prophets were (largely) warning of future doom; time remained to rectify conditions by returning to the covenant and thus averting the threatened punishments. Even the most strident of the prophets, moreover, saw punishment and exile as little more than a temporary deviation from the norm. All of them envisioned an eventual restoration, for in their view God could no more repudiate his covenantal responsibilities than Israel could. The prophet Amos, after excoriating the ten tribes for their sins, foresaw a time when:

> I will restore the captivity of My people Israel. They shall rebuild ruined cities and inhabit them; they shall plant vine-yards and drink their wine; they shall till gardens and eat their fruit. I will plant them on their land, nevermore to be up-rooted from the land I have given them, says the Lord your God.[17]

Similar passages occur in every prophetic work. Ezekiel, who witnessed the exile, assured the survivors that God "will take you from among the nations and gather you from all the countries," in order to "bring you [back] to your own land."[18] Redemption was even viewed in superlative terms, as an era of messianic bliss and human (and animal) perfection. In this future era the land of Israel would be more than just the Jews' home: It would become the center of the world and a shrine for truth and a source of teaching for all the nations of the earth.[19]

The prophecies of doom were fulfilled as first the Assyrian and later the Babylonian empires extended their influence throughout the Near East. They impinged upon and eventually overwhelmed the First Jewish Commonwealth. The exiles, however, prayed for imminent redemption. Downcast, they proclaimed, "If I forget thee, o Jerusalem, let my right hand lose its cunning."[20] But this exile, as the prophets had predicted, was of short duration and a return to *Eretz Israel* was permitted by Cyrus, the king of Persia. As the returnees travelled, they chanted the psalms known as the "Songs of Ascents," which culminated in "A Song of Ascents. When the Lord brought Zion out of captivity we were like dreamers."[21]

Land and State in Rabbinic Literature

The partial restoration in Cyrus' time led to the creation of a Second Jewish Common-wealth which was circumscribed in territory and in the degree of sovereignty possessed by its Jewish inhabitants.[22] In different eras the territory — whose name changed a number of times to reflect different perceptions — was dominated by the great powers of the age: Persia, Greece, Ptolemaic Egypt, Seleucid Syria, and finally, Rome. The latter conferred the name Palestine upon the territory after the failed Jewish revolts of the first and second centuries of the common era.

Still, throughout this era, the embers of hope for full restoration burned brightly. During the Maccabbean uprising, for instance, hopes ran high for the imminent fulfillment of all the messianic prophecies through historical and national means. This theme dominated Jewish political thinking during the revolts against Rome (66–73 and 132–135 C.E.).[23] The theme of imminent redemption played an especially prominent role in the last of these revolts, which was led by Simon Bar-Kozba (Bar-Koseva), who claimed Davidic descent and thus messianic status. This claim was supported by some of the most prominent rabbinic scholars of the era — especially Rabbi Akiva. The latter even went so far as to change Bar-Kozba's name to Bar-Kokhba in order to fulfill messianic prophecies.[24] The failure of Bar-Kokhba's rebellion, however, brought with it intense persecution (in the form of a series of decrees associated by Jews with the emperor Hadrian) and nearly resulted in the extirpation

Two Scenes From a Model of Jerusalem in the Second Commonwealth.
Authors' Collection

of remaining Jews in *Eretz Israel*.[25]

This traumatic defeat forced the rabbis, natural inheritors of the prophetic tradition, to reorient Judaism's nationalist and redemptivist ideology. Continued resistance to Rome would be futile and would, in the rabbinic view, thwart the divine plan for the world. As a result, a new, passive nationalist ideology was needed. The new attitude was reflected in a famous passage in the Talmud:

Rabbi Yose son of Rabbi Hanina taught: What are the three oaths that God caused Israel to swear?[26] One that they would not return to Israel as a wall [=by force], one that they would not rebel against the gentile nations, and one that He caused the idolatrous nations to swear: that they would not enslave [=oppress] Israel too much.[27]

The purpose of this passage, and many similar ones, was to deter any attempts to continue resistance to the Roman Empire, or the later empires that occupied *Eretz Israel*. At the same time, rabbinic literature is replete with references to a future messianic era in which Jews would be restored to their ancestral homeland. As the actual fulfillment of this expectation became less immediately expected, the messianic idea absorbed numerous supernatural elements, considered authoritative by traditional Jews but viewed by others as merely metaphorical expressions for yearnings that could not immediately be fulfilled, and resulted in a policy of always awaiting the hour of messianic redemption.[28] The clearest statement of this attitude was made by Rabbi Moses Maimonides (Rambam). In his introduction to the tenth chapter of the Mishnaic Tractate Sanhedrin, Maimonides outlined the thirteen principles that he considered basic to Judaism. The twelfth principle is: "I believe with perfect faith in the coming of the Messiah. No matter how long he may tarry, I will await his arrival every day."[29]

As already noted, this passive Jewish nationalism was always combined with a clear appreciation of the centrality of *Eretz Israel* to Judaism and of the yearning for a return to the glory days of Israel's independence. Customs, such as the groom's breaking a glass at the traditional Jewish wedding to symbolize mourning over the destruction of the temple in Jerusalem, reinforced this yearning and meant that, despite the focus on passively awaiting the Messiah, Judaism never completely lost its nationalist element.[30] A casual perusal of the Jewish prayerbook reveals repeated references to the covenant, exile, the temple, Jerusalem, and ultimately redemption. Granted, most of the prayers are derived directly or indirectly from the Bible, but the repeated repetition of these themes and of certain specific phrases does indicate the intensity and fervor with which Jews in exile hoped and (literally) prayed for redemption.[31] It is, therefore, difficult to disagree with Naomi Sarlin's statement that, "[t]he idea of Zion and the Jewish people are inseparable." or, as Sarlin continued, that "Zion is an intrinsic part of our religious belief and our historic heritage . . ."[32] In addition, numerous texts attest to Eretz Israel's beauty and its centrality to Judaism. The best known is a text from the Babylonian Talmud (Kiddushin 49b) that repeats the formula "ten measures of . . . descended to the world; nine were taken by Eretz Israel and one was taken by the rest of the world." In this way, the land of Israel is established as the most beautiful, wise, and heroic land on the planet.[33]

Two other texts round out this picture. The first is a clear Halachic comment located just before the Talmudic discussion of the three oaths, specifically, a debate on the meaning of a Mishna that reads: "All are brought up to *Eretz Israel*, but not all may leave; all are brought up to Jerusalem, but not all may leave."[34] The Talmudic gloss on this passage is that it refers to the case of family members who wish to settle in *Eretz Israel* when other members of the family do not so desire. In this case, the unwilling family member(s) may be compelled to move, even if the opponent is the head of the family. On the other hand, no Jew may ever be forced by a family member to leave Eretz Israel, even if the head of the family so decrees.[35] An even more startling statement, when viewed from the perspective of the rabbis' passive nationalism (and the supposed implications of the three oaths), was made by Rabbi Shimon ben Eliezer (a second-century Tanna): "All Israelites who live outside Eretz Israel — are [considered] Idol worshippers." Rabbi Shimon also expressed this as a general principle: "Settling in Eretz Israel is considered as [equal to performing] all the other commandments."[36]

For the next seventeen centuries most Jews remained committed to this pattern of behavior and belief. *Eretz Israel* became vital to the self-definition of the entire Jewish people just as it ceased to be a center of Jewish life. Reality, of course, was not conducive to mass immigration, even after the Arab conquest and the various autonomy arrangements that permitted Jewish life to flourish under Muslim rule throughout the Middle East.[37] And the three oaths remained the main proof text to control messianic fervor and prevent foolhardy efforts at mass migration. This does not mean that Jews did not immigrate when possible. A small number of Jews always lived in *Eretz Israel*, primarily (though by no means exclusively) in the four so-called Holy Cities of Jerusalem, Hebron, Tiberias, and Safed. These settlers were reinforced in every generation by a trickle of immigrants who came to live in the atmosphere of Jewry's land of destiny.[38]

Simultaneously, diaspora Jewry established the mind-set closely associated with any national minority living outside of its homeland. By definition, diaspora communities — regardless of their own antiquity — considered themselves as little more than outposts destined to be liquidated at the earliest opportunity.[39] This point of view recurred throughout medieval Jewish texts, especially in the poetry of Rabbi Judah ha-Levi. In one of his poems ha-Levi cried, "Jerusalem will you not enquire about the fate of your exiles?"[40] In another poem, ha-Levi despondently noted that: "My heart is in the east and I am [in] the furthest west."[41] Ha-Levi further expounded on his geo-theological view in his major philosophical

work, the *Kuzari*. Just as the Jews were God's chosen people, in ha-Levi's view, *Eretz Israel* was his chosen land. Choseness, in both cases, was seen as mutual. Land and people were appropriate for each other — a perfect land was destined for the people whose divine mission was to achieve perfection on earth (this, according to ha-Levi, was the sense in which Israel is to be a "nation of priests").[42] Ha-Levi was by no means alone in his geo-theological view of *Eretz Israel*.[43] Rabbi Moses ben Nachman (Nachmanides, or Ramban), for instance, listed "inheriting [= settling] *Eretz Israel*" as one of the 613 commandments obligatory on all Jews; many scholars agreed with Ramban's conclusion, but the sentiment was not unanimous.[44]

Among the dissenters was Maimonides, who laid down many conditions to the commandment of settling in *Eretz Israel*. In particular, Maimonides felt that an authoritative commandment to live in *Eretz Israel* (as opposed to a theoretical hope for the future) only applied and was binding on all Jews when a sovereign Jewish kingdom existed in *Eretz Israel*. Otherwise, Jews did not actually have to live in the land, especially when prevailing conditions were not conducive to a secure Jewish life. At the same time, Maimonides posited that *Eretz Israel* had an intrinsic holiness unconnected with the Jewish people, reflected, for example, in the halachot of ritual purity, tithes, the seventh year of rest (Shemittah), the Jubilee, the ritual of firstfruits, and the cities of refuge. None of these halachot appertained outside of *Eretz Israel*, even (according to Maimonides) if a Jewish state were to come into existence in any other part of the world.[45]

Maimonides' views on Eretz Israel and its holiness must be viewed in context, and in particular should be seen as part of his political philosophy. In one of his letters, Maimonides explained the Jews' suffering in exile in light of his understanding of Jewish political history:

For thus was our kingdom destroyed, our temple destroyed, and our exile has lasted to this day: for our forefathers sinned and did not study warcraft and the conquest of many lands.[46]

The counterpoint of Maimonides' understanding of the past was his view of the messianic future (his unequivocal belief in the Messiah has already been noted). Rather than emphasize the supernatural elements of the messianic era, Maimonides taught that "there will be no difference between our world and the Messianic era save that Israel will no longer be enslaved to the nations."[47] Altogether, Maimonides' position stood well within the conventional rabbinic approach: to passively await the Messiah who would surely come to redeem the Jewish people and restore them to their land of destiny.

Ideology and Praxis: Messianism

The polar opposite of the standard rabbinic approach was the repeated claim by some members of the community that the redemption was close at hand. Messianic speculation was not ipso facto contrary to the standard rabbinic approach. Indeed, some of the greatest rabbinic leaders of the Middle Ages propounded dates for the Messiah's possible arrival. In general, however, when eminent rabbis proposed such dates they selected dates well in the future. Their purpose in proposing any date was to offer members of communities whose morale was sorely tried a renewed sense of hope for a better future. Maimonides, for example, had a family tradition predicting that the Messiah would come in 1216 C.E. twelve years, as it turned out, after his death.[48]

In contrast, messianists within the community hoped, at times hoping against hope, that the hour of redemption was at hand. They used a variety of hermeneutic methods on biblical verses dealing (directly or indirectly) with the Messiah and attempted to adduce the date of the Messiah's expected arrival from them.

The problem was that these speculators expected the Messiah's imminent arrival, not his eventual arrival. In many cases they also sought a variety of quasi-pietistic means to hasten the so-called end of days that would usher in the messianic era. This expectation often led to disaster. When the expected Messiah did not arrive or when a false Messiah appeared and failed at his messianic mission (a clear sign of a messianic pretender), Jews' morale fell even lower than it had been previously. Thus, the established rabbinic leadership fought tooth and nail against such speculation and tried to discourage messianic pretenders.

At least eight nessianic pretenders appeared between the eleventh and thirteenth centuries, a period of intense upheaval characterized by the Crusades, the persecution of Jews, and intense inter-religious warfare. Indeed, the year that the First Crusade was launched (1096), was itself a messianic year, a belief derived by applying the traditional Jewish numerology system (Gematria) to the Hebrew calendar. By giving each letter and each word a numeric value, Gematria grants letters, words, and sentence fragments a hermeneutic importance that could easily be applied to speculation about the Messiah's arrival. Since the Jewish calendar operates on a cycle of nineteen years and deriving a key number from a "messianic" verse, in this case from the verse "sing with gladness for Jacob" (רנו ליעקב שמחה, Ranu le-Yaakov Simha, Jeremiah 31:7), it was assumed that the Messiah would come in the during the 256th (sing, רנו, in Hebrew has the numeric value of 256) cycle. Although the Messiah could come in any year of the cycle (which ran from 1085 to 1104), it was widely assumed he would arrive in the eleventh year of the cycle because that year was adduced by some scholars to be the millennial anniversary of the destruction of the Second Temple.[49] Far from heralding the Messiah's arrival, however, 1096 witnessed attacks by Crusader armies that decimated the Jewish communities in the Rhine River valley. The irony of a messianic year turning into a year of mass bloodletting was not lost on contemporary Jewish chroniclers who beseeched God to remember his covenant.[50]

Of the eight messianic pretenders who arose in this environment, four were active in the Middle East, three in Europe, and one in *Eretz Israel*. The latter is of special interest, despite sparse details, since his messianic pretensions show a clear nexus between messianic speculation and active attempts to restore Jewish sovereignty. In 1121 a former Norman Crusader and recent convert to Judaism named Obadiah made acquaintance with one Solomon ha-Kohen (apparently a local Jew or Karaite) who told Obadiah that he (Solomon) was the Messiah and would manifest himself in a period of two and a half months. Nothing further was heard of him.[51]

A more extensive messianic movement arose in Mesopotamia shortly thereafter, led by David Alroy. Alroy claimed to be the Messiah and called on his followers to take up arms to conquer *Eretz Israel* from both the Muslims and the Christians. Some followed Alroy and took up arms against the Caliph, but only on a small scale. Alroy's exact end is unknown, although he was reportedly murdered by his father-in-law. In any event the messianic movement perished with its leader.[52]

The three centuries after Alroy saw only three messianic pretenders, but speculation intensified again after the Jews were expelled from Spain in 1492.[53] The catastrophes of the late fifteenth and early sixteenth centuries persuaded many of the Spanish exiles (and other Jews as well) that recent sufferings were the "birthpangs of the Messiah." Compounding the sense of coming redemption was a relatively new and activist form of Kabbalah (Jewish mysticism) associated with Rabbi Isaac Luria of Safed. Lurianic Kabbala, like earlier forms of Jewish mysticism, was suffused with messianic fervor. Unlike earlier forms of Jewish mysticism, however, Lurianic Kabbala emphasized creating a mass movement and implied that human actions could hasten the Messiah's arrival. More importantly, Lurianic Kabbalists believed that the Messiah's arrival was imminent.[54]

Two major pretenders arose in the years after the Spanish expulsion. The earlier of the two, David Reuveni, claimed to be the representative of a Jewish king (alleged to be either Reuveni's brother or half-brother) who ruled in the Khaibar and was engaged

in a war against the Muslims. Reuveni offered Jews the hope of an impending mass return to *Eretz Israel*; at the same time he engaged in negotiations with Christian notables (including Pope Clement VII) over a possible joint crusade to free the Holy Land from Moslem rule. Reuveni, it must be emphasized, never claimed to possess any supernatural powers, nor did he perform any "miracles." His goal was political independence for the Jewish people, to be accomplished by military and diplomatic means. Still, Reuveni excited speculation among those who sought the long-awaited Messiah. In particular, his mission excited many Marranos — Spanish Jews who had officially converted to Christianity but remained crypto-Jews, desiring (but legally unable) to return to Judaism. One of these Marranos, Solomon Molkho became associated with Reuveni and alternately claimed to be a prophet (with a messianic prophecy) or the Messiah. Molkho returned to Judaism, an act that proved to be Reuveni's undoing. In 1532, Molkho was burned at the auto-da-fé and Reuveni imprisoned for Judaizing among Marranos.[55]

Perhaps the most infamous of the false messiahs was Shabbetai Zvi, a Jew from Smyrna (Izmir) who first claimed to be the Messiah circa 1648. He reiterated this claim after a meeting with the self-proclaimed prophet Nathan of Gaza in 1665. By 1666 Shabbetai's messianic movement spread throughout the Ottoman Empire and even reverberated in North European Jewish communities. That Shabbetai announced his imminent coronation in Jerusalem lent further credence to his claims as did the fact that the Ottoman authorities initially did not respond to his declaration. In January 1666, Shabbetai led a march to the imperial capital in Istanbul (Constantinople), claiming that he would peacefully remove the sultan's crown and thus manifest himself as the redeemer of Israel. On February 8, 1666, Shabbetai was arrested for treason, while the Ottoman authorities debated what to do with the pretender to the throne of Israel. Imprisoned for six years, Shabbetai was given the choice of conversion or death in 1672.[56] His choice of conversion, which should have ended his messianic movement, only spurred his followers to further outrageous actions. Attempting to find a mystical justification for Shabbetai's actions, some of his followers interpreted his conversion by reference to the concept of "redemption through sin" (a complete distortion of the rabbinic concept that it is impermissible to commit a sin in order to perform a Mitzva: for example, one cannot steal an animal to offer it as a sacrifice). Some indeed went so far as to follow their leader into conversion, forming a crypto-Jewish sect (known as the Dönmeh) within Islam.[57]

Shabbetai died in 1676, but that was not the end of the matter. Many Jews continued to believe in Shabbetai's messianic mission long after his death, which led to considerable recrimination and nearly tore apart the Jewish community. The Messiah, according to Jewish tradition, could not fail in his mission nor could he die before his mission was completed. Yet Shabbetai clearly had done both. As a result, a heated controversy arose between followers of Shabbetai Zvi and their opponents.[58] The lingering dispute, in turn, led to a weakening of the active messianic component of Kabbala.[59] Furthermore, fear of a new Shabbetai Zvi paralyzed many traditionally minded Jews who feared that any movement (Zionism for example) calling for restoration by human means would only excite and then disappoint Jewry. When political Zionism arose in the nineteenth century it was thus shunned by the elements of the Jewish community that, theoretically, had kept alive the ideas of a Jewish polity.[60]

On the Verge of Modern Nationalism

With the exception of the false Messiahs, the norm of Jewish passive nationalism remained unchanged for nearly 2,000 years. Conditions in the diaspora precluded any mass effort to change the status quo while religious teachings reinforced the tendency to await divine redemption. Nonetheless, the situation was not static. The expulsion of the Jews from Spain in 1492 which created a conducive environment for false messiahs (as already noted) also created the opportunity for a number of colonization efforts and ideological changes that carried Jewish hope for national restoration into the early modern era.

Probably the most important of the changes was the rise of new modes of Jewish scholarship during the Renaissance. Strongly opposed to false messianism, the new Jewish scholarship sought to explain the recent Jewish tragedies within the context of exilic history and proposed, by implication (since a direct statement of that sort could be interpreted as an attack on the traditional concept of divine punishment for sin), that crises deriving from historical causes could have historical solutions. Again, by implication, that meant that the Jews' exilic condition, deriving from historical causes, could also be undone by historical means.[61]

More traditional in his form of scholarship, Don Isaac Abravanel nevertheless represented another manifestation of this trend: he was the first scholar since Maimonides to attempt to piece together a coherent political philosophy.[62] The implication inherent in such an effort was, of course, that Abravanel believed redemption was near. Furthermore, Abravanel's sources — Jewish and non-Jewish — and his emphasis on limited monarchy provide a glimpse into his thought about the organization of a future Jewish commonwealth.[63] In Abravanel's view, only a limited monarchy could successfully provide the type of government needed to do justice and restore the type of covenantal theocracy that had existed in ancient Israel. In this case the clear presence of a divine element prevented tyranny, creating what would be considered (in contemporary terms) a mixed government with shared and reserved powers, because the king would always be aware of a higher authority to whom he was responsible (God).[64] The additional creation of a hierarchically organized court system provided a human check on unlimited royal power while providing the people with a say, albeit a limited one, in how they would be governed.[65] Altogether, Abravanel's political philosophy emphasized what may be termed a federal system of government, elements of which Abravanel (and a number of recent scholars) argued had always existed in the Jewish polity.[66]

The expulsion from Spain also provided a new incentive to re-create an active center of Jewish life in *Eretz Israel*. As a direct result of the Spanish exiles' need to reestablish themselves, they considered the possibility of reviving long-dormant settlements. In particular, a renewed settlement in the Galilee (around Safed) came to fruition during the sixteenth century. By century's end this was a flourishing community. Part and parcel of this effort was Don Joseph Nasi's attempt to organize mass resettlement in an economically revived *Eretz Israel*.[67]

In 1564, Nasi, a prominent Marrano who returned to Judaism, used his extensive contacts with the sultan — by whom he was honored as the Duke of Naxos — to obtain permission to begin a massive resettlement project in the Galilee. The goal was to create a new Jewish city that would become the nucleus for a Jewish province in the Ottoman Empire.[68] Although the proposed government of this Jewish province remains unclear — it is unlikely that any plan existed to endow the Jewish community with more than local autonomy — Nasi's extensive economic planning was prescient. In addition to agriculture, accepted as the basis for renewed settlement, Nasi sought to import silkworms in order to provide the colony with a manufacturing capability that would render it economically independent of charity from other Jewish communities.[69]

Nasi's plans were never completed and he died in 1579. Nevertheless, the Safed Jewish community continued, as did small-scale *aliya*, well into the seventeenth century. At that point the settlement collapsed: repeated Bedouin incursions, a series of natural disasters, and the economic consequences of the Atlantic's opening and the subsequent commercial revolution (which rendered the Ottoman Empire a backwater in the global economy) all contributed to the downfall of the renewed colony in Galilee. Yet it is important to recall that some Jews remained there for most of the modern era.[70]

Another turning point in the premodern history of Jewish nationalism was the rise of Hasidism. In Shabbetai Zvi's aftermath, Jewish mystics deactivated the messianic elements of Kabbala. Hasidism, which emphasized piety and articulated an optimistic worldview, arose to fill the vacuum left by Sabbateanism. Combining mystical piety with deactivated messianism that emphasized the cosmic importance of *Halacha* (Jewish law). The Hasidic masters, the *tzadikim*, followed Israel ben Eliezer, the Baal Shem Tov, in emphasizing *devekut* (devotion) and *hitlahavut* (joy) — both seen as being as important as, if not more important than, book learning. Hasidism spoke to the Jewish everyman and soon spread from the steppes of the Ukraine to the foothills of the Carpathians, central Poland and beyond.[71]

Of immediate significance was the effort by one of the *Tzadikim*, Reb Nachman of Bratslav, to reintegrate the physical presence of *Eretz Israel* into the Jewish psyche. Reb Nachman sought to do so by undertaking a pilgrimage to *Eretz Israel* and by his repeated references to Kabbalistic doctrines that derived their meaning from *Eretz Israel*. To these he added a new element, his belief that living in Israel was itself an act of repentance that permitted the resident to see the full manifestation of divine grace. This sense of grace that could only manifest itself in *Eretz Israel* suffused Reb Nachman's famous prayer "A True Desire to Come to Eretz Israel."[72] Strikingly, Reb Nachman emphasized not the idealized land of the Talmud, but the real land of "rocks and dust, a land that can be touched, [on] whose soil men tread."[73] Although he remained in *Eretz Israel* only a short time and despite the lack of a follow up to his pilgrimage, in the form of renewed *aliya*, Reb Nachman epitomized a turning point ideologically. He clearly was seen as seminal by the leaders of the Hibbat Zion movement, who incorporated many of his ideas into their program.[74]

One final settlement effort characterized early modern Jewish nationalism. In the 1740s a group of 1,000 Eastern European Jews led by Rabbi Judah he-Hasid settled in Jerusalem, hoping thereby to hasten the Messiah's arrival. Although no one in the group claimed to be the Messiah, it is clear that many of the immigrants were, in fact, secret Sabbateans. It should be further emphasized that the group were also not Hasidim in the usual sense of the term. They were, therefore, unable to attract any major wave of immigration and they built no new economic structures. Rather, they fit themselves into the already existing pattern of Jerusalem Jewry.[75] The same held true for the trickle of Jews who immigrated during the years before 1880: They augmented an already existing community and kept Eretz Israel relevant to the Jewish psyche worldwide.[76]

By way of summary we may note three elements that predated the rise of Zionism in the nineteenth century. (1) Jews in all eras considered Eretz Israel to be a national home and, more importantly, a land of national destiny to which they would ultimately return. (2) Regardless of conceptual changes in their definition of the nation and of national redemption, Eretz Israel remained central to Jewish nationalism throughout the eras. (3) Finally, although this cannot be fully elucidated here, a Jewish presence in Eretz Israel existed virtually throughout the era discussed here.

The centrality of *Eretz Israel* to the Jewish people even found an echo in non-Jewish writings in the early modern era, most prominently in Napoleon's call for Jews to return to *Eretz Israel* under the sponsorship of revolutionary France.[77] At the time, however, Jews were involved in an experiment with a different definition of redemption, namely civic emancipation and assimilation. That effort would transform the Jewish people and would, ironically, give a new impetus to a revolutionized Jewish nationalism.

Notes

All translations from the Bible and the Talmud are the authors' unless otherwise noted.

1. For an overview of the history of the Holocaust, see Abraham J. Edelheit and Hershel Edelheit, *History of the Holocaust: A Handbook and Dictionary* (Boulder: Westview, 1994).
2. Cf. Martin Sicker, *Judaism, Nationalism, and the Land of Israel* (Boulder: Westview, 1992) p. x, and, more broadly, Daniel J. Elazar and Stuart A. Cohen, *The Jewish Polity: Jewish Political Organization from Biblical Times to the Present*, Bloomington: University of Indiana Press, 1985.
3. For a more detailed discussion of the issues raised here see Avi Erlich, *Ancient Zionism: The Biblical Origins of the National Idea* (New York: Free Press, 1995) Eliezer Schweid, *The Land of Israel: National Home or Land of Destiny?* (Rutherford, NJ: Fairleigh Dickinson University Press/ Herzl Press, 1985) pt. 1, chap. 1, and W. D. Davies, *The Territorial Dimension in Judaism* (Berkeley: University of California Press, 1982).
4. Solomon Zeitlin, *The Jews: Race, Nation, or Religion?* (Philadelphia: Dropsie College Press, 1936).
5. Elazar and Cohen, *Jewish Polity*, passim, and Daniel J. Elazar, "The Covenant as the Basis of the Jewish Political Tradition," in D. J. Elazar, ed., *Kinship and Consent: The Jewish Political Tradition and its Contemporary Uses* (Ramat Gan: Turtledove Publications, 1981) pp. 21–56.
6. Genesis 17:8.
7. Respectively, Genesis 23:9–20 and 26:26–34.
8. Sicker, *Judaism*, pp. 17–19.
9. Elazar and Cohen, *Jewish Polity*, p. 63, citing Exodus 19-20, Deuteronomy 29:9-25, and Joshua 8:31; 23:6.
10. Leviticus 25:23. Although the verse refers to the actions of an individual, its implications for all Israelites are clear, as are other similar passages (dealing, e.g., with the Jubilee Year). Cf. J. D. Eisenstein, "Yovel," in his אוצר דינים ומנהגים (A Digest of Jewish Laws and Customs) (New York: Privately published, 1917, pp. 157–158.
11. Isaiah 1:27. Numerous similar references occur throughout biblical literature.
12. Exodus 19:6.
13. The clearest example of this view is expressed in the book of Jonah: The unwilling prophet seeks to escape his divine mission by traveling to Tarshish where, presumably, God cannot "find" him (Jonah 1:3). Psalm 137:4 expresses a similar sentiment: "How can we sing the Lord's song on a foreign land?"
14. Erlich, *Ancient Zionism*, pp. 59–63.
15. Exodus 20:11 as cited in Joseph Telushkin, *Jewish Wisdom* (New York: William Morrow, 1994), p. 568.
16. Cf. Aviezer Ravitsky, "הציבי לך ציונים' לציון: גלגולו של רעיון'" (Waymarks to Zion: The History of an Idea), in Moshe Hallamish and Aviezer Ravitzky, ארץ ישראל בהגות היהודית בימי הביניים (The Land of Israel in Medieval Jewish Thought) (Jerusalem: Yad Yitzhak Ben-Zvi, 1991), pp. 4–8.
17. Amos 9:14–15.
18. Ezekiel 36:24.
19. Cf. Schweid, *Land of Israel*, pp. 28–29, citing Isaiah 2:1–12.
20. Psalm 137:5
21. Psalm 126:1–2.
22. A general survey of the Second Commonwealth's history is provided by Solomon Zeitlin, *The Rise and Fall of the Judean State*, 3 vols. (Philadelphia: Jewish Publication Society, 1962–1978).
23. In addition to the relevant sections in Zeitlin, *Rise and Fall*, see Michael Grant, *The Jews in the Roman World* (New York: Scribner's, 1973), chap. 11–15.

24. JT Ta'anit 68d.

25. Grant, *Roman World*, chap. 15.

26. Song of Songs 2:7, 3:5, and 5:8. The passage refers to the traditional interpretation of the Song of Songs, that it is an allegory of the relationship between God and the Jewish people.

27. BT Ketuvot 111A. The Talmudic discussion centers on the concept of three oaths, not these specific three (as would be expected given the prominence these three oaths obtained in the last century), and various other homiletical and allegorical interpretations of the Song of Songs. In the late nineteenth and early twentieth centuries these specific oaths became the focal point for Orthodox rabbis who sought a Halachic basis for their opposition to Zionism: They used the oaths as an authoritative legal statement against any project to restore the Jews to Israel by human means, even though the passage was never meant to be more than a homiletical interpretation. Compare the statements by Orthodox anti-Zionists in Michael Selzer ed., *Zionism Reconsidered* (New York: Macmillan, 1970), pp. 1–47. For the religious Zionist interpretation of the same passage, see Mendell Lewittes, *Religious Foundations of the Jewish State* (Northvale, NJ: Jason Aronson, 1994), pp. 1–4, 157, and 211.

28. Cf. Lewittes, *Religious Foundations*, chap. 10, and Gershom Scholem, "Toward an Understanding of the Messianic Idea in Judaism," in his *The Messianic Idea in Judaism* (New York: Schocken Books, 1971), pp. 1–36.

29. Maimonides, Introduction to Perek Helek (Commentary to the Mishna, Sanhedrin 10:1), cited in A. Cohen ed, *The Teaching of Maimonides*, new ed. (New York: Ktav, 1968), p. 227.

30. Cf. Hyman Goldin comp., *המדריך* (The rabbi's guide) (New York: Hebrew Publishing, 1939) p. 21.

31. Cf. Philip Birnbaum (trans.), *The Daily Prayerbook* (New York: Hebrew Publishing, 1949) passim; and Stephen Garfinkel comp., *Zionism: Conceptual Bases in the Prayer Book* (New York: Department of Youth Activities of the United Synagogue of America, 1977).

32. Naomi Sarlin, *The Ideas of Zion: A Primer on Zionism* (New York: Hadassah, n.d.), p. 6.

33. The remainder of this text includes a discussion of what the other nations received ten measures of. Again, it must be emphasized that the statement was never meant to be taken as literal truth but as a figurative and hyperbolic statement. Nonetheless, it does reflect the importance that the rabbis attached to the Land of Israel.

34. BT Ketuvot 110B–111A.

35. See Rashi's comment on the Mishna, BT Ketubot 110B.

36. Tosefta Avoda Zara, chap. 4, in Chanoch Merhavia, *קולות קוראים לציון* (Voices Calling for Zion) (Jerusalem: The Zalman Shazar Institute for the Study of Jewish History, 1976), p. 37.

37. Cf. Norman Stillman, *The Jews of Arab Lands: A History and Sourcebook* (Philadelphia: Jewish Publication Society, 1979), pp. 22–39 and 154–158.

38. Cf. Dan Bahat et al., *רציפות הישוב היהודי בארץ ישראל* (The Continuity of Jewish Settlement in the Land of Israel) (Tel Aviv: Ministry of Defense/Chief Training Officer, 1978) chap. 2.

39. Schweid, *Land of Israel*, Pt. II, Ch. 2.

40. The poem is cited in its entirety in Merhavia, *קולות*, p. 43.

41. Ibid., p. 44.

42. Yohanan Silman, "*ארציותה של ארץ-ישראל בספר הכוזרי*" (The Earthliness of the Land of Israel in the Kuzari), in Hallamish and Ravitzky, eds., *ארץ-ישראל*, pp. 79–89.

43. We have borrowed this term from Schweid, who uses it in connection with his analysis of ha-Levi. It can, however, equally apply to Nachmanides and to some of the other rabbis of the era. Cf. *Land of Israel*, pt. 2, chap. 3.

44. Merhavia, *קולות*, pp. 48–58.

45. To fully understand Maimonides' complex perception of Eretz Israel, Schweid, *Land of Israel*, pt. 2, chap. 4 should be read, along with the contributions by Twersky and Nehorai in Hallamish and Ravitzky, eds., *ארץ-ישראל*, pp. 90–137.

46. Maimonides, "Responsum to the Scholars of Lunel," cited in Israel Halpern, ed., ספר הגבורה (The book of Jewish heroism) (Tel Aviv: Am Oved, 1942), 1:104.

47. See the sources listed in note 29.

48. Abba Hillel Silver, *A History of Messianic Speculation in Israel* (Boston: Beacon Press, 1959), p. 75

49. Ibid., pp. 58–63.

50. Cf. Shlomo Eidelberg, ed., *The Jews and the Crusaders: The Hebrew Chronicles of the First and Second Crusades*, 2nd ed. (Hoboken, NJ: Ktav, 1996), passim.

51. Elchan N. Adler, "Obadia le Prosélyte," *Revue des Etudes Juives* 69 (1919): 129–134.

52. Silver, *Messianic Speculation*, pp. 79–80.

53. Ibid., pp. 100–109.

54. Cf. Gershom Scholem, *Major Trends in Jewish Mysticism* (New York: Schocken Books, 1961), chap. 7.

55. Silver, *Messianic Speculation*, pp. 133–135, 145–150.

56. This brief sketch of the Sabbatean movement is based on the works of Gershom Scholem, especially his *Shabbetai Sevi: The Mystical Messiah* (Princeton: Princeton University Press, 1973).

57. Cf. Gershom Scholem, "Redemption Through Sin," in his *Messianic Idea*, pp. 78–141.

58. Cf. Bernard D. Weinryb, *The Jews of Poland* (Philadelphia: Jewish Publication Society, 1972), chap. 10–11.

59. Cf. Scholem, *Major Trends*, chap. 8.

60. In addition to the materials already cited from Selzer, *Zionism Reconsidered*, see Zalman Shazar, *Morning Stars*, (Philadelphia: Jewish Publication Society, 1967), pp. 37–44.

61. Cf. Elias Tcherikower, "Jewish Martyrology and Jewish Historiography," *YIVO Annual of Jewish Social Science)* 1 (1946): 17-19.

62. For a general biography of Abravanel that includes an analysis of his political philosophy, see Benzion Netanyahu, *Don Isaac Abravanel: Statesman and Philosopher* (Philadelphia: Jewish Publication Society, 1972).

63. Ibid., chap. 3.

64. Ibid., p. 165. There has been some debate over the precise terms of Abravanel's political philosophy and the sources of his argument; for a summary, see A. Melamed, "Isaac Abravanel and Aristotle's *Politics*: A Drama of Errors," *Jewish Political Studies Review* (hereafter *JPSR*) 5: 3/4 (Fall, 1993): 55–75.

65. Netanyahu, *Abravanel*, pp. 172–173, citing Abravanel's commentary on Deuteronomy.

66. Melamed, "Isaac Abravanel." Cf. Elazar and Cohen, *Jewish Polity*, passim.

67. Daniel J. Elazar, "Toward a Political History of the Sephardic Diaspora," *JPSR* 5:3/4 (Fall 1993): 16–18.

68. Cf. Cecil Roth, *The House of Nasi* (Philadelphia: Jewish Publication Society, 1948), pp. 110–115.

69. Ibid., pp. 117-118.

70. Elazar, "Political History," p. 18.

71. Cf. Gershom Scholem, "The Neutralization of the Messianic Element in Early Hasidism," in *Messianic Idea*, pp. 176–202.

72. The prayer is cited in full in Merhavia, קולות, pp. 92–93. Cf. Schweid, *Land of Israel*, pt. 3, chap. 1.

73. Ibid., p. 88.

74. Ibid., pp. 93–96.

75. Bahat et al., רציפות הישוב היהודי בארץ ישראל, pp. 112–113.

76. Ibid., pp. 113–125.

77. Napoleon's declaration is cited in Merhavia, קולות, p. 94. For an analysis of the declaration, see Franz Kobler, *Napoleon and the Jews* (New York: Schocken Books, 1976).

2

EARLY GLIMMERINGS OF REBIRTH

Enlightenment and Emancipation

The latter half of the eighteenth century spawned a series of ideological changes in Western Europe that were not directly related to Jews, but impacted greatly on their future status. In particular, the Enlightenment — generally identified with cultural and intellectual trends in France and the systematic application of rationalist principles to human affairs — and the rise of absolutist monarchies created conditions whereby concerned thinkers proposed the "civic improvement" of the Jews by granting them emancipation and citizenship in return for their joining the host nation. From the mid-eighteenth century on, a grand debate raged over the idea of emancipation, although the Ancien Régime proved unable to reform so radically. The European debate on emancipation received further impetus from the American Revolution (1776–1783), the ratification of the U.S. Constitution (1789), and the granting of citizenship to American Jewry.[1]

Within the Jewish world a new spirit was also kindled during the mid-eighteenth century. Small numbers of Jews became aware of the supposed backwardness of Jewish society and proposed remedies for all ills that kept Jews in what they saw as a cultural ghetto even while the walls of the physical ghetto were crumbling. The modernizers called themselves *Maskilim* (Enlighteners) and called their movement the *Haskala* (Enlightenment). Ideologically, this group owed its background to the teachings of Moses Mendelssohn, a German Jewish philosopher. The primary goal of the Haskala was to reeducate Jews so that they could fit into modern society. With the emancipation, the *Maskilim*, at least in Western Europe, led the way in creating "good" Jewish citizens. Adaptation of Jewish mores to the larger society became the goal. "Be a Jew in your home and a man in the street" was their motto.[2]

The French Revolution (1789) brought the debate on Jewish status to a crescendo. During the next century complete civil rights were granted to Jews throughout Western Europe, including France (1791), Italy (1869), Great Britain (1858–1871), and Germany (1871).[3] Tension often accompanied the emancipation, however, especially in France and Germany. Civil status was accorded to Jews as individuals but not to Jewish communities. In return for civil rights, Jews were asked to surrender their national identity and assimilate into the larger society.[4] Overall, emancipation reflected a fundamental shift in the Jews' political status, forcing Jews to rethink their relationship with society at large and to contemplate the state of their social, political, and religious traditions. In some cases, indeed, emancipation forced Jews to question their own sense of self.[5] On a more immediate level, the emancipation resulted in the collapse of Jewish communal autonomy in Western Europe and a basic reorientation of Jewish communal life.[6]

Under the circumstances, adaptation to and assimilation into the larger societal environment were the only means to resolve the paradox of Jewish survival while also proving that Jews had made strides in "improving" themselves in order to become deserving citizens — Israelites of French or German nationality. An obvious corollary of this line of thought was that many Jews in Central and Western Europe relinquished their belief in Jewish national identity, surrendering their hope for collective salvation and restoration in *Eretz Israel* for the hope of individual salvation in Europe.

This social and intellectual environment also led to an increasingly diverse religious environment within the Jewish community, mainly (but not only) in Germany, England, and the United States. In Germany, a number of Jews sought to radically reform Judaism in order to make it more fitting with modern society. Others saw the need for some changes but were only willing to make those changes for which they found precedents in Jewish history. Yet a third group saw no need for changes in tradition, although they too adopted a more modern worldview. The most liberal group coalesced into the Reform movement, which was guided by leaders such as Abraham Geiger, Samuel Holdheim, and David Friedländer. The more traditional group, guided by luminaries including Zechariah Frankel and Solomon Schechter, developed into Conservative Judaism. The most traditional group, led by Shimshon Raphael Hirsch, Isaac Breuer, and Azriel Hildesheimer, developed into Neo-orthodoxy, combining strict adherence to Jewish law with a modern weltanschauung.[7]

Post-Emancipation German Jewry

With the final decree of emancipation dated January 12, 1871, German Jewry entered a new stage of history. At least officially, German Jews now became full citizens of the German empire, permitted to participate in all aspects of economic, political, and cultural life. German Jewry became a shining example of the best and worst aspects of modern Jewry: great wealth coupled with intense materialism; religious freedom coupled with an attempt to flee Judaism; civic equality coupled with intense antisemitism in many circles. Throughout the nineteenth century and well into the twentieth, German Jewry remained a compact, highly urbanized middle-class or upper-middle-class element in German society. More than half of German Jews made their living in commerce (mainly small- and medium-scale retailing), banking, and manufacture. Free professionals (lawyers, doctors, dentists), represented the next largest group of gainfully employed Jews. In both cases, the percentage of Jews in these fields was disproportionate to their total population.[8] Yet, when Jewish urban concentration is considered, the amount of disproportion declines and it becomes clear that Jews did not dominate any one field of the economy.[9] Jewish political orientations in pre–World War I Germany have also been seen in a stereotyped way, that must be kept in context. Jews tended to suport the center and left primarily because the right-wing parties had been opposed to emancipation in the first place.[10]

Internally, emancipation resulted in a major transformation of German Jewry. In addition to the aforementioned rise of multiple Jewish denominations, German Jewry experienced an intense period of secularization. Increasingly, German Jews perceived themselves (and hoped to be seen) as Germans, not as Jews. When they did discuss their religious affiliation, they did so as "Germans of the Mosaic faith."[11] This was a new way of describing Judaism. Brief mention has already been made of the diversity of religious experiences among German Jewry. Yet, for a variety of reasons, all the German Jewish religious denominations, individual thinkers notwithstanding, shared a common thread: All, to a greater or lesser degree, de-emphasized the political nature of Judiasm and removed the immediate hope for restoration to

Jewry's ancestral homeland. To be sure, Orthodox and Conservative religious leaders retained the messianic concept but pushed it off to some far almost unimaginable, future. Restoration of Jewish national sovereignty in the here and now, rather than in some post-historical future, was reduced to a virtual impossibility.[12]

Reform Jews went even farther. For them Germany was the new Zion and Berlin the new Jerusalem. Those who maintained even a shred of the messianic concept, a small minority of Reform rabbis, reinterpreted and universalized Jewish messianic yearnings, totally divorcing the idea from any political implications and removing any reference to the restoration.[13] The same, it might be added, held true for individuals and small groups of radical assimilationists, who sought to abandon Jewish identity completely. They argued that the future salvation of Jewry could come only through the complete submersion of Jews into the broader society in which they lived. As a direct result, radical assimilation — which may be defined as an attempt to flee Judaism — became rampant in many segments of German Jewry.[14]

The Jewish Problem

Ironically, this new definition of Judaism spawned an entirely different, and not necessarily positive, relationship between Jews and their neighbors. Whereas prior to the emancipation Jewish distinctiveness was seen as a problem, now their attempt to enter the mainstream of European society was interpreted threateningly. Simply put, some ideologues argued that the emancipation deal did not refer to any form of continued Jewish existence — even if defined as a new and universalized Judaism — after the grant of citizenship to Jews. The result was the development of a "Jewish problem" in the minds of many Europeans.[15]

This was so for three reasons. First, because Jews had traditionally been both demonized and victimized by Christian societies seeking a scapegoat for their imperfections. Second, although the Enlightenment reduced religious antisemitism to a fringe element, the philosophes retained considerable antipathy toward Jews. This antipathy was partly rooted in the philosophes' critique of organized Christianity, which was seen as the ultimate victory of Jewish morality over Greek aesthetics. Ironically, this hatred of Jews was expressed in rhetoric that echoed traditional Christian antisemitism, paradoxically taken straight from the teachings of the same Christian church that the philosophes publicly scorned. This was especially true of Voltaire's condemnation of Jewish usury, but may also be discerned in the writings of other members of the French and German Enlightenment. Third, was the inescapable appearance of Jewish "success" in the modern world. Previously outsiders, Jews had been emancipated as a result of the changes in European politics in the eighteenth and nineteenth centuries and now entered the very heart of European society. Emancipation, was supposed to lead to the Jews' disappearance, but instead had resulted in the "Judaization" of society. In order to reach the millennium, these social critics argued, society had to be "de-Judaized," returning it to its pristine form by creating a "new" ghetto, through legislation strictly segregating Jews and protecting society at large from their harmful effects, and through a return to the old pagan Nordic values.

Such agitation put antisemitism on the political agenda in Germany and France during the last decades of the nineteenth century.[16] Between 1870 and 1900 antisemitism merged with a new and popular pseudo-science, Social Darwinism. Although most antisemites adopted racism because of their *a priori* antisemitism, and not vice versa, they adopted an ideology that had developed over the nineteenth century and turned it into a eugenic science. Basically, the racists argued, humanity was not a totality that originated from a common root. Rather, they assumed the existence of different races (much as there are different breeds of animals linked by a common genus), with one race, the Aryan (Nordic) race, being superior and the others inferior. Society was seen as diseased because of racial intermingling, which explained the Jewish rise to prominence. Jews, however, were not merely a lower race but represented an anti-race. They were identified as bacilli and cancer; just as a bacillus infects its victim, Jews infected European society and just as the only response to physical disease is to attempt to exterminate the bacilli, so too the only response to the crisis of European society was to eliminate the cause, the Jews.[17]

When combined with racism and Social Darwinism, antisemitism became a potent and potentially violent ideology. At the turn of the twentieth century a further justification was added to this ideology: the so-called Jewish conspiracy theory. As developed by the authors of *The Protocols of the Elders of Zion*, this theory holds that Jews seek world dominion, using both liberal capitalism and revolutionary socialism as tools to manipulate the political life of Europe. In addition, Jewish financiers were attempting to gain control of Europe's finances. Together, the ultimate goal of this conspiracy, variously attributed to the Rothschilds, the Bleichroders, and Theodor Herzl, was to create and cement Jewish domination over the entire world.[18]

The Jewish conspiracy theory may be seen as the ultimate development of the position of antisemites regarding the "Judaization" of society. However, one major difference existed. Whereas the critics held that society had already been "Judaized," since even Christianity (as then organized) represented the victory of Jewish morality, the conspiracy theorists held that the process of Judaization had not yet been completed. Regardless, both positions held that de-Judaization was still possible, indeed morally imperative. accomplishing the goal required the adoption of a conscious program designed to remove the Jews from all influential positions in politics, economics, and culture and to encourage them to emigrate. The creation of such a program required that antisemitism become the operative ideology of a government and resulted in the growth of antisemitic political parties as well as the

rise of professional antisemitic rabble-rousers.[19]

Failure of Emancipation in Eastern Europe

Conditions in Eastern Europe diverged widely from the Western European model for almost the entire nineteenth century. While *Haskala* took root in the Russian empire, emancipation never progressed beyond the most rudimentary stages. The failure of emancipation in Eastern Europe became most apparent after 1880. In particular, the pogroms that spread throughout Russia in 1881–1882 in the wake of Czar Alexander II's assassination by Narodnik (populist) terrorists proved to be a watershed. The government response to the pogroms, which were neither planned nor supported by the authorities in St. Petersburg (unlike later outbursts, which were government sponsored), included a series of laws designed to further limit Jewish rights.[20] These so-called May Laws essentially undermined any future possibility for emancipation on the Western European model while emphasizing the permanent second-class status of all Jews in the Russian empire.[21]

Combined with the increasing demographic and economic pressures on East European Jewry in this era, in 1900 an estimated five million Jews lived in the Russian empire under conditions of immense economic deprivation, the failure of Western-style emancipation was destined to have an important impact on the entire Jewish world. Moreover, conditions did not improve. To the contrary, the last twenty years of the czarist regime were extremely difficult for the Russian Jewish community, which faced numerous pogroms and further depredations caused by war (both the Russo-Japanese War and World War I) and revolution (the abortive Revolution of 1905 and the two revolutions of 1917). After the humiliation of the Russian army in the Russo-Japanese War (1903–1905), Jews became virtual scapegoats for all the difficulties experienced by the empire. This process culminated in the unleashing of the so-called Black Hundreds and climaxed in the Beilis trial of 1913.[22]

Mendel Beilis, a Jewish factory worker from Kiev, was accused of ritual murder in March

1911, when a young Christian boy was found killed. The boy had died in the early spring in close proximity of the Jewish holiday Passover, giving rise to rumors that Jews used Christian blood and renewing the age-old — but largely discredited — accusation that Jews murder Christian children to reenact the Crucifixion. Eschewing a proper investigation, local police authorities, acting upon Interior Ministry orders, arrested Beilis and he was placed on trial. That the Beilis trial was to be a show trial was obvious to all. All Jews were figuratively said to be sitting in the dock. Somewhat surprisingly, the Russian government chose not to air its most recently created antisemitic canard — a Jewish conspiracy to take over the world. Despite the prosecutors' best efforts, Beilis was cleared of all charges. Nonetheless, his personal victory did not augur well for Russian Jewry as a whole.[23]

From Emancipation to Auto-Emancipation

Under the circumstances, Jews in both Eastern and Western Europe were forced to respond to an ever increasing crescendo of antisemitism. Given the divided nature of Jewish communities, it is not surprising that arguments arose over the best means to respond to the crisis. Broadly speaking, Western European Jews responded to antisemitism in one of two ways: first, through complete abasement and total assimilation (which implied the complete abandonment of all forms of Jewish identity) or, second, through the defense of Jews' legal rights and an assertion of the need to foster Jewish self-respect and the right to be different.

Neither of these alternatives fit the specific circumstances facing Eastern European Jewry. Assimilation was not a realistic option, considering the large size of the Russian Jewish population and their cultural distinctiveness (despite increasing secularization during the nineteenth century). Defense of Jewish rights also proved to be a dead end, since it was impossible to defend what the Jewish community lacked almost entirely

(civil rights). Furthermore, the czarist regime proved extremely resistant to external pressure, leaving almost no other option for Jews save emigration.[24] As a result, emigration became the primary means for Jewish self-defense in the latter third of the nineteenth century. Between 1881 and 1914 emigration became a mass movement, with an estimated 2 million Jews quitting the Russian empire for America and hundreds of thousands of others leaving for other destinations.[25]

Migration offered one solution to the growing Jewish problem. But, demographic realities meant that despite mass migration, millions of Jews remained in the Russian empire and eked out a living under difficult conditions. These conditions, in turn, worsened over the last thirty years of the czarist regime. Furthermore, even if it had been possible to remove all Jews to a safe haven, such resettlement would have solved only one of the two distinct, but interrelated problems identified by Jewish thinkers in late nineteenth century Russia: the problem of Jewry — which derived from the economic, political, and physical insecurity of diaspora Jewry — and the problem of Judaism — which derived from the postemancipation effort to find a new definition of Judaism for a largely secular audience.[26]

Most contemporaries believed that the latter problem — finding a way to redefine Judaism for the modern age — was more important. The simple, and seemingly logical progression was that if emancipation and tradition were viewed as polar opposites (which they largely were), then Russian Jewry lived in a state of suspended animation. Russian Jewry had not been emacipated since the Russian government steadfastly refused to budge on Jewish rights, but it was not able to return to the traditional mores of Jewish communal life because they no longer offered meaningful answers to the questions of the day.[27] That being the case, a new definition of Judaism was needed. In this milieu Jewish intellectuals began to discuss some form of Jewish self-emancipation through a return to Jewish nationalism. As more fully developed in the last decade of the nineteenth century, this self-emancipatory trend split into three streams: Folkism, Bundism, and Zionism.

The ideology of Folkism, was developed in large part by the historian Simon Dubnow, who held that Jews are indeed a nation and that all Jews are connected by bonds of nationality. However, Jews are a spiritual nation and their national consciousness requires no specific territory. Dubnow derived his concept of Jewish nationalism from what he saw as a sociohistorical viewpoint. According to his theory all nations evolve through three stages: The first, is the tribal stage; the second is the territorial stage; the third and most developed, is the stage of a spirit nation.[28] Jewry, having attained the third stage (which all nations would certainly attain in time), could easily accept the conversion of the Russian empire into a "state of nationalities" wherein their rights would be guaranteed.[29] The upshot of Dubnow's diaspora nationalism was to emphasize the need for Jews to reorganize their communal structure on a regional and international scale while also attaining recognition of Jewry's right to cultural autonomy in Eastern Europe. "Jews in every country," it followed, would "take an active part in civic and political life [and] enjoy all rights given to citizens, not merely as individuals, but also as members of their national group."[30] Cognizant of Jewry's need for a national center, to unify and define the nation, Dubnow proposed that Russia and Poland would serve as the new center, despite the obvious problem that in no part of Eastern Europe did Jews form a majority of the population. Thus, in effect, Dubnow proposed the creation of a Jewish "state within a state," based on individual membership in the community and autonomy for the whole.[31] Dubnow did not consider — until the last years before World War II — the implications of such advocacy, particularly, that autonomism could (and did) exacerbate rather than relieve the problems faced by Jews in a hostile non-Jewish environment.

Whereas Folkism had no specific economic agenda, Bundism was a form of Jewish revolutionary socialist nationalism. Although the early founders of the Bund thought that Jewish nationalism was transitory in nature and that Jews were fated to assimilate out of existence after the advent of socialism, by the late 1890s most Bundists had adopted a posture of unqualified advocacy of diaspora nationalism. Bund ideology held that Jews are a nation whose destiny is to be an ever present minority in European society. Cultural and communal autonomy — the centerpieces of the Folkist political agenda — would be necessary to guarantee Jewish national self-expression; however, true justice for the Jews could be attained only by overthrowing capitalism and replacing it with the type of socialist society predicted by Karl Marx. The Bund, therefore, focused on preparing Jews for revolutionary activity.

Nevertheless, there were two inconsistencies in the Bund's ideology, neither of which was apparent in the 1890s. First was the problem of Socialist responses to Jewish requests for autonomy. In August 1903, a meeting of the Central Committee of the All-Russian Social Democratic Party (held in Brussels) rejected requests for autonomy made by the Poles and the Bund, meaning that for the foreseeable future the main nationalist part of the Bundist agenda was unattainable even under the best circumstances. Second, was the tension between nationalism and socialism that derived from the fact that a nationalist party must represent all elements of the national group, irrespective of their class. As a socialist revolutionary party, however, the Bund was committed to a policy of class warfare and the overthrow of all capitalists. Left unstated was the Bund's attitude toward Jewish capitalists, although the problem would not become apparent until after the 1917 Bolshevik Revolution in Russia. In 1917 many Bundists defected to the ranks of the victorious Communist Party and abandoned all pretense of a nationalistic orientation.[32]

In contrast to diaspora nationalism, Zionism viewed Jewish life in the diaspora as fundamentally untenable. Eventually a catastrophe of epic proportions would force Jews to quit Europe. In order to avert this catastrophe, Zionists argued that Jews had to do three things. First, Jews had to stop fooling themselves about the possibility of integration into European society. Instead, they had to return to a policy of strengthening Jewish communal bonds and return to a policy of communal (rather than individual) salvation. Second, as a corollary to the first, was the restoration of Jewish sovereignty, preferably in *Eretz Israel*. Third, in the interim, Jews had to fight to protect their rights in order to facilitate the accomplishment of Zionist goals.[33]

The Proto-Zionists

Even before the turning point for Jewish nationalism represented by 1881, a number of visionaries had called for the restoration of the Jewish national home. These so-called Proto-Zionists were individuals whose plans rarely went beyond the point of discussion. Still, they contributed to the rise of Zionism by keeping restoration on the Jewish agenda, even if on a very low level of priority.

Perhaps the earliest Proto-Zionist ("quasi-Zionist" might be a more accurate term) was Mordechai Manuel Noah, the American Jewish political figure and U.S. Consul General in Tunis in 1813 and 1814. After his service in Tunis, Noah returned to discover that — to his chagrin — even in tolerant America, Jews were faced with pressure to convert, adapt, and surrender their Jewishness. Additionally, perhaps extrapolating from his own experience, Noah discovered that elements in the U.S. government did not take a kind view of Jews. Antisemitism weighed heavily on his mind when, in 1818, he proposed that the world's 7 million Jews band together and "march in triumphant numbers, and possess themselves once more of Syria, and take their rank among the governments of Earth."[34] If it proved impossible for all the Jews to move at once to Syria, by which Noah apparently meant the areas of the Fertile Crescent associated with biblical Israel, then they should field an army of 100,000 men for the conquest of their ancestral homeland.[35]

Although his first scheme for Jewish restoration came to nought, Noah was undeterred. In 1844 he proposed that a Jewish national territory be created in northern

New York State, in a place he fancifully dubbed Ararat: along the Niagara River astride the U.S.–Canadian border (near present-day Buffalo, New York).[36] If Noah's earlier scheme shared much of the later Zionist movement's rhetoric, this scheme paralleled a different development that demonstrated one Zionist weakness: in his zeal to find a territory, any territory, as an asylum for tempest-tossed Jewry, Noah paralleled the late arguments over Territorialism. Insofar as Zionism sought an immediate answer for Jewish homelessness the Zionist movement would have to grapple with the question of whether a Jewish national home could exist outside of *Eretz Israel*. The argument between advocates of immediate refuge versus advocates of a singular focus on Jewry's ancestral homeland began in earnest in 1906 and culminated in the first of many schisms between Zionists and self-styled Territorialists.[37]

A year before Noah publicized his Ararat scheme, Rabbi Yehuda Alkalai, a young spiritual leader of the Jewish community in Semlin, Serbia, renewed the call for restoration to the Jewish national home. In Semlin, Alkalai witnessed a succession of events — beginning with the successful wars of independence waged by Greece and Serbia against the Ottoman Empire and culminating with the Damascus Blood Libel. The logic of events surrounding him brought Alkalai to propose a traditional but activist endeavor to restore Jewish sovereignty.

In his book *Minhat Yehuda* (Judah's offering, 1843) Alkalai set out the ideological and organizational elements needed to carry his plan through. First, Alkalai argued that Jewish action to begin the redemption, long rejected by the rabbis (because of the dangers inherent in such action and the crushing disappointment that followed the collapse of each succesive false messianic movement), was not only *Halachically* permissable but necessary. Divine intervention in the process of redemption would not, according to Alkalai's analysis, begin until at least 22,000 Jews lived in *Eretz Israel*. Divine completion of the redemption would occur only after this initial wave had settled the Holy Land.[38]

Alkalai identified this first phase of redemption with the traditional concept of Messiah Ben-Joseph, that is, an early and incomplete redemption.[39] However, even the second phase of redemption would play itself out gradually and by natural means. "This new redemption will — alas, because of our sins — be different," Alkalai wrote, "Our land is waste and desolate . . . the land must, by degrees, be built up and pre-pared."[40] Only then would the divine enter the picture, with the appearance of Messiah Ben-David, signalling Jewry's complete redemption.

If Alkalai's concept was novel in some respects, it was also completely conventional and stood well within the boundaries of traditional orthodox messianic postures.[41] At the same time, however, Alakali used this conventional veneer as a frame built around some very novel — even radical — organi-zational ideas. It was obvious to Alakali that a Jewish military campaign to liberate the Holy Land was out of the question. Instead, he proposed that Jewish notables create an agency (which he dubbed the *Keren Kayemet*, a name that was later used by the World Zionist Organization) to purchase land in *Eretz Israel* from the Ottoman Porte, thereby permitting the first stage of redemption to begin. "The organization of an international Jewish body," Alkalai wrote (almost prophetically), "is in itself the first step to the Redemption, for out of this organization there will come a fully authorized assembly of elders, and from the elders, The Messiah Son of Joseph will appear."[42]

Likewise, Alkalai proposed that Jews must reform their educational priorities. In particular, he suggested that Jews had to return to daily use of Hebrew rather than Yiddish or Ladino (a Judeo-Spanish dialect popular among Sephardi Jews living in the Balkans). Here again, Alkalai couched a radical impulse, laying the cultural foun-dations for renewed Jewish statehood, in purely religious terms. Prophecy, widely accepted as a prerequisite for the arrival of the Messianic era could not be restored until Hebrew became the Jews' daily language once again. To prove his point, Alakali quoted Joel 2:28 to the effect that in the messianic age boys and girls would prophesy. Alkalai linked this with Maimonides' well-known pronounce-ment that prophecy could only occur in Hebrew, concluding that Jews had to "redouble our efforts to maintain Hebrew and to strenthen its position. It must be the basis of [all] our educational work."[43]

Despite the intensity of his feelings, Alkalai's proposals led nowhere. His immediate impact was felt only within a limited circle of tradition-minded scholars and did not resonate within the larger Jewish community. About twenty years later, another rabbi also formulated a restorationist call based on the synthesis of Jewish tradition and modern nationalism. Rabbi Zvi Hirsch Kalischer's *Drishat Zion* (Seeking Zion, 1863) was conceptually similar to Alakali's call to action. Kalischer, like Alakali, served as a rabbi in a traditional Jewish community on the border between emancipated Western European Jewry and unemancipated Eastern European Jewry, in this case in the Polish town of Posen (then ruled by Prussia). Like Alkalai, Kalischer saw a rising nationalist tide around him and drew some obvious conclusions. Unlike Alkalai, however, Kalischer's Proto-Zionism also derived, at least in part, from another source: fear of the Reform movement.

In Kalischer's estimation, assimilation posed the greatest danger to the Jewish community. Abetted by well-meaning *Maskilim* and by re-formers bent on changing Judaism and denying its essence, assimilationists were destroying the foundations for Jewish survival. Equally prob-lematic, however, was the orthodox response to this threat — turning inward and attempting to insulate the observant community from the ill effects of modernity. Kalischer saw this effort as doomed to failure because it was a negative response to the problem, whereas a positive response was also needed. The only positive rejoinder that made sense to Kalischer was a return to *Eretz Israel*. Restoration would provide a project that would galvanize Jewry and revive the positive elements of the Jewish tradition. Moreover, assimilationist pressures would be considerably reduced in a Jewish society.

Kalischer's analysis of assimilation was novel. In his estimation, the reason Jews sought to assimilate was the perception (largely correct) that full participation in the national, social, economic, and intellectual life of the countries in which they lived was incompatible with a traditional Jewish lifestyle. Accordingly, the creation of a vibrant and modern Jewish national entity would funnel Jews' creative energies into a positive goal and reduce the tension inherent in diaspora living. Hence assimilationist tendencies would be weakened. Restoration, and only restoration, would be sufficiently powerful to draw the attention of enough Jews to make a substantial difference.[44]

Upon this foundation, Kalischer proposed creation of a fund for land purchases and settlement building, setting his ideas out in much the same way Alkalai did. Kalischer also proposed the creation of an agricultural school to train young Jews for productive labor after the creation of the Jewish national home.[45] Kalischer also went to great lengths to prove that all his proposals were consistent with traditional messianism. Instead of undermining the tradition, Kalischer asserted, his proposal was designed to hasten the Messiah's arrival. He cited selected verses from the book of Isaiah, which, he claimed, proved that:

> The redemption of Israel, for which we long, is not to be imagined as a sudden miracle . . . On the contrary, the Redemption will begin by . . . the gathering of some of the scattered of Israel into the Holy Land.[46]

An element exclusive to Kalischer's analysis — far different from Alakali and virtually unseen in the writings of Kalischer's friend and colleague Rabbi Meir Laibush Malbim — was one further justification for his Proto-Zionism: the rising tide of European nationalism.[47] The experience of nationalists fighting and sacrificing for an ideal — in Poland (whose abortive 1863 uprising Kalischer witnessed firsthand) and Italy — fired Kalischer's imagination. In a searing response to the events around him, Kalischer wrote:

> Why do the people of Italy and other countries sacrifice their lives for the land of their fathers, while we, like men bereft of strength and courage, do nothing? Are we inferior to all other peoples, who have no regard for life and fortune as compared with love of their   land and nation? . . . We should be ashamed of ourselves! All other peoples have striven only for the sake of their own national honor; how much more should we exert ourselves, for our duty is to labor not only for the glory of our ancestors but for the glory of God who chose Zion![48]

Kalischer's impassioned plea, like Alkalai's, produced no immediate impact. In 1868, Charles Netter, a leader of the Franco-Jewish Alliance Israélite Universelle (AIU), called for the creation of a Jewish agricultural school in Palestine. Although the idea echoed Kalischer's proposal, Netter never directly mentioned the Polish rabbi in his proposals.[49] The AIU followed up on Netter's proposal in 1870, overseeing the construction of an agricultural school at Mikve Israel, located near Jaffa.[50] Despite the implication that *aliya* would follow the creation of the agricultural school, no major changes took place in the orientation of most Jews. A foundation was established, perhaps, but little else.

In the same year that Kalischer published *Drishat Zion*, another author took up the cudgels for the cause of Jewish restoration. Prior to 1863 Moses Hess had been more closely associated with socialist activities, earning the nickname of "Red Rabbi Moses" or the "Red Rabbi of Berlin." From 1846 to 1848 Hess had even been a close associate of Karl Marx and Friedrich Engels, the fathers of modern communism.[51]

Hess began to reevaluate his stance after the revolutions of 1848. The revolutions in that so-called Year of Freedom had largely failed in their goal of creating democracy and freedom. Hess, exiled in Paris and living with a price on

Moses Hess
Courtesy of the Central Zionist Archives, Jerusalem

his head, began to study a range of subjects beyond the economics and materialist philosophy that were the hallmarks of "scientific socialism." In particular, he studied anthropology and ethnography, arriving at a startling conclusion: socialist internationalism was contrary to human nature. Rather, man's natural state was to be part of a national community. Following the logic of his own conclusions, Hess had to admit that:

After an estrangement of twenty years, . . . A thought which I believed to be forever buried in my heart, has revived anew. It is the thought of my nationality, which is inseparably connected with the ancestral heritage and the memories of the Holy Land, the Eternal City, the birthplace of the belief in the Divine unity of life, as well as the hope in the future brotherhood of man.[52]

Renouncing his previous abandonment of Judaism, Hess proposed a theory directly opposed to his previous internationalism — that Jews constitute a single nation. Furthermore, Jewish nationalism, in Hess's estimation, is indestructable. No matter where they reside, no matter how long they remain there, Jews will always be strangers in any land other than *Eretz Israel*.[53]

Contrary to the reformers and *Maskilim*, Hess rejected the notion that emancipation represented the end of exile. He also rejected the notion, then gaining currency in German Jewish circles (modern and traditional) that Jewry's exile was a divinely inspired Jewish "mission" to teach tolerance to the nations of the world. Hess did accept the premise that Jewry had survived in the exile because of a mission. The mission, however, could not be fulfilled in the exile. Instead, the Jews first had to restore their national home and then fulfill the terms of the mission. Thus the diaspora was not part of the mission, but was merely one aspect of the Jewish reality that had to be accounted for in planning for the mission's fulfillment; indeed, Hess could easily have argued that the mission would have remained the same even if the Jewish Commonwealth had not been detroyed by the Romans in 70 C.E.[54]

Given Hess's previous leanings, it comes as no surprise that he framed his concept of the Jewish mission in socialist terms. Specifically, he claimed that the Jews' mission is to create a new society based on equality for all classes and on the equitable distribution of wealth, without class struggle.[55] "The Jewish people," Hess averred, "will participate in the great historical movement of present-day humanity only when it will have its own fatherland."[56]

Like Alkalai and Kalischer, Hess spoke in messianic terms. Unlike his two predecessors, however, Hess used traditional Jewish messianic yearnings in a manner that was not, strictly speaking, Orthodox. For instance, though Hess paralleled Kalischer's attack on the Reform movement because of its abandonment of Jewish national identity, he did not unequivocally embrace the Orthodox position on cultural and religious issues. Instead, Hess deferred the entire issue until after the creation of a Jewish national home, citing the well-known cliche that "Rome was not built in a day."[57]

Hess did not express a conviction that all Jews would eventually live in Eretz Israel. "We do not mean to imply," he wrote, "a total emigration of the occidental Jews to Palestine."[58] Instead, Hess argued for the creation of a spiritual center for world Jewry that would refocus Jews' creative energies on Eretz Israel, thereby making the creation of a model society possible. At that point, the Jews' mission would have been fulfilled; the Jewish homeland would become "a light to the nations."[59]

Like his earlier counterparts, Hess had little immediate impact. Most Jews still sought their future security in personal salvation via emancipation rather than in some seemingly dubious national enterprise. Although the Proto-Zionists lacked an institutional framework to carry out their proposals, two critical developments transpired during the middle decades of the nineteenth century to keep the Proto-Zionist idea alive and place Jewish nationalism on a firmer (but still weak) foundation. The first, already mentioned, was the opening of the Mikve Israel agricultural school. The second had its roots in the 1840s, but culminated in the late 1860s.

In Damascus in 1840, the murder of a Cappuchin Monk under mysterious circumstances shortly before Passover led to a renewed accusation that Jews use Christian blood to bake Matzas. Although thoroughly discredited, as an utter distortion of all Jewish law, Blood Libels of this sort continued to crop up from time to time. A Jewish barber was soon arrested by the local Ottoman authorities and was subjected to torture. He subsequently confessed and implicated leaders of the Damascus Jewish community, all of whom were soon arrested and imprisoned. The police had been egged on by the French consul general, who sought to parlay the incident into greater French influence in the area during a very fluid period (the Egyptian leader Mehmet Ali had

declared independence from the Ottomans in 1839 and had invaded Syria shortly before the incident).[60] The Damascus Blood Libel soon became an international cause célèbre. The Austrians and British — both of whom sought to reduce French influence in the Fertile Crescent and increase their own — sought to intervene on behalf of the accused Jews. The British went so far as to open a consulate in Jerusalem with the consul specifically ordered to monitor the fate of the accused and, more broadly, to observe the status of Jews in the Ottoman Empire.[61] In the end, justice was done: all the accused were released when the monk's valet came foreward and confessed that the murder had been a falling out among thieves — the monk had been dealing in bogus religious artifacts.

By coincidence, renowned Anglo-Jewish financier Sir Moses Montefiore was then in the Holy Land on a pilgrimage. Shocked by the appalling poverty of the Jerusalem Jews, Montefiore sought support from other Jewish philanthropists in Western Europe for a massive development project. In particular, Montefiore proposed collecting sufficient funds to build textile mills, powered by a series of windmills, to give the Jewish community the means to "productivize." In anticipation of the project coming to fruition, Montefiore himself donated the funds to build one windmill and the first Jewish neighborhood outside the walls of the Old City (now called Yemin Moshe).[62] Between 1860 and 1880 further efforts were made by European philanthropists and by Jews in *Eretz Israel*. Among the local efforts, the organization called Avodat ha-Adama ve-Geulat ha-Aretz (Agricultural work and restoration of the land) was most significant. Founded in 1876, Avodat ha-Adama began to use some of the funds collected for the so-called *Haluka* (distribution, a form of welfare provided by European Jewish charities for the upkeep of indigent religious Jews living in the Old Yishuv) to purchase land for Jewish agricultural settlements. The first settlement thus created was in Petah Tikva in 1878.[63] However, construction was halted after Montefiore's windmill was completed and none of the factories he planned had been started when he died in 1885. Similarly, Petah Tikva, settled in 1878, was abandoned soon thereafter because of its insecure position; The "Mother of Agricultural Settlements" was not reinhabited until 1883.

Hibbat Zion

The pogroms of 1881–1882 transformed the status of Jewish nationalism as East European Jews rethought and abandoned the emancipationist ideology they had worked with for the previous half century.[64] The pogroms helped to consolidate all the forms of Jewish nationalism described above and spurred the 1884 creation of the first full-fledged Zionist movement, known popularly as Hibbat Zion (Love of Zion).[65] Hibbat Zion's ideological father was Dr. Leon Pinsker, a member of the Russian Jewish intellectual elite who had advocated assimilation as the answer to the Jewish problem in the decades before the pogroms. Pinsker, a medical doctor, was disappointed by the pogroms and, more significantly, by the positive attitude expressed by Russian intellectuals to the pogromists. In response, Pinsker wrote *Auto-Emancipation*, at once an impassioned *cri de coeur* and a plan for future Jewish action.[66]

In Pinsker's estimation, the pogroms were nothing new in Jewish history, since the "Jewish question stirs men today as it did ages ago."[67] The foundation of the Jewish problem in Pinsker's view was that the Jew "is everywhere a guest, and nowhere *at home*."[68] Pinsker's analysis had a more than passing resemblance to that of Simon Dubnow, especially in its emphasis on the spiritual nature of Jewish nationalism. However, one major difference existed in Pinsker's view, as opposed to Dubnow's. What Dubnow saw as a positive, namely, that Jews had passed the phase of territorial nationalism, Pinsker saw as a negative. Jewish disconnectedness from land was seen by the non-Jewish world as an anomaly not a higher form of nationalism. Thus, Pinsker turned Dubnow's analysis on its ear. The

"Spirit Nation" could, just as easily, be seen as a ghost nation and Pinsker easily related the fear and loathing of ghosts to the fear and loathing that characterized antisemitism. According to Pinsker's analysis, moreover, antisemitism has biological and psychological — not theological or religious — foundations. In line with contemporary psychological science, Pinsker felt that antisemitism was a hereditary disease that could be (and was) passed from generation to generation.[69] The doctor's prognosis was as simple as it was unequivocal:

> For the living the Jew is a dead man; for the natives, an alien and a vagrant; for property holders, a beggar; for the poor, an exploiter and a millionaire; for patriots, a man without a country; for all classes, a hated rival.[70]

Pinsker's straightforward analysis received an apathetic response from Western European Jews, especially the philanthropists Pinsker hoped would help realize his ideas. But, some Jews in Eastern Europe enthusiastically embraced the idea of creating a Jewish national home in some part of the globe. Although Pinsker had nowhere mentioned *Eretz Israel* in *Auto-Emancipation*, he was soon sufficiently involved in the movement that he accepted the premise that all his work (and that of the organization) ought to concentrate on the goal of restoring the Jewish people to Palestine.[71] The immediate next step was convening a conference in Kattowitz (Katowice, then Prussian Poland) on November 6, 1884, where the Hibbat Zion movement came into being.

Hibbat Zion (HZ) was dedicated to taking steps to further Jewish settlement in *Eretz Israel* with the ultimate goal of attaining some form of Jewish autonomy in the region. HZ was organized on a local level, with affiliated groups differing in size and, in some cases, ideology. Western European and the U.S. affiliates, for instance, were usually organized on a nationwide basis and concentrated on philanthropy. By contrast, Eastern European affiliates tended to be local groups and were more *aliya* oriented.[72]

Pinsker and his associates, in turn, established the Society for the Support of Jewish Farmers

Participants in the Kattowitz Conference, November 6, 1884.
Dr. Leon Pinsker is Seated in the Front Row, Center.
Courtesy of the Central Zionist Archives, Jerusalem

and Artisans in Syria and Palestine, better known as the Odessa Committee, which was recognized by the czarist authorities as a charity in 1890.[73] By the time the Russian authorities fully accredited HZ, it comprised 138 local chapters with perhaps as many as 14,000 members.[74] HZ ideology contained many nuances, but, the most basic premises of HZ doctrine were accepted by all members. As framed by Rabbi Mordechai Eliasberg, these basic premises included:

A) To establish colonies and villages, with our brother Jews working the land and guarding it . . .
B) To build factories equipped with machines to produce goods . . .

C) To develop trade in Eretz Israel and outside to export wines and oils, in addition to other fruits . . .
D) To settle there simple skilled laborers to produce items needed by all the settlers, such as houses, household items, clothes, shoes, and the like.[75]

As the organization began to crystalize, some HZ members sought to realize the call for renewed *aliya*. This group, composed mainly of college educated Russian Jewish youth, formed the movement known as Bilu — an acronym derived from the Hebrew initials of their motto, *"Beit Yaakov Lehu ve-Nelha"* (House of Jacob arise and go).[76] Hoping to lead the Jewish renaissance by personal example, the Biluim set out for *Eretz Israel*: by the time of the Kattowitz conference, Bilu had established two colonies — at Rishon le-Zion and Gedera — while other groups of Russian, Polish, and Romanian Jews had established settlements in Zichron Ya'akov (originally called Samarin), Rosh Pina, Yesod ha-Maale, and Nes Ziona.[77] Bilu managed a number of important accomplishments. By the end of the First *Aliya* (1903), almost 25,000 *olim* (immigrants) had settled in *Eretz Israel*. Jews held a total of 400,000 dunams of land in *Eretz Israel* (about 1.5 percent of the total land mass) and, beside the four traditional Jewish settlements of Jerusalem, Hebron, Safed, and Tiberias, a new Jewish community was created in the port city of Jaffa. Finally, twenty-three settlements and seven hundred independent farms held approximately 6,000 settlers.[78]

Impressive as these accomplishments were, however, many insurmountable difficulties existed for this new *Yishuv*. First, financial difficulties abounded. On September 19, 1886, Pinsker distributed a searing circular letter to all HZ societies summarizing income to that date: a mere 16,000 rubles collected and sent to the settlements. Much more had been pledged but not collected, and debts were piling up.[79] HZ's inability to distribute sufficient funds left the Bilu settlers in a precarious financial position.

Second, few (if any) of the Bilu settlers were actually prepared for the heavy burden of agricultural work. They possessed more enthusiasm than training and were, for the most part, unused to the great physical exertion demanded of agricultural workers. Furthermore, conditions in *Eretz Israel* could not have been less conducive. Two thousand years of war, backward farming methods, and erosion had left most of the country an unproductive wasteland. Far from flowing with "milk and honey," most of the country was barren desert. Malarial swamps covered whatever had not been swallowed by the desert, and disease and hardship were the daily rule of life. Furthermore, the entire country was exposed to frequent depredations by Bedouin raiders.[80] Finally, the

Ottoman authorities were another hurdle to overcome. Beset by friend and foe alike who took large chunks of Ottoman territory over the course of the nineteenth century, the Turks could hardly have welcomed the influx of Jews to a border district; the fact that most of these Jews originated in the Russian Empire, the Ottomans' traditional enemy certainly did not help matters.[81]

Of the problems faced by the Biluim, and by those who followed in their footsteps, only the financial problems were ever adequately solved, but not by HZ. The facts of *Eretz Israel*'s geographic and physical condition could not be addressed immediately; neither could the complication posed by Ottoman obstruction of *aliya*, which was lifted only when the Turks lost control of Palestine following World War I (and it should be borne in mind that unfettered *aliya* only became a reality with the creation of the State of Israel in 1948). An additional problem, Jewish relations with the Arabs of Palestine, only became clear as Bilu's settlement projects expanded and also found no immediate solution.

Again, only one of these problems was solved before HZ collapsed altogether. Although French banker and philanthropist Baron Edmond de Rothschild had originally rejected pleas to support colonization schemes in *Eretz Israel*, he eventually accepted the fait accompli and began to assist the settlers. By 1884, four of the seven Bilu settlements continued to operate only thanks to Rothschild's financial assistance. This aid was decisive — and earned Rothschild the sobriquet *ha-Nadiv ha-Yadua* (the well-known patron) — but was not without controversy. In particular the bureaucracy created to distribute funds and the heavy-handed tactics of the "advisers" that Rothschild insisted should oversee the settlements led to much friction. In Rishon le-Zion, for instance, controversy began in 1883, the same year in which Rothschild began to aid the colony. By 1887 the controversy had flared into open mutiny against both Rothschild and his overseers. Similar mutinies broke out in Zichron Yaakov (1888) and Ekron (1888–1892). The Ekron mutiny ended only when Rothschild asserted his complete ownership of the entire settlement (including the land it was built on), threatening to remove the settlers.[82]

Despite the ongoing controversies Rothschild's accomplishments cannot be underestimated. Without his assistance the Bilu settlements would have collapsed and Zionism would have remained a stillborn ideal, unfulfilled and unfulfillable. Furthermore, for all their high-handedness, Rothschild's experts did greatly contribute to the establishment of Israel's agricultural economy in its earliest years.[83] Rothschild himself withdrew from direct stewardship of the settlements in 1899 — due mainly to health considerations — and transferred them to the resposibility of the Jewish Colonization Association (better known by its Yiddish initials, ICA).[84] The resulting new body, called the Palestine Jewish Colonization Association (PICA) remained aloof from Zionist affairs, but continued its important work in settlement building and land purchase between 1900 and 1948.[85]

By the time Rothschild bowed out, neither Bilu nor Hibbat Zion existed. Bilu had been weakened as an organization after a schism in 1883 and collapsed as a settlement movement after the Turks banned *aliya* in 1891.[86] Hibbat Zion had also run its course by the early 1890s. Pinsker died in mid-1891 and the Hibbat Zion Executive collapsed because it could not find a suitable successor. As a result, the first Zionist organization completely withdrew from its main activities, settlement and land purchase, concentrating only on educational and cultural work in the diaspora.[87] The goal of attaining a Jewish *political* revival had thus suffered a setback (albeit a temporary one), but the most important interim goal had been reached: Jewish nationalism had regained its vitality and the search for a means to restore Jewish nationhood had been revived.[88]

Notes

1. The intellectual, social, and political background of European emancipation is described at length in Arthur Hertzberg, *The French Enlightenment and the Jews* (New York: Columbia University Press, 1968) chap. 4, and Jacob Katz, *Out of the Ghetto* (New York: Schocken Books, 1978) chaps. 3–6. On emancipation in the United States, see Salo W. Baron, "The Emancipation Movement and American Jewry," in *Steeled by Adversity: Essays and Addresses on American Jewish Life* (Philadelphia: Jewish Publication Society, 1971), pp. 80–105.

2. Cf. Michael A. Meyer, *The Origins of the Modern Jew* (Detroit: Wayne State University Press, 1979), chaps. 1–2.

3. Cf. Howard M. Sachar, *The Course of Modern Jewish History*, 2d ed. (New York: Dell, 1977), chaps. 3, 5–6.

4. On this aspect of the emancipation, a statement by Stanislaus de Clermont-Tonnerre has often been quoted: "All should be refused the Jews as a nation, but everything granted to them as individuals." Hertzberg, *French Enlightenment*, p. 360.

5. Michael R. Marrus, "Jewry and the Politics of Assimilation: A Reassessment," *Journal of Modern History* 49 (1977): 89–109; George L. Mosse, "Jewish Emancipation: Between *Bildung* and Respectability," in *Confronting the Nation: Jewish and Western Nationalism* (Hanover, NH: University Press of New England for Brandeis University Press, 1993), pp. 131–145.

6. Calvin Goldscheider and Alan S. Zuckerman, *The Transformation of the Jews* (Chicago: University of Chicago Press, 1984), chap. 3.

7. Joseph L. Blau, *Modern Varieties of Judaism* (New York: Columbia University Press, 1964).

8. Jacob R. Marcus, *The Rise and Destiny of the German Jew*, reprint ed. (New York: Ktav, 1973), pp. 106–120, 325.

9. Ibid., chap. 9.

10. Ibid., chap. 7.

11. George L. Mosse, *German Jews Beyond Judaism* (Bloomington: Indiana University Press, 1985).

12. For the typical German Orthodox response to modernity and its implications for Jewish nationalism, see Samson Raphael Hirsch, *Collected Works*, ed. Elliot Bondi and David Bechhofer, (New York: Philipp Feldheim, 1984) 1: 335–349, 385–391, the scattered references throughout the other seven volumes; and Hirsch's essays on the subject in the journal *Jeschurun*. Hirsch's position on redemption—which he saw exclusively in divine terms and dated to a far future—animated the ideology of Agudas Israel, the party founded (among others) by Hirsch's grandson, Rabbi Isaac Breuer. Cf. Alan L. Mittleman, "Some German Jewish Orthodox Attitudes Toward the Land of Israel and the Zionist Movement," *JPSR* 6, no. 3/4 (Fall 1994): 107–125.

13. Michael A. Meyer, *Response to Modernity: A History of the Reform Movement in Judaism* (New York: Oxford University Press, 1988) pp. 208–210 and passim; Fred Krinsky, the Renascent Jewish Nationalism: A Study of its Leading Concepts and Practices (Ph.D. diss: University of Pennsylvania, 1951), pp. 41–43.

14. Werner E. Mosse, "Problems and Limits of Assimilation: Hermann and Paul Wallich, 1833–1938," *Leo Baeck Institute Yearbook* [hereafter *LBIYB*], 33 (1988): 43–65; Hannah Arendt, "The Jew as Pariah: A Hidden Tradition," *Jewish Social Studies* [hereafter *JSS*], 6, no. 2 (1944): 99–122; and Werner Jochmann, "The Jews and German Society in the Imperial Era," *LBIYB* 20 (1975): 5–11.

15. Jacob Katz, *From Prejudice to Destruction, 1700–1933* (Cambridge: Harvard University Press), 1980, passim.

16. Cf. Alex Bein, *The Jewish Question: Biography of a World Problem* (Rutherford, NJ: Fairleigh Dickinson University Press/ Herzl Press, 1990), chaps. 5–6.

17. For an extensive study into European racism, see George L. Mosse, *Toward the Final Solution: A History of European Racism* (New York: Harper Colophon Books, 1978).

18. Norman Cohn, *Warrant for Genocide* (New York: Harper and Row, 1966); and Binjamin W. Segel, *A Lie and a Libel* (Lincoln: University of Nebraska Press), 1995 (based on a German work published in 1926), remain the standard analyses of the *Protocols*.

19. Cf. Peter J. Pulzer, *The Rise of Politcal Antisemitism in Germany and Austria*, rev. ed. (Cambridge: Harvard University Press), 1988.

20. Louis Greenberg, *The Jews in Russia: The Struggle for Emancipation* (New York: Schocken Books), 1976, 1: chaps. 3–9.

21. A complete list of the May Laws was published in Bernard K. Johnpoll, "Why They Left: Russian-Jewish Mass Migration and Repressive Laws, 1881–1917," *American Jewish Archives* 47, no. 1 (Spring/Summer 1995): 17–54.

22. This (necessarily brief) survey of Russian Jewish history is based on Greenberg, *Jews of Russia*, passim; Salo W. Baron, *The Russian Jews Under Tsars and Soviets* (New York: Macmillan, 1976); Stephen M. Berk, *Year of Crisis, Year of Hope: Russian Jewry and the Pogroms of 1881–1882* (Westport, Conn.: Greenwood Press, 1985: and John D. Klier and Shlomo Lambroza, eds., *Pogroms: Anti-Jewish Violence in Modern Russian History* (New York: Cambridge University Press, 1992).

23. Maurice Samuel, *Blood Accusation* (New York: Knopf, 1965); and Ezekiel Leikin ed., *The Beilis Transcript* (Northvale, NJ: Jason Aronson, 1993).

24. For Russian Jewry in this era, in addition to the sources cited in note 23, see: John D. Klier, *Imperial Russia's Jewish Question, 1855-1881* (New York: Cambridge University Press, 1995); Ellen S. Cannon, "The Political Culture of Russian Jewry During the Second Half of the Nineteenth Century," Ph.D. diss., University of Massachusetts, 1974. Regarding efforts abroad to convince the Russians to ease conditions for Russian Jewry, see Cyrus Adler ed., *The Voice of America on Kishineff* (Philadephia: Jewish Publication Society, 1904); and Gary D. Best, *To Free a People* (Westport, Conn.: Greenwood Press, 1982).

25. Mark Wischnitzer, *To Dwell in Freedom* (Philadelphia: Jewish Publication Society, 1948), chap. 2–4.

26. Cf. Krinsky, "Renascent Jewish Nationalism," pp. 8–9, 13–15, and Leon Simon, ed., *Selected Essays of Ahad ha-Am* (New York: Atheneum, 1962), passim.

27. In addition to Ahad ha-Am's already cited essays, see the selections of Russian Jewish intellectuals cited in Arthur Hertzberg ed., *The Zionist Idea* (New York: Atheneum, 1969), pp. 248–277. An incisive new analysis of the ideological origins of Jewish nationalism was provided by David H. Weinberg, *Between Tradition and Modernity* (New York: Holmes and Meier, 1996). For a literary perspective reflecting the alienated position of Jewish intellectuals, see Haim Nachman Bialik, "El ha-Zippor" (To the Bird), "Al Saf Bet ha-Midrash" (At the Study Hall's Doorpost), and "Ha-Matmid" (The Student), in שירים (Poems) (Tel Aviv: Dvir, 1967), pp. 9–11, 32–35, and 313–333, respectively.

28. Simon Dubnow, *Nationalism and History: Essays on the Old and New Judaism*, Koppel S. Pinson, ed. (Philadelphia: Jewish Publicaton Society, 1958), p. 76.

29. Ibid., p. 97.

30. Ibid., p. 137.

31. Ibid., pp. 48–49.

32. In addition to Weinberg, *Tradition*, chap. 2, see Nora Levin, *While Messiah Tarried: Jewish Socialist Movements, 1871–1917* (New York: Schocken Books, 1977) and Emanuel Scherer, "Bundism," in *Struggle For Tomorrow*, Feliks Gross and Basil J. Vlavianos, eds. (New York: Arts Incorporated, 1954), pp. 135–196.

33. Cf. Yitzhak Korn, *The Centrality of Israel — A National Imperative* (Tel Aviv: World Labor Zionist Movement, 1974), pp. 4–5. We have kept these formulations deliberately vague; as will be seen in the chapters that follow, almost every aspect of Zionist ideology was open to a variety of nuances and intense argumentation.

34. Noah's sermon of April 17, 1818, at the She'erit Israel Congregation, cited in Peter Grose, *Israel in the Mind of America* (New York: Schocken Books, 1983), p. 14.

35. Grose, *Mind of America*, pp. 14–15. It is not clear whence Noah derived the figure of 100,000 men.

36. A brief review of Noah's Ararat scheme was written by Tuviah P. Schapiro in 1891 and is quoted, verbatim, in Jacob Kabakoff, "Some East European Letter on Emigration," *American Jewish Archives*, 45, no. 1 (Spring/Summer, 1993): 77–80.

37. For more details on the causes and course of the schism with Territorialism, see below: pp. 50–53 and 59–60.

38. Rabbi Yehuda Alkalai, מנחת יהודה (Judah's Offering), cited in Arthur Hertzberg, ed., *The Zionist Idea: A Historical Analysis and Reader* (New York: Atheneum, 1976), p. 105. The number 22,000 was derived from BT Yevamot 64a which, in turn, analyzed the verse "Return oh Lord unto the ten thousands and thousands of Israel" (Numbers 10:36). In the view of the Talmudic interpreters the verse had messianic implications and was the answer to the question when would the Shehina (the manifestation of divine grace) return to Israel. That answer was that the Shehina would return when the verse was fulfilled: the twin plurals (ten thousands and thousands, in Hebrew, respectively רבבות and אלפי) meant that two of each numerical category had to be present in Eretz Israel for the prophecy to be fulfilled (2X10,000 + 2X1,000 = 22,000).

39. Hertzberg, *Zionist Idea*, p. 107. Alkalai's discussion was an innovation in rabbinic views of the messianic redemption, especially in his identification of Messiah Ben-Joseph with a process rather than a person. Shlomo Avineri, *The Making of Modern Zionism* (New York: Basic Books, 1981), pp. 51–52, analyzed these new elements, but failed to note the considerable agreement of contemporary Orthodox rabbis with the broad elements of Alkalai's analysis. For evidence of considerable rabbinic acceptance of the concept (if not the specific policy implications of such a belief) that redemption would only occur *after* the Jews had begun the process, see: Chanoch Merhavia, ed., קולות קוראים לציון (Voices Calling for Zion) (Jerusalem: The Zalman Shazar Institue for the Study of Jewish History, 1976), pp. 80–101.

40. Hertzberg, *Zionist Idea*, p. 105.

41. Avineri, *Modern Zionism*, pp. 51–52. Cf. Supra, pp. 5–11.

42. Hertzberg, *Zionist Idea*, p. 107.

43. Ibid., p. 106.

44. Cf. Eliezer Schweid, *The Land of Israel: National Home or Land of Destiny?* (Rutherford, NJ: Fairleigh Dickinson University Press, 1985), p. 100.

45. Avineri, *Modern Zionism*, p. 54.

46. Rabbi Zvi Hirsch Kalischer, דרישת ציון (Seeking Zion), cited in Hertzberg, *Zionist Idea*, p. 110. The specific verses that Kalischer cited were Isaiah 27:6, 12–13.

47. Malbim to Kalischer, 1867 (but otherwise undated), cited in Merhavia, קולות, p. 123.

48. Hertzberg, *Zionist Idea*, p. 114.

49. Cf. Merhavia, קולות, pp. 124–125.

50. Howard M. Sachar, *A History of Israel: From the Rise of Zionism to Our Time* (New York: Alfred A. Knopf, 1976), 1:7.

51. Meyer Waxman, introduction, Moses Hess, *Rome and Jerusalem* (New York: Bloch Publishing, 1943), pp. 21–22. We have used Waxman's edition for all quotes, except in cases where the citations were more easily labelled in Hertzberg, *Zionist Idea*.

52. Hess, *Rome and Jerusalem*, p. 43.

53. Hess repeated this theme a number of times in *Rome and Jerusalem*, e.g., pp. 43, 58–60, and 74–75. Cf. Misha Louvish, *Nineteenth Century Zionist Theories* (Glasgow: University Zionist Federation, 1933), p. 3.

54. Louvish, ibid.

55. Avineri, *Modern Zionism*, pp. 42–45.

56. Hertzberg, *Zionist Idea*, p. 137.

57. Hess, *Rome and Jerusalem*, p. 145.

58. Hertzberg, *Zionist Idea*, p. 138.

59. Hess, *Rome and Jerusalem*, p. 157.

60. For a general discussion of the Damascus Blood Libel, see: Sachar, *Modern Jewish History*, pp. 133–137, Isaiah Friedman, "Lord Palmerston and the Protection of Jews in Palestine, 1839–1851," *JSS*, 30 no. 1 (Winter, 1968): 23–41 looked at the affair from the British perspective as did Meir Vereté, "Why Was A British Consulate Established in Jerusalem?" *English Historical Review*, 85 no. 335 (April, 1970): 316–345.

61. For a full analysis of the role played by the British Consullate, see the items by Friedman and Vereté cited in the previous note along with Albert Hyamson, *The British Consulate in Jerusaelm in Relation to the Jews of Palestine* (London: HMSO, 1939).

62. Montefiore's call, dated 1875, is published in Hebrew in Merhavia, ‫קולות‬, p. 130.

63. On the settlement in Petah Tikva, see: Merhavia, ‫קולות‬, pp. 133–134 and Alex Bein, *The History of Jewish Agricultural Settlement in Palestine*, Jerusalem: Reuven Mass, 1947, pp. 5–6.

64. Cf. Michael Stanislawski, *For Whom Do I Toil? Judah Leib Gordon and the Crisis of Russian Jewry* (New York: Oxford University Press, 1988), ch. 9–10.

65. Some Russian Jewish thinkers had already been using the argument that emancipation had run its course by the 1870s; they, like the Proto-Zionists already discussed, were generally lone voices until after the pogroms. Cf. the citations by Smolenskin and Ben-Yehuda in Hertzberg, *Zionist Idea*, pp. 143–165.

66. Sachar, *History of Israel*, pp. 14–15.

67. Leon Pinsker, *Auto-Emancipation* (1882), cited in Hertzberg, *Zionist Idea*, p. 182.

68. Ibid., p. 183.

69. Ibid., pp. 184–188. Cf. Avineri, *Zionist Idea*, pp. 76–77.

70. Hertzberg, *Zionist Idea*, p. 188.

71. Avineri, *Modern Zionism*, p. 81.

72. David Vital, *The Origins of Zionism* (Oxford: The Clarendon Press, 1975), pp. 147–151.

73. Ibid., p. 175.

74. Ibid., p. 155.

75. Rabbi Mordechai Eliasberg, "‫על דבר ישוב ארץ ישראל‬" (On the matter of settling the Land of Israel, 1889), cited in David Shahar, "‫תפיסתו הציונית והדתית של הרב מרדחי אליאסברג‬" (R. Mordechai Eliasberg's Zionist and Religious Philosophy), ‫כיוונים‬, 26 (February 1985): 101.

76. The name of the movement was derived from Isaiah 2:5. Most historians have followed the convention of using the acronym Bilu when dealing with the group as a whole, reserving the full name for their motto; we too have followed this convention here.

77. Documents elucidating aspects of Bilu's history are published in: Shmuel Yavnieli (ed.), ‫ספר‬ ‫הציונות: תקופת חיבת ציון‬ (Jerusalem: ha-Sifriya ha-Zionit, 1961), vol. 2; Walter Laqueur, ed., *The Israel-Arab Reader* (New York: Bantam Books, 1970), pp. 3–4; and, Isaiah Friedman, ed., *From Precursors of Zionism to Herzl*, Rise of Israel Series, vol. 1, (New York: Garland, 1987), pp. 186–201.

78. Yosef Gorni, *From Rosh Pina and Degania to Demona: A History of Constructive Zionism* (Tel Aviv: MOD Books, 1989), p. 35.

79. Pinsker's letter cited in Friedman, *Precursors of Zionism*, pp. 203–204.

80. Ibid., pp. 209–217, contains a selection of Bilu correspondence on the multifarious problems encountered by the settlers.

81. Cf. Isaiah Friedman, *Germany, Turkey, and Zionism, 1897–1918* (New York: Oxford University Press, 1977), pp. 35–42.

82. Cf. Dan Giladi, "‫הברון רוטשיילד ומשטר החסות של הפקידות‬" (Baron Rothschild and the patronage system of his administration), in ‫ספר העליה הראשונה‬ (The Book of the First *Aliya*),

Mordechai Eliav, ed., (Jerusalem: Yad Ben-Zvi/Israeli Ministry of Defense, 1982), 1: 179–206; Shulamit Laskov, הבילויים (The Biluim) (Jerusalem: ha-Sifriya ha-Zionit, 1979), chap. 3; Simon Schama, *Two Rothschilds and the Land of Israel*, (New York: Alfred A. Knopf, 1978), chap. 3.

83. Giladi, "הברון רוטשילד," pp. 191–194, 204–206.

84. Schama, *Two Rothschilds*, pp. 134–136.

85. Theodore Norman, *An Outstretched Arm: A History of the Jewish Colonization Association* (London: Routledge and Kegan Paul, 1985).

86. Laskov, הבילויים, pp. 140–143, 155–158.

87. Cf. Vital, *Origins*, pp. 184–186.

88. Hibbat Zion continued to exist as a barely functioning organization until 1911. Most members of Hibbat Zion had joined the World Zionist Organization long before that date, however. Ibid., p. 330.

3
THE RISE OF POLITICAL ZIONISM

Ideological Developments, 1891–1896

As the organizational drama of Hibbat Zion played itself out, critical ideological developments unfolded within the Jewish nationalist movement. Perhaps the most critical was the development of the concept of Spiritual Zionism, commonly (and largely correctly) identified with Asher Ginsberg, the Russian Jewish publicist and intellectual best known by the pen name Ahad ha-Am. Reluctantly at first, Ahad ha-Am stridently criticized three aspects of Hibbat Zion. First, he argued that the leadership had not adequately considered what could be accomplished by their movement; second, he felt that such activities as had been undertaken were carried out poorly and in a disorganized fashion; and, third, that the leaders had not properly assessed the real needs in Jewry's time of crisis.[1]

Ahad ha-Am repeated these themes in two main ideological essays, *"Lo Zeh ha-Derech"* (This is not the path, 1889) and *"Emet me-Eretz Israel"* (Truth from the Land of Israel, 1891). His argument may be summarized thus. First, he held as axiomatic the premise that Jews form a nation and that Jewish nationalism is irrevocable. Second, he argued that the modern concept of Jewish nationalism arose because of two crises: the crisis of the Jews (*Zarat ha-Yehudim*) — deriving from Jewry's homelessness and powerlessness — and the crisis of Judaism

(*Zarat ha-Yahadut*) — deriving from the apparent irrelevance of Judaism in the daily lives of most Jews. Whereas Judaism — as framed by halacha and interpreted by Orthodox rabbis — had kept Jewry alive for generations, religion — especially as interpreted by the orthodox — no longer served that unifying role. Indeed, Judaism as a religious experience, far from acting as a unifying factor, played a divisive role in modern Jewry or at best played no role at all in most Jew's daily life. The former was most clearly true in Western Europe, where arguments over Reform Judaism had become ever more bitter; the latter reflected conditions in Eastern Europe where many Jews had simply abandoned Orthodoxy not for Reform but for complete secularization. In light of these conditions, it followed that Jewry's "will to live" was in great danger. Jewish nationalism — or rather the Jewish nationalist movement — had to address this problem.[2] The way to do so was to focus on *"Tehiat ha-Ruah"* (Revival of the spirit).[3]

By distinguishing between a crisis of Jews and a crisis of Judaism, Ahad ha-Am implied that there might be two different solutions to Jewish distress in Eastern Europe. Furthermore, these two solutions — while not necessarily mutually exclusive — required emphasis on one or another of the two crises: it was not possible, in his view to find one encompassing solution for both Jewry and Judaism. Since the crisis of Jewry derived from an external stimulus — antisemitism as reflected in the pogroms in

Russia — Ahad ha-Am could easily argue that a nonnationalist solution, such as mass Jewish migration to a more secure diaspora location (such as the United States), was also viable. Finding a new diaspora, however, did nothing to solve the crisis of Judaism — that was a spiruatual problem that could only be solved by the creation of a new Judaism. The crux of the matter, in Ahad ha-Am's estimation, was that the crisis of Judaism — not the crisis of Jewry — was the more pressing. Left unchecked, the crisis of Judaism would eventually lead to the collapse of the Jewish nation and no number of Jewish national homes could, by themselves, solve the problem.

In addition to his ideological concerns, which were based on concepts of nationalism and national character popular in the latter third of the nineteenth century, Ahad ha-Am saw himself as a lonely voice reminding Jewish nationalists of the many external impediments to the fulfillment of their goals. Whereas most Zionists still spoke of Israel as a land of milk and honey, the reality was far different. Most of the land was uncultivatable; much of what remained was already owned or cultivated by Arabs — they would hardly welcome newcomers by selling land to Jews. Land that could be purchased was, by and large, almost completely infertile, consisting of swampland and the like. This land could be rendered useful only after immense outlays of money and labor. Even then, Ahad ha-Am doubted that enough farm land could be salvaged to create "a permanent, mass settlement of Jews, based on cultivation of soil."[4]

In light of these realities, Ahad ha-Am concluded that the creation of a Jewish national home, even if such a goal was plausible, could never offer a complete answer to Jewry's need for physical security; in other words *Eretz Israel* could never (at least not in the foreseeable future) become a home to the majority of world Jewry. Thus, any effort to create a national home inhabited by all Jews would live would end in failure.[5] However, a clear alternative did exist, and it promised a good chance of

success: creation of a spiritual center populated by an elite segment of Jewish youth. Ahad ha-Am believed that the quality of the settlers, not their quantity, would prove critical to the Zionist undertaking.[6] What Jewry needed was a movement to settle some Jews as pioneers in *Eretz Israel*. They would work on the land and create a vibrant community which in turn would become the cultural and spiritual center for the entire Jewish world, despite the lack of opportunity for most Jews to live in *Eretz Israel*. Ahad ha-Am believed that this would come to pass in much the same way that the Second Commonwealth, which represented only a minority of the Jewish population in the Greco-Roman era, became the central focus for the entire Jewish world. Just as the half-*shekel* paid by all Jews to the Temple treasury had once unified the diaspora, so too now philanthropic work for the spiritual center would reunite the entire Jewish people. Just as *Eretz Israel* had been the center of Jewish intellectual life in the Mishnaic and Talmudic eras, becoming a source for authoritative interpretations of Judaism, so too a vibrant spiritual center would once again rejuvenate and revivify Judaism. By that means the real problem, *Zarat ha-Yahadut*, would be solved; and, by definition, if that problem was solved thus, Ahad ha-Am believed, *Zarat ha-Yehudim* would cease to be a problem.

Given his position, it is not surprising that Ahad ha-Am stressed the educational and cultural roles that he saw Zionism playing over the political and demographic roles on which other Zionists concentrated. The Jewish spirit could be revived if even a small number of Jews relocated to *Eretz Israel*, as long as this resettlement was combined with effective educational efforts.[7] Since Ahad ha-Am felt that *Zarat ha-Yahadut* was the main crisis facing Jewry, he had, in his mind, offered the solution to the problem. "The path of the spirit," he concluded, "cannot be obstructed".[8]

As controversial as Ahad ha-Am's positions were at the time, attempting to assess his role in Zionist history is more controversial still. his ideology became the touchstone of two raging controversies: First, between champions of religious Zionism — who saw his spiritual

Zionism, his rejection of Orthodoxy, and his emphasis on immediate decisions (necessarily controversial) about cultural and educational matters as undermining the Jewishness of the Jewish nationalism he advocated — and secular Zionists.[9] Second, between so-called maximalists — who saw his emphasis on cultural and educational work as detracting from the goal of creating "facts on the ground" that could be used as the basis of a Jewish national home, and minimalists, who were satisfied with creating an elite cultural center that would unify Jewry without providing opportunities for mass *aliya*.

Furthermore, historians have argued that Ahad ha-Am's position lowered "the sense of urgency, the sense of imminent — indeed, actual — catastrophe" and thus slowed Zionist growth.[10] Although this assessment is partly true, it overlooks the fact that neither Zionist weakness nor the difficulty in evacuating large numbers of Jews was caused by Ahad ha-Am. It is, thus, difficult to assess whether Spiritual Zionism was a cause for Zionist weakness or merely a symptom of a larger problem: Zionism was (as noted in the last chapter) competing with both diaspora nationalism and Jewish socialist nationalism (associated with the Bund) to define the new Jewish identity.[11] Ahad ha-Am sought a middle path between celebrating the diaspora (as Simon Dubnow did in his diaspora nationalist ideology) and calling for the diaspora's complete liquidation (which many Zionists implied or advocated outright). And it is critical to remember that Ahad ha-Am's reason for rejecting the latter was practical and utilitarian. He did not believe that it would be possible to achieve such grandiose Zionist goals, and failure would leave the diaspora nationalists and the socialists in complete control of the Jewish street — a fate that was only marginally better than the assimilationist ideology then rampant in Western Europe.[12] Furthermore, Ahad ha-Am's strictures about mass aliya were — by and large — correct. No mass migration movement developed, in part due to

conditions in *Eretz Israel*, especially after the Ottomans banned *aliya* in the early 1890s.

Zionist activities continued despite Hibbat Zion's near total institutional collapse. In particular, Zionist ideologues of various stripes continued to argue for increased activity to promote Jewish restoration. Rabbi Shmuel Mohilever, one of the earliest and most eminent Hibbat Zion supporters, for example, wondered (in 1890) why Jews "still did not see the divine hand" that inspired work for restoration.[13] Mohilever was especially clear on two points — clearer even than Rabbis Alkalai and Kalischer (who had proposed Zionist schemes in the earlier part of the 19th century) — relating to Zionism. First, Mohilever saw all the events that transpired in the Jewish world, including the rise of modern antisemitism, as deriving from a divine source. It followed, of course, that the call to return to Jewry's ancestral homeland also emanated from a divine source. Second, and perhaps more important, Mohilever argued — in stark contrast to Kalischer — that it was preferable for Jews to "live in Eretz Israel without observing the Torah properly, compared to living in the diaspora and observing the Torah properly."[14]

Other rabbis of the era largely rejected Zionism, but a number agreed with Mohilever and enthusiastically supported efforts to organize the return to Eretz Israel. This latter group of rabbis included, among others, Rabbis Yitzhak Aronowski (Kovno), David Solomon Slouschz (Odessa), and Shmuel Yaakov Rabinowitz (Liverpool).[15] Nor was Zionist activity in this era exclusively the provenance of a small group of Orthodox rabbis. All the same, Zionism would require an external stimulus to galvanize the movement and catapult it to the center of the Jewish affairs.

Theodor Herzl: The Man and His Mission

Ironically, the event that catapulted Zionism to the forefront of Jewish (and world) affairs unfolded in France in 1894. Captain Alfred Dreyfus, a Jewish artillery officer, was falsely accused of espionage, was convicted, and banished to the French prison colony on Devil's Island. Dreyfus contined to profess his innocence, although he was widely assumed guilty, even within the Franco-Jewish community. As the wheels of justice slowly turned, however, it became clear that Dreyfus was indeed innocent, the victim of an antisemitic officer corps wishing to blame a scapegoat for failure on the battlefield in order to avoid admitting defeat at the hands of a better-prepared enemy.

After years of advocacy by the pro-Dreyfusards, justice was finally served, in no small measure thanks to the efforts of the writer Emile Zola, whose essay *"J'accuse"* forced the case to be reopened, and the Socialist leader Jean Jaurès, whose spirit was offended by injustice. Nevertheless, the anti-Dreyfusards were not swept away in defeat but rather were forced underground. The position of those opposed to reopening the case helps illuminate the crisis of French society at the time. Many of the anti-Dreyfusards were willing to admit, in the face of overwhelming evidence, that Dreyfus could actually be innocent. Yet, they argued, the best thing for France would be to continue the charade of his guilt so that the army's reputation would remain untainted. For the anti-Dreyfusards, as for many European antisemites of the era, an imperfect society had to be brought to apocalyptic perfection, even against its will.[16]

While the Dreyfus affair was playing itself out, one aspect particularly impressed an Austrian Jewish journalist named Theodor Herzl who served as Paris correspondent for the liberal daily paper *Das Neue Freie Presse*: the fact that one Jew had committed a crime, but all Jews were considered guilty by the French public. Indeed, Herzl later wrote that the taunts of witnesses to Dreyfus's public degradation — "Á la mort les Juifs" (death to the Jews) — contributed greatly to his decision to write *Der Judenstaat* (The Jewish State), the booklet destined to become the Zionist classic par excellence.[17]

Born in Budapest on May 2, 1860, Herzl's path to Zionism had been a long, indirect one. Raised in a Jewish household, his education and upbringing were only slightly more than marginally Jewish, especially after his bar mitzva. Ironically, Herzl's background placed him squarely in the camp of potential Jewish nationalists (at least subconsciously). He had been born in Budapest, but his family did not originate in the Hungarian capital. They had migrated there from Semlin, Serbia, the same city where Rabbi Yehuda Alkalai, author of one of the earliest proto-Zionist works, served as spiritual leader. Herzl's grandfather, Simon Loeb Herzl, was a follower of Alkalai's and the elder Herzl may well have regaled his grandson with the eminent rabbi's teachings.[18] Nonetheless, Judaism was not central to the young Herzl's life. In 1898, Herzl reminisced about his difficulties in the supplementary classes he attended in the synagogue his parents attended, placing special stress on a thrashing he received when he could not recall details about the Exodus. In keeping with his preoccupation at the time of his reminiscence, Herzl added, "Today there are scores of teachers who would like to thrash me because I remember the Exodus from Egypt only too well."[19] Despite his ambivalence about his teachers — and about the value of a traditional Jewish education — young Herzl continued to toy with the Exodus and restoration theme. At age twelve, Herzl dreamed that "the Messiah called to Moses: It is for this child I have prayed." Then, turning to Herzl, the Messiah ordered the youth to "go, declare to the Jews that I shall come soon and perform great wonders and great deeds for my people and for the whole world."[20]

In the interim, Herzl's attentions turned to school matters. Childhood dreams of grandeur gave way to a rigorous education that culminated in Herzl's graduation as a doctor of law from the University of Vienna in 1884. This career path soured quickly and Herzl chose a new one: making a living as a writer and reporter. Yet even here Jewish affairs continued to intrude on his life, most particularly the rising tide of European antisemitism. While in Paris, Herzl confided to his diary that a solution to the Jewish problem had occurred to him: mass conversion to Christianity.[21] Herzl soon dropped that idea in favor of a return to his earlier dreams of a Jewish exodus from Europe, with himself serving as the new Moses. The importance of the Dreyfus affair on Herzl's thinking should not be underestimated — as recently as 1892, he had rejected the quasi-Zionist Midian scheme as impractical — but cannot be overestimated either — he had been long obsessed with a solution to the Jewish question. Moreover, in his writings, Herzl sought the grand and heroic — what better way to accomplish both than to restore the Jewish people to a national home?[22]

Herzl's response to the larger events around him was to turn to writing: shortly after the Dreyfus trial, around the time of the trial he wrote a play *Das Neue Gheto* (sic) (The new ghetto), which was staged for the first time shortly after the guilty verdict. Ideas were now coalescing in his mind. He sought and obtained an interview with Baron Maurice de Hirsch, the German Jewish financier who had founded the Jewish Colonization Association (ICA) and was the patron of efforts to relocate threatened Russian Jews into Argentina and Brazil. Herzl hoped that Hirsch would agree to support the creation of a Jewish state. Instead, the meeting turned into a disaster, ending with the two men engaging in a virtual shouting match.[23] Undeterred, Herzl penned his modest proposal to solve the Jewish problem, entitling his book *Der Judenstaat* (1896).

Der Judenstaat laid out Herzl's proposals fairly simply. Like Leon Pinsker, Herzl emphasized the need of the hour, given the rising antisemitic tide. Again like Pinsker, he emphasized that the Jewish problem could not be solved as long as Jews remained a minority in Europe. "The Jewish question exists," Herzl unequivocally declared, "it would be foolish to deny it."[24] This held true despite efforts, after the emancipation, by European countries and by European Jewry. The former had tried to truly absorb their Jewish communities, while the latter had sincerely tried to be absorbed. Emancipation and integration had not worked because they

An 1896 Hebrew Edition of *Der Judenstaat*.
Courtesy of the Central Zionist Archives, Jerusalem

were the wrong responses to the problem. Why had emancipation failed? Herzl stated his two premises clearly:

> To my mind, the Jewish question is neither a social nor a religious one, even though it may assume these and other guises. It is a national Question, and to solve it we must first of all establish it as an international political problem which will have to be settled by the civilized nations of the world in council.
>
> We are a people, *one* people.[25]

Given the nature of the problem, Herzl's preferred solution was unequivocal and simple: "Let sovereignty be granted over a portion of the earth's surface that is sufficient for our rightful national requirements."[26] To attain this goal, Herzl proposed creating two organizations: The society of the Jews and the Jewish company, the former dealing with all technical issues and the latter undertaking the financial arrangements necessary to ensure success.[27] In Herzl's plan, Jews would not leave Europe as a disorganized rabble, but rather as part of a well-organized exodus. All businesses would be liquidated by the Jewish company, which would use the resources thus obtained to organize the new Jewish state's economy.

Almost immediately, Herzl took up the question of location: Should the Jewish state be located in Argentina or in *Eretz Israel*? In *Der Judenstat* Herzl set out arguments for both, without drawing a clear conclusion. Instead, he argued that "the society [of the Jews] will take whatever it is given and whatever is favored by the public opinion of the Jewish People."[28] Most of Herzl's other writings of this era stress *Eretz Israel*. Yet, in light of later events, it must be noted that in his earliest manifestation as a Zionist, his focus was on the creation of a sovereign Jewish state, not where it would be located. Put differently, it is not inconceivable that Herzl's grand scheme could have taken a territorialist, rather than a Zionist, turn.[29]

The remainder of *Der Judenstaat* dealt with technical issues: how the Jewish company would operate, how it would purchase land and build settlements, and how it would organize labor and the economy. One entire chapter detailed constitutional issues and the new Jewish state's internal and external relations. Herzl foresaw the creation of a modern, democratic state organized along European lines. He did not deal with the specifics of this state, its organization, or the society and culture (except insofar as he rejected theocracy) of the future Jewish entity.[30] All other questions were to be deferred to the time when the idea of a Jewish state became a reality.[31]

Despite the lack of specifics, indeed, perhaps because of it, and even though Herzl said little that was really new (many similar ideas having been mooted by the Proto-Zionists, none of whom was known to Herzl), *Der Judenstaat* created a sensation within Jewish nationalist circles. Many Zionists echoed Chaim Weizmann's statement that the book was a "bolt from the blue." This was not because of its specific contents, but because, "the personality which stood behind them appealed to us. Here was

daring, clarity and energy. The fact that a Westerner came to us unencumbered by our own preconceptions had its appeal."[32]

This is not, of course, to imply that all readers approved of Herzl's ideas. In fact, many vociferously opposed Herzl, including Rabbis Moritz Güdemann and Hermann Adler, respectively the chief rabbis of Vienna and the United Kingdom.[33] East European rabbis by the score also denounced Herzl's scheme, as either false messianism, heresy, or both.[34] Finally, many West European Jews, though tried by antisemitism, felt that Herzl's approach would not solve their problem. Indeed, they argued, by focusing attention on Jews, Herzl might even make the problem worse.[35]

Yet, despite the negative responses, Herzl also soon found himself inundated with requests that he assume the position of the new Moses. In any event, to realize his dream of restoration, Herzl created a tentative organization and called its organizing conference — dubbed the First World Zionist Congress — which met in August 1897.

The First Zionist Congress

Herzl had recommended diplomatic activity as the sole means to achieve Zionist goals, but he also recognized that no Zionist would obtain the attention of the European powers — vital to his plan — or the Turks without a clear statement of massive Jewish public support. Such support had to be dramatic and highly visible, in other words, only a Zionist congress would suit Herzl's purposes.

In the period between publishing *Der Judenstaat* and convening the First World Zionist Congress, Herzl began his initial, tentative contacts with world leaders. His first contact, was with the Grand Duke Frederick of Baden, thanks in no small part to the Gentile Zionist, Reverend William H. Hechler. This contact would culminate in a meeting with Kaiser Wilhelm II in *Eretz Israel* in 1898.[36] In the meantime, Herzl also sought to finish two intermediate tasks: creating the Society of the Jews, and creating an organ to spread Zionist doctrine. The former task ultimately would have to await the Congress. Similarly, the Zionist organ had to be started from scratch. To be sure, Herzl tried to use his contacts — notably with his employers at *Die Neue Freie Presse* — to found a journal but these contacts proved futile and Herzl fulfilled his dream of creating a Zionist organ himself, with no other financial support. The first issue of this new journal, *Die Welt*, appeared on June 4, 1897.[37]

Herzl soon obtained a small, but ardent, circle of followers — the Kadimah Students's Society of Vienna, for example. Many members of Hibbat Zion, which had been defunct as an international Zionist movement since 1891, also joined Herzl's new movement. Still, the Jewish notables Herzl hoped would gain his entry into the halls of power remained cool to his ideas. He was received politely by Baron Edmund de Rothschild but got no farther with him than he had with de Hirsch.[38] The next step was to go directly to the Jewish masses, an idea that led directly to convening the First Zionist Congress' in August 1897.

Initially called for August 25, 1897, in Munich, the Congress was designed to bring together as many representatives of different Zionist, quasi-Zionist, and Proto-Zionist groups as possible. Interference by so-called Protestrabbiner, Reform rabbis inalterably opposed to any national definition of Jews or Judaism, forced a change of venue to Basel, Switzerland; technicalities related to the move eventually forced a delay until August 29. Worse still, invitations to the congress touched off a small-scale furor between a group of Zionists who sought quiet diplomacy, cautious rhetoric, and minimal bombast and Herzl who intended to deal with matters of substance in private but who hoped to use the congress's open sessions as a means to obtain maximum publicity for the new movement.[39] Still, despite frayed nerves, the congress duly met and soon got down to business.

The first order of business was for the 204 delegates to constitute themselves as the Zionist Congress. Herzl, naturally, was elected president of the congress and of the World Zionist Organization (WZO) that the congress spawned. Max Nordau, another literary figure originally better known for his European cosmopolitanism but recently returned to full-time interest in Jewish affairs, was elected WZO vice president. Both Herzl and Nordau addressed the congress; the former emphasized the general goals set for the WZO while the latter discussed the condition of Jewry in some detail.[40] Nordau's conclusion could well have been the WZO's motto: "The misery of the Jews cries out for help. The finding of that help will be the great task of this Congress."[41] After the plenary addresses, the Congress turned to its main immediate task, unanimously passing the resolution placed before it:

> The aim of Zionism is to create for the Jewish people a home in Palestine secured by public law.
> The Congress contemplates the following means to the attainment of this end:
> 1. The promotion, on suitable lines, of the colonization of Palestine by Jewish agricultural and industrial workers.
> 2. The organization and binding together of the whole of Jewry by means of appropriate institutions, local and international, in accordance with the laws of each country.
> 3. The strengthening and fostering of Jewish National sentiments and consciousness.
> 4. Preparatory steps towards obtaining government consent, where necessary, to the attainment of the aim of Zionism.[42]

This resolution, known as the Basel Program, became the basis for all further Congress and WZO activity. Yet there had even been a debate over the resolution's wording, almost to the last minute. Herzl, for all the rhetoric of the congress, did not want to create any more potential problems than absolutely necessary. He certainly did not want to scare away any potential partners in the world community — especially not the Turks. The problem turned on the word "law" in the preamble: the radicals demanded a clear statement on Jewish restoration by right, not as the result of Turkish

An Invitation to the First Zionist Congress
Courtesy of the Central Zionist Archives, Jerusalem

sufference. Once the word "public" was added, all parties were satisfied and work proceded.[43]

Despite the debate over the resolution's wording — again it should be emphasized that ultimately the Basel Program passed unanimously — the main issue facing the congress was organizational. The congress plenary oversaw creation of the WZO, dividing that body into a general council, better known as the Greater Actions Committee (GAK, Grosses Aktions-Komité), which acted in the congress's name when it was not in session, and the executive, initially entitled the Inner Actions Committee (EAK, Engere Aktions-Komité), which included Herzl and his immediate circle.[44] For the first seven years of the WZO's existence, the main focus was on the executive and especially on Herzl's activities. At the time, all members of the executive resided in Vienna as did, for all intents and purposes, the WZO.[45] Finally, the Congress considered, but did not act on, a proposal by Zvi Hermann Schapira to create a Jewish National Fund (this organization, better known by its Hebrew name, Keren Kayamet le-Israel, was established by the fifth Zionist congress in 1901).[46]

At first glance, the First Zionist Congress appeared to accomplish somewhat paltry results. But, it is worth recalling that the first congress put Zionism on the map institutionally. Herzl, summarizing the congress in his diary, noted,

> Were I to sum up the Basel Congress in a word — which I shall guard against pronouncing publicly — it would be this: At Basel I founded the Jewish State. If I said this out loud today, I would be answered by universal laughter. Perhaps in five years, and certainly in fifty, everyone will know it.[47]

Herzlian Diplomacy

Buoyed by the first congress, Herzl set himself to the task at hand. He had already undertaken a few tentative, and mostly abortive, steps designed to bring Zionism to the attention of world statesmen. He had hoped thereby to quickly and easily obtain the charter that would permit the Jewish state to come into existence. In May 1895, for example, Herzl wrote to former German chancellor Otto von Bismarck, hoping that Bismarck — who had brokered a peace treaty in 1878 that averted war between Russia and Turkey — might gain him entry to both the German kaiser and the Ottoman Porte. Herzl was to be disappointed, however: Bismarck (recently relieved of his position by Kaiser Wilhelm II) never replied.[48]

Following up on this first, unsuccessful, effort, Herzl placed much emphasis on meeting the kaiser. In the interim, he also sought a direct approach to the Turks, traveling in June 1896 to Constantinople in the hope of meeting Sultan Abd-Al Hamid II. In the course of his twelve-day stay Herzl met with key Ottoman leaders, including both Grand Vizier Halil Rifat Pasha and the sultan's second secretary, Izzat Bey. The latter, an Arab, was publicly cool to Zionism and prevented Herzl from meeting the sultan at this point. However, in private, Izzat Bey proved open to some of Herzl's proposals, especially those relating to Zionist economic compensation to the failing Ottoman Empire in return for *Eretz Israel*. Herzl got no farther. The sultan replied with an authoritative, negative response, telling Herzl's intermediary, Philipp de Newlinski, "I cannot sell even a foot of land for it does not belong to me, but to my people."[49] Nonetheless, Herzl had at least managed to present his case to a head of state and had obtained the attention of a major power.

Herzl then returned to Germany and stepped up his efforts to meet Kaiser Wilhelm II. Reverend William Hechler, as already noted, facilitated a meeting between Herzl and Grand Duke Frederick of Baden, the kaiser's uncle, in the spring of 1896. At this stage, a meeting with the kaiser was impossible, but Herzl left no stone unturned in an effort to obtain an audience with the sultan. In turn he met with Austrian, Portuguese, French, and British diplomats.[50] Herzl was nothing if not persistent. About seven weeks after the congress, that is in early October 1897, he renewed his contacts with Frederick of Baden. This time, Herzl presented the grand duke with a detailed report of the congress's proceedings and with an enclosure for Wilhelm.[51] Frederick did finally follow up, broaching the subject of Zionism during a conversation with his nephew in July 1898. He also admitted that he had waited until after the congress to see if Herzl could actually get his movement started. More significantly, Frederick strongly stated his belief that Zionist goals were completely compatible with Germany's and could only strengthen the German position in the Middle East.[52]

In the interim, the Second Zionist Congress met in Basel (August 28-31, 1898). Herzl had originally wanted it to meet in London, hoping thereby to interest the British government and obtain the great power support he knew the World Zionist Organization needed. The return to Switzerland — necessary to maintain the veneer of Zionist neutrality in European affairs — reflected new contacts with both Frederick of Baden and, through him, with the Kaiser.[53]

The second congress itself represented little more than an incremental advance over the first congress. To be sure, it was larger than the first — by more than 150 delegates. Larger delegations from England and the United States reflected a maturation of Zionist groups in the West, as did the attendance of Bernard Lazare, among the foremost of the Dreyfusards. A delegation of Orthodox rabbis also attended, wary of certain trends in Zionist discourse (of which more below) but seeking a hand in Herzl's enterprise. In all, the second congress was more truly representative of the Zionist element within the Jewish world, reflecting the WZO's strengths and weaknesses.[54]

Herzl again addressed the congress, concentrating on the inner logic of Zionism for the Jews, the Turks, and the great powers. Rousing Zionists to action, Herzl declared: "It is not enough for us to feel that we are a people and to recognize ourselves as such. National awareness must be followed by an awakening of the national will."[55]

Herzl continued by emphasizing the wide support for Zionism among the Jewish masses and called upon Zionists to seize the initiative in Jewish communal organizations.[56] Although his declaration of mass support is debatable — which modern Jewish political movement really had the support of the masses is an open question — given the diplomatic context into which the second congress fell, it is not surprising. Indeed, the congress plenary actually only approved two initiatives: a resolution calling on Zionists to "conquer" their communities in the masses' name, and another creating a Jewish colonial trust.[57] Finally, the congress also passed a resolution on education that, inadvertently sparked a major debate between religious and secular groups in Eastern Europe.

The original intent of the resolution was to call for a program of mass Zionist education as a means to inculcate national identity in Jewish youth.[58] Herzl sought to avoid a conflict with the traditionalists, seeing them as a necessary bridge to the Jewish masses in Eastern Europe. Even Ahad ha-Am, who sought the education resolution, did not desire a complete break between the two Zionist camps. Of course, many leaders in the traditional community already uncategorically rejected Zionism and many of the Orthodox rabbis attending the

Herzl's Visit to *Eretz Israel* in Autumn 1898: Herzl Meeting the Kaiser Near Mikve Israel (left) and With Members of the Zionist Delegation Near the Walls of Jerusalem (right).
Courtesy of the Central Zionist Archives, Jerusalem

second congress would do so in the weeks and months thereafter. Religious and cultural questions, initially seen by Herzl as something to be deferred until after the Jewish State became a reality, would continue to flare as one of a number of internal (and external) Zionist conflicts.[59]

With the major controversies still ahead of him, Herzl returned to diplomacy after the second congress. After another meeting with Grand Duke Frederick, Herzl finally attained the breakthrough he had sought: an audience with Kaiser Wilhelm II during the latter's trip to Constantinople and Jerusalem in October 1898.[60] In fact, Herzl met the Kaiser three times: In Constantinople (October 18), near Mikve Israel (October 28), and in a formal meeting at the kaiser's camp near Jerusalem (November 2).[61]

During his third audience with the kaiser, Herzl systematically set out the Zionist position. The two-thousand year dream, Herzl noted, was still alive. *Eretz Israel* was a barren land that "cries out for men to come and cultivate it." Finally, Jewish settlement would benefit both German and Turkey. "It is easy," Herzl declared, "to foresee a magnificent fructification of desolate areas, and all this will result in more happiness and culture for many human beings."[62] A direct appeal for Germany's protection, originally included in Herzl's oration, was deleted at the insistence of Reinhold Klehmet, one of the kaiser's main foreign service advisers.[63]

If Herzl really hoped for a clear and unequivocal statement of support from Wilhelm, he was severely disappointed. The kaiser listened politely to Herzl's discourse but refused to commit himself. The Germans especially refused to issue a clear statement regarding protection of Zionism or Zionists.[64] Bluntly, Germany's interest in maintaining the Ottoman Empire as a bulwark against Russia or England (or both) overrode any possible sympathy the kaiser may have had — or feigned to have — for Zionism.[65] Herzl quickly realized the reality that Germany would not sponsor Jewish restoration but maintained his contacts with Frederick of Baden and other German leaders literally until his final days. In particular, Herzl used these contacts as a means to gain entry to the czar (who was the kaiser's cousin and thus also a nephew of Grand Duke Frederick).[66] This resulted in a brief flurry of activity — letters between Herzl, Frederick of Baden, and Czar Nicholas II — and another disappointment for the Zionist leader: the czar saw no possibility for a practical application of Zionism in the near future and refused to become the movement's patron.[67]

Thus, Herzl had little to show in two years of public diplomacy. The Third Zionist Congress, held between August 15 and 18, 1899 (again in Basel), therefore proved to be more fractious: In addition to the cultural problem, which arose once more, a dispute arose between Herzl and supporters of the concept of practical Zionism who sought to organize an ad hoc exodus in the interim before attaining the international charter sought by the WZO under the Basel program.[68]

Ideology and Praxis

Given the general lack of success with the Herzlian approach to private diplomacy, it could fairly be said that Zionism had reached a critical crossroad by the summer of 1898. To be sure, Herzl claimed that between 3–4 million Jews could rapidly be relocated to *Eretz Israel* if the charter were approved.[69] However, the charter had not yet been attained. As a result, a new argument broke out within the WZO over the relative merits of Herzl's "Political Zionism" as opposed to the "Practical Zionism" proposed by some of his Zionist opponents. In essence this was a new manifestation of already existing ideological cleavages: Ahad ha-Am and the "Spiritual Zionists" on one side and Herzl and the "Political Zionists" on the other. Given that mass *aliya* was impossible under present conditions, Ahad ha-Am argued for the creation of a small spiritual center, emphasizing the quality of the pioneers rather than their quantity. In contrast, Herzl sought the aliya of the bulk of European Jewry. Since that was currently impossible, he argued for deferring settlement activities in order to concentrate on diplomacy.[70]

In effect, there were three concepts of Zionism at work. Practical Zionists sought small-scale "infiltration" as a means to create facts on the ground, hoping thereby to eventually obtain more *aliya*. Ahad ha-Am supported this position not as an end in itself: He felt that mass *aliya* was impossible and would always be so. Thus, only a few Jews should infiltrate *Eretz Israel* and create a spiritual center. Herzl, in contrast, saw neither utility nor dignity in such actions. Jews should not, he argued, attempt to return like thieves in the night, but as men of honor. "Once we reach the point where we can start to settle *Eretz Israel*," he wrote, "we must not do so in a disorganized, chaotic way, with everyone simply running there as he pleases."[71]

Nonetheless, despite Herzl's opposition, some settlement work had continued. The Second Zionist Congress, for example, had ordered the creation of a settlement committee, headquartered in London, to prepare (in conjunction with the Jewish Colonial Trust) for settlement work when the charter was achieved. In August 1903, Herzl agreed to the creation of a Jaffa branch of the Jewish Colonial Trust, the so-called Anglo-Palestine Company headed by Zalman D. Levontin. Herzl also strongly welcomed the creation of WZO branches and organizations in the colonies already existing in *Eretz Israel*.[72]

None of these steps directly assisted *aliya* on any scale, for the Ottoman ban on mass *aliya* militated against anything larger than continued infiltration. The ban, moreover, was reconfirmed during Herzl's stay in Constantinople in 1896 — he was told, more or less directly, that although Jews were welcome in any portion of the empire, the only place they could not settle en masse was Palestine.[73]

The controversy between Political and Practical Zionists continued to simmer, boiling over during the Third Zionist Congress. In particular, Herzl's style of leadership — though not the fact of his leadership — was questioned. Cultural and religious issues arose once more, and were once more deflected by Herzl's insistence that the WZO must maintain a unified face and not break into different parties.[74] Even so, the third congress proved to be a success, though a qualified one. The most important resolution, regarding the Jewish Colonial Trust, passed unanimously.[75] Herzl summarized his plan in one word: charter. As he put it:

Only when we are in possession of this Charter, which will have to include the necessary guarantees under public law, will we be able to begin large-scale practical settlement.[76]

Still, the rising tide of opposition convinced him that a success was needed quickly.

As an opening gambit, Herzl once again sought an audience with Sultan Abd-Al Hamid. As his original intermediary, de Newlinski, had passed away, Herzl turned for help to another non-Jewish supporter, Arminius Vábéry. After many months of delay, Vábéry obtained a two-hour audience for Herzl. The meeting was cordial, but there were no real results, least of all in terms of a change in Ottoman policy toward Jewish immigration.[77] Indeed, in some ways matters had taken a turn for the worse. New restrictive measures, including the so-called Red Slip and the opening of a secret police branch in Jaffa, soon followed.[78] If there was any positive result of Herzl's second visit in Istanbul, it was that contacts between the WZO president and the Grande Porte were able to continue.[79] In the end, however, these contacts came to naught.

Herzl had maintained his contacts with the Ottomans for one major reason: Complete failure of his diplomatic mission would lead to the utter collapse of the WZO. Obviously, he needed a new ally; renewed diplomacy on his part arrived in the form of an invitation to testify before the British Parliamentary committee considering a restrictive immigration bill (the Second Aliens Bill) in July 1902.[80] Herzl's testimony consisted of little more than a repetition of his demands for obtaining a charter for a Jewish National Home.

Herzl's opening remarks were telling:

> The Jews of Eastern Europe cannot stay where they are — where are they to go? If you find they are not wanted here, then some place must be found to which they can migrate without raising the problems that confront them here. Those problems will not arise if a home be found for them which will be legally recognized as Jewish.
> And I do submit that whether the Commission can directly influence that solution of the problem or not, they must not omit to consider it and give it the high value of its opinion.[81]

Thereafter, despite another brief (and once again abortive) trip to Istanbul, Herzl turned exclusively to England, hoping that His Majesty's government would fulfill Zionist goals. He approached the British at the correct time: they were in the throes of a reevaluation of their colonial policies in the Middle East. Herzl saw a possible strategy that could obtain a territory for the WZO that could, in turn, be used as a bargaining chip to (eventually) obtain *Eretz Israel*. Given Ottoman refusal to consider mass Jewish settlement in Palestine, he recognized the need for an indirect approach that would be near enough to *Eretz Israel* to be suitable.

In October 1902, Herzl approached the British regarding the Sinai Peninsula. At the time the British-controlled Egyptian government was attempting to purchase the Sinai from the Turks as a means of securing the eastern flank of the Suez Canal. Herzl directly approached members of the cabinet with a proposal to grant a charter for Jewish settlement on the Sinai's northern coast.[82] The British accepted Herzl's proposal in principle and negotiations followed.

Reluctant to accept an autonomous Jewish colony in northern Sinai, the Egyptian government still accepted the idea of mass Jewish immigration — conditional upon their acceptance of Ottoman citizenship.[83] Herzl's approval of the scheme soon followed and a tentative agreement was formulated on April 23. By then, however, the British government had developed serious reservations about the project.[84] These reservations were both technical — the difficulty in transporting water being the main hurdle — and economic: even if the area around El Arish could be irrigated, the expense would be prohibitive.[85] Additionally, security and citizenship concerns arose, as did some basic reservations regarding the propriety of bringing European Jews into the northern Sinai, especially since these Jews wanted a degree of autonomy that was unacceptable to the Turks.[86]

Although the negotiations dragged on until July, the end result was that the agreement collapsed and the El Arish scheme became another setback for Herzl. Discussions with the British relating to Cyprus came to a similar conclusion and would have involved the problem of a Jewish immigrant community being caught between Turks and Greeks.[87] In the interim, conditions in Russia deteriorated greatly, and Herzl became even more desperate to find a solution to Jewish distress.

Zionist Activity in the Shadow of Pogroms

The immediate catalyst for further Zionist efforts to find even a temporary haven outside of Eretz Israel was renewed anti-Jewish violence in the Russian Empire.[88] When the pogroms of 1881-1882 ended, the Russian government had instituted a series of policies (the so-called May Laws) that, in effect, punished Russian Jewry for the pogroms. As tensions continued to build up in the Russian empire, a new round of anti-Jewish violence began, this time sponsored by the czarist government through the agency of the "Black Hundreds," officially the Union of Russian People. The Black Hundreds' official role was to suppress anti-governmental activity; their method was to assault innocent Jews.

Between 1902, when the new pogroms began, and 1907, at least sixteen major pogroms and hundreds of minor ones struck Russian Jewry. Among the pogromists, in each and every case, were local gendarmerie and Cossacks temporarily relieved of military duty and assigned to the Black Hundreds. And while casualties were never extremely high (the pogroms never reaching the proportions of twentieth century genocides) they were certainly high enough: forty-five Jews killed in Kishinev on April 6–8, 1903; thirteen killed in Gomel, September 1, 1903; three hundred killed in Odessa during a series of pogroms between October 31 and November 4, 1905. In Bialystock on June 1, 1906, eighty Jews were executed by soldiers and gendarmes. This scene was repeated in Sedvitz on August 27, 1907, when thirty Jews were executed.[89] As noted, these were the major pogroms; minor incidents can barely be numbered, much less recounted in detail: Salo W. Baron, for example, estimates that there were 660 incidents between November 1 and 7, 1905.[90]

The reaction to the pogroms was swift and ineffectual: despite mass meetings throughout Europe and the Americas, the Russian government would not or could not be swayed off its self-destructive course. Protests were held in virtually every European country, but the protests in America were most extensive.[91] Yet the only tangible result of protests in the United States was the abrogation of a Russo-American trade treaty that had been signed in 1832. More problematic was the fact that the abrogation of this treaty had been on the American Jewish agenda since 1881.[92] In Russia itself Jewish movements offering a solution to the Jews' problems grew. Bund membership, for example, peaked in 1905 at 274 local cells with approximately 30,000 members.[93] Emigration also returned to the top of the Russian Jewish agenda. As already noted in the last chapter, more than 2 million Jews left the Russian empire prior to World War I. Almost half of them left between 1900 and 1914.

For Zionists, the pogroms represented a spur for renewed activity. Herzl had previously met with Russian authorities, in both Germany and Istanbul, since he felt that the Russians would agree that Zionism was the best possible solution for Russia's Jewish problem. For their part, the Russians

had committed themselves to nothing and never formally agreed to help the Zionists in any way. To the contrary, in June 1903, Count Vyacheslav K. von Plevhe, Russia's interior minister and the sponsor of the pogroms, circulated an aide memoire to all police prefects to the effect that they should "prohibit, immediately, all Zionist propaganda at public meetings or at gatherings of a public nature."[94]

The pogroms and the Russian government's subsequent antisemitic actions forced Herzl to act. The WZO president traveled to Russia to meet with von Plevhe in August 1903, hoping to lessen the pressure on Russian Jewry while obtaining support from the czarist government for Zionist goals. Herzl's mission must be understood in context — ex post facto arguments that Herzl hoped to somehow "use" Russian antisemitism to Zionist advantage totally misconstrue his purpose. He did not meet with von Plevhe because of any commonality of interest, and certainly not because he agreed with von Plevhe's anti-Jewish orientation, but because he understood the meaning of the recent pogroms. In effect, Herzl discovered that he needed a quick fix that would relieve Russian Jewish distress.[95] Although Herzl did meet with von Plevhe and signed an agreement that restored permission for Zionist groups to act within Russia (as long as they remained aloof from all discussion beyond emigration), he obtained little of substance from Plevhe. In return, he received a great deal of criticism from Russian Zionists who saw his meeting as nothing less than playing ideologically and politically "into Plevhe's hands by undertaking to help still the criticism at home and abroad to which the regime was now subject" by meeting with the very unscrupulous minister who had overseen the pogroms.[96] Moreover, in seeking his quick fix for Russian Jewish distress, Herzl accepted an offer from Great Britain that would nearly rend the Zionist movement asunder.

Zion or East Africa

When Herzl created the WZO, he did not anticipate the development of individual political parties — all Zionists were to define themselves as Zionists and not as members of an ideological sub-party. However, by the time of the Third Zionist Congress, certainly by the Fourth, fissures had begun to develop; these, in turn, generated political parties within the overall Zionist movement. Furthermore, some of these parties viewed themselves as being — to one degree or another — in opposition to Herzl on social or political issues.

Three groups stand out in particular. The *Mizrachi* party, founded in 1902, formulated its ideology on the basis of a fusion of Herzl's nationalism with strict religious orthodoxy. Although not opposed to Herzl's diplomatic platform, *Mizrachi* sought to prevent any WZO discussion of cultural or religious issues, hoping thereby to maintain an orthodox voice in the WZO (and in the future Jewish State) while also retaining the status quo within Eastern European Jewish communities.[97] Herzl was never viewed as *Mizrachi*'s main ideological opponent, that distinction being held by Ahad ha-Am.[98]

In contrast to *Mizrachi*, socialist Zionists did oppose Herzl's views on deferring social and economic reforms within the Jewish community until the Jewish State actually came into existence. The socialist Zionists fused Marxist ideas (then prevalent within both the Russian intelligentsia and in the Bund) with Jewish nationalism. Although they differed on many issues, most notably on Herzl's belief in the creation of a liberal Jewish state, the socialist Zionists viewed as mandatory the creation of both a Jewish and a socialist State in *Eretz Israel*. Significantly, since they most singularly confronted Bundist diaspora nationalism, socialist Zionists stood in the forefront of advocates of immediate settlement activities, even without the charter. This meant that socialist Zionists stood squarely in the Practical Zionist camp, a reality that animated the Second *Aliya*.[99]

For the time being, Herzl's most vocal critics were members of the Democratic Fraktion (Democratic Faction, DF), led by young Russian Jewish intellectuals including Chaim Weizmann, Leo Motzkin, and Martin Buber. First appearing as a distinct group during the Fifth Zionist Congress (Basel, December 26-30, 1901), the DF mainly comprised Ahad ha-Am's followers. They differed with Herzl on cultural issues and on the relative merits of diplomatic versus other Zionist activities. Granted, only diplomatic means could achieve Zionist goals. In that case, Weizmann, for example, strongly argued that there ought not be a "cult of personality" around Herzl; rather, the WZO President ought to be responsible — and (more significantly) responsive — to the WZO membership.[100] In turn, DF ideology led its leaders to emphasize what was colloquially known as Gegenwartsarbeit (work in the here and now), or, in other words, efforts on behalf of the Russian Jewish community in addition to continuing efforts to obtain the charter. As with the socialist Zionists, this position fully crystallized after Herzl's death, when it virtually became the WZO defining ideology.

These general faultlines already existed when Herzl entered into his negotiations with the British over the el Arish plan. It must be emphasized that Herzl's motivation for seeking el Arish was simple. He believed that an asylum, even a temporary one, was vitally necessary as testimony to Zionist success and as a first step toward obtaining the charter on *Eretz Israel*. Almost from the beginning, however, the British had made a parallel offer: to permit the creation of an autonomous Jewish colony in Eastern Africa (colloquially identified with Britain's Uganda Colony). Herzl initially refused to consider Uganda; he stepped back from his complete rejection of the scheme only for tactical reasons, hoping to "barter" Uganda for el Arish, Cyprus, or *Eretz Israel* at a later date.[101]

In May 1903, the el Arish scheme collapsed, as already noted, mainly because of the opposition of the Egyptian government. On May 20, 1903, however, the British renewed their offer regarding East Africa.[102] Having once rejected the scheme, Herzl now accepted it as a temporary haven for Russian Jewry. He apparently hoped that Zionist acceptance of the Uganda proposal would be followed by the creation of a committee to investigate the territory. He had every reason to believe that such a commission would conclude — much like the el Arish commission — that the territory was unfit for European habitation, after which Zionist-British negotiators would return to a discussion of a more appropriate locality.[103] Herzl particularly focused on one phrase in the offer made by the British: "If a site can be found which the [Jewish colonial] trust and his majesty's government consider suitable."[104] The implication was clearly that if no such site could be found in East Africa, efforts to find such a site would continue.

Despite understanding the subtler nuances of his own diplomatic efforts, Herzl could not — or would not — tip his hand. Rather than brief the Zionist congress on his apparent hope that this proposal would collapse, leading to further negotiations for a more appropriate Jewish national home, Herzl concentrated on the offer as a serious one. He admitted bluntly that "it [Uganda] is not and can never be Zion."[105] Rather, in his estimation, Uganda represented nothing more than "an emergency measure designed to allay the present helplessness of all the philanthropic undertakings and to keep us from losing scattered fragments of our people."[106] Nordau, who only reluctantly supported Herzl on this issue, spoke in a similar vein, dubbing the Uganda scheme a "Nachtasyl" (asylum for the night); in other words, a temporary haven to be abandoned at the first opportunity.[107] As a result, all Herzl requested from the congress was a resolution agreeing to study the plan further.[108]

Far from supporting Herzl, however, the plenary of congress delegates, constituting themselves as the GAK, fragmented into two camps: those who supported the scheme or supported Herzl completely and unquestioningly, and the so-called nein-sager (nay-sayers) who — calling themselves Zionei Zion (Zionists for Zion) — completely rejected the plan. The latter included almost the entire DF led by Weizmann and a group of Russian Zionists,

led by Yehiel Tschenlow and Menahem M. Ussishkin who had become increasingly restive under Herzl's leadership.[109] Mizrachi's leaders also temporarily joined with these self-styled Zionei Zion (Zionists for Zion), although they remained aloof from a formal alliance. Recognizing that, to a degree, Herzl had already presented the GAK with a fait accompli, the Zionei Zion turned into a fully ramified opposition, although, their only tangible initial action was to propose a resolution politely thanking the British for their offer but rejecting it as unlikely to solve the Jewish problem.[110] Haham Moses Gaster, leader of the English delegation, summarized the issue even more succinctly: The plan, he averred, was diametrically opposed to Zionism.[111]

Three days of acrimonious debate followed. The Russian Zionists — for whom the plan was ostensibly proposed — debated the issue and ended up passing a resolution (by a vote of 146 to 84) to reject the offer.[112] The matter did not quite end there. The GAK now took up the matter and, by a vote of 295 to 277, passed a resolution approving further EAK negotiations with the British, in essence giving Herzl what he wanted all along.[113] It should also be remembered that all the resolution committed the WZO to was sending a commission to East Africa to study the situation firsthand.

This victory proved phyrrhic: when the results were announced, the entire group of Zionei Zion withdrew from the congress, leaving Herzl visibly shaken.[114] Further battles within the WZO were fought over Uganda, most notably at the conference of Russian Zionists held in Kharkov November 11–14, 1903. The scheme literally dogged Herzl for the rest of his life.[115] In the interim, the British had second thoughts about the wisdom of creating an autonomous Jewish colony in East Africa.[116] By then Herzl decided to show part of his hand, thereby partially setting the stage for reconciliation within the WZO. In a letter to Sir Francis Montefiore, Herzl adopted some of the very arguments used by the Zionei Zion: only Eretz Israel could offer a solution for the Jewish problem, Herzl agreed. However, in light of conditions in Russian the magnanimous offer of a haven by a great power could not be ignored.[117] Final reconciliation did indeed come: After a five-day meeting of the GAK in Vienna (April 11-15, 1904), a resolution restating the Basel Program but permitting the Zionist Commission to investigate East Africa and another calling for an end to acrimony within the Zionist camp passed virtually unanimously.[118]

The committee duly visited Uganda and — as Herzl predicted — returned a negative report. The end of the Uganda affair, however, came too late for Herzl personally.

His health had been sapped by the infighting and now virtually failed. The first modern Political Zionist succumbed to a heart condition on July 3, 1904. He was only forty-four years old when he died — cut down in his prime. He had no equal in the Zionist movement and left no heir, but his accomplishments went beyond the personal: He had literally created a Zionist organization that proved able to withstand a terrible crisis of self-definition. That movement, in turn, would continue to develop in the post-Herzl era, working toward the goal of Jewish restoration.

Notes

1. Ahad ha-Am, "לא זו הדרך" (This is not the path), cited in David Vital, *The Origins of Zionism* (Oxford: Clarendon Press, 1975), p. 192.
2. Cf. Fred Krinsky, "The Renascent Jewish Nationalism: A Study of its Leading Concepts and Practices", Ph.D. Diss.; University of Pennsylvania, 1951, pp. 55-60; Shlomo Avineri, *The Making of Modern Zionism* (New York: Basic Books, 1981), chap. 11; and Leon Simon's introduction to *Selected Essays of Ahad Ha-'Am* (New York: Atheneum, 1970).
3. Cf. Misha Louvish, *Nineteenth Century Zionist Theories* (Glasgow: University Zionist Federation, 1933), p. 6.
4. Ahad ha-Am, "אמת מארץ ישראל" (Truth from the Land of Israel), cited in Vital, *Origins*, p. 195.
5. Ahad ha-Am, "Past and Future," in Simon, *Selected Essays*, pp. 80–90.
6. Alex Bein, תולדות ההיתישבות הציונית מתקופת הרצל ועד ימינו (A history of Zionist settlement from Herzl's time to today), 4th ed. (Ramat Gan: Masada Press, 1970) p. 13.
7. Ahad ha-Am, "The Transvaluation of Values" and "The Spiritual Revival," in Simon, *Selected Essays*, pp. 217–241 and 253–305.
8. Cited in Naomi E. Cohen, *Zion's Founding Fathers* (New York: Education Department of Hadassah, n.d.), p. 12.
9. Arthur Hertzberg perceptively described Ahad ha-Am as "the Agnostic Rabbi" in his *The Zionist Idea* (New York: Atheneum, 1970), pt. 4. On the struggle between religious and secular Zionists in this era, see Shmuel Luz, *Parallels Meet* (Philadelphia: Jewish Publication Society, 1988), pp. 77-96.
10. Vital, *Origins*, p. 199.
11. Cf. David Weinberg, *Between Tradition and Modernity* (New York: Holmes and Meier, 1996), chap. 2–4.
12. Ahad ha-Am, "Slavery in Freedom," in Simon, *Selected Essays*, pp. 171–194.
13. Rabbi Shmuel Mohilever, "מטרת נסיעתי לארצנו הקדושה" (The purpose of my journey to our holy land), cited in Chanonch Merhavia (ed.), קוראים לציון קולות (Voices calling for Zion) (Jerusalem: Zalman Shazar Center for the Study of Jewish History), 1976, pp. 177–178.
14. Ibid., p. 177.
15. Excerpts from their writings are included in Merhavia, קולות קוראים לציון, pp. 178–179 and 182–183.
16. Cf. Norman Finkelstein, *Captain of Innocence: France and the Dreyfus Affair* (New York: Putnam's, 1991).
17. The first entry in Herzl's diary makes no direct mention of the Dreyfus affair but does discuss the importance of his stay in Paris on his perceptions of antisemitism. Cf. Raphael Patai and Harry Zohn eds., *The Complete Diaries of Theodor Herzl* (New York: Herzl Press, 1960), 1:3–6.
18. Andrew Handler, *Dori: The Life and Times of Theodor Herzl in Budapest* (University of Alabama Press, 1983), passim.
19. Alex Bein, *Theodor Herzl: A Biography of the Founder of Modern Zionism* (New York: Atheneum, 1970), pp. 11–12.
20. Ibid., p. 14.
21. Cited in Howard M. Sachar, *A History of Israel* (New York: Alfred A. Knopf, 1976), p. 38.
22. See, for example, the way Herzl had his alter ego, Kingscourt, frame this idea in *Altneuland* (Haifa: Haifa Publishing, 1960), p. 31: "Do something courageous, something grand . . . Just because you have the whole world and his wife against you!"
23. On Hirsch, ICA, and their relation to Zionism, see Haim Avni, "חברת יק"א והציונית" (The Jewish Colonization Association and Zionism), in Haim Avni and Gideon Shimoni eds., הציונית ומתנגדיה בעם היהודי (Zionism and its Jewish opponents) (Jerusalem: ha-Sifriya ha-Zionit, 1990), pp. 125–144.

24. Theodor Herzl, *The Jewish State* (New York: American Zionist Emergency Council, 1946), p. 33.

25. Ibid. Emphasis in original.

26. Ibid., p. 49.

27. Ibid., p. 50.

28. Ibid., p. 52.

29. Cf. Haim Avni, "הטריטוריאליזם, התיישבות טריטוריאליסטית, וההתיישבות הציונית" (Territorialism, territorialist settlement, and Zionist settlement), in *יהדות זמננו* (Contemporary Jewry: A research annual) 1 (1983): 69–87.

30. Herzl, *Jewish State*, p. 100.

31. Ibid., p. 101.

32. Statement by Chaim Weizmann cited in Ervin Birnbaum, *In the Shadow of the Struggle* (Jerusalem: Gefen Books, 1990), p. 36.

33. Theodor Herzl, "Dr. Güdemann's *National-Judentum*," in *Zionist Writings*, Harry Zohn (New York: Herzl Press, 1973), 1:62–70.

34. Cf. Yosef Salmon, "תגובת החרדים במזרח אירופה לציונות המדינית" (The response of Eastern European Orthodoxy to political Zionism), in Avni and Shimoni, *הציונית ומתנגדיה בעם היהודי*, pp. 51–73.

35. Birnbaum, *Shadow*, p. 36.

36. Bein, *Herzl*, pp. 191–192.

37. Ibid., pp. 222–223.

38. Israel Cohen, *Theodor Herzl: His Life and Times* (London: Jewish Religious Educational Publications, 1959) pp. 12–13.

39. A detailed description of the internal Zionist negotiations leading up to the Congress was provided in Vital, *Origins*, chap. 12.

40. Both speeches are reprinted verbatim in Hertzberg, *Zionist Idea*, pp. 226–230 and 235–241.

41. Ibid., p. 241.

42. The resolution was published in German in the congress protocols, *Protokol des I.Zionistenkongress in Basel, vom 29 bis 31 August 1897*, Prague, 1911, pp. 133–135. An English translation was published shortly thereafter (and is the version cited here), in *The Jewish Chronicle*, September 3, 1897, p. 13. Cf. Cohen, *Life and Times*, pp. 15–16.

43. Vital, *Origins*, pp. 364–369.

44. We have used the common English terms for these bodies, despite the minor differences of translation and meaning: The "Inner Actions Committee" should, for instance, actually be translated as "Smaller Actions Committee," a reference to the committee's size (not its function) that would be confusing without extensive explanation. The German terminology was used until after World War I, when the terms were Hebraized: the GAK became the Va'ad ha-Poel ha-Klali (thereafter translated as the Zionist General Council) and the EAK became the Va'ad ha-Poel ha-Mezumzam (thereafter translated simply as Executive).

45. Cohen, *Life and Times*, p. 16.

46. Josef Fraenkel, *Theodor Herzl: A Biography* (London: Ararat Publishers), 1946, p. 71.

47. Herzl, *Complete Diaries*, 2: 581.

48. Vital, *Origins*, p. 245. Cf. Jehuda L. Wallach, "Bismarck and the 'Eastern Question' — A Re-Assessment," in J. L. Wallach ed., *Germany and the Middle East, 1835–1939* (Tel Aviv: Institute for German History/Tel Aviv University Press, 1975), pp. 23–29.

49. Vital, *Origins*, p. 295.

50. Birnbaum, *Shadow*, p. 39; Hermann Ellern and Bessi Ellern, comps., *Herzl, Hechler, the Grand Duke of Baden and the German Emperor, 1896–1904* (Tel Aviv: Ellern's Bank, 1961), pp. 1–27.

51. Cf. Ellern and Ellern, *Herzl*, pp. 28–30.

52. Grand Duke Frederick of Baden to Kaiser Wilhelm II, July 28, 1898, cited in ibid., pp. 32–35.

53. Herzl, *Complete Diaries*, 2:612; *Zionist Writings* 1:216–218 and 2:9–13; Ellern and Ellern, *Herzl*, pp. 36–39.

54. David Vital, *Zionism: The Formative Years* (New York: Oxford University Press, 1982), pp. 63–65.

55. Herzl, "Opening Address at the Second Zionist Congress," in *Zionist Writings* 2:16.

56. Ibid., 2:16–17.

57. On the conquest of communities, see Vital, *Formative Years*, pp. 66–68. The Jewish Colonial Trust was incorporated in London on March 20, 1899, as the Jewish Colonial Bank. The bank did not, however, begin to operate immediately due to financial complications. Thereafter the Jewish Colonial Bank incorporated a subsidiary, the Anglo-Palestine Bank (APB). In 1948 APB was again renamed, this time to Bank Leumi le-Israel. On the bank's history, see Nadav ha-Levi, *Banker to an Emerging Nation: The History of Bank Leumi le-Israel* (Haifa: Shikmona Publishing, 1981), chap. 1.

58. Vital, *Formative Years*, pp. 69–70.

59. Luz, *Parallels Meet*, pt. III.

60. Ellern and Ellern, *Herzl*, pp. 37–53; Vital, *Formative Years*, pp. 74–77.

61. Cf. Ellern and Ellern, *Herzl*, pp. 54–57 and the footnote to Theodor Herzl, "Address to the German Kaiser," *Zionist Writings*, p. 30.

62. Herzl, "German Kaiser," pp. 30–32.

63. Herzl, *Complete Diaries*, 2:719–721.

64. Cf. Herzl to Grand Duke Frederick, November 18 and December 15, 1898, in Ellern and Ellern, *Herzl*, pp. 58–64. A marking on the December letter places the reality in stark relief: where Herzl wrote of an agreement over German protection for Zionism, his reader printed a large question mark.

65. Cf. the contributions by Wallach, Trumpener, Carmel, Pick, Grunwald, and Yisraeli in Jehuda Wallach, *Germany and the Middle East*, pp. 23–29, 30–43, 45–71, 72–84, 85–101, and 142–164.

66. Herzl to Grand Duke Frederick, October 27, 1899, in Ellern and Ellern, *Herzl*, p. 75.

67. Ibid., pp. 76–80.

68. Herzl, "Opening Address at the Third Zionist Congress," in *Zionist Writings*, 2:101–108. Cf. Vital, *Formative Years*, pp. 102–105.

69. Herzl to Grand Duke Frederick, March 5, 1900, in Ellern and Ellern, *Herzl*, pp. 81–84.

70. Bein, *תולדות ההיתיישבות*, pp. 13–14; Herzl, "Practical and Political Zionists," in *Zionist Writings*, 2:129–134.

71. Herzl, "Practical," p. 133. Cf., Emanuel Neumann, *The Birth of Jewish Statesmanship: The Story of Theodor Herzl's Life* (New York: Zionist Organization of America, 1940), pp. 20–23.

72. Bein, *תולדות ההיתיישבות*, pp. 17–18.

73. Vital, *Origins*, p. 295.

74. Vital, *Formative Years*, pp. 70, 102–103.

75. Ibid., pp. 104–105.

76. Herzl, "Third Zionist Congress," p. 106.

77. Vital, *Formative Years*, pp. 109–119.

78. Cf. Neville J. Mandel, *The Arabs and Zionism Before World War I* (Berkeley: University of California Press, 1976) chap. 1.

79. Vital, *Formative Years*, pp. 119–128.

80. Bein, *Herzl*, pp. 388–391.

81. Ibid., p. 389.

82. Cf. Herzl's statement to the Sixth Zionist Congress, cited in Raphael Patai, ed., "Herzl's Sinai Project: A Documentary Record," *Herzl Yearbook* 1 (1958):108.

83. Ghali to Greenberg, February 23, 1903, ibid., pp. 114–115.

84. A copy of the draft agreement was published in full in ibid., pp. 117–119.

85. Cromer to Landsdowne, May 14, 1903; Ghali to Goldsmid, May 11, 1903; Sanderson to Herzl, July 16, 1903, ibid., pp. 119–122.

86. Vital, *Formative Years*, p. 150.

87. Ibid., pp. 146–147.

88. Two major sources for this section are Salo W. Baron, *The Russian Jews under Tsars and Soviets*, 2nd ed. (New York: Macmillan, 1976), chap. 4; and Edward Crankshaw, *The Shadow of the Winter Palace: Russia's Drift to Revolution, 1825–1917* (New York: Viking Press, 1976), passim.

89. Martin Gilbert, *The Jews of Russia: Their History in Maps and Photographs* (London: National Council for Soviet Jewry, 1976), p. 23.

90. Baron, *Russian Jews*, p. 57.

91. Cf. Cyrus Adler, ed., *The Voice of America on Kishineff* (Philadelphia: Jewish Publication Society, 1904); Eliyahu Feldman, *Russian Jewry in 1905 Through the Eyes and Camera of a British Diplomat*, Spiegel Lecture in Jewish History no.6 (Tel Aviv: Tel Aviv University Press, 1986); and the editions of the *American Jewish Yearbook* (hereafter *AJYB*) for 1902–1907.

92. Naomi W. Cohen, "The Abrogation of the Russo-American Treaty of 1832," *JSS*, 25, no.1 (January 1963): 3–41.

93. Gilbert, *Jews of Russia*, p. 27.

94. Vital, *Formative Years*, p. 243; Yitzhak Maor, התנועה הציונית ברוסיה (The Zionist movement in Russia) (Jerusalem: Ha-Sifriya ha-Zionit, 1973), pp. 220–222.

95. For a scandalized version of this part of Zionist history, see Lenni Brenner, *Zionism in an Age of Dictators* (New York: Croom Helm, 1983), passim; as a corrective, see Maor, התנועה הציונית ברוסיה, pp. 243–244.

96. Vital, *Formative Years*, p. 253.

97. See, for example, the statement by Rabbis Mohilever and Pines, in Hertzberg, *Zionist Idea*, pp. 398–415.

98. Luz, *Parallels Meet*, chap. 9.

99. Cf. Nachman Syrkin, "The Jewish Problem and the Socialist-Jewish State," in Hertzberg, *Zionist Idea*, pp. 340–350 and Maor, התנועה הציונית ברוסיה, pp. 162–167 and 335–340.

100. Maor, התנועה הציונית ברוסיה, pp. 243–244, Vital, *Formative Years*, pp. 190–198.

101. Vital, *Formative Years*, p. 159. It is necessary to repeat here (as has almost every other scholar on the subject) that the term Uganda plan was something of a misnomer, since the territory offered was located in contemporary Kenya. Nevertheless, since the term Uganda plan (or scheme) has become popular, we have used it throughout.

102. A complete history of the Uganda plan is provided in Robert G. Weisbord, *African Zion* (Philadelphia: Jewish Publication Society, 1968).

103. Cf. the documents cited in Isaiah Friedman ed., *Herzl's Political Activity, 1897–1904*, Rise of Israel Series vol. 2 (New York: Garland, 1987), pp. 289–290 and 295–327.

104. Hill to Greenberg, August 14, 1903, as read into the transcript of the Sixth Zionist Congress, cited in Friedman, *Political Activity*, p. 308.

105. Theodor Herzl, "Opening Address at the Sixth Zionist Congress," in *Zionist Writings*, p. 228.

106. Ibid., p. 229.

107. Nordau's remarks are reproduced verbatim in Friedman, *Political Activity*, pp. 328–338. Cf. Michael Heymann, "Max Nordau at the Early Zionist Congresses, 1897–1905," *Journal of Israeli History* 16, no.3 (Autumn 1995): 245–256.

108. Herzl, "Sixth Zionist Congress," p. 228.

109. Cf the introduction to Michael Heymann, ed., *The Minutes of the Zionist General Council: The Uganda Controversy* (Tel Aviv: Institute for Zionist Research, 1977), 2:5–7.

110. Ibid., p. 10.

111. Moses Gaster, "Open Letter," cited in Heymann, *Uganda Controversy*, pp. 125–126.

112. Heymann, *Uganda Controversy*, pp. 13, 289.
113. Ibid., p. 18.
114. Vital, *Formative Years*, pp. 303–304.
115. Ibid., pp. 318–320, 340–346.
116. Greenberg to Cowen, January 14, 1904, cited in Heymann, *Uganda Controversy*, p. 229. Cf. Vital, *Formative Years*, pp. 320–330.
117. Vital, *Formative Years*, pp. 326–327.
118. Ibid., pp. 345–346.

4

FROM HERZL TO BALFOUR

Ideological Developments, 1904–1914

Theodor Herzl's untimely death in 1904 represented a major setback for the World Zionist Organization and a turning point in the history of Zionism. The WZO, a mere seven years old, was now leaderless — albeit only temporarily so — since no one possessed Herzl's stature or charisma. Indeed, with no heir apparent, the WZO also seemed to be without hope: Hibbat Zion, an earlier international Zionist body, had collapsed after its leader's demise in 1891. Lacking a clear heir, the Engere Aktions Komité (EAK) elected Max Nordau — Herzl's closest companion — temporary president, a position he held only until the Seventh Zionist Congress.

On the surface, the congress, which met in Basel July 27–August 2, 1905, offered little hope for the future. Diplomatic progress was not expected and none was reported.[1] The congress elected a presidium of three to replace Herzl as leader of the Zionist movement, with the triumverate composed of Nordau, Otto Warburg, and David Wolffsohn. The latter acted as chairman of this newly-created Executive Committee (not to be confused with the EAK) and served as president in all but title.

Only two other noteworthy events took place at the congress; both were shocking and not at all reassuring about the WZO's future. First, the Seventh Zionist Congress finally and unequivocally put an end to the Uganda scheme. Second, the Congress's unequivocal rejection of Uganda led to a schism (one of many that would befall the WZO) with the Jewish territorialist movement.

Herzl's 1903 announcement of the British offer to allow the creation of a Jewish colony nearly rent the WZO asunder. However, at the Sixth Zionist Congress in 1903, a compromise was worked out, whereby the British offer would not be rejected out of hand. Instead, a Zionist commission was to study the project's feasibility.[2] This commission reached Uganda in January 1905 but returned with an overall negative response that the WZO published in May 1905.[3] The upshot of this report was that the congress, by an overwhelming majority, rejected the plan once and for all.

The Congress's rejection of the scheme was not without controversy. Zionist leaders such as Israel Zangwill and Nachman Syrkin, who had been strong advocates of settlement in Uganda, believed that the Zionists were making a mistake. They, in turn, seceded from the WZO to form the Jewish Territorial Association (better known by the abbreviation ITO, from the organization's Yiddish initials). These territorialists claimed that by rejecting Uganda the Zionist organization "lost its objective, or at least lost the objective it should have worked for."[4] Territorialists did not deprecate *Eretz Israel* as the Jews' historic homeland. They did, however, feel that work to restore Jewry there was bound to failure since the territory was unobtainable. In light of that reality, the only Zionist alternative to finding a different territory was to create a "small settlement" in *Eretz Israel*. That "small settlement," the territorialist leaders averred, could never develop into a Jewish state and could never provide a refuge for a majority of Jews. It followed that Zionism itself was bound to fail. Eventually the Jewish masses in Eastern Europe, besieged by antisemitism and disheartened by the lack of substantial relief, would be frittered away by assimilation, nonnationalist migration, or both.[5]

In the short term, therefore, the WZO was weakened but in the long term Zionism was strengthened. Territorialism — which saw Zionist efforts in *Eretz Israel* as utopian, impractical, and unlikely to succeed — proved to be all those things and more. For nearly forty years territorialist leaders sought to find a homeland for the Jewish people — a recent history has identified thirty-four different Territorialist schemes — not a single one of which ever came to fruition. Only one, the Birobidzhan scheme, imposed on Russian Jewry by Stalin in the late 1920s and early 1930s, came near to fruition. Yet, despite official Soviet support for settlement by Jews in a nominally "Jewish Autonomous Region," nothing came of the Birobidzhan scheme either. After seventy years Birobidzhan remains Jewish in name only and never replaced Zion in the hearts or minds of nationalistically minded Soviet Jews. About 56,000 Soviet Jews migrated there, but an astounding 60 percent either left for other destinations (including parts of the Soviet Far East) or returned to their points of origin.[6] Many other territorialist schemes — some with greater support, some with less — came to the same ultimate end: complete, abject failure.[7]

Within the Zionist camp, the period after Herzl's death was a time of searching for new means to accomplish the already stated goals. As already noted, Herzl was replaced by an executive committee whose dominant voice was David Wolffsohn. Much different in both style and substance when compared to Herzl, Wolffsohn nevertheless was the correct choice for the task at hand: to rebuild the WZO. Wolffsohn, it may be noted, had not originally wanted the position of chairman, but reluctantly accepted.[8]

Unlike Herzl, Wolffsohn placed relatively less emphasis on diplomacy: His only major diplomatic initiative was with the Turks and culminated in the establishment of a Zionist office in Istanbul (then still called Constantinople).[9] Desultory negotiations over permission to settle 50,000 Jewish families, in return for a hefty Zionist contribution toward the Ottoman empire's debts, seemed to offer a slim hope of obtaining a charter. These negotiations were never more than a minor step, however, their importance being temporarily magnified by the Young Turk revolution (1908) which many Zionists thought (incorrectly) would fundamentally change the Turkish government's attitude toward Zionism. In fact, Wolffsohn and the WZO executive soon gave up hope of influencing the Young Turks and the talks collapsed.[10] Nevertheless, this minor step had two important consequences. First, it brought Zionism back to the attention of the Germans.[11] Second, opening a Zionist office represented a transition from the era in which Political Zionism and Practical Zionism were viewed as polar opposites. Menahem Mendel Ussishkin, one of the leading opponents of the Uganda scheme, summarized the new WZO attitude as the realization that Zionists "had to work to attain the charter from the bottom [up] and from the top [down] simultaneously, through both practical work in Eretz Israel and continued political work in Istanbul."[12]

This new Zionist attitude, colloquially known as Synthetic Zionism, did not mean an end to ideological squabbling within Zionist ranks. On the contrary, Wolffsohn's stewardship as WZO president saw the crystalization of broad, ideological blocs into specific, narrowly construed parties that not only subdivided the WZO, but also developed local chapters wherever Zionism existed. The development of parties was a mixed blessing. Although the movement now appeared disunited and weaker at the top, membership continued to grow — by 1914, at least 127,000 Jews had joined recognized Zionist bodies — reflecting the dynamism and continuing attractiveness of Zionism on the Jewish street.[13]

Moreover, these ideological blocs already had begun to develop in the WZO during Herzl's presidency. Broadly speaking, by Wolffsohn's era these had coalesced into three parties: the General Zionists, the Mizrachi (religious Zionists), and the Socialist Zionist movement. These parties, except for Mizrachi, were further subdivided along a variety of fracture points: General Zionism (which really did not emerge as a specific party until later) was, for example, divided among those who still clung to a narrowly formulated political Zionism (little different from Herzl's), those who still followed Ahad ha-Am's exclusively spiritual focus, and those arguing for a synthesis of the two.[14] Socialist Zionists were divided between those who saw themselves primarily as Zionists adhering to a socialist ideology (whether Marxist or not) and those who saw themselves as primarily socialists working within a Jewish nationalist context (for tactical or other reasons).[15]

Two thinkers stand out as especially critical for an understanding of socialist Zionism: Nachman Syrkin and Ber (Dov Ber) Borochov. Both approached the problem of synthesizing Zionism and socialism from slightly different perspectives, although overall, their ideas were complementary rather than contradictory. A third key socialist Zionist thinker, Aharon David Gordon, developed his ideas somewhat later, but from similar sources. In light of the emphasis Gordon placed on the ideology of Labor (his ideas have come to be known as *Dat ha-Avoda*, or "the religion of labor") rather than on pure ideology, Gordon will be analyzed below in the context of the Second Aliya, whose ideological flavor owed more to him than to either Syrkin or Borochov.

Syrkin (of whom reference already has been made in the context of the territorialist schism) was the earliest of the three fathers of socialist Zionism. He was also the only one of his contemporaries to develop a systematic schema of Jewish nationalism and of Jewry's role in humanity based on broadly Marxist principles. However, it must be added that, despite his Marxist veneer, Syrkin thought of himself as a Zionist — he rejected outright the determinism and negative attitude toward Judaism (and Jewry) that characterized Marx's socialism.[16] Unlike many of his contemporaries, Syrkin did not idealize the proletariat. True, he blamed modern antisemitism mainly on the *petit bourgeois*, who sought a means to divert attention from their exploitation of the working class. But, despite this, Syrkin saw the upcoming proletarian revolution as directed mainly "against the Jews, capitalism, the monarchy, and the state."[17] Moreover, Syrkin feared that antisemitism "has the tendency to permeate all of society and to undermine the existence of the Jewish people."[18]

The only way to avoid catastrophe was for Jews to create a socialist and nationalist homeland. Syrkin's Zionism directed toward this goal developed in three stages. From 1899 until 1905, Syrkin emphasized settlement in *Eretz Israel* — although he never mentioned any specific location for the new Jewish homeland in his main ideological work, *Die Judenfrage und der sozilistische Judenstaat*. As a result of the Uganda schism, Syrkin withdrew from the WZO, entering his territorialist period. The Young Turk revolution revived Syrkin's belief that *Eretz Israel* might be obtainable. As a result, he returned to the WZO in 1909, thereafter (until his death in 1924) expounding his socialist Zionist vision and working for its fulfillment in *Eretz Israel*.

Regardless of its geographic location, Syrkin was specific on the nature of the new Jewish society, which for him summarized the two themes of Zionism: "Exodus" and "Utopia."[19] Young Jews would migrate as pioneers as part of a cooperative venture between the Jewish bourgeois and the Jewish proletariat. Private capital, donated as a matter of Jewish solidarity from the Jewish bourgeois and administered by national institutions, would permit the creation of a classless society in the new Jewish homeland. Although emphasizing cooperation with middle-class elements, Syrkin sought to limit their impact on the Yishuv: "It was a basic axiom," one historian writes of Syrkin, "that the capitalist system and the bourgeois class should not be permitted any foothold in the new society."[20] Finally, it should also be emphasized that Syrkin was emphatically not an etatist. Although the new homeland would be built on a combination of agri-cultural and industrial development, Syrkin believed that the state would be superfluous in the new society, being replaced by a "union of free producers."[21]

Broadly speaking, Borochov fit into the same ideological pattern as Syrkin. Two glaring differences stand out from an analysis of Borochov's writings. First, Borochov was much more narrowly Marxist than Syrkin, especially, but not exclusively, in his adherence to materialism and historical determinism. Then too, unlike Syrkin, Borochov remained tied exclusively to *Eretz Israel*, having entered the Zionist political arena as a protege of Ussishkin's during the Uganda affair.[22] It has been argued recently that the latter was the crux of Borochov's ideology: an effort to prove that some nationalisms could be seen as legitimate from a Marxist point of view. By use of syllogism, Borochov's goal was to prove that if that premise were true, then for empirical reasons it was obvious that a socialist Jewish homeland could only exist in *Eretz Israel*.[23] Emigration to any other destination would merely continue the present Jewish problem and extend its geographic scope — it would not offer a real solution to antisemitic agitation.[24]

It has been argued that Borochov's ideas, like Syrkin's, developed in three distinct phases. From 1901 to 1906, Borochov's thinking was mainly Zionist and only secondarily socialist. This has been regarded as his "pioneering" (or "therapeutic") phase. Between 1907 and 1914, Borochov began to focus more narrowly on socialist issues, in his "proletarian" phase. Finally, between 1915 and 1917 (when he died, at age 36) Borochov sought a synthesis of the two. During this last phase, Borochov also began to jettison (though never completely) some of the deterministic and materialistic aspects of his earlier writings.[25] The upshot of

Borochov's ideology was the creation of a socialist Zionist party, called Poale Zion. However, the party rapidly developed a bi-furcated perspective on Zionist questions, each based on a limited understanding of Borochov's dialectic. Eventually, this duality led to a breach, with Poale Zion splitting in two: Poale Zion's right wing (Poale Zion Yemin, PZY) concentrated on Borochov's earliest and last periods, emphasizing cooperation with bour-geois Zionists (much like Syrkin) and WZO membership. Poale Zion's left wing (Poale Zion Smol, PZS), by contrast, concentrated on Borochov's middle ideological era, forming itself into a dogmatically Marxist party with a Zionist veneer. PZS called for unilateral proletarian activity (class struggle) in all Jewish communities (including the *Yishuv*) against the Jewish middle class, and withdrew from the WZO. After the 1917 Communist takeover in Russia, PZS sought membership in the Third (Communist) International.[26]

Mizrachi, the religious Zionist movement, developed parallel to socialist Zionism, but, obviously, derived from a different synthesis. As will be recalled, two of the earliest Proto-Zionist thinkers, Rabbis Alkali and Kalischer, derived their ideas from traditional sources. Religiously Orthodox Jews, such as Rabbi Mohilever, also participated actively in the Hibbat Zion movement and in the WZO.[27] Orthodox support for Zionism — though by no means universal — continued into the Herzl era.[28] This group of religious supporters for the Zionist movement coalesced into the Mizrachi party after the creation of the Democratic Fraktion in 1901. Mizrachi's name encapsulated the party's entire ideology: to create a *Mercaz Ruhani* (spiritual center) for the Jewish people. To put it another way, Mizrachi's goal was to ensure that the WZO operated in a manner consistent with, or at least cognizant of, Jewish tradition.[29]

Mizrachi's leaders, harking back to concepts of Jewish identity that predated modern nationalism, rejected Ahad ha-Am's notion that *"Zarat ha-Yahadut"* existed. In their view, Judaism remained as vibrant as ever — except that some Jews, having absorbed modern notions from the non-Jewish world, now rejected the eternal covenant. The essence of Jewry as both an ethnic/national and religious group was always and would always remain the "Torah and the culture of their forefathers, or in one word tradition in its broadest sense."[30] As such, it was impossible to accept the premise that a "new" Jewish culture was needed. It followed, naturally, that Mizrachi's leaders saw the real Jewish crisis (to use Ahad ha-Am's phrase) as "*Zarat ha-Yehudim*," or the need to solve the problem engendered by Jewish homelessness as it manifested itself in modern antisemitism. Zionism, accordingly, was nothing more (and nothing less) than an effort to "find a safe haven in our ancestral homeland for the children of Israel in the diaspora."[31]

To be sure, the attitude that Zionism was little more than a response to antisemitism derived from ideological and demographic realities: Fewer and fewer Jews in Eastern Europe continued to define themselves as Orthodox. By defining Zionism in the narrow, Herzlian sense, Mizrachi's leaders eliminated any potential opposition — at least to their own satisfaction — against cooperation with "freethinkers" and heretics. At the same time, Mizrachi leaders such as Rabbi Yitzhak Yaakov Reines saw Zionism as a foretaste of an eventual return to Jewish tradition(*halacha*) by nationalistically minded Jews.[32] Nonetheless, such a hope was formulated as secondary; Mizrachi's main goal was framed as finding a secure homeland in some part of the world.

Ironically, a corollary to Mizrachi's position on antisemitism, Zionism, and the need to rescue Jewry from an impending catastrophe led Mizrachi's leaders to support the Uganda proposal. Rabbi Reines, for example, felt that Herzl had to be supported unequivocally. This was true even if Uganda held no specific meaning for Jews or Judaism.[33] Cultural Zionism detracted from the goal of creating a Jewish national home and thus was to be strongly resisted.[34] In light of this position, Mizrachi fought consistently to remove cultural questions from the Zionist agenda, fighting a rearguard action on this issue for most of the

first twenty years of the WZO's existence.[35]

Mizrachi's position in the Jewish world as a whole must be kept in context. The party faced an almost unprecedented two-front battle for most of its history, being viewed as too Orthodox by secular Zionists and as insufficiently Orthodox by religious leaders who rejected Zionism. The non-Zionist Orthodox — who later would adopt the term *Haredi* (God-fearing) to define themselves — saw Zionism (in all forms) as an anathema. "Zionism," wrote one rabbi, "itself is based on the denial of divine providence . . . and the hoped-for redeemer. The nationalism of which they speak fulfills itself in nothing other than the destruction of [our] sacred religion."[36] For religious critics of Zionism, Mizrachi represented as much of a threat, if not more of a threat, as any secular Zionist party.[37] The leader of the Lubavitch Hasidic sect, for one, condemned religious Zionism for leading "right-thinking Jews to tear from their hearts every concern with the holiness of the Torah, faith in God and the fulfillment of the active commandments . . . and has instead planted in their hearts the belief that through nationalism they are complete Jews."[38]

The relationship between religion and nationalism was destined to remain controversial throughout the history of the WZO; it certainly remains an active concern in the State of Israel today.[39] To be sure, such conflicts appeared to weaken the WZO, mainly by diverting time and energy that could be better spent elsewhere. At the same time, however, the Zionist movement's ideological diversity reflected conditions in the Jewish world as a whole, and the WZO's democratic nature left no choice except the emergence of parties. Indeed, given the limited chances for accomplishing Zionist goals at the time, the development of parties was inevitable. That these parties advocated their positions without destroying the essential unity of the movement was a tribute to the resilience of the organization that Herzl founded.

Institutional Developments, 1904–1914

Institutional factors played a pivotal role in

the evolution of Zionism between Herzl's death and the outbreak of World War I. Two features stand out as critical: the geographic growth of the Zionist movement and the emphasis on *Gegenwartsarbeit*, the taking of small steps within local Jewish communities to improve living conditions, since the possibility of attaining diplomatic success was minimal. In passing, it should also be noted that the WZO — as an institution — remained relatively stable during this entire era. Stability continued after Wolffsohn's resignation as *de facto* president at the Tenth Zionist Congress in Basel (August 9–15, 1911) and his replacement by Otto Warburg.[40]

The growth of Zionism in this transitional era may be represented by two different sets of data. The first, a public opinion survey conducted with Jewish students in Kiev in 1909, studied 520 Jewish students attending the University of Kiev or the Kiev Poly-technic Institute.[41] Of the total, more than half (55 percent to be precise) responded to a question on Jewry's future by positing a hope for continued national existence. By contrast, only 21.6 percent saw Jewry's future in assimilation.[42] Out of a total of 277 who claimed to be active members of a political party, sixty-six (23.8 percent), described themselves as Zionists; another forty-four (15.3 percent) identified as Bundists. Nearly half the students either denied membership in any party or did not respond (243 in all or roughly 46.7 percent).[43] Finally, all the Zionist students and 86 percent of the Bundist students stated their preference for the continued national survival of the Jewish people, as did half of the students who described themselves as unaffiliated. One quarter of the latter saw assimilation as Jewry's most desirable future, as did 38 percent of students identifying as non-Bundist Socialists. However, 36 percent of non-Bundist Socialists also saw Jewry's future in Jewish national terms.[44]

What can be gleaned from these figures? In analyzing them, one fact becomes immediately apparent: in the first decade of the twentieth century, the Zionist organization represented neither a majority of college educated Russian Jewish youth nor the small minority that Zionism's opponents claimed them to be. Zionists held a slim majority over Bundists (by about 3 to 2), although that may reflect the personalities of party members: as a socialist party, the Bund's membership derived from segments of the Jewish urban proletariat that were unlikely to send youth to university. Finally, however, the relatively high proportion of all students responding affirmatively to questions about Jewish national survival seems to indicate that even among those who did not actually join Zionist parties, a fairly strong reserve of sympathy for Zionism — what could possibly be seen as a "potential Zionism" — existed.

Roughly similar conclusions may be drawn from another example, that of the blossoming of Zionism in America. By 1914 Zionist federations existed in virtually every country where Jews lived. However, there were a number of critical differences between American Zionism and its European counterpart. First, the United States would not seem to be conducive to Jewish nationalism. Although antisemitism existed in the United States, Jew hatred was neither as prevalent nor as virulent as it was in Europe.[45] Furthermore, the mass Jewish immigration between 1880 and 1920 appeared to belie Zionist feelings on the migrants' part. Had they held such convictions, it could be argued, they would have moved to *Eretz Israel*. While this is an unfair generalization, it is not wholly inaccurate.[46]

The astounding fact about Zionism in the United States in the pre–World War I era, and what made American Zionism unique, was the extent to which expressions of sympathy for Zionism extended both upward and downward through American Jewry. If, for instance, Zionists in England saw themselves as having no chance to conquer their community — a reality that forced them to rely on the potentially dubious tactic of infiltration — such was not the case in the United States.[47] To be sure, many of American Jewry's grandees (the so-called *Yahudim*) opposed Zionism. But others, including the highly respected jurists Louis D. Brandeis (the first Jewish Associate Justice of the U.S. Supreme Court) and Julian

W. Mack (who served on the U.S. Circuit Court of Appeals), as well as communal leaders Horace M. Kallen, Rabbis David De Sola Pool and Solomon Schechter, and journalist Cyrus L. Sulzberger (a member of the family that owned the *New York Times*), supported Zionism and made support for Zionism appear respectable in the American and American Jewish contexts.[48]

As important as these developments were, and the significance of Zionist growth should not be deprecated, the development of ideas regarding *Gegenwartsarbeit* (work in the here and now) were more important. By the summer of 1906 it was obvious, even to the most novice WZO members, that a charter could not be achieved in the near future. That realization, when combined with the apparent, if temporary, recent successes of non-Zionist ideologies in promoting Jewish interests — especially during and after the Russian revolution of 1905 — placed Zionists in a quandary: If they did nothing, they stood to lose the loyalty of most Jews, even those whose orientation was nationalist, since the community would see its needs fulfilled by other parties.[49] On the other hand, if Zionists became involved intensively in the affairs of the local community, the possibility of diffusing Zionist strength on ephemeral goals seemed much more threatening. Nonetheless, an unofficial Russian Zionist conference held in Odessa in late July 1906 recommended concentration on communal and educational work.[50]

This approach became the WZO's official policy after the Helsingfors Conference. The Russian Zionists meeting in Helsingfors (Helsinki) December 4–10, 1906, over-whelmingly supported "work in the here and now," including demands that Zionists involve themselves in efforts to obtain Jewish autonomy in the diaspora. More significantly, the conferees realized quite quickly that no one form of Zionism had hither-tofore succeeded, nor was any one form likely to succeed in the future. As a result, they demanded a synthesis of political and practical work, with main focus (for the time being, at least) on the latter.[51]

This new policy resulted in something of a paradox. If Zionists began to work for Jewish autonomy in the diaspora, even as a temporary gesture, what distinguished them from non-Zionists? Obviously, no easy answer was available. Yitzhak Gruenbaum, one of the sponsors of the Helsingfors Conference, could only attempt to explain away the paradox by nothing that "there is no future, without a present."[52] This was a major departure from previous Zionist policy — for all intents and purposes meaning a radical departure from Herzl's ideas — but appeared to be the only option available to the WZO.[53] Hereafter, Zionists would operate on three levels: the diplomatic level (abandoned for now, but to be resumed in 1914), the communal level, and the practical level (in terms of building of the *Yishuv*).

The Yishuv's Growth, 1904–1914

Although the WZO appeared to stagnate after Herzl's death, the *Yishuv* did not. Growth, which had been slow between 1881 and 1903, was at least steady. And this growth pattern continued during the Second Aliya in the decade before World War I. The opening of a branch of the Anglo-Palestine Bank in Jaffa in 1903, and the creation of the Palastinaamt in 1905 — respectively chaired by Zvi D. Levontin and Arthur Ruppin — were thus critical developments. Equally important was the Zichron Ya'akov Conference of 1903, at which the conferees agreed to create a representative body elected by all settlers aged 18 years or older. This body, which was to meet annually, would unify the various settlements and, to the extent possible, defend their interests. Importantly, although of limited duration (the *Yishuv*-wide committee ceased to function in 1905), this was the first expression of Jewish self-government in *Eretz Israel* in modern times.[54]

A new wave of *aliya* began as a result of the pogroms in Russia in 1902–1903. This so-called Second Aliya had both similarities and differences with the First Aliya (which arrived in

Eretz Israel between 1881 and 1903). As with the earlier arrivals, most new *olim* arrived from Eastern Europe. And once again, few had any formal (or extensive informal) training in agriculture. Unlike their predecessors, however, the new *olim* were more ideologically disposed. Though raised in middle-class Jewish homes, most of the new *olim* had absorbed the revolutionary ideas and rhetoric of their time; most were also affected, to one degree or another, by the Jewish experience in the abortive 1905 Russian revolution and by Jewish self-defense efforts during that tempestuous era. Additionally, and more importantly, the land they now settled in was somewhat prepared to receive them. That fact did not, however, necessarily mean fewer travails for the new *olim*. On the contrary, in a sense the members of the Second Aliya had a more difficult struggle than their predecessors. In particular, the new *olim* had to fight against the tendency among *Moshav* members to hire Arab labor. As a result, the new *olim* spoke of a Jewish need to "conquer labor" and to emphasize *Avoda Ivrit* (Hebrew labor), by which they meant that all substantial labor — manual or otherwise — in the *Yishuv* should be performed by Jews.[55]

For all intents and purposes, the Second Aliya's motto might well have been, "*anu banu artza livnot ule–hibanot ba*" — we have come to the land to build her and be built by her. This ideology has come to be identified primarily with these newcomers, and in particular with Aaron David Gordon. Gordon framed his ideology as nothing less than a religion of labor (*Dat ha-Avoda*). Restoration of a Jewish national home *per force* required the individual Jew's regeneration through creating a bond with nature. This could only be accomplished by agricultural work. "The Jewish people," Gordon wrote in 1911, "has been completely cut off from nature and imprisoned within city walls these two thousand years."[56] Gordon continued:

We have become accustomed to every form of life, except to a life of labor — of labor done at our own behest and for its own sake. It will require the greatest effort of will for such a people to become normal again. we lack the principal ingredient for national life. We lack the habit of labor — not labor performed out of external compulsion, but labor to which one is attached in a natural and organic way. This kind of labor binds a people to its soil and to its national culture.[57]

Gordon followed the logic of his ideology in 1904 when he immigrated and took the first of a series of agricultural jobs, working as a day laborer in a vineyard. Injured in a scuffle with Arab thieves in 1907, Gordon nevertheless continued to advocate the creation of a socialist, agrarian Jewish society in Eretz Israel. In this period, he distinguished between two pairs of Zionist work: the path adopted by "realists" and the visionary path of national rebirth. Gordon identified the former with all Zionist ideologies that hoped to transfer Jews to *Eretz Israel* without having to effect any changes in the people or the land. Of these people Gordon said, "Galut is always Galut, in Palestine no less than in any other country."[58] In contrast, Gordon identified the visionary philosophy as the one that sought to totally transform the Jewish people by returning to agricultural labor.

Gordon's main impact was felt after 1912, when he joined Kibbutz Degania: his fusion of Ahad ha-Am's cultural Zionism — mainly its emphasis on *Tehiat ha-Ruah* (spiritual regeneration) — with socialism was to be of greater importance within the New *Yishuv* than Nachman Syrkin's fusion of political Zionism with socialism or even Ber Borochov's more strictly Marxist ideology (both of which have been dealt with above).[59] A direct consequence of Gordon's activities was the creation of ha-Poel ha-Zair (the young laborer). However, two notes must be added here. First, not all socialist Zionists in *Eretz Israel* agreed with Gordon's apolitical assessment. These socialist Zionists, including two activists named David Ben-Gurion and Yitzhak Ben-Zvi, formed a wing of the diaspora Poale Zion party. Second, it must be emphasized that Gordon's ideology was much less strictly socialist — and certainly less Marxist — than the socialist Zionist visions of either Syrkin or Borochov. One author, for example, chose to clearly distinguish between the "Jewish version of Marxist Socialism" á la Borochov, and the "utopian-anarchist Gordonian idea."[60]

The rise of socialist Zionist ideology was one key development during the Second Aliya; the *Kibbutz* was another, turning out to be a key to future developments in the *Yishuv*, it was a corollary to the ideological development just described. It followed, after all, that if Jews were to build a class-less society, they had to do so by creating a society based on four principles: self-reliance, social justice, pioneering (*halutziut*), and Jewish labor.[61] The *Kibbutz* — Zionism's democratically organized form of collective settlement — was the crux of socialist Zionist ideology precisely because it fulfilled those four roles perfectly.

That said, it must also be noted that much of socialist Zionism developed as a result of the founding of the early *Kibbutzim*, and not vice versa. This held true because the first collective settlements developed from financial, not ideological causes: the new *olim*, expecting a relatively easy time finding work in Jewish-owned settlements, were severely disappointed to discover that the *Biluim* preferred Arab labor. The new *olim* were "too inexperienced" and the wages they sought were too high. Additionally, they were not fully acclimatized to conditions in *Eretz Israel*. To overcome their poverty and their loneliness, these *halutzim* banded together to form collective settlements. Between 1904 and 1907, four such *Kvutzot* arose: in Rehovot, Petah Tikva (two *Kvutzot*), and Jaffa. None of these lasted longer than two years, but all of them gave rise to further experiments in collective living.[62] In 1907, a group of twelve agricultural workers approached representatives of the Jewish Colonization Association (ICA, the non-Zionist philanthropic group founded in the 1890s to assist the *Biluim*) requesting permission to build a collective settlement in ICA's Sejera training camp in the Lower Galilee. In 1909 this group moved to a small plot of land on the shores of Lake Kinneret (the Sea of Galilee) near a "preparatory" settlement planned by Arthur Ruppin, who, as already noted, headed the WZO's Palestinaamt.[63]

The new settlement, called Degania by its settlers, was an unqualified success — at least insofar as it continued to operate almost without interruption until World War I. Furthermore, Degania — which prides itself as *"Em ha-Kvutzot"* (the mother of collective settlements) — was only the first of many more to come: By 1914 twenty-eight *Kibbutzim, Kvutzot,* and *Moshav Poalim* (a less stringent form of collective settlement that retained the concept of private property, but in which all work was done collectively and for all members' benefit) were operating with 382 members.[64]

All these settlements operated on a simple set of principles: settlement in a specific location, generally at the periphery of the *Yishuv*; cooperative lifestyle, in terms of obligations (labor), rights, and property (including among other things, communal ownership of all goods); communal child care; and, to a degree, economic success, at least within the limited capabilities of the *Yishuv* at the time. Finally, it must also be noted that part of the reason for the success of the *Kibbutz* experiment was the close attention to details — for example, the technicalities relating to settlement building — that went into creating the settlements after 1910.[65]

The *Kibbutz* was one of the most important contributions associated with the Second Aliya. Moreover, despite their small size, these collective settlements represented the first glimmerings of the labor party that would lead Zionism — haltingly at first — toward its goals.[66] However, it would be wrong to assume that only socialist Zionists were represented in the Second Aliya. Quite the contrary: In a survey of 937 *olim* (644 men and 293 women) who immigrated between 1904 and 1914, a diverse membership pattern was detected, as summarized in Table 4.1.[67]

TABLE 4.1: Party Affiliations of Second Aliya Members in the Diaspora

Party	Number	Percentage
Poale Zion	188	20.06
General Zionist	149	15.90
Zeirei Zion	121	12.91
Other Socialist Zionist	37	3.94[68]
Bund	16	1.70
Social Democrats	15	1.60[69]
Social Revolutionary	12	1.28[70]
Other/Unaffiliated	399	42.56

Source: Yosef Gorni in *Ha-Zionut*, 1 (1970): 229 f.

As these figures show, a plurality of *olim* had not been politically active in the diaspora, although a clear majority of those who had been active, had been involved in socialist Zionist groups. In *Eretz Israel*, these *olim* divided their membership between four major parties (although most [482/51.4%] remained unaffiliated): ha-Poel ha-Zair (228/24.3%), Poale Zion (201/20.5%), General Zionists (22/2.4%), and Mizrachi (4/0.4%).[71]

To put the figures into perspective, although the *Kibbutz* was one of the Second Aliya's enduring legacies, the establishment of Tel Aviv, the first modern Jewish city, was another. The origins of Tel Aviv can be traced to the realities of *aliya* prior to World War I. In particular, the fact that Ottoman Palestine had only one functioning port (Jaffa) meant that most *olim* disembarked there. As more Jews immigrated, over-crowding and squalor increased in a city that was already overcrowded and suffering from slum conditions. To remedy this situation, forty-six Jewish families formed the Ahuzat Bayit Society in 1907. With a loan from the Keren Kayemet le-Israel and technical help from Ruppin — who can only be described as "ubiquitous" — sixty housing units were begun in 1909. A year later the locality was founded as a city, although its legal status at the time was that of a suburb of Jaffa (a status that was retained until 1934).[72] Over the years Tel Aviv experienced phenomenal growth becoming the social, political, and economic center of the developing *Yishuv*.

The Second Aliya also saw a major influx of Jews from Yemen into the *Yishuv*. Many have overlooked this aspect of Zionist history, concentrating instead on the European context of modern Jewish nationalism. But, between 1908 and 1912, almost 1,200 Jews left Yemen and settled in *Eretz Israel*. Their *aliya* was inspired in part by a visit by Shmuel Yavnieli, a member of Ruppin's staff at the Palestina-amt. Yavnieli's mission speeded up a process of Jewish emigration from Yemen that began parallel to the First Aliya.[73] The Yemenite *olim* also experienced difficulties in finding jobs, but, on the whole, they fit in more easily than their European counterparts. Eventually, all Jewish settlements (except for *Kibbutzim*) contained a Yemenite neighborhood.

Finally, the Second Aliya also saw the systematic development of Jewish self-defense in *Eretz Israel*. It is, of course, a myth — well-worn, but nonetheless inacurate — that Jews did not physically defend themselves during the years of the diaspora.[74] Even so, self-defense became a major issue of Jewish communal concern only after the Kishinev Pogrom, during the same period as the Second Aliya. In part, self-defense was a reflection of the new spirit within the Jewish community. This was particularly true regarding the Zionist (and Bundist) youth who participated in organized self-defense groups.[75] Some of them, in turn, immigrated to *Eretz Israel* where they continued their clandestine activities (under different circumstances).

In September 1907, ten young men met in Yitzhak Ben-Zvi's house to hear Israel Shochat, one of the leaders of the Second Aliya, discuss the implications of *Avoda Ivrit.* In Shochat's view, the concept of Zionist conquest of labor also included conquest of self-defense. Until then, Jewish settlements hired local Circassians or Druze to protect their property from marauding Bedouin or petty Arab thieves. The ten conferees formed themselves into the ha-Shomer (Watchman's) society, setting out to convince Jewish farmers to hire them as guards. This proved to be more complicated than originally expected. Still, two Shomrim were hired to provide security in Kfar Tabor (lower Galilee) in 1908. Two more settlements hired Shomrim in 1909. By 1911, ha-Shomer was responsible for security in all Jewish settlements in the Galilee.[76]

Ha-Shomer's members spoke of an intimate bond uniting Jews, the land, and the need for security. They also practiced what they preached, participating in the founding of every *Kibbutz* established between Degania and World War I. The Shomrim also tried, unsuccessfully, to form a training body called Gdud ha-Avoda. Its purpose would be to train young immigrants in both agriculture and self-defense techniques after which members would serve for at least two years in a new settlement. The idea, however, proved abortive (for the time being).[77]

Of course, ha-Shomer's immediate task was to protect Jewish settlements from attack by local Arabs who were, to one degree or another, hostile to Jewish nationalism.[78] Arab nationalists sought the creation of an Arab kingdom in Ottoman territory and, in the 1880s, had begun agitation in that direction.[79] Negib Azouri, one of the foremost Arab nationlists of the early twentieth century, went so far as to claim (in 1905) that Jewish and Arab nationalism were "destined to fight each other continually until one of them prevails over the other."[80]

This nascent conflict between two Semitic nationalisms would become central to Zionist diplomacy during the mandatory era.

Prior to World War I, the main security threat facing ha-Shomer was more prosaic. Some local Arabs would intermittently attack Jewish settlements in order to rob them. A completely different problem was posed by Bedouin bands whose depredations struck equally upon Jewish and Arab residents.[81] What complicated ha-Shomer's mission was the hope of defending Jewish settlements *while* maintaining proper (if not friendly) relations with local Arabs, in the hope that the Arabs could be won over into an anti-Ottoman alliance.[82]

In seeking to summarize the Second Aliya, it seems pertinent to emphasize the salient features associated with this wave of immigration: approximately 30,000 Jews settled in *Eretz Israel* by the eve of World War I; the expansion of the *Yishuv,* mainly into the Lower Galilee; development of the *Kibbutz* and of Tel Aviv; beginnings of Jewish self-defense; and the first, tentative steps toward Jewish self-government. To be sure, in early 1914 no one knew just how close the Zionists were to the diplomatic breakthrough they sought. Nonetheless, it was clear that the *Yishuv* had been placed on a secure foundation.

Zionism During World War I[83]

A new found sense of vibrancy within the WZO was expressed forcefully at the Eleventh Zionist Congress held in Vienna September 2–9, 1913. At the Congress the dispute between political and practical Zionists was finally laid to rest. The first test of this vibrancy, however, developed from an unexpected quarter a year after the Congress. The outbreak of war in 1914 caught Zionists in an unusual, and potentially dangerous, position. Prior to the war, WZO policy had maintained strict neutrality on all matters relating to the great powers. Thus, while negotiating with the British, French, Russians, Germans, and Turks, the WZO went to great lengths not to associate with any one power too closely. The initial Zionist response to war's outbreak was to advocate staying the course. Zionist neutrality was founded on two major strategic concerns. First, was the weak diplomatic position of the

WZO. Associating with either the Entente Powers (England, France, and Russia) or the Central Powers (Germany, Austria-Hungary, and Ottoman Turkey) could potentially close doors for Zionist diplomacy in the other camp. Moreover, since it was not by any means clear which side would win, the potential of making the "wrong" decision was high and the potential risk of such miscalculation great. Second, the fate of the *Yishuv* weighed heavily on Zionist minds, especially after the Ottoman Empire declared war on Great Britain on November 4, 1914. The subsequent massacres of Armenians by Turkish authorities and the potential for similar attacks on Jews in *Eretz Israel* were major incentives to remain neutral.[84]

The latter concern was, of course, the primary one for most Zionists. Not surprisingly, the Grosses Aktions Komité, meeting in Copenhagen in December 1914, unanimously voted to adopt a tripartite policy: strict neutrality between the powers; redoubled efforts to obtain international support for a charter and a Jewish national home; and demonstrations of complete loyalty to Turkey by all members of the *Yishuv*.[85]

The propriety of Zionist policy was most clearly demonstrated over the next few months. Within days of the Ottoman declaration of war, extensive house-to-house searches — ostensibly for illegal firearms and British agents — were undertaken in Jewish settlements on or near the coast, including Tel Aviv and Mikve Israel. The latter was under virtual military occupation for two entire days until the searches ended.[86] Simultaneously, many Zionist leaders were arrested and the activities of all Zionist agencies — including the Keren Kayemet le-Israel, the Palestinaamt, and the socialist Zionist parties — were ordered terminated.[87] Numerous Zionist activists were deported, with many of the deportees making their way to the United States.[88]

The result of these developments was to cement the official Zionist policy of strict neutrality. As a corollary, Zionist leaders,

including Ruppin, Richard Lichtheim (the WZO representative in Constantinople), and Victor Jacobson (a senior EAK member), sought, and obtained, German promises of protection for the *Yishuv*.[89] The Zionist perception, during and after the war, was well captured by a statement made by Jacob Thon (Ruppin's Deputy at the Palestinaamt):

We would have suffered irreparable harm had the mighty hand of the German government not protected us in the hour of danger . . . and thus preserved the civil(ian) population from destruction.[90]

Even with German protection the Jewish population of Jaffa was forcibly evacuated in 1917, and further evacuations were planned.[91]

Zionist behavior under the circumstances is quite clear, but German actions require some explanation. Although the Zionists' first diplomatic impulse had led to Germany, nothing substantial had developed from these contacts. In fact, both of the major territorial offers made to the WZO prior to 1914 — the el Arish and the Uganda schemes — had originated with the British. At the beginning of the war, the German policy of paying scant serious attention to the WZO began to change. The exact cause of this change is unclear, but one factor seems to stand out: German victories on the eastern front brought large numbers of Jews (in addition to Poles, Ukrainians, and other ethnic groups) into the German fold. It was widely assumed, by the Germans and the British, that most of these Jews supported Zionism and that their attitude toward the war could be swayed by either side in return for a "friendly attitude towards Zionism and its aims."[92] Senior figures in the German foreign ministry and some of the most senior field commanders expressed similar attitudes.[93] The upshot of such attitudes was pressure for a pro-Zionist declaration to be issued by the German government.

The push for such a declaration continued to mount over the course of 1916 and 1917, especially after the Germans realized that the British were also contemplating such an act.[94] However, an equally strong current within the

German government rejected, to a greater or lesser degree, such an action. Some German diplomats — especially the German ambassador to Turkey, Richard Von Kühlmann — strongly opposed any action on behalf of the Zionists. The ambassador feared that such an action would alienate the Turks.[95] Zionist leaders tried repeatedly but unsuccessfully to change German policy. By the time the Germans budged, the British had already issued the Balfour Declaration. Furthermore, the glaring inconsistencies in the German statement made it virtually meaningless, of no real significance to the WZO.[96] In July 1918 — the eve of the complete British conquest of Palestine and Syria — even the Turks changed their policy, agreeing to the creation of an autonomous "Jewish Center" in an Ottoman-controlled Middle East.[97]

Momentous changes were also occurring among the Entente powers and their attitudes toward Zionism and the Middle East. In particular, France and Britain were greatly concerned with the strategic situation in the region. Despite British acquisition of the Sinai Peninsula as a buffer for Egypt, the Suez Canal was still very vulnerable to attack. Moreover, operations against the Ottomans — in Mesopotamia (1914–1916) and at Gallipoli (1915) — proved to be spectacular failures.[98] In seeking allies to aid their operations against the Ottoman empire, Britain and France also had to consider public opinion in neutral America. Although in retrospect their positions seem greatly exaggerated, British and French politicians seriously felt that tepid American public opinion — especially within an American Jewish community widely perceived as being pro-German (though, if anything, American Jewish public opinion was really anti-Russian) — could be won over to the Entente cause by overt support for the Zionist cause.[99] A third factor existed as well. British military personnel in Egypt were convinced that an Arab military campaign against the Ottomans could provide help to hard-pressed British forces defending the Suez Canal. Eventually a military advisory mission was dispatched to Sharif Hussein of Mecca, a leading exponent of Arab nationalism. This mission, popularly identified with the British officer Thomas E. Lawrence (Lawrence of Arabia), succeeded in fanning the flames of revolt in Arabia and Trans-Jordan. Lawrence's guerilla campaign indeed was helpful to the British; the next steps would be both military and diplomatic.

In October 1915, Sir Henry McMahon, the British high commissioner in Egypt, began a diplomatic correspondence with Hussein. McMahon's proposals were based on mutual interests: British support for Arab political demands in return for further military assistance. In essence, the result was a British agreement to support moves (after the war) to create an independent Arab kingdom in the Middle East, to be ruled by Hussein (or a member of his family). Since this British promise was to become a source of controversy during the 1930s, the letter must be analyzed in some detail, even though it is of only indirect importance to developments in Anglo-Zionist relations during World War I.[100]

By the time McMahon sent his famous letter to Hussein, the negotiations were nearly a year old. First contacts had been made by the Field Marshal Lord Horatio Kitchener. Hussein responded to the British initiative reluctantly, but on July 14, 1915, he was sufficiently confident of British support to put his minimum demands in writing. McMahon responded on September 9, but only in a general way. This disappointed Hussein, who sought specific assurances from the Entente. Further correspondence culminated in McMahon's letter of October 24, which read in part:

> I have realised, however, from your last letter that you regard this question as one of vital and urgent importance. I have, therefore, lost no time in informing the Government of Great Britain of the contents of your letter, and it is with great pleasure that I communicate to you on their behalf the following statement, which I am confident you will receive with satisfaction.
> *The two districts of Mersina and Alexandretta and portions of Syria lying to the west of the*

districts of Damascus, Homs, Hama and Aleppo cannot be said to be purely Arab, and should be excluded from the limits demanded.

With the above modification, and without prejudice to our existing treaties with Arab chiefs, we accept those limits.[101]

Couched in this diplomatic language was a five-part agreement between the Arabs and Great Britain. Under the agreement's terms the British would help obtain independence for the Arab nation after World War I. For their part, the Arabs agreed to redouble their efforts to defeat the Ottoman Empire. However, part of the British commitment was destined to be controversial. In his zeal to delineate borders for the proposed Arab state, McMahon did so by listing the major population centers in Syria. That led many Arab nationalists to assume that only the regions west of the cities listed — Damascus, Homs, Hama, and Aleppo — would be excluded from the Arab state.[102] Based on the international borders current in the 1990s, the region to be removed from Hussein's control corresponded approximately to the Lebanese Republic. In other words, the British appeared to have promised Palestine to the Arabs.

Yet, in statements made as early as 1920, and most particularly in testimony before the Palestine Royal Commission (the so-called Peel Commission), McMahon testified that such had never been his intention. On the contrary, McMahon claimed that his promise to Hussein excluded all territories west of an imaginary line drawn from Aleppo southward via Homs, Hama, and Damascus, to the Gulf of Akaba and the eastern arm of the Red Sea.[103] In terms of contemporary international borders, that would have excluded Lebanon, Palestine/Israel (i.e., the territory geographers once designated Cis-Jordan), and the Jordan River Valley. Roughly speaking, the excluded territory's border could be said to run parallel with the Hedjaz to Damascus railroad.

The arguments over McMahon's actual

intentions have continued to bedevil historians and political analysts more than eighty years after the letter was originally written. Not inappropriately, some historians view the differing interpretations of the letter's territorial aspects as one of the main causes of the Arab-Israeli conflict. Further, this is more than a matter of semantics. Hussein's successors — his sons Faisal and Abdullah — did not raise the issue immediately after the war. In fact, Faisal's agreements with Zionist leaders Chaim Weizmann and Felix Frankfurter represented his acceptance of the premise that *Eretz Israel* belonged to the Jews and should be excluded from his territory. Only after Faisal was denied what he sought — control of Syria — did Arab nationalists begin to advocate their claim that Palestine/*Eretz Israel* was a twice-promised land.[104]

Furthermore, the Sykes-Picot agreement rendered the question of territorial promises to the Arabs (and later to the Jews as well) ever more complex. Representing only slightly more than a land grab by Britain and France (with inducements added for the Russians, Italians, and Greeks), the Sykes-Picot agreement was critical to further developments and must also be reviewed in detail. Broadly speaking, the agreement sought to reduce Anglo-French rivalries in a postwar Middle East by dividing Ottoman territory (assuming that a hypothetical allied victory would lead to Ottoman collapse). Initial discussions were held late in 1915 between French Middle East expert Charles Francois Georges Picot and his opposite number in England, Sir Mark Sykes. In May 1916, an agreement was worked out, whose main substance is summarized here.

In essence, the Sykes-Picot Agreement divided the Middle East into five zones: the Blue Zone under direct French control, the Red Zone under direct British control, the A Zone under French influence (as either a colony or an independent protectorate), the B Zone under British influence (as either a colony or an independent protectorate), and finally, an allied Condominium. The latter was the term used for Palestine, which, it was expected, would be ruled jointly by Britain and France.[105] In effect, the Sykes-Picot Agreement

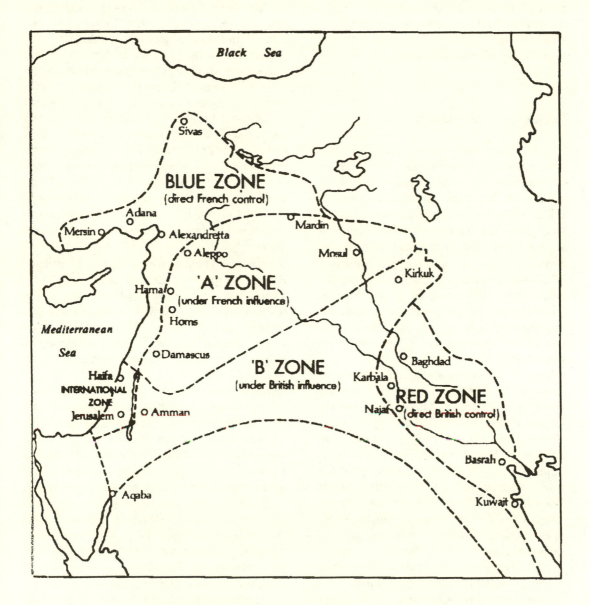

Map of the Sykes-Picot Borders, as Proposed in 1916.
From: Arthur Goldsmidt, Jr., *A Concise History of the Middle East* 5th ed.,
(Boulder: Westview Press, 1996): 190. Reprinted with permission of Westview Press.

gave Syria and Lebanon to the French and Mesopotamia (today's Iraq) and Trans-Jordan to the British.

But the British began to have reservations almost immediately, mainly over international rule for Palestine. Britain's involvement in the Middle East was based on the perceived need to protect the Suez Canal. Palestine, which bordered on the Sinai Peninsula, was seen as part and parcel of Britain's strategic interests.[106] Obtaining Palestine was therefore of paramount importance. Yet the British had promised to share Palestine with the French — and may well (by an unintended inference of vague geographic terms) have also already promised the territory to the Arabs. Further contemplation of strategic necessities would lead the British into a further promise, in this case, with the Zionists.

Forging an Anglo–Zionist Compact

The belligerent powers' actions and perceptions in the Middle East during World War I gave rise to complex political maneuvers. These perceptions led to negotiations with the Arabs and, in the guise of the Sykes-Picot Agreement, to a decision on a postwar sharing of Ottoman territory. In France (at least) a more positive evaluation of Zionism began to develop around the same time. As important as the Franco-Zionist connection may have been, however, the renewed contacts between Zionists and the British government were even more important.

Just as British leaders realized that a coincidence of interests existed between Britain's needs in the Middle East and the hopes of the WZO in that region, some Zionists began to arrive at the same conclusion. Although the WZO as a whole remained strictly neutral at this stage of the war, leaders of the English Zionist Federation (EZF) — notably Sir Herbert Samuel — did not long remain bound to WZO policy. In particular, Samuel wrote a memorandum to the cabinet in January 1915, advocating that the British army occupy Palestine and Trans-Jordan. In setting forth his belief that support for Zionist aspirations in *Eretz Israel* would help the British Empire, Samuel concentrated on two points: First, British control of *Eretz Israel* would enhance imperial security, and second, such an occupation, when combined with a policy of Jewish restoration to the Holy Land, would win the goodwill of Jews and of biblically minded people worldwide.[107]

The matter did not end there. Samuel held numerous conversations with cabinet members in an attempt to gain their support for his ideas. Samuel's diplomacy uncovered considerable sympathy for Zionism in the cabinet, but little willingness, at this stage, to actually act on the proposal.[108] The same held true for a mission of personal diplomacy undertaken by Chaim Weizmann. The latter — who had been closely associated with the WZO Democratic Fraktion as a student during the Herzl era — did not hold any official position within the WZO or the EZF. Weizmann was a somewhat respected chemistry professor whose research on the British Admiralty's behalf into smokeless gunpowder and close relationship with Charles P. Scott, the *Manchester Guardian*'s influential editor, opened many doors.[109]

Weizmann began to advocate a British-Zionist compact as early as October 1914.[110] Thereafter, he lobbied with virtually every figure in the Anglo-Jewish hierarchy and the British government: Baron James de Rothschild, Sir Herbert Samuel, Sir Arthur J. Balfour, Sir David Lloyd George, and, of course, Scott.[111]

Weizmann and Samuel were able to persuade a fairly large number of British leaders and thus built sympathy for, as Samuel stated in his memoir, "something in the nature of a British protectorate."[112] This culminated in the cabinert requesting an updated memorandum from Samuel which was presented in March 1915. While Sir Edward Grey may well have told Samuel "that a British protectorate was quite out of the question," his opinion was increasingly a minority one in the cabinet.[113] For example, the De Bunsen committee, established in 1915 to report on desiderata for the future British position in the Middle East, strongly recommended that Palestine be held within the British sphere of influence, assuming that the Ottoman Empire was not to be maintained intact.[114] Even a staunch anti-Zionist like Lucien Wolf was placed in the uncomfortable position of having to advocate a British declaration of sympathy with Zionism — if only for the sake of bringing American Jewry to support the Entente.[115] Although the British response was far from unequivocal, an important threshold had been crossed.[116]

Another important threshold would soon be crossed. After considerable study, a December 1915 proposal by Pinhas Rutenberg (a Russian Jewish leader only recently converted to Zionism), Ze'ev (Vladimir) Jabotinsky (then a celebrated author and Zionist leader), and Joseph Trumpeldor (well-known as the one-armed Jewish hero of the Russo-Japanese war) to create a Jewish legion was accepted by the British.[117] Four such battalions were created as part of the Royal Fusiliers (for administrative purposes, they fell under the command of the West Kent Regiment, commonly known as the Buffs).[118] Prior to that decision, a small Jewish auxiliary unit had been formed, the so-called Zion Mule Corps (ZMC), to provide logistical support for the Royal Army, the personnel being mule handlers who brought supplies from the rear to combat units. Deployed during the Gallipoli debacle, the ZMC's performance was considered more than sufficient by British commanders in the Middle East. Despite some reluctance in London, therefore, the legion's organization and recruitment proceeded.[119]

Further inducement for the British to "reward" the Jews as they had the Arabs came from Eretz Israel itself, in the form of an espionage ring. The culmination of ideas mooted by Aaron Aaronson, his sister Sarah, brother Alexander, and two friends, Avshalom Feinberg and Yosef Lishansky, the ring called itself Netzah Israel Lo Yishaker (the Eternal of Israel shall not lie), better known by the acronym NILI.[120] Beginning their operations in early 1916 — at approximately the end of the Gallipoli debacle — the spy ring provided considerable intelligence to the British. NILI came to a crashing end in 1917: Feinberg was killed by Bedouins during a mission in the Negev on October 1, 1917; Sarah Aaronson was arrested by Ottoman authorities almost simultaneously. Despite intense torture, she provided no useful information to the Turks, taking her own life on October 5, in order to insure an end of the torture. As noted, much important intelligence information had

by then passed to the British. Aaron, in London, and Alexander, in Cairo, capitalized on their reputation in order to help Weizmann (and other Zionist advocates) win a British declaration of sympathy with Zionism.[121]

In the interim, the four battalions of the Jewish Legion duly mustered. Volunteers came from almost every part of the Jewish world — with the notable exception (of course) of Jews from the Central Powers. A major component of the legion's personnel came from *Yishuv* settlers living in exile in the United States, most prominently David Ben-Gurion and Yitzhak Ben-Zvi. Jabotinsky — who could easily lay claim to being the legion's father — also enlisted, attaining officer's rank almost immediately. Unfortunately, the legion was organized too late to play more than a secondary role in the British campaign in Palestine. The 38th Battalion served in positions covering General Sir Edmund Allenby's southern flank during the Jerusalem campaign (November–December 1917). It continued to cover Allenby's southern and eastern flanks for the remainder of the campaign, ending the war in the Jordan River Valley (on the Trans-Jordanian side), just north of the Dead Sea. The 39th Battalion was active in Trans-Jordan as well, serving together with the 38th under Colonel John Henry Patterson's command. They did so during the critical period of the Megiddo campaign, which culminated in the complete defeat of all Turkish and German forces in Palestine and Syria. The 40th Battalion served on the Cis-Jordan side of the river during this campaign, being attached to the British XX Corps. Apparently, the 42nd Battalion saw no combat service, entering Palestine after hostilities ended.[122]

The Balfour Declaration

The creation of a Jewish Legion under British auspices represented the first major wartime breakthrough for the Zionists. Furthermore, diplomatic realities had not stagnated. The Entente still hoped to tilt American Jewry from its (perceived) pro-German stance and the British still sought to "beat" the Germans in the

A Unit of the Jewish Legion on Parade Near El Arish, 1918.
Courtesy of the Central Zionist Archives, Jerusalem

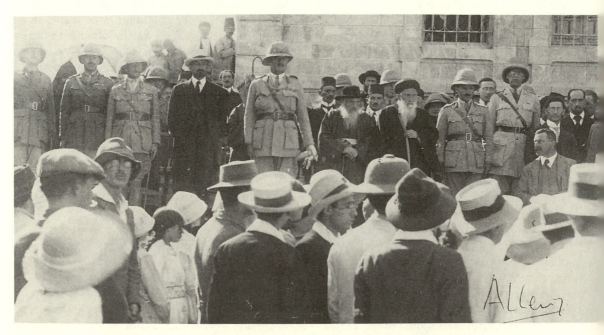

Field Marshal Allenby Meeting with Jewish Notables in Jerusalem, 1918.
Dr. Chaim Weizmann is Standing to Allenby's Right.
Courtesy of the Central Zionist Archives, Jerusalem

propaganda battle for Jewish hearts and minds. Two other factors were added to this mix by early 1917. After a series of debacles on the front in 1916, Herbert H. Asquith's liberal government foundered and was replaced (on December 6, 1916) by a government led by David Lloyd George.[123] Although not significant by itself, the new government was more decisive in its desire to obtain Jewish support for the Entente. Another impetus for such support came from Russia in March 1917 (still calculated as February by the Russians). A revolution led to the Czar's abdication and the creation of a shaky provisional government led by Alexander Kerensky. Many British statesmen, who routinely misunderstood the differences between Zionists and Jewish socialists (and communists) and just as routinely identified all the top Bolshevik leadership as Jews, naturally assumed that the best way to keep Russia in the war, thereby assuring a victory for the Entente, was to influence Russian Jewry. The latter, in turn, would influence the allegedly Jewish revolutionaries to support the Kerensky government and prevent further upheavals.[124] Added to continuing fears over a German declaration and to the deeply held British desire to obtain Palestine at a strategic bulwark for the Suez Canal's defense, the Russian Revolution was the final straw: the British cabinet finally and almost completely tilted toward the compact with the WZO.

This held true despite the fact that the Anglo-Jewish community was severely divided on the issue: While Haham Moses Gaster and Rabbi Joseph H. Hertz along with Lord Rothschild, Harry Sacher, Leon Simon, and other communal leaders supported the negotiations, an equally august group of communal leaders — including Lucien Wolf, David L. Alexander (president of the Board of Deputies), and Claude G. Montefiore (president of the Anglo-Jewish Association) — were strongly opposed.[125] This conflict, in turn, developed at a rather inopportune time — in the summer of 1917, just as the British cabinet was debating the draft declaration — but ended in a major (but not complete) Zionist victory. The Board of Deputies overwhelmingly voted to censure its own president for his anti-Zionist remarks and withdrew from the Co-Joint Foreign Committee that it had organized with the Anglo-Jewish Association.[126]

The stage was now finally set for the declaration. The immediate result was a succession of drafts and other proposals. The initial Zionist draft (July 1917), notable for its simplicity and clarity states, the following:

1. His Majesty's Government accepts the principle that Palestine should be reconstituted as the National Home of the Jewish People.
2. His Majesty's Government will use its best endeavors to secure the achievement of this object and will discuss the necessary methods and means with the Zionist Organization.[127]

Foreign Minister Arthur J. Balfour's draft incorporated most of the Zionist suggestions but weakened the second paragraph by merely expressing willingness to "consider any suggestions on the subject" made by the WZO. This draft was weakened even further in an August 1917 draft written by Lord Milner that reduced the government's commitment to a willingness to explore all opportunities to create a home for the Jewish people in at least part of Palestine.

Naturally, such an equivocal statement was unacceptable to the Zionists; in particular, a promise to explore possibilities implied that nothing would actually be done if, after "exploration," it was found to be too difficult. The give-and-take continued through the summer and into the early autumn.[128] A draft dated October 4, 1917, restored a specific promise to constitute *Eretz Israel* (or at least part thereof) as a Jewish national home. This draft also added a new wrinkle that would complicate matters in the future: the phrase "it being clearly understood that nothing shall be done which may prejudice the civil and religious rights of existing non-Jewish communities in Palestine." Further refinement of this text resulted in the final draft, which was approved by the cabinet on October 31, 1917. This draft was then incorporated into a letter sent by Balfour to Rothschild on November 2, 1917:

His Majesty's Government views with favour the establishment in Palestine of a national home for the Jewish people and will use their best endeavors to facilitate the achievement of this object, it being clearly understood that nothing shall be done which may prejudice the civil and religious rights of existing non-Jewish communities in Palestine, or the rights and political status enjoyed by Jews in any country.[129]

Given the importance of the declaration for future British-Zionist (and Arab-Jewish) relations, it is important to analyze the text carefully. A cursory reading proves that the Zionists had obtained most of what they had been seeking for the past two decades. In particular, a major power had indeed promised to use its best endeavors to help obtain an internationally recognized charter for a Jewish national home in Eretz Israel. The Balfour Declaration was thus a watershed, opening opportunities for Zionist development that were unthinkable prior to World War I.

Yet, the document was just sufficiently ambiguous to cast potential doubts on the long-term British commitment to Zionism. First, for all its promise of a charter, the text never mentioned a Jewish state. To be sure, the Zionist leaders had been as uncomfortable as the British were with the term "state," preferring to leave the Jewish national home's ultimate status for a later date. Moreover, during the 1930s Balfour insisted that his understanding of the phrase "Jewish national home" had, all along, assumed that such an entity would eventually culminate in Jewish sovereignty. Balfour's was not by any means the sole interpretation of the text, however, and much of the later strife in Palestine/ *Eretz Israel* could have been avoided with clearer phraseology.

Second, the phrase "in Palestine of" as opposed to a more direct statement "of a national home in Palestine" implied — or could be taken to imply — that the British never promised all of historic *Eretz Israel* (even when narrowly defined as Cis-Jordan) to the Jews. In a similar vein to the promise made to Hussein, the British did nothing more than promise to facilitate the creation of a Jewish entity. If the entity thus created included all of *Eretz Israel*, all the better; if it did not, the British could still claim to have fulfilled their promises to the Jewish people. Finally, and perhaps most importantly, inclusion of the phrase regarding the existing non-Jewish community could — in fact was — interpreted as contradicting the basic premises of the declaration: the Arabs could (and did) easily argue that facilitation of a Jewish national home inherently prejudiced their civil and religious rights.[130]

Despite all these caveats — whose importance would become obvious only in the 1920s and 1930s — the Balfour Declaration's significance should not be minimized. The WZO had long sought a charter and had now obtained a charter. The way was now opened to fulfill the Basel Program. Not since Cyrus of Persia had declared that Jews could return to Judea in the Sixth Century B.C.E. had such a momentous event happened in the Jewish world. Now Zionism's task would change from attaining a Jewish national home to turning the idea of a home from theory into reality.

Notes

1. The texts of the speeches by Max Nordau, Israel Zangwill, et al., are cited verbatim in Isaiah Friedman ed., *The Post-Herzlian Period, 1904-1914*, Rise of Israel Series vol. 3 (New York: Garland Publishing, 1987), pp. 1–29.

2. For more details, see above, pp. 51-53.

3. Eliahu Benjamini, *מדינות ליהודים: אוגנדה, בירוביז'אן ועוד שלשים וארבע תוכניות* (States for the Jews: Uganda, Birobidzhan, and Thirty-Four Other Projects) (Tel Aviv: Sifriat ha-Poalim, 1990) pp. 43–46. As noted above, this may have been Herzl's plan all along, a reality that renders moot Shabetai B. Bet-Zvi's extravagent claim, in his *הציונות הפוסט-אוגנדית במשבר השואה* (Post-Ugandian Zionism in the crucible of the Holocaust), Tel Aviv: Bronfman's Agency, 1977, that the WZO became "egotistical" after the Uganda affair and could not properly address Jewish needs for immediate refuge during the Nazi era.

4. Statement attributed to T. Ben-Yemini, cited in Benjamini, *מדינות ליהודים*, p. 52.

5. Israel Zangwill, *A Land of Refuge* (London: ITO, 1907).

6. As of this writing Birobidzhan is still, theoretically, a Jewish autonomous region in the Russian Republic (and in the Commonwealth of Independent States). For the history of Birobidzhan, see Benjamini, *מדינות ליהודים*, pp. 100–207, and Chaim Sloves, *ממלכתיות יהודיות בברית המועצות* (Jewish sovereignty in the Soviet Union) (Tel Aviv: Am Oved, 1980), chap. 8–15.

7. Cf., Benjamini, *מדינות ליהודים*, passim.

8. Mordechai Eliav, *דוד וולפסון: האיש וזמנו* (David Wolffsohn: The man and his era) (Jerusalem: ha-Sifriya ha-Zionit, 1977), pp. 54–57.

9. Documents on the opening of the Zionist office (which was initially disguised as a bank) are published in Friedman, *Post-Herlian Period*, pp. 319–411.

10. Jacob M. Landau, *"הערות על יחסם של התורכים הצעירים לציונות"* (Notes on the Young Turks' attitude towards Zionism), *הציונית* 9 (1984): 195–205; Walter Laqueur, *A History of Zionism* (New York: Holt Rinehart, and Winston, 1972), pp. 140-141.

11. Loytved-Hardegg to Auswartiges Amt, May 9, 1913, and Trummler to Wilhelm II, May 31, 1913, Friedman, *Post-Herzlian Period*, pp. 412–435.

12. Alex Bein, *תולדות ההיתישבות הציונית מתקופת הרצל ועד ימינו* (A history of Zionist settlement from Herzl's time to today), 4th ed. (Ramat Gan: Masada Press, 1970), p. 19.

13. Howard M. Sachar, *A History of Israel* (New York: Knopf, 1976), p. 66. This figure may not seem impressive at first glance but must be considered in light of the fact that membership in a Zionist party did not derive from direct dues payment. Rather, one became a member by "buying the shekel," which was actually a payment permitting the right to vote in WZO elections. Shekel figures are very controversial — an issue that will be addressed in detail in chapter 6 — and clearly prove only the approximate number of families willing and able to spend the money to declare their Zionist membership. Given the present state of research, however, shekel figures are the best means to estimate membership in Zionist parties. Cf. Ezra Mendelsohn, "Zionist Success and Zionist Failure: The Case of East Central Europe Between the Two World Wars," in *Essential Papers on Zionism*, ed. Jehuda Reinharz and Anita Shapira (New York: New York University Press, 1996), pp. 171–190 and W. D. Rubinstein, "From Balfour to Biltmore: Zionism from the Balfour Declaration to the Holocaust," paper read at the Australian Association for Jewish Studies Annual Conference, 1995. Professor Rubinstein has kindly made available a copy of his paper to us, a generosity that is hereby duly acknowledged.

14. Reference has already been made (in chapter 3) to the emergence of the Democratic Fraktion during Herzl's life. For studies on general Zionist ideology as it developed after Herzl, see: Gideon Shimoni, *The Zionist Ideology* (Hanover, NH: University Press of New England/ Brandeis University, 1995), chap. 3; and David Schaary, *מ"סתם ציונות" ל"ציונות כללית"* (From "plain Zionism" to "general Zionism) (Jerusalem: Reuven Mass, 1990), chap. 1.

15. In addition to the sources listed hereafter, see Shimoni, *Ideology*, chap. 5.

16. Jonathan Frankel, "Nachman Syrkin: The Populist and Prophetic Strands in Socialist Zionism," *Zionism* 1; no. 2 (Autumn 1980): 176–178, 186–187.

17. Nachman Syrkin, *The Jewish Problem and the Socialist Jewish State* (1898), cited in Arthur Hertzberg (ed.), *The Zionist Idea*, New York: Atheneum, 1970, p. 340. Syrkin's perspective on antisemitism was quoted on pp. 333-340. Cf. Frankel, "Populist," pp. 186-189.

18. Hertzberg, *Zionist Idea*, ibid.

19. Ibid., 345-350.

20. Frankel, "Populist," p. 189.

21. Ibid.

22. Matityahu Mintz, "בר ברוכוב" (Ber Borochov), *הציונות* 7 (1981): 87–89.

23. Cf. Shimoni, *Zionist Ideology*, p. 182.

24. Ber Borochov, "Our Platform," (1906) cited in Hertzberg, *Zionist Idea*, pp. 360–366.

25. Mintz, "בר ברוכוב"

26. Shimoni, *Zionist Ideology*, pp. 187–189.

27. Above, pp. 28–31 and 51–52.

28. The wide range of orthodox approaches to Zionism are summarized in Eliezer Don-Yehiya, "תפיסות של הציונות בהגות היהודית האורתודוקסית" (Views on Zionism within Orthodox Judaism), *הציונות* 9 (1984): 55–93, and Mordechai Breuer, "על המושג 'דתי-לאומי' בהיסטוריוגרפיה ובהגות יהודית" (The concept of religious nationalism in Jewish historiography and thought), *התחיה בשבילי* 3 (1988): 11–24.

29. Rabbi Meir Berlin, "לתקופת העשרים-וחמש" (On the twenty-fifth anniversary, 1923), cited in Friedman, *Post-Herzlian Period*, pp. 183–185.

30. Rabbi Isaac Nissenbaum, "מהי המזרחות?" (What is Mizrachism?), cited in Shimoni, *Zionist Ideology*, p. 131.

31. Rabbi Yitzhak Yosef Reines, *אור חדש על ציון* (A new light On Zion, 1902), cited in Eliezer Don-Yehiya, "אידיאולוגיה ומדינות בציונות הדתית: הגותו הציונית של הרב ריינס ומדיניות 'המזרחי' בהנהגותו" (Ideology and politics in religious Zionism: Rabbi Reines' orientation and Mizrachi policy under his leadership), *הציונות* 8 (1983): 114.

32. Ibid., pp. 109–110.

33. Ibid., pp. 116–117, 121–126.

34. Ibid., pp. 114–117.

35. Cf. Geula Bat-Yehuda, "שאלת 'הקולטורה' והמזרחי" (Mizrachi and the cultural question), in Mordechai Eliav and Yitzhak Raphael eds., *ספר שרגאי* (The S. Z. Shragai memorial volume), Jerusalem: Mossad ha-Rav Kook, 1981, vol. 1, pp. 66–86.

36. *ספר דעת הרבנים* (The book of rabbinic opinion, 1902), cited in Shimoni, *Zionist Ideology*, p. 137.

37. For one example of such argument, written after the State of Israel was established but using many of the arguments advanced in the nineteenth and twentieth centuries, see Urie Zimmer, *Torah-Judaism and the State of Israel* (London: Jewish Post Publications, 1961), pp. 74–82.

38. Statement by Rabbi Shalom Dov Schneerson, 1903, cited in Shimoni, *Zionist Ideology*, p. 138.

39. Ehud Luz, *Parallels Meet* (Philadelphia: Jewish Publication Society, 1988), reviews the many stormy periods in the relationship between Mizrachi and the rest of the WZO beten 1890 and 1904. For a perspective on the contemporary crisis of religion in Israel, see David Hartman, *Conflicting Vision: Spiritual Possiblities of Modern Israel* (New York: Schocken Books, 1990).

40. Eliav, *דוד וולפסון*, chap. 11.

41. Zvi Lipset, "השקפות פוליטיות של סטודנטים יהודיים בקיוב בשנת 1909" (Political views of Jewish students in Kiev in 1909), *הציונות* 2 (1971): 64–73.

42. Ibid., p. 66.

43. Ibid., p. 68.

44. Ibid., p. 70.
45. For a broad overview of American antisemitism, see the essays collected in David A. Gerber, ed., *Antisemitism in American History* (Urbana: University of Illinois Press, 1986).
46. The development of Zionism in the United States has been reveiwed a number of times, the most widely available survey being Melvin I. Urofsky, *American Zionism from Herzl to the Holocaust*, 2nd ed. (Lincoln: University of Nebraska Press, 1995).
47. Cf. Stuart A. Cohen, *English Zionists and British Jews:The Communal Politics of Anglo-Jewry, 1895–1920* (Princeton: Princeton University Press, 1982).
48. In addition to Urofsky's account, cited in note 46, see the documents in Friedman, *Post-Herzlian Period*, pp. 144–182; and Aaron S. Klieman and Adrian L. Klieman, eds., *American Zionism: A Documentary History* (New York: Garland Publishing, 1990), vols. 1–2.
49. Jonathan Frankel, *Jewish Politics and the Russian Revolution of 1905*, Spiegel Lecture in Jewish History no.4 (Tel Aviv: Tel Aviv University Press, 1982), views these developments from a broad Jewish perspective. For the Zionist perspective, see Vital, *Zionism: The Formative Years* (Oxford: The Clarendon Press), 1982, pp. 385–390.
50. Eliav, דוד וולפסון, p. 74.
51. Vital, *Formative Years*, pp. 467–475.
52. Cited in ibid., p. 475.
53. A fundamentally different interpretation is offered by Vital, ibid., pp. 476–478.
54. Bein, תולדות ההיתישבות, pp. 20–21; L. Hazan and Y. Peller, דברי ימי הציונות (A history of Zionism) (Jerusalem: Kiryat Sefer, 1969), pp. 130–131; and Yitzhak Gil-Har, "הגיבוש והעיצוב הארגוני של הישוב בראשית המאה העשרים" (The origins and political organization of the Yishuv at the beginning of the twentieth century), הציונות 6 (1981): 7–47.
55. Sachar, *History of Israel*, pp. 74–76.
56. A. D. Gordon, "People and Labor" (1911), cited in Hertzberg, *Zionist Idea*, p. 372.
57. Ibid.
58. A. D. Gordon, "Some Observations" (1911), cited in Hertzberg, *Zionist Idea*, p. 375.
59. Cf. Michael Langer, *Labor Zionist Ideology Reconsidered* (Tel Aviv: Ichud ha-Bonim, 1978), pp. 17–18.
60. Ibid., p. 18.
61. Ervin Birnbaum, *In the Shadow of the Struggle* (Jerusalem: Gefen Books, 1990), p. 52.
62. Henry Near, *The Kibbutz Movement: A History* (Oxford: Littman Library of Jewish Civilization/Vallentine Mitchell, 1992), 1:18–22.
63. Ibid., pp. 24–30, 35–37.
64. Ibid., pp. 32–34.
65. Ibid., p. 57. For a review of the often complicated planning that was needed for successful settlement building, see Derek Penslar, *Zionism and Technocracy: The Engineering of Jewish Settlements in Palestine, 1870–1918* (Bloomington: Indiana University Press, 1991), chap. 4–6.
66. Mordechai Naor, ed., *1903–1914,* העלייה השנייה (The Second Aliya, 1903-1914) (Jerusalem: Yad Yitzhak Ben-Zvi, 1985).
67. Yosef Gorni,"1904–1940 השינויים במבנה החברתי והפוליטי של העלייה השנייה בשנים (Changes in the social and political structure of the Second Aliya, 1904–1940), הציונות 1 (1970): 204–246.
68. Twenty-one of these respondents defined themselves as members of the Socialist Zionist party (The Zionist Socialist Labor Party, better known by its initials SSRP) which, despite its name, was a territiorialist party. Cf. Jonathan Frankel, *Prophecy and Politics: Socialism, Nationalism, and the Russian Jews, 1862-1917* (Cambridge: Cambridge University Press, 1981), pp. 325–328 and 346–349.
69. These respondents included members of the Russian Social Democratic Labor Party (RSDLP) without distinction of affiliation with the Menshevik or Bolshevik wings of that party. Regarding

the RSDLP's attitude toward Zionism see Mordechai Altshuler, "The Attitude of the Communist Party of Russia to Jewish National Survival", *YIVO Annual* (1969) 14: 68–86.

70. The Russian Social Revolutionary Party (SR) was a recently created party (having held its first congress in 1905). Openly revolutionary in its attitude, the SRs were mainly connected with the Russian peasant class. The SRs were violently anti-Bolshevik and were eliminated by Lenin shortly after the Bolshevik takeover in 1917. It would be interesting to speculate on the influence of SR ideas on Socialist Zionist leaders such as Gordon, but no comparative study on the subject exists to our knowledge. A brief review of SR ideology was contained in Leonard Schapiro *The Russian Revolutions of 1917* (New York: Basic Books, 1984), p. 221. For the SR's attitude toward Jews see Frankel, *Prophecy and Politics*, p. 274.

71. Gorni, "השינויים במבנה," p. 231.

72. Cf., Marc Hillel, *La Maison du Juif: L'Histoire Extraordinaire de Tel Aviv*, Paris: Librairie Académique Perrin, 1989 and Shlomo Shva, *עיר קמה* (A city rises) (Tel Aviv: Zmora, Bitan, and Modan Publishers), 1989.

73. On the Yemenite contribution to the Second Aliya, see Shalom Gamliel, *Aliya To Israel From Yemen*, English/Hebrew (Jerusalem: Shalom Research Center, 1987), chap. 1, and, more broadly, Tudor Parfitt, *The Road to Redemption: The Jews of the Yemen, 1900–1950* (Leiden: E. J. Brill, 1996), passim.

74. Cf. Israel Halpern (ed.), *ספר הגבורה* (The Book of Jewish Heroism), reprint edition (Tel Aviv: Am Oved, 1977) 3:1–229.

75. *שורשי ההגנה העצמית* (The roots of Jewish self-defense) (Ramat Efal: Yad Yitzhak Tabenkin, 1983).

76. Halpern, *ספר הגבורה*, 3:240-352.

77. Ze'ev Schiff, *A History of the Israeli Army, 1870-1974* (San Fransisco: Straight Arrow Books, 1974), p. 4. In 1920 Yosef Trumpeldor created a paramilitary unit that adopted the name Gdud ha-Avoda, but bore no relationship to ha-Shomer's proposal. The Gdud became a source of much controversy in the Yishuv, eventually splitting due to ideological pressures. Cf., Anita Shapira, *ההליכה על קו האופק* (Visions in conflict) (Tel Aviv: Am Oved, 1988), pp. 157–207.

78. For a perspective on Zionist preceptions regarding the Arabs as potential enemies or allies, see Protocols of the Meeting of the WZO GAK, June 7, 1914, Central Zionist Archive (hereafter: CZA) Z3/449 and Ruppin to EAC, July 23, 1914, CZA Z3/1457.

79. Arthur Goldschmidt, Jr., *A Concise History of the Middle East*, 5th ed., (Boulder, CO: Westview Press, 1996), pp. 179–185.

80. Negib Azouri, *Awakening of the Arab Nation*, 1905, cited in Netanel Lorch, *One Long War: Arab Versus Jew Since 1920* (Jerusalem: Keter Books, 1976), p. 3.

81. For examples, see the passages from Halpern, *ספר הגבורה*, cited in note 76.

82. Cf. the statements on Arab-Jewish relations by Moshe Eliovitz and Nahum Horowitz, cited in Friedman, *Post-Herzlian Period*, pp. 438–446.

83. Due to the profusion of sources — both primary and secondary — on the Balfour Declaration over the last thirty years, citations in the next three sections refer only to major primary sources (except in cases of direct quotes). In addition to the sources cited here, these sections have benefitted from a careful reading of the following secondary sources: Leonard Stein, *The Declaration* (London: Vallentine Mitchell, 1961); Jehuda Reinharz, *Chaim Weizmann: The Making of a Statesman* (New York: Oxford University Press, 1993); Ronald Sanders, *The High Walls of Jerusalem: A History of the Declaration and the Birth of the British Mandate for Palestine* (New York: Holt, Rinehart, and Winston, 1983); Isaiah Friedman, *The Question of Palestine, 1914–1918: British-Jewish-Arab Relations* (London: Routledge and Kegan Paul, 1973); Ibid., *Germany, Turkey, and Zionism, 1897–1918* (Oxford: Clarendon Press, 1977); Jon Kimche, *The Unromantics* (London: Weidenfeld and Nicolson, 1968); and David Vital, *Zionism: The Crucial Phase* (New York: Oxford University Press, 1987).

84. Cf., Minutes of the GAK Meeting, December 3-6, 1914, cited in Isaiah Friedman (ed.), *Germany, Turkey, and Zionism, 1914–1918*, Rise of Israel Series vol. 4, New York: Garland, 1987, pp. 109–114. A brief summary of the Armenian Massacres was provided in Abraham J. Edelheit and Hershel Edelheit, *History of the Holocaust: A Handbook and Dictionary* (Boulder, CO: Westview Press, 1994), pp. 16–17.

85. GAK Meeting, loc cit., Warburg to Jacobson, August 29, 1914, Minutes of the Zionistische Vereinigung für deutschland (ZVFD) Council Meeting, March 23–24, 1916, cited in ibid., pp. 101–108 and 115–120.

86. *Reports of the Executive of the Zionist Organization to the XII ZIonist Congress* (1921), cited in ibid., pp. 15–27.

87. Ibid., pp. 18–19.

88. Cf., Shabtai Teveth, *Ben-Gurion: The Burning Ground* (Boston: Houghton Mifflin Company, 1987), chap. 7–9.

89. See the documents cited in Friedman, *Germany*, pp. 49–100.

90. Cited, in translation, in ibid., p. vii and, in the original, on p. 359.

91. Ibid., pp. 324–363.

92. Wolff-Metternich to Bethmann-Hollweg, November 22, 1915, cited in ibid., p. 183.

93. The documents cited in ibid., pp. 126–205 should be read in conjunction with Zosa Szajkowski, "The German Ordinance of November 1916 on the Organization of Jewish Communities in Poland," *Proceedings of the American Academy for Jewish Research* 34 (1966): 111–139; and Max Bodenheimer, "The Story of the Hindenburg Declaration," *Herzl Yearbook*, 2 (1959): 56–77.

94. Von Romberg to Bethmann-Hollweg, March 2, 1917, cited in Friedman, *Germany*, pp. 243–246.

95. Zimmermann to Kühlmann, March 16, 1917; Kühlmann to Bethmann-Hollweg, March 26, 1917 and April 6, 1917; Rosen to Bethmann-Hollweg, May 3, 1917; all cited in ibid., pp. 259–262 and 266–272.

96. See the documents in ibid., pp. 273–323 and 364–437.

97. Ibid., pp. 438–440.

98. Cf. Howard M. Sachar, *The Emergence of the Middle East, 1914–1924* (New York: Alfred A. Knopf, 1969), chap. 3.

99. Cf. Isaiah Friedman ed., *France and Zionism, 1914–1920*, Rise of Israel Series vol. 5 (New York: Garland, 1987), pp. 1–11.

100. Cf. Sachar, *Emergence*, chap. 5. For a useful insight into the historiographical and methodological issues raised here, interested readers should see: Elie Kedourie, "The Chatham House Version," in *The Chatham House Version and Other Middle-Eastern Studies* (New York: Praeger, 1970), pp. 351–394; and Isaiah Friedman, "The McMahon Correspondence and the Question of Palestine," *Journal of Contemporary History* (hereafter *JCH*) 5: no.2 (1970): 83–122. Arnold J. Toynbee's comments and Friedman's rejoinder in *JCH* 5, no.4 (1970): 185–201, are also instructive.

101. McMahon to Hussein, October 24, 1915, cited in Walter Laqueur, ed., *The Israel–Arab Reader*, 2nd ed. (New York: Bantam, 1971, pp. 16–17. A slightly different version of the text is cited in Isaiah Friedman, ed., *British-Zionist Relations, 1914-1917*, Rise of Israel Series vol. 6, (New York: Garland, 1987), pp. 118-120. Emphasis added.

102. Cf. George Antonius, *The Arab Awakening* (New York: G.P. Putnam's Sons, 1946), chap. 9.

103. Cf. the documents by McMahon, Shuckburg, Churchill, Lloyd George, and Ormsby-Gore in Friedman, *Relations*, pp. 121–134.

104. Cf. Moshe Perlman, "Arab-Jewish Diplomacy, 1918–1922," *JSS*, 6, no.2 (April 1944): 123–154.

105. Sachar, *History of Israel*, pp. 92–96; Vital, *Crucial Phase*, pp. 199–206.

106. Kimche, *The Unromantics*, chap. 3.

107. Herbert Samuel, "The Future of Palestine", January 1915, cited in Friedman, *Relations*, pp. 46–50.

108. See also the documents cited in Friedman, ibid., pp. 51–59.

109. Reinharz, *Chaim Weizmann*, chap. 1–2.

110. Weizmann to Zangwill, October 19, 1914, cited in Friedman, *Relations*, pp. 1–3.

111. Friedman, *Relations*, pp. 4–36; Reinharz, *Chaim Weizmann*, chap. 3.

112. Viscount Herbert Samuel, *Memoirs* (London: Crescent Press, 1945), pp. 140–145.

113. The revised memorandum and the responses thereto are reprinted in Friedman, *Relations*, pp. 60–65.

114. Ibid., pp. 66–67.

115. Wolf's memorandum was reprinted verbatim in Friedman, *Relations*, pp. 73–89. On Wolf's ambivalent relationship with Zionism, see Marc Levene, "Lucien Wolf: Crypto-Zionist, Anti-Zionist, or Opportunist *par Excellence?*" *Studies in Zionism* 12, no.2 (Autumn 1991): 133–148.

116. Friedman, *Relations*, pp. 90-134, includes a selection of relevant documents on this transformation.

117. Documents on the legion's origins are reprinted in ibid., pp. 213–299. A careful study on the Legion's origins may be found in David Yisraeli, "The Struggle for Zionist Military Involvement in the First World War," in Pinhas Artzi ed., *Bar-Ilan Studies in History*, 1 (1978): 197–213. As a side note, it seems appropriate here to remind readers that approximately 21,000 Jewish soldiers (including many from the Yishuv) served in the Ottoman armed forces. On their experience, see Ya'akov Markovitzy, *בקף הקלע של הנאמנות: בני היישוב בצבא התורכי, 1908-1919* (A Conflict of loyalties: The enlistment of Palestinian Jews in the Turkish Army, 1908–1919) (Ramat Efal: Yad Yitzhak Tabenkin, 1995).

118. Yigal Elam, *הגדודים העבריים במלחמת העולם הראשונה* (The Hebrew battalions in World War I) Tel Aviv: Ma'arachot/IDF Press, 1973, chap. 12.

119. Ibid., pt. 1.

120. As with so many of the Zionist acronyms already mentioned, NILI's name derived from a Biblical verse, specifically I Samuel 15:29.

121. NILI's full history has yet to be written: in the interim, the best available source on the ring has to be: Walter Gribbon, *Agents of Empire: Anglo-Zionist Intelligence Operations, 1915–1919*, (London: Brassey's, 1995).

122. Elam, *הגדודים העבריים*, pt. III.

123. Vital, *Crucial Phase*, pp. 208–209: Stein, *Declaration*, pp. 309–311.

124. Isaiah Friedman ed., *Britain Enters a Compact with Zionism, Parts I and II*, Rise of Israel Series vol. 7–8 (New York: Garland, 1987), pt. 1, pp. 132–167.

125. Ibid., pp. 218–266.

126. Ibid., pp. 267–273. Cf. Cohen, *English Zionists and British Jews*, passim.

127. The various draft versions of the declaration are cited in Stein, *Declaration*, appendix A, p. 664. The diplomatic documents behind the drafts were cited in Friedman, *Compact with Zionism*, pt. 2, passim.

128. Friedman, *Compact with Zionism*, pt. 2, pp. 45–64.

129. Ibid., p. 140.

130. Antonius, *Arab Awakening*, pp. 262–275.

5

THE RISE OF A JEWISH POLITY

Formalizing the Mandate

With the Balfour Declaration and the subsequent British occupation of Palestine/*Eretz Israel*, Zionism came of age. "There is ground," Justice Louis D. Brandeis stated in a letter, "for congratulations."[1] Congratulations and self-satisfaction, however, would have been premature. The promises framed at the Balfour Declaration notwithstanding, much work remained to make the Jewish national home a reality. The first order of business was to define *Eretz Israel*'s future legal status; second, the borders of the new Jewish national home had to be drawn; finally, specific plans for immigration and development had to be laid, and carried out.

Notwithstanding the apparent clarity of the British promise to the WZO, diplomatic entanglements remained complex. Despite public support from all the Entente powers, the charter would not be accomplished easily. The French, for example, who had been "won over" to the Zionist cause in the autumn of 1917, were already backpedaling by early 1918. The French government's perceptions of its interests in the Middle East and its fears of possible adverse Arab responses to creating a Jewish national home required immediate and high-level attention from Zionist leaders.[2]

Even more complicated were relations between the WZO and the British. Despite the Balfour Declaration, some elements in the British government — especially the military leadership in the Middle East — strongly opposed the government's position on Zionism. Tension between the Zionists and the British were exacerbated by the fact that *Eretz Israel* was then ruled by the army's Occupied Enemy Territories Administration (OETA) and not by a civilian government.[3] The Arabs also had mixed feelings, at best, about future relations with both the British and the Jews; efforts to sound out Arab leaders, including Emir Faisal Ibn Hussein (who had led the Arab armies during World War I and inherited the mantle of Britain's promise to support an Arab kingdom when his father died), on a possible Arab-Jewish-Armenian entente in the postwar Middle East were met coolly. The Arabs never explicitly rejected cooperation with the Zionists (at least not in 1918–1920) but did not enthusiastically embrace the idea either.[4]

In 1919 anxiety levels in Palestine were on the rise, with both Jews and Arabs seeing themselves as aggrieved parties.[5] Part of this stress, it might be noted, resulted from intra-Arab rivalries. Faisal, the putative king of the British-promised Arab kingdom, was of Sharifian extraction (meaning, he was a Bedouin whose ancestors had held the title Sharif of Mecca); he was not Syrian and was thus considered something of an interloper by local Arab nationalists.[6] Faisal's relations with the French (of no direct relevance to the story of Zionism) must also be recalled, if only because both Faisal (citing the McMahon-Hussein correspondence) and the French government (citing the Sykes-Picot Agreement) sought to rule Syria.[7] Arab-French tension, destined to flare into open fighting during 1919 and 1920, would also negatively impact on the Yishuv's security.[8]

Decisive action to foster Arab-Jewish cooperation by the British government might have avoided unnecessary hardships later on, but the exact opposite happened. Many OETA officers seemed intent upon overturning the Balfour Declaration. One, a Colonel Gabriel, went so far as to propose settling Maltese in Palestine instead of Jews.[9] Other officers were more tactful, but no less opposed to aiding the Jews. In their view, the Arabs were a romantic people who fought with honor and deserved of respect; Jews, by contrast, were artisans and small businessmen (at best), caricatures of the poor London Jews accused of being loud, pushy, dirty — decidedly undeserving of respect. That the British attitude was more than tinged with antisemitism was never denied, least of all by the military authorities.[10] Far from encouraging Arab-Jewish cooperation, many members of OETA sought to encourage Arab fears, hoping to forestall any further actions by their government in support of Jewish aspirations.[11] This attitude was not limited to OETA — though the army officers were in a position to do the most potential damage in the short term — but infused some members of the British delegation to the Paris peace talks. Jews, in their attitude, were adherents of a "lower" religion who had given up their national rights, and especially their right to a homeland, when they committed deicide.[12]

The upshot of these problems was a continued Zionist sense of unsettlement. Relations with OETA were cool, placing Zionist leaders in the uncomfortable position of having to repeatedly complain to London about conditions in *Eretz Israel*. Making matters more difficult was the fact that decisions regarding the postwar status of the entire Near East had been deferred by the negotiators in Paris. *Eretz Israel*'s future status, obviously, could not be finalized until a peace treaty was signed

between the Entente powers and Turkey. That meant that OETA would continue to rule the country, which, in turn, translated into continuing limits on Zionist development in *Eretz Israel*. And that meant that bad relations between the Zionists and the British would continue, at least in the short term.[13]

The sundry maneuvers in Jerusalem, Paris, and London diffused Zionist attention just when focus on constructive work was needed. A Zionist commission had traveled to *Eretz Israel* in the spring of 1918, with the goal of preparing the groundwork for future practical activities. Though by no means unanimous in their appreciation of current needs, all Zionists agreed that four immediate practical goals existed: (1) reviving and enlarging *aliya* and absorption; (2) fund-raising to conserve and expand national resources (mainly water); (3) expansion of Haifa harbor; and (4) expansion of housing resources within the *Yishuv*.[14] Additional, complementary, goals included creation of a single communal organization to represent the *Yishuv* in its relations with the British; developing the educational system; and expanding the Jewish economy, mainly the agricultural sector.[15] Chaim Weizmann, chairman of the Zionist Commission, summarized the WZO's short term goals more briefly: the *Yishuv*, in his estimate, needed only "men" and "money."[16] The Zionist Commission did not achieve this goal, but it did lay the foundation for the institutions that developed into the Jewish State over the next thirty years.[17]

The Zionist Commission wrapped up its work in October 1918. Within a month, efforts were to begin on the peace treaty that would finally establish Palestine's status. This meant further maneuvering between the Zionists and the British government (as well as between the WZO and the other Entente governments) on the one hand, and a series of maneuvers between the Zionists and the Arabs on the other hand.[18] The Arabs feared displacement even as they continued to hold that Syria — which they took to include both Cis-Jordan and Trans-Jordan in addition to Lebanon — had been promised to the Arab kingdom under the terms of the McMahon-Hussein correspondence.[19] The Zionists hoped to allay Arab fears, mainly by citing that there was room enough in Eretz Israel for a Jewish population of 4–5 million "without encroaching upon the rights of the Arabs."[20]

The Zionist desire to allay Arab fears led to contacts with Faisal in December 1918.[21] These negotiations culminated in an agreement signed by Weizmann and Faisal on January 3, 1919. In nine articles and a brief Arabic annex the two sides agreed to cooperate for their mutual benefit. In essence, Faisal conceded Palestine to the Zionists, accepting the Balfour Declaration as the basis for the territory's future. Similarly, Faisal agreed that steps should be taken "to encourage and stimulate immigration of Jews into Palestine on a large scale, and as quickly as possible."[22] The Zionists agreed to protect holy sites in *Eretz Israel* and to protect Arab peasants. Finally, both sides accepted negotiations in case disagreements arose in the future.

More ominous was Faisal's annex: He made his support for Zionism virtually contingent upon his obtaining Syria; should that quid pro quo not be forthcoming, he proclaimed that he could "not be answerable for failing to carry out this agreement."[23] For now, Faisal deemphasized the negative and concentrated on the positives and the Zionists did likewise.

In March, Faisal reiterated his support for Zionist aspirations in a letter to Felix Frankfurter, an American jurist and eminent Zionist leader.[24] Zionists saw Faisal's agreements as a sign that, in Frankfurter's words, Jews and Arabs could "live side by side as friends."[25] However, as Neil Caplan has so ably pointed out, Zionist-Arab negotiations were, at this stage at least, an exercise in "futile diplomacy." Faisal, in fact, proved unwilling or unable to deliver on his promises to the Zionists. Similarly, the Zionists could not deliver Syria to Faisal, since it was not theirs to give. By November 1919, therefore, the

Emir Faisal and Dr. Chaim Weizmann During Their Fateful Meeting on January 3, 1919.
Courtesy of the Central Zionist Archives, Jerusalem

agreement had collapsed in much recrimination and, as shall be seen below (in Chapter 7), cooperation gave way to an increasingly violent Arab-Jewish conflict.[26]

One final setback awaited the Zionists and their hopes for the immediate realization of the Balfour Declaration in the short term. Tensions in Palestine convinced the Entente powers to send a committee of investigation to determine how the local populations' felt about their future governance.[27] This commission, known commonly as the King-Crane Commission (from the names of its two members, both Americans employed by the Allies), was duly sent to the Middle East. The commission's recommendations could not have been worse from the Zionist perspective. In essence, King and Crane proposed that the Balfour Declaration be repudiated, that *aliya* be severely limited, and that Syria remain undivided and part of the Arab kingdom. Fortunately for the WZO, this last-ditch effort to abort the Balfour Declaration even before it was implemented, proved to be stillborn.[28]

These events must be viewed in context. By the time the King-Crane Commission reported its finding, the Paris peace talks had already begun. After much preparation, the Zionists had submitted their basic proposal to the peace conference: (1) the borders should be as inclusive as possible; (2) the territory should be constituted as a national home, not a commonwealth or a state, so as not to unnecessarily upset the Arab population; (3) nothing would be done to affect the Muslim and Christian holy sites; and (4) *aliya* should be permitted in an unfettered manner.[29]

At the time, the issue of the Jewish national home's future borders appeared to be most important. Weizmann, for instance, demanded "sufficient elbow room," since he proposed bringing 4–5 million Jews into *Eretz Israel* in twenty-five years.[30] This need for space led Zionist leaders to propose relatively wide borders for the new homeland: *Eretz Israel* "from Dan to Beersheba" as a minimum. More realistically, the Zionists sought territory as far north as the Litani River, as far east as the Hauran (i.e., east of the Hejaz-Damascus Railway), and as far west as El-Arish.[31] Most Zionist attention was placed on the northern and eastern border, since the peace talks and the reality of British control over Egypt (which, in turn, ruled the Sinai) rendered most of the other Zionist demands moot.[32] In fact *Eretz Israel*'s northern boundary was established on an ad hoc basis: mainly drawn so as to include Jewish settlements (including Tel Hai and Kfar Giladi, two settlements attacked by Faisal's supporters in early 1920), but far south of the Litani River.

The eastern border was much more complex. Partly, the eastern border question derived from Zionist needs for water; partly, it derived from the fact that Cis-Jordan and Trans-Jordan are not geographically distinct — the two have been ruled as one territory for most of recorded history.[33] Added to the geographic and historical factors was the British fear that Trans-Jordan might be seized by the French during their campaign against Faisal (who was removed from Damascus by force in 1920). As a result the British were willing to accede, as least temporarily, to Zionist demands about *Eretz Israel*'s eastern border. As established in 1920 this border would include *all* of Trans-Jordan. It must be emphasized, however, that the border thus established was always considered temporary — at the first opportunity (in 1921–1922) Trans-Jordan was removed from mandatory Palestine.[34]

Thus, the path from the Balfour Declaration to the Mandate was a torturous one for the Zionists. While negotiations over the national home's borders were undertaken, other negotiations were being held over the mandate's constitutional terms. Here too the Zionists hoped to obtain considerable leverage but were severely disappointed. Although the WZO draft constitution emphasized the Jews' historic right to return to *Eretz Israel*, the British Foreign Office referred only to a "historic connection" between Jewry and the "Holy Land." After further talks, a new draft was submitted to the foreign office by a joint committee of British and Zionist representatives. This draft fared little better than the WZO's original. Lord Curzon (the only cabinet member to vote

Proposals for The Peace Conference.

The Peace Conference, having taken notice of the aspirations and claims of the Jewish people with regard to Palestine, hereby decides:

1) That the historic right of the Jewish people to the re-establishment of its National Home in Palestine be recognised for all times as incontestable and that all possible assistance be given to facilitate the achievement of this object.

2) That, with this ultimate purpose in view, the Country of Palestine, within its historical boundaries to be defined by a Special Commission, shall at present be entrusted to the care of Great Britain which, in its capacity of Trustee, shall place the Country under such conditions — political, administrative, economic etc. — as will lead up to the steady enlargement and development of the Jewish settlement, so that it may ultimately develop into a Jewish Commonwealth on national lines; it being clearly understood that nothing shall be done which may prejudice the civil and religious rights of existing non-Jewish communities in Palestine or the rights and political Status enjoyed by Jews in any other Country.

Zionist Proposal for the Draft Mandate, 1919.
Courtesy of the Central Zionist Archives, Jerusalem

against the Balfour Declaration in 1917), who assumed the foreign ministry portfolio in late 1919, went so far as to condemn this new draft as "a document which reeks of Judaism in every paragraph . . . It is quite clear that this Mandate has been drawn up by someone reeling under the fumes of Zionism." Curzon summed up, "I don't want a Hebrew state."[35]

Despite Curzon's rhetoric — which flirted with overt antisemitism — that was not the end of the matter. More drafts were formulated over the spring and summer of 1920, but none proved to be acceptable to one or another of the parties involved in defining *Eretz Israel*'s future. An August 1920 draft, for example, restored the clause on Jewry's historic connection to the Holy Land that the WZO demanded. Simultaneously, however, wording in other parts of this draft implied that the British might turn to an organization other than the WZO for the purpose of building the Jewish national home. By this point, both Curzon and the Zionists found the draft unacceptable.[36]

Two further incidents forced Curzon's hand. The further deterioration of security conditions in Palestine, coupled with the British decision to demobilize the Jewish Legion, led to riots in Jerusalem in early April 1920. A virtual pogrom erupted that left 5 Jews killed and 211 injured. The OETA leadership proved unable to cope with the rioting. The WZO leaders were outraged that the British had not only failed to protect innocent Jews but, even worse, by publicizing a patently false report of a Jewish attack on the mufti of Jerusalem, had actually caused the riots.[37] Even more galling was the fact the Ze'ev Jabotinsky, the ex-Jewish legion officer who organized the Jewish defense during the riots, was arrested (and later deported from *Eretz Israel*) while the

Arab nationalist leader who organized the riots, Haj Amin Al-Husseini, was not.[38] These facts led to the final collapse of the OETA, at least as far as Palestine was concerned, and forced the Foreign Office to give up its efforts to stymie the Balfour Declaration's implementation.

Moreover, despite Curzon's machinations, considerable support existed in the cabinet and in Parliament for the Zionist position. Indeed, Prime Minister David Lloyd George gently nudged Curzon into a compromise with the Zionists. So did Balfour, from his lofty position as lord president of the council.[39] The Inter-Allied Conference that met at San Remo, Italy, in April 1920, pressed the British, strongly supporting the Zionist understanding of the Balfour Declaration and other British Middle East commitments.[40] Finally, in late September, a draft was published that, although by no means perfect, was at least acceptable to all parties. In particular, the preamble now strongly noted the Jews' historic connection with Eretz Israel. The new draft also emphasized that Jews returning to Eretz Israel did so by right, not on sufferance, a point that the WZO strongly demanded. On the other hand, the rest of the document reflected Curzon's desires and, in particular, committed the British government to very little. The vagueness of this document was to be a cause for further British-Zionist conflict. But for now, the Zionists could get on with their more immediate tasks of immigration and building.[41]

Laying the Foundations, 1919–1923

With the draft mandate in hand, and with exclusive British control of Palestine approved by the allies at the San Remo conference, League of Nations approval of the mandate was virtually guaranteed. Indeed, the League's debate was virtually *pro forma*. On June 28, 1919, the League had tentatively given Palestine to the British; this was confirmed and made official on September 16, 1922.[42] The first new order of business was the appointment of an administrator (the high commissioner) who would transform the country from military to civilian rule and eventually fulfill the mandate's terms. After a short search — and another brief rearguard action by Curzon and his anti-Zionist cohorts — Sir Herbert Samuel was appointed to the post. Samuel was deemed acceptable to the Jews while also being sympathetic to the Arabs; he had the further advantage of being highly respected in Parliament and in the cabinet.[43] Still, Samuel's job was not as simple as it seemed. The history of British Mandatory Palestine/*Eretz-Israel* was one of high Zionist hopes, increasing conflict with the Arabs, frustration and disappointment in relations with the British, the horror of Jewish genocide in Europe, and, finally, a bitter conflict leading to Zionist fulfillment.

Most of these events were far off in the future as the Third Aliya began in 1919. On December 19, 1919, the ship *SS Ruslan* arrived in Jaffa, having sailed from Odessa, with 620 *olim*, they were the first of a total of 35,000 *olim* who would enter *Eretz Israel* between then and 1923.[44] Ideologically, these *olim* represented a continuation of the Second Aliya: mainly socialist in their orientation and deeply committed to settling the land. Like their predecessors, they linked Zionist fulfillment with Jewish agriculture, settling mainly in *Kibbutzim* and *Moshavot*. *Aliya* remained critical to Zionist endeavors. As Julian Mack perceptively noted in 1919:

> The powers of the world cannot create a Jewish Homeland; the powers of the world can give the Jews of the world the opportunity to create a Jewish Homeland, but the Jews themselves, only the Jewish people, can make Palestine a real Jewish Homeland.[45]

A similar appreciation animated Max Nordau's controversial 1919 plan for intensive Zionist development. Nordau, one of the few original Herzlian Zionists still alive, approached the subject from a purely political Zionist approach. In essence, Nordau argued that the revolutionary upheavals and anti-Jewish pogroms in Russia were proof positive of Herzl's approach to the Jewish question. It followed that the only means to accomplish Zionist goals was to work for mass *aliya* and the creation of a Jewish state as quickly as possible. Mass *aliya* was required both to help Eastern European Jewry and to establish a Jewish majority in *Eretz Israel*. Nordau saw a unique opportunity and suggested that Zionists strike while the iron was hot: He called for the aliya of 600,000 Jews in a maximum of two or three years.[46] Other Zionists spoke of the Jewish population in *Eretz Israel* reaching 4–5 million in the future but were willing to accept considerably less immigration in the short term. These Zionists did not share Nordau's sense of urgency, arguing for organic growth in consonance with Eretz Israel's absorptive capacity.[47] For his part, Nordau rejected any delay. He denied the existence of a long term without massive *aliya* in the short term, because delay would weaken the Zionists. The unique confluence of events in Europe, the United States, and *Eretz Israel* would pass, the British would come to rely on the Arabs to keep Palestine peaceful, and Eastern European Jewry would find some other means to safeguard their future. The Zionists would, Nordau argued, miss the boat.[48] It was also clear to Nordau that if Jews wanted to be treated as major players in world affairs, their diplomacy had to have a solid foundation. Anything less would be an exercise in futility — the diplomacy of the powerless. Nordau's foundation was simple: Only a Jewish majority in *Eretz Israel* could confer the kind of benefits Nordau was talking about.[49]

After stormy debates, the WZO decided not to pursue the Nordau plan, not because they rejected his premises nor even because they rejected his long term goals; Zionists rejected his contention that mass *aliya* could be accomplished without consideration for the *Yishuv*'s economic capacity. To do so, they feared, would result in a disaster that would undermine the very foundation that Nordau claimed was needed. It is interesting to note that Jabotinsky — who proposed a very similar plan in 1935 and whose later strident criticisms of the WZO leadership made Nordau's seem mild by comparison — utterly rejected the Nordau plan in 1920. Jabotinsky saw Nordau's plan as unrealistic and implausible, even as he rejected the naive gradualism that gripped his colleagues, including Weizmann.[50]

Rejecting the Nordau scheme did not mean rejecting *aliya*, just that the Zionist mainstream sought to operate within the boundaries of conventional growth, that is to encourage *aliya* in consonance with *Eretz Israel*'s economic absorptive capacity. The Zionists also agreed to work within a system formulated by the British to control immigration. As developed in the 1920s (and further refined in the 1930s), the system worked thus: After consultations with Jewish organizations and input by the Palestine administration's Immigration and Labour Departments, a quota was established for Jewish immigration. This quota, in turn, was reflected in a semi-annual "schedule" that represented the number of immigrant visas that could be granted during that six-month period (either April–September or October–March). Within the schedule *olim* fell into one of four categories: A, defined as capitalists (individuals already in possession of certain amounts of cash); B, individuals who would otherwise fall into category A but were not in immediate possession of such cash (for example, property owners); C, laborers; and D, dependents of legal residents or persons whose immigration was otherwise deemed desirable.[51]

It must be emphasized that the WZO initially accepted this system and that for most of the 1920s the system worked. The first schedule (1920–1921) included a total of 16,500 certificates.[52] In 1921–1922 the Zionist Executive requested 19,000 certificates for laborers, translating to a total potential *aliya* rate (in all categories) of 4,000 olim per month.[53] The government's first census (taken in 1922) found that a total of 83,794 Jews lived in *Eretz Israel*, up from the 56,000 estimated by the Zionist office to be in *Eretz Israel* in 1919. The census figure represented a growth of 27,794, or almost 50 percent.[54] But, many of the *olim* were actually returnees who had been deported by the Ottomans when World War I began. Even so, immigration was significant, considering that by 1929 the government estimated the Jewish population at 154,300, or a trebling of the Jewish population prior to World War I.[55] Jewish growth was also reflected in the proportion of Jews to the total population: circa 12.9 percent in the census of 1922 and circa 18.9 percent (again a 50 percent increase) in 1929.[56]

The Third Aliya was a critical era for developments in virtually every economic sector. Wheras in 1900 Jews cultivated approximately 119,000 dunams of land, by 1927 the figure had jumped to 463,570 dunams. Moreover, by 1927 Jewish organizations — Keren Kayemet le-Israel (KKL), the Palestine Jewish Colonization Association (PICA), and the American Zion Commonwealth Corporation — held an estimated 1 million dunams of land.[57] Similarly, almost unprecedented growth could be seen in virtually every field within the agriculture industry.[58] Electrification, begun in 1921 at Pinhas Rutenberg's initiative, also contributed to the Yishuv's growth, both potential and actual.[59]

Developments in *Eretz Israel*'s cities paralleled the critical developments in agriculture and were, in some ways, even more startling. It has been estimated that approximately 80 percent of *Eretz Israel*'s Jewish population lived in cities or towns rather than villages or collective settlements.[60] At this time, Tel Aviv really emerged as a major Jewish population center, with new settlements — partly agricultural, partly industrial — built around it.[61] Similar developments transpired in Jerusalem and Haifa, meaning that almost all sectors of Eretz Israel were experiencing growth, though not quite at the same pace.

As a result of these developments, the WZO's joint Palestine Survey Commission, established in 1928 to report on the previous ten year's developments and propose outlines for future Zionist policy, concluded its report on an overall optimistic note, which was expected to persist.[62] Still, there were difficulties to be overcome. From July 1922

to March 1927 a total of 21,020 certificates had been used. But, in the same period, the WZO received 25,860 certificates. In other words, during an intense period of Zionist growth, 4,840 certificates (nearly 18 percent) had been lost since no suitable candidates could be found to take them.[63] Similarly, until 1928 *yerida* — that is Jewish emigration from *Eretz Israel* — was high. In some cases the number of Jews leaving *Eretz Israel* exceeded the number arriving. During the period covered, for instance, 8,339 Jews (almost twice as many as the number of unused certificates) left. This slowed but never stopped the *Yishuv*'s growth.[64]

Then too, the lack of enthusiasm for Zionism among the communities whose problems the WZO had set out to solve was a severe disappointment. This was not a new phenomenon. Zionists had always claimed that they spoke in the name of world Jewry but could not prove (or disprove) that assertion. In the weeks after the Balfour Declaration was issued, most Zionists expected significant numbers of Jews to "buy the *Shekel*" signalling the final conquest of all communities. Zionist hope, however, soon turned to disappointment. The new regimes established in east central Europe led most Jewish communities to rebuild in place and not emigrate. Far from turning to Zionism, most Jews opted to support ideologies that maintained the status quo. Labor Zionist leader Moshe Beilinson, for example, argued in 1924 that the WZO's biggest enemy was not the Palestine administration but "Jewish passivity."[65] This development was clearest in Poland but had identifiable parallels throughout Eastern Europe.[66]

Institutional and Ideological Developments

Nevrtheless, the popular view of the Third Aliya remains largely correct: The four years led to critical developments that placed the *Yishuv* on a stronger foundation. Without those developments, further progress would have been difficult if not impossible. All the same, Zionist activities remained beset by repeated conflicts over issues both large and small.

Perhaps the most important issue dividing the Zionist movement was the clash between Chaim Weizmann, newly elected president of the WZO, and Justice Louis D. Brandeis, doyen of the American Zionists. The dispute had both personal and political ramifications.[67] Brandeis believed that development in *Eretz Israel* ought to be Jewish and apolitical, rather than narrowly Zionist and diplomatic. Brandeis sought WZO approval of a plan, dubbed the Zeeland program (after the ship on which Brandeis sailed to London in 1920 when he composed this scheme), that emphasized the philanthropic elements of Zionist development and deferred any new political activity. By contrast, Weizmann and his supporters saw little utility in deferring political action, fearing a repetition of the conditions in *Eretz Israel* when OETA ruled the territory.[68] Brandeis claimed, with some accuracy, that hitherto, Zionist development had been carried out willy-nilly and was characterized by great inefficiency. The European approach, Brandeis averred, was too dogmatic and squandered too many precious resources. What Brandeis sought was a dual track for Zionist development: public funds used for land purchase, immigration, and the like, with private funds used for industrial and agricultural development. Though Weizmann conceded that inefficiency had been a hallmark of previous Zionist development, he denied that the problem was systemic. Moreover, Weizmann argued that private funding for settlement activity would result in even greater inefficiency since donors might, potentially, be asked to donate funds to different fund-raisers all seeking funds for the same settlements. The only way to prevent a diffusion of Zionist fund-raising efforts would be a central fund for settlement (the Keren ha-Yesod, KHY) that would operate parallel to the KKL. Whereas the KKL would use funds collected throughout the Jewish world to buy land, KHY would use funds to build Jewish settlements on KKL land.[69]

At the London conference (1920) the Weizmann faction — with the Zionist Executive's overwhelming support — was victorious. Henceforth, Zionist policy would remain a synthesis of political and practical activity whose main focus would remain the national (public) rather than the private sector.[70] As a result of the conference decision, however, Brandeis's withdrew from any leadership posi-tion in the Zionist Organization of America, substantially weakening the American Zionists.[71]

The dispute between Brandeis and Weizmann had an ironic sequel. One aspect of the dispute had been the issue of cooperation between the WZO and American non-Zionists who, although rejecting Jewish nationalism, supported the building of a Jewish National Home. At least officially, such collaboration was rejected when the Zeeland program was rejected. However, development was so slow and adequate financing for immigration and settlement projects so difficult to find that by 1928, the Zionist Executive faced imminent bankruptcy.[72] As a result, the WZO and the Zionist Executive returned to a modified form of the very proposal that had been rejected in 1920: In 1929 the Zionist Executive was transformed, by the addition of American non-Zionist representatives, into the Jewish Agency for Palestine, a quasi-governmental institution that claimed to speak in the name of the Jews interested in creating a Jewish National home.[73]

What effect the Brandeis-Weizmann conflict had on the *Yishuv* is less clear. Growth, as has already been noted, was slow but steady for most of the 1920s.[74] Likewise, the precise impact of disunity on the WZO is almost impossible to gauge at this distance. To be sure, the Twelfth Zionist Congress — the first held since before World War I — which convened in Carlsbad, Czechoslovakia, from September 1–14, 1921, sought to project a united Zionist front. Zionist reality was, of course, different. Different parties continued to proliferate — combining, splitting, and recombining over (at times) minor ideological issues.

Weizmann's opening address reviewed both the successes and failures experienced by the WZO since the previous congress. Mainly he emphasized the new opportunities and dangers facing Zionism. Weizmann also urged his listeners to eschew either undue optimism or undue pessimism, calling on them to concentrate on the tasks ahead.[75] Nahum Sokolow followed Weizmann's speech with a similarly attuned oration summarizing recent Zionist history and the tasks ahead.[76] The subsequent debates in the plenary concentrated on two topics: financial and economic conditions and relations with the Arabs.[77] Despite some criticism of the Executive, a majority of the delegates voted to reelect the entire ruling slate with no changes.[78] Ten resolutions were passed by the Congress plenary; none was controversial. Indeed, most were simply restatements and refinements on previously adopted decisions whose motto may just as well have been "stay the course."[79]

If the Zionist congress appeared unified, the movement was far from united. Three major blocs had developed in the WZO: the general Zionist bloc, the socialist Zionist bloc, and the religious Zionist bloc. All three blocs manifested themselves at the Congress and in the *Yishuv*. Each of these blocs underwent considerable change in the 1920s, although three of these developments would be critical to the future of the WZO and the *Yishuv*. First was the emergence of Revisionist Zionism within General Zionism. Second was the further fragmenting of socialist Zionism and the emergence of a clearly Marxist left wing (including a Communist party) in *Eretz Israel*. Third was the initial manifestation of discord between the revisionists and the laborites — a schism that was to be decisive for the *Yishuv's* future.

Revisionist Zionism crystallized after Ze'ev Jabotinsky created Hitachdut ha-Zionim ha-Revisionistim (the Union of Zionist Revisionists, Ha-Zohar) in 1925. Jabotinsky, it will be recalled, was one of the Jewish Legion's fathers and had led Jerusalem's defense during the Arab riots in 1920. A talented writer and gifted orator, Jabotinsky was slightly younger than Weizmann but shared the latter's exclusively pro-British orientation. In 1919–1920 Jabotinsky had sided with the WZO majority in opposing

the Nordau plan. He also opposed any effort to defer *aliya* until some (unspecified) future date when *Eretz Israel* would be "ready." Thus, already at the outset of the mandate Jabotinsky articulated a position that differed from the WZO leadership, even though his position was still compatible with theirs.[80] In 1922 Jabotinsky went a step further, proposing his own Zionist political platform for constructive Zionist development and for relations with the Arabs. In essence, Jabotinsky proposed a parity scheme for relations with the latter, whereby Eretz Israel would be shared equally by all its national groups.[81]

By 1925, however, Jabotinsky despaired of any possibility, at least for the foreseeable future, of a peaceful accommodation with the Arabs. Simultaneously, a fiscal downturn in the *Yishuv* and the virtual drying up of *aliya* led him to question the assumptions that guided the Zionist leadership. Two of Weizmann's assumptions particularly worried Jabotinsky: his emphasis on gradual development — with no contingency plan for rapid mass *aliya* should conditions change — and his emphasis on quiet diplomacy — again, with no apparent contingency plan should conditions change. Furthermore, the rise and development of Zionist parties — what Jabotinsky dubbed "hyphenated Zionisms" — worried the Revisionist leader. Instead, Jabotinsky proposed a "monist" Zionist policy that would concentrate on fulfilling Zionist goals as quickly as humanly possible. Additionally, Jabotinsky emphasized the need for the WZO to adamantly demand that the British fulfill their promises to the Jewish people. In effect, Jabotinsky had proposed a return to an exclusive focus on Herzlian Political Zionism.[82]

Jabotinsky's multifarious positions led him to an increasingly vocal and eventually violent conflict with the socialist Zionists. This held true in part because of Jabotinsky's monism and in part because the socialist Zionists — who inherited the mantle of Spiritual Zionism from Ahad ha-Am — supported Weizmann's gradualist policy for *Yishuv* development. At this stage, most labor Zionists preferred that *aliya* be limited to *halutzim*, that is, to those who had obtained agricultural training in the diaspora.[83] By 1927, Jabotinsky was claiming that labor Zionism, in all its manifestations, was but a form of Bolshevism with a Jewish national veneer. As a result, Jabotinsky increasingly defined himself as a capitalist and saw himself in conflict with the labor Zionists. As already noted, this conflict would become violent, mainly after 1930.[84]

As ha-Zohar developed, it became even more closely identified with the personal ideology and political philosophy of its founder. Ha-Zohar soon developed a number of guiding principles, of which two stand out. The first was the principle of monism, or, as Jabotinsky termed it, *hadness* (unity). He argued that all forms of "hyphenated" Zionism should place their individual agendas on hold. No substantive decisions needed to be made regarding the policies of the Jewish state before its creation. Rather, the Jewish need of the hour was the creation of a disciplined, though not autarkic, Zionist movement. The second guiding principle was his emphasis on *hadar* (self-respect), an idealized code of aesthetics and behavior whose purpose was to create a "new Jew." According to Jabotinsky, hadar "combines various conceptions such as outward beauty, respect, self-esteem, politeness, [and] faithfulness."[85]

In practice, Jabotinsky emphasized three concrete aspects of his ideology: (1) the immediate need for Zionists to announce their ultimate goal, which he defined as the establishment of a Jewish state; (2) *aliya* "for all who want it" with the creation of an immigration policy devoid of any limitations, including supposedly objective ones such as economic absorptive capacity; and (3) the conversion of Eretz Israel into the political, social, and intellectual center of the Jewish world. By 1925, therefore, Jabotinsky defined Zionism almost exclusively in terms of sovereignty and the goal of a Jewish state.[86]

Jabotinsky's brand of Zionism has been viewed in a number of different ways. Historians have noted similarities between revisionist Zionism and the liberal nationalism of Giuseppe Mazzini. Jabotinsky repeatedly referred to the role that the Italian *Risorgimento* played in his ideological development. "All my views," he wrote, "on problems of nationalism, the state and society were developed during those years under Italian influence."[87] Socialist (and some non-socialist) Zionist opponents, however, condemned revisionism as a form of "integralist" nationalism or fascism.[88] This identification was widely used by opponents to attack Ha-Zohar and deny its legitimacy. Thus, for example, Chaim Weizmann attacked Jabotinsky, comparing him — on the basis of an incorrectly reported speech about Jewish relations with the British Empire — to Germany's Nazis.[89]

Jabotinsky strongly condemned this anti-revisionist libel. In a letter to Shlomo Y. Jacobi, he identified only one similarity between revisionism and Italian fascism — the rejection of the Marxist concept of class struggle — while also noting Ha-Zohar's complete rejection of all the antidemocratic elements of fascism. Similarly, Jabotinsky strove to explain the supposedly militaristic elements of revisionist ideology, with its emphasis on uniform and paramilitary drill (most notable in Betar, ha-Zohar's youth movement). Far from instilling a militaristic spirit, Jabotinsky believed, the uniform and drill served to instill a dignified bearing.[90] He was careful to add, however, that although militarism had intensely negative connotations, especially for Jews, there might be a positive element in the militaristic bearing; mainly the discipline instilled in Betar members. In Jabotinsky's view, this form of discipline symbolized the essential difference "between a multitude, a mob, and a nation."[91] In view of Jabotinsky's concentration on the specific goal of statehood, his focus on discipline is understandable; however, it would also contribute to the crux of an increasingly violent conflict between ha-Zohar and Mapai.

Despite his impassioned defense, the identification of revisionism with fascism remained a sore point in intra-Zionist relations throughout the 1930s and well into the 1940s. Although the fascist label did not fit Jabotinsky very well — especially in light of his essentially pro-British and liberal attitudes — the same cannot be said to hold true for all his followers. When combined with syndicalist economic theories, romantic notions about organic nationalism, and hero worship, revisionism could indeed develop into a quasi-fascism. This held especially true among some of Jabotinsky's younger followers — notably Abraham Stern and Abba Ahimeir — and was prominent among the members of a shadowy organization which called itself Brit ha-Biryonim (the Covenant of Terrorists).[92] Zvi Kolitz, a revisionist leader from Tel Aviv, wrote a biography of Benito Mussolini in 1936 that may be seen as typical; the publisher appended a small preface to the book that read in part: "Italy can teach us something. In particular, we Jews . . . should study the miracles which the Fascist movement has brought about, especially in the area of nationalism." Jabotinsky was sufficiently concerned about this trend that he condemned it strongly in an article entitled "Basta!"[93] In a letter to the editors of *Hazit ha-Am* (Ha-Zohar's daily organ) he condemned even grudging admiration for Mussolini and Hitler in no uncertain terms: "The articles and notices on Hitler . . . are to me, and to all of us, like a knife thrust in our backs. I demand an unconditional stop to this outrage."[94]

Simultaneously with the rise of Revisionist Zionism were a series of developments within the labor Zionist camp. The first of these was the rise of the Gdud Ha-Avoda (Labor Battalion) founded by Joseph Trumpeldor.[95] Based on the need to find employment for large numbers of new immigrants, the Gdud operated on a communal — critics claimed a communist — basis. Like a *Kibbutz*, all members shared their resources; unlike a *Kibbutz*, the Gdud did not operate in one locale. Members formed a mobile labor force for public works projects and the like. Gdud members also founded a number of settlements in the upper Galilee, notably Ein Harod and Tel Yosef (named in Trumpeldor's honor after he was killed during the defense of Tel Hai on March 1, 1920).[96] Despite Trumpeldor's death, the Gdud attempted to carry on. This became more difficult during the middle and late 1920s as ideological fissures (relating to communism) became more pronounced. In 1926 the Gdud split entirely, with its two wings collapsing within a year. In a final act, some of the most ideologically motivated members of the Gdud's left wing emigrated to the Soviet Union in 1928 to build a socialist Jewish homeland.[97]

By the early 1930s a full-blown Communist party had developed in the *Yishuv*. Although this movement was considered threatening by the Histadrut and the mainstream Socialist Zionist parties, it never became more than a peripheral factor in the Yishuv's politics. Moreover, by the 1930s, the Palestine Communist Party could only marginally be considered Jewish. Its unquestioningly anti-Zionist position relegated the party to the outermost fringes of Jewish society and its unequivocally pro-Arab position also did not find many sympathetic ears in a *Yishuv* built on the Zionist ideal.[98]

Two other developments within the *Yishuv's* socialist Zionist parties were of greater importance. First, in December 1920, delegates of *Eretz Israel's* three main socialist Zionist parties — ha-Poel ha-Zair, Ahdut ha-Avoda, and Poale Zion — met to found the Histadrut, which was destined to become a key foundation of socialist Zionism and of the *Yishuv*.[99] Second, nearly ten years later, ha-Poel ha-Zair and Ahdut ha-Avoda — parties committed to cooperation with nonsocialist Zionists for the fulfillment of Zionist goals — merged to form Mifleget Poale Eretz Israel (the Israeli workers' party, Mapai). By 1931, Mapai (and its European counterparts) represented a plurality with the WZO, leading to the era of Mapai's hegemony within the Zionist organization and the *Yishuv*.[100]

Ideologically both the Histadrut and Mapai were committed to three policies: *aliya* (at this stage, limited to *Halutzim*), *Avoda Ivrit* (Hebrew Labor, which meant building the *Yishuv's* economy by exclusive use of Jewish labor), and *Hityashvut* (settlement). The first and third policies were simply laborite reinterpretations of generalized Zionist goals, but were given a socialist Zionist flair. *Avoda Ivrit* was critical to the Yishuv's growth, but, was, broadly speaking, little more than a re-statement of A. D. Gordon's belief (see the previous chapter), that in order to rebuild a national home, Jews had to assume the mantle of responsibility for their economic future. Nonetheless, it should be noted that the Histadrut/Mapai ideology (they were virtually identical in light of the interlocking leadership of what were ostensibly two different organizations) was framed in a somewhat vague fashion.[101]

Mapai's unique ideological orientation manifested itself more clearly on the question of the relative importance of nationalism compared to socialism. David Ben-Gurion, who served as Histadrut general secretary between 1921 and 1935 (and who thereafter served as chairman of the Jewish Agency Executive [JAE] and Israel's first prime minister), for instance, declared openly in 1922 that "The one and only task that dominates our thoughts and deeds is to conquer the country and build it up with the aid of large immigration. All the rest is trivia and rhetoric."[102] Mapai's leaders thus remained committed to creating a mixed market economy in *Eretz Israel*, for all intents and purposes rejecting class struggle and orthodox Marxism. Further-more, Mapai's position always accepted the premise of cooperation with nonsocialist Zionist parties, notably Mizrachi and the Weizmannite wing of the General Zionists.

To further understand Mapai's position, it is worthwhile noting that, after the merger, the new party approved a platform that pledged itself to the goal of becoming "responsible for the pioneering fulfillment of the Zionist movement and a faithful mem-ber of the International Socialist Labor Movement."[103] Central to Mapai's ideology was the concept of "constructive socialism," by which was meant a fusion of the concepts of Jewish national rejuvenation and a broadly socialist weltanschauung, with the ultimate goal of creating an *Am Oved*, a laboring people. Mapai concentrated on each small step — one more settler, one more dunam of land under Jewish cultiva-tion, one more settlement. As further

developed in the 1930s by Mapai ideologues, primarily Ben-Gurion, Chaim Arlosoroff, and Berl Katznelson, constructive socialism would operate in two main stages. First was to create an *Am Oved*, which would be realized when the Jewish masses had been converted to produc-tive labor on the soil of *Eretz Israel*. At that point, Jews should strive to become an *Am Mamlachti*, a sovereign people. As formulated by Ben-Gurion, *Mamlachtiut* (statism) involved three components: (1) cooperation with non-socialist Zionists in building *Eretz Israel*, (2) abandonment of class struggle as the primary defining feature of socialist Zionism, and (3) assumption of responsibility for fulfillment of Zionist goals.[104] In his major ideological work of the 1930s, *me-Ma'amd la-Am* (From a Class to a Nation), Ben-Gurion wrote:

The time has come for our movement to cease to be one branch of the Zionist move-ment and take upon itself the yoke of, and responsibility of, the entire Zionist organi-zation . . . Our movement demands . . . [that] . . . we identify completely with the Zionist Organization, that we be a majority in the Congress and the Zionist Organization, and stand at its head. This does not mean that we must turn the Zionist Organization into a socialist organization, nor does it mean that we must abandon socialism or become less socialist than we have been.[105]

In essence, Ben-Gurion's argument was that Mapai owed loyalty to two focal points. Doing so, however, required that labor Zionists be-have responsibly within both orbits. It followed that a Marxist approach, emphasizing class struggle and internecine warfare, was not necessarily the best tactic for socialist Zionism. Instead, an evolutionary (or reformist) approach would accomplish Mapai's twin goals more efficiently.

Arlosoroff too expressed significant doubts about orthodox Marxist theories. In *Der Jüdische Volkssozialismus* (Jewish peoples' socialism), he contended that European socialists refused to permit Jews the same national consciousness that was taken for granted by all other nations. Therefore, Jews were not compelled to adopt orthodox Marxism. "For us," he stated, "Socialist struggle does not mean the struggle of one class with another. Our goal is the positive construction of a society."[106] Arlosoroff further refined his position in the early 1930s. For instance, in an article in *Davar*, he argued that the Zionists had developed *Eretz Israel* too slowly. At contemporary rates of *aliya*, Jews would need 163 years to constitute a majority of *Eretz Israel*'s population. Given the Arab population growth, the Jews would need even more time than that to develop as a majority in their national home.[107]

In contrast with Mapai, both Poale Zion Smol (PZS) and ha-Shomer ha-Zair (the young Watchman) — which was founded in 1926 by remnants of Gdud Ha-Avoda — adhered to more conventionally Marxist forms of socialism. PZS, for example, argued that class struggle was still critical to socialist Zionism. In other words, where Mapai's ideologues argued that socialism was the best means to attain Zionist goals, PZS argued that Zionism was the best way for Jews to achieve true socialism. "The construction of a Jewish Socialist Palestine," one Poale Zion document read, "can only come about in agreement with the main principles of revolutionary class struggle."[108] As a result, PZS withdrew from the WZO in 1920 and did not return until 1937.[109]

Ha-Shomer ha-Zair, whose main strength lay in its associated *Kibbutz* movement, was not much different from PZS in its analysis of the direction Zionism ought to take: Zionism was seen as a form of Jewish national liberation that was part and parcel of global efforts to overturn capitalism. Like PZS, ha-Shomer ha-Zair called for revolutionary socialism and "complete social liberation" in its most basic ideological documents.[110] Despite their similarities, there was one critical difference between PZS and ha-Shomer ha-Zair: The latter remained in the WZO throughout the 1920s and 1930s. Neither party amounted to more than nuisance opposition for Mapai; which would emerge (in the 1930s) as the central

force for Zionist development.

There were numerous other developments, both in the *Yishuv* and in the WZO, but they pale by comparison to the rise of Mapai and the Histadrut. One noteworthy development was the further refinement of Mizrachi's position with the WZO. The religious Zionist party strongly rejected the notion of a "separation of church and state" within the *Yishuv*. Instead, Mizrachi advocated a national and religious renaissance whose central theme would be educational, using education to restore as many Jews as possible to an orthodox but nationalistic lifestyle.[111] Religious Zionists continued to emphasize the need to build a Torah state. However, for the most part, they also echoed the teachings of the first Ashkenazi chief rabbi of *Eretz Israel*, Rav Abraham Isaac ha-Kohen Kook, and cooperated with secular Zionists on mutually important projects.[112] Mizrachi, it might be added, developed its own socialist offshoot, initially organized as the Torah va-Avoda movement, which eventually coalesced into ha-Poel ha-Mizrachi.[113]

The balance sheet of Zionist ideological developments in the 1920s may be summarized thus: By 1929 the *Yishuv*, its parties and its institutions, had developed sufficiently that one could begin using terms like "a state in the making" or a "quasi-state" to refer to the growing Jewish society then being built. This trend would be furthered during the next wave of *aliya*, which began in 1924.

Yishuv Developments, 1924–1929

The *Yishuv*'s growth during the 1920s was slow but steady. Some of the figures from the 1929 government estimate of the Jewish population bear repeating: In 1929, the Jewish population was estimated at 154,300, or 18.9 percent of Palestine's total population. Even so, it is important to note that the Fourth Aliya was considerably different from its immediate predecessor. Broadly, there were three major differences between the Third and Fourth Aliyas: First, the Fourth Aliya was a truly mass *aliya* that nearly doubled *Eretz Israel*'s Jewish population in six years. Second, the *olim* were not, by and large, pioneers; rather they were mainly middle-class Jews of Eastern or Central European origin who made no claim to agricultural training and had no intention of settling in *Kibbutzim*. Finally, this wave of *aliya* — colloquially known as the *Grabski Aliya* (after the prime minister of Poland at the time, Wladyslaw Grabski) — was the first to directly respond to the crisis of rising antisemitism in Europe and the closing of America as a destination for Jewish migration. Although antisemitism had been one of the catalysts for the creation of the Zionist movement, the *Yishuv* had always had to compete with the United States for immigrants. America, seen by Eastern European Jews as the "golden land," had generally won the competition. Restrictive immigration laws adopted by the U.S. Senate in 1922 and 1924, however, virtually closed that option for Eastern European Jews — hence, mass *aliya* under antisemitic pressure.[114]

Some of the political implications of the Fourth Aliya, notably ha-Zohar's creation and rise to prominence, have already been discussed. Revisionist Zionism's appeal may be partly explained by reference to the ethos of the new *olim* and the response by Zionist leaders to that ethos. Socialist Zionists, for example, claimed that middle-class *olim* drove land prices up — due to speculation in market values — without creating anything truly productive. Furthermore, Socialist Zionists appreciated more keenly than others the revolutionary elements of Zionist goals — essentially an attempt to escape the diaspora model of Jewish existence. Yet here was an *aliya* wave that, to a greater or

lesser degree, sought to re-create the diaspora ethos in *Eretz Israel*. Not only Socialist Zionists felt this way. Weizmann, for instance, told a meeting of the Va'ad ha-Poel ha-Zioni in 1924 that he opposed creating a "second Nalewki" in *Eretz Israel*.[115]

Weizmann's opponents formulated a sharply divergent position. Jabotinsky, for example, argued that mass *aliya*, regardless of the economic suitability or ethos of the *olim*, should be the Zionists' only goal.[116] For their part, the new *olim* responded by noting that they were Zionists who had paid their dues, a reflection of the fact that the *Yishuv* was still heavily dependent on philanthropy, and had as much of a right to settle in *Eretz Israel* as any of the *Halutzim*. Moreover, even some of the Socialist Zionists had mixed feelings about opposition to middle-class *aliya*; noting that mass immigration had always been central to Zionism.[117]

In the end, the business cycle, not ideological argumentation, was fated to halt the Fourth Aliya. New immigration coupled with land speculation created a financial boom in 1924–1925. By late 1925, however, the Yishuv had reached the maximum limit of financial development. A recession resulted.[118] This recession was felt in a number of ways, first, and foremost, in considerable unemployment. Figures for Tel Aviv represent the trend. Unemployment, which was virtually nonexistent in 1924, jumped to 2,000 in 1925, 5,200 in 1926, and 8,000 in 1927. Thereafter, the unemployment rate dropped to 3,000 in 1928.[119] New housing starts in Tel Aviv, summarized in Table 5.1, are another means to understand the recession.

TABLE 5.1: New Housing Starts in Tel Aviv by Square Meters

Quarter	1925	1926	Percentage Change
First	58	26.0	-55.2
Second	63	14.0	-77.8
Third	66	08.5	-87.1
Fourth	52	05.5	-89.4
Total	239	54.0	-77.5

Source: D. Giladi, in הציונות 2 (1971), p. 134.

Lord Arthur James Balfour Speaking at Hebrew University's Dedication Ceremony, 1925.
Courtesy of the Central Zionist Archives, Jerusalem

Aliya picked up again as economic conditions improved, but, to a degree, the damage had already been done. The British government, whose means for establishing *aliya* rates had been economic absorptive capacity, would henceforth be suspicious of mass *aliya* on economic grounds. When coupled with Arab riots in the summer of 1929, British efforts to control the *Yishuv's* growth led to a temporary halt in *aliya* that created more dissension within Zionist ranks and further soured relations between the WZO and the British mandatory authorities.

Despite these negative developments, the Fourth Aliya saw positive developments within the *Yishuv* during the middle and late 1920s. The Jewish population increased and considerable strides were made in the *Yishuv's* economy, both agricultural and industrial, during this era.[120] Nevertheless, it may well be that the most portentous development of this era was cultural: Hebrew University's opening.

Spiritual Zionists had long emphasized education. Indeed, according to Ahad ha-Am, Zionist educational was as important as — if not more important than — *aliya*. This was true because the *Yishuv*, in Ahad ha-Am's mind, was to be the cultural center for all world Jewry. Political Zionists also placed an emphasis on culture — though obviously less so than their Spiritual Zionist counterparts. In his utopian novel *Altneuland*, for instance, Herzl spoke extensively about its future Jewish state's first-rate education system.

The importance attached to education manifested itself in a unanimous WZO decision in 1913 to establish a university in *Eretz Israel* as soon as conditions permitted. In March 1921, a site on Mount Scopus overlooking the old city of Jerusalem and the Temple Mount was selected for the university.[121] On January 4, 1925, the new university — now formally named the Hebrew University of Jerusalem — was inaugurated. Speakers at the festive event included poet Chaim Nahman Bialik, Lord Arthur J. Balfour, and a panoply of Zionist and British public figures.[122] Moreover, the university was indeed destined to become the centerpiece of a highly developed educational system in the *Yishuv*.[123] The *Yishuv* definitely had come of age.

Notes

1. Brandeis to Gottheil, October 10, 1919, available at http.www.wzo.org.il/Blueprint, p. 24.

2. Cf. Yoram Mayorek ed., "1918 פברואר-ינואר, סוקולוב נחום של פאריס יומן" (Nahum Sokolow' Paris diary, January–February 1918), *הציונות* 16 (1991): 213–255.

3. For a perspicacious review of OETA's activites in Palestine/*Eretz Israel*, see Bernard Wasserstein, *The British in Palestine*, 2d ed. (London: Basil Blackwell, 1991), chap. 1–2.

4. Isaiah Friedman ed., *The Zionist Commission in Palestine, 1918*, Rise of Israel Series, vol. 9 (New York: Garland, 1987), pp. 105–138.

5. Isaiah Friedman ed., *Tension in Palestine — Peacemaking in Paris, 1919*, Rise of Israel Series, vol. 10 (New York: Garland, 1987, pp. 13–73).

6. Clayton to Balfour, September 21, 1918, cited in ibid., pp. 1–4.

7. Clayton to Foreign Office, March 14, 1918, cited in Friedman, *Zionist Commission*, p. 138.

8. The Franco-Syrian conflict is summarized in Leonard Stein, *Syria* (London: E. Benn, 1926).

9. Isaiah Friedman ed., *Opposition to Zionism, 1919*, Rise of Israel Series, vol. 11 (New York: Garland, 1987), pp. 50–54.

10. Note by Ormsby-Gore, February 15, 1919, in ibid., pp. 68–71.

11. Ibid., pp. 65–172 cites the relevant British and Zionist documents.

12. Ibid., pp. 55–64.

13. Cf. the diary entries for June 24, June 27, July 3, and July 19, 1919, cited in Leah Landau-Duchan ed., "זלקינד אלכסנדר "דר של מיומנו — היהודים הצירים ועד" (The Comité des Délégations Juives — As Seen From the Diary of Dr. Alexander Zelkind), *הציונות* 12 (1987): 371–399.

14. Julian Mack, "Political Status of the Zionist Movement," *Bulletin of the Zionist Society of Engineers and Agriculturists*, 1 no.2 (February 1920): 19–21.

15. Report by Ormsby-Gore, June 17, 1918, cited in Friedman, *Zionist Commission*, pp. 340–347.

16. Weizmann and Sieff to Sokolow, April 18, 1918, ibid., pp. 221–232.

17. Cf. ibid., pp. 139-402 on the Zionist Commission's other activities.

18. The Anglo-French-American maneuvering over the Near East is more fully documented in Friedman, *Tension in Palestine*, pp. 74–156.

19. Clayton to Balfour, December 6, 1918, in ibid., pp. 71–73.

20. Weizmann to Sokolow, reporting on his conversation with Balfour, December 5, 1918, in ibid., p. 106.

21. Neil Caplan, *Futile Diplomacy* (London: Frank Cass, 1983) 1:31–36.

22. Faisal-Weizmann Agreement, January 3, 1919, cited in Friedman, *Tension in Palestine*, p. 158.

23. Ibid., p. 161.

24. Faisal to Frankfurter, March 1, 1919, in ibid., pp. 240–241.

25. Frankfurter to Faisal, March 5, 1919, in ibid., p. 251.

26. Caplan, *Futile Diplomacy*, pp. 36–46, Friedman, *Opposition to Zionism*, pp. 173–195.

27. Wasserstein, *British in Palestine*, p. 39.

28. Ibid., p. 41, Friedman, *Tension in Palestine*, pp. 255–267.

29. Friedman, *Tension in Palestine*, pp. 74–91, 93–95.

30. Weizmann to Clayton, November 27, 1918, in ibid., p. 96.

31. Memoranda on Borders, by Aaronsohn and Tolkowsky, in ibid., pp. 268–289.

32. Ibid., pp. 290–356.

33. Maps reviewing the history of *Eretz Israel*'s borders are reproduced in *Carta's Historical Atlas of Israel* (Jerusalem: Carta, 1977), pp. 8, 10–11, 13, 17–18.

34. Cf. Yitzhak Gil-Har, "אחרת ראיה זווית - ישראל מארץ המזרחי הירדן עבר הפרדת שאלת" (The separation of Trans-Jordan from Eretz Israel — Another angle), *זמננו יהדות* 1 (1984): 163–177.

35. Curzon Minute, March 20, 1920, cited in John J. McTague, "Zionist-British Negotiations over the Draft Mandate for Palestine, 1920," *JSS* 42, no. 3/4 (Summer/Fall 1980): 284.

36. Ibid., pp. 286–288.

37. Wasserstein, *British in Palestine*, pp. 62–67; the riots and their international implications are documented in Isaiah Friedman ed., *Riots in Jerusalem — San Remo Conference, April 1920*, Rise of Israel Series, vol. 12 (New York: Garland, 1987), pp. 1–141.

38. Friedman, *Riots in Jerusalem*, pp. 142–198. It might be noted that Husseini was rewarded for his aggravating violence by being appointed Mufti of Jerusalem, whereas Jabotinsky, who had merely acted in legitimate self-defense, was virtually expelled from Palestine/*Eretz Israel*. During a trip to Europe in 1929 he was informed by the British that he would not be permitted to return to the country.

39. Mctague, "Draft Mandate," pp. 288–289.

40. Friedman, *Riots in Jerusalem*, pp. 199–227.

41. Mctague, "Draft Mandate," pp. 290–291; Friedman, *Riots in Jerusalem*, pp. 228–310.

42. Howard M. Sachar, *A History of Israel* (New York: Alfred A. Knopf, 1976), pp. 123–124.

43. Friedman, *Riots in Jerusalem*, pp. 311–332.

44. On the Third Aliya, see Baruch Ben-Avram and Henry Near, עיונים בעלייה השלישית: דימוי ומציאות (Studies in the Third Aliya: Image and reality) (Jerusalem: Yad Yitzhak Ben-Zvi, 1995).

45. Mack, "Political Status," p. 19.

46. Baruch Ben-Anat, "הרגע הגדול מצא דור קטן — תוכנית נורדאו, 1919–1920" (The great moment confronted a small generation — the Nordau Plan, 1919–1920), הציונות, 19 (1995): 99–103.

47. Ibid., pp. 99–100. Weizmann, for instance, spoke of an aliya rate of 20,000 per year for the foreseeable future. At that rate, it would have taken thirty years to establish a Jewish majority in *Eretz Israel* (assuming the Arab population stagnated at 600,000) and would have required an unprecedented 200 years to achieve Weizmann's long-range goal of a Yishuv with 4 million Jewish citizens.

48. Ibid., pp. 104–106.

49. Ibid., pp. 107–111.

50. Ibid., pp. 112–115.

51. The various legislative acts controlling *aliya* are reprinted in Aaron S. Klieman ed., *Practical Zionism, 1920–1939*, Rise of Israel Series, vol. 15 (New York; Garland, 1987), pp. 1–20. The "nuts and bolts" of how the immigration system actually worked are set out in Gabriel Sheffer, "Political Considerations in British Policy-Making on Immigration to Palestine," *Studies in Zionism*, 4 (October 1981): 237–274 and in Abraham J. Edelheit, *The Yishuv in the Shadow of the Holocaust: Zionist Policy and Rescue Aliya, 1933–1939* (Boulder: Westview Press, 1996), chap. 1.

52. Cited in Neil Caplan, "The Yishuv, Sir Herbert Samuel, and the Arab Question in Palestine, 1921–1925," in Elie Kedourie and Sylvia Haim eds., *Zionism and Arabism in Palestine and Israel* (London: Frank Cass, 1982), pp. 4–5.

53. Frederick H. Kisch, *Palestine Diary* (1938), cited in Klieman, *Practical Zionism*, pp. 21–24.

54. *Ten Years of Jewish Immigration into Palestine*, Statistical Bulletin 17, (Jerusalem: Keren ha-Yesod, 1929), p. 3.

55. Ibid. The 1931 census tabulated the Jewish population at 174,610 (Edelheit, *Yishuv*, p. 3).

56. *Jewish Immigration*, p. 10.

57. *Census of Jewish Agriculture*, 1927, cited in Aaron S. Klieman ed., *The Jewish Yishuv's Development in the Interwar Period*, Rise of Israel Series, vol. 16 (New York: Garland, 1987), p. 257.

58. Ibid., pp. 257–288.

59. Weizmann to Untermyer, July 28, 1921, in ibid., pp. 289–290. On Rutenberg, see: Eli Shaltiel, פנחס רוטנברג (Pinhas Rutenberg: His life and times) (Tel Aviv: Am Oved, 1990), chap. 1–2.

60. Ben-Avram and Near, עיונים, pp. 47–70.

61. On the history of Tel Aviv's suburbs, see, for example, Miriam Meshel, רמת גן (Ramat-Gan: A history) (Ramat-Gan: Avivim Press, 1991), pp. 11–21.

62. Report of the Joint Palestine Survey Commission, 1928, in Klieman, *Yishuv's Development*, p. 117.

63. Ibid., p. 39.

64. Ben-Avram and Near, עיונים, pp. 124–137, 189.

65. Beilinson's comments are cited in ibid., p. 107.

66. Cf. Ezra Mendelsohn, *Zionism in Poland: The Formative Years, 1915–1926*, (New Haven: Yale University Press, 1981), pp. 223–231.

67. Cf. Ben Halpern, *A Clash of Heroes: Brandeis, Weizmann, and American Zionism* (New York: Oxford University Press, 1987), chap. 1–3.

68. Ibid., pp. 205–218. The dispute is documented, from Weizmann's point of view, in Aaron S. Klieman, ed., *Giving Substance to the Jewish National Home, 1920 and Beyond*, Rise of Israel Series, vol. 14 (New York: Garland, 1987), pp. 123–135.

69. Sachar, *History of Israel*, pp. 140–142.

70. Halpern, *Clash of Heroes*, pp. 218–226.

71. Ibid., pp. 226–232.

72. Weizmann to Wise, May 11, 1926; to Landsberg, May 20, 1926; and to Lewis, May 24, 1927; cited in Klieman, *Giving Substance*, pp. 139–148.

73. Cf. Herbert Parzen, "The Enlargement of the Jewish Agency for Palestine: 1923–1929, A Hope Hamstrung," *JSS* 39, no.1/2 (Winter/Spring 1977): 129–158.

74. Cf the KKL and KHY reports, repectively dated 1933 (covering 1919–1932) and 1940 (covering 1921–1940) in Klieman, *Giving Substance*, pp. 308–489. A comprehensive history of the Zionist funds and their functions prior to 1948 is a great desideratum, but is (as of this writing) lacking.

75. *Report of the Twelfth Zionist Congress* (London: Central Office of the World Zionist Organization, 1922), pp. 13–16.

76. Ibid., pp. 17–30.

77. Ibid., pp. 31–218.

78. Ibid., p. 218.

79. Ibid., pp. 148–152.

80. Jabotinsky's orientation in 1919 and 1920 is set out in Yaacov Shavit, comp., "מאמרי ז'בוטנסקי 1919–1920" (Jabotinsky's articles, 1919–1920), הציונות, 6 (1981): 323–358.

81. Jabotinsky to Kioch, December 29, 1922, CZA S25/2073.

82. Cf., Yaacov Shavit, *Jabotinsky and the Revisionist Movement, 1925–1948* (London: Frank Cass, 1988), pp. 28–57, 181–202; Howard I. Rosenbloom, "A Political History of Revisionist Zionism, 1925–1938" (Ph.D. diss, Columbia University, 1986), chap. 1.

83. Cf. Edelheit, *Yishuv*, pp. 63–68

84. Ibid., pp. 22–25.

85. Cited in Joseph B. Schechtman, *The Life and Times of Vladimir Jabotinsky* (New York: Thomas Yoseloff, 1961), 2:416.

86. Cf. Zvi Adiv, "עיונים בהשקפתו הציונית של זאב ז'בוטינסקי" (Studies on Zeev Jabotinsky's Zionist philosophy), in Ben-Zion Yehoshua and Aaron Kedar, eds., אידיאולוגיה ומדיניות ציונית (Zionist ideology and politics) Jerusalem: Zalman Shazar Institute Press, 1978), pp. 115–134.

87. Zeev Jabotinsky, אוטוביוגרפיה (Autobiography) (Jerusalem: Eri Jabotinsky, 1948), p. 27; cf. Shavit, *Revisionist Movement*, p. 115.

88. The most prominent example of that approach was taken by Shlomo Avineri, *The Making of Modern Zionism* (New York: Basic Books, 1981), chap. 15.

89. Weizmann to Landesberg, December 30, 1931, cited in Edelheit, *Yishuv*, p. 21.

90. Jabotinsky to Jacobi, October 4, 1933, Jabotinsky Institute Archives (Hereafter JIA) A1/2/23/2.

91. Cited in Edelheit, *Yishuv*, p. 22.

92. Cf. Joseph Heller, *The Stern Gang: Ideology, Politics, and Terror, 1940–1949* (London: Frank Cass, 1995), chap. 1.

93. Both items are cited from Shavit, *Revisionist Movement*, p. 366.

94. Jabotinsky to Yeivin, cited in Schechtman, *Life and Times*, 2:216.

95. Cf. Anita Shapira, ההליכה על קו האופק (Visions in conflict) (Tel Aviv: Am Oved, 1988), pp.157–207.

96. On the Gdud's settlement activities, see ibid., pp. 162–170; on Trumpeldor (and his death at Tel Hai), see Shulamit Laskov, טרומפלדור: סיפור חייו (Yosef Trumpeldor: A biography), 3d ed., (Jerusalem: Keter Publishing, 1995).

97. Cf. Anita Shapira, "השמאל בגדוד העבודה והה.פ.ק.פ. עד 1928" (The Gdud ha-Avoda's left wing and the Palestine Communist party to 1928); and Shmuel Dothan, "ראשיתו של קומוניזם לאומי יהודי בארץ-ישראל" (The origins of Jewish national Bolshevism in Eretz Israel), in הציונות 2 (1971), respectively, pp. 148–168 and 208–236.

98. Sondra M. Rubenstein, *The Communist Movement in Palestine and Israel, 1919–1984* (Boulder: Westview Press, 1985), passim.

99. Cf., Ze'ev Tzahor, בדרך להנהגת הישוב: ההסתדרות בראשיתה (On the road to Yishuv leadership: The Histadrut's early years) (Jerusalem: Yad Yitzhak Ben-Zvi, 1981).

100. Cf. Yonathan Shapiro, *The Formative Years of the Israeli Labor Party: The Organization of Power, 1919–1930* (London: Sage Publications, 1976).

101. Ibid., chap. 6–7, attempts to untangle the precise relationship between the Histadrut and Mapai leadership at this point.

102. David Ben-Gurion, statement at the third Ahdut ha-Avoda convention, cited in ibid., p. 69.

103. The Mapai program, 1931, cited in Baruch Ben-Avram ed., מפלגות וזרמים פוליטיים בתקופת הבית הלאומי (Parties and political Movements during the mandatory era) (Jerusalem: Zalman Shazar Institute Press, 1978), p. 95.

104. Nathan Yanai, "Ben-Gurion's Concept of Mamlahtiut and the Forming Reality of the State of Israel," *Jewish Political Studies Review* 1 no.1/2 (Spring 1989): 151–177.

105. David Ben-Gurion, ממעד לעם (From a class to a nation) (Tel Aviv: Am Oved, 1938), p. 302.

106. Cited in Shlomo Avineri, *Arlosoroff* (New York: Grove Weidenfeld, 1989), p. 25.

107. Edelheit, *Yishuv*, p. 19.

108. Peretz Merhav, *The Israeli Left: History, Problems, Documents* (San Diego: A. S. Barnes, 1980), p. 63.

109. Ibid., pp. 67–68.

110. Kibbutz Artzi Founding Conference Resolutions, April 3, 1927, cited in Ben-Avram, מפלגות, p. 77.

111. Rabbi Meir Berlin (Bar-Ilan), "What Kind of Life Should We Create in Eretz Israel," cited in Arthur Hertzberg, ed., *The Zionist Idea* (New York: Atheneum, 1970), pp. 548–555.

112. Rav Kook is cited in ibid., pp. 419–430. Evaluations of Rav Kook's ideology abound and include, among others, Avineri, *Modern Zionism*, chap. 16, and more recently David J. Goldberg, *To the Promised Land* (London: Penguin Books, 1996), chap. 10. Rav Kook's writings have been published in numerous editions in English and Hebrew; the list is too long to enumerate here.

113. Ben-Avram, מפלגות, pp. 242–243, 253–258.

114. Cf. Yosef Gorny, *From Rosh Pina and Degania to Dimona: A History of Constructive Zionism* (Tel Aviv: MOD Books, 1989), pp. 82–85.

115. Ibid., p. 85. Ulica Nalewki was the major commercial street in Warsaw's Jewish quarter.

116. Edelheit, *Yishuv*, p. 68.

117. Gorny, *Rosh Pina*, pp. 85–86.

118. Dan Giladi, "1926–1927 המשבר הכלכלי בימי העלייה הרביעית" (The economic crisis during the Fourth Aliya, 1926–1927), *הציונות* 2 (1971): 119–147.

119. Ibid., p. 128.

120. Ten Year Report of the Palestine Economic Corporation, 1935, cited in Klieman, *Yishuv's Development*, pp. 291–304.

121. Zionist Executive, Jerusalem, to Zionist Organization, London, March 30, 1921, in ibid., p. 387.

122. Some of the speeches are reprinted in ibid., pp. 388–402.

123. Ibid., pp. 362–386.

6
ZIONISM AND JEWISH COMMUNAL POLITICS

Zionism and Modern Jewish Politics

We have already touched upon many of the salient features of the relationship between Zionism and modern Jewish politics. It should be self-evident that Zionism was by no means the only example of Jewish communal politics in modern times. Nevertheless, it should be equally self-evident that Zionism played a crucial role in shaping Jewish political orientations and defining the Jewish communal agenda. Not surprisingly, Daniel J. Elazar and Stuart A. Cohen, in their recent handbook on Jewish political history, considered the Zionist movement's meteoric rise to be one of the culminating events in Jewish history between 1648 and 1948. Elazar and Cohen chose the Holocaust and the geographic spread of Jewry since the nineteenth century to be the other two culminating events in this era.[1] This chapter seeks to survey Zionism's impact on world Jewry and after a broad review charts that impact on specific Jewish communities up to the 1930s.

As already noted (in Chapter 2) much of modern Jewish politics may be traced back to the era of Enlightenment and emancipation. In trying to fit Jews into the societies that emancipated them, the Maskilim consciously deemphasized the national and political elements in Judaism. Yet, in doing so, the Maskilim inadvertently created a modern Jewish political environment. And while this held most clearly true in czarist Russia, the same may be said for virtually every Jewish community emancipated prior to World War I.[2] Enlightenment and emancipation had one other relevant — again, largely unintended — consequence: an unleashing of considerable centrifugal forces that broke the previous veneer of global Jewish solidarity.[3]

It has been estimated that, at the minimum, twenty-two different ideologies competed on the Jewish street at the turn of the twentieth century: Assimilationism, Acculturationism, Integrationism, Socialism, Communism, Jewish Socialist Nationalism (Bundism), Socialist Territorialism, Autonomism, Internationalism, Anarchism, Hasidism, non-Hasidic Orthodoxy, at least three different forms of Socialist Zionism, Practical Zionism, Political Zionism, Spiritual Zionism, Territorialism, Orthodox Zionism, Synthetic Zionism, and Zionist Zionism.[4] Each of these ideologies, in turn, claimed to exclusively possess the one correct and all-encompassing path to salvation (individual and communal). Each further claimed that all other parties would lead Jewry to a catastrophe of epic proportions.

GRAPH 6.1: Spectrum of Jewish Political Ideology

Orientation/Focus	Diaspora	Eretz Israel
Nationalist	Bundists	
	Diaspora Nationalists	Zionists[5]
Non-Nationalist	Integrationists	Non-Zionist Orthodox[6]
	Socialists	

Despite the wide variety of parties, these Jewish ideologies can be divided into six representative categories: integrationists, socialists, Bundists, Orthodox, Zionists, and diaspora nationalists. Upon further examination, a spectrum of Jewish political ideology emerges, based on a combination of ideological orientation and geographic focus, which may be diagrammed in the manner of Graph 6.1.[7]

Even within this spectrum there were significant nuances and considerable variations; numerous schisms were recorded in the history of virtually every party, leading to a dynamism that was unprecedented by the standards of any other political community.[8] Still, it is also necessary to note that some basic presumptions permeated the entire Jewish polity during the years after World War I. Of these, three seem essential: acceptance of the fact — by all but the integrationists — that Jews constitute a nation; that this nation, like any other nation, has specific interests and needs; and, finally, that party activity should be designed to promote the nation's best interests in the short and long term.

Commonality of broad approach should not, of course, be confused with unity of purpose. The blocs (and within blocs the individual parties) differed on many significant details. To name only the most obvious, they disagreed — vehemently — on future viability of the diaspora.[9] Thus, while all Jewish parties but integrationists (a term here used to include assimilationists of various stripes as well as Jewish communists, non-nationalist socialists, and adherents of the Reform movement in Judaism) accepted the idea of Jewish nationality, only Zionists rejected the long-term viability of the diaspora; diaspora nationalists and Bundists in this case aligned themselves with the integrationists to defend a policy that became known as *doikeit* ("here"ism), or, in other words, an ideology that emphasized the diaspora's permanence.[10] Non-Zionist Orthodoxy, with its literal belief in divine messianic salvation, did not believe in the diaspora's permanence in quite the same way. Instead, the Orthodox argued that human action to terminate the diaspora was inappropriate. Until the Messiah's arrival, the diaspora would continue to exist as it had since the destruction of the Second Temple in 70 C.E. The net result, of course, was that the Orthodox attitude toward the diaspora was similar, at least in practice, to other non-Zionists.[11]

The differences on the issue of diaspora viability were more than window dressing and expressed a fundamental difference in world views between Zionists and non-Zionists: the latter based their ideologies on fundamentally optimistic worldviews. Integrationists believed that as enlightenment and interethnic tolerance spread, the Jews would benefit from a less tense and violent civilization. Socialists too, for all their belief that socioeconomic conditions would worsen in the short run, believed that the world upheaval — the revolution Karl Marx predicted — would eventually create a classless society in which nations and ethnic groups would disappear, as would the capitalist contradictions that created ethnic strife. The same held true for the non-Zionist Orthodox. True, Jews would suffer in the short run, but eventually the Messiah would arrive and the world would be perfected.[12]

In contrast, Zionists were pessimistic about Jewry's future in the diaspora. Every Zionist theory, from the far left to the far right, was based on a feeling of impending catastrophe. A somewhat ironic juxtaposition exemplifies this reality quite nicely. During the 1930s Ze'ev Jabotinsky, leader of the Revisionist Zionists and a staunch critic of Socialist Zionism, quoted as a virtual mantra Ber Borchov's statement that "we must liquidate the diaspora before the diaspora liquidates us." In the Zionist view, Jews had two choices: flee Europe or be overwhelmed.[13] This orientation, which has come to be known as "catastrophic Zionism" (or, less often, catastrophe Zionism) led Zionists to denigrate the diaspora. More significantly, Zionists also denigrated the creativity and vitality of diaspora Jewry — a concept known as *Shlilat ha-Gola* — even while they emphasized the fact that they were working on diaspora Jewry's behalf.[14]

Zionist pessimism was, of course, the mirror image of non-Zionist optimism. Both derived from the same source: a belief in Jewry's eternal existence coupled with a hope for (imminent) messianic redemption. The difference between Zionist redemptivist ideologies and their non-Zionist counterparts may be summarized as simply a matter of differing destinations. All Jewish political parties longed for the creation of a perfect society ruled by justice, righteousness, and truth; only Zionists despaired of such a society emerging in Europe in the foreseeable future. As a result, Zionists advocated restoration to the ancestral Jewish homeland to build this society as a model for the rest of humanity.[15] Even so, Zionists retained their commitment (at least on paper) to social and economic justice. They simply differed over how best to achieve security for Jewry while the "birth pangs of the Messiah" — the apocalyptic upheaval that would lead to humanity's perfection — were taking place. Again, this was an idea shared by most Jews, including those on the far left.

An example from a somewhat unusual source may place this point into stark relief. Isaac Babel's well-known short story collection *Konarmiia* (Red Cavalry) includes the story of Ghedali, a simple Hasidic Jew

with whom Babel comes into contact while operating near Zhitomir. In debating with Babel whether the revolution is good or evil, Ghedali retorts: "We are not ignoramuses. The International — we know what the International is. And I want an international of good people. I would like every soul to be taken into account and given first category rations." Babel described Ghedali's international — which he dubs variously the Fourth International or the Sabbath International — as an impossible dream. Yet, in at least two other stories in the collection, "Rabbi" and "The Rabbi's Son," we see that Babel, the "Jewish Cossack," found this dream irresistable.[16]

Any attempt to discern the role Zionism played in interwar Jewish communal politics, must consider other factors as well. Zionism — and to a lesser degree Jewish Socialist nationalism (insofar as Jewish socialists discussed personal and class dignity) — placed considerable emphasis on self-respect, honor, and dignity. The Revisionist Zionist youth movement, Betar, for example, listed *Hadar* (dignity) as one of its main objectives. Other Zionist youth of both left and center emphasized similar ideas. One definition of Zionism, formulated in interwar Poland but relevant to the entire movement, read as follows:

> Zionism wishes to raise up the Jews from their lowly state . . . Zionism must lead to the inner freedom of Jews, it must root out the traces of slavery, it must implant in the hearts and souls of Jews the desire for life, for air, for purity.[17]

Zionist emphasis on self-respect manifested in a tripartite emphasis on collective activity, heroism, and self-sacrifice. This held equally true for socialist Zionists, who emphasized pioneering and building, and for revisionist Zionists, who stressed quasi-military drill and discipline. The symbol of the "new Jew" — proud (but not arrogant), dignified, with a straight back — was a powerful image that attracted many diaspora Jews when linked with an appreciation of the heroic Jewish past (both recent and distant) and of the unsettled and dangerous present.[18] Zionism was thus a conscious attempt of a powerless people to attain power; an effort to convert Jews from a tempest-tossed object of history into a subject controlling its own destiny.[19] The issue of political power was never far from Zionist discourse: the lack of true power in diaspora Jewry was considered the main cause (and also the main symptom) of the diaspora's impermanence. Obtaining true political power was central to the future Zionist endeavor and hence was critical to securing Jewry's future.

Ideologically, Zionism aspired to the creation of a unified Jewish people. This aspiration was not unique to Zionists. The non-Zionist Orthodox, for instance, also emphasized the collective nature of Jewish identity, but the aspiration was uniquely important to the Zionist role on a communal level. Jewish socialists, including those of a nationalist temperament, spoke in class terms. To be sure, Bundist self-defense units acted on behalf of all Jews, not just party members. Nonetheless, in theory, even Bundists believed that the Socialist uprising would (or potentially could) pit Jewish proletarians against the Jewish bourgeois, which occurred in postrevolutionary Russia.[20] Similarly, the non-Zionist Orthodox spoke about *Klal Israel*, the Jewish collective; but, in practice, non-Zionist Orthodox politics concentrated on furthering the specific agenda of that community with only secondary attention to a broad, united Jewish front.[21]

Zionists used traditional Jewish terms for unity, arrogating the role of defending *Klal Israel*'s future for themselves. Jewish unity as a means to achieving Zionist goals meant slightly different things to different groups within the movement. For Zionists of the right and center, unity meant the rejection of struggles between Jews over "artificial" matters (i.e., transferring class struggle to a Jewish communal environment). For these Zionist groups, unity was a logical response to historical developments. For Zionists of the left, unity was a goal for the future that would come hand in hand with the creation of a "new Jew." The past, important as it

was, was exactly that — past. The future lay in creating a united Jewish front to build *Eretz Israel* and guarantee Jewry's eternity.[22]

Zionism in Eastern Europe

The remainder of this chapter reviews Zionist fortunes (and misfortunes) in five different communal settings: Eastern Europe, Western Europe, the United States, the Middle East, and the British empire.

Eastern European Zionism developed initially in the Russian empire and, after 1917, in the empire's successor states. For most of its history the Russian Zionist Federation found itself competing against powerful ideological rivals in the Bund and in Autonomist movements. The results of this ideological competition may be seen in the results of a 1909 study on the political orientations of Jewish university students in Kiev in 1909: sixty-six of 279 students declaring they were members of a political party (nearly 24 percent) defined themselves as Zionists; another forty-four (approximately 16 percent) declared themselves Bundists.[23] These figures must be kept in context. They reflect the reality that Zionists were *not* the majority party in the Russian Jewish community prior to World War I. Nonetheless, the figures also seem to indicate that Zionists were a majority of Jewish nationalist students and probably represented the plurality party within the Russian Jewish community.

The particular ideological makeup of Russian Zionism led to a dual emphasis on Practical Zionism, that is on the small but steady steps to build a Jewish national home, and on Gegenwartsarbeit.[24] Zionists understood

Membership Label of the Russian Poale Zion Federation, circa 1900.

Authors' Collection, via Mr. Isidore Baum

Gegenwartsarbeit to mean involvement in all activities that promoted the civil rights, human dignity, and physical security of Russian Jewry, even if such activity did not promote specific Zionist goals. The idea behind Gegenwartsarbeit was expressed most clearly at the Helsingfors conference. Meeting December 4–10, 1906, the Russian Zionists adopted a dualistic platform that demanded, in addition to continued work in *Eretz Israel*, (1) democratization of the Russian regime, (2) equality of rights for Jews, (3) guarantees for minority rights and equality for all ethnic groups, (4) recognition of Jews as a national minority, (5) convening a Jewish national council to reorganize the Jewish community, (6) official recognition of linguistic equality for the Jewish national language (either Hebrew or Yiddish — the conference did not specify), and (7) the right to rest on Saturday instead of Sunday.[25]

The Helsingfors Conference, in effect, committed Zionists to work for Jewish minority rights in the same fashion that autonomists did.[26] The conference did not emphasize massive emigration, though continued work in *Eretz Israel* was prominently mentioned in the resolutions. In sum, however, the conference reoriented Russian Zionism to an internal focus for the next ten years, a decade that was crucial to further developments. The revolutionary upheaval in Russia in 1905 was merely a forecast of impending disasters: by 1906 a counter-revolution had undone the democratic gains made during the revolution and reimposed the czarist autarchy.[27]

Further agonies awaited. The outbreak of war in 1914 found both Russia and Russian Jewry unprepared for the storm. Jews, whom the authorities considered a disloyal ethnic group, were deported en masse from the war zones. Ironically, this act undid one of the most harsh czarist limitations on Jewish rights in that it forced an end to the Pale of Settlement. Still, the overall effect was negative. Russian Jewish charities were hard-pressed to keep up with the newly created class of refugees.[28]

The year 1917 brought a series of further revolutionary upheavals that toppled the czar and initially granted considerable freedom to Russian Jewry. The Bolshevik seizure of power in November 1917 (reckoned as October in the Russian calendar) — and their subsequent victory in the civil war — reversed the trend. To be sure, Jews as individuals now obtained considerable equality and full civil rights (such as they were). However, the Communist regime rapidly clamped down on all manifestations of Zionism. By 1921 the Zionist movement was forced underground (as were the various Hasidic sects). Repeated Soviet persecutions during the 1920s and 1930s eventually silenced the Russian Zionist movement, which only reemerged after World War II.[29]

The collapse of the Russian empire, along with the downfall of the German and Austro–Hungarian empires, created a new situation in interwar Eastern Europe. A series of successor states arose in the territory vacated by the three fallen empires: Poland, reborn after a century of foreign partition; Yugoslavia, created by merging Serbia with Slovenia and Croatia; Czechoslovakia, Latvia, Lithuania, and Estonia all gaining independence under the terms of the Treaty of Versailles. These states shared common goals and problems. All favored maintaining the status quo through restoring the balance of power and collective security. All were saddled with huge national minority problems, which presented the threat of foreign subversion through the "fifth column." Only in Czechoslovakia did a semblance of democracy thrive. In each of the other successor states, social, economic, and political conditions that discouraged democracy and encouraged autocratic forms of government prevailed. Financial difficulties abounded, as did border conflicts — among the successor states and between them and Germany, the Soviet Union, or (in Poland's case), both of them.[30]

Jews experienced considerable difficulties in this new environment. Efforts to guarantee Jewish rights by international agreement met with only partial success. Following up on the legal formula established at the Congress of Berlin (1878), the League of Nations induced most of the successor states to sign national minorities treaties. In theory, the treaties guaranteed the civil rights of all national minorities. Theory did not always accord with practice, however. Each of the successor states sought to limit international intrusions into "internal affairs" while also undermining the terms of the treaties. The Poles, for example, succeeded in undercutting some aspects of the treaty by holding census counts on Saturdays. Since a majority of Polish Jews would neither write nor answer family-related questions on the Sabbath, there was an undercount of the Jewish population. As a result, the Polish government could "legitimately" set aside less money for Jewish schools and communal institutions.[31]

Moreover, antisemitism became a major factor in the political lives of virtually every Eastern European state. The Polish example can be seen as typical of all the successor states and was indicative of the direction that the Jewish problem took. Violent antisemitism was most prevalent in Poland, which also had the largest Jewish population in interwar Europe (3.5 million souls). Both organized pogroms and random attacks on Jews were relatively common, as were political, religious, and economic discrimination. In general, four eras of Polish-Jewish relations in the interwar period are discernible. During the first era, between 1919 and 1922, in the immediate aftermath of the founding of the Polish republic, Jews suffered from considerable physical violence that derived in large part from unstable conditions in the country. In the second era, between 1922 and 1925, the years of the "Sejmocracy," anti-Jewish violence abated slightly. Nevertheless, Jews found numerous obstacles placed in the path of full citizenship by an unfriendly Polish government that sought to limit the role of national minorities. In this era Jewish suffering was primarily economic, since the government sought to eliminate Jews, by direct or indirect means, from the economic life of the country. The third era, between 1925 and 1935, the years after Pilsudski's coup, for the most part represented a respite from public manifestations of antisemitism, reflected in

a reduction in pogroms and swift police action to quell anti-Jewish violence, but the respite did not improve the socioeconomic position of Polish Jewry.

The fourth era began after Pilsudski's death in 1935, when the reins of power were taken over by a troika — President Ignacy Mościcki, Marshal Edward Rydz–Śmigly, and Foreign Minister Józef Beck — and continued until the outbreak of World War II. In this era Polish Jewry was besieged. In almost every sphere, the government, its supporters from the Sanacja movement ("Recuperation," a term coined by Pilsudski, when, after the coup, he established a military regime and named himself minister of defense, but used to signify the colonels' clique that held the actual power and operated behind the scenes), and the nationalist opposition — primarily the National Democratic Party, the Narodowa Demokracja (Endecja), better known as Endeks — operated from a clearly antisemitic program. Only the small Polish socialist movement defended the Jews, whenever possible. In this period Jewish economic life was systematically undercut: Jews were treated as second-class citizens, their political rights were ignored, and the minority treaties were reduced to a sham. Whether the issue was the anti-*shechita* (ritual slaughter) bill of 1937 or "ghetto benches" in universities, the Poles pursued one policy: "Rzeczypospolita Polska dla Polakow, Żydzi do Palestini" (Poland for Poles, Jews to Palestine).[32]

Finally, it is important to recall that in Poland, and to a greater or lesser degree the other successor states in Eastern Europe, antisemitism derived from political and religious sources. Much of Polish antisemitism, for instance, was tinged with Christian symbols. Thus, August Cardinal Hlond, the primate of Poland, issued a pastoral letter on February 29, 1936, that read in part:

> A Jewish problem exists, and will continue to exist as long as Jews remain Jews. . . . One ought to fence oneself off against the harmful moral influences of Jewry, to separate oneself against its anti-Christian culture, and especially to boycott the Jewish press and the demoralizing Jewish publications.[33]

Jewish market in Bialystok

Radun. The funeral of Rabbi Hofec Chaim.

Two Scenes of Jewish Life in Interwar Poland, as Seen in Contemporary Postcards.
Authors' Collection

A similar problem arose in Lithuania, although there the economic and social pressures made antisemitic sentiments less direct. However, Lithuanians saw Jews as a Polonizing group and especially blamed the Jews for Poland's seizure of Vilna in October 1920. In both Czechoslovakia and Yugoslavia, Jews found themselves caught between two rival ethnic groups vying for control of the state. The stability of Czech democracy and the personal goodwill of President Tomas G. Masaryk kept antisemitism in check. Antisemitic feelings did exist, however, and were particularly strong in Slovakia. Jews were much less secure in Yugoslavia, where they were caught between Serbs and Croats. Both ethnic groups viewed Jews as an untrustworthy element, and both were willing to eliminate their Jews at the proper moment.

Hungarian and Romanian Jewry also found themselves besieged. The Hungarian Jewish problem may be dated to the White Terror that followed the fall of Bela Kún's abortive Communist state. To be sure, antisemitism had existed in nineteenth-century Hungary, as it had throughout Central Europe, but it had been more muted. After 1920, however, the Hungarian elite held Jews collectively guilty of treason because of the acts of a small group of communists who were only marginally Jewish. Conditions in Romania were much the same, but they derived from factors that existed well before World War I. When the Congress of Berlin created Romania in 1878, the new state was forced to guarantee the civil rights of Jews. From that time on, however, the government sought to limit Jewish rights, which were seen as deriving from foreign intrusions upon Romanian sovereignty. Conditions for Jews in Romania worsened after World War I and became especially difficult with the rise of the Garda de Fier government, led by Octavian Goga, in December 1937.[34]

These background events are important for understanding Zionist developments in interwar Eastern Europe. Conditions for Zionist success were ripe: All of the successor states were multi-national states where assimilatory pressure was minimal, all had newly established national governments that emphasized the discontinuities with previous regimes, all were relatively underdeveloped both socially and economically, all had highly nationalist majority cultures laced with intense antisemitism, and almost all were pluralistic — though not really democratic — in their governmental organization. That, of course, meant that Zionists were relatively free to organize a wide range of political activities (as were non- and anti-Zionist parties).[35]

Overall, these criteria would appear to have made interwar Eastern Europe a territory ripe for Zionist conquest. In reality, conditions were very different. In Romania and Hungary, countries whose Jewish communities were divided along a spectrum ranging from ultra-Orthodox to highly assimilated, Zionism barely took root. And although there is no single acceptable way to definitively count the number of Zionists in these countries, a rough estimate may be derived from statistics for so-called *Shekel* purchases.

A few words of caution are in order, so that the figures can be kept in context. First, a *Shekel* purchase was not actually a statement of Zionist affiliation or party membership. The *Shekel* was a form of paid franchise by which individuals expressed their desire to "vote" in elections to the biennial Zionist congresses. They did so by purchasing a *Shekel* from the party they supported. In most countries no other balloting was held; instead, a tally of all *Shekel*s sold was kept (and was duly reported to the congress); each party received a number of delegates equal to the proportion of *Shekel*s it sold. Each delegation (they were organized geographically) was organized by a party key based on the proportion of *Shekel* sales in each country to the total number of *Shekel*s sold in that year. The *Shekel* system was a controversial means of electing delegates to the Zionist congresses throughout the 1920s and 1930s. This was reflected in numerous accusations of vote fraud, repeatedly made by opponents of the Zionist leadership throughout the interwar era.[36] But inertia guaranteed that the system would not be changed. Given its limited purpose, *Shekel*s were rarely, if ever, purchased by

TABLE 6.1: Shekel Purchases in Romania and Hungary, 1931–1934

Congress	Year	Romania	Hungary
17	1931	23,136	1,500
18	1933	35,157	3,450
19	1935	53,350	5,763
20	1937	49,816	6,044
21	1939	60,013	21,562

Source: E. Mendelsohn, "Zionist Success," in *Essential Papers on Zionism* , p. 181

more than one family member. Reinforcing this trend was the fact that the *Shekel* was not inexpensive, another factor that rankled the WZO's many critics.[37]

Under these circumstances the *Shekel* can be considered nothing more than one index of support for Zionism. As such, however, *Shekel* purchases indicate the weakness of Zionist organizations in Romania and Hungary, as reflected in Table 6.1.

To place these figures into a broader context, it should be noted that the 1939 Romanian *Shekel* purchases equalled roughly 7 percent of that country's Jewish population, while Hungary's — prior to 1939 — represented merely 1 percent.[38] More precisely indicative of Zionist failure to take root in the Danubian countries was the extremely low rate of *aliya* from Hungary and Romania between 1933 and 1939. Hungarian *aliya* totaled only 1,107 *olim* (0.6 percent of the total *aliya*) while Romanian *aliya* totaled 9,458 (5.1 percent of the total).[39] Conditions in these two countries began to change just prior to World War II, mainly as a result of the un-bridled antisemitism of the fascist and quasi-fascist regimes that assumed power after 1938. Nonetheless, neither country can be considered a Zionist success in that the traditional Jewish leadership remained in control of the communities — for better or worse — during this difficult period.[40]

By no means should Zionist weakness be seen as Zionist inactivity; it merely means that the Zionist federations did not win over these communities. In Romania, for instance, a highly developed Zionist federation, along with an extensive array of Zionist parties and organizations, took root during the interwar era.[41] Zionist activity picked up considerably during the 1930s, when the democratic regime began to decline, and especially after the royal coup of February 1938. Zionists remained in the forefront of Romanian Jewry's struggle for civil rights from 1938 through the Holocaust era and up to (and after) the post–World War II Communist takeover.[42]

The situation in Poland was, to a degree, similar. *Shekel* purchases peaked in 1935 at 405,756, declining precipitously thereafter when the Revisionist Zionists withdrew from the WZO.[43] Again, this figure — which repre-sented 8.5 percent of Polish Jewry — should not be taken as an exact gauge of Zionist strength in Poland, but only as one element in such an analysis. *Aliya* figures must be con-sidered as well. Unlike the Danubian states, *aliya* from Poland totaled 83,847, or 45 percent of all *aliya* between 1933 and 1939.[44] When Polish Jews resident in other countries (mainly Germany) are included, the proportion of Polish *olim* to total *aliya* rises. Indeed, if the entire period from 1919 to 1939 is considered, Polish *olim* accounted for two-thirds of all *olim*.[45]

Another way to look at the level of support for Zionism is to consider donations to the national funds Keren Kayemet le-Israel (KKL) and Keren ha-Yesod (KHY). In 1937 and 1938 KKL collected 706,805 zlotys; KHY did even better, collecting 1,119,559 zlotys.[46] Given the crippling poverty of Polish Jewry at the time — less than 25 percent of Polish Jews were de-fined as self-sufficient in a 1936 report by the

American Jewish Congress — these figures were phenomenal and seem to reflect a wider range of sympathy for Zionism than indicated by *Shekel* purchases alone.[47] He-Halutz figures for *hachshara* (agricultural training school) graduates — who numbered more than 100,000 trained in 554 camps and farms between 1917 and 1939 — seem to indicate the same thing.[48]

Finally, it must be noted that a clear majority of Jewish politicians elected to the Sejm and Senat (respectively the lower and upper houses of the Polish parliament) came from Zionist lists. This in itself was an impressive feat (paralleled by the Orthodox anti-Zionist Agudas Israel party, which, however, was a minority within the Jewish delegations to the Polish Parliament), although it was, admittedly, not a decisive symbol of support for all Zionist goals. The Bund, in comparison, failed to obtain a single nationwide mandate, but did, paradoxically, capture a number of *Kehillot* (community councils) during the late 1930s.[49]

Thus, a summary of Polish Zionist history would have to emphasize both the substantial successes and the significant failures experienced by the movement. In the main, Zionism appears to have been strongest in the first years of Polish independence, weakening after 1926.[50] Then too the Polish Zionists experienced their greatest successes in the diplomatic sphere: mainly in relations with other minorities and, to a lesser degree, with the government. In 1922 Polish Zionist Sejm members reached an agreement with ethnic German, Ukrainian, and Belorussian parties for a joint electoral list to be submitted for the next elections. It was hoped that this joint list would strengthen the minorities' position in the Sejm, thereby pressuring the government to fulfill the national minority treaty's terms. In fact, this policy was a short-term success, although a split within the Zionist ranks in 1923 led to the agreement's lapsing in 1925.[51]

The Zionists' relationship with the Polish regime was more complex. Government support for an antisemitic (or quasi-antisemitic) policy had an ironic sidelight: Poland was one of the staunchest supporters of the Jewish national home — the *Yishuv* represented a potential target for Jewish emigration and for Polish exports — and of Jewish migratory rights throughout the world. In both cases, Polish support for Jewish rights derived from the hope to increase Jewish emigration.[52] Capitalizing on Polish governmental desire to increase emigration, in 1925 the Polish Zionist members of the Sejm reached an agreement — called the Ugoda — with the government. In essence, the Jewish representatives hoped for an improvement in the government's attitude toward the Jewish community; a reduction in the rhetoric about Jews being a surplus population, which contributed directly to antisemitism violence; and a lessening of the economic burden that was slowly crushing Polish Jewry. The Ugoda agreement was indeed signed; shortly thereafter, however, the Pilsudski coup led to its collapse and abandonment.[53] This was not the last time an agreement was sought. For most of the 1930s Revisionist Zionists saw the Polish government as an ally and actively sought to promote cooperation that would further both Polish and Zionist goals.[54]

The Zionist federation was wracked by repeated schisms over personality and ideology and never completely conquered the Polish Jewish community. Nor did the Zionists encounter unequivocal success in furthering their political agenda. And yet, viewed in context, Polish Zionism's failure is not so glaring. First, no other Jewish party — from the communists on the far left to Agudas Israel on the far right (considering Revisionists to be part of the larger, though not monolithic, Zionist bloc just for the sake of this argument) had any greater success in promoting a Jewish agenda and defending Jewish interests.[55] Second, there is no real way to accurately measure party affiliations other than for the Zionists. Such records — if they ever existed — did not survive World War II. Indeed, it is quite likely that most Polish Jews were not members of any political group, the financial burdens of such membership being greater than most individuals could shoulder. Simultaneously, personal sympathy with one or another movement cannot, at this juncture in time, be judged with any accuracy. To note one example, it was not uncommon for members of a single family to be supporters of different (competing) Jewish political parties. This hypothetical family could then be said to simultaneously support Agudas Israel, Hitahdut (Mapai's diaspora equivalent), and Betar (the Revisionist Zionist youth movement).[56] As in pre-revolutionary Russia, the Polish Zionists appear to have represented a plurality of Polish Jewry. Judged in context with the other Jewish parties, the Zionists' supposed failure in Poland actually reads more like a small success.

Much the same may be said about Czecho-slovakia. Although not as antisemitic an environment as interwar Hungary, Romania, or Poland, the multiplicity of nationalities — Czechs, Slovaks, Ruthenians, Ukrainians, Germans, and Jews, to name only the major ones — and the highly nationalistic environment in the newborn state made Zionism a viable Jewish political alternative. In particular, the cultural-national conflict between Czechs and Germans in late-nineteenth-century Bohemia allowed considerable latitude for Zionism to develop.[57]

Like Czechoslovakia itself, Czechoslovak Zionism developed unevenly: faster in Bohemia-Moravia, the more developed and progressive portion of the country, and more slowly in Slovakia, the less developed and more backward part of the country. In Slovakia, as in Hungary, ultra-Orthodox groups still held sway among Jews, resulting in a weak Zionist movement.[58]

Even in Bohemia-Moravia, the Zionist movement was relatively weak. In this case, the assimilatory pressures on Jews combined with the low levels of antisemitism, rather than the plethora of parties and movements, kept the Zionists from dominating the Czech Jewish community.[59] As a result, *aliya* from Czechoslovakia was very sluggish, totaling only 4,779 between January 1933 and September 1938.[60] Aliya picked up in the twilight era between the Munich crisis and the outbreak of war (from October 1938 to

September 1939) but by then mass emigration was virtually impossible.[61]

Like their Polish counterparts, the most prominent Czech Zionists made their reputations in the parliament and government. But this process was much less controversial, since neither the Bund nor the autonomists took root in Czechoslovakia.[62] If only for that reason, Czech Zionism appeared to be more successful than Zionist organizations throughout Eastern Europe. Albeit, success, in this case, was very shallow and came at the cost of repeated fratricidal schisms within the Czech Zionist federation.[63]

With slight variations other Eastern European Zionist movements appear to have had similar experiences. They attempted — and to a degree succeeded — in focusing Jewish attention on the need for a nationalist orientation and for activity to build the Jewish national home. Given the relatively weak nature of the Jewish communal structure at the time, however, Zionist success was often fleeting and was never (certainly not before World War II) decisive. Although the Zionists stridently warned about the diaspora's fragility, their position in the diaspora's political life was, in many respects, a symptom of the broader problems. It may thus be necessary to attribute Zionist failure more to the realities of Jewish powerlessness in the face of antisemitism than to any organizational, ideological, or individual flaws inherent in Zionism or the WZO.

Zionism in Western Europe

The Zionist situation in interwar Western Europe can, to a greater or lesser degree, be viewed as a mirror image of conditions in Eastern Europe. World War I had a much less catastrophic impact in Western Europe, leading to a less intensive Jewish crisis in the postwar era (with the exception of Germany). Nonetheless, intense antisemitism did exist in Western Europe as did, paradoxically, intense pressure to assimilate. Finally, the Jews' level of comfort in emancipated communities — Jewish emancipation was a constitutional fact in Germany twenty-seven years prior to Herzl's clarion call (in *Der Judenstaat*) that emancipation had failed — militated (to a degree) against Zionism: after all, no one wanted to "rock the boat," as it were.

Still, by 1914, a Zionist culture had emerged in Western Europe. Less intensely nationalist than its Easternropean counterpart — more closely akin to ethnicism than to pure nationalism — Zionism in Western Europe bore the marks of a "supplementary" nationality that permitted members to participate in the societies they lived in while remaining Jewish (however defined) and living happy, healthy, and normal lives.[64] This trend continued well into the 1930s. Thus Robert Weltsch (one of the key ideologues of German Zionism) could assert in 1922 that "Zionism is not above all a political movement; it is primarily a moral movement," and that assertion would likely have been accepted by a majority of Zionists.[65] For many Western European Jews, therefore, Zionism was a matter of identity, honor, and even (to a degree) manliness. Max Nordau had once spoken of the need to create a *Muskeljudentum* — a Judaism of muscularity.[66] His ideas now resonated among the West European Zionists, even if in a modified form: Zionism was seen as a means to a moral equivalent of war via a process of nation building. Instead of mass death on the battlefield that other nationalists sought, Zionists wanted to create a new, proud, erect Jew, unafraid and willing to assert his rights.[67]

Examples abound that explain the Zionist experience in Western Europe. The small Swedish Zionist movement, for example, may be seen as a case in point. From the 1890s to 1945, Zionism was a minor backwater within the Swedish Jewish community. The Swedish Zionist Union mainly attracted new immigrants, a small trickle of whom came into the country from Russia after 1881. At the same time, doctrinaire anti-Zionism also did not exist in Sweden, since the issue was largely irrelevant to the daily lives of most Jews.[68] The Zionists scored one notable success. In 1911 they were able

to control the selection process for Stockholm's chief rabbi, replacing a strongly committed anti-Zionist with a more moderate spokesman.[69] *Shekel* sales are indicative of the realities in Sweden, however: in 1910, a mere ninety *Shekels* were sold; this number fell to eighty-eight in 1911, but grew to 145 in 1912 — possibly a reflection of the new chief rabbi's influence.[70] An extensive array of other Zionist projects collapsed quickly, despite a continuing immigration after World War I. Zionism did not become a decisive voice in Swedish Jewry until after 1945.[71]

Given the unique nature and small size of Swedish Jewry (and likewise of the Jewish communities in Denmark, Norway, and Finland) a question may be raised about its relevance. Yet many of the same issues that plagued the Swedish Zionist Union also plagued other, more obviously relevant, Zionist bodies in Western Europe. Of these, two central communities must be reviewed: France and Germany.

France had long been associated with the genesis of modern Zionism. As mentioned previously, Napoleon Bonaparte issued a clarion call for Jews to return to *Eretz Israel* during his campaign in Egypt and the Fertile Crescent in 1798–1799. This was encompassed in a comprehensive but ultimately abortive proclamation by the future French emperor on April 20, 1799. Similarly, it was in France that Theodor Herzl first formulated his Zionist ideology, after witnessing intense antisemitic outbursts during Alfred Dreyfus's first trial for treason.[72]

French Jews did not, however, immediately flock to the Zionist banner. Not a single French rabbi, for example, traveled to Basel in 1897 to attend the First Zionist Congress. A few French delegates did attend the first congress and every subsequent one as well, although it is impossible to reconstruct the actual number of French Zionists at the time. The Communist party's Yiddish publication *Naie Presse*, for example, reported that the French Zionist Federation had 6,000 members in 1919. Since these figures were cited without source and without elaboration, they are dubious but may offer a benchmark. Two other sets of figures — *Shekel* sales for 1933 and for 1937 — give a better, but still imperfect picture: 1,326 *Shekel*s were sold in 1933 and 1,855 in 1937.[73]

Simultaneously, the Franco-Jewish elite largely ignored Zionism altogether or, in some cases, actually accused the Zionists of providing antisemites with new ammunition to hurl at Jews: mainly the accusation of Jewish "dual loyalty."[74] Although this situation began to change in the early 1920s, the changes were very subtle — so subtle, indeed, that many contemporaries missed them altogether.[75]

As late as the 1930s most French Jews continued to distinguish between two terms for self-identification: *Juif* and *Israelite*. The former implied an unassimilated Jew — usually a recent immigrant — who possessed a nationalist orientation, whereas the latter referred to a "native Jew" whose orientation was purely French.[76] The "Israelites" rejected Zionism (and Bundist socialist nationalism as well) as inconsistent with the bargain of emancipation. Rabbi Jacob Kaplan, who held prestigious pulpits in Mulhouse and Paris, once suggested that immersion in Torah would provide a better guarantee for Jewish identity than Zionism.[77] Moreover, it should be noted that Kaplan was considered a moderate in his views on Zionism during the 1920s and 1930s. He was viewed (correctly) as the most pro-Zionist chief rabbi of France when appointed to that position in 1955.[78]

As in Poland, Zionists in France faced two major opponents: assimilationism and Bundist socialist nationalism. The Bund had actually made inroads in French Jewry before the Zionist federation was established.[79] Both the Bund and the Zionists had a similar membership profile: recent immigrants who were not yet fully integrated into French society and felt unable to continue defining themselves on the basis of adherence to religion. Zionism, in this case, was a means to maintain Jewish identity.[80]

To a degree, the rising antisemitic tide brought many Franco-Jewish intellectuals — among whom Edmond Fleg and André Spire were probably the best known — into the Zionist fold as well. This group of new converts to Zionism were also responding to their discovery of "authentic" Judaism within the immigrant community and to their alienation from the traditional mores of the "official" community. Spire, for example, noted that after "discovering" the immigrant Jews, "French Jews who had lost all contact with Jewish life, who were ignorant of virtually all of Jewish history, began to study them with fervor."[81] Zionism was thus central to the Jewish cultural renaissance in interwar France.

Mainstream Franco-Jewish organizations, including the Consistoire and the Alliance Israélite Universelle (AIU), did not precisely jump onto the Zionist bandwagon at this juncture; they remained decidedly noncommittal, but in the non-Zionist (not anti-Zionist) camp. AIU had been an indirect supporter of virtually all Practical Zionist activity in *Eretz Israel* since the 1870s, when the organization agreed to sponsor the Mikve Israel agricultural school. AIU maintained its non-Zionist policy until World War II, as did most other Franco-Jewish mainstream organizations. At the same time Franco-Jewish leaders, even those opposed to Zionism on political grounds, found the Zionist call to a restored Jewish culture irresistible.[82]

Zionist prestige received a major boost from the French government. Although contacts between WZO leaders and the French foreign ministry were tentative, the fact that meetings took place at all and took place in very public fora — the Paris peace talks, for instance — gave the appearance of government acceptance of Zionism. That, in turn, meant that anti-Zionists could no longer hurl the dual loyalty accusation against Zionists. On the contrary, support for Zionism now appeared patriotic in many eyes. This virtually silenced the anti-Zionists: they would still assail the Zionist Federation, but in the main quietly and behind the scenes.[83]

By 1939, therefore, it can safely be said that overt sympathy for Zionism had spread (unevenly) throughout the French Jewry even if direct membership in the Zionist Federation remained tepid. Previous barriers rapidly collapsed as ad hoc cooperation between

Zionists and non-Zionists became the order of the day. In 1931, for example, France's chief rabbi accepted the honorary position of vice president of Keren ha-Yesod in France. Thereafter, cooperation on matters of mutual interest, for instance the struggle against antisemitism, grew. This should not be confused with the "conquest of communities" that WZO leaders often spoke about. Far from it; Franco-Zionist victories derived more from infiltration than from conquest and were, in the interwar era, largely limited to the cultural and philanthropic spheres.[84]

Ideologically, the response of German Jewry to the Zionist challenge was similar to that of French Jewry, at least initially. The sociopolitical milieu in which German Zionism developed was certainly the same. Here too emancipation was seen as a "bargain" in which Jews surrendered their political identity in return for civil rights. Three major Jewish thinkers of the nineteenth and twentieth centuries can (despite the differences between them) be seen as typical of the German-Jewish approach to Zionism and Jewish nationalism: Rabbi Samson Raphael Hirsch, Rabbi Abraham Geiger, and Franz Rosenzweig.

Hirsch, generally considered the father of modern Orthodoxy, may also be considered the grandfather of Agudas Israel (which was founded by Isaac Breuer, Hirsch's grandson). Ideologically, Hirsch's orientation was the polar opposite of Mizrachi's and may be summarized as the premise that Jews could only survive as Jews if they observed the complete minutiae of Torah law. However, they did not necessarily have to do so in *Eretz Israel*. Whereas, according to Hirsch, land and state were once needed to ensure the Jews' proper moral and spiritual development, this was no longer the case or, more properly, this was not the case until the metahistorical era (the messianic era) when God would miraculously redeem the scattered tribes of Israel. Since the redemption was assumed to be metahistorical, no human agency could hasten the end; in fact, human action could delay rather than speed up the process.[85]

Despite his association with Reform Judaism, Geiger's approach was similar to Hirsch's. According to Geiger, Judaism had developed in a linear progression from greater physicality to greater spirituality. For example, Geiger argued that Jews had progressed from a religion based on animal sacrifices (a physical act) to a religion based on prayer (a spiritual act) as its means for communion with the Divine. Likewise, Geiger argued, Jews had once been a physical nation needing a specific territory; now their spiritual mission to humanity could only be fulfilled by remaining in the diaspora.[86] Of course, Geiger utterly rejected the messianic idea and therefore left no possible opening for a future redemption of any sort. Still, in practice Hirsch's and Geiger's prescription for Germany Jewry was essentially the same: Stay put, become good Germans, do not act to end the exile.

Rosenzweig may be seen as occupying a compromise position between Hirsch and Geiger. Judaism, according to Rosenzweig, is pure spirituality. Spirituality and physicality cannot mix. Thus, according to Rosenzweig, it should not be considered a surprise that the essence of Judaism — the Ten Commandments and the Torah — were revealed in the desert before the tribes occupied their homeland, that is, in exile. Seen from a historical perspective — ironic because Rosenzweig generally eschewed historical methods in his revived Jewish spirituality — Judaism's greatest developments came during periods of exile, not when Jews resided in their homeland. Rosenzweig took this argument a step further. When Jews act as Jews (i.e., on a spiritual plane), they are at home anywhere in the world. However, when they seek to "live like all the nations" (i.e., on a physical plane), they are in exile and are alienated from their true selves. By this argument, Rosenzweig overturned the very essence of Zionism. He had, ultimately, created an edifice for a total and unequivocal rejection of Zionism by arguing that a Zionist *Eretz Israel* would not be a redemption but would be a new spiritual exile.[87]

The ideologies expressed by Hirsch, Geiger, and Rosenzweig were part of a broader set of developments in postemancipation German Jewry. The unexpected resurgence of anti-semitism, only a few short years after the signing of the emancipation decree, had given many German Jews pause regarding the completely assimilationist policy initially adopted. Nonetheless, German Jewish public thought between 1870 and 1897 concentrated on the defense of Jewish rights as equal citizens and not on the needs of a Jewish national minority living in Germany.[88] Much can be gleaned from the name chosen by advocates of Jewish self-defense for their agency: Centralverein deutscher Staatsbürger jüdischen Glaubens (the Central Organization of German Citizens of the Jewish Faith, CV).[89] Although never purely assimilationist, this orientation was not (and never became) consistent with support for Zionist goals. As noted previously, protests by Jewish leaders (the so-called Protest-rabbiner) even forced a change of venue for the first Zionist congress from Munich to Basel in 1897.[90]

Despite this stridently non-Zionist orientation, laced with a clear anti-Zionist streak, the Zionistische Vereinigung für Deutschland (ZVFD) was among the first of the national federations to be established. The early history of the ZVFD was marked by an attempt to infiltrate other Jewish organizations, parallel to similar efforts in France and England. By 1913, however, it was clear that these efforts had largely failed. Thereafter, to a greater or lesser degree, Zionist and non-Zionist elements in German Jewry developed in a oppositional fashion, at least until 1933.[91] The ZVFD grew — in fits and starts — from 100 members in 1897 to a peak of 57,202 in 1934–1935 (a few years prior to the organization's liquidation by the Nazis).[92] Over the course of those forty years, ZVFD member-ship represented between 2.6 and 7.9 percent of overall WZO membership, with the ZVFD's proportion within the WZO peaking at 18.2 percent in 1933–1934.[93]

That the ZVFD spoke for only a minority of German Jews was even recognized in an editorial in *Jüdische Rundschau*, the mouthpiece of the German Zionists.[94] *Aliya*, likewise, played only a minor role in the ZVFD's program, as it did for virtually all Western European Zionist federations: total *aliya* from Germany between 1919 and 1932 was 2,048 (of whom 88 were Zionists residing in Germany but holding citizenship from other countries). This represented a mere 1.6 percent of *aliya* over the same period — a minuscule number indeed.[95] Three aspects of the *aliya* situation must be kept in mind before any generalization can be derived from the figures. First, although only a small percentage of total *aliya*, the Germany *olim* arriving between 1919 and 1932 represented a major portion of *aliya* from Western countries. Since Western European Zionists were not fleeing antisemitic persecution (a reality that made migrationary pressure on Jews very low prior to the Nazi seizure of power), they represented *olim* who emigrating because of their deeply held desire for Zionist fulfillment (so-called *Hagshama* Zionism) and the numbers are actually quite impressive.[96] Second, German *olim*, although few in number, made an important contribution to the Yishuv's institutional life by creating a network of friendly societies and social self-help agencies, notably Hitachdut Olei Germania, which became a model for all *olim* after 1933.[97] Finally, it is critical to note that *aliya* from Germany rose considerably between 1933 and 1939, reaching an estimated 20 per-cent of all *aliya* for the last seven years prior to World War II. It is equally important to recall that *Eretz Israel* absorbed about one-third of all German Jewish refugees during the Nazi era.[98]

Yet, if Zionism can be said to have contrib-uted anything to German Jewry, the main con-tribution would be visible in the cultural sphere. Zionism's significance in shaping German Jewish identity — like its significance for Franco-Jewish identity — cannot be under-estimated. As Steven Poppel has observed,

> Zionism offered an escape from the demeaning pressure of antisemitism, an antidote to self-denial and self-disdain, and a solution to the dilemma of Jewish existence in a Germany that seemed to deny the Jews the right to a full life of his own.[99]

Zionist intellectuals — including Martin Buber, Gershom Sholem and Yitzhak F. Baer (to name only three) — were in the forefront of the Jewish cultural revival in Weimar Germany.[100]

By and large, Zionist fortunes in France and Germany were similar to those derived in countries such as Austria, Holland, and Belgium. Once again, the results of Zionist activity were mixed prior to World War II: basically weak political federations that were nevertheless critical to the continued vibrancy of the communities in which they operated.[101]

American Zionism

Perhaps the most intensely studied element within the Zionist movement prior to 1948, the Zionist Organization of America (ZOA), had the reputation of being the strongest Zionist federation in the world prior to the establishment of the state of Israel. Yet, American Zionism's major strengths, particularly in the diplomatic sphere, could also be seen as weaknesses when viewed within the communal sphere.[102] Specifically, actual paying membership for ZOA and Hadassah (the Women's Zionist Organization of America) represented a relatively small proportion of the total American Jewish population. ZOA membership, for example, hovered between a low of 8,484 dues-paying members in 1932 and a high of 43,453 in 1939. The average for membership, based on figures published by the ZOA, between 1920 and 1939 was 15,842. The American Jewish population grew to about 5 million just prior to World War II. In other words, average ZOA membership was a tiny portion of American Jewry. These anemic membership figures become even more glaring when dues-paying members in Hadassah, Poale Zion, and Mizrachi are added to the ZOA membership figures.[103]

The figures for Zionist membership in the United States are similar to figures in other countries already reviewed. Also similar was the response of mainstream American Jewish organizations: the American Jewish Committee, B'nai B'rith, the Union of America Hebrew Congregations, and the Central Conference of American Rabbis (CCAR) all rejected Zionism to one degree or another. On the surface, therefore, American Jewry seemed ripe for conflict over Zionism and for the same mixed results as in other communities.[104] This perception is also confirmed by *aliya* figures — American Jewry did not feel an imminent antisemitic threat in any sense (despite the often intense nature of antisemitism in the United States) and therefore developed ideologies that emphasized "staying put." The fact that most American Jews were immigrants, or descendants of immigrants, to the country widely perceived as the "golden land" reinforced this trend.[105]

But this was not the entire story. First, America's fascination with the idea of Zion, a characteristic shared by Christians and Jews, led to a deeply held sense that Jewish restoration was indeed a legitimate goal.[106] Second, the unique nature of American Jewish identity strengthened sympathy for Zionism even among those elements that did not support Zionist organizations. In particular the claim that Zionism was identical with American progressivism — a claim made stridently by Zionist leaders such as Justice Louis D. Brandeis and educator Horace M. Kallen — made sympathy for Zionism acceptable.[107] In effect, such arguments converted the communal debate over Zionism from one about patriotism to one about the best means to foster Jewish identity. As demonstrated in the French case, only the most vociferous anti-Zionists, those totally committed to a policy of complete assimilation and abnegation of Jewish identity, could resist the Zionists' appeal to Jewish unity for very long.

The attitude of Reform Judaism in America toward Zionism was a good barometer of the realities facing opponents of Zionism. As already noted, the father of classical Reform in Germany, Rabbi Geiger, rejected the concept of Jewish restoration entirely. The American Reform movement was even more explicit in its rejection of Zionism: the CCAR's Pittsburgh Platform (1885) insisted that "the object of

How the Zionist Journal *Maccabean*
Viewed Relations with the American
Jewish Establishment in 1919:
Complete, Mutual Rejection.
Courtesy of the YIVO Institute, New York

Judaism is not political nor national, but spiritual."[108] The Reform position changed from anti-Zionist to non-Zionist only slowly. In 1935 the CCAR declared itself officially neutral on the subject, a policy retained until 1942.[109] Yet by the time the CCAR declared its neutrality as an institution, most Reform rabbis (including rabbis holding prestigious pulpits such as Stephen S. Wise, Abba Hillel Silver, and James G. Heller) were either members or (in the case of the above-mentioned three rabbis), senior members of ZOA. By then, the anti-Zionists were in the clear minority within the Reform movement.

Changes in the Reform movement's attitude toward Zionism reflected a broader dynamic in American Jewry's self-definition. Whereas America was long seen as a "melting pot" of immigrants all of whom shed their ethnicity to become generic Americans, by the 1930s this process had slowed. Thereafter, an "ethnic stew" ideology began to take root (a process that was not completed until the 1970s), emphasizing the compatibility of personal ethnic identification (so-called hyphenated identities) with being American. The transition to an "ethnic stew" ideal meant that Jews had the same right as any other ethnic group to identify themselves as they saw fit. Zionism, which had always claimed that Jews should demand for themselves nothing more (nor less) than the right to be different, gained by this process mainly because of its emphasis on Jewish national pride and solidarity with *Klal Israel*. Religion, viewed as a private matter by most Americans, could not serve the same purpose since it did not parallel developments in other ethnic communities (e.g., Italian-Americans).[110]

Finally, the Zionists indirectly benefited from their access to the U.S. government. Open support for Zionism by presidents Woodrow Wilson, Warren G. Harding, Calvin Coolidge, and Herbert Hoover added to the Zionists' prestige and reinforced the idea that Zionism and Americanism were in fact completely compatible. This also held true, to a greater or lesser degree, during the stormy years of Franklin D. Roosevelt's administration (a topic to which we shall return in Chapter 9). Ironically, the Zionists thus had it both ways: Their access to the halls of power derived from the impression within administration circles that the Zionists spoke for American Jewry and could, possibly, sway elections. At the same time, they used the courting by non-Jewish public figures as a way to prove their ability — in contrast to non-Zionists — to attain the American Jewish agenda and thereby press their claim to authority within the American Jewish community. Zionists did nothing to correct the exaggerated claims regarding their power in Washington and within the American Jewish community, since they had no other real tools with which they could convert American Jewry into the decisive facilitator of Zionist goals. Indeed, the process described here was never so straightforward, and it was not until after World War II that American Zionists could forge amorphous ideas about American Jewry's global responsibilities into a cogent political weapon that resulted in the State of Israel's establishment.[111]

Lest this last point be misunderstood, it

TABLE 6.2: Performance of Zionist Funds in the U.S., 1930-1939, in Dollars

Year	KKL	KHY	Year	KKL	KHY
1930	418,226	305,000	1935	297,846	355,000
1931	332,001	465,000	1936	297,873	520,000
1932	246,890	300,000	1937	704,993	845,000
1933	144,276	195,000	1938	1,038,752	1,070,000
1934	200,379	395,000	1939	1,744,556	1,745,000

Source: Halperin, *Political World*, p. 325.

should be noted that no chicanery was involved on the Zionist side at any time during the period under consideration. When democratic means were used to establish the composition of Jewish communal organizations — the American Jewish Congress for example — Zionists tended to predominate. Furthermore, the core of sympathy for Zionism (as opposed to willingness to actively join and participate in Zionist institutions) was always strong in the United States, stronger indeed than in any other country. This can be seen most clearly from a cursory glance at Zionist fundraising in the United States: American Jewry consistently outperformed every single Jewish community for both KKL and KHY for every year from 1930 to 1948. Indeed, in all likelihood, KKL and KHY funds raised in the United States probably equaled (and may have exceeded) all other national funds combined. Furthermore, this includes neither funds obtained through American Jewish investment corporations nor the numerous funds for discrete social, educational, and religious institutions. To understand the magnitude of American Jewry's financial role in building the *Yishuv* (a subject that requires fuller treatment than can be given here), Table 6.2 sets out the amounts of money collected for the two main Zionist funds in the United States for the 1930s. This trend continued throughout the 1940s, with ever growing amounts donated by American Jewry being decisive for continued Zionist activity.

The figures have implications far beyond the mere statistics. Assuming the membership figures for ZOA and other Zionist parties were accurate, the massive outpouring of charity for the Zionist funds could hardly have come from members alone. An indeterminate proportion of KKL contributions came from the Blue Box, the small *pushke* (charity box) which most families kept and into which they dropped small change. Time and again socioeconomic analyses of American Jewry have noted the working-class and lower-middle-class nature of the community during the era under consideration.[112] To obtain millions of dollars in donations thus meant tens of thousands, perhaps hundreds of thousands, of donors. It is thus apparent that sympathy for Zionist goals was, in the United States, as in many other Jewish communities, both broader and deeper than membership figures in Zionist organizations could possibly attest to.

This is not to imply that American Zionism experienced an unambiguous string of triumphs. Successes, such as president Wilson's support for the Balfour Declaration and the passage of the Lodge-Fish Resolution (1922), by which the U.S. Congress restated its support for the creation of a Jewish national home, were often fleeting.[113] Similarly, failures were often spectacular, especially between 1933 and 1939. Yet, the American Zionists succeeded in creating a framework for what eventually developed into a decisive diplomatic weapon.

Zionism in the Middle East

As complex as the fate of Zionist federations were in the Christian world, conditions were even more complex for Jewish communities residing in the Middle East and North Africa.

The complexities derive from four factors, although it is unclear which was the most critical. First, there was no emancipation process in Middle Eastern countries and certainly no fundamental change in attitudes toward Jews and Judaism within the Muslim world to parallel the Enlightenment. Second, the impact of European colonialism and imperialism cannot be underestimated. The liberal treatment of Jews, for example, by the French in Algeria, as compared to the Arab majority (which was not treated as liberally) exacerbated already existing tensions between Jews and Arabs or created new ones. Third, the almost simultaneous flourishing of two nationalist movements (Zionism and Arabism) and their increasing conflict over *Eretz Israel* exacerbated already existing tensions and made public manifestations of Zionism dangerous in most instances.[114] Finally, it must be kept in mind that Zionism developed initially as a European Jewish movement; little if any thought was given by Herzl or his colleagues to conditions within Middle Eastern Jewish communities.

Balancing these factors was the fact that, to a large extent, Middle Eastern Jewry remained traditional in its orientation well into the twentieth century. Traditional Jewish concepts of redemption remained foremost in the minds of sizable elements in every Middle Eastern Jewish community. In turn, that meant that ideologies arguing for the restoration of Jews to their ancestral homeland would find receptive audiences in most Middle Eastern Jewish communities. It also meant, of course, that *aliya* was easier and more directly relevant to redemptivist ideology. Approximately half of Jerusalem's Jewish population derived from the Middle East in 1913, while an estimated 4,000 Yemenite Jews immigrated between 1880 and 1914.[115] The proportion of Jews from all Muslim countries living in the *Yishuv* prior to World War I has been estimated as 41 percent, at a time when their proportion or the total world Jewish population was no more than 10 percent.[116] It can be safely said, therefore, that Middle Eastern Jewry's contribution to Zionism was more practical than ideological.[117]

Sympathy for Zionist goals was both deeply entrenched and broadly spread among Middle Eastern Jewish communities. We need only note the existence of Zionist Federations — small ones to be sure, but verifiable in their existence nonetheless — in fringe communities such as Afghanistan and Bukhara.[118] Again, the broader aspects of this history can be more easily understood in reference to specific Jewish communities, in this case, Egypt, French North Africa, the Levant (Ottoman and post–Ottoman), and Yemen.

Support for Zionist causes in Egypt actually predated the rise of modern political Zionism, but such activity was severely limited in scope prior to the twentieth century. The first real Zionist society, Bar Kokhba, was established in 1896 by Russian Jewish emigrés living in Cairo. They soon succeeded in establishing links with the already existing Jewish community, such that by 1913 the Egyptian Zionist Federation sold 800 *Shekels*.[119] World War I provided a further impetus for Zionist activity: Many members of the *Yishuv* were deported to Egypt by Ottoman authorities in 1915. Hundreds of Egyptian Jews volunteered for the Zion Mule Corps; a number served in that unit and in the the Jewish Legion established in the Royal Army in 1917. On November 11, 1917, 8,000 Egyptian Jews rallied in Cairo in a public show of support for the Balfour Declaration.[120]

Most Egyptian Jews considered support for Zionism to be a basic symbol of Jewish solidarity. A small cadre of dedicated activists was able to win the majority of the Jewish community. They also sought, with less success, to convince Egyptian Arab nationalists that the latter's struggle against British imperialism was completely compatible with the Jews' efforts to rebuild their national home. As noted, this effort met with only modest results: Most Egyptian nationalists — as most Arabists in general — identified Zionism with imperialism and not with efforts to remove imperialist control.

Anti-Zionism was a factor, but only a minor factor, within the Egyptian Jewish community. Few, if any, Egyptian Jews were involved in direct anti-Zionist activities. Similarly, most Egyptian Jewish organizations were non-Zionist in their official orientation but were perfectly willing to cooperate with Zionists on a regular basis. Of far greater importance was disunity within Zionist ranks: A united federation did not exist. Instead, regional federations operated by themselves with the Zionist Federations of Cairo and Alexandria being the most important. This led to problems of coordination and weakened the overall impact of Zionist propaganda.[121] Overall, however, it appears that Zionist functioning was considerably weakened by the need to operate discreetly and to chart a course between the twin millstones of Arab nationalism and Muslim puritanism that shaped Egyptian politics from 1922 to 1939.[122]

The tension existing between Jewish aspirations, Zionist or otherwise, and Arab nationalism can be dramatically framed by reference to conditions in the French North African colonies (Algeria, Tunisia, and Morocco). French conquest of an empire in North Africa after 1830 created a ripe atmosphere for the development of an Arab nationalist movement, and the collective granting of citizenship to Jews (the so-called Crémieux decree of 1871) created the (largely mistaken) impression of Jewish collaboration with imperialism and thus soured relations between the Jewish minority and the Muslim majority.[123] Zionism complicated this already tense situation, but did not cause the problem. Indeed, Algerian Jewry had set upon a course of assimilation and Francification already prior to 1870. If anything, Zionism would have been nothing more than a response to antisemitism manifested by both the Arab nationalists and the *Pied Noir* (European colonists). Under the circumstances, however, open identification with Zionism was considered inexpedient and the Algerian Zionist movement remained inconsequential until the 1940s.[124]

Conditions were much more conducive to Zionist activities in Tunisia and Morocco. In both cases, Jews found themselves in a volatile situation, between the hammer of French imperialism and the anvil of Arab nationalism. In Tunisia virtually the entire community adopted a Zionist orientation by the 1920s. Indeed, Tunisia had the distinction of being the only Middle Eastern Jewish community to develop a widely diverse Zionist press and had the Middle East's only Revisionist Zionist party.[125]

Moroccan Zionism is also illustrative of the problems facing Jewish nationalists in the Arab world. Initial organization for Zionist endeavors began at the turn of the twentieth century. With the joint Franco-Spanish partition of Morocco into two colonies, Zionist activity initially ceased. It immediately resumed in Spanish Morocco, until the Zionist Federation was banned by the fascist Falange government in the mid-1930s. In French Morocco, Zionist activity also initially resumed, but was officially forced to halt for most of the period between 1923 and 1925. The ban resulted from increasing tension between Jews and Arabs, which had led French officials to (temporarily) ban the Zionist Federation. WZO pressure obtained a renewal of Zionist activities in 1925 and the movement flowered throughout the 1930s and 1940s.[126]

No Zionist movement *per se* existed in the Levant during the Ottoman period; the Ottoman authorities would never have permitted such a movement to come into existence. Nonetheless, some educational activities did take place and the director of AIU's school program in Syria, Yomtov Sémach, reported in 1907 that sympathy for Zionism was widespread.[127] A number of Zionist figures were temporarily exiled to Damascus by Ottoman authorities in 1915, and that may properly be considered the beginning of organized Zionism in the Levant. Syria and Lebanon — mandated by the League of Nations to France after World War I — witnessed intensive Zionist activity, mainly a reflection of the intensely nationalist environment in those countries after Faisal's defeat and the imposition of French rule in 1920.[128] On the other hand, Zionism in the French mandated territories was mostly a practical matter — concerned mostly with *aliya* and the like — and was very nonpolitical.

Throughout the 1920s and 1930s Syrian and Lebanese Zionists sought a means to achieve an accommodation between Jews and Arabs.[129]

Iraq witnessed a similar progression. The first Zionist Federation was established in the 1920s — under the guise of a literary society — but Zionist sympathies ran deep. However, Iraq witnessed a process that was similar to the Western European experience with Zionism. A Zionist Federation existed in all but name, and its activities were opposed — strongly at times — by the entrenched communal leadership. Again, the usual mixture of activist Arabism and colonial rule (in this case British rule) impacted negatively on Zionist growth, at least officially. Conditions worsened after Iraq was granted independence in 1932. Increasingly vocal Arabism coupled with the virtual extermination of the Assyrians during the mid-1930s deterred stronger Zionist activity.[130]

Conditions in Yemen were somewhat more complicated, mainly due to the disorganized political situation in the country from most of the nineteenth century. The British occupation of Aden (1839) rendered the political structure in South Arabia more clear but did not fundamentally change the Jews' status. The result was a series of *aliya* waves from Yemen that began at almost the same time as the First Aliya (see Chapter 2) and continued sporadically until 1914.[131] In 1913 a proposal had been mooted for the evacuation of 40,000 Yemenite Jews under WZO auspices but was rendered inoperative by World War I.[132]

Redemptivist beliefs connected with *Eretz Israel* ran deep in Yemen, a country whose Jewish community had a rich history of messianic speculation and false messiahs.[133] Still, no organized Zionist movement ever developed in Yemen, the country and the community were too undeveloped for such a possibility. Worsening conditions in Yemen after 1930 led to renewed calls for complete evacuation, a process completed only after the State of Israel was established.[134]

Any attempt to summarize the fate of Zionism in the Muslim world must, *ipso facto*, deal with the eventual result of the growing Arab-Israeli conflict. Although breaking the chronological scope of this chapter, the events of 1948–1952 (and thereafter) are important as a counterpoint to arguments regarding the relative success or failure of Zionism in the Jewish communal context. In particular, the mass evacuation of virtually the entire Jewish population living in Arab countries and their resettlement in the State of Israel demonstrates precisely why, apparent institutional failure notwithstanding, Zionism was indeed the most successful of all Jewish political movements in the twentieth century.

Zionism in the British Empire

Pride of place has been given in this survey to the experience of the English Zionist Federation (EZF), a reflection, of course, of the critical role Great Britain played in interwar developments in the Yishuv. It is also a reflection of the geographical spread of Zionism within the British empire, considering that Zionist Federations existed in every part of the commonwealth and empire.[135] The broad outlines of EZF history need little repetition: Zionism took root early on, but not necessarily with any great depth.[136] As in other countries, in England Zionism was often associated with the new immigrant community established after 1875, and the EZF's rising prominence has been attributed to the immigrants' entry into the center of Anglo-Jewish life during the interwar era.[137]

Still, most historians writing between the 1940s and 1970s emphasized Zionist success in Great Britain, particularly the EZF's contribution to the creation of the Jewish state.[138] Since the 1970s, however, this assumption has been questioned. In particular, historians have noted that the Anglo-Jewish community was never "conquered" — in the sense that Zionists never dominated it completely — and that the EZF was forced to resort to infiltration tactics, trying to sufficiently enter one or two major communal organizations to get Zionism onto the Anglo-Jewish agenda. According to this line of

THE TWO SIDES TO THE PICTURE.

(Specially drawn for "The Australian Jewish Herald" by L. F. Reynolds.)

Cartoon Appearing in the *Australian Jewish Herald*, March 7, 1922,
Portraying the Frustrations of Australian Jews at the Infighting
Between Zionists and non-Zionists in the British Empire.
Courtesy of Dr. William D. Rubenstein

analysis, infiltration was a sign of Zionist weakness. Furthermore, this position contends that infiltration was never a complete success because the EZF was never able to completely silence its opponents.[139]

Parallel to the Eastern European Zionists, the EZF faced two major forms of opposition. First, the traditional Jewish leadership opposed Zionism and resented the EZF's efforts to take charge of "their" organizations. Second, on the opposite extreme, the Jewish Communists, saw Zionism as a step backward for the Jewish proletariat.[140] Added to this mixture, in England at least, was a still vocal, if not particularly potent, territorialist movement that sought to create a Jewish national home outside of *Eretz Israel*.[141]

The result of all this competition was an EZF that chose infiltration as its main means to obtain its communal goals. *Shekel* sales — which have never been tabulated precisely — were certainly not stronger than in other countries, *aliya* was also anemic, and, as already noted, the English Zionists were dogged by determined anti-Zionist opposition throughout the 1920s and 1930s (these were still arguing vociferously against EZF positions as late as 1948).[142] Zionist successes thus appear to have been fleeting and based more on bluff and circumspection than on any real base of communal power.

On the surface, therefore, it seems that infiltration was a failure and the EZF would have been better off pursuing a policy of communal conquest similar to the Polish Zionists. However, this line of analysis raises at least three major questions, the answers to which do not seem consistent with the conclusions offered. First, even if we assume Zionist weakness, can we really say that other groups were more powerful? In other words, was the Zionist failure a victory for anti-Zionists or was it a victory for Jewish apathy and lethargy (from which communities in the English-speaking world were roused only by the Holocaust)? Second, implicit in the critique of Zionist methods is the sense that had the Zionists been more clearly "in control" they may have succeeded in forcing the British government to maintain its commitments. But was that really so? The very question of a Jewish vote in England — a question that is still sufficiently controversial that most communal functionaries still will not tackle it publicly — seems to imply the exact opposite: that the British government made its decisions regarding Zionism based on global strategic calculations and not on the basis of local politics.[143]

Finally, did infiltration really fail? This question, which seems cut and dried on the surface, is, in fact, quite complex. In particular, the answer cuts to the core of what defines a Zionist. Over the course of the 1930s, as Zionist influence grew (or at least appeared to grow), both of the major Jewish public bodies — the Board of Deputies of Anglo-Jewry and the Anglo-Jewish Association (AJA) — appointed senior EZF leaders to positions of prominence, the Board's new president (appointed in 1939) being Professor Selig Brodetsky and the AJA's new chairman (also selected in 1939), being Leonard Stein. To be sure, Stein's tenure at the AJA was not a happy one for the Zionists. To the contrary, he spent the six years of his tenure as a real thorn in the EZF's side, being, to say the least extremely unhelpful (contemporaries probably would have worded this analysis more forcefully). Yet can we say that he was not a Zionist? Stein's biography further complicates the matter. Prior to his tenure at the AJA he was an advisor to WZO president Chaim Weizmann. In the 1960s, Stein wrote the classic Zionist history, *The Balfour Declaration*.[144] Is it really possible

for a person to be a Zionist, change his sides entirely, and then change again, reverting seamlessly to his former position? Even if he did, what implication would that have for Anglo-Jewry and English Zionism?

To put this question slightly differently, can we state with any guarantee that the EZF had a serious alternative to infiltration? That the English Zionists were unable to influence their government begs the question. Given what we now know about the British leaders' attitudes toward their own promises to the Jews it seems unlikely that a more Zionistic Anglo-Jewry would have had any greater impact.[145] Then too, the reality that British political discourse had only recently turned from traditional patterns of limited politics to mass politics and that ideas of mass politics were alien to Anglo-Jewry militated against the likelihood of success even if the EZF had adopted a more combative policy. We may learn a lesson from events in 1947, when Zionist militancy in both *Eretz Israel* and England resulted in near pogroms across England's industrial heartland.[146] Under the circumstances, infiltration does not appear to have been a misguided failure, but to be the best means by which Zionists could influence the Anglo-Jewish community in support of *Klal Israel*. Here, most glaringly, Zionist failures did not derive from Zionist actions (or inactions), but from the essence of the Zionist argument: How else could a powerless people be restored to power?

Balance Sheet

This brief — and by no means exhaustive — review of Zionist fortunes in the interwar era seems to suggest a third path of analysis between two polar extremes in Zionist historiography. On the one hand, Zionist writings of the years immediately after the State of Israel was established emphasized the mass appeal of the Zionist movement as it moved from success to success. On the other hand, recent studies have demonstrated that Zionist successes were often fleeting and mass support little more than a mirage. Yet, even within these two extreme positions, due consideration must be given to the realities that surround the historical picture.

As already demonstrated, Zionist federations failed to obtain the mass support of most Jewish communities. Complex as the membership figures are, this conclusion is virtually unavoidable. All the same, while Zionists did appear to fail, they never did so in such a way as to destroy utterly all possibility for continued activity. Indeed, the nearest proof for the earlier ("Whig") style of Zionist historiography's validity is the existence of the State of Israel — if Zionism essentially was a failure and the WZO's history a string of unmitigated setbacks, how can the state's very existence, not to mention its vibrancy, be explained?[147]

In light of the above, it seems necessary to restate the root causes for Zionist failings. Of these, six appear to have been critical. First, the relative "newness" of modern Jewish political activity coupled with the lack of a precise frame of reference for conducting such activities. Second, the anomalous reality that Jewish nationalists were attempting to unite a widely scattered and diverse population (a situation by no means unique to Jews) in order to re-create a national and political entity in a territory where a majority of the national population did not reside and which was not even partially (until 1948) in the sovereign hands of the nationalist movement.[148] Third, the relative socioeconomic weakness of the Jewish world, which restricted the WZO's financial contingencies and forced an emphasis on slow but steady growth in the *Yishuv*. In addition to exposing Jews to potential danger, this gradualist policy had the weakness of not being "exciting" and grandiose. And as Jews came to believe that the Zionists could not offer a solution for

their individual problems, they sought solutions elsewhere. Fourth, and closely related to the first and third issues, the existence of numerous competing groups all of which argued with a nearly messianic fervor that their way offered the only path to true salvation for the entire Jewish people. The fact that a broadly accepted Jewish agenda exists now should not be read back into Jewish history. Zionism was not merely different from Bundism, Communism, Territorialism, or Assimilationism; it was based on premises that were incompatible with the other ideologies. Since it was not clear which of these ideologies would succeed, obviously participants could not know which movement better served their short- and long-term needs. Many Jews seem to have chosen the "wrong" ideology; that can hardly be blamed on the Zionists. The entire reason for analyzing Zionist failures is precisely the general framework of Zionist success; the fact that no other Jewish movement of the interwar era was crowned with greater success should indeed give pause regarding the meaningfulness of the entire debate. Fifth, disunity within Zionist ranks — between religious and secular, socialist and nonsocialist, gradualist and maximalist — also weakened Zionism's appeal. The WZO often appeared to be a ship with neither a captain nor a rudder, a perception reinforced by repeated schisms on the local level and by the two great schisms in the WZO: the defection of the Territorialists in 1906 and of the Revisionists in 1935. Finally, the restrictive *aliya* system created by the British weakened the Zionist movement as did continued conflict with the Arabs. To a reasonable observer in the 1920s or 1930s Zionism appeared to be an impossible dream that would — perhaps — be fulfilled after centuries. It is to this factor in Zionist history that we now turn.

Notes

1. Daniel J. Elazar and Stuart A. Cohen, *The Jewish Polity* (Bloomington: Indiana University Press, 1985), p. 207. The book, a handbook and gazetteer of Jewish political organization, ideology, and history from the biblical era onward has remained the best single source on the development of the Jewish polity; clearly, a synthetic text on the subject is to be desired. Cf. Abraham J. Edelheit ed., *The Literature of Jewish Public Affairs: A Ten Year Compilation* (New York: The Jewish Book Council, 1996), and the various issues of *Jewish Political Studies Review*.

2. Cf. Eli Lederhendler, *The Road to Modern Jewish Politics* (New York: Oxford University Press, 1989), chap. 5; and Martin Sicker, *Judaism, Nationalism, and the State of Israel* (Boulder: Westview Press, 1992), chap. 5.

3. Michael A. Meyer, *Jewish Identity in the Modern World* (Seattle: University of Washington Press, 1990), chap. 1.

4. Ezra Mendelsohn, *On Modern Jewish Politics* (New York: Oxford University Press, 1993), p. 3.

5. For the purpose of the graph, Zionists are defined as those exclusively focused on settling *Eretz Israel*, whereas territorialists are considered the equivalent of diaspora nationalists. This is, of course, a bit of an oversimplification, since the territorialists initially were members of the WZO. Cf. Haim Avni, "הטריטוריאליזם, התיישבות טריטוריאליסטית, וההתיישבות הציונית" (Territorialism, territorialist settlement, and Zionist settlement), in *יהדות זמננו* (Contemporary Jewry: A research annual) 1 (1983): 69–87.

6. A strong argument could be made that Orthodox groups, except Mizrachi, are not as keenly focused on *Eretz Israel* as the Zionists were, but the fact is that all Orthodox groups — even the most virulently anti-Zionist — retained a belief in a future messianic redemption that would restore the Jews to their homeland. This, of course, translated to a bifurcated political ideology: one that negated political activity in the here and now to effect a change in the status quo but that, simultaneously, negated the diaspora's future. Cf. Alan Mittleman, *The Politics of Torah* (Albany: State University of New York Press, 1996), pp. 19–20, 63–68.

7. Cf. Elazar and Cohen, *Jewish Polity*, p. 213.

8. Mendelsohn, *Jewish Politics*, chap. 3.

9. Ibid., pp. 17–23.

10. Sicker, *Judaism*, pp. 105–126.

11. Mendelsohn, *Jewish Politics*, pp. 23–27.

12. Ibid., chap. 1.

13. Abraham J. Edelheit, *The Yishuv in the Shadow of the Holocaust: Zionist Politics and Rescue Aliya, 1933–1939* (Boulder: Westview Press, 1996), p. 69.

14. Eliezer Schweid, "The Rejection of the Diaspora in Zionist Thought: Two Approaches," *Studies in Zionism*, 5 no. 1 (Spring 1984): 43–70.

15. On the comparison between Zionist and non-Zionist messianism, see Mendelsohn, *Jewish Politics*, p. 113. Similar analyses are contained in Judy E. Myers, "The Messianic Idea and Zionist Ideologies," and Eli Lederhendler, "Interpreting Messianic Rhetoric in the Russian Haskalah and Early Zionism," in *Studies in Contemporary Jewry* 7 (1991), pp. 3–13 and 14–33, respectively.

16. Isaac Babel, *Red Cavalry* (London: Alfred A. Knopf, 1929), pp. 45–50, 59–64, 253–255. The quote is from p. 63.

17. Cited in Mendelsohn, *Jewish Politics*, p. 104.

18. Ibid., pp. 104–107.

19. For three different interpretations based on these same premises, see Milton Himmelfarb, "The Jews: Subject or Object?" *Commentary* 40 no.1 (July 1965): 54–57, Yehuda Bauer, *The Jewish Emergence from Powerlessness* (Toronto: University of Toronto Press), 1979; and David Biale, *Power and Powerlessness in Jewish History* (New York: Schocken Books, 1986).

20. Cf. Joseph B. Schechtman, *Zionism and Zionists in Soviet Russia: Greatness and Drama* (New York: Zionist Organization of America, 1966), pp. 16–17.

21. Gershon Bacon, "Rabbis and Politics, Rabbis in Politics: Different Models Within Interwar Polish Jewry," *YIVO Annual* 20 (1991): 39–59.

22. Mendelsohn, *Jewish Politics*, p. 107; Edelheit, *Yishuv*, pp. 18–19. David Ben-Gurion's main contribution to Zionism, an idea dubbed *Mamlahtiut* and generally translated "etatism", fell in between the rightist and leftist idea of Zionist unity when viewed as an entirety. Ben-Gurion started his career with a definite left leaning but finished, some would argue, with a rightward tilt. Cf. Avraham Avihai, *Ben-Gurion: State-Builder* (Jerusalem: Israel Universities Press, 1974).

23. Zvi Lipset, "השקפות פוליטיות של סטודנטים יהודים בקיוב בשנת 1909" (Political views of Jewish students in Kiev in 1909), *הציונות* 2 (1971): 64–73.

24. Yehuda Ben-Avner, "ציונות ואוטונומיזם באירופה המזרחית בראשות המאה העשרים" (Zionism and autonomism in Eastern Europe at the beginning of the twentieth century), *כיוונים*, 16 (August 1982): 91–101.

25. Yitzhak Maor, *התנועה הציונית ברוסיה* (The Zionist movement in Russia) (Jerusalem: ha-Sifriyah ha-Zionit, 1973), pp. 315–319.

26. Oscar I. Janowsky, *The Jews and Minority Rights* (New York: AMS Press, 1966).

27. Maor, *התנועה הציונית ברוסיה*, chap. 18, 21.

28. Ibid., pp. 403–406; and Steven J. Zipperstein, "The Politics of Relief: The Transformation of Russian Jewish Communal Life During the First World War," *SCJ* 4 (1988): 22–40.

29. Maor, *התנועה הציונית ברוסיה*, chap. 23–25, Nora Levin, *The Jews in the Soviet Union Since 1917: Paradox of Survival* (New York: New York University Press, 1988), chap. 1–11.

30. Cf. Hugh Seton-Watson, *Eastern Europe Between the Wars, 1918–1941* (Hamden, CT: Archon Books, 1962).

31. Cf. Celia S. Heller, *On the Edge of Destruction* (New York: Schocken Books, 1980), pp. 71–76, and Harry M. Rabinowicz, *The Legacy of Polish Jewry, 1919–1939* (New York: Thomas Yoseloff, 1965), chap. 2.

32. Israel Gutman et al. eds., *The Jews of Poland Between the Two World Wars*, (Hanover, N.H.: University Press of New England/Brandeis University, 1988), passim.

33. Heller, *Edge of Destruction*, p. 113.

34. Cf., Abraham J. Edelheit and Hershel Edelheit, *History of the Holocaust: A Handbook and Dictionary* (Boulder: Westview Press, 1994), chap. 2.

35. Cf. Ezra Mendelsohn, "Zionist Success and Zionist Failure: The Case of East Central Europe Between the Wars," in Jehuda Reinharz and Anita Shapira, eds., *Essential Papers on Zionism* (New York: New York University Press, 1996), pp. 171–173.

36. Edelheit, *Yishuv*, pp. 142, 172–173.

37. Ibid., p. 183.

38. Mendelsohn, "Zionist Success," p. 181.

39. Edelheit, *Yishuv*, p. 154.

40. Raphael Patai, *The Jews of Hungary: History, Culture, Psychology* (Detroit: Wayne State University Press, 1996), pp. 507–511.

41. Cf. A. B. Yaffe et al, *יהדות רומניה בתקומת ישראל* (Romanian Jewry and the rise of Israel) (Tel Aviv: Shevet Yehudei Romania, 1992), 1:120–198.

42. Ibid., 1:201–285.

43. Mendelsohn, "Zionist Success," pp. 180–181.

44. Edelheit, *Yishuv*, 154.

45. Rabinowicz, *Legacy*, p. 109.

46. *Report of the Executive to the XXI Zionist Congress* (Jerusalem: WZO, 1939), p. 80.

47. Abraham G. Duker, *The Situation of the Jews in Poland* (New York: American Jewish Congress, 1936).

48. Rabinowicz, *Legacy*, p. 110.

49. Mendelsohn, "Zionist Success," pp. 178–179; and Robert M. Shapiro: *The Polish Kehile Elections of 1936: A Revolution Reexamined* (New York: Yeshiva University Press, 1988).

50. Cf. Ezra Mendelsohn, *Zionism in Poland: The Formative Years, 1915–1926* (New Haven: Yale University Press, 1981), passim.

51. Ibid., pp. 213–222.

52. Cf. "Colonies for Poland," *World Review*, vol. 2 (1936): 60–61.

53. Mendelsohn, *Zionism in Poland*, pp. 300–310.

54. Laurence Weinbaum, *A Marriage of Convenience: The New Zionist Organization and the Polish Government, 1936–1939* (Boulder: East European Monographs, 1993).

55. Rabinowicz, *Legacy*, chap. 7.

56. For just one example, see the notes on family members' political orientations in Hershel Edelheit, "Journal from a Lost World", unpublished memoir in authors' possession.

57. Hillel J. Kieval, *The Making of Czech Jewry: National Conflict and Jewish Society, 1870–1918*, New York: Oxford University Press, 1988).

58. Oskar K. Rabinowicz, "Czechslovak Zionism: Analecta to a History," in *The Jews of Czechoslovakia*, (Philadelphia: Jewish Publication Society, 1971): 2:24-28.

59. Kieval, *Czech Jewry*, ch. 7; Rabinowicz, "Analecta," pp. 28–29.

60. Edelheit, *Yishuv*, p.154.

61. Ibid., pp. 218–219.

62. Rabinowicz, "Analecta," pp. 30–32.

63. Ibid., pp. 35–108.

64. Cf. Michael Berkowitz, *Zionist Culture and West European Jewry Before the First World War* (New York: Cambridge University Press, 1993).

65. Robert Weltsch, writing in *Jüdische Rundschau*, December 15, 1922, cited in Michael Berkowitz, *Western Jewry and the Zionist Project, 1914-1933* (New York: Cambridge University Press, 1997), p. 194.

66. Max Nordau, "Muskeljudentum," in his *Zionistische Schriften*, 2nd ed., (Berlin: Jüdischer Verlag, 1923), pp. 424–426.

67. Berkowitz, *Western Jewry*, chap. 1–2.

68. Morton H. Narrowe, "Zionism in Sweden: Its Beginnings until the End of World War I", (DHL diss., Jewish Theological Seminary of America, 1990), pp. 143, 316–317.

69. Ibid., chap. 3.

70. Ibid., p. 74.

71. Ibid., passim.

72. Above, p. 13 and pp. 39-40. Cf. Franz Kobler, *Napoleon and the Jews* (New York: Schocken Books, 1976).

73. David Weinberg, *Community on Trial: The Jews of Paris in the 1930s* (Chicago: University of Chicago Press, 1977), p. 42.

74. The essays by Jean-Marie Delamaire, Alain Boyer, and Jean-Marc Chouraqui in Bejamin Pinkus and Doris Bensimon eds., יהדות צרפת, הציונות, ומדינת ישראל (The Jews of France, Zionism, and the State of Israel) (Kiryat Sde Boker: Ben-Gurion Research Center, 1992), pp. 5–59, review diverse aspects of Franco-Zionism prior to World War I.

75. Cf. Renée Neher-Bernheim's essay of Aharon Aharonson in ibid., pp. 60–73.

76. Phyllis Cohen Albert, "Israelite and Jew: How Did Nineteenth Century French Jews Understand Assimilation?" in Jonathan Frankel and Steven J. Zipperstein eds., *Assimilation and Community: The Jews in Nineteenth Century Europe* (New York: Cambridge University Press, 1992), p. 92.

77. Weinberg, *Community on Trial*, pp. 51–53.

78. It could, of course, also be argued that Kaplan's orientation (which was never anti-Zionist)

was changed by his experience during the Nazi occupation. For a brief biography, see: *Encyclopedia Judaica* (Jerusalem: Keter, 1972), 10: col. 750.

79. Paula Hyman, *From Dreyfus to Vichy: The Remaking of French Jewry, 1906–1939* (New York: Columbia University Press, 1979), p. 92.

80. Ibid., pp. 23, 57.

81. Ibid., pp. 44, 153–154.

82. Ibid., pp. 155–160.

83. Ibid., pp. 160–169.

84. Ibid., pp. 170–178.

85. Ze'ev Levi, "ארץ ישראל במחשבה היהודית בגרמניה מהירש ועד רוזנצווייג" (Eretz Israel in German Jewish Thought from Hirsch to Rosenzweig), *כיוונים* 4 (August 1949): 55–58.

86. Ibid., pp. 59–62. Surprisingly, Levi does not mention the parallel between Geiger's ideas and Simon Dubnow's. Both considered the Jews to be a spirit nation, although only Dubnow accepted the premise that the statement had any political meaning.

87. Ibid., pp. 62–66.

88. Ismar Schorsch, *Jewish Reactions to German Antisemitism* (New York: Columbia University Press, 1972), chap. 1–4.

89. Ibid., chap. 5–6.

90. Above., p. 43.

91. On the ZVFD's early history see Yehuda Eloni, *Zionismus in Deutschland: Von den Anfängen bis 1914* (Stuttgart: Bleicher Verlag/Tel Aviv University, 1987). A broader approach to German Zionist history is provided in Steven M. Poppel, *Zionism in Germany, 1897–1933* (Philadelphia: Jewish Publication Society, 1977). The conflict with non-Zionists is reviewed in Jehuda Reinharz, *Fatherland or Promised Land: The Dilemma of the German Jew, 1893–1914* (Ann Arbor: University of Michigan Press, 1975), chap. 3–4. A selective documentary history of German Zionism was provided in Jehuda Reinharz ed., *Dokumente zur Geschichte des deutschen Zionismus, 1882–1933* (Tübingen: J.C.B. Mohr/Leo Baeck Institute, 1981).

92. Poppel, *Zionism in Germany*, pp. 176–177.

93. Ibid.

94. *Jüdische Rundschau*, January 1, 1914, p. 1.

95. Poppel, *Zionism in Germany*, pp. 180–181.

96. Lilo Stone, "German Zionists in Palestine before 1933," *Journal of Contemporary History* (hereafter *JCH*) 32, no.2 (April 1997): 171-186.

97. Hitachdut Olei Germania's history is briefly reviewed in Edelheit, *Yishuv*, pp. 101–104.

98. Ibid., passim.

99. Poppel, *Zionism in Germany*, p. 165.

100. Cf. Michael Brenner, *The Renaissance of Jewish Culture in Weimar Germany* (New Haven: Yale University Press, 1996).

101. On Austria, see Harriet P. Friedenreich, *Jewish Politics in Vienna, 1918–1938* (Bloomington: Indiana University Press, 1991), chap. 3, 6–7. On Holland, see Ludy Giebers, *De zionistische beweging in Nederland, 1899–1941* (Assen: Van Gorcum, 1975).

102. Cf., Samuel Halpern, *The Political World of American Zionism* (Detroit: Wayne State University Press, 1961); Melvin I. Urofsky, *American Zionism from Herzl to the Holocast*, 2nd ed. (Lincoln: University of Nebraska Press, 1995); Naomi W. Cohen, *American Jews and the Zionist Idea* (New York: Ktav, 1975); and Aaron S. Klieman and Adrian L. Klieman eds., *American Zionism: A Documentary History* (New York: Garland, 1990–1991).

103. Halpern, *Political World*, p. 327.

104. Ibid., chap. 3–4.

105. Cf. Henry L. Feingold, *Zion in America: The Jewish Experience from Colonial Times to the Present* (New York: Hippocrene Books, 1974), chap. 13–16.

106. Peter Grose, *Israel in the Mind of America* (New York: Schocken Books, 1983), pp. 3–45. Reference has already been made to the fact that one of the earliest proto-Zionists was Mordechai Manuel Noah. See above, p. 23.

107. Cohen, *American Jews*, chap. 2.

108. Cited in Halpern, *Political World*, p. 72.

109. Ibid., pp. 79–80.

110. Cf. Nathan Glazer, *American Judaism* (Chicago: University of Chicago Press, 1957), chap. 6–7.

111. Melvin I. Urofsky, *We Are One! American Jewry and Israel* (New York: Anchor Press, 1978), pp. 1–176; David H. Shpiro, *From Philanthropy to Activism: The Political Transformation of American Zionism in the Holocaust Years, 1933–1945* (New York: Pergamon Press, 1994).

112. W. D. Rubinstein, *The Left, The Right, and the Jews* (New York: Universe Books, 1982), chap. 1.

113. Urofsky, *American Zionism*, p. 310.

114. We use "Arabism" to designate Arab nationalism following Elie Kedourie in Elie Kedourie and Sylvia Haim eds., *Zionism and Arabism in Palestine and Israel* (London: Frank Cass, 1982).

115. Norman A. Stillman, *The Jews of Arab Lands in Modern Times* (Philadelphia: Jewish Publication Scoiety, 1991), chap. 3–4.

116. Nitza Druyan, "על הציונות בקרב ארצות האיסלם" (On Zionism in the Muslim countries), כיוונים 28 (August 1985), p. 89.

117. Ibid., pp. 87–90.

118. Ben-Zion Yehoshua, "אהבת ציון וציונות אצל יהודי אפגניסתאן" (Love of Zion and Zionism among the Jews of Afghanistan), כיוונים 7 (May 1980): 43–57; Benjamin Ben-David, "כמה ביטויי ערגה לציון" (How many terms of longing for Zion), כיוונים 27 (May 1985): 155–164.

119. Stillman, *Arab Lands*, pp. 69–70.

120. Shlomo Barad, "הפעילות הציונית במצרים, 1917–1952" (Zionist activities in Egypt, 1917–1952), שורשים במזרח 2 (1989): 71–72.

121. Michael M. Laskier, *The Jews of Egypt, 1920–1970* (New York: New York University Press, 1992), chap. 1.

122. Ibid., chap. 2; Barad, "הפעילות הציונית במצרים," pp. 77–87.

123. Richard Ayoun, "ההתאזרחות הקולקטיבית של יהודי אלג'ריה וההתקוממות המוסלמית ב-1871" (The collective enfranchisement of Algerian Jewry and the Muslim uprising of 1871), במזרח שורשים 1 (1986): 11–35.

124. Stillman, *Arab Lands*, pp. 71–72.

125. David Cohen, "הפעילות הציונית בחברה הקולוניאלית של צפון-אפריקה בין שתי מלחמות העולם" (Zionist activities in the colonial societies of North Africa between the two world wars), שורשים במזרח 2 (1989): 211–274.

126. Zvi Yehuda, "הארגון הציוני במרוקו בשנים 1900–1948" (The Zionist organization in Morocco in the years 1900–1948) (Ph.D. diss, Hebrew University, 1981).

127. Sémach to AIU, Paris, January 14, 1907, cited in Stillman, *Arab Lands*, p. 81.

128. Cf. William L. Cleveland, *A History of the Modern Middle East* (Boulder: Westview Press, 1994), pp. 203–215.

129. Stillman, *Arab Lands*, pp. 82–84.

130. On Iraqi Zionism, see Nissim Rejwan, *The Jews of Iraq* (Boulder: Westview Press, 1985), chap. 25–28; on the Assyrians, see Ronald S. H. Stafford, *The Tragedy of the Assyrians* (London: Allen and Unwin, 1935).

131. Yehuda Nini, תימן וציון: הרקע המדיני, החברתי, והרוחני לעליות הראשונות מתימן (Yemen and Zion: The political, social, and spiritual background to early Yemenite aliya) (Jerusalem: ha-Sifriya ha-Zionit, 1982).

132. Tudor Parfitt, *The Road to Redemption: The Jews of Yemen, 1900–1950* (Leiden: E. J. Brill, 1996), p. 56.

133. Abba Hillel Silver, *A History of Messianic Speculation in Israel* (Boston: Beacon Press, 1959), passim.

134. Parfitt, *Road to Redemption*, pp. 7–10.

135. Cf. Gideon Shimoni, *Jews and Zionism: The South African Experience* (Cape Town: Oxford University Press, 1980); Hilary L. Rubinstein and W. D. Rubinstein, *The Jews in Australia: A Thematic History* (Port Melbourne: Heinemann Australia, 1991), vol. 1; and David J. Bercuson, *Canada and the Rise of Israel* (Toronto: University of Toronto Press, 1985).

136. Cf. Virginia H. Hein, *The British Followers of Theodor Herzl: English Zionist Leaders, 1896–1904* (New York: Garland, 1987).

137. V. D. Lipman, *A History of the Jews in Britain Since 1858* (New York: Holmes and Meier, 1990), chap. 5–6; David Cesarani, "The Transformation of Communal Authority in Anglo-Jewry, 1914–1940," in *The Making of Modern Anglo-Jewry* (Oxford: Basil Blackwell, 1990), pp. 114–117; and Gideon Shimoni, "Selig Brodetsky and the Ascendancy of Zionism in Anglo-Jewry," *Jewish Journal of Sociology* 22, no.2 (December 1980): 125–161.

138. Elias M. Epstein, "British Zionists' Contribution to Israel," in Israel Cohen ed., *The Rebirth of Israel* (London: Goldstein, 1953), pp. 311–323.

139. Cesarani, pp. 117–140, Stuart A. Cohen, *English Zionists and British Jews* (Princeton: Princeton University Press, 1982); Stuart A. Cohen, "Same Places, Different Faces — A Comparison of Anglo-Jewish Conflicts over Zionism During World War I and World War II," in Stuart A. Cohen and Eliezer Don-Yehiya eds., *Conflict and Consensus in Jewish Political Life* (Ramat Gan: Bar-Ilan University Press, 1986), pp. 61–78.

140. On the traditional leadership's views, see Mark Levene, "Lucien Wolf: Crypto-Zionist, Anti-Zionist, or Opportunist *Par Excellence?*" *SiZ*, 12 no. 2 (Autumn 1991): 133–148. On the Communist threat to Zionism, see: Sharman Kaddish, *Bolsheviks and British Jews* (London: Frank Cass, 1992).

141. Above, pp. 59–60.

142. Cf. Geoffrey Alderman, *Modern British Jewry* (Oxford: Clarendon Press, 1992), chap. 6.

143. Jon Kimche, *The Unromantics: The Great Powers and the Balfour Declaration* (London: Weidenfeld and Nicolson, 1968), chap. 5–6.

144. On Brodetsky, see Shimoni, "Ascendancy of Zionism"; on Stein, see *Encyclopedia Judaica*, 15: col. 356.

145. Cf. the statement by Malcolm MacDonald on the White Paper of 1939, cited in W. D. Rubinstein, *A History of the Jews in the English-Speaking World: Great Britain* (London: Macmillan, 1996), pp. 430–434.

146. Alderman, *Modern British Jewry*, p. 319.

147. Cf. Shlomo Lev-Ami, *?העם הציונות נכשלה* (Was Zionism a failure?) (NP: Ami Publications, 1988), chap. 10–12.

148. Of all the diaspora nationalisms — including the Irish, Indian, Chinese, and Malayans — only Zionism had to contend with the lack of a majority residing in the land claimed as a national home. Not surprisingly, Zionism was thus the only true example (and perforce the most successful one) of diaspora nationalism. Cf. Hugh Seton-Watson, *Nations and States* (Boulder: Westview Press, 1977), chap. 10.

7

ZIONISM, ARABISM, AND THE BRITISH

Legacies of Arab-Jewish Relations

Brief reference has already been made to the heightened tensions in *Eretz Israel* during the first years of British rule; which culminated in a series of Arab riots in 1921 and set the tone for Arab-Jewish relations for the next thirty years or more.[1] And while the deterioration of Arab-Jewish relations was largely a function of modern political realities, it is helpful to recall the broader historical background of modern Arab-Jewish relations, if only to demystify the so-called golden age of Arab-Jewish relations.

According to the myth, Jews in the Muslim world were treated with respect — if not outright deference — by Muslim rulers. Jews lived in a sort of perpetual golden age that saw the unequivocal flourishing of Jewish culture throughout the Arab empires. Only in recent times were Arab-Jewish relations tainted as a result of Zionist agitation and the close association between Jews and European imperialism.[2] There are elements of truth to this myth. In certain locations and under specific (but usually fleeting) conditions Jews were treated well by Arab/Muslim rulers. Then too, in such climates, Jewish culture did indeed develop mightily, for example the Golden Age of Spanish Jewry (8th–10th centuries) and the liberal immigration policy for Jews enacted by the Ottoman government after the expulsion from Spain (1492).[3]

Yet, despite these examples, the realities were considerably more complex. At its core, Islam has always had an ambivalent attitude toward Jews and Judaism (and to Christianity as well). One example from the *Qur'an*, Islam's premier holy book, can indicate the general nature of this problem:

> Wretchedness and baseness were stamped upon them (that is the Jews) and they were visited with wrath from Allah. That was because they disbelieved in Allah's revelation and slew the prophets wrongfully. That was for their disobedience and transgression.[4]

At least five other similarly negative passages exist in the *Qur'an*. When considered in light of Muhammed's almost complete destruction of the Jewish community of North Arabia (including the massacre of the Banu Qurayza tribe in 627), a generally negative picture of early Muslim policy toward Jews emerges.[5]

The other element in Arab–Jewish relations for the next millennium was the tolerance shown by Arab leaders after Muhammed toward Jews — as people of the book — and as established in the Pact of Omar (7th century).[6] Essentially, Jews (and Christians) agreed to a permanent second-class status in return for the right to live in Muslim-controlled territory, to worship freely, and to remain Jews. The status thus conferred, known as *al-Dhimmi* status, established clear parameters for Arab–Jewish relations with Arab/Muslim dominance always assumed.[7] Once those parameters were clearly established, a pattern of limited tolerance did exist: *Dhimmi* were permitted to retain their distinctive religion and culture.

Still, the tolerance shown to *Dhimmi* was always limited. Regulations that emphasized *Dhimmi's* permanent lower status abounded: the *Haraj*, a land tax, and the *Jizya*, a head tax, by which *Dhimmi* "bought" the sufferance to live where they lived; a complete ban on the possession of weapons, even for self-defense; regulations banning *Dhimmi* from any position of dominance over Muslims — including outright bans on government service and owning slaves; automatic invalidation of *Dhimmi* oaths in judicial proceedings against Muslims; laws regulating *Dhimmi* liturgy and places of worship (e.g., insisting that churches and synagogues had to be smaller than the smallest mosque in a location); regulations regarding dress, which had to be distinctly different from Muslim dress so that the *Dhimmi* would "never be allowed to forget that they were inferior beings"; and, finally, regulations enjoining *Dhimmi* from riding camels or horses and from walking in the path of Muslims or of ever standing erect inthe presence of a Muslim.[8]

The Pact of Omar, as well as other basic documents formulating the relationship between *Dhimmi*s and Muslims, presumed that the *Dhimmis'* lives and property would be protected by the Muslim authorities, but that was often not the case. The persecution of Jews by Muslims — though certainly less frequent than persecutions of Jews by Christians — were common during the Middle Ages. There were massive bloodlettings in Fez, Morocco, in 1033, and in Granada, Spain, in 1066. An estimated 5,000 Jews died in Fez alone. Judaism was banned in Yemen between 1165 and 1678. Repeated persecutions by the Almohades — Muslim crusaders seeking to turn back the *Reconquista* in Spain — between 1130 and 1212 ended the Golden Age of Spanish Jewry while also threatening the Jews of Morocco. Moroccan Jewry endured two other eras of mass persecution, in 1465 and 1790. Forced conversions occurred in Baghdad in 1333 and 1344 and in Persia as

late as the mid-seventeenth century.[9] And massive riots, against both Jews and Christian Arabs, broke out in Syria after the liberalizing legislation of the Second Tanzimat (Ottoman reform) was announced in 1860.[10]

In sum, the Arab/Muslim relationship with Jews (and Christians) was never unequivocally positive and often was negative. The *Dhimmi* were classified as a special class of infidels who nevertheless were not be destroyed because of their identification with the Bible. Still, *Dhimmi* were considered part of the *Dar Al-Harb* ("the world of the sword," i.e., non-Muslims) whose destiny was to be conquered and dominated for all eternity by the *Dar Al-Salaám* ("the world of peace," i.e., the community of Muslim faithful).[11] While the Dhimmi concept did not remain static (it was, for example, largely abandoned for tactical purposes by early Arab nationalists in their relations with Christian Arabs) it has significantly influenced Arab nationalists' attitude toward Jews, Jewish nationalism, and, most particularly, Zionism.[12]

Arab Nationalism

A full investigation of Arab nationalism lies well beyond the scope of this chapter (and of book), but some salient features of the history of Arab nationalism are needed to provide background for an understanding of Arab-Jewish relations and the incipient Arab-Jewish conflict. Arabism, like Jewish nationalism, arose in the mid-nineteenth century, mainly under the impact of contacts with Europeans whose nationalist ideology was transmitted and internalized by a variety of ethnic minorities in the Ottoman Empire. Despite the fact that the empire was always a Muslim state, its culture was always distinctly Turkish, not Arab. The Arabs, heirs to the caliphate established in Baghdad in the eighth century, accepted the Ottoman yoke for nearly six centuries; however, increasing opposition developed as the empire weakened.

The first manifestations of Arabism — a term coined by Elie Kedourie to denote modern Arab nationalism — were cultural, mainly focused on language and on recovering the Arab world's medieval literary heritage. The focus on language permitted Christian and Muslim Arabs to come together on an equal basis in opposition to the foreign rulers (Ottomans) who shared a common religion but not a common history, language, and culture with Muslim Arabs. Thus nationalist agitation provided an argument for including Christian Arabs in a patriotic nationalist movement. To be sure, two distinct strains of Arabism developed, although both had a common thread: nationalists active in countries occupied by European powers prior to World War I (mainly in North Africa) saw themselves as anti-imperialists; those in territories held by the Ottomans proved receptive (at least initially) to cooperating with the imperialist powers to remove themselves from Ottoman domination. Nevertheless, a single goal linked both wings of Arabism — the desire for a united kingdom linking all Arab territories "from Mesopotamia to Morocco."[13]

Arabism, as a political movement, began with the first distinctly Arabist movements during the mid-nineteenth century. A number of small secret societies dedicated to the Arabist cause arose in Beirut during the 1860s, after rioting by Muslim puritans who protested the reforms of the Second Tanzimat that slightly liberalized *Dhimmi* status. Such early movements (cells really) had all run their course by 1883.[14] Nationalist ideologies began to circulate again during the 1890s, a reflection of the charismatic leadership of Jamal al-din al-Asadabadi (also known as al-Afghani). Al-Afghani published an influential Arabic language news journal in Paris aptly entitled *al Urwa al-wuthqa* (the Indissoluble Link), which served as a forum to advocate Arab solidarity, although from a pan-Islamlic (rather than pan-Arab) perspective.[15]

As conditions in the Ottoman Empire worsened, Arabism gained strength, although with little ideological clarity or depth. By the turn of the century Arab nationalists could clearly state what they opposed, but not what they supported. They clearly opposed continuing foreign, including Ottoman, domination of historically Arab lands.[16] On almost every other issues Arabists were divided — whether to create a modern Arab state or a traditional one, whether the capital should be in Mecca, Baghdad, or elsewhere, whether the proposed entity should be a monarchy, theocracy, or republic, and, broadly, whether the Arabs should work for one entity or several.[17] World War I and the British promises to Emir Hussein of Mecca (described in Chapter 4) assisted in clarifying Arab attitudes on internal matters and gave Arab nationalism the orientations that have been central for almost eighty years: mainly its pan-Arab (rather than pan-Islamic) orientation and its desire for intra-Arab unity.[18]

Prior to 1914, Arab nationalists were divided in their attitudes toward Zionism. Many Christian Arabs held decidedly negative feelings about Jews, but prior to 1908 Arabist responses to Zionism were muted. Indeed, between 1908 and 1914 a number of initiatives to forge an Arab-Jewish alliance, or at least an entente cordiale, were made.[19] All these efforts foundered on the Arab demand to know, in advance of agreeing to an alliance, the extent of Zionist colonization plans.[20] By the outbreak of World War I a collision between the two Semitic nations was probable, though by no means inevitable.[21] In essence, the concept of pan-Arabism — by which it was hoped to create some form of Arab rule between Morocco and Mesopotamia — precluded any real possibility for a compromise over Palestine/*Eretz Israel*. In a diary entry for February 23, 1914, Marxist leader Khalil al-Sakakini wrote that:

[The Jewish people's] conquest of Palestine is as if it had conquered the heart of the Arab nation (Umma), because Palestine is the connecting link which binds the Arabian Peninsula with Egypt and Africa. If the Jews conquer [Palestine], they will prevent the linking of the Arab nation; indeed, they will split it into two unconnected parts.[22]

By July 1914 a secret society for uprising against the Zionists was advocating opposition "by all possible means, . . . among all avenues of the Arab nation in general and in Syria and Palestine in particular."[23] All Arab arguments against Zionism (mainly against immigration and land purchase) that were central to Arab propaganda in the years prior to 1948 had thus been developed by World War I.[24]

Nonetheless, a dispute exists among historians regarding when the dispute between Arabs and Jews became an actual conflict. Some historians argue that it happened during the Second Aliya. Zionist emphasis on the Jewish conquest of land and labor, they argue, led Arabs to infer that they were to be "left out" and would have no role to play in Palestine's future. In other words, Arab fears of being uprooted by Zionists turned them into opponents.[25]

While the argument has some superficial merit since it is really impossible to speak of the few incidents of Arab-Jewish confrontation prior to 1903 as a conflict. But, this interpretation fails to consider the Arabs' ideological orientation concerning the Jews' role as *Dhimmi* and Palestine/*Eretz Israel*'s importance to Arabism, which left no room for a real compromise.[26] Moreover, this interpretation posits the possibility that Zionists could have remained Zionists and yet surrendered the very essence of Zionism, *aliya*. To be sure, that was the basis for Ahad ha-Am's spiritual Zionism and for later Jewish efforts to reach a compromise with Arab nationalists. The so-called Arab question was thus by no means a "hidden one" (although it often seemed to be); the Zionist perspective is therefore worthy of recapitulation.[27]

Zionism and the Arabs

Zionist attitudes toward the Arabs were never monolithic or even consistent. In the Zionist movement's early years, many honestly believed that they were working to return Jews to an empty land. When the Arabs' existence was acknowledged, it was assumed that the economic benefits of Jewish immigration would more than offset Arab losses and lead to cooperation between the Semitic nations.[28] As theory and naive optimism gave way to hard reality on the ground, four Jewish positions developed: the integrative approach, the separatist approach, the liberal approach, and the socialist (or constructive socialist approach). Each of these must be viewed in context.[29]

In essence, the integrative approach posited that Jewish aspirations could not be fulfilled without Arab consent (or tacit acquiescence). For utilitarian reasons, therefore, Jews should seek to include Arabs in their activities while also promoting Arab national aspirations. The integrationist approach also emphasized a slow buildup of Jewish population, accepting the idea that Jews needed a spiritual center populated by a few and not a national home created by mass *aliya*. Eventually, the integrationist approach developed into a binationalist approach, culminating in the creation of Brit Shalom in 1925. This approach was, in theory, the most realistic of the Zionist approaches, since it matched limited goals to the facts on the ground and considered the Jewish world's overall weakness. But the approach ultimately failed, mainly because no Arabs stepped forward to act as partners in dual nation building.[30]

As against the integrationist approach, the separatists argued that compromise was futile because any compromise acceptable to the Arabists would eviscerate Zionism. Adherents of this approach acknowledged that nationalist competition between Arabs and Jews would eventually flare into conflict. "I know," wrote Yosef Klausner (one of the fathers of the separatist approach), "that in the long run a nation cannot be built without clashes and bloodshed, but these are not inevitable as the present moment [1908] and should be postponed as long as possible."[31] Advocates of separatism argued for unyielding firmness toward the Arabs regarding *Eretz Israel*, but supported the creation of a federal and multinational Middle East.[32] In essence this approach might be characterized as a "carrot and stick" approach that eventually (during the 1920s) crystallized into the so-called "iron wall" approach advocated by Ze'ev Jabotinsky.

Prior to World War I Jabotinsky had advocated a moderately separatist approach. He strongly believed that a Jewish *Eretz Israel* could come to terms with the Arabs in the context of a federal and multinational Middle East. By the 1920s, however, repeated Arab rioting led Jabotinsky to despair of any cooperation in the short term. He proposed that Zionists create an iron wall: a defense so strong that Arab opponents of Zionism could not breach it and therefore could pose no threat to the *Yishuv*'s development. Eventually, Jabotinsky posited, the Arabs would tire of repeated defeats and would learn to accept the Jewish State. In the interim, however, Zionists had to act quickly in order to obtain a Jewish majority and achieve at least minimal sovereignty in Eretz Israel. That way, further Jewish development work would not be dependent on British (or Arab) goodwill and could continue unmolested.[33]

Between the two polar extremes, integration and separatism, stood the liberal approach. Hoping to avoid conflict, the liberals sought a coalition among Turks, Arabs, and Jews. Like the integrationists, liberals advocated supporting Arab causes and aiding development in the socioeconomic sphere. They advocated such assistance only, however, when doing so did not harm future Zionist development. Thus, while integrationists sought to meld with the Arabs, liberals always advocated maintaining Zionist options. An example may help explain the difference. Integrationists opposed Zionist development that uprooted Arabs. Liberals also tried, as much as possible, to avoid uprooting Arabs. However, when that proved impossible, liberals refused to compromise Zionist goals for Arab comfort. The liberal position, which developed into the official policy of the WZO, was to try to negotiate when possible and to deal with reasonable Arab demands all the while insisting that Jewish demands also be taken into account. Liberals thus hoped to gradually create conditions whereby the Arabs would have no choice but to accept the reality of a Jewish national home and make their peace with it.[34] Theoretically less satisfactory than either of the alternative approaches, the liberal position proved to be the WZO's only viable option during the 1920s and early 1930s. By 1936, however, conditions had changed and this approach was modified considerably.

Also standing between the integrationist and the separatist approaches was the socialist approach, sometimes also known as the constructive socialist approach. Limited primarily to members of the growing *Kibbutz* movement, the socialist approach emphasized that conflict with the Arabs was not inevitable. In accord with Marxist theory, Arabs ought to have the same pressures of class and status that plagued other nations. Thus, the socialists argued, a common bond could be forged between Jewish laborers and their Arab counterparts. In the long run, such links would fundamentally change Arab society and permit a mutually beneficial agreement on *Eretz Israel*. In the interim, many socialists advocated ignoring the Arab problem, some because they did not believe it to be a serious threat to Zionist development and others because they did believe that conflict was inevitable.[35]

In essence, the socialist approach utilized ideas from both integrationist and separatist approaches to the Arabs. But a lack of Arab response to Jewish peace overtures stymied any possible cooperation in the short term, and the socialist Zionists' emphasis on *Avoda Ivrit* (Hebrew labor) and the *Yishuv* virtually guaranteed continued conflict. During the 1920s and 1930s the socialists emphasized the need to continue development regardless of the Arabs. As a result, many socialist Zionist groups strongly advocated that the British grant a wide range of autonomy to both ethnic communities, at the same time insisting that open *aliya* facilities be preserved throughout *Eretz Israel* for Jews. By the time the two major socialist Zionist parties — Poale Zion and Ahdut Ha-Avoda — merged to form Mapai (in 1930), the socialist position could be summarized as emphasizing the Jews' exclusive national rights in *Eretz Israel* and the right of Arabs to reside there as a national minority with their rights protected under international law.[36] In the short term this was a virtual prescription for conflict, but in the long term most socialist Zionists leaders hoped the conflict would be solved, a hope that remained unfulfilled through the 1940s. It might also be added that no correlation existed between level of Marxist orientation and view on the Arab question. For all its intensely Marxist views, ha-Shomar ha-Zair opposed unilateral Zionist concessions to Arab nationalism more strongly than most Mapai members.[37]

As Mapai gradually began to increase its influence within the WZO, the socialist and liberal approaches, which had never been very far apart to begin with, increasingly converged. Both were based on moderation and on gradual development in the hope that slow but steady Jewish immigration and land purchase would be less likely to provoke uncompromising Arab opposition. Both the liberal and the socialist approaches proved to be precipitate, since the Arabs saw conflict as their only option.[38]

Arab Riots and Jewish Defense

By and large, historians date the actual beginning of the Arab-Jewish conflict to the early mandate era. Negative interactions dating back to the 1890s and the earliest manifestations of Jewish national rebirth cannot fairly be considered a conflict in the strictest sense of the term. By 1929, however, the conflict existed and had already assumed the parameters that would define Arab-Jewish relations for more than half a century: a series of attacks by Arabs that Jews met (with greater or lesser degrees of success) by developing and expanding Jewish underground movements.

The first series of riots took place in Jerusalem in April 1920. Although they were silenced rapidly, the tension that led to these riots was never addressed and new rioting broke out in May 1921. These riots were accompanied by publication of Arab demands: abolition of the Jewish national home, a complete ban on *aliya*, and creation of an Arab nationalist government to

replace the Mandate.[39] The rioting left an impression of British incompetence and irresolution, impressions that worried the Zionists considerably. More devastating, however, was the temporary cessation of *aliya* imposed by high commissioner Sir Herbert Samuel; this was viewed as punishing the victims.[40] Samuel's actions, denounced as turning the Jewish national home into an Arab national home, set an unfortunate precedent. Thereafter the Arabs expected that if they made enough noise the British would drop their support of Zionism.

WZO leaders, who had placed much stress on Samuel's appointment because of his prominence in the Anglo-Jewish community and the high regard he was held in by the British political elite, felt betrayed and devastated.[41] Still, the Zionist response was muted. Politically, it would serve no purpose to undercut Samuel since his replacement would, very likely, return *Eretz Israel* to the type of military control that had proved so disastrous in 1918 and 1919.[42] Little else could be done publicly because of that fear. The Twelfth World Zionist Congress, for example, which met in Carlsbad on September 1–14, 1921, strongly reemphasized that the WZO sought all means to reach a compromise with the Arabs, but only in terms consistent with internationally recognized Jewish rights.[43]

The reality that they had few options for serious protest did not allay Zionist disappointment. Yitzhak Levi, a leader of the Jerusalem Sephardi community, for instance, strongly condemned Samuel, noting that the latter "will return to England and be reinstated as a minister, but *we* shall remain here — in danger."[44] Realistically, the Zionists could only turn inward and concentrate on building up their own infrastructure to withstand future Arab assaults and to guard against possible repudiation of promises by the British government. In effect, political realities in 1920 and 1921 left only one option: the development and expansion of Jewish self-defense forces in *Eretz Israel*.

The Hagana, founded as an ad hoc defense force in Jerusalem during the 1920 riots, became a more or less permanent agency within the Yishuv as a result of decisions taken by the Histadrut and the WZO Va'ad ha–Poel ha–Mezumzam in March 1921. This decision resulted from fears about renewed rioting and the seeming unwillingness or inability of British security services to cope with the riots. Further impetus for a permanent Jewish militia came when the British disbanded the Jewish Legion. Initially, the Hagana was organized as a militia, with units operating on a local basis. Hagana doctrine called for a purely defensive posture to deflect possible British accusations that the Jews behaved no better than the Arabs, meaning that an attack had to be initiated before Hagana units would respond.

For security purposes the Hagana's entire operation was placed under Histadrut oversight. Initially, there was no ideological implication to that decision. It made sense institutionally since the Histadrut was heavily involved in settlement building, defense and settlement being seen as two aspects of the same Zionist policy. However, this decision to identify the Hagana with the Histadrut (and, during the 1930s) with Mapai and the Jewish Agency (JA) was to prove controversial.[45] The March 1921 decision created a five-member high command: Israel Shohat, Eliahu Golomb, Yosef Baratz, Chaim Sturman, and Levi Skolnick (Eshkol).[46] The Hagana grew throughout the 1920s, becoming a truly nationwide organization by 1929.[47] Albeit, severe constraints existed both doctrinally and practically. In particular, the Hagana's emphasis on defense, coupled with the necessity of operating underground, limited the Hagana's options and meant that even when fully prepared, the Hagana could not always respond to Arab attacks. This weakness led to a schism within the Hagana's ranks in 1931 and was amply demonstrated during renewed Arab riots in August 1929.

The 1929 riots derived mainly from the same root causes as the 1921 rioting — Arabs' efforts to unequivocally terminate the mandate and end the Jewish national home.[48] The precipitating event that led to the riots was a dispute over holy sites in Jerusalem, specifically, the Western Wall (commonly but mistakenly called the Wailing Wall). The wall, the outer retaining wall of Herod's Temple, is considered one of the holiest Jewish sites; beyond and above it lies the Temple Mount which is the most sacred Jewish site in the world. However, the Temple Mount plays an important role in Islam as well. Muhammed is said to have ascended to heaven from there, and a mosque has existed there since the seventh century. During the middle and late 1920s, the two sites' proximity repeatedly caused frequent arguments and fights between Jews and Arabs. On Yom Kippur 5689 (September 29, 1928) a scuffle was caused by the Mufti of Jerusalem, ostensibly to protest Jews' putting up a curtain to separate male and female worshipers, resulting in police action and the desecration of Jews' holiest holy day.[49]

Although violence halted after the Jewish holidays, another violent outburst soon shattered the peace. On Friday, August 23, 1929, the Mufti preached a particularly violent sermon against the Jewish infidels. Rioting began immediately in Jerusalem (with one Jew murdered) and spread from there to Hebron and Safed. The fact that the Jewish residents of both cities were not Zionists seems (even at the distance of many years) to belie Arab claims to oppose Zionists only. Since the victims did not consider themselves to be part of the Zionist community in *Eretz Israel*, they had shunned Hagana protection. The Jewish community in Safed was hard hit, but the Hebron community was virtually destroyed. Most Jews fled with only a few returning after 1967.[50] Further rioting created more casualties within the Jewish communities in Haifa and Tel Aviv–Jaffa. Many Jews simply fled Jaffa for Tel Aviv, where they subsisted as refugees, some until 1933.[51]

Massive rioting in major cities received the bulk of attention from British and Jewish defense forces, but attacks on smaller Jewish settlements outside the major settlement areas stretched the Hagana's resources beyond its limit. Arab bands attacked the settlements of Hard-Tuv, Motza, Hulda, Be'er Tuvia, and one hundred smaller Jewish settlements.[52] The Hagana, with its ponderous organization and its multiple command levels, was unable to respond to most of these attacks in a timely fashion. Consequently, the Hagana was almost completely reorganized. First, a high command structure (general staff) was created and then the Hagana's units were reorganized and given a permanent geographic definition.[53]

Despite these changes, the Hagana's defensive doctrine remained in place, no thought of preemptive attack ever being considered. As a result, the Hagana continued to reject any possibility of operations prior to the opening of an actual assault. Whereas in 1920 and 1921 this purely defensive doctrine was universally accepted, by 1929 (certainly by 1931) such was no longer the case. After considerable internal debate, the Hagana's Jerusalem branch split. The majority remained loyal to Yosef Rochel (Avidar), who had been appointed by Eliyahu Golomb, the recently nominated chief of staff. A smaller group, styling itself the "Hagana Leumi" (Nationalist Hagana) and led by Abraham Tehomi, withdrew to form its own organization. Tehomi's group protested two aspects of Hagana policy, first, its refusal to consider offensive operations and, second, the close connection between the Hagana command and the Histadrut. Tehomi and his followers strongly believed that the Yishuv's defense should be non-partisan. WZO nonpartisanship had suffered considerably, however, since the founding of Hitachdut ha-Zionim ha-Revisionistim (Ha-Zohar, the Union of Revisionist Zionists) by Ze'ev Jabotinsky in 1925. By 1931 the rising tide of intra-Zionist partisanship had risen and had, seemingly, infected the underground defense movements as well. By the end of 1931 Tehomi's group had consolidated and would eventually crystalize into the Irgun Zvai Leumi (IZL, National Military Organization).[54]

Despite the disagreement over doctrine, the new organization initially adopted the Hagana's defensive tactics. In the interim with the end of rioting, peace was restored, at least on the surface. By October 1929, priorities for securing the Yishuv's future had been transformed from a military (or quasi-military) sphere to a fully developed diplomatic struggle over the Yishuv's future.

The British Response

Although Britain had entered into a compact with the WZO in 1917 and had agreed to League of Nations oversight in carrying out the terms of that compact in 1922, Anglo-Zionist relations were byzantine from almost the beginning. On the surface, the parameters of Britain's promises, as set out in the Balfour Declaration and the mandate, could not have been clearer. In reality, these relations were very complex and became increasingly vexatious during the 1920s and 1930s. As previously noted (in Chapter 5) the problem derived, in part, from the anti-Zionist (and to a degree antisemitic) orientation popular within the very group of British bureaucrats who were supposed to carry out the promises. Arab violence during the 1920s exacerbated the already existing problem and created repeated zig-zags in British policy toward Zionism and the Yishuv.

At the root of Britain's problem stood a paradox. While the Balfour Declaration and the Mandate had been conceived as the means to create a Jewish national home, both contained statements designed to protect (to an unspecified degree) the civil and religious rights of the already existing Arab community in Palestine/ *Eretz Israel*. Whereas the Mandate recognized that Jews seeking to return to *Eretz Israel* did so by right, not on British (or Arab) sufferance, this right appeared to contradict the Arabs' rights to national self-determination, religious expression, and personal liberty. Zionist leaders went to great lengths to prove that the two apparently conflicting sets of rights did not, in fact, contradict one another, but that view was not shared by either the Arabs or the British administration. In particular, Zionist leaders sought to prove (1) that the Arabs were not being displaced by *aliya* and (2) that the Arabs were gaining considerable economic advantage from Jewish investment in *Eretz Israel*'s infrastructure.[55]

Instead of responding with unequivocal resolve, the British equivocated. Their immediate, if temporary, response to the riots of 1921 was to halt *aliya* as a means of cooling Arab anger in the short term. But *aliya* resumed in 1921 and 1922, meaning that neither Jews nor Arabs were satisfied. Jews were upset because they felt the original ban on *aliya* was unfair while the Arabs were upset because their actions accomplished nothing of substance.[56] Unfortunately, this scene was to be repeated for the next twenty years, until 1939, as the British tried to "muddle through somehow."

British policy attempted to silence riots by police action and then sending several commissions to investigate the causes of the rioting.[57] However, the inability of the British government to solve the problem — a conflict between two apparently equal sets of rights — weakened any studies and rendered most commissions' conclusions moot. A case in point was the first of the commissions, the Haycraft Commission, led by Sir Thomas Haycraft, chief justice Palestine/*Eretz Israel*. The commission studied the causes for the 1921 riots and concluded that *aliya* was the root cause for the disturbances. Due to the controversial nature of the Haycraft Report, and given the possibility that the mandate would not be granted to Great Britain, the recommendations were never implemented. Instead, the colonial office issued a white paper signed by Winston S. Churchill (then serving as colonial secretary) which ended unfettered *aliya* in favor of a system of limited *aliya* based on economic absorptive capacity (described in Chapter 5). However, the critical points for future conflict had already been established in 1921: Arab disturbances had been partly rewarded while the Zionists were not fully abandoned. The British government had tipped its hand showing its inability to act decisively.[58]

The same pattern was repeated in 1929. After the riots a commission headed by Sir Walter Shaw was sent to investigate the impasse and propose means to bring peace to Palestine/*Eretz Israel*. The Shaw Commission carefully pondered the evidence it collected from Arab, Jewish, and British sources.[59] Two further commissions were sent to wrap up matters left unverified by the Shaw Commission. The first, the Western Wall Commission, studied conditions at the holy sites in Jerusalem; the second, the Hope-Simpson Commission (actually composed of only one member, Sir John Hope-Simpson) was to study immigration, demographics, and economy of Palestine/*Eretz Israel*. All three commissions reported that they found a single concern to be the foremost cause for Arab disturbances: fear that the Jews would undertake massive immigration and would drive them off land they had lived and worked on for twelve centuries.[60]

The result of all British reevaluations was a reversal of policy that devastated the Zionists: the new labour government's colonial secretary, Sydney Webb (Lord Passfield), issued a white paper that severely limited *aliya*. Specifically, no immigrant certificates were to be issued during the September 1930 to April 1931 schedule period and all future *aliya* was to be linked to Palestine's economic absorptive capability as expressed as an inverse ratio to the level of Jewish and Arab unemployment. Including Arab unemployment in calculating *aliya* rates was a major change and, given the divergent nature of Jewish and Arab economics, would virtually cut off mass *aliya* for the foreseeable future.[61] As threatening as the white paper's terms were, there was an even more threatening aspect to the government's position. The prime minister, the high commissioner, the colonial secretary, and other key figures all sought to justify the *aliya* stoppage as fully consistent with the mandate's terms and with Britain's commitments to the Jewish people.[62]

The Zionists had been concerned about the labour government's direction ever since the Shaw Commission was constituted. Zionist fears grew when Hope-Simpson — a noted opponent of Zionism — was ordered to prepare the report on immigration. Still, they were totally unprepared for the actual British announcement.[63] Utterly rejecting the white paper's terms, Chaim Weizmann declared that

Passfield had "gone a long way towards denying the rights and sterilizing the hopes of the Jewish people in regard to the national home."[64] As a result, Weizmann felt he had no option but to resign from the presidency of the WZO, which, in turn, was thrown into virtual chaos.

The Storm, 1930–1931

Weizmann's resignation was the beginning of an organized campaign to discredit the Passfield White Paper and have it over-turned. Leonard Stein, for instance, wrote a detailed memorandum on the white paper that refuted virtually all of the government's assertions.[65] Weizmann, although no longer president of the WZO, hammered away at the government hoping to obtain, at the least, some amelioration of the white paper's terms.[66] Weizmann continued his protests, writing to virtually anyone who could influence the government.[67]

This diplomatic effort seemed to represent Zionist weakness, but the approach was not at all ill conceived. A strong core of pro-Zionist sentiment existed throughout the British government, both in the Labour Party and the Tory and Liberal opposition, and it was to these circles that the Zionists now turned.[68] J. M. Kentworthy, a Labour M.P., provides one good example. In a letter to Weizmann, he reminded the Zionist leader that Zionists

> have many friends and sympathizers in this crisis amongst non-Jewish M.P.'s [sic] and that, speaking for myself, and I have no doubt for my friends, we shall do all we can do to repair this blunder by the C.O.[69]

British opponents of the Passfield White Paper included Jan C. Smuts, premier of South Africa and one of the Balfour Declaration's architects, former prime ministers Stanley Baldwin and David Lloyd George, and Josiah Wedgewood, a promi-nent Labour member of Parliament and un-questionably the most visible non-Jewish

supporter of Zionist (and Jewish) issues during the 1920s and 1930s.

However, the Zionists did not rely entirely on personal diplomacy, crucial as that was. They organized anti-British protest rallies throughout Europe and in South Africa and the United States. American Zionists, rejuvenated by Louis D. Brandeis's return to Zionist activism, urged a policy of economic pressure to force the British government to change the white paper.[70] The Zionists were also able to use a by-election in White Chapel (a heavily Jewish London district) to obtain support in the Labour Party for a strong stance against the white paper.[71]

Finally, when even Prime Minister Ramsay MacDonald's son Malcolm publicly threw his support behind Weizmann and the Zionists, the government relented. After a series of negotia-tions, Prime Minister MacDonald assured Weizmann that, as far as he was concerned, there was no white paper.[72] An Anglo-Jewish conference followed, meeting peripatetically between November 18, 1930, and February 4, 1931. All issues were raised, with the govern-ment slowly granting concessions to the WZO. In the end, the government agreed to undo the Passfield White Paper *de facto*. The statement of policy could not be withdrawn *de jure* with-out too much embarrassment for the govern-ment (which was already weak and would fall in August 1931 and be replaced by a national unity government led by MacDonald).[73] Still, MacDonald wrote a clear and unequivocal letter to Weizmann, which was communicated as authoritative to the League of Nations as well, stating in no uncertain terms that the Passfield White Paper would not be considered the basis for British policy in Palestine/*Eretz Israel*. Instead, immigration and land sale policy would return (in a modified form) to the status quo ante.[74]

With the MacDonald letter, the external threat to Zionist goals was (if only temporarily) quieted. Internally, however, a new storm — over the Weizmannist policy of gradual devel-opment and cooperation with the British — was brewing. The rise of ha-Zohar's maximalist Zionism, combined with the collapse of the center and the rise of Mapai, led to major changes in the makeup of the WZO. When added to Weizmann's apparent failure to obtain unequivocal British support for Zionist goals — a failure that even Weizmann admitted was exemplified by the Passfield White Paper — this new party structure led to a complete reevaluation of Zionist priorities and policies. In the long run, the eventual revisionist withdrawal from the WZO, which took place in 1935, may be traced back to the storm over Weizmannism (and over Weizmann) in 1930 and 1931.[75]

In essence, Zionists now had to decide (1) whether or not to continue the gradualist strategy and (2) whether or not Weizmann was the suitable leader to continue Zionist growth. These two choices were related but were not necessarily mutually exclusive. A continued policy of gradualism was conceivable without Weizmann's stewardship. Theoretically, the opposite also held true (though in practice it was not very likely) that a Weizmann-led WZO would abandon gradualism. Delegates at the congress, however, generally felt that Weizmann should step aside. Although gradualism might not have been completely discredited, his own personal style of diplomacy was. Moreover, the delegates felt that after two years of crisis, the time for change had arrived. Indeed, Mapai — a coalition between ha-Poel ha-Zair and Ahdut ha-Avoda (both evolutionary socialist Zionist parties) — had captured a small plurality of the votes for the congress and, for the first time ever, held the largest single bloc of delegates to the congress. Mapai appeared in position to assume the WZO's mantle of leadership.[76]

Jabotinsky also stepped into the fray. While he had been instrumental in defeating Max Nordau's maximalist plan for *aliya* in the early 1920s, by 1931 the revisionist leader had begun to advocate a policy of maximal Zionist development in the minimum of time. Jabotinsky came to this position because of his fear that continued Arab violence would erode the British commitment to Zionism. As a result, Jabotinsky emphasized replacing Weizmann, and also emphasized what he termed an

"Endziel" resolution. Jabotinsky's efforts to win election as WZO president seemed credible, given the way that gradualism had been discredited. At one point, in fact, Weizmann seems to have anticipated an incipient coalition between Mapai and the revisionists to oust him and elect Jabotinsky.[77]

Regarding the Endziel (final goal), Jabotinsky had proposed a simply worded resolution to the effect that the time had come for Zionists to define the long term goals that the WZO sought to accomplish. Specifically, Jabotinsky meant that the WZO should publicly state that Zionism sought to establish a Jewish majority and a sovereign Jewish state in *Eretz Israel*. Most delegates at the congress agreed that these were, indeed, Zionism's ultimate goals. However, most delegates also believed that tipping the WZO's hand so soon after the storm over the Passfield White Paper would be counterproductive. Such a resolution would embarrass the British, increase friction with the Arabs, and possibly spur the British to reevaluate relations with Zionism and the WZO. To be fair to Jabotinsky, it might be added that his resolution carried no timetable. Nonetheless, his Endziel resolution was considered too controversial and was rejected by the congress plenary. Pandemonium ensued, as Jabotinsky stood on a chair and dramatically tearing up his delegate card, declaring "this is not a Zionist congress anymore."[78]

By the time the tumult created by the Endziel resolution died down, the possibility of a coalition between the revisionists and Mapai had ceased. Faced, for the first time, with responsibility for the entire WZO, the Mapai leadership decided to protect the gradualist policy that had marked Practical Zionists since the Herzl era. Thus, although Weizmann was personally defeated, Weizmannism had survived.[79] The congress elected Nahum Sokolow WZO president and chose Emanuel Neumann, a moderate American General Zionist, as chairman of the newly established Jewish Agency Executive.[80]

Zionism and the WZO had weathered yet another storm, the most threatening one since the Uganda crisis. But the movement was approaching a potentially dangerous path.

Relations within the WZO were beginning to strain while relations with the British had barely been protected. The Arab factor would continue to vex Zionist leaders, with no possible settlement then in sight. Finally, events in Europe after the Nazi rise to power in January 1933 would fundamentally transform the problems facing the WZO leadership.

Notes

1. Above, p. 89-90.
2. For a typical example of the mythologized view, see: Leo Benjamin, *Arab-Jewish Brotherhood*, New York: Impress House, 1973.
3. On the Golden Age of Spanish Jewry, see Norman A. Stillman, *The Jews of Arab Lands: A History and Sourcebook* (Philadelphia: Jewish Publication Society, 1979). On the Sephardi migration to the Ottoman Empire after 1492, see Cecil Roth, *A History of the Marranos* (New York: Meridian Books, 1959).
4. *Sura* 2:61, cited in Stillman, *Arab Lands*, p. 150.
5. Stillman, *Arab Lands*, pp. 122–149.
6. Ibid., pp. 157–158. As an aside, it should be noted that the only extant text of the Pact of Omar refers exclusively to Christians; other sources verify that a similar pact existed with Jews.
7. Ibid., pp. 159–162, 165–168.
8. Bat Ye'or, *Oriental Jewry and the Dhimmi Image in Contemporary Arab Nationalism* (Geneva: World Organization of Jews from Arab Countries, 1979), p. 3.
9. Bat Ye'or, *The Dhimmi: Jews and Christians under Islam* (Rutherford, NJ: Fairleigh Dickenson University Press, 1985), pp. 60–61.
10. Salo W. Baron, "Jews and the Syrian Massacres of 1860," *Proceedings of the American Academy for Jewish Research* 4 (1932/1933): 3–31.
11. Bat Ye'or, *The Dhimmi*, pp. 113–118.
12. Ibid., pp. 119–139.
13. Cf. Hugh Seton-Watson: *Nations and States* (Boulder: Westview Press, 1977), pp. 260–262.
14. Cf. Sylvia Haim's introduction to her *Arab Nationalism* (Berkeley: University of California Press, 1964), pp. 4–5.
15. Ibid., pp. 6–15. Haim denigrated al-Afghani's role in modern Arab nationalism, while noting that most Arab writers considered him the father of Arabism.
16. Ibid., p. 21.
17. Ibid., pp. 25–34.
18. Ibid., p. 34f.
19. Neville J. Mandel, *The Arabs and Zionism Before World War I* (Berkeley: University of California Press, 1976), chap. 2.
20. Ibid., pp. 199–203.
21. Ibid., chap. 7.
22. Cited in ibid., p. 211.
23. Cited in ibid., p. 219.
24. Ibid., pp. 228–229.
25. Cf. Gershon Shafir, *Land, Labor, and the Origins of the Israeli-Palestinian Conflict, 1882-1914* (New York: Cambridge University Press, 1989).
26. For incidents prior to 1903, see Eliezer Be'eri, ‏ראשית הסכסוך ישראל-ערב‎ (Origins of the Israel-Arab conflict) (Tel Aviv: Sifriat ha-Poalim, 1985), chaps. 6, 8–10. Be'eri dates the origins of the conflict to the period after 1911.
27. For a broad overview of Jewish-Arab relations, see Israel Kolatt, "The Zionist Movement and the Arabs," in Shmuel Almog ed., *Zionism and the Arabs* (Jerusalem: Zalman Shazar Institute Press, 1983), pp. 1–34.
28. An early formulation of this idea was provided in Theodor Herzl's utopian novel, *Altneuland*, which provides an idyllic view of future cooperation, see *Altneuland* (Haifa: Haifa Publishing Company, 1960), passim.
29. This section closely follows the framework established in Yosef Gorny, *Zionism and the Arabs, 1882-1948: A Study in Ideology* (Oxford: Clarendon Press, 1987).

30. Ibid., pp. 41-49, 118–128. Cf. Susan L. Hattis, *The Bi-National Idea in Palestine during Mandatory Times* (Haifa: Shikmona Press, 1970).

31. Cited in Gorny, *Zionism and the Arabs*, p. 49.

32. Ibid., pp. 49–57.

33. Ibid., pp. 156–178. Cf. Yaacov Shavit, *Jabotinsky and the Revisionist Movement, 1925–1948* (London: Frank Cass, 1988), chap. 8.

34. Gorny, *Zionism and the Arabs*, pp. 57–66, 96–117.

35. Ibid., pp. 66–75.

36. Ibid., pp. 129–134.

37. Ibid., pp. 135–155.

38. See the documents collected in Aaron S. Klieman ed., *Arab-Jewish Relations, 1921-1937*, Rise of Israel Series, vol. 17 (New York: Garland, 1987), pp. 1–204.

39. Neil Caplan, "The Yishuv, Sir Herbert Samuel, and the Arab Question in Palestine, 1921-1925," in Elie Kedourie and Sylvia Haim eds., *Zionism and Arabism in Palestine and Israel* (London: Frank Cass, 1982), pp. 5–6.

40. Ibid., pp. 8–11.

41. See, for example, Chaim Weizmann's statement, cited in ibid., p. 11.

42. Ibid., pp. 13–15.

43. Ibid., pp. 12, 15–16.

44. Cited in ibid., p. 19. Emphasis in the original.

45. Of the vast literature on the Hagana, three items have provided the core of this section: קיצור תולדות ההגנה (Short history of the Hagana) (Tel Aviv: Ma'arachot/IDF Press, 1978), bk 2; Shlomo Lev-Ami, במעבק ובמרד (In struggle and revolt) (Tel Aviv: Ministry of Defense Publications, n.d.), pp. 15–27; and Meir Pail, התפתחות כוח המגן העברי, *1907-1948* (The emergence of Jewish Defense Forces, 1907–1948) (Tel Aviv: Ministry of Defense/Chief Education Officer, 1987), pp. 28–32.

46. Pail, כוח המגן העברי, p. 29.

47. Ibid., chap. 4.

48. Shai Lachman, "Arab Rebellion and Terrorism in Palestine, 1929-1939: The Case of Sheikh Izz al-Din al-Qassam and His Movement," in Kedourie and Haim, *Zionism and Arabism*, pp. 52–99.

49. Memorandum by the Secretary of State for Colonies on the Western, or Wailing, Wall, November 19, 1928, in Klieman, *Arab-Jewish Relations*, pp. 152–157.

50. Frederick W. Kisch, *Palestine Diary* (1938), cited in ibid., pp. 168–178.

51. Protocols of the JAE, April 9, 1933, CZA S100/14.

52. Lev-Ami, במעבק ובמרד, pp. 31–34.

53. קיצור תולדות ההגנה, chap. 10.

54. Lev-Ami, במעבק ובמרד, pp. 46–50.

55. The various arguments over Britain's promises in *Eretz Israel* are summarized in Christopher Sykes, *Cross-Roads to Israel* (London: Collins, 1965), chaps. 3–4.

56. Cf. Moshe Mossek, *Palestine Immigration Policy under Sir Herbert Samuel* (London: Frank Cass, 1978).

57. On the police aspects of British responses to Arab rioting, see Martin Kolinsky, *Law, Order, and Riots in Mandatory Palestine, 1929-1935* (London: St. Martin's Press, 1993), chaps. 3–6.

58. Bernard Wasserstein, *The British in Palestine: The Mandatory Government and the Arab-Jewish Conflict*, 2d ed. (London: Basil Blackwell, 1991), pp. 239–244.

59. The commission's full report, published in 1930, is reprinted in Klieman, *Arab-Jewish Relations*, pp. 185–390, the Zionist response being cited in ibid., pp. 391–544.

60. Cf. Aaron S. Klieman ed., *The Intensification of Violence, 1929-1936*, Rise of Israel Series, vol. 20 (New York: Garland, 1987), pp. 28–223.

61. The Passfield White Paper, October 1930, cited in ibid., pp. 224–245.

62. Statement by Prime Minister Ramsay MacDonald in Parliament, ibid., pp. 246–247.

63. Cf. the selection of Weizmann's letters from September 1929 through October 1930, cited in ibid., pp. 257–313.

64. Weizmann to Passfield, October 20, 1930, ibid., pp. 314–315.

65. Leonard Stein, Memorandum on the Palestine White Paper of October 1930, in ibid., pp. 316–405.

66. Weizmann to MacDonald, November 5, 1930, ibid., pp. 461–463.

67. Weizmann to May, July 25, 1931, cited in Aaron S. Klieman ed., *Zionist Political Activity in the 1920s and 1930s*, Rise of Israel Series, vol. 21 (New York: Garland, 1987), pp. 344–345.

68. Norman A. Rose, *The Gentile Zionists: A Study in Anglo-Zionist Diplomacy, 1929-1939* (London: Frank Cass, 1973), chaps. 1–2; Yosef Gorny, *The British Labour Movement and Zionism, 1917-1948* (London: Frank Cass, 1983), chap. 4–6.

69. Kentworthy to Weizmann, October 30, 1930, cited in Rose, *Gentile Zionists*, p. 17.

70. Rose, *Gentile Zionists*, pp. 9–17; Ervin Birnbaum, *In the Shadow of the Struggle* (Jerusalem: Gefen Books, 1990), p. 126.

71. Gorny, *Labour Movement*, pp. 91–96.

72. Rose, *Gentile Zionists*, p. 20.

73. Ibid., pp. 21–26.

74. The letter was reprinted in Walter Laqueur ed., *The Israel-Arab Reader*, 2d ed. (New York: Bantam Books, 1968), pp. 50–56 and is analyzed in Rose, *Gentile Zionists*, pp. 26–28.

75. Cf. Abraham J. Edelheit, *The Yishuv in the Shadow of the Holocaust: Zionist Politics and Rescue Aliya, 1933-1939* (Boulder, CO: Westview Press, 1996), pp. 23–24, 104–108.

76. Cf. Yaacov Goldstein, "Mapai and the Seventeenth Zionist Congress (1931)," *Studies in Zionism*, 10, no. 1 (Spring 1989): 19–30.

77. Joseph B. Schechtman, *The Life and Times of Vladimir Jabotinsky* (New York: Thomas Yoseloff, 1961), 2: 151–152.

78. *Verhandlungen der 17. Zionistische Kongress* (London: World Zionist Organization), 1931, pp. 164–194; Schechtman, *Life and Times* 2: 152–153.

79. Goldstein, "Mapai," pp. 29–30.

80. *Verhandlungen*, p. 475.

The Rising Antisemitic Tide

Renewed stability in the WZO following the stormy years between 1929 and 1931 did not immediately translate to renewed growth for the *Yishuv*. Despite the collapse of the Passfield White Paper, *aliya* did not recover immediately: A recession, coupled with the British government's decision to double the financial requirements for an immigrant certificate in the so-called capitalist A category, translated into sluggish *aliya* rates in 1931 and 1932.[1] Slow *aliya* meant less pressure on the Arab front and hence fewer problems in Anglo-Zionist relations. Nevertheless, dissension within Zionist ranks grew, flaring to virtual civil war between the revisionists and Mapai.

Even before the Seventeenth Zionist Congress convened in 1931, conflict had replaced cooperation as the defining feature of interparty relations. That spring, a Betar work company accepted agricultural work in Kfar Saba without Histadrut consent. An attempt to prevail on the Betar members to join the Histadrut failed, prompting their forcible removal from the workplace. This incident caused a violent three-way confrontation between the Histadrut, Betar, and the growers, resulting in a stalemate at the end of the harvest season. In the interim, other farmers began hiring non-Histadrut labor, and a lockout ensued.[2] The struggle

was exacerbated in the autumn of 1932, when violent clashes erupted between Betar and Histadrut members during a strike against the Froumine Biscuit Company.[3] Yet another outbreak of violence took place on the last day of Passover, April 17, 1933, when a peaceful march in Tel Aviv by uniformed Betar members was interrupted and attacked by workers, a majority of whom were Histadrut members.[4]

More fuel was added to the fire by a series of ideological clashes. In 1932, Joshua H. Yeivin, editor in chief of ha-Zohar's newspaper, *Hazit ha-Am*, published a novel containing a thinly veiled attack on both the Histadrut and Mapai, accusing socialist Zionist leaders of venality and a lust for power.[5] Ze'ev Jabotinsky also contributed to this atmosphere with his stand on Mapai's so-called *sha'atnez* (improper intermingling of ideologies). In response to the publication of David Ben-Gurion's *me-Maamad la-Am*, Jabotinsky challenged Mapai to truly place national goals ahead of class interests by surrendering the right to strike. In exchange, Jabotinsky proposed a national arbitration board to adjudicate labor disputes. Mapai leaders saw this proposal as nothing more than an attempt to defend middle-class interests, a class struggle in reverse, and an effort to deny workers the chance to better themselves. In view of the voluntary nature of *Yishuv* institutions, Jabotinsky's proposal could not be taken seriously, since even a "mandatory" arbitration board would not be able to enforce its decisions. Moreover, the entire proposal smacked of the integralist, "corporate" economics prevalent in contemporary fascist Italy. Convinced that Jabotinsky was an implacable enemy, the Histadrut rejected his proposals out of hand.[6]

In the summer of 1933 interparty strife increased markedly. On June 16, Haim Arlosoroff was murdered while walking with his wife on Tel Aviv's beach. Undoubtedly one of the most controversial crimes in Israel's history, the Arlosoroff affair has been investigated repeatedly, but without clear results. Indeed, in 1985 an Israeli government commission of inquiry con-cluded that although the suspects arrested in 1933 were innocent, Mapai's suspicions regarding possible revisionist involvement were not unfounded. Despite an intensive investigation into the confessions of two Arabs, Abdul Majid and Issa el Abrass, the committee concluded that it could not determine the identity of the murderers.[7]

At the time of Arlosoroff's murder the *Yishuv* was divided into two camps. After a brief inquest, the British Palestine police, aided by members of the Hagana, arrested three Betar leaders, Abba Ahimeir, Zvi Rosenblatt, and Abraham Stavsky. All were soon tried for the crime. The prosecution claimed that their motives were political and that the three were members of a shadowy terrorist group called Brit ha-Biryonim. As evidence, the prosecution pointed to a num-ber of Ahimeir's articles in *Doar ha-Yom*, which Mapai had interpreted as death threats against Arlosoroff.[8] The defense, on the other hand, claimed that the motive for the murder was robbery and that the accusa-tions against the three were politically motivated and false.

Mapai's leaders were unalterably con-vinced that the three accused were guilty, though Ben-Gurion initially suspected that Communists were responsible.[9] Jabotinsky and some influential nonrevisionists, in-cluding Chief Rabbi Abraham Isaac Kook, were equally adamant in believing in their innocence. Kook went so far as to sponsor a fund for Stavsky's defense. In this he was supported by the editors of *ha-Aretz*, who believed Stavsky to be guilty but felt that justice would best be served if he had the best defense.

In the immediate aftermath of the arrests, numerous voices in the *Yishuv*, including members of the conservative General Zionist Alliance (the B faction), called for the outlawing of all revisionist organizations, and especially Betar. At the Eighteenth World Zionist Congress, just three months after the murder, Jabotinsky and his wife were accosted by a group of young labor Zionists. Although threatened, Jabotinsky was able to enter the hall peacefully. After such an inauspicious beginning, ha-Zohar fared badly in the congress. All of Jabotinsky's resolutions were rejected while a Mapai resolution not to allow members of ha-Zohar onto the Presidium passed the plenum by a vote of 151 to 149.[10]

Furthermore, a WZO court, held during the congress, found Betar (and ha-Zohar) guilty of what the executive declared to be repeated breaches of Zionist discipline, primarily in relation to the Keren Kayemet le-Israel (KKL) and Keren ha-Yesod (KHY), and punished the party by withdrawing its right to obtain certificates. In response, Betar Circular no. 60 announced a new party policy: henceforth efforts would be made to obtain certificates directly from the high commissioner's reserve instead of from the JAE.

When the JAE received a purloined copy of Circular no. 60, the majority of its members viewed the newly enunciated policy as a direct threat to their authority and demanded its immediate repudiation. The JAE noted that the new Betar policy played right into the hands of the British, who at that very moment sought to justify changing the immigration statutes. Betar refused, defending the circular by noting that the JAE monopoly over certificates was unfair. It was being used to weaken nonsocialist Zionist parties by granting certificates only to those who had graduated from a hachshara. Betar also stated that the makeup of the JAE, primarily the membership of non-Zionists, was unacceptable and that it freed Betar from the responsibility of submitting to JA authority. Moreover, the Betar leadership argued, the

Immigration Ordinance of 1931 guaranteed the right to request certificates from the high commissioner.

The JAE rejected Betar's defense of Circular no. 60 as either irrelevant or unacceptable and maintained that the premises on which the Betar circular based itself constituted a breach of Zionist discipline. Since Betar was a duly recognized member of the WZO — which granted certain rights but also brought with it specific responsibilities — Betar could not claim these rights while refusing to accept its responsibilities. Moreover, the makeup of the JAE had been accepted by a majority of the delegates at the World Zionist Congresses in 1929, 1931, and 1933. Therefore, Betar's unwillingness to accept JAE authority undermined the position of the JA and harmed the Zionist cause.[11]

Although some Betar members were guilty of instigating violent clashes, neither Betar nor ha-Zohar were the only guilty party in this case. Each side justified physical attacks as part of a legitimate war against the alleged enemies of Zionism. During a stormy meeting with South African Zionists, Ben-Gurion, Eliezer Kaplan, and Yitzhak Gruenbaum analyzed two major issues separating Mapai and ha-Zohar: labor relations and Zionist discipline. Ben-Gurion and Kaplan saw Betar's efforts in the sphere of labor as an attempt to destroy the Histadrut and thereby crush the movement for *Avoda Ivrit* (Hebrew Labor), which was one of the basic premises of socialist Zionism. According to this line of analysis, Betar, and by extension ha-Zohar, reflected the position of certain Jewish bourgeois circles in Palestine who, although Zionist in orientation, placed their own economic interests ahead of national interests.[12]

For their part, the South African Zionists attempted to persuade Ben-Gurion and Kaplan to issue a public manifesto calling for an end to internecine strife, but they failed to offer convincing evidence that a manifesto would improve the situation in any way. Thus Ben-Gurion stated his agreement with the principle of intra-Zionist peace but adopted a position of uncompromising enmity toward Jabotinsky and ha-Zohar. "I tell you," Ben-Gurion stated bluntly, "that Jabotinsky will not accept any agreement except one — *the state of Hitler in Germany for Zionism.*"[13] He added: "There are some people who are bitterly complaining why cannot labour leaders be hanged in Palestine as they are doing in Vienna."[14] With these words, Ben-Gurion fell into the common trap of identifying Jabotinsky with Nazism when nothing could have been further from the truth. Despite his emphasis on military-style discipline and uniforms for Betar members, Jabotinsky was committed to a liberal and democratic vision that represented the antithesis of fascism. Ben-Gurion's words reflect the depth of hatred between the two competing blocs, and the willingness of Mapai's leaders to use terminology repudiating the legitimacy of their opponents.

To say the least, Ben-Gurion's phraseology was inopportune. Less than two months prior to this meeting, the Nazis had seized power in Germany and created a fundamentally new situation for the WZO. When coupled with the rising antisemitic tide throughout Eastern Europe, the Nazi *Machtergreifung* (seizure of power) became a central focus for Zionist crisis management and, ultimately, for a burgeoning catastrophe that led to the unprecedented murder of 6 million Jews.[15]

Nazi mass murder was far in the future and was almost completely inconceivable to most Zionist activists during the 1930s.[16] As a result, the WZO and JAE concluded that a policy of vastly increased migration, a policy which might properly be dubbed Rescue Aliya, would be the most appropriate response to the Nazi threat.[17] Given the *Yishuv*'s limited resources (and those of the WZO as well) most Zionists concentrated on constructive aid, by which they meant the maximization of *aliya* to form a rescue policy. Zionist justifications for this policy were both ideological and pragmatic. Ideological insofar as all Zionist ideologies were based on the premise of increased *aliya*, and practical because the Yishuv stood to gain considerably by the influx of German Jews who possessed wealth and technical know-how.

The political realities of 1933 limited other

A Keren Kayemet le-Israel Poster of the 1930s Emphasizes *Eretz Israel*'s Role in Rescuing German and European Jewry.

Authors' Collection

Jewish options in opposition to both Nazism and Eastern European antisemitism. Jews responding to the Nazi threat used one of four broad tactics: through the press, through legal action (the so-called Bernheim Petition), through an anti-Nazi boycott, or through aid to refugees. All of them were tried by elements of the Jewish world, and all of these policies had advocates within the *Yishuv*.[18] In practice, however, the *Yishuv*'s options were severely limited. The press, for example, could (and did) devote considerable space to reportage on the situation in Germany. Regrettably, however, the *Yishuv*'s press was limited in its influence. With the possible exception of the *Palestine Post*, the only English-language daily, none of the papers were regularly read by members of the government. And since most papers were party sponsored and were read by party members, they were writing for a majority who already accepted certain Zionist premises regarding the proper response to an antisemitic attack. This prejudice did not *ipso facto* mean the rejection of other policies, but it did establish a clear preference regarding what kind of policy a majority of the *Yishuv*, and virtually all its leaders, would support. The same held true for the Bernheim petition. Although diaspora Jewish organizations considered it to be important, the petition was not a possible anchor for the *Yishuv*'s policy of aid to German Jewry, for two reasons. First, the *Yishuv* lacked a clearly defined diplomatic status and, second, the British government refused to lend its support to these Jewish efforts. The idea of sponsoring an anti-Nazi boycott was also rejected by the majority of Zionists as "inexpedient and dangerous."[19]

Again, the direct result of the *Yishuv*'s lack of alternative policies meant that only by maximizing *aliya* could any relief, even partial relief, be found for European Jewish distress. For Rescue Aliya to be considered successful, however, it had to provide the realistic possibility of *aliya* for as many German (and Eastern European) Jews as possible. *Aliya* increased 317 percent in 1933 over 1932. Total aliya in 1932 was 9,553 and in 1933 reached 30,327. Indeed, *aliya* blossomed for the next five years, totaling 174,803 new immigrants between 1933 and 1937.[20]

Since *aliya* was restricted only by the number of certificates granted, these figures may seem low, but need to be understood in light of three considerations. First, few Zionists, and fewer still German Jewish leaders (even those who advocated emigration), spoke in terms of total evacuation. Arthur Ruppin, for instance, spoke of 200,000 emigrants in a speech at the Eighteenth Zionist Congress in 1933. Such a figure represented approximately one-third of German Jewry in 1933.[21] As late as 1937, the majority of German Jews did not see emigration as their sole recourse, even though "there was agreement on the desirability, even necessity, of facilitating the exodus of the young."[22] The second consideration was the attitude and policy of the British Palestine

תקות וחדוה בשבל ארץ ישראל

THE JEWISH AGENCY FOR PALESTINE.

77, GREAT RUSSELL STREET.
LONDON. W.C.1.

TO THE JEWS OF ALL COUNTRIES.

Jews throughout the world have been deeply moved by the tragic fate which has befallen their brethren in Germany. Their feelings have found spontaneous expression in the immediate organisation of relief work both for the refugees in neighbouring countries, and for those who remain in Germany.

Thousands of German Jews, especially among the young, see the prospect of re-starting their lives in Palestine, to which some of them have already made their way.

Palestine shows a steady development both of agriculture and industry. Its power of absorption is increasing and can be further increased. A determined and concerted Jewish effort can make it capable of providing a permanent home for a considerable part of German Jewry, to whom the rest of the world, with few exceptions, is closed.

As representatives of the Jewish Agency for Palestine, constituted under the authority of the League of Nations, by virtue of the Palestine Mandate, and recognised by the Mandatory Power, and as friends of the Jewish people and the Jewish National Home in Palestine, we appeal to all Jewish communities to take part in creating a Palestine Fund for German Jews.

It is earnestly hoped that fund-raising committees will begin their work without delay. The receipts of this fund will be applied, in co-operation with existing financial institutions of the Zionist Organisation and the Jewish Agency (the Keren Hayesod and the Keren Kayemeth LeIsrael) to purchasing land in Palestine for settlement by German Jews, assisting industrial undertakings and artisans, furnishing credits, supporting the private enterprise of persons with means, encouraging the settlement on the land of "chalutzim" (pioneers) and generally to facilitating transition to new occupations. An effort will be made to provide Jewish scholars and scientists who have had to abandon their studies in Germany, with facilities for continuing them in Palestine under the auspices of the Hebrew University, the Agricultural

Experiment Station, the Haifa Technical College, and other institutions of higher learning.

The great abilities of the German Jews, who have held so eminent a place among the Jewries of the world for many centuries, must be linked up with all the creative forces of the Jewish people in the reconstruction of the Jewish National Home. To assist them in the establishment for themselves, in Palestine, of a new existence, in freedom and honour, is a great humane task. The Jews of Palestine itself have led the way. Collections for the Palestine Fund for German Jews have already been launched in Palestine under the auspices of the Jewish Agency and with the collaboration of all sections of the Jewish population. We appeal to the Jews of all countries to emulate this example by service and sacrifice on a scale commensurate with the grave emergency.

CECIL
D. LLOYD GEORGE
HERBERT SAMUEL
J. C. SMUTS
CYRUS ADLER
MORRIS ROTHENBERG
NAHUM SOKOLOW
FELIX WARBURG
CHAIM WEIZMANN

Collections for this fund will not be made in the British Isles, where the British Central Fund for German Jews has been established, which - by arrangement with the Jewish Agency - will allocate a substantial proportion of its collection to Palestine. Also in other countries, where by similar agreements joint appeals are launched, no collection for this fund will be made.

May 29th, 1933.

Jewish Agency Proclamation Calling for Jewish Solidarity to Rescue German Jewry, May 1933.
Courtesy of the Central Zionist Archives, Jerusalem

administration. Although initially supportive, the British attitude toward Rescue Aliya rapidly became ambivalent and became increasingly hostile as time wore on. Humanitarian considerations notwithstanding, the Palestine administration existed to serve Great Britain's strategic interests. Primary among those interests was maintaining peace in Palestine/*Eretz Israel* and retaining the goodwill of the independent (or semi-independent) Arab states, especially Egypt and Iraq. Against such interests the needs of Jews were seen as secondary, at best, and they declined altogether in importance after 1936.[23]

The third consideration, finally, was Zionist rescue policy, which reflected ideologically adumbrated rescue priorities. Although this factor should not be exaggerated, it must not be ignored. Numerous disagreements arose within the *Yishuv* regarding the new *aliya* and its implications. Such disagreements were generally not over which policy to adopt but rather over how best to apply the policy already adopted. These three factors — the attitudes of German Jewry, of the British government, and of the Zionist movement — were, to different degrees, responsible for shaping Rescue Aliya's ultimate outcome.

Rescue Aliya is widely misunderstood by

writers and historians who overlook the objective conditions then prevailing in the world. To be sure, we can now see that German Jewry, the *Yishuv*, and the WZO were almost completely unprepared to meet the crisis. Furthermore, with hindsight it is easy to criticize the political naivete and lack of wisdom allegedly shown by the leaders at the time. Indeed, Zionist policy was something of a paradox. There was plenty of grandiose rhetoric used during the 1930s about rescue in the abstract, but it was coupled with an attitude of "business as usual" when concrete steps were to be taken. Consequently, some historians have distinguished between "rescue" and "salvation," claiming that the former was conceptually incompatible with the latter. Rescue always meant the immediate evacuation of German and European Jewry while salvation meant the rescue of only a "saving remnant." This line of analysis hinges on the assumption that German goals were always clear and that all Nazi actions led inexorably to the extermination of European Jewry. A careful analysis of Holocaust historiography, however, shows that such a conclusion cannot presently be upheld, especially not before the mass outburst of anti-Jewish violence that culminated on Kristallnacht.[24] Thus, when author Anita Shapira concluded that even by 1939 Zionists "had not read the writing on the wall," she was telescoping events and assuming that in 1939 (or earlier) the Final Solution was obvious to all who viewed the events properly.[25]

Although this position cannot be fully upheld, it also cannot be unequivocally rejected. Moreover, the painful paradox facing the *Yishuv* cannot be denied. Some Zionists were indeed unable to rise above their petty concerns, the same was true for virtually every other Jewish party and group at the time. Not even the most pessimistic could foresee the direction that Nazi antisemitism was taking until it was too late to save more than a remnant of European Jewry. That Zionists often used grandiose rhetoric regarding the extraordinary means needed to undertake the program of Rescue Aliya, and that an attitude of "business as usual" pervaded the program once it actually began cannot be denied. Blaming Zionists, for example accusing them of "egotism" due to their supposed unwillingness to consider mass resettlement outside of the Jewish national home, misses the point.[26] Had a sovereign Jewish state existed during the 1930s, such accusations would be valid. In reality, Britain and not the Jewish Agency ruled *Eretz Israel*. Given the *Yishuv*'s limited resources, Dina Porat's conclusion regarding Zionist responses to the extermination of European Jewry should be kept in mind:

> Israelis today have long since forgotten or are unaware of the difficulties facing the Yishuv at the time. It was a minority in a country ruled by foreigners. It was a social-national experiment in its early stages. Its resources — in manpower, money, and arms — were small. Nor do they realize that, for all its limitations — and in the face of the efficiency of the German death machine and the interference of the Allies — the Yishuv in fact did more than it was ever given credit for — either then or now.[27]

As already noted, 174,803 new immigrants entered *Eretz Israel* between 1933 and 1937. They doubled the existing Jewish population, enlarged both rural and urban settlements, and greatly expanded the economy. Even so three major impediments existed to the task of growing the Jewish national home and rescuing European Jewry. First, the sheer magnitude of the problem was staggering. In addition to Germany's 600,000 Jews, 7–8 million other Jews in Poland, Romania, Hungary, and the Baltic republics — the so-called zone of antisemitism — awaited rescue. Second, although seeking the total emigration of Jews from Germany, the Nazis, paradoxically, placed numerous difficulties in the path of would-be emigrants. Financial restrictions were especially problematic, since Jews leaving Germany (except for the few able to participate in Haavara) were effectively reduced to penury.[28] Finally, British ambivalence about rescue increased, especially as Arab opposition to *aliya* flared into violence, leading to efforts by the Palestine administration and the foreign office to slow *aliya*, even if that meant a more generous immigration policy in England proper. This policy had the disadvantage of relating only to German Jews, however, and thus did not represent a systematic effort to relieve Eastern European Jewish distress. In response, desperate Jews sought entry into *Eretz Israel*, even doing so illegally. *Aliya Bet* (the entry of Jews into the Jewish national home without the benefit of proper documentation), in turn, led to further British restrictions on *aliya*, which increased Jewish desperation and further *Aliya Bet*. By 1935 (certainly by 1936) a vicious cycle had been created relating to *aliya* that was not broken until 1948.[29]

Conditions only worsened after 1935. Almost all Zionist leaders issued clarion calls for increased *aliya* after the Nuremberg Laws were published, but conditions still militated against evacuation. For example, in November 1935 a proposal for an organized exodus was considered by the JAE. Concentrating on the approximately 73,000 Jews between the ages of seventeen and thirty-five, the plan was to finance the relocation of an initial 24,000 to *Eretz Israel* over three years, at a rate of 8,000 per anum. The plan assumed that over the same three years the other 48,000 would find refuge outside of *Eretz Israel*. Along with the unaided *aliya* of 6,000 Jews per year for the plan's duration, an escape was thus provided for 90,000 Jews, all those already in the aforementioned age range and all entering it between 1936 and 1939. "The alternative," wrote the author, "to some such scheme as this is a complete breakdown in the structural life of German Jewry, a stampede into neighboring countries . . . and a direct stimulus to the forces everywhere making for anti-semitism."[30] The plan was debated but not implemented by the JA for financial reasons. Yet, this plan remained well within the bounds of what may be labeled conventional in both the numbers quoted and the general approach used.

A radically different proposal not based on the conventional wisdom of the time was Ze'ev Jabotinsky's evacuation plan, designed to remove a minimum of 1.5 million Jews from Eastern Europe, primarily from Poland, and bring them to *Eretz Israel* over the course of ten years. The evacuation scheme was based on four premises: (1) Jews had to become a majority of the population of *Eretz Israel* in as short a time as possible; (2) only the creation of an "immigration regime" (a British administration willing to foster *aliya*) would make that goal possible; (3) reforms to the structure of the WZO and JA were necessary to further these goals; (4) the long-range goal of evacuation would be the creation of a sovereign Jewish state. Once completed, the evacuation plan would itself be only the first phase; the second phase would take place after a Jewish state came into being and would involve the repatriation of the entire diaspora.[31]

Jabotinsky's opponents utterly rejected his evaluation plan, condemning it as either unrealistic, unnecessary, or both. Yet some WZO leaders, including Ben-Gurion, adopted Jabotinsky's rhetoric for their own grand schemes. A seasoned veteran of the Second Aliya, Ben-Gurion was an activist and organizer in the Histadrut and Mapai. By 1935, he had risen through the ranks to become chairman of JAE, in effect, becoming the *Yishuv's* shadow prime minister. At the Nineteenth Zionist Congress, which met in Lucerne, Switzerland, from August 20 to September 4, 1935, Ben-Gurion spoke about mass *aliya* in terms that were similar to Jabotinsky's: a million Jews to be resettled in *Eretz Israel* as quickly as possible. Simultaneously, Ben-Gurion entered negotiations with the British government over the possibility of increasing *aliya* to a guaranteed rate of 50,000 per year. Neither of these initiatives bore fruit, thus proving the limits of the Rescue Aliya program in relation to the British.[32] Indeed, as a direct response to Ben-Gurion's request for greatly increased schedules, the British high commissioner for Palestine, Sir Arthur Wauchope, retorted, "If I grant a schedule of 20,000 certificates now, will you return in six months and request another 20,000?"[33]

Still, Ben-Gurion had put mass *aliya* on the Zionist agenda again. At a Mapai political committee meeting on March 30, 1936, Ben-Gurion evaluated the situation thus: "We face one burning question: the condition of Jews in Poland and Germany and the necessity of bringing them to *Eretz-Israel*.[34] Ben-Gurion repeated this evaluation in April:

> If we assume — and I believe this is the main assumption we must make under the present circumstances — that *Eretz-Israel* must provide an answer for Jewish suffering, if not the complete answer then at least the major portion of the answer that must be given immediately for the Jews of Germany, Poland, and other countries — then it is incumbent upon us to see our principle work in attaining the maximum [*aliya* rate] . . . barring this, not only will there be no escaping [European] Jewry's fate, but there will be no remedy for the fate of Zionism.[35]

As refuge after refuge closed, the European Jewish situation became increasingly perilous. Increasingly, Ber Borochov's statement to the effect that "we must liquidate the diaspora before the diaspora liquidates us," began to ring true even for Zionist minimalists such as Weizmann, who returned to the WZO presidency on Nahum Sokolow's death in 1935.

Boycott or Transfer?

Although the mainstream of Zionist policy in response to Nazism concentrated on *aliya*, there were two related issues of considerable import: One was the abortive Jewish effort to boycott Nazi Germany, based on the hope that economic warfare could bring down the regime or at least mute its antisemitic ardor. The second was the Ha'avara (transfer) agreement, which in part contradicted the boycott and sought to increase Jewish emigration by ensuring the export of German Jewish capital. Ha'avara was the most controversial aspect of the Rescue Aliya program and, not surprisingly, remains controversial to this day.[36]

The first urge felt by many Jewish groups, both Zionist and non-Zionist, was to establish a boycott against the Nazi regime. Spontaneous boycott groups sprang up in late February and early March 1933 as the first reports filtered out of Germany regarding individual attacks on Jews. The difficulty faced was not in declaring a boycott but in organizing it and building up sufficient support to make it work. The boycott needed to be united and to represent a clear majority of Jewish groups. It also required the support of consumers, Jewish and non-Jewish alike. Despite high hopes, however, the boycott had a limited impact, causing only minor ripples in the German economy. The boycott did not reflect a united Jewish movement against the Nazi regime. Most Jewish communal organizations, including the Board of Deputies of British Jews, the Anglo-Jewish Association, the Alliance Israélite Universelle, and the American Jewish Committee, opposed the idea of boycotting Germany altogether. Furthermore, the Ha'avara (transfer) agreement also undercut the boycott, at least in *Eretz Israel*.

Despite these impediments, an international Jewish boycott movement, of sorts, was organized. Revisionist Zionists and many like-minded groups, including such American Zionist opponents of Jabotinsky's as Rabbis Stephen S. Wise and Abba Hillel Silver, began to organize. They felt that at the very least Jewish honor demanded a boycott. Given what appeared to be the weak state of the German economy, still reeling from the catastrophic effects of the depression, a vigorously pursued boycott seemed to have a good chance of success. Some thought that the boycott, combined with diplomatic action, could result in the complete collapse of the Nazi regime or, at the minimum, in mitigating the Nazis' antisemitic campaign.[37]

But, the results were not what they hoped for. Until World War II the boycott movement in the United States (the most significant one, considering American Jewry's relative economic power compared to other Jewish communities) remained largely a sectarian issue, attracting only a small number of non-Jews sympathetic to the plight of German Jewry and failing to provide a sufficient incentive for American businesses to break their German connections. The boycott also aroused considerable criticism and suspicion. For example, an editorial in the highly influential *Christian Science Monitor*, dated April 4, 1933, stated: "Hate has begot hate, bitterness has rebounded in bitterness. Jews outside Germany have brought down trouble upon their fellows within the Reich." This editorial continued by noting that Jewish atrocity stories would be "accepted only by the gullible," and scoring the Jews' "commercial clannishness which often gets them into trouble." In the end, the *Christian Science Monitor* condemned as equally unjustified both the Nazi anti-Jewish boycott and Jewish efforts at self-defense.[38]

For their part, the revisionist Zionists continued to advocate a boycott until 1935, when they withdrew from the WZO. Thereafter, the boycott was quietly replaced by advocacy of mass evacuation (as already noted), a policy that inherently implied some form of capital transfer to be successful.[39]

Yet, it cannot be said unequivocally that a more forcefully pursued boycott would have succeeded. Jews simply did not possess sufficient economic power to adversely affect German exports in any country except, perhaps, Poland. Jews received almost no support for their boycott from consumers or retailers. Macy's, for example, stated its intention to comply with the boycott in principle, but only after all orders for German goods made before March 1, 1933, were completed.[40] It is too much to expect that a minority group composing a few percents of a population could radically affect imports to that country. During the 1930s, Germany appeared to be on the verge of economic collapse, and Nazi leaders played up this weakness. Since World War II, however, historians have concluded that the German economy, although seriously affected by the depression, was stronger than most contemporaries realized. It follows, then, that Nazi statements regarding the economy must be dismissed as propaganda designed to justify the severe economic measures that the Nazis applied. A few statistics may help to place this into context. Between 1932 and 1936, at the height of Nazi economic propaganda, Germany's gross national product grew by 43 percent (from RM58 billion to RM83 billion) while unemployment fell by 71 percent (from a height of 5.6 million to 1.6 million).

Economic growth was the order of the day in German exports as well. In 1929 Germany had a positive trade balance of only RM36 million. By 1932, at the height of the depression, Germany's positive trade balance grew to RM1.07 billion. While the balance of trade fell from that height to "only" RM667 million in 1933 (and then fell negative by RM284 million in 1934), by 1936 Germany's balance of trade was back in the black by RM55 million. The reason for this was that Germany's export economy was protected in the Balkans and Eastern Europe by a series of forty clearing agreements that replaced foreign currency payments (for German imports from the relevant countries) with barter (via the export of equivalent values in German goods).[41]

The Transfer Agreement represented a different approach to the Nazis. In essence, *Ha'avara* was a clearing agreement designed to ease restrictions on capital export for German Jews migrating to *Eretz Israel*. Originally negotiated as a private agreement between the German Zionist Federation and the Nazi regime, *Ha'avara* began operation in August 1933.[42]

Like any clearing agreement, *Ha'avara* operated on a simple set of principles. The prospective emigrant placed his assets in one of two blocked accounts (Sonderkonto I or Sonderkonto II) in either the M. M. Warburg Bank in Hamburg or the A. E. Wasserman Bank in Berlin, the two designated Paletina Truehandstelle (Paltreu) banks. In return he received a certificate of debenture from Ha'avara Ltd (Paltreu's branch in *Eretz Israel*) that entitled him and his family either to be reimbursed in goods and services or to receive the monetary equivalent of his deposit after the sale of imported German products once he arrived in *Eretz Israel*. In theory, the émigré retained a relatively large percentage of his capital. In practice, however, only about 25 percent was actually transferred. The main reason for this glaring discrepancy was Nazi export policy, specifically, the demand that transferred goods be sold at their full market value or higher, so as not to harm private German exporters in the Middle East. As a result, in order to transfer RM1 million (£P80,000), approximately twice that amount (in goods) had to be sold. German restrictions rapidly resulted in a policy of dumping goods, that is, of importing materials that were paid for by retailers who had little (if any) hope of recouping their expenses.

The inability to absorb such a large amount of goods led to financial limitations on *Ha'avara* in *Eretz Israel*. Only £P1,000 (RM12,500) was guaranteed to the *oleh*, although more than that amount was eventually paid out. Indeed, Paltreu was still making payments to investors as late as 1951. In spite of the financial difficulties

Ha'avara experienced, the agreement permitted the aliya of between 20,000 and 50,000 German Jews, meaning that it was one of the most successful of all Rescue Aliya programs.

Financial arrangements in *Eretz Israel* were overseen by the Anglo-Palestine Bank (APB), although it was not responsible for actual payments. The payments, based on a schedule of funds available divided by the number of transferees, were made by Ha'avara Ltd in Tel Aviv, organized for this purpose as a limited stock company. Jews living in Palestine could invest in Ha'avara Ltd, although the purpose of the company was neither to reap a profit nor to increase the stock value.[43]

As conditions in Eastern and Central Europe worsened the boycott became less viable as a defense, while Ha'avara — or some other form of clearing arrangement — increased in apparent value. Thus the Nineteenth Zionist Congress (held in 1935) overwhelmingly approved a JAE proposal to take over Ha'avara Ltd., which had until that time operated as a private agency representing no official Zionist body. Furthermore, crucial

Poster Expressing Opposition to the *Ha'avara* Agreement.
Courtesy of the Jabotinsky Institute Archive, Tel Aviv

support for *Ha'avara* came not only from the German Zionists, who directly benefited from the agreement, but from Polish, Romanian, and Hungarian Zionists who sought relief for millions of Jews trapped in an increasingly antisemitic environment.[44] Simultaneously, the JA engaged in a systematic effort to negotiate similar agreements with Eastern European governments as a means of rescuing as many Jews as possible with sufficient capital to permit significant building within the *Yishuv* and, as a direct result, greater possibilities of British-approved mass *aliya*.

The earliest Eastern European contacts were with the Czechs. Not unlike those that were made prior to the German *Ha'avara* agreement, they began as a series of unofficial contacts by Czech Zionists. The terms of this initial agreement differed from those of the *Ha'avara*. Instead of a deal involving goods, the transferee's money was deposited in a Prague bank and an equal sum in Palestine pounds was transferred to the Philip Mayer and Associates real estate firm in Haifa. Unlike the German *Ha'avara*, this agreement allowed the full sum to be exported. The transferred capital was then invested in land bought for Czech Jews. Thus the Czech *oleh* met the minimum financial requirements for the A-I certificate and also had a place in which to settle upon arrival. Regrettably, these talks hit a snag, although contacts continued. In September 1938 a final agreement was reached regarding the transfer of 2,500 Czech Jews with £P500,000 ($100,000) of their capital. The emigrants deposited their capital in a blocked account in the Narodni Banka (Czech national bank) and were reimbursed from the Bank of England as part of a £8 million ($40 million) loan that Britain had extended to Czechoslovakia.

After further negotiations, agreements were reached with the governments of Latvia and Lithuania. Signed on March 23, 1936, the Latvian agreement was a straight barter arrangement. In return for a guarantee that the *Yishuv* would import $500,000 in Latvian products, Latvian *olim* would be permitted to withdraw sufficient funds to qualify for a capitalist certificate. The Lithuanian agreement was identical and was signed on April 20, 1936. It is difficult to gauge the impact of these two agreements, since *aliya* from either Lithuania or Latvia never amounted to a significant proportion of any schedule.

Contacts with the Poles began in May 1936. Despite lengthy negotiations, which dragged on into 1938, no agreement was ever reached. Yitzhak Gruenbaum visited Poland on a number of occasions to try to get the talks moving, to no avail. The Poles, according to the Zionist negotiators, refused to negotiate in good faith, and the negotiations may be deemed a failure. Judging by the quantity of documents on the talks, failure to conclude an agreement cannot be blamed on the Zionist representatives.[45]

Ha'avara remained operational until World War II broke out on September 1, 1939. Throughout, the agreement was dogged by controversy that resonated throughout the entire Zionist movement. Yet, despite its controversial nature, *Ha'avara* played an important role in rescue aliya. From 1933 to 1936 it was a major means of encouraging emigration from Germany in a way that also improved economic conditions in *Eretz Israel* and thereby increased the labor schedule. Indeed, as the situation in Germany worsened (in 1938 and 1939), *Ha'avara* became the only practical means for Jewish emigration on a large scale. For that reason alone, the Zionists sought to continue the agreement and negotiated similar agreements with Eastern European countries.

The Schism

As already noted, an extremely unsettled relationship existed between the two major blocs within the Zionist movement, that is, between the WZO establishment dominated by Mapai and the revisionist Zionist movement, which acted mainly as an opposition group pressuring the WZO toward a more maximalist policy. In 1933, this schism boiled over into violence and the possibility of an inter-Zionist civil war threatened. The Zionists seemed to have only three further avenues: (1) continue the internal fighting until one side achieved total victory; (2) continue to fight fruitlessly until the entire Zionist project was consumed and collapsed; or (3) achieve a compromise between the two principle groups.[46]

Given the context, it is no surprise that both sides stepped back and tried to work out a compromise. Contacts between senior Histadrut leaders, including David Remez and Yitzhak Ben-Aharon, and senior ha-Zohar leaders in early 1934 culminated in an attempt by Pinhas Rutenberg to mediate a peace agreement. Rutenberg — now best remembered for his efforts to bring electricity to the *Yishuv* — was a highly respected figure in the WZO and was considered above partisan politics.[47] Rutenberg successfully convinced both sides that moderation and compromise were in the best interests of the WZO and the Jewish people. This, in turn, resulted in a series of face to face talks between Ben-Gurion and Jabotinsky in London in early October 1934.[48]

After some initial hesitation on both sides, frank talks were held. Ben-Gurion agreed with Jabotinsky that all issues should be aired, although he refused to consider compromising WZO discipline. On November 11, 1934, three agreements were concluded. The first governed ha-Zohar's relations with the WZO and JAE. This agreement also stipulated that when Betar's Circular no. 60 and its boycott of the KKL and KHY were rescinded, the *status quo ante* regarding Betar's right to receive immigrant certificates would be restored. The agreement did not declare either party guilty of any misdeeds, but established the grounds for peaceful coexistence. The second agreement related to internecine violence, calling on both sides to work together for the goals of Zionism. Importantly, this agreement was worded in such a way that neither Mapai nor ha-Zohar was blamed for the clashes. The third agreement dealt with relations between the Histadrut and the revisionists:

Ben-Gurion made important concessions with regard to Jabotinsky's proposal seeking arbitration, in return for concessions on strikebreaking and a hoped-for lessening of internecine violence.[49]

Despite initial skepticism, the agreements proved easier to reach than either side had expected. However, ratification was a far different matter. The revisionists, for example, bitterly examined and condemned the agreements but, in deference to Jabotinsky's impassioned defense of Zionist unity at the eighth ha-Zohar conference (Krakow, January 13, 1935) approved them. The revisionist position was ironic in that Jabotinsky was the one who had (because of the rebuffs in 1931 and 1933 over the Endzeil issue) maneuvered ha-Zohar into a position of potentially breaking Zionist unity. Indeed, the Calais compromise by which ha-Zohar remained in the WZO in 1933 had been strongly opposed by Jabotinsky.[50] Still, the agreements did contain important concessions for ha-Zohar and were approved.[51]

Matters were more complex from Mapai's perspective. Ben-Gurion, who had negotiated in good faith, did so as chairman of the JAE, not as the leader of Mapai. By a vote of 3 to 2 (with one abstention) the JAE approved the agreements.[52] However, it must be emphasized that the real issue was Mapai's relations with ha-Zohar. As a result, the JAE turned the issue over to Mapai. In turn, Mapai's executive debated the agreements and became deadlocked. Discrete majorities could be obtained for each individual agreement, but the totality of all three agreements obtained no such majority.[53] At further meetings on November 24 and December 20, the issue was removed from the party altogether and was transferred to the Histadrut. This posturing allowed a minority to impose its will on the majority. In turn, the Histadrut executive elected to place the agreements before a referendum of all members. On January 31, 1935, the Histadrut executive established the procedure for the referendum: All voting would be by secret ballot, although only those whose membership in the Histadrut dated before November 1934 would be allowed to vote; even then the format would be all or nothing. When Ben-Gurion proposed that the executive publish a letter supporting passage, he was defeated by a vote of 13 to 1. Thereafter he ceased all activity in the Histadrut executive pending the outcome of the referendum.[54]

Notwithstanding the stature of the agreement's proponents, the opponents appear to have had a better appreciation of the rank-and-file Histadrut members' views. Despite the fact that nearly 80 percent of the Histadrut's 67,570 members supported Mapai, the agreements failed during the referendum (held in early 1935) by nearly 3 to 2. Only 29,024 Histadrut members voted, with 16,474 nays and 11,522 ayes. A further 1,028 ballots were handed in empty or were otherwise disqualified.[55] Mapai's failure to ratify the agreements made further Zionist unity impossible. After a decade of trying to influence the WZO from within, Jabotinsky had accomplished little. More significantly, ha-Zohar was almost completely isolated within the WZO by 1935. At the Seventeenth World Zionist Congress (1931), Jabotinsky had torn up his delegate card in disgust after his resolution on the Endziel was shouted down. Now labor Zionists had vetoed an agreement negotiated in good faith. Rescuing the Zionist dream required decisive action; specifically, the forming of an organization dedicated to political activism and to advancing the true goal of Zionism — the creation of a Jewish state. Previously Jabotinsky's closest followers had strongly urged that he withdraw from the WZO and establish his own organization but he had been unwilling to condone such an attack on Zionist unity. Now, convinced that continuing the fight would not yield any positive results, he decided to withdraw in May 1935.

Jabotinsky's decision initiated the greatest schism in Zionism since the Uganda controversy. Following his lead, ha-Zohar and its subsidiary agencies (notably Betar) completely withdrew from the WZO. Only a small portion of the revisionist movement, associated with Meir Grossman and styled the Jewish State Party, remained within the WZO. The remainder of ha-Zohar joined Jabotinsky in the formation of Histadrut ha-Zionit ha-Hadasha (ha-Zach; the New Zionist Organization), which held its first congress in Vienna in September 1935, one month after the Nineteenth World Zionist Congress, which was held in Lucerne. In his keynote address, Jabotinsky denied creating a separatist organization and claimed to have created "the seedling for the legal development of the entire Jewish people." He believed that he was rescuing the ideals of Theodor Herzl and Max Nordau, which had been destroyed by Mapai.

Jabotinsky also briefly referred to conditions in Germany, noting the need to solve the totality of the Jewish problem, instead of concentrating on one specific aspect of it. He again offered his explanation of the crisis in Europe, saying that antisemitism was endemic and calling for evacuation as the only means of rescuing European Jewry. In essence, Jabotinsky accused the WZO leadership of missing the forest for the trees; as he observed, European antisemitism was of one cloth. Today's antisemitic outbreaks in Germany or Poland would be followed by tomorrow's in Hungary or Romania. Sooner or later, European Jewry, and the *Yishuv*, would be faced with the bitter necessity of rescuing as many Jews as possible. Therefore, Jabotinsky said, it was better to act now, while mass rescue was still feasible.

Far from ending the controversy with Mapai, the creation of ha-Zach intensified the climate of ideological disunity. Mapai election posters prepared for the Nineteenth World Zionist Congress emphasized Mapai's role in Rescue Aliya, which was a function of its control of the JAE and thus of immigration certificates. At the Congress, the revisionists were never mentioned directly, although Sokolow and Ben-Gurion referred to them in passing in their respective addresses.[56]

In the interim, ha-Zach proceeded to organize. The executive, with offices in London, Geneva, and Warsaw, was patterned on the JAE. Ten departments were established: (1) Presidium and Political Department (London), headed by Jabotinsky; (2) Finance (London), headed by Zinovy Tiomkin; (3) Organization and Passports (London), headed by Dr. Jacob

Damm; (4) Press and Propaganda and National Assembly (London), headed by Dr. Joseph B. Schechtman; (5) The Ten-Year Plan (London), headed by Dr. Stefan Klinger; (6) Representative at the League of Nations (Geneva), Dr. Harry Levy; (7) Legal Adviser (London), Samuel Landman; (8) Immigration, Training, and Economic Department (London), headed by Aron Kopelowicz; (9) Department for Organizing Orthodox Jews (Warsaw), headed by L. Ingster; (10) Passport Department for Poland (Warsaw), headed by Ingster. The Political Department also included an advisory committee consisting of Landman, Klinger, Shlomo Y. Jacobi, and M. S. Schwartzman.[57]

The next step in ha-Zach's plan to establish itself as a factor in Zionist affairs was to conduct a series of negotiations with the British and Poles regarding the Evacuation Plan, now renamed the Ten-Year Plan, as well as other Zionist issues. In September, Jabotinsky began negotiations with the Poles regarding the evacuation scheme. These negotiations created a stir among Polish Jews, with some circles accusing him of trying to sow discord within the Jewish community. From parallel Polish documentation recently published by Jerzy Tomaszewski, it is clear that sowing dissension and disunity within the Jewish community was indeed the Poles' purpose in these negotiations. Jabotinsky was not aware of this Polish trickery and undertook the negotiations in good faith.[58]

Further negotiations between ha-Zach leaders and leaders of the WZO and JAE implied that the rift was not yet permanent. In May 1936, for instance, Jabotinsky met with Chaim Weizmann, who had recently resumed the WZO presidency (after Sokolow's death). Jabotinsky directly set out his minimum demands for ha-Zach's return to the WZO, a theme he expounded on extensively during a speech in Vienna on November 20, 1936. Specifically, Jabotinsky demanded (1) adoption of a maximalist political demands, culminating in statehood; (2) adoption of the Ten-Year Plan as the basis for Zionist *aliya* policy; (3) expansion of Zionist alliances with Italy, Poland, and perhaps other states; and (4) convocation of a Jewish National Assembly elected on the basis of universal male suffrage that would supersede both the WZO and the NZO.

Jabotinsky's proposals did not become the basis for a united Zionist front. The JAE chose not to respond to his overture. The Arab revolt and the disagreement over *havlaga* (self-restraint) between the Hagana and Irgun Zvai Leumi reinforced the already existing centrifugal tendencies, meaning that substantive chances for compromise were very slim. In addition, the WZO preferred that the revisionists return to a reunited movement rather than create a new organization. Indeed, although further efforts at attaining unity were to be made in 1937, 1938, and 1939, outward unity was never really reestablished until the State of Israel came into being in 1948.[59]

The Arab Revolt

Of far greater significance than the revisionist schism for Zionist development during the 1930s were new rumblings of Arab discontent. The rioting in 1929 and the diplomatic maneuvers relating to the Passfield White Paper (summarized in the last chapter) had not satisfied either party to the imbroglio, but had left open the possibility that such violence might recur.[60] Minor incidents in the Bet Shean (Beisan) Valley and the Hefer Valley (Wadi al-Hawarith) between 1929 and 1933 proved how volatile conditions really were. In both cases the allocation of land to Arabs and Jews (worsened in the latter case by Jewish efforts to remove Arab squatters from land owned by the KKL) proved controversial, at best.[61] Increased Jewish immigration in 1933 led to brief rioting, mainly in the port cities of Jaffa and Haifa that was silenced by a quick British response.[62]

Previous British vacillation, however, had suggested to the Arabs that future rioting might lead to more concessions. As Arab frustration increased, especially after the massive increase in *aliya* in 1935 and 1936, the Palestinian Arab leadership returned to active opposition to Zionist goals in 1936. That April, a general strike was declared that had three overt goals: (1) establishment of a national (i.e., Arab) government in Palestine, (2) an unequivocal ban on *aliya*, and, (3) the termination and invalidation of all land sales to Jews.

The strike turned out to be a fiasco. With the exception of port workers in Haifa and Jaffa, Arab economic warfare had virtually no impact on the *Yishuv*. To the contrary, refusal by Arab workers to work on Jewish owned farms finally put to rest some of the conflicts over *Avoda Ivrit* that had been simmering since the Second Aliya. Even in the ports the strike had only a limited impact. Arab workers in Haifa were quickly replaced by Jews, while the Jaffa port was sidestepped by the construction of a port in Tel Aviv. On balance, therefore, the general strike failed and may actually have strengthened the *Yishuv* in the short run.[63]

The general strike's virtual collapse by October 1936 led to an almost immediate outbreak of violent rioting, encouraged by Italian and German radio propaganda, that soon flared into an all-out revolt. Statistics published by the JA in 1936 showed that there were, in the revolt's opening stages, 1,996 attacks on Jewish settlements or on individual Jews in cities and towns throughout *Eretz Israel*. Simultaneously, there were 795 attacks on British authorities (including police and military personnel), and 305 attacks by radicals (i.e., supporters of the Mufti) against moderate Arabs (including supporters of the Nashashibi clan). The statistics also broke down type of attack: 1,369 bombs were planted in 1936; 380 attacks with firearms, stones, or other weapons were directed at passengers on buses, railroads, and cars; and 895 cases of sabotage were reported against Jewish-owned property resulting in the destruction of over 200,000 trees and 17,000 dunams of crops. Finally, in 1936 alone (it bears recalling that these statistics were published at year's end and thus only reflect the first six or seven months of the rebellion) 82

Jews had been killed and 405 wounded.[64]

Furthermore, although the fighting slowed in 1937, the security situation deteriorated greatly in 1938. Unlike previously, the Arabs were better organized and better prepared, and they received both military and financial support from Arab groups (and countries) outside of Palestine/*Eretz Israel*.[65] The security forces turned the tide against the Arabs only in late 1938 and early 1939. Peace was restored, at a very high political price (as will be seen below) for the Zionists, just as European Jews (whose massive *aliya* was seen as the revolt's penultimate cause) encountered the greatest threat ever to their survival.

As in 1929, however, part of the problem was caused by the slow and inadequate British response to the general strike and the revolt. In April 1936, it should be noted, the British security forces in Palestine/*Eretz Israel* numbered less than 5,000: approximately 2,500 police, two infantry battalions (each with approximately 850 men), two Royal Air Force (RAF) light bomber squadrons, and two RAF field squadrons with armored cars. Initially, this force could receive only 900 reinforcements, drawn from the Trans-Jordan Frontier Force. Moreover, even when raised to the strength of an infantry division, the British forces were unequal to the task they faced.[66]

Consequently Jews (or rather the Jewish underground movements in *Eretz Israel*) had to accept increasing responsibility for their own defense, which further exacerbated existing conflicts between and within the two principle Jewish undergrounds, the Hagana and the Irgun Zvai Leumi (IZL). Despite ideological differences, both the Hagana and the IZL were initially committed to a policy of reactive defense. In other words, both limited their operation to the defensive sphere and both waited until Arab attackers initiated contact. This policy, known at the time as *havlaga* (self-restraint), was based on the perception among Zionist leaders that it was unwise to provide propaganda for the Arabs. Offensive operations, even when such operations could be characterized as "anticipatory self-defense," might be misinterpreted to place Zionist defenders on par with Arab attackers. By waiting to defend themselves, the Zionists hoped to protect their long term interests and to protect the Anglo-Zionist alliance.

By July 1936, However, the IZL leaders, especially Jabotinsky, were having second thoughts about *havlaga*. In their eyes a defensive posture was only a means to a strategic goal. If *havlaga* was viewed as a goal in itself, then it was (according to the IZL leadership) merely a cover for defeatism. Thereafter, the Irgun modified its policy to one of counterterror, hoping to convince the Arabs that continued assaults on Jews were futile, too costly, or both.[67]

In contrast, the Hagana officially remained committed to *havlaga* until 1939. As understood in the late 1930s, Havlaga did not necessarily mean that no reprisals would ever be carried out, although in theory, self-restraint did imply such a policy. Both the Hagana and Irgun left reprisals to the discretion of local commanders. On the night of August 17–18, 1936, for example, Hagana units in Jaffa retaliated for a hand grenade attack by Arabs on the Jaffa-Haifa railway in which a small Jewish child was killed and two women were wounded. The Hagana units, under the direct command of Eliahu Golomb, destroyed a number of Arab houses in the area of the attack, killing and wounding a large number of Arabs. Typically the Hagana undertook reprisals only in response to particularly unacceptable acts of Arab terror, and then only to prove that Jewish blood was not cheap.[68]

To be sure, Zionist leaders privately dreamed of massive revenge. One prominent example is found in a diary entry for July 11, 1935. Ben Gurion wrote that

I would welcome the destruction of Jaffa, port and city. This city which grew fat from Jewish immigration and settlement, deserves to be destroyed for wielding an ax at those who built it and made it prosper. If Jaffa went to hell, I would not count myself among the mourners.[69]

Nonetheless, the Hagana remained officially committed to a defensive policy throughout the Arab revolt.

Despite the overall defensive orientation, critical changes took place in Hagana doctrine during the Arab revolt. Additionally, a major reorganization during that same period virtually transformed the Hagana from a minor militia into an underground army.[70] Prior to the Arab revolt, the Hagana had been organized very loosely. Most Hagana members served only part-time, forming a cadre of members who lived in or close to the settlements they defended. The reorganization added a command superstructure: Battalions and brigades were organized, each still retaining a specific zone of operations, while the national command was restructured as a (shadow) general staff. The restructuring theme, known officially as Tochnit Avner (Plan Avner), also had a strategic element. For the first time, Hagana leaders considered the possibility that Jews would have to seize the initiative should the British withdraw from Palestine/*Eretz Israel*. Tochnit Avner also anticipated the Hagana's considerable enlargement to a force of 50,000 full-time personnel in addition to 17,000 regional volunteers.[71]

Tochnit Avner represented an important organizational step for the Hagana. The decision to defend settlements in an active way, to "move out beyond the fence" in Yitzhak Sadeh's words, was the parallel doctrinal change of this era. Henceforth, all available Hagana units were organized into so-called Plugot Shadeh (field companies, Fosh) or into mobile units, the so-called Nodedet (Nomad). Their mission was to intercept Arab attackers before they attacked. Ambush and preventive strikes on suspected terrorist bases were now the order of the day.[72]

The Arab revolt's ferocity forced the creation of an ad hoc alliance between British security forces, who were reluctant to aid the Jews directly but saw no other means to control the rebellion, and the Hagana. In particular, the need for mobile defense (since attacks could occur just about anywhere) led the British to legalize parts of the Hagana, mainly Fosh units and the Nodedet patrols, which were soon constituted as the Jewish Supernumerary Police (JSP, known in Hebrew as Notarim). The JSP performed vital defensive functions within the *Yishuv* and also suitably increased the Hagana's access to firearms (although that was not the British administration's goal in creating JSP). The 22,000 Notarim had approximately 8,000 rifles at their disposal, which more than doubled the Hagana's stock.[73] At the same time, the JSP created a potential problem for the *Yishuv*, specifically, the issue of loyalty. Were the Notarim primarily loyal to the *Yishuv*'s leaders or to the British? This problem, which became more pressing after the British cabinet published the White Paper of 1939, was never adequately solved. Still, on balance, it is clear that the JSP contributed greatly to strengthening the Hagana and consequently the entire *Yishuv*.[74]

The final step in the Hagana's conversion from a minor militia to a potential army came in May 1938. At that point, a junior officer named Orde Charles Wingate arrived in Palestine/*Eretz Israel* as an intelligence staff officer. Raised in a strictly religious and overwhelmingly patriotic home, Wingate was soon enamored with the *Yishuv*. Here, in the land of the Bible, Wingate suddenly felt at home. To one of his confidants, Wingate wrote:

> When I was at school, I was looked down on and made to feel that I was a failure and not wanted in the world. When I came to Palestine, I found a whole people who had been treated like that through scores of generations, and yet, at the end of it they were undefeated, were a great power in the world, building their country anew. I felt I belonged to such people.

Wingate's intense feelings were soon reciprocated. He was known throughout the *Yishuv* as *ha-Yedid* (the Friend). Furthermore, Wingate soon convinced his superiors to allow him to raise a special unit to combat the terrorists. By this point in the Arab revolt, the rebels' ability to operate in daytime had been severely curtailed. Night operations were a different matter. "The Arabs," Wingate wrote, "think the night

belongs to them. The British army huddles in its camps at night." But, he concluded, "we, the Jews, will teach the Arabs to fear the night more than they fear the day."[76] The unit Wingate raised, dubbed the Special Night Squads (SNS), set out to harry the rebels by adopting some of their tactics, most notably, by using offensive operations, mobility, and firepower to wrest the initiative from the Arab bands threatening the Jewish national home.

Wingate's operations were rapidly crowned with success. Indeed, by early 1939 the Arab Revolt was virtually broken, ground down by the Hagana, a force now fully committed to offensive mobile operations that carried the attack to the enemy, and by the overwhelming superiority of the British police and military. This moment of success, however, was crowned with personal tragedy for Wingate. His contacts with the WZO created considerable backlash with his superiors, who always mistrusted the Zionists. One went so far as to write that Wingate:

> is a good soldier, but so far as Palestine is concerned, he is a security risk. He cannot be trusted. He puts the interests of the Jews before those of his own country. He should not be allowed in Palestine again.[77]

In early May 1939, the SNS was disbanded and Wingate was transferred back to England, against his will. Heartbroken, Wingate vowed to return to complete his mission of building a Jewish army and a Jewish state. In his farewell speech he even proclaimed a readiness to return to *Eretz Israel* as a refugee. But, his dream never came true. After service in Ethiopia, and Burma, Wingate was killed when his airplane crashed in the Burmese jungle in 1944.[78]

Yet Wingate's self-appointed mission was a success. By 1939, the groundwork had been laid for the Hagana to flower from a small militia to a virtual army almost ready to accept responsibility for the defense of the Jewish national home. Though not yet powerful, the *Yishuv* was no longer completely powerless. In ten years, the force Wingate helped to mold would decisively defeat seven invading Arab powers.

The Partition Plan

Virtually from the outset of the revolt, the British government sought a nonmilitary means of ending the dispute. As with previous outbreaks, the government eventually decided to send a royal commission to investigate conditions and to propose a solution that would be equitable for all parties. In the short term, the British sought a number of schemes, none successful, to break the impasse. Of these, two were critical: a renewed proposal for a legislative council and a proposal regarding the cantonization of Palestine/*Eretz Israel*.

The legislative council had originally been mooted in 1922 and derived its authority from the Mandate's terms. The League of Nations had, in the mandates, demanded that ruling powers create so-called self-ruling institutions on behalf of the indigenous population in order to prepare them for eventual independence. The original British proposal for a legislative council foundered on Arab opposition to any council that would include Jews, even though the latter would have had only minority representation. By 1935, the British high commissioner, General Sir Arthur Wauchope, was once again proposing a legislative council, hoping that its creation would blunt Arab opposition to the Mandate and head off any further violence. The Arab revolt's outbreak lent a new sense of urgency to this work, but, Arab intransigence (since the Jews now demanded parity on the council) once again ensured its defeat.[79]

Similarly stillborn was a proposal to convert the mandate into a Swiss-style cantonal government. As proposed by Sir Archer Cust, the assistant district commissioner for Nazareth, Palestine/*Eretz Israel* would be divided into two cantons, one Jewish and one Arab. The cantons would obtain considerable autonomy and would control such controversial issues as immigration and land purchase. The British would continue to control the "federal" government, providing a bridge for contacts

between the Arab and Jewish communities should they desire to reach a peaceful settlement of outstanding differences. While offering the appearance of workability, the plan was never realistic. It did not grant either Arabs or Jews enough of what they wanted — total control over immigration — and required a degree of mutual cooperation that was not likely under the circumstances. Far from acting as a bridge between the two communities, the British would most likely have had to act as a barricade to prevent simmering hostilities from flaring into all-out war.[80]

Efforts by Brit Shalom, the liberal Zionist group dedicated to creating a binational (Jewish-Arab) state, to negotiate a *quid pro quo* also proved abortive. Although Brit Shalom's members proved more than willing to concede on *aliya* and Jewish land purchase — concessions that seriously cast into doubt the propriety of using the term Zionist in conjunction with Brit Shalom — no Arabs stepped forward to negotiate.[81] That left only one recourse: the Palestine Royal Commission headed by Lord Peel.

The Peel Commission's formation, and particularly its wide scope of investigation, worried many of the Zionist leaders, Ben-Gurion in particular. But, after careful consideration the JAE recognized that nonparticipation could only hurt the *Yishuv*. In turn, three different approaches to the commission were considered: one that would exclusively defend the *Yishuv* against Arab charges; one that would exclusively air Jewish complaints; or one that would adopt some elements of both approaches and demand that the British fulfill the terms of the Mandate.

In the end, the JAE adopted the third position. Ben-Gurion agreed that, despite the Zionist commitment to the Mandate, the League of Nations document should "neither be seen as the basis nor the source of Jewish rights in *Eretz-Israel*." In his estimation, Jewish rights had three bases, and the acceptance of all of them was vital to the Jewish future: the historical connection of Jews with the land; Jewish suffering in the diaspora; and the socioeconomic realities of the dynamic *Yishuv*.[82]

The JAE also took the precaution of preparing considerable printed material on the Mandate, the *Yishuv*, and the needs of European Jewry for the commissioners. In addition, Weizmann prepared an extensive pamphlet version of his opening remarks, which was published by the WZO under the title *The Jewish People and Palestine*. Weizmann emphasized the refugee aspect of the Jewish problem in the memorandum he wrote on behalf of the JAE for the commission. For him, homelessness was the principal Jewish problem. European Jews, he wrote, were "doomed to be pent up in places where they are not wanted, and for whom the world is divided into places where they cannot live in peace, and places into which they cannot enter." The suffering of German Jewry was not the primary threat facing Jewry. "The German tragedy," wrote Weizmann, "is of manageable proportions, and moreover, the German Jews are stronger; they can resist the onslaught much better." Of far more pressing importance was the fate of Eastern European and especially Polish Jewry. Though suffering from antisemitism and intense economic distress, the Polish Jews were unable to find a safe haven. For Weizmann, the only solution was the creation of a Jewish national home — the long-term goal of Zionism and the sole purpose of both the Balfour Declaration and the Mandate.

Such an entity did not have to be a sovereign state, although the fulfillment of Zionist goals did require a Jewish majority in Palestine. But four practical problems stood in the path of fulfillment: immigration, land, labor, and self-government. Regarding immigration, Weizmann noted that the Zionists had accepted the principle of economic absorptive capacity, even though it was disproportionate to the needs of the Jewish masses. Basically, such a concept was inconsistent with the idea of a national home, since a home "is a place to which everyone may return freely." Even though the Arab revolt had changed the atmosphere in Palestine, at least from the British perspective, Weizmann concluded his

memorandum by demanding that the British fulfill all their promises and obligations.[83]

In his direct testimony at the commission, during the eighth public session, held on November 25, 1936, Weizmann continued to testify on three inter-related themes. First, that the Jewish problem could not be solved by the Jews themselves but required the participation of the entire world. According to Weizmann, *Eretz Israel* would play the decisive role in any long term solution to Jewry's needs. Second, against claims of overpopulation Weizmann argued that no one really knew what population could actually be absorbed. He also stated that all the key documents relating to Britain's commitments toward the Jewish national home referred to Trans-Jordan, which, he maintained, should be opened for Jewish colonization but had been closed to the Jews since 1922. On the other hand, Weizmann accepted the premise of economic absorptive capacity as a determinant of yearly *aliya* rates, but only if it was used as an objective and fair criterion.

After Weizmann, a virtual panoply of JAE figures testified: Moshe Shertok, Werner D. Senator, Arthur Ruppin, Eliyahu Epstein, and Maurice Hexter, among others. Further testimony by the leaders of the Va'ad Leumi, the Histadrut, and the JA continued to hammer home the basic Zionist contention that the Mandate should be maintained and that the *Yishuv* should be granted the fullest possible opportunity to continue growing. Leonard Stein testified on the legal ramifications of the Balfour Declaration and the Mandate, concluding: "The administration is to do something positive. That positive thing is to facilitate Jewish immigration under suitable conditions."

Ben-Gurion, who testified during the forty-ninth public session in Jerusalem on January 7, 1937, ended the JA's presentation. Declaring the Bible to be Jewry's mandate, he strongly defended the Jewish people's historical right to *Eretz Israel*. In his public testimony, Ben-Gurion supported the Mandate's continuation and campaigned against Jewish statehood, saying that Zionists did not wish to be placed in a position where they could dominate and then persecute the Arabs. The implication of Ben-Gurion's public testimony was much the same as that of other Zionist leaders. Ben-Gurion's private testimony, however, supported an almost contradictory position: that the Jews would accept termination of the Mandate and the creation of a sovereign Jewish state. In his in camera testimony, Ben-Gurion also called for schedules sufficiently large to permit the aliya of 4 million Jews in twenty years.

Throughout his testimony, both public and private, Ben-Gurion seems to have attempted to manipulate the commission. He sought to maneuver it into making an offer for which he could claim responsibility if it proved popular among Jews or that he could repudiate if it proved unpopular. The commission members evidently saw through Ben-Gurion's hairsplitting, however, and negatively contrasted his testimony to Weizmann's. Yet in the end they did exactly what Ben-Gurion hoped they would, offering the Jews sovereignty in a partitioned Palestine/*Eretz Israel*. The paradox of Ben-Gurion's arguing for one set of goals publicly while hoping for a completely different outcome privately arose from his fear that the British would reject any call for sovereignty that originated with the Zionists and the corollary, that the result of such rejection would inevitably be an end to *aliya*. This would result in the erosion and ultimate evaporation of Zionism, along with the *Yishuv*'s withering. Recognizing that after going through the motions of hearing Jewish and Arab testimony, the British government would act in accordance with its own strategic interests, Ben-Gurion hoped that Arab rejection of parity with Jews and the impracticality of cantonization would lead the British to support the Zionist position. He hoped that ultimately the British would offer sovereignty to the Jews as a way to cement their strategic position in the Middle East.

For the time being, only Jabotinsky publicly contemplated a sovereign Jewish state. True to his long-held position, Jabotinsky demanded the creation of a sovereign, autonomous Jewish state on both sides of the Jordan River. He left room for

negotiations with the British, however, over the exact extent of sovereignty beyond "some indispensable amount of self-government in inner affairs." Jabotinsky also denied that Jewish sovereignty would displace Arabs. He argued that there was ample room in the whole of *Eretz Israel* for as many as 2 million Arabs, in addition to millions of Jews. Jabotinsky also spoke explicitly of the pressing need for an immediate rescue of European Jewry. During his testimony, he spoke at length about the rapidly deteriorating situation in the diaspora and admitted, that in his view, attaining sovereignty and a Jewish majority in Palestine would be only the beginning:

I am going to make a "terrible" confession. Our demand for a Jewish majority is not our maximum; it is our minimum; it is just an inevitable stage if only we are allowed to go on salvaging our people. The point when the Jews will reach in that country a majority will not be the point of saturation yet, because with 1,000,000 more Jews in Palestine today you could already have a Jewish majority, but there are certainly 3,000,000 or 4,000,000 in the East who are virtually knocking at the door asking for admission — i.e. for salvation.

Although he, like the labor Zionists, spoke in terms of "salvation," in Jabotinsky's view this "humanitarian" element distinguished him from Spiritual Zionists. He defined the view of the Spiritual Zionists "as the desire for self-expression, the rebuilding of a Hebrew culture, or creating some 'model community of which the Jewish people could be proud.'" Although publicly respectful of this position, Jabotinsky utterly rejected it, seeing Spiritual Zionism as a luxury under contemporary conditions.

On the issue of Zionist-Arab relations, Jabotinsky remained similarly unequivocal. He claimed, to the apparent chagrin of the commission members, that the lack of inter-communal peace was Britain's fault. Jabotinsky explained that by prevaricating in their support for Zionist goals that the British government had accepted as legitimate, the government had inculcated in the minds of the Arabs a belief that British support for Zionism was shallow and that pro-Zionist declarations or actions were undertaken under duress. The Arabs' past outbursts had been rewarded, rather than punished, and had culminated in the revolt, necessitating the creation of the Peel Commission. To regain peace and to guarantee a peaceful future, Jabotinsky concluded, the British had to make their support for the legitimate goals of Jewry abundantly clear via a new policy that would encourage aliya and grant sovereignty to the Jewish national home.[84] With testimony completed, the commission adjourned and began to prepare its report.

In the interim, fighting continued with only minor abatements. Shortly after the Peel Commission adjourned, Fawzi al-Kaukji, a charismatic Arab nationalist leader in Syria, led his so-called Arab Liberation Army into Palestine/*Eretz-Israel*. Kaukji's guerillas undertook two major assaults, on Tel Josef and Tirat Zvi, that were beaten off with great difficulty. Zionist fears grew when reports circulated that the Mufti of Jerusalem, Haj Amin al-Huseini, was attempting to recruit a pan-Arab army to destroy the *Yishuv* once and for all.[85]

When the Peel Commission finally issued its report on June 22, 1937, the *Yishuv* was beleaguered, demoralized, and pessimistic. The report concluded that nothing short of separation could prevent further outbreaks of Arab-Jewish violence. Therefore, the report called for partition, with the mandated territory to be divided into three zones. The Jewish state would include Palestine/*Eretz Israel*'s coastal plain from a point some twenty-five kilometers south of Rehovot north to the border of French-controlled Syria-Lebanon. This zone, however, would include neither Jaffa nor a ten-kilometer passage representing the British zone to Jerusalem. In the north, the Jewish State would include the entire Emek region except for Beisan. The fate of territory on the eastern bank of the Jordan River north of the Sea of Galilee was not clearly established. In all, the Jews received less than one-third of the territory west of the

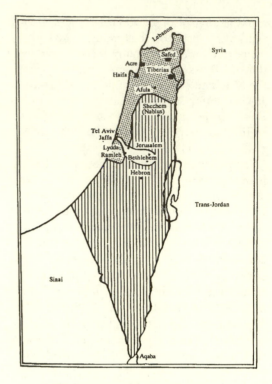

The Peel Partition Plan Map.
Palestine Royal Commission, Report, 1937
(London: His Majesty's Stationary Office, 1937)

Jordan, with the Arabs and British receiving more than two-thirds. All territories not included in the Jewish State and not retained by the British were planned to be part of the Arab state.[86]

Two Zionist parties immediately declared themselves unalterably opposed to partition: Mizrachi and ha-Zach. Mizrachi's objections were based on religious considerations: The land of the divine covenant with the Jewish people could not be divided. Ha-Zach's opposition was based on fear that the territory promised to the Jews would be insufficient to absorb the millions of Jews in dire need of rescue and out of a sense that Jewish national rights were being infringed. *Eretz Israel* was Jewry's ancestral home and could not be bartered for some chimerical state.[87]

Jabotinsky, in opposing the partition plan, repeated the gist of his testimony at the Peel Commission's hearings. He also added a new dimension, that the creation of the proposed Jewish State would increase antisemitic agitation throughout Eastern Europe, since antisemites would expect Jews to evacuate immediately despite insufficient space there for the millions of Jews rendered homeless. Having created a new "Pale of Settlement," albeit with the veneer of Jewish sovereignty, partition could make the Jewish world as a whole less, rather than more, secure.

As an alternative, Jabotinsky proposed the evacuation scheme he had first put forth in 1935, now named the "Ten-Year Plan." This variant plan contained five substantive components: maintenance of the Mandate, with minor adjustments; opening Trans-Jordan to Jewish settlement; a Jewish national loan campaign to reclaim cultivatable but unused lands on both banks of the Jordan River; creation of an immigration regime to absorb 150,000 Jews per year; and, sovereignty after ten years, when a Jewish majority existed.[88]

Positions within the WZO, except for Mizrachi's already noted inalterable opposition to partition in any form, were not quite as simple. Ben-Gurion, for example, declaimed that "in a world without evil" Jews would have to reject partition; in the real world, however, the WZO and JAE had little choice but to accept whatever could be obtained in the short run in order to guarantee *aliya* in both the short and long terms.[89]

The Zionists' accumulated fears and hopes, as well as their need to discuss the few remaining alternatives, came to the fore at the Twentieth Zionist Congress, held in Zurich August 3–16, 1937. Weizmann opened the session with a keynote address that summarized recent events in *Eretz Israel* and in Central and Eastern Europe. He finished his preoration by noting that only a limited time remained to act, since the Palestine administration had already announced the establishment of a "political maximum" capping Jewish immigration at 8,000 per year (one-third less than proposed by the Peel Commission) for the duration of the mandate.[90]

Weizmann followed with a strong speech on behalf of partition delivered on August 4, entitled, "Faith in the Future of the Jewish Nation."[91] In turn, Ben-Gurion and Shertok both spoke strongly on behalf of the partition plan. Ben-Gurion's speech, which was perceptive considering it was delivered more than a year before the Munich Conference and the Anglo-French sellout of Czechoslovakia, predicted a new world war. Moreover, Ben-Gurion warned his audience of the dire consequences that Zionism and the *Yishuv* would face if the present opportunity was missed. The phrase Ben-Gurion used, "international complications," also led him to fear for the diaspora, and he predicted the possible loss of contact with other Jewish communities, paralleling the breakdown of communications with the Jews in the Soviet Union. In view of increasing Arab strength, Ben-Gurion said, Jews had to act immediately and forcefully. Ben-Gurion did not state that partition was good but that it was necessary. Even he realized that the borders of the new state would not be adequate for the numbers of Jews seeking immigration. He explicitly rejected the rump state that the British were offering, but he hoped to negotiate for larger borders after the principles of partition and Jewish sovereignty were accepted. Moreover, Ben-Gurion was attracted to the idea of transferring the Arab population living in the area of the Jewish state to the Arab state. Only a sovereign Jewish state, in his view, could fulfill the need for mass *aliya*.

In opposition to the "yeasayers," two Zionists stood out at the Congress as "naysayers": Menahem M. Ussishkin and Berl Katznelson. Their significance increases upon recollection that the revisionists did not attend the congress at all. Contrasting Weizmann's apparent eagerness to accept the partition plan with the JAE's unwillingness to even consider the Endziel resolution at the Eighteenth Zionist Congress in 1933, Ussishkin flatly rejected partition. Ussishkin then laid out his reasons for rejecting the Peel plan, first, because he did not trust the British, and second, because partition would destroy the Zionist movement. The British, he claimed, "have placed two choices before us: either to strangle our movement or to tear our homeland to shreds. And [we have] the task of advising them as to which we prefer: strangulation or dismemberment."

Katznelson spoke in a similar vein, emphasizing the negative impact that Zionist acceptance of partition would have on the moral and ideological foundations of Zionism. Partition meant the surrender of Zionist values and, more significantly, the mortgaging of Jewry's future for a mirage. He saw partition as denying the essence of Jewish rights in *Eretz Israel*, contradicting both the Mandate and Ben-Gurion's assertion that the Bible, and not the Mandate or the Balfour Declaration, was the basis for Jewish rights.[92]

Leery about partition's implications but surely afraid that time was running out for the rescue of European Jewry, a majority of delegates (300 to 158) voted to approve the partition resolution proposed by Weizmann. The resolution granted authority to the WZO and JAE to negotiate a partition plan that would provide the Jewish State adequate borders for the immense tasks ahead. But this was not to be and the next two years would witness steadily eroding conditions in both Europe and *Eretz Israel*.[93]

Relations at a Breaking Point

As the partition debate in the WZO reached its crescendo, conditions worsened in Europe. By the time the Zionists had finally agreed to pursue the partition scheme despite the unacceptable borders offered by the Peel Commission, not only was German Jewry suffering under the Nazis' oppressive heel, but conditions in Hungary, Romania, and Poland had deteriorated as well. Poland may be used as a particularly glaring example. The year 1937 saw the severe deterioration of Jewish economic conditions and political fortunes. Pogroms returned as a factor in Polish-Jewish relations, representing a more active approach adopted by antisemitic groups enboldened by the Nazi example. Then too Polish legislation undercut the very foundations for Jewish communal life. This was most obvious in the anti-*Shechita* bill passed in 1937 but may also be seen in the various

items of economic legislation — attempts by government to create monopolies in industries identified with Jews — passed between 1935 and 1939. In this regard, it is worth noting the data presented in a 1936 study by the World Jewish Congress which found that barely 25 percent of Polish Jews could be considered economically stable. A similar number, the study averred, could be stabilized with considerable aid from outside Poland (i.e., by American Jewish philanthropy). For the remainder, conditions were virtually hopeless.[94] Even the Poles recognized what they were doing. One Polish statesman characterized antisemitism as "a necessary cruelty" — necessary to force a solution to the problem of Poland's surplus (Jewish) population.[95]

In response, Zionists sought to redouble their efforts to obtain a Jewish state, thereby hoping to obtain control of unfettered *aliya*. While partition was still on the agenda, the British had imposed a so-called political maximum on *aliya* that would remain in place until the mandate's expected termination. The political maximum must be understood in no uncertain terms. This was a definite departure from the immigration system that had existed since 1922 and had used Palestine/*Eretz Israel's* presumed economic absorptive capacity as the main criterion for establishing the schedule. From the time the Peel Commission published its report, economic absorptive capacity was no longer used as a criterion. Now, *aliya* was set on the basis of the number of *olim* considered unlikely to overly upset the Arabs while still keeping the WZO happy.[96]

As if these trends were not bad enough, the British were having second thoughts about partition. In particular, contacts with the independent Arab countries — Egypt, Iraq, and Saudi Arabia — led the newly installed Chamberlain cabinet to question partition's impact on Imperial interests in the Middle East. When combined with continuing fears for the safety of the Suez Canal, which appeared to be under imminent Italian threat (from Libya and from newly-occupied Ethiopia), the fear of an Arab-Italian-German axis considerably cooled British politicians to the wisdom of partition.[97] Appreciating that the Jews would be severely disappointed if partition was withdrawn, the British nonetheless recognized that Jews would never side with Great Britain's enemies, a reality that led, in the long run, to a British appreciation of Jewry's precarious — and weak — international position.[98] One British official went so far as to advocate creating a Jewish State "anywhere except in Palestine."[99]

The Zionists fought a valiant rearguard action to maintain partition. As during the Passfield White Paper crisis (detailed in Chapter 7), they sought to utilize every possible forum to keep the pressure on the cabinet to fulfill its promises. The sympathetic attitude of Colonial Secretary William Ormsby-Gore helped, but ultimately the Zionist were fighting a losing battle.[100] On December 8, 1937, the cabinet debated partition; two weeks later announced its intention to place the partition plan on temporary hold while studying the matter further.[108] In presenting the Zionist case, Weizmann used four interrelated themes: first, that the cabinet would embarrass itself and tarnish England's good name if it reneged on a promise; second, that violence would increase, not decrease, if the cabinet showed that it could be cowed by Arab terror; third, that Jewish need was great and that Jewish rights could not be totally ignored in this case; and, fourth, that since a general European war was not imminent, fears for Britain's strategic situation in the Middle East were greatly exaggerated.[102]

Again, it must be emphasized that Zionist diplomacy could not stem the tide of British reorientation: overruling his own misgivings, Colonial Secretary Ormsby-Gore announced on January 4, 1938, that the cabinet had decided to send a new commission to Palestine/*Eretz Israel* to study the feasibility of partition. This commission, officially known as the Palestine Partition Commission, was better known as the Woodhead Commission; Zionists derisively nicknamed it the "Repeal Commission." Ormsby-Gore charged the Woodhead Commission with considering the likelihood of a successful partition, drawing borders for the Jewish

and Arab states, and creating the means by which Britain could fulfill its obligations under the terms of the Mandate.

Unlike the Peel Commission, the Woodhead Commission held all its hearings in private, with a total of fifty-five sessions, including nine that took place in London. The first testimony came from the Palestine administration, in the form of a memorandum by outgoing High Commissioner Wauchope. Setting out his reservations about the Peel plan, Wauchope offered alternative borders for a more limited Jewish State. His proposal aroused strong indignation within Zionist circles. Weizmann, for example, accused Wauchope of insensitivity to Jewish needs.

The first to give Zionist testimony to the commission was Weizmann, who testified for three hours. Among other subjects, he touched on two primary themes: first, that support for Zionism weakened Britain's position in the Middle East, a mistaken notion that Weizmann sought to contradict, and, second, that Eretz Israel represented Jewry's only hope for the future, a line of analysis he hoped would convince the commission members. "The awesome responsibility to decide the question of life or death for the Jewish people has fallen upon you," Weizmann told the commission. Following Weizmann, the other members of the JAE testified, most of them during a single five-hour session on June 10. Ben-Gurion and Shertok closed the JA case, calling for British endorsement of mass Jewish immigration. The JA delegation was followed by Jewish religious figures (Zionist and non-Zionist) and a delegation from ha-Zach, headed by Benjamin Akzin. All of them attacked partition on one ground or another but did not encounter any substantial British encouragement for mass *aliya*.

Its work in Palestine/*Eretz Israel* done, the Woodhead Commission returned to London. There it heard testimony from British leaders on both sides of the issue, took further evidence from members of the Palestine administration, and then adjourned to consider its findings.[103]

Not surprisingly, the Woodhead Commission found that partition was not feasible, since no borders could be drawn that would be totally acceptable to Jews and Arabs. The latter in particular had made their opposition to any Jewish state very clear while the need for massive population transfers — of Arabs from the proposed Jewish state and of Jews from the proposed Arab state — were seen as a perscription for war. Despite reservations, therefore, the Woodhead Commission counseled against partition. The commission, however, failed to offer an alternative to partition, meaning that the *status quo* would remain.[104]

For Zionists, the Woodhead Commission Report was a doubly tragic turn of events: not only had the British Cabinet undone the partition plan, but the evening after the Woodhead Commission Report was issued witnessed the mass anti-Jewish pogram in Germany that has since been dubbed *Kristallnacht*.[105] Jewish desperation had reached a new crescendo, but the British would not budge. Twelve days after *Kristallnacht*, Bernard Joseph cabled Moshe Shertok to the effect that:

> Apparently, H.M.G. [sic] only concerned [to] please [the] Arabs to . . . We evidently have nothing [to] hope for from negotiations . . . And must exert what little influence we can through public opinion . . . We have nothing to lose by adopting [a more] aggressive attitude.[106]

Joseph's prognosis proved correct. Despite the great Jewish need of the hour, Rescue Aliya had virtually collapsed by the autumn of 1938. European Jewry's future lay in the hands of individuals who, despite their possible good intentions, were unable to find even a single alternative haven and had virtually precluded Palestine/*Eretz Israel* as a Jewish national home.[107] All that remained was for the British government to publicly announce its new policy.

The Eleventh Hour

Little changed in *Eretz Israel* in the aftermath of the Woodhead Commission, at least on the surface. The Mandate continued in operation and, in theory, Jewish rights to immigrate were maintained; in reality, of course, everything had changed. The political maximum *aliya* policy, enacted as a temporary measure in late 1937, now became permanent policy (until changed again in 1939). In addition, the British instituted a blockade of Palestine/*Eretz Israel*'s territorial waters. This was, it might be useful to recall, the only blockade in history undertaken during peacetime by a country over a coastal territory under its own control. This blockade served one purpose only: to prevent Jewish illegal immigration (*Aliya Bet*), which had grown immeasurably as legal immigration became increasingly difficult.

As already noted, *Aliya Bet* had begun in the early 1930s and had increased as European Jews became more desperate to flee at a time when legal *aliya* was decreasing. In 1934, ha-Zohar had founded an organization (as an autonomous section of the IZL) called Af-Al-Pi (Despite All) to organize a mass (illegal) exodus. The organization had had some striking successes, leading proponents of *aliya* at any cost within Mapai and he-Halutz to follow suit. Initially, the JAE was inalterably opposed to Aliya Bet, since illegal Jewish acts hurt relations with the British. The JAE remained convinced of this policy until 1937; at that point the pressure to assist immigration no matter what became too strong and the Hagana was ordered to create its own agency to foster illegal immigration, known as the Mossad le-Aliya Bet (Agency for Illegal Immigration). Although it began its life as a minor agency, the Mossad soon grew in importance and size, peaking in its role as the *Yishuv*'s main immigration service during the years after World War II. Willingness to undertake the arduous journey reflected Jewish desperation to escape from Europe. Although *Aliya Bet* had been a marginal factor in Zionist politics during the early 1930s, by 1937 and 1938, it had become central to continued plans from rescue from Europe.[108]

Under the prevailing circumstances, the British cabinet attempted one last gesture designed to achieve a mutually acceptable agreement between Jews and Arabs. That effort resumed in convening the London Conference of 1939 that took place in the St. James Palace. The conference was designed as a roundtable with Jewish and Arab representatives invited to attend. When added to the cabinet members and ambassadors of Iraq, Egypt, Saudi Arabia, and Trans-Jordan, the assembly was august indeed. In reality, the conference collapsed even before the first meeting was held, when the Arab delegates refused to sit in the same room with the Jews. For the duration of the conference the British acted as intermediaries, a process that led to greater intransigence (especially on the Arab side).[109] After a month of preparation, the JAE delegation arrived in London, and on February 7, 1939, the talks began. The conference opened with speeches by Prime Minister Neville Chamberlain, Weizmann, Va'ad Leumi president Yitzhak Ben-Zvi, Wise, and Lord Reading. Weizmann presented the Jewish case on February 8, citing Jewish rights in Palestine as recognized by the Balfour Declaration and the Mandate, and stressing Jewry's urgent need for a safe haven. Colonial Secretary Malcolm MacDonald responded, expressing "a great deal of sympathy with the Jewish people" but, nevertheless, exclusively presenting the Arab case. Ben-Gurion spoke next, saying that he did not regard the problem "as a case between Arabs and Jews: it was a case between the Jews and the world." He referred repeatedly to Jewish homelessness and suffering, concluding that the Jews' return to Palestine was "a restitution of the civilized world for 2,000 years of persecution." MacDonald interjected that he would "not admit for one minute that 16 million Jews had the right to go back to Palestine." To this, the JA leaders responded that they did not anticipate the immigration of all Jews but that they considered consultation with diaspora Jewry on issues affecting the Jewish national home at least as legitimate as the interference in Palestine/*Eretz Israel*'s affairs by neighboring Arab states.

Sessions held on February 13–15 and February 17–20 repeated this pattern. At every meeting the British supported the Arab position on all issues, especially immigration. Throughout, the British offered no concessions; in effect, they operated as intermediaries for the Arab delegation that refused to meet with the Jewish leaders. On February 16, the JA delegation decided to make one last effort to reach an agreement. The Zionists proposed direct negotiations with the Arab delegation on all issues except immigration. Again, the Arabs refused to sit with the Jewish delegation. As a result, the conference rapidly approached a deadlock.[110]

Further sessions, mostly of an informal nature reinforced the impression of a deadlock. Meetings in early March made it clear that government had, more or less, already decided on the policy it intended to pursue and was simply seeking the imprint of WZO or JAE acquiesence to this policy. In recognition of that reality, the JAE delegates threatened to withdraw from the conference already in late Fegruary, with the conference collapsing altogether by the end of March.[111] Continuing contacts between the WZO leadership and the British achieved little; all that remained was for the government to announce its new policy publicly.[112]

The White Paper

That the cabinet's awaited policy statement would be inimical to Zionist interests was expected during the London conference. Steadily worsening conditions in Europe further worried the Zionist leaders. *Eretz Israel* was needed as a haven now more than ever. The Zionist appreciation of danger was by no means exaggerated. When the cabinet first discussed the failure of the London conference on March 8, 1939, it was obvious that the mandatory government would have to impose a policy that suited its interests.[113] Further cabinet meetings refined the government's decision to impose a policy, the basic premise being that neither Jews nor Arabs would be totally satisfied but that sufficient openings should be left for both to keep them quiet.

As finally refined in April, the new British

policy was based on four premises: (1) *Eretz Israel* could not exclusively belong to either Jews or Arabs; (2) England would have to retain, at least for the time being, responsibility for governance and defense in the territory; (3) that Arab neutrality would be vital in any upcoming European conflict; and (4) that Jews, although severely disappointed, would have little choice but to accept the *fait accompli* since they could never form an alliance with Nazi Germany. Moreover, in a complete reversal of attitudes, the cabinet now denied — in direct contradiction of the conclusions drawn by the Peel Commission — that a promise of statehood had ever been implied in either the Balfour Declaration or the League of Nations mandate.[114]

The policy statement that resulted from these cabinet discussions was published as a white paper on May 17, 1939. Variously known as the White Paper of 1939 or the MacDonald White Paper (after Colonial Secretary Malcolm MacDonald), the new policy contained three elements: (1) Limitations on *aliya*, with a maximum rate of 15,000 Jewish immigrants per year for five years. Thereafter, no new Jewish immigration would be permitted except with Arab approval. This meant that the Jews would be reduced to permanent minority status, with the *Yishuv*'s growth limited and held at one-third the total population. (2) Limitations of the areas in which Jews could purchase new land. For the purpose of the land laws, Palestine-Eretz Israel was divided into three zones, designated A, B, and C. In the A zone, Jews would be permitted unlimited rights to purchase land. However, most cultivatable land in the A zone was already owned by Jews; the B and C zones were virtually closed to new land purchase. (3) A constitutional clause promised that Palestine would be granted independence, with the obvious implication that its majority (Arab) population would dominate the new state, in ten years.[115]

This policy repudiated all previous British commitments to the Zionists and constituted a potential death knell for both the Jewish

national home and the WZO. Condemnations by British public figures and by the League of Nations were not long in coming. Winston Churchill, for example, pointedly asked, "How can he [MacDonald] find it in his heart to strike them [the Jews] this mortal blow?".[116] After meetings held in May and June 1939, the League of Nations' Permanent Mandates Commission strongly condemned the MacDonald White Paper, declaring it to be inconsistent, at every point, with the mandate.[117]

The Jewish response to the MacDonald White Paper was also almost immediate and can be summarized as disappointment tinged with indignation.[118] Zionist indignation only grew as British government officials, particularly Malcolm MacDonald (whose decisive help for the *Yishuv* in 1931 was erased by authorship of the white paper), repeatedly asserted that the White Paper of 1939 was in Jewry's best interest.[119] The Zionists' immediate steps included publication of memoranda showing the White Paper of 1939 to be inconsistent with Britain's promises, hoping to embarrass the government into abrogating the new policy.[120] This tactic, which had worked in 1931, did not fully consider the international circumstances. The Zionists were forced (in face of mounting tensions in Europe) to argue that war was not imminent and that, therefore, Britain had acted too hastily in seeking Arab support.[121]

Conditions in Europe being what they were, this Zionist policy was bound to fail. An alternative policy had been proposed, however. In December 1938, before the London conference, Ben-Gurion predicted that Britain would abandon its commitment to the Jews. As an alternative, Ben-Gurion called on the JAE to:

convene a world Jewish conference in America and we will have to declare and carry out an *aliya* war: we shall organize *aliya* on our authority — and we shall place before the British the alternative of combating this *aliya* by force. . . . Let the British fleet fight against the tens of thousands of our youth who will set sail from the ports of Europe (and perhaps America as well) for the coast of *Eretz-Israel* and its ports.[122]

Ben-Gurion saw this as part of a larger plan to overturn the White Paper of 1939 that he dubbed *Milhemet ha-Aliya* (the aliya war). In Ben-Gurion's definition, this was "not a war for *aliya*, but a war by means of *aliya*, an *aliya* rebellion."[123]

This concept animated the JAE's manifesto of May 18, 1939, a manifesto that specifically condemned the white paper.

In this hour of unprecedented danger for the Jewish people, the English Government announces its intention to cut off Jewry's last hope and to seal off the road to its homeland.
This is a cruel blow. It is an especially hard blow because it comes from the government of a great power which had offered its hand to help the Jewish people and whose power rests on moral prestige and loyalty to international obligations.
This blow will not make the Jewish people surrender. The historical connection between Jewry and its homeland will not be cut. The Jewish people will never accept the closure of the gates of the homeland in the faces of its sons and will not allow the national home to be converted into a ghetto.[124]

May 18, 1939, also witnessed a one-day general strike throughout the *Yishuv*. In its aftermath, the JA implemented its protest strategy, in a significantly modified form.

The JAE, which had announced its intention to resign upon publication of the white paper, did not do so, fearing that such a move would create chaos. That decision cost the JAE more in the long term, since both its unwillingness to follow the precedent set by Weizmann in 1930 and its apparent sloth in protesting the white paper were widely interpreted within the *Yishuv* as cowardice, collaboration, or both. Behind the scenes, a different reality existed. On May 20, 1939, the *Yishuv* held its first internal census of military-age men, carried out with the full cooperation of ha-Zach. The next day, the JAE approved a staged plan of action by a vote of 4 to 2. Three new settlements were to be created immediately, and the Mossad le-Aliya Bet budget would be increased. Further diplomatic action in Geneva and London would be combined with these acts of defiance. If the MacDonald White Paper was not cancelled by the autumn of 1939, a prospect that Ben-Gurion alone doubted, then the Hagana would begin to undertake military operations. Ben-Gurion expected that military operations would be needed, and he instructed the Hagana high command to draw up a contingency plan, based on *Tochnit Avner*. This new plan (which apparently was given no separate name) was completed in late May.[125] Further Hagana plans called for an all-out revolt to begin after the scheduled Zionist Congress in August 1939. Once again, however, conditions in Europe were not ripe for completing Zionist plans in their original form.

Notes

1. The recession was discussed above, p. 99. On the new *aliya* regulations, see *Government of Palestine, Ordinances, 1933* (London: His Majesty's Stationary Office, 1934), pp. 102–105, and, more broadly, Abraham J. Edelheit, *The Yishuv in the Shadow of the Holocaust: Zionist Politics and Rescue Aliya, 1933-1939*, Boulder: Westview Press, 1996). Since this chapter is, in effect, a précis of that book, citations from archival material have been excluded, except in extraordinary cases. Readers interested in the sources on which our argument was based should consult the copious notes and bibliography in that work for fuller citations.

2. Meir Avizohar, ביראי סדוק: אידיאלים חברתיים ולאומיים והשתקפותם בעולמה של מפא״י (National and social ideals as reflected In Mapai) (Tel Aviv: Am Oved, 1990), pp. 97–103.

3. Edelheit, *Yishuv*, p. 24.

4. Avizohar, ביראי סדוק, pp. 104–106.

5. Howard I. Rosenblum, "A Political History of Revisionist Zionism, 1925–1938", (Ph.D. diss, Columbia University, 1986), p. 140.

6. Ibid., pp. 143–145.

7. David Bechor et al., דין וחשבון של ועידת החקירה לחקירת רצח דר. חיים ארלוזורוב (Report of the commission to study the murder of Dr. Haim Arlosoroff) (Jerusalem: Israel Government Printing Office, 1983).

8. Edelheit, *Yishuv*, pp. 104–105.

9. David Ben-Gurion, *Letters to Paula* (Pittsburgh: University of Pittsburgh Press, 1968), pp. 63–65.

10. Joseph B. Schechtman, *The Life and Times of Vladimir Jabotinsky* (New York: Thomas Yoseloff, 1961), 2: 190–193.

11. Edelheit, *Yishuv*, p. 106.

12. Ibid., p. 107.

13. Ibid., p. 108. Emphasis in original.

14. Ibid.

15. For a broad review on Nazi antisemitic policy between 1933 and 1939, see: Abraham J. Edelheit and Hershel Edelheit, *History of the Holocaust: A Handbook and Dictionary*, Boulder, CO: Westview Press, 1994, ch. 4.

16. Edelheit, *Yishuv*, p. 3.

17. Ibid., pp. 26–28.

18. Abraham J. Edelheit, "Jewish Responses to the Nazi Threat, 1933–1939: An Evaluation," *JPSR*, 6 no. 1/2 (Spring 1994): 135–152.

19. Zioniburo, London, to Jevagency, Jerusalem, March 29, 1933, CZA S49/381.

20. David Gurevich, comp., *Statistical Handbook of Jewish Palestine* (Jerusalem: Jewish Agency for Palestine, 1947), pp. 98–108.

21. *Stenographisches Protokol der Verhandlung des 18. Zionistische Kongress* (London: World Zionist Organization, 1933), pp. 198–199.

22. Max Gruenwald, "About the Reichsvertretung der Deutschen Juden," *Imposed Jewish Governing Bodies Under Nazi Rule*, New York: YIVO Institute for Jewish Research, 1972), p. 43.

23. Cf. Gabriel Sheffer, "Political Considerations in British Policy-Making on Immigration to Palestine," *SiZ* 4 (October 1981): 237–274.

24. Edelheit and Edelheit, *History of the Holocaust*, pp. 41–42.

25. Anita Shapira, "Did the Zionist Leadership Foresee the Holocaust?" in Jehuda Reinharz ed., *Living with Antisemitism: Modern Jewish Responses*, Hanover, N.H.: University Press of New England, 1987), p. 412.

26. For a more detailed review of the historiography on this issue, see Edelheit, *Yishuv*, pp. 26–28 and Edelheit and Edelheit, *History of the Holocaust*, chap. 8.

27. Dina Porat, *The Blue and Yellow Stars of David* (Cambridge: Harvard University Press, 1990), p. 262.

28. This was true because a law passed by the Reichstag during the great inflation of 1923–1924 limited the amount of currency an emigrant could take to RM50. Cf. Bruno Blau, ed., *Das Ausnahmerecht für die Juden in deutschland, 1933–1945* (Dusseldorf: Verlag Algemeine Wochenzeitung der Juden in deutschland, 1965), p. 117.

29. Edelheit, *Yishuv*, chap. 6.

30. German Jewry: A Plan for Emigration, November 3, 1935, CZA S25/9810.

31. Stefan Klinger, *The Ten Year Plan for Palestine* (London: New Zionist Organization, 1938).

32. David Ben-Gurion, זכרונות (Memoirs) (Tel Aviv: Am Oved, 1976), pp. 395–415; and Edelheit, *Yishuv*, pp. 68–70, 122–124.

33. Cited in Edelheit, *Yishuv*, p. 123.

34. Protocol of the Mapai Political Committee, March 30, 1936, Israel Labor Party Archives (hereafter: ILPA), 23/26/36.

35. Protocol of the Mapai Political Committee, April 16, 1936, in ibid.

36. Edelheit, *Yishuv*, pp. 73–92.

37. Ibid., pp. 10–13, 40–41, 86–89.

38. Ibid., p. 12. Cf. Moshe R. Gottlieb, *American Anti-Nazi Resistance, 1933–1941: An Historical Analysis* (New York: Ktav, 1982).

39. Edelheit, *Yishuv*, pp. 158–159.

40. For examples, see the various minutes of the American Jewish Congress Joint Boycott Committee held in the Israel State Archive, record group GL8586.

41. Cf. Abraham Barkai, *Nazi Economics: Ideology, Theory, Policy* (Oxford: Berg Publishers, 1990), pp. 250–255.

42. Francis R. Nicosia, *The Third Reich and the Palestine Question* (Austin: Texas University Press, 1985), chap. 3.

43. Edelheit, *Yishuv*, pp. 76–77.

44. Ibid., pp. 79–80.

45. Ibid., pp. 90–91, briefly reviewed these negotiations. However, the topic deserves a deeper treatment.

46. Ya'akov Goldstein, ללא פשרות: הסכם בן-גוריון-ז'בוטינסקי וכשלונו (Without compromise: The Ben-Gurion-Jabotinsky agreement and its failure), Tel Aviv: Hadar Publications, 1979, p. 39.

47. On Rutenberg, see Eli Shaltiel, פנחס רוטנברג (Pinhas Rutenberg) (Tel Aviv: Am Oved, 1990), passim; on his involvement in the negotiations, see ibid., 2: 431–440.

48. Goldstein, ללא פשרות, chap. 3.

49. Ibid., chap. 4.

50. Rosenblum, "Political History", pp. 125–127.

51. Goldstein, ללא פשרות, chap. 4.

52. Edelheit, *Yishuv*, p. 109.

53. Ibid., pp. 110–111; Goldstein, ללא פשרות, chap. 6.

54. Goldstein, ללא פשרות, chap. 7.

55. Ibid., p. 134.

56. Edelheit, *Yishuv*, pp. 112–113.

57. Ibid., p. 114.

58. Jerzy Tomaszewski, "Vladimir Jabotinsky's Talks with Representatives of the Polish Government," *Polin* 2 (1988): 276–293.

59. Edelheit, *Yishuv*, p. 115.

60. Haim Arlosoroff, "Our Position in Palestine," cited in Aaron S. Klieman, ed., *The Intensification of Violence, 1929-1936*, Rise of Israel Series, vol. 20 (New York: Garland, 1987), pp. 471–476.

61. Cf. W.P.N. Tyler, "The Beisan Lands Issue in Mandatory Palestine," *Middle Eastern Studies* 25 no.2 (April 1989): 123–162 and Raya Adler (Cohen), "Mandatory Land Policy and the Wadi al-Hawarith Affair, 1929-1933," *SiZ* 7, no.2 (Autumn 1986): 233–257.

62. Martin Kolinsky, *Law, Order, and Riots in Mandatory Palestine, 1928-1935* (London: St. Martin's Press, 1993), pp. 172–177.

63. Ian Black, *Zionism and the Arabs, 1936-1939* (New York: Garland, 1986), chap. 1.

64. "The Disturbances of 1936," cited in Klieman, *Intensification of Violence*, p. 517.

65. On the history of the revolt, see Yehoshua Porath, *The Palestinian Arab National Movement: From Riots to Rebellion, 1929-1939* (London: Frank Cass, 1977); and Ezra Danin and Ya'akov Shimoni, eds., תעודות ודמויות מגנזי הכנופיות הערביות במאורעות, *1936–1939* (Documents and portraits from the Arab gangs during the Arab Revolt of 1936–1939) (Jerusalem: Magnes Press, 1981).

66. Martin Kolinsky, "The Collapse and Restoration of Public Security," in M. J. Cohen and Martin Kolinsky, eds., *Britain and the Middle East in the 1930s* (London: MacMillan, 1992), p. 149.

67. Ya'akov Shavit, ed., הבלגה או תגובה? הויכוח בישוב היהודי *1936-1939* (Self restraint or response? The Jewish debate, 1936–1939) (Ramat Gan: Bar-Ilan University Press), 1983.

68. Edelheit, *Yishuv*, p. 133. Cf. Anita Shapira, *Land and Power: The Zionist Resort to Force, 1881-1948* (New York: Oxford University Press, 1992), chap. 6.

69. Ben-Gurion's diary, July 11, 1935, Ben-Gurion Research Center Archive (henceforth BGRA).

70. The changes in Hagana operational doctrine are described in קיצור תולדות ההגנה (Short history of the Hagana) (Tel Aviv: Ma'arachot/IDF Press, 1978), bk.3, and Meir Pail, התפתחות כוח המגן העברי, *1907-1948* (The Emergence of Jewish Defense Forces, 1907–1948) (Tel Aviv: Ministry of Defense/Chief Education Officer, 1987).

71. Cf. Ze'ev Schiff, *A History of the Israeli Army, 1870-1974* (San Francisco: Straight Arrow Books, 1974), pp. 15–17.

72. Ibid., p. 17.

73. Ibid. At the height of the Arab Revolt, the Hagana had 6,000 rifles, 600 automatic rifles (light, medium, and sub machine guns), and 24 medium machine guns at its disposal.

74. Gerson Rivlin, לאש ולמגן: תולדות הנוטרות העברית (In fire and defense: History of the Jewish supernumerary police) (Tel Aviv: Maarachot/IDF Publishing House, 1964), pp. 35–37, 71.

75. Cited in Schiff, *History*, p. 18. Punctuation has been added for clarity's sake.

76. Ibid., p. 20.

77. Ibid.

78. None of Wingate's English-language biographers pays sufficient attention to his Zionist contacts and his formative years in *Eretz Israel*. That is not the case in Peninah Zer, לוחמים בלילה: סיפורו של אורד וינגייט (Night fighters: The story of Orde Wingate) (Jerusalem: Yad Yitzhak Ben-Zvi, 1992); and Avraham Akavia, אורד וינגייט: חייו ופעולו (Orde Wingate: His life and Mission) (Tel Aviv: IDF Press, 1993).

79. Edelheit, *Yishuv*, pp. 125-127, Aaron S. Klieman, ed., *The Search for a Solution, 1936*, Rise of Israel Series, vol. 21 (New York: Garland, 1987), pp. 18–86, 165–169.

80. Klieman, *Search*, pp. 171–224.

81. Ibid., pp. 87–164.

82. Edelheit, *Yishuv*, pp. 135-137.

83. This material was reprinted in full in Aaron S. Klieman, ed., *Zionist Evidence Before the Peel Commission, 1936-1937*, Rise of Israel Series, vol. 23 (New York: Garland, 1987). The memoranda, which totaled 320 pages, testified to the Zionists' thoroughness if nothing else.

84. Edelheit, *Yishuv*, pp. 137–143. The text was also published verbatim in Aaron S. Klieman, ed., *The Palestine Royal Commission*, Rise of Israel Series, vol. 22 (New York: Garland, 1987, pp. 4–431. Ben-Gurion's position is elucidated in Shabtai Teveth, *Ben-Gurion: The Burning Ground, 1886–1948* (Boston: Houghton Mifflin Company, 1987), pp. 531–534.

85. Edelheit, *Yishuv*, p. 143.

86. Aaron S. Klieman, ed., *Palestine Royal Commission Report, 1937*, Rise of Israel Series, vol. 24 (New York: Garland, 1987).

87. The partition debate is discussed in Edelheit, *Yishuv*, pp. 144–151; Yitzhak Galnoor, *The Partition of Palestine: Decision Crossroads in the Zionist Movement* (Albany: State University of New York Press, 1995); and Shmuel Dothan, פולמוס החלוקה בתקופת המנדט (The Partition controversy during the mandatory era) (Jerusalem: Yad Yitzhak Ben-Zvi, 1979). Jabotinsky's view was summarized in Statement by the Presidency of the New Zionist Organization on Partition, 1937, Jabotinsky Institute Archive (henceforth: JIA), G4/14/2, p.2.

88. Memorandum on the Partition of Palestine Submitted to the Permanent Mandates Commission on Behalf of the New Zionist Organization, July, 1937, JIA G4/1/5.

89. Cf. Edelheit, *Yishuv*, p. 147, fuller documentation being provided in Aaron S. Klieman, ed., *The Partition Controversy*, Rise of Israel Series, vol. 25 (New York: Garland, 1987).

90. Edelheit, *Yishuv*, p. 148.

91. Klieman, *Partition Controversy*, pp. 436–443.

92. Edelheit, *Yishuv*, pp. 149–150.

93. Ibid., p. 151.

94. Abraham G. Duker, *The Situation of the Jews in Poland* (New York: American Jewish Congress, 1936).

95. Cf. Edward D. Wynot, Jr. "A Necessary Cruelty: The Emergence of Official Antisemitism in Poland, 1936–1939," *American Historical Review*, 76 no.4 (October, 1971): 1035–1058.

96. Edelheit, *Yishuv*, pp. 164–171.

97. See the proposals by George Rendel, July 1 and October 30, 1937, cited in Aaron S. Klieman, ed., *A Return to Palliatives, 1938*, Rise of Israel Series, vol. 26 (New York: Garland, 1987), respectively, pp. 1–4, 10-13.

98. Cf. the British documents cited in Klieman, *Return to Palliatives*, pp. 24–43 and 59–61.

99. Memorandum by Baggallay, August 13, 1937, in ibid., pp. 5–9.

100. Ibid., pp. 14–23, 49–58.

101. Ibid., pp. 62–84.

102. See the selection of Weizmann's letters cited in ibid., pp. 85–135.

103. Edelheit, *Yishuv*, pp. 187–189.

104. The Woodhead Commission Report is cited in Klieman, *Return to Palliatives*, pp. 136–458, with the relevant cabinet papers cited in ibid., pp. 459–476.

105. Edelheit and Edelheit, *History of the Holocaust*, pp. 46–49.

106. Joseph to Shertok, November 23, 1938, cited in Edelheit, *Yishuv*, p. 203.

107. Ibid., pp. 205–206.

108. For broad histories of Aliya Bet prior to 1939, see Yitzhak L. Avneri, מולוס עד טאורוס: ראשון עשור להעפלה (From Velos to Taurus: The first decade of illegal immigration) (Ramat Efal: Yad Yitzhak Tabenkin, 1985); and David H. Shpiro, לעלות בכל הדרכים (Aliya by any means) (Tel Aviv: Am Oved for the Institute to Study Aliya Bet of Tel Aviv University, 1994), chaps. 3–7. On Zionist relations in this era, see: Edelheit, *Yishuv*, chaps. 7–9.

109. Edelheit, *Yishuv*, pp. 206–213; documents on the diplomatic road to the London Conference were reprinted in Aaron S. Klieman, ed., *The Darket Year, 1939*, Rise of Israel Series, vol. 27 (New York: Garland, 1987), pp. 1–34.

110. All quotes were cited from the Stenograpic Protocol of the Meeting at St. James's Palace, CZA S25/7630. Cf. the documents in Klieman, *Darkest Year*, pp. 35–147.

111. Klieman, *Darkest Year*, pp. 148-241, Edelheit, *Yishuv*, p. 213.

112. Klieman, *Darkest Year*, pp. 242-282, Edelheit, *Yishuv*, p. 216–217, 219–223.

113. Cabinet minutes, March 8, 1939, cited in Klieman, *Darkest Year*, pp. 283–292.

114. Ibid., pp. 293–301.

115. The White Paper of 1939 and the government's explanation of its meaning were reprinted in ibid., pp. 302–322.
116. Ibid., p. 332. Additional comments by parliamentarians are reproduced in pp. 323–337.
117. Ibid., pp. 338–349.
118. Weizmann to MacMichael, May 31, 1939, in ibid., pp. 359–375.
119. Notes of a conversation with Malcolm MacDonald, May 13, 1939, in ibid., pp. 356–358.
120. Some of these documents were reproduced in ibid., pp. 376–466.
121. Cf. Wingate's February 12, 1939, telegram, reproduced in Yehuda Bauer, *From Diplomacy to Resistance* (New York: Atheneum, 1973), pp. 364–365.
122. Protocols of the JAE, December 11, 1938, CZA S100/25, p. 5.
123. Ibid., p. 16. Cf. Meir Avizohar, הציונות הלוחמת (Fighting Zionism) (Kiryat Sde Boker: Ben-Gurion Research Center), 1985.
124. Edelheit, *Yishuv*, p. 233.
125, Ibid., pp. 233–234, 241–243.

9

WAR AND CATASTROPHE

Facing the White Paper

With cabinet approval of the White Paper of May 1939, Great Britain essentially repudiated its commitment to the creation of a Jewish national home. The Zionists were facing a quandary, since the British re-evaluation of Middle Eastern commitments came just as living conditions for Jews in Nazi-controlled territory worsened. The Reich now included not only Germany but Austria (incorporated during the Anschluss on March 12, 1938) and Bohemia-Moravia (formerly Czechoslovakia, which was occupied on March 15, 1939) as well. Worse still, virtually all potential safe havens for Jews had closed; exit from the Nazi-imposed hell was virtually (but, at this stage, not totally) impossible.[1]

Efforts to find a territorialist solution to Jewish distress became even more desperate at this point, with some Zionists reluctantly accepting that rescue (without regard to the territory to which endangered Jews fled) was primary in this hour of incredible danger. Prominent Zionists who now advocated a temporary shift to territorialism included Arthur Ruppin, who had been advocating such a policy since *Kristallnacht*, and, ironically, Ze'ev Jabotinsky.[2] Yet, even such advocacy was tinged with despair. As the affair of the *SS St. Louis*, a ship carrying 936 Jews who held immigrant visas for Cuba but were denied entry and subsequently unsuccessfully sought entry into the United States, proved, the grave conditions facing European Jewry influenced few nations to adopt a strictly humanitarian immigration policy.[3] Complete WZO abandonment of Zionist goals could not, therefore, even guarantee the viability of a territorialist solution to the Jewish problem.[4]

At the same time, it was obvious to Zionists that the White Paper of 1939 had to be overturned. Limitations on *aliya* and land purchase would stifle the *Yishuv*, and the Jewish national home would wither away. Moreover, in an international emergency (which few Zionists actually saw as imminent but which they all feared) the *Yishuv*'s closure would virtually guarantee the collapse of any mass rescue scheme. Plans for a Jewish rebellion were in fact being laid almost from the day the White Paper of 1939 was approved. The Irgun Zvai Leumi (IZL) began its attacks — relatively minor pinpricks against the British administration — in the late spring and early summer.[5] Of greater significance were plans for a revolt proposed by the Hagana, if only because the Hagana was the larger of the two undergrounds. Plans for revolt were drafted in the spring with a tentative date set for early September 1939, that is, after the Twenty-First Zionist Congress.[6]

Meeting in Basel August 16–26 1939, the Twenty-First Zionist Congress was burdened by gloom and a sense of impending disaster. The Jewish Agency Executive's (JAE) report, despite a few rays of hope, could only be described as unsettling, since it appeared that not even the League of Nations could change the British cabinet's determination to implement the White Paper.[7] Nevertheless, the plenary's main debate centered on the issue of revolt.

דבר מפלגת פועלי א"י
לקונגרס הציוני הכ"א

לא נכנע!

זהו נדר העם להמשיך, להמשיך
בהתאבקותו המדינית, להמשיך
בעבודתו הקונסטרוקטיבית,
להמשיך בעליה, בסרקע,
בהתישבות, בחרושת, בהתגוננות;
להערים על פקודות ולעקוף חוקים
לשם המשך הזה, ליצור בקרם
מתיחות רוחנית, המטילה את מרות
אי-הכניעה על כל פרט והמכוונת
אליה כל מעשה וכל הליכות חיים.

Mapai Election Poster for the
Twenty-First Zionist Congress, 1939.
Courtesy of the Central Zionist Archives, Jerusalem

Rabbi Abba Hillel Silver of the United States spoke passionately against rebellion; Moshe Shertok, head of the JAE political department, spoke equally forcefully on behalf of revolt.[8]

Neither the proponents nor the opponents of revolt were convinced, since the plenary never reached an authoritative decision. Indeed, it should be noted that the congress actually broke up early. News reports regarding Polish mobilization and the possibility of Polish-German hostilities forced the congress to close down prematurely, with the delegates making their way home and vowing to meet again as soon as possible.[9] For many of the delegates that was not to be; they were swept away with the communities they represented, obliterated en masse by the Nazi moloch.

Although Zionists had used the argument that war was not imminent as a means to dissuade the British from implementing the

White Paper, in fact, hostilities broke out on September 1, 1939. A tragic sidelight to the commencement of hostilities was the arrival of the *SS Tiger Hill*, a blockade runner carrying 1,417 *Ma'apilim* which made landfall near Tel Aviv on September 3, 1939. Fired upon by British warships while landing, two of the *Tiger Hill Ma'apilim* were killed: the first persons killed by British arms during World War II.[10] The realization that this tragedy had two causes, the Nazi threat and the British White Paper, left Zionists few choices for the coming years. David Ben-Gurion, for instance, declared that Zionists had no choice but "to fight the White Paper as if there was no Hitler and to fight Hitler as if there was no White Paper."[11]

The Zionists emphasized the possibility of a truce with the British, at least for the war's duration. The reality, of course, was that Jews had no other option: despite marginal and fringe groups there was no realistic possibility of fighting against Britain since that meant fighting for Hitler.[12] In truth, despite the arguments from some British political leaders, including Winston S. Churchill (then First Lord of the admirality), and advice by the British ambassador in Washington, the cabinet realized that Jews had virtually no alternatives and proceeded to act accordingly.[13] In response to American inquiries, the British promptly implemented the White Paper's restrictions on immigration; the land regulations were not long in following.[14] Jewish issues played no role whatsoever in Britain's wartime strategic policy; to the contrary, the British government seemed intent on ignoring the Jews as long as possible.[15] This was reiterated in February 1940 when the cabinet approved a telegram to all Middle Eastern ambassadors and staffs that confirmed adherence to the White Paper.[16]

Persecution and Resistance[17]

As the British continued to emphasize their adherence to the White Paper of 1939, the Nazi persecution of Jewry intensified and took center stage. Between war's outbreak in 1939 and the definite turn of the tide toward the Allies in the spring/summer of 1943, Jewish communities continued to fall under the Nazi heel. Almost immediately the Nazis began to establish their *Naiordnung* (new order). In each occupied country they introduced Nazi legislation and administration, including the entire array of anti-Jewish laws. Hitler had, after all, in his infamous speech in the Reichstag on January 30, 1939, predicted that:

If the international Jewish financiers in and outside Europe should succeed in plunging the nations once more into a world war, then the result will not be the Bolshevizing of the earth, and thus the victory of Jewry, but the annihilation of the Jewish race in Europe![18]

As the Nazis occupied more territory, however, more Jews came into their orbit leading to plans for a comprehensive solution to the Jewish question. At first, the Nazis explored the possibility of creating a reservation for Jews in the Lublin-Nisko region of Poland. When that plan collapsed, a new colonization scheme was explored: the so-called Madagascar Plan. Reviving a 1937 Polish scheme to transport "surplus populations" (Jews) to the French colony, the Nazis considered the possibility of creating a master concentration camp containing Europe's 4 million Jews. The Madagascar Plan also collapsed; implicit in the plan all along was Great Britain's surrender. When that did not happen any possibility of mass deportation from Europe became moot to be replaced in the autumn of 1940 with a new and more ominous Nazi plan: nothing less than the total extermination of European Jewry.[19]

In the interim, the Nazi bureaucracy took a number of steps designed to simplify any long-term solution that was adopted. In Poland, the Nazis incarcerated Jews in ghettos. Some of the ghettos located in large cities were sealed with walls, barbed wire, and guard posts. Jews lived in appalling conditions in these closed ghettos. In Warsaw nearly half a million Jews resided in an area adequate for less than 100,000;

similar conditions existed in Lodz, Krakow, Tarnow, and Lublin. In addition to overcrowding, and even more important, the ghettos were allotted totally inadequate supplies of food, medicine, and fuel. In some instances, even clean drinking water became scarce. Sanitary conditions declined rapidly with overcrowding, and starvation, dysentery, typhus, and other diseases took hold.

For Jews, this phase of Nazi persecution posted a new challenge for survival. Virtually all of European Jewry was united under the heel of Nazi oppression. Yet individual Jewish communities were increasingly isolated from one another. Because of Nazi laws severely curtailing Jewish movement from one place to another on penalty of imprisonment or death, hardly any Jew knew what was going on in the next community, even if it was only a few kilometers distant. Further obstacles also existed. Eastern European Jewry in particular was doubly isolated: from the general environment and from one another. Whereas aggression by the common enemy should have instilled a sense of solidarity, in reality Jews felt abandoned by the local non-Jewish populations. Within the Jewish community itself was the possibility that communal anarchy would take hold — that instead of working collectively, individuals would attempt to save themselves and their immediate family members. Although such cases did exist on a limited scale, anarchy did not reign. Jewish communities lost much of their cohesion but they did not collapse.

Moreover, the Jews did not surrender their human dignity. They opened soup kitchens to feed the hungry and maintained clandestine schools, synagogues, and cultural activities to feed Jewish souls. The prewar Jewish political parties continued to operate underground, publishing a secret Jewish press and preparing the young members for the day of the battle. Although at first glance it would appear that Jewish disunity was maintained — each party operated on its own — a trend toward unification was also perceptible. In particular, the debate over Jewish nationalism ceased to animate as passionate an ideological struggle as it had in the prewar era. Zionists still emphasized *Eretz Israel* as the only solution for the Jewish problem in the long term. But, the problem was not the long term survival of the entire Jewish people but the short term survival of Jews imprisoned in Nazi ghettos. Even the most passionate ideological differences were relatively minor, and intraparty cooperation was considered the need of the hour.

Unity initially did not rank high on the agenda of Jewish political parties when they reconstituted in the underground. Initially, the parties strove only to continue to operate and to give members a sense of belonging and hope for the future. In that way, the parties hoped to ensure individual survival while maintaining morale and achieving party goals. However, disunity was dangerous and the Nazis did not distinguish between different ideological stripes of Jews. Moreover, few contingencies existed; *ad hoc* unification of different parties to share meager resources made sense because it guaranteed survival.[20]

Adaptability to the new conditions was a special hallmark of the Zionist youth movements. A particularly good example of this trend was the unification of all Zionist youth groups in the Będzin-Sosnowiec region of Poland into the Brit ha-Halutzim (Alliance of Pioneers) in late 1940 or early 1941. They formed the core of an opposition to both the Nazis and the Nazi-imposed Jewish leadership (the Judenrat). Zionists (and Zionist youth groups) were, in fact, among the first to organize in most ghettos (in Warsaw and Lodz, for example), a reflection of both their ideology and their commitment to national salvation and the preservation of Jewish self-respect.[21] Conditions were similar in Western Europe, with Zionist groups (again the youth movements being in the forefront) among the first to organize to defend Jewish morale and physical survival.[22]

Jewish clandestine activity in 1940 and 1941 translated into resistance activities during 1942 and 1943 (continuing through liberation in Western Europe in 1944). In every locale where Jews rose up against the Nazis, Zionists played an important and at times central role. This was true, for instance, in France, where Franco-Zionist youth movements crystallized into the Armée Juive in January 1942, but held no less true in Poland.[23] Thus, for example, although the Warsaw Ghetto's Antifascist Bloc (AFB) came into being (in March 1942) at the instigation of Jewish Communists, a plurality of the movements' members were Zionists. In turn, when AFB reconstituted itself as the Żydowska Organizacja Bojowa (Jewish Combat Organization, ŻOB) a clear majority of fighters adhered to Zionist groups. So total was the Zionist majority that a ha-Shomer ha-Zair leader, Mordechai Anielewicz, was chosen as ŻOB's commander in chief.[24] This is not to denigrate the contribution of non-Zionists to the Jewish anti-Nazi resistance. In the face of adversity, the Jewish *Kehila* was finally united (to a greater or lesser degree). However, in every case, Zionists were in the forefront of resistance activities: in the ghettos, forests, and death camps, in Eastern Europe, and in the urban and non-urban guerrilla units in Western Europe.[25]

This was, of course, an epic but unequal struggle. Virtually abandoned by their non-Jewish neighbors (especially in Eastern Europe) and by the allied powers, lacking sufficient weapons and training, and operating under conditions of extreme duress, the Jewish resistance dared to face the strongest war machine then known to mankind and won a moral victory. Although not all Jews resisted, accusations regarding a Jewish "compliance reaction" may be ignored in light of actual conditions and in light of the greater extent of Jewish resistance than was assumed in the immediate postwar years. Then too, the armed resistance that the Jews finally did effect received almost no aid from the Allies and, in Eastern Europe, little from their neighbors. Nevertheless, Jewish resisters won a moral victory. Although doomed, they dared to declare that world Jewry would live. The Jewish struggle in World War II was a stage in the Jewish emergence from powerlessness. Ultimately the Jewish war that began in April 1943 ended in May 1948. The process begun by the resistance during World War II may fairly be said to have ended only with the establishment of the State of Israel.

Jewish resistance — whether in the ghettos, camps, or forests — was also a reaffirmation of the heroic element in previous Jewish history. Throughout their long history, Jews had been attacked countless times for being born Jewish and stubbornly adhering to their forefathers' faith. They had to endure the early persecutions of the Catholic Church, the ravages of the Crusades, desecration of the Host, ritual murder, and blood libels, accusations of poisoning of wells and carrying the Black Plague, the Inquisition, the Chmielnicki massacres, and countless pogroms. They were tortured, burned at the stake, expelled, made to wander from place to place — always forced to rely on the whim of the ruling bishop or prince. Yet in many instances throughout their long journey, Jews defended themselves with whatever means were available to them and acquitted themselves honorably. Despite the harsh reality, the Jews managed to survive. Many times previously history had declared the Jews dead, yet they had survived. So too it was during the Holocaust. Jews, against all odds resisted their murderers and survived them.[26]

The Desperate Flight

As the Nazi plan to murder European Jewry unfolded in all its gruesome horror, only one avenue existed for Jews to rescue themselves: *Aliya Bet*. As noted previously, Aliya Bet had begun in earnest during the 1930s. By 1939, *Aliya Bet* was central to Ben-Gurion's concept of an *aliya* war to overturn the British White Paper of 1939. However, when World War II broke out, the *aliya* war was held in abeyance. Yet, *Aliya Bet* as a means of rescue continued and even increased in importance.

Numerous difficulties abounded. First, ships that were difficult enough to acquire in peacetime proved virtually impossible to obtain in wartime. The same held true for trained crews. Second, the financial arrangements needed to move thousands of Jews fleeing Nazi persecution, whether as *Ma'apilim* to *Eretz Israel* or elsewhere, were virtually impossible. Obtaining sufficient financial resources for mass *aliya* had proved difficult in peacetime and was infinitely more complex once the war began.[27] Finally, a new danger existed. During the already arduous voyage through an active war zone, imminent attack by either side was possible, with potentially deadly results. At least two ships were sunk as a result of hostile military action: the *SS Struma*, which went down with no survivors in the Black Sea in February 1942, apparently sunk by a Soviet submarine, and the *SS Mefkurie*, a Mossad blockade runner also sunk in the Black Sea, in this case, apparently by a German U-boat in August 1944 (although a number of historians have recently argued that the submarine was Soviet). The *Mefkurie* had only five survivors.[28]

The dangers notwithstanding, hundreds of Jews were willing to attempt the trek, seeing it as their only potential means of escape. In addition to the two ships already mentioned, three others sank. The *SS Pentcho* (sponsored by the revisionist Zionist Af-Al-Pi organization), sank near Rhodes in May 1940; the *SS Salvador*, a privately organized ship sank in the Dardanelles losing 120 of its 323 *Ma'apilim* (the others were successfully rescued by the Mossad ship *SS Darien II*); and the *SS Vitorul* which sank without loss of life in the Bosporous in October 1942.[29] Numerous other efforts by Jews in small boats and yachts, were not recorded; suffice it to say that at the peripheries of the Final Solution (in Romania, Bulgaria, and Greece), many Jews made the daring but generally unsuccessful effort to flee with their lives.

A particularly tragic and poignant example was the so-called Kladovo-Sabac group. Between January 1940 and April 1941, small groups of Jews escaped from Austria and Czechoslovakia. Making their way to Kladovo, Yugoslavia, the unfortunates intended to continue onward to the Black Sea coast in Romania. In fact, a ship was ready for them, the Mossad blockade runner *SS Darien II*.

Ma'apilim Being Helped Ashore in 1939.
Courtesy of the Central Zionist Archives, Jerusalem

Complicating matters, however, was the fact that the ship had been promised by the Hagana's intelligence service (Sherut Yediot, Shai) to the British Special Operations Executive (SOE) for a mission in the Danube basin. The *Yishuv's* leaders hoped that cooperation with British intelligence would improve postwar relations between the WZO and the mandatory government. This mission, in turn, was cancelled and some refugees were able to make their way to *Eretz Israel* from Romania. None of them were from the Kladovo group, who were stuck in Yugoslavia. When the Nazis invaded that country in April 1941, their final avenue for escape was closed. Moreover, when an anti-Nazi revolt began in Serbia, most of the men in the group were shot. The women and children were then transferred to Sajmiste, where most perished.[30]

These horrible disasters must be seen in the context of a difficult period for the *Yishuv*. As details regarding the murder of European Jewry became common knowledge, Jews (in and out of the charnal house) and sympathetic bystanders alike became more desperate to rescue at least a remnant. Yet, as Moshe Shertok noted, the attempt to flee Europe via *Aliya Bet* "revealed the abysmal poverty and frailty of our position, our utter helplessness and our lack of [political] standing as a Jewish nation."[31]

Zionist Fortunes and Misfortunes

While the tragic events were playing themselves out in Europe, the Yishuv remained in a chronic state of crisis. It had been hoped that the outbreak of war would delay implementation of the White Paper of 1939, if only for the sake of an Anglo-Zionist truce to influence American public opinion. The Zionists, stung by implementation of the immigration restrictions, particularly hoped to delay (or cancel) the land purchase restrictions.[32] This was not to be. On February 28, 1940, the land regulations were promulgated, virtually freezing the Yishuv in the territory already held by Jews.[33] Protests by the Yishuv fell on ears deafened by a deadly combination of bureaucratic inertia and overt anti-semitism.[34] The British, still hoping to appease the Arabs, were fully prepared to sacrifice relations with the Jews in the hope that they could cement an alliance with the Arabs.[35]

Zionists hoped that perhaps the change in government on May 10, 1940, specifically Prime Minister Neville Chamberlain's replacement by Sir Winston S. Churchill, whose pro-Zionist sympathies were well-known, would signal a change in their fate as well.[36] Realities were far different. Churchill's personal views notwithstanding, the government remained committed to carrying out all the terms of the White Paper of 1939.[37] Moreover, the cabinet, abetted by British military and political figures in the Middle East, continued on this path even when evidence that the alliance with the Arabs was failing and that the Arabs were more likely to be swayed by conditions on the battlefield than by British promises regarding postwar accommodations in Palestine/*Eretz Israel*.[38]

By the end of 1940, therefore, relations between the British and the Zionists had reached an impasse. The possibility that a postwar independent Arab federation in the Middle East might agree to grant autonomy to Jews in *Eretz Israel* collapsed almost as quickly as it was raised in 1941. No Arab leader of stature would agree to accept any Jewish presence in the Middle East, even if the Zionists agreed to surrender their demands for independence.[39] Despite this glaring reality, considerable effort was expended in attempting an Arab-Jewish rapproachment. In particular, British and American leaders hoped to obtain the acquiescence of King Abdul Aziz ibn Saud that Jews be granted autonomy in Palestine/*Eretz Israel* in return for Jewish support for the creation of a pan-Arab federation ruled by the Saudi leader. Ibn Saud, strongly opposed to any Jewish role in a postwar Middle East (except as *Dhimmi* tolerated by a Muslim state), refused to even consider the proposal.[40] The ominous reports filtering from Europe after the Nazis invaded the Soviet Union (June 1941) made matters worse, as did the fact that, from a Zionist perspective, Jewish needs during and after the war were perfectly clear. The only question seemed to be how to achieve Zionist goals under prevailing circumstances.[41]

Politically and diplomatically conditions appeared virtually unchanged throughout 1940 and 1941. This is not to say that conditions remained entirely static. In particular, the Axis threat to Palestine/*Eretz Israel*, inspired in 1940 and 1941 by events in Syria and Iraq and in 1942 by the successful German offensives in North Africa, required a Zionist reply. The bulk of the *Yishuv* remained loyal to Ben-Gurion's dualistic policy — fighting against the Germans while preparing for a possible struggle against the British — and ceased anti-British operations. Contingency plans were prepared for continuing to fight in case the British withdrew entirely from the Middle East.[42] From these plans, the so-called Carmel scheme (Tochnit ha-Carmel), also known as the Northern scheme (Tochnit ha-Zafon), was noteworthy for the comprehensive planning that went into producing it. The Hagana's high command had matured to the point where it felt comfortable in planning to wrest control of at least part of *Eretz Israel* and defend it against the Arabs, the Italians, and the German Afrika Korps.[43]

There was, however, an alternative view expressed by a small but vocal group that opposed the *Yishuv's* direction. Some members of the IZL high command argued that the truce declared by the *Yishuv* was a mistake. To be sure, the Nazis were enemies of the Jewish people. But they were only enemies insofar as they sought to expel the Jews from Europe. The Jews' true enemy — the power preventing Jews from fleeing Europe to a safe haven in

Eretz Israel — was not Nazi Germany, but Great Britain. It followed, then, that the Jews should fight the British and seek some form of accommodation with the Axis Powers.

Jabotinsky, who strongly opposed the quasi-fascist tendency among some of his followers, died during a visit in the United States in August 1940. One month later, IZL supporters of continued rebellion, who coalesced around Abraham Stern (whose nom-de-guerre was Yair), withdrew from the IZL and founded Lohame Herut Israel (Lehi), better known in the English speaking world as the Stern Gang.[44] As already noted, one of Lehi's first acts, and by far its most controversial, was the effort to contact Italian and German agents in the Middle East to request support for an anti-British revolt.[45] The German response to Stern's overtures is unclear, but it is certain that no actual alliance ever existed between the Axis and Lehi. Repudiated by the majority of Zionists and within the *Yishuv*, Stern and his followers were forced to adopt terrorist tactics. The British, in response, hunted Lehi down with unusual zeal. Stern was killed by British police detectives under suspicious circumstances on February 12, 1942. Thereafter, most of his followers were rounded up and imprisoned. Lehi ceased to function for more than a year; the movement only resumed operations in 1943 as further frustrations over conditions in Europe and repeated Zionist diplomatic failures led to renewed tension and pressure within the *Yishuv*'s population.[45]

However, the *Yishuv* and the Zionist movement still remained in a political limbo: unwilling to act against the British for fear of thereby indirectly aiding the Nazis but unable to obtain support for even a minor modification to the White Paper's policies, even while the cruelty of keeping *Eretz Israel* closed to Jewish refugees was becoming increasingly clear.[47] Fears for the *Yishuv*'s safety merely increased the tendency toward indecisiveness in some circles but was not a cause for the Zionists' failure. The basic cause for failure was the Zionists' (and

Jewry's) fundamental powerlessness and consequent paralysis was little more than a symptom of this reality. This distinction between root, cause, and symptom in the Zionists' malaise between 1940 and 1942 may be seen very clearly in Chaim Weizmann's appropriately entitled essay "Palestine's Role in the Solution of the Jewish Problem," which appeared in *Foreign Affairs* in April 1942.[48] In his essay Weizmann restated the classical Zionist arguments: Jewish homelessness caused the eruption of the Jewish problem. The Jewish problem's main symptom, antisemitism, had become even more cruel since Herzl's days and, as a result, solving the Jewish problem had become ever more pressing. Furthermore, a solution for the problem already existed in the form of the Jewish national home. To try to ignore the problem (as the Allies appeared to be doing) or to deny *Eretz Israel*'s centrality in solving the problem (which was the basis of the White Paper of 1939) could not work, since that merely delayed reality. Only by directly confronting the problem and, in particular, overturning the White Paper of 1939 and restoring that which was rightfully the Jews' could the Jewish problem be solved.

The Biltmore Conference

The accumulated frustrations that Zionists felt were broached publicly on May 10–11, 1942. The American Zionists, emerging in fits and starts as the key element in Zionist diplomacy, called an extraordinary conference held at New York's Biltmore Hotel. Previous efforts to mobilize American Jewry and American Zionism had failed dismally due to a combination of organizational weakness and interparty rivalries.[49] The war, reports about the dire straits of European Jewry, and British obstinacy on the White Paper of 1939 now left no alternative for Zionist leaders.

The Biltmore Conference sought to redress this situation. Attended by the leading Zionist personalities — including Weizmann, Ben-Gurion, Silver, Rabbi Stephen S. Wise, and Nahum Goldmann — the conference hoped to galvanize the Zionist Organization of America and the WZO by providing a new diplomatic initiative for the Zionist movement.[50]

Early reports of Jewish suffering in Europe elicited from the conference "a message of hope and encouragement to fellow Jews in the ghettos and concentration camps of Hitler-dominated Europe, and prays that their hour of liberation may not be far distant." The dangerous global military situation resulted in warm greetings to Jewish servicemen and servicewomen in the far-flung Allied armies. Similarly, the conferees approved a resolution offering an olive branch to the Arabs in the hope that a peaceful settlement could be attained for all.[51] The resolution's final element, however, was its most important: The conference issued an unequivocal call for the creation of a Jewish commonwealth in an unpartitioned Palestine/*Eretz Israel* after the war. Article 8 read, in full,

> The Conference declares that the new
> world order that will follow victory
> cannot be established on foundations of
> peace, justice and equality, unless
> the problem of Jewish homelessness is
> finally solved.[52]

This was, to say the least, a radical departure from WZO policy. To be sure, some Zionists (Jabotinsky, for instance) had been arguing that the Zionist movement needed to clearly formulate its ultimate goals. These figures, however, had not generally been heeded up to this point. Jabotinsky had been hooted down when he proposed a similar resolution at the Eighteenth Zionist Congress in 1931. When the Zionists had considered statehood previously (after the Peel Commission hearings) they had done so on outside (British) initiative.[53] Now, the Zionists were taking the initiative: The British repudiation of the Mandate left the Zionists no recourse but to stake out a maximalist position.

This new Zionist orientation was not obtained unanimously. To the contrary, the moving spirits behind the Biltmore Resolution — Ben-Gurion and Silver —

found themselves in a bitter conflict with more moderate figures such as Weizmann and Wise. The moderates counseled a gentler approach, one that aimed at influencing the Allies without risking the chance of alienating them. In response, the maximalists emphasized that such a gradualist policy was no longer plausible, even if it was desirable. Only public diplomacy designed to pressure the Allies into action would influence those in the corridors of power.[54] Still, even the maximalists knew that their efforts needed an amount of flexibility. Ben-Gurion, for example, was willing to accept any reasonable alternative to statehood — maintaining the Mandate, partition, Jewish sovereignty without full independence (as part of the British Commonwealth), or inclusion in an Arab federation with guarantees of Jewish autonomy — as long as conditions were those that allowed for mass *aliya* after the war. In Ben-Gurion's estimation, at least 2 million Jews would be uprooted by the war. For them, only one haven existed: *Eretz Israel*. It followed, then, that mass rescue and Zionist salvation went hand in hand.[55] Silver, Ben-Gurion's most strident partner in the maximalist position, framed the matter somewhat differently (but not radically so) during his now famous speech at the American Jewish Conference in September 1943 (see below):

> We cannot truly rescue the Jews of Europe
> unless we have free immigration into
> Palestine. We cannot have free immigration
> into Palestine unless our political rights
> are recognised there. Our political rights
> cannot be recognized unless our historic
> connection with the country is acknowledged
> and our right to rebuild our national home
> is reaffirmed. These are inseparable links in
> a chain. The whole chain breaks if one of
> the links is missing.[56]

The Biltmore Resolution was not, by any means, the complete solution to Zionist problems. To the contrary, considerable indecisiveness remained while the resolution was debated, reviewed, and finally approved by the Va'ad ha-Poel ha-Mezumzam. Furthermore, three agonizing years were to pass — with increasingly severe news about the extermination of European Jewry — before the Zionists were able to put the policies expressed by the resolution into practice.[57] Nonetheless, the Biltmore Resolution's significance cannot be minimized. It was, in effect, the Zionist's first declaration of independence and was an important first step out of the doldrums.

Zionism, the Great Powers, Wartime Rescue

After the Biltmore Conference, the Zionists again girded themselves for the diplomatic battle to amend or cancel the White Paper of 1939. The Zionist push, however, was more than equaled by British obstinacy. The cabinet dug its heels in and would not budge.[58] In this endeavor, the British received considerable assistance from the U.S. State Department. Like their British counterparts, American diplomats feared Arab enmity more than Jewish disappointment.[59] As a result, the Roosevelt administration pursued an essentially dualistic policy: assuring Jews of its support for their goals while actively seeking alternatives in secret to prevent any action on Jewry's behalf.[60]

In the interim, news was received that made Zionists and non-Zionists alike even more desperate. On August 8, 1942, Gerhard Riegner, representative of the World Jewish Congress in Geneva, cabled Wise with information he received from a German businessman relating to the planned extermination of European Jewry. By the time the so-called Riegner cable was verified, in November 1942, it was discovered that the plan had actually already been in operation for months. By December 12, 1942, the Allies were sufficiently well informed that they could confirm that more than 2 million Jews had already been murdered in cold blood.[61]

From the Jewish perspective, this information proved the twin needs for some form of immediate rescue activity and for a long-term change in the government of Palestine/*Eretz Israel*.[62] The realization that the very Jews on whose behalf Ben-Gurion had urgently called upon Zionists to redouble their efforts might be murdered before they could be rescued raised two questions: first, to what extent did long-term actions on behalf of a Jewish state impede the short-term goal of rescue? and second, to what degree could Jews act unilaterally when the Allies — mainly Great Britain and the United States — did not share the Jews' sense of urgency?

These two questions remain contentious to this day. Zionist meetings with American and British leaders in late 1942 and early 1943 obtained little or nothing that could warm their hearts on either the rescue or the diplomatic fronts.[63] This reality led to a renewed rift within the American Jewish community. Zionist maximalists insisted that rescue and cancellation of the White Paper must proceed hand in hand while non-Zionists and moderate Zionists expressed a willingness to unlink the two issues and concentrate (temporarily) on the rescue front.[64] During this period American Jewry sought a consensus that would unify the multifarious Jewish organizations thereby converting them into a single, potentially powerful, voice on behalf of the Jewish agenda.[65] The resulting American Jewish Conference met in September 1943.

Far from fostering unity, however, the Biltmore Resolution proved contentious. Initially removed from the agenda, approval of continued work on behalf of a Jewish commonwealth was accomplished only thanks to Silver's already quoted argument that rescue was impossible without mass Jewish transfer to *Eretz Israel*. In response, the American Jewish Committee withdrew from the conference and refused to cooperate in a united front, fearing that continued Zionist activism would raise the level of antisemitism in America and would hurt efforts to create an official U.S. government rescue policy.[66]

Again, it must be emphasized that these actions were and remain contentious. A wide spectrum of authors have accused the Zionists of abandoning European Jews to their fate in order to obtain some form of political benefit in the postwar era.[67] Pseudoscholarship notwithstanding, similarly framed but more mildly stated, conclusions have infiltrated the work of serious scholars who have misunderstood the context in which these events took place.[68] In reality, Silver's was the correct prognosis: given our current level of knowledge on Allied policy making relevant to Jewish affairs, it is highly unlikely that a Zionist concession — even the ultimate concession of surrender to the regime established by the White Paper of 1939 — would have changed Allied policy. The truth behind that reality is demonstrated in Allied rescue activity between December 1942 and January 1944.

Not one Allied country was willing to protect the Jews. When the Allies issued their manifesto on the Nazi murder of European Jewry (and other acts of bestiality and genocide) on December 12, 1942, they did not list any specific actions to be taken in the immediate future. The issuing governments were content to speak in generalized terms about aiding the victims and warned that those guilty of crimes against humanity would be punished after the war. In the meantime, the Allies were not willing to divert any resources away from the war in order to defend the Jews, even in cases where targets had military significance, such as the rail lines on which Jewish deportees were transported to the death camps. Only in a few cases were radio messages beamed to Europe by the BBC, warning that what the Nazis termed "resettlement" in fact meant death. Even these broadcasts were stopped by the British government so as not to create anti-Jewish resentment in the occupied territories by appearing to devote too much time to the Jews. In short, the Allies were apathetic toward the Jews. Whereas the Nazis viewed killing Jews as a paramount goal of the war, the Allies never considered the Jewish question in the formulation of their war strategy, considering it merely a side issue to be settled with the end of hostilities.[69]

This unhappy generalization especially applies to the British government. One month after the Allied manifesto of December 1942, the Foreign Office set out its position on rescue in a memorandum to members of the U.S. States Department staff. In part, this document read:

> There is a possibility that the Germans or their satelites may change over from the policy of extermination to one of extrusion, and aim, as they did before the war, at embarrassing other countries by flooding them with alien immigrants.[70]

This phraseology only makes sense when understood in light of the White Paper of 1939, humanitarian concerns here taking second place to the possibility that the British government might find itself in the embarassing position of having to find homes for Jews saved from the Nazi charnel house. Viewed another way, British policy may be likened to an ostrich policy: the government hoped that if it ignored the Jewish problem long enough it would go away. A statement wrongly attributed to Lord Moyne (Eric Arthur Guinness), the British minister resident in Cairo, but apparently made by a senior member of the British Palestine administration, indicates as much. Told unofficially of Joel Brand's 1944 mission and Adolf Eichmann's offer to ransom a million Hungarian Jews for 10,000 trucks, the Englishman responded, "But what will we do with one million Jews?" Official government opinion was little better. An anonymous cabinet member responded, on the record, to the Eichmann offer by hoping that if His Majesty's government joined the negotiations, the Germans would not "offer to unload an even greater number of Jews on our hands."

The U.S. government approached the Jewish problem in much the same way, that is, that rescue was never viewed as an urgent topic needing immediate high-level attention. To be sure, State Department officials framed administration policy around a public sense of concern, assuring the press and populace that everything possible was being done to rescue European Jewry. The Roosevelt administration's primary argument, however, was that a speedy Allied victory would be the best way to effect rescue. Far from being effective, administration policy was actually a prescription for inaction. Allied inaction was most apparent on April 19, 1943. On the same day that the Warsaw ghetto uprising began, representatives from Britain and the United States met at the Bermuda Conference. The conference's ostensible goal was to investigate means of rescue. While the small remnant of Warsaw Jewry, the ground literally burning under them, fought their last battle, the gentlemen in Bermuda exchanged trivial pleasantries; their real goal was to deflect public pressure by appearing to do something while making no real policy changes.

Not until 1944, when political pressure at home increased during an election year, did the Roosevelt administration act. Even then decisive action was undertaken only after secretary of the Treasury Henry Morgenthau became involved. In late December 1943 Morgenthau had instructed two of his assistants, Randolph Paul and John Pehle, to investigate the State Department's handling of rescue issues. In January, Paul and Pehle reported back in a scathing memorandum entitled "The Acquiescence of This Government in the Murder of European Jews." Morgenthau proceeded to take this document to Roosevelt and suggested the creation of a U.S. rescue agency. Roosevelt agreed, signing an executive order on January 22, 1944. The creation of what came to be known as the War Refugee Board (WRB) finally brought the rescue issue to the fore, at least on paper. In reality, the creation of the WRB came too late to save most European Jews and in practice accomplished very little.[71]

Wartime Anglo-American diplomacy on Palestine/*Eretz Israel* was similarly frustrating for the Zionists. After the Biltmore Conference, almost nothing changed. A joint Anglo-American initiative in 1943, relating to a joint statement that would guarantee the White Paper's permanent implementation, although representing some movement on the diplomatic front, could hardly have warmed the hackles of the Zionists' hearts. The defeat of this proposal

turned out to be the only significant Zionist accomplishment for 1943 — a clear but minor victory. The joint statement was not canceled but was only postponed until after the war.[72] Moreover, the same agrument that was used by the Zionists to defeat the joint statement could potentially be a double-edged sword. They had argued that it was inopportune to undertake any initiatives in the Middle East until after hostilities ceased, an argument that could just as easily be turned against them.

Further initiatives from Washington and London repeated the same pattern. Zionist pressure in the U.S. Congress resulted in the introduction of parallel pro-Zionist resolutions in the Senate and House of Representatives in February 1944. Overwhelming bipartisan congressional support existed for the nonbinding resolutions that called for administration assistance in creating a Jewish commonwealth after World War II. Yet, administration delaying tactics, mainly Secretary of War Henry L. Stimson's comment that the resolution would cause Arab attacks on American servicemen in the Middle East, left the resolution stillborn.[73] By the time the resolution was reintroduced, during the presidential election campaign in the autumn of 1944, it was so watered down as to be virtually meaningless.[74] To add insult to injury, after a February 1945 meeting with King Ibn Saud of Saudi Arabia, President Roosevelt made a remark that he had learned more in five minutes about the Palestine/*Eretz Israel* problem than he could "in the exchange of two or three dozen letters." Although he later backpedaled in a conversation with Wise in March, Roosevelt had already done considerable damage to his credibility and to the Zionist cause he claimed to support.[75]

The lack of diplomatic progress led to considerable cleavages within the Zionist ranks, in particular, a rift between minimalists like Weizmann and maximalists like Ben-Gurion.[76] Realistically, however, the Zionists had few options. Weizmann's meeting with Soviet ambassador Ivan Maisky opened up the slim hope of Stalin's support for Zionist aspirations after the war but had no immediate impact on conditions in *Eretz Israel*.[77] Nearly five years of Zionist efforts had come to virtually nothing, although contacts and efforts to change the *status quo* continued until war's end.[78]

One final abortive initiative originated in London. After lengthy arguments over the White Paper of 1939, the British commitment to Jewry, and the need to do justice in Palestine/*Eretz Israel*, the Churchill government had (at Churchill's initiative) frozen implementation of the constitutional clause contained in the White Paper. On April 18, 1943, just after the German surrender in North Africa rendered Arab support for the Allies no longer necessary, Churchill informed his colleagues that he did not consider himself bound by the White Paper of 1939. Over the next ten weeks a series of memoranda sketched out a new policy whose main point was a return to partition and the creation of a Jewish state within a broader Arab Middle Eastern federation.[79] Although most of Churchill's cabinet remained skeptical, a sufficiently strong plurality emerged to place the proposal on the war cabinet's agenda.[80] Had this plan been carried out, it is not unlikely that much of the unhappiness in the Middle East in recent years could have been averted. However, a confluence of unrelated events halted Churchill's plan before implementation, and continuing opposition by British administrators and bureaucrats in the Middle East slowed the project down. Final cancellation followed Lehi's assassination of Lord Moyne, on November 5, 1944. At this point, the cabinet decided to withhold any further action until after the expected Allied victory was completed. By then, of course, Churchill was no longer prime minister and the entire process, tragically, began again from the beginning.[82]

The Civil War

The Moyne assassination must be viewed in context. Accumulated Zionist frustrations had been building to a point where senior British military and police leaders considered a Jewish revolt plausible, if not likely.[83] Simultaneously, Lehi's revival led to a renewed cycle of anti-British violence at the fringes of the *Yishuv*. The attack on Moyne was merely the most glaring; was not the only one and not necessarily the most militarily or politically significant one.

Lehi, after all, was a tiny, revolutionary offshoot of the IZL, formed when the latter agreed to a truce with the British during the dark days of 1940. At the time, the IZL leadership was following a similar policy to the rest of the *Yishuv*. However, a major diference existed. Whereas the JA (and the Hagana and Palmah) had agreed to a truce until World War II was over, the Irgun's declaration had been much narrower. Specifically, the IZL's truce had been formulated for as long as *Eretz Israel* remained under threat. Thereafter, the IZL would reevaluate its position, in light of conditions in *Eretz Israel* and relations between the Zionists and the British. In 1942, a well-known revisionist Zionist leader from Poland, Menahem Begin, arrived in *Eretz Israel*. Begin assumed IZL leadership in early 1943 and began to consider the organization's options. On February 1, 1944, IZL also declared a revolt against the British, opening with a series of pinprick attacks on the police.[84]

These attacks had only limited impact on the *Yishuv*, which was still preoccupied with conditions in Europe and the apparent immobility on the diplomatic front. To be sure, JA and WZO leaders resented actions by the IZL and Lehi, which were seen as irresponsible, at best, and bent on a policy that would lead to disaster. Moreover, at a time when Jewish unity was vital, IZL and Lehi insisted on operating by themselves without even token regard for Zionist discipline.[85] The *Yishuv*'s policy changed radically after the Moyne assassination. In a statement to Parliament, Prime Minister Churchill bared his own disappointment at the killing:

If our own dreams for Zionism are to end in the smoke of assassins' pistols and our labours for its future to produce only a new set of gangsters worthy of Nazi Germany, many like myself will have to reconsider the position we have maintained so consistently and so long in the past.[86]

The implication of Churchill's words — that the JA must act to remove the dissidents — resounded clearly with the Zionist leadership. In a controversial move the JAE on November 12, 1944 (a week after the assassination) delegated the task of silencing the dissidents to the Hagana. Even though the IZL had not been implicated in the Moyne assassination, it became the main target for what has become known as the Hunting Season, mainly because it was larger than Lehi and thus represented a greater threat in the Zionist leaders' eyes. Under the JAE's original orders, the Hagana was to operate against the dissidents as independently as possible; however, if that proved impossible then captured dissidents might be handed over to the British police. The latter point was the source of controversy. While disagreeing with the dissidents' tactics, many Hagana and Palmah troops shied away from any act that resembled collaboration with the authorities in an operation against other Zionists, who, though misguided, were acting in what they considered the Jewish people's best interest.

For four months the Yishuv teetered on the brink of total war, with the concomitant possiblity that the entire Zionist movement might collapse. The Hunting Season even surpassed the worst period of intra-Zionist violence during the 1930s: eventually, even posting a legal party banner became potentially dangerous. Hagana and Palmah troops fulfilled their orders, even if somewhat reluctantly, and attacked IZL personnel in order to capture and imprison them. The IZL fighters, for their part, resisted every effort to capture them. Scuffles led to gun battles and, as already noted, civil war.[87]

After four months of internecine struggle that had accomplished little other than squandering precious resources, the Hunting Season was called off. Meetings held in March 1945 between leaders of the different underground movements at Kibbutz Yagur led to a fragile truce. Further Hagana operations against the dissidents were cancelled while the latter agreed to desist from any operations that would embarass

the JA and WZO leadership. This truce was destined to be a brief one. By November the truce had become a complete alliance that broke down again in July 1946. Like the political bodies they represented, the underground movements were to cooperate only under limited conditions, and then mainly when external crises forced them together.

The Yishuv's War Effort

One aspect of the Yishuv's history during World War II deserves special attention: the effort to establish a Jewish military unit as part of the Allied cause. Immediately after World War II began, the Zionist leaders pledged their support for the Allied war effort.[88] The upshot of these offers was a specific commitment on both sides for the creation of a Jewish division to fight the Nazis, along with preparation for other joint efforts, overt and covert, that would synchronize Jewish/Zionist capabilities with British/Allied strategic needs.[89] The Zionists pinned great hopes on military cooperation, hoping to derive similar benefits as had accrued from the Jewish Legion raised in World War I. This was even true despite the unfortunate arrest, by British military police, of forty-three Hagana officers who were on a training exercise — an act that showed just how ambivalent the British were to cooperation with the Zionists.[90]

As with the diplomatic front, the military experience during the war was to prove very frustrating for the Zionists. Agreement having apparently been reached on the Jewish division in December 1939, disappointment set in only a month later when the British announced a policy of equal recruitment for Jews and Arabs, and even then mainly as auxiliaries to supplement the existing British garrison.[91] The truth was that many British leaders opposed the establishment of a Jewish army altogether: Colonial Secretary George Lloyd went so far as to opine that "any whisper of such a bargain would set the Middle East ablaze."[92] The cabinet, however, felt it inexpedient to discuss such matters in so open a fashion. Instead, a variety of excuses, mainly in connection with the army's reputed lack of resources (especially after the withdrawal from Dunkirk), was used to repeatedly delay implementation of the Division's creation.[93]

That a lack of sufficient resources was an excuse may be gleaned from the fact that despite opposition to creating the Jewish division, opponents fully supported the anonymous individual recruitment of *Yishuv* members into the British armed forces.[94] Furthermore, the British recognized the propaganda utility, at least in the United States, of continuing to discuss the Jewish army even without implementing it.[95] As a result, the issue was debated, back and forth, between opponents and proponents with no specific conclusion reached through the summer of 1940.[96]

Italian entry into the war and its invasion of Egypt in September 1940 rendered the matter critical, since the *Yishuv* was now faced with a tangible security threat.[97] The result of Zionist fears was a new series of negotiations that led to agreement on both recruitment and parity with the Arabs but brought the cause of a Jewish army no closer to fruition than it had been in September 1939.[98] By the end of 1940, a side issue had been raised regarding the use of Zionist military units — mainly the JA's desire that such units be used first and foremost to defend the Yishuv.[99] But, such disagreements were not the cause for the delay in creating the Jewish division, which was now dubbed a "Palestine" division and was to be recruited in equal proportion from Jewish and Arab communities.[100]

New opposition by British military and political leaders in the Middle East and Great Britain again led to a delay, this time bluntly called a postponement, and collapse of the Jewish division scheme.[101] This held true despite Prime Minister Churchill's insistence that he would "see the thing through" even though another postponement was greatly distressing to the Zionists.[102] Again, the delay mainly reflected British fears about Arab responses, about the potential need to repay the Jews (after World War II) for their loyalty by canceling the White Paper of 1939, and about the chance that a Jewish army could lead to the Zionist conquest of *Eretz Israel* after the war.[103]

In the interim *Yishuv* youth answered the call to colors, volunteering in unprecedented numbers for recruitment into the Royal Armed Forces. Recruitment in the *Yishuv* totaled slightly less than 30,000 personnel (men and women), of whom 5,258 served in all-Jewish units (the Buffs and the Jewish Brigade, see below) and 1,100 were volunteers from outside Palestine/*Eretz Israel*: seven hundred of the latter were Egyptian Jews who served in the Jewish Brigade. *Yishuv* personnel served in every unit and on every front from North Africa and Europe to India and Burma. In 1940 and 1941, many of the volunteers served in pioneer units — units that combined engineering and infantry functions in support of both offensive and (given the circumstances faced by the Allies, mainly) defensive operations. This was true during the French campaign and continued in North Africa, Greece, and Crete.[104] One such unit made an epic stand near Mechili, North Africa, during the desperate summer of 1942, holding out until relieved by elements of General Pierre Koenig's Free French Brigade, and withdrawing from Bir Hakheim to El Alamein.[105]

An entirely different but no less important role was played from 1942 onward by Jews who recently immigrated to *Eretz Israel* and who served in the ranks of British secret services, commando units, and other special forces. Mainly relevant to the recruitment and evolution of the Palmah, the Hagana's so-called strike companies (derived from the abbreviation words Plugot Mahatz, strike companies), which was formed in 1940 as a mobile, offensive, element in the Hagana order of battle. The Palmah, in turn, was divided into companies that were trained for commando or irregular operations; when not on active duty the companies were based for financial reasons in various *Kibbutzim* and *Kvutzot*.[106] Within this special force, two companies were even more special: the Arabist Company, composed of Middle Eastern Jews who could easily blend in with the local population, and the Germanist Company, composed of Jewish refugees from

להגנת עם ומולדת

התגייס לחיל הנוטרים!

Wartime Recruitment Poster for the Jewish Supernumerary Police:
"For the Defense of Our People and Homealnd/Join the Police Force."
Courtesy of the Central Zionist Archives, Jerusalem

the Reich who were available for operations behind German lines.[107]

In 1940, the JA reached an agreement with the British Special Operations Executive (SOE) for cooperation on secret operations in Europe and the Middle East. This agreement recognized *inter alia* that aid to diaspora Jewry should be part and parcel of any joint operation. SOE officials went so far as to promise "not to interfere" in operations that were not approved by the Palestine Administration or the Colonial Office.[108] This cooperative agreement worked well during the allied invasion of Syria, when Palmah units spearheaded, with mixed success, the Allied invasion forces. Additionally, the Palmah

German Company was incorporated into an ultrasecret British force dubbed the Special Interrogation Group (SIG) that specialized in operating behind German lines in North Africa in German uniforms. Operational experience was mixed, the spectacular failures being more publicized today than the successes, but there is no question about the heroism displayed by personnel who knew that they could expect no quarter from the enemy.[109]

A basic dichotomy was inherent in these operations and in all others during the war years: the JA saw the Jewish aspects of the war — including possible use of commando forces to rescue Jews in the Balkans from the Nazis — as critically important, if not paramount.[110] In contrast, the British continued to express considerable reservations regarding the wisdom and utility of creating forces that could, after the war, be used to foment a Jewish rebellion in *Eretz Israel*.[111] This dichotomy of approaches led to considerable frustration for the JA, the Palmah, and (to a lesser degree) the SOE, and resulted in much time and effort being expended for a very little gain. After excruciating negotiations, a decision was taken to send thirty-two Jewish paratroopers into the Balkans to assist intelligence gathering, promote anti-Nazi guerrilla forces, and rescue any Jews who could be saved. The story of the paratroopers is well-known and does not need detailed recapitulation here. Militarily their mission was a failure since most were unable to undertake any substantial military operations against the Nazis. Likewise, few had the opportunity to undertake systematic rescue opeartions. However, from the purely Jewish perspective, the mission was a (qualified) success. Jews hunted by the Nazis throughout Europe heard of the thirty-two heroes and heroines who sacrificed their lives to save a remnant and shepherd them home. The mission is perhaps best summarized by a poem by paratrooper Hannah Szenes, composed just prior to her embarkation for Hungary, where she was captured, tried, and executed:

Blessed is the match,
  That is consumed in kindling flame
Blessed is the flame,
  That burns in secret fastness of the heart
Blessed is the heart,
  with the strength to stop beating
  for honor's sake
Blessed is the match,
  That is consumed in kindling flame.[112]

Clandestine cooperation did not bring any movement on plans for the Jewish division. To the contrary, each passing month brought new delays and, finally, on October 14, 1941, the plan was abandoned altogether.[113] Instead, a Palestine regiment was raised as part of the West Kent infantry regiment, to so-called Buffs. The Buffs had been the parent unit of the Jewish Legion during World War I; on the surface, therefore, a semblance of concession to Zionist sensibilities could be claimed by the war cabinet. In reality, the Buffs created during World War II bore no resemblance to their earlier counterparts since recruitment was to be equally spread between Arabs and Jews. Arab recruitment lagged behind Jewish recruitment and although a few battalions of the Buffs saw limited (mostly rear area) duty, the plan virtually fell apart.[114]

The Jewish army idea appeared to be stillborn, but the concept resonated in the Jewish world. Considerable effort was thus expended, mainly in the United States, to pressure the British to reverse their decision.[15] The Yishuv's right to defend itself returned to the forefront of the Zionist struggle in the summer of 1942. Serious British reversals in North Africa posed a grave danger to the entire Allied position in the Middle East until Field Marshal Erwin Rommel's Afrika Korps was halted at El Alamein in August. Even then, Rommel's forces were less than seventy miles from Alexandria and the capture of the Suez Canal appeared imminent. Under the circumstances, Zionists once again pleaded for the right to defend themselves. Once again, a Jewish division was proposed, debated, and — as soon as the threat passed — rejected by the cabinet.[116]

Zionist advocacy kept the idea of a Jewish fighting force alive during 1943, although no substantive actions were taken by the British or the WZO to revive the idea.[117] Instead, the Zionists concentrated on further refining the Palmah into the seedling for an independent military force that would fight the decisive battle coming after World War II. To be sure, difficulties abounded in such a policy, particularly in regard to the Palmah troopers, who had been extensively trained for action but were not immediately deployed to the battlefield. Except insofar as they were settled on *Kibbutzim*, they seemed to be doing nothing of any significance. Moreover, agricultural labor seemed to belie their special military training and thus led to low morale and many requests for transfers. In response, the Hagana general staff decided to reorganize the Palmah. A cadre of companies, the barest minimum needed for defensive action, were kept on permanent service. The rest were placed in a ready reserve pool that could be mobilized rapidly in case of an emergency.[118] After the reorganization, the Palmah could continue to grow in both size and importance, becoming a major factor in the Yishuv's plans for defense. By 1945, the Palmah could field a force of some 1,900 men and women who would be put to good use during the critical battles waged between 1945 and 1949.[119]

Renewed pressure on the British government to allow the Jews to participate in European liberation finally and belatedly bore fruit. In March 1944, the WZO again requested that Jews be mobilized under their own banner to fight the Nazis. Again the matter was debated in the British cabinet; this time, tentative approval of the scheme was received in July.[120] By this time, the Jewish force was considerably pared down, a single brigade being proposed. Final approval of the brigade was given in August and mobilization began immediately.[121]

The Jewish Brigade Group (Hativa Yehudit Lohemet or HIL in Hebrew) mustered near Alexandria in October 1944. On completion of basic training under Brigadier Ernest F. Benjamin, a Canadian Jew, HIL was transferred to Italy. Intense combat training commenced once the brigade reached Italy, with the first units entering the line in March 1945. HIL's major operation was the daylight assault crossing of the Senio River on April 9, 1945. This complicated operation was successfully accomplished and the pursuit of retreating German forces commenced. HIL units followed the battle's progress northward, participating in the liberation of Bologna in late April. War's end found HIL encamped near Taravisio.[122]

The shock of combat was followed by an even greater shock for the brigade's troops. Meetings with Holocaust survivors, especially after HIL was transferred to occupation duties in Belgium and Holland in July 1945, seared many of the troops. Early on, therefore, HIL became a focal point for Zionist efforts to rescue the surviving remnant of European Jewry and to aid Jewish survivors' rehabilitation in Jewry's ancestral homeland. Growing tensions caused by *Briha*, *Aliya Bet*, and the revolt that flared in *Eretz Israel* led to the Brigade's disbandment in 1946, but by then it may be said that the seeds for a conventional Israeli army had been sown.[123]

Perfidy or Powerlessness?

With the end of World War II, a long nightmare ended for world Jewry. With the horror fully exposed, the brutal murder of 6 million Jews finally entered the world's consciousness. This unprecedented catastrophe represented a nadir for Zionist fortunes. Powerless to effect their own fate, Jews both inside and outside the Nazi sphere could only watch the unfolding tragedy with horror and prepare for the denouement of the struggle for Jewish survival that was bound to happen.

In recent years, this reality has been largely forgotten and accusations of perfidious behavior have been hurled at the JA and WZO leadership. Such accusations are unfair and inaccurate. Given the actual conditions facing European Jewry and the *Yishuv*, it is difficult to see what might have been done that was not tried at the time. The wartime failure to effectively respond to the Nazi threat did not derive from a Zionist problem but from the fact that the British controlled *Eretz Israel*.

Indeed, the Holocaust represented the final, decisive proof that Zionist predictions of catastrophe had been prescient. It stood to reason that only one lesson could properly be learned from the events that took place between 1939 and 1945: A Jewish state must come into being in order to prevent a similar catastrophe from ever happening again. Viewed from a different perspective, it might be said that the Holocaust provided the clearest example of Jewish powerlessness (and also highlighted all the dangers inherent in Jewish powerlessness) while also representing a watershed in the history of the Jewish people that culminated in Jewry's ultimate emergence from powerlessness.

Notes

1. For developments in Europe in the last five months prior to World War II, see: Abraham J. Edelheit and Hershel Edelheit, *History of the Holocaust: A Handbook and Dictionary* (Boulder: Westview Press, 1994), pp. 49–50.

2. On Ruppin, see Abraham J. Edelheit, *The Yisvuv in the Shadow of the Holocaust: Zionist Politics and Rescue Aliya, 1933-1939* (Boulder: Westview Press, 1996), p. 206; on Jabotinsky, see Howard I. Rosenblum, "A Political History of Revisionist Zionism", (Ph.D. diss, Columbia University, 1986), chap. 7.

3. Saul Friedländer, *Nazi Germany and the Jews* (New York: HarperCollins, 1997), 1:299–300.

4. A very different line of argument was adopted by Shabtai B. Bet-Zvi, הציונית הפוסט-אוגנדית במשבר השואה (Post-Ugandian Zionism in the crucible of the Holocaust) (Tel Aviv: Bronfman's Agency, 1977), passim. Bet-Zvi argues that Zionist concentration of *Eretz Israel* prevented successful rescue because mass rescue implied abandoning the Zionist goal of achieving salvation for the Jewish people. This argument fails to consider that the British, not the Zionists ruled *Eretz Israel* at the time, does not sufficiently account for Zionist calls for mass emigration prior to the Nazi seizure of power, and does not address the numerous failed territorialist rescue schemes proposed at the time. Fundamentally, Bet-Zvi has missed the point: that no country placed as much emphasis on rescuing Jews as the Nazis placed on killing them.

5. Shlomo Lev-Ami, במאבק ובמרד (By struggle and revolt) (Tel Aviv: Ministry of Defense Publication, n.d.), pp. 131–132.

6. Oded Messer, תכניות אופרטיביות של ההגנה, *1937-1948* (Hagana operational planning, 1937–1948) (n.p.: Tag Books, 1996), pp. 25–27.

7. The JA documentation from this period was cited in Aaron S. Klieman, ed., *The Darkest Year, 1939*, Rise of Israel Series, vol. 27 (New York: Garland, 1987), pp. 467–545; and M. J. Cohen, ed., *Implementing the White Paper, 1939-1940*, Rise of Israel Series, vol. 28 (New York: Garland, 1987), pp. 7–40.

8. Both speeches were reprinted in Joseph Heller, ed., במאבק למדינה (The struggle for a Jewish state) (Jerusalem: Zalman Shazar Center Press, 1984), pp. 264–271.

9. A poignant description of these events was provided in Zorach Warhaftig, פליט ושריד בימי שואה (Refugee and Survivor During the Holocaust), Jerusalem: Yad Vashem, 19884, ch. 1.

10. Edelheit, *Yishuv*, p. 286.

11. Ibid., p. 247.

12. Weizmann to Smuts, October 18, 1939, and Weizmann to Churchill, December 14, 1939, in Cohen, *Implementing*, pp. 41–42, 65–67.

13. Lothian to Foreign Office, November 24, 1939 and Churchill to War Cabinet, December 25, 1939, in ibid., pp. 45–64, 74–75.

14. Ibid., pp. 76–85, 90, 97–106.

15. Williams to Foreign Office, November 25, 1939, in ibid., pp. 43–44, lists the "desirable" and "undesirable" themes for British wartime propaganda, prominent among the latter being any mention of the Jews.

16. Ibid., pp. 91–96.

17. A detailed history of the Holocaust cannot be provided here, but documents relevant to the subject were cited in M. J. Cohen, ed., *The Holocaust and Illegal Immigration, 1939–1947*, Rise of Israel Series, vol. 30 (New York Garland, 1987). Interested readers should see Edelheit and Edelheit, *History of the Holocaust*, passim.; Leni Yahil, *The Holocaust: The Fate of European Jewry* (New York: Oxford University Press, 1990); Raul Hilberg, *The Destruction of the European Jews*, rev. ed. (New York: Holmes and Meier, 1985), and the issues of *Yad Vashem Studies* that have appeared since 1957.

18. Edelheit and Edelheit, *History of the Holocaust*, pp. 51–52.

19. Ibid., pp. 52–53, 57–61.

20. Ibid., pp. 55–57.

21. Yahil, *The Holocaust*, pp. 209, 213.

22. Ibid., pp. 226–229.

23. Edelheit and Edelheit, *History of the Holocaust*, p. 401.

24. Ibid., p. 403.

25. Cf., Marie Syrkin, *Blessed is the Match*, rev. ed. (Philadelphia: Jewish Publication Society), 1976, pts. IV–VI.

26. Yehuda Bauer, *The Jewish Emergence From Powerlessness*, Toronto: University of Toronto Press, 1979, pp. 26-40.

27. Edelheit, *Yishuv*, p. 250.

28. The circumstances of both sinkings are still open to widely varying interpretations. Cf. Dalia Ofer, *Escaping the Holocaust: Illegal Immigration to the Land of Israel, 1939-1944* (New York; Oxford University Press, 1990), pp. 149–171, 195–198; and Ze'ev Venia Hadari (Pomerantz), צומת קושטא: שליחות כנגד כל הסיכויים (Crossroads Istanbul: against all odds) (Tel Aviv: Ministry of Defense Publications, 1992), pp. 62–63, 72–74, 85–90.

29. Hadari, צומת קושטא, p. 75.

30. Dalia Ofer and Hannah Weiner, *Dead-End Journey: The Tragic Story of the Kladovo-Šabac Group* (Lanham, MD: University Press of America, 1996).

31. Press release, March 11, 1942, cited in Ofer, *Escaping the Holocaust*, p. 175.

32. Weizmann to Churchill, February 23, 1940, cited in Cohen, *Implementing*, p. 97.

33. Ibid., pp. 98–106.

34. Cf. the documents in ibid., pp. 107–121, and especially the April 27, 1940, minute by Sir John Schuckburgh that reeks with antisemitic venom (pp. 111–112). Documents such as this one give lie to the notion that the Allies "did all they could" to rescue Jews during the Holocaust. For a radically different interpretation, based only on secondary sources, see W. D. Rubinstein, *The Myth of Rescue* (London: Routledge, 1997).

35. Cohen, *Implementing*, pp. 126–134; M. J. Cohen, ed., *Palestine and the Arab Federation, 1938–1945*, Rise of Israel Series, vol. 32 (New York: Garland, 1987), pp. 67, 78–91; M. J. Cohen, ed., *The Zionist Political Program, 1940–1947*, Rise of Israel Series, vol. 31 (New York: Garland, 1987), pp. 5–12.

36. Cf., Ben-Gurion's memoranda on the new government in Cohen, *Zionist Political Program*, pp. 1–4 and Cohen, *Implementing*, pp. 122–125.

37. Cf. Nethanel Katzburg, מדיניות במבוך: מדיניות בריטניה בארץ ישראל, 1940-1945 (The Palestine problem in British Politics, 1940–1945) (Jerusalem: Yad Yitzhak Ben-Zvi, 1977), chap. 1–2; and Gavriel Cohen, צ'רצ'יל ושאלת ארץ ישראל, 1939-1942 (Churchill and the Palestine problem, 1939–1942), Jerusalem: Yad Yitzhak Ben-Zvi, 1976, chaps. 3, 5.

38. Cohen, *Implementing*, pp. 135-214.

39. In addition to the documents in Cohen, *Arab Federation*, pp. 100–165, see Philip J. Baram, *The U.S. State Department in the Middle East* (Philadelphia: University of Pennsylvania Press, 1978), chaps. 13–14.

40. Cohen, *Arab Federation*, pp. 166–246. Cf. Yehoshua Porath, "Weizmann, Chruchill and the 'Philby Plan,' 1937–1943," *Studies in Zionism*, 5 no. 2 (autumn 1984): 239–272.

41. The Zionists' assessment was reflected in the documents by Ben-Gurion, Weizmann, and others, cited in Cohen, *Zionist Political Program*, pp. 13–64; and Heller, במאבק למדינה p. 273–296. Jabotinsky's analysis was virtually identical to his ideological opponents' at this stage. See Jabotinsky's *The War and the Jew*, new ed. (New York: Altalena Press, 1987), pp. 234–250.

42. Uri Brenner, נוכח איום הפלישה הגרמנית לארץ ישראל (Under the German threat of invasion of Eretz Israel) (Ramat Efal: Yad Yitzhak Tabenkin, 1981); Yoav Gelber "מצדה": ההגנה על ארץ ישראל במלחמת העולם השנייה ("Masada:" The Defense of Eretz Israel in World War II) (Ramat

Gan: Bar-Ilan University Press, 1990).

43. Yehuda Bauer, *From Diplomacy to Resistance* (New York: Atheneum, 1973), pp. 195–203.

44. Joseph Heller, *The Stern Gang: Ideology, Politics, and Terror, 1940–1949* (London: Frank Cass, 1995), chap. 3.

45. The two critical documents on Lehi's plan are cited in Heller, למדינה במאבק, pp. 308–311; they are interpreted in Heller, *Stern Gang*, pp. 78–79, 85–91.

46. Heller, *Stern Gang*, chap. 5.

47. Bauer, *Diplomacy*, chap. 2.

48. Cohen, *Zionist Political Program*, pp. 50–64.

49. David H. Shapiro, *From Philanthropy to Activism: The Political Transformation of American Zionism in the Holocaust Years, 1933–1945* (Oxford: Pergamon Press, 1944), chap. 1–2.

50. Ibid., chap. 4.

51. "The Biltmore Resolution," cited in Walter Laqueur, ed., *The Israel-Arab Reader*, 2d ed., (New York: Bantam Books, 1971), pp. 78–79.

52. Ibid., p. 79.

53. Supra pp. 169–174.

54. Cf. Zvi Ganin, "Activism Versus Moderation: The Conflict Between Abba Hillel Silver and Stephen Wise during the the 1940s," *Studies in Zionism*, 5 no. 1 (Spring 1984): 71–95. Documents concerning the rift were reproduced in Cohen, *Zionist Political Program*, pp. 66–74, 76–89.

55. Bauer, *Diplomacy*, pp. 230–242.

56. Abba Hillel Silver, *Vision and Victory* (New York: Zionist Organization of America, 1949), pp. 13–21.

57. Bauer, *Diplomacy*, chaps. 7–9.

58. Halifax to Foreign Office, May 20, 1942, Giles to Chief Secretary, Oct. 12, 1942, cited in Cohen, *Zionist Political Program*, pp. 65, 90–93.

59. Halifax to Foreign Office, July 1, 1942, in ibid., p. 75.

60. Cf., Monty N. Penkower, *Franklin D. Roosevelt and the Palestine Imbroglio* (New York: Touro College, 1996).

61. Monty N. Penkower, *The Jews Were Expendable: Free World Diplomacy and the Holocaust* (Urbana: University of Illinois Press, 1983), chap. 3.

62. Weizmann to Dugdale, January 8, 1943, Cohen, *Zionist Political Program*, pp. 94–98.

63. Ibid., pp. 103–105, 113–134.

64. Ibid., pp. 136–138.

65. Ibid., pp. 99–102, 106–112.

66. On the history of the American Jewish Conference, see Melvin I. Urofsky, *We Are One! American Jewry and Israel* (Garden City, NY: Doubleday, 1978), pp. 22–33.

67. For two examples of such literature, see Ben Hecht, *Perfidy* (New York: Robert Speller, 1961); Lenni Brenner, *Zionism in an Age of Dictators* (London: Croom Helm, 1983). An analysis of this genre was provided in Edelheit, *Yishuv*, p. 28.

68. David S. Wyman, *The Abandonment of the Jews* (New York: Pantheon Books, 1984), appendix B.

69. Edelheit and Edelheit, *History of the Holocaust*, pp. 132–133.

70. Cited in Bernard Wasserstein, *Britain and the Jews of Europe, 1939-1945* (Oxford: Clarendon Press, 1979), p. 184.

71. Edelheit and Edelheit, *History of the Holocaust*, pp. 135–138, 367–368.

72. Monty N. Penkower, *The Holcoaust and Israel Reborn: From Catastrophe to Sovereignty* (Urbana: University of Illinois Press, 1994), chap. 4.

73. *Hearings Before the Committee of Foreign Affairs of the House of Representatives on H. Res. 418 and H. Res. 419, Resolutions Relative To the Jewish National Home in Palestine*, Reprinted with an introduction by Ben Halpern (New York: Ktav, 1970).

74. Penkower, *Israel Reborn*, pp. 221–223.

75. Ibid., pp. 224–226.

76. Cohen, *Zionist Political Program*, pp. 137–138, 147–148.

77. Ibid., p. 136.

78. Ibid., pp. 149–154; Heller, *במאבק למדינה*, pp. 350–381.

79. Gavriel Cohen, *הקבינט הבריטי ושאלת ארץ ישראל, אפריל-יולי, 1943* (The British cabinet and Palestine, April–July, 1943) (Tel Aviv: ha-Kibbutz ha-Meuchad for Tel Aviv University Press, 1976), pp. 39–72.

80. Ibid., pp. 72–82.

81. On the Moyne assassination, see Heller, *Stern Gang*, chap. 6; and Gerold Frank, *The Deed* (New York: Avon Books, 1963).

82. Katzburg, *מדיניות במבוך*, chaps. 4–7. The Churchill partition plan is documented in M. J. Cohen, ed., *The British Return to Partition, 1943–1945*, Rise of Israel Series, vol. 33 (New York: Garland, 1987), pp. 1–245.

83. M. J. Cohen, ed., *Jewish Resistance to British Rule, 1944-1947*, Rise of Israel Series, vol. 34 (New York: Garland, 1987), pp. 1-52; Yoav Gelber, "המדיניות הבריטית והציונית בצל החשש מהתקוממות יהודית, 1942-1944" (British and Zionist Policy in Eretz Israel in Shadow of a possible Jewish Revolt, 1942–1944), *הציונות* 7 (1982): 342–396.

84. J. Boywer Bell, *Terror Out of Zion* (New York: St. Martin's Press, 1977), pp. 104–119.

85. Lev-Ami, *במאבק ובמרד*, chap. 8.

86. Winston S. Churchill, statement to Parliament, November 17, 1944, cited in Cohen, *Jewish Resistance*, p. 31.

87. Lev-Ami, *במאבק ובמרד*, chap. 9, Bauer, *Diplomacy*, pp. 323–333.

88. Weizmann to Chamberlain, August 29, 1939, cited in M. J. Cohen, ed., *The Jewish Military Effort, 1939-1944*, Rise of Israel Series, vol. 29 (New York: Garland, 1987), pp. 1–2; Yoav Gelber, *תולדת ההתנדבות* (A history of Palestinian Jewish volunteering in the British army during World War II), 4 vols. (Jerusalem: Yad Yitzhak Ben-Zvi, 1979–1984).

89. Cohen, *Military Effort*, pp. 12–29; Gelber, *תולדת ההתנדבות*, 1; chap. 3.

90. Cohen, *Military Effort*, pp. 7–11.

91. Ibid., pp. 30–40.

92. Ibid., pp. 41–56 cites Lloyd's statements, the quote being repeated twice (on pp. 47, 56).

93. Lloyd to Halifax, June 3, 1940, in ibid., pp. 57–66.

94. Lloyd to Weizmann, June 15, 1940, in ibid., pp. 69–70.

95. Weizmann to Brendan Bracken, June 11, 1940, in ibid., pp. 67–68.

96. Ibid., pp. 71–89.

97. Ibid., pp. 90–97.

98. Ibid., pp. 98–109. Cf. Arye B. Saposnik, "Advertisement or Achievement? American Jewry and the Campaign for a Jewish Army, 1939–1944: A Reassessment," *Journal of Israeli History* 17 no.2 (Summer 1996): 193–220.

99. Cohen, *Military Effort*, pp. 110–113.

100. Ibid., pp. 114–136.

101. Ibid., pp. 137–157.

102. Ibid., pp. 158–160.

103. Ibid., pp. 161–163.

104. Gelber, *תולדת ההתנדבות*, 1, chaps. 4–7.

105. Pierre van Paassen, *The Forgotten Ally* (New York: Dial Press, 1943), pp. 191–198.

106. Bauer, *Diplomacy*, pp. 139–142.

107. On the "Arabists" see Zvika Dror, *המסתערבים של הפלמ"ח* (The Arabists of the Palmah) (Tel Aviv: ha-Kibbutz ha-Meuchad, 1986). No similar source exists on the German company, but details may be found in widely scattered sources on British special forces during World War II

and in Gelber, *תולדלת ההתנדבות*, passim.

108. Bauer, *Diplomacy*, p. 113.

109. Ibid., pp. 153–161, 199–202.

110. Cf. Yehuda Bauer, *"הצנחנים ותוכנית ההתגוננות"* (The paratroopers and the defense plan), *ילקות מורשת* no.1 (1963): 86–94.

111. Wasserstein, *Jews of Europe*, chap. 7.

112. The paratroopers' mission has been summarized many times, most notably in Gelber, *תולדלת ההתנדבות*, 3: chap. 2. Szenes's poem, also reprinted many times, was cited from Syrkin, *Blessed is the Match*, frontis.

113. Cohen, *Military Effort*, pp. 164–214.

114. Gelber, *תולדלת ההתנדבות*, 2: chap. 1. Arab participation during the war and their preference for cooperation with the Axis, are set out in: Lukasz Hirszowicz, *The Third Reich and the Arab East* (London: Routledge and Kegan Paul, 1966) and Antonio J. Munoz, *Lions of the Desert: Arab Volunteers in the German Army, 1941–1945*, 2d ed., (Bayside, NY: Axis Europa, 1996).

115. Saposnik, "Advertisement or Achievement."

116. Cohen, *Military Effort*, pp. 215–239.

117. Ibid., pp. 240–245.

118. Bauer, *Diplomacy*, pp. 292–304.

119. Ibid., p. 333.

120. Cohen, *Military Effort*, pp. 240–271.

121. Ibid., pp. 272–274.

122. Gelber, *תולדלת ההתנדבות*, 2, chaps. 6–7.

123. Yoav Gelber, *גרעין לצבא עברי סדיר* (The seeds of a Jewish army) (Jerusalem: Yad Yitzhak Ben-Zvi, 1986), chaps. 1–2.

10
REVOLT AND REBIRTH

Liberation and Survival

In 1945 the horrifying experience of European Jewry during World War II was finally laid bare for the entire world to see. In six years, 6 million Jews, nearly one-third of the world Jewish population, had been brutally murdered by the Nazis and their henchmen. In particular, the Zionists' great demographic reservoir, Eastern European Jewry, was almost completely destroyed. Polish Jewry was especially hard hit losing an estimated 90 percent of its prewar population.[1] The survivors, who likened themselves to the *She'erit ha-Pleta* (saving remnant) of biblical prophecy, made simple physical survival their first priority, followed by communal rehabilitation, education of youth, and preparation for emigration.

Although Allied policymakers had focused their wartime planning on completely restoring Jews to their countries of origin once the Nazis had been defeated, that plan unequivocally worked only in Western Europe. Conditions in Eastern Europe, by contrast, were conducive only to the creation of temporary communities whose long-term objective was finding a suitable haven for emigration and resettlement. Given the continuing restrictions on immigrants in most countries, that reality meant that most Jews sought to leave Europe for *Eretz Israel* (although the United States and Great Britain might have been equally acceptable

destinations had either been willing to accept a mass influx of Jewish refugees).

The small remnant of Polish Jewry was faced with a double dilemma. It was hard enough to stay in blood-soaked Poland, where each step Jews took reminded them of Polish Jewry's great losses and wherever they stepped, they encountered a cemetery. It was harder still to conceive that after surviving the Holocaust they would be hunted again for the simple reason that they had dared to survive. The years of Nazi occupation of Poland, which had brought pain, humiliation, and suffering for the Polish masses, seem to have done little to change their attitude toward Jews. Antisemitism, which should logically have ceased with the demise of Nazi Germany, was instead advocated overtly or covertly by a majority of Poles. Between November 1944 and October 1945, at least 351 Jews were murdered in Poland by other Poles. At the time there were fewer than 80,000 Jews living in the country, in addition to some 175,000 Polish Jews then in the Soviet Union. Postwar Polish antisemitism reached its height on July 4, 1946. A blood libel after the disappearance of a Christian child led to a pogrom in the city of Kielce. In the resulting attack on the Jewish community building, forty-two Jews were murdered.[2]

Under the circumstances, reconstruction proved impossible in Poland. In response, Polish Jews began to leave the country spontaneously, initially in a disorganized fashion, ending up in Displaced Persons (DP) camps established by the Allies in their zones of occupation in Germany, Austria, and Italy. Conditions in the Danubian republics and the Balkans echoed conditions in Poland, although violence was never as intense as in Poland. In this case, the rise of Communism significantly undercut Jewish security and created conditions ripe for a mass exodus.[3] Willy-nilly, the survivors thus became a critical catalyst in postwar Zionist politics and played a crucial role in the creation of the State of Israel.

As conditions worsened in Eastern Europe, the spontaneous trickle became a torrent, soon dubbed *Briha* (flight). Initially, this movement organized itself, being led by former Jewish partisans including (among others) Abba Kovner, Yitzhak Zuckerman, and Zivia Lubetkin. At this point, *Briha* was organized and with the help of *Shelihim* (emissaries) from the *Yishuv. Briha* operated along two major routes: from Lodz west to Poznan and Szczecin, thence to the American or British zones in Germany; and from Lodz south to Katowice or Krakow through Czechoslovakia, Hungary, or Austria to either Italy or Yugoslavia. A smaller proportion of the potential émigrés ended up in the Black Sea ports of Varna (Bulgaria) or Constanta (Romania). Groups ending up in Italy were, in 1945 and the first half of 1946, escorted in part by members of the Jewish Brigade for Palestine, a Jewish unit of the Royal Army. Simultaneous with Briha, thousands of liberated Jewish concentration camp survivors in Germany and Austria were also moved with the help of the Jewish Brigade. Taken from their miserable camp environment in small groups and temporarily housed in refugee shelters nearer the Italian border, they were secretly integrated into large transports of Italian prisoners of war returning from the Soviet Union; once in Italy, they were gradually transported (again, with the help of the Jewish Brigade) to the south to await transportation to *Eretz Israel*.[4]

For its part, the British rejected any link between the fate of Jewish refugees and the postwar status of *Eretz Israel*. Although the war cabinet had considered a new partition plan in 1943 and 1944, this plan (as noted in the previous chapter) proved to be abortive. The possibility of partition returned to the forefront of British policy briefly in 1945, but no action was taken prior to the end of World War II. At that point the caretaker government led by Winston S. Churchill debated the issue but took no decisions. The newly elected Labour government led by Prime Minister Clement Atlee and Foreign Minister Ernest Bevin also debated the issue after assuming power in August 1945. Previous promises by Labour to cancel the White Paper of 1939 notwithstanding, (promises made, for example, during the election campaign in 1945), the cabinet rejected partition as impractical and dangerous to imperial interests. Instead, the cabinet hoped to retain the White Paper of 1939, at least temporarily, with one concession to the WZO. Certificates that had not been issued but that had been promised under the White Paper's terms (almost half of the original 75,000 certificates) would continue to be available for limited *aliya* even though their term had expired. This was, of course, nothing more than a sop, since no new certificates were to be made available once these were used up.[5]

Throughout this extremely trying period the cabinet concentrated on the means needed to effect Jewish resettlement in Europe, primarily by inducing Jewish DPs to return home.[6] Although well aware that these decisions would satisfy neither the Arabs nor the Jews, the cabinet also saw this as a stopgap measure until a substantive policy on Palestine/*Eretz Israel* could be formulated. Thus, when the cabinet took this decision (in September or October 1945) it was already looking for a new long-term policy that could win the acceptance (or at least the acquiescence) of both Jewish and Arab communities and thus guarantee a continued British role in Palestine/*Eretz Israel*.[7]

While the British cabinet fiddled with its Palestine/*Eretz Israel* policy, the Zionists did not remain idle. True to government prediction, the WZO was not satisfied with the plan to continue the White Paper policy, a decision criticized as unfair and inhumane.[8] An extraordinary Zionist conference held in London in

August 1945 stated the Zionists' minimum demands: the immediate entry into *Eretz Israel* of 100,000 Jewish DPs and the removal of all restrictions on Jewish land purchase. In other words, the Zionists demanded the unequivocal revocation of the White Paper of 1939, although for now they decided to forgo further demands related to the Jewish commonwealth that had been demanded by the Biltmore Resolution of 1942 (see previous chapter). The Zionists hoped that by conceding on statehood they might provide room for the cabinet to manifest some flexibility, thereby creating a sound basis for further negotiations.[9]

Meetings in September and October between WZO leaders and members of the Labour government dampened any optimism the Zionist leaders might have felt. Foreign Minister Bevin stated bluntly that he opposed the creation of a Jewish state. Similarly, in response to the request for 100,000 certificates, Colonial Secretary George Hall made what he considered the most generous offer to the Zionists that was possible at the time: 3,000 certificates to be made available to the JA for the next schedule period (October 1945 to April 1946).[10] At that rate the immigration of 100,000 DPs would have taken thirty-four years. Presumably, in the interim the DPs would have struck roots in the lands of their temporary resettlement — quite possibly the British plan all along — although the

parallel with the biblical story of the Exodus (which took forty years) could not have been missed by the discussants. Obviously, with the two parties so far apart, Zionist flexibility was virtually meaningless. It could not promote a compromise, since the Zionists were unable to extricate even half of what they wanted from a British cabinet intent on maintaining the status quo. Reluctantly, therefore, the Zionists' were forced to undertake active measures to change British policy. The revolt, planned for the autumn of 1939 but aborted by the outbreak of World War II, now became the Zionists only option.

The Revolt

Even before the WZO and JAE committed themselves to a policy of resistance, Jewish undergrounds in Eretz Israel, notably the Irgun Zvai Leumi (IZL) and Lohame Herut Israel (Lehi), had renewed their attacks on the British. In 1944 and early 1945 this policy led to a series of confrontations between these dissident groups and the JA militia, the Hagana (and its offshoot, the Palmah).[11] To be sure, the dissidents were not able to strike at the British in a meaningful way, initially satisfying themselves with pinprick attacks on the police and military. Moreover, by the summer of 1945, opposition between the Hagana and the dissidents gave way to cooperation in an anti-British revolt undertaken by a coalition of

Two scenes From an anti-British Protest by Holocaust Survivors in Milan, Italy, Summer 1946.
Authors' Collection

Jewish undergrounds now organized under the banner of Tenuat ha-Meri ha-Meuhad (the United Resistance Movement). Tenuat ha-Meri did not actively plan operations and in fact had no institutional existence. Instead, it provided coordination for each of the different movements in order to prevent the duplication of operations and to defer internal disagreements among the undergrounds so as to avoid clashes within the united Jewish front. In particular, the JAE saw Tenuat ha-Meri as a way to control IZL and Lehi and reduce their tendency toward spectacular but outwardly irresponsible attacks on high profile targets.[12]

Tenuat ha-Meri remained a viable coalition between November 1945 and July 1946. During that period, despite lingering disagreements, the undergrounds cooperated in anti-British operations. The opening salvo of this struggle came on November 1, 1945, when operational groups from all the undergrounds (acting under the Tenuat ha-Meri banner) attacked Palestine/*Eretz Israel*'s British-operated railroad system. Service throughout the country was disrupted almost entirely, although most lines were back in service in a matter of days.[13] A few similar operations were carried out, although in practice, each underground approached the tactical problem of how best to strike at the British in a different fashion. Thus cooperation was forced and collapsed entirely after the IZL attack on the King David Hotel on July 22, 1946.

The King David Hotel served as the nerve center for Britain's Palestine administration. As a result, the committee overseeing Tenuat ha-Meri (the so-called X Committee) initially approved the plan to destroy part of the building. Diplomatic developments, mainly connected to the Anglo-American Committee (see below) made the attack less urgent to the JAE, which still sought a compromise with the British. When the attack went on as planned and resulted in nearly a hundred deaths (mainly civilians, including seventeen Jews), the JAE found a pretext for breaking Tenuat ha-Meri. Thereafter, de facto

cooperation continued (mainly insofar as the different groups tried to avoid clashes), but each underground attacked targets as it saw fit.

The attack and its aftermath, however, point to the fundamental difference in tactics (and, to a lesser degree, strategy as well) alluded to previously. Whereas the IZL and Lehi saw themselves as national liberation movements waging a guerrilla campaign to which diplomacy was an auxiliary, the Hagana and Palmah saw armed struggle as a means to attain a diplomatic goal; in effect, each went about revolt as a mirror image of the other.[14]

In light of their overall diplomatic orientation, the Hagana and Palmah generally eschewed guerrilla tactics, concentrating on *ha'apala* ("illegal" immigration) and on attempting to publicize the plight of refugees in order to gain universal support for Jewish aspirations. *Briha* and *Aliya Bet* thus played crucial roles in the Hagana's revoltionary strategy since they were highly visible and were mainly seen as moral and humanitarian issues. The Hagana adopted this strategy because it did not believe that the British could be decisively defeated in a direct military struggle: The British armed forces were too strong and too experienced for that. It stood to reason, therefore, that the JAE saw guerrilla warfare (central to the IZL/Lehi strategy) as a path to sure defeat unless combat was strengthened by a diplomatic weapon that the British could not counter: the moral weapon wielded by unarmed Jewish Holocaust survivors who sought to go home.[15]

As during the Arab Revolt in 1936, the British were initially caught unprepared for fighting in 1945. Furthermore, the local administration did not believe that most Jews supported the new activist policy and would eventually meekly submit to British rule. Throughout cabinet discussions in late 1945 and early 1946 no official ever hinted that giving in to Zionist demands regarding the 100,000 DPs might be a possible means to end the Jewish revolt.[16] To be sure, the British realized that there were nuances to the different Zionist approaches and policies. The government could clearly distinguish Ben-Gurion and the JAE from Menahem Begin and the IZL: the former was at particular pains to dissociate the official Zionist organization from operations characterized as terrorist.[17] Nevertheless, JAE moderation was seen as a sign of weakness rather than as an opening for diplomacy and thus did not lead to any concessions from the British until it was too late.[18]

Part of the problem was the fact that the British cabinet misread the international situation almost completely. The cabinet, and especially Foreign Minister Bevin, considered Jews in general (and American Jews in particular) to be vocal but not very powerful. Thus, it was assumed that American Jewish pressure would eventually "blow over" and would not influence President Harry S. Truman. In fact, however, Truman was under considerable pressure from almost every corner of the American Jewish community to do something positive on behalf of the Holocaust survivors.[19] This British misperception of potential Jewish diplomatic power virtually ruled out any possiblity of a realist compromise at precisely the moment that many Zionists thought that one was both possible and desirable.[20]

As a result, the security situation deteriorated rapidly and continued to deteriorate after the failure of the Anglo-American Committee. Terror and retaliation became the order of the day, with the rebels slowly gaining the initiative. In mid-June, for instance, the Palmah destroyed every bridge leading out of Palestine/*Eretz Israel* in a single night and with no losses to the operational groups.[21] In response, the cabinet ordered an all-out assault on the JAE and WZO as a means of striking at the Hagana and Palmah. This operation, known as Operation Agatha, took place on Saturday, June 29, 1946. Over the course of the operation, JAE headquarters were occupied by British troops and all JAE members then in *Eretz Israel* were arrested. Much of the JA staff was likewise imprisoned. This was, in Chaim Weizmann's term, a virtual declaration of war on Jewry, not just on the terrorists, and as such was a failure.[22]

To be sure, the JAE leaders concluded that direct assaults on the British would be useless after this operation (which came to be known in Jewish circles as "Black Sabbath"). As already noted, however, the JAE had always been mistrustful of guerrilla operations and this proved to be little more than an incentive to concentrate on those operations already expected to bring decisive results. Additionally, the JAE had already decided to withdraw from Tenuat ha-Meri (doing so after the King David Hotel incident a few weeks prior to Operation Agatha) in order to concentrate on *Aliya Bet*.[23] Still, British actions did not ease the security situation; to the contrary, British actions fed Jewish resentment and thus strengthened the revolt, arousing sympathy among the population for operations by the IZL and Lehi that might otherwise not have existed. The cycle of violence and counterviolence, along with a stream of unfortunate statements by the British military commander in Palestine/*Eretz Israel*, General Evelyn Barker, continued literally until the United Nations decided to terminate the mandate and create a Jewish state. At that point the struggle against the British ceased and transformed into an Israeli struggle for independence waged against the local Arab population and Israel's Arab neighbors.[24]

American Intervention

Independence was still in the future in December 1945, when Weizmann proposed to President Truman that the latter send a committee to investigate the European Jewish situation and propose a means to break the Anglo-Zionist deadlock.[25] Weizmann's proposal culminated nearly five months of U.S. government interaction with Jewish DPs and a variety of Zionist (and non-Zionist) lobbying efforts in Washington. President Truman was already intimately acquainted with the DP problem, thanks to the report prepared on the subject by his personal representative, Earl G. Harrison, in August 1945.[26]

The Anglo-American Committee, officially tasked with an investigation into the "problems of European Jewry and Palestine," was duly constituted early in 1946. Instead of the all-American committee that Weizmann had proposed, an English delegation was added to ensure balance and to secure (or so it was hoped) acceptance of the committee's recommendations by the Britsh cabinet. The committee was composed of six members, three Americans and three Englishmen, with a staff of researchers and secretaries. Testimony was heard beginning on January 4, 1946, and was completed by April 20 of that year. By then, the committee members together or in groups had visited three continents (North America, Europe, and Asia); had collected testimony from Arab heads of state, British administrators, Zionist ideologues of all stripes, and Holocaust survivors; and had seen the realities on the ground in both the European DP camps and the *Yishuv*.[27] The Zionists, still committed to the entry of 100,000 DPs, also carefully prepared a detailed report for the committee that covered virtually every aspect of Zionist and Jewish history.[28] Having wrapped up the investigation, committee members proceeded to prepare their recommendations in late March.

The Anglo-American Committee report exemplifies precisely the British problem at its simplest level: an inability to grapple with the new conditions created by the Holocaust and an unwillingness to adjust Middle Eastern policy in accordance with the new realities. Specifically, the cabinet had agreed to the committee's creation only reluctantly and only as a means to allay President Truman's disquiet about the DPs. Given the committee's composition, it was assumed that a unanimous recommendation would be difficult, if not impossible, to achieve. Therefore, the cabinet had magnanimously announced that any recommendation arrived at unanimously would be implemented without reservation. In all honesty, Bevin appears to have assumed that he could strike a pose as an honest party seeking a true compromise while avoiding any actions that would threaten continued British rule in Palestine/*Eretz Israel*. Furthermore, the British realized their dependence on American goodwill (and economic assistance as well) but hoped to coopt the Truman administration into support for continued implementation of the White Paper of 1939.[29]

It was with intense chagrin, therefore, that the cabinet responded to the Anglo-American Committee's unanimous recommendation that 100,000 Jews be permitted to enter Eretz Israel immediately.[30] To be sure, the Zionists were not completely satisified with the committee's recommendations, since the report ignored or rejected virtually every aspect of the Biltmore resolution and the idea of a Jewish common-wealth. Nonetheless, although seen as a virtual defeat by the Zionists, the recommendations were viewed as vindicating short-term (and minimalist) Zionist goals without necessarily endangering long-term aspirations. As a result, Zionists accepted the report without protest.[31]

In reality, matters were not that simple and the committee's recommendations were never implemented. On May 1, 1946, Bevin declared that implementation of the recommendation — which he had previously assured President Truman would be unconditional for any recommendation that was unanimous — would now be made conditional, specifically, the 100,000 certificates would be issued only if the Jewish undergrounds in *Eretz Israel* completely disarmed and (by definition) ceased all operations.[32] Beside the obvious dilemma posed by Bevin's changing his commitment on the fly, this proposal was not realistic. For the Jews to disarm completely would have been suicidal. Arab enmity meant that any such surrender would have necessitated the permanent perpetuation of British rule in the Jewish national home with no guarantee that any *aliya* would have been resumed in the future. Whereas most Zionists were willing to accept the committee recommendations because they did not prevent future implementation of goals that the committee had not unanimously accepted (i.e., statehood) to accept the new British condition would have closed the future on a Jewish state entirely and was not acceptable even to the most minimalist of the Zionist leaders.

Further contacts between May and September 1946 refined the two positions but clearly proved that another impasse had been reached. The Zionists continued to base their position on the minimal implementation of the *aliya* of 100,000 DPs as a precondition for any further discussions.[33] Some Zionist leaders (Weizmann and Nahum Goldmann, for example) would have been willing to compromise on virtually all other demands, especially on the maximalists demand for Jewish statehood. However, in order to convince the WZO that such a compromise was worthwhile, a quid pro quo was needed.[34] The British cabinet's unwillingness to fulfill its own commitments made compromise impossible and, ironically, played directly into the maximalists' position.

The consequence of British intransigence was five months of futile diplomacy and the creation of another committee to investigate the matter: the so-called Morrison-Grady Commission.[35] Formulated as a committee of experts on the Middle East, the committee was actually composed of only two members (who had access to four staff members): Sir Herbert Morrison, appointed by the Foreign Office, and Henry F. Grady, appointed by the State Department. After a brief investigation Morrison and Grady proposed that Palestine/*Eretz Israel* be divided into three autonomous (not independent) cantons. Under this plan, the Jewish canton would extend from Haifa to Tel Aviv, with the Negev and Jerusalem comprising the British canton (an area wherein the British Mandate would remain in force). All other territory would be ceded to the Arab canton. Upon acceptance of this scheme by both Jews and Arabs, the British cabinet assured all interested parties that 100,000 certificates would be made available. Even then, however, mass *aliya* would not be permitted; instead, the British would control *aliya* to the Jewisg canton, using economic absorptive capacity as the criterion for annual schedules until the 100,000 certificates were used up. Further *aliya* at that point was not specified, nor was the meaning of Jewish autonomy clear, given that the British would have exclusive control over immigration to the Jewish canton (it being highly unlikely that the Arab canton would permit any *aliya* at all). *Aliya* to the British-controlled territory was likewise unclear: Would Jewish settlement in British-controlled parts of the country be permitted? Would that be counted as part of the 100,000 or would that be considered independently?[36]

These questions aside, it is clear that the Morrison-Grady scheme was doomed from the start. Had the British proposed some similar scheme in 1945, it is highly likely that the Zionists would have been forced to accept it. They could not have refused the opportunity to help the DPs, even if the help would be dragged out over the course of an unspecified number of years. By the summer of 1946, however, conditions had changed radically. Events in Eastern Europe, especially the Kielce Pogrom of July 4, 1946, had opened a floodgate of Jews fleeing to the American and British zones of occupation in Germany and Italy. There were now many more than 100,000 DPs, and an *aliya* of 100,000 would not solve the problem. And there was no end in sight for *Briha*: Jewish flight did not slow down until late 1948 when the newly established Communist regimes banned emigration.[37] Moreover, the maturation of American Jewish lobbying brought considerable pressure to bear on the Democrats, especially on President Truman.[38] British efforts to persuade the Zionists that the Morrison-Grady scheme was nothing more than a basis for further negotiations rang hollow after the experience with the Anglo-American Committee. Thus, by September 1946, the Morrison-Grady scheme was abandoned for one final attempt at diplomacy.[39]

The Diplomatic Offensive

The diplomatic developments of September and October 1946 were conditioned by a number of key events. First, the Jewish uprising continued unabated in *Eretz Israel*. Despite considerable fluctuations in the revolt's intensity, the IZL and Lehi guerrilla campaigns continued and in some cases intensified.

Second, the same held true for the JA (and, by definition, for the Hagana and Palmah) despite its withdrawal from Tenaut ha-Meri. In this case, the main emphasis was on *Aliya Bet*. Through September 1946, the Mossad had sent twenty-three ships with nearly 15,000 *Ma'apilim* aboard to run the British blockade. Although almost all of the ships were captured and the *Ma'apilim* interned (from August 1946, including internment in camps on Cyprus), they generated positive publicity for the Zionists and negative publicity for the British.

A case in point was the so-called La Spezia ships, which never sailed. On May 13, 1946, two ships, the *Eliahu Golomb* and the *Dov Hoz*, were impounded by Italian police authorities while docked in La Spezia (near Rome), at the instigation of the British secret service. In the aftermath of the incident, for which Britain was resoundingly condemned, the Palestine administration was forced to allow the La Spezia internees into *Eretz Israel* legally. The Mossad ships proved to be the Zionists' crucial weapon.

Whenever a ship set sail, Mossad agents alerted the foreign press, giving all pertinent details. Although such information might have been useful to the British, the agents realized that maximum publicity on the plight of the *Ma'apilim* was their only weapon. In any case, the Mossad agents were not giving the British any information they could not easily obtain from other sources. Indeed, the British were able to infiltrate agents onto a number of blockade runners. Try as they might, however, there was one thing the British could not do — break the spirit of the *Ma'apilim* or their escorts from the Hagana and Palmah.[40]

Finally, it is worth noting that a survey taken in the United States in late 1945 unovered the following information: 53 percent of the Americans (Jews and non-Jews) had heard about Zionism, Zionist goals, or the *Yishuv*. Of those, nearly 60 percent claimed that they supported Zionist goals and 42 percent agreed with the proposition that the Truman administration should act to help achieve Zionist goals.[41]

These circumstances reinforced President Truman's already strong commitment to Zionist and Jewish causes during the congressional elections in 1946.[42] And although the Republican electoral victory in the election weakened the president's domestic position, it further eroded the State Department's case against supoporting the Zionists.[43]

A British concession in late summer or early fall 1946 might have eased the pressure on opponents of Zionism in the White House and State Department. That was, for example, the view of the British ambassador to Washington and was similar to arguments put forward by members of the opposition, including Winston S. Churchill, who condemned the Labour government's "squalid war" against Jewish refugees.[44] Instead of following this sage advice, the Labour cabinet repeatedly condemned President Truman's "betrayals" — a smoke screen to cover their own intentions not to fulfill their commitments — while acting in such a way as to ensure that the Jewish refugee problem remained on the front burner. This was most particularly obvious in the British decision to exile and imprison *Ma'apilim* in Cyprus. To be sure, the British hoped that imprisonment would stem the tide of *Aliya Bet*, maintain their control of Palestine/*Eretz Israel*'s territorial waters, and permit them to claim they were behaving in a civil fashion toward refugees.

In reality, what transpired was a rather sad spectacle: British soldiers forcibly removing *Ma'apilim* and then shipping them off in boats that were little better that the ones in which they arrived, to concentration camps in Cyprus. While these camps were not at all like the Nazi camps liberated by the Allied armies in 1945; nevertheless, they were concentration camps and the very idea behind the deportations created adverse publicity for the British. Had Joseph Goebbels, the Nazi propagandist, not committed suicide in the Hitler bunker on April 30, 1945, and been imprisoned instead, he might well have scored a propaganda victory like the one gained after the Evian Conference fiasco of 1938.

For the *Ma'apilim*, exile on Cyprus had one small compensation: After serving a period of detention, *Ma'apilim* could immigrate to *Eretz Israel* legally. As a goodwill gesture, the British government agreed in October 1946 to resume granting up to 1,500 immigrant certificates per month, with some of those certificates to be set aside for internees.

Externally, the camps were run by the Royal Army; theoretically, the army also supervised the internal running of the camps. To prevent escapes, Royal Army patrols guarded the perimeters of the camps, which were surrounded by barbed wire fences mounted with search towers. Internally, however, the camps were run autonomously, with a Central Committee established to administer daily affairs. The Central Committee acted in concert with appointed representatives of American Jewish philanthropic agencies, primarily the American Jewish Joint Distribution Committee (JDC), and with *Shelihim* from *Eretz Israel*. Most of the latter were members of the Hagana, the Mossad, or both. To help rehabilitate the detainees and to prepare them for their new lives in *Eretz Israel*, special classes were established in DP camps throughout Europe, and the Organization for Rehabilitation and Training (ORT), with the help of the JDC, established vocational training schools.

Surprisingly, there were relatively few mass escape attempts from the Cyprus camps. Because any escape attempt involved numerous dangers, mass escapes were especially discouraged by the Zionist leadership. In fact, the only mass breakout was after a tunnel had been dug through which some three hundred *Ma'apilim* escaped. Individual escapes, however, were encouraged by the Mossad because they were simpler and less dangerous. Approximately 8,500 *Ma'apilim* were even spirited away through the use of forged documents, a program called Aliya Dalet.[45]

These were the overall conditions when, in October 1946, President Truman declared his intention to make a public pronouncement on the Palestine/*Eretz Israel* problem as part of his Yom Kippur letter to the American Jewish community.[46] In his statement, President Truman again emphasized the need to find a secure home for the suffering DPs. Strongly focused on humanitarian issues, the letter was less strongly so on the Zionist political agenda. The president mentioned recent Zionist offers regarding partition, but also mentioned the discredited Morrison-Grady Plan as a potentially viable option. Although the Zionists stood to gain from Truman's statement (although not attaining all they wanted), the statement was greeted with considerable consternation in Zionist circles.[47] The same held true for the British, who considered the statement to be nothing more than preelection posturing and nothing less than a betrayal of Anglo-American cooperation on the Palestine/*Eretz Israel* issue.

Another flurry of diplomatic maneuvering ensued, resulting from fractures in the WZO between proponents (the Goldmann faction) and opponents (the Silver–Ben-Gurion faction) of partition. But by November 1946, virtually nothing had changed. At least, that was how matters appeared in public. Behind the scenes, considerable changes had taken place; in particular the British cabinet finally, painfully, began to inch away from its insistence that partition was not possible. This meant that a compromise satisfactory to a majority of Zionists might still be possible.[48]

In the interim, the Twenty-second Zionist Congress convened in Basel (December 9–24, 1946). The congress witnessed a complete victory for the maximalists: Weizmann was not reelected to the presidency (a position that was kept empty). Rabbi Stephen S. Wise was replaced as head of the JA American Section by the more forceful Rabbi Abba Hillel Silver. The Twenty-second Congress also witnessed the revisionists' return to the WZO, a move that clearly strengthened the pressure on the British government. In response, the cabinet proposed another Arab-British-Zionist conference to meet in late January 1947. It was hoped that the conference would lead to a compromise acceptable to all parties, with Britain retaining overall control of *Eretz Israel*, but granting autonomy to both Jews and Arabs and permitting renewed *aliya*.[49]

When the conference opened on January 27, 1947, it was seen as a last chance to avoid open conflict between Jews and Arabs.[50] Unfortunately, what was on the table led to an immediate impasse: The British proposed a U.N. trusteeship that would permit the *aliya* of 96,000 Jews over two years. Thereafter negotiations would begin over the final status of Palestine/*Eretz Israel*. This was unacceptable to the Zionists since a renewed British trustee government could halt *aliya* after two years. In effect, the British had proposed a refined version of the Morrison-Grady scheme, which created a miniature Pale of Settlement for Jews in their own national home. The Arabs also opposed the new British plan, since they rejected any *aliya*. Deadlock ensued and the conference collapsed entirely on February 14, 1947.[51]

Faced with the utter failure of what it considered its final effort to solve the problem peacefully, the British government decided to divest itself of Palestine/*Eretz Israel* altogether. On February 14, 1947, the day on which the conference collapsed, the British announced their intention to refer the matter to the United Nations (U.N.), in effect, the first step in a complete withdrawal from the territory.[52] Zionist leaders accepted the change of venue, even though they were initially less than sanguine about the amount of support they could expect from the General Assembly.[53] But, the die had been cast and a new chapter was about to open.

The United Nations

When the British cabinet informed the United Nations of its intention to refer the matter to the General Assembly, it did so without recommending a policy for the U.N. to pursue. As a result, the General Assembly dedicated a two-month special session to the subject of Palestine/*Eretz Israel* that culminated in the creation of a United Nations Special Commission on Palestine (UNSCOP). A new reality now

existed and Zionists shifted the focus of their diplomacy from London and Washington to Lake Success (the first home of the U.N.) and to UNSCOP.[54]

Focusing on the U.N. did not mean that Zionists could ignore either England or the United States. The latter wavered in its position on Zionist goals between intense support from President Truman and intense opposition by the State Department.[55] The same was true of the Soviet Union, which had not been a factor in Middle East politics up to this point. Ideologically, the Soviet regime was inalterably opposed to any manifestation of Jewish nationalism, except in connection with the Jewish National Soviet (Jewish autonomous region) in Birobidzhan.[56] In February 1945, Josef Stalin reiterated his regime's opposition to Zionism. Thereafter, however, Stalin's position had softened somewhat. At the General Assembly session on May 14, 1947, Soviet Foreign Minister Andrei Gromyko announced that, although a binational state was preferable, the Soviets would accept partition as a reasonable alternative.[57]

At the outset of discussions members of the General Assembly appeared either undecided or decidedly negative about the Zionist cause. At the time, almost the entire membership — including the United States and the Soviet Union — could be charaterized as undecided. Indeed, only the Arab bloc, whose position on the possible creation of a Jewish state was decidedly negative, had a clearly unequivocal position in the matter.[58]

UNSCOP immediately began its enquiry into the Palestine/*Eretz Israel* imbroglio. The committee's eleven members were selected from U.N. members not directly connected to the issue, specifically, Australia, Canada, Czechoslovakia, Guatemala, Holland, India, Iran, Peru, Sweden, Uruguay, and Yugoslavia. UNSCOP'S chairman was the Swedish representative, Emil Sandström. Testimony was taken in Europe and the Middle East beginning in May 1947. The committee's investigation culminated in an intensive period of hearings held in Jerusalem between June 16 and July 24. By the time UNSCOP completed its work, almost every Jewish spokesman had testified, as had representatives of most of the Arab states (only Trans-Jordan and the Palestinian Arabs refused to cooperate in the hearings).[59]

Critical support for a Jewish state came from virtually all Zionist advocates, who now finally presented a united front, and, ironically, from the Lebanese Maronite community. The latter saw a Jewish state as a means to break up the Muslim stranglehold on the Middle East, a result that could only help the besieged Christian Arab community in the former French-mandated territory.[60] The most graphic testimony came in the European DP camps where Holocaust survivors openly advocated opening the gates to *Eretz Israel* so that they could go home.[61] And if the survivors' verbal testimony was not enough, the Mossad developed a plan to graphically exemplify the Jews' unhesitating determination to leave Europe for rehabilitation in *Eretz Israel*.

Aliya Bet had not slowed in the interim, but the Mossad's most ambitious projects, the *Exodus 1947* came to the fore now. The largest blockade runner sent to date, the *Exodus*, a former Chesapeake Bay steamboat named the *SS President Warfield*, set sail from Marseilles, France, on July 1, 1947. The ship was captured by the British after a brief struggle and was impounded. The JA and Mossad both expected, as per usual British practice, that the *Ma'apilim* would be interned on Cyprus — an act of cruelty that would impress the UNSCOP members. No one could anticipate what came next. Instead of imprisoning the *Exodus Ma'apilim* on Cyprus, the British cabinet ordered them returned to their country of departure.

Upon arrival in three deportation ships, however, the would-be immigrants refused to disembark. In response, the French government declared that they could not admit anyone entering France against their will. This seemed to leave the British no options other than Cyprus or *Eretz Israel*, with pressure mounting

Members of UNSCOP Alight From One of the Deportation Ships Holding *Exodus Ma'apilim*.
Courtesy of the Central Zionist Archives, Jerusalem

to allow the *Ma'apilim* into the latter legally. The cabinet, however, had one more option, and removed the *Exodus Ma'apilim* to a DP camp in the British zone of occupation in Germany. This was accomplished on September 8, 1947. After pumping the deportation ships with tear gas, riot clad British troops forcibly removed the *Ma'apilim* and transported them to camps near Poppendorf and Amstau, Germany.[62]

This was a hollow victory for the British. In full view of the media they proved that the British could deploy overwhelming force to compel unarmed Jews to act according to their orders. However, they also unquestionably proved the bankruptcy and inhumanity of British policy on Palestine/*Eretz Israel*. Indeed, it was obvious for all to see that the British mandate was no longer viable and had to be terminated. Logically, that could only mean one thing: a return to Jewish sovereignty through the creation of a Jewish state. Arab opposition, however, was bound to be fierce, leading a majority of UNSCOP members to partition as the only solution. Three members dissented, calling instead for a binational state to be based on a cantonal system with the central government run cooperatively by Jews and Arabs with U.N. assistance. Given the Arabs' previous unwillingness to accept parity with Jews, the minority scheme did not seem reasonable. Nonetheless, the majority agreed to incorporate one idea from the minority proposal: internationalizing Jerusalem. Since the committee deadlocked, in September two proposals were submitted to the General Assembly: the majority scheme that called for partition and the minority calling for a binational state.[63]

When the debate began, it was not clear which, if any, of the proposals would be accepted. Although the British cabinet repeatedly insisted that it intended to relinquish the mandate, many observers suspected that Bevin would have been happy if the U.N. requested, in essence begged, the British to stay permanently, especially if the debate on UNSCOP's reports became deadlocked.[64] Further complicating matters was the fact that U.S. policy repeatedly veered between President Truman's avowedly pro-Zionist position and the State Department's efforts to delay, or prevent, the creation of a Jewish state.[65] Soviet policy was also unclear, although in practice, it appeared likely that the Soviet bloc would vote for the mandate's termination.[66] Even with the Soviet bloc states, however, partition seemed to have little chance of obtaining the necessary two-thirds majority in the General Assembly.[67]

Intense Zionist lobbying with the major powers (the United States and Soviet Union) and with lesser members of the U.N. (e.g., Argentina) turned the tide. Using arguments that included promoting guilty feelings about insufficient rescue activity during the Holocaust and concentrating on the need to resettle the thousands of Jewish DPs, the Zionist lobbyists also implied that U.S. financial assistance might be obtained more easily in return for support for a Jewish state. Some diplomats resented the Jewish efforts (the Liberians and Haitians complained about it to the secretary general), but most proved responsive, including almost all of the Latin American delegates.[68] In many cases, they did feel guilty about their nations' wartime failure to rescue Jews (including cases where governments repudiated documents that they had issued themselves that could have saved lives) and hoped thereby to make amends.[69] Thus, on November 29, 1947, a unique coalition emerged to ensure victory for partition and creation of a Jewish state. Thirty-three states, including the entire Soviet bloc, most of the British Commonwealth (but not Britain itself), and the bulk of South American countries voted for partition; thirteen countries, mainly in the Middle East, voted against; eleven abstained. The resolution accordingly passed with the needed two-thirds majority.[70] A Jewish State had finally come to be a reality, with the struggle against Great Britain ending and a war for independence and survival beginning.

The Road to Independence

Although the General Assembly resolution called for termination of the British mandate

JAE Chairman David Ben-Gurion Briefs the Va'ad Leumi on the U.N. Partition Vote.
Courtesy of the Central Zionist Archives, Jerusalem

by the end of August, 1948, the path to Jewish statehood was not that simple. Within days of the resolution, the Jewish and Arab communities in Eretz Israel were in a virtual state of war. While Zionists rejoiced at the prospect of a Jewish state, even if that meant accepting partition, the Arabs remained unalterably opposed to both partition and Jewish statehood. Rioting ensued within hours of the resolution and spread, with intercommunal violence rapidly approaching a civil war. The British response to this development can only be described as tepid. While the British retained responsibility for internal and external security until the mandate's last moments, in May 1948, British combat troops and police in Palestine/*Eretz Israel* maintained a posture that was described by one observer as "benevolent neutrality."[71]

Renewed Arab-Jewish violence led to a brief and ultimately abortive reevaluation of U.S. policy regarding partition. In January 1948, members of the State Department staff recommended resurrecting a proposal President Franklin D. Roosevelt had made in 1943 to convert the mandate to an international trusteeship under U.N. supervision.[72] By February, these staffers were openly advocating the partition could not be carried out peacefully, maintaining that U.S. troops would be needed to prevent an all-out war. They, therefore, proposed a complete reversal in U.S. policy regarding Zionism and partition.[73]

Such talk worried Zionists immensely and required immediate countermeasures. More significantly the discussions, which were leaked to the press, embarrassed and angered President Truman, who saw his foreign policy being undermined by advisers widely perceived to be in an unprecedented mutiny.[74] Discussions of this new plan rapidly took on a life of their own, literally continuing into the hours just prior to Israel's declaration of independence.[75] By then the trusteeship proposal was only one weapon that the State Department sought to use in order to prevent the declaration. Rapid action by Truman, including the now famous meeting with his former business partner Eddie Jacobson and Chaim Weizmann, halted this last-ditch effort and finally set the stage for the Jewish State to become a reality.[76]

In the meantime, fighting continued and intensified. Jewish efforts to calm Arab fears and obtain the neutrality of neighboring Arab states failed almost entirely. Some Arab leaders girded for an full-scale confrontation. Declaring the Jews to be nothing more than the "sons of death" mentioned in the *Qur'an*, these leaders called for pushing the Jews into the sea. Compromise was not even considered.[77] Apparent (but limited) British willingness to arm Arabs encouraged the radicals into believing that they were, in fact, unstoppable. In response, the *Yishuv* began an unprecedented and frenzied campaign to purchase or produce enough arms to counter this new Arab threat.[78]

Zionist diplomats also attempted to obtain agreements with the neighboring Arab kingdoms (mainly Trans-Jordan, Iraq, and Egypt), hoping to keep them out of the war. This effort was not crowned with much success. A tentative agreement reached with Emir Abdullah of Trans-Jordan soon collapsed. The basic problem was that Abdullah was playing a dual game and hoping to obtain the maximum benefit for himself. On the one hand, Abdullah repeatedly assured the Jews of his good intentions and proposed a federation betwen Trans-Jordan and the U.N. proposed Arab

state that would terminate any hostilities before they began. This plan, or so Abdullah argued, would leave the radical Palestinian Arab leadership (especially the Mufti of Jerusalem) with no choice but to negotiate with the Israelis and would prevent all-out war. Simultaneously, Abdullah was reassuring members of the Arab League of his intentions to help forestall a Jewish state by any means, including all-out war. Somewhat disingenuously, Abdullah also promised the Arab League that he would not negotiate with the Zionists at precisely the negotiating a possible timetable for Trans-Jordanian troops to enter Palestine/*Eretz Israel* and capture the areas promised by the U.N. for the Arab state.[79]

This dual policy had an unfortunate set of consequences. Abdullah had kept his contacts with the Zionists secret and had permitted a vicious propaganda campaign to begin in Trans-Jordan that whipped up hysteria for intervention. At first, the Arab Legion was transferred into Palestine/*Eretz Israel* only to prevent total Arab collapse and to gain control of the territories Abdullah coveted. However, once the Arab Legion was in the former mandated territory, clashes could not be avoided with Jewish forces. As a result, the Trans-Jordanians found themselves (albeit reluctantly) involved in direct combat with the Hagana (and later Zva ha-Hagana le-Israel). Months of bitter fighting followed, as did behind-the-scenes efforts to find a lasting peace between Israel and Trans-Jordan.[80]

By March and April 1948, the fighting had become intense. Gush Etzion, a group of settlements that protected Jerusalem's southern flank, was entirely surrounded and numerous other settlements throughout the country were isolated. Jerusalem, slated to be internationalized under the U.N. resolution, was besieged. On the evening of March 25–26, a convoy to the city was decimated, with only a few trucks and precious supplies reaching the Jewish garrison. An even worse misfortune struck in the northern sector: Operation Yehiam, a task force assembled to break out of besieged Haifa to bring supplies to embattled settlements in the Lower Galilee was ambushed and annihilated.[81]

Shortly thereafter, the Hagana began a thorough reevaluation of its operational plans and methods. To that point, the Hagana had continued to operate like an underground militia, albeit one with nation-wide responsibilities. As independence appraoached, such a policy no longer made sense. The Hagana now had to fulfill the tasks of a conventional military force that was to protect the newborn state of Israel. After careful study, a new operational plan, dubbed Tochnit D (Plan D) was proposed. Tochnit D included six doctrinal points: (1) defense against Arab regular and irregular forces would be given equal footing; (2) first priority in planning operations was to be placed on gaining control of means of communication and supply (mainly the road network); (3) second priority was to be given to capturing forward bases (as the British abandoned them) in order to prevent their use by the Arabs; (4) deterring Arab attacks by besieging their villages and destroying the Arab community's economic infrastructure; (5) once that was accomplished, priority would be given to destroying Arab guerrilla bands; (6) high priority was to be placed on capturing government institutions and installations located inside the Jewish state's borders.[82]

Slowly, almost inperceptibly, the initiative changed. By the end of April 1948, the road to Jerusalem was temporarily reopened. Haifa, Safed, Tiberias, and Jaffa were in Jewish hands, thus providing the soon-to-be-declared state with a secure base of operations. Outlying Jewish settlements such as Mishmar ha-Emek and Tirat Zvi had beaten off coordinated attacks by Fawzi al-Kaukji's self-styled Arab Liberation Army, thereby fleshing out the Jewish State's borders. During this period, the single most significant battle took place at Kastel, a ruined Crusader fortress and Arab settlement that dominated the road to Jerusalem. Kastel was considered so critical that a Palmah task force was assembled for this mission only. On April 6, 1948, the Palmah force was able to occupy Kastel and held it for nine days. A major Arab counterattack on April 15 pushed the Jewish forces out of Kastel, but the fortress was in Jewish hands (permanently) twenty-four hours later. In addition to heavy casualties, the Arab forces lost perhaps their best resource. Abdel Kader al-Husseini, the Mufti's nephew and possibly the Arabs' best field commander, who was killed during the battle.[83] As against these positive developments, there was one major Israeli loss, Kfar Etzion, which fell in early May, meaning that the direct route to attack Jerusalem from the south was in Arab hands.[84]

These military developments had important diplomatic consequences. In particular, the *Yishuv's* ability to hold its own against the Arab onslaught strengthened the position of those Zionist leaders, including Ben-Gurion, who advocated declaring independence immediately upon the mandate's termination and weakened those who advocated delaying or cancelling the declaration altogether.[85] The military developments in April also resulted in the quick dispatch of one final U.S. State Department effort to undermine President Truman's stated intention to recognize the Jewish State when it declared independence by having the General Assembly impose a trustee-ship on the former British mandate.[86]

Efforts to negotiate a truce also came to naught. It had been hoped, mainly by the U.N. Security Council, that the transition from mandate to independent state would be peaceful.[87] Obviously, that was not to be: a truce implied a compromise and, again, the Arabs were in no mood to compromise. To the contrary, the fighting turned gruesome as atrocities (by Arabs and some overly zealous Jewish forces as well) began to proliferate. On April 13, an unarmed convoy of medical personnel en route from Jerusalem's city center to the Hadassah Hospital on Mount Scopus was attacked and massacred. Four days earlier, IZL and Lehi units operating in coordination with (but not under the command of) the Palmah during the assault on Kastel attacked the Arab village of Deir Yassin. Recently the village had been quiet, although previously considerable gunfire had been directed at Jewish neighborhoods from the village, which was a legitimate military target. Indeed, Iraqi irregulars had been based in the village and had prompted the decision by the Jerusalem garrison commander (David Shaltiel) to permit the dissidents' attack. During the course of the operation the attackers killed some 250 Arabs, including 110 civilians. Although the local IZL commander declared that the civilians had been killed accidentally during the course of military operations, British representatives (who also publicized reports about sexual assaults by Jewish troops subsequently disproved) and by Arab leaders characterized the attack as a massacre. The Israeli government entirely repudiated the operation, in effect apologizing for an act that it was not responsible for, certainly a unique undertaking in the annals of international relations and one that was not reciprocated by Arab leaders openly advocating genocide.[88]

Deir Yassin and the massacre of the Hadassah convoy represented a further deterioration, if that was possible, in Arab-Jewish relations. A corollary to this worsening relationship was the beginning of mass flight by Arabs from Palestine/*Eretz Israel* after April 1948. In recent years, a debate has raged as to the precise origins of this refugee problem, which is, tragically, still a component in Middle Eastern affairs. In this debate, three schools have emerged. One school claims that the Arab refugees fled as an unintended consequence of the war, a second school claims that the Arab noncombatants fled more or less willingly under orders from their leaders in order to render the war against the Jews easier, and the third school claims that the Arabs were essentially chased out as part of a conscious and systematic Israeli policy to reduce the potential for fifth column activities within the Jewish State's borders.[89]

This debate, which hinges upon the careful interpretation of statements contained in documents that are not fully available (Arab archives, for instance, have never been opened to the public), cannot be fully analyzed here. Nonetheless, some points may be made with clarity about all three of the different hypotheses. First, apparent conclusions drawn from faulty research into the Israeli documents notwithstanding, no systematic Israeli policy of expulsion ever existed. In effect, the Provisional Israeli government (which existed as the Minhelet ha-Am from March 1948 until constituted as the provisional government in May) never formulated such a policy. There was a series of *ad hoc* decisions by local military commanders who did, in some cases, seek to chase Arab civilians from their operational areas. That this policy was never systematic is demonstrated by the fact that Arabs in some areas were encouraged by the Israelis to leave (e.g., the so-called Little Triangle of the Galilee) but in other areas the Israeli government directly appealed to the Arabs to stay (e.g., in Haifa). Second, there does not appear to have been any systematic Arab plan to remove the civilian population in order to render easier the possibility of massacring Jews, even though it should be emphasized that most Arab leaders spoke in uncertain terms about their genocidal intentions (e.g., throwing the Jews into the sea). Some Arab leaders did make statements that could be interpreted as ordering local Arab civilians to leave. For instance, in his memoirs then Syrian prime minister Khaled el-Azm stated that "since 1948 we have been demanding the return of the refugees to their homes. *But we ourselves are the ones who encouraged them to leave.*"[90]

Since neither interpretation covers all the refugees who left, the only reasonable conclusion is that most Arabs who left did so as an unintended consequence of the fighting. Wars, especially modern wars with their heavy firepower and massive collateral damage to targets not involved in the fighting, tend to create many refugees. The Middle East fighting has not been an exception to that general rule, especially in light of the brutality of the fighting and the vicious hatred between the warring sides.[91]

Final efforts to impose a truce under Security Council auspices prior to the mandate's termination collapsed in late April and early May. By then the Zionists felt that they had no alternative to an unequivocal declaration of independence, even though that virtually guaranteed an Arab invasion and all-out war.[92] By May 13, 1948, all final preparations had been made. As British forces completed their withdrawal on Friday, May 14, 1948, JAE chairman David Ben-Gurion would declare independence. And that is precisely what happened. At 4 P.M. (local time), in a solemn ceremony at Tel Aviv's Mann Auditorium, Ben-Gurion read a proclamation declaring Israel's independence. Fifty-one years after the First Zionist Congress, Herzl's dream of a Jewish state had come into being. American recognition of Israel followed within a few hours. The Jewish State was a reality.[93]

The War of Independence

Within minutes of Ben-Gurion's declaration, Tel Aviv was struck by the first Arab air raid; the ground invasion followed within twenty-four hours as five armies assisted by units from three other states poured into the Jewish State. Egypt, Trans-Jordan, Syria, Lebanon, and Iraq sent their armies while the Saudis, Moroccans, and Yemenis sent troops who fought under Egyptian command. Whereas the Israelis had wrested military initiative from the Arab irregular forces led by the Mufti and his followers, the regular Arab armies were another matter. Recent studies seem to have proved that the military disparity between the forces was not as great as appeared at the time, but the Israeli forces were nearly swamped.[94] On almost every front the Israelis had to concede territory, trading precious space for time in the hope that a counterattack could be organized to restore the situation. On the positive side, Israeli defensive operations exacted a heavy toll from the invaders, thus lessening Arab fervor for military operations.

By June the Arab armies had reached their high-water mark: Tel Aviv was threatened by the Egyptians; Jerusalem was besieged by the Arab Legion; and the Syrians, Lebanese, and Iraqis (operating in an uncoordinated fashion) had almost cut off the Galilee from the rest of Israel.[95] Still, the Israelis had managed to stabilize the front. They had staved off complete defeat and, unlike the invaders, were becoming stronger with each passing hour. There were a number of interrelated reasons for this. First, despite the fact that most U.N. members adhered to the Secuirty Council arms embargo, the Israelis were able to scour battlefields in Europe for World War II surplus weapons that had been abandoned. Second, sympathetic governments, such as Czechoslovakia agreed to look the other way while the Israelis transferred arms and equipment (some of which was smuggled) purchased throughout the world to Israel. The Czechs actually went a step farther, selling surplus aircraft to the fledgling Israel Air Force.[96]

More significantly than the purchase of weapons was the availability to Israel of manpower resources that the Arabs lacked, especially the Jewish and non-Jewish volunteers who composed Mitnadve Hutz la-Aretz (Mahal), men who had gained considerable combat experience during World War II and brought their expertise to the Israelis. Mahal included such figures as Colonel David "Mickey" Marcus, the American Jewish officer who commanded the Jerusalem front until his death just prior to the first truce; Al Schwimmer, another American Jew who later founded Israel's aircraft industry; Ben Dunkelman, a Canadian Jew who commanded Israel's first mechanized battalion; and George F. "Screwball" Beurling, Canada's highest scoring ace during World War II and a non-Jew who came to Israel for the adventure.[97] At the other end of the scale, Israel also obtained manpower from Jewish DPs in Europe (and, to a lesser degree on Cyprus) who formed a conscript army known as Giyus Hutz la-Aretz (Gahal). Though poorly trained and, in many cases, still suffering the after-effects of Nazi persecution, Gahal troops were generally well motivated. They were fanatically committed to creating a homeland that would erase the dishonor of the Holocaust and ensure that Jews were never again victims. Their fanaticism infused them with a sense of purpose; many Gahal troops were fated never to see the country they fought to establish.

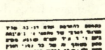

Special Edition Newspaper Published By the WZO to Mark the
Declaration of Israel's Independence, May 14, 1948.
Courtesy of the Central Zionist Archive, Jerusalem

Finally, Israel had one other advantage over its Arab enemies. Whereas the latter were united only by their unalterable opposition to a Jewish state, they had no specific purpose beyond preventing Israel's establishment, and they did not cooperate on operations. The Israelis faced no such problem. On May 28, 1948, the Israeli Provisional Government ordered all the underground movements to disband and to unite into Zva ha-Hagana le-Israel (Zahal). The IZL disbanded only reluctantly and then only after civil war threatened during the Altalena affair and the Palmah viewed dissolution as a politically motivated (rather than militarily necessary) decision. Both the IZL and Palmah protested and held out as long as possible, but unification into a single military entity was completed by mid-June.[99] In turn, organizational unity permitted Zahal to concentrate on preparations for the upcoming battles.

Renewed fighting was not long delayed. The two U.N. mediators Count Folke Bernadotte and (after Bernadotte's assassination by Lehi gunmen) Ralph Bunche had negotiated a truce that lasted from June 11 to July 9, 1948. Both sides used the truce to prepare for renewed fighting, but the Israelis had worked out a systematic plan of operations in case the truce broke down. In mid-July, these plans were set into motion. Remaining in a defensive posture against the Egyptians, Zahal units undertook a series of swift, mobile campaigns that broke the back of the Lebanese, Syrians, and Arab irregular forces besieging the Galilee. Simultaneously, the Israelis pushed the Jordanians back on the central front, occupying the crucial towns of Ramle and Lod. Both were strategically important since they sat astride the approaches to the road to Jerusalem (which was still blocked); Lod was also important for its airport.

A renewed effort was also made to open the road to Jerusalem. Repeated attempts to capture Latrun from the Arab Legion failed; the position was a natural defensive asset and could not be conquered easily. That meant that direct communications with the besieged city were still almost impossible. However, in the interim Israeli units probed the Trans-Jordanians' flanks and discovered a difficult but not impossible route around the main line of Arab resistance. This route, covered from direct observation, was also considered to be free of Trans-Jordanian fire, meaning that almost any type of vehicle could make the journey. Dubbed the Burma Road (in honor of the road built during World War II to bring Allied supplies from India to China), the route was improved (if that word could be used in the context of something that is still a dirt track) by Zahal engineers. Soon sufficient supplies were pouring over the Burma Road to break the siege.

The military initiative once again passed to the Israelis and Zahal planned to commence operations on the Egyptian front. These operations were halted by the Secuity Council, which imposed a new truce on July 18 that lasted until October.[100] Militarily the battles in July 1948 were significant for the pattern they set: Zahal attacked and grabbed the initiative while Arab forces tended to wait for the coming blows.

The second truce had been part of a larger U.N. effort to end fighting altogether. Again, fighting ceased, this time for a span of three months, but peace was not brought any closer since the Arabs refused to concede. Both sides once again used the truce to prepare for further fighting. When renewed fighting broke out, instigated by the Egyptians, Zahal was ready for them and began another series of moves designated Operation "Ten Plagues" (also known as Operation Yoav). Initially holding a defensive posture on the northern and central fronts, Zahal concentrated on the Egyptians, liberating Jewish settlements in the northern Negev. These settlements had been surrounded by the Egyptians since the war began. Most had been kept supplied by the Israel Air Force, but the end game was about to unfold.[101]

Zahal put Operation Yoav into effect on October 15, 1948, after the Egyptians fired on an unarmed food convoy passing, as permitted by the truce, near the town of Faluja. Testifying to the rapidity with which Zahal had matured into a professional army from a collection of motly undergrounds, Operation Yoav was undertaken entirely by mobile forces. Despite heavy fighting, Zahal prevailed: the Egyptian lines were broken, the Negev settlements were liberated, and Israeli sovereignty was established all the way to Elat, Israel's outlet on the Red Sea. Significantly, Zahal operations turned the tables on the Egyptians, completely surrounding considerable Egyptian forces in the so-called Faluja Pocket. Further operations on the northern, central, and southern fronts culminated in the brief Israeli occupation of El Arish (in the northern Sinai) and left no question about the war's outcome: Zahal, and Israel, had emerged victorious.[102]

Zionism Since 1948

Armistice talks began on the Island of Rhodes on January 13, 1949. Agreements were difficult but were reached: with Egypt on February 24, Lebanon on March 1, Trans-Jordan on March 11, Iraq (an agreement actually signed by Trans-Jordanian representatives acting as plenipotentiaries for the Iraqi king) on March 15, and Syria on July 20. Not only was the Israeli-Syrian armistice the most difficult to negotiate, but it was also the most fragile, collapsing within months of signing.[103] The armistice agreements, however, were viewed as nothing more than interim agreements to a comprehensive peace, which did not follow. To the contrary, the Middle East has seen repeated Arab-Israeli confrontations over the years. Only since 1979 has any glimmer of hope for peace emerged and, only recently have direct, face-to-face negotiations become the basis for what may be a true accommodation between all Arab states, the Palestinian Arabs, and Israelis. These tentative steps are only that: the peace that has hopefully begun to emerge is, as of this writing, far from irreversible.

With the establishment of the State of Israel, the Jewish world entered a new phase of history. For 2,000 years the Jews had been a tempest-tossed object of forces largely beyond their control, but now at least part of Jewry had crystalized into a sovereign state, a subject of history, a nation like all others. Yet, in summarizing the role Zionism has played in the Jewish political history of the twentieth century, one question remains: what, if any, meaning has Zionism had since Israeli statehood? After the recent anniversaries — the Zionist movement's centennial (1997) and the State of Israel's jubilee (1998) — the question becomes even more intriguing. In light of recent decisions, taken just prior to the Thirty-third Zionist Congress in 1997, that have led to the World Zionist Organization's virtually ceasing its functions by the end of 1999, it is painfully obvious that there is no simple answer to this question.[104] At the simplest level, the temptation exists to echo the sentiments of one author who ended his recent history of Zionism with, "Zionism is dead, long live the State of Israel."[105]

In fact, the situation is much more complex. Institutional existence notwithstanding, Zionism still has a continuing role to play, both culturally and politically, within the contemporary Jewish community. Concentrating only on the issue of Jewish identity, or as currently framed by Jewish communal leaders, Jewish continuity, for instance, yields the possibility that the Zionist mission is far from being successfully completed. Quite the contrary, the very existence of neo-Canaanism in Israel and the rising tide of apathy in diaspora communities seems to indicate, that much more has yet to be done by Zionists and Zionism to create a new Jewry that is both consistent with Jewish tradition and comfortable with all its components.[106] This new Zionism will have to manifest itself in a new organizational model, one that will fit the contemporary modes of Jewish life. Zionism is thus not dead. As Ahad ha-Am argued over a century ago, Jewish nationalism is indestructable; it has merely taken on a new series of tasks for the foreseeable future. The history of Zionism since 1948 is also impossible to distinguish from the history of the State of Israel; that, however, is a different story entirely.

Notes

1. Abraham J. Edelheit and Hershel Edelheit, *History of the Holocaust: A Handbook and Dictionary* (Boulder: Westview Press, 1994), pp. 145–150, 226.

2. Ibid., p. 149.

3. See the essays by Dobroszycki, Katzburg, and Ancel in Yisrael Gutman and Avital Saf, eds., *She'erit Hapletah, 1944-1948: Rehabilitation and Political Struggle* (Jerusalem: Yad Vashem, 1990), pp. 1–16, 117–142, 143–167.

4. Edelheit and Edelheit, *History of the Holocaust*, pp. 150–151.

5. M. J. Cohen, ed., *The British Return to Partition, 1943-1945*, Rise of Israel Series, vol. 33 (New York: Garland, 1987), pp. 250–277.

6. Ibid., pp. 288–296.

7. Ibid., pp. 278–287.

8. David Ben-Gurion, "Reply to Bevin," (1946) cited in M. J. Cohen, ed., *The Zionist Political Program, 1940–1947*, Rise of Israel Series, vol. 31 (New York: Garland, 1987), pp. 185–206.

9. Ibid., pp. 155–165.

10. Ibid., pp. 166–167.

11. Supra, pp. 197–198.

12. Shlomo Lev-Ami, במאבק ובמרד (By struggle and revolt) (Tel Aviv: Ministry of Defense Publications, ND), pp. 267–269, 286–287. For a review of intra-Zionist relations in this period, see Shimon Golan, מרות ומאבק בימי מרי (Allegiance in the struggle) (Ramat Efal: Yad Yitzhak Tabenkin, 1988), chaps. 2–3.

13. Lev-Ami, במאבק ובמרד, pp. 269, 271–271. M. J. Cohen, ed., *Jewish Resistance to British Rule, 1944–1947*, Rise of Israel Series, vol. 34 (New York: Garland, 1987), pp. 56–73.

14. Thurston Clarke, *By Blood and Fire* (New York: G. P. Putnam's Sons, 1981), passim; Golan, מרות ומאבק, ch. 5-6.

15. Cf., Saul Zadka, *Blood in Zion: How the Jewish Guerrillas Drove the British out of Palestine* (London: Brassey's, 1995), passim.

16. A selection of British cabinet documents on the revolt is included in Cohen, *Jewish Resistance*, pp. 74–93.

17. Ben-Gurion to Cunningham, January 1, 1946, in ibid., p. 94.

18. Cunningham to Colonial Office, February 19, 1946, in ibid., pp. 95–96, in which the normally moderate Moshe Shertok is accused of sedition.

19. Cohen, *Zionist Political Program*, pp. 173–184 and Arieh J. Kochavi, "British Assumptions of American Jewry's Political Strength, 1945–1947," *Modern Judaism*, 15, no. 2 (May 1995): 161–182.

20. Cohen, *Zionist Political Program*, pp. 173–184, Yosef Heller, במאבק למדינה (The struggle for a Jewish state), (Jerusalem: The Zalman Shazar Center, 1984), pp. 424–437, 443–446, 453–460.

21. Cohen, *Jewish Resistance*, pp. 106–113.

22. Ibid., pp. 116–133.

23. Ibid., pp. 114–115, 133–135.

24. Ibid., pp. 136–264 includes documents on virtually every aspect of the security situation between July 1946 and August 1947. For an authoritative review of the documents, see Bruce Hoffman, *The Failure of British Military Strategy Within Palestine, 1939–1947* (Ramat Gan: Bar-Ilan University Press, 1983), pp. 17–33.

25. Weizmann, Report of a meeting with President Truman, December 4, 1945, cited in Heller, במאבק למדינה, pp. 471–473.

26. On the genesis of the Anglo-American Committee, see M. J. Cohen (ed.), *The Anglo-American Committee on Palestine, 1945–1946*, Rise of Israel Series, vol. 35 (New York: Garland, 1987), pp. 13–119. On American Jewish lobbying efforts in North America, see Cohen, *Zionist Political Program*, p. 236.

27. Cf. Amikam Nachmani, *Great Power Discord in Palestine* (London: Frank Cass, 1987) and Allen H. Podet, *The Success and Failure of the Anglo-American Committee of Inquiry, 1945–1946* (Lewiston, NY: Edwin Mellen Press, 1986).

28. Cohen, *Anglo-American Committee*, pp. 120–135; *The Jewish Case before the Anglo-American Committee of Inquiry on Palestine as Presented by the Jewish Agency for Palestine*, reprint ed. (Westport, Conn.: Hyperion Press, 1976).

29. Christopher Sykes, *Cross-Roads to Israel* (London: Collins, 1965), ch. 12.

30. The Committee report is reprinted in Cohen, *Anglo-American Committee*, pp. 136–218; British responses are cited on pp. 225–228, 233.

31. Ibid., pp. 219–224, 229–232, 234–237.

32. Ibid., p. 238.

33. Ibid., pp. 239–240, 250–251, 253–255.

34. Cf. the documents cited in Cohen, *Zionist Political Program*, pp. 237–241, 248–254.

35. Cohen, *Anglo-American Committee*, pp. 241–249, 252, 256–278, 290–298.

36. Ibid., pp. 299–324.

37. Cf. Ephraim Dekel, *B'riha: Flight to the Homeland* (New York: Herzl Press, 1972), chaps. 6–13, 18.

38. Cohen, *Anglo-American Committee*, pp. 325–331, Kochavi, "British Assumptions," pp. 162–163, 167–169.

39. Cohen, *Anglo-American Committee*, pp. 332–345.

40. Cf. Edelheit and Edelheit, *History of the Holocaust*, pp. 151–152, and Ze'ev Venia Hadari, *פליטים מנצחים אמפריה: פרשיות עליה ב', 1945-1958* (Refugees defeat an empire: Chapters in the history of *Aliya Bet*, 1945–1948) (Kiryat Sde Boker: Ben-Gurion University of the Negev, 1985), pt. 2.

41. Kochavi, "British Assumptions," p. 163.

42. Ibid., pp. 167–170; Zvi Ganin, *Truman, American Jewry, and Israel* (New York: Holmes and Meier, 1979), chap. 2–5.

43. Kochavi, "British Assumptions," p. 173.

44. Ibid., p. 170, 175. For Churchill's statement, see Martin Gilbert, *Exile and Return* (Philadelphia: Lippincott, 1978), pp. 301–302.

45. Nahum Bogner, *אי הגרוש: מחנות המעפילים בקפריסין, 1946–1948* (The island of exile: Illegal immigrant camps on Cyprus, 1946–1948) (Tel Aviv: Am Oved for the Center to Study *Aliya Bet*, 1991), pt. 6–7.

46. Cohen, *Zionist Political Program*, pp. 255–264.

47. Ibid., pp. 265–271, Ganin, *Truman*, ch. 7.

48. Cohen, *Zionist Political Program*, pp. 272–293.

49. Ganin, *Truman*, chap. 8, M. J. Cohen (ed.), *The British Decision to Evacuate Palestine, 1947–1948*, Rise of Israel Series, vol. 36 (New York: Garland, 1987), pp. 6–59.

50. On the direction taken by Zionist–Arab diplomacy during this period, see: Heller, *במאבק למדינה*, pp. 483–495.

51. Cohen, *British Decision*, pp. 60–117.

52. Ibid., pp. 118–142, 155–164, 171–192.

53. Ibid., pp. 143–144, 165–170.

54. M. J. Cohen (ed.), *United Nations Discussions on Palestine, 1947*, Rise of Israel Series, vol. 37 (New York: Garland, 1987), pp. 1–48.

55. Ibid., pp. 49–51; Michael T. Benson, *Harry S. Truman and the Founding of Israel* (Westport, Conn.: Praeger, 1997), chaps. 4, 6, 8.

56. Cf., supra, p. 60 and Abraham J. Edelheit, "The Soviet Union, The Jews, and the Holocaust," *Holocaust Studies Annual*, 4 (1990): 113–134.

57. Heller, *במאבק למדינה*, pp. 511–522.

58. David Horowitz, "The Holocaust as Background for the Decision of the United Nations to Establish a Jewish State," *Holocaust and Rebirth: A Symposium* (Jerusalem: Yad Vashem, 1973), pp. 144–145.

59. Cohen, *United Nations*, pp. 49–56, 61–63.

60. Ibid., pp. 57–60.

61. Horowitz, "The Holocaust," pp. 147–149.

62. Aviva Halamish, אקסודוס: הסיפור האמיתי (Exodus: The full story) (Tel Aviv: Tel Aviv: Am Oved for the Center to Study *Aliya Bet*, 1990); Hadari, פליטים מנצחים אמפריה, pp. 260–309.

63. For the terms of the UNSCOP report, see *Report to the General Assembly by the United Nations Special Committee on Palestine* (London: His Majesty's Staionary Office, 1947). For analyses of the report, see Cohen, *United Nations*, pp. 64–93.

64. Cohen, *United Nations*, pp. 105–109, 113–116, 135–137.

65. Ibid., pp. 99–104, 110–112, 117–119, 44–158.

66. Ibid., pp. 128–131.

67. Ibid., pp. 132–134.

68. Ibid., pp. 159–160, 196–221.

69. For one example of successful Jewish lobbying written by a South American diplomat who viewed the process in a positive light, see Jorge Garcia-Granados, *The Birth of Israel* (New York: Alfred A. Knopf, 1948).

70. Cohen, *United Nations*, pp. 161–192.

71. Netanel Lorch, *Israel's War of Independence, 1947–1949* (Hartford, Conn.: Hartmore House, 1968), pp. 46–59; Uri Milstein, *History of the War of Independece* (Lanham, Md: University Press of America, 1996), 1:175–189; and Gedalia Yogev (ed.), *Political and Diplomatic Documents, December 1947 – May, 1948* (Jerusalem: Israel Government Printing Office, 1979), pp. 20–21.

72. M. J. Cohen (ed.), *The American Trusteeship Proposal, 1948*, Rise of Israel Series, vol. 38 (New York: Garland, 1987), pp. 1–77.

73. Ibid., pp. 78–93.

74. Ibid., pp. 94–143.

75. Ibid., pp. 144–251.

76. M. J. Cohen (ed.), *The Recognition of Israel, 1948*, Rise of Israel Series, vol. 39 (New York: Garland, 1987), pp. 1–106, Melvin I. Urofsky, *We Are One! American Jewry and Israel* (Garden City, N.Y.: Doubleday, 1978), pp.165–166, 186–189.

77. Lorch, *War of Independence*, pp. 17–26, Yogev, *Diplomatic Documents*, pp. 25–30.

78. Cf., Yogev, *Diplomatic Documents*, pp. 36–37, 39–42, 69–74; and Lorch, *War of Independence*, pp. 33–35.

79. Cf., Yoav Gelber, *Jewish-Transjordanian Relations, 1921–1948* (London: Frank Cass, 1997), chaps. 11–13.

80. Ibid., chap. 14.

81. Lorch, *War of Independence*, pp. 54–70.

82. Ibid., pp. 89–90.

83. Ibid., pp. 91–136.

84. Ibid., pp. 137–144.

85. *Cohen*, Recognition, pp. 106–169, Yogev, *Diplomatic Documents*, pp. 123–561.

86. Yogev, *Diplomatic Documents*; pp. 562–571, 579–624, 628–629.

87. Ibid., pp. 572–573, 625–627, 632–646.

88. On the Hadassah incident, see ibid., pp. 648–650. On Deir Yassin, see: A. Joseph Heckelman, *American Volunteers and Israel's War of Independence* (New York: Ktav, 1974), chap. 3.

89. For an example of the traditional Israeli argument, see *The Arab Refugees* (Jerusalem: Government of Israel, 1953). For the revisionist historians' interpretation, see Benny Morris, *The Birth of the Palestinian Refugee Problem* (New York: Cambridge University Press, 1987); and the

essays by Ephraim Klieman, Nafez A. Nazzal, and Avi Shlaim, in Ian Lustick, ed., *Triumph and Catastrophe: The War of 1948, Israeli Independence, and the Refugee Problem* (New York: Garland, 1994), pp. 124–140, 196–214, and 290–302 respectively.

90. El-Azm's statement was cited in Chaim Herzog, *The Arab–Israeli Wars* (New York: Randon House, 1982), p. 38, emphasis added.

91. Cf. the essays by Syrkin and Teveth in Lustick, *Triumph and Catastrophe*, pp. 303–310 and 328–363.

92. Yogev, *Diplomatic Documents*, pp. 677–785.

93. Ibid., pp. 786–794, Cohen, *Recognition*, pp. 170–193, 207–210.

94. Amitzur Ilan, *The Origin of the Arab-Israeli Arms Race* (London: MacMillan, 1996), passim.

95. Lorch, *War of Independence*, pt. IV.

96. Cf. Leonard Slater, *The Pledge* (New York: Simon and Schuster, 1970).

97. Heckelman, *American Volunteers*, pt. II, David J. Bercuson, *The Secret Army* (New York: Stein and Day, 1984).

98. Hanna Yablonka, ‫אחים זרים: ניצולי השואה במדינת ישראל, 1948–1962‬ (Foreign brothers: Holocaust survivors in Israel, 1948–1952) (Jerusalem: Yad Yitzhak Ben-Zvi, 1994), chaps. 6–8.

99. Lorch, *War of Independence*, pp. 298–304; Lev-Ami, ‫במאבק ובמרד‬, pp. 413–422; Anita Shapira, ‫מפיטורי הרמ"א עד פירוק הפלמ"ח‬ (From the discharge of the staff to the disbandment of the Palmah) (Tel Aviv: ha-Kibbutz ha-Meuhad Publishing House, 1985).

100. Lorch, *War of Independence*, pp. 311–352.

101. Ibid., pp. 383–400.

102. Ibid., pp. 401–530.

103. Itamar Rabinovich, *The Road Not Taken: Early Arab-Israeli Negotiations* (New York: Oxford University Press, 1991), chap. 2.

104. Cf. the coverage in the *New York Jewish Week* for December 1997 and January 1998.

105. David J. Goldberg, *To the Promised Land: A History of Zionist Thought* (London: Penguin Books, 1996), p. 251.

106. Hillel Halkin, *Letters to an American Jewish Friend: A Zionist Polemic* (Philadelphia: Jewish Publication Society, 1976) and "After Zionism: Reflections on Israel and the Diaspora," *Commentary*, 103, no. 6 (June 1997): 25–31.

PART 2
DICTIONARY OF ZIONIST TERMS

David Ben-Gurion Proclaiming Israel's Independence, May 14, 1948.
Reprinted from Bernard Reich and Gershon R. Kieval, *Israel: Land of Tradition and Conflict*, Boulder: Westview Press, 1993, p. 63. With permission of Westview Press.

Abba [אבא, H] "Father": Post–World War II Hagana code name for the city of Vilna. The term was used to designate one of the terminal points from which Briha operated. The identification of Vilna with Abba derived from the critical role played by Abba Kovner, who had led the Vilna Jewish partisans during the Holocaust, in the Briha movement and the high regard with which he was held in the *Yishuv*: Vilna was said to be "Abba's city." > see also: **Briha**.

Ada [PN]: Mossad le-Aliya Bet code term for Italy, derived from the name of the key Mossad agent in Rome, Ada Sereni. Italy was "her" country. > see also: **Aliya Bet; Paratroopers, Palestinian**.

Agami [אגמי, H] "Mr. Pond": Mossad le-Aliya Bet code name for Moshe Auerbach (who later adopted this nom de guerre as his Hebrew name). Since Agami mainly operated from Romania, this also became the code name for the entire country, that is, "Agami's country." > see also: **Aliya Bet**.

Agricultural Settlement(s)

1. Scope and Definition
   Zionism has always emphasized, to one degree or another, a Jewish return to the land and to agricultural work. Although styles and emphases differed, most Zionists — deriving their ideas from European romantic thought and its ideology of a return to the "natural life" — saw European Jewry as too urbanized and too heavily involved in small-scale trade or professions. Of special importance, in this regard, was Aaron David Gordon (1856–1922), who emphasized the need to return Jews to productive work before a national renaissance could occur. Zionists who followed Gordon's ideas advocated a Zionist revolution to return Jews to the land politically (i.e., by establishing a Jewish national home) and physically as well. Until the late 1920s virtually all *olim* entering *Eretz Israel* did so as recruits for agricultural settlements; this emphasis lessened during and after the Fourth Aliya but never ended completely. In the 1930s, continuing emphasis on agricultural settlement became a source of controversy deriving from the massive need to rescue European Jewry. Agricultural settlement, however, was open to a number of differing approaches regarding the question of private or communal property. As a result, a number of different types of agricultural settlements were developed. > see also: **Hachshara; Halutz; Halutzic Aliya**.

2. Types of Agricultural Settlements
   Kibbutz (קיבוץ), voluntary collective settlement, also known as a *Kvutza* (קבוצה), unique to the *Yishuv* and the Zionist movement. Kibbutzim initially developed as the result of two factors: the difficult (physical and financial) conditions facing settlers around the turn of the twentieth century and the (at times bitter) conflict over Arab labor between members of the Second Aliya and previously settled

members of the First Aliya. Additionally, continuing conflicts between settlers and the Jewish Colonization Association and the WZO led the latter to grant a small parcel of land to a group of recent *olim* in 1909. They, in turn, established Kvutzat Degania, which was to be the first of the Zionist collective settlements. Over the next five years, a small number of *Kibbutzim* were established; development boomed after 1920 as the WZO, JAE, and Histadrut focused on *Halutzic Aliya* and settlement building.

Kibbutzim were organized from the beginning as collectives, with members sharing personal possessions and work responsibilities. Typically, a Kibbutz was (and still is) managed by an elected committee, with all adult members able to vote and be elected. As a result of ideological differentiation within the labor Zionist camp, four nationwide *Kibbutz* federations were organized, each seeking to give member *Kibbutzim* support beyond what the individual group could possibly do for itself. In order of creation, these federations were: Hever ha-Kibbutzim (1921, initially associated with Ahdut ha-Avoda and later with Mapai); ha-Kibbutz ha-Meuhad

(1927, associated with Mapai but leaning toward its Siya Bet); Kibbutz Arzi (1927, associated with ha-Shomer ha-Zair); and ha-Kibbutz ha-Dati (1935, associated with ha-Poel ha-Mizrachi). > see also: **Yishuv, Yishuv Organizations**.

Kibbutz members primarily engaged in agricultural work, although a degree of light industry developed in some *Kibbutzim* after 1930. All work on a *Kibbutz* was done by the members, from the most menial tasks to the most technically critical ones. Members also engaged in guard duty on a rotating schedule. This latter task also accentuated another of the *Kibbutz*'s roles in Zionist settlement policy. New *Kibbutzim* established during the mandate era were situated with a strategic purpose: establishing "facts on the ground" while also making maximal use of settlements as a means to protect outlying Jewish controlled areas. Therefore, every *Kibbutz* was designed to be a small fortress capable of holding out until relieved if attacked. Moreover, after 1940, *Kibbutzim* were used to house Palmah units: troops thereby earned their keep and bolstered the local defenses. In 1948, forty-one *Kibbutzim* housed a total of 2,000 Palmah troops. > see also: **Homa u-Migdal**; N.

Settlers at *Kibbutz* Kinneret, circa 1910.
Courtesy of the Central Zionist Archives, Jerusalem

TABLE A.1: Kibbutz Population in Selected Years

Year	Population	Percent Growth	Year	Population	Percent Growth
1920	800	N/A	1935	9,400	241
1925	2,300	288	1940	26,550	282.4
1930	3,900	169.6	1945	36,900	138.9

Source: S. Maron, "Centrality of the Kibbutz Family," *Jerusalem Quarterly* 39 (1986): 80.

Graph A.1: Trends in *Kibbutz* Population, 1920-1945

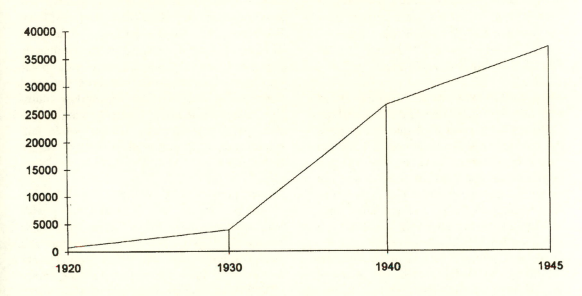

Moshav (מושב), 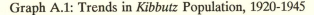 smallholders cooperative deriving from the era of the Second Aliya. *Moshav* members retained their private property, including their own plot of land, but acted as a cooperative corporation for financial purposes, mainly in purchasing items needed for work and in selling products together. As in the *Kibbutz*, all work in a *Moshav* was done by *Moshav* members; the main difference between the two types of settlements lay in the *Moshav* members' holding title to the land they worked. The first *Moshav*, Ein Ganim, was founded in 1907. The number of *Moshavim* increased slowly but steadily until 1948. Until the 1930s *Moshav* members worked exclusively in agriculture; thereafter, German and other Central European *olim* introduced small-scale industry to many *Moshavim*. A national council of *Moshavim*, Tnuat ha-Moshavim, was established in 1925.

Moshava (מושבה), private farming village in *Eretz Israel*. The first *Moshava*, Petah Tikva, was established in 1878. Unlike the *Kibbutz* or *Moshav*, there was no collective element to the *Moshava*. Members banded together for fellowship and security but did not undertake any joint economic activities. All *Moshava* members owned the land they worked and did so as they saw fit. Thus, it was not unusual for individual *Moshava* members to own land which was worked by hired, Jewish or Arab, labor.

Moshav Ovdim (מושב עובדים), original name for the type of settlement that is better known as a *Moshav*, that is, a cooperative settlement in which each member owns and works a private piece of land but in which all members act as a cooperative in financial matters.

Moshav Shitufi (מושב שיתופי), cooperative smallholders settlement that is a combination of the *Kibbutz* and *Moshav* styles of settlement. Like a *Kibbutz*, all land on the *Moshav Shitufi* was owned by the collective, as were all tools. All work was done jointly, as in *Kibbutz*. Unlike a *Kibbutz*, members of a *Moshav Shitufi* did not live collectively and did not share personal possessions. Instead, each household drew a fixed percent from the *Moshav Shitufi*'s budget that could be spent as they saw fit. The first *Moshav Shitufi*, Kfar Hittim, was founded in 1936.

Ahad ha-Am [אחד העם, H] "One of the People": Nom de plume of Asher Ginsburg (1856–1927), Zionist ideologue who fathered the concept of Spiritual Zionism. Ginsburg based his Zionist views on the Russian populist movement rather than on western or central European nationalist movements. As a result, Ginsburg used the populist form in signing his name. This emphasis on populism led Ahad ha-Am to emphasize the need for a spiritual, cultural, and intellectual rebirth of the Jewish people via a renewed Jewish nationalism. This rebirth became necessary in his eyes because, in modern times, Judaism (as a religious tradition) no longer served the needs of Jews seeking their place in the world. Therefore, Ahad ha-Am argued that the goals of Zionism should principally be spiritual. In contrast to Political Zionists, he believed that the Jews needed to build a cultural center in *Eretz Israel* and did not need a state per se. This cultural center would unify the Jewish people but would not necessarily absorb the majority of the diaspora's population. Instead, a small, select group of pioneers would migrate to the cultural center and would become the main focus of world Jewish attention, thereby uniting the disparate elements in diaspora Jewry. Ahad ha-Am's ideas were very influential, especially among more moderate groups (including many of the socialist Zionist parties), but not in a

pure form. After World War I, Spiritual Zionism was combined with Political Zionism to create a new ideology, popularly called Synthetic Zionism. > see also: **Zionut, Forms of Zionism**.

Ahavat Zion [אהבת ציון, H] "Yearning for Zion": Term reflecting the historical attachment of the Jewish people to their ancestral homeland. This attachment was traditionally reflected in the prayer book, in wedding customs, and in rituals connected with the observance/nonobservance of certain *Halachot* (traditional laws) that are dependent on being in the Land of Israel. The term *Ahavat Zion* was intimately connected with (and may be seen as the polar opposite of) the hoped for future resolution of *Galut* and with *Shivat Zion*. In modern times, the concept of *Ahavat Zion* has lost much (but not all) of its religious linkage, while still retaining deep cultural roots. > see also: **Galut; Shivat Zion**.

Ahuzat Bayit [אחוזת בית, H] "Housing Property": Name of the first all-Jewish neighborhood north of Jaffa in what later became Tel Aviv. The neighborhood was established in 1907 by sixty families who bought a parcel of land for some 400,000 francs (F300,000 of which came from the Keren Kayemet le-Israel and the rest from private sources or from the members) and the first dwellings were completed in 1910. The neighborhood's name emphasizes Jewish property rights in *Eretz Israel*, rights further guaranteed by purchasing land for new settlements.

Aliens Act: Legislation enacted periodically in England during the twentieth century and designed to limit, or halt altogether, immigration by groups considered "undesirable." When used in a specific context, the term refers to the Aliens Act of 1905, enacted by the government of Prime Minister Arthur J. Balfour. The bill was designed to keep Eastern European Jews out of England; indirectly, efforts to redirect Jewish imigration animated Balfour's interest in Zionism. > see also: **Gentile Zionism; Balfour Declaration**.

Aliya [עליה, H] "Immigration to *Eretz Israel*":

1. Scope and Definition

Jewish immigration to the Holy Land was one of the primary goals of the Zionist movement and was at the center of all Zionist ideologies. Prior to the establishment of the State of Israel, five waves of *aliya* came to *Eretz Israel*: the First Aliya lasted from 1882 to 1903, the Second Aliya lasted from 1904 to 1914, the Third Aliya lasted from 1919 to 1923, the Fourth Aliya lasted from 1924 to 1928, and the Fifth Aliya lasted from 1929 to 1939. Each of these *Aliyot* contributed to the general building of the Jewish national home, while each also had a unique characteristic. The First Aliya, for instance, laid the foundation for later settlement building and also concentrated heavily on agricultural colonization. The Second Aliya brought the first socialist Zionists to *Eretz Israel* and also contributed to the flourishing of independent Jewish self-defense organizations. The Third Aliya continued the trend of the Second, in terms of class of *olim*, but also witnessed the first attempt at industrial immigration. The

Fourth Aliya witnessed the resurgence of middle class *aliya* and is thus known as the "shopkeepers' *Aliya*." Finally, the Fifth *Aliya* was the first truly mass immigration and saw calls for the rapid establishment of both a Jewish majority and Jewish sovereignty in *Eretz Israel*.

Free Jewish immigration was guaranteed by the terms of the League of Nations mandate for Palestine/*Eretz Israel*, granted to Great Britain on July 24, 1922. The mandate further stipulated that Jews immigrating to *Eretz Israel* did so by right and not by sufferance. Even so, immigration became a constant struggle between the Zionists, the British, and the Arabs. In 1933 the high commissioner for Palestine/*Eretz Israel*, General Sir Arthur Wauchope, slightly liberalized immigration facilities for European Jewry, but this policy was reversed in 1936 as a result of the Arab Revolt. In 1939 the British government decided to break its commitment to Zionism, issuing a white paper that limited Jewish immigration to 15,000 a year for five years. After that no further *aliya* would be permitted without Arab consent. > see also: **Aliya Bet; Beit Yaakov Lehu ve-Nelha; Israel, State of; Biltmore Resolution; White Papers, White Paper of 1939**.

Graph A.2: Population Trends During the Five Aliyot

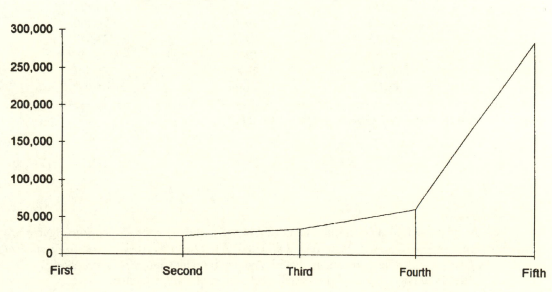

Note on statistics

The following tables present all available information on *aliya*, with emphasis on the mandatory period. The statistical information relating to the Jewish population in *Eretz Israel* during the Ottoman era is simply too incomplete to be tabulated. Then too, astute readers will note the glaring differences in the numbers cited in Tables A.3, A.4, and A.5. The major differences derive from the ways that Jewish immigration was counted and recorded from 1919–1948, in particular, from the counting of "illegal" immigrants and tourists, some of whom remained in Palestine/*Eretz Israel* after their visas expired.

TABLE A.2: The Five Aliyot

Aliya	Years	Olim
First	1882–1903	20,000–30,000
Second	1904–1914	20,000–30,000
Third	1919–1923	35,000
Fourth	1924–1928	62,000
Fifth	1929–1939	285,000

Source: David Gurevich, comp., *Statistical Handbook of Jewish Palestine* (Jerusalem: Jewish Agency for Palestine) 1947, pp. 90– 91.

Table A.3: Legal Jewish Immigration, 1919–1949: By Year[1]

Year	Olim	Year	Olim
1919	1,806	1935	61,854
1920	8,223	1936	29,727
1921	8,294	1937	10,536
1922	8,685	1938	12,868
1923	8,175	1939	27,561
1924	13,892	1940	8,398
1925	34,386	1941	5,886
1926	13,885	1942	3,733
1927	3,034	1943	8,507
1928	2,178	1944	14,464
1929	5,249	1945	13,121
1930	4,944	1946	17,760
1931	4,075	1947	21,542
1932	9,553	1948	118,993[2]
1933	30,327	1949	239,141[3]
1934	42,359	Total	779,271

Source: *Statistical Abstract of Israel* 1 (1948–1950): 29.

---

[1] This and the next two tables cover only the period of the mandate since all previous figures are approximations and have never been fully tabulated. Cf. David Gurevich, comp., *Statistical Handbook of Jewish Palestine* (Jerusalem: Jewish Agency for Palestine, 1947), pp. 90–91.

[2] Of these, 102,428 immigrated after the Israeli declaration of independence.

[3] *Aliya* after the establishment of the State of Israel is included for comparative purposes, but is reflected in the grand total.

TABLE A.4 Legal Jewish Immigration, 1919–1948: By Region

Region	Olim	Percentage
Europe	377,487	78.2
Asia and Middle East	40,776	8.4
Americas and Oceania	7,579	1.6
Africa	4,053	0.8
Unknown	52,982	11.0
Total	482,877	100.0

Source: *Israel Statistical Abstract* 39 (1988): 161.

TABLE A.5 Legal Jewish Immigration, 1919–1948: By Country of Origin

Country	Olim	Country	Olim
Argentina	238	Italy	1,554
Austria	7,748	Libya	873
Australia/New Zealand	72	Netherlands	1,208
Bulgaria	7,057	Poland	170,127
Canada	316	Romania	41,105
Czechoslovakia	16,794	Russia/USSR	52,350
France	1,637	South Africa	259
French N. Africa	994[1]	Turkey	8,277
Germany	52,951	United Kingdom	1,574
Greece	8,767	United States	6,635
Hungary	10,342	Yemen	15,838[2]
Iran	3,536	Yugoslavia	1,944
		Other/Unknown	17,679

Source: Ibid.

Aliya Bet [עליה ב', **H]** "Illegal Immigration":

1. Scope and Definition

Despite the Balfour Declaration and the League of Nations mandate for Palestine/ *Eretz Israel* that committed Great Britain to assist in the building of a Jewish national home, the mandatory administration sought a retrenchment from its commitments as a means to ensure Arab quiescence in the Middle East. As a result, increasingly severe restrictions were placed on *aliya* during the years after the Arab riots of August 1929. In response, Zionists began a policy of *Ha'apala* (literally, striving), or immigration without the benefit of an immigrant certificate. Whereas the British termed such immigration illegal, the Zionists referred to it as *Aliya Bet*, second-type *aliya*, as opposed to regular (legal) *aliya*.

Systematic *Aliya Bet* began in the mid-1930s in response to the steadily worsening situation in Europe. By 1937 both the revisionist

---

[1] Includes Algeria, Tunisia, and Morocco.
[2] Includes Aden.

Zionists, followers of Ze'ev Jabotinsky, and the Hagana, the underground militia under the authority of the Jewish Agency Executive, established agencies to foster *Aliya Bet*. The revisionist agency Af-Al-Pi (Despite All) was founded in 1937 and the Hagana's agency, the Mossad le-Aliya Bet (Agency for Illegal Immigration; commonly known as the Mossad), began to operate in 1938.

During World War II *Aliya Bet* became a primary means for rescuing Jews from the Nazis, although operations were severely hampered by a lack of ships, difficulties in finding trained crews, the continuing British blockade of *Eretz Israel*, and the generally unsafe conditions in the war zones and in the waters around them. After the war,

Aliya Bet became the principal weapon in the Zionist rebellion against the Mandatory government. Using public opinion as its main tool, *Aliya Bet* succeeded in displaying the bankruptcy of British *Eretz Israel* policy and provided a major cause for the United Nation's ultimate decision to create a Jewish state.

While the major focus of *Aliya Bet* was the blockade runners that brought *ma'apilim* to the shores of *Eretz Israel*, two variants on *Aliya Bet* must also be mentioned: *Aliya Gimmel*, or as *Aliyat Kenaf* (airborne *aliya*), in which aircraft replaced ships for three missions that brought 150 *ma'apilim*, and *Aliya Dalet*, the use of forged immigrant certificates by which means some 8,500 *ma'apilim* entered *Eretz Israel*, primarily from Cyprus. > see also: **Aliya**; **Briha**; **White Paper of 1939**.

TABLE A.6: Aliya Bet Ships

Ship	Party	No. of Olim	Sailed From	Date	Result[1]
Prewar					
Velos I	H	350	Pireaus	7/34	Landed Tel Aviv
Union	R	117	Pireaus	8/34	Landed Tel Aviv
Velos II	H	350	Varna	9/34	Captured/Returned
Af-Al-Pi	R	15	Pireaus	4/37	Landed Herzliya
Af-Al-Pi II	R	54	Dorado	9/37	Landed Binyamina
Poseidon A	H	65	Lorion	1/38	Landed Mizpe ha-Yam
Af-Al-Pi III	R	96	Fiume	3/38	Landed Tantura
Artemisia A	R	128	Pireaus	4/38	Landed Tantura
Poseidon B	R	65	Pireaus	5/38	Landed Tantura
Artemisia B	R	157	Pireaus	7/38	Landed Tantura
Af-Al-Pi IV	R	156	Pireaus	8/38	Landed Binyamina
Af-Al-Pi V	R	38	Pireaus	9/38	
Draga A	R	180	Shusak	10/38	Landed Tantura
Atarto A	M	300	Bari	11/38	Landed Shefayim
Draga B	R	550	Constantsa	12/38	Landed Netanya
Ely	R	340	Galatz	12/38	Landed Netanya
Gepo A	R	734	Tulcea	12/38	Landed Netanya

---

[1] The following abbreviations are used to designate parties: H = he-Halutz (Mapai's youth division in the diaspora); M = Mossad le-Aliya Bet; Mi = Mizrachi; P = Private; R = Revisionist Zionists (ha-Zohar or ha-Zach). Details of journey, such as port of departure and result, given when known.

Delphi	R	250	Constantsa	12/38	
Atarto B	M	300	Ancona	1/39	Landed Shefayim
Katina	R	800	Baltzec	2/39	Landed Netanya
Atarto C	M	300	Naples	2/39	Landed Tel Aviv
Atarto D	M	378	Shusak	3/39	Landed Tel Aviv
Sandu	P	270	Romania	3/39	Captured/Returned
Assimi	Mi	470	Romania	3/39	Captured/Returned
Gepo B	R	750		4/39	Sank, *olim* rescued
Aghia Dezioni	R	400	Fiume	4/39	Landed Nebi Ruben
Atarto E	M	408	Shusak	4/39	Landed Herzliya
Atarto F	M	337	Brindisi	4/39	Landed Herzliya
Ostia	R	699	Italy	4/39	Landed Herzliya
Agia Nicolaus A	P	800	Burgas	5/39	Landed Netanya
Karliza Maria	P	350		5/39	
Atarto G	M	400	Constantsa	5/39	Captured/Detained
Demetrius	M	244	Greece	6/39	Captured
Liessel	R	921	Constantsa	6/39	Captured/Detained
Colorado I	M	379	Constantsa	6/39	
Astir	R	724	Rani	6/39	Landed Majdal
Los Perlos	R	370	Constantsa	7/39	
Nikko	R	560	Fiume	7/39	Landed Netanya
Colorado II	M	377	Constantsa	7/39	Captured/Returned
Rudnichar A	P	305	Varna	8/39	Landed Netanya
Dora	M	480	Flisingen	8/39	Landed Shefayim
Rim	R	600	Constantsa	8/39	Sank, *olim* rescued
Agia Nicolaus B	R	745	Constantsa	8/39	Landed Netanya
Parita	R	850	Constantsa	8/39	Captured/Detained
Osiris	R	650	Varna	8/39	
Cartova	R	650	Varna	8/39	
Tripoli	R	700	Varna	8/39	

Wartime

Prosola	P	654	Varna	9/39	Trans. to *Tiger Hill*
Tiger Hill	M	1,417	Constantsa	9/39	Landed Tel Aviv[2]
Rudnichar B	P	371	Varna	9/39	Landed Herzliya
Naomi Julia	R	1,130	Constantsa	9/39	Captured/Returned
Rudnichar C	P	457	Varna	11/39	Captured/Detained
Hilda	M	728	Baltzec	1/40	Captured/Detained
Rudnichar D	P	505	Varna	1/40	Captured/Detained
Sakarya	R	2,400	Constantsa	2/40	Captured/Detained
Pentcho	R	500	Bratislava	5/40	Sank[3]
Libertad	P	700	Varna	7/40	Landed Zichron Yaacov

---

[2] As the *Tiger Hill* unloaded, it was fired upon by British gunboats; two *olim* were killed.

[3] The *Pentcho* passengers were picked up by the Italian navy and were interned on Rhodes; many were later deported to death camps in Poland.

Pacific	M	1,100	Tulcea	11/40	⎤ Captured and
Milos	M	671	Tulcea	11/40	⎦ transfered to *Patria*[4]
Atlantic	M	1,880	Tulcea	11/40	Captured/Deported
Salvador	P	327	Varna	12/40	Sank[5]
Darien II	M	800	Constantsa	3/41	Captured/Detained
Struma	P	769	Constantsa	2/42	Sank[6]
Vitorul	P	120	Constantsa	9/42	Landed Turkey[7]
Europa	P	20	Constantsa	10/42	Landed Turkey
Milka A	M	239	Constantsa	3/44	Landed Turkey[8]
Marissa A	M	224	Constantsa	4/44	Landed Turkey
Milka B	M	517	Constantsa	5/44	Landed Turkey
Marissa B	M	318	Constantsa	5/44	Landed Turkey
Kazbek	M	735	Constantsa	7/44	
Morina	M	308	Constantsa	8/44	
Bulbul	M	410	Constantsa	8/44	Landed Turkey
Mefkurie	M	344	Constantsa	8/44	Sank[9]
Salah-al-Din	M	547	Constantsa	11/44	
Taurus	M	948	Constantsa	12/44	

Postwar

Dahlin	M	35	Barletta	8/45	Landed Caesarea
Netuna I	M	79	Bari	9/45	Landed Caesarea
Gabriella	M	40	Pireaus	9/45	Landed Caesarea
Pietro I	M	168	Chiatone	9/45	Landed Shefayim
Netuna II	M	73	Bari	10/45	Landed Shefayim
Pietro II	M	171	Chiatone	10/45	Landed Shefayim
Berl Katznelson	M	211	Greece	11/45	Captured after landing
Hanna Szenesh	M	252	Savona	12/45	Landed Nahariya
Enzo Sereni	M	900	Vado	1/46	Interned in Atlit
Orde Wingate	M	238	Palestrina	3/46	Interned in Atlit
Tel-Hai	M	736	France	3/46	Interned in Atlit
Max Nordau	M	1,666	Constantsa	5/46	Interned in Atlit

----

[4] After the British announced that the *Patria* was to be sailed to the Mauritius Islands, the Hagana attempted to sabotage the ship. The *Patria* sank in Haifa harbor as a result of the explosion with 260 *olim* killed.

[5] The *Salvador* sank in the Dardanelles and 120 *olim* drowned; the remainder later transferred to the *Darien*.

[6] The *Struma* was sunk by a Soviet submarine in the Black Sea; there was only one survivor.

[7] The ma'apilim from these two (and possibly other) ships were later transferred to Cyprus at Jewish Agency expense.

[8] The *olim* from ships that landed in Turkey during 1944 were permitted to enter Palestine/*Eretz Israel* legally.

[9] The *Mefkurie* was sunk by a German or Soviet submarine that attacked with automatic weapons while surfaced; only five passengers survived.

Eliahu Golomb	M	1,014	⌐ La Spezia	5/46	⌐ Ships impounded by
Dov Hoz	M		⌙		⌙ Italian authorities[10]
Haviva Reich	M	462	Greece	6/46	Interned in Atlit
J. Wedgewood	M	1,257	Vado	6/46	Interned in Atlit
Biriya	M	999	France	7/46	Interned in Atlit
Hagana	M	2,678	Yugoslavia	7/46	Interned in Atlit
Hayal ha-Ivri	M	510	Belgium	7/46	Interned in Atlit
Yagur	M	754	France	8/46	Interned on Cyprus
H. Szold	M	536	Greece	8/46	Interned on Cyprus
Katriel Jaffe	M	604	Bocca di Magra	8/46	Interned on Cyprus
23 Yorde haSira	M	790	Bocca di Magra	8/46	Interned on Cyprus
A. Shochat	M	183	Bocca di Magra	8/46	Landed Caesarea
Arba Heruyot	M	1,024	Bocca di Magra	9/46	Interned on Cyprus
Palmach	M	611	Bocca di Magra	9/46	Interned on Cyprus
Bracha Fuld	M	806	Bocca di Magra	10/46	Interned on Cyprus
Latrun	M	1,275	France	11/46	Interned on Cyprus
Knesset Israel	M	3,845	Yugoslavia	11/46	Interned on Cyprus
Rafiah	M	785	Yugoslavia	12/46	Sank
La-Negev	M	647	France	2/47	Interned on Cyprus
Maapil Almoni	M	746	France	2/47	Interned on Cyprus
H. Arlosoroff	M	1,348	Trelleborg	2/47	Landed Bat Galim
Ben Hecht	R	600	Port-de-Bouc	3/47	Interned on Cyprus
S. Lewinski	R	823	Metaponto	3/47	Landed Nizzanim
Moledet	M	1,563	Metaponto	3/47	Interned on Cyprus
T. Herzl	M	2,641	France	4/47	Interned on Cyprus
She'ar Yashuv	M	768	Boliasco	4/47	Interned on Cyprus
Hatikva	M	1,414	Boliasco	5/47	Interned on Cyprus
Morde haGetaot	M	1,457	Mola di Bari	5/47	Interned on Cyprus
Yehuda haLevi	M	399	Algiers	5/47	Interned on Cyprus
Exodus 1947	M	4,530	Marseilles	7/47	Returned to Germany
Gesher A-Ziv	M	685	Milliarino	7/47	Interned on Cyprus
Shivat Zion	M	411	Algiers	7/47	Interned on Cyprus
Af-Al-Pi-Chen	M	434	Formia	9/47	Interned on Cyprus
Geula	M	1,388	Burgas	10/47	Interned on Cyprus
Jewish State	M	2,664	Burgas	10/47	Interned on Cyprus
Kadima	M	794	Palestrina	11/47	Interned on Cyprus
Aliya	M	182	France	11/47	Landed Nahariya
HaPorzim	M	167	France	12/47	Landed Tel Aviv
Lo Tafhidenu	M	850	Civitavecchia	12/47	Interned on Cyprus
29 November	M	680	Girolata	12/47	Interned on Cyprus
The U.N.	M	537	Civitavecchia	1/48	Interned on Cyprus

---

[10] The *Eliahu Golomb* and the *Dov Hoz* were impounded by the Italian police at the instigation of the British before either could sail. The international crisis that followed forced the British to permit all 1,014 of the *olim* (who would have sailed aboard the two ships) to enter Palestine/*Eretz Israel* legally.

Pan York	M	7,623	Burgas	1/48	⎤ Mossad agreed to
Pan Crescent	M	7,616	Burgas	1/48	⎦ sail to Cyprus[11]
HaLamed Heh	M	274	Palestrina	1/48	Interned on Cyprus
Yerushalayim	M	670	Civitavecchia	2/48	Interned on Cyprus
La Komemiyut	M	699	France	2/48	Interned on Cyprus
Bonim	M	1,002	Yugoslavia	2/48	Interned on Cyprus
Yehiam	M	769	Gaeta	3/48	Interned on Cyprus
Tirat Zvi	M	798	Italy	4/48	Interned on Cyprus
Mishmar Emek	M	782	France	4/48	Interned on Cyprus
Nachson	M	550	France	4/48	Interned on Cyprus
LaNizahon	M	189	Brindisi	5/48	Landed Tel Aviv[12]
Medinat Israel	M	243	Brindisi	5/48	Landed Tel Aviv
Emek Ayalon	M	706	Brindisi	5/48	Landed Tel Aviv

TABLE A.7: Aliya Bet: Statistical Summary

Period	Ships	Ma'apilim
1933–1939	47	18,968
1939–1945	28	18,522
1945–1948	65	69,856
Total shipborne	137	107,326
Aliya Kenaf	3	150
Aliya Dalet	NA	8,500
Grand total *ma'apilim*		115,996

Source: A. J. Edelheit: *The Yishuv in the Shadow of the Holocaust: Zionist Politics and Rescue Aliya, 1933-1939* (Boulder, CO: Westview Press, 1996).

Aliyat ha-Hasidim [עלית החסידים, H] "Hasidic Aliya": Term for four waves of East European *olim* that came to *Eretz Israel* before the rise of Zionism: (1) Around 1700, a group of Jews led by Rabbi Judah he-Hasid, a popular and charismatic leader, settled in Jerusalem as a means to hasten the Messiah's arrival. The settlement collapsed shortly after arrival amidst acrimonious accusations of Sabbatianism. (2) A group of followers of Israel ben Eliezer, the Ba'al Shem Tov, arrived in 1764. This group was organized by Rabbi Menahem Mendel of Peremyshlyany and settled in Jerusalem, thereby establishing the first Ashkenazi community in the city. (3) Another group of Hasidim, three hundred in all, arrived in 1777, under the guidance of Rabbi Menahem Mendel of Vitebsk, also a disciple of the Ba'al Shem Tov. These Jews settled in the upper Galilee, mainly in Safed. Further Hasidic migration over the next twenty years augmented this group. (4) A fourth group followed the third, but settled in Hebron in 1808. These Hasidim were followers of Rabbi Schneur Zalman of Lyady, founder of the Lubavitch Hasidic dynasty.

Alljüdisch [G] "Pan-Jewish": Term for the Zionist policies in Germany and Austria that

[11] Given the large number of *olim* on the *Pan*s, and especially out of concern that resistance would be met with deadly force, the Mossad agreed to sail the ships directly to Cyprus.
[12] The last three ships arrived after the State of Israel had become independent.

emphasized the participation of all Jews, especially non-Zionists, in activities designed to promote Jewish solidarity, communal cohesion, and self-defense. Such activities were formulated and "nonnationalist" in their veneer so as not to scare away non-Zionists but were actually intended as a means of obtaining support for Zionist goals from institutions that would otherwise not support Zionist goals. These activities were thus parallel to Anglo-American Zionists' efforts to "infiltrate" their communities and were part and parcel of the policy of conquering communities that was basic to all Zionist ideologies. > see also: **Conquest of Communities**; **Infiltration**.

Alt-Neuland [G] "Old New Land": Title of Theodor Herzl's utopian novel of a restored Jewish state in *Eretz Israel*. The book is at once a continuation of Herzl's *Der Judenstaat* and a correction of the latter's omissions. Specifically, in *Alt-Neuland* Herzl emphasized that any Jewish rebirth must take place in Jewry's ancestral homeland. At the same time many critics — including many Zionists — noted that *Alt-Neuland* assumed that the Jews would eventually obtain a national home but nowhere explained how this process would come about; in light of Herzl's diplomatic failures the book was viewed as little more than a utopian rumination. > see also: **Der Judenstaat**.

Altalena [I] "Swing": Pseudonym of revisionist Zionist leader Ze'ev (Vladimir) Jabotinsky. Jabotinsky's use of this pen name actually predated his Zionist activity. He already signed articles and feuilletons with that name in 1898 when he was Rome correspondent for the Russian liberal newspaper *Odesskiya Novosti*. Jabotinsky continued to use this pseudonym, albeit less frequently, until his death in 1940. In June 1948 the Irgun Zvai Leumi gave the name *Altalena* to a ship bringing arms and immigrants to Israel. After disagreements over the ship's unloading led to a near civil war, units of the Israel Defense Forces sank the *Altalena*. > see also: **Altalena Affair**.

Altalena Affair [HT]: Common name for the near civil war that broke out between remnants of the Irgun Zvai Leumi (IZL) and Zva ha-Hagana le-Israel (Zahal) on June 18, 1948. The IZL had acquired a large amount of weapons and ammunition that were brought to Israel in an old American vessel bought in France and renamed in Ze'ev Jabotinsky's honor. When the ship approached the coast, a tentative agreement was worked out whereby the provisional government would permit it to land at Kfar Vitkin, where it would be unloaded. The arms were to be handed over to the newly formed Zahal, created on May 31, 1948, to supersede all the underground movements active in the Yishuv. Upon arrival, however, IZL leaders sailed the vessel to Tel Aviv in a move widely perceived (though apparently not originally planned) as a challenge to the provisional government's authority. A brief fight ensued during which the *Altalena* was sunk and following which the last IZL units integrated into Zahal. > see also: **Altalena**; **War of Independence**; **Zva ha-Hagana le-Israel**.

Anashim [אנשים, H] "People": Code name used by the Af-Al-Pi organization and the Irgun Zvai Leumi for crew members of *ha'apala* ships they organized. > see also: **Aliya Bet**; **Yishuv, Yishuv Organizations (Underground Organizations)**.

Angola Plan [GN]: Territorialist scheme for mass Jewish resettlement in the Portugese colony of Angola. Initially conceived in 1886, the plan proceded no further than a mere proposal until taken up by the Jewish Territorial Organization (ITO) in 1910. ITO leaders hoped to convince the newly established Portugese Republic to permit mass immigration to Angola by Russian and Romanian Jews who would establish autonomous agricultural colonies in the country. The Portugese government discussed the plan extensively throughout 1912 and finally approved a modest settlement scheme in August 1913. By then, however, ITO was having difficulty in obtaining the £250,000 initially needed to finance the project. The outbreak of World War I terminated all further discussion of the plan in this form. In 1940 a similar but non-territorialist scheme was proposed by U.S. Presidential Adviser Bernard Baruch who saw Angola as a possible refuge for German Jewish refugees. The scheme was not adopted by any government or refugee aid organization and was quietly dropped soon thereafter. > see also: **Territorialism.**

Anshei Yosef [אנשי יוסף, H] "Josef's Men": Mossad Le-Aliya Bet code name for Soviet or Communist agents active in postwar Bulgaria. The term derives from Soviet dictator Josef Stalin and may also be translated as "Stalin's men." The Mossad was very careful to try to keep its distance from the Communist activists, since they could easily disrupt its operations (just as the Yevsektsias had disrupted Zionist activities in postrevolutionary Russia). > see also: **Lubricating Expenses.**

Antisemitismus [G] "Antisemitism": Term coined in 1879 by Wilhelm Marr and used to signify the pathological hatred of Jews. Antisemitism played an important but not decisive role in the creation of Zionism, since many of the early Zionists claimed that their turn to Jewish nationalism derived from experiences (direct or not) with antisemitism. The relationship between antisemitism and Zionism was most obvious in the cases of thinkers such as Leon Pinsker and Theodor Herzl: the former responded to the pogroms in Russia in 1881–1882 and the latter to antisemitic outbursts during the Dreyfus Trial in 1894 by proposing the creation of a Jewish national home. Albeit, antisemitism played only a partial role in the rise of Jewish nationalism, since many Jewish thinkers had already turned to some form of nationalism before the massive outburst of antisemitism in last third of the nineteenth century, deriving their ideas from internal sources rather than external stimuli. > see also: **Zionut; Hibbat Zion.**

Insofar as antisemitism may also be viewed as a denial to Jews of rights granted to other peoples, anti-Zionism may be viewed as a form of antisemitism. This holds true because anti-Zionists fundamentally deny the Jewish right to national self-identification and, consequently, deny legitimacy to the creation of a Jewish state. Ironically, many Jewish anti-Zionists may thus flirt with antisemitism, the dividing line between antisemitism and anti-Zionism being a very fine one. > see also: **Anti-Zionism.**

Anti-Zionism [HT]: Jewish opposition to Zionism and, in some cases, to all manifestations of Jewish nationalism. Before the founding of the state of Israel, anti-Zionism derived from four disparate sources: (1) from elements of the Orthodox community (mainly but not exclusively in Eastern Europe) who viewed any human act toward Jewish redemption to be rebellion against God; (2) from assimilated Western European Jews (including members of the Reform movement) who no longer considered Jews to be a national community but merely a religious identification; (3) from Jewish socialists and socialist nationalists who believed that a return to Zion was a step backward and that Jews had to participate in the great class struggle (with proper guarantees for Jewish cultural rights in the diaspora) in order to gaurantee a better future for mankind; and (4) from those individuals and groups who agreed that Jews constitute a nation but did not consider *Eretz Israel* a viable option in the short or long term. Any or all of these groups used a variety of arguments, including the argument that Zionists fueled antisemitism by admitting that Jews cannot be integrated into non-Jewish society. Additionally, assimilationist critics of Zionism charged that Zionism created accusations of "Dual Loyalty" for otherwise patriotic Jews. Anti-Zionism was strongest in Eastern Europe and America before the Nazi rise to power in 1933. In fact, Zionists were a small but vocal minority in many Jewish communities for most of the period from 1897 to 1933. The Holocaust, however, proved anti-Zionism to be bankrupt and marginalized most nonreligious anti-Zionists. Orthodox anti-Zionism continues in some circles but is a marginal political philosophy. > see also: **Zionut; Nationalism; Autonomism; Bundism; Conquest of Communities Judaism and Zionsim; Territorialism.**

Apotroposim [אפורטופוסים, Aramaic] "Representatives": Mossad Le-Aliya Bet term for British pounds sterling, which could be used to buy the tacit or active co-operation of bureaucrats in the countries from which *Ha'apala* ships originated. > see also: **Lubricating Expenses.**

Arabs

1. Scope and Definition

Although Zionism claimed to be the national liberation movement of the Jewish people, it was by no means the only nationalist movement arising in the last third of the nineteenth century with claims against the Ottoman Empire. The Zionist vision of returning a homeless people to an empty homeland turned out, in reality, to be the precursor for a nationalist struggle that has lasted nearly a century and is only marginally closer to a solution now than it was when it began. The first tentative steps to achieve peace between the two Semitic nations were taken only twenty years ago, and no comprehensive peace agreement has been signed as of this writing. > see also: **Aretz bli Am, le-Am bli Aretz.**

Arab agitation against Jewish immigration to Palestine began almost simultaneously with the First Aliya, although in some cases simple robbery and not ideological opposition animated many attacks upon Jewish settlements in this era. Arab nationalist opposition to Zionism began to grow after the turn of the twentieth century, despite efforts (in 1908 and 1913, for instance) to rally Zionist support for Arab aspirations of independence from the Ottoman Empire. During World War I it briefly appeared that an Arab-Jewish alliance might indeed become a reality. This hope culminated in two agreements signed by the Emir Faisal and WZO President Chaim Weizmann and

American Zionist leader (later Supreme Court Justice) Felix Frankfurter. These agreements were designed to reduce friction in Palestine but were also based on Faisal's assumption that the Zionists would risk their alliance with Great Britain (whose government, in any case, did nothing to support an Arab-Jewish rappoachement) in order to obtain Syria's inclusion in an independent Arab kingdom. > see also: **Faisal-Weizmann Agreement; Faisal-Frankfurter Correspondence; Sykes-Picot Agreement.**

Hope for peaceful accommodation was soon dashed, however: Arab nationalists in Palestine and in the neighboring countries refused to consider any accommodation with Zionism, which represented little more than a form of European inperialism in their eyes, and refused to grant that Jews had any rights to return to their ancestral homeland. The latter point was critical, since the Arabs viewed Jewish immigration not as a repatriation of exiles but as an illegal and immoral invasion of the Arab nation's sacred land by members of a foreign group bent on domination. Arab nationalists also rejected the notion that Jews constituted a nation possessing the same rights to self-expression as the Arab nation, seeing Jews instead as a religious group possessing limited rights to live as a minority in Muslim countries. This Arab view meant the uncategorical rejection of the Zionist notion of a "right of return," which was (and still is) central to Zionist ideology. Finally, Arabs viewed Jews as little more than Dhimmi, members of a protected religious minority, having no right to rule over Arabs. > see also: **Nationalism; Dhimmi; Anti-Zionism.**

Arab rejection of Zionism periodically boiled over into violence, culminating in several periods of intense rioting (1921, 1929, and 1933). After 1933 Arab nationalists, egged on by fascist and Nazi propaganda and adopting fascist-style political ideologies, increasingly turned to violence in hopes of breaking the Anglo-Zionist entente. This process culminated in the Arab Revolt of 1936–1939, a military failure but (because of then-prevailing British strategic concerns) a political success that resulted in the White Paper of 1939 by which the British government repudiated its commitments to Zionism. Despite government repudiation of Britain's role in creating a Jewish national home, most Arab nationalist leaders supported the Axis during World War II. Indeed, the Mufti of Jerusalem, Haj Amin al-Husseini, spent most of the war years in Berlin attempting to gain Arab/Muslim support for the Nazis and their war to rid the world of the Jews. Finally, Arab rejection of compromise after the U.N. decision to partition Palestine led to all-out fighting between the Arab and Jewish communities, followed by the invasion of Israel by seven Arab regular armies on May 14, 1948. The resulting War of Independence represented the first of many abortive Arab efforts to destroy the Jewish state: as already noted progress toward real peace in the Middle East has only taken its first, tentative steps. > see also: **Meoraot**; **Mufti of Jerusalem**; **Fascism, Arabs and**; **World War II**; **United Nations**; **War of Independence**.

2. Major Arab Organizations

Arab Higher Committee (AHC), quasi-governmental agency established by the leaders of the main Arab clans and nationalist organizations in Palestine on April 25, 1936. Created to coordinate activities, the AHC was, almost from its inception, dominated by the Mufti of Jerusalem, Haj Amin al-Husseini. The AHC program was, therefore, similar to his and was based on a complete unwillingness to compromise with Zionism in any way, shape, or form. The AHC offered broad command of Arab forces during the revolt against Great Britain that began on the same day which the AHC was created. As a result, the AHC was banned by the government on October 1, 1937; it was revived again after World War II but collapsed entirely as a result of the crushing defeat faced by the Mufti's troops during Israel's War of Independence. > see also: **Mufti**; **Meora'ot**.

Arab League, common name for the association of independent Arab states created on March 22, 1945. The Arab League's creation was encouraged by Great Britain, which viewed the development as a means to retain influence in the Middle East. From its inception, the Arab League acted as a lobbying group against Jewish goals in Palestine, at times following the British lead in anti-Zionist pronouncements. It was the Arab League that threatened violence if the United Nations agreed to partition Palestine and that resolved on February 9, 1948, to prevent the creation of the State of Israel. > see also: **Arabs**; **United Nations**; **War of Independence**.

Arab Legion (AL), popular name for the armed forces of the Hashemite Kingdom, founded in 1923 when the country was still called Trans-Jordan. Initially, the AL was created to protect the volatile border between Trans-Jordan and Syria. The AL, in turn, was a conglomerate of previously established units composed of Arab personnel commanded by British officers. In 1939, an Englishman, Sir John Bagot Glubb (Glubb Pasha), was named overall AL commander. Although significantly understrength during World War II, the AL had the distinction of being the only Arab army to remain loyal to the Allies throughout the war. After the war, the AL expanded greatly, to a total strength of 6,000 men, and invaded Israel on May 15, 1948. The AL proved to be the toughest of the Arab armies facing Israel, successfully closing the road to Jerusalem and nearly splitting Israel in two. Theoretically, the Jordanian armed forces are still called the Arab Legion, although that title has not been used in public since 1956. > see also: **War of Independence**.

Arab Liberation Army (ALA), irregular force of Arab freebooters from Syria, Lebanon, and Palestine, organized in late December 1947. Armed and trained in Syria, the ALA was commanded by Fawzi Al-Kaukji, who hoped to help local Palestinian Arab forces dominate the Upper Galilee and destroy all Jewish settlements there. The ALA infiltrated Palestine on January 10, 1948, but failed in its initial attack (on Kfar Szold). An ALA attack on Tirat Zvi in February also failed but an ALA attack on Mishmar ha-Emek on April 4, 1948, placed the settlement under siege. The Hagana launched a sharp counterattack against the ALA, relieving Mishmar ha-Emek on April 22. Further defeats led to increasing desertions and the ALA collapsed entirely as a result of Zahal's operation Hiram in October 1948. > see also: **Zahal; War of Independence**.

Greenshirts, Colloquial name for paramilitary units established in 1936 by the Mufti of Jerusalem, Haj Amin al-Huseini. Their name derived from the color of the tunics that all members were supposed to wear during operations. Green was selected for its identification with Islam and with the earth; the latter was parallel to fascist use of brown and reflected the clear influence of both Italian fascism and German Nazism on the Mufti. Aspiring to nationwide status, the Greenshirts may be seen as the Arab equivalent of the Hagana. In reality, the Greenshirts were only marginally more than an armed rabble engaged in anti-Jewish (and at a later stage anti-British) terrorism. > see also: **Arab Revolt; Mufti**.

Arab Revolt [HT]: General term for the all-out effort by Palestinian Arabs to uproot the *Yishuv* and force the mandate's termination, undertaken between 1936 and 1939. The revolt must be seen as part of the continuing cycle of violence undertaken by the Arabs in an effort to convince the British government that continuing support for Zionism was contrary to Britain's imperial interests, especially insofar as the British required peace in the Middle East in order to counter Italian (and later German) efforts to encroach upon the Suez Canal. The revolt began as a general strike in April 1936, but the strike had no impact on the Yishuv and little overall impact on economic conditions in Palestine. As a result, the Arab Higher Committee approved a turn to violence that soon flamed into an uprising against British rule in Palestine. The revolt may be divided into four stages: (1) From April to October 1936, when Jewish settlements and institutions bore the brunt of Arab attacks. (2) From November 1936 to September 1937 (when the Peel Commission Report calling for partition appeared), a lull occurred in

the fighting. (3) From September 1937 to January 1939, when the main targets for Arab attack were British troops and institutions. (4) Between January and May 1939, a period when British efforts to find a diplomatic solution to the impasse led to the revolt's winding down. Although militarily a failure, the Arab Revolt led the to a major reassessment of British strategic interests and the eventual effort by the British cabinet to repudiate its promises to the Jews, as reflected in the White Paper of 1939. > see also: **Arabs; Me'oraot; Committees of Investigation, Peel Commission; White Papers, White Paper of 1939**.

Aretz bli Am le-Am bli Artez [ארץ בלי עם לעם בלי ארץ, H] "A Land without People for a People without Land": Zionist slogan reflecting both the romantic attitude toward Palestine and the pressing sense of Jewish homelessness. The slogan implies the clear benefits to be derived, for Jewry and humanity, from a Jewish renaissance in Palestine, but virtually ignores the existence of the Arabs. > see also: **Arabs**.

Arlosoroff Affair [HT/PN]: Popular name for the incident on June 16, 1933, in which Dr. Haim Arlosoroff, a prominent Mapai member and head of the JA Political Department, was killed. Arlosoroff had just returned to Palestine from Germany, where he was involved in early negotiations relating to the *Haavara* Agreement. He and his wife were strolling on the Tel Aviv beach when they were approached by three men, one of whom fatally shot Arlosoroff. Thereafter, two different reconstructions of the crime emerged. Mapai leaders claimed that Arlosoroff was killed by members of the shadowy revisionist Zionist underground, the Brit ha-Biryonim. They thus claimed that the murder was, in essence, a political assassination. For their part, the revisionists claimed that the murderers were Arabs whose motive was robbery or sexual assault.

After a brief investigation, the British police arrested three reputed members of Brit ha-Biryonim: Abba Ahimeir, Abraham Stavsky, and Zvi Rosenblatt. All were charged with the crime, the bill of indictment specifically naming

Stavsky as the shooter. Rosenblatt, a minor, was acquitted of the crime, as was Ahimeir, who, in any case, had only been accused of incitement due to an article he wrote condeming Arlosoroff as a traitor. Stavsky, however, was convicted on June 8, 1934, and was sentenced to death. On July 19, 1934, Stavsky's sentence was commuted to life in prison, due to a quirk of Palestine's legal code: Palestine law did not permit the execution of a suspect on the basis of testimony from a single eyewitness. Stavsky's conviction was later overturned on the same basis and he was released.

The case has remained controversial since the 1930s. In 1981 the Israeli government established a commission to investigate the incident. After reviewing all pertinent data, the commission concluded that while the three accused men probably were innocent, unnamed revisionist Zionists had probably been involved in some way. The main body of Israeli archival material on the affair has been sealed until at least 2017.

Armistice Agreement(s) [HT]: Legal term for the interim treaties signed between Israel and the Arab confrontation states (Egypt, Jordan, Lebanon, and Syria) in 1949. These armistice agreements were negotiated after a set of bilateral peace talks held on the island of Rhodes under U.N. auspices. Although the agreements were supposed to be temporary, another twenty-eight years (and four wars) passed before an Arab country — Egypt — signed a peace treaty with Israel.

Table A.8: The Armistice Agreements

Date	Country
February 24, 1949	Egypt
March 23, 1949	Lebanon
April 3, 1949	Trans-Jordan
July 20, 1949	Syria

Source: Hershel Edelheit and Abraham J. Edelheit: *Israel and the Jewish World* (Westport, CT: Greenwood Press, 1995).

Arnevet [ארנבת, H] *"Rabbit":* Code name used by the Hagana intelligence service (Shai) for wiretapping operations in Arab neighborhoods in Jerusalem during the War of Independence. The term derived from a rabbit's long ears, i.e. its ability to hear well and thus obtain information, in this case parallel to Shai's efforts to obtain information on Arab intentions. > see also: **Yishuv, Yishuv Organizations (Underground Organizations, Sherut Yediot).**

Arzi [ארצי, H] *"My Land":* Hagana and Mossad le-Aliya Bet code name for Shaul Avigur, a senior commander of the former and founder of the latter. The term was used in Avigur's connection between 1920 and 1948. During the 1940s the term also came into general use to designate the Mossad le-Aliya Bet. > see also: **Yishuv, Yishuv Organizations (Underground Organizations).**

As A Leads to Z, so Argentina Shall Lead to Zion: Statement in support of Baron Maurice de Hirch's plan to settle Russian Jews in the Argentine Pampas, by Hibbat Zion leader Rabbi Samuel Mohilever. Mohilever's statement came in an 1894 letter to Colonel E. W. Goldsmid, a Hibbat Zion leader in England, and was based on realities: Hibbat Zion could not then obtain land in *Eretz Israel* (due to a Turkish government ban on *aliya*) and Hirsch's plan, at least, had a nationalist veneer that (Mohiliver hoped) would eventually lead the colonists to Zionism. > see also: **Territorialism.**

Assembly: Hagana term for the armoring of private cars thereby making them useful for military purposes during the War of Independence. Cars were acquired from a variety of sources, including legal purchases outside of Palestine/*Eretz Israel*. These cars were then bought to the main Hagana armory in Ramat Gan, where they were converted. > see also: **Sandvichim; Yishuv, Yishuv Organizations (Underground Organizations, Ta'as).**

Assimilation: General sociological term for the absorption of external stimuli by a population. In general, assimilation is used to denote the conscious or subconscious adoption by a minority group of the mores associated with the majority among whom they live. The mildest forms of assimilation are indistinguishable from mere acculturation, and include adoption of language and dress styles. More radical forms of assimilation imply further levels of surrender of minority characteristics, including, ultimately, the total abnegation of unique self-identity by the individual(s) and complete immersion into the general society. In the specific case, assimilation is the term used to represent Jewish adoption of European mores during the era of emancipation.

Moderate assimilation (acculturation) reflected the tendency of Jews to adopt the language, dress, and general cultural norms of the countries in which they lived. More radical assimilationists ceased to be Jews altogether, styling themselves as "Europeans of the Mosaic persuasion." These assimilationists denied the very existence of a Jewish nation, arguing that Judaism is a religion only and that no bonds — other than those of a common faith — link the Jewish world. In this context, the most radical assimilationists entirely abandoned Judaism, opting to convert to Christianity.

Although Zionism was formulated as a means to regulate Jewish relations with the non-Jewish world and, to a degree, as an effort to make Jews "like all the other nations" (classically an assimilationist concept), Zionists opposed assimilation as treason to the Jewish people. Zionists saw their movement as a bulwark against assimilation, especially for those Jews who sought to preserve their identity in an era of intense secularization. Zionism also offered a means by which Jews who no longer observed the minutae of Jewish law could join with moderate Orthodox Jews in defense of Jewish continuity. Paradoxically, Orthodox anti-Zionists opposed Jewish nationalism precisely because it offered a defense of Jewish identity with little reference to Jewish tradition. > see also: **Judaism and Zionism**.

Assimilant(en) [G] "Assimilationist(s)": > see also **Assimilation**.

Astronomers [slang]: Term used by members of the Irgun Zvai Leumi to designate members of Lohame Herut Israel (Lehi). The term derives from the fact that astronomers look at stars; in Hebrew the term for star is kochav, which in turn may be translated into Yiddish as stern: Abraham Stern founded Lehi in 1940. It is unclear whether the term was used in a derisive or derogatory fashion. > see also: **Yair; Yishuv, Yishuv Organizations (Underground Organizations)**.

Athalta de-Geulta [אתחלתא ד'גאולתה, Am] "Beginning of the Redemption": Religious Zionist slogan that places Zionism into the context of traditional redemptivist ideology. In this formulation, Zionism is not a human usurpation of messianic redemption, but rather a necessary precursor that is part and parcel of the divine plan. The phrase itself was derived from the Talmudic discussion (BT Megilla 17b) of the traditional prayer (repeated thrice daily in the Amida service) for divine redemption. One of the sages hypothesized that "war is also the beginning of redemption." Hence, it follows that human activity to begin the redemption is both necessary and appropriate.

Auch-und-Bauch Judentum [G] "Also-and-Belly Judaism": Derisive term coined by Max Nordau to reflect his feelings about Jewish opponents of Zionism. He saw them as passive, cowardly, degenerate, and lazy. Although they claimed to speak in the name of Judaism, they did not take it seriously and merely used it as a cover for their own failings. In contrast, Nordau saw Zionists as exactly the opposite: active, heroic, virile, and industrious. The latter represented the true Jew of the future. > see also: **Muskeljudentum**.

Auto-Emancipation [G] "Self-Emancipation": As a proper noun, the term is the title of Leon Pinsker's 1882 pamphlet suggesting a Zionist solution to the Jewish problem. The pamphlet was written in the aftermath of the pogroms of 1881–1882 and suggested that anti-semitism was an endemic psychological problem deriving from the fear of ghosts. Since Jews are a spiritual nation lacking a definitive territorial base they are hated, resented, and feared. Pinsker argued that this fear would only lead to worse tragedies in the future unless immediate steps to re-vive a Jewish national home in the Land of Israel were undertaken. *Auto-Emancipation* influenced the creation of the Hibbat Zion movement and also influenced the first pioneers who traveled to Israel in the 1880s. When used in a general sense, the term designates the goal of all Zionist ideologies.

Autonomism, Jewish [HT]: Non-Zionist ideology popular among elements of Easternr Euopean Jewry in the last decade of the nineteenth century and the first three decades of the twentieth century. Auto-nomism is commonly associated with historian and political activist Simon Dubnow. In essence, Dubnow argued that Jews constitute a spiritual nation that needs no specific territory to manifest its national identity. According to Dubnow, Jews do, however, need an organizational infra-structure to ensure cultural continuity and to guarantee political rights. Dubnow and his supporters, therefore, suggested that Jews seek the creation of national minority treaties in the post–World War I successor states and emphasized the need for a new supracommunal agency parallel to the Council of the Four Lands active in Poland and Lithuania from the sixteenth to the eighteenth centuries. > see also : **Nationalism**; **Organizations, non-Zionist (Folkspartei)**.

Avi Geula [אבי גאולה, H] "Father of Redemption": Code name used by and about David Ben-Gurion in sensitive JAE documents written between 1935 and 1948. The phrase reflected Ben-Gurion's intensive activities to accomplish Zionist goals in that period but also derived from his daughter's name. In light of the former, this phrase

also may be translated "Father of the country." Including Avi Geula, Ben-Gurion used twenty other code names at various times (and in various contexts) after he assumed the JAE chairmanship. > see also: **Ha-Zaken**; **Ha-Yevani**; **Hercules**.

Avlad al-Meta [Ar] "Children of Death": Derisive Arabic term for Jews, especially popular prior to World War I. The term reflected the generally low esteem in which Jews were held by Arabs (both Muslim and Christian), being perceived as cowards and children of the devil. The term especially implied Jewish cowardice. Jews were thought to be unable or unwilling to protect themselves, ready to flee at the first sign of Arab resistance. > see also: **Dhimmi**.

Avlei Zion [אבלי ציון, H] "The Mourners of Zion": Term for the Jewish sect that, after Simon Bar Kokhba's defeat (ca. 135 C.E.) foreswore any physical symbols of happiness to pray for a speedy divine redemption. Marking the destruction of Jerusalem at all times, Avlei Zion adopted numerous Jewish mourning rituals, including wearing sackcloth and ashes even on the Sabbath. In the ninth century, some Avlei Zion joined with parts of the Karaite sect (sectarians who rejected the authority of the oral law) and settled in Jerusalem. Once there they spent their days praying for redemption, generally praying by the ruins of the Western Wall of the Temple, giving rise to the common mistranslation Wailing Wall. > see also: **Kotel ha-Maaravi**.

Avoda Ivrit [עבודה עברית, H] "Hebrew Labor": Socialist Zionist concept reflecting the goal of self-reliance that the labor Zionist movement hoped to foster in the *Yishuv* and which, it was hoped, would create a "new Jewish man." The idea derived from romantic ideas about national vitality that were popular during the middle and last third of the nineteenth century. As developed by leaders such as Dov Ber Borochov and Aaron David Gordon, *Avoda Ivrit* emphasized that Jews should not "merely" return to *Eretz Israel* to become a colonial ruling class but ought to reorganize their economic life to do all manual labor (especially in agriculture) themselves. By that means, Jewish society would be entirely transformed and a new (socialist and nationalist) Jewish society could be created. Although controversial, *Avoda Ivrit* became the operative ideology of almost all Zionist parties during the 1920s and 1930s, not just of the leftist ones. Concentrating all labor in Jewish hands was seen as means of rapid state building. This policy risked alienating the Arabs, but relations between the Jewish and Arab communities were so bad by the time of the British mandate that the *Yishuv*'s economic policy could hardly have made conditions any worse. > see also:

Agricultural Settlements; Kibbush ha-Avoda; Dat ha-Avoda.

A'yān [Ar] "Urban Notables": Arabic term for wealthy individuals who wielded considerable economic and political power in the Ottoman Empire. Under the terms of the Tanzimat land law reforms (passed in 1858), these notables were able to acquire a large proportion of the arable land in the Levant. Thereafter, they acted as absentee landlords who collected rent from the fallahin. The A'yān were among the first Arabs to willingly sell land to Jews — at inflated prices — generally without informing either the tenants or the new landlords of the other's existence. > see also: **Land Ownership.**

Ba'al Shoshanat Goshen [בעל שושנת גושן, H] "The Egyptian Rose's Husband": Hagana and Jewish Agency code name for Aubrey (Abba) Eban, used during World War II. At the time, Eban was a staff officer attached to the Special Operations Executive in Cairo while also acting as an adviser to the London JAE's Political Affairs Committee. The term derives from Eban's private life. His wife, who was born in Egypt, was named Rose. > see also: **World War II**.

Bad [בד, H] "Cloth": Abbreviation for Ben-David, sometimes used as a code name for Menaham Begin. > see also: **Ben-David**.

Badim [בדים, H] "Solitary (Ones)": Mossad le-Aliya Bet code term deriving from the Hebrew word *boded* (בודד, solitary or single), used to designate children sailing (by themselves or along with parents) on blockade runners. The term was apparently used only in 1946.

Balfour Declaration:

1. Scope and Definition
British declaration of sympathy for Zionist goals, issued in the form of a letter to Lord Lionel Rothschild from Foreign Minister Arthur James Balfour. Dated November 2, 1917, the declaration was actually based on a series of prior drafts that date back to summer 1917. Scholars have offered a number of hypotheses to explain the British cabinet's actions, none of which can be decisively proved; one — that the British made the declaration to repay Chaim Weizmann for his scientific research — can be decisively disproved. The other hypotheses can be grouped into three categories: (1) fear that the Germans would issue a similar declaration, thereby gaining significant diplomatic advantages; (2) hope to gain support from American Jewish financiers to speed up U.S. entry into World War I; and (3) hope to gain the support of Jewish Bolsheviks to keep Russia in the war. Again, it must be emphasized that all three of these hypotheses are reflected in parts of the cabinet discussions of 1917.

The wording of the declaration was a source of contention and disagreement almost from the beginning. While the cabinet promised to use its "best endeavors" to help Zionists settle in Palestine/*Eretz Israel*, British authorities almost immediately acted to prevent mass *aliya*. Similarly, the wording "in Palestine of a national home for the Jewish people" rather than a more straightforward formulation ("of a Jewish national home in Palestine") could be (and in fact was) interpreted by later British governments to mean that the British only promised part of Palestine to the Jews. The clause regarding protecting the rights of local Arab population also was used to inhibit the Yishuv's growth, since virtually anything done on behalf of Jews could be interpreted as impairing Arab rights. Finally, many British leaders denied that the Balfour declaration ever promised the Jews sovereignty, the term "national home" being held to imply considerably less than a sovereign state, despite Balfour's statements — made as early as a month after the declaration — that such was his intent. The sum total of all these conflicts led to very stormy relations between the British and the *Yishuv* virtually from the beginning of the mandate and ultimately contributed to the expansion of the Arab-Jewish conflict. > see also: **Hindenburg Erklärung; Yishuv; Mandatory Palestine**.

2. Major Textual Variants

Cabinet Draft, July 1917, 1. His Majesty's Government accepts the principle that Palestine should be reconstituted as the national home of the Jewish people. 2. His Majesty's Government will use its best endeavours to secure the achievement of this object and will discuss the necessary methods and means with the Zionist Organisation.

Balfour Draft, August 1917, His Majesty's Government accepts the principle that Palestine should be reconstituted as the national home of the Jewish people and will use their best endeavours to secure the achievement of this object and will be ready to consider any suggestions on the subject which the Zionist Organisation may desire to lay before them.

Milner Draft, August 1917, His Majesty's Government accepts the principle that every opportunity should be afforded for the establishment of a home for the Jewish people in Palestine and will use its best endeavours to facilitate the achievement of this object and will be ready to consider any suggestions on the subject which the Zionist organisation may desire to lay before them.

Milner-Avery Draft, October 1917, His Majesty's Government views with favor the establishment in Palestine of a national home for the Jewish race and will use its best endeavors to facilitate the achievement of this object, it being clearly understood that nothing shall be done which may prejudice the civil and religious rights of existing non-Jewish communities in Palestine or the rights and political status enjoyed in any other country by such Jews who are fully contented with their existing nationality and citizenship.

Final Version, November 1917, His Majesty's Government views with favour the establishment in Palestine of a national home for the Jewish people and will use their best endeavors to facilitate the achievement of this object, it being clearly understood that nothing shall be done which may prejudice the civil and religious rights of existing non-Jewish communities in Palestine, or the rights and political status enjoyed by Jews in any country.

Bank/Bank Drafts/Promisory Notes: Euphemisms used by JAE representatives in London to represent *Yishuv* enlistment into the Royal Armed Forces during World War II. The term implied that the *Yishuv* hoped to gain political benefit by being recognized as an Allied Power. > see also: **World War II**.

Bashan [GN]: Geographic term used to designate a region in historical Trans-Jordan. During the 1930s, the term was used by the JA as a code for (1) Emir Abdullah, the ruler of Trans-Jordan, and (2) Colonial Minister William Ormesby-Gore. The latter use was based on the closeness of the Hebrew transliteration part of Ormesay-Gore's last name (Gore) to Gur, a city in the Bashan mentioned in Jewish sources.

Basic Law(s): Term for the constitutional system used in Israel. Since a written constitution was deemed unacceptable by the religious parties, the draft constitution drawn up between 1947 and 1949 was never ratified. Instead, the Knesset passed a series of fundamental regulations, known officially as basic laws, which define specific powers of the government and its relationship to the rights and responsibilities of the Israeli citizenry and to world Jewry. The first of these basic laws was published in 1958. The process has been virtually completed as of this writing, thereby giving Israel a constitution in all but name. > see also: **Small Constitution**.

Programm

Handwritten Copy of the Basel Program.
Courtesy of the Central Zionist Archives, Jerusalem

Basel Program [GN]: Statement of Zionist goals issued by the First Zionist Congress in August 1897. The program, which passed the congress plenary session unanimously, committed Zionists "to create for the Jewish people a home in Palestine secured by Public law." Sometimes also known as the Basel Declaration, the statement neither specified the borders desired by Zionists nor discussed specific Zionist goals past the creation of a Jewish national home. > see also: **World Zionist Congress(es)**; **Endziel**.

Batlan [בטלן, H] "Idler": Hagana term for a British police officer, used mainly after World War II. Derivation is unknown.

Bayit [בית, H] "House": Mossad le-Aliya Bet code term for (1) A boat (used between 1938 and 1940) and (2) Italy (used after World War II). It is not clear what, if any, relationship exists between the two usages, except insofar as both related to *Ha'apala*. > see also: **Aliya Bet**.

Bayit Leumi [בית לאומי, H] "National Home": Zionist term for Palestine incorporated into the Balfour Declaration and subsequent international documents. Although Theodor Herzl had expressed Zionist goals as the attainment of a Jewish state, he never defined the level of sovereignty that the entity would possess. Moreover, the First

Zionist Congress reformulated Herzl's statement into the more general concept of a national home in order not to frighten the Turkish government, with whom he was already negotiating over Palestine/*Eretz Israel*. Thereafter, most Zionists continued to use the more general term rather than the politically explicit concept of statehood, even while they claimed to be working toward the ultimate goal of statehood. Conditions in the 1930s forced a reevaluation of this ideologial position — which has since come to be known as gradualism — and many Zionists began to advocate a stronger and more explicit statement of Zionist goals. While Ze'ev Jabotinsky and the revisionist movement were the most passionate advocates of what they described as an "Endziel" resolution, the Biltmore Resolution of 1942 finally ended all disputes over immediate Zionist goals by demanding the creation of a Jewish commonwealth after World War II. > see also: **Basel Program**; **Balfour Declaration**; **Biltmore Resolution**; **Endziel**; **Gradualism**.

Bayit Shlishi [בית שלישי, H] "The Third Commonwealth": Literally meaning the Third House, a reference to the hoped-for future Temple that the Messiah will build, the term has been used in some circles to refer to the State of Israel. The precedent was that the two previous eras of Jewish sovereignty were referred to in this manner: Bayit Rishon (בית ראשון, i.e., the First Commonwealth) and Bayit Sheini (בית שני, i.e., the Second Commonwealth). The term has redemptivist overtones but is not prevalent among religious Zionist circles, since it implies that the final redemption has already happened. > see also: **Athalta d'Geulta**; **Shivat Zion**.

Be-Dam va-Esh Yehuda Nafla, be-Dam va-Esh Yehuda Takum [בדם ואש יהודה נפלה, בדם ואש יהודה תקום, H] "By blood and fire Judea fell, by blood and fire Judea shall arise": Slogan of the ha-Shomer defense organization created in 1909. The slogan reflected the romantic notions about the need for Jews to return to militancy as the first step on the road to national sovereignty. Despite the desire for military adventurism implicit in the slogan, ha-Shomer observed a strictly defensive posture for its entire history. > see also: **Yishuv, Yishuv Organizations (Underground Organizations, ha-Shomer)**.

Begadim [בגדים, H] "Clothes": Hagana code term used after World War II for secret arms factories. The term may derive from the close identification of Jews with the needle trades, although that derivation is unclear. > see also: **Ta'as**.

Beit Gisi [בית-גיזי, H/PN] "Gisi's House": Briha and Mossad le-Aliya Bet code term for Slovakia, named after Gisi Fleischmann, a Zionist leader and underground rescue activist during the Holocaust. Fleischmann, who had been involved in negotiations to ransom the surviving remnant of European Jewry from the Nazis (the so-called Europa plan) was murdered in Auschwitz in October 1944. After World War II, Briha routes through Slovakia — and thence the entire territory — were named in her honor.

Beit Hanna [בית-חנה, H/PN] "Hanna's House": Briha code name for Budapest, named after the Palestinian paratrooper Hanna Szenes. Sent during World War II on a mission to Hungary to rescue Jews, Szenes was captured by the Hungarian fascist authorities, tried for treason, and executed. > see also: **Beit Madleket ha-Gafrur; Paratroopers, Palestinian**.

Beit Holim [בית-חולים, H] "Hospital": Code term used by a number of the *Yishuv's* underground movements with a variety of meanings. In particular, the term was used during the 1930s by the Hagana and the Irgun Zvai Leumi to represent a prison. After 1945, the term was used (as part of the phrase "leaving the hospital") by the Mossad le-Aliya Bet to represent the sailing of a blockade runner.

Beit Madleket ha-Gafrur [בית מדלקת הגפרור, H] "House of the Match Lighter": Hagana code term for Kibbutz Sdot Yam (near Ceaserea), a major reception area for *Ma'apilim*. The term derives from the fact that Hanna Szenes had been a member of Sdot Yam before her final mission to Europe during World War II (while on the mission, Szenes wrote her famous poem, "Blessed Is the Match"). This term is another reflection of the heroic deeds of the thirty-two Palestinian paratroopers and was a tribute to Szenes's heroism. > see also: **Beit Hanna; Paratroopers, Palestinian**.

Beit-Nuri [בית-נורי, H/PN] "Nuri's House": Hagana and Mossad le-Aliya Bet code name for Iraq, derived from Prime Minister Nuri Al-Said. During and after World War II, Iraq was a major source for "illegal" Jewish immigration to *Eretz Israel*, a reflection of the unsettled conditions faced by Iraqi Jewry.

Beit Yaakov Lehu ve-Nelha [בית יעקב לכו ונלכה, H]: House of Jacob arise and go up" (Bilu): Biblical quotation (from Isaiah 2:5) used as a motto by the first group of Hovevei Zion immigrants to *Eretz Israel*. The motto's use represented the fact that the group sought an immediate remedy to Jewish distress in the Russian empire, no matter how defined, by a policy of *aliya*. From 1882 onward, the abbreviated form of the group motto was also used as the group's name. Bilu also operated under two other Hebrew names: Daber el Bnai Israel va-Yisa'u (Dabiu, דבר אל בני ישראל ויסעו, i.e., "Speak unto the Children of Israel, That They Go Forward," Exodus 14:16) and Shivat ha-Heresh veha-Masger (Sahu, שיבת החרש והמסגר, Return of the Carpenter and Metalworker). The latter name represented the urban element of Bilu, that is, those Bilu members who settled in Jerusalem and worked in light indiustry. > see also: **Yishuv, Yishuv Organizations; Aliya; Agricultural Settlement(s)**.

Bejahung [G] "Affirmation": Term coined by Martin Buber before World War I to characterize the goals of Zionist education in Western and Central Europe: to create conditions whereby each individual Jew would recognize and strengthen his or her ties to the

Jewish people, embrace a Jewish ethos (including learning Hebrew), and try to live a Jewish life. Buber saw Zionism as a means to foster a positive identity (hence the term) and to increase the German Jews' recognition of Jewish uniqueness.

Ben-Boullion [Slang]: Derisive nickname for Jewish Agency Executive (JAE) chairman David Ben-Gurion used by his chief rival, revisionist Zionist leader Ze'ev Jabotinsky. The play on Ben-Gurion's name was meant to convey the sense that the JAE chairman was wishy-washy and was leading the Zionist movement to disaster. Jabotinsky used the term only in internal ha-Zach correspondence, principally after the failure of the Ben-Gurion–Jabotinsky agreement of 1934.

Ben-Hadad [PN/HT]: Hagana code name for Tuvia Arazi, a Hagana leader who served in the Trans-Jordanian Frontier Force in the 1920s. In the 1930s, Arazi headed the Shai (intelligence service) Arab Bureau, and commanded the joint Hagana-British intelligence mission in Vichy-controlled Syria during World War II. Arazi was captured by Vichy police twice but escaped both times. > see also: **Yishuv, Yishuv Organizations (Underground Organizations, Sherut Yediot)**

Bernadotte Plan [PN]: Name for the peace plan submitted on September 16, 1948, by U.N. mediator Count Folke Bernadotte as a means to end Israel's War of Independence without further bloodshed. In addition to demanding the internationalization of Jerusalem, the Bernadotte plan called on Israel to relinquish the Negev to the Arabs and Haifa to the U.N., and permit the repatriation of all Arab refugees to their homes. In return, Israel was to receive sections of the Galilee that had been apportioned to the Arab state in the U.N. partition plan but had been occupied by Jewish forces during the war. Bernadotte was assassinated in Jerusalem after submitting the plan; in any case it was rejected as impractical by the U.N. General Assembly in December 1948. > see also: **Partition Plans**.

Between Washington and Pinsk: Term used by Chaim Weizmann to explain the almost unbridgeable chasm between himself and Louis D. Brandeis in the 1920s. The term reflected more than just a difference in tactics; it reflected Weizmann's belief that two totally opposite and ultimately incompatible views of Zionism were clashing. As a result of his perception, Weizmann further believed that the future of the Zionist organization and the destiny of the Yishuv were at stake. > see also: **Brandeisists; Zeeland Program**.

Bevingrad [Slang/PN]: Popular name for the British government compound in Jerusalem at the height of the Jewish revolt in Palestine/ *Eretz Israel* (1945–1947). The name derived from Britain's resoundingly hated foreign minister, Ernest Bevin. The term was used as a derisive joke. Although the British had fortified themselves in the city center, hoping to create a miniature Stalingrad that would be the core of retained British power in Palestine, Bevingrad turned out to be the center of the Labour government's Waterloo. Bevingrad was abandoned when the mandate ended and was almost immediately occupied by Hagana forces.

Bevin Plan: Proposed settlement for the Palestine impasse announced by British Foreign Minister Ernest Bevin in late January 1947. The plan was a response to recent British diplomatic setbacks and may be seen as a last effort by the Labour government to maintain the mandate. In particular, the plan was a response to President Harry S. Truman's Yom Kippur letter of 1946, seen by the British government as an election year gambit that unfairly tilted U.S. government policy toward a pro-Zionist position. As a result, Bevin proposed to modify the White Paper of 1939 for an interim period of five years. During that time the mandate would continue as a trusteeship (still to be held by Great Britain). For the first two years of the trusteeship *aliya* would be fixed at a rate of 4,000 persons per month (thus almost reaching the 100,000 *olim*

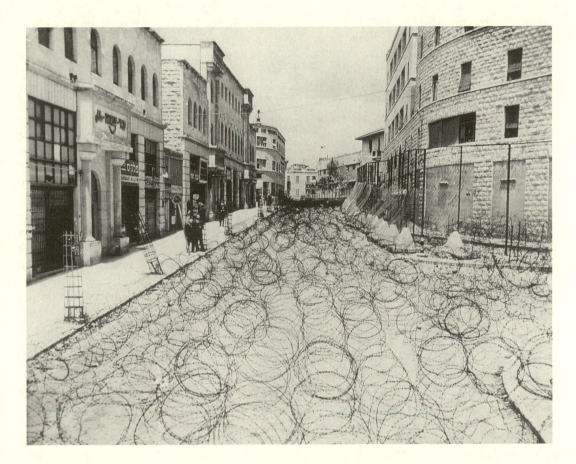

Bevingrad at the Height of the Revolt.
Courtesy of the Central Zionist Archives, Jerusalem

demanded by the Anglo-American Committee of Enquiry), after which *aliya* rates would be based solely on Palestine/ *Eretz Israel*'s economic absorptive capacity (the basis for *aliya* rates during the 1920s and 1930s). In addition both Jewish and Arab communities would be granted considerable autonomy. Simultaneously, the British government would work for an agreement between the Jews and Arabs, thereby reducing intercommunal tension and leading to a peaceful transition to independence at the end of the trusteeship. Although the plan might have obtained Jewish acceptance in 1945, when Bevin announced his plan the *aliya* section was

seen as a cruel joke and the entire scheme was condemned as a barely disguised attempt to permit Great Britain to hold on to the mandate. The plan was therefore rejected out of hand by the Arabs, the Zionists, and the Truman Administration. > see also: **Yom Kippur Letter; Committees of Inquiry, Anglo-American Committee of Enquiry Regarding the Problems of European Jewry and Palestine.**

Biltmore Resolution: Declaration of Jewish goals adopted at the Extraordinary Zionist Conference held in New York in 1942. The resolution explicitly advocated the establishment of a Jewish commonwealth in Palestine.

The conference, so named because it took place in New York's Biltmore Hotel, was attended by many Zionist leaders, including Chaim Weizmann, Abba Hillel Silver, Stephen S. Wise, David Ben-Gurion, Israel Goldstein, and Nahum Goldmann. The resolution marked the first time that a majority of Zionists called openly for the establishment of Jewish sovereignty as the ultimate goal of Zionism. The resolution became central to the activities of the American Zionist Emergency Council.

Bilu > see also: **Beit Yaakov Lehu ve-Nelha**.

Bina [בינה, H] "Intelligence": Hagana code term for its intelligence service, Sherut ha-Yediot (Shai), used in documents not likely to fall into unfriendly hands. The term was a simple translation (in Hebrew the word also implies "wisdom") and was thus considered too easy to decipher.

Binationalism [HT]: Term for the semi-Zionist ideology that sought an accommodation with the Arabs via the creation of a joint Arab-Jewish state in Palestine/*Eretz Israel*. Binationalists based their arguments on three elements, first, that Jews represented a small minority of Palestine's total population; second, that Arabs had indeed lived there for hundreds of years; and, third, that unless a consensus was reached between Jews and Arabs conflict would last forever. In theory binationalists remained Zionists. However, their argument that Zionists had to accept less than the full measure of their demands placed most binationalists outside of the Zionist mainstream. Despite their willingness to compromise on elementary Zionist demands regarding *aliya* and land ownership, binationalists were never able to find an equivalent element in the Arab community with whom to seriously discuss a compromise. > see also: **Yishuv, Yishuv Organizations (Political Organizations, Brit Shalom)**.

Binaum [בינאום, H] "Binationalization": Term used for the status of Jerusalem in the U.N. partition resolution passed on November 29, 1947. In light of Jerusalem's importance to Jews, Muslims, and Christians, the General Assembly decided not to include the city in the general partition plan. Instead, Jerusalem was to be internationalized and was to remain under General Assembly supervision; day-to-day affairs in the city were to be controlled by a U.N. appointed high commissioner. Neither the Jews — who otherwise accpted partition — nor the Arabs — who rejected the plan altogether — accepted the internationalization of Jerusalem, resulting in a bitter seven-month battle for the city (December 1947–June 1948). For a long period, Jerusalem was besieged by the Arab Legion. After the fighting ceased, the U.N. attempted to assert its control over an internationalized city, but that was impractical: the de facto partition of Jerusalem (with the "old" city held by Trans-Jordan and the "new" city by Israel) rendered internationalization impossible. On July 26, 1948, the Israeli Provisional Government declared Jerusalem to be Israel's eternal capital, despite the continuing Jordanian occupation of the "old" city. Jerusalem was reunified as a result of the Six Day War of 1967. > see also: **War of Independence**.

Black Letter: Term used by some Arabs for the letter sent by Prime Minister Ramsay MacDonald to WZO president Chaim Weizmann on February 13, 1931. In his letter, MacDonald revoked the most glaringly anti-Zionist elements of the Passfield White Paper, especially in regard to *aliya*. The Arabs decried MacDonald's apparent surrender to Jewish pressure, even though the White Paper had itself been a capitulation to Arab violence and *aliya* was guaranteed by the League of Nations mandate. > see also: **White Paper(s), Passfield White Paper**.

Blackstone Memorial [PN]: Proto-Zionist petition presented on March 5, 1891, by William Blackstone, a well-known American Methodist layman, to President Benjamin Harrison. Signed by 413 prominent Americans — including political, religous, economic, and communal leaders — the petition called upon the U.S. government to purchase Palestine from the Ottoman Empire in order to facilitate the Jews' return to the Holy Land. Although framed in Christological terms, the petition claimed that the Second Coming could not occur until the Jews had returned to their land, the petition prefigured many of the ideas formulated by the First Zionist Congress. > see also: **Gentile Zionism**.

Blue Box(es): Common name for the charity collection box(es) distributed by the Keren Kayemet le-Israel (KKL, also known as the Jewish National Fund). The boxes were designed to be kept in Jewish homes where charity — usually a few coins — was collected and sent to the KKL for land purchases in Palestine. The money thus collected barely covered minimal KKL expenses, but the point of the boxes went beyond charity collection. The idea was to have all Jews — young and old, religious and secular, men and women — participate in the Jewish national rebirth. > see also **Organizations, Zionist Organizations (International; Keren Kayemet Le-Israel)**.

Blue Eyed Arab(s) [Slang]: Slang term used among American Zionists in the 1940s to refer to the British. The term was a reflection of the pro-Arab tilt of Britain's Middle Eastern policy after the White Paper of 1939 was issued and was also an ironic response to the apparent racial preferences (bordering on antisemitism) expressed by the British. To many of the Englishmen in the Palestine administration, the Arabs were a romantic people, whereas Jews were an accursed and despicable race even though both were of Semitic origins. > see also: **Indians**.

B'nai B'rit [בני ברית, H/Slang]: Jewish Agency code term, used during and after World War II for American dollars. The term was used principally in the context of fund-raising for *Aliya Bet* activities. The term may derive from the name of the American Jewish (and international) social organization (usually spelled B'nai B'rith)

and may reflect the importance placed by *Yishuv* fundraisers on American Jewish organizations.

Bnai Eliahu [בני אליהו, H] "Sons of Eliahu": JA code term, used in sensitive documents during World War II for members of the Hagana. The term derives from Hagana chief of staff Eliyahu Golomb, who — figuratively speaking — was the troops' father.

Bnai Hananiah [בני חנניה, H] "Hanania's Sons": Lehi term for members of the Irgun Zvai Leumi who did not join Abraham Stern when he seceded in 1940. The term as stated was neutral, but two derivatives of it were not: Bach and Bachnikim — the former an abbreviation of Ben-Hanania (the Hebrew name of IZL commander David Raziel's father), the latter a derisive diminutive derived from the former. > see also: **Yishuv, Yishuv Organizations (Underground Organizations)**.

Bogrim [בוגרים, H] "Graduates": Term used in Zionist youth movements, especially those of a socialist leaning, for members who had "aged out" and had graduated, either becoming members of the party or moving on to other organizations.

Borochovism [PN]: Socialist Zionist ideology popularized by Poale Zion and deriving from the writings of Dov Baer Borochov (1881–1917). Borochov, who studied Marx as a youth, attempted to apply the concepts of historical materialism to the Jewish case. Socialism can only be attained, according to Borochov, when a majority of the group attains class consciousness. Jews, however, were never able to do so because of the anomalous Jewish condition in the diaspora. The only way to normalize Jewry — even in the Marxist sense — would be for a mass Jewish return to a Jewish state, after which Jews could develop like any other nation. Borochov's synthesis of Marxism with Zionism was the basis for all socialist Zionist ideologies, although many (including especially Mapai) developed an evolutionary, rather than revolutionary, approach to both socialist and Zionist questions. > see also: **Zionut**.

Boycott, Anti-Nazi: Jewish defense mechanism in reaction to the Nazi persecution of German Jewry. On March 19, 1933, the Jewish War Veterans of America announced that its members would boycott German goods and services. Similar boycott groups arose in Poland, the Yishuv, and France. Ze'ev Jabotinsky, president of Ha-Zohar, declared his support for the boycott in May 1933 and in October organized the Center for Economic Defense in Paris. Following the anti-Jewish boycott in Germany, anti-Nazi groups in the United States and other countries joined the boycott. The American Jewish Congress issued its own boycott declaration in August 1933 and founded the Joint Boycott Council with the Jewish Labor Committee in 1935. Despite widespread support among Jewish communities, the boycott was opposed by many important Jewish organizations, including the American Jewish Committee, B'nai B'rith, the Board of Deputies of British Jews, and the Alliance Israélite Universelle. Because of this disunity, the boycott met with only limited success. Within the Yishuv, support for the boycott was mixed as a result of the Transfer (Ha'avara) agreement. > see also: **Ha'avara**.

Boycott, Arab: Term for the Arab use of economic warfare to thwart the *Yishuv/* Israel. The first boycott against business dealings with Jews was declared in April 1936 by the Arab Higher Committee. This boycott, which encompassed only the Palestinian Arabs, was a resounding failure, a fact that derived from the marginal role Arabs played in mandatory Palestine's economic growth. On December 2, 1945, the Arab League unanimously voted to initiate a boycott on all goods produced by the Yishuv. This boycott was supplemented in 1946 when the Arab League created a permanent boycott committee and extended the boycott to all dealings with companies that did business with the *Yishuv* (the so-called secondary boycott). The boycott continued and took on a so-called tertiary boycott (against companies that did business

with companies blacklisted in the secondary boycott) after the State of Israel was established. > see also: **Arabs, Arab Organizations**.

Brandeisists [Slang]: Common name for the American Zionist faction that sided with Justice Louis D. Brandeis in his dispute with Chaim Weizmann. Although many issues — including clashing personalities — were in dispute, three issues animated the main conflict: (1) The issue of continued political work, rejected by the Brandeisists because they sought to present the British with the fait accompli of massive Jewish development on the ground before making any overt political moves; (2) the issue of permitting private development and concentrating on middle-class immigration, which the Brandeisists supported, against exclusively public development and *Halutzic Aliya*; and (3) The issue of "American" versus "Palestinian" methods of planning and fund-raising. Of the three issues, the second was undoubtably the main one dividing the two camps. In 1926, the Va'ad ha-Poel ha-Zioni overwhelmingly voted against the Brandeisists' proposals, and they temporarily withdrew from the WZO. > see also: **Zeeland Program**; **Halutzic Aliya**.

Briha [בריחה, H] "Flight": The postwar movement of Holocaust survivors from Poland to Displaced Persons' camps in Germany, Austria, and Italy. The avowed aim of *Briha* was for Jews to reach the coasts where they would embark on vessels of the Mossad le-Aliya Bet for the journey to *Eretz Israel*. Spontaneous *Briha* began in 1944 and increased as each new Jewish community, or rather the survivors thereof, was liberated. The term applies both to the movement and to the organization that oversaw the operation. In late 1945 the Mossad le-Aliya Bet and the Hagana began oversight of the *Briha* program. > see also: **Aliya Bet**.

Brihnikim [בריחניקים, H/Slang]: Untranslatable term used by the Hagana for individuals involved in *Briha*. > see also: **Briha**.

Briskai [בריסקאי, H] "The Man from Brest-Litovsk": Hagana code term in use after 1942, to designate Menahem Begin, commander of the Irgun Zvai Leumi. The term alluded to to Begin's birthplace, Brest-Litovsk, better known to Jews by the Yiddish name Brisk.

Brodetskis [Slang/PN]: Hagana code term used in the late 1930s and the 1940s for British currency (pounds sterling). The term derived from Dr. Selig Brodetsky, a member of the London JAE and a distinguished Anglo-Jewish leader.

Bulgarians [Slang/GN]: Code name for Palmah units used in internal Hagana documents in 1948. It is not clear why the term was used; a number of other terms had been previously used to designate Palmah units between 1945 and 1947. All of the terms, however, seem to have been chosen completely at random. > see also: **Yishuv, Yishuv Organizations (Underground Organizations, Plugot Mahatz)**.

Bulim [בולים, H] "Postage Stamps": Af-Al-Pi code term used in the late 1930s for (1) The small ships used by the organization to transport *ma'apilim* to *Eretz Israel* and (2) the *ma'apilim* carried aboard such ships. Both meaning were used simultaeously but appear limited to Af-Al-Pi's Romanian bureau. > see also: **Aliya Bet; Yishuv, Yishuv Organizations (Underground Organizations, Af-Al-Pi)**.

Bundism [HT]: Ideology associated with the Jewish Socialist party the Bund (the Jewish Socialist Bund of Russia, Lithuania, and Poland). Founded in 1897, the Bund did not initially enunciate any form of nationalist ideology, seeing its role as inculcating Jews with a Marxist revolutionary ardor and leading them to join the Russian Social Democratic Party. The Bund's message was Jewish in form but socialist in content and emphasized the need for Jews to assimilate into the postrevolutionary classless (and presumably secular) society. The assimilationist element of the Bund's message was

muted almost from the beginning. By the turn of the twentieth century, Bund leaders were forcefully arguing on behalf of Jewish cultural autonomy while remaining strongly opposed to any form of Jewish nationalism, especially Zionism, which was seen as a reactionary force on the Jewish street. Bundist anti-Zionism became more strident during the 1920s and 1930s. Simultaneously, leading Bundists increasingly adopted the diaspora nationalist ideas of the autonomist camp. > see also: **Organizations, Non- or Anti-Zionist (Eastern Europe, Yiddisher Arbeiter Farband fun Russland, Lite, un Poilin); Autonomism; Socialism and Zionism; Communism and Zionism; Daism**.

Burgundy: Hagana/Palmah code name for Dan Laner, a member of the Palmah German Company and one of the thirty-two Palestinian paratroopers dropped in Eastern Europe to try to fulfill British intelligence missions and rescue Jews during the Holocaust. Laner was captured by the Nazis but managed to escape and established a small partisan army in the Austrian Alps. Laner rose to the rank of battalion commander in the Palmah during Israel's War of Independence and eventually retired from Zahal with the rank of general. > see also: **Parachutists, Palestinian**.

Business Zionism: Derisive term used by Haim Arlosoroff in 1923 to designate what he anticipated would be the ultimate result of *Yishuv* development based only on private capital: creation of a few small settlements along with the purchase of large parcels of land for speculation and investment, resulting in an overall failure to accomplish Zionist goals. Despite his opposition to unfettered private investment, Arlosoroff did not oppose the infusion of private capital into the *Yishhuv*. Instead, he wanted such capital to be used for public purposes, especially connected with his ideas about "contructive socialist Zionism," in order to fulfill Zionism's short- and long-term goals.

C

Cantonist(s) [HT/Slang]: Term for Jewish children kidnapped into the czarist Russian army prior to the mid-nineteenth century, that was embedded into Jewish memory as a horrifying experience — boys thus drafted remained in the army for up to twenty-five years and were always under intense pressure to convert. In 1944 and 1945 the term was applied to another tragic group: Irgun members kidnapped by the Hagana and Palmah during the so-called hunting season. Although originating with the Irgun, the term seems to have gained wide usage throughout the *Yishuv*. > see also: **Ha-Saizon**.

Cantonization [HT]: Plan for the partition of Palestine short of granting full independence and proposed by the Morrison-Grady Commission in July 1946. The plan revived a 1936 proposal that had been rejected by the Peel Commission to create a federal Palestine. Central government under the cantonization plan would be provided by the British, under a U.N. trusteeship that would replace the League of Nations mandate. Jews and Arabs would be granted a wide degree of self-government within their cantons, and two other cantons would continue under direct British rule, at least temporarily. Each cantonal government would be free to set immigration and land sales policy, thereby terminating restrictions on the *Yishuv* imposed by the British White Paper of 1939. However, the Jewish canton was slated to include only a small part of Palestine/ *Eretz Israel* — an area slightly smaller than proposed by the Peel partition plan of 1937. Since the territory offered was inadequate to deal with the massive number of European Jewish refugees needing a home, the WZO utterly rejected the Morrison-Grady scheme. The Arabs also rejected the scheme, refusing to consider a Jewish state of any size. The Truman administration also rejected this proposal since it was inconsistent with the commitment to accept to the Anglo-American Committee's report that the Atlee government had made in early 1946. As a result, the proposal was quietly dropped. > see also: **Committees of Investigation; Partition Plans**.

Capitulations [HT]: Term for the extra-territorial rights under international law granted by certain countries, generally weaker states desperate to preserve even nominal sovereignty, to major European powers during the nineteenth century. The Ottoman Empire signed capitulation agreements with most of the European powers (including Great Britain, France, Germany, and Austria-Hungary) that gave considerable latitude to citizens of those countries who lived or conducted business in Ottoman territory. For example, most capitulation agreements incorporated the right of a foreign citizen accused of a crime in the Ottoman Empire to be tried under the laws of his or her homeland and by a jury of citizens of that country. Some of the capitulation agreements also included the right of the European power to offer protection to national or ethnic minorities in the empire. Notable among these was French protection for Maronite Christians and British protection of Jews in *Eretz Israel* and Syria (e.g., during the so-called Damascus Blood Libel). Jewish citizens of countries having capitulation agreements with the Ottomans therefore enjoyed numerous rights and had an easier time purchasing land and settling in *Eretz Israel*. This did not help the bulk of *olim* during the nineteenth century, however, since most came from Russia, a country that did not have a capitulation agreement with the Turks. Moreover, the Turks, who feared the infiltration of masses of foreigners who would dilute Ottoman control of imperial territory, sought to limit the impact of the capitulations on *aliya*. The Ottoman Porte finally canceled all capitulation agreements when World War I broke out. > see also: **Damascus Blood Libel; Hitotmanut.**

Certificates [HT]:

1. Scope and Definition

Common name for the legal travel documents issued by the Palestine Administration's Department of Immigration and made available to the Jewish Agency for distribution (by local British passport control officers) to new *olim* or tourists. In addition to obtaining certificates from the JA, Jews could apply directly to British consulates. The document represented the bearers' right to enter Palestine/*Eretz Israel* legally and remain there. The different categories of certificates were established as a result of the Colonial Office's adoption of the principle of "economic absorptive capacity" as the criteria for establishing the twice-yearly immigration quota (better known as the Schedule). Exact criteria for each category of immigrant were established under the Palestine Immigration Ordinance of 1922 and were ammended twice: in 1925 and 1933. > see also: **Schedule; Aliya Bet; Arabs; Sochnut Yehudit; Passport Control Officer(s).**

TABLE C.1: Palestine Immigration Certificates, 1933–1939

A Capitalists
- A-I   Persons with at least £P1,000 in capital
- A-II   Persons with at least £P500 in capital
- A-III Persons with at least £P250 in capital
- A-IV   Persons with an income of £P4 or more per month
- A-V   Persons with £P500 and demonstrated ability to support self

B Immigrants whose self-sufficiency is secured
- B-I   Orphans in publicly supported institutions
- B-II   Religious functionaries
- B-III Students

C Workers

D Persons whose immigration is requested by resident(s)
- D-I   Relatives of immigrant/resident
- D-II   Workers with special skills

Source: *Government of Palestine, Ordinances, 1933* (London: HMSO, 1934), pp. 102–105.

Charter [HT]: Term used by early Zionists, especially Theodor Herzl, to signify the legal means by which they hoped to obtain the Holy Land. The Basel program, for instance, spoke of Jews obtaining a charter "secure under public law." Zionists sought this charter as a means to obtain international guarantees recognizing the inalienable Jewish right to all *Eretz Israel*.> see also: **Balfour Declaration; League of Nations.**

Bond Issued To a Labor Schedule Immigrant.
Courtesy of the Histadrut Archives/Machon Lavon, Tel Aviv

Cold Pogrom [HT]: Term for anti-Jewish actions short of direct violence. During the nineteenth century the term was used principally in reference to the so-called May Laws, that the czarist government issued to punish the Russian Jewish community after the pogroms of 1881–1882. The term was later used to designate Nazi and Nazi-inspired persecutions of Jews in the 1930s, but before the mass outbreak of violence on *Kristallnacht*. > see also: **May Laws**; **Sufot ba-Negev**; **Holocaust**.

Colonization Regime [HT]: Revisionist Zionist term for the type of British mandatory administration they prefered, specifically, one truly willing to assist in creating a Jewish state and thereby fulfilling the terms of the Balfour Declaration and the League of Nations mandate. The colonization regime would encourage *aliya* by six

means: (1) transferring all unowned or uncultivated land (whether owned or not) to a state land reserve; (2) approving a government loan to reclaim unusable lands, which would then become part of the land reserve, and to improve water resources; (3) enacting protective legislation on behalf of local industry; (4) encouraging *aliya*; (5) maintaining peace and security in Palestine/*Eretz Israel*; and (6) holding off political reforms in Palestine/*Eretz Israel* until the creation of a stable Jewish majority. The British rejected the idea of a colonization regime out of hand, although it remained central to Ze'ev Jabotinsky's Zionist ideology from the 1920s until his death. > see also: **Evacuation Plan**; **Tochnit Ha-asor**; **Palestine, Mandatory**; **Aliya**; **Land Owership**.

Columbus Platform [GN]: Statememt on Zionism and Judaism issued by the Union of American Hebrew Congregations at its Fiftieth

Annual Conference. The Columbus Platform replaced the Pittsburgh Platform (1885), especially in significantly modifying the latter's strongly anti-Zionist stance. The Columbus Platform therefore affirmed the obligation of all Jews to help in the building of the Jewish national home. > see also: **Judaism and Zionism.**

Committee of Eighteen [HT]: *Yishuv* defense committee established in May 1941 to consider various strategies for fighting the White Paper of 1939 during wartime. The committee had a secondary but obviously important subsidiary goal of defending Zionist interests on the global level. The committee was composed of eighteen members (hence its name), half of whom were appointed by the JAE and the other half by the Va'ad Leumi. Among the latter were four nonsocialists who represented the political parties then present in Assefat ha-Nivharim, including the revisionists. Moshe Shertok was elected chairman of the committee by unanimous decision at the first meeting. Shertok held this position for the duration of the committee's existence. In 1946, the Committee of Eighteen was eclipsed by the so-called X Committee. > see also: **Yishuv, Yishuv Organizations; White Paper(s), White Paper of 1939; X Committee.**

Committees of Investigation:

1. Scope and Definition
   Virtually from the day that the British government accepted the League of Nations mandate, the Palestine Administration and the Colonial Office faced intense pressure to fulfill apparently contradictory promises made to Jews and Arabs during World War I. In an attempt to find an equitable solution to both sides — and invariably as a response to outbursts of Arab violence — committees were established to investigate conditions in Palestine and report on possible solutions. Eleven such commissions were created between 1919 and 1947: six derived their authority from the British

government, one did so on the authority of the U.S. government, two were joint British-American, and one each derived authority from the League of Nations and the United Nations.

   Each of these committees investigated the "root causes" for intercommunal violence and for the burgeoning conflict between Arabs and Jews. All proposed solutions based on one of three possible broad approaches: (1) unequivocal support for the Arab case advocating a complete suspension of Jewish immigration and land purchase; (2) division of the country in a manner that did not grant independence (i.e., cantonization) with limits placed on Jewish and Arab rights; or (3) partition of the country into two independent states, with or without their federation into a larger entity. The first option was unequivocally accepted by the Arabs, but was only rarely accepted by the British cabinet since it directly contradicted the mandate's guarantees about *aliya*. The remaining two options thus became a major focus for committees and their diplomatic efforts. Due to the vast divergence of Arab and Jewish positions, no committee's proposal was ever accepted by all parties. > see also: **Mandatory Palestine; League of Nations; United Nations; Arabs; Cantonization; Partition Plans.**

2. Investigating Committees
   King-Crane (1919), established under joint Anglo-American authority to report back to the Paris Peace Conference on political conditions in the Middle East. Composed of two Americans — H. C. King and C. R. Crane. Although not focused solely on Palestine/*Eretz Israel*, they recommended that Syria be kept whole and be granted independence under the authority of Emir Faisal. They thus negated the possible creation of a Jewish national home. The proposal was never officially submitted to the Peace Conference and was not published until 1947. > see also: **McMahon-Hussein Correspondence; Faisal-Weizmann Agreement; Faisal-Frankfurter Correspondence.**

   Haycraft (1921), established by order of High Commissioner Sir Herbert Samuel after the Arab riots of May 1921 and composed of Sir Thomas Haycraft and two other British adminstrators. The committee placed exclusive blame for the riots on the Arab community but called for the Jews to surrender their goals of immigration as a means of allaying Arab fears. The committee also called for the convening of a round table discussion between Jews and Arabs, although no such meeting ever took place. In practice, the British government ignored the committee's recommendations, although limits (as opposed to a complete halt) were placed on *aliya* by the Churchill White Paper, which enacted "economic absorptive capacity" as the maximum limit for Jewish immigration. > see also: **Economic Absorptive Capacity**; **White Papers, Churchill White Paper**.

Shaw (1929), established by Colonial Secretary Sydney Webb (Lord Passfield) in response to Arab riots in August 1929. Composed of Sir Walter Shaw and three other members of Parliament. Blamed the incidents of violence throughout Palestine/ *Eretz Israel* on Arab instigation, but nevertheless, indirectly proposed a complete halt to *aliya*, which was temporarily enacted into the Passfield White Paper.

Western Wall (1930), created by the League of Nations Permanent Mandates Commission as a follow up to the Shaw-Committee. Composed of three members — the representatives of Holland, Sweden, and Switzerland — and tasked with studying the Western Wall incident of 1929. The committee placed complete blame for the incident on the Arabs, who refused Jews access to the holy site, but also called for restrictions on Jewish access to the same. > see also: **Kotel ha-Ma'aravi**.

Hope-Simpson (1930), fact-finding mission comprising Sir John Hope-Simpson, who was tasked by the Colonial Office to report on means to carry out the Shaw Committee's findings. Hope-Simpson did not collect any new material but did directly call for the end to *aliya* that was implied in the Shaw Committee report. His ideas were directly formulated into the Passfield White Paper, which halted *aliya* in 1930 and 1931. > see also: **White Papers, Passfield White Paper**; **Aliya**; **MacDonald Letter**.

French (1931), as a further follow-up to the

Shaw Committee, the Colonial Office set Louis French, a well-known English agronomist, to Palestine to study patterns of Arab displacement by Jewish settlement. After intensive investigation, French concluded that only 1,000 Arabs had actually been displaced by Jewish agricultural settlements, as had a small but undisclosed number of Jews. French proposed that the government grant each displaced Arab a small parcel of land from the government reserve, even though he noted that most such land was unsuitable for agriculture. Approximately 350 Arabs were relocated as a result of French's proposal but relocations ceased after 1931.

Palestine Royal Commission (1937), more commonly known as the *Peel Commission* (after the name of its chairman), established as a response to the outbreak of the Arab revolt, the commission was given wide ranging investigative powers to uncover the "root causes" for the revolt and to propose any definitive solution to the problem. Recognizing that the intent of the Balfour Declaration had always been the creation of a Jewish state and noting that fulfillment of Britain's promises to the Jews was incompatible with that declaration's promise to protect the "civil and religious rights of existing non-Jewish communities," the Peel Commission proposed that Palestine/*Eretz Israel* be partitioned into Jewish and Arab states. > see also: **Balfour Declaration**; **Partition Plans, Peel Plan**.

Palestine Partition Commission (1938), more commonly known as the *Woodhead Commission* (after the name of its chairman), created as a result of Jewish and Arab complaints about the unfairness of the Peel partition plan's borders, the Woodhead Commission actually represented a British attempt to withdraw from its promises to create a Jewish state in *Eretz Israel*. After investigating all possible border configurations, the committee reported that there was no feasible way to partition Palestine fairly and recommended that new diplomatic efforts be undertaken to end the Arab revolt and achieve peace between the Jews and the Arabs. > see also: **Repeal Commission**; **Partiton Plans**; **Conferences, International, St James' Palace (1939)**.

Anglo-American Committee of Inquiry Regarding the Problems of European Jewry and Palestine (1946), established under the joint authority of British prime minister Clement Atlee and U.S. president Harry S. Truman, the committee was organized to investigate means of finding a permanent haven for European Jewish refugees and represented an effort to respond to the Holocaust and to Jewish unrest in *Eretz Israel*. The committee was composed of six English and six American representatives. Before hearing testimony in *Eretz Israel*, the Committee members visited many Jewish refugees in Eastern and Central Europe. Contrary to British expectations that the committee would deadlock, it unanimously proposed the immediate admission of 100,000 Jewish refugees to Palestine and termination of aliya restrictions of the 1939 White Paper. After publication of the committee's report, Foreign Minister Ernest Bevin reneged on Atlee's promise that the Labour government would abide by any unanimous decision. He sought to link any new aliya with the surrender of Jewish underground movements and a complete disarming of the *Yishuv*. This proved unacceptable to the *Yishuv* and the Truman administration. > see also: **Displaced Persons, Jewish; Harrison Report; Yom Kippur Letter; Yishuv, Yishuv Organizations (Underground Organizations).**

JAE Chairman David Ben-Gurion Testifying
Before the Anglo-American Committee, Jerusalem, 1946.
Courtesy of the Central Zionist Archives, Jerusalem

TABLE C.2: Composition of the Anglo-American Committee of Inquiry

Frank Aydelotte	American	Frederic Legget	British
Frank W. Buxton	American	R.E. Manningham-Butler	British
Wilfred P. Crick	British	James G. McDonald	American
R.H.S. Crossman	British	Herbert Morrison	British
Bartley C. Crum	American	William Phillips	American
Joseph Hutcheson	American	John Singelton	British

Source: Central Zionist Archives.

Members of the Anglo-American Committee Arriving in Jerusalem.
Courtesy of the Central Zionist Archives, Jersalem

Morrison-Grady (1946), two-member committee created by the British government in collaboration with the U.S. State Department. The two members were Sir Herbert Morrison and Henry F. Grady (a senior State Department official). The commission was ostensibly created to realize the terms of the Anglo-American Committee's proposals, but Morrison and Grady were actually tasked with overturning the proposal altogether. After brief investigations the committee reported that Palestine/*Eretz Israel* should be cantonized, with one canton being Jewish, another being Arab, and two others being held by the British. Free *aliya* would be permitted only in the Jewish canton (which represented 17 percent of *Eretz Israel's* land mass) and then only if economic absorptive capacity, as defined by the overall British administrator of the territory, permitted new immigration. Accepted eagerly by the British, the plan was rejected out of hand by President Truman and by the Zionist leadership. > see also: **Economic Absorptive Capacity; Yom Kippur Letter.**

United Nations Special Committee on Palestine (UNSCOP), eleven-member committee created by the U.N. General Assembly on April 12, 1947, to report on the Palestine/*Eretz Israel* problem and to suggest possible solutions to the Arab-Jewish impasse. UNSCOP held hearings in Jerusalem between June 16 and July 24, 1947, and afterward continued to gather evidence in Cairo, Germany, and England. Unable to come to a unanimous conclusion, UNSCOP submitted two reports to the General Assembly. The minority report, proposed by the Yugoslav representative but rejected by the General Assembly, called for the creation of a single state equally divided between Jewish and Arab cantons and overseen for the time being by a trusteeship to be answerable to the U.N. The majority report called for partition with Palestine/*Eretz Israel* divided into independent Arab and Jewish states and the area around Jerusalem internationalized and placed under U.N. administration. The majority report was approved by a two-thirds majority of the General Assembly on November 29, 1947. Although reluctant to accept the borders proposed by UNSCOP, the JAE accepted partition and agreed, officially at least, to Jerusalem's internationalization. The Arabs, however, rejected partition out of hand and began a military campaign to destroy the Jewish state before it was born. > see also: **United Nations.**

Commonwealth, Jewish: Term for statehood used by American Zionists as a means of avoiding a direct statement that Jews demanded complete sovereignty for the *Yishuv.* Though the distinction was more imaginary than real, the purpose of using the term was to avoid any statement that might prejudice American Jewish non-Zionists, whose support was considered vital. As used at the time, the term was considered "softer" than the term "state," since a commonwealth implied that some British participation in *Eretz Israel's* future was possible. > see also: **Shem ha-Meforash; Biltmore Resolution.**

Communism and Zionism: Deriving its attitude toward nationalism from a Marxist viewpoint, by which national identity was assumed to be "merely" a capitalist construct used to divide the working class and weaken their natural solidarity, Communism inalterably rejected all forms of Jewish nationalism. The Communist position derived mainly from Karl Kautsky, an Austrian Marxist theoretician, who argued before World War I that Jewish identity was only a response to antisemitism. Left to themselves, Jews would naturally assimilate into the larger national or economic group in which they lived. In following this line of analysis, Communists distinguished between "natural" and "artificial" nationalities; Jews were assumed to be in the latter category. Following this line of analysis, Communist leaders including both Vladimir I. Lenin and Josef Stalin rejected any possiblity of Jewish national existence and decried Jewish nationalism — even that of the Socialist-Nationalist Bund — as inherently and inalterably reactionary.

Communist theory was put into practice in

the Soviet Union after the 1917 Bolshevik putsch. Zionists were persecuted in all areas of the former Russian empire that fell into Soviet hands after the civil war. Zionism as such was pronounced to be a form of imperialism and Zionists were condemned as both class enemies and agents of the British empire who sought to overthrow the workers' paradise. Communist movements outside of the Soviet Union, mainly in Western Europe and the Americas, followed this party line slavishly, engaging in frequent ideological battles to win the hearts and minds of Jews and convert them (especially Jewish youth) to communism. Additionally, the Communist orientation entailed a complete rejection of Jewish diaspora nationalism and Territorialism. Jews were fated under communism to one destiny: assimilation and submersion into the "natural" nationalities among whom they lived.

Communist theory and practice notwithstanding, both Lenin and Stalin dabbled in a number of quasi-nationalist schemes as a means of obtaining Jewish support for communism and financial support from American Jewry for the Soviet Union. Lenin, for instance, created so-called Yevsktsias (Jewish national soviets) to inculcate Russian Jews in communism. The Yevsektsias, however, were Jewish in form and Communist in content; in any case their activities were severely circumscribed and they were eliminated when Stalin believed they no longer served their purpose. Stalin similarly used Jewish identity to increase the bolshevization of Russian Jewry and obtain support from the West. In 1928 Stalin created a Jewish autonomous region in Birobidzhan as an alternate to the Jewish national home in *Eretz Israel*. Stalin also entered into negotiations with the American Jewish Joint Distribution Committee (JDC), mainly the JDC's subsidiary Agro-Joint, over the creation of Jewish agricultral colonies in Crimea. These actually atracted wide, though temporary, attention in the Jewish world: a number of socialist Zionists (mainly members of Poale Zion Smol) actually left the *Yishuv* to settle in Crimea to create a

Jewish and socialist framework. Finally, during World War II, Stalin permitted the creation of a Jewish Anti-Fascist Committee (JAFC), which existed to give Soviet Jewry a cohesive voice in promoting anti-Nazi and pro-Soviet propaganda within American Jewry. The JAFC also acted as a communal body during and immediately following the war.

To one degree or another, however, all these efforts proved abortive or temporary. Birobidzhan remained only nominally Jewish and could hardly be expected to have the same emotional pull as the historic Jewish homeland. The Crimean projects were decimated by the Nazis and were used by Stalin as proof of Jewish disloyalty after the war. The fact that the Crimean colonies were supposed to be semi-autonomous was magnified into a Jewish nationalist conspiracy to cut off Crimea from the Soviet Union as a base for imperialist and capitalist subversion. The same JDC that Stalin took money from in the 1920s was condemned as a tool of the Central Intelligence Agency at the height of the Cold War. The JAFC, similarly, was used to prove the existence of reactionary Jewish circles that led directly to a purge of Jewish culture in 1947 and 1948. Stalin planned further purges (under the pretext of the so-called Doctors' Plot) but died before they could begin.

For their part, Zionists (with only a few exceptions) saw communism as a hostile and malevolent opponent. All major Zionist leaders condemned communism as a threat that would sap Jewish youth of their nationalist identity and diverted them from true national goals. Fear of Communist infiltration did not, however, prevent some radical socialist Zionist groups from flirting with communism and the Soviet Union. These groups included, in addition to the already mentioned Poale Zion Smol, ha-Shomer ha-Zair and its associated groups. Additionally, a Palestine Communist Party (PCP) was created (evolving into the Israeli Communist Party after 1948) in the *Yishuv*. Albeit, the PCP can only marginally be considered a Jewish party, since by Soviet dictates at least half the members had to be Arabs. The PCP was always marginal in the *Yishuv*; Communist sympathizers were more numerous but never had a decisive impact on *Yishuv* development and never altered the overall anti-Communist orientation of most Zionist organizations.

Communist enmity to Zionism continued after the State of Israel was established in 1948. Ironically, this was true despite the decisive role played by the Soviet Union in Israel's establishment. Stalin's actions in 1948 must, of course, be kept in context: The Soviet leader supported Israel's creation not so much as a manifestation of support for Zionism but as a means to weaken British power in the Middle East. Anti-Zionist agitation after 1948 — including the use of Zionism as a means to accuse Jewish Communists (in the Soviet Union and in Communist bloc countries) of disloyalty and treason — proves how shallow Stalin's support for Israel actually was on an ideological level. Thereafter, the Soviet Union became the main supporter of Israel's enemies, in both physical and

ideological terms. Indeed, Communist anti-Zionism became so visceral after 1948 that it approached the border between mere
rejection of Jewish nationalism and anti-semitism and, in fact, crossed that border after 1967. > see also: **Nationalism; Autonomism; Daispora Nationalism; Yevsektsia(s); Organizations, Non- or Anti-Zionist (United States, Joint Distribution Committee); Territorialism, Territorialist Schemes; Yishuv, Yishuv Organizations (Political Parties and Organizations); Socialism and Zionism**.

Conferences, International:
Cairo, Held March 12–13, 1921 at the instigation of Colonial Secretary Winston Churchill. The coneference agenda included a thorough study of England's strategic, political, and economic interests in the Middle East. Main accomplishments included the reorganization of Iraq, granted to the Emir Faisal, and Trans-Jordan, which was separated administratively from Palestine and was placed under the

Statesmen Meeting in Jerusalem After the Cairo Conference: From Left to Right
Emir Abdullah, Herbert Samuel and Winston Churchill.
Courtesy of the Central Zionist Archives, Jerusalem

control of Emir Abdullah. In addition, Churchill rescinded the ban on *aliya* imposed in 1920 and enacted the system of "economic absorptive capacity" that became the basis for all *aliya* regulations until the late 1930s. > see also: **White Papers, Churchill White Paper**; **Aliya**; **Economic Absorptive Capacity**.

Evian, held in Evian-les-Bains, France, July 6–15, 1938, with delegates from thirty-two countries who had been invited by President Franklin D. Roosevelt. The conference was convened to facilitate the emigration of Jewish refugees from the Reich and to create an organization to solve the refugee problem. As the conference proceeded, state after state denied its ability to accept further refugees. Only the Dominican Republic volunteered to contribute unspecified areas for agricultural colonization in return for hefty financial contributions from world Jewry. The conference thus had only one concrete result: the creation of the Intergovernmental Committee on Refugees.

עוויאן ... עוויאן ...

... פליטים צוגעהכמן — מהיכי־היתי! אבער יענער ...

A Cartoon From the Zionist Newspaper *Haynt* Parodies the Evian Conference: Each of the delegates Is Pointing a Finger At the Other To Highlight Responsibility for Helping Refugees.

Courtesy of the YIVO Institute for
Jewish Research, New York

Lausanne, held in Lausanne, Switzerland, April 27–May 12, 1949, under U.N. auspices and composed of a series of bilateral talks between Israeli and Egyptian, Jordanian, and Syrian delgations. The Arab Higher Committee also sent representatives but did not participate directly in the talks. The conference was supposed to deal with two primary issues: return of refugees (mainly Arab refugees) to lands they lived on prior to Israel's War of Independence and conclusion of permanent peace accords between Israel and its Arab neighbors to replace the interim armistice agreements. The conference was a disaster from the beginning, with the parties unable even to agree on an order for the agenda of topics. Divergent Arab demands for Israeli territiorial "adjustments," seen as the only means to solve the Arab refugee problem, led to a multiplicity of proposals that soon went out of control. As a result, no two sets of conference protocols contain the same recommendations, leading to repeated arguments over the correct set of protocols. Finally, three fundamentally different sets of draft agreements were signed on May 12, 1949; it soon became apparent that they differed completely on all major points. Instead of promoting Arab-Israeli peace, the Lausanne talks actually spurred continued conflict, since both sides felt that they had been swindled. > see also: **Armistice Agreements**.

Paris, International peace conference held in Versailles (a Paris suburb) in 1919 and 1920. In addition to attempting to make peace between the powers that fought World War I, the conference focused considerable attention on the conditions in former Ottoman territory, with an eye to preparing both Arabs and Jews for eventual statehood in territories promised to them by the British and French. Zionist proposals to the peace conference were of special significance, since much resistance had been encountered from within the British government to fulfilling the terms of the Balfour Declaration. In the end the Paris Peace Conference was unable to conclude the complicated work of redrawing the Middle East; that task was left to the follow-up conference held in Sam Remo in 1920.

Potsdam, held in East Berlin on July 17–August 2, 1945, with Winston Churchill, Joseph Stalin, and Harry S. Truman. Mainly concerned with postwar inter-Allied relations. During the conference Truman approached Churchill about the possibility of England canceling the White Paper of 1939 and permitting Jewish refugees to enter Palestine freely. British elections held during the conference resulted in Churchill's replacement by Clement Attlee and the cancellation of all discussions of Palestine's future.

St. James Palace (1939), held in London February 7–20, 1939 with British, Jewish, and Arab representatives. The purpose of the conference was to find a peaceful solution to the Palestine problem. Arab refusal to meet with Jewish delegates and British insistence on exclusively defending Arab interests brought about a Jewish withdrawal from the talks and ultimately led to the British White Paper of 1939.

San Francsisco, held April 25–June 26, 1945, and resulting in the founding of the United Nations. Although not officially on the conference agenda, the Palestine/*Eretz Israel* issue intruded into the earliest U.N. conferences. The newly created Arab League sought, unsuccessfully, to have the U.N. remove recognition (dating back to the League of Nations) of the Jewish Agency as a non-governmental institution, thereby disbarring the Zionists from the General Assembly. Simultaneously, the Jewish Agency and American Jewish organizations tried to use the U.N. as a means to force the British to open the gates of *Eretz Israel*. These efforts were rebuffed and the U.N. did not deal officially with Palestine/*Eretz Israel* until the issue was refered to the General Assembly by the British in February 1947. > see also: **United Nations**.

San Remo, meeting of the victorious Allied powers held in Italy on April 19–26, 1920, to settle diplomatic problems arising from the Versailles Treaty. Among other topics discussed at the conference was the problem of conflicting wartime British promises of postwar territorial divisions in the Middle East. After a brief debate, the conference reconfirmed the Balfour Declaration's promises to Jewry and led to British assumption of the League of Nations mandate for Palestine/*Eretz Israel*. > see also: **Balfour Declaration; McMahon-Hussein Correspondence; Sykes-Picot Agreement; League of Nations; Mandates**.

Conferences, Zionist:

1. Scope and Definition
Zionism was born in a grand congress (the First Zonist Congress) convened in Basel in 1897. Thereafter, meetings, conferences, and congresses came to characterize much of Zionist political activity, especially internally. This held as true on an international level as on the local level: Zionist politics often took on the character of a debating society. This was especially true in periods when little or no progress was made on the diplomatic front or in periods of intense crisis for the Zionist movement. The following list makes no claims of completeness. It is merely a compilation of available data about a selection of the more important regional and international Zionist conferences between 1880 and 1948 (exact dates of conference meeting being included when known). > see also: **Jahreskonferenz; World Zionist Congress(es)**.

2. Major Zionist Conferences
Anglo-Jewish Conference, general title for a series of joint conferences held between senior British government officials and members of the WZO executive between November 1930 and February 1931. These meetings were organized to end the impasse in Anglo-Zionist relations created by the Passfield White Paper. The negotiations resulted in the MacDonald letter of February 14, 1931, that overturned the white paper's terms. > see also: **White Papers, Passfield White Paper; MacDonald Letter**.

Berlin (1913), extraordinary conference held jointly by the Zionistische Vereinigung für Deutschland (ZVFD) and the Centralverein deutschen Staatsbürger jüdischen Glaubens (CV) on May 1, 1913. The conference was an attempt to head off a potential conflict between

Dr. Chaim Weizmann addressing the Biltmore Conference, May 11, 1942.
Courtesy of the Central Zionist Archives, Jerusalem

the ZVFD and the CV: the CV annual conference (held shortly before the conference) had passed — by a large majority — an anti-Zionist resolution. As a result of failed negotiations, the ZVFD adopted an oppositional approach to the CV and sought directly to conquer the German Jewish community. > see also: **Conquest of Communities; Organizations**.

Berlin (1916), three-day conference sponsored by the Zionistische Vereinigung für Deutschland (ZVFD) and held between on 24–26, 1916. The main point on the conference agenda was Zionist cultural work during World War I, with the specific issue being how best to further Zionist goals in formerly Russian territory then occupied by the Germans. > see also: **Hindenburg Erklärung**.

Berlin (1936), last national conference called by the Zionistische Vereinigung für Deutschland (ZVFD) and held on February 2–4, 1936. The main topics on the agenda were relations with the Nazi regime and

emigration, with emphasis on the latter. This was the last conference held by the ZVFD before the organization was closed by the Gestapo in 1938.

Biltmore, International Zionist emergency conference, held in New York City on May 10–11, 1942. The conference included 653 delegates (of whom 67 came from abroad) and represented almost all major Zionist organizations in the United States. Ominous news from Europe combined with the continuing struggle over the British White Paper of 1939 and almost total political failure in the U.S. led the conference to unanimously adopt a resolution calling for the creation of a Jewish commonwealth in *Eretz Israel* after World War II. > see also: **Biltmore Resolution**.

Bingen, founding conference of the Zionistische Vereinigung für Deutschland (ZVFD), held on July 11, 1897. Among the topics discussed at the conference was the upcoming First Zionist Congress and organizational issues related to the ZVFD. The conference was later considered the first of the so-called Delegiertentage (Delegate Days) held by the ZVFD.

Boulogne, emergency conference of Hitahdut ha-Zionim ha-Revisionistim (ha-Zohar) held on April 5–6, 1931 to deal with the implications of revisionist defeat during the Zionist Congress in 1929 (when ha-Zohar sought to scuttle the enlargement of the JA). The conference worked out a compromise stating that, should the upcoming Zionist congress fail to pass an Endziel resolution, ha-Zohar would withdraw from the WZO. A follow-up conference held in Calais in September 1931 (just after the Zionist Congress) overturned the Boulogne Compromise and nearly tore ha-Zohar apart. > see also: **World Zionist Congress(es)**; **Endziel**; **Organizations, Revisionist Zionist**; **Conferences, Zionist (Calais)**.

Brno, second annual conference of the Czech Zionist Federation, meeting on March 26–27, 1921. Main topic of discussion was future organizational trends in the federation, and particularly means to increase activities in Slovakia. Dr. Jacob Rufeisen was elected president of the federation, a position he held until his retirement in 1938.

Brussels, international Jewish conference sponsored by the WZO and comprising representatives of major Jewish philanthropies, meeting between January 29 and February 1, 1906. Dedicated to finding some means to relieve Russian Jewish suffering, the conferees concentrated mainly on emigration. Nonetheless, the WZO failed to obtain the hoped-for resolution supporting mass *aliya* and did not obtain guarantees of support from the major philanthropies.

Calais, emergency conference of Hitahdut ha-Zionim ha-Revisionistim (ha-Zohar) held on September 10–11, 1931. The conference had one item on its agenda: the question of revisionist secession from the WZO. By a narrow margin, the Calais conference voted to remain in the WZO for a brief time (ha-Zohar withdrew from the WZO in 1935). > see also: **Organizations, Revisionist Zionist**; **Revisionist Schism**.

Cleveland, American Zionist conference held on June 5–6, 1921, as a follow up to the London conference of 1920. The main topic of discussion was the relationship between the Zionist Organization of America and the WZO, a subject that had created considerable friction between the American Zionists (the so-called Brandeisists) and their opponents. The result was a defeat for Brandeis's camp and his temporary withdrawal from Zionist activities. > see also: **Zeeland Program**; **Between Washington and Pinsk**; **Brandeisists**.

Druskieniki, held as a follow-up to the Kattowitz conference and meeting on June 16–20, 1887. The main issue on the conference agenda was the slow pace of development in *Eretz Israel*, a troubling reality reinforced by the anouncement (just days before the conference convened) that the Russian government refused to incorporate Hibbat Zion's proposed Jewish Corporation to Settle *Eretz Israel*. A secondary issue at the conference was religious observance in the *Yishuv*. Neither issue was resolved, a symptom of the organization's increasing inability to accomplish its stated goals and the increasing frustration of Hibbat Zion's members. > see also: **Hibbat Zion**.

Frankfurt-am-Main, Zionistische Vereinigung für Deutschland (ZVFD) conference, held on September 11–12, 1932. In addition to discussion of Zionist themes, including the swirl of diplomatic events since 1929, the conferees explored the situation of German Jewry as conditions in the country worsened. The possibility that the Nazis might seize power and the implications of such a regime for German Jews were major topics of discussion.

Hamburg, fifth conference of the Russian Zionist movement, held on Decmber 23–24, 1909. The conference met in Germany because Russian authorities refused to grant permits for the meeting. The conference dealt with the implication of the reactionary policies that were adopted after the failure of the Revolution of 1905. In particular, the conferees dealt with the impact of new government policies, including open support for the pogromists of the so-called Black Hundreds, on the status of the Jewish community and the Zionist movement. Recognizing that any movement toward attainment of Zionist goals was unlikely for the foreseeable future, the conference reaffirmed the decisions taken at the Helsingfors Conference. > see also: **Gegenwartsarbeit**.

Helsingfors, third conference of Russian and Polish Zionists, held in Helsinki (then part of the Russian empire and known as Helsingfors) on December 4–10, 1906. The conference dealt with the question of how Zionists should respond to communal questions (such as education reform or demands for communal autonomy) and specifically dealt with the issue of Gegenwartsarbeit. The conference called on all Zionist organizations to work within the local *Kehilla* as a means to conquer the communities. > see also: **Gegenwartsarbeit; Conquest of Communities**.

Kattowitz, founding conference of the Hibbat Zion movement, held in Katowice, Poland (then part of the German empire and called Kattowitz) on November 6, 1884. Thirty-five representatives attended and unanimously decided to create an agency to encourage aliya. > see also: **Hibbat Zion; Bet Yaakov Lehu ve-Nelha**.

Kharkov, Conference of Russian members of the WZO Greater Actions Committee, held on November 11–14, 1903. The conference agenda included only one item: how best to ensure that the WZO rejected the Uganda scheme. > see also: **Uganda Scheme; Zionei Zion**.

London (1920), annual conference of the WZO held in the British capital on July 7–22, 1920. The main subject for consideration was the growing dispute between WZO leaders Chaim Weizmann and Louis D. Brandeis: primarily the latter's so-called Zeeland Program to severey curtail the WZO's activities in favor of a non-partisan Jewish committee to finance the building of the *Yishuv*. The conference resulted in an overwhelming victory for Weizmann and his supporters and the consequent withdrawal of the Brandeisists from the WZO. > see also: **Brandeisists; Zeeland Program; Between Washington and Pinsk**.

London (1945), extraordinary Zionist conference held in August 1945, just as World War II was ending. The conference met to set out Zionist goals in light of recent events in Europe and the Middle East, especially the Nazi murder of two-thirds of European Jewry and the need to find a safe haven for the survivors. The conference accepted as its minimal position the conclusions of the Harrison Report and demanded that 100,000 Jewish displaced persons be permitted to enter Palestine. Although temporarily taking off the table Jewish demands for sovereignty, the conference ended by demanding an end to the White Paper of 1939. > see also: **Biltmore Program; Displaced Persons Jewish; Harrison Report; White Papers, White Paper of 1939**.

Minsk, second national conference of the Russian Zionist movement, held in late September 1902. The conference dealt with the growing fragmentation in the Zionist movement. Although all speakers called for Zionist unity, the Minsk conference was a microcosm of the larger problem, with the Russian Zionist movement splintering into different parties shortly after the meetings ended.

Moravská Ostrava (Märisch Ostrow), twelfth and last annual conference of the Czech Zionist Federation, held on March 6–7, 1938. Main topics for discussion included the Jewish fate in Nazi- threatened Europe, *aliya*, and the progress of talks for a Czech-*Eretz Israel* transfer agreement. > see also: **Ha'avara**.

Petrograd, seventh (and final) conference of the Russian Zionist movement, held in the Russian capital on June 6–12, 1917 (under the calendar system then in use in Russia, May 24–30). The conference dealt with the new conditions for Zionism since the February Revolution and with relations between the Jewish community and the provisional government led by Alexander Kerensky. The conference issued a declaration calling on Zionists to redouble their efforts in Russia.

Pittsburgh, annual convention of the Zionist Organization of America (ZOA), held in 1918. The convention witnessed an attempt to systematically redefine American Zionism and to bring ZOA into consonance with both American and Zionist realities. The convention approved a six-point program that concentrated equally on building Jewish identity in the diaspora and on building the *Yishuv*.

Posen, German Zionist conference held in early June 1912. The conference reflected a significant disagreement between radicals and moderates within the Zionistische Vereinigung für Deutschland (ZVFD) over the relative importance of *aliya* as opposed to philanthropic work. The conference unanimously approved a resolution emphasizing the centrality of *aliya* to Zionism and calling on members to prepare for emigration. > see also: **Philanthropic Zionism; Aliya.**

Prague (1918), one-day Zionist conference meeting on October 22, 1918, that founded both the Czech Zionist Federation and the National Committee of Czech Jewry. Although overlapping, the two bodies acted as the representatives of a Czech Jewry that had to be created from the disparate parts of the newly independent Czechoslovakia.

Prague (1919), first annaul conference of the Czech Zionist Federation held on July 26–27, 1919. Main topics of discussion included future Zionist work in *Eretz Israel* and the diaspora. Ninety-seven delegates attended, mainly from Bohemia-Moravia.

Pressburg, Mizrachi conference held on August 16–19, 1904, and dedicated to considering the means to carry out Mizrachi's ideology. Additionally, the conferees considered Mizrachi's role within the WZO and called upon activists to work toward the goal of creating a Jewish national home consistent with Halacha (Jewish law).

Salonika, founding conference of the Greek Zionist Federation held in early May 1919. The conference brought together all existing local Zionist chapters from thoughout Greece and united them under on banner. Because of their more intense activities, the Salonika Zionists (who established eighteen local clubs between 1908 and 1924) dominated the conference and all future Zionist activities in Greece.

Stockholm, founding conference of the Swedish Zionist Union, held on January 5–6, 1913. Conferees emphasized the need to organize Zionist groups in order to ensure Jewish ethnic survival in Sweden.

Vienna (1920), fifth annual conference of the Poale Zion (PZ) movement, held during July 1920. Two topics of discussion were key to the agenda: relations between PZ and the WZO and the PZ attitude toward communism. This conference represented the final schism between PZ's left and right wings (the latter of which eventually matured into Mapai in *Eretz Israel* and the Ihud movement in the diaspora). > see also: **Communism and Zionism; Socialism and Zionism; Organizations, Zionist.**

Vienna (1935), first congress of the New Zionist Organization (NZO), held on September 7–11, 1935. In addition to creating the NZO, the congress also discussed a renewed proposal by Ze'ev Jabotinsky for mass Jewish evacuation from Eastern Europe. > see also: **Organizations, Revisionist Zionist (Histadrut ha-Zionit ha-Hadasha).**

Vilna (1889), Hibbat Zion conference meeting in August 1889 in response to Leon Pinsker's announcement that he intended to retire as soon as a replacement could be elected. The conference soon degenerated into a battle between religious and irreligious supporters of Hibbat Zion. Two specific issues were raised, first, should Pinsker appoint his own successor or should Pinsker's successor be elected by a plenary session of members of the movement? Second, to what degree should Hibbat Zion limit its support for colonies in *Eretz Israel* only to those who observed Jewish law? The Vilna conference represented the beginning of Hibbat Zion's institutional collapse, although the religious issues continued to plague all Zionist groups for much of their history. > see also: **Hibbat Zion; Judaism and Zionism, Orthodoxy and Zionism.**

Vilna (1902), founding conference of the Mizrachi Religious Zionist Organization, held on March 4–5, 1902. The conference called on Orthodox Jews worldwide to support a return to Jewry's land of destiny but specifically called for the creation of a religious bloc in the Zionist movement to counter the cultural Zionism of the so-called Democratic Fraction led by Chaim Weizmann.

Vilna (1905), conference organized by the *Zionei Zion* held in Russia January 1–4, 1905.

The conference dealt with the continuing implications for Zionism of the Uganda plan. At the end of the conference, Russian supporters of mass Jewish settlement outside of *Eretz Israel* withdrew from the Zionist organization and formed their own territorialist organization. > see also: **Territorialism; Zionei Zion; Uganda Plan**.

Warsaw (1898), first national conference of the Russian Zionist movement designed to consolidate the orgaization's communal position and to provide East European Zionists with a voice at the upcoming Second World Zionist Congress. The conference was the first at which a split between Practical Zionists, who emphasized settlement activity, and Political Zionists, who emphasized diplomacy, appeared.

Warsaw (1919), founding conference of the he-Halutz movement in Poland held on May 14–16, 1919. Officially billed as a preliminary conference (difficulties in obtaining necessary transportation left most of the thirty-two delegates, representing twenty localities and more than 1,100 members, unable to attend) the preconference de facto was the founding conference of Poland's he-Halutz movement. The main items on the agenda were organization of he-Halutz activity and the organization's relationship with the WZO.

Conquest of Communities:

1. Scope and Definition

Term for the short-term goal of diaspora Zionist organizations: to convert communal institutions to Zionism as completely as possible. Control of communities had two major benefits for the Zionists. First, it allowed all energy — espeecially all fund-raising energy — to be focused on the goal of collecting capital for *Eretz Israel*. Second, the conquest of communities played an important role in Zionist diplomacy. Since Zionist leaders claimed to be speaking on behalf of the entire Jewish people, unified support would strengthen their hand in any negotiations with the Ottomans, Germans, British, Americans, and others. The conquest of communities was usually (but not always) carried out by Zionists creating a conflict within communal bodies and then proceding (or threatening) to "go over the head" of the existing leadership by taking the issue at hand directly to the Jewish masses. Zionist weakness, especially in Western Europe, led some Zionist federations, notably the English Zionist Federation, to eschew conflict and seek conquest through consensus building. Zionists began their attempts to conquer communities already in 1897, but by 1939 only a minority of communities had actually been conquered. Other ideologies that competed with Zionism

TABLE C.3: Kehila Mandates for Major Polish Communities, 1936, By Party

Party	Mandates	Percent
Agudas Israel	218	32.0
Zionists/Ihud	107	15.6
Bund	81	11.8
Mizrachi	62	9.1
Poale Zion Right	50	7.3
Revisionists	30	4.3
Poale Zion Left	12	1.8
Folkspartei	9	1.3
Other/Unaffiliated	115	16.8

Source: Robert M. Shapiro, *The Polish Kehile Elections of 1936* (New York: Yeshiva University Press, 1988).

slowed down the process, as did the general inertia that permitted many communal leaders to simply ignore the "will of the masses." The fact that Zionists did not always represent the will of the masses also hindered Zionist goals. But the Holocaust galvanized all Jews and thereafter conquest of communities was no longer necessary as non-Zionists joined the Zionist bandwagon and most anti-Zionists were swept aside. > see also: **Infiltration**.

Conservative Judaism and Zionism > see also: **Judaism and Zionism**.

Constructive Socialism [E]: Socialist Zionist ideology associated with the leadership of Mapai during the 1930s. According to Mapai's main ideologues, Haim Arlosoroff, David Ben-Gurion and Berl Katznelson, constructive socialism represented the fusion of socialism and Zionism with the ultimate goal of creating, first, an *Am Oved* (laboring people) and thereafter an *Am Mamlahti* (sovereign nation). Constructive socialism meant the abandonment of class struggle as an element in Mapai's ideology as well as cooperation with non-Zionists in efforts to create and build the Jewish National Home. > see also: **Mamlahtiut**.

Copenhagen Manifesto [GN]: Popular name for the declaration issued by the WZO's executive bureau in Copenhagen on October 28, 1918. The manifesto called upon Zionists to aid the creation of a Jewish national home and, in light of the promises encapsulated in the Balfour Declaration, set out the basic Jewish/Zionist demands from the great powers in any upcoming peace conference: (1) Confirming the Jews' right to return to *Eretz Israel* and to organize a Jewish national home; (2) granting full civil equality to Jews in all countries; and (3) granting communal autonomy to Jewish communities that demanded such a right. The manifesto became the central document of Zionist policy in 1918–1919 and its terms were eventually encapsulated in the League of Nations mandate for Palestine/*Eretz*

Israel and the so-called National Minorities Treaties signed by the Eastern European successor states (under League of Nations auspices) in 1919 and 1920. > see also: **World War I**; **Balfour Declaration**; **League of Nations**; **Organizations, Zionist (Denmark, Copenhagen Bureau)**.

Corpus Separatum [L] "Separate Entity": Legal terminology used by the United Nations for the status of Jerusalem under the terms of the 1947 partition plan. The term implied that Jerusalem would not be part of either the Jewish or Arab states but would be an independent entity under U.N. auspices. > see also: **Bernadotte Plan**; **Partition Plans, United Nations Plan**.

Crémieux Decree [PN]: Decree issued by the French government in 1870 announcing the emancipation of Jews in Algeria. Algeria had been occupied by the French in a campaign that started in 1830 and ended in 1857. In the interim, Algera was declared a province (department) of France — rather than a colony — although military rule continued in most of the country. Algeria's dual status thus meant that European colonists entering Algeria (the so-called Pied Noir) could rule themselves. The Crémieux decree granted French citizenship to Algeria's 150,000 Jews, making them part and parcel of the French colonial regime and converting them into a touchstone for local resistance to French rule. Pogroms resulted during revolts in 1871, 1879, and 1884. > see also: **Arabs**.

Crimea Scheme > see also: **Territorialism, Territorialist Schemes**.

Cult of the Cow [Slang]: Derisive term used by revisionist Zionist leader Ze'ev Jabotinsky (in a number of variants) to denounce what he saw as the utopian elements in socialist Zionism. In this case Jabotinsky used one of Mapai's common slogans — that *Eretz Israel* could only be built one settler, one dunam, and one cow at a time — to delegitimize the socialist Zionist goals. He, in effect accused them of placing more emphasis on rescuing the cow than on rescuing East European Jewry, then in dire need of mass *aliya*. The phrase was unusual: in addition to its reference to the Mapai slogan, this was also an indirect reference to the biblical prophecy (Hosea 13:2) "They who sacrifice people, kiss the calves." > see also: **Little Zionism**; **Fata Morgana Land**; **Monism**; **Gradualism**.

Cultural Conflict: Common name for two internal conflicts within the Zionist movement before World War I. Although viewed as one unified conflict over the future Jewish national home's cultural and intellectual life, actually two conflicts existed: between religious and secular Zionists, and between so-called Germanists and Hebraists. Considerable overlap existed within the different positions; for example, many secularists were dedicated to the revival of Hebrew and vice versa. Both conflicts derived from the question of how best to inculcate Jewish youth with a sense of national identity. Although all Zionists agreed on the need for education, the means and goals of such education were open to searing disagreements. Religious Zionists saw nationalist education as a means to restore the status of Jewish tradition, which had been ravaged by modern secularist ideologies. Secular Zionists, by contrast, saw nationalist education as a means of creating a new Jewish identity that would dispense altogether with the trappings of rabbinic Judaism. Similarly, Hebraists saw the revival of Jewry's ancestral mother tongue as part and parcel of the revival of the ancestral homeland; Germanists did not view favorably the effort to revive a long-dead language and argued that Jews should adopt a modern European language as their new national tongue. Although Theodor Herzl sought to steer clear of these types of arguments, since he saw them as premature and dangerous from the standpoint of Zionist unity, both conflicts repeatedly cropped up in the years before World War I. In 1899 the WZO agreed to create a cultural commission but was unable to move either party of either conflict to a compromise. In the end, Germanists accepted the

fait accompli of Hebrew use in the *Yishuv* while religious issues were regulated by a series of ad hoc compromises worked out in the 1930s. These compromises (most of which are still in force in Israel today) granted religious Zionists dominance in certain areas without creating more than a veneer of traditional Jewish observance within the WZO. > see also: **Judaism and Zionism**; **Hebrew, Revival of**; **Organizations, Zionist (Cultural Commission)**.

Cyprus, Detention Camps:

1. Scope and Definition
British authorities held *Ma'apilim* — most of them survivors of the Holocaust trying to enter Palestine/*Eretz Israel* — in detention camps on Cyprus after a cabinet decision of August 7, 1946. The British hoped that this decision would deter *Aliya Bet* and thereby weaken the Jewish rebels in Palestine, without using more force than world public opinion would permit. The Royal Army opened the first camp on August 13 and remained responsible for administration and security; throughout their existence the camps were run as though they held prisoners of war. In all the British built some twelve camps: five so-called summer camps (all located near Famagusta) in which detainees lived in tents, and seven winter camps (in the Dekalia/Larnaca region) in which detainees lived in tin huts. Despite British efforts, the camps were continually overcrowded, a reflection of the policy's failure to deter would-be *Ma'apilim*.

The detainees in the Cyprus camps were relatively young, and most were members of pre-war Zionist youth movements. This meant that they were both spirited and disciplined. Internal camp affairs were organized by the Zionist Youth Movements in conjunction with the American Jewish Joint Distribution Committee and ORT. Officially, the detainees were permitted only political and educational institutions. Representatives of both the Hagana and the Mossad le-Aliya Bet, however, were also active in the camps and some of the detainees thus also received preliminary military training.

Exile on Cyprus offered one glimmer of hope

for the *Ma'apilim*: as long as legal immigration continued (even at a small pace) the JAE always earmarked some certificates for the detainees. This situation ended on February 10, 1949, when the last group of detainees left for Israel. A total of 52,000 Jews were detained on Cyprus, some for more than a year; 2,700 children were born to families in the camps, but they were destined to grow up in an independent Jewish state.

TABLE C.4: Age Distribution of Detainees in Cyprus, 1947

Age-Group	Number	Percent
1-12	1,033	5.9
13-18	2,961	16.8
19-35	11,334	64.2
36-50	1,759	10.0
51+	538	3.1
Total	17,625	100.0

Source: D. Ofer, "Holocaust Survivors as Immigrants," *Modern Judaism* 16, 1 (February 1996): 4.

One of the detention camps for *Ma'apilim* on Cyprus
Courtesy of the Central Zionist Archives, Jerusalem

D

D: Mossad le-Aliya Bet term for the use of forged documents as a means to get *Ma'apilim* into Palestine/*Eretz Israel* after World War II. Although some individual *Ma'apilim* may have used this device before the war, the Mossad's operation was the only systematic effort to forge documents and use them. In all, some 8,500 *Ma'apilim* entered Palestine/*Eretz Israel* this way between 1945 and 1948. > see also: **Aliya Bet**.

Damascus Blood Libel [GN/HT]: Also known as the Damascus Affair. Popular name for the false accusation that Jews use Christian blood for their religious ceremonies. The affair originated in imperialist clashes in the Middle East, specifically in the conflict between France and England over the future of the Ottoman Empire. Whereas the British sought to defend the empire's territorial integrity, the French supported the efforts of Mehmet Ali, military governor of Egypt, to rebel against the Ottomans and destroy the empire. The French supported Ali's invasion of Syria in 1839, and his forces captured Damascus in early 1840. Jews became involved in this situation on February 5, 1840, when a Cappuchin Monk and his Muslim valet disappeared. A witness claimed that the two had been abducted and killed by Jews (their exact fate has not been established, although the monk was known to be involved in a variety of shady business dealings). Eight Jews were arrested and under torture a number of them admitted killing the monk in order to use his blood in baking matzot for Passover. The French consul supported the Syrian government's claim that justice was done in the case, but the British — prodded by Sir Moses Montefiore who was then on a pilgrimage to the Holy Land — and the Austrians strongly protested this miscarriage of justice. After two Jews died because of the torture police applied, the case became a cause celebré in England and America. On Augest 28, 1840, the Syrian government officially repudiated its own investigation of the matter and the remaining Jewish prisoners were freed. Ramifications of the affair included Montefiore's abortive attempts to spark *aliya* by building a windmill and textile mill in Jerusalem and in the founding of the Franco-Jewish Alliance Israélite Universelle, a defense agency dedicated to protecting Jewish rights throughout the world. > see also: **Organizations, Non- or Anti-Zionist (France)**.

Damascus Protocol [GN]: Name of the demands issued by Syrian Arab nationalists in December 1915, principally that the Allies create an independent Arab kingdom in the Fertile Crescent in return for which the Arabs would help Britain drive the Turks from the Middle East. > see also: **McMahon-Hussein Correspondence**.

Daniel Deronda: Title of a proto-Zionist book written by George Elliot (pseud. Mary Ann Evans) and published in serial form between

1874 and 1876. The story is a simple one and appears to have been based loosely on the career of Colonel A. E. W. Goldsmid (who discovered that he was Jewish only in his late twenties). An eminent English political leader named Daniel Deronda discovers his Jewish identity and decides to leave England for Palestine in order to help revive Jewry's ancestral homeland. The last of Evans's major fiction works, the book greatly influenced such Zionist writers as Eliezer Ben-Yehuda and Peretz Smolenskin. > see also: **Gentile Zionism; Altneuland; Hebrew, Revival of**.

Dat ha-Avoda [דת העבודה, H] "The Religion of Labor": Philosophical concepts popular among Labor Zionists, especially after the Second Aliya. The religion of labor was a key element in Aharon David Gordon's philosophy, and from him the idea spread throughout the Labor Zionist movement: Jews can only be reborn — spiritually and politically — if they return to the land and only if they also return to working the land. Agriculture, according to Gordon, connects the individual with both nature and his or her soul. Thus a return to agricultural work would restore the Jews' collective soul and their national creativity. This ideology was meant both as a break with the past (it was framed as a "new" Judaism) and as a return to the biblical ethos of agricultural work. > see also: **Avoda Ivrit; Agricultural Settlement(s)**.

David [PN]: WZO, JAE, and Hagana code term for the Jewish Agency and especially for the Jewish Agency Executive. Used after 1935, the term obviously derives from JAE chairman David Ben-Gurion.

Davidka [דוידקה, H] "Little David": Popular name (no official name existed) for Zahal's home-manufactured mortar, a weapon used during the War of Independence and then quickly retired from service. The weapon was

The Davidka Memorial in Jerusalem Today.
Authors' Collection

named after David Lebowitz, its developer. Although the Davidka nominally had a 65 MM bore, and some had a 76 MM bore, its bomb was much smaller. Using a combination of gunpowder, fertilizer, and rifle cartridges as propellant, the Davidka gave off an extremely loud noise whenever fired. In light of the small bomb thrown, it may fairly be said that the Davidka's "bark" was much larger than its bite. Additionally, the combination of explosives also had a tendency to explode prematurely, making the Davidka almost as dangerous to its firers as it was to the enemy. As a result, the Davidka was more often used for psychological effect than for actual destruction of targets, with modest success. > see also: **War of Independance**.

Declaration to the Seven [HT]: British governmental declaration of Middle East policy made in 1918 in response to queries by seven Egyptian notables. The notables made inquiries of the British regarding apparent contradictions in British promises to Arabs, Jews, and other Allied powers in, respectively, the McMahon-Hussein correspondence, the Balfour Declaration, and the Sykes-Picot Agreement. In response, the British government emphasized its interpretation that the three agreements did not contradict and renewed their vow to help create an independent Arab kingdom. Furthermore, the declaration reiterated British intention to use the "consent of the governed" as the sole criterion for any changes made to already existing commitments. > see also: **Arabs; McMahon-Hussein Correspondence; Balfour Declaration; Sykes-Picot Agreement**.

Degel [דגל, H] "Flag": The earliest modern proposal for a Zionist flag was made in the 1880s by members of the Hibbat Zion movement; their proposal was for a plain white flag struck with a blue star of David centered by the word Zion. Theodor Herzl proposed a

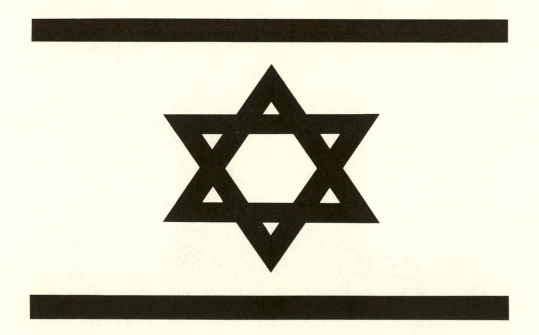

Degel: The Israeli Flag.
Authors' Collection

more elaborate flag in 1896, calling for a white background struck with six gold stars aligned to form one large star of David. In another version of Herzl's proposal the larger star held the smaller stars within its points and was surmounted by a rampant lion of Judea. The First Zionist Congress (1897) adopted a simpler version of Herzl's proposal (although the Hibbat Zion influence may also be felt here) being a white flag struck with two horizontal blue stripes (derived from the traditional Jewish prayer shawl, the *talit*) above and below a blue star of David. Although accepted as the symbol of Zionism, it might be noted that this flag did not become official until the Eighteenth Zionist Congress (1933); this eventually became the flag of the State of Israel as well. During World War II the Jewish Brigade Group, a Jewish unit founded within the Royal Army, used a modified form of this flag: two vertical blue stripes surounding a single white stripe surmounted by a yellow (or gold) Star of David. The color yellow was chosen precisely because the Nazis had used that color as a badge of shame for Jews but was here converted into a badge of honor. > see also: **Israel, State of; World War II, Jewish Military Units (Hativa Yehudit Lohemet).**

Delphi [Gr]: Term for an oracle derived from Greek mythology and used by the Hagana as a code term for its intelligence service, the Sherut Yediot (Shai). > see also: **Yishuv, Yishuv Organizations (Underground Organizations, Sherut Yediot).**

Democratic Fraction [HT]: Popular name for the oppositional party formed within the World Zionist Organization (WZO) after the Fourth World Zionist Congress, and led by Chaim Weizmann. In particular, the Democratic Fraction opposed Theodor Herzl's apparent surrender to religious groups in the WZO that manifested itself in his unwillingness to publicly discuss cultural questions. In this, Weizmann showed himself to be a student of Ahad ha-Am. However,

Weizmann was not a complete follower of the concept of Spiritual Zionism. Instead, he advocated a synthetic Zionism that combined the best of Herzl's and Ahad ha-Am's ideas. > see also: **World Zionist Congress; Zionut.**

Democratic Revisionists [HT]: Term used by supporters of Meir Grossman to define their position in ha-Zohar: they stood for institutional democracy and continued membership in the WZO. Grossman's use of the term implied that ha-Zohar President Ze'ev Jabotinsky was less committed to democracy than he was and also reflected the intense maneuvering that occurred within the Revisionist movement in the early 1930s. Nonetheless, Jabotinsky's supporters resented the very implication. Moreover, the collapse of the Bolougne and Calais compromises prior to and immediately after the Eighteenth World Zionist Congress, when the issue of secession from the WZO emerged as the defining question within ha-Zohar, reinforced the Grossmanites' use of the term. When ha-Zohar did in fact withdraw from the WZO (in 1935), the term fell into disuse as the Grossmanites reorganized themselves into a WZO faction called the Jewish State Party. > see also: **Revisionist Schism; Organizations, Revisionist Zionist; Conferences, Zionist.**

Derech Burma [דרך בורמה, H/GN/Slang] "(the) Burma Road": Popular name for the roadway built to outflank Latrun and open a supply line to Jerusalem during Israel's War of Independence. The need for such a road became patently clear to Zahal's commanders after the failure to eject units of the Jordanian Arab Legion from the police fort and town of Latrun in late May 1948. Aluf (general) David "Mickey" Marcus — the American volunteer who commanded Israeli forces trying to open the road — proposed building the road to outflank the Jordanians and suggested using the name in honor of the road built by Allied forces during World War II to help keep the flow of supplies to China open. Probes by Palmah forces discovered a clear path, that could be improved for heavy vehicular traffic on May 31. The route was shielded from the Jordanians and work commenced immediately,

Memorial to *Derech Burma*.
Authors' Collection via Carol Ann Stein Edelheit

with construction work being completed shortly after Marcus was killed. The first units — a convoy of Palmah jeeps carrying ammunition and medical supplies — passed over the road on June 1, even before the path had been completely prepared. The road remained in use until the Israeli-Jordanian armistice agreement of April 3, 1949. Thereafter, parts of the Burma Road were incorporated into the main access road to Jerusalem, although a large portion of the path was left as a national monument to the siege breakers.

Der Judenstaat [G] *"The Jewish State"*: Title of Theodor Herzl's 1896 Zionist tract. Herzl argued that the only way for Jews to normalize their relations with non-Jews was to create a Jewish state, though he never defined the precise meaning of the term. Herzl had begun writing the book only to abandon it, but the Dreyfus Affair and the rising tide of antisemitism in Central Europe filled Herzl with a renewed sense of purpose. He completed the text and had it published in 1896. The book caused an immediate stir, and led directly to the creation of the WZO and the convening of the First World Zionist Congress in Basel, Switzerland, in 1897. Critics, including many Zionists, have noted a number of glaring gaps in the argument. First, *Eretz Israel* is nowhere mentioned as the territory in which the Jewish state is to come into being; and second, Herzl was never specific about the Jewishness of the Jewish state. As a result, even in Herzl's era, the Zionist movement was beset by considerable ideological infighting. > see also: **Zionut**; **Territorialism**; **Cultural Conflict**.

Detroit [GN]: Code term used by Israeli purchasing agents for the United States in 1948 and 1949. These agents, sent on a desperate mission to acquire arms (especially warplanes) for the newborn State of Israel — used the term "automobiles" for the needed weaponry. Since the center of the U.S. automobile industry was in Detroit, the term was an obvious one. Likewise, arms purchasing missions sent to Central and South America used the term "Latin Detroit" for their destinations. > see also: **Rechesh**; **Sonnenborn Institute**.

Deutsche Staatsbürger Jüdischen Glaubens [G] "German Citizens of the Jewish Faith": Term associated with German Jewish non-Zionists who saw themselves primarily as Germans and only secondarily as Jews; they sought assimilation as the answer to the "Jewish question" and strongly opposed any effort to define Jews as members of a national minority. > see also: **Assimilation**; **Deutschtum und Judentum**; **Protestrabiner**.

Deutschtum und Judentum [G] "Germanness and Jewishness": Term for the synthesis of two historical identities, mainly (though not exclusively) identified with German non-Zionists. German Jews sought a symbiosis between their identity as German citizens and their identity as members of the Jewish faith (regardless of how they defined the latter). In this sphere, most German Jews sought a moderate form of assimilation (really acculturation) by fusing the best elements of both identities. German Zionists rejected this synthesis, since they saw themselves as Jews by both religion and nationality, and viewed their "Germanness" as nothing more than a (temporary and accidental) fact of citizenship. Even so, German Zionists argued for a distinctively "German" goal for their movement: to create a Jewish national home for those in need of asylum and an entity that fostered Jewish national pride, but where all German Jews would not necessarily reside. > see also: **Assimilation**.

Dhimmi [Ar] "Protected Minority": Muslim legal term dating to the medieval era and denoting the relationship between believers and so-called People of the Book. Dhimmi status basically guaranteed the latter the right to practice their religion while also protecting their lives and property. In return, Dhimmi recognized the complete superiority of Muslims in all other spheres; not the least of which was the political sphere. Dhimmi were, for example, enjoined from owning Muslim slaves or from having any form of dominion (even indirectly) over Muslims. This could be exemplified by matters as minor as accepting the rule that no house of worship could be built taller than a locality's shortest mosque to matters as major as paying the poll tax (Jizya) to earn residency permission from rulers. In net effect, Dhimmitude legislated second-class status for Jews and Christians (at least until modern times). Dhimmi status was officially terminated in the Ottoman Empire during the Tanzimat era (mid-nineteenth century). However, many Arabs have continued to use arguments based on Dhimmitude to reject Zionism and all forms of Jewish nationalism. They thus deny that Jews (Christian Arabs no longer being considered part of the "out group") constitute a legitimate nation, but are "merely" a community of faith that may (or may not) be tolerated by Muslims if they behave correctly. > see also: **Arabs**; **Anti-Zionism**.

Diaspora [Gr] "Dispersion": Common term for the dispersal suffered by the Jewish people after the Roman destruction of Jerusalem in 70 C.E. > see also: **Galut**; **Gola**.

Diaspora Nationalism [HT]: Non-Zionist concept of Jewish nationalism that emphasized Jewish continuity in Europe. Diaspora nationalists sought to create a regime of Jewish autonomy in Eastern European Jewish population centers. Although clearly articulating a non-Zionist position, diaspora nationalists were not necessarily anti-Zionists; they certainly had no ideological opposition to Jewish nationalism. Zionists and diaspora nationalists cooperated on efforts to obtain international guarantees for Jewish minority rights in the East European countries during the first third of the twentieth century. Zionists saw these as a means to an end while diaspora nationalists saw such guarantees as an end in themselves; hence the difference between the two positions. > see also: **Gegenwartsarbeit; Autonomism**.

Diplomatic Zionism [HT]: Term coined in 1945 or 1946 by David Ben-Gurion to characterize Zionist gradualism, that is, the form of Zionism that eschewed conflict with the British at all costs. Ben-Gurion used the term derisively to attack the policies advocated by WZO president Chaim Weizmann and he contrasted this brand of Zionism with his own "Fighting Zionism." > see also: **Zionut Lohemet; Gradualism**.

Displaced Persons, Jewish

1. Scope and Definition
   With the end of World War II the Allied powers discovered that the Nazis had uprooted between 7 million and 9 million people. Even during the war, however, Anglo-American policy emphasized the repatriation of these displaced persons (DPs), and by late 1945 more than 6 million had returned to their homes. Still, that left 1.5 million to 2 million DPs who either refused or were unable to return to their countries of origin. Nearly 100,000 Jewish DPs were among those still in camps at the end of 1945. Many survivors were not prepared to return to their countries of origin and felt unable to resume their lives in blood-soaked Eastern Europe. Because of the rising tide of antisemitic violence in postwar Eastern Europe, including the Kielce Pogrom, a great number of Jewish refugees soon joined the DPs as they fled Eastern Europe with the Briha. Attempts to resettle the DPs became part of the struggle for a Jewish state after World War II, and the DP problem was only solved after the creation of the State of Israel on May 14, 1948. > see also: **Aliya Bet; Briha; She'erit ha-Pleta**.

TABLE D.1: Jewish DPs in the U.S. Zone in Germany, 1945

Camp	Number	Camp	Number
Dachau	2,190	Geretsried	1,800
Ebensee	1,438	Landsberg	5,000
Feldafing	3,309	Munich-Freiman	1,544
Fohrenwald	1,000	Total	16,281

Source: *Department of State Bulletin*, September 30, 1945, pp. 456–463.

TABLE D.2: Jewish DPs in 1946

Zone	Germany	Austria	Italy
American	175,960	22,000	18,000
British	28,000	4,000	NA
French	1,500	1,000	NA
Berlin	10,000	Vienna 7,000	NA
Total	215,460	34,000	18,000

Source: Z. Warhaftig, *Uprooted: Jewish Refugees and Displaced Persons* (New York: World Jewish Congress, 1946).

3. Jewish DP Organizations

Ihud [איחוד], "Unity," political organization established in September 1945 by the leadership of the Landsberg DP camp. Led by Samuel Gringauz and David Treger, Ihud operated as both an intermediary between DPs and the U.S. Army and as a pressure group for DP emigration to *Eretz Israel*. Ihud also operated in close contact with the Jewish Agency Executive, especially after David Ben-Gurion's visit to Landsberg on October 22, 1945.

Kibbutz Buchenwald, agricultural training center established at the Buchenwald DP camp in June 1945. Designed to train young survivors for placement in *Kibbutzim* in the *Yishuv*, Kibbutz Buchenwald was modeled on prewar *Hachshara* programs. The *Kibbutz* also served as a center for Jewish political activity on behalf of the *Yishuv* in the U.S. zone of occupation. > see also: **Hachshara**.

Kibbutz Nili, agricultural training center established on the grounds of Nazi party leader Julius Streicher's former estate near Pleikershof, Germany, in mid-1945. In addition to its agricultural training program, the Kibbutz operated a complete DP school program for young survivors.

Merkaz la-Gola [מרכז לגולה], "Center for the Diaspora," agency founded in 1945 by the JA and operated under the auspices of the Briha. The primary aim of this organization was to move Jews from Germany and Austria to Italy, pending a resolution of further transit plans, usually, their embarkation on a Mossad blockade runner. To move the Jewish DPs, the Merkaz used the Jewish Brigade Group, which was stationed in northern Italy and southern Germany.

4. DP Publications

Dos Fraye Vort [דאס פרייע ווארט], "The Free Word," weekly Yiddish newspaper published at the Feldafing DP camp in the U.S. zone of occupation in Germany. Operating under the auspices of a Zionist, Bundist, and Agudas Israel coalition, *Dos Fraye Vort* was edited by M. Gavronsky and appeared from 1945 to 1948.

Front Page of the
Landsberger Lager–Cajtung, October 5, 1945.
Courtesy of the YIVO Institute for
Jewish Research, New York

Landsberger Lager Cajtung, "Landsberg Camp Newspaper," weekly newspaper published at the Landsberg DP camp in the U.S. zone of occupation in Germany. The paper appeared from January 8, 1946 until 1948 and was edited by Rudolph Valsonok. The *Landsberger Lager–Cajtung* was written in Yiddish but printed in Latin script; the paper was considered the most influential DP newspaper.

Landsberger Szpigel [לאנדסבערגער שפיגעל] "Landsberg Mirror," Yiddish newspaper published in the Landsberg DP camp and printed in Yiddish script. The newspaper was not distributed per se; instead copies were posted at strategic gathering posts throughout the camp.

Unzer Stimme [אונזער שטימע], "Our Voice," organ of the Jewish DPs in Bergen-Belsen. Began publication in August 1945 and continued uninterrupted until the camp closed in 1950. *Unzer Stimme* also used its printing facilities to publish books, pamphlets, and educational materials for DPs throughout Germany.

Unzer Velt (אונזער וועלט, UV), "Our World," bilingual (Hebrew/Yiddish) weekly appearing between 1945 and 1950 at the instigation of Betar in the U.S. zone of occupation in Germany. The first four issues were circulated as a mimeographed bulletin entitled *ha-Medina* (המדינה); all other issues (196 in all) were printed on a standard press. UV reached every corner of the Jewish DP community in Germany but was most influential among Betar members in Germany. Publication ceased after the last staff members left for Israel in 1950. Editors: Mordechai Kronowski (1945-1948), Moshe Halpern (1948-1949), Mordechai Zandberg (1950).

Unzer Ziel (אונזער ציל, UZ), "Our Goal," bilingual (Hebrew/Yiddish) weekly published in Linz by the renewed Betar branches in Austria and appearing between 1946 and 1948. UZ claimed a circulation of 6,000, although this probably included readers in DP camps throughout Europe. UZ was widely considered the most sophisticated and most influential of the postwar revisionist Zionist organs. Publication ceased after the State of Israel was established because the entire editorial staff emigrated. Sole editor: Aharon Edelstein.

Doism [דאָיזם, Y] "Hereism": Term expressing opposition to emigration used by many Jewish leaders in pre-Holocaust Eastern Europe. The term was especially popular within the Bund, but other non- (and anti-) Zionist Jewish socialist groups used it as well. Doism represented a complete rejection of Zionism and implied that Jews should stay in Eastern Europe if only as guardians of sacred sights associated with Jewish history. The emigré was viewed as one who abandoned his or her communal responsibilities or was a coward who lacked the courage to fight for Jewish rights. > see also: **Bundism; Folkism**.

Dreyfus Affair [PN]: Common name for the antisemitic affair that rocked France in the last years of the nineteenth century and first

years of the twentieth. Captain Alfred Dreyfus, a French Jewish artillery officer, was falsely accused of espionage in 1893 and was convicted and punished for that crime by banishment to the French prison colony on Devil's Island. Although continuing to profess his innocence, Dreyfus was widely assumed guilty, even within the Franco-Jewish community. As the wheels of justice slowly turned, however, it became increasingly clear that Dreyfus was indeed innocent, the victim of an antisemitic officer corps wishing to blame a scapegoat for failure on the battlefield in order to avoid admitting defeat at the hands of a better-prepared enemy. Of more immediate significance was the fact that when Dreyfus was publicly humiliated prior to his exile a Paris mob called for violence against all Jews. This incident was witnessed by Austrian Jewish journalist Theodor Herzl, who had clear proof of the precarious nature of Jewish existence in post-Emancipation Western Europe. His realization that assimilation would not end antisemitism led Herzl to renew his interest in the Jewish Question and convinced him to publish his book, *Der Judenstaat*. > see also: **Antisemitismus**; *Der Judenstaat*.

Drishot [דרישות, H] "Demands": Polish Jewish term for D-I (relatives) certificate, used to unify families. In order to qualify for a D-I certificate, the person requesting had to be able to prove that he or she had a close relative who was living legally in Palestine/*Eretz Israel* and was gainfully employed. > see also: **Certificates**.

Dual Loyalty [HT]: Canard used by anti-Zionists and antisemites to describe their vision of what may be termed Zionism's original sin: They believe that Jews who have not assimilated (or who cannot assimilate because Zionists will not allow them to do so) constitute a "state within a state." In turn, these Jews have a divided loyalty, ostensibly to the nation they live in but really to the Jewish entity (be it the Zionist movement or some other entity). Anti-Zionists accused Zionists of fostering antisemitism, claiming that non-Jews used these arguments because Zionists encouraged this perception by constantly arguing for the creation of a Jewish state. Following this logic, antisemitism could only be strengthened by Zionist success, since the creation of a Jewish state would ultimately call into question the loyalty of all Jews who continued to live in the diaspora. Anti-Zionists who used this argument were at a loss to explain why antisemities had been using the accusation of Jewish dual loyalty even before the Zionist movement existed (the concept of divided loyalty reflected in Jewish unwillingness to fully assimilate had been used in Germany since the 1870s, whereas Zionism developed after the 1880s), but in reality the accusation reflected the anti-Zionists' fears about their own future status to a greater degree than it ever explained antisemitism. The canard of dual loyalty has continued in use since the State of Israel was established in 1948. It resurfaced during the Pollard Affair of the 1980s and the Gulf War of 1990–1991, despite the fact that the antisemitic basis of this false accusation has become increasingly clear. For their part, Zionists have denied altogether that their goal is to foster Jewish disloyalty, claiming that Jews have a dual duty to the state in which they live and to the entire Jewish people. > see also: **Anti-Zionism; Antisemitismus**.

East Africa Scheme [GN]: Official title for the Uganda plan of 1903, which repesented a British offer to create a Jewish colony in parts of eastern Africa, specifically in today's Kenya and Tanzania. The plan began after the earlier El Arish scheme hit a snag. The British cabinet, desiring a friendly European population in East Africa (thereby halting German and French colonial encroachment in an area considered vital to British interest) also sought to help Russian Jews who were then suffering through a period of antisemitic pogroms. > see also: **Uganda Plan; El Arish Plan**.

Economic Absorptive Capacity [E]: Term used by the British goverment and, reluctantly, by Zionists to refer to a set of objective criteria that limited *aliya* to mandatory Palestine/*Eretz Israel*. In theory, the mandatory government's department of immigration was to estimate the number of new jobs that would be created in the upcoming schedule period. That number, added to all forms of capitalist immigration, repesented Palestine's economic absorptive capacity. The term was first used in the Churchill White Paper of 1922 and established the parameters of Jewish immigration to Palestine at any given time. Although the mandate had spoken of Jews returning to *Eretz Israel* "of right, not by suffrance" — a concept that implied free and unfettered immigration — WZO president Chaim Weizmann did not protest the new policy since the alternative (as encapsulated in the Haycraft Commission report) was a total end to *aliya*. Economic absorptive capacity worked as a fair way to define *aliya* quotas only as long as *aliya* requests remained stable and the criteria were adhered to objectively. Once *aliya* began to boom (especially after the Nazi rise to power in 1933) and the British Palestine administration began to interpret economic absorptive capacity in a subjective manner, the policy began to break down. The policy was replaced altogether in 1937 by a so-called political maximum that dictated how many Jews would be permitted into Palestine/*Eretz Israel* based on how many the Arabs might be willing to accept (in other words, once the British sought to find the absolute minimum way to fulfill the mandate's terms while still keeping Jews as a minority in Palestine/*Eretz Israel*) regardless of how many jobs were available. Once it was obvious that the Arabs sought to reduce *aliya* to zero, the British replaced the policy of a political maximum as well. > see also: **Aliya; Aliya bet; Mandatory Palestine; Certiticases; Schedule; White Paper(s)**.

Edomi [אדומי, H] "Edomite": General term used in the *Yishuv* after World War II for any Englishman. In Hebrew the term has negative connotations deriving from Jewish traditions about the unbridled hatred felt by the Edomites, descendants of Isaac's son Esau, toward descendants of Isaac's other son, Jacob. The usage may have started in the Hagana but soon spread throughout the entire Jewish community. A related term, *Edomi ba-Madim* (אדומי במדים, "an Edomite in uniform") was used to refer to British soldiers. > see also: **Blue Eyed Arab(s)**.

Education

1. Scope and Definition

Prior to the rise of Zionism, a widely ramified Jewish education system existed throughout the diaspora and in *Eretz Israel*. Within the Old *Yishuv*, education was concentrated in the operations of a small number of Yeshivot, Talmud Torahs, and Hadarim located in the "four holy cities" that provided for the educational needs of community members. The expansion of Jewish settlement areas after 1870, along with the arrival of the Bilu pioneers (after 1881) led to the expansion of this educational system. In particular, the establishment of the Mikve Israel agricultural school, financed by the Alliance Israélite Universelle, opened new vistas in education within the *Yishuv*. Even so, the schools of this era were mainly religious and were not, by and large, nationalist in their orientation. The same was true for the schools initiated after 1881 by secular European Jewish institutions such as the Anglo-Jewish Association and the Hilfsverein der deutschen Juden. These schools sought to modernize *Eretz Israel*'s Jewish community with mixed successes that, in many ways, paralleled conflicts over education in diaspora communities during the emancipation era.

As a greater proportion of secular Zionists arrived in *Eretz Israel* (mainly but not exclusively, after the Second Aliya) education became an increasingly public conflict between the Old and New *Yishuv*s. By the turn of the twentieth century this boiled over into a conflict between Zionists (both religious and secular), non-Zionist European Jews, and anti-Zionist Orthodox elements within the *Yishuv*. An additional layer of conflict existed within the Zionist camp; mainly between religious Zionists seeking to preserve and enhance tradition, and secularists seeking to create a "new" Jewish civilization in Jewry's ancestral homeland. Among other conflicts on cultural and religious question, the issue of education led directly to the creation of the Mizrachi (religious Zionist) party in 1902.

The various conflicts over education (and the bitterness over them should not be underestimated) were not resolved by the outbreak of World War I. Under the mandate regime, the power to regulate education devolved to the Jewish Millet, which was reorganized as the Knesset Israel. In the interim, the WZO approved a 1918 proposal to permit a dual track educational system to exist in the *Yishuv*. One, run by Mizrachi, was suited to religious Zionist elements within the *Yishuv* (after 1948 this was transformed into the Dati Mamlahti, i.e., religious public school system); the other was suited to secular elements within the *Yishuv* (after 1948 this crystalized as the Mamlahti, i.e., public school system). In 1926, a third track, mainly suited to socialist elements and run by the Histadrut, was established. Yet a fourth track operated outside of the system created by the Knesset Israel/Va'ad Leumi: this was the Haredi school system created by surviving elements of the anti-Zionist Orthodox elements from the Old *Yishuv*.

Until 1929, the three Zionist education tracks were overseen by the WZO through the Knesset Israel and the Zionist Commission. In 1929 responsibility for education passed to the newly reorganized Jewish Agency and fell under the responsibility of the latter's Education Department. After the 1931 rationalization of the *Yishuv*'s governing bodies, the JA turned over responsibility for education to the Va'ad Leumi. The education system was further refined in 1938, by which time a fully developed system of schools covering all levels of education from kindergarten to university existed. This four-track educational system, it might be noted in passing, still exists in the State of Israel to this day and is still the touchstone of conflict between religious and secular parties. > see also: **Old Yishuv/New Yishuv; Yishuv; Cultural Conflict; Millet System; Israel, State of; World Zionist Organization**.

TABLE E.1: Total Number of Pupils in Jewish Schools, 1920-1949[1]

Year	Students	Year	Students
1920	12,830	1940	58,692
1925	16,243	1945	79,441
1930	22,533	1949	129,688
1935	39,701	Total	359,128

Source: *Statistical Abstract of Israel*, 1967, p. 525.

Eitan/Eitanim [איתנים/איתן, H] "Enduring Person(s)": Hagana code name for Teddy Debres, a French volunteer who fought in Israel's War of Independence. The plural form of the term referred to any volunteer from France or to French members of Giyus Hutz la-Aretz. In an unrelated usage, the name Eitan was used by the Irgun Zvai Leumi to designate the head of its delegation in the United States during World War II, Peter Bergson (A.K.A. Hillel Kook). > see also: **Zahal**; **Giyus Hutz la-Aretz**.

El Arish Plan [GN]: British territorial offer made to the WZO in 1902. The plan centered around the possibility of Jewish settlement around El Arish, on the Sinai Peninsula's northern coast. Although technically not part of the historic *Eretz Israel*, El Arish was close enogh to Palestine/*Eretz Israel* to be considered by Zionists as a good first step toward completion of the Basel Program. Additionally, the entire Sinai was richly associated with Jewish history and an argument of the plan's relevance to Jewish redemptivist ideologies could be made. From the British perspective, Sinai was a vital buffer between Ottoman-controlled Syria/Palestine and the Suez Canal; the settlement of a friendly population in the Sinai could thus enhance imperial security. WZO president Theodor Herzl therefore entered into detailed negotiations with Colonial Secretary Joseph Chamberlain over the El Arish plan almost as soon as the offer was made. The British-controlled Egyptian government placed a number of important hindrances in the plan's path and British purchase of the entire Sinai from the Turks in 1903 rendered the plan moot. However, the plan did help to stimulate British cabinet interest in solving the Jewish problem, by restoring Jews to their ancestral homeland while also safeguarding Britain's imperial interests. > see also: **Uganda Plan**; **Mesopotamia Scheme**; **Balfour Declaration**.

Eleventh Commandment: Term coined in 1939 by American agronomist and Gentile Zionist Walter Clay Lowdermilk. The eleventh commandment, in Lowdermilk's usage, was a divine order to preserve the land by judicious use of natural resources in concert with the use of modern technologies to improve agriculture and make deserts bloom. Lowdermilk used this concept as the centerpiece for his Zionist advocacy, especially during World War II, and incorporated it into his plan for a "Jordan Valley Authority." > see also: **Lowdermilk Plan**; **Gentile Zionism**.

---

[1] The following school types were included: kindergartens, elementary schools, high schools, vocational schools, and teacher training colleges. Academic institutions (including Yeshivot Gedolot) were included only in the figures for 1949.

Members of the Zionist Commission Studying the Prospects for Jewish Settlement in El Arish.
Courtesy of the Central Zionist Archives, Jerusalem

Emaliye [T] "Forced Labor": Hebraized form of a Turkish term used in the *Yishuv* to depict the status of Jewish soldiers serving in the Ottoman military during World War I. Although equality was guaranteed by the Ottoman constitution of 1894, all non-Muslim troops were removed from combat units when the Porte declared the war to be a *Jihad*. Soldiers thus removed from duty were not, however, released from the army. Instead they were used as slave laborers mainly to construct fortifications. They were not permitted to carry firearms and were treated as virtual prisoners of war. In light of the great need for workers, the Ottomans extended the Emaliye during 1916 to include all men between the ages of forty-five and fifty-five, thus almost depopulating the *Yishuv*. > see also: **World War I**.

Emancipation [HT]: Term for the grant of civil rights to disenfranchised groups during the nineteenth century. In the European context, the term is used to represent actions taken between 1789 and 1870 that, cumulatively, led to the entry of Jews into the social and political lives of the countries they resided in. Emancipation was thus the culmination of nearly a century of activity that derived from major changes in social, political, economic, and cultural structures in European and European Jewish societies. In general, emancipation proceeded in more modernized countries and may also be seen as part of the process whereby the Ancien Régime was toppled. Emancipation was completed in Western Europe by 1870 and resulted in rapid assimilation by Jews. Assimilation, in turn, led to an effort to downplay Jewish distinctiveness and, in some circles, the outright denial that Jews constituted a nation. The complete failure of emancipation in Eastern Europe (where Jews did not obtain equality of rights until after World War I) combined with the rise of modern antisemitism led to calls by Jewish nationalists for a policy of "autoemancipation," leading directly to the creation of the Zionist movement. > see also: **Assimilation; Antisemitismus; Nationalism; Zionut**.

Em ha-Kvutzot [אם הקבוצות, H] "The Mother of the Collective Settlements": Popular name for Degania, the first collective settlement in *Eretz Israel*. Degania, the first *Kvutza*, was established in 1909 by ten settlers who had previously worked in Hadera, Petah Tikva, and Ben-Shemen. The idea of creating a collective settlement derived from their desire to permit each member to work while also caring for their personal needs. The idea was later widely adopted, forming the basis for the *Kibbutz* movement. > see also: **Agricultural Settlement(s)**.

Em ha-Moshavot [אם המושבות, H] "The Mother of Settlements": Popular nickname for Petah Tikva, the first Jewish agricultural settlement established in *Eretz Israel* in modern times. Petah Tikva was established in 1878 by members of the Jerusalem Jewish community in order both to revive the old *Yishuv*'s economic life and provide new housing for Jerusalem's burgeoning Jewish population. The leaders of the Petah Tikva settlement project included Rabbi Joel M. Solomon, David Gutman, Yehoshua Stampfer, and Judah Rab. They hoped that Petah Tikva would ultimately reduce the Jewish community's reliance on Haluka (charity from abroad) and thereby strengthen the *Yishuv*. Initially they purchased 3,400 dunams; additional plots totalling 8,500 dunams were added on to the settlement in the late 1880s. Security and other problems led to the abandonment of Petah Tikva in 1882; the settlement was renewed in 1883 with the arrival of dozens of Bilu members from Romania. In 1937 Petah Tikva was granted city status by the mandatory authorities. > see also: **Old Yishuv/New Yishuv; Halukka; Bet Yaakov Lehu ve-Nelha; Agricultural Settlement(s)**.

Endziel [G] "Final Goal": Term for Zionism's ultimate goal: the establishment of a sovereign Jewish state. Early Zionist leaders, including Theodor Herzl, never explicitly formulated long-term goals for the WZO out of fear that such a statement might imperil efforts to obtain a charter for *Eretz Israel*. Nonetheless, the WZO's unstated goal was always understood to be a sufficient amount of self-government to allow for open mass immigration and secure Jewish land purchase. With the Balfour Declaration and the British acceptance of the League of Nations mandate, the time seemed ripe to discuss long-term goals, as was advocated by revisionist Zionist Leader Ze'ev Jabotinsky. The latter began advocating that the WZO issue such a statement at the Eighteenth Zionist Congress (1931); the Nazi *Machtergreifung* in 1933 made his calls even more passionate. Fear for European Jewry's safety and an unwillingness to directly create a rift with the British caused Jabotinsky's opponents to oppose a call for Jewish sovereignty with equal passion. Zionist "gradualists" accused Jabotinsky of being an irresponsible demagogue. Albeit, indirectly, some of Jabotinsky's opponents (such as Mapai chairman David Ben-Gurion) began to adopt similar (though not identical) ideas, especially after the Peel Partition plan was announced in 1937. In May 1942, the Extraordinary Zionist Conference (the so-called Biltmore Conference) placed the WZO officially on record as demanding a Jewish state after World War II. > see also: **Gradualism; Shem ha-Meforash; Biltmore Resolution; Zionist Congress(es)**.

Eretz Israel [ארץ ישראל, H] "(The) Land of Israel": Traditional Jewish name for the territory known as the Holy Land, Palestine, or (in its geographic designation) Cis-Jordan. This territory is considered the inalienable possession of the Jewish people, a fact emphasized in the name. As used in Biblical literature, the term meant those territories in which the twelve tribes of Israel settled. As used in postbiblical Jewish literature, the term has an additional redemptivist overtone which carried over into Zionist use of the term in the nineteenth century. In the twentieth century the term has taken on two radically different meanings. It was used by Zionists for the territory known as mandatory Palestine (or more correctly, Palestine/*Eretz Israel*), a term which reflected the renewed Jewish settlement. The term was (and still is) used as well by Orthodox Jewish anti-Zionists who insist on using the geographic term in order to deny legitimacy to the State of Israel. > see also: **Ha-Makom**; **Ha-Aretz**; **Palestine/Eretz Israel**.

Evacuation Plan [HT]: Visionary *aliya* proposal suggested in 1935 by revisionist Zionist leader Ze'ev Jabotinsky and designed to remove a minimum of 1.5 million Jews from Eastern Europe, primarily from Poland, and bring them to *Eretz Israel* over the course of ten years. The plan was based on four premises: (1) Jews had to become a majority of the population in Palestine/*Eretz Israel* in as short a time as possible; (2) only the creation of an "immigration regime" (a British administration willing to foster *aliya*) would make that goal possible; (3) reforms to the structure of the WZO and JA were necessary to further these goals; and (4) the long-range goal of evacuation would be the creation of a sovereign Jewish state. Once completed, the evacuation plan would itself be only the first phase; the second phase would take place after a Jewish state came into being and would involve the repatriation of all diaspora Jews who desired to settle in the Jewish state. The evacuation plan must also be viewed within the context of time. By 1935 living conditions for Jews in Central and Eastern Europe, especially, but not exclusively in Nazi Germany, Poland, Romania, and Hungary, had become almost impossible. Yet, the very numbers of Jews encompassed by these communities (nearly 6 million Jews in 1933) meant that ordinary means of rescue were insufficient. Now Jews had only one choice: to flee or to be overwhelmed. Although rejected by the majority of the Zionist establishment, some of Jabotinsky's ideas and his rhetoric on the evacuation plan was incorporated into the ideas of other Zionist thinkers, notably David Ben-Gurion. The British never considered the idea as a basis for *aliya* policy. > see also: **Aliya**; **Tochnit ha-Asor**; **Halutzic Aliya**.

Ezba ha-Galil [אצבע הגליל, GN] "The Finger of Galilee": Colloquial term for the sliver of territory in Northern Israel in the vicinity of Kiryat Shmona that juts into southern Lebanon like a finger. This specific area was not clearly demarcated by the San Remo conference; as a result its inclusion in the Palestine mandate was a matter of conjecture. This confusion, coming at a time of unsettlement in Syria (and pitting the French against local Arab nationalists), led to a bloody conflict between Jews and Arabs. When the French attempted to assert their control over the region, the local Arab bands rose up. Under the pretext of clearing the area of French soldiers they attacked the Jewish settlements of Kfar Giladi and Tel Hai. During the defense of the latter, the famous Jewish soldier Joseph Trumpeldor was killed. As a result, the settlements had to be abandoned. In the long run, however, the defense of Ezba ha-Galil was not in vain — the territory was ceded to Palestine/*Eretz Israel* once peace was restored in Syria. > see also: **Tel Hai**; **Meora'ot**.

F

Faisal-Frankfurter Correspondence [PN]: Common name for the diplomatic maneuvers associated with American Zionist leader Felix Frankfurter and the Arab nationalist leader Emir Faisal (later King Faisal I of Iraq). Framed as a series of letters — the first from Faisal to Frankfurter and the second from Frankfurter to Faisal — the undertaking developed in March 1919. In his letter, Faisal reemphasized the commitments he had earlier made to Chaim Weizmann and once again strongly expressed his support for *aliya* and for the re-creation of a Jewish national home. Faisal failed to mention his other contacts with Weizmann over Zionist support for his claim to the Syrian throne, a fact that later led him to repudiate the agreement altogether. > see also: **Faisal-Weizmann Agreement**.

Faisal-Weizmann Agreement [PN]: Diplomatic arrangement signed in London on January 3, 1919, between Arab nationalist leader Emir Faisal (later King Faisal I of Iraq) and Zionist Commission chairman Chaim Weizmann. Faisal, the son of Sharif Hussein of Mecca and leader of the Arab forces that fought the Ottomans in alliance with Great Britain during World War I, welcomed the Jews back to their ancestral homeland and pledged his support for the creation of a Jewish national home. For his part, Weizmann promised to honor and protect Muslim holy sights in Cis-Jordan and

The First Page of Faisal's Letter to Felix Frankfurter, January 3, 1919.
Courtesy of the Central Zionist Archives, Jerusalem

permit freedom of religion in the Jewish national home. Both sides agreed to cooperate at the upcoming Paris peace conference.

Although the agreement was an important one, it is now clear that Faisal had an ulterior motive for signing. He sought Weizmann's support (and hence the WZO's support) for his claim to be the legitimate ruler of Syria, which he claimed in his father's name (as a result of the 1915 McMahon-Hussein correspondence) but which the French now also claimed (as per the terms of the Sykes-Picot Agreement). When Weizmann proved unable to "give" Syria (which was not his in the first place) to Faisal, the latter continued a dual policy, denying to Arab audiences that he had ever signed the agreement while secretly promising the Jews that he would abide by its terms if they did. The agreement collapsed altogether when Haj Amin al-Huseini was appointed Mufti of Jerusalem. This act reduced Faisal's influence on the Palestinian Arab nationalist movement and placed an implacable foe of Jews and Zionism in a position of great power. Further efforts to avert the Arab-Jewish conflict foundered thereafter; it was not until 1979 that an Arab state (Egypt) signed a peace treaty with Israel. > see also: **Faisal-Frankfurter Correspondence; McMahoh-Hussein Correspondence; Sykes-Picot Agreement; Arabs; Mufti.**

Fallah [AR] "Peasant": Common term for a simple village resident, usually a farmer. The term is somewhat derogatory, even though the fallahin formed the core of most modern Arab nationalist movements. > **Arabs.**

Faluja Pocket [GN]: Popular name for the territory occupied by Egyptian forces and surrounded by Zahal in October 1948. Located near the main highway between Ashkelon and the Negev, Faluja was occupied by the Egyptians early in Israel's War of Independence and was used as a staging area in the abortive assault up the Mediterranean coast. During the Israeli counterattack in late October, Faluja was cut off from the main Egyptian line of retreat and 3,000 troops were bottled up there. The pocket was cleared in December 1948, when all organized resistance ceased. Egyptian prisoners of war included the local commander, Colonel Gamal Abdel Nasser (later president of Egypt), who was

repatriated in February 1949. > see also: **War of Independence; Zva ha-Hagana le-Israel.**

Fata Morgana Land [Slang]: Untranslatable term used by Ze'ev Jabotinsky to deride his opponents' plans for developing the *Yishuv*. Instead of trying to build an actual Jewish state, based on mass *aliya*, they were trying to create the illusion of a grand "cultural center" that would look good but would offer no real benefit to most of European Jewry. > see also: **Sionisme de Luxe.**

Filastin Biládná [Ar] "Palestine Is Ours": Arab nationalist slogan originating in 1918 and used thereafter to represent a complete refusal to even negotiate with the Zionists. To the extent that local Arab notables were aware of his efforts to reach an agreement with the WZO, the term also reflected the nationalists' repudiation of Emir Faisal. The term has pan-Arabist implications and was most popular in the territory claimed as "greater Syria." > see also: **Arabs; Pan-Arabism; Faisal-Weizmann Agreement.**

Five Piastre Regiment [HT/Slang]: Common term for the Jewish units of the Palestine Regiment (the so-called Buffs) raised during World War II. The term derived from the fact that the unit's insignia was of the same copper color as the five piastre coin (called the five agora piece in Hebrew) then in use in *Eretz Israel*. > see also: **World War II.**

Folkism/Folkist [HT]: Common term for any of a number of Jewish diaspora nationalist ideologies, mainly those of a non-Socialist orientation, and/or the parties advocating such an ideology. > see also: **Autonomism; Diaspora Nationalism.**

Furmanim [פורמנים, Y] "Wagoneers": Hagana code term used early in Israel's War of Independence to designate Palmah units tasked with convoy escort duties. In particular, the term was used for units that escort convoys on the heavily defended and dangerous road to Jerusalem. Precise derivation of the term is unknown.

Galut [גלות, H] "Exile": Traditional term for the Jewish experience in the diaspora. Even before the advent of Zionism, the term had negative connotations, being linked with persecution and degradation. Zionist ideologues further added to the negative implications of the term by assumimg that any Jewish presence in the diaspora would lead to internal disintegration and external annihilation. > see also: **Gola; Shlilat ha-Gola.**

Gar'in [גרעין, H] "Kernel": Commonly used term for the group that founded a settlement or organization. In particular, the term was (and still is) used for the initial group of settlers in a *Kibbutz*. > see also: **Agricultural Settlement(s).**

Gegenwartsarbeit [G] "Work in the Here and Now": Zionist ideological term popular after Herzl's death and before World War I. Gegenwartsarbeit emphasized the need for Zionist activists to concentrate on goals that could be obtained, such as the "conquest of communities," and put off unobtainable goals, such as obtaining the right to settle *Eretz Israel* en masse, to some time in the distant or not-too-distant future. Further, Gegenwartsabeit called for Zionists to work on enhancing or defending Jewish rights throughout Europe. > see also: **Conquest of Communities; Kahal.**

Geistige Judennot [G] "Jewish Spiritual Distress": German Zionist term for the problems suffered by Western European Jews: not physical distress, but the lack of a spiritual anchor for those who in the name of emancipation had abandoned Jewish tradition. Alienated from Judaism, these Jews were also alienated from the societies in which they lived. Zionism offered these Jews a new sense of belonging and a new means to define Jewishness. > see also: **Materielle Judennot; Emancipation.**

Gelt un Assmilatsye Yidn [געלט און אסימילאציע יידן, Y] "Wealthy Assimilated Jews": Derisive term used by socialist Zionists in the United States to designate their main enemies: Jewish plutocrats who tended toward assimilation and opposed all forms of Zionist activity. Despite the antagonism expressed by the term, the Zionists were willing to cooperate with these same Jews on endeavors that accomplished broader Jewish goals, for instance, in the American Jewish Congress.

Gentile Zionism [HT]

1. Scope and Definition
Despite the obvious identification of Zionism with Jewish nationalism, a surprising number of non-Jews have also argued — at times forcefully — on behalf of Jewish restoration. This urge had four major roots, first, the close connection many Christians have felt with the Bible and with the restorationist prophecies therein. Second, and closely connected with the first, was the millenarian impulse associated primarily (though by no means exclusively) with

pietistic and revivalist Protestant denominations. In particular, the popular idea that the Second Coming of Christ could not happen until the Jews once again resided in their ancestral homeland provided an impetus for Zionist (or quasi-Zionist) activities. Third, the influence of modern Christian Hebraism, a phenomenon closely connected with the prior two, helped build up considerable sympathy for the Jewish people in Western Europe. Finally, guilt feelings over the impact of antisemitism, mainly manifest after the Holocaust, but also felt in some circles during the 1930s, and the perceived need to "right the two-millenia wrong" done the the Jewish people by the church led to support for Jewish causes in general and Zionism in particular.

All these causes have one common denominator: all deal with the support shown by individuals for Jewish restoration. Another cause, which can only be considered Gentile Zionism in the broadest sense of the term, was perceived national self-interest. Many governments and statesmen couched their support for Zionism in altruistic terminology but used the ideas generated by Gentile Zionists for broader national purposes: generally to secure interests (or perceived interests) in the Middle East by helping the Jews obtain a national home. In this case, support for Jewish aspirations derived mainly from the hope for a quid pro quo from the Jews, for example, in providing a friendly population for imperial interests in an area critical to the major European powers. In an ironic way, some statesmen of the pre-1948 era actually supported Zionism for antisemitic reasons, mainly, their belief in the existence of a cohesive Jewish body like the one alleged (with great exaggeration, it was admitted) by the author of the *Protocols of the Elders of Zion*, which could be "bought off" at the price of support for Jewish restoration. Variants on this theme included British support for Zionism during World War I and, in some cases, support by politicians in the United States for Jewish causes during and after World War II, seen as a means to obtain Jewish votes.

Most Gentile Zionists did not concern themselves with grand strategy or with politics. They advocated Jewish restoration for a multiplicity of reasons. Some, for example, used their Zionist advocacy as thinly veiled camouflage for efforts to convert Jews. Most Gentile Zionists advocated Jewish restoration because they truly believed that justice, fairness, and truth demanded the re-creation of a Jewish national home. > see also: **Blackstone Memorial; Balfour Declaration; Prokololle der Weissen von Zion; Nationalism; Vatican and Zionism; Zionut.**

2. Major Gentile Zionists

Amery, Leopold S. (1873–1955), English parliamentary leader and eminent cabinet member during World War I. Amery was an early and ardent advocate of Zionism. He drafted one of the earliest versions of what eventually became the Balfour Declaration and was essential to the creation of the Jewish Legion. Between 1924 and 1929, Amery served as colonial secretary, a period considered the most peaceful in the Yishuv's history. Amery continued to support the Zionist cause long after the alliance with the Jews was considered passe in the British cabinet; Amery was a forceful opponent of the White Paper of 1939 and strongly supported the Zionist cause before the Anglo-American Committee in 1946.

Balfour, Arthur J. (1848–1930), eminent British statesman and author of one of the most important documents in Zionist history. Balfour came to Zionism through an indirect route. As prime minister, Balfour sponsored legislation (the so-called Aliens Bill) to halt open immigration to Great Britain for Eastern and Southern Europeans (mainly Jews). Thereafter, Balfour remained interested in the Jewish problem: he supported efforts to find a homeland for the Jews in British East African, in Cyprus, and in the northern Sinai. When he joined the war cabinet in 1915 as first lord of the admiralty, he was in contact with Anglo-Zionist leaders; this culminated in his authorship of the cabinet statement of sympathy with Zionism (the Balfour Declaration) when he was foreign minister in the Lloyd George cabinet. > see also: **Balfour Declaration.**

Blackstone, William E. (1841–1935), American evangelist and preacher. Already in his earliest book, *Jesus is Coming* (1878), Blackstone argued that the millennium could not come until the Jews were restored to Palestine. Blackstone became further convinced of this argument after a pilgrimage to the Middle East in 1888–1889. On his return to the U.S., Blackstone authored a memorandum to President Benjamin Harrison advocating government action to turn this dream into a reality. Although this so-called Blackstone Memorial was signed by 413 leading Jewish and Christian personalities, it was not acted upon by the U.S. government. Moreover, accusations that Blackstone's agenda included overt proselytizing led to the collapse of his movement. In 1917, Blackstone urged President Woodrow Wilson to issue a statement of support for the Balfour Declaration; this memorandum apparently did indeed exert some influence on Wilson. > see also: **Blackstone Memorial**.

Borchsenius, Poul (1897–1983), Danish theologian and author. Borchsenius was intimately involved with the rescue of Danish Jewry during World War II; after the war he became an ardent convert to Zionism. His many works concentrated on Jewish history and the theme of toleration: Borchsenius was one of the earliest Christian theologians to publicly advocate that Judaism was as valid a means of salvation as Christianity.

Borges, Jorge L. (1899–1986), Argentine author. Descending from a well-known Marrano family, Borges sought to assimilate his "old" and "new" identities in his writings. Biblical themes pervaded Borges's short stories and were especially prominent in his collection, *El Aleph* (1949). He influenced a generation of Argentine writers into a philosemitic and pro-Zionist orientation.

Cazalet, Edward (1827–1883), British industrialist. Cazalet, whose company was involved in import-export business with czarist Russia was an early advocate of mass Jewish migration from Russia to the Holy Land. In 1881 Cazalet sent one of his Jewish representatives to Istanbul in an attempt to purchase land for a Damascus to Baghdad railway on which he hoped to settle masses of Russian Jews.

Cazalet, Victor Alexander (1896–1943), grandson of Edward Cazalet and an eminent British parliamentarian. Following his grandfather's lead, Cazalet advocated mass resettlement schemes for Russian Jewry, mainly in the Middle East. Cazalet was a close friend of Chaim Weizmann and was one of the few advocates of rescue to make his case publicly at the beginning of the Holocaust.

Churchill, Winston L. S. (1875–1965), British statesman, prime minister, and author. Churchill's Zionism derived from his intense Christianity as well as his understanding of human and Jewish history. Churchill opposed the Aliens Bill and established himself as a powerful defender of Jewish rights. He publicly advocated a Zionist solution to the Jewish question as early as 1906, although he initially tended toward territorialism rather than Zionism. As first lord of the admiralty during World War I, Churchill supported the establishment and deployment of Jewish military units. During his tenure as colonial secretary (1921–1922), Churchill established a mixed reputation. He staunchly opposed any efforts to restrict *aliya*, but his white paper did create clear limits to Zionist growth (including establishing economic absorptive capacity as the sole criterion for *aliya*). During his years out of power, Churchill repeatedly defended Britain's promises to the Jewish people. Because he felt that Britain's commitment was a sacred bond, Churchill zealously condemned the White Paper of 1939. Churchill's record on Jewish affairs was once again mixed after he returned to the premiership in 1940: he acted to prevent any further damage to the Jewish national home and advocated rescue activities, but achieved little in the way of rescue due to cabinet intransigence. After World War II Churchill returned to his unmitigated advocacy of Zionism, strongly condemning the Atlee government's actions against Jewish refugees and supporting the creation of a Jewish state.

Deedes, Wyndham (1883–1956), British military leader. Serving as an intelligence officer in the Mediterranean theater of operations in the Royal Army during World War I, Deedes became intimately involved with efforts to obtain a statement of British support for Zionism. Deedes remained a supporter of the WZO, acting as an adviser to the Zionist Commission in 1918 and as chief secretary to High Commissioner Sir Herbert Samuel from 1920 to 1923. He continued to support British fulfillment of the Balfour Declaration as a member of Parliament. In 1943 Deedes founded the British Association for a Jewish National Home (which became the Anglo-Israel Friendship Association in 1948), an organization he chaired until his death in 1956. > see also: **World War I**.

Dugdale, Blanch E. C. (Baffy, 1890–1948), English political activist and adviser to WZO president Chaim Weizmann. Dugdale was a niece of British foreign secretary Arthur James Balfour and became involved in Zionist activities almost simultaneously with her uncle. A staunch supporter of Britain's promises to the Jews, Dugdale was a tireless activist on the *Yishuv*'s behalf in the corridors of power in Whitehall. From 1940 to her death in 1948, Dugdale served as chairwoman of the Political Department of the Jewish Agency London Executive. Dugdale was also a strident advocate of immediate activity to rescue European Jewry during the Holocaust. > see also: **Sochnut Yehudit**.

Eliot, George (pseud. Mary Ann Evans, 1819–1880), English novelist and prominent proto-Zionist. Evans's most important Jewish work was the last novel she completed, *Daniel Deronda* (serialized 1874–1876). The book tells the story of an English political leader who, upon discovering his Jewish identity, emigrates to *Eretz Israel* in order to revive Jewry's ancestral homeland. Furthermore, Evans was a energetic enemy of antisemitism, for example, in her essay "The New Hep-Hep" (1878). Although her influence was limited to literary circles, her books inspired Jewish authors including Eliezer Ben-Yehuda and Peretz Smolenskin, among others. > see also: *Daniel Deronda*.

Finn, James (1806–1872), British politician and diplomat. One of the earliest modern pioneers of Jewish restoration in Great Britain, Finn served as consul general in Jerusalem between 1845 and 1862. A devoted philosemite, Finn saw his role as protecting the Jews from Ottoman persecution while also promoting British imperial interests in the Middle East. Although his Zionist commitment derived from his belief that Jews would ultimately convert to Christianity, his retirement was greeted with sadness in the Jewish community in Jerusalem. They sent a profound letter of thanks to the British Foreign Ministry for his services. A volume of his writings on the Jews of *Eretz Israel* was published posthumously as *Stirring Times* (1878).

Frederick of Baden (1826–1907), German statesman and grand duke of Baden. Frederick inherited his father's throne in 1852 and ruled until his death. Expressing sympathy for the Zionist cause from the beginning, Frederick acted as a go between for Theodor Herzl and Kaiser Wilhelm II (who was his nephew). Frederick remained a supporter of Herzl's throughout and was the main reason Wilhelm II agreed to meet the WZO leader in 1898.

Galaction, Gala (pseud. Grigore Pişculescu, 1879–1961), Romanian novelist. Considered one of Romania's greatest literary figures, Galaction included sympathetically drawn Jewish characters in almost all of his writings: two of his novels, *Roxana* (1930) and *Papucii lui Mahmud* (1932), dealt with antisemitism and the persecution of Jews by (respectively) Christians and Muslims; *Scisori către Simforoza* (1930) dealt with the future of the Jewish national home. An early supporter of Theodor Herzl's, Galaction continued his support for Jewish and Zionist causes during the fascist regime, when such positions were dangerous.

Grauel, George (b. 1917), American cleric. Grauel's family was active in the Catholic Church, and he was ordained into the priesthood in 1943. As a young clergyman, Grauel was shocked at news of the extermination of European Jewry that increasingly appeared in the U.S. press toward the end of World War II. In late 1944 he attended an American Zionist conference vowing that he would dedicate himself to Zionist fulfillment; thereafter he worked as a recruiter for the Hagana (1945–1946) and as an emissary for the Mossad le-Aliya Bet. In 1947, Graule joined the crew of the *Exodus 1947*, earning the unofficial title of chaplain to the *Ma'apilim*. Grauel has remained active in Israel-related causes since 1948, although he retired from the pulpit in 1977. > see also: **Aliya Bet**.

Hay, John (1838–1905), U.S. statesman. Hay served as secretary of state during the McKinley and Roosevelt administrations (1898–1905). During his tenure, he took an active role in protesting Russian and Romanian antisemitism. Hay also pursued an active interest in Jewish restoration to the Holy Land, seeing that as one way to solve the Jewish problem in Eastern Europe.

Hechler, William H. (1845–1931), Anglo-German religious figure and author. The son of Christian missionaries (his father was German and his mother English) working in India, Hechler also chose the life of a missionary upon graduation from seminary in 1871. After a three-year ministry in

William Hechler, Christian Missionary and Gentile Zionist.
Courtesy of the Central Zionist Archives, Jerusalem

Nigeria, he returned to Germany and became the tutor to Frederick of Baden's children. Between 1885 and 1910 Hechler served as chaplain to the British embassy in Vienna. During this period he developed a strong conviction that the messianic era was imminent and that the messiah's arrival required that Jews live in *Eretz Israel*. His apocalyptic position led Hechler to strongly support Hibbat Zion and, later, Theodor Herzl. In 1884 Hechler wrote *The Restoration of the Jews*, in which he predicted that the messiah would come in 1897 or 1898. Herzl's movement seemed to fit that prediction, convincing Hechler that further action was needed. Hechler used his influence to obtain a meeting with Frederick of Baden for Herzl, with the further hope of an eventual meeting with Kaiser Wilhelm II. Hechler attended all the Zionist congresses of the Herzl era and was a frequent contributor to the WZO's publication, *Die Welt*. Hechler joined Herzl for the latter's meeting with the kaiser in Jerusalem in 1898 and was with Herzl when he died. Hechler continued to support Zionist causes until his own death. Interestingly, despite Hechler's mystical approach and his missionary background he never appears to have tried to use his contacts with Zionists as a forum for proselytizing among Jews.

Koenig, Marie Pierre (1898–1970), French military leader. An early and ardent supporter of continued French resistance to the Nazis, Koenig became commander of Free French forces in North Africa in 1942. During the disastrous debacle that spring and summer, Koenig's troops held out in their fortress of Bir Hakheim until forced to withdraw. At that time Koenig came into contact with Jewish military units from the *Yishuv*. Impressed with their heroism in the common anti-Nazi struggle, Koenig became a dedicated supporter of Jewish causes. In 1944 Koenig served as a corps commander, his units being the first to enter liberated Paris on August 25, 1944. In 1945 and 1946 Koenig served as commander in chief in the French zone of occupation in Germany. As such he permitted the Briha and Mossad le-Aliya Bet to operate openly in this part of Germany, thus helping to build further pressure on the British to open the gates of Palestine/*Eretz Israel*. > see also: **World War II; Aliya Bet; Briha**.

Lie, Trygve (1896–1968), Norwegian statesman and political leader. Elected to parliament as a Labor party representative in 1935, Lie was an earnest opponent of fascism and antisemitism in all their manifestations. Lie fled Norway during the Nazi occupation and served as acting foreign minister for the Norwegian government in exile. In 1946 Lie was elected the first secretary-general of the U.N. General Assembly. As such, he oversaw the creation of the U.N. Special Committee on Palestine (UNSCOP) which proposed partition in November 1947. Lie strongly supported the Zionist case at the U.N. and was willing to forgive Jewish lobbying efforts that some delegates found heavy-handed. Lie also oversaw the abortive U.N. effort to mediate Israel's War of Independence in 1948 and efforts to create a real Arab-Israeli peace after the war ended in 1949. Lie resigned from the secretariat in 1953 after a dispute with the Soviet delegation over the Korean Conflict. > see also: **United Nations**.

Lloyd George, David (1863–1945), British statesman and prime minister. A leading light of the Liberal party, Lloyd George served in a variety of cabinet posts prior to World War I, ascending to the premiership after the Asquith cabinet fell in 1916 (after the so-called Munitions Scandal). Lloyd George was an early and ardent supporter of Zionism, support that manifested itself during his tenure as prime minister. The proposal for the cabinet to sponsor a declaration of support for Zionism had previously stalled but was renewed almost immediately after Lloyd George took office. Lloyd George was convinced that a Jewish national home was a historic necessity and that every opportunity should be granted to Jewry to re-create a Jewish state. Lloyd George's position paralleled that of his foreign minister, Arthur James Balfour, and led to the Balfour Declaration issued on November 2, 1917. Lloyd George continued to support the Zionist cause after his public

career ended in 1922. In particular, his testimony before the Peel Commission in 1937 led that body to propose the creation of a Jewish state in a partitioned Palestine/*Eretz Israel*. > see also: **Balfour Declaration; Committees of Investigation, Peel Commission**.

Lowdermilk, Walter C. (1888–1974), American agronomist and author. Widely acclaimed as an expert on soil preservation, Lowdermilk served as assistant chief of the U.S. Soil Conservation Service for most of the 1940s. In 1944 Lowdermilk was commissioned by the American Zionist Emergency Council to undertake a study of soil and water resources in Palestine/*Eretz Israel*. He did so, publishing his findings as *Palestine: Land of Promise*. In the book, Lowdermilk proposed creation of a "Jordan Valley Authority" (patterned on the Tenessee Valley Authority) to allocate water resources and aid in irrigation. The book was important to Zionists mainly because Lowdermilk estimated that, if properly irrigated, *Eretz Israel* could maintain a population of approximately 10 million, meaning that Arab claims of hardship caused by *aliya* were wildly exaggerated. Lowdermilk continued to work on behalf of the Zionist movement and the State of Israel after 1948. > see also: **Eleventh Commandment**.

Lyne, Joseph L. (Father Ignatius, 1837–1908), English Catholic leader and monastic organizer. Father Ignatius used his oratorical skill as an ardent supporter of Hibbat Zion and, after 1897, Theodor Herzl's World Zionist Orgaization.

Masaryk, Jan G. (1886–1948), Czech political leader and statesman. The only son of Thomas G. Masaryk, Czechoslovakia's founding father, Masaryk inherited his father's charisma and dedication to democratic government; he also inheritted his father's close and friendly relationship with Jews and especially the Zionist movement. From 1925 to 1938 Masaryk served as Czech ambassador to England, a post he used to help defend the *Yishuv*'s interests. In 1938 Masaryk resigned after the Munich Conference, when the Anglo-French coalition pressured the Czechs to make unilateral concessions to Nazi Germany in order to prevent a war (that broke out one year later). He predicted dire consequences for Jews from the Allied policy of appeasement, a prediction that largely came true when the Germans overran Czechoslovakia, Europe headed toward war, and most countries closed their doors in the face of desperate Jewish refugees. Masaryk served as foreign minister of the Czech government in exile (1940–1945), a position that allowed him to closely monitor the murder of European Jewry. The Holocaust further convinced Masaryk of the justice of the Zionist cause and he remained a close ally of Zionist leaders throughout the war. Masaryk retained the position of foreign minister in the provisional coalition government created in 1945. In this post Masaryk was extremely helpful to the Zionist cause, since it was he who ordered Czech border guards to ignore the Briha movement, thereby allowing Jews fleeing Eastern Europe to get to safety in preparation for *aliya* (legal or illegal). Masaryk was killed on March 10, 1948, apparently by Communist activists intent on completing their takeover of Czechoslovakia. > see also: **Briha**.

Masaryk, Thomáš G. (1850–1937), Czech educator and statesman. Widely respected as a statesman, Masaryk is widely considered Czechoslovakia's father. He was appointed president pro tem of the Czechoslovakian provisional government upon its creation in 1918. Masaryk was reelected to the Czech presidency three times, and he personally oversaw the flourishing of democratic principles in the Czechoslovak republic. He was also a earnest philosemite and supporter of Zionism and other Jewish causes. Masaryk retired from the Czech presidency in 1935 because of ill health.

McDonald, James G. (1886–1964), American educator and diplomat. McDonald gained prominence as the president of the Foreign Policy Association, a public educational body that was dedicated to breaking America out of its isolationist orientation, between 1919 and 1933. In 1933 he was appointed high commissioner for refugees by the League of Nations, a position that brought McDonald into direct

contact with the Jewish problem. McDonald resigned his post in 1935 as a protest against the apathy of the world to the plight of the Jewish refugees; in his letter of resignation he also accused the Germans of planning a racial war against Jewry. During his tenure as high commissioner, McDonald came into contact with Zionist leaders and was impressed with the important role the *Yishuv* was prepared to play in aiding refugees. He frequently advocated opening the doors of *Eretz Israel* as the only way to solve the European refugee crisis. McDonald remained a staunch critic of U.S. rescue policy during World War II, repeatedly calling for bold action to rescue Jews. After the war, McDonald served on the Anglo-American Committee of Inquiry, where he advocated the immediate entry of 100,000 Holocaust survivors to *Eretz Israel*, a proposal that the committee adopted. McDonald continued to support the Zionist cause at international fora in 1947 and 1948. He was nominated to be the first U.S. ambassador to the new State of Israel, a post he held until retirement in 1951. Thereafter he devoted most of his time to the sale of Israel bonds. McDonald's memoirs, *My Mission to Israel*, were published in 1953. > see also: **Committees of Inquiry, Anglo-American Committee**.

Meinertzhagen, Richard H. (1878–1967), British military administrator and officer. Meiertzhagen served in various staff positions during World War I, ending the war on General Edmund Allenby's staff during the Palestine campaign (1917–1918). After the war Meinertzhagen acted as senior political officer to the Occupied Enemy Territories Administration (OETA) for Palestine/*Eretz Israel* and Syria. In this capacity Meinertzhagen witnessed firsthand both Zionist development of the *Yishuv* and the duplicity of OETA officers charged with helping to build a Jewish national home but actually subverting the Balfour Declaration's promises. When OETA was disbanded, Meinertzhagen remained in *Eretz Israel* as a military affairs adviser to High Commissioner Sir Herbert Samuel. Retiring from that position in 1924, he then served as a Middle East affairs expert in the Colonial Office, where he helped to overturn the

Passfield White Paper in 1931. Meinertzhagen continued to support Zionist causes after his retirement from public service. He published a memoir, *Middle East Diary, 1917–1956* (1959), that set out to correct much of the misinformation about British policy toward the Jewish national home. > see also: **Occupied Enemy Territories Administration**.

Niebuhr, Reinhold (1892–1971), German/American Lutheran theologian. Hitler's rise to power and the persecution of German Jewry had a powerful impact on Niebuhr who was born in Germany but was forced to flee his homeland. Niebuhr was perhaps best known for his argument that Jews, like other people, had two sets of rights: the right to citizenship in the state of their residence and the right to organize their collective (ethnic) identity as they saw fit. Active in promoting rescue efforts for persecuted European Jews during the 1930s, Niebuhr came to support the creation of a Jewish national home as a means of ending Jewish homelessness. He did not, however, support the creation of a Jewish state and ceased active support for Zionism after the State of Israel was created.

Newlinski, Philipp M. (1841–1899), Polish journalist and diplomat. Born in Austrian Poland, Newlinski was trained as a journalist but served as a staff member at the Austro-Hungarian embassy in Constantinople (Istanbul). In 1880 Newlinski left diplomatic service, returning to journalism in Paris and Vienna. In Vienna Theodor Herzl first contacted Newlinski, hoping to use his contacts in the Turkish capital as a means to obtain a meeting with the sultan. Newlinski agreed and also acted to obtain support for Zionism in the Vatican and in German diplomatic circles, with little success. He did manage to arrange meetings between Herzl and senior Ottoman officials in 1898, but these did not open *Eretz Israel* to mass Jewish settlement as Herzl had hoped. Newlinski was engaged in yet another diplomatic initiative in Constantinople, and had returned to Europe to brief Herzl on the little progress that he had made, when he died suddenly.

Oliphant, Lawrence (1829–1888), English scholar and explorer. The author of a series of popular travel books, Oliphant became interested in the Middle East in the wake of the Russo-Turkish war that was ended by the Congress of Berlin in 1878. Simultaneously, Oliphant became aware of the increasing pressure on Eastern European Jewry. Concluding that Turkey had to be supported in order to prevent Russian domination of the Near East, Oliphant proposed settling Jews in Ottoman territories en masse. He felt that such settlements would revive the Ottoman Empire's failing economy while providing a haven for persecuted Jews. Oliphant's plan, which he dubbed the Gilead Scheme, was based on the premise of Jewish settlement on both sides of the Jordan River in the northern parts of what today are the State of Israel and the Hashemite Kingdom of Jordan. Oliphant's scheme was originally proposed in 1879 but was rejected by Sultan Abdul Hamid III. The pogroms in Russia in 1881 merely convinced Oliphant that his ideas were sound. The pogroms also brought him into contact with the Hibbat Zion movement, which he supported for the rest of his life. In his last years Oliphant settled in Haifa, living and working to bring his dream to reality until the very end.

Parkes, James W. (1896–1977), British scholar and theologian. Parkes was ordained by the Church of England in 1926 and witnessed the rise of antisemitism firsthand. Parkes' most significant scholarly contributions were his studies on antisemitism and on the church's role in persecuting Jews during the Middle Ages. Parkes's appreciation of antisemitism led him to a keen support for Zionism. He never wavered in his belief that *Eretz Israel* belonged to the Jewish people and that a Jewish state was a necessity to right the historic wrong created during two millennia in which Jews were mistreated by their non-Jewish neighbors (Chrisitian and Muslim alike). Parkes set out his views on Zionism and the State of Israel in his book *Whose Land? A History of the Peoples of Palestine* (1970).

Patterson, John H. (1867–1947), British military commander and author. Of Protestant Irish descent, Patterson was raised with a strong belief in the Bible. Entering the army, Patterson served in command positions during the Boer War and World War I. In 1915 he was appointed commander of the Zion Mule Corps and later of the Jewish Legion. Seeing the Jewish legionnaires at their best impressed Patterson with the heroic nature of Jewish nationalism, to which cause he became immediately and strongly attached. After the war Patterson maintained close connections with the Zionist leadership and particularly with Ze'ev Jabotinsky. Patterson strongly opposed the British policy changes of the 1930s, which he saw as abandoning Britain's sacred promises to the Jews, and he condemned the White Paper of 1939 in unequivocal terms. During World War II Patterson used his influence to gain cabinet approval for independent Jewish military participation, advocacy that culminated in the creation of the Jewish Brigade Group in 1944. > see also: **World War I**; **World War II**.

Scott, Charles P. (1846–1932), British journalist and editor. Scott served in Parliament as a Liberal between 1895 and 1906, a period of intense agitation in England to limit immigration (mainly Jewish immigration) from eastern and southern Europe. While serving as an MP, Scott also edited the liberal daily, *Manchester Guardian*. Scott first became aware of the Zionist movement during a dinner party for Chaim Weizmann in September 1914; he later became thoroughly convinced of the justice of the Zionist cause and its compatibility with Britain's imperial interests. Scott used his contacts within the Liberal party to arrange meetings between Weizmann and many of the key British political leaders of the day, including David Lloyd George (who assumed the premiership in 1917) and Arthur J. Balfour. Scott ardently supported the creation of the Jewish Legion and used his newspaper as a means to enlist wide support for Zionism in British public circles. Scott remained committed to his Zionist position until his death and was mourned as a staunch defender of the *Yishuv*.

Smuts, Jan C. (1870–1950), South African military and political leader. A leader of the Boers during the war against Great Britain, Smuts was one of the leading negotiators during the peace talks held in 1902. In 1910 he was appointed minister of defense in the dominion government led by Louis Botha. During World War I, Smuts led the Anglo-Indian forces in East Africa and was appointed to the Imperial War Conference (IWC) in 1917. Apparently while participating in the IWC, Smuts came into contact with the Zionist idea and he became an ardent supporter of a Jewish national home. He strongly advocated the Balfour Declaration and continued to support British assistance in creating a Jewish national home during the 1920s and 1930s. Smuts fervently advocated action to rescue European Jewry during the Holocaust and opposed the White Paper of 1939. During World War II, Smuts acted as an adviser to Prime Minister Winston S. Churchill and sought to move the latter to support overturning the white paper. After World War II Smuts continued to support Zionist calls for the creation of a Jewish state and was largely responsible for South Africa's strong backing of the U.N. partition resolution in 1947.

Truman, Harry S. (1884–1972), American statesman, political leader, and thirty-third president of the United States. Truman became involved in Democratic party politics at a relatively mature age, becoming a senator in 1934 (at age fifty). Franklin D. Roosevelt chose Truman as his running mate in 1944, and he succeeded to the presidency upon Roosevelt's death in April 1945. Despite claims that Truman's support for a Jewish state after World War II was nothing more than an electoral ploy (a canard that was already propounded by the British government in 1947 and 1948) the evidence is that Truman supported Zionism out of conviction. His humanitarian impulse led him to champion activities to rescue European Jewry from the Nazis, while his contacts within the Kansas City Jewish community led him to early and active opposition to antisemitism. These two impulses also created Truman's feeling of sympathy for Zionism and his willingness to help promote the establishment of a Jewish state in 1948. It is now widely accepted that Truman's repeated interventions against his own State Department and his immediate recognition of Israel on May 14, 1948, prevented anti-Zionist and Arabist advocates in the U.S. foreign service from aborting the creation of the State of Israel. > see also: **Hershel Ish Emet**.

Van Paassen, Pierre (1895–1968), Dutch-American journalist. Van Paassen was perhaps the most fervent Gentile Zionist of his era. A fervent Calvinist, van Paassen obtained his first ideas about Jewish restoration from the Bible. He became strongly attached to the modern Zionist movement after a 1925 trip to *Eretz Israel*. His lifelong commitment to the Zionist cause manifested itself especially during the 1930s and 1940s, when van Paassen worked tirelessly to rouse sympathy for Jews suffering from Nazi and Nazi-inspired persecution. Van Paassen strongly believed that the only way to solve the refugee problem was to open the gates of *Eretz Israel* for mass *aliya*. Van Paassen's book, *The Forgotten Ally* (1943), brought considerable pressure to bear on the Allies to create an independent Jewish fighting force that culminated in the creation of the Jewish Brigade Group. > see also: **World War II**.

Wedgwood, Josiah C. (1872–1943), British statesman, political leader, and author. Wedgwood became aware of the Zionist movement during World War I. While serving at Gallipoli, Wedgwood met troops of the Zion Mule Corps and was impressed by the arguments on behalf of a Jewish national home. After the war, Wedgwood remained a staunch supporter of Zionist causes. Closely identified with Ze'ev Jabotinsky, Wedgwood nonetheless steered clear of internal Zionist politics. Active in Parliament (where he served as a Labour representative), Wedgwood led the fights against the Passfield White Paper in 1930–1931 and the MacDonald White Paper in 1939. During the 1930s, Wedgwood proposed that Britain take the initiative in establishing an independent Jewish state that would become England's "seventh dominion" and would help anchor British imperial interests in the Middle East. In addition to his Zionst advocacy, Wedgwood was one of the staunchest advocates of rescuing German Jewry during the Nazi era. > see also: **World War I**; **Seventh Dominion Scheme**.

Wilson, Woodrow (1856–1924), American educator, statesman, and twenty-eighth president of the United States. Wilson was elected president in 1912 and was reelected in 1916. Wilson was a supporter of many liberal causes and was especially opposed to anti-semitism. Wilson appointed Justice Louis D. Brandeis to the U.S. Supreme Court, and it is apparently from Brandeis that Wilson first learned about Zionism. Once the United States entered World War I (in April 1917), Wilson became aware of the British cabinet's discussion of a possible pro-Zionist pronouncement. Wilson supported such an act by the Entente, seeing the creation of a Jewish national home as a means to right the historic wrong of Jewish homelessness. He used his popularity among Europeans to ensure, among other things, that the Jewish issue was not ignored at the Paris Peace Conference in 1919. Wilson hoped to obtain U.S. membership in the League of Nations as a means to promote human rights and peaceful relations between countries, but his hopes were dashed in 1919. Wilson suffered a stroke in October 1919 and retired from public office after the Republicans won the presidential election in 1920. > see also: **Balfour Declaration; League of Nations**.

Wingate, Orde Charles (1903–1944), British military officer. Considered one of the greatest modern British practitioners of irregular warfare, Wingate was born in India and served as a staff officer in Palestine during the Arab Revolt (1936–1939). Wingate, who had been shunned as eccentric by many peers, soon found a deep bond with the *Yishuv*, the Zionist movement, and the Jewish people. In 1936 he convinced his superiors to allow him to organize the Special Night Squads (SNS) to combat Arab marauders who struck while regular British troops were huddled in their barracks. The SNS was composed of a core of British officers leading Jewish personnel.

Many of the Hagana's senior commanders considered Wingate their mentor, a reality that soon earned him the nickname "ha-Yedid." Changing attitudes within the British high command in Palestine/*Eretz Israel* meant that Wingate's Zionist contacts were soon considered a liability. He was transferred out of the country early in 1939, vowing to return to lead the Jewish state's army in the future. Wingate served with distinction as commander of Gideon Force, a commando unit composed of many of his Jewish cronies from the SNS that fought the Italians in Ethiopia, and as commander of the Chindits, the long-range penetration force that fought in Burma. Wingate was killed in an airplane crash on March 24, 1944, during the second Chindit operation in Burma. > see also: **Gideon Force**; **Ha-Yedid**; **Special Nights Squads**; **Yishuv, Yishuv Organizations (Underground Organizations, Hagana)**.

Geula [גאולה, H] "Redemption": Traditional Hebrew term used as the polar opposite of both *Gola* and *Galut*. The term implies an end of the exile and a return to Zion; it also implies a complete restoration of Jewish sovereignty in *Eretz Israel*. The term resonates throughout Jewish ritual and prayers, representing the long-held Jewish hope for eventual restoration. The Zionist movement used the term to reflect its main goal: liquidation of the diaspora and a Jewish return to the council of nations. > see also: **Galut**; **Gola**.

Ghaffir [גפיר, T/Slang] "Copper": Turkish slang term for a police officer used by the *Yishuv* in the 1920s and early 1930s to designate the Jewish Supernumerary Police (JSP). The JSP were auxiliary police recruited, mainly from the Hagana's ranks, to assist in defending isolated Jewish settlements from Arab marauders. The term derived from the Turkish-style uniforms issued to the JSP, specifically, referring to the fez hat that topped the uniform. After 1936 the JSP was greatly expanded, although the term *Ghaffir* was used more rarely by that time, being

replaced in common usage by the Hebrew term Noter (police officer). > see also: **Notrim**; **Yishuv, Organizations (Underground Organizations, Hagana)**.

Gideon Force [HT]: Colloquial name for the unit of British and other personnel assembled by Major Charles Orde Wingate to participate in the liberation of Ethiopia. Gideon Force's major component was a troop of Hagana members who had been trained by Wingate and fought under his command in the Special Night Squads during the Arab Revolt. Wingate named the unit after the biblical judge, Gideon, who saved the Israelites from a Midianite invasion by using guerrilla warfare tactics. Wingate, whose own interests lay in unconventional operations, saw himself as an heir to Gideon and also saw the name as emphasizing his close connection with Jews and Zionism. Gideon Force was used in 1941 as a guerrilla force operating behind Italian lines and was successful in liberating Addis Ababa on April 5, 1941. Despite this success, Gideon Force's history was a source of deep personal frustration for Wingate. He was not permitted to return to Palestine/*Eretz Israel* and the force was disbanded after the Ethiopian campaign ended. > see also: **Ha-Yedid**; **Special Night Squads**; **Gentile Zionism**.

Giyus Hutz la-Aretz [גיוס חוץ לארץ, H] (Gahal, גח"ל) "Foreign Conscription": Official term for the conscription into the fledgling Zva ha-Hagana le-Israel (Zahal) of some 19,000 European and North African Jews. The bulk of Gahal conscripts were Holocaust survivors, mainly survivors of concentration camps, but also a sprinkling of former Jewish partisans. A miniscule proportion of Gahal conscripts were personnel who had served in Allied armies (mainly the Soviet Red Army) during World War II. The latter included personnel who had been liberated from German prisoner of war camps and were still in western or southern Europe. Most Gahal troops were poorly trained and even more poorly equipped, but they made up for their lack of military skills with a considerable degree of fortitude and high degree of fanaticism. They saw themselves as avenging the Holocaust and thereby vindicating Jewish honor. Many of the conscripts gave their lives on behalf of a country they were fated never to even see. The use of such conscripts reflected the dire straights in which Israel found itself during the early days of the War of Independence — conditions that required the immediate use of personnel not otherwise ready for combat. As a result, casualties were high but should not be exaggerated. At its height Gahal represented one-fifth of the available Zahal personnel. > see also: **Mitnadvei Hutz la-Aretz; Zva ha-Hagana le-Israel; War of Independence**.

Gola [גולה, H] "Diaspora": Traditional term for Jewish existence outside of *Eretz Israel*. Although less prejorative than the parallel term, *Galut*, *Gola* nevertheless retains strongly negative implications. In particular, *Gola* implied both personal alienation and communal powerlessness. > see also: **Galut; Shlilat ha-Gola; Zionut**.

Golden Book [HT]: Keren Kayemet le-Israel (KKL) term for the book(s) in which key events in the donors' lives (and the lives of their families) were recorded. Each key date was recorded by a donation to the KKL; the donor and the honoree were recognized in the golden book. The idea was to establish a means for regular donations by Jews who sought recognition for their assistance and were able afford to more than just the few coins most donors were able to put into the KKL's blue boxes. Although no longer arranged as an individual book, the KKL continues to accept this type of donations to this day. > see also: **Blue Box; Organizations, Zionist (International, Keren Kayemet le-Israel)**.

Golusjude [G] "Diaspora Jew": Derisive Zionist term used (with minor linguistic variations) by activists to identify the "old" style of Jew who needed fixing. In particular, Zionists argued that Jews living in the diaspora were unable to show self-respect, slavishly appeasing the Gentile society in which they lived while concentrating in a few relatively limited and nonproductive fields of economic endeavor. This policy, however, had the opposite effect than the one hoped for: instead of bringing pity and compassion, the Jews' behavior brought out enmity, scorn, and the epithet "parasites." As an alternative to this ultimately self-destructive Jewish lifestyle, the Zionists proposed the creation of a "new" Jew who would abandon the traits of the diaspora entirely. The "new" Jew would be proud, unafraid to defend himself or herself, and would work in productive economic activities (mostly agriculture). In net effect, therefore, Zionists proposed the creation of a virtually new Jewish civilization that would eliminate all of the diaspora's ill effects on Jewish youth. > see also: **Shlilat ha-Gola**.

Gradualism: Zionist policy adopted during the mandatory era by supporters of a moderate pace of Zionist development. Gradualism meant that the Jewish National home should should be built at a steady but initially slow speed. After many decades, Jews would constitute a majority of *Eretz Israel*'s population and then demand a more rapid pace of development. Supporters of gradualism, most notably Chaim Weizmann, hoped that this policy would mute any potential conflict of interest between the *Yishuv* and the British administration while also giving Arabs "adequate" time to to come to terms with Jewish statehood. Opponents, including Ze'ev Jabotinsky, argued that the very timetable implied Zionist abandonment of responsibility for saving European Jewry before a catastrophe (which Jabotinsky had predicted since 1915) struck. A majority of Zionist parties and leaders supported Weizmann's approach during the 1920s. By the 1930s conditions had changed so much, especially after the Nazi rise to power, that many Zionists (e.g., David Ben-Gruion) abandoned part or all of the gradualist approach. After the 1942 Biltmore Conference, gradualism ceased to be a tenet of Zionist policy. > see also: **Biltmore Resolution; Shem ha-Meforash**.

Grand Sanhedrin [F] "Great Sanhedrin": Official name for the seventy-one-member

Jewish body convened by Napoleon Bonaparte between February 4 and March 9, 1807. The Sanhedrin's purpose was to confirm the prior assembly of notables' responses to Napoleon's questions about Jewish assimilation, acculturation, and nationalism. The Sanhedrin verified that Jews do not consider themselves a national group but did not clearly repudiate the idea of Jewish unity as a religious community. The terms of the Sanhedrin's decisions, however, deterred later Zionist development in France and Western Europe. > See also: **Emancipation; Assimilation.**

Gush [גוש, H] "Bloc": Hebrew term used for a group of settlements. After the 1929 Arab riots, when Hagana forces proved unable to respond to the threat, Zionist settlement policy changed radically. Instead of building a single settlement and letting it develop, henceforth a group of nearby settlements were all built simultaneously (thus creating a bloc effect) and in sufficiently close proximity to be mutually supporting. In particular, Hagana units in any part of the bloc could respond rapidly to threats from any quarter. Threatened sectors could thereby be rapidly reinforced without depleting the Hagana's small mobile reserve. The Hagana was entirely reorganized into blocs between 1938 and 1941, but was further reorganized thereafter to emphasize mobility. Nonetheless, settlement in blocs continued well after the establishment of the State of Israel.

Gush Etzion [גוש אציון, H] "The Etzion Bloc": Name for the bloc of Jewish settlements in the Hebron mountains, located fifteen miles (24 KM) south of Jerusalem. The bloc's four settlements were Kfar Etzion, Ein Zurim, Revadim, and Masu'ot Yizhak. All were established during World War II on the site of a previously abandoned Jewish settlement. Because of its strategic location on the Jerusalem-Hebron road, Gush Etzion became a major battlefield during Israel's War of Independence. Arab irregulars who ambushed a supply column (the so-called Lamed Heh) on January 15, 1948, thereafter besieged the settlements. Communication between the settlements and Jerusalem were severed completely om March 27, 1948. Kfar Etzion fell to Arab irregulars supported by armored cars of the Arab Legion on May 13, 1948, and resulted in the massacre of 250 Jewish soldiers and civilians. To prevent further massacres, the remianing settlements surrendered to the Arab Legion on May 14. The Gush Etzion settlements were rebuilt after the Six Day War. > see also: **Lamed-Heh; War of Independence.**

Gustav [PN/Slang]: Post-Holocaust Mossad le-Aliya Bet code term for Sweden, derived from the name of Sweden's King Gustav VI Adolph. The term may also have been applied (in the plural) to Swedish currency used by Mossad agents to purchase ships in Sweden. The Mossad was active among Jewish refugees in postwar Sweden, despatching the blockade runner SS *Haim Arlosoroff* with 1,348 *Ma'apilim* in February 1947.

H: Hagana term for sabotage, used primarily during the period of the revolt against Great Britain. The letter Het (ח) also was used to signify explosives. Both usages seem to derive from the Hebrew word for sabotage, *Habala* (חבלה). > see also: **Ha-Mered**.

זעקה לצבור !

רצוצים ומדוכאים אנו קבוצת יהודים הבלתי לגליים הנמצאים בארץ כבר שנים אחדות, פונים לצבור הרחב בזעקה גדולה ומרה, תקשיבו לזעקתנו זעקת אנשים מיואשים, נרדפים ומעונים. אנו מנותקים מנשינו וילדינו זה שנים. מכריזים שלא נוכל יותר לחיות בתנאים כאלה. עד מתי תמשך הצרה הזאת של עניינו ?

׳ זעקתנו היא זעקת אנשים מיואשים ואומללים, נשינו וילדינו סובלים יסורי גיהנם – הילדים אינם מכירים את אבותיהם, משפחות נשמדו ונהרסו במשך השנים הללו.

יהודים !

הזדעזעו לשמע הצרה הגדולה והאיומה הזאת ותעזרו לנו. אנו לא נוכל לשבת בחבוק ידים. מצב כזה לא יוכל להמשך. ואנו הכרזנו מהיום יום א׳ ל׳ גיטן (1 במאי) משע״ג 12

שביתת רעב

עד שינתן לנו רשיונות עליה

נפגין את אסוננו וידע הצבור כלו על עניינו׃

Call for Support in a Hunger Strike Organized by *Ma'apilim* **Seeking Immigrant Certificates.**
Courtesy of the Central Zionist Archives, Jerusalem

Ha'apala [העפלה, H] "Striving": Alternative Zionist term for "illegal" immigration. Unlike the term *Aliya Bet*, which emphasizes organized activity, *Ha'apala* is used to encompass both organized and spontaneous activity. Furthermore, *Ha'apala* emphasizes the actions of the *Ma'apilim* as actors in their own rescue. > see also: **Aliya Bet**.

Ha-Aretz [הארץ, H] "The Land": Common Hebrew term for *Eretz Israel*, used without any more than the implied geographic specificity: "The Land" must be the Land of Israel much as "The Book" must be the Bible. The term obviously also implies the close connection between the Jewish people and *Eretz Israel*, again with no need for more than implied specificity. > see also: **Ha-Makom**.

Ha-Askola ha-Yerushalmi [האסקולה הירושלמי, H] "The Jerusalem School": Term used by cultural historians to distinguish the first generation of scholars and faculty members at Hebrew University's Institute for Jewish Studies. Active from the 1920s to the 1940s, the term offers ex post facto recognition to the fact that this particular group of faculty — which included Max Margolis (Bible), Yitzhak F. Baer (medieval Jewish history), Joseph Klausner (literature and ancient Jewish history), Hanoch Albeck (rabbinics), and Gershom Scholem (Jewish mysticism) — undertook scholarly activity both as an intellectual pursuit and as a derivative of their Zionist views. Mainly they saw the creation of a vibrant Jewish culture in *Eretz Israel* as part and parcel of Jewish national rebirth. The term is used as a parallel to the so-called Frankfort School of German academia of the ninteenth century (identified, for example, with Professor Leopold von Ranke). Like the Frankfort School, the Jerusalem School was identified with philosophical positivism and with an attempt to fuse scholarship and national culture. Unlike the Frankfort School, no single form of scholarship predominated in Jerusalem, exemplifying the wide range of interests of the Hebrew University Faculty. > see also: **Hebrew University**.

Ha'avara [העברה, H] *"Transfer"*: The agreement between German Jewish leaders and the treasury of the Third Reich under which Jews could emigrate to Palestine/ *Eretz Israel* and receive a percentage of their capital in the form of German-produced goods. Signed in August 1933, the agreement met with stiff opposition from Jewish groups that advocated an economic boycott of Nazi Germany. German Jews, however, supported the agreement, since it was the only way for them to get out of Germany without being reduced to penury. In 1935 the World Zionist Congress debated the Ha'avara agreement and decided to maintain it, although thenceforth it was placed under the oversight of the Jewish Agency Executive. It has been estimated that as many as 50,000 Jews entered Palestine under the Ha'avara agreement between 1933 and 1939. Even so, the Ha'avara corporation experienced considerable difficulties in meeting its payments and was still reimbursing its German Jewish investors as late as 1951.

Ha-Bayit ha-Adom [הבית האדום, H] *"The Red House"*: Nickname for the building on ha-Yarkon Street in Tel Aviv that served as Hagana headquarters during the early stages Israel's War of Independence. The building had previously housed Mapai's Tel Aviv branch. The name derived from a coat of red paint applied to the walls sometime in

Sample *Ha'avara* Certificate.
Courtesy of the Jabotinsky Institute Archive, Tel Aviv

the 1940s. It did not, as is often hypothesized, derive from opponents' derisive remarks about Mapai members being secret Communists. The Hagana general staff moved into the building in 1947, but did not remain there for long. Just after the U.N. vote on partition, Hagana headquarters was moved to a building in Givatayim (a suburb of Tel Aviv). The building was demolished in the 1960s and the site is currently occupied by a hotel. > see also: **Zva ha-Hagana le-Israel**.

Ha-Biryonim [הבריונים, H] *"The Brigands"*: Hebrew term with no real translation, used in Hagana slang for former members of the Irgun Zvai Leumi (IZL) who returned to the Hagana after 1937. The term was used derisively, since it implied that the returnees had been members of a shadowy terrorist cell calling itself Brit ha-Biryonim but had lost their nerve for such tactics. > see also: **Yishuv, Yishuv Organizations (Underground Organizations)**.

Ha-Bo'er [הבוער, H] *"The Burning One"*: Hagana code name for Moshe Kleinbaum (Sneh) who served as chief of staff between

1941 and 1946. The term came from the biblical passage regarding the burning bush (Exodus 3:2). Since Kleinbaum used Sneh (= bush) as another of his code names the derivation made sense.

Hachshara [הכשרה, H] "Training program": Zionist term for an agricultural training school organized to prepare *halutzim* (pioneers) for eventual settlement in *Eretz Israel*. Each Zionist party established its own training programs, with the number of *Hachsharot* operating dependent on the number of youth group members in each specific locality. After 1920, *Hachsharot* fell under the authority of he-Halutz, in effect placing all Zionist youth movements under Mapai's supervision. This move, designed to standardize the training in all *Hachsharot*, led to considerable controversy. This was also reflected in the frequent protests over the way in which the JAE distributed immigrant certificates to *Hacshara* graduates. > see also: **Halutz**; **Halutzic Aliya**; **Bogrim**; **Certificates**; **Organizations, Zionist**.

Ha-Dabran [הדברן, H] "The Speaker": JA code name for Rabbi Abba Hillel Silver, the fiery leader of militant American Zionists and a JA representative at the U.N. founding conference in San Francisco. The term derived from Silver's well-known oratorical skills.

Hagana [הגנה, H] "Defense": > see also: **Yishuv, Yishuv Organizations (Underground Organizations, Hagana)**.

Hagana Temidit u-Peula Yeshira [הגנה תמידית ופעולה ישירה, H] "Continuous Defense and Direct Action" (HTPY, התפ"י): Slogan used by members of the *Yishuv* near the end of World War I to designate the future defensive needs of the Jewish national home. The decisions represented by HTPY were

Members of the *Hacshara* in Berdichev, Russia,
Before the Training Farm was Closed by Soviet Authorities in 1919.
Courtesy of the Central ZIonist Archives, Jerusalem

taken at a conference attended by members of ha-Shomer and an ad hoc group of watchmen from Tel Aviv-Jaffa (the so-called Jaffa group). Both groups agreed that the *Yishuv* needed a permanent defensive capability. Ha-Shomer, however, sought a localized agency while the Jaffa group wanted a centralized, *Yishuv*-wide defensive organization. Thus, despite agreement on principles, no organizational agreement was reached at this time. > see also: **Ha-Kevuza ha-Yafoit**; **Yishuv, Yishuv Organizations (Underground Organizations)**.

Hagana V, a code name for the Gdud ha-Avoda founded by Joseph Trumpeldor and used by that organization. > see also: **Yishuv, Yishuv Organizations (Underground Organizations, Gdud ha-Avoda)**.

Hagana Yemanit [הגנה ימנית, H] "Rightist Defense": One of numerous terms used by and about the Irgun Zvai Leumi (IZL) before it adopted its better known name. This term referred to disagreements between what eventually became the IZL and the Hagana over the latter's close relationship with the Histadrut. The special relationship was viewed as too partisan by many Betar members who therefore joined IZL. Other similar terms included Hagana Leumit (הגנה לאומית, Nationalist Hagana), Hagana B, and Irgun B (Organization Two), all of which implied that IZL was a dissident breakaway group from the Hagana. > see also: **Porshim**; **Yishuv, Yishuv Organizations (Underground Organizations)**.

Hagira [הגירה, H] "Migration": Hebrew term used in the sense of any Jewish migration not to Eretz Israel, regardless of whether or not the migrants were animated by a nationalist orientation. > see also: **Aliya**; **Territorialism**.

Ha-Givah [הגבעה, H] "The Hill": Hagana and Zva ha-Hagana le-Israel term for the building that housed the general staff during

the War of Independence. This building replaced the so-called Red House as operational headquarters in late 1947 and was located in Givatayim (a Tel Aviv suburb), near the border with Ramat Gan. In 1949 the building reverted to civilian use; it was converted into a high school shortly after the war ended. > see also: **Ha-Bayit ha-Adom**.

Hagshama Azmit [הגשמה עצמית, H] "Self-Fulfillment": Conceptual goal popular among Zionist youth groups, especially those representing pioneering movements. In this concept, broadly defined Zionist goals that speak of acting on behalf of all Jewry are reduced in relative importance as compared to the goal of making the individual member "whole." Talk of individualism and of personal fulfillment was most important to Zionist youth movements in Western Europe and the Americas. All talk of individual accomplishment was couched in terms of actions that would also help the collective, mainly *aliya* and settlement in a *Kibbutz*. > see also: **Halutz**; **Halutzic Aliya**.

Haham Bashi [T] "Chief Rabbi": Honorary title for the chief rabbi of Istanbul, ex officio the chief spiritual leader of the Jewish millet during the Ottoman Empire. The term is sometimes incorrectly identified with the term *Rishon le-Zion*, which properly referred only to the Sephardi chief rabbi of Palestine/*Eretz Israel*. > see also: **Millet System**; **Tanzimat**; **Rishon le-Zion**; **Rabanut Rashit**.

Ha-Hazan [החזן, H] "The Cantor": Hagana code name for Ahmed al-Imam, deriving from his last name (an imam is a Muslim religious leader who can lead prayer services). Al-Imam was close to the Mufti of Jerusalem but in 1948, provided information on Arab military dispositions to the Hagana's Sherut Yediot. > see also: **Arabs**.

Ha-Heder [החדר, H] "The Classroom": Hagana code name applied to several of the secret manufacturing facilities that constituted Ta'as, mainly those involved in producing hand grenades. Apparently the term was in use between 1933 and 1943 and came from the Jewish term for a traditional one-room school. Why this term was chosen to designate the Hagana's hand grenade factories is unclear. In all, four factories existed, located in the Tel Aviv and Givatayim. An explosion in the fourth factory on November 25, 1943, in which one person was killed, forced the Hagana to relocate its facilities and apparently also brought about a change in code terms. > see also: **Yishuv, Yishuv Organizations (Underground Organizations)**.

Ha-Lamed-Heh [הל״ה, H] "The Thirty-Five": Popular Israeli term for the platoon ambushed and slaughtered on January 15, 1948, during an abortive attempt to resupply the isolated settlements in Gush Etzion. The platoon was composed entirely of volunteers from the Hagana, Palmah, and Heyl Sadeh (Hish), most of whom were religious. Attempting to infiltrate Arab positions, the platoon was spotted by an elderly Arab shepherd. Although the troops did not harm him because he was a noncombattant, he raised the alarm and a pitched battle ensued. Fighting until their ammunition gave out, the survivors were killed in a vain attempt to surrender. > see also: **Gush Etzion; War of Independence**.

Haltstelle [G] "Station": Term used by Theodor Herzl's moderate supporters to explain their position on the Uganda scheme. Although appearing to be a setback for Zionism and a deviation from the Basel Program, Uganda was nothing more than a station along the path to a Jewish national home in *Eretz Israel*. > see also: **Nachtasyl; Notbau; Uganda Plan**.

Haluka [חלוקה, H] "Distribution": Term for the distribution of charity to Jews living in *Eretz Israel* before the advent of Zionism. Since many of the Jewish inhabitants of the Holy Land had come to study Jewish law and lore, the *Haluka* was a form of stipend provided by wealthy Jewish philanthropists living in the diaspora. Indirectly, *Haluka* also encouraged the continuing settlement of Jews in *Eretz Israel* and reflected Jewish concern with the territory's future. Nevertheless, *Haluka* was severely criticized by Zionists of all stripes, since it created a class of dependent Jews who could not live except by foreign (even if Jewish) charity. *Haluka* was seen as leaving the Jewish community at the mercy of rich philanthropists without creating a means to expand the Jewish economy or to create a national home. This stood precisely in opposition to everything Zionists claimed to believe in: the need to create a vital and vigorous Jewish society that would be able to care for itself without the need for charity. Zionists were not the only critics of *Haluka*; indeed, some of the rabbis overseeing the charity distribution recognized the negative aspects of *Haluka* and used some of the monies to purchase the land that became *Moshav* Petah Tikva. > see also: **Em ha-Moshavot; Agricultural Settlement(s)**.

Halutz [חלוץ, H] "Pioneer": Popular term for the young Zionists who moved to *Eretz Israel* in the years before Israel's independence. Prior to World War I, most *olim* were *halutzim*, that is, pioneers who settled on small agricultural settlements. These individuals saw themselves as an avant garde of Jewish national rebirth and also as the first generation of a new Jewish people who would return to the soil and to manual labor. During the period of the mandate, continued emphasis on *Halutzic Aliya*, especially within the *Kibbutz* movement, led to considerable controversy between socialist and nonsocialist Zionists: mainly between those who sought to limit *aliya* only to the young and healthy and those who sought the complete evacuation of European Jewry. > see also: **Halutzic Aliya; Aliya; Agricultural Settlement(s); Evacuation Plan; Hachshara**.

Halutzic Aliya [עליה חלוצית, H/Slang] "Pioneering Immigration": Neologism adapted from the two Hebrew words for pioneer and immigration and used in both English and Hebrew to designate a fundamental debate that wracked the Zionist movement during the 1920s and early 1930s: whether immigration to *Eretz Israel* ought to be limited to the young and healthy pioneers who could be trained for agricultural work or whether *aliya* ought to be available to any Jew regardless of age and health, regardless of the possible contribution (if any) of the *oleh* to the *Yishuv*. Broadly speaking, socialist Zionists and their allies adopted the former position while the revisionist movement adopted the latter view. Albeit, considerable crossover did exist between the two camps, especially after the Nazi seizure of power in 1933 increased Jewish emigrationary pressure from Central Europe. The subsequent worsening of living conditions in Eastern Europe reinforced the trend, to the extent that by the mid-1930s the actual positions held by opposing Zionist leaders, such as Ze'ev Jabotinsky and David Ben-Gurion, had become virtually identical. > see also: **Aliya; Evacuation Plan; Halutz**.

Halutziyut [חלוציות, H] "Pioneering": Zionist term for the pioneering spirit that sought to return the Jewish people to their ancestral homeland while creating a new Jewish people who would be rooted in productive, that is, agricultural, labor. > see also: **Agricultural Settlement(s); Dat ha-Avoda; Halutz**.

Ha-Ma'amad [המעמד, H] "The Deputation": Internal code name used by members of the Irgun Zvai Leumi (IZL). The term was derived from the organization of laymen who served in the Temple in ancient Israel. All available adult males were divided into twelve groups, each one of which served in the Temple for one month. Each *Ma'amad* was seen as representing the entire Jewish people and hence the IZL use of the term: IZL members saw themselves as fighting for Jewry's national home and national existence. > see also: **We Fight Therefore We Are**.

Ha-Ma'avak [המאבק, H] "The Struggle": Popular term for the Zionist struggle to obtain Israel's independence between 1945 and 1947. Given the term's chronological limits, it has come to exclusively refer to the struggle against Great Britain and

encompasses all means used at the time: military, economic, political, and diplomatic. The struggle encompassed multiple strands of Zionist activity during the postwar era, including (but not limited to) armed insurgency, "illegal" immigration (*Aliya Bet*), and diplomacy. Whereas all three of these elements were clearly needed to obtain independence, Israeli historians have (for the most part fruitlessly) debated which was the most important element in the struggle. > see also: **Aliya Bet; War of Independence**.

Hamaeya [T] "Foreigner": Term used by Turkish civil and military authorities to designate any person residing in the Ottoman Empire who was not an Ottoman subject. The term included all foreigners, both temporary residents and new immigrants, as well as those locals who resided in imperial territory but had acquired foreign citizenship (by birth or other means). As a result of the Ottoman policy of capitulations, foreigners obtained privileges that made foreign citizenship attractive to Ottoman subjects (mainly Jews and Christian Arabs). Prior to World War I, therefore, most of the *Yishuv*'s Jewish population fell into this category, since most *olim* (especially from the Russian empire) had retained citizenship from their countries of origin. The extraterritorial status implied in *Hamaeya* status was a matter of grave concern to the Ottoman government, which sought means to limit foreign encroachment. In December 1914, the Grand Porte decided to begin to deal with the problem by voiding the residency rights of all Jews living in *Eretz Israel* who were not Ottoman subjects. In 1915 this resulted in the deportation of all military-age foreign males from *Eretz Israel*. > see also: **Hitotmanut; World War I**.

Ha-Makom [המקום, H] "The Place": Traditional Jewish term for God, used in some Zionist circles as a pseudonym for *Eretz Israel*. This dual usage derived from the idea that God, as creator of the universe, had apportioned each people its own ancestral homeland, an idea that was furthered by the promises to the forefathers that *Eretz Israel* would belong to their descendents in perpetuity. In light of this dual meaning, the term has a transcendent and abstract meaning, even when used in the mundane sense of referring to *Eretz Israel*. As a result, the term also refers to Jewish messianic expectations and may be rendered "the land where we dwell in safety," a concept originating with the idea that only in the messianic age will the world be restored to its proper order. > see also: **Galut; Gola; Mashiach; Ha-Aretz**.

Ha-Melech [המלך, H] "The King": Briha code name for French General Marie Pierre Koenig, commander of Allied forces in the French zone of occupation in Germany. The term was a direct translation of Koenig's name (which means king in German). Koenig was very sympathetic to Jewish suffering, a fact that most historians trace to his years as commander of the Free French forces in North Africa. He was among the first military commanders to order his troops to look aside when Jews fleeing Eastern Europe entered his command. > see also: **Briha**.

Ha-Nadiv ha-Yadua [הנדיב הידוע, H] "The Well-Known Benefactor": Nickname for Baron Edmund de Rothschild, the Franco-Jewish philanthropist, respectfully referring to his role in early Zionist settlement activities in *Eretz Israel*. When it appeared that *Moshavot* founded by members of the First Aliya might fail, Rothschild provided financial subsidies and agricultural training for the Halutzim. This aid, which began in 1882, was critical to the success of the first settlement projects. Ill-health led Rothschild to transfer support of colonies to the Palestine Jewish Colonization Association (PICA), which he served as president until his death in 1934. Rothschild was seen as cool to Political Zionism, but he did work behind the scenes during World War I to change French policy from neutrality to support for the Jewish Legion and the Balfour Declaration. Rothschild's reputation within Zionist circles, even among the settlers he aided, was always mixed. All Zionists were very glad to accept his financial support, but some resented the heavy-handed way he controlled (or sought to control) the settlements.

Hankin Project [PN]: Colloquial term for a tentative agreement signed on March 26, 1920, between Yehoshua Hankin, a senior member of the WZO, and Arabs claiming to be leaders of the Syrian nationalist movement. The latter agreed to publicly and privately support the Zionist cause in Palestine in return for financial support to help Faisal retain the crown of Syria against the French. The deal fell through when it became clear that the Arabs had misrepresented their identities and were merely seeking to enrich themselves. > see also: **Faisal-Weizmann Agreement**.

Harish Politi [חריש פוליטי, H] "Political Plowing": Zionist term for efforts to plant crops on disputed parcels of land as a means of establishing Jewish ownership of that specific parcel. Although the term derived from a later date, the first attempt to at political plowing dated to the Ottoman era, for example, at Merhavia in 1911. The term itself was born in the 1930s, apparently at the height of the Wadi al-Hawarith (Emek Hefer) affair. After passage of the British Land Purchase Regulations in 1940, this type of plowing was used as a means to resist British attempts to limit the *Yishuv*'s growth. > see also: **Wadi al-Hawarith Affair; White Paper(s), White Paper of 1939**.

Harrison Report [PN]: Popular name for the report issued by presidential adviser Earl G. Harrison regarding the treatment of Jewish Displaced Persons (DPs) in the American zone of occupation in Germany, published on September 29, 1945. Harrison was empowered to study conditions in DP camps by President Harry S. Truman after a series of scuffles between Holocaust survivors and U.S. military police in occupied Germany. Secondarily, Harrison was asked to suggest means whereby overcrowding in the DP camps could be reduced. After numerous meetings with DPs, with U.S. military and civilian relief workers, and with Jewish communal leaders, Harrison issued his report, which contained two major

Ha-Nadiv ha-Yadua, Baron Edmund de Rothschild, During a Trip
to Visit the Settlements in *Eretz Israel*.
Courtesy of the Central Zionist Archives, Jerusalem

recommendations: U.S. military personnel should be withdrawn from the DP camps, allowing the residents to govern themselves (while leaving the military police responsible for internal and external security), and the camps should be emptied by emigration. Specifically, Harrison recommended that 100,000 Jewish DPs be permitted to legally enter Palestine/*Eretz Israel* immediately. That, he suggested would clear virtually all DPs out of the U.S. Zone while also granting the survivors their wish — to migrate to the Jewish national home. The Truman administration made this proposal central to its Middle East policy, but the Atlee-Bevin government rejected it out of hand. > see also: **Displaced Persons, Jewish**; **Briha**.

Ha-Saizon [הסזון, H] "The Hunting Season": Popular term for the intra-Zionist civil war that broke out between the Hagana and the so-called dissident underground movements, mainly the Irgun Zvai Leumi (IZL). The Hunting Season began in November 1944 and was officially a response to the assassination of Lord Moyne (the British minister resident in Cairo) by members of Lohame Herut Israel (Lehi). Nonetheless, although sparked by a Lehi action, the season's main target, as already noted, was the IZL. In essence the Hunting Season was an effort to enforce discipline on a movement that was seen as threatening Zionist diplomacy by its irresponsible attacks on British troops and installations. The original plan called for Hagana and Palmah units, operating on the JAE's direct authority, to disarm and detain IZL suspects; in rare instances they were to be handed over to the British. Although the plan did not call for any combat, violence quickly broke out as the intended prey defended themsleves.

The Hunting Season was destined to be controversial from the beginning. Some JAE leaders and many of the Palmah troops deployed to crush the IZl saw the operation as a personal vendetta against the revisionists. They could not understand why resources that could be better used fighting the Nazis, the Arabs, or the British were being used (and squandered) fighting against other Zionists. Efforts at indoctrination of the troops were almost completely unsuccessful, while considerable backlash developed in the *Yishuv*. For these reasons, the JAE and the Hagana high command agreed to terminate the operation in March 1945. Although conflict was soon replaced by cooperation between the underground movements, the Hunting Season left a reservoir of considerable ill will among members of the *Yishuv*'s various political movements that lasted well into the early years of the State of Israel. > see also: **Yishuv, Yishuv Organizations (Underground Movements)**.

Ha-Saizon ha-Sheini [הסזון השני, H] "The Second Hunting Season": Appelation sometimes used for the conflict between the Hagana and Palmah on the one hand and the Irgun Zvai Leumi (IZL) and Lohame Herut Israel (Lehi) on the other after the United Hebrew Resistance movement collapsed in July 1946. Although never as dangerous to Zionist unity or to the broader accomplishment of *Yishuv* goals as the first "Hunting Season," this period of friction did lead to a direct confrontation between the newly created Zva ha-Hagana le-Israel (Zahal) and Irgun members when the latter brought the arms-laden S.S. *Altalena* to Israel in June 1948. > see also: **Altalena Affair**; **Ha-Saizon**.

Ha-Seminar [הסמינר, H] "The Seminar": Code term used by the Hagana high command for a wide-ranging institutional analysis and reform undertaken in 1947 at David Ben-Gurion's orders. The reform took its name from the briefing Ben-Gurion received when he assumed full responsibility for defense after the Twenty-Second Zionist Congress: Ben-Gurion took so many notes at the briefing that he was said to resemble a seminar student. The reform's goal was to convert the Hagana from an underground movement into a conventional army capable of confronting the Arab armies in the event of an all-out war when the State of Israel came into being. > see also: **Zva ha-Hagana le-Israel**; **Yishuv**; **War of Independence**.

Ha-Shlish [שליש, H] "The Third": Common nickname, used by the Mapai executive and the JAE to designate Mapai's *Siya Bet* (Faction B) — the faction that opposed the direction that the party had taken during the 1930s and 1940s. The term derived from Siya Bet's relative strength within the party, representing approximately one-third of party members. In 1944 *Siya Bet* withdrew from Mapai altogether and formed the Ahdut ha-Avoda party. > see also: **Yishuv, Yishuv Organizations (Political Parties)**.

Ha-Shlishia [השלישיה, H] "The Triumvirate": Irgun Zvai Leumi code term for the executive body of the Af-Al-Pi organization, which operated from London. This triumvirate was composed of Eri Jabotinsky, Arye Ben-Eliezer, and Yitzhak Ben-Ami and was responsible for all revisionist-sponsored *Aliya Bet* activities. > see also: **Aliya Bet**; **Yishuv, Yishuv Organizations (Underground Organizations, Af-Al-Pi)**.

Hashmonaim [חשמונאים, H] "The hashmoneans": Historical term designating the ruling strata of the Second Jewish Commonwealth (during the period between 168 and 37 B.C.E.). During the late 1940s the term was used by the Irgun Zvai Leumi (IZL) high command to designate IZL members. In addition to its historical connotations, use of the term may derive from the fact that many of the IZL fighters were graduates of the religious Zionist Bnai ha-Hashmonaim youth movement. > see also: **Yishuv, Yishuv Organizations**.

Hasidim: General term for ultra-Orthodox Jews, used in the 1930s and 1940s as a code term for members of Sherut Yediot (Shai), the Hagana intelligence service, who had infiltrated the Irgun Zvai Leumi or Lohame Herut Israel in order to report back on the dissidents' activities. Precise derivation of the term is unknown. > see also: **Porshim**.

Hasidism and Zionism: > see also: **Judaism and Zionism**.

Haskala [השכלה, H] "Enlightenment": Eighteenth and nineteenth century movement and philosophy seeking to modernize Jewish communal and educational institutions to permit the Jews to enter the European mainstream. Customarily dated as originating with Moses Mendelssohn (mid-eighteenth century), the Haskala has generally been seen as antinationalist in its orientation. This is true, especially for *Maskilim* in Western and Central Europe, and is mainly a reflection of the fact that the Haskala called for a thorough reevaluation of most aspects of traditional Judaism, including traditional Jewish hope for restoration in *Eretz Israel*. In contrast, East European *Maskilim* retained a more positive attitude toward the idea of Jewish nationalism and eventually formed the core of the nascent Zionist movements that arose toward the end of the nineteenth century. > see also: **Zionut; Nationalism**.

Ha-Tikva [התקוה, H] "The Hope": Poem written in 1878 by Naftali Hertz Imber (published in 1886). The poem was inspired by news of the founding of Petah Tikva, the first major Jewish agricultural settlement outside of

כָּל עוֹד בַּלֵּבָב פְּנִימָה
נֶפֶשׁ יְהוּדִי הוֹמִיָּה,
וּלְפַאֲתֵי מִזְרָח קָדִימָה
עַיִן לְצִיּוֹן צוֹפִיָּה -

עוֹד לֹא אָבְדָה תִּקְוָתֵנוּ,
הַתִּקְוָה בַּת שְׁנוֹת אַלְפַּיִם,
לִהְיוֹת עַם חָפְשִׁי בְּאַרְצֵנוּ,
אֶרֶץ צִיּוֹן וִירוּשָׁלַיִם.

Ha-Tikva, Israel's National Anthem.
Author's collection, via the Keren Kayemet le-Israel

the four holy cities. Imber visited *Eretz Israel* in 1882 and read the poem to settlers at Rishon le-Zion; shortly thereafter one of them set the poem to the music of a well-known Romanian folk song. *Ha-Tikva* became the unofficial anthem of the Zionist movement very early on: it was already sung in public at the Second Zionist Congress (1898). *Ha-Tikva* was officially adopted as the Zionist anthem at the Eighteenth Zionist Congress in 1933; since 1948 the song has served as Israel's national anthem.

Hativa Meguyeset [חטיבה מגוייסת, H] "Mobilized Brigade": Unofficial term used in Hagana documents to designate the brigades of the Palmah. These were the only permanently mobilized units available to the Yishuv. > see also: **Yishuv, Yishuv Organizations (Underground Organizations, Plugot Mahatz).**

Hauptsitz [G] "Main Office": Term used by Theodor Herzl in his analysis of German antisemitism. In Herzl's view, antisemitism was a global phenomenon, affecting all aspects of the relationship between Jews and non-Jews. Since the modern antisemitic movement had originated in Germany, the Jewish problem was more prevalent there, although it had spread throughout the globe. For this reason, Herzl thought that the German government would be in the forefront of efforts to find a solution to the Jewish problem and would thus be a natural ally for the Zionist movement. > see also: **Antisemitismus.**

Ha-Va'ad ha-Odesai [הועד האודסאי, H] "The Odessa Committee": Another name for the Hibbat Zion organization, deriving from the fact that it was headquartered in Odessa. > see also: **Hibbat Zion.**

Havazelet [חבצלת, H] "Fleur-de-Lis": Code term used in sensitive Hagana and JAE documents to represent the Yishuv's main intelligence service, the Sherut Yediot (better known by its Hebrew intials, Shai) that was founded in 1929. The term's origins

are unclear, although it was used early in Shai's history. > see also: **Yishuv, Yishuv Organizations (Underground Movements, Sherut Yediot).**

Havlaga [הבלגה, H] "Self-Restraint": Controversial Hagana policy adopted during the 1920s. *Havlaga* emphasized the purely defensive nature of the *Yishuv*'s military effort. This policy was adopted out of fear in WZO and JAE circles that any form of retaliation or preemptive operation would cause more harm to the Yishuv than to the Arabs because the British would view Arab attack and Jewish defense as essentially the same. In light of these fears, the Hagana's doctrine stressed that operation could not commence until after an attack had begun. The policy of self-restraint was accepted by all parties during the 1920s; by the time of the Arab Revolt (1936–1939) conditions had changed radically. Hagana doctrine, however, had not kept pace with new developments (notably the infiltration of Arab fighters from neighboring Arab states) leading to considerable controversy. Although the Hagana remained committed to *Havlaga*, the Irgun Zvai Leumi (IZL) abandoned the policy in mid-1936. A schism ensued with more moderate members of the IZL leaving that organization and more radical members of the Hagana beginning to chafe under the restrictions that surrendered all military initiative to the Arab attackers in return for almost no political benefit to the *Yishuv*. As the revolt continued, Hagana policy began to change. More openly aggressive defensive techniques were adopted with the creation of the Special Night Squads, the Hagana's Field Force (Heyl Sadeh, Hish), and, in 1939, the Hagana's Peulot Meyuhadot (POM, Special Operations). By the end of the Arab revolt, havlaga had been abandoned in all but name. > see also: **Arab Revolt; Yishuv, Yishuv Organizations (Underground Movements).**

Hayal ha-Tenua [חייל התנועה, H] "A Soldier of the Movement": Term used by members of Lohame Herut Israel (Lehi) to designate themselves. They saw themselves as soldiers in a liberation army whose goal was to liberate the

Jewish people by liberating its ancestral homeland from the British occupiers, who, by definition, were the Jews' oppressors. > see also: **Yishuv, Yishuv Organizations (Underground Movements, Lohame Herut Israel)**.

Hayalim Almonim [חיילים אלמונים, H] "Anonymous Soldiers": Another self-defining term used by members of Lohame Herut Israel (Lehi) to designate themselves: they recognized that they would receive no accolades for their acts of self-sacrifice and might be condemned as terrorists (as indeed they were). The term derived from a poem written by Lehi's founder, Abraham Stern, and became Lehi's virtual motto after his death under mysterious circumstances while in British custody. > see also: **Yishuv, Yishuv Organizations (Underground Movements, Lohame Herut Israel); Yair.**

Ha-Yedid [הידיד, H] "The Friend": Zionist nickname for Orde Charles Wingate, a British army officer stationed in *Eretz Israel* in 1936. Wingate, sent to the Middle East as a junior staff officer during the Arab Revolt, soon became an ardent champion of the Zionist cause, much to the embarrassment of his superiors. In May 1936, Wingate received permission to raise a specially trained unit to combat terrorist attacks in the lower Galilee. Using Hagana personnel and British noncommissioned officers, Wingate trained his unit to operate as a mirror image of the terrorists, who were then plaguing the British-owned Haifa to Habyana oil pipeline. In particular, Wingate insisted that the unit be able to operate at night, a policy that won the unit the name of Special Night Squads (SNS). Wingate also insisted on a high degree of training and skill, instilling a sense of professionalism in the Hagana personnel attached to the SNS. Many of them, indeed, went on the senior posts in the Hagana and (after 1948) in Zva ha-Hagana le-Israel. Wingate's close contact with the WZO and JAE leadership led to his dismissal in 1939 and his return to England. Dreaming that one day he would

return to *Eretz Israel*, he received a promise that he would lead the army of a future Jewish State. His dream was not fated to be fulfilled: after service as commander of Gideon Force, a unit composed of many of his SNS comrades that fought against the Italians in Ethiopia in 1940 and 1941, Wingate was promoted and given command of the Chindits fighting in Burma. Wingate was killed in an air accident while overseeing the second Chindit campaign in Burma in 1944. > see also: **Gideon Force; Special Night Squads; Yishuv, Yishuv Organizations (Underground Organizations, Hagana); Gentile Zionism.**

Ha-Yevani [היוני, H] "The Greek": One of the twenty code names used by or for David Ben-Gurion during his tenure as chairman of the JAE. As with other code names, this one reflected an aspect of Ben-Gurion's personal life, in this case, the fact that he learned classical Greek in order to read Homer in the original. > see also: **Avi-Geula; Ha-Zaken; Herucles.**

Ha-Yishuv ha-Meurgan [הישוב המאורגן, H] "The Organized Settlement": Term used to designate the totality of Jewish political and social life in the *Yishuv* during the mandatory era. > see also: **Yishuv.**

Hayka/Tossia [PN]: Two Briha code names for Poland, derived from two leaders of the ghetto undergrounds during the Holocaust: Hayka for Hayka Grossman (Bialystok) and Tossia for Tosssia Alterman (Warsaw). > see also: **Briha.**

Ha-Zakan [הזקן, H] "The Beard(ed one)": Lohame Herut Israel (Lehi) code name for Yitzhak Yezernitski (later Shamir), one of Lehi's three commanders after Abraham Stern was killed. The term derived from the disguise Yezernitski adopted after he escaped from a British prison, specifically a beard that he wore while masquerading as "Rabbi Shamir." > see also: **Yair.**

Ha-Zaken [הזקן, H] "The Old Man": Another popular code name used to designate David Ban-Gurion between 1935 and 1948. As with similar names, ha-Zaken was used in documents that were sensitive or in cases where identification of the subject might cause embarrassment to the JAE or WZO. Ha-Zaken was the most popular of the names for Ben-Gurion and its use became widespread after the establishment of the State of Israel. > see also: **Avi-Geula; Ha-Yevani; Hercules**.

Hazon [חזון, H] "Vision": Popular Zionist term for the Jewish vision of the future — one in which the Jewish people lived securely and with dignity in their restored homeland. Although derived from the Bible (where it was used in the sense of prophecy) and sometimes connected with the messianic idea (to the extent that the term is sometimes cited as Hazon Meshihi, חזון משיחי, messianic vision) the term has also been used in a secular context by a diverse group of Zionist authors. The term has an additional, somewhat narrower, meaning, as a designation for the planning needed to carry out Zionism's short- and long-term goals. > see also: **Alt-Neeuland; Mashiah**.

Hebrew, Revival of: Zionism sought not only the physical regeneration of the Jewish people but their cultural and social revival as well. Part and parcel of this planned renaissance was the attempt to revive Hebrew as the Jews' daily language. Despite mythology, it should be borne in mind that Hebrew had never been totally forgotten. Although it had ceased to be a language of daily use, Hebrew remained the language for both prayer and scholarly discourse in most Jewish communities around the world. Early Maskilim, for example, had written almost completely in Hebrew and had done so in a very clear and flowery style. Efforts to revive Hebrew as a daily language began in earnest in the late 1870s and early 1880s. These efforts are largely, but not exclusively, associated with the activities of Eliezer Ben-Yehuda (Pearlman). A leading advocate of Hibbat Zion, Ben-Yehuda doubted that a Jewish national home could develop without a return to a Jewish national language. Of necessity, Ben-Yehuda adopted Hebrew.

Only Hebrew was associated with periods of previous Jewish statehood, and Yiddish and Ladino were too closely identified with the diaspora. Although Ben-Yehuda's orientation met with considerable skepticism, even within Zionist ranks, his predictions proved to be essentially correct. It is, indeed, highly unlikely that the State of Israel could have emerged from the *Yishuv* had there been no cultural development; the *Yishuv*'s culture, in turn, was completely dependent on the revival of Hebrew. > see also: **Cultural Conflict**.

Hebrew University (HU): Premier educational institution in the *Yishuv* (and in the State of Israel), established in 1925. The establishment of such a university was a major goal for Spiritual Zionists. In so doing they hoped to renew *Eretz Israel*'s role as the cultural and spiritual center of world Jewry. In reality, HU did not initially fulfill that goal; it did, however, fill the need for an institution of higher education in the *Yishuv*. The campus was dedicated in 1925 and courses began the next school year. HU continued to grow, especially after 1933, when the influx of educated German Jews (including many univeristy professors) boosted HU's status as a scholarly institution. The original campus was located on Mount Scopus, but that had to be abandoned after the War of Independence. Although the HU campus was in Israeli hands, the enclave was completely surrounded by Arab-held territory. A new campus was built for HU on Givat Ram (in West Jerusalem) with construction completed in 1968. By that time, the old campus had been liberated (during the Six Day War) and work began on restoring the original campus to use. Currently, both campuses are in use, although the Mount Scopus campus is once again considered to be the "main" institution. > see also: **Education**.

Hefez ha-Kiyum [חפץ הקיום, H] "Will to Live": Zionist term for the instinctive desire of national or ethnic groups to survive. According to this line of analysis, which relied heavily on organic conceptions of nationalism that were popular during the last third of the nineteenth century, ethnic groups seek to survive in order to pass their cultural and national ideals to another generation. The thought that nations have a will to live was central to Ahad ha-Am's Cultural Zionism. He sought the creation in *Eretz Israel* of a center that would focus world Jewry's attention and would thus provide the direction to revive Jewry's will to live. > see also: **Ahad ha-Am**; **Nationalism**; **Zionut**.

He-Hanut [החנות, H] "The Store": Code name for a clandestine Hagana arms factory located in downtown Tel Aviv that operated between 1939 and 1947. The factory was located two blocks from the central bus station and operated under the cover of being a plumbing supply shop, whence the name derived. The factory primarily produced small arms ammunition. > see also: **Yishuv, Yishuv Organizations (Underground Organizations, Ta'as)**.

Hercules [Gr]: Another of the code names used for David Ben-Gurion in JA and Hagana documents. In similar vein to code names such as "Avi Geula" and "ha-Yevani," Hercules had a double meaning. It reflected Ben-Gurion's deep interest in ancient Greek literature and was also an admission of the Herculean task Ben-Gurion had set for himself — the accomplishment of Zionist goals through the creation of the State of Israel. > see also: **Avi Geula**; **ha-Yevani**; **ha-Zaken**.

Hershel Ish-Emet [איש-אמת הערשיל, Y/H/Slang]: JA code name used to designate U.S. President Harry S. Truman. The term is an elaborate Hebrew and Yiddish pun: Hershel is the Yiddish equivalent for Harry, Ish means man, and Emet means true (or in this case, Tru-) in Hebrew.

Hesder [הסדר, H] "Agreement": Code term used by the Hagana and JAE in 1945 and 1946 for the agreement whereby all Jewish undergrounds united to fight the British. Since the War of Independence the term has been used to designate the program of

combined yeshiva study and military service permitted to groups of nationalist orthodox Israeli youth. > see also: **Yishuv, Yishuv Organizations (Underground Movements, Tenuat ha-Meri ha-Ivri)**.

Hevrei ha-Makhela [חברי המקהלה, H] "Members of the Choir": Internal code term used by members of the Irgun Zvai Leumi to designate themselves. A similar term was Makhela (מקהלה, "choir"), which was used to designate the Irgun itself. In both cases, the derivation is unknown.

Hevrat Bituah [חברת ביטוח, H] "Insurance Company": JA code term, used during World War II, for the British defense ministry. Derivation is from the fact that the Hebrew term for insurance and defense are similar, while a company could also be a ministry. A similar term was Hevrat Anthony (חברת אנטוני, Anthony's Company), a reference to Minister of Defense Sir Anthony Eden.

Hibbat Zion [חיבת ציון, H] (HZ) "Love of Zion": Official name of the first modern Zionist organization and for its ideology. Members of HZ called themselves Hovevei Zion (Lovers of Zion, חובבי ציון) and the organization was sometimes also known by that name. HZ was founded in response to the profound shock produced by the Russian pogroms of 1881–1882 and was the direct outcome of Leon Pinsker's seminal Zionist work, *Auto-Emancipation*. Pinsker had called on Jews to return en masse to their ancestral homeland, rebuild it, and restore it to its place as the center for Jewish physical and spiritual life. Pinsker's writings attracted a panoply of Russian Jewish intellectuals to HZ, including (among others), Ahad ha-Am (Asher Ginsburg), Moses Leib Lilienblum, Menahem Mendel Ussishkin, and Rabbi Samuel Mohilever. HZ ideology emphasized that the Jews had no long-term future in the diaspora, certainly not if they wanted to maintain their distinctive cultral and ethnic identity.

Organizational development of HZ was rapid after the Katowicz Conference (1884), which laid the foundation for future HZ operations.

HZ chapters spread throughout the Russian empire (which included Poland and Lithuania, both centers of dense Jewish population) and Romania. In 1890, HZ established permanent headquarters in Odessa; by then the organization had some 14,000 members. Once fully organized, HZ began to operate in three spheres: (1) education to inculcate a nationalist orientation in Russian Jews; (2) collection of funds to purchase and build on land in *Eretz Israel*; and (3) sending colonists to begin the first wave of settlement. Financial and institutional difficulties abounded and meant that only a slow pace of development in *Eretz Israel* was ever possible. Although HZ was primarily responsible for the Bilu settlements during the First Aliya, by 1890 the organization had run its course. Support for HZ eroded rapidly and the entire organization collapsed after Pinsker's death in 1891. > see also: **Ahad ha-Am**; **Autoemancipation**; **Bet Ya'akov Lehu ve-Nelha**; **Conferences, Zionist, Katowicz.**

Hindenburg Erklärung [G] "Hindenburg Declaration": German statement of support for Jewish (and Zionist) goals issued as a means of gaining Jewish support for Germany in World War I. Although most Russian Jews viewed the German army as liberators, because the Germans freed them from the oppressive czarist regime, some senior German military leaders hoped to derive extra benefit from an encompassing statement of sympathy with Zionism. Officers holding this view included Field Marshal Paul von Hindenburg, who saw it as a means to gain active Jewish cooperation in the occupation of eastern Poland and other territories seized from the Russians. As a result, Hindenburg issued a very general statement in 1914 and tried to convince the German foreign ministry that a more specific declaration was needed. However, Hindenburg failed to convince the foreign ministry that the benefit to be gained from such a statement would outweigh the loss of support from the Ottoman Empire that a declaration of sympathy with Zionism was

bound to cause. Late in 1917, when the course of the war had changed, the German foreign ministry relented and considered issuing a comprehensive, explicit declaration but by the time it was issued it had been eclipsed by the Balfour Declaration. > see also: **Balfour Declaration; World War I.**

Histarvut [הסתערבות, H] "Arabization": Hagana and Palmah code term for an undercover operative who lived as an Arab, or for the operation in which the agent participated. The term was usually used in the context of operations by the Palmah's Arabic Company (also known as Plugat ha-Shahar). This unit comprised Palmah members with appropriate physical features and sufficient command of Arabic to be able to pass as Arabs during infiltration missions. Ha-Shahar was used in intelligence gathering, psychological warfare, and other special operations. During World War II, for instance, ha-Shahar served as the Yishuv's primary source of intelligence about neighboring Arab countries and about developments in the Palestinian Arab community. In this capacity, ha-Shahar worked closely with the Hagana's intelligence service (Shai), the JA Political Department, and, through them, the British Middle East Intelligence Center (MEIC). Ha-Shahar operatives were also active in organizing overland *Aliya Bet* from Iraq between 1942 and 1948. > see also: **Yishuv, Yishuv Organizations (Underground Movements, Palmah); World War II.**

Historical Providence [HT]: Term used by David Ben-Gurion to represent the universal wisdom that would inevitably help fulfill Zionist goals. To an extent, Ben-Gurion used this term as a replacement for God, although he used other terms more obviously derived from the religious sphere as well, most notably, "Rock of Israel" (צור ישראל).

Historic Coalition [HT]: Ppopular name for the three party coalition that dominated the *Yishuv's* institutions during the 1930s and, with some variations, dominated the State of Israel's political life between 1948 and 1977. The coalition was composed of Mapai, which was the dominant socialist Zionist party in the *Yishuv*, Mizrachi, the religious Zionist movement, and the General Zionist Alliance, followers of the gradualist policies espoused by Chaim Weizmann. The coalition was based on the premise, accepted by all three parties, that compromise and cooperation — especially on divisive religious and political issues — was the only means to attain Zionist goals. > see also: **Status-Quo Agreement; Sochnut Yehudit; Yishuv**.

Hito′tmanut [התעותמנות, H] ″Ottomanization″: Jewish term for the forced acceptance by Jews in *Eretz Israel* of Ottoman citizenship after Turkey joined the Central Powers during World War I. Prior to the war, most Jewish settlers had maintained citizenship from their countries of origin, mainly Russia. Since Russia and Turkey were now at war, this situation was potentially dangerous: all foreigners could theoretically be deported as enemy aliens. It is clear that the Turks considered the *Yishuv* a potential fifth column. They thus enacted a series of decrees that had the goal of forcing Jews to either accept Ottoman citizenship, which implied their commitment to uphold all Ottoman laws (including those restricting Jews′ rights to purchase land in *Eretz Israel*), or face expulsion. Zionist leaders called upon the *Yishuv′s* population to accept Ottoman citizenship, seeing that as the only way to protect the results of thirty years of painstaking efforts and hoping that the Ottomans would not persecute a seemingly cooperative Jewish population. The Ottoman authorities were, however, ambivalent about the decree, acting slowly on most citizenship requests. Many of the most prominent Zionist leaders who requested citizenship, such as David Ben-Gurion and Yitzhak Ben-Zvi, were rejected and were expelled from Ottoman territory in May 1915. > see also: **World War I**.

Hityashvut ha-Elef [התיישבות האלף, H] ″Settlement of the Thousand″: Plan to rapidly settle 1,000 Jewish agricultural workers in *Eretz Israel* in an extraordinary settlement operation. Instead of settling the *olim* as groups in new settlements — a process that took considerable time and scarce resources — the plan was for the 1,000 to pay their own carfare (with loans available for those in dire need) and then to join already existing settlements. Approved tentatively by the Sixteenth Zionist Congress (1929), the plan was not actually carried out until 1932 due to the Arab riots and consequent political fallout from the Passfield White Paper (1931). Between 1932 and 1936, a total of 432 labor schedule *olim* had settled in this fashion; by then, however, the plan′s basic premises (mainly relating to speeding up *aliya*) were no longer valid and the operation ceased. The plan was not a total failure, despite its inability to reach its initial goal. This was the first time that private capital was used for *Yishuv*-wide development to any extensive degree.

Hok ha-Shvut [חוק השבות, H] ″Law of Return″: Official title of the Basic Law passed unanimously by the Knesset on July 5, 1950. The law confers potential Israeli citizenship on any Jewish person, regardless of place of residence, citizenship, or personal status. A few exceptions to the general rule do exist, but the broad parameters of the law fulfill its main purpose: to consciously link Israel with the entire Jewish world, thereby fulfilling Zionism′s main dream of creating a united Jewish people.

Holocaust [HT]: Generally used term for the European Jewish catastrophe that developed during the Nazi era, between 1933 and 1945. During this period some 6 million Jews were systematically persecuted and murdered as part of a Nazi plan to permanently rid Europe of Jews. Just three years after the liberation of European Jewry, the State of Israel was reborn. Both historians and theologians have noted an intimate connection between these two seminal events of twentieth century Jewish history. On the historical level the Holocaust and the rise of the State of Israel are linked chronologically and by sharing a clear, if not unequivocal, cause-and-effect relationship. Although a Jewish state would eventually have emerged despite Arab opposition and British obstruction, the Holocaust and the fate of European Jewish survivors considerably speeded up the process. This was especially clear during the hearings of the United Nations Special Committee on Palestine in the summer of 1946 and the subsequent U.N. discussions on the *Eretz Israel* problem. The horrific events in Europe influenced many Latin American states, which otherwise would have chosen neutrality or even hostility to Jewish aspirations, to support partition and the creation of a Jewish state. > see also: **World War II**; **United Nations**.

The Holocaust plays an important role in both everyday life and ideology in Israel to this day. Israeli sensitivity to national security derives, in part, from fears of powerlessness that can be traced back to the dark years of World War II when the *Yishuv* was forced to watch European Jewry being mercilessly ground to dust while unable to offer any realistic assistance. This sense of the new state arising to correct a historical injustice has played a prominent role in Israel's political ethos since 1948, examples of which abound but are outside the scope of this work. In general Israelis have come to accept the premise that an attack, or even the threat of an attack, on Jews — because of their Jewishness — should not go unpunished. Indeed, for this reason, many Israeli leaders deny the validity of distinctions between antisemitism and anti-Zionism. Ultimately both deny to Jews those rights naturally granted to other nations. > see also: **Yom ha-Shoa**; **Antisemitismus**; **Anti-Zionism**.

On a theological level, a number of Jewish philosophers, including Emil Fackenheim, Ignaz Maybaum, Irving Greenberg, and Eliezer Berkovits, have concentrated on the dialectical relationship between *Hurban* (destruction) and redemption. This theme, which has parallels in the Bible and throughout Jewish thought, recognizes two polar extremes in Jewish history: destruction, as represented by the pharaonic persecution, the destruction of the First and Second Temples, and, finally, the Holocaust, and rebirth, as represented by the Exodus, the return from Babylon in the Persian era, and the creation of the State of Israel. In each case, moreover, both destruction and the subsequent redemption were framed in the form of a renewed covenant between the Jewish people and God and within the Jewish community. > see also: **Yishuv**; **Israel State of**.

Holy Cities, Four [HT]: Term used to designate the four cities in *Eretz Israel* that, as a result of their historic and religious significance, always had considerable Jewish populations: Jerusalem, Hebron, Safed, and Tiberias. Before the rise of Zionism, the bulk of Palestine's Jewish population — estimated at just under 25,000 in 1880 — resided in the four cities. > see also: **Old Yishuv/New Yishuv**.

Homa u-Migdal [חומה ומגדל, H] "Stockade and Tower":

1. Scope and Definition

Term for a type of settlement used extensively in the Yishuv during the 1930s and 1940s. Such settlements were built within a wall and were guarded by, among other defenses, a series of watchtowers. The *Homa u-Migdal* type of settlement was necessitated by increasingly violent Arab guerilla attacks on Jewish settlements, particularly during the Arab revolt of 1936–1939. In theory, the entire settlement was prefabricated and could be assembled in a single evening. In reality, just the tower and stockade were completed in one evening, with further buildings being erected as time permitted with settlers taking turns at guard duty. As the name implies, the tower and stockade were the principle defenses, but almost all such settlements made extensive use of barbed wire and trench systems to slow down attackers and provide covered firing positions for defenders. The settlers were, after all, expected to defend themselves against attack until the arrival of Hagana or British reinforcements. In all, 118 Homa u-Migdal settlements were established between 1936 and 1939.

TABLE H.1: Major Homa u-Migdal Settlements, 1936-1939

Settlement	Year	Settlement Type	Location
Afek	1939	Kibbutz	Akko Plain
Alonim	1938	Kibbutz	Jezreel Valley
Amir	1939	Kibbutz	Hula Valley
Bet Oren	1939	Kibbutz	Carmel Hills
Bet Yehoshua	1938	Moshav	Sharon Plain
Bet Yosef	1937	Moshav	Bet Shean Valley
Dafna	1939	Kibbutz	Hula Valley
Dalia	1939	Kibbutz	Manassa Hills
Dan	1939	Kibbutz	Hula Valley
En Gev	1937	Kibbutz	Kinneret Valley
En ha-Mifratz	1938	Kibbutz	Zevulun Valley
En ha-Shofet	1937	Kibbutz	Manassa Hills
Eylon	1938	Kibbutz	Upper Galilee
Ginnosar	1937	Kibbutz	Kinneret Valley
Hamdia	1939	Kibbutz	Bet Shean Valley
Hanita	1938	Kibbutz	Upper Galilee
Ha-Zor'im	1939	Moshav	Lower Galilee
Kfar Glickson	1939	Kibbutz	Sharon Plain
Kfar Masaryk	1938	Kibbutz	Zevulun Valley
Kfar Menahem	1937	Kibbutz	Coastal Plain
Kfar Netter	1939	Moshav	Sharon Plain
Kfar Ruppin	1938	Kibbutz	Bet Shean Valley
Kfar Szold	1937	Kibbutz	Hula Valley
Ma'ale ha-Hamisha	1938	Kibbutz	Jerusalem Hills
Ma'ayan Zvi	1938	Kibbutz	Carmel Hills
Mahanayim	1939	Kibbutz	Upper Galilee
Maoz Haim	1937	Kibbutz	Bet Shean Valley
Masada	1937	Kibbutz	Lake Kinneret
Mesilot	1938	Kibbutz	Bet Shean Valley
Moledet	1937	Moshav Shitufi	Lower Galilee
Negba	1939	Kibbutz	Coastal Plain
Nir David	1936	Kibbutz	Bet Shean Valley
Sde Eliahu	1939	Kibbutz	Bet Shean Valley
Sde Nahum	1937	Kibbutz	Bet Shean Valley
Sha'ar ha-Golan	1937	Kibbutz	Kinneret Valley
Shavei Zion	1938	Moshav Shitufi	Akko Plain
Shdemot Devora	1939	Moshav	Lower Galilee
Tel Yitzhak	1938	Kibbutz	Sharon Plain
Tel Zur	1939	Moshav	Sharon Plain
Tirat Zvi	1937	Kibbutz	Bet Shean Valley
Zur Moshe	1937	Moshav	Sharon Plain

Source: *Archion Toldot ha-Hagana.*

Horgim [חורגים, H] "(Step) Brothers":
Code term used by members of the Irgun
Zvai Leumi (IZL) to refer to members of
Lohame Herut Israel (Lehi). The term
reflected the origin of both underground
movements from within the revisionist
Zionist camp but also reflected the
considerable tension between the two movements during World War II when the IZL
declared a truce with the British in order to
fight the Nazis. > see also: **Yishuv, Yishuv
Organizations (Underground Organizations).**

Hovevei Zion: > see also: **Hibbat Zion.**

Ideological Collectivism [HT]: Term used by *Kibbutzim* associated with ha-Shomer ha-Zair to explain their orientation. In this concept, the *Kibbutz* played a triple role as a collective settlement, a social partnership, and an ideological collective. After discussions among all *Kibbutz* members, the group was supposed to choose which stream of socialist Zionism it would adhere to. This statement then became binding on all members with no deviations allowed. Ideological collectivism paralleled many of V. I. Lenin's ideas, for example about "democratic centralism," and touched off a major debate within the *Kibbutz* movements. In turn, this debate politicized settlement work, thereby increasing controversy within socialist Zionist ranks. Partly, the controversy reflected ha-Shomer ha-Zair's efforts to differentiate itself from Mapai; however, the controversy also derived in part from ha-Shomer ha-Zair's attitude toward Marxism and the Soviet Union, an attitude that was far more positive than Mapai's. > see also: **Yishuv, Yishuv Organizations (Political Parties); Agricultural Settlement(s)**.

"Illegal" Immigration [HT]: British term for all immigration to Palestine/*Eretz Israel* without the benefit of legal documentation. In British usage there was no differentiation between *Ma'apilim*, individuals who contracted false marriages in order to bring a "spouse" along with them (thereby obtaining the benefit of two immigrants on the same certificate), and tourists who overstayed their visas (accidentally or otherwise). > see also: **Aliya Bet; Ha'apala**.

Indian [Slang]: Code term used by the Hagana's Sherut Yediot (Shai, Intelligence Service) to represent any Englishman who worked for Shai either directly or indirectly. Derivation of the term is unknown. > see also: **Yishuv, Orgaizations (Underground Organizations, Sherut Yediot)**.

Immigration [HT]: > see also: **Aliya; Aliya Bet**.

Infiltration [E]: Term for the means used by some Zionist groups in the process of "conquering communities." The term is most often associated by historians with the English Zionist Federation (EZF). As a tactic, infiltration eschewed controversy. Instead of creating conflicts that would lead them to overturn the existing communal order by reference to the Jewish masses, Zionists created consensus within existing communal bodies on issues not directly related to Zionism, thus permitting their participation in and (they hoped) eventual domination of these same institutions. Infiltration has been viewed by historians as a tactical success but a strategic failure. Because of the time needed to create consensus within Jewish communities, the EZF's infiltration tactics created broad support for generalized Zionist goals but did not create deep or active support under crisis conditions like those existing during World War II. Moreover, infiltration never led to the defeat of non- or anti-Zionist ideologies, as happened in other communities. It is not clear, however, if the EZF could have adopted any other tactic given the specific conditions within Anglo-Jewry and the accomplishments that infiltration did gain were by no means minor. > see also: **Conquest of Communities**.

Irgun B′ [׳ב ארגון, H] "Second Organization": Another name for the Irgun Zvai Leumi, used mainly during the 1930s to distinguish it from the Hagana. > see also: **Yishuv, Organizations (Underground Organizations, Irgun Zvai Leumi)**.

Irgun ha-Makbil [המקביל אירגון, H] "The Parallel Organization": Hagana term for the Irgun Zvai Leumi (IZL) during negotiations on reunification held in fits and starts during the 1930s. The term emphasized the common goals held by both organizations while glossing over the differences in strategy and tactics between them. The term was seldom used in internal Hagana documents, in which the usual reference to the IZL was *Porshim* (dissidents), a term that had more negative connotations. > see also: **Porshim**.

Irgun Zvai Leumi be-Eretz Israel [ארגון ישראל בארץ לאומי צבאי, H] "National Military Organization in the Land of Israel": Original name for Lohame Herut Israel (Lehi), used from approximately 1940 to 1942 and designed to distinguish Lehi from its parent organization, the Irgun Zvai Leumi. > see also: **Yishuv, Organizations (Underground Organizations, Lohame Herut Israel)**.

Ish Zahav [זהב איש, H/PN] "Man of Gold": JA code term for Nahum Goldmann, based on a literal translation of his family name into Hebrew. It is not clear precisely when the term was used, but it is unlikely to have been used in sensitive documents since the reference would have been too obvious.

Israel, State of:

1. Scope and Definition

On May 14, 1948, JAE chairman David Ben-Gurion addressed a solemn assembly of *Yishuv* notables in Tel Aviv's Mann Auditorium and declared the State of Israel's independence. Coming three years after the end of World War II and the Holocaust, the creation of the State of Israel was an epic redemptive moment in Jewish history and was viewed as such by most contemporary witnesses. Sadly, within minutes, the new state was plunged into a fight for its existence in the War of Independence. Over the course of nearly six months of bloody fighting, during which nearly 1 percent of the *Yishuv*'s population perished, the new State of Israel was placed on a firm, although by no means secure, footing. *De jure* or *de facto* recognitions by thirty-two states and membership in the United Nations (in 1949) cemented Israel's diplomatic position, although a lack of final peace treaties with the Arab states meant that Israel was isolated in its own region of the world. > see also: **Yishuv**; **World War II**; **War of Independence**; **Armistice Agreements**.

The significance of the State of Israel for the Zionist movement cannot be underestimated. Even before the WZO came into being in 1897, proto-Zionists had been urging Jewish restoration for nearly fifty years. When the First World Zionist Congress convened, it unanimously approved a resolution calling for the establishment of a Jewish national home, an act that Theodor Herzl characterized in his diary as laying the foundations for a sovereign Jewish state. To be sure, the terminology used at the time was deliberately vague in order to keep the Zionists' negotiating options open and not shut out any potential partners prematurely. Zionists remained true to their broad goals despite sometimes virulent disagreements over strategy and tactics, since, in the broadest perspective, only statehood could achieve all the subsidiary goals that the WZO set for itself. > see also: **World Zionist Congress**; **Basel Program**; **World Zionist Organization**; **Gradualism**; **Shem ha-Meforash**.

The *Palestine Post*'s Headline for May 16, 1948
Courtesy of the New York Public Library Jewish Division

The redemptive achievement associated with the State of Israel's independence must be viewed in historical and philosophical context: it brought the Jewish world into a new era. For nearly two millenia prior to 1948, Jews had been objects of history, tempest tossed by events they could not control, insecure, homeless. But with the emergence of the Jewish State, Jews became a subject of history. They now assumed responsibility for securing their future as well as for preserving the memory of their past. This brought about a massive change in the Jews' fate and future, which holds equally true for Jews living outside of Israel. It may be safely said that independence is almost unprecedented in all of history.

2. Provisional Government Agencies

Constituent Assembly (CA), preparliament convened by the Provisional State Council on November 18, 1948. The initial idea was to hold elections for the CA in early 1949, after which it would meet to write a constitution for the new state. Elections were held on January 25, 1949. However, opposition to a written constitution by religious parties led to the idea of a new constitution being discarded. As a result, the CA passed only one piece of legislation: the Transition Law of February 16, 1949, by which the CA reconstituted itself as the Knesset (parliament). That same day the CA unanimously elected Chaim Weizmann to be Israel's first president. > see also: **Basic Laws; Small Constitution.**

TABLE I.1: Composition of the Constituent Assembly

Party	Representatives	Percentage
Mapai	46	37.7
Mapam	19	15.6
United Religious Front	16	13.1[1]
Herut	14	11.5
General Zionists A	7	5.7
General Zionists B	5	4.1
Sephardim	4	3.3
Maki	4	3.3
Arab List	4	3.3
WIZO	1	0.8
Yemenites	1	0.8
Fighters Party	1	0.8
TOTAL	122	100.0

Source: *Israel and Middle East*, October–November, 1948, p. 33.

Joint Emergency Committee (JEC), name under which the Jewish Agency and Va'ad Leumi joined in November 1947 to organize for Israel's upcoming independence. The JEC established the parameters for Jewish self-government, operating as a *de facto* provisional government prior to the mandate's termination. The JEC also assumed sole responsibility for defense and for the creation of the fledgling state's administration. The JEC was replaced by Minhelet ha-Am in April 1948.

Minhelet ha-Am (מנהלת העם), "National Administration," official term for the Israeli provisional government, created in April 1948 by combining the twelve member Jewish Agency Executive with fourteen members of the Va'ad Leumi and eleven other representatives of Jewish parties in *Eretz Israel*. By this means, all parties except the revisionists were represented in the provisional Government. Minhelet ha-Am continued to operate until March 1949, by which time Knesset elections had taken place and permitted the establishment of the first coalition government.

Moezet ha-Am (מועצת העם), "Popular Assembly," another name used in official documents for the Israeli provisional government. > see also: **Israel, State of, Provisional Government Agencies (Minhelet ha-Am)**.

Moezet ha-Medina ha-Zmanit (המדינה מועצת הזמנית), "Provisional State Council," (PSC) interim legislature created by the reorganization of the Moezet ha-Am immediately after Israel's declaration of independence. Composed of thirty-seven members, the PSC was, in effect the Moezet ha-Am operating under a new title. Given the emergency conditions under which the PSC was created, it wisely adopted a hands-off policy, leaving virtually all British regulations from the mandatory era untouched. The PSC's main initiatives related to *aliya* and to preparing for the provisional government's replacement with a permanent establishment. The PSC met between May 14, 1948, and February 10, 1949, at which time it transferred all authority to the Constituent Assembly.> see also: **Israel, State of, Provisional Government Agencies (Constituent Assembly)**.

---

[1] A coalition of religious parties created for election purposes and including Mizrachi, ha-Poel ha-Mizrachi, and Agudas Israel representatives. URF members of the provisional cabinet have been identified (below) by original party affiliation.

TABLE I.2: Composition of the Provisional Government

Name	Party	Portfolio[1]
David Ben-Gurion	Mapai	Prime Minister & Defense
Moshe Shertok	Mapai	Foreign
Eliezer Kaplan	Mapai	Finance
Hayim M. Shapira	Mizrachi	Immigration & Health
David Remez	Mapai	Communcations
Mordechai Bentov	Mapam	Labor and Public Works
Aharon Zisling	Mapam	Agriculture
Fritz Bernstein	General Zionists	Trade and Industry
Yitzhak Gruenbaum	General Zionists	Interior
Fritz Rosenblüth	General Zionists	Justice
Yehuda L. Fishman	Mizrachi	Religious Affairs
Itzhak M. Levin	Agudas Israel	Social Welfare
Behor Shitrit	Sephardim	Minorities & Police

Source: *Israel and Middle East*, October–November, 1948, p. 33.

TABLE I.3: Israel's Diplomatic Relations as of May 1, 1949

Country	Date	Country	Date
Albania	04/18/49	Honduras	11/09/48
Argentina	02/16/49	Hungary	06/03/48
Austria	03/16/49	Iceland	02/09/49
Belgium	01/30/49	Ireland	02/13/49
Bolivia	02/24/49	Italy	01/27/49
Brazil	02/08/49	Luxembourg	01/30/49
Bulgaria	11/28/48	Niceragua	05/19/48
Colombia	02/02/49	Norway	02/05/49
Cuba	01/15/49	Phillipines	04/20/49
Czechoslovakia	05/18/48	Poland	05/18/48
Denmark	02/03/49	Romania	06/13/48
Ecuador	02/03/49	South Africa	05/24/48
El Salvador	09/17/48	Switzerland	01/29/49
Finland	06/12/48	Turkey	03/29/49
France	01/20/49	United States	05/14/48
Great Britain	01/30/49	Uruguay	05/19/48
Guatemala	05/19/48	USSR	05/18/48
Holland	06/02/48	Venezuela	05/27/48

Sources: *New York Times*; *American Jewish Yearbook*.

---

[1] Ampersands (&) have been used to designate persons holding more than one portfolio.

Va'ad ha-Bitahon (ועד הביטחון, VHB), "The Defense Committee," JA committee established in November 1947, pending the U.N. vote on partition. It was empowered to prepare the *Yishuv*'s defenses in case of all-out war. VHB replaced the so-called X Committee, which had set priorities for the anti-British struggle after 1946. VHB took one major decision: to organize the army that would come into existence after independence along the lines of a conventional rather than a guerrilla army. > see also: **X Committee.**

J

Jahreskonferenz [G] "Annual Conference": Term for meetings held by the Grosses Aktions-Komité of the WZO between 1902 and 1922, principally, regular conferences held when no Zionist congress was in session. The annual conferences (actually held biennially) became necessary after the congress format was changed from annual to biennial at the Fifth World Zionist Congress (1910). Jahreskonferenzen were held until 1922; the 1924 conference was canceled and the Fourteenth World Zionist Congress abolished them altogether. Thereafter meetings between congresses were usually organized as meetings of the WZO Va'ad ha-Poel. > see also: **World Zionist Congress; World Zionist Organization**.

TABLE J.1: The Jahreskonferenzen

Year	Dates	Location	Year	Dates	Location
1902	October 28–30	Vienna	1910	June 27–29	Berlin
1904	August 17–19	Vienna	1912	September 1–3	Berlin
1906	August 28–31	Cologne	1920	July 7–22	London
1908	August 11–13	Cologne	1922	August 25–September 1	Karoly Vary

Source: Central Zionist Archive

Jargon [Slang]: Linguistic term used by some Zionists as a derogatory name for Yiddish. They felt that Jewry would only experience a rebirth when it abandoned its diaspora culture and returned to the daily use of the national tongue, Hebrew. > see also: **Hebrew, Revival of; Language Conflict; Yiddishism**.

Jerusalem Program [GN]: Name used for the Biltmore resolution after it was approved by the Va'ad ha-Poel ha-Mezumzam in late 1942. > see also: **Biltmore Resolution**.

Jihad [Ar] "Great Effort": Arabic term for a divinely ordained holy war, presumably one to spread Islam, in which all Muslims must participate. Death in a *Jihad* guarantees soldiers a future place in heaven. Although the Jihad is not usually associated with a specific territory, the concept is closely connected to the belief that Muslims should never cede ground to infidels (even so-called People of the Book, i.e., Jews and Christians). As a result, the term *Jihad* has had great usage in the Arab-Israeli conflict, with Arab leaders repeatedly calling for a Jihad to eliminate the Zionist endeavor. > see also: **Arabs**.

342

Jordan Valley Authority [GN]: Proposed name for the water-sharing agency that was central to Walter C. Lowdermilk's plan for development in Palestine/Eretz Israel and Tans-Jordan. > see also: **Lowdermilk Plan; Eleventh Commandment**.

Judaism and Zionism

1. Scope and Definition

Although Zionism viewed itself as a movement for Jewish national rebirth, its attitude toward — and relationship with — Jewish tradition was mixed. On the one hand, Zionism drew from the wellspring of traditional sources to justify its call for re-creating a Jewish national entity in *Eretz Israel*. Thus, it was not unusual for Zionist leaders of all ideological persuasions to use biblical texts or the bible as a whole to "prove" their assertions. The most radical such usage (ironic in that its author was not personally religious) was by David Ben-Gurion who proclaimed, on numerous occasions, that "the Bible is our mandate." The importance of drawing items from Jewish tradition cannot be underestimated. It offered an unbroken Jewish link to *Eretz Israel* to a nationalist movement, the bulk of whose members resided in the diaspora.

Nevertheless, Zionism also saw itself as an essentially secular movement with the subsidiary goal of creating a new Jewish identity; as it were, to create "a new Jewish man." Insofar as Zionism offered a modern effort at defining Jewish identity, its goal was to reduce the obvious differences between Jews and non-Jews by creating a Jewish national home that "was like all the nations."

As a result of these diverse goals, each of which was open to greatly nuanced individual approaches, Zionism invariably brought to the fore (and sometimes exacerbated) already existing religious and cultural tensions within the Jewish community. Such tension did not always derive from Zionism. Changes in religious identification that developed in the first half of the nineteenth century — notably the rise of Reform Judaism — also had the same effect and impacted on the way which communities responded to the Zionist call. > see also: **Zionut; Cultural Conflict; Conquest of Communities**.

2. Denominational Attitudes Toward Zionism[1]

Conservative Judaism emphasized the need to retain a positive view of Jewish history and Jewish tradition without being restricted by either. Since that position is similar to the classical Zionist point of view, Conservatives (as a movement) always strongly supported Zionist goals. The earliest student Zionist groups in the United States and Canada were associated with or founded by alumni of the Jewish Theological Seminary of America. Conservative support for Zionism was strengthened during the 1930s and 1940s as prominent Conservative rabbis, including Israel Goldstein, accepted senior positions in the Zionist Organization of America.

Hasidism generally opposed Zionism, despite the intense feeling of imminent redemption that is central to Hasidic thought. Most Hasidic leaders of the nineteenth century resisted the Zionist movement, since it sought to hasten redemption by means other than divine action. Additionally, most Hasidic courts opposed the Zionists' secular orientation. Opposition to Political and especially to Spiritual Zionism did not decrease Hasidic interest in *Eretz Israel*, however, and a small but steady stream of Hasidim migrated there throughout the period prior to the State of Israel's establishment.

Orthodox Judaism accepted the premise that Jewish law and tradition retain continued relevance in the modern era; as a result, Orthodoxy found itself divided in its attitude toward Zionism. Deep attachment to, and hope

---

[1] These statements are broad generalizations of each group's attitude toward Zionism and are not meant to reflect all nuances and opinions. Differing attitudes toward the State of Israel are not included.

for redemption in, *Eretz Israel* was balanced by fear of Zionism's secularizing and heterodox trends. Therefore, it is not possible to speak of one Orthodox attitude, but, broadly speaking, two opposing trends which reflected in Orthodox organizations formed in the early twentieth century: (1) Support for Zionist goals, combined with the hope of influencing Zionists to return to tradition, the approach adopted by the Mizrachi (religious Zionist) movement. (2) Outright rejection for reasons similar to those used by the contemporary Hasidic courts of any manifestation of Zionism (including religious Zionism), an approach that was adopted by Agudas Israel. > see also: **Historic Coalition**.

Reconstructionist Judaism an offshoot of Conservative Judaism, retained Conservatism's strong support for Zionism. Indeed, Mordechai M. Kaplan, the "father" of Reconstructionism, made the re-creation of Jewish national and cultural life, as reflected by Zionism, central to his concept of Judaism. Kaplan's concept of Judaism, it might be added, bore a strong resemblance to the ideas of Ahad ha-Am. > see also: **Zionut, Types of Zionism (Spiritual Zionism)**.

Reform Judaism as manifested in early and mid-nineteenth century Germany and the United States, saw Judaism in exclusively religious terms and thus strongly opposed Zionism and all other forms of Jewish nationalism. Opposition to Zionism was articulated most clearly in the 1885 Pittsburgh Platform adopted by the Central Conference of American Rabbis (CCAR) that utterly rejected the notion of a Jewish nation. Reform opponents of Zionism also succeeded in forcing a change of venue for the First World Zionist Congress, from Munich to Basel. This position muted slowly. Notwithstanding official opposition to Zionism many younger Reform rabbis — such as Stephen S. Wise and Abba Hillel Silver in the United States and Ignaz Maybaum in Germany (and later Great Britain) — became forceful supporters of the Zionist movement. By 1935, conditions in the Jewish world had changed to such a degree that the CCAR was forced to change its position, adopting, in its Columbus Platform, a neutral attitude toward Zionism. Thereafter, activity on behalf of Zionism was left to each rabbi and his conscience. That position was further eroded as a result of the Holocaust. By 1943 the CCAR was openly supporting the movement to create a Jewish state in postwar *Eretz Israel*. This led to a schism within the CCAR, with diehard opponents of Zionism withdrawing to form the American Council for Judaism. > see also: **Organizations, Non- or Anti-Zionist (United States, American Council for Judaism)**.

Kahal [קהל, H] "Community": Jewish political term denoting both the community and its governing board (technically known as the *Kehila*). In the preemancipation era the *Kahal* was the focus of Jewish autonomy; after the emancipation, however, its role was limited to religious and cultural activities. Zionist interest in the *Kehilot* centered on the legitimacy that could be derived from being seen as the "successor" to diaspora Jewish institutions and from the potential economic benefits that could derive from communal taxation. As a result, local Zionist federations in almost every country and major locality sought to "conquer" the community by taking over the *Kahal*'s leadership. > see also: **Conquest of Communities; Infiltration.**

Kaiserjuden [G] "King's Jews": Derisive term for German Jewry coined by Chaim Weizmann before World War I. The term emphasized the high degree of German Jewish assimilation, even among Zionists, and the inflated (in Weizmann's eyes) German patriotism imbuing the entire German Jewish community.

Kaplansky Program [PN]: Popular name for the binationalist scheme for Palestine/*Eretz Israel*'s future proposed in 1941 by Technion director Shlomo Kaplansky. A well-known Zionist, Kaplansky had joined Mapai at its inception and served as director of the JA Settlement Department between 1927 and 1929. He was tasked with chairing a committee on Arab-Jewish relations by the Twenty-First Zionist Congress (1939) and was ordered to report his findings to the Va'ad ha-Poel ha-Mezumzam as soon as possible. Kaplansky issued his report in 1941. He sought to create a scheme that would assuage Arab fears while permitting continued (but limited) *aliya* and Zionist development. In effect, he proposed a system of "dual sovereignty" and full parity between Jews and Arabs in a joint government. Rejected out of hand by the Arabs and never really considered by the British, Kaplansky's proposal was repudiated by Mapai as inconsistent with Jewish needs of the hour during the debate over the Biltmore Program. Nonetheless, the plan became central to ha-Shomer ha-Zair's ideology for most of the 1940s. > see also: **Binationalism; Biltmore Program.**

Kayak(s): Slang term used by the Mossad le-Aliya Bet for the small motor launches it used to shuttle *Ma'apilim* during rescue operations from the Dodacanese Islands (which were then under Nazi occupation) during World War II. Each boat could carry twenty to thirty *Ma'apilim* and safely transport them to ports in Turkey where they were permitted to request certificates for legal entry into *Eretz Israel*. By this means some 850 Greek Jews were rescued in between September 1943 and September 1944. > see also: **Aliya Bet.**

Kenufiyot [כנופיות, H] "Bands": Zionist term for the groups of armed Arabs who attacked

Jewish settlements. The term did not really distinguish between organized attackers who operated for basically political goals, that is, those seeking to disrupt the development of the *Yishuv*, and robbers seeking plunder. Before 1929 robbers represented the greatest threat to the *Yishuv*. Thereafter, the politically organized bands (some actually small private armies) posed the greater threat. > see also: **Arabs**; **Meora'ot**.

Kfar [כפר, H] "Village": Hebrew term for a settlement, generally used to designate a *Moshav* or *Kibbutz*. The term is directly parallel to the Arabic term Kafr and has been used in conjunction with many place names; for example, Kfar Etzion. > see also: **Agricultural Settlement(s)**; **Gush**.

Kfilim [כפילים, H] "Doubles": Slang term used by men of the Jewish Brigade Group who remained in Europe after their term of service expired to assist in the rescue and rehabilitation of Jewish displaced persons. The term derived from the fact that by remaining in Europe, these men created slots for the Mossad le-Aliya Bet to sneak *Ma'apilim* into *Eretz Israel*, literally under the noses of the British high command. In all, 130 men volunteered to stay behind so that some refugees could get to *Eretz Israel* more quickly. > see also: **World War II, Jewish Military Units (Hativa Yehudit Lohemet)**.

Kibbush ha-Avoda [כיבוש העבודה, H] "Conquest of Labor": Socialist Zionist term deriving from the period of the Second Aliya and expressing the belief that national rebirth could only be accomplished by means of Jewish labor in *Eretz Israel*. Socialist Zionists viewed the transformation of Jewry as part and parcel of the Zionist goal; in light of contemporary populist ideas they concentrated on the ideal of a people living and working its own land. This was the basis for the idea of *Kibbush ha-Avoda*, that is, the idea that Jews could only control their destiny if they transformed themselves from an urban (or semiurban) society working in

"nonproductive" economic areas to an agricultural society working the land. As a corollary, *Kibbush ha-Avoda* implied that Jewish landowners should refrain from hiring Arabs to do their work for them. > see also: **Zionut**; **Avoda Ivrit**; **Halutz**; **Halutzic Aliya**; **Agricultural Settlement(s)**.

Kibbutz [קיבוץ, H] "Collective Settlement": > see also: **Agricultural Settlement(s)**.

Kibbutz Galuyot [קיבוץ גלויות, H] "Ingathering of the Exiles": Talmudic term for the messianic era when all Jews will return to the Holy Land. The term was used by Zionists of all political stripes to designate the stream of *olim* that would come to *Eretz Israel* once the Jewish national home was established on a firm foundation. In many cases, however, this use of the term was a rhetorical tool rather than a specific plan; in this case the term was used more to describe a hoped-for eventual result, rather than a specific long-term goal. During the Holocaust the term took on a tragically ironic further meaning. The Nazis concentrated all Jews in one place (Poland) in order to kill them. In some cases, the Nazis pacified their victims with the story that they were to be transported to Palestine/*Eretz Israel*. In 1947, the term was used as the code name for the Mossad blockade runner SS *Pan York*. > see also: **Aliya**; **Aliya Bet, Ships**.

Kibbutznik [קיבוצניק, H/Slang]: Term for a member of a Kibbutz. > see also: **Agricultural Settlement(s), Types of Settlements (Kibbutz)**.

Kindertransporte [G] "Children's transports": Convoys of trains or trucks made up entirely of Jewish children from Germany or other occupied countries that were able to leave Europe for temporary or permanent shelter (e.g., Youth Aliya transports to Palestine). > see also: **Teheran Children**.

King David Hotel Incident [HT]: Popular name for the bombing carried out by members of the Irgun Zvai Leumi (IZL) on July 22, 1946. The attack was the culmination of a series of attacks begun by IZL under the auspices of the United Hebrew Resistance Movement (a loose coalition of the IZL, Lohame Herut Israel, and the Hagana) against British installations in *Eretz Israel*. The first such attack, on May 25, 1945, destroyed a portion of the Haifa to Kirkuk oil pipeline and was soon followed by a series of attacks on police stations and other installations. The attack on the King David Hotel was to be the culmination of this campaign, as the building's south wing served as adminstrative headquarters for the Palestine government's military and political commands. The attack was carried out in broad daylight. While a diversionary incident took place outside, IZL members dressed as Arabs brought five milk cans of explosives into the hotel kitchen. The bombs were exploded shortly after 12:30 P.M. A telephone warning by the IZL at 12:20 P.M. was apparently ignored by security officials, who thought it was a false alarm. As a result, the building was not evacuated when the bombs went off, resulting in ninety-six deaths. Among those killed were fifteen Jews, mainly employees of the hotel. Sensing that the attack had been counterproductive, the JAE distanced itself from the IZL and broke with the United Hebrew Resistance Movement. A brief return of civil war between the Hagana and IZL ensued — the so-called Saizon Sheini — but was soon called off. Despite the loss of life, a number of historians argue that the destruction of the King David Hotel was central to the British decision to refer the Palestine/*Eretz Israel* issue to the United Nations. > see also: **Yishuv, Yishuv Organizations (Underground Organizations, Tenuat ha-Mered ha-Ivri); Ha-Mered; Shabbat ha-Shahor; Saizon Sheini.**

Klal Israel [כלל ישראל, H] "The Entirety of Israel": Term emphasizing the unity of the Jewish people, their common origins, and their linked destiny. Klal Israel first developed as a religious concept that designated the covenantal relationship between Jews both vertically (i.e., over history) and horizontally (i.e., in all lands).

Zionists incorporated this idea, giving it a more explicit political content and deemphasizing the term's religious basis. Zionists also used the idea of *Kklal Israel* as a means to distinguish themselves from non- or anti-Zionists. Zionists emphasized (and strove to fulfill the needs of) Jewish unity, whereas their opponenets were accused (in most cases correctly) of abandoning the idea of Jewish unity altogether.

Klaniot [כלניות, H] "Anemones": Hebrew slang term used to designate troops of the British Sixth Airborne Division during their service in Palestine between 1946 and 1948. The term was partly derogatory, although it derived from a value-free source: the color of the paratroopers' maroon berets was likened to a coral sea creature.

Kna'an [כנען, H] "Land of Cana'an": One of the biblical names for the Land of Israel, derived from the aboriginal inhabitants of the central highlands. The term was used in restorationist literature of the seventeenth and eighteenth centuries but was rarely used in modern Zionist discourse. During the 1940s a splinter group calling themselves *Kna'anim* (Cana'anites) advocated the abnegation of Zionism's Jewish origins and its assimilation into the Semitic Middle East. > see also: **Kna'anim.**

Kna'anim [כנענים, H] "Cana'anites": Name of the intellectual circle active in *Eretz Israel* during the late 1940s and thereafter as a response to reputed post-Zionist alternatives for the Jewish national home or (after 1948) the State of Israel. The *Kna'anim* were mostly young writers and artists who rejected Israel's Zionist and Jewish roots, arguing for the abnegation of any identification between the Hebrew state (Israel) and world Jewry. Instead, they advocated Israel's asssimilation into the Semitic Middle East in order to attain peaceful relations with the Arabs. The roots of *Kna'anism* may be traced back to World War II, a period of intense upheaval during which some Zionists militants (from both the radical left and right) argued that the *Yishuv* should seek to broaden its anti-British posture into an anti-imperialist posture, thereby linking the *Yishuv*'s future with the broader Semitic nation(s) — including the Arabs, Druze, Kurds, and Maronites — and aiding them in their struggle for independence. *Kna'anism* peaked in its appeal between 1948 and 1953; it declined thereafter (although the underpinning ideology never completely disappeared and has recently resurfaced in the guise of "post-Zionism") mainly due to the increasingly genocidal nature of Arab hostility toward Israel.

Knesset [כנסת, H] "Assembly": Official name of Israel's parliament and the official seat of Israeli government.

Knesset Israel [כנסת ישראל, H] "Assembly of Israel": Official term for the Jewish community of Palestine/*Eretz Israel* under the mandate. Knesset Israel (KI) was the communal framework created by the British for Jews in the Jewish national home. A parallel Arab body was supposed to come into being but was never fully organized due to Arab refusal to consider the possibility of sharing the territory with Jews. KI was organized in 1920; legislation regulating its operations was promulgated by the British in 1928, at which point KI superseded the Jewish millet that had been created by the Turks prior to World War I. KI included all Jews as members, including non- and anti-Zionists, although it was possible to withdraw from the body. Officially, KI oversaw the functions of both the Va'ad Leumi and Assefat ha-Nivharim. In practice, both bodies were dominated by Zionists and operated under the WZO's authority. > see also: **Millet System; Mandate, League of Nations; Organizations; Yishuv.**

Kofer ha-Yishuv [כופר הישוב, H] "Settlement Tax": Official title for the tax system created by the JA and the Va'ad Leumi (VL) from July 24, 1938, to September 1948. Collected by the VL, the tax was used for defense purposes, including financing the *Homa u-Migdal* settlements and purchasing weapons for the Hagana. In light of its illicit

purposes, the *Yishuv*'s institutions did not rely on British aid in collecting the tax; rather, it was framed as a voluntary contribution by the *Yishuv*'s population. Despite its voluntary nature, considerable social pressure to comply meant that most individuals agreed to pay their assessments. During World War II, additional uses were found for the taxes, including providing funds to help enlistment in the British army (the "enlistment fund") and aiding efforts to rescue European Jews (The "rescue fund"). During its existence the tax raised a total of £P150,000 ($750,000), or roughly three quarters of the Hagana's budget. Kofer ha-Yishuv ceased to function in September 1948, its functions being absorbed into the provisional government's Ministry of Finance. > see also: **Yishuv; Sochnut Yehudit; Homa u-Migdal.**

Kotel ha-Ma'aravi [כתל המערבי, H] "Western Wall": Proper name for the surviving wall of the Second Temple in Jerusalem that was destroyed in 70 C.E. by the Roman army comanded by Titus. Scenes of Jews praying at the wall and a complete misunderstanding of Jewish prayer rituals led the wall to be dubbed the "Wailing Wall" in English, a term that does not correctly translate the Hebrew words. Because the Temple (and especially the section known as the Holy of Holies) was traditionally considered Jewry's holiest site, great reverence has continued for the wall. Regular worship services were held there between the tenth century and the present day, interrupted only during the Jordanian occupation of the Old City between 1948 and 1967. During the 1920s and 1930s, the wall and the approaches to it became the scene of numerous violent clashes between Jews and Arabs.

Kumsitz [קומזיץ, Y] "Gathering": Slang term used by members of the Palmah for an informal party, usually in camp around a campfire, during which unit members shared stories, songs, and food. The term derived from two Yiddish words, *Kum* (come) and *Sitz* (sit down) but the concept was unique to the *Yishuv*.

Kvutza [קבוצה, H] "Collective Settlement Group": > see also: **Agricultural Settlement(s).**

Two views of the Western Wall: As it appeared in the 1920s (top) and in the 1990s (bottom)
Courtesy of the Central Zionist Archives, Jerusalem (top); Authors' Collection (bottom)

Kvutzat Hitnagdut [קבוצת התנגדות, H] "Opposition Group": Mossad le-Aliya Bet term for the teams of *Ma'apilim* — generally younger and healthier individuals — tasked with offering resistance to British boarding parties on blockade runners.

Generally, the teams had specific locations in different parts of each ship. They were expected to offer at least token resistance but were to desist from any form of opposition if it seemed likely that the British would respond with deadly force. > see also: **Aliya Bet**.

Kvutzat Kibbush [קבוצת כיבוש, H] "Conquest Group": Term for the team of pioneers that preceded settlers to the site of a new settlement prior to its erection. The team staked out the perimeter of the camp and secured the region prior to the arrival of the settlers and their escorts.

Labor Wing [HT]: Common 1920s term for those elements in Poale Zion or Ahdut ha-Avoda (prior to their 1930 merger to form Mapai) that opposed the use of private capital for Jewish settlement building in *Eretz Israel*. The labor wing's members did not uncategorically reject the inflow of capital from private sources. Instead, they argued that such capital should be donated to the WZO and used for national, rather than private, purposes. Most socialist Zionists agreed, to one degree or another, with this line of reasoning; specifics were open to widely differing interpretations (e.g., whether middle-class Jews should ever be admitted to the *Yishuv* or whether *aliya* should be limited to *Halutzim*) that led to considerable dynamism within the labor wing, frequent schisms, and ultimate collapse after the parties merged. > see also: **Halutzic Aliya**.

Land Ownership:

1. Scope and Definition

Although Zionists claimed an inalienable link between the Jewish people and their ancestral homeland, actual possession of *Eretz Israel* was, before 1948, largely in Arab hands. Jews hoping to expand the area of settlement (even prior to the rise of Zionism had to grapple with the need to purchase land, often from nonresident landlords who charged exorbitant prices for miniscule parcels of land. After 1881, when Zionist settlement began, the problem of ownership became even more critical. Clashes over possession of lands, and especially over rights to wells, were frequent already at the turn of the century. Fear that wealthy Jews would buy the entire territory and thereby threaten the Ottoman Empire's security led the government to ban land sales to Jews altogether in 1908.

After World War I, Jewish land purchase again became (along with *aliya*) a sore point in Arab-Jewish relations; specifically, Arabs rejected the right of Jews to purchase land in the same way that they rejected the Jewish right to a national home, claiming that Jewish land purchases led inexorably to dispossession of Arab farmers who had possessed the land without interruption for the previous 1,300 years. In fact, Arabs claims were greatly exaggerated. Far from dropping (as would be expected in cases of mass dispossession), the Arab population of mandatory Palestine/*Eretz Israel* grew steadily between 1922 and 1947 — in some localities by a rate much greater than the potential natural increase. Furthermore, according to some estimates, only 4,000 Arab families were displaced by Jewish land settlement during the entire mandatory era.

In any case, Jews were in possession of only a small portion of the Palestine landmass during the mandatory era. In 1939, the MacDonald White Paper promised to limit Jewish land purchase, a promise that was enacted into legislation with the land regulations of 1940. This new legislation divided Palestine/*Eretz Israel* into three zones. In zones A and B (respectively 64 and 31

Table L.1: Jewish Land Purchases, 1878–1939[1]

Year	Dunams Purchased	Total in Jewish Hands
1878–1890	67,073	67,073
1891–1900	60,218	127,291
1901–1914	118,290	245,581
1920–1922	103,137	348,718
1923–1927	199,678	548,396
1928–1932	92,432	640,828
1933–1936	41,150	681,978
1937–1939	84,820	766,798

Source: Yehoshua Porath, "The Land Problem in Mandatory Palestine," *Jerusalem Quarterly* 1 (Fall 1976): 20–21.

percent of *Eretz Israel*'s landmass) Jewish land purchase was severely restricted; only in zone C — where Jews already owned a majority of the arable land — Jews would have free purchase rights. The regulations immediately became a touch point in Jewish resistance to the white paper, although such acts were not effective until the very end of the mandate.

Throughout the period Zionist land purchases were primarily conducted by two agencies, although individuals could (and did) buy land for themselves: the Keren Kayemet le-Isreal (KKL, Jewish National Fund) was the agency responsible for acquiring funds and purchasing land while the Keren ha-Yesod (KHY, Settlement Fund) was responsible for oversight of settlement building on KKL lands. > see also: **A'yān; Simsār; White Paper(s), White Paper of 1939.**

Landspolitik [לאנדספוליטיק, Y] "Land Politics": Zionist term for Jewish political activity in the diaspora (whether by Zionists or by other Jewish political parties) not on behalf of the *Yishuv*. The term had a negative implication as if such activities produced little or no benefit and wasted effort that could be better used in settlement building. > see also: **Gegenwartsarbeit; Conquest of Communities.**

Landsverbände [G] "Territorial Organizations": Term for the national Zionist federations organized and chartered by the WZO. Each national federation was subdivided into local chapters based on the needs and geography of each individual country. In addition, each Zionist federation, chapter, and cell invariably further subdivided by parties, blocs, and factions. It may thus be fairly said that no two Zionist federations were identical. > see also: **World Zionist Organization; Sonderverbände.**

---

[1] Only land purchased directly from Arabs is included in this table; other land purchases (mainly from the government) raised Jewish held land to between 1,305,000 dunams (according to the JA) and 1,420,000 dunams (according to the government). Cf. *Statistical Abstract of Palestine* (Jerusalem: Government of Palestine, 1940), p. 174.

Law of Return [HT]: > see also: **Hok ha-Shvut**.

League of Nations [HT]: International body created after World War I to replace war by enhancing collective security through the mobilization of peace-loving nations against aggression. The league was intimately involved with the Palestine/*Eretz Israel* issue, and with other Jewish issues, with its founding on January 10, 1920. In particular, the league's Permanent Mandates Commission oversaw the mandate for Palestine/*Eretz Israel* granted to Great Britain on July 24, 1922. Albeit, oversight of the mandate was neither close nor careful. As a result, resolutions relating to alleged and actual cases of British deviation from the mandate's terms — especially crippling limits on *aliya* (stated by the mandate to be a Jewsh right not dependent upon British or Arab sufferance) — did little more than offer words of support for aggrieved Zionist activists. The league dedicated two special sessions to the Palestine problem: one in 1930, after the Passfield White Paper terminated *aliya*, and the other in 1937, in response to the Peel partition plan. In both cases the British were criticized for deviations from the mandate's terms, but no further action was taken. The league was also directly involved in protecting Jewish minority rights in Eastern and Southern Europe, accomplished through oversight of a series of national minority treaties that the East European successor states had to sign. These same countries used every opportunity to deny Jews (and other minorities) the rights thus granted, and the entire chapter points out the league's fundamental weakness: its inability to enforce its resolutions. On August 17, 1939, the Permanent Mandates Commission unanimously ruled that the British White Paper of 1939 was in conflict with the mandate's terms and suggested that the mandate be granted to a different country. Before any further action could be taken, World War II broke out and rendered the entire matter moot. The League of Nations

ceased to function on April 19, 1946, its diplomatic and political functions being absorbed by the United Nations. > see also: **Mandate, League of Nations; Committees of Investigation; White Papers, White Paper of 1939; United Nations**.

Legion ha-Am [לגיון העם, H] "The National Legion": Proposal by Michael Halperin, one of ha-Shomer's founders, to create a nationalist Jewish legion under British command to conquer *Eretz Israel* from the Turks. Halperin's idea was based on the premise that the British would carry out their El Arish scheme and that mass Jewish settlement near *Eretz Israel* would then be possible. Halperin's plan called for the military campaign to complete Zionist goals next. Although completely unrealistic when proposed (in 1903) Halperin's plan prefigured the creation of the Jewish Legion in World War I. > see also: **World War I**.

Legionism [HT]: Popular term for Ze'ev Jabotinsky's intitial defensive ideology, which placed great emphasis on the existence of the Jewish Legion. Jabotinsky felt that the Arabs would only come to an accommodation with Zionism if they were certain that the Zionists and the British were serious about their commitment to turn *Eretz Israel* into a Jewish national home. To convince the Arabs, it was necessary to appear strong and especially to appear willing to use force to defend Jewish interests. The legion would have a special role to play in this scheme as the main symbol of Jewish military strength. When the British disbanded the legion in 1921–1922, Jabotinsky was severely disappointed and turned to the task of creating Jewish self-defense forces in *Eretz Israel*. > see also: **World War I**.

Legislative Council: 1922 British proposal for a legislative body to respresent Palestine/*Eretz Israel*'s entire population, Arabs and Jews, in order to fulfill the terms of article 4 of the League of Nations mandate that called for creating "self-governing institutions." Although the council was never intended to have more than consultative powers, with actual authority remaining vested in the high commissioner's hands, the idea frightened Zionists, since a council elected on any basis other than intercommunal parity (equal representation for Jews and Arabs despite the difference in population) would guarantee an Arab majority. The initial proposal was to create a council with twelve elected members (eight Muslims, two Christian Arabs, and two Jews) and thirteen appointed members (one each from the three religious communities and ten appointed by the high commissioner) meant that even if the high commissioner only appointed Jews to the council (an unlikely event), an automatic majority aganist *aliya* and Zionist land purchase would exist and would thereby contradict the terms of both the Balfour Declaration and the mandate. Arab refusal to sit on a council including any Jewish members delayed implementation of the couincl until 1936. At that point the Arab revolt precipitated cancellation of the council altogether, although an all-Arab legislative council was explicitly promised in the constitutional clause of the White Paper of 1939. > see also: **Palestine, Mandatory; White Paper(s)**.

Le-Shana ha-Ba′a be-Yerushalayim [לשנה הבאה בירושלים, H] "Next year in Jerusalem": Traditional prayer used at the end of services on Yom Kippur and at the closure of the Passover seder(s). The phrase is suffused with messianic and redemptivist overtones; its purpose is to emphasize the close Jewish religious and cultural connection to *Eretz Israel*. Since the nineteenth century the term also carried political overtones, since Zionists used the term in a more literal sense, hoping that the goal of restoring the Jewish people to its homeland would come soon.

Leyl ha-Gesharim [ליל הגשרים, H] "Night of the Bridges": Underground term for the events of June 17–18, 1946. As an act of defiance against British rule, Hagana and Palmah units attacked and destroyed all the bridges leading into Palestine/*Eretz Israel*. Eleven bridges were destroyed in all and, although all were quickly rebuilt, the action proved embarrassing for the British high command. In response the British undertook operation Agatha, the mass arrest of JAE leaders. > see also: **Leyl ha-Rakavot; Shabbat ha-Shahor**.

Table L.2: Bridges Destroyed on June 17–18, 1946

Bridge	Location	Bridge	Location
Achziv Rail Bridge	Lebanese border	Damiya Bridge	Trans-Jordan
Achziv Road Bridge	Lebanese border	Gaza Rail Bridge	Egyptian border
Al-Haava Bridge	Upper Galilee	Gaza Road Bridge	Egyptian border
Allenby Bridge	Trans-Jordan	Metula Rail Bridge	Lebanese border
Bnot Yaakov Bridge	Upper Galilee	Metula Road Bridge	Lebanese border
Sheikh Hussein Bridge	Trans-Jordan		

Source: Hershel Edelheit and Abraham J. Edelheit comps., *A World in Turmoil: An Integrated Chronology of the Holocaust and World War II* (Westport, CT: Greenwood Press, 1991).

Leyl ha-Rakavot [ליל הרכבות, H] "Night of the Railroads": Underground term for the mass sabotage operation carried out under the auspices of the Tenuat ha-Meri ha-Ivri on November 1, 1945. As an act of defiance against British rule, elements of the Hagana, Palmah, Irgun Zvai Leumi, and Lohame Herut Israel undertook a coordinated series of attacks to disrupt Palestine/*Eretz Israel*'s

railroad communications. In 153 discrete attacks, saboteurs successfully cut the rail lines at fifty different locations. The result was temporary disruption of all railroad service and further embarrassment for the British high command. > see also: **Leyl ha-Gesharim**.

Leyl Wingate [ליל וינגייט, H/PN] "Wingate's Night": Official name for the Hagana/Palmah operation on March 24, 1946, connected with the arrival of the Mossad le-Aliya Bet blockade runner SS *Orde Wingate*. The ship, carrying 238 *Ma'apilim*, was the second largest sent until that time and was the subject of concerted efforts to land the *Ma'apilim* and hide them from British police and military units. Hagana's efforts notwithstanding, most of the *Ma'apilim* were captured and interned at the Atlit prison. Yet, by publicizing the plight of Jews in post-Holocaust Europe and their desperation to find a haven in *Eretz Israel*, the operation can be considered a political success. > see also: **Aliya Bet**.

Little Zionism [HT]: Derisive nickname used by revisionist Zionist Leader Ze'ev Jabotinsky in reference to the gradualist policies adopted by WZO president Chaim Weizmann. In Jabotinsky's estimation, Weizmann's policies represented a deviation from classical Zionism because they created no opportunity for timely mass *aliya*. Thus, according to Jabotinsky, gradualism would never result in a Jewish state, only in a "garden for show." > see also: **Gradualism**; **Fata Morgana Land**; **Cult of the Cow**.

Lodge-Fish Resolution [PN]: Colloquial name for Joint Resolution 73 passed unanimously by both houses of the U.S. Congress on September 21, 1922. Named after its sponsors, Senator Henry Cabot Lodge and Congressman Hamilton Fish, the resolution expressed strong U.S. support for the Balfour Declaration, the League of Nations mandate, and, more broadly, for the idea of a Jewish national home. Although officially committed to a policy of isolationism, the resolution expressed considerable interest in and support for Zionism in the United States.

Lohameiel/Shomreiel [לוחמיאל/שומריאל, H] "God's Fighters/God's Watchmen": Names proposed by Rabbi Akiva Joseph Schlesinger for a Jewish army that would conquer *Eretz Israel* and thereby hasten the messianic era. Rabbi Schlesinger made the

proposal shortly after his *aliya* in 1870, although the exact date is unknown. The Lohameiel were to be a mounted offensive cavalry while the Shomreiel were to be an infantry force that would defend areas captured by the cavalry. Despite its fanciful nature (perhaps because of it) nothing came of the scheme. > see also: **Proto-Zionism**.

Lowdermilk Plan [PN]: Economic development plan associated with Walter Clay Lowdermilk, who had served in the soil conservation division of the U.S department of agriculture. In 1942 Lowdermilk visited Palestine/*Eretz Israel* to research agricultural development. Upon his return to the United States, he proposed a threefold scheme to irrigate the entire Middle East and bring peace between Jews and Arabs. Lowdermilk's plan, as set out in his 1944 bestseller, *Palestine: Land of Promise*, was based on creating a Jordan Valley Authority (similar to the American Tennessee Valley Authority) to harness the Jordan's waters. By using a series of strategically placed dams and pipelines, Lowermilk hoped that the entire land mass of Palestine/*Eretz Israel*, including the Negev, could be irrigated. The Arabs would thus have nothing to fear from Jewish immigration since there would be enough arable land for everyone. Embraced by the Jewish Agency (mainly because it opposed the concepts behind the British White Paper of 1939), the Lowdermilk plan was never actually implemented. Instead, parts of the plan were incorporated into the plan for Israel's national water carrier system, the Movil Artzi, completed in May 1964.

Lubricating Expenses [HT/Slang]: Euphemistic expression used by agents of the Mossad le-Aliya Bet for bribes paid to officials in order to facilitate the exodus of Jews who might otherwise experience difficulty in leaving their homes. Between 1945 and 1948 the term was primarily used in reference to Eastern European countries and reflected the desperate measures needed to guarantee the continuation of *Briha* in countries that were rapidly being taken over by the Communists. Most bribes were paid to midlevel officials involved in border control in Czechoslovakia, Hungary,

Romania, and Bulgaria. After 1948 the same term was applied to bribes paid to officials in Muslim countries (e.g., Iraq and Iran) that had opposed the creation of the State of Israel. > see also: **Aliya Bet; Briha**.

Luftgesheft(en) [G]: "Self-debasing Profession(s)": Labor Zionist term referring to the supposedly unnatural concentration of diaspora Jews in certain "nonproductive" professions (such as small-scale trade). Some of the earliest Zionist (and proto-Zionist) thinkers called for Jews to return to the land and to agricultural labor as a means to create an ideal Jewish entity and begin a Jewish national renaissance. This condemnation of Jewish professions went hand in hand with *Shlilat ha-Gola*, especially among more radical and ideologically motivated socialist Zionists and *Kibbutz* members. Condemnation of Luftgesheften was also manifested in movements (again, principally, but not exclusively, the various *Kibbutz* movements) that emphasized *Halutzic Aliya*. The Holocaust put an almost complete end to such discussions; after World War II all Zionists emphasized rescuing as many Jews as possible regardless of their professions. > see also: **Shilat Ha-gola; Halutzic Aliya**.

Luftmensch(en) [(לופטמנש(ן, Y] "Dreamer(s)": Literally "man (men) of air," the term was a derogatory expression for Eastern European Jews who, lacking gainful employment, were reduced to dreaming up schemes to rescue the Jewish people. > see also: **Luftgesheft(en)**.

Ma'abara/Ma'abarot [מעברה/מעברות, H] "Transit Camp(s)": Popular name for the temporary housing accommodations made for the thousands of new *olim* who came to Israel in the first years of independence. Conditions in the camps were chaotic, a result of both poor planning and lack of facilities. These intolerable conditions manifested themselves primarily in a scandalous lack of sanitary facilities. Although many critics of the Israeli government claimed that these conditions derived from a lack of sensitivity to the *olim* (most of whom came as refugees from Middle Eastern countries) on the part of Zionist leaders of European descent, such was not the case. Indeed, most of the glaring deficiencies of the *Ma'abarot* were cleared up during the early 1950s and by the end of the decade the last transit camps had closed down entirely as their inhabitants found housing in permanent settlements.

Ma'amadiut [מעמדיות, H] "Classism": Labor Zionist term for the concentration on class-related issues and proerty ownership. Derived from the concepts of contemporary European socialists, *Ma'amadiut* represented an attempt to synthesize Zionism and socialism to create a classless society in a revived Jewish national home. Notwithstanding its explicit nature, *Ma'amadiut* was never viewed exclusively in European terms. In particular, the reformist wing of the labor Zionist movement (represented by Mapai and by such leaders as David Ben-Gurion, Haim Arlosoroff, and Berl Katznelson) saw *Ma'amadiut* as a temporary phase in the history of Jewish national rebirth. Zionism, they claimed, needed to concentrate on its laboring wing in order to fulfill its goals, after which the Jewish national home would develop into a sovereign entity that represented all Jews. On the other hand, many socialist Zionists (such as ha-Shomer ha-Zair and the Communists) took the idea of *Ma'amadiut* literally and advocated class struggle within the *Yishuv* and the WZO. > see also: **Mamlahtiut; Halutz; Halutzic Aliya.**

Ma'apil(im) [מעפיל(ים), H] "Climbers": Popular *Yishuv* term for Jews undertaking the arduous trek to *Eretz Israel* as "illegal" immigrants. Used without regard to whether the *Ma'apil* was part of a group or acted as an individual, the term emphasizes his or her active role in *Aliya Bet*. > see also: **Aliya Bet; Ha'apala.**

Maccabiah [מכביה, H]: Official name of the quadrennial Jewish athletic competition held in Israel. First proposed by Joseph Yekutieli in 1923, the games were conceived as a "Jewish Olympics" that would showcase the new-found athletic skills possessed by nationalistically oriented Jewish youth wordwide. Yekutieli emphasized the fact that Zionism always called for the reinvigration of world Jewry and a renewal of the Jewish sense of physicality and strength that were signs of a "healthy" nation. The WZO soon sponsored the games, the first

Maccabiah being held in 1932. A second set of games was held in 1935. Although a special village, Kfar ha-Maccabiah, was built in 1938, conditions in *Eretz Israel* did not permit any further games until after the State of Israel was established in 1948.

MacDonald Letter [PN]: Common name for the February 13, 1931, letter sent by British prime minister Ramsay MacDonald to WZO president Chaim Weizmann. In effect, the letter was an attempt to withdraw from the government's previous decision to repudiate commitments to Zionism and thereby limit the damage done to MacDonald's coalition government by the Passfield White Paper. Although the letter was thus a Zionist victory — *aliya* was protected in the short term — in actuality, all the letter did was to reinterpret the Passfield White Paper in such a way as to permit continued *aliya*. MacDonald did so only because the white paper was viewed in Britain and abroad as an abrogation of the mandate. He did not expand *aliya* and did not restore the previous certificate values (which were doubled in the 1930 Palestine Immigration Regulations). Indeed, the letter could be interpreted as replacing the policy of using Palestine/*Eretz Israel*'s economic absorptive capacity as a means to decide the *aliya* schedule with a "political maximum" of *aliya* that would be permitted at any time. > see also: **White Paper(s)**, **Passfield White Paper**; **Economic Absorptive Capacity**; **Political Maximum**; **Aliya**.

Magen David [דוד מגן, H] "Shield of David": Six-pointed star — two super-imposed triangles — that has come to be identified as one of Jewry's national symbols. Though used as a symbol at least since the third century C.E., the Magen David was widely used by Jews as a symbol only after the thirteenth century. The WZO adopted the Magen David as one of its symbols in 1897 and used it as the basis for the Zionist flag (now the Israeli flag). Albeit, the menora is actually the official symbol of the State of Israel. > see also: **Degel**; **Menora**.

Mahala/Terufa [מחלה/תרופה, H] "Disease/Medicine": Hagana code terms respectively standing for an Arab attack on Jews and a retaliatory strike by the Hagana on suspected Arab attackers. The term carried over into general use in Zva ha-Hagana le-Israel during Israel's early years. > see also: **Me'oraot**.

Mamlahtiut [ממלכתיות, H] "Etatism": Conceptualization of Zionism associated David Ben-Gurion and formulated by him in the 1930s. In Ben-Gurion's estimation, Zionist fulfillment required a two-step process, first, the creation of an *Am Oved* (laboring nation) via the creation of an economically viable *Yishuv* and, then, the creation of an *Am Mamlahti* (sovereign nation) by the creation of a Jewish majority in *Eretz Israel*, which would culminate in the creation of a Jewish state. Ben-Gurion's etatist ideology led him to eschew strictly Marxist socialist principles, even though when it suited him he defined himself strictly as a socialist (and even, on occasion, as a Leninist). He consistently called for socialist Zionist cooperation with any group — capitalist or not — that would further the goals of creating the *Am Mamlahti*. Despite his willingness to cooperate with other parties, Ben-Gurion's position was always based on the idea of Mapai domination of the *Yishuv* and hegemony over its political life. He saw Mapai as the only agency capable of fulfilling Zionist goals in the long term. Ben-Gurion continued to adhere to his *Mamlahti* position throughout the period of his premiership, viewing it as the only pragmatic way to defend Jewish statehood. > see also: **Constructive Socialism**.

Managam: Name of an unarmed British yacht, officially owned by the Khedive of Egypt but impressed for service by the Royal Navy, that was used to communicate with the Nili spy ring during World War I. Nili members knew the ship by the code name *Menahem*. In 1917 the HMS *Managam* undertook a number of secret missions to the coast of *Ertez Israel* to pick up information. On its last mission (September 25, 1917) the ship's captain offered Sarah Aaronson an opportunity to escape the ever tightening vise of Ottoman security, but she refused. Shortly thereafter, Aaronson was arrested, and the Nili ring was broken up.

Mandate, League of Nations:

1. Scope and Definition

Legal term for the framework under which Great Britain ruled Palestine/*Eretz Israel* between 1920 and 1948. The mandate system was created by the League of Nations as a means to control imperialism, at least theoretically, by forcing colonizing powers to act on behalf of the indigenous populations in colonies seized after World War I. In accepting the mandates, European countries (and in the Pacific, the Japanese) committed themselves to creating self-governing institutions that would lead the mandated territories to eventual independence. Again, the purpose of this system was to reduce international tensions that derived from untrammeled imperial conquest and sought to give European colonialism a kinder face. Mandates were granted to imperialist powers in consonance with article 22 of the League of Nations charter which, in turn, formed part and parcel of the Treaty of Versailles. > see also: **League of Nations**.

Middle Eastern mandates were carved out of former Ottoman territories occupied by the Allies as a reult of the successful British campaign during 1917 and 1918 but were complicated by the three apparently contradictory compacts that the British undertook with the French, the Arabs, and the Jews. Nonetheless, the British received mandates for Palestine/*Eretz Israel* (which initially included Trans-Jordan) and Iraq while the French received mandates over Syria and Lebanon at the San Remo conference in April 1920. In 1922, the British modified their mandate by separating Trans-Jordan from Palestine/*Eretz Israel* to create an independent entity, the Emirate of Trans-Jordan (which was granted independence in 1946). The history of Middle Eastern mandates was mixed. The British experienced outward success in Iraq, where a constitutional monarchy was created in 1926. However, the newly independent state never lived up to the spirit (not to mention of the letter) of the League of Nations charter under which it was created. The failure of constitutionalism in Iraq was pointedly proved in the case of the Assyrian massacres of the 1930s. The same held true for Trans-Jordan, a state carved out of an ill-defined territory and almost entirely dominated by the personality of the Emir Abdullah. The French mandates were also not notable successes. The French were hard-pressed in both cases to impose their rule on Arab nationalists who sought immediate independence. As a result, the French did not even attempt to fulfill the terms of the mandates and made no efforts to create the self-governing institutions that article 22 demanded. > see also: **Conferences, International, Sam Remo; White Paper(s), Churchill White Paper; Arabs; MacMahon-Hussein Correspondence; Sykes-Picot Agreement**.

The mandate in Palestine/*Eretz Israel* was an even unhappier failure. The British defined their role in the Holy Land as seeking to accomplish two totally contradictory goals: to create a Jewish national home while also protecting the rights of the local Arab population. Such an undertaking would have been difficult enough had the British been uniformly concerned with being fair to both communities. Such was not the case, however, and from the inception of the mandate the Zionists faced repeated struggles in London and Geneva to obtain in practice the elements needed to build the *Yishuv* that had been promised (free *aliya* and reasonable land purchase regulations) and had been unanimously guaranteed by the League of Nations. As a result, the twenty-seven-year history of the British mandate was a story of repeated conflicts between Jews and Arabs and between both of them and the British government. Broadly speaking, therefore, the mandate's history may be summarized as a sequence of Arab attack, appeasing British response, Jewish counterresponse, and resumption of the status quo ante under circumstances that satisfied no one. This vicious cycle was not broken until the termination of the mandate on May 14, 1948. > see also: **Balfour Declaration; Aliya; Aliya Bet; Land Ownership**.

Still, it should also be noted that the era of the mandate witnessed the greatest period of development within the *Yishuv* in every sphere: economic, demographic, social, educational, and political. In mandatory *Eretz Israel* Jewish self-government was truly created to an extent that was unprecedented, and which formed the basis for the State of Israel. Although the WZO was the first Jewish experiment in self-government in the modern era, it is clear that Jewish political life (at least of the Zionist persuasion) matured during the years of the mandate. It can truly be said that the political parties and blocs active in the State of Israel have their origins in the *Yishuv* during the mandate era. > see also: **Yishuv; Sochnut Yehudit; World Zionist Organization.**

TABLE M.1: British High Commissioners in Palestine/*Eretz Israel*

Name	*Tenure*	*Prior Service*
Herbert Samuel	July 1920–August 1925	Parliament
Herbert O. Plumer	August 1925–November 1928	Royal Army
John Chancellor	November 1928–November 1931	Royal Army
Arthur Wauchope	November 1931–March 1938	Royal Army
Harold MacMichael	March 1938–October 1944	Colonial Office
Vereker J. Gort	October 1944–November 1945	Royal Army
Alan G. Cunningham	November 1945–May 1948	Royal Navy

Source: Central Zionist Archives

Mandelbaum Gate [PN]: Popular name for the walled-off area on the border between Israeli West Jerusalem and Jordanian East Jerusalem between 1948 and 1967. The "gate" — actually two walls (one on each side of an alley) and two buildings used for customs and security posts — was built on the site of the dormitories of a yeshiva founded by Rabbi Baruch Mandelbaum (hence the name) in 1927. The yeshiva had been the scene of fierce fighting during the War of Independence and was relocated in 1949. The buildings of the former yeshiva were located at the point where Israel and Jordanian-occupied territory came together and (to a degree) overlapped. The gate served as the only open line of communications between Israel and the Israeli garrison on Mount Scopus and as the meeting site between Israeli and Jordanian military leaders on those occasions when exchanges had to take place (e.g., of prisoners of war). After the Six Day War (1967) the gate was demolished. > see also: **War of Independence.**

Mashiah [משיח, H] "Messiah": Redemptivist Jewish belief in a perfect future that will be brought into existence by a divinely inspired savior who will manifest himself by causing the Jews' return to the Holy Land. The messianic concept may be traced back to the prophetic books of the Bible and was considerably embellished during the years of the diaspora. As a religious ideology, Jewish messianism had an activist wing that called for human deeds to hasten the Messiah's arrival and a passive wing that emphasized waiting until the moment of divine redemption was at hand. Although more satisfying emotionally, active messianism generally ended in disaster when false messiahs were exposed as frauds. Passive messianism, on the other hand, helped foster Jewish survival by giving hope for a better future (for Jews and for all mankind). In the modern era, some elements of the messianic posture were secularized and formed a basis for the Zionist call to return to *Eretz Israel*; most notably, the messianic yearning for the homeland and for redemption. > see also: **Galut; Gola; Geula; Judaism and Zionism.**

Maskilim [משכילים, H] "Enlighteners": Term for Jews who sought to encourage changes in Jewish communal and religious life in the late eighteenth and early nineteenth centuries. Mainly identified with the followers of Moses Mendelssohn, the *Maskilim* had ambivalent feelings about the concept of Jewish nationalism. > see also: **Haskala**.

Materielle Judennot [G] "Jewish Material Distress": German Zionist term for the persecution and stark poverty suffered by Jews in the Russian empire. Material distress was considered one major reason for the Jewish turn to Zionism: Jews could never improve their lot as long as they remained in Europe. However, conditions in Western Europe were far different, requiring a different approach to national issues. > see also: **Geistige Judennot**; **Nachtasyl**.

Mauritius Islands, Exile in [GN]: Location of the first deportation camps for *Ma'apilim* created by the British government in 1940. Although previous British policy had been to return illegal Jewish immigrants to their point of origin, such a policy was considered inopportune during World War II. Likewise, it was considered impossible to keep such immigrants in prisons in *Eretz Israel*, since that would (theoretically at least) permit the illegals to legally enter the country at a later date (as long as certificates still remained). As a result, in 1940, the British began to deport *Ma'apilim* to the Mauritius Islands, located east of Africa in the Indian Ocean. Approximately 1,600 *Ma'apilim* were held in detention camps (women) and prisons (men) on the island. Many contracted malaria while there and 124 died during the five years of their internment. A bloc of 150 exiles from Czechoslovakia managed to obtain freedom by joining the Czechoslovak Legion, which fought the Nazis as part of the Allied armed forces.[1] Another fifty joined the Jewish Brigade Group and fought in Italy in 1944 and 1945. Although the British government had announced that the Mauritius exiles would never be permitted into *Eretz Israel*, on August 26, 1945, the newly elected Labour government reversed this decision, allowing all remaining internees into the country legally. > see also: **Aliya Bet**; **World War II**; **Cyprus Detention Camps**.

Mauschel [G] "Little Moses": Diminutive German term derived from the Hebrew name Moses (Moshe) and specifically referring to a Jewish merchant. The term, which is reminiscent of the German word for a mouse (Maus), had antisemitic overtones and was invariably used derisively. Kaiser Wilhelm II, for instance, in discussing Zionism with his nephew the Grand Duke Friedrich of Baden, used the term as a means to disparage the possibility of Jews returning to re-create a national home in *Eretz Israel*. The verb Mauscheln, to speak (German) with an accent was derived from the noun and also had (and still retains) antisemitic overtones. > see also: **Hindenburg Erklärung**.

May Laws [HT]: Common name for a group of anti-Jewish laws adopted by the czarist government on May 3, 1882. Prinicpally framed around strictly regulating Jewish residence and property rights in the Pale of Settlement, the laws were the Russian government's response to the pogroms of 1881–1882. The May Laws resulted in mass expulsions of Jews from cities in the pale and a general lowering of the Jews' standard of living. By adopting an antisemitic policy, the Russian government increased the already perceptible shift toward nationalism within the Russian Jewish community. > see also: **Pale of Settlement**; **Sufot ba-Negev**.

---

[1] For more details on the Cezchoslovak Legion, see: Abraham J. Edelheit and Hershel Edelheit, *History of the Holocaust: A Handbook and Dictionary*, Boulder, CO: Westview Press, 1994, p. 247.

Mayofespolitik [מהיפותפוליטיק, Y/Slang] "(The) Politics of Supplication": Neologism, generally derisive in use, coined by Jewish nationalists to designate traditional forms of Jewish diaspora political activity. According to this view, Jews had traditionally been suppliant "yes-men" who obtained benefits by flattering foreign rulers and abbasing themselves. The term derived from the Hebrew words *ma yafe* (literally, "how goodly") as pronounced in Yiddish. In contrast, Jewish nationalists, both Zionists and non-Zionists, argued that Jews should abandon such policies and adopt relationships with rulers and states based on self-respect and, when needed, opposition to policies inimical to the Jewish community.

McMahon-Hussein Correspondence [HT]: Designation used by historians for the eight letters exchanged by Sir Henry McMahon, the British high commissioner in Egypt, and Sharif Hussein of Mecca, leader of the Arab revolt against the Turks, during World War I. McMahon's letters were meant to sway Hussein by offering British military support for the Arabs as long as they continued to oppose the Turks, thereby helping British forces in the Middle East. As an additional encouragement, McMahon spoke of British support for the creation of an Arab kingdom in the Middle East as part of any postwar settlement. Yet, McMahon was not specific in regard the borders of this future state and he also did not inform Hussein about concurrent negotiations between British and French representatives over a future partition of Ottoman territory. That fact, coupled with McMahon's vague use of towns in Syria and Lebanon as bordering the area to be excluded from the Arab state, led to considerable conflict after the war, since the Arabs interpreted McMahon's promises as including *Eretz Israel*. McMahon denied such an intention in 1917 (and continued to deny it as late as 1937), but the idea of a twice promised land has remained a touch stone for the Arab-Israeli conflict ever since. > see also: **Sykes-Picot Agreement; World War I; Balfour Declaration**.

Mea Shearim [מאה שערים, H] "The Hundred Gates": Name of a north Jerusalem neighborhood, now known for its ultra-Orthodox community. *Mea Shearim* was one of the earliest Jewish settlements outside the walls of the Old City, being built on land purchased in 1875. From its inception, most residents rejected Zionism and identified themselves with the so-called Old *Yishuv*. > see also: **Old Yishuv/New Yishuv**.

Mechutonim [מחותנים, Y] "In-laws": Bitter Polish-Jewish term for the British mandatory government that indirectly aided the Nazis by preventing Jews from entering Palestine. Jews had thought that the British accepted the League of Nations mandate in order to help build the Jewish National Home, but they discovered that Britain cared little for the victims of Nazism.

Medina ba-Derekh [מדינה בדרך, H] "State in the Making": Popular Zionist term for the *Yishuv* and its institutions as they matured throughout the 1920s and 1930s: they were said to be a state in the building. Although an accurate description of developments during the mandate era, the term was only used ex post facto (i.e., after the State of Israel was established) and thus loses much of its immediacy and meaning. A related term, *Zva ha-Medina ba-Derekh* (The Army of the State in the Making, **צבא המדינה בדרך**), has sometimes been used to characterize the Hagana in a similar fashion. > see also: **Yishuv**.

Megillat ha-Azma'ut [מגילת העצמאות, H] "Scroll of Independence":

1. Scope and Definition
Official title of the parchment document containing Israel's declaration of independence that was read by David Ben-Gurion at a solemn meeting of Israel's Provisional Government in Tel Aviv's Mann Auditorium at 4:00 P.M., Friday, May 14, 1948 (Hebrew date 5 Iyyar 5708). After the reading, the scroll was signed by all members of the Provisional Government. The government's next official act was to nullify all British laws restricting the

Jewish national home, especially the notorious White Paper of 1939 that limited *aliya* and land purchase.

The text placed a heavy emphasis on traditional Jewish and Zionist themes. A preamble, for instance, fervently recalled the close connection between the Jewish people and *Eretz Israel* to set the stage for the Jewish claim to national sovereignty. Then too Ben-Gurion's insistence on mentioning the "Rock of Israel" was meant to bring religious Zionists (and religious non-Zionists) into the Israeli orbit without a direct confrontation over the issue of religion in the new state. Finally, the declaration set out the new state's goals and hopes; including most particularly an in-gathering of the Jewish diaspora and a peaceful transition from mandate to state-hood. Particular attention was paid to offering an olive branch to the Arabs (in Israel and in neighboring states).

Unfortunately, the hope for peace was dashed almost immediately. Arab irregulars stepped up their campaign to destroy the new state while the neighboring Arab states girded for a war to "throw the Jews into the sea." Indeed, minutes after the declaration was read, Egyptian aircraft bombed Tel Aviv. Twenty-four hours later, Israel was invaded by seven Arab armies and was plunged into a war for survival. > see also: **Israel, State of; War of Independence**.

2. Text of the Declaration

The land of Israel was the birthplace of the Jewish people. Here their spiritual, religious and national identity was formed. Here they achieved independence and created a culture of national and universal significance. Here they wrote and gave the Bible to the, world.

Exiled from Palestine, the Jewish people remained faithful to it in all the countries of their dispersion, never ceasing to pray and hope for their return and the restoration of their national freedom.

Impelled by this historic association, Jews strove throughout the centuries to go back to the land of their fathers and regain their statehood. In recent decades they returned in masses. They reclaimed the wilderness, revived their language, built cities and villages and established a vigorous and ever-growing community with its own economic and cultural life. They sought peace yet were ever prepared to defend themselves. They brought the blessing of progress to all inhabitants of the country.

In the year 1897 the First Zionist Congress, inspired by Theodor Herzl's vision of the Jewish State, proclaimed the right of the Jewish people to national revival in their own country.

This right was acknowledged by the Balfour Declaration Of November 2, 1917, and reaffirmed by the Mandate of the League of Nations, which gave explicit international recognition to the historic connection of the Jewish people with Palestine and their right to reconstitute their National Home.

The Nazi holocaust, which engulfed millions of Jews in Europe, proved anew the urgency of the reestablishment of the Jewish state, which would solve the problem of Jewish homeless-ness by opening the gates to all Jews and lifting the Jewish people to equality in in the family of nations.

The survivors of the European catastrophe, as well as Jews from other lands, proclaiming their right to a life of dignity, freedom and labor, and undeterred by hazards, hardships and obstacles, have tried unceasingly to enter Palestine.

In the Second World War the Jewish people in Palestine made a full contribution in the struggle of the freedom loving nations against the Nazi evil. The sacrifices of their soldiers and the efforts of their workers gained them title to rank with the peoples who founded the United Nations.

On November 29, 1947, the General Assembly of the United Nations adopted a Resolution for the establishment of an independent Jewish State in Palestine, and called upon the inhabitants of the country to take such steps as may be necessary on their part to put the plan into effect.

This recognition by the United Nations of the right of the Jewish People to establish their independent State May not be revoked. It is, moreover, the self-evident right of the Jewish People to be a nation, as all Other nations, in its own sovereign State.

Accordingly, we, the members of the National council, representing the Jewish people - in Palestine and the Zionist movement Of the world, met together in solemn assembly today, the day of the termination of the British mandate for Palestine, by virtue of the natural and historic right of the Jewish and of the Resolution of the General Assembly of the United Nations,

Hereby proclaim the establishment of the Jewish State in Palestine, to be called **ISRAEL.**

We hereby declare that as from the termination of the Mandate at midnight, this night of the 14th and 15th May, 1948, and - until the setting up of the duly elected bodies of the State in accordance with a Constitution, to be drawn up by a Constituent Assembly not later than the first day of October, 1948, the present National Council shall act as the provisional administration, shall constitute the Provisional Government of the State of Israel.

THE STATE OF ISRAEL will be open to the immigration Of Jews from all countries of their dispersion; will promote the development of the country for the benefit of all its inhabitants; will be based on the precepts of liberty, justice and peace taught by the Hebrew Prophets; will uphold the full social and Political equality of all its citizens, without distinction of race, creed or sex; will guarantee full freedom Of conscience, worship, education and culture; will safeguard the sanctity and inviolability of the shrines and Holy Places of all religions; and will dedicate itself to the principles of the Charter of the United Nations.

THE STATE OF ISRAEL will be ready to cooperate with the organs and representatives of the United Nations in the implementation of the Resolution of the Assembly of November 29, 1947, and will take steps to bring about the Economic Union over the whole of Palestine.

We appeal to the United Nations to assist the Jewish people in the building of its State and to admit Israel into the family of nations.

In the midst of wanton aggression, we yet call upon the Arab inhabitants of the State of Israel to return to the ways of peace and Play their part in the development of the State, with full and equal citizenship and due representation in its bodies and institutions - provisional or permanent.

We offer peace and unity to all the neighboring states and their peoples, and invite them to cooperate with the independent Jewish nation for the common good of all.

Our call goes out to the Jewish people all over the world to rally to our side in the task of immigration and development and to stand by us in the great struggle for the fulfillment of the dream of generations - the Redemption of Israel.

With trust in Almighty God, we set our hand to this Declaration, at this Session of the Provisional State Council, in the city of Tel Aviv, on this Sabbath eve, the fifth of Iyar, 5708, the fourteenth day of May, 1948.

Source: Israel Provisional Government, *Official Gazette*, May 14, 1948.

Menora [מנורה, H] "Candelabra": Another traditional Jewish symbol used by Zionists to focus attention on the continuity of Jewish nationalism. In this case, the symbol was the seven-branched candelabra mentioned in the Bible and intimately associated with the Temple. In 1948 the menora was declared to be the official symbol of the State of Israel.

Meora'ot [מאורעות, H] "Events":

1. Scope and Definition
Popular term for Arab rioting that periodically boiled over during the mandatory era. Although intercommunal tension was almost always present after the beginning of modern Jewish settlement in *Eretz Israel*, conditions were generally quiet even after the adoption of the mandate and the international commitment to create a Jewish national home. Nonetheless, the peace was broken during periods of tension

and particularly during four extensive periods of rioting: spring 1920, spring 1921, summer 1929, and spring 1936. The latter riots, fanned by Italian and German radio propaganda, flared into the all-out Arab Revolt, which lasted until 1939. > see also: **Arabs; Arab Revolt.**

Broadly speaking, Arab rioting represented an effort to pressure the British on two fronts, first, to create political and military instability in the Middle East, thereby threatening Britain's strategic interests, and to create pressure from such instability to convince the British to cancel their promises to the Jews. In particular, riots were used to protest *aliya* and Jewish land purchase, that is, against the very elements that Zionists considered central to the creation of a Jewish national home. The Arabs viewed rioting as the only means to pressure the British in this regard, since they believed that the Balfour Declaration and the mandate were manifestations of Jewish diplomatic pressure on His Majesty's government, diplomatic pressure that could be countered easily by military means. Second, the rioters hoped to dissuade Jews from risking their lives in settlements outside a few enclaves, hoping thereby to foil the Zionist plan regardless of British policy. Finally, rioting was seen as a source of potential military and political power that could lead to the creation of an Aran nationalist government (dominated by the Mufti of Jerusalem) at the expense of more moderate circles who were willing to compromise with the Jews and the British. > see also: **Arabs.**

The *Yishuv* repsonded to Arab rioting in three ways: first, by redoubling efforts to bring in immigrants and to build settlements and thereby convince the Arabs that rioting was futile and eventually bring them to the peace table. Unfortunately, insofar as the British repeatedly limited *aliya* (or halted it altogether) after each outbreak of rioting, this policy was not successful. Second, most Zionists adopted a purely defensive strategy that emphasized the Jews' right to defend their lives and property, while signaling that the *Yishuv* would not concede even an inch

to rioters. This policy, known as *Havlaga* (self-restraint) was also not completely successful, since it gave the rioters the initiative to strike whenever and wherever they desired without fear of preemptive attack, but was viewed as the only expedient means for Zionists to respond to the rioting. Finally, a minority of Zionist leaders and activists, mainly (but not exclusively) supporters of the revisionist movement, advocated a policy of active defense combined with retaliation in kind — a policy of attacking Arab bands before they struck or, if that was not possible, then attacking Arab settlements in retaliation for attacks on Jewish settlements. The policy of retaliation was rejected by the majority of the *Yishuv* for political reasons: the fear that the British would equate the morality of Jewish response and Arab provocation to the detriment of the Zionist movement. Nevertheless, Arab rioting did not cause the wholesale abandonment of Jewish settlements and was thus unsuccessful at its primary goal, which was to uproot the *Yishuv*. > see also: **War of Independence.**

2. Major Eras of Arab Rioting/Revolt

1920: Rioting connected with the Syrian revolt against France began in Palestine/*Eretz Israel* on March 1, 1920, with an attack on the settlement of Tel Hai. Rioting spread soutward from the Galilee with sporadic attacks on other Jewish settlements, reaching their high water mark on April 4. On that day, the Muslim feast of Nebi Musa, anti-Jewish riots broke out in Jerusalem. Rioting continued for two days, although martial law was imposed on April 5. As a result of these riots, Ze'ev Jabotinsky and nineteen other Zionist leaders in Jerusalem organized the Hagana as a Jewish defense militia. > see also: **Yishuv, Yishuv Organizations (Underground Organizations).**

1921: Rioting broke out in Jaffa in May and spread from there to Jerusalem and, briefly, to other cities in Palestine/*Eretz Israel*. Some forty-seven Jews died during the rioting and scores were injured. A temporary halt in *aliya* led to renewed peace. *Aliya* was resumed (in limited fashion) after the Churchill White Paper of 1922. > see also: **White Paper(s), Churchill; Economic Absorptive Capacity.**

1929: Rioting broke out in Hebron and Jerusalem in late July and early August, spreading throughout the country before dying down in the autumn. More than 130 Jews were killed — most of them anti-Zionists living in Hebron — and 400 were injured. The Hebron Jewish community was destroyed entirely and was not rebuilt until 1969. The riots brought another temporary halt to *aliya* and a swirl of controversy between the Zionists and the British government that ended in 1931. > see also: **White Paper(s), Passfield; MacDonald Letter**.

1933: Brief rioting broke out in the spring in response to German Jewish *aliya*, but was halted by rapid British police action.

1936–1939: Rioting accompanied the Arab general strike declared in April 1936; when the strike collapsed, a general revolt ensued against British rule and the Jewish national home. By October 1936 the rioting spread throughout Palestine/*Eretz Israel*, creating a tense security situation that was worsened by Italian and German radio propaganda that encouraged the Arabs and by the infiltration of Arab volunteers from neighboring states. Although a military failure, the Arab Revolt convinced the British cabinet of the need to appease the Arabs in order to win their support (or at least their neutrality) in an upcoming confrontation against the Nazis. As a result, the cabinet reevaluated the commitments under the mandate and issued the White Paper of 1939, which restricted aliya and Jewish land purchase, thereby giving the Arabs a political victory. > see also: **Arab Revolt; White Paper(s), White Paper of 1939; World War II**.

1947: Arab rioting broke out immediately after the U.N. decision to partition Palestine/*Eretz Israel* was announced on November 29, 1947, and became, in effect, the first step toward Israel's War of Independence. > see also: **United Nations; War of Independence**.

Mered ha-Aliya [מרד העליה, H] "Aliya Revolt": Zionist policy formulated in late 1938 by David Ben-Gurion and forming the core of his concept of "fighting Zionism." Ben-Gurion's plan was to use *Aliya Bet* coupled with an intensive global Jewish propaganda campaign to undermine any British policy that abandoned promises made to the Jews in favor of appeasing the Arabs. Given that the *Yishuv* had few options if the British decided not to implement the terms of the mandate, Ben-Gurion felt that Zionists would have to seize the initiative in a way that did not discredit Zionism in the eyes of the general public in Great Britain and elsewhere (mainly, the United States). This plan was accepted by the JAE as a basis for its response to the British White Paper of 1939, with a target date of September 1939 as the beginning of the revolt. The outbreak of World War II put the *aliya* revolt on temporary hold, although it became the centerpiece for JAE and WZO resistance to continued British rule after 1945. > see also: **Milhemet ha-Aliya; Aliya Bet; Zionut Lohemet**.

Mesopotamia Scheme [GN]: Popular name for a territorialist settlement scheme broached by the Jewish Territorialist Association (ITO) in early 1909 and based on settling Russian Jews in Mesopotamia (Iraq). This plan was based on earlier schemes, some dating to the early 1890s, proposed in Germany (including by leaders of the Antisemitenbund), the United States, and Turkey. Indeed, WZO president Theodor Herzl had discussed this scheme, as part of a broader plan to settle Jews in the Ottoman Empire with Sultan Abdul Hamid III in 1902 and 1903. The ITO scheme derived from British sources, who sought the creation of a buffer state between the Ottoman Empire and the (British-controlled) Suez Canal but was otherwise identical and was similar to earlier British proposals in connection with settling Jews around El Arish in the northern Sinai. ITO seriously considered the possibility of having its settlement arm, the Jewish Colonization Association (ICA), purchase a parcel of land in upper Chaldea that totaled 3,125 square miles (5,000 KM^2) or approximately 1.3 million acres. ICA estimated that the settlement costs for such a parcel of land would reach £8,000,000 but also assumed that the territory was large enough for nearly 1 million Jews. In addition, it was assumed that agricultural produce by the settlers would eventually yield an income for the Ottomans and ICA in excess of £17,000,000. Thus, the scheme appeared to be a no-lose proposition; it was further expected to succeed since the Jewish connection with Mesopotamia, in general, and Chaldea, in particular, ran deep: Mesopotamia (Babylonia) had a Jewish settlement since the destruction of the First Temple (586 B.C.E.) while Chaldea was the traditional origin point (mentioned in the Bible) for the patriarch Abraham. Even so, the plan collapsed due to international circumstances, mainly the change in Ottoman orientation from pro-British to pro-German. Cooperation with an organization that appeared to work for British interests no longer was acceptable to the Turks. > see also: **Territorialism**; **Sinai Plan**; **El Arish Plan**.

Michael [PN]: Nom de Guerre used by Yitzhak Yezernitski (Shamir) from 1941 to 1945. Yezernitski adopted the name to commemorate Michael Collins, the Irish Republican Army leader and tactician whom Yezernitski hoped to emulate in order to attain Jewish independence. > see also: **Rabbi Shamir**.

Mif'al u-Binyan [מפעל ובנין, H] "Industrial Enterprise and Construction": Antisocialist slogan associated with revisionist Zionists and popular during the 1920s and 1930s. In effect, the slogan was an attack on the socio-economic and *aliya* policies adopted by the Histadrut, Mapai, and the JA. Instead of emphasizing the creation of a "new" Jewish society based on agriculture the revisionists called for an emphasis on industrial development that would create economic conditions for mass *aliya* and the evacuation of most of Eastern European Jewry. > see also: **Halutzic Aliya**.

Mifleget ha-Lohamim [מפלגת הלוחמים, H] "The Fighters' Party": Short-lived political manifestation of Lohamei Herut Israel (Lehi) after 1948. Winning one seat in the Knesset in 1949, the party merged with the Herut bloc (formed by veterans of the Irgun Zvai Leumi) shortly after the election. > see also: **Yishuv, Organizations (Underground Organizations, Lohamei Herut Israel)**.

Milhemet ha-Aliya [מלחמת העליה, H] "Aliya War": Proposed Zionist policy dating to early 1938 and associated with JAE chairman David Ben-Gurion. In response to increasingly harsh British restrictions on *aliya*, mainly the so-called political maximum, Ben-Gurion proposed an unarmed insurgency campaign based on Aliya Bet to force the British to return to an even-handed policy in relation to the Yishuv. When the British issued their White Paper of 1939, Ben-Gurion's proposal was approved by the JAE with operations slated to commence in the autumn of 1939. The *aliya* war was postponed, however, because of World War II and did not become central to Zionist efforts to undermine British rule until 1945. > see also: **Political Maximum**; **Mered ha-Aliya**; **Aliya Bet**; **Ha-Mered**.

Millet System [HT]: Term for the system of religious and communal organization instituted throughout the Ottoman Empire during the reforms of the nineteenth century. Although modern in structure, the millets were based on preexisting institutions and were, in effect, a modernized form of the communal autonomy possessed by Dhimmi in Muslim countries. The Jewish millet was established by a royal decree in 1856. The decree stipulated that the Haham Bashi, as chief Jewish clergyman, would henceforth control all Jewish cultural and religious institutions throughout the empire. Although granted a wide geographical domain, the Haham Bashi's powers were limited and mainly concentrated on providing for Jews' religious needs. The British retained the millet system in Palestine/*Eretz Israel* for the duration of the mandate era, dividing the population into three millets: one each for Jews, Muslims, and Christians. Each of these was further subdivided as needed, for example into denominations for the Christian millet and into Ashkenazi and Sephardi sections (each headed by a chief rabbi) for the Jewish millet.

Technically all members of an ethnic group belonged ipso facto to the appropriate millet; in reality, individuals or groups could withdraw from the millets altogether and petition the government directly for the financial and other elements needed to care for their religious needs. Indeed, the anti-Zionist Neturei Karta withdrew from the Jewish millet in 1920 (i.e., upon its foundation) and did not join any other entity in *Eretz Israel*. > see also: **Haham Bashi**; **Rabbanut Rashit**; **Yishuv**; **Organizations**.

Mishmar Na [נע משמר, H] "Mobile Watch": Another term for mobile Hagana patrols, organized during the Arab Revolt of the 1930s. > see also: **Nodedet**.

Mishpahat Alter [אלטר משפחת, H/PN] "Alter's Family": Code name for the Jewish socialist nationalist Bund, used mainly by the JA rescue delegation in Istanbul during World War II. The usage derived from Wiktor Alter, a leader of the Polish Bund who was executed (along with Alexander Ehrlich) at Josef Stalin's orders in 1941. Although anti-Zionist in its orientation, the Bund cooperated with the JA delegation in Istanbul on an ad hoc basis during the war, mainly in relation to sharing information on Nazi efforts to exterminate European Jewry.

Mitnadve Hutz la-Aretz [לארץ חוץ מתנדבי, H] "Foreign Volunteers" (מח"ל, Mahal):

1. Scope and Definition
Official name for the military personnel who volunteered (or, in some cases, who fought as mercenaries) in Israel's War of Independence. Although the Hagana had developed from a militia into a quasi-army during the 1930s and 1940s, the Jewish forces still lacked experience with many of the more techinical aspects of modern warfare. In particular, fighter pilots and naval personnel were in short supply. To fill this gap, the Hagana (and to a lesser degree the other underground movements as well) attempted to recruit foreigners with military experience starting in late 1947 and early 1948. Although an exact number cannot be given for Mahal volunteers, it appears that the total was between 3,000 and 5,600. Not all the volunteers were Jews: many were non-Jews with needed military experience who volunteered out of sympathy with the Jewish cause or for adventure. Mahal's contribution was most significant in the Israeli air force, the Israeli navy, and in the armor and artillery branches of the ground forces. The majority of volunteers left Israel in 1949, although a few notable exceptions remained in the country; approximately six hundred "experts" were retained through the early 1950s.

Table M.2: Mahal Volunteers, by Country of Origin

Country	Volunteers	Country	Volunteers
United States/Canada	1,500	France	500
England/Commonwealth	1,500[1]	Western Europe	500
South Africa	1,000	Latin America	600
		TOTAL 5,600	

Source: A. J. Heckelman, *American Volunteers and Israel's War of Independence*, New York: Ktav, 1974, pp. 235-248.

---

[1] Includes all Commonwealth members and colonies, except Canada and South Africa.

2. Prominent Mahal Personalities

Arazi, Yehuda (pseud. Yehuda Tenenbaum, 1907–1959), one of the founders of Rechesh and of the Hagana intelligence service (Shai). Joining the Hagana shortly after his aliya in 1924, Arazi was seconded to the British police during the early 1930s. In 1936 he undertook a vital mission to Poland where he set up one of the first clandestine arms acquisition agencies for the Hagana. At the outbreak of World War II Arazi returned to the *Yishuv* and was appointed head of Shai, a position he held until 1945. Thereafter, he returned to Europe and helped to run the operations of *Briha* and the Mossad le-Aliya Bet. During Israel's War of Independence, Arazi was involved in purchasing weapons, mainly in the Balkans and Czechoslovakia, and transporting them and Mahal volunteers to the new state. > see also: **Rechesh**.

Avriel, Ehud (1917–1980), one of the founders of the Mossad le-Aliya Bet and its chief activist in the Danube basin prior to World War II. From 1943 to 1945, Avriel headed the JA's Rescue Committee in Istanbul while also operating as chief of the Mossad station there. After the war, Avriel was active in arms acquisition and in recruitment and transport of Mahal and Gahal (Giyus Hutz la-Aretz) volunteers in Czechoslovakia. In 1970 he published a volume of memoirs, *Open the Gates!* > see also: **Aliya Bet; Yishuv, Yishuv Organizations (Underground Organizations); Sochnut Yehudit.**

Beurling, George F. (Buzz) (1921–1948), top Royal Canadian Air Force (RCAF) ace of World War II. Beurling was credited with destroying more than thirty German aircraft and had received the Distinguished Flying Cross, Medal, and Bar while serving with the RCAF in the Mediterranean and Europe, where he earned the nicknames "Buzz" and "Screwball." In 1945 he returned to Canada but soon became bored with civilian life. In 1948 Beurling volunteered to fly with the fledgling Israeli air force and was sent to the Mahal center in Rome. He was killed while on a transport mission to Israel (his first Mahal flight) when the Noorduyn Norseman he was piloting crashed and burned on takeoff.

Dunkelman, Benjamin (1913–1998), Canadian Jewish military officer and Israeli career soldier. Raised in a Zionist and Jewish atmosphere, Dunkelman was well acquainted with conditions in the *Yishuv* even prior to World War II, since he had briefly lived in *Eretz Israel* during the 1930s. During World War II, Dunkelman served in the Canadian army, rising to command a battalion in the Queen's Own Royal Rifle Regiment of Canada (QRRC) from D-Day until VE-Day. Returning to Canada after the war, Dunkelman became involved in Zionist activities, including efforts to purchase arms for the fledgling Jewish state prior to the War of Independence. Dunkelman was one of the first Canadian volunteers to heed the call to the colors issued by the provisional government. He arrived in Israel in June 1948 and was immediately given command of the 72nd Mechanized Battalion of the Seventh Brigade. He assumed command of the entire brigade on July 5, 1948, and retained that post until released from active service in 1949. In 1976 he published his memoirs, *Dual Allegiance*.

Kollek, Theodore (Teddy, b. 1911), Israeli public figure. Kollek was born in Vienna and settled in Eretz Israel in 1934. Active in he-Halutz and Mapai, he also served in a number of capacities in the JA Political Department between 1940 and 1947. His assignements included a stint with the Hagana's intelligence service (Shai) and with the JA Rescue Committee in Istanbul. In 1947 and 1948 Kollek represented the Hagana in the United States, including primary responsibility for the Mahal recruiting office in New York City. Kollek remained in public service after the State of Israel was established and is best remembered for his tenure as Jerusalem's mayor between 1965 and 1990.

Marcus, David (Mickey, 1902–1948), American military figure and perhaps the best-known Mahal figure. Marcus graduated from the U.S. Military Academy at West Point in 1924 and received further training in the law while on active duty. When he left military service in 1927, he took positions at the U.S. Attorney's office in New York City and later with the New York Department of Corrections under Fiorello LaGuardia. The latter appointed Marcus director of the Corrections Department in 1940, a post he held only briefly. He returned to active military service because of the growing crisis in Europe. Initially assigned to the Judge Advocate General Division, Marcus was promoted to lieutenant-colonel and served in the Civil Affairs Division. In this capacity he was intimately involved in setting the policies implemented on liberation of enemy-occupied territory; inter alia this policy included plans to restore civil rights to Jewish displaced persons. Despite his lack of paratroop training, Marcus volunteered to jump into Normandy with the U.S. 101st Airborne Division on D-Day. After the war Marcus hoped to return to civilian life, but events in *Eretz Israel* soon caught his attention. Marcus travelled to *Eretz Israel* at the JAE's request in January 1948; while there he acted as a consultant to JAE chairman David Ben-Gurion on issues connected with transforming the Hagana into a conventional army. In *Eretz Israel*, Marcus used the nom de guerre Michael Stone in order to avoid potential embarrassment for the JA, the U.S., and the British government. Marcus returned to America in April, but was soon back in *Eretz Israel*, this time traveling openly, when independence was declared. Among his other duties was translating U.S. Army field manuals into Hebrew, thus providing the fledgling army with its first professional training materials. On May 28, 1948, Marcus was appointed *Aluf* (general), a new rank that he was the first to receive, and was given command of the Jerusalem front. Failing to break the Jordanian siege of Jerusalem by capturing Latrun, Marcus contemplated his next move: a broad flanking maneuver on a path he dubbed the Burma Road that provided food and supplies to the besieged city. While supervising operations on the road, Marcus was accidentally killed by a nervous sentry who did not recognize him. > see also: **Derech Burma**.

Schwimmer, Adolph W. (Al, b. 1917), American aeronautical engineer and the father of the Israel Aircraft Industries (IAI). Schwimmer grew up with aircraft and served in the U.S. Army Air Force (USAAF) during World War II. In 1948 he was recruited for Mahal while also working for Rechesh: in one of his more memorable incidents, Schwimmer purchased three former USAAF B-17 Flying Fortress bombers and flew them to Israel with the Federal Bureau of Investigation hot on his tail. Schwimmer served as chief of the Israeli air force engineering department during the War of Independence, helping to keep the fledgling air arm's multifarious aircraft flying under appalling technical conditions. Schwimmer briefly came back to the United States in 1950, in part to serve a prison sentence in connection with the B-17 incident, but returned to Israel in 1952 to found IAI.

Mixed Armistice Commission(s) (MAC) [HT]: Term for the committees created under U.N. authority in 1949 to monitor and police the armistice agreements signed by Israel and the Arab confrontation states. Four MACs were created: one each for Israel's borders with Egypt, Trans-Jordan, Lebanon, and Syria. The plan was to use the MACs to prevent military confrontations to allow the armistice regime time to consolidate. It was hoped that under those circumstances a comprehensive peace accord might develop. Unfortunately, only the Egyptian-Israeli MAC operated as originally conceived, with frequent meetings by regional military commanders and U.N. officials, even though it was totally ineffective in preventing raids into Israel and Israeli retaliation that frequently flared into all-out combat. The Lebanese-Israeli and Jordanian-Israeli MACs hardly ever met, although both continued to operate (at least officially) until 1956. The Syrian-Israeli MAC collapsed immediately, its first and last major meeting being held in 1951. > see also: **Armistice Agreements**.

Mizug Galuyot [מיזוג גלויות, H] "Mixing of the Exiles": Sociocultural term used in the *Yishuv* (and, after 1948, in the State of Israel) for the need to blend the disparate elements of world Jewry into a single cohesive unit in order to mold an Israeli cultural identity. The term's use reflected the reality that different parts of the Jewish world had developed at different paces. It also reflected the reality that differing customs, in some cases radically differing customs, and mores could potentially disrupt the nation building process. Under the terms of mixing, efforts were to be made to maintain customs that promoted unity while eliminating those that created difficulties (such as polygamy, which was still practiced by Yemenite Jews prior to their mass *aliya*) and blending those that could most singularly create a Jewish national culture. > see also: **Shlilat ha-Gola**; **Kibbutz Galuyot**.

Moledet [מולדת, H] "Homeland": Term for *Eretz Israel* popular among Zionists and used to reflect the close connection between the Jewish people and their historic homeland. > see also: **ha-Aretz**.

Monism [HT]: Term for ideological purity used by revisionist Zionist leaders, mainly Ze'ev Jabotinsky, to contrast with the supposed ideological sha'atnez (admixture) practiced by other Zionist groups. Jabotinsky saw any form of what he termed hyphenated Zionism as problematic; however, he reserved particular ire for the mixture of Zionism and socialism practiced by the labor Zionist movements. Jabotinsky used the term monism in the sense of a disciplined movement possessing a clear set of goals and a clear sense of how to achieve those goals. In this specific case, Jabotinsky identified three goals: mass *aliya*, creation of a Jewish majority in *Eretz Israel*, and the attainment of Jewish sovereignty. Zionists, Jabotinsky argued, should concentrate on those goals only, leaving open the diverse opinions on the way that a future Jewish state should be organized until the state actually came into existence. Socialist Zionists utterly rejected Jabotinsky's idea, seeing it as nothing less than a means to silence them and defer their agenda until an undefined future period that could not be

predicted. As a result, Jabotinsky's orientation became one of the touch stones for his many conflicts with the socialist Zionists. > see also: **Sha'atnez**.

Mordechai [HT]: Mossad le-Aliya Bet code name for Iran, deriving from the biblical book of Esther and its hero, Mordechai. The term's use may be attributed to the fact that the book of Esther was set in the ancient Persian empire, whose territory included modern Iran (a country that was still known as Persia until the 1920s).

Morenu ve-Rabbenu ha-Goy [מורינו ורבינו הגוי, H] "Our Teacher and Mentor the non-Jew": Phrase used by revisionist Zionist leader Ze'ev Jabotinsky to characterize his attitude toward the non-Jewish world. In his estimation, Jews ought to learn lessons of patriotism and nationalism from the non-Jew and apply them to Zionsim.

Moskub [Ar] "Muscovites": Slang Arabic term used for *olim* of the First and Second Aliyot, a reflection that most came from Russia. The term was apparently used with any connotations, either positive or negative. > see also: **Filastin Biládná**.

Mufti [AR] "Religious Leader": Untranslatable Arabic term for a Muslim authority capable of issuing a *fatwa* (a religio-legal ruling). In modern times, most muftis have sought to avoid political entanglements, although the Mufti of Jerusalem — Haj Amin al-Huseini (appointed in 1921) — used his position as a religious leader to further his political goals. In particular, he used religious arguments to foster Arab nationalist opposition to Zionism, with the goal of, as he put it, "throwing the Jews into the sea." His further goal was the creation of an Arab state in Palestine, of which he would, presumably, be head of state. Al-Huseini spent the better part of World War II in Germany and Italy, attempting to obtain Axis support for his goals. > see also: **Arabs**.

Muskeljudentum [G] "Muscular Jewry": Concept framed by Max Nordau at the Second

World Zionist Congress (1898). Nordau argued that Jewry had lost its physical element during the nearly two millenia of its exile. Part of Zionism's goal, therefore, was to restore this missing physical component by creating a heroic atmosphere that would encourage Jewish self-confidence. Nordau earnestly argued for the inclusion of regular sporting events in the programs of all Zionist youth movements, hoping thereby to build both character and physical strength. > see also: **Auch-und-Bauch Judentum; Hadar.**

N: Hagana term for the layout of Jewish settlements in the *Yishuv* in the middle and late 1930s. Viewed on a map, the settlements were laid out to resemble a letter N, which reflected the concentration of Jewish settlements in certain areas of the country. Thus, the zone from Tel Aviv to Haifa formed the left-hand bar of the N, the Emek and lower Galilee formed the connecting bar, and the Sea of Galilee/Tiberias/upper Galilee region formed the right-hand bar of the N.

Nachtasyl [G] "Night Shelter": Neologism created by Max Nordau in support of the Uganda scheme. In his view Russian Jews needed a temporary haven where they could live in peace prior to the final creation of a Jewish state in *Eretz Israel*. This night shelter, Nordau claimed, would only be temporary but would provided Jews with the practical training in statecraft that they needed. > see also: **Uganda Plan**.

Nahshonim [נחשונים, H/PN] "Courageous": Hagana term, derived from name of the biblical figure who led the tribe of Judah, for *Yishuv* personnel who had served in the Allied (mainly British) armed forces during World War II and who were organized into their own special reserve unit upon demobilization. The Nahshonim remained part of the Hagana reserve attached to Heyl Sadeh (Hish) until they were mobilized in late 1947. > see also: **World War II**.

Nakba [Ar] "Disaster": Palestinian Arab term for the Arab defeat in the Israeli War of Independence and the subsequent exodus of thousands of Palestinian Arab refugees. The term implies a tragedy, but it also reflects the continuing Arab inability to grapple with Israel's existence. The tragedy was not so much a reflection of what Israelis did, but the fact that Israel exists that is the disaster. > see also: **Arabs**

Nalewki [GN]: Street in Warsaw used by Polish Zionists as a derogatory term for diaspora Jewish life and deriving from the many small, Jewish-owned shops on that street. > see also: **Shlilat ha-Gola**.

Napoleonchik [נפוליונצ'יק, Slang] "Napoleon": Popular Hebrew name for the first artillery pieces obtained by Zva ha-Hagana le-Israel during the War of Independence: five antiquated 65MM mountain guns that arrived from Italy aboard the SS *Boreah* on May 13, 1948. Impounded by the British, the weapons were returned to the Israelis on May 15, after the mandate's termination. Although derisively named for Napoleon Bonaparte (and often misidentified as nineteenth century weapons), the initial five weapons were actually of Italian manufacture and dated to the World War I era. A total of fifty simlar weapons, this time mostly of French design, were purchased during the War of Independence. > see also: **Zva ha-Hagana le-Israel; War of Independence; Davidka**.

National Home [HT]: Term used in the Balfour Declaration to describe the Jewish entity that the British promised to assist. The term was also widely used by Zionist leaders after the mandate was adopted in 1922. The term was deliberately vague, since the Zionists were unsure about the level of support they would obtain by a more explicit declaration of goals. Thus, "National Home" could easily be interpreted as a cultural entity, an autonomous political zone permitting a quasi-independent life for a protected minority, or a sovereign state expressing the will of a Jewish majority. Repeated disagreements over the term's precise meaning were a source of continuing tension in British-Zionist relations and was a source of conflict between differing Zionist interpretations. > see also: **Shem ha-Meforash; Gradualism; Endziel; Commonwealth, Jewish; Balfour Declaration**.

Nationalism [HT]: Political concept that spread throughout Europe and the Americas in the nineteenth century and throughout the rest of the world to one degree or another in the twentieth. Nationalism basically holds that the individual leads a meaningless life unless and until he or she becomes part of a larger collective (and at times organic) body — the nation — which at the suitable time manifests itself as a nation-state. The nation, in turn, is defined as a collective group that shares a common language, common land (regardless of whether or not a majority of the population actually reside in the homeland), a common historical and cultural legacy, and is conscious of its national identity. Modern nationalism developed from Enlightenment ideas about popular sovereignty and the need of the masses to have a say in their government.

Generally speaking, historians distinguish two eras in the history of nationalism. The earlier era, usually dated to 1848, is seen as an era of "liberal nationalism," which, despite its emphasis on patriotism and national self-determination, maintained a cosmopolitan attitude and emphasized the equality of different nations despite their differences. After 1848, nationalism became illiberal entering a phase of "national egotism." This new ideological trend developed from the notion that one's own nation represents the pinnacle of all that is good and pure. National egotism also acted as the justification for national demands for respect from other nations and for attempts by the nation to "find its place in the sun" through a policy of territorial expansion. National egotism, therefore, also justified a jingoistic and militaristic form of hyperpatriotism. No longer cosmopolitan, nationalism now tended to be exclusive and to emphasize the inherent superiority of some nations over others.

Both Jews and Arabs imbibed this nationalist spirit beginning in the mid-nineteenth century. Although most Jewish ideologies emphasized emancipation and assimilation, external pressure (principally in the form of antisemitism) and internal religious and social developments led some Jewish thinkers to propose a nationalist self-definition for postemancipation Jewry. Over the course of the next half-century three different forms of Jewish nationalism emerged: Folkism, Bundism, and Zionism. Folkism accepted the premise that Jews represent a single nation but argued that they were a "spirit nation" that needed no territory. The Folkists argued for a renewed supracommunal structure with international gurantees for Jewish autonomy. Bundism operated in a similar diaspora nationalist context, accepting virtually all of the Folkists' ideas but adding a Jewish commitment to revolutionary socialism. Only in a classless society organized along Marxist lines, the Bundists argued, could Jewry's rights ever be defended. In contrast, Zionists argued that Jews could guarantee their future only by re-creating their national home in Palestine/*Eretz Israel* and thereby solving both their internal and external problems. > see also: **Antisemitismus; Assimilation; Autonomism; Bundism; Emancipation; Hibbat Zion; Spirit Nation; Zionut**.

Ne'eman [נאמן, H] "Trustworthy": Another Yishuv nickname for President Harry S. Truman, reflecting the great trust that Zionist leaders had for the president's integrity and commitment to Zionism. Indirectly the term is also a play on Truman's last name, since a person who is "true" would be considered "trustworthy." > see also: **Hershel Ish-Emet**.

Neinsager [G] "Naysayers": Common term for those WZO members who opposed the Uganda plan, viewing the creation of even a temporary haven outside of Palestine/*Eretz Israel* as inconsistent with the major tenets of Zionism. The Neinsager argued that the WZO should concentrate on action to obtain a Jewish national home even if that meant temporary pain for one or more Jewish communities. The term Neinsager was used again in the 1930s to indentify those Zionists who opposed the Peel partition plan on the grounds that it too sacrificed long-term Zionist goals for an illusory short-term benefit. > see also **Uganda Plan; Zionei Zion; Partition Plans, Peel Plan**.

Nish'arim [נשארים, H] "(The) Remnants": Slang term for the young men who remained in Tel Aviv after the Ottomans ordered the deportation of virtually the entire Jewish male adult population in April 1917. These youths took upon themselves the task of protecting Jewish property, initially clandestinely and later with the tacit acquiesence of the Turkish authorities. The group operated for approximately six months, that is, until the British captured Tel Aviv. > see also: **World War I**.

Nodedet [נודדת, H] "Nomad": Term for units of the Hagana or the Jewish Supernumerary Police (JSP) that operated with some form of mobility. In general, the *Nodedet* was a patrol mounted on trucks or semiarmored cars and organized for the purpose of protecting strategically important targets from marauding Arab bands. The first such patrols were organized on an ad hoc basis in 1933, but the patrols did not last long. The idea of a permanently established mobile unit of the Hagana able to reinforce settlements or engage Arab bands before they attacked Jewish settlements became widely accepted only after the Arab Revolt of 1936. The size and intensity of attacks on Jewish settlements at that point literally swamped the Hagana and stretched its resources to their limits. In response, the Hagana began to rethink its exclusively defensive doctrine and returned to the idea of a mobile unit, which was established in Jerusalem in early June 1936 with a strength of eighty men. Yitzhak Sadeh (Landowberg), who had previously served as an officer in the Red Army, was given command of this unit. He trained his men to operate under virtually any conditions. That autumn, the *Nodedet* was enlarged and transferred to the JSP, which for all intents and purposes was the legal arm of the Hagana. Due to the *Nodedet's* success, the Hagana high command decided to create an even larger reserve force, called Plugot Sadeh (Field Companies, Fosh) in 1937. > see also: **Arab Revolt; Yishuv, Yishuv Organizations (Underground Organizations); Notrim**.

Nordau Plan [PN]: Proposal made after World War I by Max Nordau and designed to transfer a relatively large number of Jews to Palestine/*Eretz Israel* in a short time. Nordau based his plan on two premises: that Zionists had to move rapidly after the Balfour Declaration in order to create a Jewish majority before Arab or British opposition to Zionism could crystalize and that Eastern European Jewry (suffering from pogroms in the aftermath of the Russian empire's collapse) needed immediate refuge. Both of these assumptions led Nordau to call for mass *aliya*. Specifically, he proposed that the WZO oversee the transfer of 600,000 Jews to Palestine/*Eretz Israel* in a matter of months. When Nordau first proposed his plan in 1921, it appeared unrealistic and unduly pessimistic and was therefore rejected by the WZO. In the mid-1930s a similar plan was proposed by revisionist Zionist leader Ze'ev Jabotinsky and some establishment Zionist leaders, notably David Ben-Gurion, adopted similar mass migration schemes during the 1930s and 1940s under the impact of the Nazi persecution of European Jewry. > see also: **Evacuation Plan; Tochnit ha-Asor**.

Notar(im) [(נוטר(ים, H] "Guardians":

1. Scope and Definition

Hebrew term dating to the mandatory era and used to designate personnel assigned, temporarily or permanently, to the Palestine police either as supernumeraries or as police officers. In effect, these individuals (and some entire units) represented a legal arm for the Hagana, especially after the outbreak of the Arab Revolt in 1936. Although they contributed greatly to the Yishuv's security, the *Notarim* also represented a potential conflict of interest, specifically, when needs of the Jewish undergrounds came into conflict with orders from British police commanders. > see also: **Arab Revolt; Yishuv, Yishuv Organizations (Underground Organizations, Hagana)**.

Recruitment to the *Notarim* began in June 1936 with an initial group of 2,550; of them some 1,800 were deployed to isolated Jewish settlements. The *Notarim* peaked in the spring of 1939 at a force of 22,000 men, organized into settlement police units, a mobile patrol (the *Nodedet*), a border fence patrol unit, the Special Night Squads, and other units. After publication of the White Paper of 1939 the British administration began to slowly reduce the number of *Notarim*, since they were considered potential security risks. In May 1939 the force was established at a total manpower of only 14,600. The number continued to decline, however, as individual *Notarim* resigned, joined other units, or were recruited for military service during World War II. By 1945, only 4,200 *Notarim* continued to serve. > see also: **Special Night Squads**.

2. Special Police Units

Notarei Geder ha-Zafon (נוטרי גדר הצפון), "Northern Fence Police," defense unit established in May 1938 to guard workers building the Northern Fence, a fortification measure installed the Palestine/*Eretz Israel* border with Syria as a means to prevent infiltrations by Arab bands. The force numbered three hundred men, of whom two hundred were Hagana recruits. The force was divided into two companies, each commanded by a British army officer with a Jewish noncommissioned officer as his second in command. Upon completion of the fence, in September 1938, the unit was disbanded. > see also: **Northern Fence**.

Notarei ha-Hof (נוטרי החוף), "Coastal Police," defense unit established as part of the *Notarim* in the summer of 1942. The unit was created in response to the possibility of Axis units infiltrating (or invading) Palestine/*Eretz Israel* from the sea. The unit was multiethnic, although Jews and Arabs did not serve together: five hundred Jewish *Notarim* served in lookout posts from Rosh ha-Nikra in the north to Nebi Reuven in the south and two hundred Arab guards served in mounted units south of Nebi Reuven (i.e., in the area now known as the Gaza Strip). In 1943 the Jewish *Notarim* were established as a separate part of the Palmah (thereby creating the Palyam), and the unit was disbanded entirely in 1945, with many of the veterans joining the Jewish Brigade Group. > see also: **World War II**.

Notarei ha-Rakevet (נוטרי הרכבת), "Railroad Police," defense unit established in the summer of 1938 to protect sensitive or exposed areas of the Palestine/*Eretz Israel* railway system. Initially, the force numbered four hundred Jewish *Notarim*, who were provided with small railcars (colloquially known as trolleys) for transporation. In 1939 the force was doubled in size, with a small number of Arab police officers attached. Over the course of World War II, the number of Jewish officers was steadily reduced and Arab personnel took their place; by 1945, virtually no Jewish *Notarim* remained in the unit. > see also: **World War II; Leyl ha-Rakavot**.

Notarei Hevrat ha-Hashmal (נוטרי חברת החשמל), "Electric Company Police," privately created defense unit, considered to be part of the police by Jews even though the officers' salaries were paid by the Palestine Electric Company. Their tasks included protecting the generators and the high voltage wires of the Mahanayim generation plant throughout the *Yishuv*. Similar private police units were established during the Arab Revolt, including one created to protect the Palestine Potash

Works, plant near Sdom, and total personnel numbered five hundred-fifty officers. Most of these units were disbanded during World War II.

Notarei Mahanot ha-Ma'azar (נוטרי מחנות המעצר), "Internment Camp Police," elite defense unit established during World War II and tasked with guarding the camps in which German civilians were interned when the war broke out. Many of the guards were of Central European origin and could thus be a source of political intelligence. At its height the unit numbered three hundred men, including seventy assigned to guard internment camps for Axis citizens in Australia. > see also: **World War II**.

Notarei Mifa'l ha-Mayim (נוטרי מפעל המים), "Water Works Police," police detachment numbering sixty Jewish officers temporarily assigned in 1938 to defending the water pipeline to Jerusalem. Headquartered at the pipeline's main source at Rosh ha-Ayin (twenty-four officers), the substations were located in Latrun, Sha'ar ha-Gai, and Saris (twelve officers each). The *Notarim* served under British command.

Notarei Sdot ha-Teufa (נוטרי שדות התעופה), "Airport Police," defense detachment established to guard Palestine/ *Eretz Israel*'s airports. Created in September 1938, the unit was initially assigned to protect the airport in Lod (Lydda, now Ben-Gurion International Airport) and the smaller airport in Tel Aviv (Sde Dov). A mixed unit, the proportion of Jews to overall personnel was approximately 50 percent. In 1942 the unit numbered four hundred officers, but it was expanded to a peak of 1,200 over the course of 1943. In addition to protecting aircraft and airport facilities from sabotage, the unit had a secondary task of anti-aircraft defense in case of Axis air raids. The unit was reduced to three hundred officers in 1945, mostly Arabs serving under British command. > see also: **World War II**.

Notbau [G] "Emergency Building": Term coined by Max Nordau during his defense of the Uganda plan at the Sixth World Zionist Congress (1903). Although he was not convinced that Zionist support for mass Jewish settlement in Uganda was a good idea, Nordau emphasized the great need for a temporary haven in the emergency conditions engendered by pogroms in Russia. Once Eastern European Jewry was out of harm's way, future Zionist efforts could concentrate on obtaining the true goal of a Jewish national home in *Eretz Israel*. > see also: **Haltstelle; Nachtasyl; Uganda Plan**.

Northern Fence: Official name for the defensive measure installed by the British in 1938 along *Eretz Israel*'s border with Syria as a way to prevent infiltrations by bands participating in the Arab Revolt. The fence is often associated with Charles Teggart, the British officer responsible for its construction. The fence was actually constructed by Solel Boneh, the Histadrut's construction firm, and was protected by a British garrison augmented by local Hagana units. The fence was completed in July 1938 and immediately cut down the number of infiltrators entering Palestine from Syria. In turn, the fence and its defenders became targets for frequent terrorist attacks that were generally unsuccessful. > see also: **Arab Revolt; Yishuv, Yishuv Organizations (Underground Organizations, Hagana)**.

O

Occupied Enemy Territories Administration (OETA):

1. Scope and Definition

Term used for the British governmental agency created in 1917 to organize the transfer of formerly Ottoman territory to civilian government after World War I. As such, OETA was planned as a temporary agency prior to adoption of mandate or other civilian regimes. However, the delays experienced in negotiating the peace treaty with Turkey led to a situation whereby OETA became a semipermanent fixture in the Middle East between 1918 and 1920. OETA was further beset by an almost permanent state of crisis, at least in its administration of Palestine/*Eretz Israel*. This derived from the fact that most OETA officers, especially the senior ones, were strongly anti-Zionist and, in some cases, overtly antisemitic. They sought consciously or otherwise to foil the creation of a Jewish national home through a combination of bureaucratic roadblocks and in some cases the encouragement of tension between Jews and Arabs. OETA's actions were exposed as a result of the riots in Jerusalem in 1920, which led to the complete collapse of the military government and the establishment of a civil administration, headed by High Commissioner Sir Herbert Samuel. Some historians have concluded that much of the tension among the British, the Jews, and the Arabs during the interwar era may be traced back largely to the damage done to British credibility by OETA. > see also: **World War I**; **Mandate, League of Nations**; **Me'oraot**.

Table O.1: Chiefs of OETA in Palestine/*Eretz Israel*, 1918–1920

Name	Highest Military Rank	Tenure
Arthur Money	Major General	March 1918–August 1919
Henry H. Watson	Major General	August–December 1919
Lewis J. Bols	Major General	December 1919–July 1920

Source: Bernard Wasserstein, *The British In Palestine*, 2d ed. (Oxford: Basil Blackwell, 1991).

Odessa Committee [GN]: Popular nickname for the Hibbat Zion governing board. > see also: **Ha-Va'ad ha-Odesai**; **Hibbat Zion**.

Old Yishuv/New Yishuv [HT]: Historiographic term distinguishing the two broad eras in the modern history of *Eretz Israel*: the "old" *Yishuv* was a nonpolitical entity that existed before the advent of Zionism, whereas the "new" *Yishuv* was the entity created by Zionist settlers beginning in 1881. Although the chronological distinction between these two archetypes is somewhat artificial, the ideological distinction is not. The "old" *Yishuv* was composed principally of religious individuals who came to *Eretz Israel* to study and/or die (in the latter case in response to the Jewish belief that in the messianic era persons buried in the Holy Land would be resurrected before those buried in the diaspora). By and large, the members of the "old" *Yishuv* did not occupy themselves in productive labor and depended on a charitable system known as *Haluka*. In contrast, the "new" *Yishuv* represented a conscious effort to create a Jewish polity without reference to religion. In fact, many of the Zionist *Halutzim* were nonreligious or antireligious. Almost from the beginning of Zionist settlement, conflicts broke out between members of the two communities. Despite the establishment of a *modus vivendi* between religious and secular forces when the State of Israel was created, the conflicts continue to bubble near the surface of the Israeli polity to this day. > see also: **Yishuv; Judaism and Zionism; Status Quo Agreement; Israel, State of.**

Oleh [עולה, H] "Immigrant": Hebrew term for a new immigrant to Israel. > see also: **Aliya.**

Olei Bulgaria [עולי בולגריה, H] > see also: **Bulgarim.**

Operation Agatha [PN]: British code name for the massive, systematic military effort to crush the Jewish revolt in *Eretz Israel* undertaken on Saturday, June 29, 1946. On that day the better part of the leadership of the *Yishuv*, including virtually the entire membership of the JAE, was arrested by British soldiers and police. As a counterinsurgency measure, Operation Agatha was a total failure. The military leaders by and large evaded capture, as did some of the *Yishuv*'s

most militant political leaders (including David Ben-Gurion, who was in Paris when the arrests commenced). Moreover, by operating on the Jewish Sabbath, the British incurred the wrath of many religious leaders who might otherwise have remained neutral on the Palestine issue. Nevertheless, the operation was not a complete failure. As a result of Operation Agatha, the JAE withdrew its support for Hagana and Palmah cooperation with the Irgun Zvai Leumi and Lohame Herut Israel. > see also: **Shabbat ha-Shahor; Ha-Mered; Yishuv, Yishuv Organizations (Underground Organizations, Tenuat ha-Meri ha-Meuhad).**

Operation Ali Baba [HT]: Another code name for the semiclandestine operation that brought Iraqi Jews to the new State of Israel. > see also: **Operation Ezra/Nehemia.**

Operation Ezra/Nehemia [HT]: Code name for the two-year mass exodus of Iraqi Jews. Between 1950 and 1952, the Iraqi government permitted the exit of 130,000 Jews on the proviso that they were not permitted to fly directly to Israel. Over the course of operation, the emigrés flew from Iraq to Cyprus on aircraft chartered in the United States and England; they were then transferred to Israeli aircraft for the final stage of their journey home.

Operation Igloo [HT]: British code name for the first deportation of *Ma'apilim* to camps in Cyprus. The operation took place in August 1946, when the Mossad le-Aliya Bet ships *Yagur* and *Henrietta Szold* were captured by the Royal Navy (RN). The 1,290 *Ma'apilim* aboard the two blockade runners were brought to Haifa, their only contact with the land they sought to enter, where they were transferred, under armed guard, to RN transport ships that transported them to Cyprus. > see also: **Cyprus Detention Camps; Aliya Bet.**

Operation Magic Carpet [HT]: Popular name for the JA operation to transfer the Jews of Yemen to Israel between 1948 and 1950. Conditions for Jews in Yemen had been worsening throughout the 1930s. Conditions worsened even more after the State of Israel was established and a decision was made to evacuate as many Yemenite Jews as possible. The first flights commenced in December 1948. Aircraft were used because of the unavailability of shipping and the need to make a broad circle around hostile territory (including Saudi Arabia, Trans-Jordan, and Egypt). Only long-range transport aircraft could make the nonstop flight, which covered 1,760 aerial miles and took eight hours. The Yemenite Jews first had to travel to the British-controlled Aden Protectorate (200–300 miles) and then were transferred to Israel in flights of 90–145 persons. In all, 430 flights carried 48,818 Yemenite Jews, 1,100 from Aden, and 400 Jews from Djibouti and Eritrea back to their ancestral homeland. > see also: **Operation Ezra/Nehemiah**.

Organizations

1. Scope and Definition

Historians have long noted that the Jewish community was (and remains) one of the most highly organized ethnic communities in the world. Jewry has been served by a highly diversified set of communal bodies. These agencies often differed vociferously on three issues: (1) how best to serve the interests of their communities, (2) how to relate the Jewish community to the larger society in which it existed, and (3) what degree of national self-identification was appropriate for Jews in a postemancipation era. All three of these questions manifested themselves (to one degree or another) in institutional attitudes toward Zionism. What follows is a listing of some of the major Jewish organizations existing throughout the world between 1897 and 1948. The list is by no means an exhaustive list of Jewish organizations, Zionist or otherwise. Instead, this entry provides a brief look into the organizational dynamics of the Jewish community as it related to the national question. Many organizations were not included because insufficient data was available to reconstruct their history. Similarly,

information on membership and leadership have been provided when available; in some cases leaders have been listed only for parts of an organization's history. Again, this reflects the tentative nature of some of the research.

Finally, two caveats are in order. First, this list supplements and complements the one included in our *History of the Holocaust: A Handbook and Dictionary* (pp. 350–365), although some of the overlapping entries in this volume include new material. Second, readers should remember that all of the nationwide Zionist federations (landesverbände) listed below were divided into numerous parties and blocs. Data on the latter have been included only when sufficient material warranted inclusion or where names were sufficiently different to potentially cause confusion.

2. Zionist

Argentina
  Associación Mutual Israelita Argentina (AMIA), "Jewish Mutual (Aid) Association of Argentina," friendly society linking Argentine Jewry developed in 1893 on the basis of the Ashkenazi Hevra Kadisha (Burial Society). AMIA operated a wide range of activities, ranging from philanthropic to educational, with special emphasis on helping maintain communal cohesion and assisting the integration of new immigrants. Initially neutral on the Zionist issue, AMIA moved closer to the Zionist federation in the early 1930s and came to support Jewish statehood in the 1940s.

  Delgación de Associaciones Israelitas Argentina (DAIA), "Council of Argentine Jewish Organizations," Central communal organization of Argentine Jewry established in 1934. DAIA was a charter member of the World Jewish Congress and strongly supported the creation of a Jewish state in *Eretz Israel*. In terms of Argentine politics, DAIA was a strident defender of Jewish rights in the face of the rising antisemitic tide of the 1930s and also made sharp, but ultimately unsuccessful, efforts to open Argentina as a refuge for European Jews. DAIA's support for Zionism was most pronounced after 1945. At that point almost the entire Jewish community (including the considerable community of territorialists in Argentina) came to support the creation of a Jewish state. DAIA sponsored a mass rally in Buenos Aires in December 1947 to protest the government's decision to vote against partition in the United Nations. Presidents: Moises Goldman; Jose Ventura; Abraham Mibashan; Isaac Goldenberg.

Federación Sionista Argentina (FSA), "Argentine Zionist Federation," national umbrella organization for Zionist activity, headquartered in Buenos Aires. Founded in 1897, FSA theoretically operated as a coalition of Zionist political parties, all of which were parallel to the parties in the WZO. In reality, however, FSA was dominated by the general Zionists and witnessed many of the same ideological fractures that weakened the entire WZO during the 1930s. In particular, the withdrawal of the revisionists in 1935 considerably weakened FSA'a activities. This rupture was not repaired until after World War II when, in cooperation with Delgación de Associaciones Israelitas Argentina, FSA galvanized the entire Argentine Jewish community in support of Jewish statehood.

Australia

Zionist Federation of Australia and New Zealand (ZFANZ), national federation of Australian Zionists; although the name implies that New Zealand Zionists were part of the federation, in fact, the latter had their

Delegates to the Second Conference of ZFANZ, May 19–22, 1929.
Courtesy of the Australian Jewish Historical Society, Victoria

own regional federation. ZFANZ emerged in 1927 as a coalition of five regional societies in the commonwealth of Australia, some of which were founded as early as 1900. ZFANZ joined the WZO in 1929 and adopted its name (which has been used here for identification purposes) in 1939. ZFANZ was especially active in promoting Jewish and Zionist causes during and after World War II even though there are no definitive statistics about membership. Still, ZFANZ must be deemed an overall success, especially in light of the strong support given the Yishuv by the Australian government in 1946 and 1947. Presidents: Rabbi Israel Brodie (1927-1937), Rabbi Ephraim M. Levy (1937-1938), Leon Jona (1938-1940), Bernard Cowen (1940-1941), Alec Masel (1941-1945), Rabbi Max Schenk (1945-1947), Horace B. Neuman (1947-1949).

Austria

Ahavat Zion (אהבת ציון, AZ), "Love of Zion," colonization society founded in Vienna in 1881 as a parallel to Hibbat Zion in Russia. Mainly oriented toward fund-raising, AZ was organized to help purchase land and provide resources for colonists but did not directly participate in *aliya*. Initially successful in its endeavors, AZ dissolved in 1885 due to dissension over religious issues. Presidents: Reuben Bierer, Peretz Smolenskin. > see also: **Hibbat Zion**.

Allgemeine Hebräische Sprachverein (AHS), "United Hebrew Language Organization," Zionist educational and cultural fraternity founded by university students in Vienna in 1899. AHS was dedicated to promoting Hebrew as Jewry's national language and to cultivating a nationalist Jewish cultural orientation. AHS was more focused on cultural issues than other contemporary Zionist fraternities (the so-called Color and Dueling Organizations) but was no less fervently dedicated to the Zionist cause. Mainly active in Vienna, AHS ceased to function after World War I.

Binyan ha-Aretz (בנין הארץ), "Building the Land," short-lived Austrian branch of a Zionist organization founded in Germany in 1920 and in Austria in 1933. Binyan ha-Aretz rejected all Zionist activities that were not connected with practical actions to build the *Yishuv*, a position similar to Justice Louis D. Brandeis's, in opposition to the policies espoused by WZO president Chaim Weizmann. The Austrian branch operated from 1933 to 1938, peaking with 925 members in 1937. Binyan ha-Aretz ceased to function during the Nazi era.

Jüdischer Nationalrat für deutschösterreich (JNFD), Jewish National Committee for German Austria," short-lived body dedicated to recasting Austrian Jewry in a nationalist mold and defending their rights, founded in Vienna on November 4, 1918. JNFD was composed of four major elements: (1) the Zionists (including both members of the national federation and representatives of the local Poale Zion organization), (2) Orthodox (in practice, only representatives of Mizrachi, since Agudas Israel refused to join), (3) socialists (local Bundists), and (4) other nationalistically oriented Jews who did not belong to one of the other categories. JNFD had hoped to broaden its base of membership in order to become the national representation of Austrian Jewry. This, in turn, was seen as a potential way to "conquer" the community, since after the partition from Hungary and the loss of Galicia to Poland, Austrian Jewry was much more concentrated geographically and culturally. JNFD was partially successful in this endeavor, given the highly antisemitic environment of interwar Austria, but the slow erosion of the JNFD coalition (by which JNFD became almost coterminous with the Zionist federation) led to the organization's collapse in the early 1920s.

Jüdische Volkspartei (JVP), "Jewish People's Party," the political arm of the Austrian Zionist movement, founded in 1906. During the 1920s, JVP candidates ran in all Austrian elections. Its major aim was to protect Austrian Jewry's rights while furthering the Zionist agenda within the Jewish community. JVP was abolished in 1934 by order of the Austrian fascist government. Publication: *Wiener Morganzeitung*.

Kadimah (קדימה), "Forward," Jewish nationalist student society established in Vienna in 1882. Kadimah's main goals included fighting antisemitism and combating assimilation through a strengthening of Jewish identity. The Kadimah group did not initially identify itself as Zionist in orientation but did collectively join the WZO in 1897. Thereafter, Kadimah operated as a so-called sonderverband until its operations were halted by the Nazis in 1938.

Landeskomité Zion (LKZ), "Zionist National Committee," official name for the Zionist federation of Austria-Hungary and, after 1918, of the Austrian Republic. LKZ was founded in Vienna in 1900, but at the time was unique in its Zionist role since WZO president Theodor Herzl and the entire Engere Aktions-Komité (Inner Actions Committee) resided in Vienna. As a result, LKZ was responsible for internal matters only and not for political or diplomatic activities. This meant that LKZ was largely responsible for propaganda and educa-tion in Austria and in Austrian possessions. It should be noted that although Hungary was officially linked to the Habsburg empire, it had its own national federation. Internally, LKZ was organized into six districts committees, each having its center in the major city of the province: Oberösterreich, centered in Vienna; Bohemia, centered in Prague; Moravia, centered in Brünn (Brno); Galicia, centered in Lemberg (Lwow); Bukovina, centered in Czernowitz (Chernovtsy); Westösterreich (ie, all other provinces except Hungary and its possessions), centered in Graz. LKZ functioned in this fashion until 1918 when the breakup of the Austro-Hungarian empire and the loss of Bohemia-Moravia (to Czechoslovakia), Galicia (to Poland), and Bukovina (to Romania) led to reorganization. LKZ was a founding member of the Jüdischer Nationalrat für Deutsch-österreich in 1918. In November 1918, LKZ changed its name to Zionistischen Landes-organization Österreich to reflect the new situation in the Austrian Republic and con-tinued to operate under this name until the Nazi occupation in 1938 forced a halt to all Zionist activities.

Zionistische Federation von Österreich (ZFÖ), "Zionist Federation of Austria," successor to the Zionistischen Landesorganization Österreich, founded in Vienna in 1948. ZFÖ operated as a coalition representing the different Zionist streams and coordinated Zionist activities in the country. Given the nature of the Jewish community — highly compact (almost 90 percent of all Jews lived in Vienna) and composed largely of transient Holocaust survivors who saw Austria as a temporary way station (17,000 Jews left the country between 1945 and 1948) — ZFÖ had a local focus and thus differed from most postwar federations that were active in political matters. If ZFÖ can be said to have had a main focus, that would have been *aliya*, which was closely coordinated with the local JA offices. Chairman: Gustav Leitner.

Zionistische Landesverband in Österreich (ZLÖ), "Zionist National Federation in Austria," clearinghouse for the various general Zionist parties in Austria. Despite its name, ZLÖ was not the national federation for postwar Austrian Zionists, though it was intended to fill that role when initially established in 1945. ZLÖ also published postwar Austria's only functioning Zionist periodical. As a result of its narrow political orientation, ZLÖ was superseded in its national role by the Zionistische Federation von Österreich. Chairman: Wolf Herzberg (1945–1948). Publication: *Die Stimme*.

Zionistische Mittelschul-Verbindung Jedidaea (ZMVJ), "Yedidia Zionist High School Student Society," fraternity of Jewish high school and seminary students established in Vienna in 1909. ZMVJ sought to provide a friendly environment for like-minded Jewish youth whose orientation was Zionist. Activities focused on the educational and cultural (in contrast to some of the Zionist university fraternities that concentrated on duelling and "colors") as a means to promote Jewish identity and pride. ZMVJ continued to operate throughout the 1920s and 1930s, ceasing all operations when the Nazis occupied Austria in 1938.

Belgium

Comité Belgique-Palestine (CBP), "Belgium-Palestine Committee," nationwide entity founded in 1929 to support the activities of the enlarged Jewish Agency in Belgium and *Eretz Israel*. CBP was formed as a coalition of Zionist parties and non-Zionist groups interested in building the *Yishuv*. Activities focused on fund-raising and educational activities to foster Zionist and Jewish identity among Belgian Jewish youth. CBP also sought to promote *aliya* and land settlement.

Federation Sioniste de Belgique (FSB), "Belgian Zionist Federation," national umbrella organization for Zionist activities founded in Brussels in 1900. Initially, FSB was mainly active in Zionist educational and cultural activities. FSB conducted its educational program chiefly through youth groups such as Zeirei Zion. Although it did not represent a majority of Belgian Jews, FSB was a growing force within the community and particularly appealed to the many new immigrants arriving in Belgium after 1881. Just prior to World War I, FSB numbered 1,300 member families (based on *Shekel* sales) and membership grew throughout the interwar era. The Nazi occupation of Belgium during World War II disrupted FSB's public activities, but many Zionists were active in the Belgian Jewish underground. In particular, Zionists played a critical role in founding the Comité de Defense Juive, the main Belgian Jewish underground movement. FSB renewed its activities after World War II and successfully lobbied for Belgian government support at the United Nations in 1947 and 1948. Presidents: Jean Fischer (1900–1926), Numa Torczyner (1926–1940), Yitzhak Kubowitzki (1945–1948). > see also: Abraham J. Edelheit and Hershel Edelheit, *History of the Holocaust: A Handbook and Dictionary* (Boulder: Westview Press, 1994), p. 401.

Bolivia

Federación Sionista Unida de Bolivia (FSUB), "United Zionist Federation of Bolivia," umbrella group for Zionist activity founded in La Paz in 1943. FSUB was always a tightly knit federation of factions and associations representing the entire spectrum of Zionist parties. However, the nature of the Bolivian government during the 1930s and 1940s — a quasi-fascist dictatorship that had close ties to Nazi Germany — severely limited FSUB's activities in the political sphere. As a result, FSUB concentrated on cultural and educational activities. Membership peaked in at 250.

Brazil

Kadima (קדימה), "Forward," Zionist youth group founded in Rio de Janiero in 1924. Although short-lived, Kadima was active in promoting cultural activities and in fund-raising for Hebrew University. Many Kadima graduates went on to assume positions of importance in the Brazilian Jewish community. The group disbanded in 1929.

Biblioteca ha-Tikva, "Ha-Tikva Library," cultural and educational institution founded in Rio de Janiero in 1928 and dedicated to fostering Jewish and Zionist identity among Brazilian Jews. Despite its name, ha-Tikva was more than just a library. Regular classes in Hebrew language and Jewish history as well as lectures and cultural events were held there. Additionally, ha-Tikva helped to promote *aliya* of qualified *Halutzim*, with an initial group leaving Brazil in 1934. Ha-Tikva was disbanded in 1937 when the quasi-fascist government of Getúlio Vargas banned all Zionist activity in Brazil.

Histadrut ha-Ahida (הסתדרות האחידה), "The United Federation," umbrella organization for Brazilian Zionists, also known in Portuguese as Organisation Sionista Unificada (United Zionist Organization), founded as a coalition of the different Zionist parties when renewed activity was permitted after the quasi-fascist Vargas government fell in 1945. The federation was able to activate considerable latent sympathy for Zionism in Brazil and was especially active in championing the Zionist case before Brazil's foreign ministry. In 1946 and 1947 the federation waged a successful campaign to obtain Brazilian support for the U.N. resolution on partition and the creation of a Jewish state. When the Israeli War of Independence began, the federation also began recruitment in the Jewish community for Mitnadve Hutz la-Aretz (Mahal). At its height, the federation numbered six hundred members. Chairman: Jacob Schneider; Secretary-general: Samuel Malamud.

Bulgaria

Carmel (כרמל), first Zionist organization founded in Bulgaria, established in Plovdiv in August 1895. Carmel was originally founded to facilitate the publication of a Ladino (Judeo-Spanish) and French Zionist periodical of the same name that appeared in 1895 and 1896. The journal failed, but the idea of having an active Zionist league caught on and the Plovdiv society remained in operation. A second chapter was begun in Sofia in 1896 and four more chapters were inaugurated in 1897 and 1898. In 1898 all six societies joined with other Bulgarian Zionist societies (such as the Theodor Herzl Society, founded in 1897) to form the Histadrut ha-Zionist ha-Klalit. > see also: **Publications, Zionist (Bulgaria, Carmel)**.

Ezrat Ahim (EA, עזרת אחים), "Help to Brothers," friendly society founded in Sofia in 1895. In addition to social and cultural activities, EA purchased a small parcel of land in *Eretz Israel* in 1896 and settled ten families there; this colony later grew into *Moshav* Hartuv. EZ joined the WZO in 1898, becoming a founding member of the Bulgarian Zionist federation.

Histadrut ha-Zionit ha-Klalit (HHK, הסתדרות הציונית הכללית), "General Zionist Federation," despite its name, this was the national umbrella organization for all Zionist activities in Bulgaria, established on December 27, 1898. Initially headquartered in Plovdiv, HHK moved to Sofia in 1904. Due to the predominance of advocates of Western European-style emancipation and assimilation within the Bulgarian Jewish community, HHK developed slowly. Even so, growth was steady. In 1924, HHK was composed of forty-two regional chapters and societies. World War II disrupted HHK's activities, but the organization was reformed and reorganized in 1945. After reorganization, the federation assumed the title Histadrut ha-Zionit ha-Meuhad (HZM, United Zionist Federation). HZM was destined to be short-lived: its activities were severely curtailed by the new Communist authorities in 1949. Publications: *ha-Shomer* (Bulgarian/Ladino, 1901–1941); *Zionista Trybuna* (Bulgarian, 1944–1949).

Ivria (עבריה), "The Hebrew," Zionist publishing house established in 1913, initially to facilitate publication of a journal by the same name. Six issues of the journal appeared between 1913 and 1918, but the venture was a failure. Thereafter, Ivria published Jewish and Zionist literature in Ladino and Bulgarian translation. The corporation became a cooperative in 1921 but appears to have gone out of business before 1939.

Canada

Canadian Jewish Congress (CJC), Canadian branch of the World Jewish Congress, founded (as a counterpart of the American Jewish Congress) in 1919. Unlike the American Jewish Congress, CJC did not operate as an agency in its own right; instead it worked to facilitate the operations of a variety of social, cultural, educational, and political bodies in Canada. During the 1930s and 1940s, CJC established two priorities for operations: rescue of Jews from Nazi persecution and fulfillment of Zionist goals in *Eretz Israel*. CJC lobbying was effective in obtaining Canadian support for the creation of a Jewish state in 1948.

Zionist Organization of Canada, umbrella agency for Zionist organizations in Canada, founded in 1892. Dedicated to organizing Canadian Jewry for the creation of a Jewish commonwealth in mandatory *Eretz Israel*. The organization acted as a full member of the WZO and cooperated closely with the Zionist Organization of America. Chairman: Michael Garber. Publication: *The Canadian Zionist*.

Chile

Federación Sionista de Chile (FSC), "Zionist Federation of Chile," umbrella group founded in Santiago in 1919 to unite all Zionist activities in the country. In 1926 the local branch of the Women's International Zionist Organization (WIZO) joined FSC; by that time literally every Zionist body in Chile adhered to the main federation. With its 1,500 members the WIZO group, it might be added, was the single largest bloc in the FSC. FSC unity was retained throughout the 1930s and

1940s; the local revisionist Zionists did not withdraw when the main group left the WZO in 1935. Even so, FSC's activities were dominated by a coalition of general Zionists and Mapai (each of whose local unions had 1,000 members in 1948). By contrast, the local revisionist union had only 120 members that year, while Mizrachi had only eighty. Since Chilean Jewry was organized only on a local level, FSC doubled as a de facto national representative body in communal relations with the government. That may partly explain the success Zionists experienced in getting the Chilean government to support partition at the United Nations 1947 and 1948.

China

Shanghai Zionist Association (SZA), local Zionist organization created in 1904 by Jewish refugees and immigrants living in the city. Since virtually the entire Jewish population of China lived in Shanghai, SZA was, de facto, the Zionist federation for the entire country. Despite the small number of Jews living in China at the time, the entire community having only 600 members in 1914, SZA was successful as a lobbying agency, obtaining support from the Chinese nationalist movement. Among the prominent Chinese public figures who strongly supported Zionism was Sun Yat-Sen, founder of the Guomindang (nationalist) movement and first president of the Chinese Republic. The Guomindang strongly supported the Balfour Declaration and the British assumption of a League of Nations mandate to build a Jewish national home in *Eretz Israel*. SZA continued to grow in strength as increasing Jewish distress brought many refugees to Shanghai: by 1937 the community had ballooned to nearly 20,000. The eruption of the Sino-Japanese War in 1937 and the war's spread after the Japanese attacked Pearl Harbor on December 7, 1941 disrupted SZA activities. After World War II SZA, which by then also represented Zionists and Jews in Harbin and Tientsin as well, resumed its activities, primarily to help evacuate the Jewish community to America or, after May 14, 1948, to the State of Israel. When the Chinese Communist party led by Mao Tse-Tung (Zedong) defeated the Guomindang in

1949 the new authorities clamped down on Zionist activities. SZA terminated all its operations in 1950 when the last *olim* from China reached Israel. > see also: **Communism and Zionism**.

Costa Rica

Centro Israelita Sionista (CIS), "Zionist Jewish Center," national Zionist federation and, de facto, the only governmentally recognized Jewish communal organization in Costa Rica. CIS was founded in 1934. Given the small size of Costa Rica's Jewish community (1,200 souls in 1948), no other nationwide communal bodies existed or emerged and CIS was thus able to unify the entire community. Despite persistent anti-semitism in Costa Rica in the 1940s, CIS was able to translate its agenda into effective political action. Costa Rica strongly supported partition in 1947 and was one of the first countries to recognize the new State of Israel in 1948. President: Salomon Shifter (1934–1948).

Cuba

Unión Sionista, "Zionist Union," united Zionist federation for Cuba, established in Havana in 1924, as an amalgamation of already existing Zionist parties and organizations. The union was very successful among Ashkenazi Jews living in the country, most of whom were recent immigrants from Eastern Europe, but failed to attract any large-scale membership among Cuba's Sephardi community. Additionally, a large body of Jewish Communists active in Havana remained aloof from Zionist activities. Despite these impediments, the union undertook a number of highly successful fundraising campaigns for the Keren Kayemet le-Israel and Keren ha-Yesod. Membership in the union grew with the entry of numerous refugees from Europe during the Nazi era, but this increase was balanced by the increased emigration of these same people, mainly to the United States. In 1948 the union had 375 dues-paying members while the local Women's International Zionist Organization (WIZO)

branch numbered approximately 1,350 members. Some 250 Cuban Jews emigrated to Israel between 1948 and 1959.

Czechoslovakia

Barissia, Jewish student union and dueling fraternity founded in 1893 and active through the 1930s. In its latter incarnations, Barissia acted less as a college fraternity and more as a conduit for Zionist educational activity throughout Czechoslovakia. Barissia's influence was felt throughout the entire Czech Zionist federation. Publication: *Barissen Blätter*.

Bar Kochba (BK), Jewish student union and the first Zionist organization founded in the historic Czech lands. BK was initially founded as *Maccabaea* in 1892 and operated under that name until 1898. The group called upon Jews to abandon assimilation and return to Jewish national identity. BK joined the WZO en masse in 1897 and adopted its final name at the Second World Zionist Congress. Thereafter, BK became identified with the practical Zionist wing of the WZO, that is, the younger opposition to Theodor Herzl's exclusively political approach. BK declined after 1918. The alumni association merged with similar organizations in 1929 and BK ceased to function altogether in 1935.

Ben-Guria, Jewish nationalist college fraternity established in Bratislava in 1931. It sponsored the El Al Zionist high school society and focused mainly on foreign Jewish students studying in Czechoslovakia, Ben-Guria was active in all facets of Zionist activities and by 1933 was the largest Jewish fraternity in Slovakia. In 1933, Ben-Guria graduates founded the Ahavat Zion society in Bratislava. Both organizations functioned until the Nazi occupation.

Hitahdut (התאחדות), "Unification," socialist Zionist entity founded in Prague by members of the local branches of ha-Poel ha-Zair and Zeirei Zion in 1920. The merger, which prefigured the later merger that founded Mapai in *Eretz Israel*, was designed to strengthen the socialist Zionists in relation to Zemský svaz sionistický (the local federation). Hitahdut operated independently until 1924. Thereafter, as the socialist Zionists came to increasingly dominate the federation, they ceased their independent operations. > see also: **Yishuv, Organizations (Political Parties, Mifleget Poale Eretz Israel)**.

Jewish Transport and Colonization Company, Slovakian Jewish organization established in 1939 to facilitate Jewish emigration from Slovakia with part of their property. The agency was responsible for overseeing the operation of the transfer agreement between Slovakia and Palestine/ *Eretz Israel* that superseded the Zionist agreement with the Czech government of September 1938. When the British issued the White Paper of 1939 they rendered further activities moot and the company disbanded shortly thereafter. > see also: **Ha'avara**.

Jüdischer Soldatenrat, "Jewish Soldiers' Committee," short-lived militia established at the initiative of the Veritas Zionist student society in October 1918. At the time, Czech independence had just been declared and the outbreak of pogroms seemed possible. Combining students with Jewish veterans to create a militia seemed to be the best way to ensure the community's security. When the threat of pogroms passed, the militia was reorganized into the *Jüdischer Volksrat* (Jewish People's Council) in Brno.

Theodor Herzl (TH), Zionist student union founded in Prague in 1909. Because of the small Jewish student population, TH grew only slowly prior to Czech independence. TH saw Zionism as a force to prevent assimilation and did not deeply enter into Zionist ideological disputes. As a result, many TH members were also members of other Zionist political groups; this reality gave TH a unique nonpartisan ambiance that attracted many students who might not have otherwise joined a Zionist union. During the 1930s, under the impact of Nazism, TH began to emphasize *aliya* and agricultural training for *Halutzim*. TH ceased to function shortly after the Nazi occupation of Prague in March 1939. Publication: *Listy židovské mládeže*.

Volksverein Zion (VVZ), "Zionist People's Union," friendly society established in Prague prior to World War I. VVZ functioned mainly as an adult educational tool, promoting Jewish identification with Zionist goals while also providing members with an opportunity to meet in a congenial atmosphere. VVZ chapters spread rapidly into Bohemia and Moravia, with ten established outside of Prague by 1918.

Zemský svaz sionistický (ZSS), "Zionist Territorial Union," national federation of Czech Zionists, officially established as a separate entity on January 5, 1919 (previously Czech Zionists had been part of the West Austrian federation). ZSS unified all local Zionist federations and unions, both local and county-wide, in Bohemia and Moravia, Slovakia, and Ruthenia. ZSS was organized centrally but operated mainly through its regional chapters. As with all other nationwide Zionist federations, ZSS was divided into numerous factions: every political party active within the WZO was represented in ZSS at one or another time. A nationwide census of Czech Zionists prior to the World Zionist Congress in 1921 established ZSS membership (calculated by *Shekel* sales) at 8,685. Growth in the 1920s and 1930s was slow but steady, peaking at 23,140 in 1933.

Zionist Realists (ZR), Zionist party founded in Brno in 1924 as an opposition movement to Zemský svaz sionistický (ZSS, the local federation). The ZRs took their name from the party founded by Czech president Thomas G. Masaryk prior to World War I. Masaryk had argued that Czech nationalists had to be realistic about what they could accomplish; ZRs likewise argued that much Zionist rhetoric was exaggerated and that the WZO had to approach problems more realistically. The ZRs argued for fundamental institutional change in the WZO, mainly in the format of elections by paid franchise (the *Shekel*), and in Zionist diplomatic and propaganda activities. ZR influence peaked in 1926 when their proposals for reforming the ZSS reached the plenary of the federation's annual convention. However, the ZR proposals were defeated and the group moved to the margins of Czech Zionism.

Danzig

Zionistische Vereinigung in Danzig (ZVD), "Zionist Federation of Danzig," citywide federation recognized as an independent landesverband on January 1, 1920. Previously, Danzig Zionists had been members of the German Zionist federation. They requested WZO recognition as an independent organization due to Danzig's unique international status: under the Treaty of Versailles the city had been removed from German sovereignty but had not been given to Poland. Instead, it was organized as "free city" under the supervision of a League of Nations high commissioner. In addition to the usual dimensions of internal Zionist politics ZVD also oversaw the operation of the Jewish school system (in association with the Polish Tarbut school movement) and a Jewish public bank. Leaning toward the liberal wing of the WZO, ZVD strongly supported Chaim Weizmann's approach to most issues. As the local Nazi party gained influence in Danzig, ZVD became increasingly involved in plans for evacuation of the Jewish community. Most Danzig Jews escaped the Nazi takeover in 1939 and ZVD ceased to function. Since Danzig — renamed Gdansk — was attached to Poland after World War II, no independent Zionist federation emerged. > see also: **Organizations, Zionist (Poland)**.

Denmark

Copenhagen Bureau, name for the WZO Engere Aktions-Komité (Inner Actions Committee, i.e., executive) during its brief hiatus in Denmark between 1915 and 1918. The bureau was opened because Zionist leaders feared that any appearance of favoring one side or the other during the war could open Jewish communities in enemy states to accusations of dual loyalty and potentially harm Zionist projects. The potential danger was hammered home to Zionists after the Ottoman Empire entered the war in alliance with Germany on November 4, 1914. Too close an association with Great Britain or the other Entente powers was seen as a potential threat to the

Yishuv. Simultaneously, it was feared that too close an association with Germany or the other Central Powers would alienate the only country (Great Britain) that had ever entered into serious territorial negotiations with the WZO. From inception, the bureau acted as a clearinghouse for information and communications between Zionist federations in the warring nations and also functioned as a diplomatic center, mainly in 1916 and 1917. At the time, some German Zionists were expressing considerable chagrin over the contacts made by Chaim Weizmann, Ze'ev Jabotinsky, and Nahum Sokolow and the Entente governments; these German Zionists, led by Leo Motzkin (who headed the bureau in 1915) sought contacts with the German foreign ministry to obtain support for a German statement of sympathy with Zionism. The bureau also sought German assurances of protection for the *Yishuv* after the first reports regarding the Armenian massacres were published. Although the latter effort was successful, the former was a complete failure: by the time the Germans issued a tepid declaration, the British Balfour Declaration had already been issued and had promised clear help in creating a Jewish national home. After the war, the Copenhagen Bureau ceased to function with the WZO executive (now renamed ha-Va'ad ha-Poel ha-Mezumzam) moving to London. Chairmen: Leo Motzkin (1915), Victor Jacobson (1916-1918). > see also: **World War I; Hindenburg Erklärung; Balfour Declaration**.

Dansk Zionistenforbund (DZF), "Danish Zionist Union," national federation for Zionist affairs founded in Copenhagen in 1902. DZF acted as a minor participant in WZO affairs (it only sold enough *Shekel*s to qualify for two delegates to the World Zionist Congress in 1903) and did not enjoy the support of the majority of Danish Jewry. DZF's position improved somewhat after 1904, when Jewish refugees from the Russian empire began to arrive in Copenhagen, thereby enlarging the Jewish community. Although most of the new immigrants were socialist in their orientation, enough of them espoused Zionism to strengthen the federation. DZF was further strengthened during World War I, when the

WZO Engere Aktions-Komité (Inner Actions Committee) moved to Copenhagen as a way to symbolize Zionist neutrality in the European war. Nevertheless, DZF remained a relatively weak federation and merged with the Zionist organizations of Finland, Norway, and Sweden in 1935. This coalition of Scandinavian Zionist federations collapsed during the Nazi occupation of Denmark and Norway during World War II. After World War II, DZF was reconstituted and successfully lobbied for Danish government support at the United Nations in 1947 and 1948. Presidents: Louis Frankel, Josef Nachemson, Benjamin Slor.

Ha-Koach (הכח), "The Strength," Jewish sports association affiliated with the world Maccabi organization and active in Denmark after World War II.

Jdisk Kvinderening (JK), "Jewish Women's Association," semi-Zionist organization of Danish Jewish women, established in 1931. Initial emphasis was on social, cultural, and educational activities to encourage Jewish identification in Denmark. As a result of JK's activities, the organization came to support the Zionist cause during the late 1930s and was active in fund-raising for Youth Aliya. JK was compelled to halt its activities during the Nazi occupation and did not resume after 1945. Instead, the local organization was replaced by a Danish chapter of the Women's International Zionist Organization (WIZO). > see also: **Organizations, Zionist (International; Women's International Zionist Organization).**

Dominican Republic

Unión Sionista de la República Dominicana (USRD), "Zionist Union of the Dominican Republic," nationwide Zionist federation working within one of the smallest Jewish communities in the Caribbean. USRD arose at about the same time the organized Jewish community did, that is, after World War I. Given the community's small size, USRD faced little opposition and was able to count on almost universal support within the Jewish community. On the other hand, the community's small size, coupled with its weak overall position in Dominican society, meant that USRD never exercised any influence outside a small circle of political leaders. Thus, for example, USRD was not involved in the Sossua refugee resettlement project, even though the influx of German Jewish refugees (500 by 1942) strengthened USRD and increased its activities.[1] One USRD member, Max Henríques Ureña served as the Dominican ambassador to the United Nations and he was chosen to deliver the welcoming address when Israel was admitted to membership. USRD virtually ceased to function in 1948, although its offices still existed (on paper) into the 1950s.

Ecuador

Asociacion de Beneficience Israelita (ABI), "Jewish Social Service Association," charitable body created in Quito in 1938 to aid in the settlement of Jewish refugees (more than 80 percent of Ecuador's Jews immigrated between 1933 and 1943). ABI supported a wide range of activities, including vocational training and education for new immigrants. Pro-Zionist in orientation, ABI was a founding member of the Federacion Sionista del Ecuador. Membership peaked at four hundred fifty-six with a further sixty persons supported by ABI in 1948.

Federacion Sionista del Ecuador (FSE), "Zionist Federation of Ecuador," nationwide federation for Zionist activities, established in Quito in 1941. Given the small Jewish population, the majority of whom arrived as refugees in the 1930s and 1940s, FSE was able to rapidly rally the community in support of Zionist goals. Peaking at two hundred twenty members in 1948 (with another three hundred forty paying dues to the local WIZO branch), FSE worked

---

[1] For more details on the Sossua project, see: Edelheit and Edelheit, *History of the Holocaust,* p. 129.

closely with other Jewish communal bodies all of which supported the Zionist platform.

Egypt

Bar Kokhba, Zionist friendly society founded in 1897 by Jewish immigrants from Russia. Although the society's founders were all Jews of European, origin its message of Jewish national identity and self-respect resonated within the community, especially within the groups of educated middle-class Jews. By 1901, therefore, the society had three hundred members. Internal disputes and the general inexperience with communal affairs among the leadership led to the society's collapse in 1906. Presidents: Joseph M. Baruch, Jacques Harmalin.

Ha-Tehiya (התחיה), "The Revival," Zionist educational and cultural institution founded in Cairo in 1932. Seeking to instill Jewish values into Egyptian Jewish youth, ha-Tehiya operated a Hebrew club and library. In addition, extensive courses in Hebrew language and Jewish history were offered. Ha-Tehiya ceased to function in the late 1930s, when manifestations of intense anti-Zionism among the Egyptian Muslim population made public activity dangerous.

Zionist Federation, official name for two abortive efforts to create a national framework for Zionist activities in Egypt. The first attempt to create a federation came in 1913, when the Zionist federations of Alexandria and Cairo agreed to merge. This federation lasted until 1917. In 1944 another effort was made to unite all local Zionist entities in Egypt. This effort failed due to the intense parochialism of Egyptian Jewry coupled with the intensity of Muslim opposition to Zionist activities. As a result, all Zionist activities, which despite organizational diffculties were quite extensive, remained organized at the local level only.

El Salvador

Organización Sionista de El Salvador (OSES), "Zionist Organization of El Salvador," umbrella group for Zionist and Jewish activity, organized in early 1945 on the basis of local societies in San Salvador (where the country's entire Jewish population of 300 souls resided) that dated back to 1943. Initial membership was only thirty-five, but OSES was the only communal body in existence until after World War II ended. OSES was mainly active in education and cultural activities but was also successful in lobbying the government to support partition in 1947. Founding President: Ernesto Liebes.

Finland

Ha-Merkaz ha-Zioni be-Finland (המרכז הציוני בפינלנד), "The Zionist Center in Finland," national Zionist federation founded in Helsinki in 1920. Although Finland had previously had a close connection with Zionist affairs (being, for example, the site of the Helsingfors Conference in 1906), the country had earlier been ruled by Russia and did not have its own Zionist federation. Given the small size of Finnish Jewry, the Merkaz was always small: it did not merit a single delegate to any Zionist Congress prior to 1931. Nonetheless, Zionist feelings always ran deep among Finnish Jewry who, for instance, had the highest per capita rate of pledges to the Keren Kayemet le-Israel every year between 1920 and 1948. In 1935, as a means of strengthening the federation, it joined a coalition of Scandinavian Zionist federations with the federations of Denmark, Norway, and Sweden. This coalition collapsed during World War II, at which time the Merkaz resumed independent operations, the only Zionist party allowed to function unhindered in any Axis state. In 1948, twenty-seven Finnish Jews volunteered for service in the Israeli army through Giyus Hutz la-Aretz.

France

Conseil Représentatif des Juifs de France (CRIF), "Representative Council of French Jewry," Jewish communal body established semi-secretly in 1943 as the Fédération des Sociétiés Juives de France. The name CRIF was adopted in 1944 when Franco-Jewish socialists agreed to join what was, until that point, a Zionist organization. CRIF's purpose was to unify all segments of French Jewry, protect Jewish rights in France, and represent Jewish interests in France and abroad.

Although not exclusively Zionist, CRIF had a strongly nationalist orientation, paralleling the American Jewish Congress, on which CRIF was modeled. After World War II, CRIF was a strong supporter of Zionist goals within French Jewry and in the halls of government. In 1945 CRIF joined the World Jewish Congress and has been the de facto French section of that organization.

Éclaireurs Israélites de France (ÉIF), "Jewish Scouts in France," social and educational organization founded in February 1923 by Robert Gamzon. Officially a-political, the ÉIF became increasingly Zionist in its orientation during the 1930s. In 1930 ÉIF had 1,200 members, doubling its membership by 1940. In 1937, ÉIF played a decisive role in unifying all Franco-Zionist youth movements under the banner of the Fédération de la Jeunesse Sioniste et Pro-Palestine. During World War II, ÉIF operated underground, providing many members for all-Jewish and mixed maquis. After the war, ÉIF continued its educational work and also assisted in the operations of the Mossad le-Aliya Bet. In 1946, ÉIF graduates founded *Kibbutz* Neve Ilan in the Jerusalem hills.

Fédération de la Jeunesse Sioniste et Pro-Palestine (FJSPP), "Federation of Zionist and Pro-Palestine Youth," coalition of Zionist youth movements founded in Paris in 1937. By the outbreak of World War II, FJSPP consisted of forty-seven constituent agencies with a total membership in excess of 5,000, making it by far the premier Zionist organization in France. FJSPP members were active in every Franco-Zionist organization and throughout the Franco-Jewish community. As a result, Franco-Jewry was almost completely transformed into a community in which the Zionists played a major, if not decisive, role.

Fédération Sioniste de France (FSF), "French Zionist Federation," national umbrella organization for Zionist affairs founded in 1901. FSF operated as a decentralized federation, with each of its eight constituent groups autonomous in their own region. At the time, FSF was relatively weak, since most native Jews supported assimilationism while most immigrants gravitated toward the socialist parties. Attention paid to FSF (and to Zionism in general) by the Entente powers during World War I increased FSF's prestige and membership was energized by the Balfour Declaration. Nonetheless, during the interwar period, FSF remained a relatively weak element within the Franco-Jewish community. The first glimmer of change came in 1923, when the Association of French Rabbis, previously anti-Zionist in its orientation, strongly supported settlement in *Eretz Israel* during its annual convention in Strasbourg. World War II and the Holocaust catapulted FSF into the forefront of Franco-Jewry. FSF was one of the founding members of the Fédération des Sociétiés Juives de France, which later adopted the name Conseil Représentatif des Juifs de France. Additionally, FSF youth groups provided the cadre for maquis that included the Armée Juive, the premier Jewish resistance movement in France. As a result, after World War II, virtually all Franco-Jewish organizations came to strongly support the movement to establish a Jewish state. In 1947, FSF changed its name to Union Sioniste Française (The Union of French Zionists). All Zionist organizations operating in France or its colonies were included in this new umbrella organization. > see also: **Assimilation**; **World War I**; **World War II**.

Ha-Tikva (התקווה), "The Hope," Franco-Zionist youth movement, founded in Strasbourg in 1917. Unlike other Zionist groups in France, which were mainly concerned with political developments or with personal growth, ha-Tikva was an *aliya*-oriented organization. Indeed, the bulk of French *olim* prior to 1939 were alumni of the group. World War II disrupted ha-Tikva's operations, which were not resumed in 1945.

Ligue des Amis du Sionisme (LAS), "League of Friends of Zionism," Zionist educational organization founded in 1917 as a means to diffuse the Zionist idea among the educated strata of French society. Founded by André Spire, Roger Lévy, and Henri Franck, LAS was mainly composed of French intellectuals — Jews and non-Jews — who accepted the idea of Jewish national rebirth in *Eretz Israel*. Active throughout the interwar years, LAS ceased to operate during World War II and was not revived thereafter. Sole president: Maurice Vernes. Publication: *La Nouvelle Palestine*.

Mouvement de la Juenesse Sioniste (MJS), "Movement of Zionist Youth," umbrella agency for all still-operating Zionist youth movements, founded in secret in December 1941. At the time, the Nazi occupation of northern France had disrupted the activity of almost all Franco-Jewish organizations. As a result, MJS concentrated its activities in southern France, then ruled by the collaborationist government in Vichy. Early in its history, MJS decided to focus on activities likely to promote awareness of Jewish nationalism and Jewish self-defense. Inter alia, this meant smuggling Jews from Nazi-occupied areas (which included the Vichy zone after November 1942) to safety in Switzerland and Spain. MJS also aided Franco-Jewish resistance organizations and was among the organizations that helped to found the Armée Juive.

Union des Dames Juives (UDJ), "Union of French Women," fraternal and charitable organization founded in 1923 to promote Zionist awareness among Franco-Jewish women. UDJ's main strength was in Alsace-Lorraine, and for most of its history UDJ was headquartered in Strasbourg. In 1935, UDJ merged with Union des Femmes Juives de France pour la Palestine, thereby becoming the local branch of the Women's International Zionist Organization. UDJ ceased to operate as a separate entity and moved its operations to Paris.

Union des Femmes Juives de France pour la Palestine (UFJ), "Federation of Jewish Women of France for Palestine," the French federation of the Women's International Zionist Organization established in 1924. > see also: **Organizations, Zionist (International; Women's International Zionist Organization)**.

Union Régionale des Sionistes de l'Est de la France (URSLF), "Regional Zionist Union of Eastern France," local Zionist federation for Alsace-Lorraine, founded in Strasbourg in November 1925. Given the nature of Alsatian Jewry, which was much less assimilated than Jews in the rest of the country, URSLF was able to attract a much larger proportion of the Jewish community than the Fédération Sioniste de France (FSF). In fact USRLF membership was greater than FSF membership in 1939. As a result, USRLF did not join FSF until after World War II. In 1945, USRLF joined the Union Sioniste Française, thereby bringing all French Zionist groups under one unified banner. Sole president: Léopold Metzger. Publication: *Le Juif*.

Union Universelle de la Jeunesse Juive (UUJJ), "Universal Union of Jewish Youth," Zionist youth movement established in Salonika in 1921. UUJJ transferred its operations to Paris in 1923. There it developed into the preeminent Sephardi youth movement. UUJJ was always committed to the unity of the Jewish people, the centrality of *Eretz Israel* to Jewish life, and a nondenominational orientation on religious questions. Chairpersons: Charles Néhama, Jacques Matalon. Publication: *Chalom*.

French North Africa

Fédération Sioniste de Tunisia (FST), "Zionist Federation of Tunisia," nationwide Zionist federation founded in Tunis in 1920 as a coalition of local Zionist organizations operating within the French colony. FST's main office also acted as the local JA office and provided *aliya* certificates for German Jewish refugees who arrived in Tunisia during the 1930s. In addition to FST, many Tunisian Zionists joined the Fédération Sioniste de France, which acted as a mother agency for subsidiaries in the colonies. During the 1930s the rising tide of Arab nationalism, inflamed by German and Italian propaganda, began to develop a violently antisemitic strain, which was met by FST with efforts to organize Jewish self-defense units. FST ceased to function between November 1942 and April 1943, during the Nazi occupation of Tunisia. Operations were resumed upon liberation and from then until the State of Israel was established, FST placed most of its emphasis on *aliya*.

Sha'are Zion (שערי ציון), "Gates of Zion," friendly society active in Morocco after 1901. Organized locally, the society had three major branches: Fez, Tangier, and Tetuán. When France and Spain partitioned Morocco in 1912 the societies lost contact with one another. Thereafter, the Fez society associated itself with Fédération Sioniste de France (FSF) and operated as a subsidiary of that agency until 1920. A French law banning the existence of any political parties (promulgated to prevent the organization of Muslim nationalist associations but applied to the Jewish case as well) forced Sha'are Zion to publicly cease its operation. In 1922 FSF and the WZO obtained a release from the French government and Sha'are Zion was able to resume its activities. By 1948 fifteen local branches existed in French Morocco and Zionist activities continued unabated until Morocco's independence. The Sha'are Zion societies in Spanish Morocco fared better in the short run, since their activities were left uninterrupted throughout the 1920s and early 1930s. The Spanish Civil War and the fascist victory that ended the war led to a disruption of all Jewish communal activity, which was not resumed until 1948.

Union Sioniste Algérienne (USA), "Algerian Zionist Union," de facto nationwide federation operating in French colonial Algeria. USA did not have the same status within the WZO as other national federations because of Algeria's unique legal situation. The territory was considered a department of France rather than a colony. As a result, Algerian Zionists could also legitimately join the Fédération Sioniste de France and most did so. Further weakening USA was the fact that assimilation was very strong in Algeria, where Jews had been emancipated by French government decree (the so-called Cremieux Decree) since 1870. After World War I, USA developed rapidly and was finally recognized as a landesverband by the WZO. Nonetheless, growth was slow and USA did not become a major factor in Algerian Jewry until after the establishment of the State of Israel.

Germany

Binyan ha-Aretz (בנין הארץ), "Building the Land," nonpolitical Zionist federation founded in Germany in 1920. Binyan ha-Aretz rejected all forms of political Zionism, recommending instead that diaspora Zionists should concentrate on philanthropic and other projects that would promote economic growth in the *Yishuv* and thus permit greatly expanded *aliya*. In effect, Binyan ha-Aretz was the German agency for supporters of Justice Louis D. Brandeis in his controversy with WZO president Chaim Weizmann. In turn, the German organization spawned a number of offshoots, notably in Austria and Czechoslovakia. The German and Czech branches ceased to function when the Brandeisists were defeated at Zionist conferences in London, Hanover, and Cleveland. > see also: **Brandeisists**.

Blau-Weiss (BW), "Blue-White," premier Jewish youth movement founded in Berlin in 1912. Also known in the Hebrew-speaking world as "Tehelet-Lavan," which is a simple translation of the German name. BW was chosen as the name to reflect the Zionist orientation of the group when it was founded. Initially, BW functioned in the same way as the so-called wanderfogel groups did among non-Jewish German youth, although BW always placed much greater emphasis on education and culture than the parallel organizations did. Thus BW emphasized communal celebration of Jewish holidays and Hebrew use. BW did not focus on *aliya* prior to 1933. BW's membership peaked in the early 1920s when all chapters had a combined total of 3,000 members. Most BW chapters ceased to operate after 1929; in 1933 the remaining active chapters joined with Brit ha-Olim and the Arbeiterkreis to found ha-Bonim-Noar Haluzi which did place most of its emphasis on *aliya*. Branches of BW also existed in Austria and Czechoslovakia (founded prior to World War I, when both countries were united in the Austro-Hungarian empire) but they ceased to function when the Nazis occupied their countries in 1938 and 1939.

B'nai Brith (בני ברית), "Sons of the Covenant," society founded in Germany on May 8, 1882, with the aim of assisting Jewish settlement in *Eretz Israel* by purchasing land.

In particular, the land on which Zichron Ya'akov was later built was purchased by the German organization. Despite its name, the organization was not initially associated with the international Jewish fraternal order B'nai B'rith. Rather, this B'nai Brith was a charter member of the Hibbat Zion movement. In 1884–1885 the Zionist B'nai Brith did join the international fraternal organization, becoming the Concordia Lodge of B'nai B'rith. At that point, however, it ceased to function as a Zionist body. Publication: *Der Colonist* (1882–1884). > see also: **Organizations, Non- or Anti-Zionist (International, B'nai B'rith).**

Brit ha-Olim (ברית העולים), "Union of Immigrants," socialist Zionist body founded in Berlin in 1925 to educate German Jewish youth and prepare them for a pioneering life in *Eretz Israel*. Affiliated with Dror and Gordonia, the union was a founding member of the ha-Bonim youth movement and operated in cooperation with he-Halutz, ha-Kibbutz ha-Meuhad, and Mapai. The first group of Brit ha-Olim members founded *Kibbutz* Givat Brenner in 1928. Further groups left Germany thereafter, although none founded their own settlements. In 1933 Brit ha-Olim merged with Blau-Weiss and the Arbeiterkreis to form ha-Bonim-Noar Haluzi. With the merger, the new movement united most of the Zionist youth groups in Germany with a total membership of 3,300. Because the new organization emphasized Jewish emigration, its activities were tolerated by the Gestapo and operated almost unimpeded. All functions ceased after Kristallnacht, however, and the ha-Bonim group was not revived after World War II.

Bund Jüdischer Corporationen (BJC), "Union of Jewish Fraternities," Zionist movement active among university students in Germany's major cities, founded in 1901. BJC initially was a coalition of four Jewish fraternities at the universities in Berlin, Breslau, Leipzig, and Munich that started out as dueling clubs (so-called Turnvereine) and adopted a broadly Zionist worldview. By 1914 nine more fraternities had joined, although two of the founding member fraternities had ceased to function. In July 1914 BJC merged with the Kartell Zionistische Verbindungen to found the Kartell Jüdische Verbindungen.

Bund Zionistischer Verbindungen (BZV), "Union of Zionist Leagues," Zionist fraternal organization active in German universities. BZV was founded in 1920 by members who withdrew from the Kartell Jüdischer Verbindungen. It is unclear what led to the schism, since both organizations were Zionist in their orientation. BZV was never a large fraternity and ceased to function altogether with the Nazi rise to power in 1933.

Colonisations-Vereien für Palästina (CVP), "Colonization Society for Palestine," proto-Zionist federation founded in Frankfurt am Oder in 1860. CVP brought together three of the best known proto-Zionists of that era: Rabbi Judah Alkali, Moses Hess, and Rabbi Zvi Hirsch Kalischer. Indeed, CVP was instrumental in arranging publication of the latter's book, *Drishat Zion*, in 1863. However, the call to restore Jews to their ancestral homeland did not then resonate in German Jewry and CVP ceased to function in 1864.

Esra Verein (EV), "Ezra Organization," German league to support Hibbat Zion, established on January 26, 1884. EV operated mainly as a fund-raising agency, buying land on which early settlers lived. In 1886, EV had 2,000 members; membership peaked at 5,000 in 1899. By then Hibbat Zion no longer existed. EV's operations were slowly being transferred to the WZO, a process that was completed shortly after the turn of the century. EV ceased to function on the eve of World War I. Nonetheless, its accomplishments were many, including purchasing the land on which the settlements of Rehovot, Motza, Be'er Tuvia (Kastina), and Mahanayim were built.

Jüdische Jugendhilfe (JJ), "Jewish Youth Help," social and educational agency created by Recha Frier in 1932. Initially organized for vocational training, the agency became the German arm of Youth Aliya in 1933. In the latter capacity, JJ was organized as a coalition of German Zionist youth movements, although non-Zionist youth were welcome to join. As with Youth Aliya, JJ never saw itself as acting solely on behalf of children. Almost all German Zionists saw the emigration of young people as a first, vital, step toward the removal of those elements in German Jewish society for which no future existed under the Nazi regime. Long-range plans called for the eventual reunification of families, although in most cases this was not accomplished. Because of its emphasis on emigration, JJ was permitted to operate, with increasing Gestapo interference, until 1938. > see also: **Yishuv, Yishuv Organizations (Educational and Cultural Organizations, Aliyat Yeladim va-No'ar).**

Jüdischer Verlag, "Jewish Publishing (House)," publishing house created by the Fifth Zionist Congress to further the Zionist cause by publishing books and pamphlets on the subject. As a mouthpiece publishing house, the company took considerable time to develop because it never had sufficient funds for most of its projects. The company flourished during the Weimar era but ceased functioning at Gestapo orders in 1938.

Jung Juda, "Young Judea," Zionist youth group active during and shortly after World War I. Membership never exceeded thirty, but most of the members later assumed senior positions in the German Jewish community, the Zionistische Vereinigung für Deutschland, or the *Yishuv.* In the mid-1920s about half the Jung Juda group emigrated, forming the nucleus for Kibbutz Bet Zera in the Jordan Valley. Publication: *Blauweisse Brille* (Blue-White Spectacles).

Kartell Jüdische Verbindungen (KJV), "Federation of Jewish Fraternities," Zionist student union founded when the Bund Jüdischer Corporationen (BJC) merged with the Kartell Zionistischer Verbindungen (KZV) in July 1914. KZV had originally been founded by Jewish university students who supported BJC's nationalist goals but sought a more explicitly Zionist forum for their activities. By 1914, BJC had adopted an overtly Zionist platform and continued competition no longer made sense. KJV was an immediate success. It had more than a dozen member fraternities at founding and

continued to grow throughout the 1920s. Virtually the entire leadership of German Zionism were graduates (at one level or another) of KJV (or its predecessors), such that KJV could lay claim to being the most influential Zionist organization in Germany.

Kommittee für den Osten (KDO), "Committee for the East," German Zionist organization founded during World War I to protect Jewish rights in Eastern European territory newly captured by the German army. KDO hoped to mute the problems facing Jews in the epicenter of combat between the Central Powers and the Russians while also furthering the Zionist conquest of communities in the region. Furthermore, the KDO hoped that by appearing to help solidify German control in the region, Zionists would be rewarded with a statement of sympathy from the German government after the war. KDO's political goals were an almost complete failure, especially in terms of overtures to the German government. Still, KDO did offer considerable philanthropic assistance to Jewish communities in the throes of disaster, especially in 1916 and 1917. KDO was especially active in funneling funds from the United States to needy Jewish communities. KDO collapsed after World War I. > see also: **Hindenburg Erklärung.**

Zionistische Vereinigung für Deutschland (ZVfD), "German Zionist Organization," founded in October 1897 as the official Zionist federation in Germany. Like all other landesverbände, the ZVfD was composed of different groups that accepted basic the tenets of Zionism but differed on specific nuances of Zionist goals. For much of its history, ZVfD concentrated on internal matters: re-creating a Jewish national identity in a community suffused with assimilationist attitudes. Unlike Eastern European Zionists, ZVfD did not concentrate on *aliya* until the 1930s. ZVfD cannot be said to have truly "conquered" the German Jewish community. Prior to 1933 membership was a mere 10,000 (out of a total Jewish community of approximately 575,000 souls), while membership peaked in 1935 at 22,500. Yet ZVfD's prognosis proved to be ultimately correct in that only a national solution to the "Jewish question" would provide Jews with the security they needed to survive in the modern world. In 1933, ZVfD leaders were in the forefront of negotiating the controversial *Ha'avara* (transfer) Agreement. Presidents: Max I. Bodenheimer (1897–1910), Arthur Hantke (1910–1920), Felix Rosenblüth and Alfred Klee (copresidents, 1920–1921), Felix Rosenblüth (1921–1923), Alfred Landsberg (1923–1924), Kurt Blumenfeld (1924–1933), Siegfried Moses (1933–1937). Publication: *Jüdische Rundschau*. > see also: **Ha'avara Agreement**.

Greece

Agudat B'nai Zion (ABZ, אגודת בני ציון), "Sons of Zion Association," First overtly Zionist organization in Salonika, established in 1908, when the city was still ruled by the Ottoman Empire. After the first Balkan war (1912–1913) Salonika fell to the Greeks. Because of the demographic preponderance of Salonika's Jews, who represented three-quarters of Greek Jewry prior to World War II, ABZ functioned from 1914 onward as the national federation for all of Greece and was recognized as such by the Greek government. ABZ operated uninterrupted from 1908 to 1941, promoting the Zionist cause in all communal forums with mixed success. Although many Salonika Jews emigrated to *Eretz Israel* as their situation worsened (especially after antisemitic outbursts in 1922 and 1934), most emigrants left for Egypt, France, Belgian Congo, and the United States. Zionism was considerably weaker in Greece proper, although numerous local societies operated for varying lengths of time throughout the country. ABZ ceased to function when the Nazis occupied Greece in April 1941 and was not revived after the war.

Hevrat Kadima (חברת קדימה), "Forward Society," Hebrew language and cultural society founded in Salonika in 1899. Although not explicitly Zionist in orientation, the Hevra's emphasis on Hebrew language and Jewish culture encouraged support for Jewish identity and nationalism among Salonika's Jewish youth.

Guatemala

Organisation Sionista de Guatemala, "Zionist Organization of Guatemala," local federation for Zionist activities founded in 1947. Membership was small, even compared with other Jewish communities in Central America, and peaked at 140 in 1948. A local branch of the Women's International Zionist Organization added a further eighty members to the federation. Sole president: E. W. Heineman.

Hungary

Ha-Gedudim ha-Zioniim (הגדודים הציוניים), "The Zionist Battalions," self-adopted name for self-defense units composed of Jewish war veterans led by Jewish army officers and placed to defend Jewish communities during the period after the Hungarian central government collapsed at World War I's end. Between 1918 and 1920, no less than three governments rose and fell: the legitimate prewar government, Bela Kuhn's Budapest Soviet, and the restored Social Democratic government that arose after the White Terror that brought Kuhn's government down. Because Jewish communists were heavily in Kuhn's government (he himself was of Jewish origin), many Hungarians adopted an antisemitic view that could easily be whipped up to a fever pitch by rabble rousers. Violence ensued. The battalions sought to protect Jewish communities and institutions, rising eventually to a total of 17,000 men under arms. In 1920 when peace was restored, the battalions voluntarily disbanded.

Magyar Cionista Szervezet (MCSz), "Hungarian Zionist Federation," national federation for Zionist affairs founded provisionally in 1902. MCSz held its first national congress in Pressburg in 1903 which was considered the official founding date for the organization. Nevertheless, at this stage MCSz was not legally recognized by the Hungarian royal government; recognition did not follow until 1911. Prior to World War I, MCSz was organized into five regional sections: Slovakia, Sub-Carpathia, Transylvania, South Hungary (Bosnia and Croatia), and Hungary. Headquarters was initially in Pressburg: central Hungary was considered infertile soil for Zionist development until after the antisemitic upheavals that followed World War I. Even after the war, when MCSz was reorganized to operate only in Hungary, the movement was relatively weak. Most Hungarian Jews espoused either a belief in assimilation or in traditional Orthodoxy; in neither case was Zionism considered central to Jewish needs and, in some cases, it was actively opposed as detrimental to Jewish survival. MCSz continued to operate throughout the 1920s and 1930s, gaining strength as Hungary's government increasingly adopted an anti-semitic policy. The Hungarian Zionists hoped to weather the Nazi storm, but the deportations decimated all Hungarian Jews. Attempts to renew Zionist activities in postwar Hungary were severely hampered by the new Communist regime and MCSz ceased to function.

Makkabea, student Zionist organization founded in Budapest in 1903. For part of its early history Makkabea also functioned as an ad hoc Zionist federation for all of Hungary, mainly while the Magyar Cionista Szervezet was being organized. Makkabea primarily focused on the cultural and educational aspects of Zionist affairs. It was not completely successful at these activities because the Hungarian Jewish community was generally apathetic to the Zionist cause until the 1930s. Makkabea continued to function until 1944, when all Zionist activities ceased due to the Nazi occupation.

Va'ad ha-Ezra veha-Hazala (ועד העזרה וההצלה), "Aid and Rescue Committee," Hungarian Zionist body chaired by Rudolf (Rezo) Kasztner and officially dedicated to rescue activity on behalf of Balkan Jewry during World War II. Kasztner was involved in one of the war's most controversial diplomatic effort, the "Blood for Wares" negotiations with Adolf Eichmann. > see also: Edelheit and Hershel Edelheit, *History of the Holocaust*, p. 85.

Vívó és Atlétikai Club (VAC), "Fencing and Athletic Club," youth wing of the Magyar Cionista Szervezet, founded in 1906 (prior to the federation obtaining government sanction for its activities). VAC concentrated on fostering a Zionist attitude among Hungarian Jewish youth through encouragement of physical fitness, sports prowess then being considered as central to healthy nationalism. VAC's combination of sports and Zionism was the model for many other Zionist sports federations throughout Europe in the early part of the twentieth century.

International

B'nai Akiva (בני עקיבא, BA), "Sons of Akiva," international Jewish youth movement founded in 1922 by a coalition of Mizrachi and ha-Poel ha-Mizrachi. BA's ideology may be understood by reference to its slogan: Tora ve-Avoda (Jewish tradition and labor). In other words, BA was dedicated to the re-creation of a Jewish national home that would combine adherence to Orthodox Jewish practice with modern Jewish nationalism. BA operated mainly in the diaspora to prepare Jewish youth for *aliya* and settlement in a *Kibbutz*. As such, BA cooperated closely with ha-Kibbutz ha-Dati, with Mizrachi and ha-Poel ha-Mizrachi, and with he-Halutz. After World War II, BA became more active in settlement building, founding its first two *Kibbutzim* in 1946: at En Tzurim (Gush Ezion) and Birya (lower Galilee). The latter settlement was the focus of an intense struggle against the British that had important international repercussions. BA activities have continued and have grown since 1948.

Brit Olamit Ahdut ha-Avoda-Poale Zion (ברית עולמית אחדות העבודה-פועלי ציון), "World Union of Unity for Labor and Workers of Zion," federation of left-leaning socialist Zionist parties founded in 1946. The union was an amalgamation of the Ahdut ha-Avoda party (founded in 1944 from the remnants of Mapai's Siya Bet) and Poale Zion Smol branches in *Eretz Israel* and the diaspora. More heavily influenced by socialist doctrines than Mapai, the new party was pro-Soviet in orientation (in stark contrast to Mapai's pro-Western orientation). Complete amalgamation only took place in the *Yishuv* and then only for the Twenty-Second World Zionist Congress; the diaspora branches of both parties remained separate until 1948. At that point, all branches joined with ha-Shomer ha-Zair to form Mifleget ha-Poalim ha-Meuhad (Mapam).

Ha-Noar ha-Zioni (הנוער הציוני), "Zionist Youth," multinational federation of Zionist youth groups founded in Lwow in 1931. Initially, the federation represented general Zionist youth in eight countries: Belgium, *Eretz Israel*, Hungary, Iraq, Luxembourg, Poland, Romania, and the U.S. The federation was, in turn, a conglomerate of three previously existing multinational youth federations — ha-Shomer ha-Leumi, ha-Noar ha-Ivri, and ha-Noar ha-Zioni (whose name was adopted for the new coalition) — that decided to pool their resources. During the 1930s, further youth groups joined the movement, representing Zionist youth in Austria, Czechoslovakia, France, Latvia, and Lithuania. All of the continental branches ceased to function during the Holocaust. Only the branches in America and the *Yishuv* were able to continue to operate without interruption. After the war, branches were reestablished in Belgium and France while new affiliates joined in Latin America, Holland, and the United Kingdom.

He-Halutz (החלוץ), "The Pioneer," Zionist training movement for young adults associated with the moderate socialist Zionist party that eventually emerged as Mapai. The initial impetus for organization came from *Halutzim* in Poland who began to organize on a local level as early as December 1918. A national conference for he-Halutz met in Warsaw on May 14, 1919. The international he-Halutz movement was formed in the 1920s, uniting regional he-Halutz federations from around the world, mainly including the federations from Poland and *Eretz Israel*. Ideologically, he-Halutz was indistinguishable from Mapai. The federation emphasized the need to build *Eretz Israel* as a Jewish national home and concentrated on the specific steps that *Halutzim* needed to take in order to turn the Zionist idea into a reality. Like Mapai, he-Halutz emphasized a gradualist development policy, emphasized the need for *Halutzim* to be in the forefront of Zionist development, and rejected orthodox Marxist ideas about class conflict, preferring the concept of "constructive socialism." In practice, that meant that he-Halutz saw its role as providing agricultural training that would facilitate *aliya* by permitting *Halutzim* to qualify for labor certificates to Palestine/*Eretz Israel*.

Mizrachi (מזרחי), "Easterner" (actually the name derived from the abbreviation *Merkaz Ruhani* מרכז רוחני, "a spiritual center"), religious Zionist party, founded in 1902. At the 1906 Pressburg conference, Mizrachi's ideology was largely formulated: mainly advocacy of the creation of a Jewish national home consistent with Jewish tradition and *Halacha*. Mizrachi's motto was, "The Land of Israel, for the People of Israel, by way of the Law of Israel." During the Herzl era, Mizrachi felt itself more comfortable with Political Zionists, since they tended to downplay cultural questions; Mizrachi supported Herzl's call for Zionists to accept the British offer to settle Jews in East Africa. In the post-Herzl era, however, the party articulated a palestinocentric ideology. In 1919 ha-Poel ha-Mizrachi, a religious but socialist offshoot, was founded. During the 1930s and 1940s Mizrachi participated in a coalition with Mapai in the Jewish Agency and World Zionist Organization, despite some affinities with the revisionist movement: mainly in regard the defense of *Eretz Israel*'s unity and uncompromising opposition to partition. > see also: **Historic Coalition**.

Poale Zion (פועלי ציון, PZ), "Workers of Zion," socialist Zionist party founded as a separate union within the WZO in 1901. Initially, the party was a loose amalgamation of proletarian supporters of the Jewish national movement. PZ was heavily influenced by its founder, Ber Borochov, and the party's diverse factions reflected parts of his ideology. As PZ developed, it branched into three distinct wings: the Russian Jewish Social Democratic Workers Party Poale Zion (usually known by the Russian abbreviation ZS), which turned into a territorialist party in the years after Borochov's death. The remainder of the party split in 1920 into two major factions, Poale Zion Yemin (Right Workers of Zion, PZY) and Poale Zion Smol (Left Workers of Zion, PZS), which split over the issue of cooperation with nonsocialist parties in building the *Yishuv*. PZY developed a reformist ideology that gave equal weight to both socialism and nationalism. The party joined with Ahdut ha-Avoda in 1930 to form Mifleget Poale Eretz Israel (Mapai) and its diaspora affiliates joined to form the Hitahdut. PZS, in contrast, developed an ideology that emphasized socialism and saw Zionism as a means to create a socialist entity in the Jewish world. PZS went in and out of the WZO until 1946, when its joined with Mapai's *Siya Bet* (which had, by that time, adopted the name Ahdut ha-Avoda) to form the Brit Olamit Ahdut ha-Avoda-Poale Zion and, in 1948, Mifleget ha-Poalim ha-Meuhad (Mapam).

Radical Zionists, short-lived faction popular in Germany and Poland and existing as a clear faction at the Zionist congresses from 1923–1933. The radicals saw themselves as heirs of the "Democratic Fraction" that had opposed Theodor Herzl during the WZO's early years. In their era, they opposed WZO president Chaim Weizmann but were not comfortable with either the socialist or revisionist blocs. They advocated democratization of the election system used for the Zionist Congress and opposed the enlargement of the JA, fearing that adding non-Zionists would weaken the JA's commitment to Zionist political goals. Unlike the revisionists, who supported similar positions, however, the radicals did not subscribe to maximalist ideas on *aliya* and on the so-called Endziel issue. As a reflection of how their approach differed from the revisionists, it is useful to note that in 1929, when the "enlarged" JA became a reality, the radicals declared their willingness to co-operate with the new body. The increasing polarization of the WZO in the years between 1930 and 1932 forced the radicals to choose membership in a more established bloc (most joined the World Union of General Zionists). The party collapsed after the Eighteenth Zionist Congress (1933).

World Jewish Congress (WJC), international Jewish defense agency founded in 1936. The WJC was organized around the postulate that Jews constitute one nation; the organization set its task at defending Jewish interests against Nazism and antisemitism and encouraging the creation of a Jewish national home in *Eretz Israel*. Of prime importance to the operations of the WJC was the American Jewish Congress, led by Rabbi Stephen S. Wise. During World War II, the WJC operated largely from the United States and was active in promoting rescue and other relief proposals. The WJC was also active in protesting the restrictions established on the *Yishuv* by the British White Paper of 1939. A strong supporter of Jewish national aspirations, the WJC collectively joined the WZO after the Biltmore Conference. (CASE)

Women's International Zionist Organization (WIZO), international Jewish Zionist women's

TABLE O.2: Functioning WIZO Branches in 1948

Algeria	Curacao	Mexico
Argentina	Denmark	Netherlands
Australia	Ecuador	New Zealand
Austria	El Salvador	Panama
Barbados	Finland	Paraguay
Belgian Congo (Zaire)	France	Peru
Belgium	Greece	Sweden
Brazil	Guatemala	Switzerland
Chile	Italy	United States
Colombia	Jamaica	United Kingdom
Costa Rica	Kenya	Uruguay
Cuba	Luxembourg	Venezuela

Source: Simon Federbusch, ed., *World Jewry Today* (New York:Thomas Yoseloff, 1959).

Staff Members of the World Jewish Congress, Montreaux, Switzerland, June, 1948.
Authors' Collection

organization established in London on July 11, 1920. During the 1930s WIZO grew to have chapters in some sixty-two countries worldwide. Thirty-six of these chapters were still active in 1948. WIZO established subsidiary agencies for fund-raising and political activity in many countries. During the 1930s and 1940s WIZO actively pursued rescue goals in and out of Europe. In order to maintain Jewish unity, WIZO became a member of both the WZO and the World Jewish Congress. Membership peaked at 250,000 in fifty federations.

World Union of General Zionists (WUGZ), amalgamation of all nonsocialist, non-revisionist, non-Orthodox Zionist parties formed in 1929. When Theodor Herzl founded the WZO, he had not taken into account the possibility that separate parties might emerge within the Zionist movement. Even as parties were established (Poale Zion in 1901, Mizrachi in 1902), the majority of Zionists did not consider themselves members of a bloc but as simply Zionists (in Hebrew known as "Stam Zionim," סתם ציונים). However, as the individual parties began to proliferate and even came to dominate the WZO, the general Zionists began to organize and founded the WUGZ. Nonetheless, the party was always deeply riven by ideological and personal divisions: one faction (the so-called General Zionist A Faction) supported WZO president Chaim Weizmann, supported gradualism and Zionist minimalism, and advocated cooperation with socialist Zionists. In contrast, the other major faction (the so-called General Zionist B Faction) opposed Weizmann, supported a maximalist Zionist orientation, and opposed the hegemony of Mapai. The two factions split after 1931, reunited temporarily during the early 1940s, and split permanently after World War II.

Iran

Comité Central de l'Organization Sioniste en Perse (CCOSP), "Central Committee of the Zionist Organization in Persia," first major Zionist organization in Iran, founded in Teheran in 1919. CCOSP began very auspiciously, with 3,500 members organized into eighteen branches. However, the government of Shah Reza Pahlavi I was hostile to Zionism and ordered CCOSP to cease operations in 1926. Zionist activities resumed secretly during the early 1930s and publicly after Reza I was deposed by the Anglo-Russian alliance in 1941. The new shah, Mohammed Reza I (who reigned between 1941 and 1979, with a brief interlude in 1953–1954), was more kindly disposed to Jews and Jewish issues, permitting Zionists to resume their public activities in the guise of the local JA office.

Iraq

Aguda Zionit be-Bagdad (AZB, אגודה ציונית בבגדאד), "Zionist Association of Baghdad," short-lived Zionist federation founded in 1914 to promote the Zionist cause in Mesopotamia (then part of the Ottoman Empire, now Iraq). Organized by three Baghdadi Jews — Maurice Fattal, Menashe Hakim, and Raphael Horesh — AZB collapsed in November when Turkey declared war on Britain. Efforts were made to revive AZB in 1921, when Iraq was a British mandated territory ruled by King Faisal I with British assistance. These efforts collapsed when the competent Iraqi authorities refused to issue the needed licenses for AZB to operate in public. The AZB continued to operate, albeit secretly, until 1924 when it merged into the newly formed (but equally unlicensed) Aguda Zionit le-Aram Naharayim.

Jamiyya Israeliyya Adabiyya (JIA), "Jewish Literary Society," cover name for the first major Zionist organization founded in interwar Iraq, established on July 15, 1920. JIA sought to accomplish three stated goals: (1) to encourage Jews to study their culture and history, (2) to foster Jewish national identity and support for the Jewish

national home, and (3) to promote better understanding between Jews and Arabs. JIA continued to operate in the educational and cultural role until 1924, when it openly espoused a Zionist affiliation by adopting the new name Aguda Zionist le-Aram Naharayim (Zionist Association for Mesopotamia, אגודה ציונית לארם נהריים). The new organization operated without a license, since the competent Iraqi authorities refused to grant one until 1932. Thereafter, the intensely antisemitic atmosphere in independent Iraq, coupled with the rise of quasi-fascist forms of Iraqi nationalism, made public Zionist activities dangerous. Zionist activity continued in private until the 1940s, when a government sympathetic to Nazism forced the Zionists to begin a secret exodus from Iraq that was completed in 1949. > see also: **Operation Ezra/Nehemia**.

Ireland

Daughters of Zion (DOZ), Zionist women's organization founded in Dublin in 1900. DOZ had the distinction of being the first Zionist organization active in Ireland, when the country was still ruled by Great Britain. DOZ continued to operate independently after the Irish Republic (Eire) was proclaimed in 1921. Albeit, throughout its history, DOZ acted in coordination with the Federation of Women Zionists of Great Britain and Ireland (which also encompassed the six counties of Northern Ireland). DOZ was a founding member of the Women's International Zionist Organization, after which it ceased to function as a separate body. Chairwomen: Rose Leventhal (1900–1940); Ethel Freedman (1940-1951).

Dublin Zionist Commission (DZC), local federation for Zionist affairs founded in 1901. From 1901 to 1921, DZC operated as an autonomous arm of the English Zionist Federation (EZF). After independence, DZC operated as an independent federation (though coordinating activities with the EZF) operating throughout Eire. In 1937, DZC was thoroughly reorganized due to the withdrawal of the revisionists, who were proportionally more powerful in Ireland than in any other country except Poland. Given the small size of Ireland's Jewish population, DZC was a relatively weak federation, but it did contribute greatly to the *Yishuv*'s growth and successfully lobbied for Irish support for a Jewish State in 1947 and 1948.

Italy

Comitato Italia-Palestina (CIP), "Italy-Palestine Committee," Zionist group established in 1928 to facilitate contacts between Italy and the Yishuv. Membership included many Jewish communal leaders and a small group of influential members of the Partito Nazionale Fascista. The CIP ceased to function after 1938. Chairman: Leone Carpi.

Federazione Giovanile Ebraica d'Italia (FGEI), "Federation of Italian Jewish Youth," coalition of Zionist youth groups founded in Florence in 1948. FGEI operated both in the educational/cultural and in the camping/sport fields, attempting to create well-rounded Jewish youth committed to Zionism and the Jewish community. On founding, FGEI had centers in Ancona, Bologna, Casale, Ferrara, Florence, Genoa, Milan, Naples, Prugia, Pisa, Rome, Trieste, Turin, and Venice. Publication: *Ha-Tikvah*.

Federazione Sionistica Italiana (FSI), "Italian Zionist Federation," national federation for Zionist affairs established in Modena on October 20, 1901. FSI developed very slowly at first, since most Italian Jews were comfortable with an assimilationist stance. Nonetheless, even the most ardent assimilationists in Italy supported Zionist philanthropies, meaning that the FSI had fewer difficulties within its community than most Zionist federations. Similarly, FSI had the almost continuous support of the Italian rabbinate, which saw Zionism as a way to strengthen Jewish identity. FSI gained considerable prestige after World War I, thanks in no small measure to the Italian government's support for the Balfour Declaration. When the Fascists seized power in Rome in 1922, FSI was not immediately effected by the change in regime. To the contrary, between 1922 and 1938, Italian premier

Benito Mussolini sought to establish himself as a potential WZO ally. Highly publicized meetings between Mussolini and WZO leaders including Chaim Weizmann and Nahum Sokolow reinforced that perception. However, conditions changed after 1938, as Mussolini's government drew closer to the Nazi regime in Germany and introduced a series of anti-Jewish laws. In turn, new government policies culminated in FSI operations being suspended for the rest of the Fascist era. FSI resumed its activities after a reorganizational conference held January 12–13, 1945. Greater emphasis was now placed on *aliya* and on political work in conjunction with the *Yishuv*. As is well known, postwar Italy was a major site for the Mossad le-Aliya Bet, whose activities were greatly facilitated by the FSI. Presidents: Felice Ravenna (1901–1921), Alberto Viterbo (1921–1938, 1944–1948). Publication: *L'Idea Sionnista* (1901–1911); *Israel* (1916–1938; 1944f).

Japan

Zionist Organization (ZO), name for several attempts to found a unified Zionist federation for Japan. The first such effort came in 1920 at the initiative of Israel Cohen, a leader of the English Zionist Federation then visiting the Far East. At the time, approximately two-hundred Jews lived in Japan — mostly refugees from Russia — with the major community in Kobe. Zionists among this group organized the ZO, which added further subsidiaries throughout the country intermittently during the 1920s and 1930s. Of the latter only two, in Tokyo and Yokohama, remained active by 1939. The authorities did not interfere with ZO activities during the war, although as enemy aliens most Jews living in Japan were deported to the Shanghai ghetto. The ZO ceased to function during the war due to wartime conditions in Japan and Japanese-occupied China. Postwar efforts to organize a new Zionist federation were initiated by American Jewish military and civilian personnel stationed in Japan but generally were of a transient nature.

Latvia[1]

Bar-Kokhba, unified Zionist youth movement founded in Riga in April 1920. Initially conceived as an educational and sporting organization, similar to boy and girl scout movements throughout Europe, Bar-Kokhba took on a more pioneering attitude after 1922 and operated as a *Hachshara* movement from then until World War II. In 1925 all nonsocialist Zionist youth movements withdrew from Bar-Kokhba, which moved pronouncedly to the left and soon became identified with the ideology of ha-Shomer ha-Zair. To reflect the new political orientation, Bar Kokhba changed its name to Noar Zioni Halutzi (נוער ציוני חלוצי, Pioneering Zionist Youth) but was better known as Nezah (from the Hebrew abbreviation, נצ״ח). In this guise, Nezah continued to operate until the Soviet occupation of 1940, when all public Zionist activities were severely curtailed.

Eretz Israel Ovedet (ארץ ישראל עובדת, EIO), "League for Labor Palestine," coalition of moderate socialist Zionist parties active in the Baltic republics (a similar coalition was established in the U.S.). Mainly, EIO composed two parties: Poale Zion Yemin and Zeirei Zion. In Latvia the two joined in 1930, following the amalgamation of their parallel parties in *Eretz Israel* to form Mapai. EIO rapidly became the most important Zionist party in Latvia, but its activities were severely curtailed when Karlis Ulmanis led a right-wing coup that installed an authoritarian government. EIO disappeared altogether after the Soviet occupation of 1940, when all Zionist activities were banned.

Zion (ציון), first Zionist organization founded in Daugavpils in late 1897, when Latvia was still part of the Russian empire. At the time, Zion functioned as part of the Russian Zionist federation. In 1905 czarist authorities clamped down on all Jewish political parties, leading Zion to temporarily suspend its activities. In 1918 Zion resumed its activities, now as the national federation for the newly independent Latvian republic. Zion's activities became more difficult after Karlis Ulmanis led a coup on May 15, 1934, that installed an authoritarian government in 1934 and ceased altogether after the Soviets seized Latvia in 1940.

Lithuania

Eretz Israel Ovedet (ארץ ישראל עובדת, EIO), "League for Labor Palestine," coalition of moderate socialist Zionist parties active in the Baltic republics (a similar coalition was active in the U.S.). EIO was parallel to Mapai, comprising diaspora parties that were similar in their orientation to the groups which founded that organization. Although most Lithuanian Zionists supported one of the general Zionist parties, the coalition greatly strengthened socialist Zionism in the Baltic republics. Active throughout Lithuania, EIO's center was in Riga (which became the capital when the Poles seized Vilna in 1922). EIO operated until the Soviet occupation, when all Zionist activity in Lithuania was officially terminated.

Ha-Brit (הברית), "The Covenant," general Zionist federation founded in Lithuania after the 1931 schism that broke the unity of the World Union of General Zionists. Ha-Brit members tended toward the more conservative B faction of the general Zionist movement,

---

[1] Organizations listed under Latvia, Lithuania, and Poland include Zionist organizations that were active primarily in those countries while they were still provinces of the Russian empire. Organizations active throughout the empire are listed under Russia/Soviet Union. Organizations listed under Poland include specific federations active in Galicia during the years of Austrian rule but not organizations that operated throughout the Austro-Hungarian empire. It should be recalled that Latvia and Lithuania were independent only between 1918 and 1940, when they were incorporated into the Soviet Union, and they did not regain their independence until 1991–1992. Finally, it should also be noted that there was apparently no Zionist organization of consequence in Estonia for which the foregoing otherwise would appertain.

being more likely to confront rather than support WZO president Chaim Weizmann. Ha-Brit rejected the idea of being the middle class Zionist party, propounding four policies for the WZO: (1) unification of all Zionist resources to build the *Yishuv*; (2) equal access to Zionist institutions and to the *Yishuv* for all members, regardless of their age, gender, or skills; (3) creation of a united Zionist educational system in the diaspora that would not reflect the values of any particular party or bloc; and (4) complete separation between religion and culture in the *Yishuv* and the WZO. While the first two points were clearly formulated in opposition to socialist Zionists, the latter two were formulated against Mizrachi. Ha-Brit operated in a number of guises until all Zionist activities came to a halt during the Soviet occupation in 1940. > see also: **World Zionist Organization, Subsidiary Bodies (Political Parties, World Union of General Zionists)**.

Hitahdut (התאחדות), "Unification," general Zionist federation founded in Lithuania after the 1931 schism that broke the unity of the World Union of General Zionists. Hitahdut members tended to be strong supporters of Chaim Weizmann's policies. Thus, for example, Hitahdut members supported the idea of a single labor organization (Histadrut) for the *Yishuv* and supported *Haluzic Aliya*. In contrast, Hitahdut members also supported the concept of private investment in *Eretz Israel* and rejected class struggle, calling for co-operation by all parts of the WZO. > see also: **World Zionist Organization, Subsidiary Bodies (Political Parties, World Union of General Zionists)**.

Landesverband Lite (לאנדעספארבאנד ליטע, LL), "Lithuanian National Federation," national Zionist federation established as an independent body in 1920 (i.e., after Lithuania became independent). Previously, Lithuanian Zionists had been members of the Russian Zionist federation. LL was overwhelmingly general Zionist in orientation, a factor that weakened the federation as Mapai came to dominate the WZO and JA after 1930. LL ceased to function after the Soviet occupation of Lithuania (1940) and was not resumed after World War II.

Ohavei Zion (אוהבי ציון), "Lovers of Zion," first Hibbat Zion federation, founded in Vilna (the part of the Russian empire) in 1882. Almost immediately, the organization ran afoul of the Russian authorities and their restrictions on Jewish communal life. In order to comply with regulations that virtually banned Jewish political organization, the name was changed to Tikvat Ani'im (Hope for the Poor) in 1883. Operations continued under this new name, which the Czarist police assumed was a charitable body, and the federation became one of the founding bodies of the Hibbat Zion movement. Ohavei Zion continued to operate even after Hibbat Zion ceased to function in 1891 and joined the WZO in 1897, functioning thereafter as part of the Russian Zionist federation. Sole president: Samuel Joseph Finn (1882-1897).

Mexico[1]

Zeirei Yehuda (צעירי יהודה), "Young Judea," Zionist youth organization founded in 1927 to foster Jewish identity and Zionist attitudes among Mexican Jewish youth. The unified movement apparently splintered along ideological lines during the 1930s.

---

[1] Mexico's United Zionist Federation was organized in 1949 and thus falls outside the chronological limits for inclusion in this book. The late emergence of a united federation reflected the polarity of specific Zionist parties that were unable to unite due to political inertia that magnified the ideological divisions within the Zionist movement and prevented Mexican Zionists from working together for common goals.

Netherlands

Nederlandsche Zionistenbond (NZB), "Dutch Zionist Union," national Zionist federation, established in 1899. As with many other Zionist federations, NZB initially experienced opposition from members of the communal elite and the rabbinate. As a result, growth was slow but steady. By 1914, NZB had branches in all of Holland's cities and in many towns as well. World War I spurred further development. The headquarters of the Keren Kayemet le-Israel moved to The Hague from Berlin in 1915, remaining there until 1920. After the war, NZB was among the first Zionist groups to call for the creation of a World Jewish Congress. Although composed of widely disparate parties (as were most Zionist federations) NZB experienced an unprecedented degree of ideological unanimity. This reflected itself, for example, in NZB's en bloc opposition to the Peel partition plan in 1937 and in NZB's unanimous decision to remain in the WZO at the same time. Between 1933 and 1940, NZB was active in aiding German Jewish refugees and especially in hosting *Hachsharot* to provide agricultural training to potential Olim. NZB ceased to function during the Nazi occupation (1940–1945) and a considerable proportion of its membership perished during the Holocaust. Albeit, NZB was revived in 1945 and actively lobbied the Dutch government to support partition and the creation of a Jewish state in 1947 and 1948. NZB members were also active in assisting Aliya Bet, and many volunteered to serve in the Israeli armed forces during the War of Independence, both in Mitnadve Hutz la-Aretz (Mahal) and in Giyus Hutz la-Aretz (Gahal). Publications: *De Joodse Wachter* (1905–1940, 1945–1967), *De Zionistische Stem* (1918–1920).

Nederlandsche Zionistische Studentorgnisatie (NZSO), "Dutch Student Zionist Organization," fraternal organization of Zionist high school and college students, founded in Amsterdam in 1906 and affiliated with the Nederlandsche Zionistenbond. NZSO was active in both the educational, cultural, and *aliya* aspects of Zionist activities. Indeed, enough NZSO alumni settled in *Eretz Israel* to establish their own fraternity, known as Netaim (נטעים, "Planters"). NZSO membership was slightly over 250 in 1938 in five main branches: Amsterdam, Groningen, Rotterdam, Leiden, and Utrecht. Publication: *Zionistisch Studentenjaarboek* (1910–1924, 1931–1941).

New Zealand

Zionist Council of New Zealand (ZCNZ), national federation for Zionist affairs, organized in 1943. Prior to that date all Zionist activity in New Zealand had been local, with the various parties and movements affiliated individually with the Australian Zionist federation. Zionism was never a controversial issue within the New Zealand Jewish community, but ZCNZ also never gained more than a few hundred members, mainly in Auckland and Wellington (the latter society having been founded in 1903). Nonetheless, ZCNZ successfully obtained government support for partition in 1947 and raised considerable sums of money for Keren Kayemet le-Israel and Keren ha-Yesod. Publication: *New Zealand Jewish Chronicle* (1943f).

Norway

Norsk Zionistenforening (NZF), "Norwegian Zionist Federation," landesverband for Zionist affairs founded initially in 1912. NZF was not fully organized until 1917, when its executive came into being in Oslo. A second NZF branch was organized in Trondheim, also in 1917. Growth was extremely slow; by 1927 NZF was virtually defunct. Reorganized in 1931, NZF had only one branch for most of the 1930s, located in Oslo. Still, this branch managed to accumulate some three-hundred members by 1937. In order to increase Zionist activity throughout Scandinavia, NZF joined with the Zionist federations of Denmark, Finland, and Sweden in 1935 to create a unified Zionist coalition for all of Scandinavia. This coalition lasted until 1940, when the Nazi occupation of Denmark and Norway forced its collapse. NZF was reorganized for a second time in 1945, but membership remained low. Zionism has never been a major issue for Norwegian Jewry, but support for Jewish statehood has always been intense. Presidents: Moritz Dsenselsky (1917–1921), Elais Feinberg (1921–1923, 1925–1927), Arthur Pagel (1924–1925), Louis Benjamin (1927–1931), Isser Braude (1945– 1947), Leopold Bermann (1947–1949). Publication: *Jødisk Tidende* (1918).

Poland

Ahiasaph, Zionist publishing house founded in Warsaw in 1893 and named after a biblical character. Dedicated to spreading Hebrew language and modern Jewish education, Ahiasaph was ideologically close to Ahad ha-Am's Spiritual Zionism. In 1896 Ahad ha-Am was named director, a position he retained until 1902. In addition to numerous books, Ahiasaph published two notable periodicals: *ha-Shiloah*, a monthly appearing between 1896 and 1914, and *ha-Dor*, a weekly appearing between 1901 and 1923. Ahiasaph ceased operations due to financial difficulties in 1923, but a number of its serials continued to appear thereafter.

Al ha-Mishmar (על המשמר), "On Guard," faction of the Polish general Zionist movement founded by Yitzhak Grünbaum in 1923. Grünbaum founded the faction during the first debate over the possibility of enlarging the Jewish Agency to include non-Zionist representatives as a means of increasing financial support for the *Yishuv*. Opposing that idea, Grünbaum called for his faction to guard the essence of Zionism and thus chose the name. Once JA expansion became a fait accompli in 1929, Grünbaum turned to other issues, but he did not disband his faction. In Congress Poland (i.e., the part of the country formerly under Russian rule) the faction became autonomous after the collapse of the World Union of General Zionists in 1931. Grünbaum's *aliya* in 1933 (when he was appointed to the JAE) deprived Al ha-Mishmar of its best-known leader but did not end its activities. During the 1930s the faction tended toward the left on many Zionist issues and supporter the Mapai-led coalition. Grünbaum emphasized *aliya* above

all other Zionist considerations and was willing to concede on issues such as a legislative council for Palestine/*Eretz Israel* that would be dominated by the Arabs if unfettered *aliya* would be the quid pro quo. Albeit, Al ha-Mishmar's survival owed more to the ideologically charged Polish Zionist atmosphere than to its popularity: its membership was always minuscule. Al ha-Mishmar ceased to function when World War II began. > see also: **Sochnut Yehudit; Legislative Council**.

Bnai Zion (בני ציון, BZ), "Sons of Zion," first Zionist society, founded in Warsaw in July 1897. Most members of BZ had previously been involved with the Hibbat Zion movement. A second BZ branch was established in Lodz in August; within a year, further branches had been added in Kalisz and Piotrkow Tribunalski. Still, BZ's activities were limited to Congress Poland (i.e., the part of the country ruled by Russia) and the organization agreed to affiliate with the Russian Zionist federation. At its height, BZ had between 4,000 and 5,000 members. BZ split because of the Uganda controversy. A small majority of the members rejected the proposal, joining the so-called *Zionei Zion*, while supporters of settlement in East Africa withdrew from the movement. BZ came to a complete halt after the counterrevolution reinstalled the czarist autocracy in 1905–1906. At that point, all public Zionist activities were halted at government order. BZ was not revived in independent Poland, but its impact on the Polish Zionist movement could be measured by the fact that all major leaders of Zionism in Poland were, at one time or another, members of BZ.

Dror (דרור), "Freedom," socialist Zionist society founded in Poland in 1922. Dror had originally been established in Russia as a framework for Zionist activity on behalf of those who supported Zionism but did not find a comfortable position in any of the existing Zionist groups. In Poland, Dror developed into a movement emphasizing *aliya* and Zionist commitment. This meant that the movement sought to be an avant garde and did not seek mass membership. Instead, the leaders hoped that the depth of Dror's activities would ultimately percolate throughout Polish Jewry, leading to the community's complete transformation. Given that this process would take years (if not generations) Dror's leaders concentrated on working with Zionist youth, hoping to create an ideologically committed elite within the Polish he-Halutz. Dror assiduously avoided becoming a political party per se, retaining its independence throughout the years of its operation. Despite its elitist orientation, Dror cooperated with other moderate socialist Zionist organizations (mainly with the Hitahdut). Dror continued to operate until World War II forced an end to its directly Zionist activities. During the Holocaust, Dror members were in the forefront of Jewish resistance movements throughout Poland. A number of Dror cells were reestablished in 1945, mainly to give surviving members a framework for renewed activities, including *Briha* and *Aliya Bet*.

Et Livnot (עת לבנות), "A Time to Build," faction of the general Zionist movement in Poland founded during the early 1920s. Et Livnot was created as an alternate to Yitzhak Grünbaum's Al ha-Mishmar faction. The Et Livnot faction (which represented the majority of Polish general Zionists) supported enlargement of the JA, reasoning that development in the *Yishuv* had been so slow, mainly because of a lack of financial resources, that the infusion of capital from non-Zionists was vital to the future of the Zionist endeavor. During the 1930s the relative positions of Al ha-Mishmar and Et Livnot changed. The former moved to the left in coalition with Mapai while the latter moved to the right, reflecting a clearly middle-class orientation. Et Livnot strongly opposed the limiting *aliya* to *Halutzim*. However, Et Livnot's opposition was not so strident as to lead the faction to withdraw from the WZO. Et Livnot continued to operate until destroyed by the Nazis during the Holocaust. Sole president: Leon Levite.
> see also: **Sochnut Yehudit; Halutzic Aliya**.

Gordonia (גורדוניה), Pioneering youth movement founded in Galicia in 1923. The movement's official name, Histadrut ha-Noar ha-Amamit ha-Halutzit — Gordonia

(The People's Pioneering Youth Association — Gordonia) was rarely used since the movement was named after (and widely associated with) socialist Zionist pioneer Aharon D. Gordon. From Galicia, Gordonia spread throughout Poland and into Romania, Western Europe, and the United States. Membership was estimated at 40,000 worldwide in 1939. Gordonia was clearly socialist in orientation but not necessarily Marxist in ideology. Indeed, Gordonia's founders were drawn from members of ha-Shomer ha-Zair who disagreed with the latter organization's overt Marxism. Institutionally, Gordonia was supported by the Hitahdut, a moderately socialist Zionist diaspora party that paralleled Mapai in *Eretz Israel*. In 1932, Gordonia merged with Makkabi ha-Zair, thus opening branches in Czechoslovakia and Germany. The new movement retained the Gordonia name throughout its remaining years. Despite these developments, Gordonia's hub remained in Poland. A Gordonia branch was founded in *Eretz Israel* in 1937 by *olim* who graduated from the movement in Poland and their children. European branches of Gordonia were hard hit by the Holocaust, although a few surviving cells briefly reemerged in Poland and Romania in 1945. These stood in the forefront of *Briha* and *Aliya Bet* activities but were dismantled shortly after the State of Israel came into being in 1948.

Ha-koordinatzia ha-Zionit le-Geulat Yeladim ve-Noar be-Polin (הקואורדינאציה הציונית לגאולת ילדים ונוער בפולין, KZG), "The Zionist Coordinating (Committee) to Liberate Children and Youth in Poland," survivors' organization active in Poland between 1946 and 1949. KZG was dedicated to finding, rehabilitating, and educating Jewish youth who had managed to survive the Holocaust in hiding. Among the committee's most important and searing work was retrieving Jewish children who had been raised by non-Jews and who had only dim recollection (if even that) of being Jewish. Organized as a coalition of Zionist groups, the moving factors behind the committee were the Ihud Olami and he-Halutz. Operations ceased in 1949 when the Communist authorities accused the committee's chairman of espionage.

Hitahdut (התאחדות), "Unity," coalition of moderate socialist Zionist parties founded in Poland in 1920. In practice, Hitahdut was a coalition of two major parties: ha-Poel ha-Zair and Zeirei Zion. Similar coalitions emerged in other countries, the most notable being the merger of Poale Zion and Ahdut ha-Avoda in *Eretz Israel* in 1930 to form Mapai. Ideologically and institutionally, Hitahdut played the same role in Poland that Mapai did in the *Yishuv*: arguing for Zionist unity, cooperation with nonsocialist Zionist parties, and rejection of narrow Marxism and class struggle in order to concentrate efforts on building the Jewish national home. In 1932 the relationship between Hitahdut and Mapai was formalized in the guise of the Ihud Olami (World Union), which linked all similar Zionist parties around the world. Hitahdut also sponsored the activities of the Gordonia youth movement. Most of Hitahdut's branches collapsed during the Holocaust. However, surviving members reemerged after the war, operating in Displaced Persons camps in Germany, Austria, and Italy under the Ihud Olami banner. > see also: **World Zionist Organization, Parties (Ihud Olami); Yishuv, Organizations (Political Parties, Mifleget Poale Eretz Israel)**.

Jidisze Socjalistisze Demokratisze Arbeter Partaj Poale Zion in Pojlen, "Jewish Social Democratic Workers's Party Poale Zion in Poland," full (but rarely used) name for the Poale Zion Smol (PZS, Left Poale Zion) branch that operated in interwar Poland. Poale Zion had been founded in 1906, but the unified party began to split over attitudes toward the Bolshevik seizure of power in 1918. This schism became permanent in 1921, when two factions emerged: Poale Zion Yemin (Right Poale Zion), which remained true to the movement's Zionist orientation, and PZS, which saw itself as using Zionism to foster socialism within the Jewish nation. Both parties claimed to have inherited the mantle of responsibility for socialist Zionist ideology from Ber Borochov, although each wing based itself on an interpretation of one era in Borochov's evolution as a socialist Zionist. In 1922, PZS withdrew from the WZO and sought membership in the Comintern (the so-called Third International). This effort collapsed in 1924 when the Communists unequivocally rejected any form of Zionism or Jewish national identity. Despite this setback, PZS spread throughout the entire Jewish world, remaining strongest in Poland. Nonetheless, PZS never developed into a major factor in Jewish politics and its influence waned with each passing year. In 1939, after more than a decade of isolation within the Jewish community, PZS returned to the WZO and continued to operate in Poland until the war broke out. The party's youth movements were active in Jewish resistance during the Holocaust, but most surviving members joined the Polish Communist party after the war.

Kolo Żydowskie (Kolo), "Jewish Caucus," Jewish parliamentary caucus founded in the Sejm and Senat (respectively the upper and lower houses of the Polish parliament) in 1922. The Kolo was dominated by the Zionists, the only other party having elected representatives being Agudas Israel. Among its other tasks, the Kolo attempted to better the position of Polish Jewry by ensuring government adherence to the national minority treaties that Poland had signed. In 1925 the Kolo sought to negotiate an agreement with the government of Premier Witold Grabski (the so-called Ugoda) that would obtain Kolo support for the government in return for a lessening of economic and other pressure on Polish Jewry. This agreement was canceled when the Grabski government was overthrown by the coup inspired by Josef Pilsudski. Although the Kolo continued to operate thereafter, its credibility had been considerably damaged.

Organizacje Sjonistyczne w Polsce (OSP), "Zionist Organization of Poland," national Zionist federation founded in Warsaw in 1922. General Zionist in orientation, OSP had a very difficult gestation period and never completely overcame the complex causes for its own weakness, mainly, the need to create a single Jewish political movement in a country that had been divided for more than a century among its larger neighbors (Russia, Austria, and Germany). Indeed, OSP's role as a landes-verband was itself something of a legal fiction, since it was a coalition of the three regional federations that had existed in Polish territory prior to independence: the Zionist Organization of East Central Poland (the area ruled by Russia generally known as Congress Poland), the Zionist Organization of Galicia (comprising the territories in southern Poland that had previously been ruled by Austria and Russia), and the Zionist Federation of Little Poland (the areas previously ruled by Germany). Further confusion derived from the fact that the Galician subfederation was divided into eastern and western subfederations for most of the 1920s. OSP did not untangle its institutional makeup until the 1930s. Even then, however, the Zionists remained highly divided on ideological grounds (e.g., on the relative merit of fighting for Jewish minority rights in Poland versus mass evacuation) with parties and factions splitting and re-combining often. The increasingly severe restrictions placed on *aliya* by the British (especially in 1930–1931 and 1937–1939) also weakened OSP in relation to other Jewish parties in Poland. This resulted in mixed outcomes during *Kehila* elections and meant that Zionists never fully conquered Polish Jewry. Nonetheless, a majority of Jewish parliamentarians in Poland were OSP members. Despite its weaknesses, OSP continued to operate until 1939. The Holocaust severely disrupted OSP operations and the federation was not reestablished after World War II.

Tarbut (תרבות), "Culture," Zionist school system established in Eastern Europe before World War I that flourished in interwar Poland. By 1939, the Tarbut school system included 75 kindergartens, 149 primary schools, 12 high schools, and 6 teachers seminaries. Approximately 1,000 teachers were employed in Tarbut schools and the system educated approximately 25,000 students per year. All instruction in Tarbut schools was done in modern Hebrew and

the curriculum was based on a synthesis of secular and Jewish studies. The latter raised some controversy because Jewish subjects were generally taught from a secular perspective.

Żydowska Rada Narodowa (ŻRN), "Jewish National Council," Jewish communal body established in 1918 to oversee the transition from foreign rule for Polish Jewry. ŻRN's main task was to obtain national minority rights for Jews in the new Polish republic. In this task, ŻRN cooperated closely with the American Jewish Congress and the Comité des Délégations Juives. Although not officially a Zionist organization, the council was dominated by the Zionists, who were the largest and most active party in Poland. With Polish acceptance (albeit reluctant) of the minorities treaty, ŻRN lost its raison d'etre. Its communal functions were transferred to other bodies while its role in defending Jewish rights before the government was taken over by the Kolo Żydowskie.

Romania

Asociatia Tineretului Sionişti (AST), "Association of Zionist Youth," federation of Zionist youth movements founded in 1919. Initially nonpartisan in orientation, AST included all Zionist youth movements in Romania except he-Halutz (which was founded by Ukrainian Jewish refugees in 1920). During the 1920s a series of ideological rifts led to repeated schisms within AST and by 1927 the movement was virtually identical with the ha-Shomer ha-Zair branch in Romania. Despite the repeated schisms, however, AST continued to grow, with branches throughout the country. In 1939 AST remained the single largest youth movement in Romania, with its main strength concentrated in Bessarabia and Bukovina. In 1940 AST was forced to cease operations by government decree and was never revived. Still, AST alumni were in the forefront of Jewish self-defense efforts in Romania during World War II and in *Aliya Bet* from Romania after the war.

Hashmonaea – Societatea Studentilor Universitari Sionişti (HSSUS), "Hasmonea – University Student Zionist Society," Zionist student fraternity founded in Bucharest on

March 26, 1914. Organized to encourage Jewish identity and Zionism among Jewish university students, HSSUS also sought to combat antisemitism. HSSUS cooperated closely with the Romanian Zionist federation, especially during the 1930s. Activities were disrupted during the fascist era but resumed briefly between 1944 and 1948. Under intense Communist pressure, HSSUS ceased to function in late 1948. Publication: *Revista Hashmonaea* (1915–1940).

Organizaţia Sionistă din România (OSR), "Zionist Organization of Romania," national federation for Zionist affairs founded in Galaţi in April 1897. Previously, OSR had been the local Hovevei Zion federation. OSR joined the WZO en masse and with little debate. OSR's main strength derived from poor and middle-class Jews, with little support coming from the wealthy segments of Romanian Jewry. OSR grew rapidly in the prewar years, from twenty-six chapters in 1897 to nearly one hundred in 1914. World War I disrupted OSR's activities, but the federation was revived at war's end. In 1919, OSR transferred its headquarters to Bucharest, remaining there until closed by the Communist authorities in 1949. During the 1920s and 1930s, OSR tried to remain aloof from Romanian politics, concentrating on educational and fund-raising activities. *Aliya* was not a major factor in OSR's activities during this period, despite the increase in Romania's Jewish population as a result of treaties that awarded Bessarabia, Bukovina, and Transylvania to Romania. OSR's activities became more difficult after the brief reign of the Garda de Fer (the Romanian Fascist party) in 1938 and culminated in an outright ban on OSR activities imposed by Ion Antonescu in 1940. OSR was permitted to resume its activities in 1941, but conditions remained tense. Romania's close alliance with Germany, the intense nature of Roamian antisemitism, and the government's participation in the Endlösung all destabilized Jewish life in Romania and impacted negatively on Zionist activities. During this period, OSR operated in a near-constant state of crisis that was relieved only when Antonescu's government fell in 1944. For the next five years, Zionists concentrated on *aliya*, especially on *Aliya Bet*, activities that were tacitly supported by the Romanian Communists. Cooperation ended in 1949 when all Zionist activities in Romania were suppressed by the government. > see also: **Bet Yaakov Lehu ve-Nelha**; **Hibbat Zion**; **Paratroopers, Palestinian**; **World War II**.

Russia/Soviet Union

Bnai Moshe (בני משה, BM), "Sons of Moses," semisecret order created within the Hibbat Zion movement in 1889. Guided by Ahad ha-Am, BM saw itself as an elite within the Hibbat Zion movement, aiming to create a cadre of individuals who worked toward the fulfillment of Zionist goals on a full-time basis. BM never numbered more than one hundred members, the majority of whom lived in Odessa (where the main office was located). Other offices existed in Warsaw and in Jaffa. In addition to cultural and educational work, these two offices were involved in direct settlement activity. The Warsaw office oversaw creation of the settlement in Rehovot while the Jaffa office oversaw the establishment of the first Zionist elementary school in *Eretz Israel*. Prior to 1893 BM had been a secret society, with all the trappings of a Masonic lodge. These affectations were dropped in 1893. BM ceased to exist altogether in 1897, when the entire membership joined the WZO.

He-Haver (החבר), "The Friend," Russian Zionist student fraternity, established in Bern, Switzerland, in March 1912. At the time, public manifestations of Zionism were severely restricted within the Russian empire. As a result, all he-Haver activity in Russia proper had to be undertaken clandestinely. Despite the illegal nature of the organization, it grew to some seven hundred members on the eve of World War I. He-Haver maintained a general Zionist orientation for most of its existence, although in 1917 it briefly merged with Zeirei Zion (which later became a founding member of he-Halutz). After the first Russian Revolution in 1917, he-Haver was briefly permitted to operate legally. When the Bolsheviks seized power, they prevented almost all Zionist activities in Russia. He-Haver resumed its clandestine operations after 1920, culminating in the merger of all Zionist fraternities in 1924. However, Josef Stalin's rise to power and his completion of the police state begun by Vladimir Ilyich Lenin decimated the Russian Zionist movement which was almost completely destroyed after the purges of the 1930s. Publication: *Yevreiski Student*. > see also: **Communism and Zionism; Yevsektias**.

Hovevei Sfat Ever (חובבי שפת עבר) "Lovers of the Hebrew Language," Zionist cultural organization established in the Russian empire in 1907. Mainly focusing on Russian Jewry's need for education, the organization sought Jewish national rebirth through cultural means. The organization founded schools and teachers seminaries throughout the Pale of Settlement in which all instruction was in the Hebrew language. In 1917, Hovevei Sfat Ever changed its name to Tarbut. Tarbut was banned in the Soviet Union as a result of the anti-Zionist orientation of the new government but continued to operate in Poland up to World War II. > see also: **Organizations, Zionist (Poland, Tarbut)**.

Lishkat ha-Doar (לשכת הדואר), "The Post Office," cover name for the Zionist propaganda bureau established as part of the national federation at the Warsaw conference in 1897. The need for a cover name derived from the generally negative attitude of the czarist administration to Jewish political organizations. Initially designed as a means to ensure communications between the widely scattered local Zionist branches, the office became more of a clearinghouse for information between the Second and Third World Zionist Congresses (in 1898–1899). This move was controversial but was attuned to the needs of Russian Zionism. Many Jews seeking relief from their plight would have been happy to join the Zionist movement if only they could obtain information on that movement. The office ceased operation after the counterrevolution in 1905, when all overt Zionist activity was banned in the Russian empire.

Zionistische Organizatsye in Rusland (ציוניסטישע ארגאניזאציע אין רוסלאנד, ZOR), "Zionist Organization in Russia," the first major Zionist national federation, founded in response to Theodor Herzl's clarion call in 1897. ZOR was organized on the basis of previously existing societies, mostly remnants of the Hibbat Zion movement (which became defunct in 1891). Expansion was rapid but difficult. ZOR was strongly opposed by many elements in Russian Jewry, including much of the Orthodox community, the established Jewish communal leadership (traditional or assimilationist in orientation), and nascent Jewish socialist movements (including the socialist-nationalist Bund, which was also founded in 1897). Moreover, the poverty in which most Russian Jews lived meant that only a fraction of supporters could actually join the movement. Despite these impediments, ZOR grew rapidly and the delegation was the largest of all federations attending all Zionist congresses after the First World Zionist Congress. Membership peaked at 300,000 in 1,200 local groups in 1917. Between 1902 and 1907, the Czarist government actively interfered in Zionist activities, making ZOR's activities come to a virtual standstill. ZOR was able to weather that storm but had its activities completely halted by the Communist authorities who seized power in October/November 1917. Although some Zionist societies continued to operate underground, by the 1930s almost all had been uprooted.

South Africa

Binyan (בנין), "Building," Zionist mortgage bank founded in 1922 as a means for South African Jews to invest in the *Yishuv*. Binyan provided low interest loans for South African Jews who emigrated, thereby allowing them to buy their own plots of land or providing them with the financial wherewithal to build on Keren Kayemet le-Israel lands. Additionally, Binyan collected funds from Jews who were not them-selves interested in *aliya* but still wanted to contribute to the *Yishuv*'s growth. Binyan continued to operate after 1948 and provided a considerable boost of capital into the new State of Israel in its earliest years.

Dorshei Zion Association (DZA), Zionist friendly society founded in Cape Town on September 3, 1899, and in effect the first Zionist organization in South Africa. Although founded in the British-controlled Cape Colony, DZA branches spread rapidly throughout South Africa, a process that speeded up considerably after the Boer War (1899–1902). In fact, the war seems to have increased South African Jews' sense of national identity. DZA peaked at 620 members in 1902 and was a founding member of both the South African Zionist Federation (SAZF) and the South African Jewish Board of Deputies.

Ha-Bonim, local federation of the International Zionist youth movement, founded in 1931. > see also: **Organizations, Zionist (United Kingdom, Ha-Bonim)**.

South African Zionist Federation (SAZF), political body established in 1905. Organized geographically, the SAZF was always an outspoken supporter of Zionist and Jewish unity and Jewish statehood. The Holocaust considerably strengthened the SAZF, which peaked in membership at 15,000. Major activities included propaganda, fund-raising (via the United Appeal) youth and education, and sports. Unlike other communities, virtually every element in South African Jewry supported the SAZF regardless of other political orientations. Similarly, SAZF remained united when other Zionist federations splintered during the hectic 1930s: in particular, the revisionist movement did not withdraw from the federation. Zionist unity along with the deep sympathy for Zionism within South African governing circles translated into considerable success for SAZF's lobbying efforts on behalf of the *Yishuv* between 1945 and 1948. Publications: *Zionist Record* (1908–1959), *Zionist Record and South African Jewish Chronicle* (1959–1978).

Scandinavia

Skandinavische Landesgruppe (SLG), "Scandinavian National Group," federation of Zionist organizations active in northern Europe, initially established in 1903. SLG initially came together to link local Zionist chapters in Malmö and Lund, Sweden, with the slightly larger chapter in Copenhagen, Denmark, in order to obtain greater representation for the upcoming Sixth World Zionist Congress. Since it was never meant to be a permanent coalition, SLG disintegrated shortly after the congress. The idea of a federation remained, however, mainly because of the weak nature of the Zionist national federations and the small Jewish populations in Scandinavian countries. In 1935, SLG was reactivated as a coalition of the national federations of Denmark, Finland, Norway, and Sweden. By pooling their resources and membership, SLG hoped to be able to increase Zionist activities in all four countries. This second coalition was somewhat successful, especially during the latter part of the decade. It collapsed as a result of the Nazi occupation of Denmark and Norway in 1940 and was not renewed after World War II.

Sweden

Hebreiska Klubben (HK), "Hebrew Club," Zionist cultural and educational institution for youth and young adults, founded in Stockholm in 1925. Aiming to promote Hebrew language education, HK also hoped to thereby instill a Zionist orientation among Swedish Jewish youth. HK built a considerable following in certain circles, notably Jews who remained traditional in their religious orientation, and has continued to function since its founding.

Judiska Vandrareföreningen Blau-Weiss (JVFBW), "Jewish Hiking Society Blue White," branch of the German Zionist youth movement Blau-Weiss, founded in Stockholm in May 1915. Appealing to many Swedish Jewish youth, JVFBW grew rapidly (more rapidly, in fact, than the Swedish Zionist federation). By 1920, JVFBW ceased to be a hiking society, concentrating instead on educational and cultural aspects of Zionist youth work. However, as JVFBW increasingly attracted membership of non-Zionist youth, the Zionist message became more diffused. In 1925, JVFBW changed its name to Judisk Ungdom (Jewish Youth Club) and lost its Zionist character.

Malmö Zionistförenings (MZF), "Malmö Zionist Society," first Zionist organization established in Sweden and active between 1900 and 1903. MZF acted more as a friendly society than as a political body but never had a large membership. With MZF on the verge of disintegration, its members merged with the small Zionist society in Lund, Sweden, and the Zionist federation in Copenhagen, Denmark, to form a temporary Scandinavian Zionist federation in 1903. When this collapsed, so did MZF. Efforts to renew MZF after 1904 apparently came to naught. > see also: **Organizations, Zionist (Scandinavia).**

Stockholms Zionistförenings (SZF), "Stockholm Zionist Society," local Zionist association founded in the Swedish capital by Jewish immigrants from Russia in 1910. Growth was very slow, by 1914 SZF had only one hundred members, and the organization acted as the de facto Zionist federation for all of Sweden. World War I strengthened SZF, mainly because of the country's proximity to the center of WZO activities after the Copenhagen Bureau was opened in 1915. General Zionist in orientation, SZF did not include the Swedish Poale Zion union that was founded in 1917 and functioned until 1919. On December 25, 1933, SZF was reorganized as the Svensk Zionistförenings (Swedish Zionist Society, retaining the abbreviation SZF) and henceforth acted as the official national federation for Zionist affairs in Sweden. In 1935, SZF joined with the national federations of Denmark, Finland, and Norway to form a Scandinavian Zionist union, hoping thereby to strengthen all the small federations by pooling their resources. The Scandinavian union lasted until World War II and was broken up by the Nazi occupation of Denmark and Norway. SZF was very active in promoting refugee settlement in Sweden and *Eretz Israel* during the Nazi era and was particularly active in resettling Danish Jews in Sweden after their rescue in October 1943. In 1945, SZF aided in the rehabilitation of eight hundred Jewish youth rescued from Nazi concentration camps by Swedish diplomats. Never a large movement, SZF enjoyed considerable support from Swedish political leaders. Publications: *Zionisten* (1913), *Jidische Folkschtime* (1917).

Switzerland

Comité des Délégations Juives (CDJ), "Committee of Jewish Delegations," Jewish public body founded in 1919 to represent Jewish interests at the League of Nations. During the 1930s the CDJ was active in defending German Jewish interests, for example, by sponsoring the Bernheim Petition, defending the rights of Eastern European Jewry, protecting the League's minority rights treaties, and seeking safe havens for Jewish refugees. In 1936 the CDJ became a founding member of the World Jewish Congress. At that point the CDJ ceased to function, becoming the Swiss section of the WJC. > see also: **Organizations, Zionist (International, World Jewish Congress).**

Schweitzerischer Zionistenverband (SZV), "Swiss Zionist Union," national Zionist federation founded in Diel in 1900. SZV held its first conference on October 12, 1901, and began its actual operations thereafter. Up to 1919, SZV was general Zionist in orientation, although a Mizrachi federation cooperated with the union. SZV moved its headquarters to Zürich some time prior to World War I and has remained there ever since. The war increased Zionist activity in Switzerland but caused many rifts between pro-German and pro-British elements in SZV. After the war, these rifts crystalized into a number of different camps active within SZV for the entire interwar era. Unlike many other Zionist federations, SZV did not split during the ideologically charged 1930s. In 1919, SZV was a founding member of the Comité des Délégations Juives and was a ardent supporter of the movement to create a World Jewish Congress. During the Nazi era, SZV was active in trying to convince Swiss authorities to open their borders to Jewish refugees. Unsuccessful for most of the 1930s, limited successes were attained in a number of cantons during the war. Since Switzerland eschewed membership in any international political body (such as the U.N.), lobbying played a relatively less important role in SZV's activities than it did in other federations. Conversely, fund-raising and *aliya* (especially arranging *aliya* for Jewish refugees) played considerably greater roles than in other Western European federations. Membership peaked at 3,500 in 1948 and has remained relatively steady since then.

Syria/Lebanon

Club National Israélite (CNI), "Jewish National Club," Zionist cultural organization founded in Damascus in 1924 and acting as the de facto Zionist federation for French-controlled Syria and Lebanon. Due to the intensity of Arab nationalism in the Levant, CNI felt it prudent to mask its political activities under the guise of a cultural club. Despite this precaution, CNI came under considerable pressure from local Arab leaders and moved its headquarters to Beirut in the late 1920s. CNI continued to operate from Lebanon until 1948, although activities were increasingly difficult for most of the 1930s. From 1939 onward, almost all Zionist activity in Syria and Lebanon was undertaken in close coordination with the *Yishuv* and concentrated mainly on *aliya* — both public and clandestine (*Aliya Bet*).

He-Halutz (החלוץ), "The Pioneer," branch of the international Zionist youth movement, secretly founded in Damascus in 1943 at Rachel Yanait Ben-Zvi's initiative. The Syrian he-Halutz branch also included Lebanon in its activities, mainly, in its *aliya* program that secretly evacuated Syrian and Lebanese Jews from areas of intense Arab nationalist agitation to the *Yishuv*. It is estimated that 1,350 Jewish youth entered the *Yishuv* from Syria and Lebanon in this way from 1943 to 1945. > see also: **Aliya Bet**.

Turkey

Anglo-Levantine Banking Company (ALBC), arm of the WZO founded in Istanbul (then still known as Constantinople) in 1908 and often called simply the Istanbul office. ALBC was a wholly-owned subsidiary of the Jewish Colonial Trust and, as such, operated as both a financial and a political institution. ALBC's main role was to engage in negotiations with the Ottoman Porte over offers for a substantial Jewish loan (to offset the Porte's immense expenses) in return for a charter permitting autonomous Jewish settlement in *Eretz Israel*. Secondarily, ALBC acted as a Zionizing agency within Ottoman Jewry. ALBC was not successful at either task but did succeed in maintaining a Zionist presence in the Ottoman capital at a critical juncture in the history of Zionism. After World War I, ALBC's functions were taken over by the Anglo-Palestine Bank. > see also: **World Zionist Organization, Subsidiary Agencies (Jewish Colonial Trust); Yishuv, Organizations (Miscellaneous, Anglo-Palestine Bank).**

Fédération Sioniste d'Orient (FSO), "Zionist Federation of Asia," Zionist national federation founded in Istanbul in 1919. FSO was organized as a coalition of Zionist friendly societies and other local organizations that had been founded in the waning years of the Ottoman empire (mainly after 1908). Since most of these organizations were cultural and educational in their nature, FSO concentrated on those types of Zionist activities. Conversely, since Turkey no longer ruled *Eretz Israel*, FSO eschewed political activity almost entirely. FSO membership peaked in 1920 at 4,000. Many more Turkish Jews supported the Zionist cause but did not join FSO, as was demonstrated by the mass *aliya* of Turkish Jews when the State of Israel was founded.

United Kingdom

Board of Deputies of British Jews, Jewish representative body founded in 1760. As the official representative body of Anglo-Jewry, the board also sought to safeguard Jewish interests in England and abroad. Among its multiple activities, the board also oversaw the chief rabbinate of England. Between 1897 and 1917, the board followed a strictly non-Zionist orientation, although individual members joined the WZO. Strongly supporting the Balfour Declaration, the board became increasingly active in Zionist affairs thereafter. In 1936 the board became a founding agency of the World Jewish Congress and thereafter cooperated with the Jewish Agency for Palestine. Chairmen: Joseph Sebag-Montefiore (1895–1903),

David L. Alexander (1903–1917), Stuart Samuel (1917–1922), Henry S. Q. Henriques (1922–1925), Lionel Rothschild (1925–1926), Osmond E. d'Avigdor-Goldsmid (1926–1933), Neville Laski (1933–1939), Selig Brodetsky (1939–1948).

Central British Fund for German Jewry (CBF), philanthropic agency established in May 1933. Dedicated to financing the resettlement of German Jewish refugees, primarily (though not exclusively) in the *Yishuv*. All Anglo-Jewish organizations were affiliated with the fund, which succeeded in raising considerable sums. Sole chairman: Lionel de Rothschild.

English Zionist Federation (EZF), founded in 1897 as a component of the WZO. Although there already was a Zionist national body in England (the Order of Ancient Maccabeans, OAM), EZF superseded OAM's role as the landesverbande for England but did not completely replace OAM until the 1960s. Due to conditions within the Anglo-Jewish community, EZF eschewed any effort to "conquer the community" from the beginning. Instead, EZF leaders pursued a policy they designated as infiltration, that is, becoming involved in numerous communal activities with the hope of eventually leading them toward Zionism. This policy was not completely successful, but it did create the opportunity for cooperation with bodies such as the Board of Deputies of British Jews that otherwise might not have been receptive to Zionism. General Zionist in orientation, EZF tended toward the moderate wing of the Zionist movement. Strongly supporting Chaim Weizmann's gradualist policies, the EZF was hard-pressed by the Nazi persecution of European Jewry. During the 1920s, EZF leaders emphasized the commonality of interests between the British empire and the WZO (so-called patriotic Zionism). However, as the refugee crisis grew and the British government began to restrict *aliya* increasingly, EZF had no effective means to protest its own government's actions. In 1933, the EZF became one of the sponsors of the Central British Fund but continued to emphasize the need to create an open-door policy for *aliya*. EZF became radicalized during the Holocaust but was never really able to overcome the limitations imposed upon its activities within Anglo-Jewry and the British political environment.

Federation of Women Zionists of Great Britain and Ireland, social welfare organization founded in 1919 to coordinate philanthropic activities on behalf of the *Yishuv*. The federation also sought to give women a voice within the English Zionist Federation. In 1920 the federation was in the forefront of the movement to found the Women's International Zionist Organization (WIZO) and the latter organization held its founding conference in London. Thereafter, the federation acted as the British affiliate of WIZO. Took leading role in organizing and giving aid to German and Austrian Jewish refugees. Helped to establish the Women's Appeal Committee; oversaw children and Youth Aliya; helped organize the Central British Fund for Jewish Refugees; sponsored the entry into Britain of 1,000 boys and girls from the German Zionist movement; and set up and maintained the Whittinghame Farm School for 200 children. Membership peaked at 13,000 shortly after the state of Israel was proclaimed. Publication: *The Jewish Women's Review*.

Ha-Bonim (הבונים), "The Builders," Commonwealth branch of the international Zionist youth movement, founded in 1928. Britain's ha-Bonim came under the aegis of the English Zionist Federation in 1932. In addition to its educational work, ha-Bonim in England was involved in helping to care for Jewish refugees fleeing the Nazis during the 1930s and 1940s. In 1941 all ha-Bonim groups in the British Commonwealth were united into one body with their executive branch, the Contact Office, being in Kfar Blum, *Eretz Israel*. Kfar Blum was, it might be added, a settlement built by members from England and South Africa.

Order of Ancient Maccabeans (OAM), Jewish friendly society, established in London in 1891. Although not initially Zionist in orientation, OAM quickly adopted a pro-Zionist attitude. OAM was one of the first Western European Jewish organizations to host Theodor Herzl;

his passionate lecture on Zionism in 1896 brought OAM to join the WZO in 1897. Originally, it was planned that OAM should function as the landesverbande for the United Kingdom. However, that role fell to the English Zionist Federation (EZF) and OAM accepted its role as a separate union (sonderverband) recognized by the WZO. OAM and EZF formed the Joint Zionist Council in 1912 to coordinate all Zionist activities in England. Membership peaked in 1948 at 4,261 in 22 local branches. OAM continued to operate until the 1960s when it completely merged with EZF's successor.

Professional and Technical Workers Aliyah (PATWA), professional organization operating within the English Zionist Federation and created in 1943 to promote *aliya* by persons with special skills needed in the *Yishuv*. PATWA operated in two directions: (1) providing information on the *Yishuv*'s needs to appropriately trained specialists and (2) providing information on British citizens with appropriate training to *Yishuv* institutions that needed technical assistance. After Israel's declaration of independence PATWA merged with the JA Youth and He-Halutz Department. By then, PATWA had branches in eight other countries as well: Argentina, Australia, Belgium, Canada, France, India, South Africa, and the United States. Chairman: Dr. Eli Davis (1943–1949).

UK/British Colonies[1]

Bombay Zionist Association (BZA), local Zionist association founded in 1920. For the first twenty years of its existence BZA also functioned as the de facto national federation for Indian Zionists. Although numerous local Zionist organizations functioned within the Anglo-Jewish, Iraqi, and Bene-Israel communities, they did not form a single federation until 1950. BZA aimed to create a framework for Zionist activity in India. Prior to 1947, BZA concentrated on the cultural and educational aspects of Zionist activity. With the partition on India and the emergence of the independent states of India and Pakistan, a swell of antisemitism swept the subcontinent and led BZA to seek allies among the ruling Congress Party. This was not wholly successful, with Israel and India maintaining cool diplomatic relations until the 1990s.

Kenya Zionist Association (KZA), Zionist nationwide association founded in 1909 by Jewish residents of the colony of British East Africa and initially known as the Zionist Society. Located in Nairobi, the original society was moribund almost from the outset. KZA, which claimed to be its successor, was founded in 1934, again by British Jews living in the colony. KZA was strengthened by a trickle of Central European Jewish immigrants during the Nazi era. However, KZA ceased to function during World War II since most of its members were draft-age men. Attempts to revive KZA after the war met with little headway, although a Zionist Council was formed with help from the South African Zionist Federation in 1951.

Rhodesian Zionist Society (RZS), regional confederation of Zionist organizations in Northern and Southern Rhodesia (now Zambia and Zimbabwe), founded in Bulawayo, Zambia, on September 18, 1898. Given the small number of Jews in British Rhodesia, Zionism was never a controversial topic within the community. To the contrary, given the nationalistic environment in which Rhodesian Jews lived, anti-Zionism was always a marginal ideology. On the other hand, the small Jewish population (only two hundred Jews lived in both colonies in 1901) meant that RZS was only a marginal actor in Zionist affairs. In 1902, RZS merged with the South African Zionist Federation as a means of increasing Zionist activities in Southern Africa. After the amalgamation, RZS

---

[1] Organizations that operated in Great Britain's overseas dependencies are listed here only when they operated in colonies that were not independent. For Zionist Organizations active in the Dominions, see entries under Australia, Canada, New Zealand, and South Africa.

remained autonomous; this relationship remained in force until the two colonies obtained their independence in the 1960s.

United States

American Christian Palestine Committee (ACPC), agency for the expression of Christian support for Zionism founded in 1941. In particular, ACPC sought to overturn the White Paper of 1939 and bring about the creation of an independent Jewish commonwealth in postwar Palestine/*Eretz Israel*. At its height, ACPC had 20,000 members, including many prominent political and religious leaders, among whom Senator Robert F. Wagner (D–New York), who was among the ACPC's founders, stood out. Chairmen: Senator Owen Brewster (R–Maine), Senator James M. Mead (D–New York), Reverend Daniel A. Poling.

American Committee for Relief of Yemenite Jewry (ACRYJ), North American affiliate of the Yemenite friendly society in the *Yishuv*, organized in January 1938. Major goals included fund-raising on behalf of Yemenite *aliya* and for relief for Yemenite Jews remaining in Yemen (which included the adjacent, British-held Aden territory). Membership peaked in 1948 at 8,000 members; activities continued until Operation Magic Carpet ended with the evacuation of virtually all of Yemenite Jewry. Chairmen: Moses I. Feuerstein, Lawrence G. Selinger.
> see also: **Mivza Marbad ha-Ksamim**.

American Economic Committee for Palestine (AECP), nonprofit agency conceived and organized in 1932 to promote capital investment in the *Yishuv*. Organizers hoped that by increasing capital investment, the *Yishuv*'s economic absorptive capacity would be increased, allowing larger *aliya* schedules. AECP operated as a stock company, selling shares in industries in *Eretz Israel* to interested Americans of all ideological stripes. Operations were undertaken in two offices, one in New York and the other in Tel Aviv. The latter focused mainly on putting investments to good use, mainly in schemes to increase *aliya*. The Tel Aviv office ceased to function after publication of the White Paper of 1939 and was closed that summer. The New York office continued to act on behalf of *aliya* until 1942. By then, AECP's focus changed to acting as a clearinghouse for industries in the *Yishuv* or for American investors interested in helping those industries. AECP continued to operate as a clearinghouse until 1951, when its functions were absorbed into the JA New York office. Presidents: Israel B. Brodie, Robert Szold.

American Fund for Palestine Institutions (AFPI), joint fund-raising agency created in December 1940 to coordinate activities on behalf of eighty-nine cultural, religious, social welfare, and educational institutions. AFPI operated independently of the United Palestine Appeal, even though both shared many board members. Sole Chairman: Felix M. Warburg. Publication: *American Fund News*.

American Jewish Conference, umbrella organization for American Jewry, established in August 1943 at the initiative of Henry Monsky of B'nai B'rith in an effort to unite American Jewry. The conference convened in September with three items on its agenda: a proposal to rescue the Jews of Europe, plans for Jewish postwar relief, and a resolution to support the creation of a Jewish commonwealth in *Eretz Israel* after the war. After the conference passed a resolution approving the Biltmore resolution by a majority of 477 to 4 (with 20 abstentions), the American Jewish Committee withdrew from the conference. Despite this setback to Jewish unity, the conference continued to operate until it disbanded (to form the Conference of Presidents of Major American Jewish Organizations) in 1949.

American Jewish Congress, self-defense agency founded in 1917. Dedicated to the defense of Jewish rights and interests in the United States and throughout the world. The congress was always a strong supporter of Zionism, advocating free *aliya* throughout the 1920s. The congress was electrified into further action by the rise of the Nazis in 1933. Among Congress activities was support for the anti-Nazi boycott and advocacy of an open-door policy for Jewish refugees. In 1936, the congress became the catalyst for the creation of a World Jewish Congress. At the same time, the congress supported the British plan to create a Jewish state in a partitioned Palestine/*Eretz Israel* and, in 1939, sought American intervention to cancel or mute the white paper restrictions on *aliya* and land purchase. During World War II the congress continued its support for rescue operations, although it was hampered by disputes within American Jewry regarding Zionism. As of 1948 it was organized into a plenary (which also obtained membership in the WZO) and seven departments: Commission on Community Interrelations, Commission on Law and Social Action, Community Service Bureau, Institute of Jewish Affairs, Office of Jewish Information, Organization and Finance Department, Public Relations Department. Chairman: Stephen S. Wise (1917–1949). Publications: *Congress Bulletin, Congress Record, Congress Weekly, Law and Social Action, News of the Month.*

American Palestine Trading Corporation (AMPAL), agency created in 1942 to promote trade between the *Yishuv* and the United States and also to facilitate American investment in *Eretz Israel*. AMPAL also furnished assistance to public, semipublic, and cooperative enterprises in the *Yishuv*. As of 1948, AMPAL had 8,000 shareholders in the United States and Canada.

American Red Mogen David for Palestine, fundraising agency established in 1941 to collect funds for the *Yishuv's* main first aid organization. President: Louis Lipsky. > see also: **Yishuv, Yishuv Organizations (Social Service, and Immigrant Aid Organizations, Magen David Adom).**

American Trade Union Council of the National Committee for Labor Palestine (ATUC), organization founded by the May 1947 amalgamation of the Trade Union Committee for Palestine and the National Committee for Labor Palestine's Trade Union Commission. ATUC was created to organize trade union members in support of of Mapai and the Histadrut. Honorary chairman: William Green; Chairman: Joseph Breslaw. Publication: *Histadrut News.* > see also: **Yishuv, Yishuv Organizations.**

American Zion Commonwealth (AZC), fundraising and land purchase agency founded in 1914 with the goal of providing sufficient funds to allow individual homesteaders to settle in Eretz Israel and become productive. Although founded on the eve of World War I, AZC was not incorporated until 1924 and it began to function shortly thereafter. AZC operated on a mixture of private and collective principles: each homesteader invested his or her own money to buy shares (with AZC assistance) for a settlement, although 10 percent of any land purchased was to be set aside for communal purposes. Not all investors intended to settle in *Eretz Israel*, leading to some opposition among socialist Zionist circles to what they characterized as land speculation, but AZC was able to obtain respectable holdings within a relatively short period of time: 36,000 acres of land on which the settlements of Afula, Balfouriya, and Herzliya were built. In addition, AZC held a controlling interest in the Haifa Bay Development Company (which in turn controlled the port facilities). In 1931 AZC sold its assets to Keren ha-Yesod and ceased its operations. Presidents: Bernard Rosenblatt, Solomon J. Weinstein, David Freiberger.

American Zionist Emergency Council (AZEC), Zionist lobbying group originally founded in 1939 as the American Emergency Committee for Zionist Affairs. AZEC's main goal was to promote the Zionist cause in the United States both in relation to the U.S. government and American Jewry. Initially, AZEC sought administration assistance in overturning the White Paper of 1939; thereafter AZEC concentrated on obtaining support for the postwar creation of a Jewish commonwealth in Palestine/*Eretz Israel*. Despite the intense polarization of American Jewry during World War II, AZEC was able to retain the membership of a wide range of American Zionist organizations. Chairmen: Rabbi Stephen S. Wise (1939–1945), Rabbi Abba Hillel Silver (1942–1947). > see also: **Biltmore Resolution.**

American Zionist Youth Council (AZYC), educational agency designed to disseminate the Zionist idea within American Jewish youth while also assisting in the youth-related activities of Hadassah, the Women's Zionist

Organization of America, established in 1940. AZYC was actually a coalition of four other agencies: the Intercollegiate Zionist Federation of America, Junior Hadassah, Masada, and Young Judea. As such, the AZYC had only fifty-eight members. Membership was open only to directors and other high-level members of the affiliated organizations that retained their own membership. Affiliation with AZYC implied a coordination of activities, not the abandonment of independence. Executive director: Rabbi Amram Prero.

Americans for Hagana, nonsectarian organization created in 1947 to disseminate pro-Zionist propaganda in the United States and to rally American (and American Jewish) support for the fledgling State of Israel. In addition to its legal activities, Americans for Hagana also operated as a clandestine recruiting agency for Mitnadve Hutz la-Aretz (foreign volunteers) who served in the Israeli armed forces and facilitated for arms acquisition in North America. Chairman: Bartley C. Crum; President: Abraham Feinberg. Publication: *Hagana Speaks*. > see also: **Mitnadve Hutz la-Aretz; Rechesh; Sonnenborn Institute**.

Avukah, intercollegiate Zionist student society established in 1925. Avukah operated as a loose coalition of regional and local chapters, all of which were (independently) associated with the Zionist Organization of America. Officially neutral on intra-Zionist affairs, Avukah actually was very supportive of Mapai and the Histadrut, with many members leaning toward the left wing of Mapai (*Siya-Bet*). Avukah sought to foster Jewish identification and nationalist consciousness among American Jewish university students by three means: publications, social and cultural activities, and summer camps for high school and college students. At its height in 1940, Avukah had

sixty-five affiliated chapters. Activities declined, however, as more members were drafted into the armed services during World War II. Avukah ceased operations in 1943. Publications:[1] *Avukah Bulletin* (New York, 1929–1937); *Avukah Student Action* (New York, 1938–1943), *Avukah Rostrum* (Philadelphia, 1928–1929), *The Torch* (Chicago, 1934).[2]

Bnai Zion (BZ), "Sons of Zion," fraternal society organized on July 2, 1907, to foster the Zionist idea within American Jewry. BZ saw itself as having a dual role: promoting the Americanization of new immigrants while also protecting their Jewish identity. BZ's goals were accomplished by a combination of educational activities and financial assistance (including life insurance) provided to members. Among the significant educational activities was the BZ-sponsored camp, Ohavei Zion. BZ also played a major role in Zionist fund-raising in the United States, especially (though by no means exclusively) for Keren ha-Yesod. Presidents: Judah L. Magnes (1907–1908), David Blaustein (1908–1909), Joseph Bluestone (1909–1911, 1927–1928, 1929–1930), Leon Zolotokoff (1911–1913), Joseph Barondess (1913–1917), Jacob S. Strahl (1917–1922), Abraham Shomer (1922–1923), Nathan Chasan (1923–1925), Sol Friedland (1925–1927), Max Perlman (1928–1929), Isaac Allen (1930–1933), Joseph Kraemer (1933–1938), Harris J. Levine (1938–1940), Harry Grayer (1940–1942), Harry A. Pine (1942–1944), Louis Lipsky (1944–1946), Abraham A. Redelheim (1946–1948). Publication: *Bnai Zion Voice*.

Federation of American Zionists (FAZ), first Zionist umbrella organization established in the United States, founded in 1898. FAZ was open to all supporters of Zionism's basic goals but, in practice, Political Zionists dominated the federation. FAZ faced financial crises for most of its existence and could hardly have been said to have conquered American Jewry. At its height in 1914, FAZ numbered only 15,000

---

[1] Since most Avukah publications were decentralized, only the major titles have been included; data as to place and dates of publication have been added as well.

[2] Some issues of *The Torch* may have appeared under the title *The Avukah Torch*.

members. In 1918 FAZ was thoroughly reorganized, changing its name to the Zionist Organization of America. > see also: **Organizations, Zionist (United States, Zionist Organization of America).**

Federation of Palestine Jews, friendly society founded in 1929 to assist in the return to the *Yishuv* of Jews uprooted by World War I. In addition, after 1929 the Federation assisted in fund-raising for the Va'ad Leumi and supported educational and other social activities in the *Yishuv*. President: Rabbi Joseph Gabriel. Publication: *Artzenu*.

Ha-Bonim-Labor Zionist Youth, educational and social organization founded in 1915 as the Young Poale Zion Alliance. Dedicated to assisting in the building of a Jewish national home by providing agricultural and other training for American Jewish youth. From 1935 the American branch of ha-Bonim functioned as the central organization for ha-Bonim groups in Canada as well. The North American branches were not associated with the Contact Office in Kfar Blum and operated autonomously from the international organization, but they cooperated with the world ha-Bonim federation on educational and other activities. In 1948 ha-Bonim had 4,000 members in the United States and Canada. Departments: Aliya; Camping Association; Cooperative Enterprises; Education; Habonim Institute; Organization. Publications: *Furrows, ha-Boneh.*

Hadassah, the Women's Zionist Organization of America, women's Zionist social, political, and fundraising body established in 1912. Dedicated to fostering Zionist ideals in the diaspora, developing medical, social and educational facilities in the *Yishuv,* and assisting Youth Aliya. At the end of World War II, Hadassah numbered some 120,000 members. Publication: *Hadassah Newsletter, Hadassah Magazine.* > see also: **Yishuv, Yishuv Organizations (Educational and Cultural Organizations; Aliyat Yeladim ve-Noar).**

Ha-Shomer ha-Dati, North American branch of the Kibbutz ha-Dati organization in *Eretz Israel,* organized in 1935. Mainly dedicated to educational activities, ha-Shomer ha-Dati had 2,300 members in 1948.

Histadrut Ivrit of America, educational agency dedicated to encouraging use of Hebrew, established in 1916. In addition to its direct educational role, the Histadrut Ivrit sought to promote Hebrew literature throughout the world and to cement the cultural ties between American Jewry and the *Yishuv.* Presidium: Alexander Dushkin, Boris Margolin, Samuel J. Borowsky. Publications: *Sefer ha-Shana le-Yehudei America* (1916–1922), *ha-Doar* (1921f).

Jewish National Workers' Alliance of America, friendly society created in January 1913 and affiliated with the Labor Zionist Organization of America-Poale Zion and with Pioneer Women. Mainly focused on mutual aid, the alliance also acted to foster socialist Zionist education among American Jewish youth and to collect funds for the Histadrut. In 1948 the Alliance had 30,000 members. President: David Pinski. Publication: *Farband Shtime.*

Labor Zionist Organization of America-Poale Zion (LZOA-PZ), socialist Zionist organization founded in 1905 and reorganized in 1921. In effect, the LZOA-PZ was the American branch of Mapai. In addition to its political goals, the LZOA-PZ sponsored the Jewish National Workers' Alliance of America and ha-Bonim. The latter's educational activities were considered central to socialist Zionist work in the United States. In 1948 the LZOA-PZ had 65,000 members. President: Baruch Zuckerman. Publications: *Jewish Frontier* (1934f); *Yiddisher Kempfer* (1906f).

Land and Labor for Palestine (LLP), Hagana front organization operating as a recruiting agency. Founded in 1946, ostensibly to promote *aliya* by American Jews, LLP actually sought Americans (Jews and non-Jews) with military skills that were unavailable in the *Yishuv* at the time. In addition to its main office in New York, LLP had subsidiary branches in Boston, Baltimore, Chicago, Cleveland, Detroit, Miami, Philadelphia, and Pittsburgh. The exact number of recruits LLP brought to the Hagana, the Mossad le-Aliya Bet, and Zva ha-Hagana le-Israel is not known. > see also: **Shu Shu Boys; Mitnadve Hutz la-Aretz.**

League for Labor Palestine, socialist-Zionist organization founded in 1932 as an affiliate of Poale Zion. Dedicated to assisting the operations of the Histadrut and promoting moderate labor Zionism. LLP sought to portray Zionism as a form of American progressivism, in other words, in terms that could win the support of Jews who might not otherwise support Jewish nationalism. The League was reorganized in 1921 as the Labor Zionist Organization of America-Poale Zion.

League for Religious Labor in Palestine, American affiliate of ha-Poel ha-Mizrachi, organized in 1941. Mainly involved in educational and fund-raising activities on behalf of religious *Kibbutzim*. The league had 3,000 members in 1948. President: Isaac Rivkind.

Masada, Young Zionists of America, educational and cultural organization founded in 1933 as part of the World General Zionist movement. Masada was affiliated from the outset with the Zionist Organization of America (ZOA) and was, for all intents and purposes, the ZOA's youth movement. In 1948 Masada had slightly more than 5,200 members. President: Jacob M. Snyder.

National Conference on Palestine (NCP), research arm of the United Palestine Appeal founded in 1940 in order to develop contingency plans for future fund-raising activities. The NCP was especially active in promoting the notion of Jewish sovereignty after World War II as the only means to solve the Jewish problem.

National Council for Labor Palestine (NCLP), socialist Zionist fund-raising agency for North and South America founded in 1924. The NCLP was essentially the North American arm of the Histadrut and was also part and parcel of Mapai. However, some *Arbeiter Ring* (Workman's Circle) branches affiliated with the NCLP, as did ha-Shomer ha-Zair in North America. The NCLP also financed the publication activity of the Labor Zionist Organization of America-Poale Zion. Precise membership data is unknown, but the NCLP claimed to have 3,000 affiliated

branches and organizations in 1948. National chairman: Joseph Schlossberg.

National Young Zionist Actions Committee (NYZAC), umbrella organization of Zionist youth groups formed in January 1944. NYZAC was established to coordinate the activities of its eleven member agencies, mainly in education but also in political activity on behalf of the Jewish national home. NYZAC had no members per se; membership was retained in the individually affiliated groups that came together mainly to coordinate their activities. National chairman: Joseph Blanc. Member Organizations: Habonim-Labor Zionist Youth; ha-noar ha-Ivri; ha-Shomer ha-Dati; ha-Shomer ha-Zair; he-Halutz ha-Zair; Intercollegiate Zionist Federation of America; Junior Hadassah; Junior Mizrachi Women; Masada-Young Zionists of America; ha-Noar ha-Mizrachi; and Senior Judea.

Palestine Development Council (PDC), financial body created in 1921 to funnel American Jewish investments into the Yishuv. Operating through a series of Palestine Development Leagues (PDLs), the PDC attempted to finance a wide range of projects. However, the PDC eschewed philanthropy, operating instead as an investment agency, for instance, by offering potential profits on investments. The PDC was converted into the Palestine Economic Corporation in 1926.

Palestine Economic Corporation (PEC), fund-raising agency established on January 18, 1926, as a means to funnel American Jewish investment into the *Yishuv*. Operating on the assumption that many individuals would support Zionist work in Palestine in return for financial gain, PEC was organized as a limited stock company. Capital thus obtained were invested in one of twenty-five affiliated corporations (including banks, utilities, a textile plant, and a food processing plant) in Palestine. PEC's 2,000 stockholders, in turn, were promised (and received) a solid return on their investments. Honorary chairman: Governor Herbert H. Lehman (D–NY); Chairman: Robert Szold.

Palestine Lighthouse, charitable organization established in December 1927 to raise funds in America to assist organizations that offered shelter, training, and rehabilitation for vision-impaired Jewish orphans in the *Yishuv*. During the 1930s the organization expanded its activities to include adults, especially refugees fleeing the Nazis.

Palestine Youth Conference, coalition of Zionist and non-Zionist youth groups established in August 1947. The conference's stated goal was to increase awareness of Zionist and Jewish issues among American Jewish teenagers and college students. Operating under the auspices of the National Jewish Welfare Board, the conference also oversaw the Volunteer Service to Palestine agency, whose goal was to send American Jewish youth for short periods (less than six months) of volunteer work in the *Yishuv*. Member Organizations: B'nai Brith Youth Organization; National Jewish Welfare Board; National Young Zionist Actions Committee; Young Peoples' League. Chairmen: Joseph P. Sternstein, Daniel Fliderblum, Meyer Bass, Rabbi Joseph Elgart, Rabbi Max Vorspan.

Pioneer Women – Labor Zionist Women's Organization of America, women's Zionist body, parallel to the Labor Zionist Organization of America (LZOA), founded in August 1925. Ideologically identical to the LZOA, Pioneer Women was mainly active in fund-raising and educational activities. Membership peaked at 28,000. President: Bert Goldstein. Publication: *Pioneer Woman* (Yiddish/ English, 1926f).

Plugat Aliya, American affiliate of the he-Halutz, the Mapai-oriented youth movement that placed its main stress on preparing young persons for *aliya*. Founded in 1946, Plugat Aliya had two hundred members at its height. Chairman: Arye Greenberg.

Provisional Executive Committee for General Zionist Affairs (PEC), temporary umbrella organization founded in 1916 to coordinate all Zionist activities in the U.S. during World War I. PEC reached its zenith during the postwar peace conference in Versailles, when the American Zionists were able to obtain a considerable number of their demands from the Great Powers. > see also: **Conferences, International, Paris**.

United Jewish Appeal (UJA), philanthropic agency formed in 1939 by merging the fund-raising campaigns of the United Palestine Appeal (UPA) with the non-Zionist National Coordinating Committee for the Aid of Refugees and the American Jewish Joint Distribution Committee (JDC). Although there had been previous efforts to unite the funds, mainly in order to avoid competition for scarce money, they ideological grounds. As a result of Kristallnacht and the British White Paper of 1939, however, ideological differences were put aside. A corollary to the UJA's creation was its emergence as a major factor in American Jewish communal politics and the centrality now accorded to action on behalf of Zionist goals (financial and political) in the community.

United Labor Zionist Party (ULZP), North American branch of the Poale Zion Smol party founded in 1920 and dedicated to the creation of a socialist homeland in *Eretz Israel*. ULZP was not a member of the Zionist Organization of America and its attitude toward the WZO varied between enmity and apathy, depending on the prevailing attitude in the mother party. ULZP membership peaked in 1948 at 2,000. General Secretary: Paul L. Goldman. Publication: *Unzer Veg*.

Women's League for Palestine, philanthropic agency founded in 1928 as the American arm of Moezet ha-Poalot, a pioneering socialist Zionist women's organization. Mainly oriented toward fund-raising in order to assist in vocational training, rehabilitation (when needed), and housing of recent immigrant young women. The league also maintained three dormitories for recent immigrants, one each in Tel Aviv, Haifa, and Jerusalem.

Young Judea (YJ), nonpartisan and non-denominational Zionist youth group founded in 1909 as an arm of the Zionist Organization of America. YJ fell under the responsibility of Hadassah and was used primarily as a means of inculcating American Jewish teenagers with a Zionist spirit. Seen mainly as a means to bolster American Jewish identity, YJ placed less stress on *aliya*. In 1948 YJ peaked at 15,000 members, organized into local and statewide chapters. National chairwoman: Rose Halpern; executive director: Norman Schanin.

Zionist Organization of America (ZOA), umbrella agency for all Zionist bodies in the United States, founded as the Federation of American Zionists in 1898. ZOA emerged from a complete overhaul of the earlier federation (which had never experienced much success in any case) in 1918. The Balfour Declaration greatly enhanced ZOA's prestige, as did the highly public support for Zionism given by such respected individuals as Justice Louis D. Brandeis. Dedicated to the creation of a Jewish national home in *Eretz Israel*, ZOA was a microcosm of the pressures, difficulties, failures, and successes of world Zionism. In particular, the ZOA was fractured and weakened considerably during the famous dispute between Brandeis and WZO president Chaim Weizmann during the 1920s. ZOA regained its stature as a major factor in the American Jewish community during the 1930s and was able to galvanize the movement on behalf of a Jewish state after World War II. Publications: *Dos Yidishe Folk*, *Inside Palestine*, *The New Palestine*, *ZOA Newsletter*. > see also: **Organizations, Zionist (United States, Federation of American Zionists)**; **Zeeland Program**; **Brandeisists**; **Between Washington and Pinsk**.

Uruguay

Comité Uruguayo Pro-Palestina (CUPP), "Uruguayan Pro-Palestine Committee," lobbying arm of the Uruguayan Zionist federation, founded in 1944. CUPP, which also acted as the de facto branch of the JA in Uruguay, was headquartered throughout its existence in Montevideo. CUPP lobbying efforts were successful, as evidenced by the earnest support for partition given by the government in 1947 and 1948. Sole president: Dr. Jacobo Hazan.

Organización Sionista Dr. Teodoro Herzl, "Zionist Organization (in honor of) Dr. Theodor Herzl," Sephardi Zionist federation founded in 1918; reorganized during World War II as Organización Sionista Sefaradí (OSS, Sephardi Zionist Organization). Centered in Montevideo, OSS was active within Uruguay's Sephardi community and was successful in bringing most of the community into the Zionist fold. Prior to World War II, OSS mainly operated in the cultural and social spheres. The Nazi persecution of European Jewry combined with increasing Nazi-inspired activity in Latin America (but not specifically in Uruguay) led to the wartime reorganization and a concentration on political activity. OSS was one of the founding members of the Comité Uruguayo Pro-Palestina, when the latter organization was founded in late 1944.

Union Sionista, "Zionist Union," umbrella body of Uruguayan Zionist federations, created in 1918. The union was composed of all Ashkenazi Zionist organizations active in Uruguay, Sephardim having their own separate federation. Until 1934, the union was unified and maintained a general Zionist orientation. The splintering of the WZO in 1935 also affected the union but did not rend it asunder. Although ideological fissures became significant at this time, the local revisionist Zionist section remained in the union throughout. Ideological fragmentation, which resulted in the organization of a local branch of almost every party then active in the WZO, did not weaken the union. To the contrary, it was able to continue its activities and even expanded its influence in the Uruguayan government. Until the war, the union's orientation was mostly social and cultural. The perceived need to undertake political lobbying led to the creation of the Comité Uruguayo Pro-Palestina in late 1944.

Yugoslavia

Savez Cijonista Jugoslavije (SCJ), "Yugoslavian Zionist Federation," national Zionist federation founded in 1919 as the successor of previously existing Zionist unions in Serbia, Croatia-Bosnia (which had been ruled by Austria prior to World War I), and Montenegro. SCJ was weakest in the Serbian regions of the newly created kingdom; given the highly nationalistic atmosphere in the region (where World War I had been started), and especially in Croatia, it is hardly a wonder that Jews gravitated toward nationalism as a solution to their problems in non-Serbian regions of the country. Since much of

Yugoslavia's Zionist population lived in Croatia, SCJ was founded in Zagreb and stayed there for its entire existence. Nonetheless, SCJ was a relatively weak federation, a reflection of the small size of the Jewish population, its precarious position in Yugoslav society, and the fractured nature of Jewish communal politics in the country. Membership was 4,719 in 1922, peaking at 10,223 (14.28% of the total Jewish population) in 1939. *Aliya* did not play an important role in SCJ activities per se, although Yugoslavia was always used as a way station for *olim* (both legal and "illegal") from Eastern Europe for most of the 1930s. World War II disrupted SCJ activities. Instead of reorganizing, most surviving Yugoslav Zionists emigrated when the State of Israel was established. Publication: *Židov* (1917–1941).

Savez Židoskih Omladinskih Udruženja (SŽOU), "Federation of Jewish Youth Associations," coalition of Zionist youth groups organized in 1919 as a parallel to the Savez Cijonista Jugoslavije. SŽOU included all Zionist youth groups active in the country except Betar, which did not join. SŽOU concentrated mainly on educational and social activities with only secondary emphasis being placed on *aliya*. Like its parent body, SŽOU found its activities completely disrupted by World War II and the federation was not renewed in 1945.

3. Revisionist Zionist

Austria

Herut (חרות), "Freedom," world union of Jewish war veterans founded in Innsbruck on June 20, 1921. Active in Jewish self-defense, Herut members were in the forefront of calling for a more activist policy that would lead to Zionist fulfillment. In 1922, Herut called on Jews to unite to build *Eretz Israel* and to conquer it by force if need be. Shortly thereafter, the movement collapsed over its attitude toward the WZO executive. An effort to revive the union in 1923 failed and led Betar to take over most of Herut's functions.

Irgun Yehudim Lohamim (ארגון יהודים לוחמים, ILY), "Organization of Jewish Fighters," Jewish veterans organization founded in late 1945 by former Jewish partisans who had made their way to the American zone of occupation in Austria. IYL, in turn, was a component of Betar and ha-Zohar, which had been reconstituted slightly earlier in the year. IYL was active in *Briha* and *Aliya Bet*: initially independently and then when the revisionists rejoined the WZO in conjunction with the Hagana and Mossad le-Aliya Bet.

Unitas, "Unity," unified revisionist Zionist student fraternity founded in late 1923 or early 1924. Initially designed as an international student fraternity, only the Austrian chapter was active after 1924. Unitas operated among Jewish university students and had some successes but collapsed under fascist pressure in the early 1930s.

Belgium

Jawne we-Jodephat (JWJ), "Yavne and Yodefat," student fraternal organization named after two sites made famous during the Jewish rebellion against Rome (66–73 C.E.). JWJ was founded in Antwerp in 1934 and was active among university students and recent immigrants to Belgium. Most JWJ members appear to have previously been members of Betar, although that cannot be definitively verified. Membership apparently peaked at one hundred in 1936 and a branch was initiated in Amsterdam, Holland, in that year. However, little else is known about JWJ or its activities thereafter.

Cyprus

Radio Betar, colloquial name for the news service active in the Cyprus internment camps between 1946 and 1948. The service was actually a megaphone smuggled into one of the camps that was used to "broadcast" news bulletins and party slogans to the inmates. Betar's use of the megaphone was so successful that other parties soon copied the idea, the "broadcasts" being an important source of news for inmates who otherwise had no information about conditions in Europe and *Eretz Israel*. > see also: **Cyprus, Detention Camps.**

France

Rassviet Group, colloquial name for the members of the ha-Zohar/ha-Zach executive who lived and worked in Paris. The group combined two functions: overseeing the daily operations of the world revisionist Zionist movement and simultaneously directing the affairs of the local revisionist federation. The Rassviet Group became even more important after the withdrawal from the WZO, since Paris became the headquarters for all of Ze'ev Jabotinsky's diplomatic activities. World War II and the Nazi occupation of France disrupted the group's work and forced ha-Zohar's executive to permanently move to London, thus ending the Rassviet Group's activities per se.

Union des Sionistes-Revisionistes de France (USRF), "Union of Revisionist Zionists of France," ha-Zohar federation in France, founded in Paris in the summer of 1924. Operating under the patronage of Max Nordau's widow, Anna, USRF was an active member of both ha-Zohar and the WZO. In calling for the abandonment of gradualism, USRF was among the first revisionist organizations to articulate Ze'ev Jabotinsky's major criticisms of Chaim Weizmann's stewardship of the WZO. USRF's membership was mainly composed of recent immigrants and Jewish students studying at French universities; most of them had previously been members of Betar or similar youth groups. Although active in French Zionist circles, USRF was not a predominant component of ha-Zohar until the withdrawal from the WZO, when the newly formed ha-Zach executive was activated in Paris.

Germany

Hativa ha-Betarim ha-Lohamim (חטיבה הבית׳דים הלוחמים, HBL), "The Brigade of Fighting Betarim," military formation founded in 1945 within the ranks of Betar's renewed German branch. HBL was conceived as a means of providing trained personnel, many of whom had served in partisan detachments during the war, for the Irgun Zvai Leumi (IZL). In all, eight hundred personnel were recruited into HBL; they were fully trained and ready to fight by 1948. At that point, however, their emigration was blocked at British instigation and by the time they reached Israel, IZL had been disbanded. Most nonetheless served in the Israeli army. > see also: **Yishuv, Organizations (Underground Movements, Irgun Zvai Leumi)**.

Masada (מסדה), Revisionist Zionist youth movement founded in 1946 and active in the Displaced Persons (DP) camps in Germany. Masada was in effect, if not in name, a branch of Betar; it is unclear what (if any) differences led to the use of a different name, since a Betar branch had been revived in Germany in 1945. Masada was active in both the American and British zones of occupation, dissolving when the last DP camps were closed in 1953.

Staatszionistische Organisation (SZO), "State Zionist Organization," framework for continued operation formed by Georg Kareski from the remnants of the revisionist Zionist union in Germany in 1934. Previously, Germany had had an active branch of ha-Zohar. This body collapsed in 1933 due to a combination of internal ideological pressures exacerbated by a complex set of maneuvers between the German ha-Zohar branch, the ha-Zohar executive in Paris, the WZO, and the Zionistische Vereinigung für Deutschland and the impact of the Nazi takeover in 1933. When formed, SZO had to deal with both the increasingly harsh policies of the Nazi regime and the opposition of most German Zionists to revisionism. These factors combined to almost completely isolate SZO from other Zionist institutions in and out of Germany. Ideologically, SZO was closest to the ha-Zohar faction that had formed around Meir Grossman (which crystalized into the Jewish State Party in 1935). SZO was able to continue to operate, with increasing Nazi interference, until 1938, when all Jewish institutions were closed by the Gestapo.

International

Brit Trumpeldor (ברית תרומפלדור), "Covenant of Trumpeldor," international revisionist Zionist youth movement, better known by its acronym, Betar (בית״ר). Betar was founded in Riga, Latvia, in 1923 and constituted a major section of ha-Zohar when the latter was founded. Betar's ideology was a reflection of Ze'ev Jabotinsky's Zionist conception, emphasizing *Hadar* (self-respect), *Had-ness* (monism), activism, paramilitary discipline, and total commitment to the Jewish people and the Zionist idea. Betar grew rapidly between 1923 and 1935, especially in Eastern Europe. During the 1930s, Poland increasingly became the center for Betar's activities, a reflection of the fact that the plurality of members lived there. The first Betar cells were formed in *Eretz Israel* in the late 1920s, with a national executive formed in 1934. Betar viewed its emphasis on paramilitary drill as nothing more than a means to the goal of creating a disciplined movement, but many opponents (mainly on the Zionist left) condemned what they saw as a Jewish form of fascism. This perception was reinforced in many minds by Betar's use of a tan/brown uniform that seemed similar to the colors used by the Nazis. Ideological opposition, in turn, led to repeated violent clashes, mainly (but not exclusively) in the *Yishuv*. In some locations, Betar members retaliated against their opponents by disrupting rallies for the Keren Kayemet le-Israel and Keren ha-Yesod. This cycle of internecine violence culminated in a WZO decision in 1933 to deny Betar further access to *aliya* certificates until it accepted the discipline expected of all WZO member bodies. Far from ending conflict, the decision fueled Betar efforts to undertake independent *aliya* ("illegal" immigration) and a further cycle of ideological clashes resulted. Similarly contentious was Betar's involvement in the anti-Nazi boycott, since the majority of Zionists had adopted a different policy. Betar joined the majority of ha-Zohar in withdrawing from the WZO in 1935, functioning as ha-Zach's youth movement until all revisionists rejoined the WZO in 1946. Betar was hard hit by the Holocaust. Most Betar branches were destroyed, although many members served in Jewish underground movements throughout Europe. In Warsaw, surviving Betar members created their own resistance movement, the Żydowski Związek Wojskowy. By 1945, only the Betar branches in North America, *Eretz Israel*, and Tunisia remained intact. Betar branches were reconstituted after the war in Austria, Czechoslovakia, Germany, Hungary, Italy, Romania, and Poland. Most of these, especially the ones in the newly Communist countries of Eastern Europe, were short-lived and were created in large part to assist in *Briha* activities. On the other hand, in Germany, Austria, and Italy Betar was mainly concerned with educational and political activities in Displaced Persons camps in the American and British zones of occupation. Virtually the entire Betar movement in Europe ceased to exist by the 1950s. The movement is still active in many countries, notably Israel and the United States.

TABLE O.3: Countries with Active Betar Chapters in 1939[1]

Country	Membership	Country	Membership
Austria	400	Italy	
Belgium		Latvia	75 (1928)
Bulgaria	1,500	Poland	9,000
Eretz Israel	2,000 (1933)	Romania	
France		Tunisia	
Germany	400 (1931)	United States	1,000 (1934)
Holland		Lithuania	350 (1929)

Source: J. Schechtman and Y. Benari, *History of Revisionist Zionism*, vol. 1 (Tel Aviv: Hadar, 1970).

[1] Membership data given, when known. Where no date is cited, the data refer to 1939.

Histadrut ha-Zionit ha-Hadasha (הסתדרות הציונית החדשה), "The New Zionist Organization," international revisionist Zionist body established when ha-Zohar seceded from the WZO in September 1935 and better known by its acronym ha-Zach (הצ"ח or NZO). Ha-Zach originated with Ze'ev Jabotinsky and his followers, who opposed the gradualist course adopted by the ruling WZO coalition and sought a more vigorous Zionist policy. Repeatedly rebuffed by the WZO majority, Jabotinsky hoped he could accomplish more by operating independently. In fact, ha-Zach almost immediately began a multinational diplomatic campaign to gain support for the so-called Evacuation Plan, which would remove 1.5 million Jews from Eastern Europe in ten years. This plan was designed to create a Jewish majority after a decade and would culminate in the creation of a Jewish state. Jabotinsky was able to obtain some support for the plan, but, in reality, ha-Zach's successes were few and fleeting. Ironically, ha-Zach's secession from the WZO came at a time when the latter body was itself reevaluating its gradualist policies and a new generation of leaders, notably David Ben-Gurion of Mapai, adopted many ideas that were similar to Jabotinsky's. There is little doubt that ha-Zach's secession weakened the WZO, although it is not at all clear that, given the prevailing diplomatic situation in the Middle East, a unified WZO would have been able to prevent the British government's reevaluation of its promises to the Jewish people. Ultimately, therefore, ha-Zach failed to achieve any of its goals. World War II brought the organization to a virtual halt, since the movement was strongest in precisely those countries that were destined to become mass graveyards for European Jewry. After the war, efforts to coordinate diplomatic strategy led ha-Zach to rejoin the WZO; the former officially ceasing to exist as of the Twenty-Second World Zionist Congress (August 1946). > see also: **Gradualism; Revisionist Schism; Evacuation Plan.**

Hitahdut ha-Zionim ha-Revisionistim (התאחדות הציונים הרביסיוניסטים), "Union of Zionist Revisionists," international Zionist political party, better known by its acronym, ha-Zohar (הצה"ר) founded by Ze'ev Jabotinsky in Paris in 1925. Ha-Zohar was initially formed as a coalition of nonsocialist Zionists who hoped to influence the WZO to adopt activist and maximalist policies. Since the lobbying tactics initially espoused by ha-Zohar failed, the organization increasingly took on the character of an oppositional movement, actively contesting elections for all of the Zionist congresses between the fourteenth (1925) and eighteenth (1933). Ha-Zohar's ideology was virtually identical to Jabotinsky's and could be summarized by three points: (1) the need to convert the mandate into a "colonization regime" that would actively encourage Jewish immigration; (2) the need to build the Jewish population in *Eretz Israel* rapidly and to attain a majority as soon as possible; (3) the attainment of Jewish sovereignty (no matter how defined) as soon as Jews represented a majority of the population. Thus, both Jabotinsky and ha-Zohar saw the need for an immediate and explicit statement on the Zionists' Endziel (final goal). Ha-Zohar reached its zenith in 1931 when the gradualist policies espoused by Chaim Weizmann appeared to have run their course. However, Jabotinsky's uncompromising maximalism and his increasingly antagonistic relationship with the leaders of Mapai led to a defeat at the Seventeenth World Zionist Congress from which ha-Zohar never really recovered. Internally, ha-Zohar was becoming factionalized with a distinct bloc crystalizing around Meir Grossman by 1933. Unable to influence the WZO any further, Jabotinsky withdrew ha-Zohar from the WZO to form Histadrut ha-Zionit ha-Hadasha (the New Zionist Organization) in 1935. The Grossman faction, which utterly rejected secession, simultaneously withdrew from ha-Zohar, remaining in the WZO and re-constituting itself as the Jewish State Party. > see also: **World Zionist Organization; World Zionist Congresses; Gradualism; Revisionist Schism.**

Jewish State Party (JSP), coalition of revisionist Zionists that crystalized around Meir Grossman during the early 1930s. Grossman strongly disagreed with ha-Zohar's leaders (mainly Ze'ev Jabotinsky) over the issue of secession from the WZO. Although the majority of revisionists saw such a move as vitally necessary to the defense of Zionism — whose chances for success they saw as increasingly threatened by the gradualist policies adopted by the WZO — Grossman saw secession as foolhardy and as an admission of defeat. JSP was formed as a clearly defined group during the first secession crisis in 1933 and the bloc remained in existence after the so-called Calais Compromise. In 1935 when Jabotinsky agreed to secede, Grossman led JSP out of ha-Zohar. The party remained in the WZO as a sonderverband. Despite its withdrawal from ha-Zohar, JSP retained most of its revisionist ideology, including especially the belief that Zionism required uncompromising work to achieve a Jewish state in all of historic *Eretz Israel*. JSP had its own youth wing in Eastern Europe, known as Brit ha-Kanaim. When JSP withdrew from ha-Zohar/ha-Zach in 1935, Brit ha-Kanaim withdrew from Betar as well. In 1937, JSP split over the Peel partition plan, with a minority of members withdrawing and joining Mapai. World War II paralyzed the party and JSP never really recovered. In 1946 when the revisionists agreed to rejoin the WZO, JSP ceased its separate operations, becoming part of the renewed Revisionist Union.

Keren Tel-Hai (קרן תל-חי, KTH), "Tel Hai Fund," revisionist Zionist fund-raising organization founded in 1929. KTH was not originally planned as a separate fund; indeed, for the first years of its existence, KTH acted as a supplementary fund that did not compete with the WZO's national funds (the Keren Kayemet le-Israel and Keren ha-Yesod). However, as relations between ha-Zohar and the WZO worsened, KTH increasingly became a competing fund. This, in turn, further eroded the relationship between the WZO executive and the leaders of ha-Zohar. In 1935, when the revisionists withdrew from the WZO entirely, KTH began to function as the main fundraising body for the newly created ha-Zach. Major beneficiaries of KTH funds were Betar, ha-Zach, and (after 1931) the Irgun Zvai Leumi. KTH continued to operate as a private fund for Betar members after the revisionists returned to the WZO.

Latvia

Hashmonai (חשמונאי), "Hashmonea," revisionist Zionist youth movement active in Riga between 1923 and 1934. Considered to be part and parcel of the world Betar movement, it is not clear why Hashmonea operated under a different name. Hashmonai peaked at seventy-five members in 1928. In addition to its youth movement activities, Hashmonai operated as a *hachshara* for revisionist youth in Latvia and oversaw the operations of the Betar naval academy in Latvia.

Lithuania

Brit ha-Kanaim (ברית הקנאים), "Covenant of Zealots," Zionist youth movement, better known by its acronym, Barak (ברק, Lightning). Founded in 1933, Barak initially operated as the youth wing of the faction of ha-Zohar that identified with Meir Grossman. As such, Barak operated as an autonomous entity within the Betar youth movement. In 1935, when Grossman withdrew from the revisionist movement (because the latter had withdrawn from the WZO) Barak withdrew from Betar and assumed the position as the youth movement for the Jewish State Party. Membership was 1,200 on founding and peaked at 2,000 organized into thirty-one local branches in 1939. Barak ceased to operate during World War II. Publications: *El ha-Matara*; *ha-Kvutza*; *Be-Ohalei Barak* (Kovno branch).

Poland

Brit ha-Hayal (ברית החיל), "The Covenant of the Soldier," revisionist Zionist paramilitary organization founded by a group of Jewish veterans of the Polish army in the 1930s. Active in self-defense and *Aliya Bet*, Brit ha-Hayal members were active particpants in ghetto undergrounds during the Holocaust.

Ha-Shahar (השחר), "The Dawn," revisionist Zionist youth movement, the prototype for Betar, founded in the early 1920s. Non-socialist in its orientation, ha-Shahar fused Jewish nationalism, and physical conditioning (including emphasis on military drill and discipline). When Betar was founded in 1926, ha-Shahar became one of its first member organizations and ceased to function under its earlier name. > see also: **Organizations, Revisionist (International, Betar)**.

Ha-Shomer ha-Leumi (השומר הלאומי), "The Nationalist Guardsman," short-lived nonsocialist Zionist youth movement founded in Poland in the early 1920s. Modeled on the socialist ha-Shomer ha-Zair organization, ha-Shomer ha-Leumi placed more emphasis on Jewish nationalism and on building a new Jewish society in *Eretz Israel*. By the mid-1920s ha-Shomer ha-Leumi had run its course. It merged with Betar when that organization was founded in 1926. > see also: **Organizations, Revisionist (International, Betar)**.

Romania

Hebronia (חברוניה), "Hebronite," Jewish student fraternity active in Cernauti (Czernowitz) and founded after World War I. For the first years of its existence, Hebronia was active in the WZO and was officially nonpartisan. However, in 1926, Hebronia's one hundred twenty members joined ha-Zohar en masse, remaining part of the revisionist organization even after the withdrawal from the WZO in 1935. Hebronia ceased to function during the fascist era and was not revived after World War II.

Zeireinu (צעירינו), "Our Youth," Zionist youth movement founded in Cernauti (Czernowitz) in the early 1920s. Zeireinu was initially a member of the international ha-Shomer ha-Zair organization. Zeireinu's leaders quickly soured on the larger organization, mainly due to the increasingly socialist orientation it adopted during the late 1920s. In 1927, Zeireinu withdrew from ha-Shomer ha-Zair and joined Betar, acting

as the Romanian national branch of the latter movement until disbanding during the Holocaust. Zeireinu was not revived after the war.

United States

Hebrew Committee for National Liberation (HCNL), Zionist front group founded in 1939 as the Committee for a Jewish Army of Stateless and Palestinian Jews (CJA). Officially dedicated to promoting a variety of Jewish interests, HCNL was in reality the American arm of the Irgun Zvai Leumi. In 1942 the CJA became the Emergency Committee to Save the Jewish People of Europe (ECJSPE), which was active in publicizing Nazi atrocities and worked tirelessly for the creation of the War Refugee Board. In 1944 ECSJPE was transformed into the HCNL, which also oversaw the activities of the American Friends of a Jewish Palestine. Chairman: Hillel Kook (Peter H. Bergson, pseud). Publication: *The Answer*.

New Zionist Organization of America (NZOA), Zionist political party founded in 1926 as the American wing of ha-Zohar. In 1935 the NZOA (as did all other revisionist Zionist groups) withdrew from the WZO to become a charter member of Ha-Zach. Active in promoting an anti-Nazi boycott during the 1930s and a maximalist policy for *aliya* and Jewish statehood, NZOA was not considered a mainstream Zionist organization. Ironically, the NZOA also did not cooperate with the Hebrew Committee for National Liberation. Publication: *Zionews*.

Palestine Emergency Fund (PEF), American arm of the Irgun Zvai Leumi and the final culmination of the so-called Bergson Boys, established on November 3, 1945. PEF originally was founded to raise funds for the underground, with the limitation being that no direct military assistance was (officially) offered since that would have been illegal. In reality, PEF provided the funds for weapons purchases in Europe and helped indirectly to equip the Irgun ship *Altalena*. After Israel's War of Independence, PEF continued to operate as the fund-raising arm of the Herut party. At its height, PEF had 5,000 contributors. Chairmen: Konrad Becovoci, Yitzhak Ben-Ami.

4. Non- or Anti-Zionist

Argentina

Comité Popular Contra el Antisemitismo y el Fascismo (CPCAF), "People's Committee Against Antisemitism and Fascism," Jewish Communist front organization founded in 1933. CPCAF articulated a virulently anti-Zionist orientation but simultaneously hoped to use Zionist communal organizations (notably the Delgacion de Associaciones Israelitas Argentina) as a means of taking over the Jewish community. CPCAF also operated under a number of other names, including Organización Popular Contra el Antisemitismo y el Fascismo and El Comité Contra el racismo y el Antisemitismo de la Argentina, but remained an appendage of the Argentine Communist party throughout the interwar era. CPCAF's influence peaked just prior to World War II, although exact membership figures are unknown. The Nazi-Soviet pact of August 1939 that doomed Poland made a mockery of CPCAF's supposed anti-fascism and the movement collapsed altogether during the political turmoil in Argentina after 1941.

Austria

Allgemeine Österreichische Israelitische Bund (AÖIB), "United Austrian Jewish Organization," communal umbrella organization established in 1898 and aspiring to be the representative body for all Austrian Jewry. AÖIB failed to attain more than marginal status within the community, mainly because the Austrian Jewish community was riven by numerous divisions prior to World War I; the major schisms being geographic, religious, and ideological. Had AÖIB accepted Jewish nationalism as a basic defining feature of its work, the organization might have been more successful in uniting elements within the community; as it was, AÖIB was moribund almost from its inception and collapsed altogether in 1918.

Allianz Israelitische zu Wien (AIW), "Association of Viennese Jews," social aid organization founded initially as an arm of the Franco-Jewish Alliance Israélite Universelle. AIW gained independence after 1873, although it retained its parent organization's overall orientation. AIW remained solidly non-Zionist throughout its existence, a position that was only modified during the 1930s. AIW ceased to function on Gestapo orders shortly after March 1938. President: Joseph von Werthemer. Publication: *Jahrbuch der Israelitische Allianz im Wien.*

Österreichisch-Israelitisch Union (ÖIU), "Union of Austrian Israelites," Jewish communal and self-defense organization, established in 1886. ÖIU was established with two goals in mind: protecting Jewish rights in postemancipation Austria-Hungary and defending the honor of the Jewish community against antisemitic slander. Although officially adopting a neutral stance on Austrian politics, the ÖIU leaned toward the liberal parties, since the latter were opposed to the same conservative elements that opposed Jewish emancipation. ÖIU viewed Zionism as a dangerous utopian ideology and saw any effort to define Jews as a nation as contrary to Austrian Jewry's best interests. Since facilitating Jewish integration into Austrian society was a major ÖIU goal, anti-Zionism was pursued in an uncompromising fashion. ÖIU collapsed after the breakup of the Austro-Hungarian Empire, although similar ideologies continued to proliferate in the interwar era.

Cuba

Kulturfarain–Unión Cultural Hebrea (KF–UCH), "Jewish Cultural Union," Cuban branch of the Polish-Jewish Bund organized in 1925. Vehemently anti-Zionist in orientation, KF–UCH was much closer to the Communist position on Jewish issues than to the standard Bundist position. KF–UCH was forced underground after an anti-Communist sweep by the Cuban government but remained active as a clandestine group for most of the 1930s.

Egypt

Jam'iyat al-Shubbán al-Yahúd al-Misriyin, "Association of Egyptian Jewish Youth," anti-Zionist organization founded in Cairo in 1935, better known by its French name Association de la Jeunesse Juive Egyptienne (AJJE). AJJE sought to encourage Egyptian Jews to accept their dual identity as Jews and Egyptians. By doing so, AJJE hoped that European-style emancipation would be possible and would relieve the growing antisemitic threat. AJJE operated under the slogan "Fatherland, Faith, and Culture," which was taken to mean that Jewish identity should be limited to the religious sphere. AJJE failed at its main goals, since neither the Egyptian government nor Egyptian Jewry could ignore events in *Eretz Israel*. Publication: *al-Shams* (Arabic/ French, 1935–1948).

Ligue Juive contra la Sionisme (LJCS), "Jewish League Against Zionism," Jewish Communist front organization founded in May 1947. LJCS was the culmination of nearly twenty years of Communist activity in Egypt by Ezra Harari, the most prominent of the Jewish Communists in Egypt. Framing its position around standard Soviet formulas by which Jews are not considered to be a true nation, LJCS condemned Zionism as an "unnatural" nationalist movement. Furthermore, all Jewish nationalism was seen as nothing more than the creation of Western Imperialists who thereby created an excuse for British intervention in the Middle East. LJCS was closed at the instigation of the Egyptian authorities after one month, but Harari reorganized and continued to operate under different guises until the Nasser era. > see also: **Communism and Zionism**.

France

Alliance Israélite Universelle (AIU), "Universal Jewish Alliance," social aid organization founded in 1860 to aid Jews in distress throughout the world, headquartered in Paris. AIU maintained a consistently non-Zionist approach that derived from its position as a philanthropic agency. Most AIU leaders rejected the notion of Jewish nationality, seeing Jews as an exclusively religious community. Despite its rejection of Jewish nationalism, however, AIU also retained an appreciation for the need to foster

Jewish solidarity and worked tirelessly to help build up the *Yishuv*. AIU's paramount activity was its sponsorship of the Mikve Israel agricultural school (opened in 1870 by AIU president Charles Netter). AIU retained this position of helping build the Jewish national home without adhering to political Zionism until 1948. AIU was especially active in aiding German Jewish refugees during the 1930s. World War II disrupted AIU activities, although some branches continued to operate. AIU resumed its full activities in 1945, including efforts to resettle Jewish displaced persons in *Eretz Israel*.

Consistoire Central des Israélites de France (CCIF), "Central Consistory of Jews of France," Jewish religious and communal organization established in 1808. In 1935 CCIF numbered seventy-two communities. Deriving its authority from the decisions of the Napoleonic Sanhedrin, CCIF remained ideologically opposed to Zionism from the inception of the movement until the eve of World War II. CCIF's attitude included conducting an independent diplomatic policy at the Paris Peace Conference (1919) in conjunction with British and American non-Zionists. Even in this era, however, French leaders never expressed their opposition as virulently as Jewish leaders in the United States or Great Britain. Moroever, CCIF's position on Zionism softened to a position of active neutrality during the 1930s, largely under the impact of the antisemitic assault by the Nazis (and the French Fascists). During the 1930s CCIF turned its attention to the aid of Jewish refugees. CCIF activities in northern France ceased in June 1940 and in the Vichy zone in November 1942. When CCIF was reorganized in 1945, its position on Zionism had changed from neutrality to outright support.

Palestine Jewish Colonization Association (PICA), autonomous arm of the Jewish Colonization Association (ICA), established in Paris in 1899. PICA's roots can be traced back to the 1880s, when Baron Edmund de Rothschild agreed to offer financial and technical aid to the settlements that had been established at the beginning of the First Aliya. Illness convinced Rothschild to hand day-to-day control of the settlements to others; instead of turning to the WZO, however, he turned to ICA, a philanthropy dedicated to a territorialist solution to Jewish distress. Rothschild retained the honorary title of president until his death in 1934. He was followed in this role by his son James, who held the presidency until his death in 1957. At that point, PICA ceased to function, after transferring its assets to the Israeli government. Throughout its history PICA retained a clearly non-Zionist orientation. In particular, PICA's founders and leaders rejected political Zionism, a position that did not change until the 1930s. Notwithstanding its alignment, however, PICA was intimately involved in virtually every major project that built the *Yishuv* from 1919 to 1948. During the 1920s, PICA cooperated closely with the WZO and the Zionist Executive. One of the considerations behind the enlargement of the JA in 1929 was, in fact, facilitating the cooperation of PICA and other interested non-Zionist bodies in building the *Yishuv*. In addition to numerous settlements, PICA was involved in projects as diverse as the Palestine Electric Corporation (built by Pinhas Rutenberg) in Mahanayim, the Dagan Flour Mills in Haifa, and the King David Hotel in Jerusalem, as well as most of the educational and cultural institutions in the *Yishuv*. > see also: **Territorialism; Ha-Nadiv ha-Yadua; Yishuv; Sochnut Yehudit.**

Germany

Centralverein deutscher Staatsbürger Jüdischen Glaubens (CV), "Central Union of German Citizens of the Jewish Faith," founded 1893 as a self-defense organization. Because of its emancipationist and assimilationist ideology, the CV always opposed Zionism ideologically. Opposition did not always flare into active opposition, for much of its history the CV could be considered non-Zionist rather than anti-Zionist, but after 1913 relations with the Zionists worsened, leading to a complete break between nationalist and nonnationalist elements in German Jewry. Transformed into the Centralverein der Juden in Deutschland by Nazi order in 1935, the CV was entirely disbanded on November 10, 1938. Membership (1924) 72,500. Publication: *CV Zeitung*.

Deutscher Vortrupp Gefolgschaft deutscher Juden, "German Vanguard of German Jewish Followers," German Jewish anti-Zionist organization founded by Hans Joachim Schöps in 1933. Considering themselves Jews by religion only, the Vortrupp hoped to protect Jewish rights in Germany by proving Jews to be an integral part of the German Volk. As a response to Nazi anti-Jewish propaganda that Jews are only in the professions or business, Schöps also promoted a plan to have Jewish youth work in agriculture. The efforts proved futile, however, since the Nazis sought the total elimination of the Jewish role in German society.

Hilfsverein der deutschen Juden (HDJ), "Relief Organization of German Jews," philanthropic agency founded in 1901 to meet the needs of Eastern European Jews migrating en masse to Germany. HDJ policy was to attempt to make the migrant's stay as short as possible to avoid arousing antisemitism. To this end the HDJ cooperated with organizations in other countries that were more positively oriented toward immigrants. Among others, HDJ closely cooperated with the Jewish Colonization Association (ICA) and consistently advocated a non-Zionist orientation. Despite this orientation, HDJ never acted in an anti-Zionist manner, even when its efforts in 1913 to ensure that all instruction at the Haifa Technion would be in German (rather than Hebrew). HDJ continued to operate as a migrant relief agency after World War I, obtaining indirect representation on the JAE when the latter was "enlarged" in 1929. HDJ ceased to function, for all intents and purposes, in 1933. > see also: **Ostjuden; Territorialism; Cultural Conflict; Sochnut Yehudit.**

Verband National deutscher Juden, "Association of National-German Jews," assimilationist organization established in 1921. The Verband advocated a right-of-center political platform and supported the total assimilation and denationalization of German Jewry. Leaders of the Verband also argued that Jews ought to accept the truth of antisemitic accusations.

The Verband was liquidated by order of the Gestapo in late 1935. The Verband had an associated youth group, called Das Schwarzes Fähnlein (the Black Squad). Chairman: Max Naumann. Publication: *Der National-deutscher Jude*.

International

Agudas Israel (אגודת ישראל), "Association of Israel," Orthodox anti-Zionist party founded in Poland in 1912; a subsidiary agency, Poale Agudas Israel, was founded in 1922. Aguda rejected the concept of Jewish secular nationalism, insisting that a Jewish state could only be created by divine agency and not human activity. Despite this fundamental ideological anti-Zionism, Aguda supported Jewish immigration to the *Yishuv* throughout the 1930s. As the Nazi persecution of European Jewry intensified, Aguda strongly urged rescue operations via the creation of temporary havens in any country possible. Representatives of Aguda served in the provisional government of the State of Israel in 1948 and 1949.

Folkspartei (פאלקספארטיי) "People's Party," Jewish Populist Party founded in Russia in 1906. The party's ideology was formulated mainly by Simon Dubnow who argued for a diaspora national orientation. The basis of Folkspartei activity was obtaining autonomy for Jews in the form of a renewed supranational Jewish communal structure, within a federation of Eastern European nations. The Folkspartei opposed Zionism on grounds that non-nationalist emigration was not a viable solution to the Jewish problem while no territory was available for the creation of a Jewish national home. Dubnow, of course, believed that since Jews were a spiritual nation, no territory was necessary to define Jewish nationalism. The Folkspartei was augmented by a group of autonomist-socialists which merged with the main body in 1911. The Russian Folkspartei was legalized in 1912, but ceased to exist after the Bolshevik victory in the civil war. Offshoots in Poland and the Baltic Republics were founded in 1918 and continued to operate until the outbreak of World War II. The radicalization of Jewish communal politics that resulted from severe antisemitism drew increasing numbers of Jews to Zionist or revolutionary socialist nationalist parties (mainly the Bund) and considerably reduced support for the Folkspartei during the 1930s. Publications: *Folkistishe Heften* (Warsaw), 1932-1933.

Latvia

Kultur Liga (קולטור ליגע), "Culture League," youth movement operated jointly by Poale Zion Smol and the Jewish section of the Latvian Communist party. Although claiming to be a Zionist organization, the league was, in fact, a Communist front organization, Poale Zion Smol's claim to be a Zionist party being very dubious under the circumstances.

Lithuania

Ha-Lishka ha-Shehora (הלשכה השחורה), "The Black Office," unofficial name used for the coalition of Orthodox opponents of Zionism that crystalized around Rabbi Ya'akov Lifshitz and the leader of the Lubavitch Hasidic sect, Reb Shalom Dov Schneerson. Between them, the two leaders represented both the major streams of traditional Orthodoxy in Eastern Europe: the Yeshiva world (Lifshitz) and the Hasidic community (Schneerson). Both opposed Zionism because of its secular and modern nature and both stridently condemned it as a form of false messianism. The organization created by this coalition lasted only two years (1899–1900) being beset by an existential paradox. In order to fight a modernizing movement within the Jewish community the rabbis and their followers had to adopt the tactics used by their opponents. That meant organizing a political party. Yet doing so would legitimize the Zionists' actions and would imply that modernity was not incompatible with a strict life according to Jewish law. The inability to grapple with this paradox led to the office's collapse, but its remnants later joined the groups that would form Agudas Israel in 1912.
> see also: **Organizations, Non-/Anti-Zionist (International, Agudas Israel)**.

Poland

Agudat Ahim (אגודת אחים, AA), "The Brotherhood," assimilationist organization founded in Galicia in 1880 and active throughout Austrian Poland. AA's ideology concentrated on Jewish integration into the Austrian nation and the organization was active in the cultural and educational spheres. Germanizing Galician Jewish culture was expected to facilitate integration and thus ameliorate antisemitism. By the late 1880s AA's assimilationist ideology had run its course. Many student members began to rally around the Hibbat Zion cause and, by 1897, AA ceased to exist.

Agudat ha-Ortodoksim (אגודת האורטודוקסים), "The Orthodox Association," anti-Zionist organization founded in Warsaw in 1916 with the help of German Jewish chaplains. At the time, non-Zionist Orthodox had no modern political organizations and were virtually silent in Jewish communal affairs. Orthodox rabbis serving with the German military copied the model of Agudas Israel (the German Orthodox anti-Zionist organization founded in 1912), incorporating modifications needed to make the organization more appropriate for the Polish context. After World War I, Agudat ha-Ortodoksim merged with the German Agudas Israel to found the international movement known by the latter name. > see also: **Organizations, Non- or Anti-Zionist (International, Agudas Israel).**

Poale Agudas Israel (פועלי אגודת ישראל, PAGI), "Workers Association of Israel," quasi-socialist Orthodox institution founded as a subsidiary of Agudas Israel in Poland in 1922. Although founded as a workers' organization, PAGI was not socialist by any definition of the term. Rather, PAGI called for the use of Halacha (traditional Jewish law) as a means of obtaining social justice for the Jewish proletariat. From its inception, PAGI was interested in building a renewed Jewish *Yishuv* in *Eretz Israel* and thus was more positively oriented toward Zionism than its parent body (and would thus be considered non-Zionist, not anti-Zionist). Due to its uncompromisingly religious nature, PAGI could not (and never did) join the WZO. That said, it should be noted that PAGI cooperated more closely with both the WZO and the JAE than Agudas Israel did throughout the 1930s. Prior to World War II PAGI had spread from Poland to Hungary, Romanian, Czechoslovakia, and France. PAGI opened its own *Hachshara* in Poland in 1923. Ten years later, the first graduates founded *Kibbutz* Hafetz Haim (near Rehovot). The Holocaust drew PAGI closer to the WZO and JAE than ever before: the need to rescue millions of Jews led to cooperation on *Aliya Bet* and on political planning during and after the war. When the State of Israel was established, PAGI joined the provisional government as part of the United Religious Bloc. > see also: **Organizations, Non- or Anti-Zionist (International, Agudas Israel).**

Zjednoczenie, "Unity," assimilationist union composed mainly of Jews who had served in Josef Pilsudski's Polish Legion during World War I. Overwhelmingly middle class, these veterans were steeped in Polish culture and considered themselves patriotic; it followed (in their eyes) that they were "Poles of the Mosaic faith" and not members of a national minority. Politically, the union was aligned with the Polish left, mainly the liberal and social democratic parties (with which Pilsudski was also affiliated at this time). Active between 1915 and 1935, the union collapsed after Pilsudski's death, a period in which antisemitism almost completely dominated Polish-Jewish relations.

Związek Polaków Wyznania Mojżeszowego (ZPWM), "Union of Poles of the Mosaic Faith," assimilationist organization founded in Warsaw as a coalition of three diverse groups: Związek Niezawisłych Żydów (Union of Independent Jews), Kolo Mlodzieży Polskiej im Berka Joselowicza (The Berek Josselowicz Circle of Polish Youth), and Związek Mlodzieży Studenckiej 'Zagiew' (The Zagiew Students' Union). Strongly opposed to Zionism, ZPWM was also opposed to any form of Jewish nationalism and national autonomism. ZPWM was oriented toward an integrationist policy, hoping for emancipation on the Western European model and seeking to define Judaism as a religion only. ZPWM faced increasing difficulty during the 1930s as antisemitism in Poland reached a crescendo, and collapsed altogether on the outbreak of World War II. > see also: **Assimilation; Emancipation**.

Russia/Soviet Union

Algemeiner Yidisher Arbeiterbund in Lita, Poilen un Rusland (אלגעמיינער יידישער ארבייטער באנד אין ליטע, פוילן, און רוסלאנד), "General Jewish Workers' Union in Lithuania, Poland, and Russia," anti-Zionist but nationalistically oriented Jewish socialist party, established in the Russian empire in 1897 and better known by the shortened form of its name, the Bund. The Bund's position on Jewish nationalism underwent a number of transformations prior to 1914. Initially, Bund leaders denied that Jews were a national group, based on a strictly Marxist analysis of nationalism and Jewish history. Later, Bund leaders modified that approach to incorporate the possibility of Jewish cultural nationalism; they then adopted the central theme of Bundist national demands: that Jews be granted cultural and political autonomy in the diaspora. Although nationalist in orientation, the Bund was totally and irreversibly opposed to Zionism, which it saw as a reactionary phase in the development of the Jewish nation. There was, however, an inherent dichotomy in the Bund's philosophy, specifically relating to the attitude toward the Jewish bourgeois. On the one hand, if the Bund saw itself primarily as a nationalist movement, then it had to incorporate the defense of all Jews (regardless of class) into its ideology. In contrast, if the Bund saw itself primarily as a socialist organization, then it had to incorporate class struggle within the Jewish community to eliminate the Jewish bourgeois. This paradox did not become evident until the Bolshevik coup. The Bund in Russia collapsed entirely, integrating into the newly formed Bolshevik regime; Bund branches in interwar Poland and Lithuania grappled with the same problems, however, and eventually came to a nationalist solution to the problem.

Nonetheless, the Bund never abandoned its inherently anti-Zionist position. From Poland and Lithuania, the Bund spread to France, Argentina, and the United States (as the Arbeiter Ring/Workman's Circle). By 1939 there were branches of the Bund or its subsidiary organizations in every country that had a Jewish proletariat (except *Eretz Israel*). World War II destroyed the Bund's European branches, surviving groups integrating into the postwar Communist parties in Eastern Europe, and muted the anti-Zionist stance of the one surviving major Bund branch, that in the United States. > see also: **Doism; Socialism and Zionism; Communism and Zionism; Anti-Zionism; Autonomism; Diaspora Nationalism**.

Evreiskii antifashistkii komitet, "Jewish anti-Fascist Committee" (JAFC), umbrella group created at Joef Stalin's orders in late 1941 as a means to mobilize Jewish support for the USSR in the free world. The JAFC functioned as an ad hoc Jewish communal agency during the war and briefly thereafter. The JAFC was careful to pursue a non-Zionist orientation, although its members supported the theoretical idea of international Jewish solidarity. Despite the JAFC's nonnationalist orientation, it became the focal point for hopes within Soviet Jewry that a postwar national rebirth might be possible. JAFC was forcibly disbanded by the Soviet secret police in 1947 and many of its senior members were imprisoned or killed during a purge in 1947.

Turkey

Mūsevi Uhuvvet Cemiyeti (MUC), "Jewish Brotherhood Society," anti-Zionist association founded in Istanbul in 1909. Reflecting the attitudes of the so-called unionists — Jews who sought to reform the Ottoman Empire and bring about Western European-style emancipation — MUC stridently opposed all aspects of Zionist ideology and activity. Although it was small, MUC was supported by the upper strata of Ottoman Jewry and by most of the rabbis at the empire's center. World War I brought MUC activities to a halt and the organization was not revived in the Turkish republic.

United Kingdom

Anglo-Jewish Association (AJA), non-Zionist communal body established in 1871. Dedicated to the protection of Jewish rights in England and abroad, AJA opposed the hierarchical organization of the Board of Deputies. AJA was a sponsor of the Jewish Colonization Association and was opposed to Zionism, although that opposition moderated slightly in the mid-1930s. Chairman: Leonard Stein (1939–1949). Publications: *AJA Annual Report, AJA Review*.

Jewish Fellowship (JF), anti-Zionist organization established in London on November 7, 1944. Parallel to the American Council for Judaism, JF sought to define Jews exclusively as a religious group and denied the need for a Jewish state. JF collapsed in November 1948, since the newly established State of Israel rendered the political orientation of the JF irrelevant.

Joint Foreign Committee (JFC), popular name for the two committees created by the Anglo-Jewish Association (AJA) and the Board of Deputies of British Jews to assist in carrying out Anglo-Jewry's defense of Jewish rights abroad. The earlier of the two committees, called the Conjoint Foreign Committee (CJC), was founded in 1878, initially to monitor Romanian compliance with the terms of the Treaty of Berlin that resulted in Romanian Jewry's emancipation. CJC collapsed in 1917 over recriminations regarding the publication in the *London Times* of a virulently anti-Zionist letter written by AJA leaders and opposing the Balfour Declaration. The Board of Deputies, which supported the declaration, broke off all relations with the CJC and AJA for the duration of the war. A new committee, dubbed the JFC, was founded in 1933 to monitor the situation in Nazi Germany. The JFC disbanded in 1943 because of disagreements about the Biltmore Resolution. Once again, the AJA took the anti-Zionist position while the Board of Deputies strongly supported the diplomatic maneuvers to create a Jewish state. Relations between the AJA and the Board of Deputies remained strained until after the establishment of the state of Israel.

League of British Jews (LBJ), anti-Zionist organization formed in 1917 to protect British Jews from the accusation of dual loyalty that had been feared by many opponents of the Balfour Declaration. LBJ concentrated on proving that Judaism is a religion only and that Jews share no common bonds of nationality. LBJ's leadership was drawn from amongst the old, elite families traditionally associated with the ruling elements of the Anglo-Jewish community (the so-called cousinhood): Leonard Montefiore, Laurie Magnus, Marcus S. Bearsted (Lord Bearsted), and Samuel Montagu (Lord Swaythling). LBJ ceased to function in 1929 because British acceptance of the League of Nations mandate over Palestine/ *Eretz Israel* made Zionism appear patriotic. However, a similar organization, the Jewish Fellowship, was established in 1944.

United Synagogue (US), communal body created in 1870 to ease the operations of Ashkenazi synagogues in London. Basically US acted as a facilitator to permit synagogues to coordinate fund-raising and other activities. Shortly after its creation, US also became responsible for overseeing selection of the chief rabbi of the British empire and the operations of his various committees and boards. US did not focus on Zionism at all during its early years, and the body took no official position on the subject. This position did not change after the Balfour Declaration: US never operated as a pro-Zionist or as an anti-Zionist organization. This held true despite the prominent role that individual leaders in the US played in the English Zionist Federation and may be attributed to the narrowly construed charter under which US operated. Presidents: Nathan M. Rothschild (1879–1915), Leopold de Rothschild (1915–1917), Lionel de Rothschild (1918–1942), Robert Waley Cohen (1942–1952).

United States

American Council for Judaism (ACJ), anti-Zionist organization established in 1942 by breakaway elements of the Central Council of American Rabbis (CCAR) who opposed the CCAR's stand on the Biltmore Resolution.

ACJ supporters continued to claim that classical Reform Judaism was incompatible with any ideology that viewed Jews as more than a community of faith. They rejected all forms of Jewish nationalism and opposed any action that would draw specific attention to Jews. The ACJ also opposed the creation of a Jewish army to fight the Nazis and did not articulate a specific response to the Nazi murder of European Jewry. Chairmen: Elmer Berger, Lessing Rosenwald. Publication: *Issues* (1946–1969).

American Jewish Committee, self-defense agency founded in 1906. Dedicated to protecting Jewish rights throughout the world. Originally moderately anti-Zionist in its orientation, the committee moved to a non-Zionist position during the 1920s and 1930s. Active in efforts to cancel the White Paper of 1939, the committee opposed Jewish statehood until 1948. Publications: *American Jewish Yearbook* (since 1899), *Contemporary Jewish Record* (1940–1945), *Commentary* (monthly since 1945).

American Jewish Joint Agricultural Corporation (Agro-Joint), subsidiary arm of the American Jewish Joint Distribution Committee (JDC, or Joint), founded in 1924. Dedicated to promoting Jewish agricultural settlements and to aiding in the resettlement of Jewish refugees in the USSR. Agro-Joint was never anti-Zionist in ideology, although in practice its position was closer to that of the territorialists than the Zionists. Agro-Joint operations ceased by order of the Soviet government in 1934, by which time it had settled some 60,000 to 70,000 Jews in collective farms in Crimea and Ukraine.

American Jewish Joint Distribution Committee (JDC, popularly known as the Joint), philanthropic agency founded in 1914. Dedicated to providing aid and assistance to suffering Jews, primarily in Eastern Europe, the JDC also financed Agro-Joint. For most of its history the JDC operated with a non-Zionist orientation that was committed to exclusively legal methods. Nevertheless, JDC was in fact active in building the *Yishuv*, primarily through the semiterritorialist

Palestine Jewish Colonization Association (PICA). When the JA was enlarged in 1929, the JDC received one representative on the JAE, for most of the period from 1929 to 1945 that representative being Dr. Werner D. Senator. During the Holocaust, local JDC representatives continued to funnel resources into Jewish communities, in some cases against explicit JDC orders to desist from "illegal" actions. Simultaneously, the JDC central office in New York was heavily engaged in attempting to promote rescue by seeking havens for Jews throughout the world. After the war, the JDC's position changed from passive to active support for Zionism and the creation of a Jewish state. For example, the JDC provided a considerable proportion of the finances for the Mossad le-Aliya Bet after 1945. Moreover, between 1948 and 1950, the JDC provided the Israeli government with most of the money it obtained to help absorb the massive influx of *olim* from Europe and the Middle East. Publication: *JDC Digest*. > see also: **Territorialism**.

Arbeiter Ring (ארבייטער רינג, AR), "Workman's Circle," Jewish socialist friendly society organized in New York in 1900 as a branch of the Russian Jewish Bund. Mainly dedicated to social welfare and educational activities, AR was less overtly political than its parent body. Additionally, as a friendly society, AR's by-laws permitted members to hold membership in other bodies, including socialist Zionist parties. Still, AR was anti-Zionist at its inception, a policy that began to change during the 1920s. By the 1930s, AR had moved to a non-Zionist position. Officially this remained AR's ideological stance until 1948. In practice, however, AR was a vocal supporter of efforts to create a Jewish state after 1939. This transformation resulted in part from developments in Europe and in part from changes in attitude among AR's rank and file. > see also: **Organizations, Non- or Anti-Zionist (International, Algemeiner Yidisher Arbeiterbund in Lita, Poilen, un Rusland)**.

Federated Council of Palestine Institutions, philanthropic agency established in July 1940 to collect funds for institutions in the *Yishuv* not receiving funds from the WZO. Most funds were raised for religious and other institutions not affiliated with the Knesset Israel.

Freiland League for Territorial Settlement, anti-Zionist settlement organization founded in 1941. Dedicated to the acquisition of territory for large-scale Jewish colonization, primarily in southern Africa or Australia. Publication: *Oifn Shvel*.

Jewish Labor Committee (JLC), American Jewish socialist organization founded in New York in 1934. JLC was an amalgamation of elements of the Bund, Poale Zion Smol (technically a Zionist party, but in many cases only nominally so), and unaffiliated American Jewish Socialists. JLC was created shortly after the Nazi *Machtergreifung* in Germany and the organization was rapidly immersed in efforts to rescue enemies of the fascist regime: Jews, socialists, and pacifists. Despite Bundist influence on JLC, the latter was never anti-Zionist in its orientation. To the contrary, JLC closely cooperated with American Zionist organizations in the ant-Nazi boycott, in the World Jewish Congress, and in the Conference of Jewish Organizations. JLC was non-Zionist in its orientation until the 1940s. After joining the American Jewish Conference in 1943, JLC began to work for the establishment of a Jewish state in *Eretz Israel*.

Orthodoxy and Zionism: > see also: **Judaism and Zionism**.

Oscar [PN]: Mossad le-Aliya Bet code term used after World War II to designate (1) The city of Berlin; (2) the Soviet zone of occupation in Germany, (3) Poland, and (4) the Mossad's main office in Paris (1947–1948). The frame of reference and derivation for the term are unknown. Indeed, it is not clear if the designations were used simultaneously and, if they were, how users distinguished one meaning from the other. > see also: **Aliya Bet**.

Ostjuden [G] "Eastern Jews": Derisive German Jewish term for Jews originating in Eastern Europe. The term was supposed to distinguish between "cultured" German Jews and the newer immigrants who were accused of causing antisemitism. > see also: **Yahudim**.

Oxfords: Popular name for a group of twenty-nine Oxford University theological students and faculty who helped to defend Jerusalem during the Arab riots of 1929. The students, who were visiting the Middle East as part of their course of study, were deputized by the regional commissioner for Jerusalem shortly after the riots broke out. He feared that an insufficient number of police and troops were available and had called on all English citizens to volunteer to help the defense forces. The Oxfords, who had brought automobiles with them, were issued firearms and formed a mobile patrol in the streets of Jerusalem. > see also: **Me'oraot**.

Packing Up [E]: Term popular among Royal Army officers in Palestine during the summer of 1947. The term implied the British intention to get out of the territory no matter what the U.N. decision on Palestine/*Eretz Israel* would be. > see also: **Committees of Investigation, UNSCOP**.

Palästina Amt [G] "Palestine Office": Term for the local office of the WZO or JA within a Jewish community, often abbreviated as Palamt. The first such office was established in Warsaw, Poland, in 1917, as a means of having permanent supervision of the practical components of Zionist work — distribution of immigrant certificates — in each community. After World War I ended, the Warsaw model was copied by all other WZO/JA regional offices. The Palamt, in turn, supervised nationwide Zionist activities and oversaw the actions of provincial branch offices (fifty-four such offices existed in Poland, for example). Positions in each office were offered on the basis of a party key, with local modifications to account for specific conditions in each country. Broadly, the Palamt undertook five activities: (1) distributing *aliya* certificates, (2) facilitating *Hachsharot* or other training facilities in cooperation with he-Halutz, (3) registering technical workers who wished to emigrate, (4) recruiting so-called capitalists for investment in the *Yishuv* or *aliya*, and, (5) training prospective *olim* in Hebrew and other skills that would be useful after their *aliya*. Almost all of the Palämter in Europe were closed as a result of World War II, but those in Western and Central Europe resumed operation in 1945.

Pale of Settlement [HT]: Common name for the territory, including a total of twenty-five provinces, in czarist Russia to which Jews were restricted by decree of Czarina Catherine II in 1794. The pale's borders included (roughly) Poland, Lithuania, Belorussia, Ukraine, Crimea, and Bessarabia. Jewish residence outside the pale was limited to certain groups of so-called productive Jews; they could live outside the Pale only with special permission. In 1882, Jewish residence rights were further restricted — they were expelled from a number of cities, from the border regions, and from most rural areas. Residency restrictions for Jews were effectively terminated when World War I broke out and the Pale of Settlement was abolished altogether in 1917. > see also: **Sufot Ba-Negev; May Laws**.

Palestine Conciliation Commission (PCC): International committee created on December 4, 1948, by the U.N. General Assembly and tasked with seeking a means to end Israel's War of Independence. Chaired by American representative Ralph Bunche, the PCC failed at its main mission despite a flurry of activity after hostilities ceased in 1949. In particular, the PCC sought to bring the two sides together for a conference in Lausanne, Switzerland, in order to replace the armistice agreements with a

Set of British-Issued Postage Stamps for Use in Palestine/*Eretz Israel*. The Legend
Bearing the Term (in Hebrew Only) is On the Lower Left Hand Corner of Each Stamp.
Authors' Collection

comprehensive peace treaty. Theoretically, the PCC still exists, even though its last meeting was held in Lausanne on October 2, 1962. > see also: **United Nations; War of Independence; Conferences, International, Lausanne Conference**.

Palestine/Eretz Israel [פלשתינה/ארץ ישראל, H/E]: Full formal name for mandatory Palestine used on all official documents, including currency and postage stamps, produced during the mandatory era. All documents contained the word "Palestine" in English, Hebrew, and Arabic; the abbreviation for Eretz Israel (E.I.) was used only in the Hebrew name. > see also: **Mandate, League of Nations**.

Palestine Express [Slang]: Nickname for the underground escape organization operating in Paris led by Haim Victor Gerson, who was code named "Captain Vic" by the British. The name derived from the fact that Gerson and many of his agents were active Zionists, a fact that they pointed out

in an especially glaringly way to all British airmen whom they helped to escape. The Nazis made an all-out effort to capture Gerson and succeeded in capturing some of the members of the organization. Nonetheless, Gerson eluded the Gestapo and the "express" continued to operate until liberated in 1944.

Panama Scandal [HT]: Name of the antisemitic scandal that developed in France in 1892. The Panama Society, created in 1869 to build a canal between the Atlantic and Pacific Oceans across the isthmus of Panama, went bankrupt. The Society's failure was blamed on Jewish financiers, even though the Society had not permitted Jews to purchase stock in the corporation. Antisemitic and clerical press in France continued to blame the corporation's mismanagement on Jews. This scandal was replaced in popular imagination by accusations of treason leveled at Captain Alfred Dreyfus. > see also: **Dreyfus Affair**.

Parallel Immigration [slang]: Hagana code term for *Aliya Bet* used after 1938 for the activities of the Mossad le-Aliya Bet. The term was used to reflect the parallel between legal and illegal immigration. > see also: **Aliya Bet**.

Paratroopers, Palestinian

1. Scope and Definition

As early as November and December 1942, the Jewish Agency Executive and the leadership of the Hagana and Palmah advocated using military means to rescue European Jewry. Thus, for example, a defense plan was proposed in 1944 under which Jewish volunteers would be infiltrated into northern Romania to form a guarded camp for Jews escaping the Nazi death machine. Since the Hagana lacked the resources to carry out the mission alone, approval and support had to come from the British or the Americans, neither of whom were willing to sponsor such a mission. Shortly after the defense plan was canceled, however, the British Inter-Service Liaison Detachment (ISLD), an arm of the Special Intelligence Service, approached the JAE with a proposal to train a group of volunteers who would be deployed in the Balkans on espionage and other missions. Additionally, ISLD agreed that the paratroopers would be able to fulfill their Jewish and Zionist missions in terms of rescuing Jewish survivors.

Of two hundred fifty volunteers, the thirty-two were chosen. The majority of members came from the German and Balkan sections of the Palmah, composed almost entirely of Jewish refugees and recent *olim* living in the *Yishuv*. Of those sent to Europe, twelve fell into Nazi hands; seven of them died in captivity or were executed as spies. Although the mission of the paratroopers thus did not live up to either its military or rescue potential, it did serve as an important rallying point for European Jews. It proved that despite the apathy of the world, one group — the *Yishuv* — cared enough to risk life and limb to rescue even a remnant. Since the end of World War II, the mission of the paratroops has attained near legendary status in Israel and among Jewish communities throughout the world. > see also: **Yishuv**.

TABLE P.1: The Paratroopers and Their Missions

Barberman, Sara (Yugoslavia)	Kanner, Uriel (Romania)
Ben-Ephraim, Yitzhak (Romania)	Laner, Dan (Austria)
Ben-Yaakov, Zvi (Slovakia)	Lupsko, Ricco (Romania)
Ben-Yosef, Aaron (Bulgaria)	Mekarisko, Yitzhak (Romania)
Berdicev, Abba (Slovakia)	Nussbacher (Palgi), Joel (Hungary)
Berger, Dov (Romania)	Reik, Haviva (Slovakia)
Dafni, Efra (Italy)	Reis, Raphael (Slovakia)
Dafni, Reuven (Yugoslavia)	Rosenberg, Peretz (Yugoslavia)
Doroguer, Zadok (Italy)	Rosenfeld, Yona (Yugoslavia)
Finzi, Shalom (Yugoslavia)	Sereni, Haim Enzio (Italy)
Fishman, Arye (Romania)	Szenes, Hannah (Hungary)
Gokowski, Lova (Romania)	Testa, Nessim (Yugoslavia)
Goldstein, Peretz (Hungary)	Trachtenberg, Szaika (Romania)
Jablodowski, Rehavam (Yugoslavia)	Varon, Yosef (Bulgaria)
Kamacz, Haim (Slovakia)	Wilander, Haim (Austria)
Kaminker, Baruch (Romania)	Zohar, Eli (Yugoslavia)

Source: Hagana History Archive (ATH), Paratrooper Collection

Labels Issued To Honor the Seven Jewish Paratroopers Who Fell During World War II.
Authors' Collection

2. The Seven Who Fell

Ben-Ya'akov, Zvi (1922–1944), captured near Banska Bystrica, Slovakia, October 30, 1944; executed by the Gestapo at Kremnica.

Berdicev, Abba (1918–1944), killed near Bratislava, Slovakia, while trying to lead a group of escaped Allied prisoners of war to safety.

Goldstein, Peretz (1923–1944), captured crossing the Hungarian border and deported to KL Oranienburg, where he was executed under the Nacht und Nebel Erlass.

Reik, Haviva (1914–1944), captured near Banska Bystrica, Slovakia, October 30, 1944, and executed by the Gestapo at Kremnica.

Reis, Raphael (1914–1944), captured near Banska Bystrica, Slovakia, October 30, 1944, and executed by the Gestapo at Kremnica.

Sereni, Haim Enzio (1905–1944), captured in Tuscany, Italy, May 15, 1944, and deported to Mauthausen, where he was executed on November 18, 1944, under the Nacht und Nebel Erlass.

Szenes, Hannah (1921–1944), captured June 7, 1944, and executed after a trial for treason in Budapest on November 7, 1944.

Parosh [פרעוש, H] "Flea": popular name for the Israeli-manufactured copy of the British 2-inch mortar that was the standard infantry support weapon during Israel's War of Independence. Manufactured by the same factory that turned out the Davidka, the Parosh was a better weapon but suffered from many of the defects that plagued the Davidka, mainly poor manufacturing quality and poor ammunition. These reduced overall effectiveness, even though the weapon was basically sound and was less prone to explode during use than the Davidka. > see also: **Davidka**.

Parrout présent et faire face [Fr] "Be present everywhere and stand up": Armée Juive motto, coined by David Knout, one of the founders of the underground. As teacher and ideologue for the Jewish resistance in France, Knout felt that the underground served a role beside fighting the Nazis. That role, as expressed in this motto, was to foster a sense of Jewish solidarity and a willingness to become involved in Jewish communal affairs.

Parteitag [G] "Party Day": Term for a local Zionist conference used in German-speaking countries. Such conferences were constituted when needed to decide issues specifically facing the local organizations. A Parteitag was an authoritative forum for regional decision-making, since the WZO tried not to interfere in local Zionist affairs. > see also: **Conferences, Zionist**; **Jahreskonferenz**; **Landesverbände**.

Partition Plans

1. Scope and Definition

Although early Zionist plans for Palestine/ *Eretz Israel* had presumed that the entire land, including Trans-Jordan, would be available for mass Jewish settlement, demographic realities, specifically the presence of a large Arab population, meant that the goal of a complete land of Israel under Jewish control could not be realized immediately. Furthermore, the wording of the Balfour Declaration could be taken to imply that the British did not promise all of *Eretz Israel* to the Jews and the territory could be partitioned to satisfy the needs of its two nationalities.

Partition as a solution to the Arab-Israeli conflict was tried twice, in 1936–1937 and in 1947–1948. On both occasions, Jews reluctantly accepted partition while Arabs rejected out of hand any plan that included a Jewish state. In addition, plans short of partition — mainly recommending that Palestine/*Eretz Israel* be divided into autonomous cantons — were also recommended. However, no plan for cantonization ever reached the advanced planning stage. > see also: **Committees of Investigation**; **Repeal Commission**; **United Nations**.

2. Major Partition Plans

Peel plan, proposed by the Palestine Royal Commission (the Peel Commission) on July 7, 1937, divided *Eretz Israel* into three zones: a Jewish state stretching from Tel Aviv northward to Haifa with an attached zone in the lower Galilee, an Arab state that was to include upper Galilee, Samaria, Judea (less Jerusalem) and the Negev, and a British enclave including Jerusalem and a path to Jaffa (which was included in the Arab state). The plan collapsed due to Arab unwillingness to negotiate and the tenuous nature of the proposed borders, which were rejected by Jews and Arabs alike.

TABLE P.2: Votes on the Partition Debate at the 20th Zionist Congress

Party	Yes	No	Abstained	Total
Mapai	181	0	1	182
General Zionists A	79	20	4	103
Mizrachi	0	66	0	66
General Zionists B	10	28	1	39
Ha-Shomer ha-Zair	0	23	0	23
Jewish State Party	0	9	0	9
Others/Unknown	18	6	0	24
TOTAL	288	152	6	446

Source: *Protocols of the Twentieth Zionist Congress* (Jerusalem: World Zionist Organization, 1937).

Woodhead Commission, Plan C, proposed as the minority proposal of the Palestine Partition Commission (the Woodhead Commission) on November 9, 1938, the proposal divided Palestine/*Eretz Israel* into three zones: a Jewish state stretching from Tel Aviv to Haifa, an Arab state in Samaria, Judea (less Jerusalem), and Gaza from the Egyptian border to Jaffa (inclusive), and British zones in the Galilee, Jerusalem, and the Negev.

UNSCOP Plan, proposed by the U.N. Special Committee on Palestine and approved by the U.N. General Asembly on November 29, 1947, the plan divided Palestine/*Eretz Israel* into three zones: (1) a Jewish state stretching along the coastal plain from Tel Aviv to Haifa, the lower Galilee, and the Negev; (2) an Arab state in Judea, Samaria, upper Galilee (including Acre), and the coastal plain from Gaza to Jaffa; and (3) an international enclave in Jerusalem to be under U.N. control. > see also: **Bernadotte Plan; United Nations.**

Patria Incident [HT]: Popular name for the tragic *Aliya Bet*–related incident in Haifa Bay in November 1940. Over the course of a few weeks, three Mossad le-Aliya Bet blockade runners — the S.S. *Atlantic*, *Pacific*, and *Milos* — were captured and their *Ma'apilim* were interned. Some 1,800 of the *Ma'apilim* (from the *Pacific* and *Milos*) were transferred to the S.S. *Patria*, a French ship chartered by the British

government, prior to their transfer to the Mauritius Islands. In order to prevent the deportation, the Hagana smuggled explosives aboard the Patia. The plan was to disable the engines in the hope that the deportation order would be canceled. However, the Hagana sappers who planted the explosives miscalculated conditions on board the Patria. Instead of sinking slowly in shallow water, with little or no loss of life, the ship broke in two and sank rapidly. An estimated 760 *Ma'apilim* perished when the ship went down. The survivors were indeed permitted to remain in Palestine/*Eretz Israel* — they were interned in the Atlit Prison until their release over the course of 1941. The *Atlantic Ma'apilim*, who had not been transferred to the *Patria*, were deported to Mauritius on December 9, 1940, remaining there until released (and permitted to immigrate legally) in 1945. >see also: **Aliya Bet; Mauritius, Expulsions; Aliya.**

Patriotic Zionism: English Zionist concept dating to the 1920s and attempting to obtain support for Zionist goals within the wider, non-Jewish community. Hoping to attract support, Zionists argued that Zionism was nothing or anything less than a Jewish means to guarantee Britain's wider imperial interests. Although popular among some Gentile Zionists in the 1920s, by the mid-1930s Arab resistance to Jewish immigration proved the concept fallacious and brought about a very wide divergence between Jewish and British interests in the Middle East. >see also: **Gentile Zionism.**

Peel Commission [PN]: Popular name for the Palestine Royal Commission formed in 1936 and named after its chairman, Sir William R. Peel. > See also: **Committees of Investigation, Palestine Royal Committee**.

Philanthropic Zionism [slang]: Derisive term used by Zionist radicals to condemn the timidity of their middle-of-the-road adversaries, generally before World War I. When first used, the term was an attack on those who felt that creating a Jewish national home was a good idea for certain "other" (i.e., Eastern European) Jews but not for themselves. The radicals thus accused them of reducing Zionism to the act of "one Jew collecting money from a second Jew to send a third Jew to Palestine." In the interwar era the term changed to a condemnation of those Zionists who seemed to argue that token financial contribution absolved them from any other activity on behalf of threatened Jewry. > see also: **Ostjuden; Diplomatic Zionism**.

Philby Plan [PN]: Common name for a diplomatic scheme to solve the Palestine impasse associated with British orientalist Henry St. John Philby. First proposed in 1937, the Philby plan anticipated the creation of an Arab federation including Iraq, Syria, and Trans-Jordan that would also include the Arab portion(s) Palestine and would be under the tutelage of King ibn Saud (of Saudi Arabia). Under this scheme, Jews would be permitted continued *aliya* but would give up any demands for sovereignty outside of those parts of Palestine/*Eretz Israel* in which they were the majority. Proposed repeatedly by Philby, especially during World War II, the plan (with sufficient modifications to allow considerably more *aliya* than Philby had anticipated) briefly gained the support of Prime Minister Winston S. Churchill. Arab refusal to compromise on even the small territory that Jews controlled led to the collapse of negotiations in late 1943. Some elements of the plan, notably the idea of an Arab federation, were retained in later British (and

American) initiatives in the Middle East.

Phoenician Zionism [HT]: Term used by some Lebanese Maronite Christians during the 1930s and 1940s to characterize their nationalist movement. The Maronites hoped to convert Lebanon into Christian enclave (in their view parallel to Jewish attempts to convert Palestine/*Eretz Israel* into a Jewish enclave) in order to protect their interest. In 1945–1946 it appeared that a Lebanese-Israeli alliance might be created, but this did not come to fruition.

Pinsker [פינסקר, GN] "The (man from) Pinsk": Irgun Zvai Leumi code term for Chaim Weizmann, used after World War II, and deriving from Weizmann's birthplace. Ironically, although this usage was derogatory, Pinsker also recalled one of the founders of Hibbat Zion (Leon Pinsker) and thus could be construed as a back handed compliment.

Pittsburgh Platform [GN]: Official name for the November 18, 1885, statement of policy by the Union of American Hebrew Congregations (UAHC), the rabbinic body of the Reform movement in the United States. The platform contained the first systematic formulation of American Reform Judaism. Inter alia, the platform unequivocally rejected the idea that Jews constitute a nation and thus became the central basis for anti-Zionism within the Reform movement. > See also: **Judaism and Zionism, Reform Judaism; Anti-Zionism**.

Pittsburgh Program [GN]: Popular name for the program of Zionist work adopted by the annual conference of the Federation of American Zionists on June 25, 1918. The program proposed concentrating on practical Zionist development designed to promote Jewish settlement in *Eretz Israel*. Additionally, the platform called upon Zionists to undertake systematic settlement work, unlike the haphazard settlement building of the previous thirty years, since the Balfour Declaration promised assistance in promoting the Zionist cause. Although there was very little in the platform that could be viewed as controversial (indeed the platform was unanimously adopted by the WZO executive at the London conference in 1920) it prefigured the later dispute between Louis D. Brandeis and Chaim Weizmann. Inplicit in concentrating on the practical Zionist agenda was the virtual abandonment of all (or most) political work. > see also: **Zeeland Program**.

Plishtim [פלישתים, H] "Philistines": Hagana code term for homemade armored cars. The term derives from the biblical verse "and they had iron chariots" (Judges 1:19). Although the verse does not refer directly to the Philistines, this was a popular association in the *Yishuv* at the time. In 1948 all such vehicles were renamed "sandwich cars." > see also: **Sandvitchim**.

Plugot ha-Esh [פלוגות האש, H] "Fire Companies": Another Yishuv term for the Special Night Squads, commanded and led by Captain Orde Charles Wingate. > see also: **Special Night Squads**; **Ha-Yedid**.

Pogrom [R] "Attack": Commonly used term for physical attacks on Jews, usually accompanied by the destruction of property, murder, and rape, especially the physical attacks visited upon Jews in czarist — and revolutionary — Russia and Eastern Europe since 1881. Historians have noted three eras of pogroms in Russia: (1) 1881–1884, after Narodnik terrorists assassinated Czar Alexander II; (2) 1903–1906, when the Russian government used pogroms as a means to release revolutionary tensions building up in Russian society; and (3) 1919–1921, when dislocations caused by the Russian civil war permitted Russians, especially those associated with the counterrevolutionary "Whites," to act without fear of arrest. Since 1921, the term has meant any attack on Jews, systematic or spontaneous, in any country. Interwar Poland was particularly prone to spontaneous pogroms, very often started when members of Endecja student groups attempted to force Jewish students in the Polish universities to sit on "ghetto benches." The systematic Nazi assault on German

Jewry during the night of November 9–10, 1938 (Kristallnacht) is possibly the best-known pogrom of the twentieth century. In addition, the Nazis used pogroms, especially in occupied Soviet territory, as a cover for murder operations against Jews. Pogroms were also encountered in postwar Poland and other parts of Eastern Europe, when a handful of survivors sought to return to their former homes. > see also: **Sufot ba-Negev**; **Briha**.

Polani [פולני, H] "(The) Pole": Hagana code term for Menahem Begin during his tenure as head of the Irgun Zvai Leumi. The term was derived from Begin's birthplace and from his service with the Polish army in exile prior to his arrival in Palestine/*Eretz Israel* in 1942. The term may also have been used to designate Irgun members who were thus the "Pole's men." > see also: **Yishuv, Yishuv Organizations (Underground Organizations, Irgun Zvai Leumi)**; **World War II**.

Political Maximum: Term used by the British to refer to the maximum number of Jewish immigrants who would be allowed into Palestine/*Eretz Israel* regardless of the country's economic absorptive capacity. The political maximum was unofficially instituted in 1937 as a means of quieting Palestine's Arabs, who were then involved in a general revolt against the League of Nations mandate, by controlling more carefully the main source of Arab unrest, mass *aliya*. The policy became official in 1938, to the intense dismay of Zionists seeking relief for the massive refugee crisis in Europe. The political maximum was never framed as anything but subjective, being the number of Jewish immigrants that the high commissioner estimated Arabs would be willing to tolerate. The policy was a complete failure, since the Arabs were unwilling to tolerate any *aliya* while Jews complained that the political maximum was inconsistent with the terms and spirit of the mandate. Nevertheless, the concept was written into the British White Paper of 1939, which permitted only 75,000 Jewish immigrants in the next five years. > see also: **Aliya**; **Economic Absorptive Capacity**; **Mandatory Palestine**; **White Papers**; **Aliya Bet**.

Politicide [L/E] "Destruction of a Polity": Term popular among political scientists for Arab policy toward Israel — complete annihilation. This could easily also be said to have been the Arabs' principle response to Zionism, echoing the Mufti's infamous call to "throw the Jews into the sea." > see also: **Arabs; Jihad; Mufti of Jerusalem.**

Porshim [פורשים, H] "Dissidents": Common term used during the 1940s by the JA, the Hagana, and (especially) the Palmah to refer to the Irgun Zvai Leumi and Lohame Herut Israel. The latter two movements were considered dissident insofar as they did not operate under JA command and were considered "irresponsible" in their acts of anti-British resistance. The term also reflects the intense disagreement over Zionist tactics that divided the Zionist underground movements, despite the short-term unity created when the Tenuat ha-Meri ha-Ivri existed in 1945–1946. > see also: **Yishuv, Organizations (Underground Movements).**

Prager Richtung [G] "Prague Orientation": Term for the Czech-style Zionist politics that became dominant within the WZO between Theodor Herzl's death 1904 and World War I. Though known by its Czech name, this style of Zionist politics was popular among all Central European Zionists, especially the German Zionists. The Prague orientation primarily emphasized the cultural and spiritual aspects of Zionism and, relatively speaking, deemphasized the political element. Additionally, the Prague orientation placed special emphasis on Gegenwartsarbeit, — work on behalf of diaspora Jewry (pending progress on long-term Zionist goals) — as a means of gaining communal support for the WZO. > see also: **Gegenwartsarbeit; Conquest of Communities.**

Productivization [HT]: Term associated with the socioeconomic reforms proposed by nineteenth-century Jewish activists, both nationalist and nonnationalist. Basing their analysis on populist concepts that had recently become popular, advocates of productivization claimed that Jews were in an odd economic position. Whereas in most countries, a majority of workers tilled the soil, almost no Jews did so; conversely, few members of most "normal" nations worked in commerce, but most East European Jews worked in some form of commerce. Put differently, these advocates distinguished between a primary economy, in which the worker produced actual goods, and a secondary economy, in which the worker marketed goods someone else produced. The former was viewed as "healthy," whereas the latter was viewed as essentially unhealthy. As a result of this type of advocacy, virtually every strain of Jewish nationalism included some form of proposal for productivization via a Jewish return to the soil. Incidentally, the same held true for many assimilationist proposals to reform Russian Jewry before and after World War I. As late as the 1930s the American Jewish Joint Distribution Committee's Agro-Joint subsidiary was financing Jewish agricultural settlements in the Crimea and Ukraine as a way to productivize Soviet Jewry and enlarge Jewish settlement areas. Zionism — especially labor Zionism — placed great emphasis on productivization through a return to the soil. From 1881 onward, the first priority for Zionists was the creation of agricultural settlements by hardworking *Halutzim* who tilled the soil and thus would lead to the Jewish national rebirth. > see also: **Agricultural Settlement(s); Halutz; Halutzic Aliya; Zionut.**

Proportional Representation: Electoral system whereby voters vote for a party list rather than for a specific candidate. Under such a system each party submits a list of candidates and votes are tallied for all parties. The percentage of total votes received by the party (with fractions decided by a key) is the percentage of representatives that the party has in the elected body. This system was used in the Weimar Republic and in pre- (and post-) Fascist Italy. It has also been used by the WZO and, more significantly, in the *Yishuv* for elections to the Va'ad Leumi. Although democratic in nature, proportional representation tends to encourage factionalism within parties and gives a disproportionate strength to marginal parties. Absolute majorities are very hard obtain under proportional representation, giving smaller parties great power in making or breaking coalition governments. Proportional representation was (and is) used for parliamentary elections in Israel since 1948 although in 1992 the Knesset (parliament) passed a bill for the direct election of prime ministers beginning with the 1996 elections. > see also: **Shekel**.

Protestrabbiner [G] "Protest Rabbis": Term used by Theodor Herzl to signify those German rabbis whose intense anti-Zionism forced him to change the locale for the First Zionist Congress from Munich to Basel. The rabbis, mostly members of the Reform movement, claimed that Zionism was antithetical to Judaism and would also increase antisemitism by raising the specter of Jewish "dual loyalty." After 1897 this position was consolidated within the Reform movement, a position that changed only in the 1930s. > see also: **Religion and Zionism**.

Protokolle der Weissen von Zion [G] "The Protocols of the Elders of Zion": Infamous antisemitic forgery produced by the czarist secret police and first published in 1911. The text purports to be the protocol of a secret meeting held during the First World Zionist Congress and is variously attributed to Theodor Herzl or the Rothschild or Bleichröder families. The speaker details a conspiracy to use liberalism and communism as means to attain Jewish domination of the entire world. The text was reprinted in many different editions and languages. The German and English editions were probably the most influential. In recent years, an Arabic edition has been published by the Saudi Arabian government.

Proto-Zionism [HT]:

1. Scope and Definition

Term used to represent early, mostly utopian, schemes for the return of Jews to the Land of Israel. The term also covers thinkers (known ex post facto as proto-Zionists) who proposed such schemes. By and large, historians use the term to refer to all Zionist schemes prior to Theodor Herzl's publications of the *Der Judenstaat* in 1896. The unifying factor in historians' understanding of proto-Zionism is that these proposals were either impractical, not widely disseminated in the Jewish world, or both. An argument could be made, of course, to remove Leon Pinsker, author of *Auto-Emancipation* (1882), from the category of proto-Zionist, since the movement he created was neither utopian nor esoteric.

In general, proto-Zionism is viewed as a precursor of the Zionist movement. Authors of proto-Zionist schemes are viewed as visionaries who (well before such ideas gained currency even within the Jewish world) saw that only a return to Jewish nationalism could offer a response to the malaise faced by Judaism and Jewry in the postemancipation era. Perhaps even more than the mainstream Zionist movements (as developed after 1897), proto-Zionists appear heavily influenced by the rise of nationalism in Central and Eastern Europe during the mid-nineteenth century while also seeking a response to a general crisis of Jewish identity once religion ceased to act as a unifying force within the Jewish community.

To admit that proto-Zionist schemes failed to influence Jewish political efforts in their own era is not to deprecate the importance of such schemes. Historians have long noted that a visionary message needs both a messenger and a community prepared to act on the message. Clearly, as long as hopes for individual salvation through emancipation animated the majority of Jewish public discourse, any Zionist message was premature. But, in the aftermath of the pogroms of 1881–1884 and the rise of antisemitism in Central and Western Europe, a Zionist message was no longer premature. > see also: **Hibbat Zion; Emancipation; Zionut; Nationalism**.

2. Major Proto-Zionist Thinkers

Noah, Mordechai M. (1785–1851), American Jewish public figure. In 1825, Noah proposed the creation of a Jewish colony in northern

New York, an area he dubbed Ararat. The project failed to interest Jewish financiers in Europe, after which Noah turned to proposals for Jewish restoration in *Eretz Israel*.

Alkali, Yehuda (1798–1878), rabbi in Sarajevo and Semlin (then part of Ottoman Turkish–controlled Serbia). In his 1841 book *Minhat Yehuda*, he proposed that Jews had to begin the process of redemption by themselves, after which they would receive divine assistance.

Kalischer, Zvi Hirsch (1795–1874), rabbi in Posen (Prussian Poland). In 1863, Kalischer published *Drishat Zion*, a call for Jews to return to Israel. His main argument that Jews should defend their ancestral homeland as zealously as Polish nationalists defended theirs. Interestingly, Kalischer's plan included some aspects later used by Pinsker and Herzl, specifically, that Jews should create an international fund-raising agency to collect sufficient funds to purchase *Eretz Israel* from the Ottoman Porte.

Hess, Moses (1812–1875), German socialist activist who abandoned Jewish interests during his early adult years. Hess later returned to Judaism and in *Rome and Jerusalem* (1862) suggested that Jews return to Israel in order to create a model society that would be a "light for all the nations."

Schlesinger, Akiva Joseph (1837–1922), Hungarian rabbi and communal leader. In 1870 Schlesinger immigrated to *Eretz Israel* and shortly thereafter began to evolve a series of proposals for the restoration of Jewish sovereignty in the Holy Land. By doing so, he hoped to reverse the trend toward religious reform and assimilation among European Jewry. Among his most important ideas was the emphasis on Jewish agricultural settlement in *Eretz Israel*. Schlesinger opposed the secular trend in the WZO and supported efforts by religious Jews to create their own settlements.

Smolenskin, Peretz (1842–1885), Russian Jewish literary figure. One of the most prolific publicists of the Russian Haskala, Smolenskin broke with the emancipation idea and suggested a broadly Zionist notion in his anthology *Et li-Zroa* (*A Time to Plant*, 1881) published during the pogroms in Russia.

Publications

1. Scope and Definition

The Jewish world has been served by an extensive press network over the last century. Literally thousands of periodicals have been published in every venue in which an organized Jewish community exists or existed. Within the pages of these publications major issues affecting Jewry were reported, debated, or proposed. Periodicals could be found to suit almost every political orientation that was represented, on a local or national level, within the community. Given the nature of the subject, it is virtually impossible to review all the Zionist press, let alone the entire gamut of Jewish press and publications. What follows is a brief selection with all data available about some key publications given in detail. Readers should note that this listing supplements the one provided in *History of the Holocaust: A Handbook and Dictionary* (Boulder: Westview Press, 1994), which should also be consulted. In this list, as in the earlier one, Hebrew transliterations of titles have been provided only if the periodical was published in Hebrew or bore a Hebrew title on the cover.

2. Zionist

Argentina

Davar (דבר), "The Word," literary monthly published by the Hebrew language society of Buenos Aires between 1945 and 1970. Primarily focused on educational and cultural issues, mainly of a Zionist nature, after 1948, the journal appeared in a bilingual Hebrew/Spanish format.

Eretz Israel (ארץ ישראל), "The Land of Israel," illustrated bulletin of Keren ha-Yesod in Argentina, published in Buenos Aires between 1943 and 1960. *Eretz Israel* was the first fully illustrated, full-color Jewish magazine published in Latin America and its circulation spanned the entire continent. Concentrating on Jewish issues, the magazine's content was mainly focused on developments in the *Yishuv* and, after 1948, in the State of Israel. Stress was placed equally on political, social, and intellectual developments.

Di Idishe Tseitung (די ײדישע צײטונג, DIZ), "The Jewish Newspaper," Yiddish language daily newspaper published in Buenos Aires between 1914 and 1973. Zionist in orientation, DIZ operated as a nonpartisan forum for Jewish concerns. Content was of high quality and DIZ was considered the most influential Jewish periodical in all of Latin America. Publication ceased after a majority of Argentine Jews stopped reading Yiddish; the community could no longer sustain a daily newspaper in that language.

Widerkol (װידערקאל), "The Echo," short-lived independent Zionist weekly of which only three issues appeared in March 1898. *Widerkol* had the distinction of being the first Jewish periodical published in Argentina and bore a clearly Zionist editorial line. Financial difficulties terminated the journal after less than a month of publication. Sole editor: Michael ha-Cohen Sinai.

Di Yiddishe Hofnung (די ײדישע האפנונג, DYH), "The Jewish Hope," Yiddish fortnightly published in Buenos Aires beginning in 1908. Initially published as an independent Zionist journal, DYH was taken over by the Argentine Zionist federation in 1917 as a replacement for the defunct *Der Zionist*. DYH's periodicity then changed to weekly and the title was changed (in early 1918) to *Di Yiddishe Velt* (די ײדישע װעלט, The Jewish World). The journal has continued to appear under that title.

Der Zionist (דער ציוניסט, DZ), "The Zionist," official organ of the Argentine Zionist federation, published biweekly in Buenos Aires between 1900 and 1914. General Zionist in orientation, DZ also included considerable news content on events in the Jewish world as a whole. Between 1904 and 1906, a Spanish edition appeared under the title *El Sionista*. The Spanish edition did not generate enough circulation and was quickly terminated. Publication of DZ ceased just before World War I for financial reasons. Although efforts

to revive DZ were apparently made during the war, none came to fruition. Sole editor: Jacobo S. Liachovitzki.

Other Argentine Zionist Publications:
Das Arbeiterwort (Buenos Aires), Yiddish, Weekly, 1924–1930.
Mundo Israelita (Buenos Aires), Spanish, Weekly, 1923–1949.
Die Naje Zeit (Buenos Aires), Yiddish, Monthly, 1919–1968.

Australia

Jewish Herald (JH), independent fortnightly published in Melbourne (with an edition appearing in Sydney as well) between 1879 and 1968. Initially published as a monthly, JH built up a sufficient circulation early in its publishing run to switch to a fortnightly format in 1884. Widely disseminated throughout Australia, JH also served the Jewish communities of Australasia and South-East Asia, notably New Zealand, Singapore, and Hong Kong. In 1920, the title changed to *Australian Jewish Herald* (AJH). Two orientations dominated the JH/AJH editorial line for its entire history: modern orthodoxy and Zionism. The latter was especially important since JH/AJH —— despite a fling with territorialism in 1904 —— did not deviate from its Zionist position for nearly sixty years. AJH's unwavering support for Zionism and the WZO was especially important during the period between 1939 and 1948.

Austria

Ha-Shahar (השחר), "The Dawn," Hebrew annual published in Vienna between 1868 and 1884. Oriented toward the concerns of Eastern European Jews and published on their behalf, the journal developed a Zionist orientation after the pogroms of 1881–1882. Sole editor: Peretz Smolenskin.

Jerusalem (ירושלים), Hebrew annual published in Vienna between 1882 and 1919. Initially published on behalf of Hibbat Zion, *Jerusalem* continued to publish after that organization collapsed. Although not a WZO subsidized journal, *Jerusalem* was very supportive of the WZO's goals and retained a religious and Zionist editorial line throughout.

Jüdische Zeitung (JZ), "Jewish Newspaper," German language weekly organ of the Austrian Zionist federation, published in Vienna between 1907 and 1921. Initially JZ represented only one segment of the Austrian Zionists, specifically those in Vienna and West Austria (until 1918, the federation was divided into four subfederations). After the collapse of the Habsburg empire, JZ became the mouthpiece for the entire Austrian Zionist movement. Publication ceased, however, for financial reasons: the federation could not finance both JZ and the *Wiener Morgenzeitung* and decided to focus on the latter.

Die Neue Welt (DNW), "The New World," Zionist weekly published in Vienna between 1927 and 1938 as a successor to the WZO official organ *Die Welt*. Despite its official effort to identify with the earlier journal and with the WZO mainstream, DNW actually was an independent journal leaning toward the Zionist right. Between 1927 and 1935, DNW served as ha-Zohar's official organ in Austria. Even then, DNW forged its own independent editorial line, being identified with the Grossman faction of ha-Zohar. When ha-Zohar withdrew from the WZO in 1935, DNW's editors joined the Grossman faction in founding the Jewish State party. Publication was terminated in March 1938, when shortly after the *Anschluss* the Gestapo ordered all Jewish publications to cease. Sole editor: Robert Stricker. > see also: **Organizations, Revisionist (International, Jewish State Party).**

Selbst-Emancipation, "Autoemancipation," proto-Zionist weekly published in Vienna between 1885 and 1892. Sole editor was Nathan Birnbaum, who authored the poem "ha-Tikva" (which later became Israel's national anthem). The editorial line concentrated on the need for socioeconomic revival through the "productivization" of Jewish youth, mainly by focusing them on agricultural work. Publication ceased in 1892 when the newspaper was renamed *Jüdische Volkszeitung*.

Die Welt, "The World," premier Zionist weekly which served as the official organ of

Cover of *Selbst-Emancipation*
for February 1, 1892.
Courtesy of the Central Zionist Archives, Jerusalem

the WZO between 1897 and 1914. *Die Welt* was published in Vienna between 1897 and 1904, moving to Cologne with the Engere Aktions-Komité (EAK), appearing there between 1904 and 1911. When the EAK moved to Berlin in 1911, *Die Welt* followed suit, appearing there until 1914. Yiddish and Hebrew editions of *Die Welt* appeared simultaneously with the better-known German edition from 1907 onward. *Die Welt's* importance transcended its value as a newspaper (whose content was equally divided between political and cultural news about far-flung Jewish communities) because the newspaper acted as a catalyst for Zionist activities in almost every community it reached. Publication was suspended during the Austro-Serbian crisis of July 1914 with the hope that it might soon be resumed. This did not come about, however, and regular publication was not resumed after World War I. Instead, limited editions of *Die Welt* (and in the 1930s its Hebrew equivalent, *ha-Olam*) were published as daily fact sheets during the Zionist congresses only and for the benefit of the delegates.

Wiener Morgenzeitung (WMZ), "Vienna Morning Newspaper," German-language Zionist daily newspaper, the only daily Jewish newspaper published in Central Europe. WMZ was the brainchild of Robert Weltsch, who had previously edited Vienna's *Jüdische Zeitung.* WMZ appeared between 1919 and 1927, with five issues appearing per week. Officially billed as a Jewish daily for "politics, political economy, and literature," WMZ concentrated mainly on the political situation in Austria and the grave implications for Austrian Jewry inherent in the country's instability. Publication ceased when Weltsch moved to Berlin in 1928. Sole editor: Robert Weltsch.

Other Austrian Zionist Publications:
Jeruba'al (Vienna), German monthly, 1918–1919.
Der Jüdische Arbeiter (Vienna), German monthly 1898–1899.
Die Jüdische Jugend (Vienna), German monthly, 1928–1938.
Palästina: Zeitschrift für den Aufbau Palästinas (Vienna), German monthly, 1904–1938.
Die Stimme (Vienna), German Weekly, 1928–1938.
Yiddishe Arbeiterjugend (Vienna), Yiddish monthly, 1927–1938.

Belgium
L'Avenir Juif (LAJ), "The Jewish Current," French-language fortnightly published by the Belgian Zionist federation, replacing *ha-Tikva* (which ceased publication during World War I) and carried on the latter's numbering. Publication of LAJ began in the early 1920s and continued until 1940, when it ceased due to the Nazi invasion. Political Zionist in orientation, LAJ nonetheless supported the WZO and JAE on most major internal Zionist issues.
Eretz Israel (ארץ ישראל), "The Land of Israel," bilingual French/Yiddish fortnightly published in Brussels between 1928 and 1940. Initially the journal appeared as the official organ of the Agudat Zion (general Zionist) wing of the Belgian Zionist

federation. However, in 1936, publication was transferred to the Keren ha-Yesod, after which the journal appeared only in Yiddish. Publication ceased in the spring/summer of 1940, just after the Nazi occupation of Belgium.
Ha-Tikvah, official publication of the Belgian Zionist federation, appearing monthly between 1904 and 1914. Published in German, with a few articles in French, *Ha-Tikvah* adopted a general Zionist editorial line that focused mainly on the cultural and educational activities needed to raise Belgian Jewry's national consciousness. Publication ceased with the outbreak of World War I and was resumed under the title *L'Avenir Juif.* In 1932, the Poale Zion-Zeirei Zion Federation of Belgium began to publish a journal with the same title (but did not continue the previous *ha-Tikvah* numbering). The new journal appeared entirely in French and adopted an editorial line supportive of Mapai. This new *ha-Tikvah* remained in print until World War II, when publication ceased and was not resumed.
Unzer Front, Yiddish language monthly published by the Betar movement in Brussels and operating as the nationwide mouthpiece for Betar and the Union of Zionist Revisionists in Belgium. Publication ceased during the Nazi occupation.

Other Belgian Zionist Publications
Bar-Kokhba (Antwerp), Flemish monthly, 1922–1940.
Darkenu (Antwerp), Flemish monthly, 1926–1940.

Bulgaria
Carmel, official journal of the Carmel Zionist society published in Plovdiv and appearing in French and Ladino monthly from September 1895 to January 1896. *Carmel* was the first Zionist publication in Bulgaria and sought to arouse the Jewish public in support of Zionism and in opposition to the Jewish notables. The publication was not a success and when the society temporarily ceased to function, it halted publication. Sole editor: Joseph Marcou Baruch.
El Dia (איל דיאה), "The Day," Ladino weekly published as a Zionist journal between 1897

and 1901 and as a nonpartisan journal of Jewish affairs between 1901 and 1914. In its first series, *El Dia* represented the radical wing of the Bulgarian Zionist federation. In its second manifestation, the editorial line was softened, although remaining Zionist. However, throughout, *El Dia* voiced considerable opposition to the Jewish notables who controlled the Jewish community. Publication slowed after 1910 due to financial difficulties and ceased altogether on the eve of World War I.

El Sionisto (איל ציאוניסטו), "The Zionist," Ladino organ of the Zion-Joseph Marcou Baruch Society of Sofia published between 1903 and 1907. Initially published as a weekly, after 1905 the journal appeared irregularly. Its editorial line tended to support the Practical Zionist position. However, after 1904 *El Sionisto* turned to a territorialist editorial line and ceased to be a Zionist journal. > see also: **Territorialism.**

Ha-Shofar (השופר), "The Ram's Horn," official weekly organ of the Bulgarian Zionist federation, published between 1901 and 1941. Initially published in Ladino with one page in Bulgarian, after 1913 the language content was reversed. Publication ceased during World War I but was resumed in 1918. Mainly reflecting a general Zionist perspective, *ha-Shofar* strongly advocated democratic reforms within the Jewish community while also defending Jewish rights in the Bulgarian state. Publication ceased by government decree (along with virtually the rest of the Jewish press in Bulgaria) in June 1941. Editors: Marcou Romano (1901-1910), A. Capoun (1910-1911), Preseido Romano (1911–1913), Albert Romano (1913–1941).

La Tolerencia (לה טולירינסייה), "Toleration," official Ladino organ of the Theodor Herzl society of Sofia published in 1907–1908. Despite its title, the editorial line was strongly Zionist and combatted those groups in Bulgarian Jewry —— both among the communal elite (including the chief rabbi of Sofia) and the Jewish socialists —— who opposed Zionist fulfillment. Publication ceased due to financial difficulties after one

year. Editors: Haim Farhi and Yosef ha-Levi.

Poale-Zion (PZ), "Zionist Worker," official Bulgarian-language publication of the Poale-Zion, appearing biweekly in Sofia between 1930 and 1939. Publication was halted at government order from February 1939 to October 1944. Publication resumed until July 1948, when the entire staff emigrated to Israel after the government seized PZ's press. PZ's editorial policy tended toward the left on internal Zionist affairs but supported Mapai and the JA on external issues. Editors: Joseph Reuven (1930–1939); Shabbetai Ashkenazi (1944–1948).

Razviet, official Bulgarian-language publication of ha-Zohar and (after 1935) of ha-Zach in Bulgaria, appearing in Sofia between 1927 and 1940. In addition to its party functions, *Rasviet* served as a mouthpiece of the Betar movement in Bulgaria. From 1932 on, *Rasviet* appeared as a weekly. Publication was suspended as a result of a government decree in 1940 and was not renewed after World War II.

Yevreiski Glas (YG), "Jewish Call," political Zionist journal published in Sofia in Bulgarian and Ladino. The first series appeared as a weekly in 1896 and 1897, but folded after only seventeen issues were printed. This series of YG was not helped by its confrontational tone nor did the fact that Sofia's chief rabbi pronounced a ban of excommunication on any Jewish reader help to promote circulation. In October 1917, a new series under the same title, but not continuing the first series's numbering, appeared as a monthly, again in Sofia. This second series published in Bulgarian only until May 1920, when the journal again folded for financial reasons. Editors: Yehoshua Caleb (1896–1897), Levi Hizkiah (1917–1920).

Yevreski Ratz, "Jewish Voice," independent Bulgarian language Jewish monthly published in Sofia between March 1932 and June 1941. Its editorial line was general Zionist but did not reflect any specific party orientation. Initially given special permission to publish after the government ordered the Jewish press to cease in 1940, *Yevreski Ratz* was halted after the adoption of the Bulgarian racial laws in June 1941. Editor: Albert Michael.

Zionista Trybuna (ZT), "Zionist Tribune," official Bulgarian weekly of the postwar

Bulgarian Zionist federation, published in Sofia between 1944 and 1948. A Hebrew-language edition also existed, published under the title *Bama Zionit* (במה ציונית, Zionist Forum). Both versions sought to include all Zionists, and all Bulgarian Jewry, in their purview, concentrating on political and social problems and on the means to fulfill the Zionists' national goals. Publication of both versions was stopped by the Bulgarian Communist government in 1948 and most of the editorial staff left the country for Israel shortly after the State of Israel was established. Editors: Vitaly Haimov (1944–1945), Emico Margolis (1946–1948).

Other Bulgarian Zionist Publications:
La Berdad (Sofia), Ladino weekly, 1925–1926.
Nova Palestina (Ruse/Sofia), Ladino/ Bulgarian monthly, 1922–1924.
Ha-Shomer ha-Zair (Sofia), Hebrew bi-weekly, 1926–1928.
Ha-Tikva (Sofia), Ladino weekly, 1928–1932.
Yevreiski Trybuna (Ruse), Bulgarian bimonthly, 1926–1929.

Canada
Canadian Jewish Chronicle (CJC), premier Canadian Jewish weekly, published in Montreal and Toronto between 1914 and 1974. In 1966, CJC merged with its archrival, the *Canadian Jewish Review*, appearing thereafter as the *Canadian Jewish Chronicle Review*. Initially limited in focus to events in the local Jewish community, CJC was transformed into a major factor in the Anglo-Jewish press by A. M. Klein, who edited the journal for almost a quarter of a century. Under Klein's aegis, CJC also became a passionate advocate of Canadian and Canadian Jewish action to rescue threatened European Jewry and to fulfill the goals of Zionism. Editors: A. A. Roback (1914–1917), Ida Seigler (1917–1925), Harry Wolofsky (1925–1936), Rabbi Charles Bender (1936–1938), A. M. Klein (1938–1959). > see also: **Publications, Non-/Anti-Zionist (Canada, Canadian Jewish Review)**.

Jewish Standard (JS), weekly Canadian Jewish magazine, founded by Hadassah leader Rose Dunkelman and published in Toronto between 1931 and the 1980s. In attempting to supplant the *Canadian Jewish Review*, JS failed. However, it brought Zionism to the forefront of Canadian Jewry's public agenda. The early issues also set Jewish journalism and publication quality on par with secular weeklies such as *Life* and *Time*. The JS attitude to Zionism derived from its editorial board, which read like a who's who of Canadian Zionism. Indeed, between 1938 and 1948, JS acted as the mouthpiece for the Zionist Organization of Canada. Editors: Meyer Weisgal (1931– 1932), Meyer Steinglas (1932–1933), Oscar Cohen (1933–1934), Moses Frank (1934–1938), Julius Hayman (1938–1975).

New Voice (NV), socialist mouthpiece published by the United Jewish People's Order, a Canadian Communist front organization, that appeared in Toronto between 1946 and 1948. Despite its party affiliation. NV formulated a strongly pro-Zionist line, both as a means to obtain mainstream Jewish support for Communism and as a logical consequence of the editors' anti-imperialism. Publication ceased for financial reasons. Editors: Sam Lipshitz, Nathan Cohen.

Other Canadian Zionist Publications:
Canadian Jewish Yearbook (Montreal), English annual, 1939–1942.
The Canadian Zionist (Montreal), English/ Yiddish monthly, 1938–Current.
Der Keneder Adler (Montreal), Yiddish daily, 1907–1966.
Undzer Weg (Downsview), Yiddish/Englsih quarterly, 1932–Current.
Der Yiddisher Journal (Toronto), Yiddish daily, 1914–1959.

Chile
Mundo Judío (MJ), "The Jewish World," Spanish-language weekly organ of the Chilean Zionist federation, published in Santiago de Chile since 1935. General Zionist in orientation, MJ's purview has included a wide range of Jewish and Zionist subjects, making it the premier journal of Chilean Jewry.

Czechoslovakia

Allgemeine Jüdische Zeitung (AJZ), "General Jewish Newspaper," Orthodox weekly published in German and Yiddish in Slovakia from 1933 to 1939. Publication ceased at the demand of the Tiso government and was never resumed. Pro-Zionist in orientation, AJZ reflected the position of the Mizrachi party. Editors: David Gross, Moshe Müller.

Blätter für die jüdische Frau (BJF), "Pages for the Jewish Woman," monthly supplement to the Czech Zionist journal *Selbstwehr* and focused on women's issues within the Jewish community and the Zionist movement. Published from 1925 to 1939, BJF was subsidized by the Czech chapter of the Women's International Zionist Organization (WIZO). Sole editor: Hanna Steiner.

Jüdisches Volksblatt (JVB), "Jewish People's Pages," Zionist weekly appearing in Moravská Ostrova (Märisch-Ostrow) between 1919 and 1922. More attuned to the Jewish communities lying outside of Prague but in the Czech lands (Bohemia and Moravia), JVB maintained a general Zionist orientation for its entire publication run. In 1922 financial difficulties forced a merger between JV and *Selbstwehr* and publication ceased. Sole editor: Hugo Hermann.

Jüdische Volksstimme (JVS), "Jewish People's Voice," Zionist weekly published in German in Brno between 1901 and 1939. JVS began its publishing run as a general Zionist publication, representing the more overtly political wing of Czech Zionism prior to World War I (when Bohemia-Moravia was part of the Austro-Hungarian empire). In the interwar era JVS veered to the right, becoming the de facto mouthpiece for ha-Zohar's Czech branch. JVS was the first revisionist Zionist organ to advocate withdrawal from the WZO. Following its own advice, JVS supporters withdrew from the Czech Zionist federation in 1932. Publication ceased upon the Nazi occupation and was not resumed. Editors: Max Hickl, Hugo Gold.

Ha-Ma'avar la-Bogrim (HMLB), trilingual publication in Hebrew, German, and Magyar published in Žilina between 1932 and 1939 as the mouthpiece for ha-Shomer ha-Zair in Slovakia. Publication was halted by the Slovak government upon the breakup of the Czechoslovak Republic (that is, when the Nazis occupied Prague in March 1939).

Morgenpost (מארגנפאסט), "Morning Post," Yiddish language weekly appearing in Ruthenia between 1924 and 1925. The content consisted of a compilation of materials culled from other Jewish newspapers, principally from the moderately revisionist Vienna daily *Wiener Morgenzeitung*, that were translated into Yiddish. The weakness of Zionist groups in Ruthenia (whose Jewish population was overwhelmingly Orthodox) caused financial difficulties from almost the first day of publication and led to collapse after only one year.

Selbstwehr, "Self-Defense," Zionist weekly published in Prague in German and Czech from 1918 to 1938. Considered one of the most prominent Zionist publications in Central Europe, *Selbstwehr* published articles on a wide range of Jewish topics. Editors: Felix Weltsch, Hans Lichtwitz.

Tel Hai, monthly publication of the Betar movement in Slovakia, appearing in German and Yiddish. Published in Bratislava between 1929 and 1935, publication ceased due to financial difficulties. Editors: Julius Grosz, Pali Wetzler.

Other Czech Zionist Publications:

Das Arbeitende Erez Israel, (Brno), German weekly, 1928–1939.

He-Chalutz (Moravská Ostrova), German monthly, 1929–1939.

Der Jüdische Sozialist (Brno), German weekly, 1919–1921.

Jüdisches Volksblatt (Moravská Ostrova), German bi-weekly, 1919–1922.

Jüdische Volkszeitung (Bratislava), German weekly, 1919–1939.

List Židoské Ženy (Prague), Czech monthly, 1927–1939.

Yiddishe Shtime (Mukačevo), Yiddish weekly, 1929–1939.

A Zsionö (Uzhorod), Hungarian weekly, 1929–1939.

Egypt

La Revue Sioniste, "The Zionist Review," official organ of the Egyptian Zionist federation, published in French between 1918 and 1924. Despite a circulation of over four-hundred, the journal never appeared regularly due to technical difficulties, mainly the high level of disorganization among Egyptian Zionists. Despite repeated discussions about revival, publication ceased altogether in 1924.

Israël, independent journal for Zionist thought published in Cairo by Albert Mosseri between 1920 and 1933. *Israël* appeared in three identical editions in Hebrew, Arabic, and French, and reflected a moderate general Zionist position. After Mosseri's death in 1933 his wife, Mazal M. Mosseri, continued to publish the French edition only until she returned to *Eretz Israel* (where she was born) in 1939. Publication ceased thereafter.

France

Affirmation, monthly published by a coalition of Zionist youth groups in Paris. Apparently, the journal appeared only for a short time, possibly January to August 1939. Its main orientation was the need to recast Franco-Jewry along nationalist lines.

Parisier Haynt (פאריזער הײַנט), "Paris Today," Yiddish-language daily published between 1928 and 1940 as a French subsidiary of the Warsaw *Haynt.* Main readership was new immigrants from Poland. Editorial line tended toward the center-left on the Zionist spectrum but vocally supported the JAE and WZO on most issues. Publication ceased just prior to the German invasion of France. > see also: **Publications, Zionist (Poland,** *Haynt).*

La Terre Retrouvée (LTR), "The Recovered Land," Keren Kayemet le-Israel monthly bulletin published in Paris between 1928 and 1949. Nonpartisan in orientation, LTR served as both a fund-raising tool and an information bulletin on developments in the *Yishuv.* Publication was disrupted by World War II but was resumed between 1945 and 1949.

Unzer Vort (אונזער װארט, UV), "Our Word," Yiddish-language socialist Zionist organ published in Paris in two series. The first series appeared from 1933 to 1936 as a weekly under the auspices of the Poale Zion-Hitahdut branch in Paris. In 1936, the journal's name changed to *Di Naye Zeit* (די נײַע צײַט, The New Times, DNZ), under which title it appeared until suspended during World War II. Editorial line of both UV and DNZ vocally supported Mapai. DNZ was particularly in the forefront of those Zionist voices calling for adoption of a more activist orientation within Socialist Zionism. As noted, this series ceased publication when World War II broke out. The second series of UV, also published in Paris and sometimes cited by its French title, *Notre Parole,* appeared between 1945 and 1996. Its editorial line was also supportive of Mapai and the JA, especially during the critical period between 1945 and 1948. Contents covered a wide range of subjects but emphasized events in the *Yishuv* and Franco-Jewry. Publication ceased for financial reasons, mainly connected with the virtual disappearance of a Yiddish reading public in continental Europe. Sole editor: Marc Jarblum.

Other Franco-Zionist Publications

Cadimah (Paris), French irregular, 1896–1897.
Chalom (Paris), French Monthly, 1921–1935.
L'Echo Sioniste (Paris), French weekly, 1900–1921.
Le Peuple Juive (paris), French weekly, 1907–1922.
Rassviet (Paris), Russian weekly, 1905–1935.
Der Yid (Paris), Yiddish monthly, 1912–1914.

Germany

Der Colonist, "The Colonist," German-language bulletin of the B'nai B'rith society in Germany, appearing between 1882 and 1884. Despite the sponsoring agency's name, it was not initially affiliated with the international Jewish fraternal order B'nai B'rith (which in that period was non-Zionist in orientation); when the two did merge, B'nai B'rith ceased to function. Initially published as a monthly, *Der Colonist* appeared as a weekly in 1883 and 1884. The journal ceased publication after the merger. Mainly attuned to obtaining support for land purchases in *Eretz Israel*, *Der Colonist* was among the first journals in Western Europe to be entirely dedicated to Zionist affairs. Sole editor: Selig Freuthal.

Israelitisches Familienblatt (IFB), "Jewish Family Page," German-language independent Jewish weekly published between 1898 and 1938. IFB was founded in Hamburg and was published there until 1935. From 1926 to 1935, distinct editions of IFB also appeared in Berlin and Frankfurt am Main. These local editions contained the same editorial content but also included items of local interest. In 1935, the editorial offices moved to Berlin; from then until termination only one version was published for the entire country. Publication ceased at Gestapo order after Kristallnacht. Throughout its publication run, IFB remained committed to modern Orthodox Judaism. Although officially neutral on matters of internal Jewish politics, IFB leaned toward Zionism and maintained an especially positive orientation to the Mizrachi movement. IFB's support for Zionism became explicit after 1933. In 1935, circulation totaled 36,500.

Ha-Ivri (העברי), "The Hebrew," official weekly organ of the world Mizrachi movement, published between 1912 and 1921. Initially published in Berlin, publication was transferred to New York during World War I. Despite being a party organ, *ha-Ivri* attracted a wide range of Hebrew writers, both Zionist and non-Zionist. Still, the use of Hebrew as a medium of communication restricted the readership to more traditional or more educated elements in the Jewish community leading to financial difficulties that culminated in the cessation of publication. Sole editor: Meir Berlin (Bar-Ilan).

Der Jude, "The Jew," German-language intellectual journal published as a monthly between 1916 and 1928. *Der Jude* sought to publish articles that would stimulate Jewish intellectual activity and national self-awareness among educated German Jews. Although Zionist in orientation, the editorial line was always aligned with concepts of Ahad ha-Am's Spiritual Zionism. Moreover,

Der Jude rarely discussed practical topics, such as *aliya*, operating on a theoretical and intellectual level. Contributors included a panoply of German-Jewish intellectuals, including, inter alia, Gershom Scholem, Max Brod, Adolf Böhm, Robert Weltsch, N. M. Gelber, and Nahum Goldmann. Changes in the intellectual makeup of German Jewry during the latter years of the Weimar Republic led to the journal's collapse, although it was seen as a critical influence for an entire generation of academically trained German Jews who turned away from assimilation during this critical period. Sole editor: Martin Buber.

Jüdische Rundschau (JR), "Jewish Observer," official weekly of the Zionistische Verein für Deutschland (ZVFD), published between 1897 and 1938. Editorial line may be defined as general Zionist, although JR was always open to differing opinions. Indeed, its openness to debate on major Zionist issues made JR one of the most respected Zionist periodicals of the time. publication ceased at Gestapo order just after Kristallnacht. JR circulation peaked at 37,000 between 1933 and 1937. In 1939 and 1940 JR was replaced by *Jüdische Welt-Rundschau*, a short-lived weekly published in Paris and printed in Tel Aviv.

Der Jüdische Student (DJS), "The Jewish Student," monthly organ of the Kartell Jüdischer Verbindungen, the main Zionist association of university students in Germany. DJS appeared in Berlin between 1902 and 1932. Passionately Zionist, DJS stridently opposed assimilation but was not (initially) particularly *aliya* oriented. Instead, DJS saw Zionism as a means of shoring up German Jewish identity and protecting Jewish morale from the depredations of antisemitism.

Ha-Magid (המגיד), "The Messenger," Hebrew weekly published between 1856 and 1903 initially in Lyck (Prussian Poland) then in Berlin, and, finally, in Krakow (Austrian Galicia). In its final form, the journal was designated *ha-Magid ha-Hadash* (The New Messenger) or *ha-Shavua* (The Week). Mainly oriented toward the problems of Eastern European Jews, the journal was published in Germany or Austria in order to avoid Russian censorship regulations. *Ha-Magid* was an early and vocal supporter of Jewish nationalism and of renewed Jewish settlement in *Eretz Israel*. Publication ceased due to financial difficulties in 1903. Editors: Eliezer L. Silberman and David Gordon (1856–1880); David Gordon (1880–1886); Dov Gordon (1886–1890); Jacob S. Fuchs (1890–1903).

Other German Zionist Periodicals:

Altneuland (Berlin), German monthly, 1904–1906.

Die Arbeit (Berlin), German monthly, 1919–1924, 1928.

Blau-Weiss Blätter (Berlin/Prague), German monthly, 1913–1919, 1924–1925.

Hed Betar (Berlin), German fortnightly, 1929–1933.

Herzl-Bund Blätter (Berlin), German monthly, 1913–1918.

Die Jüdische Moderne (Berlin), German fortnightly, 1897–1898.

Das Jüdisches Echo (Munich), German Weekly, 1913–1938.

Volk und Land (Berlin), German weekly, 1919–1920.

Zion (Berlin), German monthly, 1895–1899, 1929–1935.

Greece

Bayit Yehudi (BY), "The Jewish Home," Greek fortnightly published in Athens between 1948 and 1962. Officially independent, BY was zealous in its support for Zionist and Jewish causes in Greece and Israel. For much of its publishing run, BY was the only Jewish publication to appear throughout Greece, making it a powerful voice in the community. However, publication ceased due to financial difficulties. Sole editor: Raphael Constantinis.

Pro-Israël, bi-lingual (French/Ladino) weekly published in Salonika between 1917 and 1934 by a conglomerate of independent Zionists. Considered to be the premier Zionist journal in Greece, *Israël* wielded considerable influence within the Salonika Jewish community. Committed to ardent support for Jewish nationalism, the journal also fought for Jewish rights in Greece. Publication ceased when the editor and most of the financial backers left Salonika for *Eretz Israel*. Sole editor: Abraham S. Recanati.

La Renassencia Judea (לה רינאסינסייה ג׳ודיאה, LRJ), "The Jewish Renaissance," Ladino weekly published in Salonika in two series. The first series of LRJ appeared between 1917 and 1921. This series was published by a group of young Socialist Zionists who sought a dynamic journal that would influence Jews to join the Zionist movement while also fighting anti-Zionist tendencies within the community. In particular, LRJ focused much of its ire on Jewish Communists who were emboldened by the Bolshevik revolution in Russia to try to take over the Jewish community. This series ceased publication in 1921, apparently for financial reasons. In 1926, the title (but not the numbering of the original series) was revived as the official weekly organ of the Greek Zionist federation. Under this banner, LRJ continued to appear until 1941. In 1922 LRJ began to publish a Greek-language supplement. LRJ was not revived after the World War II.

Hungary

Mult es Jövö (MEJ), "Past and Future," Zionist monthly appearing in Budapest between 1911 and 1944. In its prime, MEJ was considered the most prestigious Zionist periodical in the Danube basin. General Zionist in orientation, MEJ concentrated on cultural affairs and on the need to renew Jewish culture — through Zionism — as a bulwark against assimilation and antisemitism. Banned by the Gestapo after the German invasion of Hungary, MEJ was not revived after the war. Sole editor: József Patai.

Zsidó Néplap (ZN), "Jewish People's Newspaper," short-lived Zionist weekly published in Budapest between 1903 and 1905. ZN was the first major journal published in Hungarian to voice a positive opinion of Zionism. At the time, Hungarian Jewry was divided between the strictly Orthodoxy and the so-called Neologs, who advocated assimilation. Unable to find sufficient readership, ZN folded after two years. In 1907 ZN's editor attempted to revive the journal under the title *Zsidó Elet* (Jewish Life), but this fared no better and the magazine folded after a few issues. Editor: Armin Bokor.

Zsidó Saemle (ZS), "Jewish Review," official organ of the Hungarian Zionist federation, published from 1911 to 1944. Initially published as a monthly, ZS converted to a fortnightly format in 1918 and to a weekly in 1925. Publication was temporarily suspended in 1919 during the Communist regime of Belá Kuhn but was quickly resumed. General Zionist in orientation, ZS was mainly attuned to obtaining support for Zionism from a largely apathetic Jewish community. Publication ceased during the Nazi occupation and was not revived thereafter.

Other Hungarian Zionist Publications:

Cheruth (Budapest), Hungarian monthly, 1928–1944.

Magayr Cionista Szerveret (Budapest), Hungarian monthly, 1908–1909.

Ungarländische Jüdische Zeitung (Budapest), German weekly, 1908–1914.

India

India and Israel, short-lived independent monthly published in Bombay between 1948 and 1952. *India and Israel* sought to foster a closer link between the new newly established states and former British colonies. Disinterest on the Indian side led the publication to collapse in its fourth year.

Jewish Advocate, official mouthpiece of the Bombay Zionist Association published monthly from 1930 to 1951. Since the Bombay association acted as the de facto Zionist federation for the entire subcontinent, *Jewish Advocate* was considered one of the most influential Jewish magazines in the country. Its editorial line was passionately Zionist, but financial difficulties forced the publication to cease after twenty-one years.

Italy

Il Corriere Israelitico (ICI), "The Jewish Courier," independent Jewish monthly published in Trieste between 1863 and 1915. Although Trieste was then part of the Austro-Hungarian empire, ICI was published in Italian and was mainly attuned toward the Italian Jewish community. ICI was officially neutral on Jewish nationalism, but the editors agreed to provide an open forum for Zionist leaders to promote their ideas. In its prime, ICI was considered the premier opinion-maker of Italian Jewry, a fact that increased the importance of the editors' willingness to publicize Zionism. Publication ceased after Italy joined the Entente powers during World War I: shortages in materials made continued publication impossible and postwar realignments made resumption unprofitable.

L'Idea Sionista (LIS), "The Zionist Idea," monthly Zionist organ published in Rome in two series. The first series, appearing between 1909 and 1911, was the official organ of the Italian Zionist federation. This series regularly published the federation's records, but failed for financial reasons. The second series of LIS was published by ha-Zohar/ha-Zach in Rome between 1933 and 1938. More overtly political than its predecessor, this version of LIS was also one of the most outspoken revisionist Zionist journals. Publication ceased after the Italian government introduced its anti-Jewish laws in 1938.

Israel, Italian Zionist weekly published in Florence from 1916 to 1938. Seeking to replace the highly respected *Il Corriere Israelitico*, which ceased publication in 1915, *Israel* rapidly became one of the two main journals of Zionist opinion in Italy. General Zionist in orientation, *Israel* strongly supported the WZO and JAE on most Zionist issues. Initially permitted by the Fascist government to publish without interference, *Israel* fell victim to the anti-Jewish laws instituted in 1938. Publication was resumed in December 1944, after Florence was liberated, and continued into the 1960s.

La Rassegna Mensile di Israel (LRMDI), "The Monthly Review of Israel," Zionist monthly published in Florence between 1925 and 1938. With *Israel*, LRMDI was one of the two most prestigious Zionist periodicals published in Italy during the interwar period. Unlike *Israel*, LRMDI focused almost entirely on educational and cultural issues, advocating Zionism as an antidote to assimilation and communal apathy. LRMDI did not express a clear opinion on Zionist political issues and (as with most contemporary Italian Jewish publications) remained completely neutral on Italian politics in the Fascist era. Despite LRMDI's neutral stance, the Fascists banned it with all other Jewish periodicals when the anti-Jewish laws were initiated in 1938. Publication resumed in 1948 and continued to 1981.

Latvia

Dos Folk (דאס פאלק), "The People," Yiddish daily newspaper published in Riga between 1920 and 1927. *Dos Folk*'s editorial line was general Zionist, but of a moderate persuasion. The local Mizrachi branch also supported the newspaper for most of its publishing run. Circulation is unknown, but the print run was 300 copies in 1920, rising to 6,000 copies in 1926 and 1927. Despite these successes, *Dos Folk* was plagued by financial difficulties that led to collapse.

Nazionalzeitung (נאציאנאלצייטונג), "National Newspaper," Yiddish daily published in Riga during the month of August 1907. Riga was then still part of the Russian empire and this was the first journal attuned to Latvian Jewry. Editorial line was broadly Jewish nationalist, without distinguishing between Zionism, territorialism, and diaspora nationalism. *Nazionalzeitung*'s main accomplishment was placing Jewish nationalism on Latvian Jewry's public agenda.

Unzer Weg (אונזער וועג, UW), "Our Path," Yiddish-language socialist Zionist daily, also appearing under the title *Der Weg* (דער וועג), published in Riga between 1922 and 1924. Associated with the Poale Zion–Z.S. Party (which wavered between Zionism and territorialism in the interwar era), UW was initially published in direct competition with *Dos Folk*. In particular, UW's editors felt that a Zionist periodical should express its ideology more clearly. In fact, few readers agreed and UW soon collapsed. In 1931, an abortive effort to revive UW in a more moderate socialist Zionist garb was made, but failed after only four issues.

Other Latvian Zionist Publications:
Alija (Riga), Hebrew/Yiddish monthly, 1937–1939.

Freimorgan (Riga), Yiddish daily, 1926–1934.
Liboyer Folksblatt (Liepaja), Yiddish weekly, 1931–1934.
Tora va-Avoda (Riga), Hebrew monthly, 1934.

Lithuania

Arbeter Zeitung (ארבייטער צייטונג, AZ), "Worker's Newspaper," Yiddish weekly published under the auspices of Poale Zion Smol in Kovno between 1921 and 1926. Considered to be on the far left of Jewish publications, AZ's editorial line was virtually identical with the positions espoused by Lithuanian Jewish Communists, except on the question of Jewish national identity. Publication was terminated by order of the nationalist government that seized power in December 1926.

Der Moment (דער מאמענט), "The Moment," revisionist Zionist daily published in Kovno between 1933 and 1937. Somewhat more narrowly focused than the Polish journal of the same name, the Lithuanian *Moment* was much more polemical in its attitude toward the leadership of the WZO and JA. Publication ceased due to financial difficulties.

Dos Vort (דאס ווארט, DV), "The Word," socialist Zionist daily published in Kovno between 1933 and 1940. Many issues of DV in 1933 were published under the alternate title *Unzer Vort* (אונזער ווארט, "Our Word"), with the title stabilizing after 1934. DV represented the position of the Hitahdut, that is, socialist Zionists who supported Mapai's position. Publication ceased during the first Soviet occupation of Kovno (1940–1941), but an effort to revive the publication as a clandestine publication was made in the Kovno ghetto.

Die Yiddishe Shtime (די יידישע שטימע, DYS), "The Jewish Voice," Yiddish-language daily published in Kovno from 1919 to 1940. General Zionist in orientation, DYS operated under the auspices of the Lithuanian Zionist federation almost from its inception. For parts of its publication run, DYS published weekly editions in Lithuanian and Hebrew that were digests of the daily version. Combining wide-ranging news coverage with in-depth analysis, DYS was considered the most prestigious of the Lithuanian Jewish newspapers. Publication ceased during the Soviet occupation.

Yidnshtat in Eretz Israel (ייִדנשטאַט אין ארץ ישראל, YSEI), "A Jewish State in Eretz Israel," weekly organ of the so-called Grossman faction of ha-Zohar, published in Kovno between 1934 and 1936. In 1935 and 1936, YSEI was published by the Lithuanian branch of Brit ha-Kanaim, the Jewish State Party's youth movement. Activist in orientation, YSEI opposed ha-Zohar's secession from the WZO. Publication ceased after the editor's *aliya*. Sole editor: Herzl Rosenblum.

Di Zeit (די צייט), "The Times," title used by two different Zionist serials published almost simultaneously during the 1920s and 1930s. The briefer of the two was published in Kovno as a weekly in 1932 and 1933. This series appeared under the auspices of the local Poale Zion Smol branch, but ceased publication for financial reasons after a very short run. The second series was published in Vilna between 1921 and 1939. This series appeared under the auspices of the Vilna Zionist society and began its run when the city was still held by the Lithuanians. The Polish seizure of Vilna in 1922 did not effect publication. Considered very influential in Vilna and its immediate environs, *Di Zeit* played only a minor role in Zionist politics in interwar Poland. Publication ceased on the outbreak of World War II.

Di Zukunft (די צוקונפט, DZ), "The Future," revisionist Zionist daily published by supporters of the Grossman faction in Kovno in 1933 and 1934. DZ originally appeared as a one-time publication during the election campaign for the Eighteenth Zionist Congress. This publication proved so popular that regular series publication was begun after the congress. As a daily, DZ did not enjoy financial success and publication ceased in early 1934.

Other Lithuanian Zionist Publications:
Arbeter Lebn (Kovno), Yiddish weekly, 1920–1926.
Ha-Hayim (Vilna), Hebrew weekly, 1920.
Ba-Maaracha (kovno), Hebrew weekly, 1938–1939.
Der Nayer Veg (Kovno), Yiddish monthly, 1937–1939.

Unzer Ruf (Kovno), Yiddish fortnightly, 1925–1926.
Unzer Veg (Kovno), Yiddish fortnightly, 1923–1927.

Netherlands
Ba-Derech, "On the Way," Dutch-language organ of the Federation of Jewish Youth, published as a monthly between 1925 and 1938. Due to financial difficulties, the journal appeared irregularly for many years. General Zionist in orientation, *ba-Derech* tended to shy away from overtly political posturing, concentrating instead on educational and cultural work. In 1938, with new financing available, the title was changed to *Cheroetenoe* (Our Independence), which appeared monthly until 1940 when it permanently ceased. Editors: A. Ehrenfeld, A. A. Adler, A. J. Herzberg (1925–1938), S. Kleerekoper, J. Melkman (1938–1940).

Dewar ha-Chaloets, "The Pioneer's Word," mimeographed German-language organ of he-Halutz in Amsterdam, published between 1935 and 1940. Editorial line was nonpartisan, with the journal's primary goal being to prepare members — mostly German refugees — for *aliya* and life in the *Yishuv*. Just prior to the German invasion of the Low Countries, the title was changed to *Diwrei Chaloetsiem* (Pioneers' Words), under which title it appeared for one year.

Kadima, "Forward," weekly mimeographed journal of the Tilburg Jewish community published in 1940. Unique among communal bulletins was *Kadima's* clear Zionist orientation. Publication ceased because of the Nazi occupation.

Ha-Jardeen (הירדן), "The Jordan," Dutch-language organ of the Betar branch in Amsterdam, apparently also serving as the official organ for Betar throughout the country. The journal appeared as a monthly in 1935 but appears to have been published irregularly thereafter. Publication ceased in 1940.

De Joodse Wachter (DJW), "The Jewish Watchman," Dutch-language monthly of the Nederlandsche Zionistische Beweging, published between 1905 and 1940. Considered to be the most prestigious of the Zionist journals in Holland (and perhaps in all of Western Europe), DJW presented a wide range of information on Jewish communal affairs. Publication was interrupted by World War II but resumed in 1945, continuing until 1966. In 1967 DJW merged with the *Nieuw Israëlitisch Weekblad* (NIW), which had been anti-Zionist in orientation until 1939. The resulting weekly, which retained NIW's title and numbering, is officially nonpartisan, but strongly pro-Zionist.

Zionistisch Studentenjaarboek, "Zionist Students' Yearbook," annual publication of the Nederlansche Zionistische Studentorganisatie, published in two series. The initial series appeared in Delft between 1909 and 1924. Although called an annual, this series appeared less frequently: only three issues appeared between 1909 and 1915 and only three more from then until 1924. The second series, which did appear annually, was published in Amsterdam between 1931 and 1941. Publication ceased during the Nazi occupation.

Other Dutch Zionist Publications:

Het Beloofde Land (Amsterdam), Dutch monthly, 1922–1940.

Blauw en Wit (Amersfort), Dutch/German monthly, 1908.

Derech le-Tsion (Eindhoven), Dutch monthly, 1930.

Dewar ha-Tsofeh (Amsterdam), Dutch monthly/irregular, 1938–1939.

Iton Macbi (Harlem), Dutch monthly, 1936–1939.

De Joodsche Staat (Amsterdam), Dutch fortnightly, 1933–1934.

De Joodsche Volksstem (Amsterdam), Dutch monthly, 1918.

Mageen David (Amersfort), Dutch monthly, 1937–1940.

Mizrachie (Amsterdam), Dutch/Hebrew monthly, 1916–1940, 1949–1951.

Pitchon Peh (Amsterdam), Dutch weekly, 1939–1940.

Poland

Chwila, "Moment," Polish-language daily published by the Zionist organization in

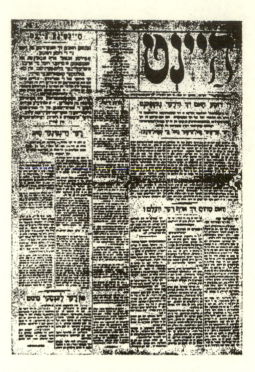

An Issue of *Haynt* From January 1908.
Courtesy of the New York Public Library Jewish Division

Lvov between 1919 and 1939. Highly regarded, the newspaper was respected by non-Zionists and by Zionists of all ideological stripes. Publication ceased due to World War II and was never resumed. Editor: Henryk Hescheles.

Haynt (היינט), "Today," Yiddish-language daily published in Warsaw between 1908 and September 22, 1939. In 1920, *Haynt* merged with *Dos Yiddishe Folk* (which ceased publication) and became the Polish Zionist federation's official organ. *Haynt's* editorial line tended toward the center-left on Jewish and Zionist issues, being correctly seen as the mouthpiece of Mapai and the JAE. Originally, *Haynt* appeared as a morning newspaper. From 1929 to 1939 an afternoon supplement entitled *Hayntige Nayes* (הײנטיגע נײעס, Today's News) was published. From 1928 to 1940 *Haynt* also published a subsidiary in Paris under the title *Parisier Haynt* (פאריזיער הײנט).

Lodzer Tagblatt (לאדזער טאגבלאט), "Lodz Daily Page," Yiddish daily published in Lodz in two series. The first appeared between 1908 and 1914, when the city was ruled by the

Germans. This series ceased publication during World War I. The second series appeared between 1925 and 1939, but was not a continuation of the earlier series. Its editorial line was similar in both series: general Zionist, moderate, and supportive of the WZO and JAE.

Ha-Mizpe (המיצפה), "The Watchtower," religious Zionist weekly appearing in Krakow between 1904 and 1921. Publication was steady except during World War I, when the lack of materials forced the newspaper to shut down. Publication was resumed in 1919. Throughout its publishing run, *ha-Mizpe* adhered to an editorial line that supported the Mizrachi party and ardently attacked the opponents of Zionism, among the assimilationist and the Orthodox camps.

Moment (מאמענט), Yiddish-language daily published in Warsaw between 1910 and 1939. Zionist in alignment, *Moment* tended toward the center-right on Jewish issues. In 1938 and 1939, *Moment* adopted an overtly revisionist Zionist orientation, in part as a means to attract readership by differentiating itself from its main competitor, *Haynt*. Circulation peaked at 60,000 just before World War II.

Nasz Przegląd (NP), "Our Review," Polish-language daily published in Warsaw between 1923 and 1939. Officially independent, NP was published with the financial assistance of *Haynt*. As a result, NP's editorial line that was similar to *Haynt*'s but was less overtly partisan. Contributors represented the entire spectrum of Polish Jewry's intelligentsia, including, among others, Florian Sokolow, Meyer Balaban, Emmanuel Ringelblum, Fishel Rotenstreich, Joseph Opatoshu, Joseph Klausner, and Janusz Korczak. The latter edited NP's weekly youth supplement (*Maly Przegald*). From 1928 to 1933, NP also published a weekly women's edition, entitled *Ewa* (Eve) which was edited by Pauline Appenszlak (wife of the then editor, Jacob Appenszlak). Circulation reached 40,000 just prior to World War II and included many non-Jewish subscribers — an unprecedented accomplishment for a Polish-Jewish journal. Ironically, NP's last issue was published on

September 1, 1939. Editors: Nathan Szwalbe, Saul Wagman, Jacob Appenszlak, Samuel Wolkowicz.

Nowy Dziennik (ND), "New Day," independent daily published in Krakow, appearing in Polish between 1918 and 1939. For technical reasons, all of the issues for 1918 and many of the issues for 1919 were printed in Moravska-Ostrava, Czechoslovakia. ND's editorial line strongly supported Zionism and was the first newspaper published in independent Poland to do so. ND's editorial line supported the moderate and gradualist policies espoused by Chaim Weizmann and in Poland by Osias (Joshua) Thon and the Galician Zionists. Publication ceased when the Nazis occupied Krakow in early September 1939. Editors: David Berkelhammer, Eliahu Tisch, Ignacy Schwarzbart, David Lazar.

Ha-Sharon (השרון), "The Sharon," short-duration Hebrew biweekly published in Lvov in 1895. Orthodox and nationalist in orientation, the journal failed to attract sufficient readership and folded after on seven issues had been printed. Ideologically, *ha-Sharon* was close to what would later develop into the Mizrachi party. Sole editor: Gershom Bader.

Der Tat (דער טאט), revisionist Zionist Yiddish-language daily published in Warsaw between 1935 and 1939. Publication began after ha-Zach was founded and the editorial line represented the most radical branch of Polish revisionism. In particular, this meant public support for the Irgun Zvai Leumi and for *Aliya Bet*. Publication ceased on the eve of World War II. Editors: Samuel Merlin, Nathan Yellin (Yellin-Mor), Abraham Stern.

Trybuna Narodowa (TN), "National Tribune," Polish-language revisionist Zionist weekly published in Warsaw between 1934 and 1939. Mainly issued as a polemical device, TN presented the revisionist worldview in stark contrast to that of the WZO. TN also published a youth version entitled *Trybuna Betaru* (Betar Tribune). Plagued almost from the beginning by financial difficulties, TN ceased to publish on the eve of World War II.

Tygodnik Żydowski (TŻ), "Jewish Weekly," title of three unrelated Polish-language serials, all of which shared a moderate general Zionist orientation. The first TŻ was published in Warsaw as a weekly, appearing in 1919 and 1920. The second TŻ was published by the ha-Shahar Zionist youth movement branch in Bielsko between 1924 and 1939. This version was bilingual, appearing in German and Polish. The third TŻ appeared simultaneously with the second but was unrelated, being published in Tarnów as a supplement to the *Yiddishe Wochenzeitung*.

Dos Vort (דאס װארט), "The Word," Yiddish-language daily published in Warsaw in 1933 and 1934 by the Poale Zion federation of Poland. Ideologically in the camp of Mapai supporters, *Dos Vort* appealed to the same readers as *Haynt*. Given the latter newspaper's more established position, *Dos Vort* could not compete and ceased publication after eleven months. In 1935, the journal was revived under the title *Dos Naye Vort* (דאס נייע װארט, The New Word) which was, in effect, a Yiddish version of the Yishuv daily *Davar*. This series survived into 1937 when publication ceased, again for financial reasons.

Dos Yiddishe Folk (דאס ייִדישע פֿאלק, DYF), "The Jewish People," Yiddish-language Zionist daily published in Warsaw. Publication commenced in 1913 as the organ of the Warsaw Zionist federation and, de facto, as the organ for all Zionist associations in Congress Poland (i.e., the territory ruled by Russia). The outbreak of World War I disrupted DYF publication almost completely. When publication resumed in 1918, DYF had become the official Zionist organ for all associations in the newly established Polish republic. However, the same institutional difficulties that plagued the Polish Zionist federation (which was being unified from previously existing regional federations) also plagued DYF and rendered its publication schedule highly eratic. To rectify the situation, DYF merged with *Haynt* in 1920 and ceased publication.

Ha-Zefira (הצפירה), "The Dawn," Hebrew weekly published in Warsaw (in 1862 and from 1910 to 1931) and then in Berlin (between 1874 and 1910). During its second Polish publication run, *ha-Zefira* appeared as a daily. *Ha-Zefira* was Zionist in orientation throughout its publishing run and always maintained a general Zionist editorial line. *Ha-Zefira* also obtained the support of Poland's Mizrachi movement, one of the few Zionist organs able to bridge the gap between Orthodox and non-Orthodox Zionists. One of *ha-Zefira*'s editors was Nahum Sokolow, who served as WZO president between 1931 and 1935. Editors: Haim Z. Slonimski, Nahum Sokolow, Yosef H. Haftman, Rabbi Isaac Nissenbaum, Fischel Lachover, Yitzhak Gruenbaum, Shmuel Rozenfeld, Natan Azriel.

Other Polish Zionist Publications:

Arbeiter Zeitung (Warsaw), Yiddish weekly, 1918–1919.

Folksblatt (Warsaw), Yiddish daily, 1939.

Der Folksfriend (Sanok), Yiddish weekly, 1909–1914.

Ha-Mizpe (Krakow), Hebrew weekly, 1904–1922.

Ha-Mizrach (Krakow), Hebrew monthly, 1903–1904.

Narod (Warsaw), Polish Monthly, 1928–1930.

Nasz Kurier (Warsaw), Polish daily, 1920–1923.

Nasz Życie (Lodz), Polish/Hebrew monthly, 1928–1932.

Nowe Slowo (Warsaw), Polish monthly, 1931–1932.

Der Telegraph (Warsaw), Yiddish daily, 1905–1906.

Der Weg (Warsaw), Yiddish daily, 1905–1906.

Der Yid (Krakow), Yiddish weekly, 1899–1903.

Romania

Al Hamüsmar (על המשמר), "On the Watch," title of two serials published by ha-Shomer ha-Zair in Romania and appearing in Bucharest. The first series was published as a mimeographed monthly in 1935 (according to some sources in 1934 and 1935). This title ceased publication for unknown reasons but was revived in 1944 as a typeset monthly that appeared until banned by the Communist authorities in 1948.

Drumuri Nouă (DN), "New Direction," monthly organ of ha-Zohar in Romania published in Bucharest in Romanian between 1926 and 1933. DN's editorial line was stridently critical of the WZO and JAE leadership. In the summer of 1933, in preparation for the elections to the Eighteenth Zionist Congress, DN was replaced by a biweekly journal entitled *Cuvîntul Evreiesc* (The Jewish Word). The latter ceased publication after only a few issues.

Hashmonaea (חשמונאי), "The Hashmonean," monthly organ of the Bucharest Student Zionist Society published in 1915. Publication was suspended when Romania joined the Entente powers during World War I but was resumed in 1919. A regular monthly publication schedule was begun in 1920 and continued until the title was banned by the Garda de Fier government in 1940. Publication was not resumed after the Holocaust. Although it never had a wide circulation, *Hashmonaea* played an important role in cultivating Zionist youth, most of whom played a prominent role in the Romanian Jewish community. Editors: Samu Stern, Samu Singer, Leon Mizrachi.

Renasterea Noastra (RN), "Our Rebirth," Romanian-language weekly published in Bucharest between 1925 and 1948. General Zionist in orientation, RN tended toward the radical Zionist position typified by Yitzhak Gruenbaum. RN had the largest circulation of any Romanian Jewish daily and thus wielded considerable influence within the community. This was especially true of educated readers to whom RN (which was founded by a group of Jewish university students and academicians) catered. Publication ceased by order of the Garda de Fier government in 1942 but was resumed in 1944. Publication was permanently ceased by the Communist government in 1948. Editors: Samu Stern (1925–1933), L. B. Wechsler (1933–1942), Moshe Moskowitz (1944–1948).

Uj Kelet (UK), "The New East," Hungarian-language Zionist daily published in Cluj, Transylvania (which was ruled by Romania in the interwar years), from 1918 to 1940. Initially published as a weekly, UK converted to a daily format in 1920. General Zionist in orientation, UK was a valiant fighter for Jewish rights in the Danubian basin. When the Hungarians regained control of Transylvania in 1940, UK was banned along with virtually the entire Jewish press in the region. In 1948, a new serial with the same title (but not continuing the original UK's numbering) was begun in Tel Aviv, catering to recent Hungarian *olim*. This serial is still in publication. Editors (Transylvanian series): Béla Székely (1918–1919), Ernö Marton (1919–1927), Ferenc Jámbor (1927–1940).

Ha-Yoez (היועץ), "The Adviser," independent Yiddish serial published in Bucharest between 1876 and 1920. Initially published as a weekly, in 1885 *ha-Yoez* converted to a biweekly format. Adopting an independent editorial line, *ha-Yoez* fought against Romanian antisemitism, for Jewish rights, and for Jewish self-respect. The editors' stand on the latter issue led them to support Hibbat Zion and, after 1897, the WZO. Superseded by other publications after World War I, *ha-Yoez* ceased publication in late 1920.

Other Romanian Zionist Publications

Arbeiterzeitung (Cernauti), Yiddish weekly, 1921–1940.

Erd un Arbet (Chişinău), Yiddish fortnightly, 1920–1938.

Neue Jüdische Rundschau (Cernauti), German weekly, 1925–1926.

Ostjüdische Zeitung (Cernauti), German daily, 1918–1940.

Uj Cor (Cluj), Hungarian/German fortnightly, 1919–1923.

Russia

Ha-Am (העם), "The People," Hebrew serial published in Moscow as a daily in 1917 and 1918. Earnestly Zionist, the editorial line was nonpartisan. Nevertheless, the editors' chose to emphasize *aliya*. They had a premonition that the revolutions of 1917 did not bode well for the long-term security of Russian Jewry. This premonition was reinforced by Communist efforts to close the newspaper, efforts that resulted in a temporary suspension in late October (November) 1917. Publication was finally and permanently halted by the Moscow Yevsektsia in June 1918. Circulation peaked at 15,000. Sole editor: Benzion Katz.

Ha-Melitz (המליץ), "The Advocate," Hebrew weekly published between 1860 and 1904 in Odessa and Petersburg. Initially concentrating on ideas of interest to *Maskilim*, *ha-melitz* advocated an assimilationist worldview prior to 1881. As a result of the pogroms, *ha-Melitz* reversed its editorial line and began to strongly support Zionism. Contributors included Y. L. Gordon, Joseph Klausner, and Ahad ha-Am. Editors: Alexander Zederbaum (1860–1893); Aaron I. Goldenblum (1893); Leon Rabinowicz (1893–1904).

Pardes (פרדס), "Plantation," Hebrew literary annual published between 1892 and 1896 (three bound volumes). Oriented toward Spiritual Zionism, the journal was strongly influenced by the Bnai Moshe movement. Publication ceased due to a combination of Russian censorship and financial difficulties. Sole editor: Y. H. Ravnitzki.

Rassviet, "Dawn," title used by three unrelated Russian-Jewish serials published in Odessa. The first two serials were short-lived weeklies (appearing 1860–1861 and 1879–1883) that advocated assimilation and Russification. In 1907 the Russian Zionist federation revived the title as its official organ, again as a weekly. This edition was published in Odessa until 1918. After the revolutions and the massive changes transpiring in Russian Jewry, publication was transferred to Moscow in 1918. Publication ceased by order of the Communist government in 1919. Publication was resumed again, this time by Russian Zionist émigrés living in Berlin in 1922 and 1923. In 1924, the editorial offices moved to Paris, where *Rassviet* appeared until publication finally ceased altogether in 1935. Publication ceased due to a combination of shrinking readership (the number of Russia speaking Jews living outside Russia and *Eretz Israel* shrivelled rapidly) and financial difficulties. While in Russia, *Rassviet*'s editorial line was general Zionist but radical in tone. During the two years of publication in Berlin, this general line remained, with a more activist edge. By the time *Rassviet* was transferred

to Paris, it had become a mouthpiece for ha-Zohar and especially for Ze'ev Jabotinsky. Considered to be the most authoritative revisionist journal, *Rassviet*'s articles were frequently translated and reprinted in other Zionist periodicals. Editors (Zionist series): Abraham Idelson (1907–1918), Ze'ev Jabotinsky (1922–1935).

Ha-Shiloah (השילוח), "The Envoy," Hebrew monthly published by a conglomerate of Ahad ha-Am's supporters. Between 1896 and 1907, *ha-Shiloah* was published in Berlin (to avoid Russian censorship) and had to be smuggled into the Russian empire. As a result of changes in press regulations that followed the Revolution of 1905, *ha-Shiloah*'s offices were transferred to Odessa in 1907. This series continued to appear until halted by the Communist authorities in 1919. After the Communist takeover, publication was transferred to Jerusalem, with regular publication between 1920 and 1926. Publication ceased due to financial difficulties in an already crowded field of Zionist publications in *Eretz Israel*. Throughout its existence, *ha-Shiloah*'s editorial line closely followed the Spiritual Zionism espoused by Ahad ha-Am, a reflection of his stewardship of the journal in its infancy. Editors: Ahad ha-Am (1896–1902), Joseph Klausner (1903–1926).

Yiddishe Folksblatt (ייִדישע פֿאָלקסבלאַט, YF), "Jewish People's Paper," Yiddish language weekly appearing in St. Petersburg between 1881 and 1890. Initially published as an independent periodical, the editorial line quickly adopted a position supporting the Hibbat Zion movement. By mid-decade, YF had become a virtual mouthpiece for the movement and was its most widely circulated periodical. Publication ceased in 1890 due to the collapse of Hibbat Zion.

Other Russian Zionist Publications:

Der Arbeiter Zionist (Minsk), Yiddish irregular, 1903.

Eretz Israel (Moscow), Russian monthly, 1918.

Makkabi (Odessa), Russian monthly, 1917.

Molodaya Yudeya (Irkutsk), Russian monthly, 1905.

Yevreiski Slovo (Harbin, Mongolia), Russian irregular, 1917–1918.

Yevreiski Student (St. Petersburg), Russian fortnightly, 1915–1917.

Der Yid (Minsk), Yiddish weekly, 1917–1918.

Zion (Drohobycz), Hebrew irregular, 1885–1888.

Zionistkoje Obosrenje (Elizabethgrad), Russian monthly, 1902–1903.

South Africa

The Jewish Herald (TJH), revisionist Zionist weekly published as the organ of ha-Zach in Johannesburg from 1937. Early issues were printed under the title *The Eleventh Hour*, with the changeover to TJH starting as of the November 26, 1937, issue. From then until 1948, TJH was a zealous supporter of ha-Zach. After the State of Israel was established, TJH converted to an independent, right-leaning weekly that remained in print until the 1980s.

Our Future, monthly organ of Mizrachi in South Africa, published between August 1942 and March 1951. For most of its publishing run the journal was bilingual, published in English and Yiddish. The first issue was trilingual (English/Yiddish/Hebrew) but no further Hebrew supplements were published. In 1951 the title was changed to *South African Jewish Observer*.

South African Jewish Chronicle (SAJC), premier organ of South Africa Jewry published as a parallel to the London *Jewish Chronicle* and appearing between 1902 and 1959. Like its namesake, SAJC appeared weekly. SAJC initially was published in Johannesburg, but in 1928 the editorial offices were moved to Cape Town. This move also represented a change in status. Previously independent (but clearly pro-Zionist), from 1928 onward, SAJC was published as an official organ, initially of the Dorshei Zion Society (1928–1953) and then of the South African Zionist Federation (1953–1959). In August 1959, SAJC merged with the *Zionist Record*, appearing thereafter as the *Zionist Record and South African Jewish Chronicle*.

South African Jewish Frontier (SAJF), socialist Zionist monthly appearing in Johannesburg since 1941. During its first five years SAJF appeared as *The Labour Zionist*; the title changed in March 1946. Publication was temporarily suspended for technical reasons between September 1948 and July 1949 but was resumed regularly thereafter. Supporting Mapai on most Zionist concerns, SAJF sought to propagate moderate socialist Zionism within South African Jewry.

Di Yiddishe Fahn (די ייִדישע פאָן, DYF), "The Jewish Standard," Yiddish-language independent Zionist journal published in Johannesburg from 1909 to 1913. Initially published as a biweekly, DYF converted to a weekly format on August 17, 1909. Between May and July 1913, DYF appeared daily. Financial difficulties forced the publisher to return to a weekly format in August, but DYF ceased publication after only a month. Strongly committed to Zionism, DYF influenced an entire generation of South African Jews to support the Jewish national movement. In 1912, DYF began to publish a weekly supplement in English. This was incorporated into the *South African Jewish Chronicle* (SAJC) when DYF ceased publication. SAJC remains in publication. Sole editor: Benzion Z. Hersch.

Zionist Record (ZR), monthly organ of the South African Zionist Federation published in Johannesburg between 1908 and 1959. From 1923 onward, ZR was South Africa's largest circulation Jewish periodical and was also considered to be South African Jewry's most authentic voice. ZR's editorial line was consistently general Zionist, leaning toward the more conservative B-Faction of the world movement and very close to Zionist factions that sought a more activist policy from the WZO and JAE. In 1959 ZR merged with the *South African Jewish Chronicle*, the new periodical being dubbed the *Zionist Record and South African Jewish Chronicle*, but publication ceased due to financial difficulties in 1978.

Other South African Zionist Publications:

Ha-Binyan (Johannesburg), English bimonthly, 1934–1945.

Ha-Cochav (Johannesburg), Hebrew/Yiddish weekly, 1903–1907.

Darkenu (Johannesburg), English monthly, 1948, 1950–1954.

Etzion (Johannesburg), English monthly, 1948–1955.

Ivri (Johannesburg), English quarterly, 1930–1936.

Judaea (Cape Town), English quarterly, 1915–1918.

Ba-Negev (Johannesburg), Hebrew monthly, 1942–1943.

On Guard (Johannesburg), English quarterly, 1939–1958.

Ha-Shomer ha-Zair (Johannesburg), English/Hebrew bimonthly, 1946–1955.

South African Jewish Times (Johannesburg), English weekly, 1936–1976.

Unzer Weg (Johannesburg), Yiddish monthly, 1919–1921.

Di Yiddishe Post (Johannesburg), Yiddish weekly, 1937–1938.

Sweden

Jidische Folkschtime (JFS), "Jewish People's Voice," Yiddish language organ of the Scandinavian Zionist Union, published in mid-1916 and early 1917. Published in Stockholm, most of the thirteen issues that appeared were printed in Copenhagen. Originally planned as a weekly, JFS initially appeared as a biweekly and then ceased publication. The last issue appeared on April 27, 1917. JFS adopted a strictly neutralist stance on World War I, mirroring the official WZO position but alienating the many Zionists of Russian origin then in Sweden.

Zionisten, "The Zionist," Swedish-language organ of the Swedish Zionist Union, published in 1913. Originally planned as a monthly, only five issues appeared. Editorial line was oriented toward synthetic Zionism and toward providing a forum for Zionist ideas to develop in Sweden. The journal collapsed due to financial difficulties deriving from the lack of mass subscriptions. Most supporters of Zionism in Sweden prior to World War I were recent Russian immigrants and they had difficulty reading the journal. Sole editor: Leopold Turitz.

Tunisia[1]

Cahiers du Bétar (CB), "Notebooks of Betar," revisionist Zionist monthly published in French by Betar's Tunis branch and appearing between 1938 and 1946. CB replaced *ha-Ivri*, which had published seven issues after its founding in 1937. Although CB was not as influential as its predecessor, it did serve an important educational role in Tunisian Jewry and was one of the most *aliya*-oriented Zionist journals in North Africa. Sole editor: Alfred Louzoun.

La Gazette d'Israël, "The Gazette of Israel," revisionist Zionist weekly published as a replacement for the defunct *La Réveil Juif* and appearing in Tunis in French between 1938 and 1951. One of the longest-running journals in Tunisian Jewish history, the gazette combined political advocacy and news with an earnest concern for *aliya*.

Ha-Ivri (העברי), "The Hebrew," short-lived monthly published by Betar in Tunis between December 1937 and July 1938. Editorial line emphasized three elements in Zionism: national rebirth, linguistic renaissance, and renewal of the land. Although only seven issues of *ha-Ivri* appeared, Betar was the largest single Jewish youth organization in Tunisia at the time. *Ha-Ivri*'s influence was thus far-reaching and the publication was replaced almost immediately by *Cahiers du Bétar*.

Kol Israel (קול ישראל), "The Voice of Israel," bilingual Hebrew and Judeo-Arabic weekly published as the official organ of the Tunisian Zionist federation. Appearing between 1919 and 1925, *Kol Israel* was possibly the most influential Jewish periodical published in North Africa. Publication ceased, however, due to financial difficulties and was never resumed.

La Réveil Juif (LRJ), "The Jewish Renaissance," revisionist Zionist French-

---

[1] Tunisia had the most active Zionist organization in all of French North Africa and the most diversified Jewish press in any French colony. Most of the periodicals listed here also circulated throughout Morocco and Algeria, neither of which communities produced any major Zionist publications.

language weekly published in Sfax between 1924 and 1934. LRJ was an outspoken critic of the WZO executive and was one of the staunchest supporters of independent activity by ha-Zohar. Among others, LRJ was the first to suggest that Keren Tel Hai directly compete with the Keren Kayemet le-Israel. Publication ceased on the eve of the schism but was resumed in Tunis under the title *La Gazette d'Israël*. Editor: Félix Allouche. > see also: **Revisionist Schism.**

La Voix Juive, "The Jewish Voice," French-language Zionist periodical published in Tunis in two series. The first series appeared between 1920 and 1922 and was oriented toward Zionist educational and cultural issues. The second series appeared between 1944 and 1946 but used only the title; it did not continue the earlier numbering or editorial line. Instead, the second series was published to organize Zionist political activity and promote *aliya*. Editors (first series): Henri Maarek; (second series): M. J. Saada, Félix Allouche, Moïse Madar.

United Kingdom

Jewish Chronicle (JC), independent Anglo-Jewish weekly, published in London since 1841, with a brief hiatus between 1842 and 1848 when the title appeared as *The Voice of Jacob*. JC's position on Zionism varied, mainly being a reflection of the editor at any given time. Under Abraham Benisch's guidance (1854–1869), for instance, JC supported a number of proto-Zionist settlement schemes. After Benisch, JC moved to a non-Zionist position, returning to the Zionist fold, permanently, after Leopold J. Greenberg bought the newspaper in 1907. In the 1930s, JC moved to the right on the Zionist spectrum, supporting activist positions (including those of ha-Zohar's leaders) against the gradualist policies espoused by Chaim Weizmann and the English Zionist Federation. Albeit, JC remained open to all positions within the Anglo-Jewish community and was (and still is) widely regarded as the authoritative voice of the Anglo-Jewish community. Circulation

peaked at 60,000 in 1945.

Jewish Standard (JS), English-language fortnightly published in London between 1888 and 1945. JS took no official opinion on Zionism until 1897 but was thereafter generally supportive. Officially independent, during the 1930s JS adopted a revisionist Zionist orientation that was retained throughout the remaining years of publication. Editor: Abraham Abrahams (1933–1945).

Jewish World (JW), Anglo-Jewish weekly launched in 1873 as a rival to the *Jewish Chronicle* and published in London until 1934. JW approached the subject of Jewish nationalism from much the same point of view as its competitor: largely supportive with certain periods of apathy. Given the similarity of their approaches, it was obvious that only one newspaper could survive and that one was the *Jewish Chronicle*. JW was purchased by the owners of the *Jewish Chronicle* in April 1913 but continued to publish as a midweek supplement until 1934.

Di Tsayt (די צייט), "The Times," Yiddish-language daily appearing in London between 1913 and 1950. Pro-Zionist in orientation, the editorial line supported Mapai and the Jewish Agency. In 1944 the newspaper switched to weekly publication. Highly influential on London's East End, *Di Tsayt* halted publication after a majority of Anglo-Jews ceased to read Yiddish.

Der Yiddisher Proletarier (דער ייִדישער פּראָלעטאַריער, DYP), "The Jewish Proletarian," irregular Yiddish journal published in 1905 by the Poale Zion party branch in London. Two different versions existed: one on standard paper for distribution to members in the United Kingdom and one on thin paper for clandestine distribution in the Russian empire. Having only a brief publication run, only one issue survives (November 1905). One source implies that DYP also appeared in 1906.

Zionist Review (ZR), official monthly organ of the English Zionist Federation (EZF), published between 1917 and 1952. ZR adopted a moderate general Zionist editorial line but failed to generate any degree of enthusiasm even within the EZF. Critics maintained that ZR concentrated on communal affairs to a degree that was inconsistent with its ostensible role as a Zionist political medium. In contrast, defenders noted that ZR's problems were similar to the EZF's and reflected the generally weak position of Zionism within Anglo-Jewry. ZR was a diligent advocate of Zionism, but it reflected all the strengths and weaknesses of its sponsor. Peak circulation was 16,000 in 1948. Publication ceased in 1952 when ZR was replaced by the *Jewish Observer and Middle East Review*.

Zionistische Korespondents (ציוניסטישע קאָרעספּאָנדענץ, ZK), "Zionist Correspondence," official Yiddish-language weekly organ of the English Zionist Federation. Appearing in 1902 only, ZK was not successful. Most recent immigrants (who read Yiddish) tended toward socialism rather than Zionism, whereas the more anglicized Jews (who supported Zionism as a means to protect the Jewish community from Communism) did not read Yiddish. Sole editor: Jacob de Haas.

Other Anglo-Zionist Publications:

Freie Yiddishe Tribune (London), Yiddish monthly, 1943–1948.

Der Kotel Ma'aravi (London), Yiddish fortnightly, 1902.

Ha-Meorer (London), Hebrew monthly, 1906–1907.

Palestina (London), Yiddish quarterly, 1892–1898.

Pioneren un Helfer (London), Yiddish quarterly, 1932–1937.

Unzer Weg (London), Yiddish fortnightly, 1919–1923.

Dos Yiddishe Folk (London), Yiddish weekly/monthly, 1934–1935.

Di Yiddishe Freiheit (London), Yiddish monthly, 1904–1905.

Di Yiddishe Zukunft (London), Yiddish monthly, 1904–1908.

United States

Congress Weekly (CW), official organ of the American Jewish Congress published since 1933. Initially entitled *Congress Bulletin*, the title CW was adopted in 1935.

The format and title changed in 1941 to *Congress Bi-Weekly*. This series appeared as a fortnightly until 1974, when the format and title again changed, this time to a monthly. Reflecting the attitudes of the American Jewish Congress, CW and its progeny were consistent in enunciating vocal support for the WZO and the *Yishuv*.

Hadassah Newsletter (HNL), organ of Hadassah, the Women's Zionist Organization of America, published since 1914. The early issues appeared as *Hadassah Bulletin*, which was changed to HNL in September 1917, when the journal appeared as a bimonthly. In addition to news about Hadassah projects and branches, HNL devoted considerable space to conditions in the *Yishuv* and European Jewry. HNL was an early and consistent supporter of Youth Aliya, which virtually became a pet project of the Hadassah organization. Zionism was always viewed by HNL as a spiritual, social, and philanthropic endeavor; little attention was ever paid to political matters and HNL's editorial line remained consistently nonpartisan. In April 1961, HNL again changed its title to *Hadassah Magazine*, which is now published in a monthly format.

Jewish Frontier (JF), monthly organ of the Labor Zionist Organization of America and the League for Labor Palestine published since 1934. Some of the early issues appeared under the title *Labor Palestine*. Focused equally on cultural and political affairs, JF consistently supported Mapai's position on Zionist issues, seeking a synthesis between Jewish nationalism and democratic socialism without compromising either goal. Considered one of the key Zionist journals of the 1930s and 1940s, JF attracted a wide range of Jewish intellectuals who filled its editorial and correspondent roles with sensitivity and alacrity.

The Jewish World (JW), independent weekly published in New York between June 1902 and 1904 in a bilingual Yiddish/English format. Published under the auspices of Louis Marshall, JW was seen as a means to Americanize recent immigrants from Eastern Europe. JW's editorial line on Zionism was bifurcated, the Yiddish section being very supportive and the English section being almost equally adamantly opposed to Zionism. Financial difficulties, combined with serious ideological disagreements between Marshall and the editorial staff, led the former to divest himself of JW in May 1904. Publication ceased altogether that December. Sole editor: Hirsch Masliansky.

The Maccabean, monthly organ of the Federation of American Zionists (until 1913) and then of the Zionist Organization of America (ZOA). The journal appeared in New York and was published entirely in English from 1901 to 1920. A Yiddish edition was published briefly in 1902. General Zionist in orientation, the *Maccabean* focused entirely on events in the *Yishuv*, the WZO, and the ZOA. Publication was suspended in November 1920 when the editorial offices moved to Washington, D.C. When publication resumed, the title was changed to *New Palestine*.

Menorah Journal (MJ), organ of the Intercollegiate Menorah Association, a Jewish fraternity with Zionist leanings, appearing between 1915 and 1962. MJ officially appeared bimonthly, although issues after 1930 tended to be less regular. Mainly literary and cultural in orientation, MJ remained staunchly nonpartisan but clearly pro-Zionist. Zionism was viewed as any other Jewish issues: after careful analysis from all possible angles, the editor concluded that Zionism was an important feature in Jewish survival. Publication ceased when Harry Hurwitz, the founding (and sole) editor, died.

New Palestine (NP), official bimonthly organ of the Zionist Organization of America, published in Washington, D.C., between 1921 and 1948. Initially published as a news bulletin, in 1941 it expanded to include essays and analysis on contemporary Zionist and Jewish issues. At the same time, NP began to appear as a fortnightly. In 1944 the format changed, with two issues per month, one containing a compilation of brief news reports and the other containing longer analysis articles. In 1947 the format changed again, with the two different issues merged into a single monthly issue. In 1951 the title was changed to *The American Zionist*. The journal still appears as *The American Zionist*, however, publication returned to New York in the 1950s.

Der Tog (דער טאג), "The Day," Yiddish-language daily newspaper published in New York between 1914 and 1953. Officially independent, *Der Tog* was published by a conglomerate that included a number of well-known Zionists. As a result, *Der Tog* reflected a moderately pro-Zionist editorial line, the first Yiddish paper in America to do so. In seeking to remain nonpartisan, *Der Tog's* editors concentrated on the travails of new immigrants to the United States and the increasing volatility of Jewish life in Eastern Europe. The suffering of East European Jewry during the 1930s and 1940s pushed *Der Tog* explicitly into the Zionist camp. From 1919 onward an English segment was included in every issue and by 1945 this had burgeoned into an entire page. Nonetheless, *Der Tog's* circulation fell as the generation of Yiddish-reading immigrants faded. In 1953 *Der Tog* merged with the *Morgen Journal* and ceased publication. Peak circulation was reached in the late 1920s, with approximately 118,000 subscribers for weekday issues and 86,000 for the Sunday issue.

Der Yiddisher Kempfer (דער יידישער קעמפער, DYK), "The Jewish Fighter," Yiddish-language socialist Zionist organ published since 1906. Initially published in Philadelphia, DYK's editorial offices moved to New York in 1907. From founding to 1920, DYK appeared as a weekly. Dedicated to socialist Zionism, DYK's editorial line supported Poale Zion's right wing, eventually dovetailing into the ideology espoused by Mapai. Still, DYK was seen by its editors as an educational tool and not a political weapon. Financial difficulties caused a suspension of publication between 1920 and 1924. Between 1924 and 1932 the journal was published in a biweekly format as *Der Yiddisher Arbeiter* (דער יידישער ארבייטער, The Jewish Worker). However, in 1932 DYK resumed its original title and weekly format. In 1934 DYK spawned an English-language monthly entitled *The Jewish Frontier*. Considered one of the most literate of the Yiddish journals published in America, DYK is still in print.

Der Yidisher Legioner (יידישער לעגאָנער דער, DYL), "The Jewish Legioneer," Yiddish-language monthly published by members of the *Yishuv* who had been exiled by the Turkish authorities and had taken up temporary residence in New York. DYL appeared during 1918 only and served as a recruiting device for the Jewish Legion. > see also: **World War I**.

Other American Zionist Publications:

American Jewish Chronicle (New York), English weekly, 1916–1918.

The Blue and White (Philadelphia), English monthly, 1906–1907.

The Jewish Star (Atlanta), English weekly, 1909–1912.

Ha-Leumi (New York), Hebrew/English weekly, 1888–1889.

Der Pinkas (New York), Yiddish monthly, 1906–1907.

Di Zeit (New York), Yiddish monthly, 1897–1898, 1920–1922.

The Zion Messenger (Chicago), English monthly, 1904–1906.

Der Zionist (New York), Yiddish monthly, 1897.

Uruguay

Di Nazionale Shtime (די נאַציאָנאַלע שטימע, DNS), "The National Voice," short-lived Zionist journal published in Montevideo in 1928, focusing on the *Yishuv* and local Jewish issues. DNS ceased publication after only a few issues appeared, due to financial difficulties.

Uruguayer Yiddishe Prese (אורוגוייער ייִדישע פּרעסע, UYP), "Uruguayan Jewish Press," Yiddish weekly published in Montevideo between 1929 and 1931. Although officially independent, UYP was strongly pro-Zionist and forthrightly published information on antisemitism around the world.

Yugoslavia

Gideon, Serbo-Croatian monthly oriented toward Jewish youth published in Zagreb from 1910 to 1926. First appearing when the Austrians ruled Croatia, publication continued after Croatia merged with Serbia to form Yugoslavia. General Zionist in orientation, *Gideon* sought to implant a feeling for Jewish culture and nationalism in Yugoslav Jewish youth. In 1926 *Gideon* was replaced in serial publication by *ha-Noar* (הנוער, Youth) which, despite its Hebrew title, was also published in Serbo-Croat. Like its predecessor, *ha-Noar* concentrated on culture, deemphasizing both political Zionism and *aliya*. Publication was temporarily suspended in 1933, but resumed in 1937. This series ceased altogether when the Nazis invaded the country in 1941.

Židov, "The Jew," Zionist weekly published in Zagreb, Croatia, from 1917 to 1941. Published in Serbo-Croat, *Židov* served as the de facto organ of the Zionist federation of Yugoslavia (whose main strength lay in Croatia in any case). Additionally, *Židov* served the entire Yugoslav Jewish community and was the most respected Jewish periodical in the country. Publication ceased after the Nazi invasion of Yugoslavia.

Other Yugoslav Zionist Publications:

Malhut Israel (Novy Sad), Hebrew/Serbo-Croat weekly, 1923.

Yevreiski Glas (Sarajevo), Serbo-Croatian weekly, 1928–1941.

Zsido Élet (Novy Sad), Hungarian weekly, 1928–1941.

Zsidovska Smotra (Zagreb), Serbo-Croat biweekly, 1907–1914.

Zsidovska Svijet (Sarajevo), Serbo-Croat weekly, 1919–1927.

3. Yishuv Publications

General Circulation Publications

Al ha-Mishmar (על המשמר), "On Watch," daily organ of ha-Shomer ha-Zair, published in Tel Aviv since 1943 (since 1948, of Mifleget ha-Poalim ha-Meuhad, Mapam). *Al ha-Mishmar*'s editorial line was much more Marxist than *Davar*'s, in fact, publication commenced in order to offer Histadrut members an alternative to the reformist orientation then dominant in Mapai. In addition to its Marxist viewpoint, the editorial line was initially very pro-Soviet, a position that only changed in the late 1950s.

Dapim, German language weekly published in Tel Aviv by Mapai between 1946 and 1952. The periodical was designed as a mouthpiece to influence the more integrated German *olim* and obtain their support for Mapai and the JA.

Davar (דבר), "Word," Hebrew daily published in Tel Aviv by the Histadrut and Mapai since 1925. Reflecting the ideology of Mapai's majority, *Davar* expressed a reformist rather than a revolutionary socialist orientation and strongly supported efforts to build a wide coalition of Zionists on behalf of the *Yishuv*. Editors: Berl Katznelson (1925–1944), Zalman Shazar (1944–1949).

Doar ha-Yom (דואר היום), "The Daily Mail," independent daily published between 1919 and 1936. Initially founded by Eliezer Ben-Yehuda and edited by his son, Itamar Ben-Avi, *Doar ha-Yom* initially served the *Yishuv* as a nonpartisan news forum. These early issues were credited with introducing modern journalistic styles into the *Yishuv*'s press. In the mid-1920s *Doar ha-Yom*'s editorial line abruptly changed to an anti-Zionist course that was retained until 1928. In its final transformation, *Doar ha-Yom* became a mouthpiece for the most radical elements of ha-Zohar in *Eretz Israel*. Although moderating its tone after 1933, publication ceased entirely in 1936.

Ha-Ahdut (האחדות), "Unity," socialist Zionist organ published in Jaffa and Tel Aviv between 1910 and 1914. *Ha-Ahdut* began its publishing run as a monthly, switching to a weekly format in 1911. Its editorial line supported Poale Zion, and especially the right wing of that party. Publication ceased in December 1914 by order of the Ottoman authorities. Editors: David Ben-Gurion, Yitzhak Ben-Zvi, Rachel Yanait Ben-Zvi.

Ha-Aretz (הארץ), "The Land," independent daily published since 1919, and considered the most respected of all Israeli dailies. *Ha-Aretz* adopted a general Zionist editorial line and maintained that line throughout the 1920s and 1930s. Even so, *ha-Aretz* was very careful never to act as a mouthpiece for any particular Zionist party, thus remaining independent in a highly politicized press atmosphere in the *Yishuv*. *Ha-Aretz* was probably the most sophisticated of the *Yishuv*'s dailies, with a network of correspondents throughout Europe and the Middle East. Editors: Moshe Glickson (1922–1937), Gershom Schocken (1937–1977).

Ha-Boker (הבוקר), "The Morning," independent daily published in Tel Aviv between 1935 and 1965. General Zionist in orientation, *ha-Boker*'s editorial line was more adversarial toward the Histadrut, JA, and WZO executives, reflecting the perspective of the so-called B-faction of the general Zionist party. In this, *ha-Boker* adopted a position that stood between the moderate editorial line adopted by *ha-Aretz* and the outright revisionism adopted by *Doar ha-Yom* in its last years. After the State of Israel was established, *Ha-Boker* became the official organ of the Liberal party.

Ha-Mashkif (המשקיף), "The Observer," daily organ of ha-Zach in Tel Aviv — also serving ha-Zach branches throughout *Eretz Israel* — published between 1938 and 1948. Representing ha-Zach's right wing, *ha-Mashkif* nonetheless repudiated the Irgun Zvai Leumi and Lohame Herut Israel during World War II for reasons of legality. Even so, the editors bitterly attacked the British Palestine administration, for betraying sacred promises made to the Jewish people, and the JA and WZO leadership, for adopting too conciliatory a policy in response to the White Paper of 1939. In 1948, after the establishment of the State of Israel, *ha-Mashkif*'s title was changed to *Herut*.

Ha-Poel ha-Zair (הפועל הצעיר, HPHZ), "The Young Worker," organ of the Polae Zion party in Eretz Israel, published from 1907 to 1970. Initially it appeared in Jaffa as a mimeographed bulletin, and regular publication began in Tel Aviv in a biweekly format in 1908. In 1913 and 1914 HPHZ appeared in a weekly format, but publication was disrupted by World War I. Publication resumed in 1918, on a weekly basis until publication ceased altogether. From 1918 to 1930, HPHZ represented the right wing of Poale Zion that adopted the name ha-Poel ha-Zair. In 1930 this group merged with the Ahdut ha-Avoda wing to form Mapai, and HPHZ immediately became the new party's organ. Reformist and etatist in orientation, HPHZ supported the JAE on all major Zionist issues.

Ha-Yarden (הירדן), "The Jordan," revisionist Zionist weekly published between 1934 and 1941. *Ha-Yarden* was initially published in Jerusalem as a daily, but the editorial offices soon moved to Tel Aviv in 1936 and the format changed to weekly publication. During the Arab Revolt, *ha-Yarden* was stinging in its criticism of the British government, the JAE, and the Hagana, which led to numerous cessations in publication when the British police imposed bans on the newspaper. In 1941 publication ceased altogether.

Ha-Zofe (הצפה), "The Seer," religious Zionist daily published since 1937 and acting as the mouthpiece for the Mizrachi party. Initially it appeared three times a week in Jerusalem. Publication was transferred to Tel Aviv in early 1938 after which a daily format was instituted. Although reflecting Mizrachi's ideology, *ha-Zofe* contained full coverage of items of Jewish and Zionist interest. Since 1948, *ha-Zofe* has been the mouthpiece of the Miflaga ha-Datit ha-Leumit (Mafdal).

Ha-Zvi (הצבי), "The Hart," Hebrew weekly published between 1884 and 1901 as a forum for Zionist ideas and for the renewal of the Hebrew language; between 1908 and 1915 *ha-Zvi* appeared as a daily. Editorial line may be described as general Zionist, although the actual position adopted by the editor was much narrower: There could be no Jewish national rebirth unless Hebrew was revived as the spoken language of the Jewish people. There was a gap in publication between 1901 and 1907, with publication ceasing altogether in 1915. Between 1897 and 1899 *ha-Zvi* also published an agricultural supplement, under the title *ha-Ikar ha-Yehudi*. Sole editor: Eliezer Ben-Yehuda.

Hazit ha-Am (חזית העם), "The National Front," radical revisionist Zionist weekly published in Jerusalem between 1932 and 1934. Reflecting the activist wing of ha-Zohar, *Hazit ha-Am*'s editorial line was vehemently opposed to the JAE, the WZO, and the Histadrut. The newspaper's tone often bordered on incitement, especially in the tense period prior to Haim Arlosoroff's murder. Indeed, *Hazit ha-Am*'s editors were accused of inciting Arlosoroff's killers, although that accusation remains unproved. Even so, publication ceased as a result of the adverse publicity from the incident; *Hazit ha-Am* was then replaced with *ha-Yarden*.

Jüdische Welt-Rundschau (JWR), "Jewish World Observer," Zionist weekly that replaced the *Jüdische Rundschau*. Published in Paris and printed in Tel Aviv, JWR ceased publication after the Nazi occupation of France.

Ketuvim (כתובים), "Writings," weekly organ of the Writers' Association of *Eretz Israel*, published in Tel Aviv between 1926 and 1933. Mainly focused on cultural issues, the journal was completely nonpolitical. Combining the best in old and new Hebrew literature, *Ketuvim*'s editors sought to participate in creating a Jewish national home by creating a new Jewish culture.

Kunteres (קונטרס), "Notebook," title of two Labor Zionist serials published in Tel Aviv. The earlier one was the weekly organ of the first Ahdut ha-Avoda party, published between 1919 and 1929. Publication of this serial ceased when Ahdut ha-Avoda merged with ha-Poel ha-Zair to form Mapai. The second series was published as a Histadrut publication between 1943 and 1945.

Le-Ahdut ha-Avoda (לאחדות העבודה), "For the Unity of Labor," weekly organ of Mapai's *Siya Bet*, published between 1944, when *Siya Bet* seceded from Mapai, and 1948, when the new party (also called le-Ahdut ha-Avoda) merged with ha-Shomer ha-Zair to form Mifleget ha-Poalim ha-Meuhad (Mapam). Its editorial line differed from *Davar*'s mainly on foreign policy issues, notably its attitude to the Soviet Union. Circulation was always very small, but the party was very vocal in its opposition to Mapai's policies.

Ma'ariv (מעריב), "Evening," independent afternoon daily published since 1948. Although independent of any party, the editorial line would be considered moderately right of center. Founding editor: Azriel Carlebach.

Mitteilungblatt, Wochenzeitung des Irgun Olej Merkas Europa, "Communications Page, Weekly Magazine of the Organization of Central European Immigrants," German-language newsletter published by Hitachdut Olei Germania (since 1938 Irgun Olei Mercaz Europa) and appearing in Tel Aviv since 1933. Initially printed as a mimeographed newsletter, MB has been published as a regular weekly since 1939. MB was designed as a journal to keep new *olim* in touch with the organization and its activities while also speeding their integration into the *Yishuv's* society. Between 1935 and 1948 MB also functioned as a de facto mouthpiece of the Ahdut ha-Am party. After World War II the title was shortened to *Mitteilungsblatt*.

Palestine Bulletin, original title of the *Palestine Post* during its publication run prior to 1932. > see also: **Publications, Zionist (Yishuv, Palestine Post)**.

Palestine Post (PP), independent, but pro-Mapai, English-language daily published in Jerusalem from 1932 to 1950; PP superseded the *Palestine Bulletin* (which appeared between 1929 and 1932) and was superseded by the *Jerusalem Post* in 1950. Nominally independent, PP vocally supported Mapai on most issues effecting the *Yishuv*. Editor (to 1950): Gershon Agronsky (Agron).

Palnews, multilingual digests of news and statistics, published at varying intervals by the Palnews Agency, an independent news agency located in Tel Aviv, between 1933 and 1947. In addition to the weekly *Palnews* survey (which appeared in both English and German editions) publications included the *Palnews Economic Annual of Palestine*, which appeared in English between 1935 and 1939 and in German in 1935 and 1936.

Yediot Aharonot (ידיעות אחרונות), "The Latest News," independent afternoon daily published in Tel Aviv since 1939. The first afternoon newspaper in *Eretz Israel, Yediot Aharonot* was also the first tabloid-style newspaper published there. General Zionist in orientation, its editorial line has leaned to the center-right of the Israeli political spectrum. Editors: A. Carlebach (1939–1948), Jerzl Rosenblum (1948–1971).

Underground Publications

Alon ha-Palmah (עלון הפלמ"ח, AHP), "Palmah Newsletter," irregular organ of the Palmah published between 1941 and 1948. Publication began as a mimeographed internal bulletin for and by members of the First Palmah Company. In the autumn of 1942, the venue changed, AHP now being available to all Palmah members, although the semiclandestine nature of the publication meant that AHP still could not adhere to a regular publication schedule. For much of 1943 AHP served as the de facto publication of the Hagana as well as the Palmah. In addition to articles on military affairs, AHP contents included items on the *Yishuv*, Zionism, and the Jewish world. Publication ceased in November 1948, shortly after the Palmah was disestablished. > see also: **Yishuv, Organizations (Underground Movements, Plugot Mahatz)**.

Anu ha-Homa (אנו החומה), "We Are the Wall," Yiddish language publication of the Hagana branch in Germany after World War II. The journal was directed toward veteran Hagana personnel as well as new recruits throughout Europe, including those who joined the ranks while in Displaced Persons camps. > see also: **Giyus Hutz la-Aretz**.

Eshnav (אשנב), "Peephole," Hagana-sponsored newspaper published between 1941 and 1947. Printed either weekly or biweekly, *Ashnav* was available to all members of the *Yishuv*. Contents were gleaned from other periodicals, specifically from items that British censors ordered deleted for one reason or another. Circulation peaked at 30,000 just after World War II ended. Editors: Berl Katzenelson (1941–1944), Eliezer Liebenstein (1944–1947).

Ba-Mahane (במחנה), "In the Camp," monthly publication of the Hagana's cultural department. Attuned toward members' cultural and educational needs, *ba-Mahane* included both information and gossip about local branches and their activities. Publication began in 1934, although prior to 1948 all issues were handwritten and mimeographed. The first printed issue appeared on December 12, 1948, by which time publication was taken over by the chief education officer of Zva ha-Hagana le-Israel (Zahal). Publication has continued

Front Page of *ba-Mahane* for
February 8, 1941.

Courtesy of Archion Toldot ha-Hagana, Tel Aviv

since 1949 under Zahal auspices, with *Ba-Mahane* now appearing as a weekly. > see also: **Zva ha-Hagana le-Israel**.

Ha-Hazit (הַחֲזִית), "The Front," irregular organ of Lohame Herut Israel (Lehi), published between 1943 and 1948. Officially published as a monthly, it appeared irregularly due to Lehi's legal status and almost continuous involvement with the police. *Ha-Hazit's* editorial line was extremist, with the British and the JAE receiving most of the editor's ire. Publication ceased when the Lehi movement disintegrated during the War of Independence. Sole editor: Israel Scheib (Eldad).

Ha-Homa (הַחוֹמָה), "The Wall," Hagana news bulletin appearing after World War II and designed to provide information to the general public in the Yishuv. Issues were plastered on walls as a means of avoiding British censorship and ensuring that a maximum number of people saw the bulletins.

Ha-Ma'as (הַמַעשׂ), "The Deed," internal bulletin of Lohame Herut Israel (Lehi) published irregularly between 1944 and 1948. This edition was published in a mimeographed format. In 1949 and 1950 the surviving Lehi members tried to publish *ha-Ma'as* as a regular monthly journal but the project collapsed for financial reasons. Representing the most radical Zionist

viewpoint, *ha-Ma'as* was equally opposed to the British and the JAE/WZO leadership. Sole editor: Israel Scheib (Eldad).

Igeret la-Noter (אִיגֶרֶת לַנוֹטֵר), "Letter to the Supernumerary," monthly Hagana bulletin for personnel serving in auxiliary police roles or in the Jewish Supernumerary Police (JSP) as part of the so-called Legal Hagana. Published between 1943 and 1945, *Igeret la-Noter* was a means to maintain the contact between the JSPs and the Hagana, thereby avoiding the possibility that the former might "go over" to the British. Publication ceased shortly after World War II ended, by which time most Jews had been released from police service. > see also: **Notar(im)**.

La-Hayal (לַחַיָּל), "For the Soldier," daily newspaper published between 1944 and 1946 by the Hagana and the JA for Jewish personnel serving in the Royal Army in Europe during World War II. *La-Hayal* was mainly dedicated to the personnel of the Jewish Brigade Group but was also available to *Yishuv* personnel serving in other units. Initially appearing in Italy, the publication apparatus moved with the brigade to Belgium in August 1945. Publication ceased when the brigade was disbanded.

Ma'arachot (מַעֲרָכוֹת), "Campaigns," monthly Hagana publication appearing since 1939. *Ma'arachot* was the first publication ever issued under Jewish auspices to deal exclusively with military affairs. A professional journal, it includes topics such as contemporary and historical investigations into the *Yishuv*, Zionist strategy, and military and political conditions in the Middle East and Europe. Since 1948, *Ma'arachot* has been published by the Israeli army's chief education officer.

Other Yishuv Zionist Publications:
Ha-Herut (Jerusalem), Hebrew fortnightly, 1909–1917.
Ha-Tor (Jerusalem), Hebrew weekly, 1920–1935.
Hed ha-Mizrah (Jerusalem) Hebrew weekly, 1942–1951.
L'Actualité Palestinienne (Jerusalem), French fortnightly, 1935–1939.
Luah Yerushalayim (Jerusalem), Hebrew Annual, 1940–1951.

Mizrah u-Ma'arav (Jerusalem), Hebrew monthly, 1919–1932.

Palestine Weekly (Jerusalem), English weekly 1920–1929.

Palestine Illustrated News, English weekly, 1933–1947.

Palestine Review, English weekly, 1936–1948.

4. Anti-/Non-Zionist[1]

Austria

Me-Mizrah ume-Ma'arav (ממזרח וממערב), "From East and West," Hebrew monthly appearing between 1894 and 1899, initially in Vienna and then in Berlin. The journal's editorial line rejected Hibbat Zion and later the WZO because they were insufficiently "humanistic." Nonetheless, the journal was not necessarily opposed to Jewish diaspora nationalism. Editor: Reuven Brainin.

Bulgaria

Bratsvo, "Brotherhood," biweekly of the Jewish section of the Bulgarian Communist Party, published in Bulgarian between August 1, 1921 and September 1, 1923. Zealously anti-Zionist, *Bratsvo* advocated total Jewish assimilation. Sole editor: Reuven Oliver.

Il Echo Judaico (איל איקו ג'ודאאיקו), "The Jewish Echo," Ladino-language weekly published by anti-Zionist supporters of Sofia's chief rabbi, Rabbi Mordechai Ehrenpreiss. Published between 1901 and 1907. For part of its publication run, the journal appeared as the organ of the Bulgarian chief rabbinate. Opposed to Zionism on religious grounds, its editorial line was equally opposed to assimilation.

Canada

Canadian Jewish Review (CJR), non-Zionist Canadian Jewish weekly published in Ontario and Montreal from 1921 to 1966. CJR's editorial line may be described as actively non-Zionist, rather than anti-Zionist, but in practice the distinction meant little. Thus, for example, during World War II CJR supported the idea of rehabilitating Jewish communities in Europe. Similarly, the establishment of the State of Israel was barely reported by CJR, whose focus was extremely parochial. In 1966 CJR merged with the *Canadian Jewish Chronicle* (to form the *Canadian Jewish Chronicle Review*), after which its editorial line reversed completely. Editors (CJR): George Cohen (1921), Florence F. Cohen (1922–1966).

France

Di Naye Presse (די נייע פרעסע), "The New Press," Franco-Jewish Communist daily, published in Yiddish in Paris between 1934 and 1939. In 1934 and 1935 the paper followed Communist policy regarding Jews and Judaism, viewing both as archaic and expressing special opposition to Zionism. Articles repeatedly attacked the organized Jewish community. This policy changed with the adoption of the Popular Front in 1936 and was most singularly represented by the editors' belated support for the Jewish anti-Nazi boycott. Publication ceased for unknown reasons on the eve of World War II.

Germany

CV Zeitung, "CV Newspaper," official monthly of the Centralverein Deutscher Staatsbürger jüdischen Glaubens, published between 1895 and 1935. Enunciating an assimilationist and

---

[1] The following section makes no claim at comprehensiveness, being only an initial investigation into the subject matter. It should be clearly noted that a considerable portion of the Jewish press prior to World War II was non- or anti-Zionist with this category likely representing the majority of Jewish periodicals in any given locale. Citations included here represent only a sample of the more interesting titles.

anti-Zionist orientation, the *CV Zeitung* was closed at Gestapo orders. Its editorial position on Zionism may be divided into three periods. From 1897 to 1912, the editors were non-Zionist but tried to enunciate their position in a temperate fashion. From 1913 to 1933, editorial orientation became more markedly anti-Zionist, although that was never the journal's main focus. In its last years, the editors advocated emigration of German Jewish youth, including *aliya*.

Der Israelit, "The Israelite," Orthodox Jewish weekly published between 1860 and 1938. From 1912 on, *Der Israelit* served as the official organ of Agudas Israel. The newspaper rejected Zionism as inconsistent with Orthodox Jewish belief in the Messiah. From the late 1920s onward, the editors supported building the *Yishuv* while still rejecting Zionism and Zionists. Publication ceased just before *Kristallnacht*.

Hungary

Egyenlöség, "Equality," Hungarian-language weekly published in Budapest between 1882 and 1944. Supporting an assimilationist editorial line, *Egyenlöség* was both anti-Zionist and Neolog (non-Orthodox) in orientation. Unlike numerous similar Hungarian Jewish periodicals, however, *Egyenlöség* retained its anti-Zionist orientation literally until the end. Publication was terminated when the Nazis occupied Hungary in March 1944.

International

Ha-Levanon (הלבנון), "The Lebanese," first ever Hebrew newspaper published in Eretz Israel, appearing in 1863. *Ha-Levanon* ceased publication after one year but was revived in Paris, where it was published between 1865 and 1870. Further moves brought the periodical to Berlin, between 1871 and 1882, and finally to London, between 1883 and 1887. Publication ceased entirely after 1887. Orthodox in its orientation, *ha-Levanon* never supported Zionism and was a critic of Hibbat Zion during its later Berlin years. Opposition to the Zionist movement softened considerably

during its years of publication in London, but the editorial line never changed to unequivocal support. *Ha-Levanon* is now remembered mainly as the father of the Hebrew press in *Eretz Israel*. Sole Editor: Yehiel Brill.

Latvia

Jungvarg (יונגווארג), "Young People," Yiddish weekly published by the Jewish Communist section in Riga in 1934 and oriented toward youth movement members. Publication ceased after the quasi-fascist government seized power. *Jungvarg's* editorial line was consistently pro-Soviet and anti-Zionist.

Netherlands

ITO, official monthly organ of the Jewish Territorial Association branch in Amsterdam. Published in German, *ITO* appeared in two series, the first between 1911 and 1914 and the second between 1916 and 1918. Both expressed a territorialist editorial line. Unlike their parent organization (which was then headquartered in London) both were virulently anti-Zionist. Publication ceased entirely after World War I, since the territorialist claim that *Eretz Israel* was unobtainable had been proven incorrect.

Nieuw Israëlietisch Weekblad (NIW), "New Jewish Weekly," among the oldest Jewish periodicals published in Amsterdam, appearing from 1865 to 1940 and from 1945 to the present. Representing the attitudes of Amsterdam's Orthodox community, NIW was stridently anti-Zionist until 1939; after World War II began the editors moderated their tone. Publication was interrupted during the German occupation of Holland but resumed in 1945. At that point, its editorial line reversed completely, with NIW expressing a position similar to that of the Mizrachi religious Zionist movement. In 1949 NIW merged with the Zionist weekly *De Joodse Wachter*, retaining its pro-Zionist orientation. > see also: **Publications, Zionist (Netherlands, De Joodse Wachter)**.

Poland

Folkstsaytung (פאלקסצייטונג), "People's Paper," official Yiddish daily organ of the Bund published between 1921 and 1939. Vehemently opposed to Zionism, editorial line was, nonetheless, nationalist. The editors advocated participation of Jewish socialists in the creation of a classless society and the attainment of Jewish national and cultural autonomy. Considered the key record of the Bund's ideological development in the interwar era. Legal publication ceased in October 1939, but it continued underground irregularly until 1943. Resumed publication as *Naye Folkstsaytung* from 1945 until taken over by Communist authorities in 1948. Editors: Alexander Ehrlich, Wiktor Alter.

Mahzikei ha-Dat (מחזיקי הדת) "Defenders of the Faith," Hebrew weekly appearing in Lemberg/Lwow (Russia/Poland/Ukraine) between 1879 and 1914. The editorial line was oriented toward Eastern Galicia's ultra-Orthodox community as was, at times, strongly anti-Zionist. Publication ceased due to World War I and was not resumed. Editors: Simon Sofer; Joshua Lipsker.

Tunisia

L'Egalité, "Equality," French-language weekly published by the Alliance Israélite Universelle (AIU) in Tunis between 1912 and 1940. Initially non-Zionist in orientation, the editorial line shifted to a strongly anti-Zionist position during the 1920s and then softened after the Nazi rise to power in Germany. Publication ceased by order of Vichy authorities in late 1940.

La Justice, independent French weekly published in Tunis between 1915 and 1934. Although officially dedicated to communal defense, its editorial line had definite assimilationist leanings. The editors, for instance, opposed *aliya* and passionately urged Jews to acquire French citizenship. Publication ceased when the editor died. Sole editor: Mordechai Smaja.

United Kingdom

Jewish Guardian (JG), weekly organ of the League of British Jews, published in London between 1919 and 1931. JG's editors claimed that they sought to free the Anglo-Jewish community from the domination of Zionists and particularly sought to break the *Jewish Chronicle*'s monopoly on the press. JG challenged the latter's claim to comprehensively represent the Anglo-Jewish community. JG's virulent anti-Zionism was, however, only popular with a narrow stratum of the Anglo-Jewish community and the newspaper's overall tone did not fit well with the editors' self-avowed patriotism (especially in an era when the British were considered to be helping build the Jewish national home and Zionism could be considered patriotic). Financial difficulties after the stock market crash in 1929 brought a cessation of publication. Circulation peaked at 1,200 in 1929. > see also: **Patriotic Zionism**.

United States

Arbeiter-Zeitung (ארבייטער-צייטונג), "The Worker's Paper," Yiddish-language weekly, published by American Jewish socialists between 1890 and 1902. Narrowly socialist in orientation and dogmatically Marxist, the journal always maintained an anti-Zionist editorial line. Attitudes toward the issue of Jewish nationalism and other ideological fissures created a schism in the editorial staff that culminated in the emergence of two rival newspapers using similar titles in 1897. Shortly thereafter, one of the two adopted the title *Forverts*. The remaining *Arbeiter-Zeitung* continued publishing for another five years and remained emphatically anti-Zionist.

Forverts (פארווערטס), "Forward," Yiddish daily published in New York since 1897, with an English edition appearing in the 1990s. Socialist in orientation, *Forverts*'s editorial line initially followed the Bundist position and opposed Zionism. This position began to mellow in the 1920s, moving from anti-Zionism to non-Zionism. A further reorientation came after World War II, when the *Forverts* supported efforts to create a Jewish state. Peak circulation reached 200,000 after World War I but fell to 80,000 in the 1940s. In the 1930s *Forverts* opened a radio station, WEVD.

Yishuv

Ha-Homa (החומה), "The Wall," not to be confused with the Hagana publication of the same title, this was an organ of Neturei Karta, the

extremely Orthodox anti-Zionist sect headquartered in Jerusalem's Mea Shearim
neighborhood. Beginning in 1944 issues of
the anti-Zionist *ha-Homa* started to appear,
being plastered on walls as an informational
broadsheet (hence the title). This version of
ha-Homa still appears from time to time,
generally to condemn Zionists for their acts
of presumed apostasy in creating a Jewish
state prior to the Messiah's arrival.

Havazelet (חבצלת), "Fleur-de-Lis," second
Hebrew newspaper published in *Eretz Israel*
(after *ha-Levanon*) appearing in Jerusalem
between 1863 and 1911. Initially published as
a monthly, *Havazelet* appeared as a weekly
from its third volume (1870) onward. The
editorial line reflected the values of
Jerusalem's Sephardic and Hasidic
communities and was thus strongly anti-
Zionist. Editors: Israel Beck (1863-1874),
Israel D. Frumkin (coeditor, 1870–1874,
editor, 1874–1911).

Kol ha-Am (קול העם), "Voice of the
Nation," Communist party Hebrew daily
published between 1947 and 1975. Published
in Tel Aviv, the early issues were mimeographed rather than printed on a standard
press. This reflected the Palestine
Communist party's fluctuating status during
the mandate period. Regular publication
began after the State of Israel was
established. Although edited and published
by Jews, the newspaper initially adopted the
Soviet position on Jewish nationalism and
thus must be considered an anti-Zionist
journal.

Kol Israel (קול ישראל), "The Voice of
Israel," organ of the Agudas Israel branch in
Jerusalem, published weekly between 1921
and 1949. In its early years, the editorial line
was distinctly anti-Zionist but always
supported the idea of Jewish restoration to
Eretz Israel. The editors moderated the anti-
Zionist tone during the Holocaust and
mildly supported Jewish statehood in 1948.
When Aguda joined the provisional
government, *Kol Israel* supported the move.

5. Research Journals on Zionism and Israel

Israel Affairs, quarterly published since 1994
by Frank Cass, London and dedicated to the
study of Israeli political history and current
events. Sole editor: Efraim Karsh.

Israel Studies, semiannual published since
1996 by the Ben-Gurion Research Center and
the Ben-Gurion University of the Negev. Dedicated to studying Israeli social, political, and
economic history in all their ramifications,
emphasis is on events after 1948. Sole editor: S.
Ilan Troen.

Journal of Israeli History (JIH), quarterly
published since 1994 by Frank Cass, London,
for Tel Aviv University's Research Institute on
the History of Zionism in Memory of Chaim
Weizmann. JIH continued the numbering of
Studies in Zionism, which it replaced. Themes
include all aspects of Zionist history and the
history of the State of Israel up to 1967.
Editors: Ronald W. Zweig, Michael B. Oren.

Studies in Zionism (SIZ), semiannual publication of Tel Aviv University's Research
Institute on the History of Zionism in Memory
of Chaim Weizmann appearing between 1979
and 1993. In 1994 the title was changed to
Journal of Israeli History and is still in print.

Ha-Zionut (הציונות), "Zionism: A Research
Annual," annual scholarly journal on the history
of Zionism published since 1970 by Tel Aviv
University's Research Institute on the History
of Zionism in Memory of Chaim Weizmann.
Emphasis has been on the history of the
Yishuv, although attention was given to all
aspects of Zionist history. Since 1979, *ha-
Zionut* has had a complementary English-
language journal, *Studies in Zionism* (since
1994, *Journal of Israeli History*), although the
contents were never identical.

Pushke [פושקע, Y] "(Charity) Box": Popular
name for the Blue Box used by all East
European Jews to collect donations for the
Keren Kayemet le-Israel or for other charities.
In most cases, charity meant a few coins
deposited before the Sabbath for buying land in
Eretz Israel. > see also: **Blue Box**.

Q

Q, R, S [Slang]: Hagana code names for the three main secret Ta'as weapons factories, established in great haste in 1947 and 1948. Located in sheds in Givatayim (a Tel Aviv suburb), the three factories mainly turned out small arms and ammunition. The reasons for the names are unknown, except for S: in that factory, Sten submachine guns were assembled from parts manufactured at other sites. The three Givatayim facilities produced considerable quantities of ammunition, mortar bombs, and some 5,000 submachine guns. > see also: **Yishuv, Organizations (Underground Organizations, Ta'as).**

R

Rabbanut ha-Rashit [רבנות ראשית, H] "Chief Rabbinate": Official term for the religious leadership placed in control of the Jewish millet in *Eretz Israel*. The office of the chief rabbi was created by the British in 1921 when they reorganized the millet system that they inherited from the Turks. Previously the position had fallen to the Haham Bashi of the Ottoman Empire. The chief rabbi's responsibilities included oversight of all religious and ritual matters for the Jewish community (known as Knesset Israel) and was considered, ex oficio, an officer of the community. Initially the plan was for one chief rabbi to represent all Jews. Ritual differences between Jews of European (Ashkenazi) and Mediterranean (Sephardi) Jews led to pressure for reform. In 1928, the Va'ad Leumi (which oversaw Knesset Israel's daily affairs) agreed to modify the rabbinate so as to permit the selection of two chief rabbis — one Askenazi and the other Sephardi — who otherwise were considered of equal status. > see also: **Millet System**; **Haham Bashi**; **Judaism and Zionism**.

Rabbi Benjamin [PN]: Pen name of Israeli journalist Yehoshua Radler-Feldman (ha-Talmi) (1880–1957). Radler-Feldman was born in Galicia and moved to London in 1906, migrating to *Eretz Israel* in 1907. After World War I he was active in Mizrachi, the religious Zionist party, and adopted his pseudonym. Rabbi Benjamin was one of Brit Shalom's founders and he maintained a binationalist postion on Arab-Israeli issues until his death.

Rabbi Shamir [PN]: Nom de guerre of Yitzhak Yezernitzki, now better known as former Israeli prime minister Yitzhak Shamir, adopted by him during his period as a fugitive from the British in 1946 and 1947. He apparently picked the name at random and has retained it ever since.

Radical Zionists [HT]: Common term for the diverse general Zionist elements that emerged in the WZO in the mid-1920s and early 1930s in dual opposition, on the one hand to WZO president Chaim Weizmann and on the other to revisionist Zionist leader Ze'ev Jabotinsky. Theoretically, the Radicals represented all

Table R.1: The Chief Rabbis

Ashkenazi Rabbis	Sephardi Rabbis
Abraham Issac ha-Kohen Kook, 1921–1935	Ya'akov Meir, 1928–1945
Isaac ha-Levy Herzog, 1936–1959	Benzion Hai Uziel, 1945–1953

Source: *Encyclopedia Judaica* (Jerusalem: Keter Books, 1972).

those who considered Weizmann too liberal but could not support Jabotinsky's over-heated (in their eyes) rhetoric. In reality, the radicals were concentrated in Poland, Czechoslovakia, Austria, and *Eretz Israel*. In the former, the radicals were able to coalesce into the Al ha-Mishmar faction; elsewhere, the radicals rallied around a few individuals: Nahum Goldmann, Moshe Glickson (the highly respected editor of *ha-Aretz*), and Robert Stricker. The latter was previously associated with the revisionist movement and in 1935 was one of the Jewish State Party's founders. The radicals suffered from one major weakness: united by what they opposed, it was difficult for them to define precisely what they stood for. More importantly, none of them could articulate a coherent alternative to Weizmann's gradualist policies that did not borrow from Jabotinsky's more radical maximalist approach. The radicals had their greatest success at the Seventeenth World Zionist Congress (1931), where they were able to remove Weizmann from the WZO presidency. However, their success had significant limits, since the congress elected Nahum Sokolow president, thereby ensuring that gradualism would remain WZO policy even without Weizmann. In 1933 most radicals joined the World Union of General Zionists (the so-called B Faction) that continued to oppose gradualism as a Zionist policy. > see also: **Gradualism; World Zionist Organization; Organizations, Zionist (Poland, Al ha-Mishmar)**.

Reaction Committee, The: Popular name for the committee established in early 1942 by the editors of *Eretz Israel*'s major Jewish newspapers. The committee's main goal was to present a unified front against British censorship while also adhering to principles of proper journalism. The committee continued to operate through 1948, when it changed its name to the Editors Committee.

Rechesh [רכש, H] "Acquisition": Popular term for Zionist efforts to purchase weapons in order to defend the *Yishuv*. The British,

who permitted the *Yishuv* to have only a limited number of firearms, considered *Rechesh* to be illegal, forcing Zionists to use a variety of means to smuggle weapons into Palestine/*Eretz Israel*. The illicit entry of weapons continued until after Israel's War of Independence when the U.N. arms embargo was finally lifted. > see also: **Sonnenborn Institute**.

Reconstructionism and Zionism: > see also: **Judaism and Zionism**.

Red Diplomat, The [Slang]: Nickname used by members of Brit ha-Biryonim in reference to Haim Arlosoroff, head of the JA Political Department between 1929 and 1933. The term derived from Arlosoroff's membership in Mapai but was clearly derogatory. In essence, accused him of working for Communism rather than Zionism. By delegitimizing Arlosoroff's work the term may have incited violence, specifically, Arlosoroff's murder on June 7, 1933. > see also: **Arlosoroff Affair**.

Reform Judiasm and Zionism: > see also: **Judaism and Zionism**.

Repeal Commission [Slang]: Colloquial name for the Woodhead Commission sent to Palestine/*Eretz Israel* in June 1938 and tasked with attempting to either draw fair boundaries for the proposed Jewish and Arab states or to suggest another means to break the impasse. The name may also be seen as a cruel pun. The Woodhead Commission undoing the work of the Peel Commission, or, as it were, repealing it. > see also: **Partition Plans**.

Research Institutes, Zionist:

Archion Toldot ha-Hagana (ארכיון תולדות ההגנה, ATH), "Hagana Historical Archive," Israeli research center dedicated to the history of the Hagana, founded in 1948. Initially held at Bet Eliyahu, the Hagana Museum, in 1969 ATH was incorporated into the Zva ha-Hagana le-Israel's (Zahal) archives as part of a series of Zahal museums dedicated to the undergound struggle for independence.

Archion Zioni Merkazi (ארכיון ציוני מרכזי) "Central Zionist Archive," (CZA) established as an arm of the WZO in 1919 and tasked with collecting and preserving documentation about the Zionist movement and its activities. The CZA initially was headquartered in Berlin but moved to Jerusalem in 1932. From 1932 to 1970 the CZA was housed in the JA buliding, but in 1970 it moved into a new building dedicated for the exclusive use of the archive. The CZA's collection includes a wide range of Zionist sources emanating from the WZO, the JA and all subsidiary organizations. Almost all of this material is available to researchers, as is the extensive photograph collection. In 1993 the CZA incorporated the archival material previously held in the Zionist Archive and Library in New York, reinforcing its position as the premier Zionist research center.

Central Archive for the History of the Jewish People (CAHJP), originally founded in 1939 as the General Archive for Jewish History, CAHJP was reorganized in 1969 with help from the Israeli government and the Central Zionist Archive. Located at Hebrew University's Givat Ram campus and dedicated to the collection of material on Jewish communities worldwide. Record groups are organized geographically with important collections on key individuals in the Zionist movement.

Centre de Documentation Juive Contemporaine (CDJC), "Contemporary Jewish Documentation Center," Franco-Jewish research center founded in Grenoble in 1943 to collect and preserve documentation on the Nazi persecution of French Jewry. Since the Holocaust, the CDJC has extended its field of research to include Franch Zionism and Franco-Jewish demography.

Ganzah ha-Medina (גנזח המדינה), "Israel State Archives," (ISA) organized as part of the prime minister's office in Jerusalem and in existence since 1948, the ISA has an extensive (but incomplete) collection of material on precursors to the Jewish State, including major holdings of the Ottoman and British administrations. Materials relating to the Israeli military (and its precursors) are organized into a separate archive, known as *Archion Zahal* (The IDF Archive, which incorporated the Hagana Archive in 1969) and is located in Givatayim.

Israel Labor Party Archives (ILPA), located at the Bet Berl Teachers College, ILPA is the main (though not exclusive) repository for material on Mapai and on socialist Zionism. In addition to material on Mapai, ILPA holds the archives of the Poale Zion world movement, the Ihud Olami, and of Berl Katznelson.

Machon Jabotinsky (מכון ז'בוטינסקי), "The Jabotinsky Institute (Archive)," (JIA) founded in 1932 as the Betar Archives, JIA is the central repository for all materials relating to the revisionist Zionist movement. Special sections of the archive refer to the Jewish Legion of World War I and to the history of the Irgun Zvai Leumi. JIA also oversees the Museum of Jewish Fighters and Partisans, an institution dedicated to recording manifestations of Jewish armed resistance in modern times.

Machon Lavon le-Toldot ha-Histadrut (מכון לבון לתולדות ההסתדרות), Lavon Institute, Archives and Museum of the Israeli Labor Movement," archives and research institute dedicated to the history of the Histadrut, located in Tel Aviv. Founded in 1932, the institute moved into its present home in the 1980s. In addition to being a repository of material on the Histadrut, the institute also holds archival material on the Poale Zion party and on Mapai.

Machon Moreshet Ben-Gurion (מכון מורשת בן-גוריון), "Ben-Gurion Research Center," (BGRC) archive and research center located at Kiryat Sde Boker and organized as an annex to the Ben-Gurion University of the Negev in Beersheba. Dedicated to historical research on Zionism and Jewish public affairs as seen through the perspective of Israel's first prime minister. Ben-Gurion's private papers (particularly his extensive diary) is the centerpiece of the BGRC.

Weizmann Archives (WA), located on the campus of the Weizmann Institute of Science, in Rehovot and founded in 1951. The WA holds an extensive collection of material relating to Israel's first president and to the

Zionist movement in the twentieth century. The correspondence files, which hold copies of 21,000 of Weizmann's letters and thousands of letters to him, is the WA's central holding and provides a personal glimpse into Zionist history.

Zionist Archive and Library (ZAL), founded in New York in the 1940s, the ZAL was a repository for material on the American Zionist movement in all its ramifications. Additionally, the ZAL held a considerable library available to researchers. In 1993, the ZAL archival collection was moved to Israel and was incorporated into the Central Zionist Archive. The library reading room is, however, still in operation.

Restoration Movement [HT]: Common term for the Christian ideology that emphasized the need to restore Jews to their ancestral homeland in order to facilitate the Second Coming of Christ. > see also: **Gentile Zionism**.

Revisionist Schism [HT]: Term used for the withdrawal of ha-Zohar from the WZO in 1935. After a complex series of maneuvers, ha-Zohar's leaders decided that remaining in the WZO was no longer effective. They could not obtain a majority in the organization and could not hope to influence the growing socialist Zionist majority toward what they defined as an activist Zionist policy. The seeds of secession were sown in 1931 when, at the Seventeenth Zionist Congress, a revisionist-sponsored resolution on the Zionist Endziel was vetoed by a large majority. The schism was the worst in the history of the WZO, far worse in its implications than the withdrawal of the territorialists in 1906, for a number of reasons. First, after withdrawing, the revisionists set up a rival organization, Histadrut ha-Zionist ha-Hadasha (ha-Zach, the New Zionist Organization). Second, ha-Zohar had a considerable following. Not large enough, to be sure, to capture control of the WZO or of any of the national federations, but large enough to give credibility to the revisionists' claim to speak for a large part of the Zionist public.

Finally, the schism occurred at just the point in time when Zionist unity was needed to protect the *Yishuv* from a British reassessment of Middle East policy. And while it is not clear that a unified Zionist movement could have prevented the resulting British abandonment of commitments to Zionism, it is clear that the fractured Zionist movement was too weak to prevent the White Paper of 1939. Seen as part of a larger ideological splintering within the WZO, the schism was not undone until the late 1940s when ha-Zach agreed to return to the WZO. > see also: **Organizations, Revisionist Zionist; World Zionist Organization; Endziel**.

Rezini [רצִינִי, H] "Serious One": JA code term, and derisive nickname, for British foreign minister Ernest Bevin. The term is a play on words, since another way of translating the Hebrew term would, in fact, be "Ernest."

Rhodes Talks [GN]: Popular name for the negotiations that led to the Arab-Israeli armistice agreements of 1949, based on the venue of the negotiations. > see also: **Armistice Agreements**.

Rishon [ראשון, H] "First (one)": JA code name used mainly during the 1940s for Winston Churchill and, apparently, deriving from the fact that Churchill was an early British supporter of Zionism. The term Ben-Rishon (בן ראשון, First Son), was used to designate Randolph Churchill when he was in Palestine/ *Eretz Israel* as a journalist and (sometimes) agent of British military intelligence.

Rishon le-Zion [ראשון לציון, H] "First of Zion": Title of the Sephardi chief rabbi of *Eretz Israel*. The title was initially granted as an honorarium to the chief Jewish spiritual leader of Jerusalem and was a means to distinguish him from the Haham Bashi (the chief rabbi of Istanbul). > see also: **Rabbanut Rashit**.

Rosolam [רוזעולם, Slang]: Code term used by the JA for President Franklin D. Roosevelt. The term is a pun on Roosevelt's name, since "velt" means "world," as does the Hebrew word Olam. > see also: **Hershel Ish-Emet**.

Sabbateans [slang]: Common name for the followers of seventeenth-century messianic pretender Shabbetai Zvi. In the nineteenth century Orthodox leaders applied the phrase in a condemnatory sense against Zionism. Just as Shabbatei Zvi had been a false messiah whose actions resulted in apostasy and suffering for Jews, so too Zionism offered a false hope that could only end in divine punishment.

Sachyan [שחיין, H] "Swimmer": Hagana, and later Israeli Air Force (IAF), code name for Al Schwimmer, an American volunteer active in forging the IAF and, after the War of Independence, the Israeli Aircraft Industry. The code derived from the meaning of Schwimmer's last name, which was simply translated into Hebrew. > see also: **Mitnadve Hutz la-Aretz**.

Sakin [סכין, H] "Knife": Israeli Air Force slang for the Messerschmidt BF-109 fighter purchased in 1948 from the Czechs. The term was a direct translation fo the first part of the designer's name ("Messer" is "knife" in German). Actually, the purchased aircraft were a Czech variant on the BF-109, officially known as the Avia S-199; these differed from the German original only in the engine that they mounted. The aircraft were retired almost immediately after the War of Independence. > see also: **Zahal**.

Sandvitchim [סנדביצ'ים,H] "Sandwich Cars": Slang name for the ad hoc armored cars and armored personnel carriers put together with great speed at the beginning of Israel's War of Independence. Basically, the sandwich car was a truck chassis onto whch a square (or rectangular) body was welded. Although technically armored, the sandwich car was barely bullet proof, except around the driver's seat. There was no standardized weaponry or portage capabilities, since each car was basically a single item. Sandwich cars served in every battlefront, providing the Hagana — and later Zva ha-Hagana le-Israel — with an important mobile component. Their jury-rigged nature meant that all of the cars were removed from service as soon as possible. > see also: **Zva ha-Hagana le-Israel**; **War of Independence**.

School [E/Slang]: Term used by members of the Sonnenborn Institute for the Hagana. Derivation is unknown. However, the Irgun had earlier used the term in its Hebrew form, Beit Sefer (with emphasis on the last word that literally translates to book) as a code term for underground press.

Sefer ha-Ma'al [ספר המעל, H] "(The Book of Treachery": Colloquial Zionist name for the British White Paper of 1939. Viewed as a grave breach of Britain's commitment to Zionism, the white paper was resoundingly condemned. The title *Sefer ha-Ma'al* was also used by

David Ben-Gurion as the title for his analysis of the white paper, a booklet published in May 1939. > see also; **White Paper(s)**.

Selbschutz (G) "Self-Defense": Generic term for self-defense used by Jews principally to refer to acts of organized, physical defense against antisemitic attacks usually during pogroms. The term has gained use mostly in the context of Eastern European Jewry during the latter part of the nineteenth and early twentieth centuries. Self-defense was justified in Zionist terms as a defense of Jewish honor and was seen as an important step in re-creating a sense of Jewish self-respect and unity. Zionist leaders therefore encouraged self-defense activities as a first step, or at least an early step in forging a new Zionist Jew.

Separate Union(s) [HT]: WZO term for members groups organized internationally and thus considered independent from but still answerable to the regional Zionist federations. > see also: **Sonderverbände**.

Settlements: > see also: **Agricultural Settlement(s)**.

Seventh Dominion Scheme [HT]: Plan drawn up by, and associated with, Josiah Wedgwood, the eminent British parliamentarian and Gentile Zionist. Wedgwood first proposed that Palestine/*Eretz Israel* be converted into the Commonwealth's seventh dominion in 1926, after a trip to the country convinced him that anti-Zionism was endemic to the mandatory administration. In Wedgwood's plan, the British government would reassess its position on *aliya*, permitting massive Jewish immigration until Jews represented a clear majority of the population. Thereafter, the territory could follow the pattern established by Canada, Australia, and South Africa to independence as a dominion within the British Commonwealth. According to Wedgwood, this plan would permit Britain to permanently anchor its position in the Middle East (against

possible encroachments by Italy or France) and right the injustice done to the Jews. The plan was never endorsed by the British government and was neither officially endorsed nor ever officially repudiated by the WZO leadership. However, the plan was avidly embraced by Ze'ev Jabotinsky and the revisionist Zionist movement. Parts of the plan were central to all revisionist planning during the 1930s and 1940s. > see also: **Gentile Zionism; Evacuation Plan; Tochnit ha-Asor**.

Sfarim Latiniim [ספרים לטיניים, H] "Latin Books": Mossad le-Aliya Bet code term for *aliya* using forged documents, especially including forged immigrant certificates, after World War II. The term apparently was used to designate both the documents and those possessing such documents. Exact derivation is unclear, but seems to relate to the fact that most such *olim* were concentrated in Italy. > see also: **Aliya Bet**.

Sha'atnez [שעטנז, H] "Forbidden Mixture": Biblical term for an impermissible mixture (of seeds, animals, or cloth) that was forbidden by divine commandment (Deuteronomy 22:11). The term was used during the 1930s by Ze'ev Jabotinsky to decry hyphenated forms of Zionism, mainly socialist Zionism, that he claimed were diffusing the WZO's strength by diverting attention from real goals (mass *aliya* and sovereignty) by focusing on goals that were not central to Zionist or Jewish needs. > see also: **Monism**.

Shabbat ha-Shahor [שבת השחור, H] "Black Sabbath": Jewish term for the events of Saturday, June 29, 1946, known in British military parlance as Operation Agatha. In an effort to destroy the Jewish resistance movement, more than 100,000 British troops and police personnel undertook a series of raids against the Jewish Agency, Histadrut, and the Hagana and Palmah. Twenty-eight settlements were simultaneously raided and searched (for weapons and *Ma'apilim*) while the headquarters of the JA and Histadrut, in Jerusalem and Tel Aviv respectively, were searched and ransacked by troops looking for documents to prove complicity in the anti-British revolt. The British seized considerable amounts of weaponry at *Kibbutz* Yagur, for example, 396 rifles, forty-six pistols, five submachine guns, fifteen machine guns, and ninety-two mortars were uncovered. British operations forced the JAE to reconsider its active participation in a direct confrontation with the British and culminated in the Hagana and Palmah withdrawing from the Tenuat ha-Meri ha-Ivri in July 1946. However, as a means to break the revolt, Operation Agatha was a failure. The Hagana and Palmah continued to operate in support of the Aliya Revolt while direct military confrontations with Irgun Zvai Leumi and Lohame Herut Israel increased. > see also: **Yishuv; Yishuv Organizations (Underground Movements); Mered ha-Aliya; Aliya Bet**.

Shabbetai [שבתאי, PN]: Hagana and Mossad le-Aliya Bet code term for Izmir, Turkey, used during and after World War II. The term derived from Shabbetai Zvi, the messianic pretender from Izmir, who was active in the latter third of the seventeenth century. Izmir was a destiny of choice for Jewish refugees. It was a safe haven from the Nazis and was close enough to *Eretz Israel* that continuing the trip toward the ultimate destination was plausible. > see also: **Aliya Bet**.

Shadow Government [HT]: Term used by some historians to designate the *Yishuv*'s political institutions prior to the establishment of the State of Israel. In the main, the term is used to identify JA activities that paralleled those of a government, such as diplomatic relations, defense, and *aliya*. The term implies that the JA was organized to be a parallel government capable of governing the *Yishuv* but not yet posessing the necessary elements of sovereignty to do so prior to 1948. The same, it may be added, was true for the Va'ad Leumi and, to a lesser degree, for the WZO as well. > see also: **Medina ba-Derekh; Sochnut Yehudit; Yishuv; Israel, State of**.

Shaliah/shelihim (שליח/שליחים, H) "Emissary/emissaries": Generic term for representatives of the Zionist parties sent from *Eretz Israel* to Europe to inculcate nationalist ideals and party loyalty among Jewish youth groups before and after World War II. The term also refers to anyone carrying out a mission on behalf of the movement or the Jewish people.

Shaliah de-Rabbanan [שליח ד'רבנן, H] "Rabbinic Emissary": Traditional term for an emissary sent in modern times by institutions of the Old *Yishuv* to collect charity in the diaspora. Usually abbreviated as Shadar, these emissaries maintained contact between the Jewish world and *Eretz Israel* and thus kept alive the hope for the eventual restoration of a Jewish national home. Shadarim continued to operate even after the rise of Zionism, although their missions usually received less attention than those of Zionist emissaries, reaching an apex just before the Holocaust.

Shark: Name of the Palyam ship used by both the Palmah and the Mossad le-Aliya Bet for special operations in Cypriot waters during the period after the British began to deport *Ma'apilim* to that island. > see also: **Yishuv, Yishuv Organizations (Underground Organizations); Aliya Bet; Cyprus, Detention Camps**.

Shaul [שאול, PN]: Hagana code name for the Mossad le-Aliya Bet, deriving from the name of the agency's founder, Shaul Avigur. Although apparently used only in 1948, the term may be translated as "Saul's boys." > see also: **Aliya Bet**.

She'erit ha-Pleta (שארית הפליטה, H) "The Surviving Remnant": Biblical phrase (I Chronicles 4:43) used during and after World War II to denote survivors of the Holocaust. > see also: **Displaced Persons, Jewish; Briha**.

She'erit ha-Tikva (שארית התקוה, H) "Remnant of Hope": alternative term for the *She'erit ha-Pleta* that emphasized the Jews' hope to evacuate postwar Europe for a permanently haven, a Jewish state in *Eretz Israel*, at all costs. > see also: **Yetziat Europa; She'erit ha-Pleta**.

Shekel [שקל, H] "Coin":

1. Scope and Definition

Biblical term for coins or currency, that the Zionist movement used as a term for the membership document purchased by dues-paying members of the WZO. *Shekel* prices were set by the WZO presidium, with the *shekel* also serving as a voting certificate. After 1921 all *shekels* sold in Palestine/*Eretz Israel* were counted twice (the so-called double *shekel*), giving the *Yishuv* a disproportional number of delegates at the Zionist Congress. This policy created controversies because of price and because of the presidium's possible undemocratic manipulation of what was, in essence, a paid franchise. This criticism was based on the fact that the WZO allocated delegates to the Zionist congresses based on the proportion of *shekels* sold by each party in each region or country. The *shekel* was abandoned as a voting tool by the WZO in 1960, although it has been retained as a certificate of membership in most countries. In 1981 the Israeli government replaced the Israeli lira (IL) with the *shekel*. > see also: **World Zionist Organization**; **Proportional Representation**.

TABLE S.1: Total Shekel Sales, 1899-1946

Congress	Year	Shekels Sold
Third	1899	114,400
Fourth	1900	96,500
Fifth	1901	96,600
Sixth	1903	232,600
Seventh	1905	137,000
Eighth	1907	164,300
Ninth	1909	182,800
Tenth	1911	175,900
Eleventh	1913	217,200
Twelfth	1921	855,600
Thirteenth	1923	958,000
Fourteenth	1925	938,300
Fifteenth	1927	631,200
Sixteenth	1929	604,600
Seventeenth	1931	627,200
Eighteenth	1933	843,600
Nineteenth	1935	1,216,600
Twentieth	1937	1,222,200
Twenty-first	1939	1,400,200
Twenty-second	1946	2,159,840

Source: Central Zionist Archives.

Shelihut [שליחות, H] "Mission": Hebrew term for the *Yishuv*'s representation, by temporary emissaries, in the diaspora. Conceived of as an educational tool, the emissaries were not usually tasked with any political goals, other than "conquest of the communities" in which they were stationed. Instead, the shaliach was responsible for preparing youth for *aliya* and settlement and overseeing *hachshara* programs. Additionally, emissaries in countries considered sensitive or important were tasked with sending reports back to the *Yishuv* on political, ideological, and social developments (regarding both the Jewish community and the country as a whole) in their station. > see also: **shaliach/shelichim**.

Shem ha-Meforash [שם המפורש, H] "The Ineffable Name": Zionist code word, used especially during the early 1940s to designate the goal of statehood. Deriving from the Jewish tradition of not pronouncing the four letter divine name (generally transliterated as YHWH), the term reflected a change in Zionist attitudes. The goal that had previously been considered unspeakable was now central to Zionist activity. > see also: **Biltmore Resolution**; **Endzeil**.

Shivat Zion [שיבת ציון, H] "The Return to Zion": Redemptivist Jewish term associated historically with the beginning of the Second Commonwealth and theologically with the future redemption of the Jewish people. The historical term derives from permission granted to exiled Judeans by King Cyrus of Persia to return to the Holy Land (539 B.C.E.) and may be derived, in part, from Psalm 126:1 "A Song of Ascents. When the Lord brought Zion out of captivity, we were like a people in a dream." The term was used after the Roman destruction of the Second Temple (70 C.E.), to refer to a future redemption of the Jewish people by divine agency. The term was used by modern Zionists in this redemptivist meaning but was devoid of much of its theological content. > see also: **Ahavat Zion**; **Bayit Shlishi**.

Shlilat ha-Gola [שלילת הגולה, H] "Rejection of the Diaspora": Ideological term reflecting Zionist denial of the viability of diaspora Jewish existence. According to this formulation, under the best possible circumstances, Jewry will disappear because of assimilationist pressures in countries that have granted Jews emancipation; under the worst circumstances, Jewry will be swallowed up in a catastrophic wave of persecution. In its most radical formulation, therefore, the ideology is extremely pessimistic about the Jewish future. More moderate ideologies incorporating *Shlilat ha-Gola* also existed. These specifically emphasized the need for a "spiritual center" in the Jewish national home that would bolster diaspora Jewry from both internal decay and external persecution. Regardless of how radical or moderate a formulation, however, *Shlilat ha-Gola* was a foundation for almost all Zionist ideologies.

Shnat Sherut [שנת שרות, H] "Year's Service": Term for the voluntary program of national service for high school graduates instituted in the *Yishuv* in 1942. At the time, restrictions on *aliya* combined with the draft for wartime service, into the Royal Army or the Hagana, created a labor shortage in *Eretz Israel*. Those too ill to work, those already employed in any sector of the *Yishuv's* economy, and those joining the Palmah or the British army were automatically exempt. Everyone else was expected to volunteer, and high school graduates were offered a series of inducements to do so. This wartime national service represented the first time that the *Yishuv* as a whole attempted to mobilize its manpower. The experiment was continued after World War II but ceased when the State of Israel was established, since all high school graduates were thereafter liable for mandatory military service. > see also: **World War II**.

Shoa (שואה, H) "Catastrophe": Hebrew term for the destruction of European Jewry, deriving from a biblical term that referred to the destruction of ancient Israel (e.g. Isaiah 10:3). The term occurs only rarely in postbiblical Jewish literature. Some Zionists used it as early as 1915, to refer to the systematic destruction of Jewish life in Eastern Europe during World War I, although using such quotes to prove premonitions of the impending Holocaust is probably an exaggeration. Since the 1940s the term has been used in Israel to refer to the Holocaust. In this usage it reflects the attempt both to link the modern catastrophe to a biblical antecedent and, given the unprecedented scope of the Nazi persecution of European Jewry, to find a term for destruction that is sui generis. Since 1951 the term has semiofficial status in Israel because the Knesset designated the twenty-seventh day of the Hebrew month Nissan (ca. April) as Yom ha-Shoa.

Shokel(im) [(שוקל(ים, H]: Untranslatable term for persons who bought the Zionist *shekel*. > see also: **Shekel**.

Shtadlan(ut) [(שתדלנ(ות, H] "Intercessor/ Interceding": Traditional Jewish term for the individual who, due to business or other contacts, was in a position to intervene with Gentile authorities when the local Jewish community was threatened. Zionists viewed shtadlanut as a dishonorable and cowardly way to defend Jews, likening it to begging for mercy. > see also: **Shlilat ha-Gola**; **Mayofespolitik**.

Shtilim [שתילים, H] "Seedlings": Hagana code term used at various times to describe (1) firearms, especially those purchased in Europe, (2) youth movement members, mainly those in transit on *Ha'apala* ships, and (3) displaced persons. The first usage was popular during the 1920s and reflected the diffuse nature of Hagana units, which also undertook agricultural activities. The latter two came into vogue after World War II and may have been used simultaneously.

Shu-Shu Boy [slang]: American nickname, popular among sailors, for representatives of the Mossad le-Aliya Bet who approached asking for assistance in organizing blockade runners after World War II. The term's origin and precise meaning are obscure but apparently reflect the Israelis' efforts to keep things quiet (i.e., the Mossad representatives were constantly shushing their interlocutors). > see also: **Mitnadvei Hutz la-Aretz**.

Sicarii [L]: One of the major anti-Roman rebel groups active in Judea and Galilee in the first and second century C.E. The name derived from the Latin name for a form of dagger that the Sicarii carried. Sicarii was also one of the unofficial names for the shadowy underground group active in the early 1930s and better known as Brit ha-Biryonim. > see also: **Yishuv, Organizations (Underground Movements, Brit ha-Biryonim)**.

Simsār [AR] "Broker": Extremely derogatory term for a land dealer, especially one who sells land to Jews, regardless of whether that individual sold his own land or merely acted as a middleman in a deal with an absentee landlord. By the late 1930s resentment of land sales was such that Arab dealers planning to conduct any business with Jews did so only in secret, maintaining a veneer of strong anti-Zionism for public consumption. > see also: **A'yān**.

Sinai Plan: > see also: **El Arish Scheme**.

Sionisme de Luxe [P/slang] "Deluxe Zionism": Term used by revisionist Zionist leader Ze'ev Jabotinsky to deride his opponents' Zionist vision. Instead of providing Jewry with what it needed — mass evacuation to *Eretz Israel* and the creation of a Jewish state — his opponents emphasized a Zionist program that Jewry could ill afford. > see also: **Fata Morgana Land**; **Halutzic Aliya**; **Endziel**.

Sittlich Judennot [G] "Jewish Moral Distress": Term coined by Max Nordau in his oration to the First Zionist Congress (1897). Although most Zionists had distinguished between the physical problems plaguing Eastern European Jewry and the spiritual problems plaguing Western European Jewry, Nordau saw both as two sides of the same coin. The Jewish problem unified Jewry despite apparent differences, since both the physical and spiritual problems derived from Jewish homelessness and powerlessness. > see also: **Materielle Judennot**; **Geistige Judennot**.

Six Piastre Regiment: Slang nickname for the Palestine Regiment based on the copper color of the unit's insignia, which resembled a local coin. > see also: **World War II, Yishuv/Jewish Military Units**.

Sjonizm Albo Eksterminacja [P] "Zionism or Extermination": Term used in 1940 by Polish underground leader (and former ambassador to Berlin) Roman Knoll to describe his analysis of Polish Jewry's future. Acccording to Knoll, Polish Jewry had no future except mass emigration to Palestine/*Eretz Israel* because Jews would not be able to return to their former residences and businesses after liberation. > see also: **Evacuation Plan**.

Small Constitution: Slang term for Israel's unwritten constitution. Although a constituent assembly was called in 1949 and a proposed constitution was written it was never ratified. Fear of inciting a civil war between religious Israelis, who saw *Halacha* as the only permissible constitution, and secularists led the constituent assembly to simply reconvene itself as the Knesset (Parliament), which set out to legislate "basic laws" to cover major constitutional issues. > see also: **Basic Laws**.

Sochnut Yehudit [סוכנות יהודית, H] "Jewish Agency" (JA):

1. Scope and Definition

Quasi-governmental organization of *Yishuv* that formed the basis for Israel's provisional government in 1948. Under article 4 of the League of Nations mandate, the British were obligated to create self-governing institutions for both Jewish and Arab communities of the mandated territory. Initially, however, the function of a Jewish agency was filled by the executive of the WZO. In 1929 the committee that fulfilled the terms of article 4 was enlarged to include representatives appointed by American and British philanthropists who had financial interests in the building of the Jewish national home, but were not members of the WZO. The result of this enlargement was renamed the Jewish Agency (JA) and functioned as the primary representative institution between the *Yishuv* and the British administration. As a result, the JA was organized like a shadow government with its departments parallel to a cabinet and its ministers being members of the Jewish Agency Executive (JAE).

In 1931, the JA's functions were further refined after an agreement was worked out with the Va'ad Leumi (VL), another quasi-governmental agency created under the terms of the mandate and officially recognized as the political representation of

the Jewish millet (religious community) in Palestine/*Eretz Israel*. Thereafter, the JAE assumed all political functions, including responsibility for relations with the British, defense matters, fund-raising, *aliya*, settlement building, and relations with other Zionist and non-Zionist institutions. The VL, in contrast, held primary responsibility for all social, cultural, and religious functions within the *Yishuv*, including social services and education. This compromise, which concentrated all real political power in the JAE was considerably simplified by the fact that one party, Mapai, the moderate social democratic party, held dominant pluralities in both agencies. > see also: **Yishuv, Yishuv Organizations (Self-Governing Institutions, Va'ad Leumi)**.

JA relations with the British government were contentious almost from the day that the enlargement was announced. In particular, fears that increasing *aliya* would lead to Arab unrest caused the British to restrict Jewish immigration. Thus, although the JAE was responsible for requesting the number of certificates to be made available in the twice annual immigration quota — the so-called Schedule — the British never granted more than 40 percent of the JAE's requests. For the better part of the 1930s, as increasingly desperate European Jews began to look at *Eretz Israel* as their only possible haven, the average schedule grant was only 25 percent of the JAE request. British restrictions on legal immigration led Jews to take matters into their own hands, resulting in *Aliya Bet* ("illegal" immigration) which deepened the British government's distrust of the Zionists, leading to further restrictions on legal immigration. Thus, a vicious cycle was created that was only broken when the British withdrew from Palestine/*Eretz Israel* in 1948. Sour as relations were, they worsened in 1938, when the British government adandoned all pretense of objectivity in creating immigration quotas and announced the implementation of a "political maximum" beyond which *aliya* would not be permitted. The White Paper of 1939 represented the final break between the British government and the JA. Although relations were proper, from May 1939 the JAE worked to end British rule over Palestine/*Eretz Israel*.

The JA's relations with the *Yishuv's* diverse political parties varied. Mapai, Mizrachi, and the General Zionists formed the so-called Historic Coalition that dominated the JAE from 1929 until 1948. Other socialist Zionist parties considered themselves to be in opposition to Mapai, including Mapai's methods of governance in the JAE. But their small size (relative to Mapai) meant that their opposition was relatively shallow. This was not the case with the revisionist Zionist movement, established in 1925 to promote a more vigorous effort to accomplish Zionist goals. In particular, the revisionists believed that the JAE was too timid in their approach to the British and too reliant upon British good will. The revisionists insisted that the JAE take the lead in demanding mass *aliya* (especially after 1935) and in clearly stating Zionism's ultimate goal as attainment of sovereignty. The revisionists' inability to get the JAE to accept their terms in this debate led to the 1935 schism in the Zionist movement and resulted in the creation of the New Zionist Organization. > see also: **Organizations, Revisionist Zionist (International, ha-Histadrut ha-Zionit ha-Hadasha).**

During World War II the JAE reacted with horror as the Nazi persecution of European Jewry developed into a policy of mass extermiantion. Given its relatively meager resources, however, the JAE did not believe that the Yishuv could enunciate a rescue policy independent of the Allied governments. David Ben-Gurion, the JAE chairman, framed what many considered to be the only possible Zionist response to the war in 1939: "We shall fight the White Paper

is if there were no Hitler," he declared, "and we shall fight Hitler as if there were no White Paper." Wartime developments convinced the Zionist leaders of the necessity of stating Zionist goals for the postwar era. The JAE therefore unanimously adopted the Biltmore Resolution and its call for the creation of a Jewish commonwealth in *Eretz Israel* as the basis for all further Zionist political work.

After the war, the JAE led the *Yishuv* in a three-year struggle to remove the British from Palestine/*Eretz Israel* and to attain sovereignty. At first, this meant cooperation, through the Hagana and Palmah, with underground movements that did not necessarily accept JAE authority — the Irgun Zvai Leumi and Lohame Herut Israel. From mid-1946, however, the JAE ended its cooperation with these groups and undertook its own strategy of defiance against British power. In particular, while the other two groups concentrated on guerrilla warfare against the government, the JAE preferred an unarmed (or semiarmed) insugency, via mass *Aliya Bet*, to undermine worldwide support for continued British rule. After the U.N. decision to partition Palestine/*Eretz Israel* was announced on November 29, 1947, the JAE was again enlarged, this time by representatives of the VL, and renamed itself Minhelet ha-Am (National Administration). On May 15, 1948, Minhelet ha-Am, in turn, declared itself to be the provisional government of the newly created State of Israel. The Jewish Agency still exists as a voluntary agency that helps with the absorption of *olim*. > see also: **World Zionist Organization; Yishuv; Israel, State of; Zionut; Historic Coalition; World War II; Aliya; Aliya Bet; Biltmore Resolution; Mandatory Palestine.**

TABLE S.2: Chairmen of the Jewish Agency Executive, 1929–1948

Years	Name	Party
1929–1931	Louis Marshall	non-Zionist
1931–1933	Emmanuel Newmann	General Zionist
1933–1935	Arthur Ruppin	General Zionist
1935–1948	David Ben-Gurion	Mapai

Source: Central Zionist Archive.

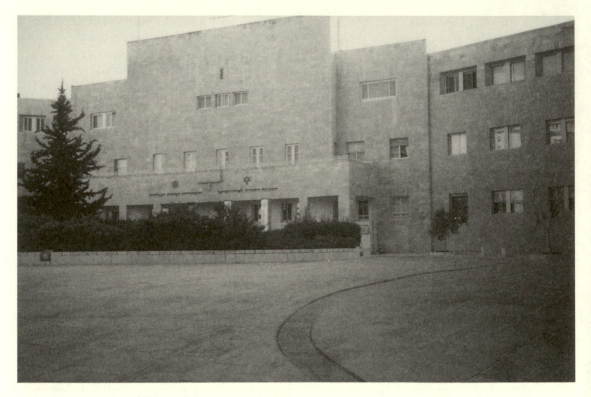

The Jewish Agency's Headquarters as it Appears Today.
Authors' Collection, via CASE

TABLE S.3: Major Jewish Agency Departments

Department	Years	Comments
Agricultural Settlement	1918–1948	
Economic Affairs	1931–1948	
Education	1913–1932	Functions transferred to Va'ad Leumi.
German	1933–1955	Oversaw all aspects of Central European *aliya*.
Housing	1944–1948	
Immigration	1919–1948	
Information Office	1938–1948	
Labour	1921–1948	
Marititme and Fisheries	1935–1948	
Organization	1933–1948	Oversaw day-to-day operations.
Political Department	1921–1948	The JA "foreign ministry."
Press Office	1924–1927	
Settlement of ex-Servicemen	1944–1948	
Statistical	1926–1948	
Trade and Industry	1922–1948	
Treasury	1918–1948	

Source: Central Zionist Archive.

2. Jewish Agency Subsidiaries

Agricultural Research Institute (ARI), founded by the WZO in 1925 and taken under JA auspices in 1929, ARI was originally located in Tel Aviv. In 1927, the ARI main office moved to Rehovot, where it still operates (as the Volcani Institute for Agricultural Research). ARI's principal task was to develop techniques that would allow a wider range of Jewish settlement, thereby increasing the *Yishuv*'s potential to absorb new immigrants.

Archion Zioni Merkazi (ארכיון ציוני מרכזי), "Central Zionist Archives," main repository for all WZO and JA documentary material. > see also: **Research Institutes, Zionist**.

Committee for the Jews of Occupied Europe (CJOE), also known as the Joint Rescue Committee, rescue department of the Jewish Agency Executive, established in January 1943. The CJOE reflected the *Yishuv*'s intense concern about events in Europe after information on the Final Solution emerged. However, continued British obstruction and a lack of sufficient funding prevented the CJOE from carrying out more than a token rescue task. Chairman: Yitzhak Gruenbaum (1943–1945).

Digest of Press and Events, weekly roundup of news and views on events in (or having an impact on) the *Yishuv* and the WZO, published by the JA Information Office. The *Digest* began publication in 1943 and remained in print until 1957 (when superseded by the *Israel Digest*). Despite being a mouthpiece, the *Digest* was remarkably objective in covering events in the *Yishuv*.

Keren ha-Herum (קרן החרום), "Emergency Fund," ad hoc Zionist fund created under JA auspices in the U.S. and England in 1929. The fund was tasked with collecting money for relief of individuals who had been attacked during the Arab riots of 1929. Uses included both providing health care for the injured and housing for those forced to flee their homes or settlements. Any capital remaining after individual distributions was to be consigned to the JA land purchase fund for settlement building and fortification.

Lishkot Giyus (לשכות גיוס), "Recruitment Offices," JA department established during 1941 to speed up recruitment in the *Yishuv* for the British armed forces during World War II. The recruitment offices acted in concert with the JA political department and thus had no central office of their own. Instead, the offices operated on a local level, recruiting personnel for all branches of the service. The British did not specifically recognize the JA's offices and in 1943 sought to close them down. The resulting stoppage of recruitment in May and June 1943 convinced the British to permit the offices to reopen; they remained functioning until 1945. > see also: **World War II**.

London Executive, common name for the section of the JAE permanently based in London after 1929 and acting as a coordinating office for JA affairs in England and Western Europe. In addition to two permanent members, the London Executive usually was augmented by JAE members from the Jerusalem Executive who spent longer or shorter periods of time in the British capital.

Mossad Bialik (מוסד ביאליק, MB), "Bialik Institute," Zionist publishing house founded jointly by the WZO and JA in 1935 and named after the Jewish national poet Haim Nahman Bialik. MB's corporate headquarters was (and remains) located in Jerusalem. Its main duty was to assist in creating a vibrant Jewish national culture in the *Yishuv* through a program of publishing significant works of Hebrew literature (or of foreign literature in Hebrew translation).

New York Executive, common name for the JAE office operating in New York from 1929 and responsible for all JA and related activities in the Western Hemisphere. In addition to activities in the United States, the office was responsible for overseeing the activities of the JA's Latin American branch. During the 1940s the JA New York Executive comprised seven members: two non-Zionists, a representative of Hadassah, and four representatives of the Zionist Organization of America. Because of the distances involved and U.S. laws preventing foreign lobbyists from directly approaching American political leaders, the New York JAE operated autonomously with few members of the Jerusalem JAE ever present. However, all activities were closely coordinated with Jerusalem and the New York JAE never pursued its own approach without prior consultations.

Palestine Office(s), local JAE offices operating in diaspora countries. > see also: **Palästinaamt**.

Socialism and Zionism: Unlike communism, which has articulated a consistently anti-Zionist position, modern socialism has not formulated a single, authoritative ideological orientation on the question of Jewish nationalism. Orthodox Marxists — members of the First and Second Internationals — tended to deny the legitimacy of Jewish nationalism and called for Jewish assimilation and integration within the (future) socialist world. This view derived exclusively from the application of Karl Marx's concepts of nationality and from his hostile statements about Jews, Judaism, and Jewry. Socialist opposition to Zionism reached it speak in the era just before World War I and may be exemplified by the inalterable opposition of such socialist leaders as Karl Kautsky, Rosa Luxembourg, and Otto Bauer (the latter two, socialists of Jewish origin) to any positive manifestation of Jewish national identity, ironically, including a rejection of Bundist socialist nationalism.

An alternative attitude to Zionism was formed by a number of socialist leaders during the late nineteenth and early twentieth centuries. In particular, so-called revisionist socialists led by Eduard Bernstein (also of Jewish origin) rejected Marx's uncompromising hostility to national minorities and accepted Zionism as part of a natural yearning of Jews to be free. The Dreyfus Affair similarly convinced French Socialists Bernard Lazare and Jean Jaures that antisemitism could not simply be willed out of existence and had to be fought by all means possible, including Zionism. Lazare, who became a major factor in the rise of the French Zionist movement, was especially adamant on this point.

As a result of the schism that led to the collapse of the Second Socialist International after World War I most Socialist and Social Democratic ideologues adopted the pro-Zionist orientation associated with Bernstein, Lazare, and Jaures. Although this was not true of all Socialists, it did hold for most of them. When the Third International was created, Mapai, the *Yishuv*'s main socialist Zionist party, was accepted as a member party. In contrast to the Comintern, which opposed Zionism at every turn, the Third International gave considerable support to the *Yishuv*, particularly after 1933. Socialist leaders in almost every European country strongly supported the creation of a Jewish national home and, after the Holocaust, the creation of a Jewish state. Mapai (now the One Israel Party) has maintained its membership in the Third International until this day. > see also: **Communism and Zionism; Zionut; Bundism; Autonomism**.

Sommerreise-Zionisten [G] "Sunshine Zionists": Derisive term used in 1901 by Chaim Weizmann to describe the majority of delegates at previous Zionist congresses who eschewed any form of controversy in the name of "not creating disunity" and thereby accomplished nothing. In Weizmann's mind, these Zionists sought only demonstrative actions that would not lead to any success for the WZO.

Sonderverband [G] "Special Organization": Term used by the WZO after the Tenth World Zionist Congress (1911) to refer to any international bloc that was recognized as a part of the WZO. Until then, all organizations were chartered through the national Zionist federations (the Landesverbände). In the interim, however, a number of political parties had crystalized that were multinational in membership but linked by ideology. Of these, Poale Zion and Mizrachi were the earliest to be recognized as Sonderverbände, being the parties that brought the issue to the WZO in the first place. A Sonderverband had to meet strict membership requirements, had to coordinate its activities with the national federation (acting as an autonomous entity within each federation), and had to be recognized by the WZO executive.

Sonnenborn Institute [PN]: Popular name for the group of prominent American Jews who met with David Ben-Gurion on July 1, 1945, to assist in the creation of the State of Israel. The institute was created by (and bore the name of) Rudolf G. Sonnenborn, a Jewish businessman from Baltimore. Mainly, the institute assisted the JA and the Hagana. This aid took two forms: between 1945 and 1948, most aid was financial and political; in 1948 and 1949, the institute's members concentrated on obtaining badly needed arms for the newly created Zva ha-Hagana le-Israel despite the U.N. arms embargo. The Sonnenborn Institute ceased to function late in 1949. > see also: **Rechesh.**

Special Night Squads (SNS): Official name for the joint British-Jewish unit created by Captain Orde Charles Wingate to combat Arab terrorists and infiltrators during the Arab Revolt (1936–1939). While Arab bands almost always operated at night, neither the Royal Army, whose troops remained in their barracks, nor the Hagana, which was tied to an exclusively defensive doctrine, were able to prevent attacks. The defenders, in effect, surrendered the initiative to the attackers without obtaining any tactical benefit. Wingate, a keen student of irregular warfare, hypothesized that an aggresively led, well-trained, and well armed force could seize the initiative back from the Arabs. The British high command approved Wingate's suggestion and created the SNS to test it in practice. Initially, SNS was organized to defend the sections of the Trans-Arabian Pipeline that crossed the Galilee to Haifa. In this operation, as well as many others, the SNS was a complete success, writing a new page in counterinsurgency theory while also providing important operational experience for the Hagana high command. British reassessments of Middle Eastern policy led to the disbanding of the SNS in 1939. Conceptually, however, the Hagana adopted the SNS idea in its Plugot Sadeh (Fosh) and in the Palmah. > see also: **Ha-Yedid; Yishuv, Organizations (Underground Movements, Hagana); Arab Revolt; Gideon Force;**

Special Treatment [HT]: British term used in connection with the imprisonment of Jewish political offenders in the *Yishuv*. In particular, the term referred to certain priviledges that such prisoners (mainly members of Jewish undergrounds) had as compared to Arabs or common criminals. Privileges included the right to sleep on a cot rather than on the floor, the right to reading materials and paper, the right to receive food from outside the prison, and exemption from labor while incarcerated. Special treatment was granted by the court martial at the time of trial and could be withheld as punishment for recalcitrance.

Spencer [PN]: JA term for former prime minister Winston S. Churchill, used after 1945. The code name derived from Churchill's middle name and was almost immediately obvious to any reader. As a result, the phrase was used only in documents not considered likely to cause embarrassment for him or the JAE.

Spirit Nation [HT]: Concept used by a number of folkist and proto-Zionist thinkers to define the Jewish nation. Among the earliest to use the concept was Leon Pinsker. In his book *Auto-Emancipation*, Pinsker argued that the reality of Jewish spiritual nationalism, which he defined as Jewish cosmopolitanism, was a source of fear and hatred. What Jews saw as a more advanced form of nationality — identity divorced from territory — non-Jews saw as a cause for alarm. Pinsker explained antisemitism in clinical terms as deriving, in part, from humanity's fear of ghosts (spirits with no firm grip in the real world, i.e., a spirit nation). Accordingly, the only solution to the Jewish problem, according to Pinsker, was to return Jews to the status of a territorial nation by creating a national home in *Eretz Israel*. Simon Dubnow, by contrast, used a similar concept in a purely positive sense, recommending that the spirit nation could not return to the status of a territorial nation. Instead, Dubnow argued for the creation of a set of international guarantees for Jewish cultural and communal autonomy. > see also: **Autonomism; Auto-Emancipation; Hibbat Zion; Nationalism.**

State Within a State [HT]: Antisemitic canard claiming that Jews constituted an independent entity within the European polity and therefore failed to live up to their part of the emancipation "bargain." The canard was somtimes used against the Zionists, mainly by Jewish anti-Zionists who accused Jewish nationalists of creating an opportunity for antisemitic rabble rousing. > see also: **Antisemitismus; Anti-Zionism; Dual Loyalty**.

Status-Quo Agreement: Common term for the agreement made between JAE chairman David Ben-Gurion and relligious leaders in the *Yishuv* on the eve of Israel's independence. The agreement harked back to previous agreements between religious and secular Zionists to protect the Jewish nature of the *Yishuv* (defined in this case as permitting religious Zionists to live full lives while participating in the *Yishuv*'s affairs) and permit freedom of conscience at the same time. In essence, the agreement stipulated that all previous agreements would remain in force, for example, that all government institutions would serve only kosher food while granting the chief rabbinate considerable latitude in personal matters (marriage, divorce, births, and funerals). > see also: **Historic Coalition; Judaism and Zionism**.

Stavsky Trial [HT/PN]: Popular name for the trial of one of the three suspects arrested in connection with the murder of Haim Arlosoroff in June 1933, specifically the Betar leader Abraham Stavsky. Stavsky, along with co-defendents Abba Ahimeir and Zvi Rosenblatt, proclaimed his innocence throughout the trial held in late May and early June 1934. On June 8, the court announced its decision: Stavsky was convicted, Ahimeir was acquitted, and Rosenblatt was released due to his age (he was a minor when the incident ocurred). Simultaneous with his conviction, Stavsky was sentenced to death, a sentence that raised storms of protests even among opponents of the revisionist Zionist

movement. On July 19, 1934, however, the Palestine Court of Appeals vacated Stavsky's conviction since the evidence was based solely on the testimony of a single eyewitness (Arlosoroff's wife, Sima) and the death penalty required confirmation by a second witness. > see also: **Arlosoroff Affair**.

Stephen [PN]: (1) Term for assets of the Hagana's intelligence service (Shai) that operated publicly and legally in cooperation with the British during World War II. (2) Postwar JA code name for the United States, derived from the first name of American Zionist leader Rabbi Stephen S. Wise. Further derivatives included Stephen's Brother, which designated Canada, and Stephen's Wife, which designated Latin America. These usages exemplified Wise's fame, in that the United States was immediately identifiable with his name, but should not necessarily be taken as a sign of respect or admiration. > see also: **World War II; Yishuv, Organizations (Underground Movements, Sherut Yediot); Detroit**.

Sufot ba-Negev [סופות בנגב, H] "Southern Storms": Jewish term for the pogroms of 1881–1884 that spread throughout the Russian empire. The term reflects the fact that the pogroms began in the southern Ukraine as a spontaneous response to alleged Jewish involvement in the assassination of Czar Alexander II. From there, pogroms spread northward throughout the Pale of Settlement (the restricted area in which Jews were permitted to live). The pogroms resulted in many Jewish intellectuals despairing of Western-style emancipation, attuning some toward Jewish nationalism and others toward revolutionary socialism. > see also: **Pale of Settlement; Bund(ism); Hibbat Zion(ism); Zionut**.

Suriya al-G'enobiyah [Ar] "South Syria": Arab nationalist term for *Eretz Israel* (i.e., Cis-Jordan) and Trans-Jordan, reflecting the belief that these territories should be part of a "Greater Syria." Implicit in the term is the pan-Arabist notion that all the territory from Mesopotamia to Morocco should be part of a single Arab empire. Also implicit in the term was a complete rejection of any possiblity of compromise with Jewish nationalism, except, perhaps, in granting Jews a limited degree of autonomy in an Arab-ruled empire.

Sykes-Picot Agreement: Popular name for the secret diplomatic agreement calling for the division of the Ottoman Empire among the Entente powers, officially known as the Asia Minor Agreement. The agreement was worked out in 1916 between Sir Mark Sykes and George Picot, representing, respectively, the British and French Foreign Offices. The agreement called for the virtual elimination of the Ottoman Empire and its partition into seven zones. Of the seven zones, four were so-called colored zones, apportioned as follows: Red (British), covering Mesopotamia from Basra to Bagdhad; Blue (French), covering the coastal strip from just north of Haifa to north of Alexandretta: Green (Italian), southern Turkey; and Brown (Russian), northern Anatolia. These colored zones were to be placed under the direct control of the named powers. Two other zones, designated "A" and "B," were created between the French and British zones. These two zones were to be under the indirect control of the French (Zone A) and the British (Zone B). Finally, *Eretz Israel* was to be placed under the control of an international condominium. After World War I, the agreement could not be carried out as originally planned, causing complications that were only cleared up by the San Remo Conference. > see also: **Conferences, International (San Remo)**.

Ta'amulat Lahash [תעמולת לחש, H] "Silent Propaganda": Term popular in the Hagana and Zva ha-Hagana le-Israel referring to a series of psychological warfare techniques used during Israel's War of Independence. This type of propaganda was designed to intimidate local Arab populations, hoping thereby to obtain their quiescence. In a few cases Hagana intelligence officers planted false stories of Jewish atrocities as a means to encourage local Arabs to flee a region entirely.

Ta'as [תע"ש, H] "Manufacture": Israeli term for the semisecret Hagana organization tasked with producing weapons and ammunition for Jewish self-defense prior to the establishment of the State of Israel. Given the generally underdeveloped nature of heavy industry in *Eretz Israel* at the time, Ta'as concentrated mainly on producing ammunition for, or copies of, weapons already in the Hagana's arsenal. Of special importance, in this respect, were the copies of the British Sten submachine gun and the 2-inch mortar produced in the 1940s. After Israel's declaration of independence, Ta'as operated in the open and produced, among other weapons, the Davidka mortar and the so-called sandwich cars (homemade armored cars used during the War of Independence). The term Ta'as is still used colloquially for the Israeli Military Industries. > see also: **Yishuv, Organizations; War of Independence; Zva ha-Hagana le-Israel.**

Tancred [Slang]: Nom de combat used by Theodor Herzl between 1881 and 1883 when he was a member of the University of Vienna's Albia dueling fraternity. The name was derived from Benjamin D'Israeli's 1847 novel about a young English aristocrat who helps to revitalize the Church of England after a pilgrimage to the Holy Land. The story's details have led many historians to hypothesize that Herzl's choice may have prefigured his later Zionist endeavors. Herzl resigned from the fraternity after an antisemitic incident on Febraury 13, 1883.

Tanzimat [T] "Reorganization": Official name for efforts made during the nineteenth centruy to reform government in the Ottoman Empire. Broadly, reforms were carried out in two periods. The First Tanzimat derived from a "noble rescript" of 1839 and the Second, from an "imperial rescript" of 1856. The effect of these reform efforts was to modernize the empire, redefining subjects as citizens, calling for an end to tax farming, and ending graft. The Second Tanzimat also declared all citizens to be equal, regardless of religion. The rescripts were issued in the hope that reforms would tie Ottoman citizenry, especially in restive border regions, to the empire and thus prevent the empire's dissolution. Ironically, by whetting the appetites of some national minorities for reform, the Tanzimat may have actually hastened the development of nationalist movements that speeded up the empire's decline.

Teddy [PN]: JA code term for the United States, used between 1946 and 1948 and derived from the name of the JA and Hagana representative in New York: Teddy Kollek. > see also: **Detroit; Stephen.**

Tefuzot [תפוצות, H] "Dispersion": Hebrew term for the diaspora, that is for all Jewish communities outside *Eretz Israel*. > see also: **Diaspora; Galut; Gola; Geula.**

Tegart Fence [PN]: Popular name for the defensive fence built along Palestine/*Eretz Israel*'s northern border and named after its designer, Sir Charles A. Tegart. > see also: **Northern Fence.**

Teheran Children [HT]: Popular name for a group of eight hundred Jewish refugee children who managed to escape the Nazis and, after three years of wandering, arrived in Iran's capital in the autumn of 1942. The children's flight began in 1939 when the group crossed from Poland into the Soviet Union. Initially held as potential counter-revolutionaries, the children and their adult escorts were freed as aprt of the Russo-Polish agreement of 1942. The Mossad le-Aliya Bet arranged for the group's transfer from Soviet territory and from there to *Eretz Israel*, via India and Egypt. The children finally arrived safely in *Eretz Israel* in February 1943.

Tehiat ha-Ruah [תחיית הרוח, H] "Revival of the Spirit": Term used by Ahad ha-Am to explicate his Zionist ideology. In his view, two crises existed in tandem — the crisis of Jews (colloquially viewed as the "Jewish problem") and the crisis of Judaism. These two crises were separate but their solution was related. The Jewish problem derived from non-Jewish attitudes toward Jews and its solution required a means to establish a new equilibrium in these relations, including Jewish emigration from antisemitic countries. The question of Judaism, however, derived from the internal decay wrought by too long an exile and made worse by the splintering of Jewish religious

and communal institutions (and ideologies) in the *Haskala'*s aftermath. While the Jewish problem required a physical solution, the problem of Judaism required a spiritual solution, which Ahad ha-Am termed the creation of a new *torah*. In both cases Ahad ha-Am believed that Jews needed a nationalist movement that would organize a partial return to the Holy Land. Ahad ha-Am's spiritual Zionism, however, did not view Palestine/*Eretz Israel* as capable of solving the entire Jewish problem (except indirectly), meaning that Jews seeking refuge from antisemitic persecution would need other refuges as well. Moreover, Ahad ha-Am did not view the creation of a Jewish national home in political terms, viewing Zionism's goal as the creation of a spiritual center that would unify the entire Jewish world while raising the Jews' status in non-Jewish eyes. > see also: **Ahad ha-Am; Antisemitismus; Haskala; Bayit Leumi; Zionut, Types of Zionism (Spitirual Zionism).**

Tel [תל, H] "Mound": Hebrew term for a hill created by human means, specifically by the repeated building of new settlements on previously inhabited localities. This process creates a layer of new settlement upon layers of ruins, thus raising a small, artificial rise over surrounding territory. The term is used with a similar connotation in Arabic. In contemporary Israel, the term "tel" is also used in the name of a number of settlements and towns, most notably Tel Aviv (i.e., "hill of spring"). > see also: **Kfar; Gush.**

Tel Hai [תל חי, GN]: Jewish settlement in the Finger of Galilee, that was attacked by Arab marauders in early February 1920. > see also: **Ezba ha-Galil.**

Tel Napoleon [GN/PN]: Name for a small mound located near the Ramat Gan/Tel Aviv border just south of the Yarkon River. Here, it is claimed, Napoleon Bonaparte had his headquarters during his campaign in the Middle East in 1798–1799. According to the folklore, it Napoleon directed the siege of Jaffa and composed his call on Jews to return to *Eretz Israel* here. > see also: **Grand Sanhedrin.**

Tender [E/Slang]: British term for a small truck, used by the Hagana to designate any vehicle used by the Jewish Supernumerary Police (JSP) to transport the so-called Nodedet (the JSP's mobile unit) during the Arab Revolt of 1936–1939. Seventy such vehicles were purchased by the JA for the Hagana; some continued in use until 1948. > see also: **Sandvitchim; Nodedet.**

Territorialism

1. Scope and Definition

Term for the ideology of those supporters of a Jewish national home who disagreed with the selection of Palestine/*Eretz Israel*, preferring some other territory. Their nationalist orientation led most territorialists to join the World Zionist Organization (WZO) when Theodor Herzl founded it in 1897, and many attended the First World Zionist Congress. The split between Zionism and territorialism occurred in 1903 when the British offered WZO territory in East Africa (generally known as the Uganda plan). Most Zionists rejected the scheme out of hand, styling themselves "Zionists for Zion," but territorialists, led by the Anglo-Jewish author Israel Zangwill, felt that the offer should be given due consideration, if only as a temporary haven. The territorialists withdrew entirely from the WZO in 1906 when the latter rejected Uganda as entirely unsuitable for Jewish mass settlement and formed the Jewish Territorialist Organization (known by its transliterated Yiddish acronym ITO). Territorialists viewed *Eretz Israel* as nothing more than an unobtainable dream until the British issued the Balfour Declaration. The ITO continued its competition with the WZO until 1925 when it disbanded. Other anti-Zionist territorialist organizations, however, continued to propose schemes for mass Jewish resettlement that became increasingly unrealistic as the *Yishuv* grew. As an ideology, territorialism ceased to have any meaning with the creation of the State of Israel. > see also: **Uganda Plan; Zionei Zion; Nachtasyl.**

2. Territorialist Organizations

Allgemeine Jüdische Kolonisations Organisation (AIKO), "United Jewish Colonization Organization," German territorialist body founded in 1908 by Zionists who feared that the WZO's overtly political orientation would harm the possibilty of mass *aliya* after the Young Turk revolution. Unlike some other territorialist organizations, AIKO concentrated on settling Jews in the Middle East, principally in the Sinai, Syria, Mesopotamia, and *Eretz Israel*. Unlike the WZO, AIKO framed its requests for permission to settle Jews in Ottoman territory exclusively in humanitarian terms and did not include any demands for autonomy for the settlements. But AIKO completely misunderstood the Young Turk revolution (as did many Zionists at the time). Far from easing immigration, the new rulers were not interested in any form of mass immigration, thus closing off most of the settlement possibilities that AIKO sought. Similarly, negotiations with the British to reopen the El Arish plan (first broached with the WZO in 1902) also failed. The Balfour Declaration and negotiations for the mandate left AIKO without a mission. In 1920, therefore, the organization dissolved and many members then rejoined the WZO. Sole president: Alfred Nossig.

Am Olam (עם עולם), "Eternal People," federation of Jewish organizations seeking mass emigration from the Russian empire during the last decades of the nineteenth century. The Am Olam movement itself was territorialist, insofar as it deprecated *Eretz Israel* as a destination for migration, emphasizing immigration to the U.S. instead, but it was not specifically political in its orientation. As a result, some chapters spoke about creating autonomous Jewish provinces in the U.S. and some were even strongly socialist in orientation. Neither of these characteristics pertained to the federation itself. Instead, the federation concentrated on seeking to move as many Jews as possible to sparsely populated areas in the American West and Southwest. No major Am Olam project came to fruition, however, despite the creation of some colonies in Texas, New Mexico, Arizona, and Oregon. Am Olam ceased to operate in 1890; a number of former members joined the WZO in 1897.

Binn, "Bee," socialist Jewish youth movement founded in Vilna in 1929 spreading throughout Poland in the years prior to World War II. Binn originated with the students and faculty of the Jewish Teachers Seminary in Vilna. Originally a scouting movement, Binn adopted an increasingly socialist orientation during the 1930s. Eventually, Binn moved so far to the left that it became a front organization for the Jewish section of the Polish Communist party. At that point, Binn adopted a policy that emphasized Jewish national settlement in Birobidzhan.

Freeland League (FLL), international Jewish non-Zionist nationalist organization founded in London on July 26, 1935, and dedicated to finding a safe haven for Jews outside of the *Yishuv*. Given the nature of Jewish distress in the mid-1930s — with masses of Jews imperiled by Nazi and Nazi-inspired antisemitism — FLL did not see itself as competing with the WZO but rather sought to supplement *aliya* with a number of safe havens (permanent or temporary). Only one FLL project progressed past the stage of initial contacts, that being the plan to settle Jews in Kimberley, Australia. Even the Kimberley scheme ended in disappointment and no other settlement plan came as close to fruition as that one. Although FLL was a well-meaning organization (which in theory still exists), it wasted precious resouces on chimerical schemes that had little relevance to the people it sought to help.

International Jewish Colonization Society (IJCS), short-lived federation of territorialist organizations founded in Amsterdam in 1938. Reacting to the worsening situation in Germany and Eastern Europe where Jewish distress increased daily and British support for Zionism steadily eroded, IJCS sought to find secure temporary havens for Jewish refugees. The outbreak of World War II led to the complete collapse of IJCS, without its having seen even a single scheme to attainment. Some of the settlement schemes were taken up after the war by the Freeland League.

Jewish Colonization Association, philanthropic agency promoting a territorialist solution to the Jewish problem, better known by the acronym ICA (from the organization's Yiddish initials). ICA was founded in 1891 by Baron Maurice de Hirsch to provide a means of mass Jewish emigration from the Russian empire to a suitable and stable haven. Hirsch sought to direct the stream of Jewish emigration into relatively undeveloped countries such as Argentina. Hirsch hoped that Jews would be welcomed as pioneers making a positive contribution to the host country, which would offset their influx in large numbers and would not generate antisemitism. Argentina proved initially receptive and was the destination of Hirsch's greatest single success, settling some 20,000 Jews between 1890 and 1930. ICA also sought to make Jewish life more productive in Europe, hoping thereby to slow emigration, and to that end began setting up vocational training schools in major Jewish population centers. In 1899 Baron Edmond de Rothschild transferred control of the settlements he was sponsoring in *Eretz Israel* to ICA, although he continued to act as the indirect benefactor of the colonies for many years thereafter. In 1923 ICA separated its *Eretz Israel* subsidiary into a new organization, henceforth known as the Palestine Jewish Colonization Association (PICA). Although both ICA and PICA were territiorialist in orientation, neither was anti-Zionist, despite the legacy of Hirsch's utter rejection of Political Zionism and very low opinion of Theodor Herzl. After the Balfour Declaration, PICA began to coordinate its activities in the *Yishuv* with the WZO and JAE, mainly in terms of land purchase and settlement. In 1929, ICA and PICA jointly founded EMICA, the Emergency Jewish Colonization Association, to help resettle Jewish refugees created by Arab rioting. Finally, in 1924, ICA (and indirectly PICA) joined with the American Jewish philanthropy HIAS and the Russian Emgidirect Agency to form HIAS-ICA-Emigdirect, better known as HICEM, which was active in obtaining the release of Jews from the Soviet Union and (between 1933 and 1939) in coordinating efforts to rescue German Jewry.

PICA divested itself of its holdings, which were transferred to the Israeli government, in the early 1950s; ICA's activities continued into the 1960s, winding down in the 1970s. Theoretically, ICA still exists, with its main offices in Tel Aviv, although it is now a body without a mission.

Jewish Territorialist Organization, premier international Jewish non-Zionist nationalist organization, better known by the acronym ITO (from the organization's Yiddish initials). ITO was founded in August 1905 by Israel Zangwill and forty other dissident delegates at the Seventh World Zionist Congress. ITO's supporters believed that the WZO had erred in rejecting the British offer of Uganda. They felt that since *Eretz Israel* was unobtainable, rejecting an offer of settlement elsewhere was tantamount to abandoning any hope for finding a secure haven for oppressed Eastern European Jews. Moreover, ITO argued, WZO concentration on *Eretz Israel* was nothing short of utopian and was bound to fail. Throughout its existence, ITO was headquartered in London and was active in seeking homelands for Jews throughout the world. Although ITO's creation intially weakened the WZO, the new organization proved to be everything its proponents had accused the WZO of being: a utopian agency composed of luftmenschen who were unable to seriously aid the people they sought to succour. ITO was never able to obtain a single territory for mass Jewish settlement and early on had to jettison the pretense of negotiating for the creation of autonomous Jewish settlements. In 1925, with the *Yishuv* providing a stable basis for a Jewish national home, ITO dissolved.

Liga für Jüdische Kolonisation (LJK), "League for Jewish Colonization," refugee relief agency established in Paris in 1934 by German Jewish émigrés and a number of moderate Jewish socialists of Eastern European origin. LJK was loosely associated with the Freeland League. Not anti-Zionist in orientation, LJK nevertheless rejected *Eretz Israel* as a solution for the entire Jewish problem and especially rejected the idea that the *Yishuv* could (or should) be a cultural center for the Jewish world. Prominent LJK supporters included Chaim Zhitlowsky and Julius Brutzkus, both of whom had connections to numerous other territorialist organizations.

Zion, Bulgarian Zionist fraternity founded as a friendly society in 1904. Zion sought to educate Bulgarian Jewry in Jewish nationalism but was not necessarily committed to any particular territory for the future Jewish national home. Zion operated on a local level with autonomous societies. Early on some societies adopted the name Zion — Joseph Marcou Baruch, in honor of the Jewish adventurer who was considered to be the father of Bulgarian Zionism. Most Zion societies apparently supported the Uganda scheme and withdrew from the WZO around 1905. The national fraternity disappered shortly thereafter, with most local elements collapsing prior to World War I.

3. Territorialist Schemes

Alaska, plan proposed by the Alaska Development Committee in 1938 to resettle an unstated number of Jewish refugees in semi-autonomous colonies in Alaska (then a U.S. territory, later admitted as the forty-ninth state). Mooted until 1940, the plan never proceeded beyond the planning stage.

Angola, ITO proposal dating from 1912 to settle Jews in Portuguese East Africa. An investigative committee sent to assess the feasibility of the scheme reported that up to 13 million Europeans could be accommodated in Angola, which led to further interest in Jewish and Portuguese circles. World War I disrupted the settlement project but did not lead to its complete cancellation. In 1934, a similar proposal was mooted by the Freeland League and Angola was again suggested as a possible refuge for German Jews by presidential adviser Bernard Baruch in 1940. However, nothing developed from the latter two proposals.

Argentina/Pampa, plan proposed by Baron Maurice de Hirsch, the Russian Jewish philanthropist and president of ICA, to find a haven for Russian Jewry by mass resettlement in Argentina. In 1891, Hirsch initiated the scheme by using ICA funds to purchase land in

Argentina's Santa Fe province. For the next twenty years, ICA continued to finance new settlements in Argentina. By 1913, ICA settlements contained 197,000 hectares of land with 26,648 colonists. Thereafter the project declined as the Argentine government became suspicious of all Eastern European immigrants. Early on the planners intended that the colonies attain autonomy, but the government refused to grant more than local authority to the colonists. > see also: **As A Leads to Z, So Argentina Will Lead to Zion.**

Baja, ITO scheme proposed in 1905 to settle Jews in Lower California (Mexico), a territory popularly known as (and geographically identical with) the Baja Peninsula. Some Jews of Eastern European descent had already settled in the region after 1880. Nonetheless, a commission of inquiry was sent by the ITO, with full support of the Mexican government, to report on conditions in the area. The commission's negative report led to the scheme's abandonment in 1910.

Birobidzhan, Jewish autonomous region established by Stalin in 1928 in a remote Asian corner of the Soviet Union. Conceptually, Birobidzhan was exactly the opposite of previous Communist policy on Zionism and Jewish nationalism. Stalin had rejected Jewish nationalism, advocating radical assimilation, because Jews (he claimed) were a nation held together by the negative impact of "capitalist contradictions." However, in order to undercut the autonomist ideology of the Bund and to attract young Jews (who might otherwise adopt Zionism as their ideology) to Communism, Stalin agreed to the creation of a Jewish region and encouraged Jews to settle there. Relatively few did so, although many who did were involved in movements that filled the ideological chasm between Communism and Zionism. Among them were small groups of Poale Zion Smol members who despaired of creating socialism in the *Yishuv* and emigrated in 1929 and 1930 to help create a Jewish socialist homeland. > see also: **Communism and Zionism.**

British Guyana, British governmental proposal issued in early June 1939 to permit the creation of Jewish settlements in British-controlled South America. The plan was little more than a fig leaf designed to obfuscate the damage done to reufgee relief efforts by the White Paper of 1939 which severely limited Jewish immigration to *Eretz Israel*. Shortly after the white paper was published, the Chamberlain cabinet sent a commission to study the possibilities of European settlement in Guyana. The commission report suggested that Guyana was underpopulated and proposed that as much as 90 percent of the territory's landmass be opened for refugee immigration. The commission did admit, however, that most of the arable land in Guyana was already in use. Consequently, the plan was held up as a smokescreen and was then quietly dropped in July or August 1939.

Crimea, popular name for the abortive effort to create autonomous Jewish collective agricultural settlements in southern Ukraine and the Crimean Peninsula during the early years of Josef Stalin's rule. The plan, which was financed largely by the American Jewish Joint Distribution Committee's (JDC) Agro-Joint subsidiary, was based on the perceived need to change Jewish settlement patterns while also helping to find productive labor for Soviet Jewry. The scheme was semiterritorialist insofar as it sought to concentrate Jews in a particular area. From the Soviet perspective, this plan aided in the struggle against Zionism, since it offered a seemingly nationalist veneer to Jewish resettlement while strengthening Communist rule in an area that strongly resisted collectivization. The plan was also acceptable since it generated much needed hard currency for the regime. In the end, thirty-eight Jewish collective settlements were established; a few were composed almost entirely of workers who had left *Eretz Israel* to create a socialist Zionist haven in the Communist homeland. Most of the settlements were destroyed by the Nazis during World War II and most of the settlers were murdered. Ironically, many of the survivors were persecuted by Stalinist authorities after World War II on the pretext that the JDC was really a front organization for American and British imperialists who sought to remove Crimea from the Soviet Union as a base for a future counterrevolution. > see also: **Communism and Zionism; Organizations, Non- or Anti-Zionist (United States, Joint Distribution Committee)**.

Cyrenaica, ITO plan dating to 1909 to settle European Jews in Ottoman-controlled North Africa (now Libya). Generally positive reactions to the plan from European and Turkish circles led to intense efforts to obtain mass Jewish immigration to a territory that was (indirectly, at least) associated with previous Jewish history. The Italian invasion of Libya in 1911, however, put an end to the scheme, which was never revived.

Ecuador, scheme associated with Franco-Jewish figures and proposed in 1935 as a means to assist in the settlement of German Jewish refugees. The ITO became involved in the scheme after initial contacts with the Ecuadorian government proved positive. Ecuadorian stipulations that settlers had to be widely separated, which was inconsistent with the level of autonomy requested by the ITO, led to the plan's being shelved in 1937. In 1955, however, the Freeland League revived the scheme as a means to oversee mass Jewish migration to South America. Nothing further came of the later plan.

French Guiana, Freeland League plan dating to 1936 to settle Jewish refugees in the French South American colony. The proposal seemed attractive, since the French government had only recently closed the borders of metropolitan France to new refugee immigration. French interest led to an investigative committee, which reported that as many as 10,000 refugees could settle in the territory. No further action was taken at the time. The proposal was too similar to contemporary Polish efforts to buy Madagascar from the French as a colony for "surplus" Polish Jews and the league's directors did not want to be accused of pandering to antisemitism. Nevertheless, the scheme was proposed again in 1946, and remained on the league's agenda throughout the 1950s.

Galveston, semiterritorialist scheme to settle large numbers of Jews fleeing opression in the Russian empire in the southern United States, proposed in 1906. The plan was to redirect the masses of Jewish immigrants from the Northeast to southern and western states, where many jobs were available and where, it was assumed, the new immigrants would not cause congestion and antisemitism. The project became politicized when Israel Zangwill and the ITO temporarily lent its name to recruitment efforts in Europe. However, the recruitment of immigrants, a felony under U.S. law, led to the plan's curtailment and eventual collapse.

Kimberley, scheme proposed in 1938 jointly by the Freeland League and Dutch and Swedish refugee agencies as a means of settling 25,000 Central and Eastern European Jews in a semi-autonomous territory in Northwest Australia. Similar plans had been previously mooted by the ITO but had never proceeded. In this case, the scheme received some support in Australia and was duly considered by the local and federal governments. Planning was halted when the Japanese entered World War II, although the final decision to cancel the scheme entirely was not taken by the Australian federal government until 1944.

Lower Silesia, scheme to settle Holocaust survivors in an independent state in parts of eastern Germany, first mooted in 1945. At the time, some 150,000 to 250,000 survivors who had little desire to return to their former homes were concentrated in Poland. Settlement work began in June 1945; by September 1946, almost 70,000 Jews had been settled in Lower Silesia. By then, however, efforts to establish as an autonomous Jewish region (as well as similar plans for Bavaria) had come to nought. Lower Silesia was granted to Poland by the Paris peace Conference (1946). Unwilling to live under Polish rule, most Jews moved to the U.S. zone of occupation in western Germany, hoping to further migrate either to the U.S. or to Israel. > see also: **Displaced Persons, Jewish**.

New Caledonia/New Hebrides, Freeland League schemes first proposed in 1935 to settle Jewish refugees on the main island of the French Oceana Territory, 937 miles (1,500 Km)

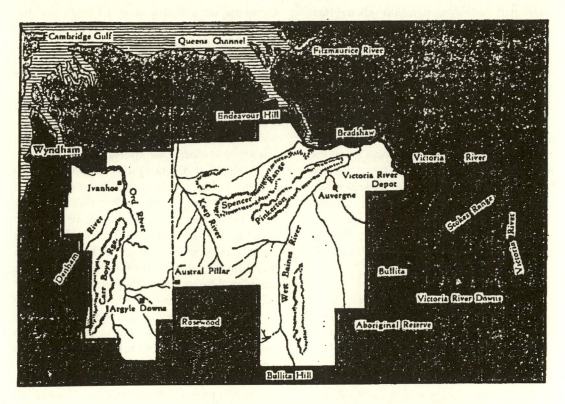

Proposed Area of the Kimberly Settlement Scheme, As Published
In S. Stedman, *A Jewish Settlement in Australia* (Sydney, 1940).
Courtesy of Professor William D. Rubinstein

north of Australia. The Freeland League sent a commission to New Caledonia with French approval in 1937. In addition to studying conditions in New Caledonia the commission reported that mass Jewish settlement was possible on the nearby islands of the New Hebrides chain. Despite these positive reports from the commission, no further action was taken.

Peru, scheme proposed by Jewish territorialist leader Haim Zhitlowsky in 1931. Positive contacts with the Peruvian government led to agreement between Zhitlowky and the Peruvians in 1934, but nothing further came of the proposal.

Surinam, also known as the Dutch Guiana Scheme, the plan was mooted by the Dutch delegation at the Evian Conference on refugees in July 1938. This plan revived a 1903 ITO proposal (that was abandoned before it progressed very far) to settle Jews in Dutch-controlled South America. Although the territorialist aspect of the scheme was absent from the 1938 Dutch proposal, this was one of the few schemes that actually resulted in some activity: some Jews managed to escape Europe for Dutch Guiana between 1940 and 1943. In 1947, the Freeland League revived the proposal yet again, requesting Dutch permission for the resettlement of as many as 500,000 Jews. Although an agreement was indeed signed between the league and the Dutch government in late 1947, that plan covered only 3,000 Jewish displaced persons. Moreover, by the time the agreement was sigend the United Nations had already approved the partition of Palestine/*Eretz Israel* and the creation of a Jewish state. As a result, the agreement was never carried out.

Tasmania, scheme considered in 1940 as a supplement to (and later as an alternative to) the Kimberley scheme. The intention was to divert part of the immigration scheme then planned for Northwest Australia to the island of Tasmania off Australia's southeast coast. Planning continued until 1945, when it became obvious that the plan was neither feasible nor desirable.

The Son: JA and WZO code term for Colonial Secretary Malcolm MacDonald, author of the White Paper of 1939, and son of former colonial secretary Ramsay MacDonald. The younger MacDonald's inheritance of his father's position explains the term. Initially the name was used in a positive light, but after 1939, Zionist disappointment with MacDonald led to its prejorative use.

Tiyul [טיול, H] "Trip": Coded term for the small-scale but systematic escape of Polish and Slovakian Jews to Hungary between 1940 and 1942. In 1944 the Va'ad ha-Ezra veha-Hatzala in Budapest organized the "re-Tiyul" program whereby Jews from Hungary were smuggled into Slovakia and Romania.

Tochnit Avner [תוכנית אבנר, H] "Plan Avner": First systematic operational plan for the Hagana, formulated in June 1937. In some documents this plan was referred to as Plan A (Tochnit A). The plan presumed a unilateral British withdrawal from Palestine/ *Eretz Israel*. Acting on this premise, the Hagana laid plans to seize control of the country's infrastructure while protecting Jewish settlements from Arab marauders, thereby permitting the creation of a Jewish state.

Tochnit AZ [תוכנית א'צ, H] "Plan AZ": Hagana defensive plan proposed during the invasion scare of June–July 1942, when Field Marshal Erwin Rommel's Afrika Korps was a mere seventy miles (112 Km) from Alexandria and total British collapse in North Africa appeared imminent. Tochnit AZ represented a modified version of Tochnit A of 1937 and was designed to counter an Arab revolt in case of German airborne or seaborne invasion. When the Germans were defeated at El Alamein, the plan was shelved. > see also: **Tochnit Avner**; **Tochnit ha-Carmel**.

Tochnit B [תוכנית ב, H] "Plan B": Hagana plan formulated during World War II and envisioned as a follow-up to Tochnit A and AZ. Tochnit B was framed toward the end of the war when the direct threat of invasion had passed but before JAE approved a rebellion against the British. Since there was no unanimity on the *Yishuv*'s next steps, the plan did not deal with strategy, but merely with organization. Under the plan, the *Yishuv* was divided into four military districts. Three of these were to be reinforced by a single Palmah battalion while the fourth (the coastal plain) was to be reinforced by an entire Palmah brigade to aid *Aliya Bet* activities. No further plans were definitively set down at this time. Instead, the plan was offered as a defensive contingency in case of a renewed Arab revolt. When this did not transpire in 1945, the plan was shelved.

Tochnit D [תוכנית ד, H] "Plan D": Hagana defensive plan proposed in December 1947 based on the assumption of an invasion of *Eretz Israel* by Arab armies on the termination of the mandate. In order to provide the *Yishuv* with a strong defensive base in the event that predictions of Arab behavior proved correct, the plan concentrated on obtaining control of lines of communications linking Tel Aviv, Haifa, and Jerusalem. The plan placed greatest emphasis on securing the latter. As JAE chairman David Ben-Gurion noted, the new State of Israel could afford to lose one of its three main cities, as long as the one that was lost was not Jerusalem. To this end, an offensive was planned to break through Arab villages on the road to Jerusalem while other fronts would remain in a defensive posture until Jerusalem was secured. Tochnit D was put into effect officially on March 10, 1948 and met with its greatest successes on its flanks: Haifa and Jaffa were rapidly secured thus anchoring the new state's borders. However, results on the Jerusalem front were mixed, with Jerusalem's new city being secured at the loss of the old city. > see also: **War of Independence**.

Tochnit Eretz Israel [תוכנית ארץ ישראל, H] "The Land of Israel Plan": Hagana contingency plan for continued resistance to a Nazi invasion force or a joint Nazi/Arab occupation force in the event of a British collapse in the Middle East during World War II. Initially proposed in autumn 1941, the plan was approved under the name Tochnit ha-Carmel. > see also: **Tochnit ha-Carmel**.

Tochnit G [תוכנית ג, H] "Plan G": Hagana operational plan proposed in May 1946 and partially implemented in 1947. The plan was premised on the need to prevent a renewal of Arab disturbances under circumstances of less than complete British withdrawal. The plan assumed that the British would seek to maintain their bases in *Eretz Israel* but would adopt a policy of neutrality in Arab-Jewish fighting. As a result, planners emphasized three items: (1) protecting Jewish settlements and population centers; (2) protecting Jewish institutions and property; and, (3) seizing the initiative from the Arabs as quickly as possible to bring rioting to an end. Tochnit G was not implemented in its pure form since by the time it became relevant, the British had already declared their intention to withdraw from *Eretz Israel*. However, some of the plan was used to wrest the initiative from Arab irregular forces prior to Israel's declaration of independence. > see also: **War of Independence**.

Tochnit H [תוכנית ה, H] "Plan H": Tentative Hagana operational plan proposed in late 1942 or early 1943 to infiltrate Jewish commandos into Nazi-occupied Europe to aid Jewish resistance movements and rescue Jews from Nazi extermination. Given the *Yishuv*'s general lack of resources, the plan (also known as Tochnit ha-Hagana, the Defense Plan) needed a considerable amount of outside assistance, mainly from the British. Initially, such aid was not forthcoming meaning that the plan had to be shelved for most of 1943. Only in 1944, when most of those whom the plan was designed to save were already dead, did the British agree to send thirty-two paratroopers of Europe to assist in resistance and rescue operations. > see also: **Paratroopers, Palestinian**.

Tochnit ha-Asor [תוכנית העשור, H] "The Ten-Year Plan": official name for the revised evacuation plan proposed by revisionist Zionist leader Ze'ev Jabotinsky in 1937. Jabotinsky saw his plan as a viable alternative to the British-proposed partition of *Eretz Israel* into Jewish and Arab states. If 1.5 million Jews would immigrate in ten years, by 1947 the Jews would constitute an absolute majority in the country and a Jewish state could be founded in an unpartitioned Palestine/*Eretz Israel*. As with the original plan, this plan was framed around phased emigration; the very premise required a degree of British acquiescence or support that was far beyond what the British were willing to provide. As a result, Jabotinsky's plan proved abortive.

Tochnit ha-Carmel [תוכנית הכרמל, H] "The Carmel Plan": Short-lived Hagana defensive contingency plan formulated in the spring of 1942. At the time, the British faced numerous threats from German or German-inspired Arab forces in the Middle East. In April 1942, the Hagana high command prepared a plan to defend the *Yishuv* based on the premise that British land forces would suffer a catastrophic defeat and *Eretz Israel* would be occupied by the Germans or Axis allies. In that event, the plan called for the creation of a fortress complex in the Carmel mountain range, centered around the port of Haifa, to which the entire Jewish population of the *Yishuv* would be evacuated. The Hagana planners presumed that this fortress could hold out as long as the Royal Navy continued to operate in the eastern Mediterranean. Although generally defensive in orientation, the Carmel plan also included contingencies for a protracted guerrilla campaign by the Palmah to keep occupying forces off balance and assist a British counterattack. Despite fears of imminent invasion in the summer of 1942 — when German forces were halted at El Alamein, less than seventy miles

(112 KM) from Alexandria — the Carmel plan never had to be activated. > see also: **Tochnit AZ.**

Tochnit ha-Zafon [תוכנית הצפון, H] "The Northern Plan": Code name for two distinct Hagana contingency plans. The first, proposed in 1939, was an operational plan to carry out JAE chairman David Ben-Gurion's call for *Mered ha-Aliya.* This plan called for a massive program of *Aliya Bet* from Germany and Eastern Europe that would undermine the White Paper of 1939. The second plan was a contingency plan for defense in case of British withdrawal, proposed in 1942 and later renamed Tochnit ha-Carmel. > see also: **Mered ha-Aliya; Tochnit ha-Carmel.**

Tochnit Mezada [תוכנית מצדה, H] "Masada Plan": *Yishuv* defense plan named after the fortress that saw the last stand against Rome during the Jewish rebellion of 70 C.E. The plan envisioned guerrilla operations by the *Yishuv's* undergrounds in case of a Nazi occupation but was not optimistic about their chances of success (hence the name). > see also: **Tochnit ha-Carmel.**

Tochnit Yefet [תוכנית יפת, H] "Plan Yefet": Tentative Hagana proposal for a series of attacks on British military personnel and government leaders in Palestine/*Eretz Israel,* proposed in 1946. Apparently, the plan was submitted in the aftermath of Shabbat ha-Shahor, — the systematic assault by British security forces against the JAE. The plan presumed that the Hagana should retaliate in kind for British attacks on the *Yishuv's* leadership. After a brief debate, the plan was rejected. > see also: **Shabbat ha-Shahor.**

Tochnit Yerushalayim [תוכנית ירושלים, H] "Jerusalem Program": Hebrew name for the Biltmore Resolution named thus for the fact that it was approved by the JAE and the Va'ad ha-Poel ha-Zioni in Jerusalem in the autumn of 1942. The JAE narrowly approved the call for a postwar Jewish state in late October, while the Va'ad ha-Poel

approved it (by an even more narrow majority) on November 10, 1942. By these actions, the program with its call for Jewish sovereignty in an unpartitioned Palestine/*Eretz Israel* became the centerpiece of Zionist diplomatic activity until 1947, when the JAE accepted the U.N. partition plan as an alternative to continuation of the British mandate. > see also: **Biltmore Resolution; Conferences, Zionist, Biltmore Conference.**

Tohar ha-Neshek [טוהר הנשק, H] "Purity of Arms": Hagana term for its self-imposed code of honor, mainly connected to the idea that might does not make right and force was not to be used for the sake of force. The Hagana fighter was to eschew blind hatred, revenge, or other manifestations of inappropriate behavior, a policy that in theory differentiated Hagana members from the so-called dissidents (the Irgun Zvai Leumi and Lohamei Herut Israel) who were accused of believing in counter-terrorism. *Tohar ha-Neshek* was intimately connected to the Zionist policy of *Havlaga* (self-restraint). In both cases the idea was to show that the *Yishuv* was acting at a level above the Arabs, for example by not initiating combat and by engaging in violence after an Arab attack had commenced. In practice, this policy could not always be adhered to and eventually was limited only to the idea that civilians should not be subject to indiscriminate attack. > see also: **Havlaga.**

Tony [PN]: Hagana and JA code name for Lieutenant Colonel Anthony (Tony) Simmonds. Simmonds had been Orde Wingate's executive officer in 1937–1938 when the latter had commanded the Special Night Squads. Like his commander, Simmonds shared a pro-Zionist outlook and was transferred out of Palestine/*Eretz Israel* in 1938. He returned in 1940 as the head of the Special Operations Executive (SOE) training center in Haifa. In that capacity, Simmonds helped cement cooperation between the *Yishuv* and British secret services. In 1941, Simmonds was transferred to Egypt, where he took command of A Force, the SOE's Balkan branch. While there, Simmonds advocated the use of *Yishuv* volunteers that ultimately culminated in the mission of the thirty-two Palestinian paratroopers. > see also: **Special Night Squads; Paratroopers, Palestinian; World War II.**

Tragt ihn mit Stolz, den Gelben Fleck! [G] "Wear It with Pride, the Yellow Badge": Title of an article by Robert Weltsch in the German Zionist newspaper *Jüdische Rundschau* on April 4, 1933. Weltsch called on German Jews not to surrender but to bear the upcoming dark days with pride and dignity.

Transnistria Plan [GN]: Romanian World War II proposal to ransom some 70,000 Jews who had been deported to Transnistria, the section of Romanian-occupied Ukraine that was organized in 1941 as a "reservation" for Jews, by "selling" them to the JA at a price of $5.00 per person. By the time of the offer (September 1942), nearly 100,000 Jews had died in Transnistria in addition to the preexisting Jewish communities that had been decimated by German and Romanian murder squads in 1941. The plan was stillborn because of financial difficulties on the Jewish side, Allied refusal to negotiate a ransom agreement, and Nazi intervention to prevent the scheme's completion.

Trumpeldor(im) [(ים)טרומפלדור, H/slang] "Trumpeldor(s)": Slang Israeli term for any soldier injured in the arm, popular after the War of Independence. The term is obviously a reference to Joseph Trumpeldor, the Russian Jewish war hero and Zionist pioneer who lost his arm while serving in the Russian army during the Russo-Japanese War (1903–1905). Trumpeldor later participated in the creation of Jewish military units in the British army during World War I. After the war, he and a group of comrades established Tel Hai, a settlement in the north designed to protect the upper Galilee from inclusion in French mandated Syria. Trumpeldor died on March 1, 1920, protecting Tel Hai from Arab marauders — an act that assumed almost legendary proportions and explains the background

to the term and its usage. > see also: **Ezba ha-Galil.**

Trusteeship Proposal [HT]: Name for the last-minute initiative undertaken by the U.S. State Department to prevent the partition of *Eretz Israel* and the creation of a Jewish state. On March 19, 1948, Secretary of State George C. Marshall announced that, in light of uncompromising Arab opposition to partition, the U.S. no longer supported partition as the only possible solution to the future of *Eretz Israel*. In place of partition, Marshall proposed a U.N. Trusteeship that would replace the mandate. He hoped that the trusteeship would be temporary, lasting only until an accomodation would be reached between Jews and Arabs. The U.N. would then withdraw and *Eretz Israel* would become an independent, binational state. Marshall's plan, which reflected the values of State Department Arabists who sought to abort a Jewish state at all costs, neglected three vital considerations. First, a temporary trusteeship would need a trustee (none was specified in the proposal, but it was understood that the U.S. would not send troops to the Middle East) that was willing to send troops to impose peace on the warring parties. Second, the proposal did not offer a solution to the pressing problem of Jewish Displaced Persons who had been the cause of the impasse in the first place. Finally, Marshall was too optimistic about the possibility of an Arab-Jewish accommodation. He failed to consider that thirty years of British rule had failed to create an accommodation and that, with the Arabs threatening to "throw the Jews into the sea," relations between the communities had reached a point of no return. The proposal created a diplomatic firestorm. American Jewish leaders felt betrayed, as did President Harry S. Truman, whose support for Jewish statehood was unequivocal. As a result, the State Department was forced to backtrack and partition proceeded as per the U.N. resolution of November 1947.

TTG [HT]: Initials used by *Yishuv* servicemen for secret missions that they were to perform on behalf of the Hagana, the Mossad le-Aliya Bet, or Sherut ha-Yediot during the course of their military service. Apparently, the initials stood for nothing, but all *Yishuv* personnel knew the meaning and sense of the letters. TTG operations included, inter alia, secretly transferring weapons abandoned on battlefields or stolen from magazines in North Africa or Europe to Hagana caches, helping transport Jews fleeing antisemitic violence in Eastern Europe via *Briha*, or helping Jewish displaced persons get to ports where they could board Mossad blockade runners. > see also: **Briha; Aliya Bet; Displaced Persons, Jewish; Yishuv, Yishuv Organizations (Underground Organizations, Hagana)**.

Turkish Solution: Zionist proposal of 1938 to create an alliance between Turkey and Great Britain proposed by WZO president Chaim Weizmann. The proposal was a response to the British reassessment of Middle Eastern policy, especially in light of increasing tension in Central and Eastern Europe. Weizmann's proposal was for the Zionist movement to secretly pay off Turkey's debts, thus lessening German influence in the country. He hoped, thereby, to delay or cancel Britain's increasingly anti-Zionist policy by securing Turkish neutrality in any upcoming European war. The JAE rejected this proposal since it offered no guarantee that Britain would respond positively to the secret Zionist initiative while linking Zionist agencies and the *Yishuv* exclusively to Britain's Imperial interests.

Two/Three: When used by the Af-Al-Pi organization, the number two represented "yes" and the number three represented "no." More particularly, the numbers meant that the possibility for a safe landing of *Ma'apilim* did (two) or did not exist (three). In the latter case, the term also meant "return to port of origin." > see also: **Aliya Bet; Yishuv, Organizations (Underground Organizations, Af-Al-Pi)**.

Uganda Plan [GN]: East African territorial offer made to the WZO by the British in 1903. Despite the name, the territory actually comprised parts of today's Kenya and Tanzania, not Uganda. In light of the recent pogroms, WZO president Theodor Herzl accepted the British proposal eagerly but tentatively. Although it is not clear exactly what Herzl thought about the project at the time, he later claimed that he saw the offer as a temporary expedient until *Eretz Israel* became available for unrestricted Jewish immigration. Herzl, therefore, brought the plan to the attention of the Sixth World Zionist Congress. He was stunned, however, when instead of approving the plan unanimously, most Eastern European Zionists (the very people Herzl hoped to aid) — calling themselves "Zionists for Zion" — vociferously opposed the scheme. As it was, the congress by a slim majority approved sending a commission to East Africa to study the feasibility of Jewish settlement there. By the time the commission returned from its investigations, the offer had been withdrawn. In the interim, proponents of the scheme withdrew from the WZO, organizing themselves into the Jewish Territorialist Organization. > see also: **East African Plan; El Arish Scheme; Nachtasyl; Territorialism; Zionei Zion.**

Ugoda [P] "Agreement": Official term for the secret coalition agreement signed between the Polish government and the Kolo, the Jewish parliamentary caucus, and ratified in July 1925. The agreement stipulated that the Polish Zionists would henceforth support the fragile coalition government led by Stanislaw Grabski (hithertofore they had been in the opposition) and would tone down their part in the international campaign to force Poland to live up to its commitments under the national minorities treaties. In return, the Poles promised to help build the Jewish national home (something the Polish government did anyway), promised to quiet rhetoric emanating from semigovernmental circles that incited antisemitism, and promised to alleviate the economic burden that was rapidly destroying Polish Jewry's ecoonomic life. The agreement never came into full operation. The Polish Zionist federation split over the agreement, while the Pilsudski coup of 1926 terminated parliamentary democracy in Poland for all intents and purposes. > see also: **Gegenwartsarbeit; League of Nations; Kahal.**

Ulpan [אולפן, H]: Untranslatable term for an intensive Hebrew language immersion program, usually one for new immigrants. Ulpanim were the key means for mass acculturation of the many new *olim* in Israel's first years of existence. Intensive Hebrew instruction was viewed as the only way to forge a single nation out of the widely scattered remnants of world Jewry arriving in Israel between 1948 and 1952.

United Nations: International agency created in 1945 with fifty-one members as the successor to

TABLE U.1: The November 29, 1947 UNGA Vote on Palestine/*Eretz Israel*

Country	Vote[1]	Country	Vote
Afghanistan	No	Iraq	No
Argentina	Abstained	Lebanon	No
Australia	Yes	Liberia	Yes
Belgium	Yes	Luxembourg	Yes
Belorussia	Yes	Mexico	Abstained
Bolivia	Yes	Netherlands	Yes
Brazil	Yes	New Zealand	Yes
Canada	Yes	Niceragua	Yes
Chile	Abstained	Norway	Yes
China	Abstained	Pakistan	No
Colombia	Abstained	Panama	Yes
Costa Rica	Yes	Paraguay	Yes
Cuba	No	Peru	Yes
Czechoslovakia	Yes	Philippines	Yes
Denmark	Yes	Poland	Yes
Dominican Republic	Yes	Saudi Arabia	No
Ecuador	Yes	Sweden	Yes
Egypt	No	Syria	No
El Salvador	Abstained	Turkey	No
Ethiopia	Abstained	Ukraine	Yes
France	Yes	Union of South Africa	Yes
Greece	No	USSR	Yes
Guatemala	Yes	United States of America	Yes
Haiti	Yes	United Kingdom	Abstained
Honduras	Abstained	Uruguay	Yes
Iceland	Yes	Venezuela	Yes
India	No	Yemen	No
Iran	No	Yugoslavia	No

Source: *New York Times*, November 30, 1947.

the League of Nations. Like its predecessor, the United Nations (U.N.) has operated for more than fifty years on the premise of collective security as a means of preventing or muting wars. The U.N. has been involved with the Palestine/*Eretz Israel* issue almost from its inception, although initially its involvement was indirect. The U.N. became directly involved in the issue on April 2, 1947 when the British government turned the matter over to the General Assembly after the Morrison-Grady plan collapsed. On May 15, the General Assembly ordered the creation of a special committee, the United Nations Special Committee for Palestine (UNSCOP) and charged UNSCOP with proposing a long-term solution to the impasse. UNSCOP's eleven members reported back to the General Assembly in the summer of 1947 but did not approve a unanimous report. Instead, a majority report proposing partition and a

[1] Yes = voted for partition, No = voted against partition (irrespective of opinion on the minority report).

minority report proposing a federal but binational Palestine/*Eretz Israel* were delivered. On November 29, 1947, the General Assembly voted to accept the majority report and propsed partition, by a vote of thirty-three yes, thirteen no, and ten abstentions. Consequently, the State of Israel came into being on May 14, 1948.

Arab refusal to accept the Jewish state, however, led to violence and to Israel's War of Independence. Israel was admitted to the U.N. on May 11, 1949. > see also: **League of Nations; Committees of Investigation, United Nations Special Committee on Palestine; Partition Plans; Binationalsim; Israel, State of; War of Independence**.

Vatican and Zionism, The [HT]: Relations between the Vatican and the Zionist movement (after 1948, with the State of Israel) were never cordial, although they could be defined as proper. The Vatican's policy on modern Jewish nationalism was enunciated by Pope Pius X in a meeting with WZO president Theodor Herzl on January 15, 1904. The pope told his interlocutor that while the Church could not prevent the Jews from attempting to return to their ancestral homeland, it would neither sanction nor assist the creation of a Jewish national home in any way. Vatican policy was based on three interrelated doctrinal considerations: (1) The Church, having supplanted the Jewish people, was the "new" Israel and there could be no other Israel beside the Catholic Church; (2) the Jews, having rejected Jesus' messianic mission, had rejected salvation and had been cursed by God to eternal wandering across the face of the earth; and (3) the only way Jews could achieve salvation (personal and national) would be through embracing Christianity, an act that would bring about the Messiah's "second coming." Given the development of Church doctrine in the twentieth century, no change in this attitude was possible and none was forthcoming until the early 1990s.

In addition to Church doctrine, the Vatican's approach to Zionism (and during the 1930s and 1940s to the possibility of Jewish statehood) was based on practical considerations that varied from period to period. Primary among these concerns was the desire to protect Christian holy sites in the Middle East and fears over the effect that Zionist activity would have on the fate of non-Muslim Arabs. Whereas these two considerations abetted the Vatican's overall negative attitude towards Zionism, the need to appear to consider humanitarian needs, for example, in relation to finding a safe haven for Jewish refugees, tended to soften the Vatican's approach. Still, it must be emphasized that the Vatican's opinion was generally negative and was expressed in opposition to the Balfour Declaration, the League of Nations mandate, the Peel partition proposal, and the U.N. partition plan.

Notwithstanding official Church policy many clerics (especially in the United States) supported the Zionist cause, some in very active ways. They did so out of a desire to right a historic wrong, out of ideological commitment to Jewish statehood, out of sympathy with the plight of Holocaust survivors, or out of a combination of the three. Among numerous individual Catholic clergymen who helped the Zionist cause, a few stand out: Fathers Edward H. Flannery, John M. Oesterreicher, and George Grauel of the United States and Fathers Joseph L. Lyne and Roland de Vaux, of Engalnd and France respectively.

Although the Vatican was ideologically disposed to an staunchly anti-Zionist position, it has responded to the emergence of the State of Israel from both theological and pragmatic political perspectives. The Vatican eschewed diplomatic relations with the State of Israel until 1993. Whether or not this represents an actual change in the Catholic Church's attitudes towards Jews and Judaism remains to be seen. > see also: **Gentile Zionism**.

Velt-Folk [װעלט-פֿאָלק, Y] "World People": Diaspora nationalist term used to justify opposition to Zionism. By implying that Jews were at home anywhere in the world, the perceived need for a specific Jewish territory was considerably reduced, thus rendering Zionist ideology meaningless. Conversely, the concept could also be used as a strong condemnation of Zionism's "narrowness," which sought to return the Jews to ghettolike isolation from the rest of the world. > see also: **Doism**

Villa [Slang]: Post-1945 Hagana, Palmah, and Mossad le-Aliya Bet code term for any radio transmitting station operated by the Gido'nim. Principal transmitting stations were located in La Spezia (Italy), France (Marseilles and Paris), Romania (Constantsa), Bulgaria (Varna), and North Africa (Tangier and Algiers). > see also: **Zevulun**; **Yishuv, Yishuv Organizations (Underground Organizations, Gido'nim)**.

Vojo Novo [Esperanto] "New Way": Popular name for the group of Jewish settlers, members of the Gdud ha-Avoda and Poale Zion Smol, who left *Eretz Israel* in 1928 to settle in a Jewish communal settlement in the Soviet Union. The group's emigration had been a propaganda coup for the Soviets, who thus proved that Zionism and socialism were incompatible. The group settled on land made available by the government and developed in coordination with the American Agro-Joint philanthropy. Vojo Novo remained in existence for some seven years. In 1935 Stalin banned the last of the Zionist (or quasi-Zionist) parties and the settlement was broken up. Thereafter, the settlement was converted into a nonsectarian

kolkhoz and the members were scattered throughout the country. > see also: **Communism and Zionism**.

Volk/Volkism [G] "Nation/Nationalism": > see also: **Nationalism**; **Zionut**.

Volksbewegung [G] "People's Movement": Pre-World War I German Zionist term for the Zionist Organization, emphasizing the popular appeal of Jewish nationalism in the highly volkish atmosphere of Wilhelmian Germany. > see also: **Nationalism**; **Zionut**.

Volunteers/Volunteerism: > see also: **Halutz**; **Mitnadve Hutz la-Aretz**; **World War II**.

Vulcan: Name of a U.S. Navy auxiliary used to transport food and other vitally needed supplies to the *Yishuv* during World War I. At the time, the *Yishuv* was under a virtual siege: Martial law was introduced in November 1914 and the Turks expelled all male Jews of military age who were not Ottoman citizens shortly thereafter. Food prices doubled between 1914 and 1916 and fears of mass starvation led U.S. Consul General in Jerusalem Otis Glaysbrook to propose to Ambassador Henry Morgenthua that a ship be sent with supplies. Since the United States was neutral, sending such a ship would not be interpreted as a hostile act and could be used as a means to exert influence to mute the Turkish persecution of the *Yishuv*. The German government, then trying to influence American Jewry toward an anti-British path, encouraged Glaysbrook and Morgenthau, convincing the Porte to permit the ship's sailing. The U.S.S. *Vulcan* sailed from Philadelphia on March 14, 1915, arriving in Jaffa on April 21. The supplies delivered by the *Vulcan* prevented mass starvation but their impact was temporary. Additionally, the *Vulcan* represented the first direct intervention in Jewish affairs by the Wilson administration and gave a unique opportunity for American Zionists and non-Zionists to cooperate in a matter of humanitarian activity.

Wailing Wall [HT]: Commonly used, but in-correct English term for the Western Wall of Herod's Temple, Jewry's holiest site. The term derived from the misinterpretation by European visitors of Jewish prayer services, held in front of the wall, which were thought to be manifestations of Jewish mourning. > see also: **Kotel ha-Ma'aravi**.

War of Independence [HT]:

1. Scope and Definition

Israel's War of Independence came as the culmination of Jewish efforts to end the British mandate for Palestine/*Eretz Israel*. These efforts culminated in the November 29, 1947, U.N. decision to partition the territory into Jewish and Arab states (with Jerusalem to be held as an enclave under U.N. control). With the British announcing their intention to leave before August 1948, attention shifted from the Jewish struggle against the mandatory administration to the growing civil war between Jews and Arabs. Fighting escalated into all out-war between the new State of Israel and its Arab neighbors within hours of the the declara-tion of independence on May 14, 1948: the new-born state was in-vaded by units from five neighboring Arab armies (Egypt, Trans-Jordan, Syria, Iraq, and Lebanon) obtaining financial and other assistance from the Arab League. > see also: **Ha-Mered**; **United Nations**; **Arabs**.

Bitter fighting marked the entire war, with the Arabs proclaiming their intention to "throw the Jews into the sea." The Jewish forces were not prepared for conventional fighting and did not have the equipment necessary for sustained combat. The Jewish forces did have the advantage of better leadership and commitment to a cause, to which must be added the effect of desperation on morale: whereas the Arab conventional armies knew that defeat in the field would not effect their countries, the Israelis sufficiently believed Arab statements to fear for their lives. Atrocities were commited by both sides, although by and large, Jewish forces attempted to reduce the number of civilian casualties, a desire that did not animate their Arab opponents. Arab irregulars, and regular troops as well, often massacred the en-tire populations of Jewish settlements that they captured — for instance, the massacre of Jewish prisoners of war by the Trans-Jordanian Arab Legion at Gush Etzion — but only one alleged case of massacre has ever been attributed to Jews: the Deir Yassin incident (April 9, 1948). It is indicative of the combatants' different goals that while the Israeli provisional government strongly condemned this incident, no Arab power (then or since) has ever condemned atrocities committed by their forces. For their part, the Israelis were satisfied to instill fear in the local Arabs and increase their proclivity to flee.

In the main, historians have divided the War of Independence into four phases. In the first phase, from December 1947 to May 1948, the war was essentially a civil war and the Israelis

Memorial Service for the Defenders of Jerusalem, Held On
the Thirtieth Anniversary of the Lifting of the Siege.
Authors' Collection

held the initiative (except for isolated Jewish settlements that were attacked by Arab irregulars) in what was essentially a battle to control the roadways between the *Yishuv*'s major cities. The primary events of this phase of the fighting were the Hagana's efforts to open secure road communication with Jerusalem and the capture of Haifa and Jaffa, which provided the *Yishuv* with secure flanks for further operations.

In the second phase, from May 15 to June 10, 1948, the neighboring Arab states invaded and nearly destroyed the new State of Israel. Israeli forces were put on the defensive but were able to hold most of the territory they controlled. Communications were effectively cut between Jerusalem and the rest of Israel; Jordanian forces failed to capture the city, however, and a prolonged siege ensued. Egyptian and Syrian threats to Tel Aviv and the Galilee respectively were checked. This phase of the war ended in a virtual stalemate with both sides accepting a U.N.-brokered ceasefire (the first truce).

The third phase lasted from July 9 to 18, 1948, the so-called Ten Days, a period when the truce broke down. During this phase of the fighting the Israelis once again gained the initiative. Zva ha-Hagana le-Israel (Zahal) forces succeeded in reopening a tenuous supply line to Jerusalem and were able to contain and throw back the Syrians and Lebanese, thereby securing the Galilee. This phase of the fighting again ended in a U.N.-brokered ceasefire (the second truce) which lasted until October 10.

The final phase of the war, from October 10, 1948 to March 10, 1949, saw Israeli forces pitted against the Egyptian army for dominance of the Negev. This phase ended after a series of lightning-fast mobile operations by Zahal secured the Negev and completed the removal of all enemy forces from Israeli territory. Thereafter, a series of armistice agreements were signed between the Arabs and Israel, although these did not result in true peace. > see also: **Armistice Agreements**.

2. Major Zahal Operations

An-Far, abbreviated code name for an operation undertaken on July 8–9, 1948, whose full name was Anti-Farouk and whose goal was to seize the juncture of the north-south and east-west roads through the Negev that passed between Majdal and Faluja. Central to the plan was capturing the Iraq-Suweydin police fort, which had withstood seven previous assaults and dominated virtually all communications between central Israel and the Negev. The operation, which took place during the ten days between the first and second truces, witnessed bitter fighting, especially in and around the police fort. While the fort remained in Egyptian hands, Israeli forces seized the vital crossroads and the high ground around both.

Asaf, follow-up operation to Operation Yoav and dedicated to clearing the last pockets of Egyptian resistance in the western Negev. Carried out in successive stages between December 5 and 15, 1948, the first step was preventing an expected Egyptian counterattack toward Beer-Sheva. Using mobile tactics and strking swiftly with armored forces, Zahal successfully forced all Egyptian forces back into the Gaza Strip.

Avak, airborne supply operation between Israeli-held territory and isolated Jewish settlements in the Negev, begun on August 23, 1948. Utilizing the capabilities of recently acquired C-46 Commando transports, the Israeli Air Force flew all missions at night, with the aircraft returning to bases near Tel Aviv before dawn. To facilitate unloading, a temporary airstrip was built near *Kibbutz* Shoval. Flights terminated when Zahal was able to open a land corridor to the Negev settlements, by which time 2,200 tons of supplies and 2,000 fresh troops had been flown into the Negev.

Ayin, another code name for Operation Horeb. > see also: **War of Independence, Major Zahal Operations (Horeb)**.

Balak, two operations to transport weapons and equipment from Europe to Israel by Air. Operation Balak I (March 31, 1948) saw the delivery of considerable ground equipment transported via Zatec,

Czechoslovakia. Operation Balak II (May 12, 1948) saw the delivery of the first twelve fighter aircraft, Avia S-199s (modified Messerschmidt Bf-109s), from Zatec. The first aircraft were dismantled and shipped in recently purchased cargo aircraft. On arrival, the aircraft were reassembled, with the first fighter becoming available on May 29.

Barak, operation by the Hagana's Givati Brigade undertaken between May 4 and 15, 1948, to clear the southern approaches to Tel Aviv and the Sharon plain. Secondarily, the operation was designed to secure communications between Rehovot and Be'er Tuvia. The operation was mostly successful but was halted when regular Arab armies invaded on May 15. The mission was later resumed under the name Operation Kitor.

Ben-Ami, Zahal operation to regain contact with isolated settlelments in the western Galilee undertaken between May 14 and 20, 1948. The operation was undertaken in three stages, first, an assault from Haifa toward Acre to isolate and disrupt Arab forces still in the latter city. Second, a series of supply columns fought their way northward and eastward to the major settlements in the region. Finally, an attack from Naharayim cleared all remaining pockets of resistance to the Lebanese border.

Ben-Nun, two operations to capture the police fort and village of Latrun and thereby open a secure road to Jerusalem. Operation Ben-Nun I was undertaken on May 25, 1948, with a task force composed of Zahal's Alexandroni and the Seventh Brigades. Despite early progress, the attackers could not breach the police fort's defenses and the assault soon bogged down. A flanking attack on Hill 315 (north of Latrun) also failed and an Arab Legion counterattack soon occupied Radar Hill, thereby forcing the Israelis back to their starting positions. Operation Ben-Nun II began five days later (May 30, 1948) and saw one task force attempt to outflank the police fort by a southerly route and succeed in clearing a number of villages before faltering at Deir Ayoub. Simultaneously, a mechanized force led by a flamethrower mounted on a half-track attacked the police fort. Although the mechanized force actually breached the fort's defenses, poor coordination between armored and infantry units left the former unsupported. On May 31, the Arab Legion counterattacked again, and forced the Israelis to withdraw.

Brosh, operation to clear the Syrians from the Hula Valley, undertaken between July 8 and 18, 1948. Three task forces operated during the ten days between the first and second truces, attacking from Yesud Ma'ale, Ayelet ha-Shahar, and Mahanayim. By the end of the operation, all Syrian forces in Israeli territory north of the Sea of Galilee had been driven back across the international border.

Dani, Zahal mobile operation designed to secure Tel Aviv from the east, to open the approaches to Jerusalem, and to draw the Trans-Jordanian Arab Legion away from the besieged city by engaging them in a set-piece battle in the Lod-Ramle-Yahudiya area. Undertaken between July 9 and 19, 1948, Operation Dani was mostly successful. Arab regular and irregular forces were cleared from the entire region, thereby providing the Israelis with a secure base for future operations. Additionally, the Mobile Commando Battalion commanded by Moshe Dayan captured the international airport in Lod, providing another entry point for supplies. However, the Arab Legion decided not to reinforce this area, and thus the siege of Jerusalem was not lifted.

Dekel, operation to clear out the western Galilee, mainly the Nazareth region, undertaken between July 9 and 18, 1948. The operation's main objective was to separate Fawzi al-Kaukaji's Arab Liberation Army from the Syrians, thereby isolating both Arab armies. Crowned with complete success, Operation Dekel ended with the decisive defeat of Kaukaji's forces and their withdrawal from the central Galilee.

El ha-Har, ancillary operation to Operation Yoav, designed to clear Egyptian forces from the Hebron mountains and thus open the road corridor south of Jerusalem. Undertaken between October 18 and 22, 1948, the operation saw units of the Harel Brigade attacking from the areas occupied during Operation Dani. Considerable territory was taken during the operation, which also protected the southern flank of the newly built "Burma Road." However, Israeli units were not able to take the vital cities of Hebron and Bethlehem, nor were they able to retake Gush Etzion. > see also: **Derech Burma; Gush Etzion; War of Independence, Major Zahal Operations (Yoav)**.

Eser Makot, another code name for Operation Yoav. > see also: **War of Independence, Major Zahal Operations (Yoav)**.

Gayis, abbreviated operational code name derived from the names of two of the Brigades involved (Givati and Yiftah) and the nickname of the Negev Brigade's commander (Sergei). Undertaken between July 26 and 31, 1948, the operation was supposed to resupply settlements in the northern Negev while occupying Faluja before the Egyptians could. The resupply operation was partly accomplished, but the Egyptians were able to occupy Faluja and fortify the area, thus denying it to the Israelis.

Hametz, Hagana operation undertaken on April 27 and 28 to clear Arab irregular forces from positions east and southeast of Tel Aviv. Units of the Hagana's Givati, Alexandroni, and Kiryati Brigades were involved in the operation, the Hagana's largest concentration of troops to date. An uncoordinated operation by the Irgun Zvai Leumi cleared Jaffa, leading to the city's surrender. The operation was crowned with almost complete success, and the approaches to Tel Aviv were securely held by the Israelis on the eve of independence.

Harel, Hagana operation to push a convoy through the blocked main highway to Jerusalem, undertaken between April 15 and 21, 1948. The plan called for the Palmah's Harel Brigade to strike from the newly captured fortress of Kastel and suppress all Arab defenses on the road to Tel Aviv. Simultaneously, a force from Tel Aviv was to meet Harel's units near Latrun and, if possible, occupy the police fort. The attack, however, bogged down at Bet-Jis and was called off due to the worsening situation in Jerusalem proper.

Hasida, experimental aerial operation to land a single planeload of supplies at Kibbutz Be'er Tuvia in the northern Negev on the evening of April 1, 1948. The operation was a complete success, but the amount of equipment and troops that could be landed by a single aircraft was deemed insufficient; thereafter, supply efforts were to be undertaken on a much larger scale.

Hiram, sixty-hour Zahal operation undertaken between October 29 and 31, 1948, and designed to eliminate Fawzi al-Kaukaji's Arab Liberation Army as a fighting force. Following up on previous operations, the plan called for simultaneous attacks northward fron Nahariya, northwest from Tiberias, and west from Rosh Pina. Hugely successful, the operation culminated in the liberation of the entire area south of the Lebanese border, ending when the so-called Finger of the Galilee was occupied on October 31.

Hissul, one-day operation originally designed to tighten the Israeli grip on the Faluja pocket. Planned for December 28, 1948, the operation was seen as part of Operation Horeb. The operation was successful beyond the Israelis' imagination and culminated in the surrender of all Egyptian forces in the pocket on December 29 — after their last supply base (at El Auja) fell to Israeli units. > see also: **War of Independence, Major Zahal Operations (Horeb)**.

Horeb, final Zahal operation to defeat the Egyptians undertaken between December 22, 1948, and January 7, 1949. Designed from the outset as a mobile operation, the plan sought to bring the war into Egyptian territory as a means to force the Arabs into peace talks. The operation was a complete success. All remaining Egyptian forces in Israeli territory were bottled up in the Faluja Pocket while Israeli forces entered the Sinai and threatened El Arish, Rafa, and Abu Agheilla. Operations ceased after a clash between Israeli and British air force units; the Israeli government feared that this presaged full-scale British intervention. Armistice talks did indeed begin shortly thereafter.

Kedem, operation to break into the Old City of Jerusalem on the eve of the second truce, attempted on July 17, 1948. The plan

called for an attack by units of the Irgun Zvai Leumi and Lohame Herut Israel (which were still independent, but which coordinated their operations with Zahal's high command) from inside the walls simultaneous with an attack by the Etzioni Brigade from outside the walls. The former was to break through the so-called New Gate in the northern part of the Jewish Quarter while the latter was to break through the Zion Gate in the southern portion. Unknown to the planners, however, the Trans-Jordanian Arab Legion had also planned an operation in the same general area to capture the Jewish Quarter before the truce took effect. Operation Kedem failed to break through to the Jewish Quarter, which surrendered to the Arab Legion shortly therefater.

Kilshon, operation to seize British-controlled sectors in Jerusalem's New City upon the termination of the mandate, undertaken on May 14–15, 1948. Basically, the operation was a race between Jewish and Arab forces to seize fortified buildings or blocs of buildings that had been used by the British military during the last years of the mandate. As British troops withdrew, the Israelis successfully seized the area known derisively as Bevingrad, in addition to the Russian Compound, the Notre Dame Monastery, and the King David Hotel. The Arabs took the railroad station, the printing press, and other government buildings in Abu Tor, and the Allenby and El Alamein barracks. Further operations forced Arab irregular units out of the railroad station and Abu Tor, while the units in the barracks later withdrew.

Lot, operation to liberate the eastern Negev, deriving from the successes of Operation Yoav, carried out between November 23 and 25, 1948. The operational task force was ordered to push from Beer-Sheva to Sdom, liberating settlements that had been abandoned in May and occupying the region around the Dead Sea. Little direct resistance was encountered during the operation, which was a complete success.

Maccabee, Hagana operation to open a supply corridor to Jerusalem, undertaken between May 8 and 18, 1948. Although previous operations had failed to completely open the road, they had weakened the Arab irregular forces that were preventing a free flow of supplies.

It was felt that another attack might succeed. During the first phase of operations, Hagana forces attacked Deir-Ayoub and Bet-Mahsir. Simultaneously, a force set out from Hulda to outflank Latrun from the north, by occupying Abu-Susa, El-Kubab, and Deir Amwas. These moves were partly successful, but the major Arab garrisons remained intact. Poor coordination and a lack of heavy weapons meant that the Israelis were forced into costly frontal assaults that were defeated. The main effort of the operation was halted on May 15, 1948, although attempts to get a convoy through persisted until May 18. At that point, the siege of Jerusalem started.

Malkia, three operations undertaken between May 20 and 29, 1948, launched to isolate the Lebanese front from Syrian forces, to block Syrian efforts to reinforce Lebanese forces besieging *Kibbutzim* Misgav Am and Yiftah, and to open a supply corridor to Rosh Pina. After heavy fighting, on both sides of the Lebanese-Israeli border, the operation was halted with only partial success.

Matatea, operation to clear Arab irregular forces from the area betwen the Hule Valley and the Sea of Galilee, undertaken on May 4, 1948, in coordination with Operation Yiftah. Mostly successful, the operation ended with Israeli forces holding a line parallel to the international border. > see also: **War of Independence, Major Zahal Operations (Yiftah).**

Mavet la-Polesh, operation undertaken on July 17 and 18, 1948, to seize the initiative from Egyptian forces and open a road to the Negev. Undertaken by the Givati Brigade, the operation was not well coordinated and many of the objectives were not attained. Israeli forces, however, acted aggressively and were able to wrest the initiative from the Egyptians.

Nahshon, major Hagana operation to breach the road to Jerusalem, undertaken between April 3 and 15, 1948. The plan called for occupying a corridor two to six miles wide (3.2–9.6 KM) around the road in order to permit convoys to pass undisturbed by Arab irregular forces. Initial successes were lost due to British intervention. The evacuating forces did not want the growing civil war between Jews and Arabs to threaten their forces and were afraid of Arab attacks in case of Jewish successes. As a result, most of the corridor was not cleared of Arab forces and the road to Jerusalem was not secured. Even so, some of Operation Nahshon's objectives were met, notably, the capture of the fortress of Kastel after a two-day pitched battle. Moreover, Arab losses at Kastel were more grievous than the mere loss of territory would indicate, as the Arab irregulars' most capable field commander, Abdel Kader al-Husseini (the Mufti's nephew) was killed during the fighting.

Pleshet, abortive operation to clear Egytian forces from the Ashdod area. The operation was undertaken in fits and starts between June 1 and 3, 1948. Initial attacks failed on the first day of operations, leading to new plans for an attack on the next day. False reports of a ceasefire led to the second day's attack being postponed and then canceled altogether. On June 3, Zahal forces undertook an all-out attack, coordinating the ground elements with as intensive an air bombardment as was possible at the time. Nonetheless, Zahal forces were inferior in both armor and artillery and were unable to achieve their main objectives. Further attacks in this region were called off.

Shmona, operation for the capture of the police fort at Iraq-Suweydin, preparatory to Operation Horev. The Israelis had a great deal of respect for the fort and its defenders. It had withstood eight previous attacks (including one in which two Israeli tanks managed to breach the main gate but had to be abandoned for lack of supporting infantry). As a result, the plan called for an unprecedented amount of firepower to be poured into the defenses prior to the attack on November 9, 1948. After two hours of artillery bombardment, the defenses crumbled, and the Israelis occupied the fort without any casualties.

Shoter, Zahal operation to clear the so-called Small Triangle of settlements in the Carmel Hills (north of Haifa), undertaken between July 24 and 26, 1948. Although undertaken during the second truce, this operation did not run afoul of the United Nations. The territory in question had been assigned to the State of Israel in the partition resolution and was completely surrounded by Israeli-held land. In effect, this was a police action (hence the name) to clear the last pockets of resistance in the region. Despite bitter fighting, the operation ended successfully with the last traces of Arab resistance in the Haifa region broken.

Tinok, evacuation of all noncombatants from settlements in the Negev, carried out as a Hagana operation between May 18 and 21, 1948. In all, six settlements in the northern Negev were evacuated: Gal-On, Gat, Gezer, Kfar Menahem, Negba, and Nizanim. Although one of the convoys was fired upon by Egyptian forces, the evacuation proceded without any casualties.

Uvda, last operation of Israel's War of Independence, planned to secure complete Israeli control of the eastern and southern Negev. Undertaken between March 5 and 10, 1949, the plan was to send a mobile task force from Beer-Sheva through the Arava in order to occupy the port of Elat. At the same time, Israeli forces fortified positions in the Hebron Hills, south of the territory held by the Trans-Jordanians. Operation Uvda met no resistance and was a complete success.

Velveta, aerial operation to transfer Supermarine Spitfire fighters purchased in Czechoslovakia to Israel, undertaken in two phases on September 24 and 27, 1948. Although the aircraft had been available since August, their transfer had been held up by technical difficulties, mainly connected with the Spitfire's short range. Without wing-mounted fuel tanks the flight would be impossible. Six suitably equipped Spitfires took off from Zatec air force base in Czechoslovakia as part of Operation Velveta I (September 24) and arrived at a refueling station in Yugoslavia, where one of the aircraft was damaged and abandoned. The other five arrived in Israel on September 25. On September 27, five more Spitfires left Zatec as Operation Velveta II. These aircraft were to fly directly to Israel, but only

three fighters completed the flight. The other two experienced fuel problems and were forced to land on the Island of Rhodes. The aircraft were impounded by the Greek government, although the pilots were freed in mid-October.

Yakum Purkan, aerial operation begun in December 1947 by the Hagana Sherut Avir (which became the Israel Air Force in May 1948) to use cargo aircraft purchased in the United States to transport combat aircraft and other military supplies to the nascent State of Israel during the War of Independence. The operation had four legs: (1) the flight from America to the Czech airbase at Zatec, (2) from Zatec to makeshift bases in France or Italy, (3) from the makeshift European bases to Israel, mainly (but not exclusively) to the Sde Dov airport north of Tel Aviv, (4) the return trip to Zatec, from which operations continued until all the supplies were transferred. By this means, the Israel Air Force obtained its first combat aircraft. > see also: **Rechesh**.

Yehiam, operation by partly mobile Hagana force to open a path from Nahariya to _Kibbutz_ Yehiam undertaken on the night of March 27–28, 1948. The unit was ambushed before it arrived and was virtually wiped out: twenty-eight troops were killed and almost all the others were wounded after a ten-hour battle. This failure led to a reassessment of Hagana tactics on the eve of the Declaration of Independence.

Yekev, subsidiary operation undertaken on October 20, 1948, as part of Operation Yoav and designed to protect the main force's flanks, mainly by occupying the Arab village of Bet-Juala. Although most of Operation Yekev's initial goals were met, stiff resistance and the precarious positions held by Zahal forces led to their withdrawal on October 21 to a point just south of the Lod-Jerusalem railroad tracks.

Yevusi, three-phase attack in and around Jerusalem undertaken by the Hagana between April 22 and May 1, 1948. Phase one of the operation saw a series of Hagana attacks on Arab villages that threatened northern Jerusalem, mainly Nebi Semwal, Bet Iksa, and Shuafat. This part of the operation was mostly successful with Bet Iksa and Shuafat captured. Hagana forces in the latter village were forced to withdraw when the assault on Nebi Semwal failed. Phase two of the operation was the attempt to clear the Sheikh Jarrach neighbor-hood in Jerusalem. Although mostly successful, Israeli forces were forced to redeploy out of the neighborhood (thereby allowing Arab irregulars to return to their prior positions) by the British, who saw Sheikh Jarrach as part of the route for their final withdrawal from Jerusalem on termination of the mandate. Phase three was the Israeli occupation of the Katamon neighborhood in western Jerusalem. This part of the operation was the only completely successful part of Operation Yevusi. Henceforth western Jerusalem was solidly in Israeli hands.

Yiftah, operation undertaken between May 6 and 10, 1948, to secure Safed and the western upper Galilee. Despite severe manpower shortages, the Zahal units outmaneuvered their opponents and obtained almost complete success.

Yoav, also known as Operation *Eser Makot* (Ten Plagues), the operation to break through the Egyptian front lines, liberate isolated Jewish settlements, and gain control of the northern Negev undertaken between October 15 and 22, 1948. Operation Yoav was planned during the second truce, but no immediate plan was made to carry out the operation. An Egyptian attack on an unarmed food convoy that traveled under U.N. protection provided Zahal with the impetus to open the attack. A series of swift mobile blows struck the Egyptian forces. Although not all were successful, one decisively changed the war in the Negev: one column occupied Beer-Sheva, thus giving Zahal almost complete control of the Negev's hub. This attack also cut off Egyptian forces in the Hebron Hills and south of Jerusalem, forcing them to retreat. Additionally, communications were restored with the northern Negev settlements. Finally, Operation Yoav gave Zahal the military initiative for the remainder of the war.

Yoram, final operation to occupy Latrun and the vital police force dominating the road to Jerusalem, undertaken on June 9, 1948. The task force for the operation comprised units of the Yiftah and Harel Brigades plus newly conscripted members of Giyus Hutz la-Aretz (Holocaust survivors who had recently arrived in Israel). Despite the bravery of the Israeli troops they were unable to progress against the Arab Legion's fortifications and the attack failed. Ground gained in the first hours was lost again during a Trans-Jordanian counterattack that signaled the end of Operation Yoram. With this failure, Zahal's commanders approved the plan to build the so-called Burma Road. > see also: **Giyus Hutz la-Aretz; Derech Burma**.

Zippora, code name for the occupation of the airport in Lod as part of Operation Dani. > see also: **War of Independence, Major Zahal Operations (Dani)**.

Weapons Trials [HT]: Term used for the trials conducted by the British mandatory administration during and after World War II to uproot Jewish underground movements. Trials were conducted before military courts and, in general, did not adhere to normal evidentiary procedures. The purpose of the trials was not merely to find and convict guilty parties but to embarrass the Hagana and the JA. The British always publicized the trials out of proportion to the actual "crimes" and invariably stiff sentences were meted out: not one defendent was ever acquitted by a court martial. Numerous searches and siezures of weapons were also used by the British as a means to weaken Jewish undergrounds, although neither method was wholly successful in uprooting them. To the contrary, this policy may have further eroded Jewish support (especially in the United States) for a compromise after World War II.

We Fight Therefore We Are [HT]: Term used by Menahem Begin when he was commander of the Irgun Zvai Leumi to reflect his concept of Zionism: the acquiring of Jewish military capability (through anti-British revolt) was seen as an existential necessity without which the Jewish people could not survive. Begin's usage was an obvious allusion to Rene Descartes' famous dictum "cogito ergo sum." Begin's phraseology seems to suggest a response to Jewish powerlessness as represented by the

Holocaust combined with a nearly messianic view of the power of individual will to overcome adversity. Although considered radical at the time, Begin's ideas were similar to those of other Zionist thinkers in both the nineteenth and twentieth centuries. > see also: **Lohameiel/Shomreiel**; **Zionut Lohemet**.

Weizmannism [PN]: Another term used to designate the gradualist policies advocated by the WZO prior to 1933. The term reflected the close association of the policy of gradualist development with the person of WZO president Chaim Weizmann. > see also: **Gradualism**; **Shem ha-Meforash**.

Weizmannism without Weizmann [HT]: Term used in 1931 to explain the actions of the Seventeenth World Zionist Congress. Although Chaim Weizmann was removed from the presidency of the WZO, mainly by a coalition of opponents who saw the events in *Eretz Israel* and in London between 1929 and 1931 as series of unmitigated disasters for Zionism, the newly elected executive remained committed to a policy of gradual development. > see also: **Weizmannism**.

Wenn Ihr Wolt, Ist Est Kein Märchen [G] "If You Will It, It Is Not a Legend": Epigram of Theodor Herzl's utopian Zionist novel, *Altneuland*, and, to a degree, an apt summary of Herzl's work. The novel was a fantasy set in a future Jewish state; Herzl sought to create a Jewish state, knowing that its achievement would be anything but utopian. Still, Herzl's critics and his ideological opponents argued that the dream of Jewish sovereignty was utopian — a dream that was impossible to accomplish. Herzl defied his opponents, contending that with sufficient will and discipline, the Jewish people could accomplish as much as (if not more than) any other nation in Europe. > see also: **Altneuland**.

Western Wall > see also: **Kotel ha-Ma'aravi**.

White Paper(s) [HT]:

1. Scope and Definition
   Term for an official statement of British government policy on major issues, so named because the cover was usually white. Generally, a white paper offered proposals for legislation or other government action to solve a major crisis. Additionally, white papers established directions for governmental policy (e.g., on defense expenditure). Most of the time, white papers were issued after a thorough investigation by a government appointed committee that proposed the legislation or government action. White papers — or the legislation derived from a white paper — usually required Parliamentary approval, although the nature of the British system was (and is) such that any majority government could ususally obtain approval for a white paper.
   During the mandate era the British issued three white papers that affected policy toward the Jewish national home. All were issued in response to Arab violence and investigations by royal commissions. All three white papers placed some limits on *aliya*, with the last two limiting it so severely as to be considered dangerous to continued Zionist development. Zionist protests about the white paper's terms led to the cancellation of the Passfield White Paper, while the MacDonald White Paper of 1939 represented a complete abandonment of Britain's promises to the Jewish people and can thus be seen as the beginning of the end of British rule in *Eretz Israel*. > see also: **Committees of Investigation**.

2. Major White Papers
   Churchill White Paper (1922), issued as a result of the Arab riots of 1921 and the Cairo Conference. The Churchill White Paper modified the mandatory regime in two ways: it split Trans-Jordan from *Eretz Israel* and instituted the concept of "economic absorptive capacity" as a limitation on *aliya*. Under Churchill's concept, *aliya* was to be encouraged, with the *Yishuv*'s ability to assimilate new immigrants the only criterion limiting Jewish immigration. > see also: **Conferences, International, Cairo**.

Passfield White Paper (1930), issued as a result of the recommendations of the Shaw, Hope-Simpson, and French commissions that were sent to investigate conditions in *Eretz Israel* in the aftermath of Arab rioting in 1929. The Passfield White Paper ended *aliya* and was thus the first major effort by a British government to repudiate commitments made in the Balfour Declaration. The Passfield White Paper was cancelled in 1931 by Ramsay MacDonald's government after a storm of protests by Zionists throughout the world and after considerable lobbying by Jews and their supporters in Parliament. However, as a result of the white paper the monetary requirements for capitalist *aliya* were doubled, thus making that form of *aliya* more difficult. > see also: **MacDonald Letter; Committees of Investigation; Certificates**.

MacDonald White Paper (1939), issued after the Arab Revolt and the failure of the St. James Palace Conference, the MacDonald White Paper (also known as the White Paper of 1939) set severe limitations on the growth of the *Yishuv*. First, the White Paper limited *aliya* to a total of 15,000 individuals per year (including 5,000 refugees) for a period of five years, after which no new Jewish immigration would be permitted without Arab consent. Second, the White Paper of 1939 strictly limited Jewish land purchase in more than two-thirds of the landmass of *Eretz Israel*. Third, the White Paper of 1939 promised that Palestine/*Eretz Israel* would be converted into an Arab state after ten years had elapsed. Given its terms, the *Yishuv* viewed the White Paper of 1939 as a direct threat to Jewish rights and, with regard to Jewish refugees fleeing Nazi-occupied Europe, to Jewish survival. These harsh terms and Britain's uncompromising execution of them led the Jewish Agency to turn to an independent policy, as represented by *Aliya Bet* and the Biltmore Resolution of May 11, 1942. > see also: **Conferences, International, St. James Palace; Conferences, Zionist, Biltmore; Aliya Bet; Biltmore Resolution; World War II; Sefer ha-Ma'al; The Son**.

William Tell [PN]: Zahal code name for Colonel Abdallah al-Tel, commander of the Trans-Jordanian Arab Legion forces in the Jerusalem front during Israel's War of Independence and Trans-Jordan's representative at the armistice talks in Rhodes. The term is based on the similarity of Tel's family name to the legendary Swiss national hero. This identification was so obvious that in some documents Tel was identified only as William, with the family name being assumed. > see also: **Arabs, Major Arab Organizations (Arab Legion); War of Independence; Armistice Agreements**.

Wilson Declaration(s) [PN]: Two statements of support for Zionism issued by President Woodrow Wilson during and shortly after World War I. The earlier of the two declarations was issued in October 1918 and was merely a restatement of the Balfour Declaration. This was an important step since Wilson's action placed his considerable prestige squarely in support of Zionism. Wilson's second declaration, of March 2, 1919, was even more explicit, clearly putting the president on record as supporting the creation of a Jewish commonwealth. > see also: **Balfour Declaration; Lodge-Fish Resolution; Commonwealth, Jewish**.

Woodhead Commission [PN]: Popular name for the Palestine Partition Commission, established by the British government in 1938 to propose new borders for a postpartition Palestine's Jewish and Arab states and named after its chairman, Sir John Woodhead. > see also: **Committees of Investigation, Palestine Partition Commission; Repeal Commission**.

World War I [HT]:

1. Scope and Defintion

The commencement of all-out war in Europe in August 1914 initially appeared to have no direct relevance to the WZO and no bearing per se on the future of Jewry or Zionism. In most cases, Jews responded to the war's outbreak not as Jews but as citizens of the countries in which they lived. Within days of the declarations of war thousands of Jews were mobilized for military service in the countries of their citizenship and many were killed in the ensuing four years of combat: 12,000 German Jews alone gave their life in the "war to end all wars."

While the European powers traded declarations of war, the WZO declared itself to be strictly neutral, seeing the issues being fought over as irrelevant to the fulfillment of Zionism. Strict neutrality did not last long, however. In November 1914, when the Turks declared war on the Entente (Great Britain, France, and Russia), WZO neutrality became both more pressing and more difficult. Fears for the future of the *Yishuv*, especially after the Ottomans deported all military-aged foreign Jewish males, counterbalanced the possibility that some sort of diplomatic gain might be obtained. Nevertheless, the WZO's initial reaction was to emphasize the continuing policy of neutrality, especially after rumors (that turned out to be true) regarding the massacre of Armenian civilians by Turkish military authorities began to circulate. The possibility that the *Yishuv*, now bereft of its male population and thus vulnerable to attack, might also be decimated by Turkish troops was a sufficient deterrent to any WZO diplomatic initiative throughout 1915.

The pressure for diplomatic action, nonetheless, proved very strong, mainly because the British were actively pursuing military operations to defend the Suez Canal and secure their imperial interests in the Middle East. Thus, although the WZO remained officially neutral, many individual Zionists sought to obtain a statement of support from the Entente for a Jewish national home. Similar attempts were also made in Germany and Austria-Hungary. European diplomats steeped in antisemitic (or quasi-antisemitic) ideas about a Jewish world government viewed Zionist neutrality not a reflection of Jewish powerlessness but as a manifestation of a Jewish desire to obtaim maximum benefit before supporting one side or the other. Negotiations were undertaken in London, Paris, and Berlin. By the spring of 1915 both France and Germany had virtually given up the idea of

making a statement. Negotiations with the British continued, however, and culminated in the Balfour Declaration of November 1917. > see also: **Hindenburg Erklärung; Balfour Declaration**.

The Balfour Declaration must be viewed in its diplomatic context. In addition to making promises to the Jewish people, the British government also signed agreements with the Arabs and with the French regarding the postwar distribution of formerly Ottoman territory. More significantly, the three promises thus made appeared to contradict one another. The Arabs were promised an Arab kingdom in the Fertile Crescent and the Jews were promised a national home in *Eretz Israel*, all while the imperialist powers planned to divide Ottoman territory among themselves. To say the least, this dualistic policy led to considerable conflict in the postwar era and certainly exacerbated the trend toward Arab-Jewish disagreement. > see also: **McMahon-Hussein Correspondence; Sykes-Picot Agreement**.

Despite the initial appearances, therefore, World War I proved to be decisively important to the Zionist movement and the *Yishuv*. The war provided the first opportunity for the emergence of a Jewish national home, which could (and did) develop into a Jewish state, while also witnessing the first modern harnessing of Jewish manpower in a military organization for a Jewish national goal. The creation of the Jewish Legion represents an important watershed in Jewish and Zionist history.

2. Jewish Military Units

Jewish Legion (JL), military unit established in 1917 as part of the British army in the Middle East. JL's nucleus was a cadre of personnel from the Zion Mule Corps that had survived the battle of Gallipoli. When the Mule Corps was disbanded, the men remained in uniform and were transferred initially to London to join the regular army. The original plan was to disperse the Mule Corps veterans into badly depleted combat units on the Western Front. However, continued advocacy of the creation of an armed Jewish force by Colonel John Henry Paterson (who had

Soldiers of the Jewish Legion Encamp on the Tel Aviv Beach, 1918.
Courtesy of the Central Zionist Archives, Jerusalem

commanded the Mule Corps) and by Zionist figures such as Joseph Trumpeldor and Ze'ev Jabotinsky led the British government to decide on August 23, 1917, to create a Jewish regiment, known as the Jewish Legion. Intially, JL was organized into a single battalion, the 38th Royal Fusiliers; two further battalions (the 39th and 40th) were added in 1918. In all, 2,000 men served in JL, including volunteers from the *Yishuv*, the United States, Canada, and Argentina. Another group of 2,300–2,900 men had volunteered for service but was not mobilized until after the war ended. The men chose as their regimental symbol a menora surmounting the word Kadima (forward) and this remained in use for JL's entire existence. Although JL remained in *Eretz Israel* at the end of hostilities, anti-Zionist officers in the Occupied Enemy Territories Administration (OETA, the military government that existed in the

formerly Ottoman territories until 1920) sought to have JL dismissed. This was completed in 1921, when the last battalion was disbanded and replaced by regular British units. JL served an important role in the *Yishuv*'s development, however, since much of the leadership strata that later governed the State of Israel, including Israel's first prime minister, David Ben-Gurion, served in JL. > see also: **Occupied Enemy Territory Administration**.

Jewish Militia, abortive 1915 proposal to raise an auxiliary force within the *Yishuv*. This force would have operated in conjunction with Turkish military and paramilitary forces in *Eretz Israel* and Trans-Jordan but would not have served on the front lines. Instead, the militia would have assumed internal security roles thereby freeing Turkish troops for conventional military operations against the British. Given Ottoman fears about potential Jewish disloyalty, however, the proposal was never seriously considered by the Grand Porte.

Indeed, within months the idea was rendered moot when the Turks decided to deport all military-age Jewish males who were not Ottoman citizens. > see also: **Hamaeya; Hitotmanut**.

NILI (ניל״י), Jewish spy ring founded in 1915 by members of the Aaronson family and acting on behalf of the British. The name was actually an abbreviation of the biblical phrase, "Nezah Israel lo Yishaker" (the eternal of Israel will not lie, I Samuel 15:29). Throughout its existence, the British referred to Nili as the "A Organization," a designation derived from the Aaronsons' first initial. Nili was founded to help the British conquer *Eretz Israel* by providing them with information on Turkish military forces that threatened the Suez Canal. Tha Aaronsons believed that the Turks might apply the same measures to the Jewish population of the *Yishuv* that they had to the Armenians; as a result, any aid that could be given to the British and that would hasten removal of Ottoman control was beneficial to the *Yishuv* and to the WZO. Regular contact with the British high command in Cairo was established after a number of false starts in February 1917. Turkish authorities in Damascus became aware of Nili's activities in October of that year. One month later, the Turks arrested a number of Nili operatives, including Sarah Aaronson, and severely curtailed Nili's activities, although such activities were never altogether halted. The information provided by Nili proved to be critical to General Edmund Allenby's successful campaign in Palestine/*Eretz Israel* in 1918. More significantly, Nili brought a great deal of respect for the Zionist endeavor among many British political and military leaders.

Zion Mule Corps (ZMC), auxiliary military unit established within the British army in 1915. ZMC was composed of military-age Jews who had been expelled from *Eretz Israel* by the Turks, reinforced by volunteers from the United States and Great Britain. ZMC's father, Russian Jewish war hero Joseph Trumpeldor, hoped that the British would create a Jewish legion to conquer *Eretz Israel*. This the British initially would not do. Instead, they accepted the idea of a Jewish military force to be organized as part of their supply train in the Middle East. ZMC was organized in Egypt and placed under Colonel John Henry Paterson's command; Trumpeldor was commissioned as an officer in ZMC as well. ZMC was permitted to choose its own emblem, with the men selecting a Magen David in a round background. In April 1915, ZMC participated in the ill-fated Gallipoli operation and suffered heavy casualties. ZMC was withdrawn in late 1915 and was transferred to London with the intention of using survivors to fill depleted infantry units on the Western Front. In 1916 ZMC was therefore disbanded. However, as an alternative to the planned use of ZMC veterans as fillers, the British government agreed to use it as the basis for a Jewish Legion that was established in 1917.

World War II [HT]:

1. Scope and Definition

The commencement of war in September 1939 represented a new level of crisis for the *Yishuv*, still reeling from the complicated diplomatic maneuvering surrounding the White Paper of 1939. To be sure, conditions differed greatly from the period before World War I. Foremost among Zionist considerations was the fact that the *Yishuv's* neutrality could not seriously be sustained when due consideration was given to the nature of the enemy — the Nazi regime that had begun its assault on German Jewry almost as soon as it had seized power in January 1933. Counterbalancing the need to fight the Germans, however, was the fact that the British had issued the White Paper of 1939 that represented a repudiation of their commitments to the Jews. Indeed, the *Yishuv* had been preparing for the initial stages of a revolt against the white paper when the war began. Diplomatic realities of the time meant that the *Yishuv*, even if somewhat reluctantly, had no alternative but to support the Allies. All Zionists, except fringe movements like Lohame Herut Israel (Lehi), thus supported (in deeds, if not in words) the analysis of the Zionist situation provided by

JAE Chairman David Ben-Gurion: "We shall fight the White Paper as if there were no Hitler, and we shall fight Hitler as if there were no White Paper." > see also: **Yishuv; White Paper(s), White Paper of 1939**.

In practice, it was impossible to do both. JA plans for a revolt by *aliya* were shelved, as were plans for military action prepared by both the Hagana and the Irgun Zvai Leumi (IZL). The IZL declared a truce with the British until Allied victory was assured, and consequently split into rival factions, those opposing a truce and advocating continued hostilities with the British crystallizing as Lehi. Although the war forced a suspension of full-scale rebellion, it did not prevent the Zionists from working in four spheres to prepare for a potential postwar confrontation with the British, the Arabs, or both. First, *Aliya Bet* activities continued. Since this was the only means by which the *Yishuv* could possibly rescue some of the threatened Jews of Europe, a complete halt to *Aliya Bet* was never considered. Second, the *Yishuv* strove to obtain the creation of an armed Jewish force that would represent world Jewry in the anti-Nazi struggle. The creation of a "Jewish Army" under Allied auspices was considered to be very important since the symbolic act of creating a Jewish armed force would provide a morale boost for Jews living in countries occupied by the Nazis and would place the *Yishuv* on a par with other minor Allied powers, thereby providing diplomatic benefits after the war. Third, the WZO continued its diplomatic offensive to obtain the white paper's revocation. This activity culminated in the 1942 Biltmore Resolution which was virtually a Zionist declaration of independence. Fourth, undertakings were continued to bolster the *Yishuv* both militarily and economically. In the former case, all of the *Yishuv*'s undergrounds made concerted efforts to obtain weapons and ammunition in preparation for postwar contingencies. Economically, the creation of a Middle East Supply Center bolstered the *Yishuv*'s productive power and continued the growth that had been experienced (albeit in fits and starts) during the 1930s. > see also: **Aliya Bet; Mered ha-Aliya; Biltmore Resolution**.

Harrowing news after 1942 regarding the murder of European Jewry by the Nazis merely reinforced these trends, providing an especially convincing argument to those who sought an abandonment of traditional Zionist gradualism and supported the assumption of statehood as soon as possible after the war. That said, it should be noted that rescue efforts were hampered by the lack of Allied priority, the lack of resources, and the serious possibility that the *Yishuv* itself might be attacked by the Axis or by Arabs aligned with the Axis. It seemed plausible that the British might not be able to defend the *Yishuv*, for example during the short-lived crisis in 1940 after the Italian invasion of Egypt. There were two particular periods when an invasion seemed imminent.

Colonel Frederick W. Kisch, Former JAE Member in his Royal Army Uniform During the North African Campaign. Kisch Was Killed in Action During a Mine Clearing Operation in Tunisia in Early 1943.

Courtesy of the Central Zionist Archives, Jerusalem

In 1941, when Field Marshal Erwin Rommel's Deutsches Afrika Korps launched first offensive simultaneous with upheavals that occurred in French-controlled Syria and independent Iraq, many in the *Yishuv* began to prepare for the worst. The same held true in 1942, prior to Rommel's forces being halted at El Alamein. Indeed, at the time, the Germans were a mere seventy miles (112 KM) from the Suez Canal and could, hypothetically, have reached Palestine/*Eretz Israel* in a matter of days. > see also: **Tochnit AZ**; **Tochnit ha-Carmel**.

By the time Allied victory was ensured, most of European Jewry had been cruelly slaughtered: the biological reserve of Zionism in Eastern Europe had literally gone up in smoke. Still, the Zionists persisted in their efforts to obtain a change in British policy toward Jewry and toward Zionism. In 1944, a Jewish Brigade Group was fielded as part of the British army operating on the Italian front. Further efforts to cancel the White Paper of 1939 having failed, however, the last year of the war represented a period of waiting for the proper time to settle accounts. In this regard, a statement attributed to an IZL commander may fairly be cited to summarize the *Yishuv*'s temperament: "For us, V-E Day is D-Day." After the war, the efforts to salvage a saving remnant of European Jewry and to rescind the White Paper of 1939 led to the establishment of the State of Israel on May 14, 1948. > see also: **Shoa**; **Displaced Persons, Jewish**; **She'erit ha-Pleta**; **Israel, State of**.

2. Jewish Military Units

Armée Juive (AJ), "Jewish Army," resistance organization founded in Toulouse, January 1942, by Abraham Polonski and Lucien Lublin. At its height the AJ numbered some 2,000 fighters. In 1943 AJ commenced operations, primarily concerned with getting members across the Pyrenees into Spain. From there they continued to *Eretz Israel*, with the ultimate goal of joining the Jewish Brigade Group of the British army. In 1944 AJ concentrated on creating Maquis that participated in the operations of the Forces Françaises de l'Intérieur in southern France. In addition to its combat operations, AJ undertook a highly successful rescue operation, using funds provided by the American Jewish Joint Distribution Committee to save Jewish children threatened with deportation. After World War II, AJ acted as the Hagana's French arm, being heavily engaged in arms purchases and in training personnel that eventually formed part of the Giyus Hutz la-Aretz. > see also: **Yishuv, Yishuv Organizations (Underground Organizations, Hagana)**; **Giyus Hutz la-Aretz**; **Eitan/Eitanim**.

Hagana Gazim ve-Avir (הגנה גזים ואוויר, Haga (הג"א)), "Defense Against Gas and Air (Attack)," voluntary air defense unit established in the *Yishuv* upon the outbreak of World War II in 1939. Officially Haga operated under the Va'ad Leumi's authority; in actuality, Haga was entirely staffed by Hagana members. Haga undertook air and civil defense activities until 1945. During the Israeli War of Independence, the initials Haga were used for Zahal's regional defense forces.

Hativa Yehudit Lohemet (חטיבה יהודית לוחמת, HIL (חי"ל)), "(The) Jewish Brigade Group," military force created within the British army but composed of Palestinian and stateless Jews. HIL was established in September 1944 and played an active role in the Italian campaign. In 1945, HIL was transferred to occupation duties in Germany and Austria. The location of HIL units enabled them an ability to aid Holocaust survivors, and one of their more important tasks was in facilitating the *Briha*. HIL was disbanded by the British in 1946 but provided the core of the soon-to-be-established Israeli army. > see also: **Aliya Bet**; **Briha**; **Displaced Persons, Jewish**; **She'erit ha-Pleta**; **Yishuv**.

Kaf-Gimel Yordei ha-Sira (כ"ג יורדי הסירה), "The Twenty-Three Who Went by Boat," popular name for the unit of Palmah and Hagana operatives, most with special operations experience, who were selected for a special mission into Vichy-controlled Lebanon on behalf of British intelligence in May 1941. The twenty-three were tasked with sabotage and intelligence gathering missions, being landed by small boat on May 18. Contact was lost with the ship almost immediately, and no precise data has ever come to light on their fate. In August 1946, the Mossad le-Aliya Bet named a blockade runner in their honor. > see also: **Yishuv, Yishuv Organizations (Underground Organizations); Aliya Bet.**

Mahlaka ha-Balkanit (מחלקה הבלקנית), "The Balkan Section," Palmah special unit recruited among *olim* of Balkan descent, mainly from Bulgaria, Yugoslavia, and Greece. The unit was raised in 1940 when it appeared that the British might need to use a commando force in the Balkans to draw off German forces threatening to invade England. The Balkan Section was also recommended for use in the Danube basin in attacks designed to strike at Germany's petroleum supplies. However, political considerations prevented the mounting of even a single operation. As a result, the Balkan Section was demobilized after its personnel completed their training. Most later volunteered for service in the special *Yishuv* paratroop unit sent to Europe in 1944. > see also: **Paratroopers, Palestinian.**

Mahlaka Meyuhedet (מחלקה מיוחדת, MM), "The Special Section," special force unit established in the Hagana in 1940 for joint operations with the British Special Operations Executive (SOE). MM members were trained in commando and intelligence-gathering operations of mutual interest to both the *Yishuv* and the British. In the event, despite close relations between the Hagana and the SOE, few of the missions were carried out. As a result, MM was transferred to exclusive Hagana control and formed the cadre for the Palmah. > see also: **Yishuv, Yishuv Organizations (Underground Organizations, Plugot Mahatz).**

Misrad le-Hakira (משרד לחקירה), "The Research Office," (RO) joint intelligence-gathering unit established in June 1940 by the JA and the British Foreign Ministry. RO was apparently independent of the Middle East Intelligence Center (MEIC) established by the Royal Army. RO's main source of information were *Ma'apilim* who managed to reach *Eretz Israel* and Jewish refugees who

managed to flee Nazi-occupied Europe for neutral Turkey. The latter generally came into contact with the RO through the JA's office in Istanbul. Ironically, *Ma'apilim* became a major source of political and economic intelligence for the same people trying desperately to keep Jewish refugees out of *Eretz Israel*. Albeit, RO collected a considerable amount of information until it ceased to function in 1945.

Nokmim (נוקמים), "Avengers," self-adopted name for the unit of Palmah and Jewish Brigade Group personnel active in Europe after World War II to avenge the Holocaust. The Nokmim operated on the highest authority of the *Yishuv* and WZO and were not answerable to the regular Hagana command structure. Composed mainly of veterans of the Palmah German Company, the unit was assigned the task of hunting down and discreetly eliminating Nazi war criminals. Assisted by men of the Hativat ha-Seridim, the Nokmim were intially successful in a number of operations. Their activities were curtailed in late 1945 and 1946, however, as the JAE began to place higher priority on the *Briha* and *Aliya Bet*. > see also: **Shoa; Yishuv, Yishuv Organizations (Underground Movements); World War II, Jewish Military Units (Pluga ha-Germanit).**

Notarei ha-Hof (נוטרי החוף), "Coastal Police," > see also: **Notar(im).**

Notarei ha-Rakevet (נוטרי הרכבת), "Railroad Police," > see also: **Notar(im).**

Notarei Mahanot ha-Ma'azar (נוטרי מחנות המעצר), "Internment Camp Police," > see also: **Notar(im).**

Pluga ha-Germanit (פלוגה הגרמנית), "The German Company," special unit of the Palmah composed entirely of personnel originating in the Grossreich (i.e., the Nazi German state established after the occupation of Austria and Czechoslovakia) raised in May 1942. The company was composed of approximately sixty men, all of whom were fluent in German. In addition to standard Palmah training, the "Germanists" (as they were commonly known) also received intensive instruction in commando operations and in German weaponry and tactics. Their intended tasks included operations behind enemy lines in German uniform (hence the extra training), in addition to reconnaissance, interrogation of prisoners of war, and miscellaneous tasks. Originally raised when fears were high about a possible German invasion, some parts of the company were deployed to North Africa, where they formed the Special Interrogation Group. Given the nature of their operations, the Germanists could not consider any possibility of quarter if captured: they would most likely be killed as spies. Yet, not a single member of the unit requested a transfer in its existence. The company was mauled n North African operations, with the remnants being incorporated into the Jewish Brigade Group in 1944. The Germanists also formed the basis for the postwar Avengers. > see also: **World War II, Jewish Military Units (Nokmim)**.

Special Interrogation Group (SIG), title of the Palmah Germanist company when under British command in North Africa. The idea behind SIG initially was to infiltrate Jews of Central European origin into prisoner of war camps as a means of obtaining intelligence (hence the title). Initially raised in 1942, the SIG was commanded by Royal Army Captain Herbert Buck, who was fluent in German. Early on, the SIG also obtained a special operational mission, specifically in operating for reconnaissance and commando missions behind German lines in North Africa. SIG men generally operated in small groups and were thoroughly trained in German military techniques. A typical operation would see the SIG men escorting a larger party of Allied troops into German lines on the pretext of being a German unit transporting Allied prisoners to the rear. SIG was virtually destroyed in the Tobruk raid of September 14, 1942, and was not reconstituted. Most SIG veterans were later incorporated into the Jewish Brigade group. > see also: **World War II, Jewish Military Units (Pluga ha-Germanit)**.

Va'adat Hadira (עדת חדירה), "Penetration Committee," arm of the Hagana tasked with liaison with British (and, to a lesser degree, American) intelligence organizations. The unit oversaw penetration of Jewish agents into Axis-occupied or Axis-allied territories, including Syria, Lebanon, and the Balkans. As such, the committee oversaw the missions of the twenty-three naval commandos lost during a mission in Lebanon and the thirty-two paratroopers sent into the Balkans in 1944. The committee was composed of four members: Eliahu Golomb, ex-officio chairman of the committee because of his status as operational chief of the Hagana, Reuven Zisling (Shiloah), who represented the Jewish Agency, and Enzo Sereni and Zvi Yehieli, who jointly represented the Mossad le-Aliya Bet. After Sereni's disastrous mission to Italy, the committee was reorganized with only three members. The committee ceased all functions in 1945. > see also: **Paratroopers, Palestinian**.

TABLE W.1: *Yishuv* Volunteers in the British Forces by Arm of Service

Branch	Number	Branch	Number
Infantry	5,258	Artillery	802
Transportation	4,407	Port Operations	544
Engineering	4,361	Medical	397
Pioneer Corps	3,222	Ordnance	250
Women's Army Corps	3,155	Home Guard	200
Royal Air Force	2,652	Signals Corps	193
Royal Navy	1,146	Other/Unknown	290
Quartermasters Corps	1,043	Non-Palestinian Jews	1,100[1]

Source: Archion Toldot ha-Hagana (ATH)

[1] This figure includes 700 Egyptian Jews serving in various British units and 400 European and Middle Eastern Jews serving in the Jewish Brigade Group.

World Zionist Congress(es) (WZC) [HT]:

1. Scope and Definition

When Theodor Herzl began to organize the WZO, an essential part of his plan was the convening of a Zionist congress. This First World Zionist Congress, which met in Basel, Switzerland, in August 1897, laid the groundwork for all further Zionist activities while also establishing the pattern for all future congresses: a public forum designed to garner publicity for the movement while also permitting Zionists to air all issues relating to the creation of a Jewish national home. The WZC thus filled two roles in the WZO. First, the congresses served as a political tool to find the common ground between different and sometimes competing Zionist visions. Second, the congresses also fulfilled an important educational role in displaying (in carefully choreographed medium) Zionism for the general public, both Jewish and non-Jewish. In general, the early congresses were less political and were not convened to establish Zionist policies. Instead, they were convened to approve the initiatives that Herzl had undertaken and to provide maximim publicity for a movement that desperately wanted to be taken seriously. After Herzl, the WZC became a tool for legitimizing different interpretations of Zionism, debating goals, and finding a consensus that represented WZO policy.

The WZC's role as policymaker and final arbiter of what was —— and was not —— to be considered legitimate Zionist policy came to the fore at the Sixth Zionist Congress (the so-called Uganda Congress), wherein the territorialist faction of the WZO was rejected by a clear majority. The WZC's centrality was reinforced at the Twentieth Zionist Congress, which dealt with the Peel partition plan. Again, distinct groups vied for position in order to establish both the short- and long-term goals of the entire WZO. While these two particular congresses dealt with controversial issues at major turning points in the history of Zionism, even less spectacular congresses could (and did) witness acrimonious debates during the open congress sessions. If only for educational purposes, the debate during open sessions became one of the keystones of the WZC. This was considered the best means to air ideas, "score" ideological points, and inform the Zionist public about WZO goals, hopes, and desires. For all these reasons (and many more) the WZC becam a decisive Zionist institution and the published stenographic protocols of each congress became among the most important WZO publications.

For all of the WZC's importance to the WZO, it is important to note that the delegates were not elected by an open franchise. The vote was open only to those WZO supporters who "bought the *Shekel*," that is who paid dues to a Zionist party or to the Zionist federation in the country of their residence. Mandates were distributed to each country based on the percent of all *shekel*s sold and were subdivided among the appropriate parties based on a key, again based on the proportion of membership dues paid (*shekel*s "bought") for the party as compared to the entire country. This form of franchise was very controversial and became even more so during the 1920s and 1930s when the revisionist Zionists repeatedly accused other parties of voter fraud. Despite intense criticism of the process by almost every Zionist bocy that studied the matter, no changes were made in the way the WZC's delegates were elected until after the establishment of the State of Israel. > see also: **Shekel**.

In addition to its role in setting general Zionist policies, the WZC functioned in three other important spheres: First, the WZC set the WZO's annual budget. Second, the WZC appointed members to both the Zionist General Council (also known as the Greater Actions Committee) and to the WZO executive (also known as the Inner Actions Committee), thus establishing the direction that the WZO would take between congresses. Finally, the WZC elected (or generally re-elected) the WZO president. Although this was usually a pro forma matter, the presidency held great symbolic importance; electing the president was thus the congresses' most significant single public action. > see also: **World Zionist Organizations; Organizations, Zionist.**

2. World Zionist Congresses, 1897–1946

First, 1897, Basel, established the World Zionist Organization and laid the foundations for the Zionist movement.

Second, 1898, Basel, called for the intensification of Zionist work in Palestine/*Eretz Israel* and the diaspora. Created the Jewish Colonial Trust (later known as the Anglo-Palestine Bank).

Third, 1899, Basel, first clash between Political Zionism (represented by Herzl) and Practical Zionism (represented by Ahad ha-Am). Additionally, clashes over culture animated the congress. > see also: **Zionut**

Fourth, 1900, London, persecution of Jews in Romania and Russia led to renewed emphasis on accomplishing Zionist goals.

Fifth, 1901, Basel, creation of organized opposition to Herzl and establishment of the Keren Kayemet le-Israel (Jewish National Fund). > see also: **Democratic Fraction**.

Sixth, 1903, Basel, responded to Kishinev pogrom and to the Uganda scheme, overwhelmingly rejecting the latter proposal. This was Herzl's last Congress. > see also: **Uganda Scheme; Zionei Zion**.

Seventh, 1905, Basel, elected Max Nordau as temporary WZO president. Renewed call for creation of a Jewish national home in *Eretz Israel*.

Eighth, 1907, The Hague, founded the Palestine Office under Arthur Ruppin to oversee land purchase. Witnessed call by Chaim Weizmann to create a "Synthetic Zionism," a combination of ideas of both Political and Practical Zionism, in order to promote Jewish unity. > see also: **Zionut**.

Ninth, 1909, Hamburg, social and economic issues dominated, as did opposition to new WZO president David Wolffsohn. First appearance of labor Zionists at the Congress.

Tenth, 1911, Basel, first systematic raising of the Arab issue at a Zionist forum. Final approval of the Synthetic Zionist position advocated by Weizmann.

Eleventh, 1913, Vienna, called for the establishment of a Hebrew University in Jerusalem. Debated practical issues, mainly relating to new settlements.

Twelfth, 1921, Carlsbad, first congress held after World War I. The Balfour Declaration and British mandate were the major issues. Chaim Weizmann elected WZO President. Founded Keren ha-Yesod in order to finance settlement building. Agreed to move WZO headquarters to London.

Thirteenth, 1923, Carlsbad, debated issues related to the mandate and to the creation of a Jewish Agency for Palestine (but took no action on the latter). Renewed call for creation of a Hebrew University.

Fourteenth, 1925, Vienna, private versus public capital in settlement building was the major issue, newly prominent labor parties called for concentration on the latter.

Fifteenth, 1927, Basel, unemployment in the *Yishuv* and slowing of *aliya* were major issues of discussion.

Sixteenth, 1929, Zurich, created the "enlarged" Jewish Agency for Palestine, a partnership of Zionist and non-Zionist representatives. Other discussions focused on the continuing economic crisis in the *Yishuv* and the new flare-up of Arab violence.

Seventeenth, 1931, Basel, debated the implications of the Passfield White Paper and the failure of Zionist diplomacy during the previous two years. Chaim Weizmann was removed as president of the WZO, and was replaced by Nahum Sokolow, but the WZO's gradualist orientation did not substantially change. The congress overwhelmingly rejected Ze'ev Jabotinsky's call for a resolution on the "Zionist Endziel." > see also: **Weizmannism without Weizmann; Endziel**.

Eighteenth, 1933, Prague, debated, often with bitter recriminations, the issue of minimalism versus maximalism, in the backdrop of efforts to rescue German Jewry and avert an all-out civil war between Mapai and the revisionist movement in the *Yishuv*.

Nineteenth, 1935, Lucerne, first congress held after the revisionists seceded from the WZO. Debate centered on the best means to aid increasingly besieged Jewish communities in Eastern Europe and culminated with Chaim Weizmann's reelection as WZO president after the death of Nahum Sokolow. > see also: **Revisionist Schism**.

Twentieth, 1937, Zurich, debated the Peel partition plan and the possibility of Jewish statehood. While rejecting the borders of the proposed state, the congress approved further negotiations with the British government. > see also: **Partition Plans**.

Twenty-First, 1939, Geneva, debated the best means to counter the British White Paper of 1939, mainly regarding the newly enacted restrictions on *aliya*. The congress adjourned early because of increasing tensions between Germany and Poland. > see also: **White Papers**; **World War II**.

Twenty-Second, 1946, Basel, first postwar congress and the last held prior to the State of Israel's establishment. In addition to approving the Biltmore Resolution as the basis for Zionist policy, the congress welcomed the revisionist movement back into the WZO and demanded that the British permit the immediate immigration of 100,000 Holocaust survivors into *Eretz Israel*. > see also: **Biltmore Resolution**.

Delegates to the First World Zionist Congress.
Courtesy of the Central Zionist Archives, Jerusalem

TABLE W.2: Delegates to the First Zionist Congress by Country of Origin

Country	Delegates	Country	Delegates
Algeria	1	Netherlands	2
Austria	51[1]	Ottoman Empire	4[2]
Belgium	1	Romania	11
Bulgaria	6	Russian Empire	63[3]
France	12	Serbia	2
Germany	42	Sweden	1
Great Britain	11	Switzerland	23
Hungary	7	United States	5
Italy	3	Unknown	1

Source: *Die Welt*, #14, September 3, 1897.

Graph W.1: Where the Delegates to the First World Zionist Congress Came From, By Percent.

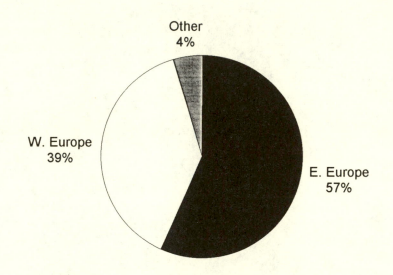

World Zionist Organization (WZO)

1. Scope and definition

Premier Zionist instrument, created by Theodor Herzl in 1897. The WZO was formed at the First Zionist Congress and was tasked by the latter with accomplishing the stated goal of Zionism: "To create for the Jewish people a home in Palestine secured by public law." The WZO thereafter acted as the administrative arm of the Zionist movement, while the congress acted as its legislative arm. Until 1914 the WZO sought to attain a "charter" on *Eretz Israel*, meaning that the main

---

[1] Including Bohemia-Moravia and Galicia.
[2] All of whom were from *Eretz Israel*.
[3] Including delegates from Poland, Finland, and the Baltic republics.

focus of WZO activity was in the diplomatic sphere. However, successes were few and fleeting, at least prior to World War I. Indeed, some Zionists despaired of the possibility (and, in many cases of the desirability) of obtaining *Eretz Israel*. These self-styled Territorialists advocated the establishment of a Jewish national home in any country that would accept mass Jewish immigration. The territorialists became enboldened after the British government offered the possibility of mass Jewish settlement in East Africa but seceded from the WZO when the latter rejected this Uganda plan. This was the first of a number of schisms that weakened the WZO but did not fundamentally damage organization's ability to operate. > see also: **World Zionist Congress**; **Basel Program**; **Territorialism**; **Uganda Plan**.

The WZO was organized both vertically and horizontally. It was organized vertically into a hierarchy from the WZO presidency through the Inner Actions Committee and the Greater Actions Committee to the Congress. It was organized horizontally into national federations that represented Zionist affairs and undertook Zionist activities in most of the world's Jewish communities. Each federation, in turn, was organized in a similar fashion to the main body, having a national leadership as well as local branches. Finally, both the WZO and the national federations were subdivided into political parties and blocs, each one of which represented a particular vision of what the future Jewish national home should be like. In theory all of these parties and federations accepted the discipline that devolved upon member organizations. In reality, discipline was hard to enforce, especially in light of the WZO's voluntary nature. Schisms in federations and parties or blocs were frequent, with a near constant shuffling of coalitions and shifting allegiances making Zionist politics very difficult. Organizationally, the difficulties increased after World War I, when it seemed that Zionism's basic goals were close to attainment, but when arguments over the last steps became overwhelming. This process reached its nadir

with the secession of the revisionist movement in 1935. Just as Zionist unity was vitally needed to concentrate efforts on rescuing European Jewry, the WZO was rent asunder. Even so, the fact that the WZO did not collapse altogether was testimony to the resiliency of the basic organization. > see also: **Organizations, Zionist**; **Revisionist Schism**.

The WZO's basic goals were partly fulfilled during and after World War I: with the Balfour Declaration and the adoption of the League of Nations mandate, the major European powers seemed to have agreed to the charter that Zionists had always sought and pledged to help facilitate the building of a Jewish national home. Thereafter, the WZO was transformed from a body advocating a Jewish national home into a body that was building the national home. This meant, first and foremost, consolidating the *Yishuv* and expanding it through *aliya* to a point where a Jewish majority and Jewish sovereignty might become plausible. Diplomatic activity (which did not cease until the State of Israel was established) was therefore supplemented by financial activity to purchase land, build settlements, and absorb immigrants. Nonetheless, the path from the Balfour Declaration to Israel's independence was not a peaceful one. Arab opposition combined with frequent British reassessments of imperial interests in the Middle East led to complications and many setbacks. Agonizing delays, for example, at the height of the crisis during the Holocaust era (1933–1945) did lead to ultimate success. Three years after the Holocaust and World War II, the State of Israel was established as the ultimate denouement of Zionist and WZO goals. > see also: **Mandate, League of Nations**; **Arabs**; **World War II**; **Israel State of**.

Presidents of the WZO were Theodor Herzl (1897–1904), David Wolffsohn (1904–1911), Otto Warburg (1911–1920), Chaim Weizmann (1921–1931), Nahum Sokolow (1931–1935), Chaim Weizmann (1935–1946).

2. WZO Subsidiary Agencies

Bet Din ha-Kongress (בית דין הקונגרס), "Congressional Court," term for any ad hoc judicial agency created during a World Zionist

Congress to adjudicate disputes between specific parties within the WZO. In theory, the court's main mandate was to ensure that each party received a number of delegates at the Congress equal to the number of *Shekel*s it had sold. Actually, given the fractious nature of Zionist politics, the courts were primarily used to maintain WZO discipline; this was especially true of the courts convened during the 1930s to rein in the revisionist Zionists. A Congressional Court could also operate as a "court of honor" in matters dealing with the relationship between individual WZO members or between members and the WZO executive. > see also: **World Zionist Congress(es)**.

Board of Arbitration, ad hoc committee created by the WZO to arbitrate disputes between and within Zionist bodies, mainly (though by no means exclusively) regarding accusations of voter fraud in connection with delegates to the Zionist Congress. If needed, the board could, in turn, convene a Congressional Court. Although the latter was voluntary, it had the status of the only official disciplinary body of the WZO. The board became increasingly politicized during the 1920s and 1930s, as the *Shekel* and other issues began of polarize the WZO. > see also: **Shekel; World Zionist Organization, WZO Subsidiary Agencies (Bet Din ha-Kongress)**.

Common Inquiry Commission (CIC), temporary committee established by the WZO in 1927 and ordered to recommend future priorities for economic development in the *Yishuv*. CIC comprised four members: Alfred Mond (Lord Melchett), Felix M. Warburg, Oskar Wasserman, and Lee K. Frankel. In turn, they were aided by panels of experts. CIC's recommendation was to continue emphasis on agricultural settlement but advocated building *Moshavot* rather than *Kibbutzim* as a means of engaging private capital in the Zionist building project. Criticized by the labor Zionist wing of the WZO, which saw *Kibbutzim* as the primary means to hegemony within the *Yishuv*, most of CIC's proposals were not implemented. However, the committee's report was an important turning point in interesting non-Zionists in *Yishuv* developments and thus led directly to the expansion of the Jewish Agency in 1929. > see also: **Agricultural Settlement(s); Sochnut Yehudit**.

Cultural Commission, fifteen-member committee created by the Third Zionist Congress to propose future cultural and educational activities for the WZO. In particular, the commission concentrated on the need to inculcate Jews in the Hebrew language; its only substantive proposal was for subsidies to produce textbooks for Jewish students in Zionist-oriented schools. Despite its wide membership, the commission was inadvertently controversial, since many religious Zionist members were concerned that secularists would seek to unfairly orient Zionist cultural activities away from traditional Jewish values. The commission ceased to function after the Fourth Zionist Congress in order to prevent the cultural dispute from disrupting more important Zionist activities. > see also: **Hebrew, Revival of; Cultural Conflict**.

Engere Aktions-Komité (EAK), "Inner Actions Committee," original name for the Zionist executive, known in Hebrew as the Va'ad ha-Poel ha-Mezumzam. > see also: **World Zionist Organization, WZO Subsidary Agencies (Va'ad ha-Poel ha-Mezumzam)**.

Grosses Aktions-Komité (GAK), "Greater Actions Committee," original name for the Zionist General Council. > see also: **World Zionist Organization, WZO Subsidary Agencies (Va'ad ha-Poel ha-Gadol)**.

Hevrat hachsharat ha-Yishuv (חברת הכשרת הישוב), "Company for Purchasing the *Yishuv*," WZO organ established in 1908 but better known as the Palestine Land Development Corporation (PLDC). PLDC was responsible for using resources obtained through the Zionist funds or from private sources to purchase land on which new settlements could be built. After World War I, PLDC shared the latter duties with the Keren ha-Yesod, and was mainly responsible for capital improvements that would make settlements possible: improving water resources, paving roads, and improving communications. PLDC also used funds to relocate Arabs (mainly squatters) living on land purchased from absentee Arab landlords. Most PLDC funds were used to build *Moshavot*, although many capital improvement projects were undertaken in *Eretz Israel*'s cities. Managing directors: Arthur Ruppin (1908–1932), Yehoshua Hankin (1932–1941), Ya'akov Thon (1941–1948).

Keren ha-Geula (קרן הגאולה, KHG), "Redemption Fund," financial arm of the WZO founded in January 1918 to provide the capital needed for expanded work in the *Yishuv*. KHG operated for only three years; in 1920 it was transformed into the Keren ha-Yesod and continued to operate until 1948. KHG was primarily responsible for financing infrastructure improvements that would permit increased settlement building, but it also underwrote social welfare programs in the *Yishuv* and *Hachsharot* in the diaspora. During its brief existence, KHG transferred £891,684 ($4,458,420) to the WZO, more than half of which was collected in the United States.

Keren ha-Yesod (קרן היסוד, KHY), "Settlement Fund," organization established on July 26, 1920, and dedicated to raising the funds neded to build the Jewish national home. In effect the KHY complemented the Keren Kayemet le-Israel (KKL) in acting as the WZO's financial arm. KHY funds were mainly used to purchase the land on which the KKL built settlements, although KHY funds were also used for education, health services, industrial development, and (from the late 1920s onward) creation of a nationwide electrical grid. As a partner to the KKL, the KHY reached into every corner of the Jewish world. Together the two national funds literally financed the creation of the State of Israel.(CASE)

Keren Kayemet Le-Israel (קרן קיימת לישראל, KKL), "Jewish National Fund," premier Zionist fund-raising organization, first proposed in 1897 and finally established at the Fifth Zionist Congress in 1901. KKL was tasked with purchasing land and (until 1918) with making all capital improvements to help settlements succeed. Land purchased by the KKL was held in perpetuity by the organization, acting as the agent of the entire Jewish people. In theory, settlements were leased to the settlers for fifty years, although in practice no settlement (or Jewish settler) was ever forcibly removed by the KKL from its land. KKL's contribution to the Zionist movement cannot be overstated. Without its action to create "facts on the ground," Zionist political and diplomatic efforts had little meaning and less chance of success. KKL used two highly successful means to obtain funds from Jewish masses who could not afford to donate millions: the organization furnished thousands of so-called blue boxes —— charity boxes (pushkes) in which Jewish families contributed small amounts of change toward the purchase of land —— and the sale of unofficial postal stamps (in actuality, printed labels) that had no value as legal tender but represented a public manifestation of the individual's commitment to Zionism. Subjects covered on KKL labels included numerous Jewish and Zionist themes; their subject combined with their beauty made them sought after by collectors and supporters alike. In fact, however, KKL had one fund-raising tool beyond all others. The idea of redemption in *Eretz Israel* atracted many traditionally minded Jews who might not otherwise have supported Zionist political goals. KKL may well have been one of the most successful philanthropic endeavors of the twentieth century. The KKL still exists, now being active in afforestation and environmental education in Israel. Chairmen: Jonah Kreminetzky (1902–1907), Max Bodenheimer (1907–1919), Nehmia de Lieme (1919–1922), Menahem M. Ussishkin (1922–1942), Berl Katznelson, Rabbi Meir Berlin (Bar-Ilan), and Abraham Granott (1942–1944), Abraham Granott (1944–1961).

Reorganization Committee, WZO commission set up in 1920 to report on the means to carry out Zionist activities in the most efficient fashion, in light of new political and financial realities. The committee comprised three members: Julius Simon, Robert Szold, and Nehemia de Lieme. After studying conditions in the *Yishuv*, the committee issued a report that was very critical of the methods by which Zionist activities were carried out. In particular, the committee members criticized the way in which land was purchased without any strategic goal. They noted, for instance, that recent purchases were located in the Jezreel Valley, far from the center of Jewish settlement in *Eretz Israel*. Instead, they recommended concentrating on the area around Jerusalem. Further, the committee scored the way in which the WZO executive carried out its tasks, particularly criticizing the focus on the political rather than practical. This criticism put the committee squarely into the ranks of Justice Louis D. Brandeis's supporters and in explicit opposition to WZO president Chaim Weizmann. The Twelfth Zionist Congress rejected the committee's report, leading Simon and de Lieme to resign their positions on the Zionist executive.

Va'ad ha-Poel ha-Gadol (ועד הפועל הגדול), "Greater Actions Committee," Hebrew name for the WZO governing body initially known as Grosses Aktions-Komité (GAK) but more popularly known as the Zionist General Council (ZGC). ZGC was founded at the First Zionist Congress, along with the rest of the WZO apparatus, and acted as the principal WZO decisionmaking body between Zionist congresses. In particular, the ZGC had two major powers: it nominated the Zionist executive and it set the WZO annual budget. Both of these activities were accomplished at annual meetings held (usually in March) during years in which no congress met. The ZGC varied in size and composition, with each Zionist congress setting both as needed. > see also; **Jahreskonferenz; World Zionist Congress(es)**.

Va'ad ha-Poel ha-Mezumzam (ועד הפועל המצומצם), "Smaller Actions Committee," Hebrew name for the Zionist executive, in use from 1921 to 1948; previously, the executive had been known under the name given at the First Zionist Congress, Engere Aktions-Komité (Inner Actions Committee). The executive was tasked with implementing Zionist policies between each meeting of the Zionist congress. In carrying out its tasks, the executive acted in coordination with the Va'ad ha-Poel ha-Gadol (the Zionist General Council) and the president. The former had decisionmaking powers while the latter was ex-officio chairman of the executive. Prior to 1921 the executive's size and makeup varied. In 1921, the Twelfth Zionist Congress consolidated the executive, establishing a committee of between nine and fifteen members who were organized in two subcommittees: one meeting in Jerusalem (which, in 1929, became the JAE) and the other meeting in London. Since the WZO was then headquartered in London, the latter executive carried the main burden of diplomatic operations while the Jerusalem executive carried out all other tasks.

X [Slang]: Term used by the Irgun Zvai Leumi (IZL) and Lohame Herut Israel (Lehi) for the expropriation of funds, mainly through bank robberies. The first such expropriation was undertaken by IZL gunmen on September 16, 1940. They robbed an Anglo-Palestine Bank branch in north Tel Aviv, getting away with LP4,400 ($22,000). > see also: **Yishuv, Organizations (Underground Movements)**.

X Committee: Code name for the joint committee established in 1945 by representatives of the JA and the underground movements to coordinate operations by the Tenuat ha-Meri ha-Ivri. In theory, no attack could be carried out without the X Committee's explicit approval. The committee disbanded after Shabbat ha-Shahor. > see also: **Ha-Mered; Yishuv, Organizations (Underground Organizations, Tenuat ha-Meri ha-Ivri); Shabbat ha-Shahor**.

Yad Vashem [יד ושם, H], "Holocaust Martyrs' and Heroes' Remembrance Authority": Israel's national institution commemorating the Holocaust, established in 1953 in Jerusalem. Yad Vashem contains both a research center and an educational institute, in addition to the museum. The archive, with its millions of pages of documentation, is at the center of the Yad Vashem research institute. Since 1968 Yad Vashem has also been a center for international scholarship on the Holocaust era. Every four years since then Yad Vashem has sponsored an international scholars conference on topics related to Holocaust studies. Important as an educational institution, Yad Vashem represents the critical role that remembering the Holocaust plays in daily life in Israel.

Yahasenu me-Ever la-Yarden [יחסנו מעבר לירדן, H] "Our Relative(s) Across the Jordan": Early code term for the Emir Faisal, reflecting Zionists' intense desire to reach an agreement with him that would satisfy Arab nationalists, permit Zionist development, and allow the mandate to begin peacefully. Despite initially high hopes, buoyed by the agreements Faisal signed in 1919 with Chaim Weizmann and Felix Frankfurter, relations between Jews and Arabs soured rapidly. Despite this setback, the Zionists continued their contacts with Faisal and, later, with his brother Abdullah (later King Abdullah I of Trans-Jordan). > see also: **Arabs; Faisal-Frankfurter Agreement; Faisal-Weizmann Agreement.**

Yahudim [Slang] "Uptown Jews": Derisive American Zionist expression for assimilated American Jews. Figuratively speaking, these opponents of Zionism were Jews who lived uptown and were divorced from authentic Jewish life, which centered on the lower east side of Manhattan. In contrast, the so-called Greenhorns — new immigrants — were Zionists or were sympathetic to Zionist goals. The term was used in the sense of mimicking the uptowners' Americanized pronunciation of Yiddish/Hebrew and had an ironic twist: Those who considered themselves to be the "best Jews" were, in fact, the least Jewish element within the community. > see also: **Assimilation; Conquest of Communities.**

Yair [יעיר, PN]: Nom de guerre of Abraham Stern, a commander of the Irgun Zvai Leumi (IZL) between 1937 and 1940. Stern, who had a theory of revolutionary action that was much more radical than that of the majority of IZL members, broke with that organization in September 1940, creating Lohame Herut Israel (LEHI). Stern was killed by British police in 1942. > See also: **Yishuv, Yishuv Organizations (Underground Organizations).**

Yavne [יבנה, GN]: Code name for the Sherut Yediot (Shai) office in Jerusalem and, ipso facto, for the regional intelligence officer that headed the Shai office. > See also: **Yishuv, Yishuv Organizations (Underground Organizations, Sherut Yediot).**

Yerida [ירידה, H] "Descent": Israeli term for one leaving the Land of Israel. The *yored* viewed as the diametrical opposite of an *oleh* (immigrant), one who ascends to the Land of Israel. Although some *Yerida* always existed, in the premandatory, Mandatory, and postmandatory eras, it has almost always been more than counterbalanced by the *aliya* rate. > See also: **Aliya; Oleh.**

Yetziat Eropa [יציאת אורופה, H] "Exodus from Europe": Slang Hebrew term for the *Briha*, tapping in on the historical Jewish experience of the Exodus from Egypt. The parallelism with previous Jewish experience played an important psychological and ideological role among the survivors and animated many of their activities.

Yevsktsia(s) [R] "Jewish Committee(s)": Popular name for the Jewish Soviets created after the 1917 Bolshevik takeover in Russia. The Yevsektsias were composed of prominent Jewish Communists and were organized to instill a Bolshevik spirit into the Jewish community. This process entailed uprooting all manifestation of bourgeois Jewish ideology — primarily Zionism. The Communist leaders realized that such a policy could not derive from the central government but had to seem to be a grassroots Jewish movement. Hence, the formula used for Yevsektsia activities: they were to be Jewish in form but Communist in substance. > see also: **Communism and Zionism; Anti-Zionism.**

Yiddishism [ייִדישיזם, H/Y]: Untranslatable ideological term prevalent in Eastern Europe and among Eastern European Jewish émigrés worldwide prior to World War II and implying a commitment to the Yiddish language and culture. Yiddishism flourished especially between the two world wars, as Yiddish literature and culture and East European Jewry enjoyed their last years of prominence before being destroyed by the Nazis. The term also had political connotations, since most Yiddishists were also anti-Zionist in their orientation. They viewed diaspora Jewry as viable and considered emigration nothing less than desertion from communal responsibilities. For their part, most Zionists rejected Yiddishism, viewing Yiddish as a mere "jargon," and emphasized the need for the Jewish renaissance to procede in tandem with the rebirth of Hebrew. > see also: **Bundism; Daism; Folkism; Cultural Conflict; Hebrew, Revival of.**

Yishai [ישי, PN]: Code name used at various times during the 1930s and 1940s for David Shaltiel, one of the Hagana's senior field commanders. The name derived from an indirect biblical reference: David was the son of Yishai; since Shalteil's first name was David, the connection was logical. The connection was also sufficiently obscure to be unclear to anyone not "in" on the code name.

Yishuv [ישוב, H] "Settlement":

1. Scope and Definition

Hebrew term for the quasi-independent Jewish political entity existing in Palestine/*Eretz Israel* before the establishment of the State of Israel. Historians distinguish between two different eras in the *Yishuv's* history. The term "Old *Yishuv*" is used to represent the Jewish community that existed in *Eretz Israel* (mainly in the four holy cities of Jerusalem, Hebron, Safed, and Tiberias) prior to the advent of Zionism. By contrast, the term "New *Yishuv*" is used to represent the entity created by the influx of Zionist *olim* after 1881. Relations between the two branches of the *Yishuv* were never more than cordial although, at the same time, their feuds rarely (if ever) went far beyond mutual name calling and recrimination. > see also: **Old Yishuv/New Yishuv.**

The new *Yishuv* (hereafter "the *Yishuv*") was, of course, self-consciously nationalist in its orientation. At a time of great ferment for Jewish communities around the world, members of the *Yishuv* saw themselves as the avantgarde of a Jewish national renaissance and as founders of a Jewish national home. The precise nature of the *Yishuv*'s future was not sketched out at this stage for the simple reason that its population was a miniscule portion of the total world Jewish population. The the Jewish population of *Eretz Israel* was also small in comparison with the local Arab popultaion. Rising *aliya* rates substantially increased both the total number of Jews and their proportion to the overall population, but this process took many years. Indeed, it would not be an exaggeration to state that the *Yishuv* could have been uprooted at any time prior to World War I. Neither its population nor its largely undefined legal status would have permitted Zionists to claim that the national home existed on anything like a stable basis. > see also: **Aliya**.

World War I fundamentally altered the legal status of the *Yishuv* but did not immediately impact on the demographic picture. When the British government issued the Balfour Declaration, it became the first country to publicly recognize Zionist claims as legitimate and to commit itself to helping facilitate the creation of a Jewish national home. However, despite clarion calls for massive *aliya* and investment, the reality was that Jewish development in *Eretz Israel* was slow. Development was hampered by a lack of consensus on Zionism within the Jewish world, by the relative poverty of most of the Jewish communities in which Zionism was strongest, by Arab opposition, and by periodic reassessments by the British of the role that Jews might play in guarding their imperial interests in the Middle East. Of course, one fact must be emphasized: at no time between the granting of the mandate by the League of Nations (1920) and the establishment of the State of Israel (1948) did the Jewish national home ever entirely govern itself. > see also: **World War I; Balfour Declaration; Arabs; Meora'ot; Committees of Inquiry; League of Nations; Mandate, League of Nations**.

Despite these impediments, the *Yishuv* continued to grow throughout the 1920s and 1930s. Even if growth was slow, it was steady. The worsening situation in Europe beginning with the Nazi rise to power in Germany in 1933 considerably speeded up developments. The Nazi persecution of European Jewry elicited a strong response from the *Yishuv*, and it found its main expression in a policy of constructive aid known as *Rescue Aliya*. The direct result was a massive wave of immigration (both legal and "illegal") that more than doubled the *Yishuv*'s population in under ten years. Similarly, as Jewish philanthropies began to seek an encompassing solution to the distress of Eastern European Jewry, financial resources that were previously unavailable were obtained for new development. Finally, a new spirit — partly a reflection of fears that time was running out on the Zionist endeavor — animated much of the *Yishuv*'s political discourse. Whereas during the 1920s it was rare for Zionists to discuss statehood (and if they did, the generally used euphemistic expressions to do so), during the 1930s such discussions were primary. The *Yishuv*, which had always been organized as a "state in the making," now became conscious of its potential and began to take the necessary steps to turn that potential into reality. > see also: **Gradualism; Shem ha-meforash; Medina ba-Derech**.

This is not to imply that the *Yishuv*'s growth during the interwar era was a succession of victories. To the contrary, many failures occurred and numerous obstacles were placed in the way of Zionist fulfillment. Still, after twenty years of development, the *Yishuv* existed on a much more secure foundation than it ever had before. When the British repudiated their commitments under the mandate in 1939, the Zionists were thus able to answer in kind. After World War II ended, the Zionists also repudiated the mandate and demanded that the Jewish people be given the opportunity to take its rightful place in the world community. A three-year struggle ensued, that culminated in the U.N. decision to partition *Eretz Israel* into Jewish and Arab states. The stage was thus set for the "sate in the making" to become a state in relaity. > see also: **World War II; White Papers; United Nations; War of Independence; Israel, State of**.

TABLE Y.1: Growth of Jewish Population in Eretz Israel, 1882–1948[1]

Year	Jews	Total Population	Percentage
1882	24,000	450,000	5.3
1914	85,000	685,000	12.4
1922	84,000	752,000	11.2
1931	175,000	1,033,000	16.9
1935	355,000	1,308,000	27.1
1940	464,000	1,545,000	30.0
1945	554,000	1,810,000	30.6
1948	650,000	806,000	80.6

Source: *Statistical Abstract of Israel* 1 (1948–1950).

2. Major Yishuv Organizations

Self-Governing Institutions

Assefat ha-Nivharim (אספת הנבחרים, AHN), "Elected Assembly," elected Jewish self-governing body organized in 1920 and recognized by the British in 1928. AHN was composed of seventy-one members, a conscious effort to echo the Sanhedrin that was the self-governing body of Jews in *Eretz Israel* during the Greco-Roman era. AHN was elected by proportional representation, with all adult members of Knesset Israel having the right to vote. Theoretically, AHN was elected every four years; in practice elections were held much less frequently. Furthermore, AHN had only two major responsibilities: to elect members to the Va'ad Leumi and to set the latter organization's annual budget. Both these tasks were performed during a single meeting of AHN, usually held in the spring. Although AHN was more representative of the *Yishuv*'s population than the Jewish Agency, it did not reflect all Jews' attitudes. Agudas Israel, which joined the Knesset Israel withdrew from AHN in 1920 over the issue of suffrage for women. Similarly, ha-Zach withdrew from AHN in 1944, ten years after it withdrew from the WZO. AHN ceased to function in late 1947, in preparation for its absorption into the provisional government.

Histadrut ha-Shotrim ha-Ivriim (הסתדרות השוטרים העבריים), "Federation of Hebrew Police," short-lived national federation of Jewish guards, police officers, and others involved in security. Formed in the summer of 1918, the federation hoped to assume responsibility for all internal security matters, seeing control of police functions as critical to the development of the Jewish national home. Despite a wide range of support for the federation within the *Yishuv*, nothing came of its proposals, and when the British established their own police system in Palestine/*Eretz Israel*, the federation ceased to function.

Knesset Israel (כנסת ישראל, KI), "Assembly of Israel," official name for the Jewish millet in mandatory Palestine/*Eretz Israel*. Founded in 1920 and reorganized in 1926, KI theoretically represented all Jews living in the Yishuv. KI embodied both the membership of the Jewish community and the organizations that represented the Jewish population in contact with the British government, its legislative arm being the seventy-member Asefat ha-Nivharim and its executive arm being the Va'ad Leumi.

Sochnut Yehudit (סוכנות יהודית), "Jewish Agency," executive arm of the Yishuv, founded as the Zionist Executive in 1922 and renamed

---

[1] Figures for 1948 include only territory granted to Israel under the UN partition plan and reflect conditions as of May 14, 1948.

after enlargement in 1929. > see also: **Sochnut Yehudit**.

Va'ad ha-Ir (ועד העיר), "The City Council," local arm of Jewish self-government in Jerusalem, established shortly after the British occupied the city in 1918. The committee was a coalition comprising Sephardi communal leaders, representatives of the Ashkenazi Orthodox community, businessmen and merchants, and the local Zionist office. They hoped to present an already existing organization to the British in order to maximize Jewish self-government in the city. Elections to the committee were held in 1918, after which an eleven-member executive committee came into existence. Shortly after this auspicious beginning, however, the Ashkenazi representatives separated and ultra-Orthodox members of the community entirely withdrew from the Va'ad. In 1920 the Va'ad was absorbed into Knesset Israel, becoming its Jerusalem branch and operating until 1948. Although Jews represented a clear plurality of Jerusalem's population, the British selected an Arab mayor for the city (Regib Bey Nashashibi). Sole chairman: Jacob Thon.

Va'ad ha-Zirim (ועד הצירים), "Committee of Delegates," body established to act as a liaison between the WZO and the British army in 1918; also known as the Zionist Commission (ZC). The committee was established to help realize the promises framed in the Balfour Declaration in terms of creating a Jewish national home. The ZC's composition was overwhelmingly British; one French and two Italian members initially rounded out an otherwise entirely Anglo-Jewish committee. When ZC's composition was established, it had been intended that Russian Jewish representatives would also join, but they were unable to leave the newly established Soviet Union. In 1919, in order to make the committee appear more representative, an American Zionist

Last Meeting of the Va'ad Leumi Prior to Its
Incorporation Into the Israeli Provisional Government.
Courtesy of the Central Zionist Archives, Jerusalem

delegate was added. ZC initially operated as an independent organization, but in October 1919 it merged with the WZO's Jaffa office. Thereafter, the organization operated as the ZC until 1921, when its name was changed to the Zionist Executive (and, later still, to the Jewish Agency) to reflect its role as the key element of Jewish self-government in mandatory *Eretz Israel*. Throughout its existence, the ZC's activities were hampered by British duality. Repeated promises from London to fulfill the Balfour Declaration were continually being undercut by the British military and political leadership in the Middle East. The ZC was therefore unable to fulfill its main goals but was important for laying the foundations of self-government in the Jewish national home. Initial composition: Chaim Weizmann (chairman), Joseph Cowan, M. David Eder, Leon Simon, Israel M. Sieff, James de Rothschild (England), William Ormesby-Gore (Royal Army), Sylvain Lévi (France), Angelo Levi-Bianchini, Giacomo Artom (Italy). > see also: **World Zionist Organization; Sochnut Yehudit; Occupied Enemy Territories Administration; Mandate, League of Nations; Balfour Declaration.**

Va'ad Leumi (ועד לאומי, VL), "National Council," executive arm of Knesset Israel and one of the major arms of Jewish self-government during the mandatory era. The fact that the VL derived its authority from the most inclusive and democratic institutions in the *Yishuv* should have led it to be the key component in of Jewish self-government. In reality, the VL was oriented toward internal developments, such as health care, education, religion, and social wlefare, leaving all political activity in the hands of the JAE. The main reason for this division of labor was the fact that the JAE derived its authority directly from the WZO (despite the JA's 1929 "enlargement" to include non-Zionists) and thus was more global in scope. Despite the potential for friction between the two bodies, after 1931 both came to be dominated by Mapai and the division of labor between them worked advantageously.

Va'ad Zemani (ועד זמני, VZ), "Provisional Council," Jewish governing body established during the early years of British rule in *Eretz Israel* that was intended as an interim agency operating until the mandate and its constitutional arrangements were fully developed. VZ operated in 1919 and 1920, simultaneously with the Va'ad ha-Zirim, until its legislative functions were absorbed by Assefat ha-Nivharim and its executive functions by the Va'ad Leumi in 1921. Sole chairman: Ya'akov Thon.

Zionist Executive, name for the WZO entity permanently in Jerusalem and representing the Va'ad ha-Poel ha-Mezumzam. The executive was responsible for carrying out day-to-day operations in *Eretz Israel* from 1921 to 1929. At that point, the executive was "enlarged" and was transformed into the Jewish Agency Executive. > see also: **Sochnut Yehudit; World Zionist Organization, WZO Subsidiary Agencies (Va'ad ha-Poel ha-Mezumzam).**

Political Parties and Organziations

Achdut ha-Am (אחדות העם), "Unity of the Nation," ethnic party of German Zionists in Palestine, founded in 1938. Leaning toward the liberal wing of the Zionist movement, Achdut ha-Am advocated rescue action for Jewish refugees in concert with binationalism. In 1942, Ahdut ha-Am was reorganized as the Aliya Hadasha party. However, its main ideological orientations and its overtly ethnic orientation were retained.

Ahdut ha-Avoda (אחדות העבודה, AHA), "Unity of Labor," name adopted by two distinctly different socialist Zionist parties active in *Eretz Israel*. The first manifestation of AHA was formed in 1919 and existed until 1929. This party was socialist in worldview, but reformist in strategy. That meant that AHA sought to create a Jewish national home based on collective principles through an emphasis on pioneering settlement and *halutzic aliya*, but did not oppose cooperation with nonsocialist parties in attainment of this goal. Moreover, this AHA rejected Marxist concepts of internationalism and class struggle, seeing them as irrelevant to the Jewish problem. In 1929 AHA agreed to merge with ha-Poel ha-Zair to form Mifleget Poale Eretz Israel (Mapai), and one year later AHA ceased to function. The second party to use the AHA name was founded in 1944 and derived from the internal opposition in Mapai known as *Siya Bet* (Faction Two). This AHA was more narrowly socialist in orientation than its parent party and viewed the needs of a Jewish national home in Marxist terms. In 1946 this AHA merged with Poale Zion Smol to form Ahdut ha-Avoda-Poale Zion and in 1948 further merged with ha-Shomer ha-Zair to form Mifleget ha-Poalim ha-Meuhad (Mapam).

Al-Domi (אל דמי), "Do Not Keep Silent," nonpartisan pressure group founded in 1942 by leading Zionist intellectuals who called upon the *Yishuv* to articulate a rescue policy for European Jewry and dedicate all resources to that goal. Al-Domi concentrated on the steps needed to get the JA to establish a rescue committee, despite awareness that the *Yishuv* was too weak to offer substantial aid to threatened European Jews. Although the results were disappointing, Al-Domi's members continued to advocate rescue until the end of World War II.

Aliya Hadasha (עליה חדשה, AH), "New Immigration (Party)," ethnic German Jewish political party that grew out of Ahdut ha-Am. AH was founded in 1942 to fill the needs of recent Central European *olim* for a political party that did not necessarily fit the mold of other parties in the *Yishuv*. AH was a middle-class party, being progressive but capitalist in ideology while maintaining the tendency among German Zionists to support the twin political goals of continued *aliya* and Arab-Jewish accommodation. AH was also commited to democratic structure, being the chief architect of the 1944 Asefat ha-Nivharim elections (the previous elections having been held in 1933). In early 1948 AH joined the Israeli provisional government, merging with groups of General Zionists to form the Progressive party that September.

Brit Shalom (ברית שלום), "A Covenant of Peace," binationalist society founded in Jerusalem in 1925 to promote Arab-Jewish understanding in Palestine/*Eretz Israel*. Most Brit Shalom members were Zionists who accepted the need to create a Jewish national home. However, the demographic realities in the *Yishuv* meant that accomplishing that goal would either take many years, involve considerable bloodshed, or both. Although Zionists might prevail in the long run, they would incur the Arabs' wrath for an interminable period. The only way to be consistent with Jewish and humanist ideals, therefore, was to concede something to the Arabs that would make Jewish immigration palatable: surrendering the Zionist goal of Jewish statehood. In reality, of course, the Arabs were unwilling to accept *aliya* even if Jews agreed to joint rule in Palestine/ *Eretz Israel*, a fact that made Brit Shalom's ideology little more than hollow utopianism. As a result, most of the *Yishuv*'s parties and leaders shunned the organization and its ideas. > see also: **Binationalism**.

Ha-Poel ha-Zair (הפועל הצעיר, HPHZ), "The Young Workman," socialist Zionist party founded in Jaffa in 1905. HPHZ was dedicated, first and foremost, to the concept of *Kibbush ha-Avoda* (the conquest of labor). Members felt that the first step in creating a Jewish national home was the creation of an organic link between Jews and the economy. This led the HPHZ leadership to emphasize Practical Zionism and the activity of *Halutzim*. HPHZ was clearly a socialist organization, retaining its membership in the Second International throughout its existence, but was not necessarily a Marxist party. Ideological socialism for HPHZ extended only as far as advocating that the Zionist movement should collectively own all land in *Eretz Israel*, holding the land in trust for the entire Jewish people. HPHZ did emphasize the creation of collective settlements and workers' and producers' co-operatives but did not view them as necessarily the end goal of Zionism while also rejecting most Marxist concepts. It may be fairly said that HPHZ saw socialism as the best means to attain Zionism where other, more socialist parties advocated Zionism as the best means to attain socialism in the Jewish world. During World War I, HPHZ advocated a pro-Turkish policy, seeing that as the only way to protect the *Yishuv*. This policy quickly turned into support for the Balfour Declaration and for the creation of a Jewish national home. In the 1920s, HPHZ acted to found institutions, such as the Histadrut and the "enlarged" JA, that were seen as a means to serve the best interests of the entire Jewish people in connection with the national home. In 1929 HPHZ began negotiations with Ahdut ha-Avoda, a like-minded socialist Zionist party, and the two merged in 1930 to for Mifleget Poale Eretz Israel (Mapai).

Histadrut ha-Ovdim ha-Kelalit shel ha-Ovdim be-Eretz Israel (הסתדרות העובדים הכללית של העובדים בארץ ישראל), "General Federation of Workers in the Land of Israel," more commonly known simply as the Histadrut, socialist Zionist labor organization associated with Mapai and founded in 1920. From a membership of 4,000 in 1920, the Histadrut grew to 67,000 in 1935, and 100,000 on the eve of World War II. Main Histadrut ideologies were *Avoda Ivrit* and the creation of a "working community" in *Eretz Israel*. The Histadrut adhered to an ideology of *Halutzic Aliya*, meaning that *aliya* should be limited to those with agricultural training (mainly through Mapai's diaspora youth group, he-Halutz). This attitude began to change during the 1930s, under the impact of pressure for mass *aliya*. Throughout, Histadrut ideology emphasized the "idea and the deed," that is, the all-encompassing nature of socialist Zionist ideology as a means to create a Jewish workers' state. The Histadrut was frequently the scene of bitter and divisive schism, especially during the 1920s and 1930s. Moreover, the organization was one of the main sore points in relations between Mapai, which greatly benefited from the Histadrut's role in the *Yishuv* economy, and the revisionist movement. The Histadrut was one of the major foundations upon which the *Yishuv* and hence the State of Israel were built.

Delegates at the Founding Conference of the Histadrut, Haifa, 1920.
Courtesy of the Central Zionist Archives, Jerusalem

Histadrut ha-Ovdim ha-Leumit (הסתדרות *העובדים הלאומית*, HOL), "Nationalist Workers Federation," nonsocialist labor body established in 1934 in direct opposition to the socialist Histadrut. HOL accused the earlier body of hegemonistic policies that were designed to help one party (Mapai) dominate the *Yishuv* but which were not necessarily best for the Jewish national movement. HOL rejected strikes and opposed efforts by the Histadrut to obtain control of major industries. Instead, HOL supported binding arbitration in labor disputes and called for the creation of cooperatives to eliminate sources of economic dissension. Although technically independent of ha-Zohar, HOL reflected the revisionist orientation on labor issues; furthermore, most HOL members were members of revisionist organizations. Independently of the Histadrut, but parallel to it, HOL ran its own sick fund (Kupat Holim le-Ovdim Leumiim), a mutual aid society (Kupat Amal), and other supporting institutions. HOL continued to operate independently after the State of Israel was established.

Ihud (אחוד), "Unity," Jewish binationalist party established in August 1942 to promote union with the Arabs. Ihud was a coalition of Brit Shalom, ha-Shomer ha-Zair, Poale Zion Smol, the Socialist League, and the League for Arab-Jewish Cooperation. Brit Shalom's members dominated the new body, which maintained almost verbatim the earlier party's call for a joint Arab-Jewish commonwealth in *Eretz Israel*. The government of this hypothesized state would be based on power sharing but would guarantee the right of free immigration for Jews. The party's ideology left it in limbo. Arabs refused to support any idea that included power sharing and *aliya*, while most Zionists were committed to the Biltmore program of a Jewish state in all of an unpartitioned *Eretz Israel*. Nonetheless, Ihud continued to operate until the United Nations decision on partition in November 1947. Sole chairman: Judah L. Magnes. Publication: *Ner* (monthly). > see also: **Binationalism**.

Irgun Olim Bilti Legali'im (ארגון עולים *בלתי ליגליים*), "Organization of Illegal Immigrants," founded in the early 1930s. The organization advocated unlimited Jewish immigration to Palestine and, as a more immediate measure, the "legalization" of all *Ma'apilim* already in the country. > see also: **Aliya Bet**.

League for Arab-Jewish Cooperation (LAJC), political advocacy group founded in 1930 and calling for closer cooperation between the Semitic nations in *Eretz Israel*. LAJC called for closer integration between the *Yishuv* and the Arab community, primarily in the economic and political spheres. Although not officially binationalist in orientation, LAJC's ideology was binationalist in practice. LAJC operated from the a priori assumption that the Arabs had to recognize Jewish national rights (in the form of accepting *aliya*) while Jews had to work for the Arab agenda (by creating a united Palestine/*Eretz Israel* that would not need British imperialist protection). LAJC's Jewish members did not receive much encouragement from the Arabs: not a single Arab leader of any stature joined LAJC.

Legion ha-Avoda (לגיון *העבודה*), "The Labor Legion," short-lived effort begun in 1909 by members of the ha-Shomer defense organization to fulfill Zionist goals by promoting the exclusive use of Jewish labor throughout the *Yishuv*. It was hoped that the legion could be organized into labor battalions that would found settlements (undertaking all labor connected with such settlements) and defend themselves. However, only two *Kvutzot* joined the legion, Sejera and Hadera, and by 1910 the idea had run its course. All members then returned to full-tme defense activities and the legion ceased to function. > see also: **Yishuv, Yishuv Organizations (Underground Organizations, ha-Shomer)**.

Mifleget Poale Eretz Israel (מפלגת פועלי *ארץ ישראל*, Mapai מפא'י), "Workers Party of the Land of Israel," socialist Zionist party, founded on January 5, 1930, by the merger of Ahdut ha-Avoda and ha-Poel ha-Zair. Almost immediately after its founding, Mapai became the dominant party in the *Yishuv*. In 1933, for instance, nearly 80 percent of all Histadrut members were affiliated with Mapai; the remaining 20 percent were affiliated with all other parties combined. Mapai's dominant position must be at least partly attributed to the party's ideological orientation: a blend of non-Marxist socialism with a reformist orientation and a nationalist outlook on Jewish issues. A majority of the JAE's leaders were from Mapai, including David Ben-Gurion, Haim Arlosoroff, Moshe Shertok (Sharett), and Eliezer Kaplan. Mapai similarly dominated the Va'ad Leumi, in which Yitzhak Ben-Zvi served as president for most of the era from 1930 to 1948. Mapai's ideology was termed Constructive Socialism. It was based on socialist principles such as collective ownership of land and of means of production but it rejected class struggle and Marxist internationalism. Furthermore, Mapai emphasized cooperation with nonsocialist Jewish parties in attainment of Zionist goals. Rifts within the *Yishuv* — the conflict between Mapai and the revisionists during the 1930s — and within the party itself — connected with the development (and eventual secession) of *Siya Bet* — forced Mapai to apply its ideology in a dynamic fashion. Thus, Mapai emphasized the socialist elements of its ideology during the conflict with the revisionists, but moved closer to the revisionists on national goals (such as mass *aliya* and statehood) during the late 1930s and 1940s. Mapai continued to dominate politics in the State of Israel after independence and represents a major element in the current One Israel party. Chairman: David Ben-Gurion (1930–1948). Publication: *Ha-Poel ha-Zair* (weekly, 1930f).

Mifleget ha-Poalim ha-Meuhad (מפלגת הפועלים המאוחד, Mapam, מפ"ם), "United Workers' Party," socialist party founded in January 1948 as a coalition of the new Ahdut ha-Avoda, ha-Shomer ha-Zair, and Poale Zion Smol. The newly established party framed itself as a clearly socialist alternative to Mapai. Mapam's ideology emphasized the need to create a Jewish state but fused Zionism with Marxist socialism, including, inter alia, with an ideology of class struggle. For much of the period prior to independence, Mapam also formulated a binationalist orientation toward the Arabs. Finally, in contrast to Mapai's clearly pro-Western orientation, Mapam saw itself as an advocate of alliance with the Soviet Union. Despite its differences with Mapai, Mapam agreed to join the Israeli provisional government, with two members serving on the provisional cabinet.

Mifleget ha-Poalim ha-Socialistim (מפלגת הפועלים הסוציאליסטים, MPS), "Socialist Workers Party," early name for the Communist movement in Palestine/*Eretz Israel*, established in Vienna in 1920. MPS never amounted to a major movement in the *Yishuv*, although it repeatedly sought to infiltrate the mainstream socialist Zionist parties. MPS advocated a stridently non-Zionist approach, calling for a joint Arab-Jewish revolution against imperialism and capitalism. MPS was broken up by the British in July 1921, being absorbed into the Palestine Communist Party in September 1922.

Neturei Karta (נטורי קרתא, NK) "Guardians of the City," ultra-Orthodox anti-Zionist party established in 1935 as part of Agudas Israel and oriented to promoting the Orthodox position that *Eretz Israel* could only be rebuilt by divine command. NK split from the main body of Aguda in 1937 because the latter was seen as too accommodating in its position on Zionism — Aguda having moved to a more non-Zionist position under the impact of events in Europe. NK's members adopted the name associated with the group in 1938. NK ideology is based on an uncategorical rejection of any human activity to restore Jews to their ancestral homeland prior to the Messiah's arrival. NK, which since World War II has become increasingly identified with the Satmar Hasidic sect, has remained staunchly anti-Zionist to this day. > see also: **Anti-Zionism; Judaism and Zionism; Organizations, Non- or Anti-Zionist (International, Agudas Israel)**.

Palestine Communist Party (PCP), extreme leftist organization that inherited the mantle of Communist activity in the *Yishuv* from Mifleget ha-Poalim ha-Socialistim in September 1922. The PCP was never more than a minor irritant to Zionist activity in *Eretz Israel* but was a cause for some concern within socialist Zionist circles. The latter feared that the PCP would slough off support for Jewish goals among Eretz Israel's youth. The PCP operated under the exclusive control of the Comintern. As a result, PCP leadership was evenly divided between Jews and Arabs, despite the fact that PCP membership was overwhelmingly Jewish. > see also: **Communism and Zionism**.

Poale Zion Smol (פועלי ציון שמאל, PZS), "Left Workers of Zion," wing of the world socialist movement, whose strength lay in Poland. The PZS wing in *Eretz Israel* was founded in 1920. Adhering to a more narrowly socialist ideology than most other socialist Zionist parties, PZS rejected any form of cooperation with bourgeois Zionists and called for class struggle within the *Yishuv*. Never more than a minor player in the *Yishuv* — whose political life was dominated by Mapai — after Mapai's *Siya Bet* seceded, PZS merged with the new party in 1946 to found Ahdut ha-Avoda-Poale Zion.

Siya Bet (סיעה ב'), "Faction Two," popular name for the internal socialist opposition in Mapai. Whereas Mapai was a coalition of two mainly reformist, non-Marxist, socialist Zionist parties, both the original entities and Mapai itself contained individuals whose ideology was more narrowly Marxist as compared with the rest of the party. These individuals were first galvanized during the 1930s and coalesced into a clear faction just prior to World War II. During the war, *Siya Bet* was in the forefront of mobilizing the *Yishuv* on behalf of the Soviet Union. However, internal pressure mounted in Mapai to eliminate all factions, leading to *Siya Bet's* secession from the party in 1944 to found the new Ahdut ha-Avoda Party. > see also: **Yishuv, Yishuv Organizations (Political Parties and Organizations, Ahdut ha-Avoda)**.

Socialist League, The (TSL), party allied with ha-Shomer ha-Zair and reflecting its values, established in 1936. TSL sought to provide a voice for urban workers in party that was dominated by the *Kibbutz* movement. Like ha-Shomer ha-Zair, TSL emphasized a socialist attitude adn an overall binationalist orientation. TSL existed independently for ten years, merging directly into ha-Shomer ha-Zair when the latter began to form Mifleget ha-Polaim ha-Meuhad (Mapam).

Underground Organizations

Adumim (אדומים), "Reds," subsidiary underground organized with two hundred members as part of the Irgun Zvai Leumi (IZL) and raised in 1939. The Adumim operated as an "underground within an underground," being kept separate from the rest of the IZL. Members were trained in demolitions, intelligence gathering, and other forms of irregular warfare. In turn, the Adumim were divided into two sections: *Shahor* (black), dedicated to anti-Arab operations, and *Lavan* (white), dedicated to anti-British operations. The Adumim began a series of attacks in the early summer of 1939, but suspended their operations when World War II broke out. The unit was apparently not revived after the war.

Af-Al-Pi (עף-על-פי), "Despite All," revisionist Zionist agency for *Aliya Bet*, established in March 1937 as part of the Irgun Zvai Leumi. Previously, efforts at "independent immigration" were undertaken under the auspices of Betar. Af-Al-Pi operated in two distinct spheres against the increasingly harsh British policy that resricted legal *aliya*, and against JA and WZO decisions that severely limited the size of Betar *aliya*. In spite of its clearly partisan orientation, Af-Al-Pi did not discriminate between members and nonmembers when organizing convoys and manning ships. Af-Al-Pi was most active in 1938 and 1939, when it oversaw the sailing of two dozen blockade runners. World War II curtailed Af-Al-Pi's activities and it did not resume independent operations in any systematic way after the war. > see also: **Aliya Bet**.

Aguda le-Shemira Azmit (אגודה לשמירה עצמית), "Association for Self-Defense," short-lived self-defense force established in Rosh Pina in 1883, mainly to protect the settlement's water supply from Bedouins. After one major clash with armed settlers, the assaults ceased.

Agudat Ahim (אגודת אחים, AA), "Union of Brothers," self-defense force established secretly in Rehovot in 1891. Also known as Agudat ha-Asarot (אגודת העשרות, the Union of Tens), AA saw itself as the seedling for an eventual Jewish army in *Eretz Israel*. Shortly after the organization began operating in Rehovot, a branch was established in Nes Ziona. AA members defended the settlements they lived in and also engaged in agricultural work. All branches ceased to function in 1897, after the Turks enacted restrictions on *aliya*.

Am Lohem (עם לוחם, AL), "A Fighting Nation," coalition of like-minded former members of the *Yishuv*'s underground movements, founded in November 1943. The main group of AL members came from the Irgun Zvai Leumi; they were disheartened by the schism in the Irgun and were demoralized by the lack of clear action against the British. Another group came from the Hagana. They too were disppointed that the fight against the White Paper of 1939 had been virtually halted because of the exigencies of fighting the Nazis. The new underground, calling itself AL, was created as a coalition of these two other groups. In their first plan for a mission, AL proposed kidnapping the British high commissioner for Palestine/*Eretz Israel*. At the last minute, the commanders of both the Irgun and the Palmah refused to cooperate with AL and this scheme was never carried out. Thereafter, AL collapsed.

Aviron (אווירון), "Airplane," private aviation company founded in 1936 that served as a front for the Hagana's air service. Having no combat aircraft, the Aviron flew a small number of liaison, reconnaissance, and light transport missions during the Arab Revolt and in the early years of World War II. In 1944, responsibility for Aviron was transferred by the Hagana to the Palmah; as a result the name was changed to Palavir. In 1948, Palavir was transferred back to the Hagana, becoming the Sherut Avir (Air Service) and, after the establishment of Zva ha-Hagana le-Israel, the Heyl ha-Avir (air force).

Bar-Giora (בר-גיורא), Zionist self-defense organization founded on September 29, 1907, and named after the leader of the Jewish revolt against Rome in 66 C.E. Bar-Giora's founding took place in Yitzhak Ben-Zvi's apartment in Jaffa. At this meeting, the members accepted the need for Jews to defend themselves and to protect Jewish property as one step in the direction of *Kibbush ha-Avoda* (the conquest of labor). Bar-Giora was active in only one settlement, Sejera, where a collective had been established. In 1909, Bar-Giora ceased its clandestine activities, thereafter operating in public under the name ha-Shomer. > see also: **Yishuv, Yishuv Organizations (Underground Organizations, ha-Shomer).**

Brit ha-Biryonim (ברית הביריונים, BB), "The Covenant of Terrorists," circle of radical Betar members living in the *Yishuv* and seeking to spark a general uprising by the Jewish population that would lead to the creation of a Jewish state. BB's exact relationship to the revisionist movement and especially with the Irgun Zvai Leumi has never been precisely established. Similarly, BB's membership — beyond Abba Ahimeir and a handful of his associates — is almost completely unknown. BB's leaders were clearly influenced by the guerrilla campaign waged by Michael Collins after the abortive Easter Uprising in Ireland and sought to model themselves on the Irish Republican Army. BB may also have been influenced by Italian syndicalist and fascist ideas about "action for action's sake," an orientation that garnered strong condemnation from Ze'ev Jabotinsky and other ha-Zohar leaders. Widely suspected in the murder of Haim Arlosoroff and treated as outcasts by most of the *Yishuv*, BB nevertheless continued to exist until the mid-1930s, operating on the *Yishuv*'s peripheries. > see also: **Arlosoroff Affair.**

Brit ha-Noar ha-Mored (ברית הנוער המורד, BNM), "Covenant of Rebelling Youth," short-lived circle of Betar members founded on April 18, 1936, and dedicated to instilling a more activist orientation in the revisionist movement and the Irgun Zvai Leumi (IZL). At the time, only a few days after the Arab revolt broke out, both ha-Zohar and IZL were officially commited to a policy of defense. BNM called for a policy of retaliation in kind and some members were involved in random acts of counterterrorism against Arabs in Tel Aviv and Jaffa. The result was a split in the IZL in 1937. Those opposed to BNM's ideology left and returned to the Hagana, while the majority of IZL members adopted BNM's activist doctrine. > see also: **Havlaga**.

Gdud Bnot Lohamot (גדוד בנות לוחמות, GBL, גב"ל) "Battalion of Fighting Girls," female auxiliary formed in 1941 by the Hagana branch in Haifa in order to increase women's participation in the *Yishuv*'s defense. Although the intention was to raise a number of similar units, only the Haifa GBL battalion was organized. This unit had 250 members. GBL members were trained in first aid, small arms use, and basic military drill. While the unit per se saw no combat, a number of GBL members volunteered and were accepted into the parachute unit sent into the Balkans in 1944. After World War II, GBL was disbanded, with its members being distributed among other Hagana units in the Haifa/Carmel region. > see also: **Paratroopers, Palestinian**.

Gdud ha-Avoda (גדוד העבודה), "The Labor Battalion," underground body founded in 1920 and inspired by Josepf Trumpeldor. The latter saw the Zionist leadership of his day as too timid. Trumpeldor therefore set out with a few followers to settle new areas, working the land while defending it. At the time, most WZO leaders preferred to concentrate settlements in areas that could be easily defended. In contrast, Trumpeldor sought to expand the *Yishuv*'s borders by settling its peripheries. Gdud leaders hoped to undertake a massive campaign of settlement but in fact were severely limited (due to financial and other difficulties) in the number of settlements they could actually build. Trumpeldor himself was killed in February 1920, defending the settlement of Tel Hai. Thereafter, the Gdud bore Trumpeldor's name, becoming Gdud ha-Avoda al Shem Yosef Trumpeldor (the Labor Battalion in Honor of Joseph Trumpeldor). Arab rioting in 1920–1921,

and the generally inadequate response of the British authorities to violent outbursts led the Gdud's leaders to join with members of ha-Shomer to found the Hagana. The Gdud remained a distinct element in the latter organization until 1926, when it split: The "right" wing ceased to exist as a separate entity while its "left" wing joined the incipient Communist party and abandoned its Zionist orientation.

Gdude Noar (גדודי נוער, Gadna גדנ"ע), "Youth Battalions," paramilitary scouting movement founded by the Hagana on May 15, 1941. Gadna's purpose was preparation for membership in the Hagana; members were expected to undertake preliminary training to develop the skills needed for underground operations. The Gadna training program emphasized unarmed self-defense, sports, first aid, marching, and military drill. No firearms training was undertaken until members graduated and joined the regular Hagana. Gadna was open to youths — both boys and girls — aaged fifteen and over, although in some cases fourteen-year-olds were also accepted. Gadna members were supposed to join the Hagana after three years in the program, and most did so. Although never intended to perform a combat role, during the War of Independence, some Gadna units fought, especially on the Jerusalem front. Gadna continues to exist today, fulfilling the same role for the Israeli army that it did for the Hagana. > see also: **Yishuv, Yishuv Organizations (Underground Organizations, Hagana); War of Independence; Zva ha-Hagana le-Israel**.

Gid'onim (גדעונים), "Gideonites," name for the Mossad le-Aliya Bet's clandestine radio network and for the radio operators. The network was created in 1938 to assist blockade runners in their task: Gid'onim escorted the vessels and provided communications with Hagana headquarters. Gid'onim also provided services for Hagana and Mossad offices in Europe after World War II. Usually, Gid'onim were trained in wireless telegraphy, although voice communications were also used. After the war, the Gid'onim established a training center in Bari, Italy, which was their operational base until 1948. > see also: **Aliya Bet**.

Hagana (הגנה), "Defense," underground militia founded in 1920. Organized geographically, the Hagana operated under the command of the Histadrut, with the support and authority of the JAE. During its early years, the Hagana was dedicated to a purely defensive doctrine that included a refusal to intercept Arab marauders before they commenced their attacks on Jewish settlements. As a result of the Arab Revolt of 1936–1939, Hagana doctrine changed and began to place a greater emphasis on mobile operations. The Hagana cooperated with the British during World War II but became a central focus of anti-British activities during the postwar Jewish revolt. Most importantly, the Hagana provided the foundation for Zva ha-Hagana le-Israel (Zahal), which was established as the regular Israeli army on May 31, 1948. Chiefs of Staff: Eliyahu Golomb (1920–1937), Yohanan Ratner (1937–1939), Ya'akov Dostrovsky (Dori, 1939–1945), Yitzhak Sadeh (1945–1947), Ya'akov Dori (1947–1948). > see also: **Arab Revolt**; **Havlaga**; **World War II**; **War of Independence**; **Zva ha-Hagana le-Israel**.

Ha-Huliya (החוליה), "The Detail," unit of the Palmah created to assist the Mossad le-Aliya Bet in its overland operations between 1943 and 1945. The main goal of the unit was to aid Jewish immigrants coming into *Eretz Israel* from Syria and Lebanon via the overland route (i.e., across the Golan Heights), regardless of their point of origin. Ha-Huliya operated from two bases: *Kibbutz* Ayelet ha-Shahar and *Kibbutz* Hanita. In 1945, this mission was passed to the Palmah's Ninth Company and ha-Huliya was disbanded.

Ha-Huliya ha-Yamit (החוליה הימית), "The Naval Detail," nickname for the Palyam unit tasked with destroying British gunboats — and thereby assisting the Mossad le-Aliya Bet's blockade runners — after World War II. Ha-Huliya ha-Yamit was founded on November 2, 1945, which was also the date of its first operation. Thereafter, between five and eight Palmah personnel formed ha-Huliya ha-Yamit and were actively engaged in operations to destroy British gunboats.

Additionally, ships used to deport *Ma'apilim* to Cyprus were also sabotaged, although none were sunk. During the War of Independence, ha-Huliya ha-Yamit was expanded into a frogman detachment and a detachment operating Italian-made Explosive Motor Boats (EMBs) in attacks on Egyptian shipping. Ha-Huliya ha-Yamit later formed the basis for Zahal's Naval Commando.

Ha-Kibbutz (הקיבוץ), "The Collective Settlement," secret organization founded by former ha-Shomer members who sought to continue "their" style of operations even after the Hagana was founded. Ha-Kibbutz members opposed the Hagana's exclusively defensive doctrine and its centralized organization, withdrawing to found their own body in 1922. These dissidents were the first to conduct *Aliya Bet* activities and were the first to recommend abandoning the WZO's pro-British stance. However, the new organization was never monolithic: some members, who had previously been associated with Gdud ha-Avoda were pro-Soviet while others sought alliances with Italy or Poland. Ha-Kibbutz ceased to function in 1927 after internal dissension tore the organization apart. It did, however, lay the groundwork for future schisms in the Hagana and set the pattern of inalterable Hagana opposition to dissident undergrounds.

Ha-Magen (המגן), "The Defender," watchman's association, comprising members who withdrew from ha-Shomer in 1915, after the latter appeared to abandon settlements in Judea. Most of the members were candidates who had hoped to join ha-Shomer but whose membership was held up by the outbreak of World War I. At its height, ha-Magen had twenty members, the recognized leader of whom was Joseph Leshinsky. None of the other members knew that Leshinsky was actually working for the Nili spy ring and that the defense organization was merely a cover to give him a reason to visit different settlements. Ha-Magen collapsed when Nili was exposed and Leshinsky was hanged by Turkish authorities. > see also: **World War I**.

Ha-Shomer (השומר), "The Watchman," Jewish self-defense organization founded as a public body by members of the clandestine Bar-Giora

A Group of ha-Shomer Members, 1910.
Courtesy of the Central Zionist Archives, Jerusalem

TABLE Y.2: Ha-Shomer Members Killed in the Line of Duty

Abraham Berdizchewski	Israel Korngold
Devorah Derchler	Reuven Kuraiken
Ya'akov Feldman	David Levitan
Yehuda Friedlander	Arye Mirtenbaum
Shmuel Friedman	Israel Romerstein
Moshe Gurman	Moshe Segalovitch
Aharon Z. Gushansnki	Shulamin Ya'akov

Zohar, Mordechai

Source: Archion Toldot ha-Hagana.

society in April 1909. Unlike the previous organization, ha-Shomer's members sought legal recognition as the *Yishuv's* sole security agency. This was a slow process, but on the eve of World War I, ha-Shomer members were guarding most of the Jewish settlements in *Eretz Israel*. At its height ha-Shomer numbered one hundred twenty members, of whom fifteen were killed in battle with Arab, Bedouin, or other marauders. World War I disrupted ha-Shomer's operations: the Turkish authorities were sufficiently suspicious of the *Yishuv*, despite the WZO's official policy of neutrality, to deport almost all Jewish males who were citizens of other countries (mainly, Russia). Although ha-Shomer strictly adhered to the WZO policy of neutrality, it was forced underground by the

Turks. Ha-Shomer was reestablished after the war, but its small size and loose organization no longer served the needs of the *Yishuv*. As a result, ha-Shomer was absorbed into the Hagana on May 18, 1920.

Herev le-Amenu ule-Arzenu (חרב לארצינו לעמינו, Halul (חלו"ל), "Arms for Our People and Our Land," short-lived self defense group founded by Michael Halperin, one of the leaders of the First Aliya, in 1891. Halul's goal was to prepare members for both agricultural work and self-defense, with a long-range goal of preparing arms and ammunition in case an opportunity to overthrow the Turkish government ever presented itself. Halul lasted for less than a year, but some of its members later joined ha-Shomer.

Heyl ha-Am (חיל העם), "People's Militia," national volunteer service organization established by the Hagana in 1939 for non-members. Fears about an impending war in Europe and the possibility that such a war might force the British to withdraw troops and leave the *Yishuv* vulnerable to attack by Arab or Axis forces led the Hagana high command to organize paramilitary units in the *Yishuv*. In Tel Aviv alone, some seventeen battalions of volunteers, each with seven hundred members, were raised. However, these units had little military value: they had nearly no weaponry (the Hagana had barely enough for its regular units) and little training, due to a dearth of qualified instructors. Morale in the volunteer units fell even further when the British banned public military drill, using the excuse that such activities upset the Arabs. In the end, the Hagana was forced to constrict the volunteer units, reducing the force to five battalions which were incorporated into the regular Hagana during 1941 and 1942.

Heyl Mishmar (חיל משמר, Him), "Guard Corps," Hagana division established in 1939 to incorporate the lessons of the Arab Revolt into the underground's organization. Prior to the revolt, all Hagana units were organized to defend specific localities, with few reserves available. The revolt proved this system to be unworkable, since any local unit would be too weak to defend its settlement for any length of time without reinforcements. Incorporating this lesson and the new aggressive spirit of active defense that had been tried successfully during the revolt, in 1939, the Hagana high command grouped all defensive units into one section, known as Him. All Hagana members over the age of thirty-four were to be organized into Him units and then would be subdivided geographically. This force initially numbered some 16,000 men, who were supplemented by 3,500 members of Heyl ha-Am after World War II began. By 1945, Him had more than 24,000 personnel under arms, being organized into regional brigades that bore the brunt of fighting during the early days of the War of Independence. > see also: **War of Independence; Zva ha-Hagana le-Israel.**

Heyl ha-Sadeh (חיל השדה, Hish), "Field Force," Hagana division, established in 1939 to incorporate the lessons of the Arab Revolt into the underground's organization. Unlike the Heyl Mishmar (Him), Hish was designed from the outset to be a mobile reserve capable of defensive operations anywhere in *Eretz Israel*. Hish replaced the Plugot Sadeh (Fosh) that had been based on similar tactical ideas but had been less carefully organized. Initially, Hish was supposed to be staffed by all Hagana members between the ages of eighteen and twenty-six; members aged twenty-six to thirty-four either served in Hish or in Him as local conditions required. This translated to an initial force of some eleven battalions with 7,800 men. Of the battalions, seven were stationed in cities, the others being held in rural areas. However, Hish forces were considerably weakened by the outbreak of World War II: many volunteered for service with the British armed forces while others were recruited into the Palmah. Thus, by 1945, Hish had been reduced to only 4,600 men, many of whom served on a part-time basis. Steadily reinforced thereafter, Hish was reorganized for the upcoming battle in late 1947. In February 1948, Hish strength rose to twenty-two battalions, organized into six brigades. These forces formed the main striking force of the Israeli army during the War of Independence. > see also: **War of Independence; Zva ha-Hagana le-Israel.**

Identification Card Issued By
the Irgun Zvai Leumi.
Authors' Collection via Mr. Isidore Baum

Irgun Zva'i Leumi (ארגון צבאי לאומי, IZL אצ״ל), "National Military Organization," underground movement founded in 1931 by dissident Hagana members and members of Betar. Initially, the dissidents only criticized the way the the Hagana was organized. They claimed that the association with the Histadrut, even if undertaken for security reasons, unnecessarily made the *Yishuv*'s defense appear partisan in nature. As the 1930s progressed, IZL members also criticized the Hagana's exclusively defensive doctrine. The Hagana was committed to a policy of not operating until an attack had begun, a policy that granted tactical initiative to Arab marauders. Instead, the IZL argued for a policy of anticipatory self-defense, if not outright retaliation in kind. When the Arab Revolt began, the IZL also began a policy of selective retaliation that split the movement. In 1937, some of the former Hagana members, who rejected retaliation, withdrew from the organization and returned to the Hagana (which, in the interim, had begun to advocate active defense). The IZL, now virtually an arm of the revisionist movement, continued on its path, advocating active defense and retaliation in kind. In 1937 the Irgun formed the Af-Al-Pi organization to promote "independent" *aliya*. Although the Hagana had always opposed dissident underground organizations, it did nothing to subvert the IZL's existence prior to the schism in 1937. Thereafter, concerted efforts were made to broker an agreement between the Hagana and IZL that would place the latter under the discipline of the former. The first such agreement collapsed in 1938, due to insistence by JA leaders that the IZL cease to function entirely. When World War II broke out, the Irgun declared a truce in its operations against the British, and Irgun members participated actively in all anti-Nazi operations of the *Yishuv*. The truce split the IZL, with members opposed to halting anti-British operations forming Lohame Herut Israel (Lehi). However, unlike the rest of the *Yishuv*, the IZL high command regarded its truce as only temporary; once it was clear that the Nazis had been defeated, the IZL felt it could act according to Jewish interests as it saw them. Therefore, in late 1944 the IZL high command issued orders for the resumption of military operations against the British. Coming on the heels of the assassination of Lord Moyne by Lehi members, the IZL's actions could only lead to conflict. The result was a systematic effort by the Hagana and Palmah to eliminate the IZL — the so-called Hunting Season. The policy of fighting the IZL was a failure that wasted considerable resources. In the spring of 1945 the Hunting Season was called off; by that autumn, the Hagana, Palmah, IZL, and Lehi were cooperating in Tnuat ha-Meri ha-Ivri. Again, however, differences in tactics and approaches led to dissension: after the IZL destroyed the British military headquarters located in the King David Hotel in Jerusalem in June 1946, the Hagana and Palmah suspended cooperation with the dissident organizations. The IZL continued to operate as an independent body until Israeli independence was declared. At that point, the IZl agreed to integrate all units, except those in Jerusalem, into the newly established Zva ha-Hagan le-Israel (Zahal). IZL entirely ceased to function after the near civil war that erupted during the so-called Altalena affair. All IZL units disbanded and the high command organized the Herut party. Commanders: Abraham Tehomi (1931–1937), David Raziel (1937–1941), Ya'akov Meridor (1942–1943), Menahem Begin (1943–1948).

Kol Israel (קול ישראל) "Voice of Israel," name of the Hagana's secret broadcasting network that began operation in 1940 as a form of protest against the land purchase restrictions imposed under the White Paper of 1939. Broadcasts were terminated for the duration of World War II after Italian entry into the war (June 1940) but were resumed on October 4, 1945. Although Kol Israel claimed to be broadcasting from one location, in fact, the clandestine radio broadcasts took place from many locations throughout the *Yishuv*: after a brief stay in one location the entire operation was packed up and moved elsewhere. By that means, Kol Israel was able to maintain operations throughout the period of revolt and never lost a broadcaster (or any equipment) to British police. In addition to the Hagana's broadcasts, the Irgun Zvai Leumi (IZL) and Lohame Herut Israel (Lehi) also had their own clandestine radio networks: Kol Herut Israel (IZL, 1939–1948) and Kol Zion ha-Lohemet (Lehi, 1941).

Lohame Herut Israel (לוחמי חרות ישראל, Lehi לח"י), "Fighters for the Freedom of Israel," splinter group of the IZL led by Abraham "Yair" Stern, which disagreed with the truce declared in 1940. Lehi's most controversial proposal during the Stern period was a 1940 offer of an alliance between Lehi and the Italian Fascists. Lehi members also attempted to contact the Germans with a proposal for support against the British. Given the Nazi attitude toward Jews, they never followed up on Lehi's proposals. As a result, Lehi remained at the fringes of the *Yishuv* while continuing its military campaign. Stern himslef was killed by British police detectives in April 1942, an act that shut down Lehi until late in 1943, when it was renewed. This "new" Lehi differed little from its predecessor; the organization still advocated action against the British to obtain a response that would spark a spontaneous *Yishuv*-wide revolt. Whereas Stern's Lehi had been more homogeneous ideologically, the new Lehi ran the gamut from far-right to far-left ideologies. Lehi's assassination of Lord Moyne, the British minister resident in Cairo, nearly sparked a *Yishuv*-wide civil war, but this action (the "Hunting Season") was mainly fought between the Hagana and Palmah against the Irgun. After World War II, Lehi came closer to the *Yishuv*'s center but was never a key player in the political or military events that unfolded. Lehi ceased to exist after the assassination of U.N. mediator Count Folke Bernadotte by individuals associated with the movement. A number of former Lehi members founded the short-lived Fighters party that was represented in the First Knesset, others integrated into the newly formed Herut Party, and others still joined a variety of left-wing parties, including the Israeli Communist party.

Mishmar ha-Am (משמר העם, MHA), "National Guard," volunteer paramilitary unit established in September 1947 by the Hagana's Jerusalem branch. MHA was formed on the assumption that the United Nations would terminate the British mandate; the personnel were needed to help keep order during the transition from British rule to Jewish sovereignty. MHA members were selected from those who could not otherwise serve in the Hagana. After the U.N. decision in November 1947, another MHA unit was mobilized in Haifa to help protect the port and other key facilities. In addition to policing duties, MHA members distributed rations during the siege of Jerusalem, helped to fortify Jewish neighborhoods, and evacuated civilians from combat zones. Its services were no longer needed after the War of Independence, and MHA was disbanded in 1949.

Mishmeret Zalahim ba-Gola (משמרת צלחים בגולה, MZB מצ"ב), "Crossing Guards of the Diaspora," name for the Hagana's European branches proposed by David Ben-Gurion in 1945. The name was meant to symbolize the identification between the *Yishuv* and Holocaust survivors while alos emphasizing the fact the MZB's main goal was the liquidation of communities in countries where Jewish life had been rendered tenuous. It is not clear whether the name was actually ever used. Hagana documents refer to members serving in Europe simply as members serving abroad and Jewish volunteers were identified as "foreign" draftees. > see also: **Giyus Hutz la-Aretz.**

Misrad Modi'in (משרד מודיעין, MM), "Information Service," semiclandestine intelligence service created by the Zionist Commission in 1918 to monitor developments in the Arab communities in *Eretz Israel*, Trans-Jordan, and Syria. MM also provided bodyguards for the Zionist Commission members and for High Commissioner Sir Herbert Samuel when he arrived. MM members were drawn from the veterans of the Nili spy ring, ha-Shomer, and the Jewish Legion. MM ceased to function when the Hagana was founded in 1920, although in 1929 the idea was revived as the Sherut Yediot. > see also: **World War I**; **Yishuv, Yishuv Organizations (Underground Organizations, Sherut Yediot)**.

Mossad le-Aliya Bet (מוסד לעליה ב'), "Agency for Aliya Bet," illegal immigration arm of the Hagana, founded in 1937 in response to increasing British restrictions on *aliya*. Although calls to organize a campaign of illegal immigration had been made within the *Yishuv* already during the 1920s, the JA and WZO leadership did not believe that the number of *olim* who could be brought in independently was worth the risk of creating a rift with the British. This policy of cooperation to attain maximum *aliya* peaked in 1935 and 1936 when *aliya* rates reached unprecedented highs. Thereafter, however, British reevaluations of conditions in the Middle East led to the imposition of a political maximum on legal *aliya*. At that point, the JA gave its approval for the creation of an organization to make *Aliya Bet* systematic. A minor player in illegal immigration during the 1930s, as compared to the revisionist organizations, the Mossad reached maturity during World War II. Despite the difficulties in obtaining ships and crews and in face of the dangers inherent in sea travel in a war zone, the Mossad's blockade runners became the only practical way to rescue some Jews from the Nazis. After the war, the Mossad became the core of an "*aliya* rebellion" that sought to force the British to either abandon the White Paper of 1939 or leave *Eretz Israel* altogether. > see also: **Aliya Bet**; **Mered ha-Aliya**.

Palavir (פלאוויר), acronym for Palmah Avir, the air section of the Palmah. Founded in 1944, the name was adopted in 1947. Acting as a fledgling air force for the soon-to-be created State of Israel, Palavir undertook a variety of missions. However, its initial order of battle was paltry: a handful of light liaison aircraft and a few transports without a single actual combat aircraft. In late May 1948 responsibility for the air service was transferred from the Palmah (which disbanded shortly thereafter) to Zva ha-Hagana le-Israel and Palavir became Heyl ha-Avir, Israel's air force. > see also: **Zva ha-Hagana le-Israel**.

Palmah (פלמ"ח), common name for the Plugot Mahatz — the Hagana commando companies. > see also: **Yishuv, Yishuv Organizations (Underground Organizations, Plugot Mahatz)**.

Peulot Meyuhadot (פעולות מיוחדות, POM, פו"ם), "Special Operations," Hagana commando unit established in 1939 and initially based in Haifa. POM was organized to undertake those missions that regular Hagana units were unable to accomplish: retaliations against Arab terrorists and (after May 17, 1939) operations to undermine the White Paper of 1939. POM members received special training in night operations and weapons use, especially demolitions. As the *Yishuv* prepared to rebel against the white paper in the summer of 1939, each regional Hagana command was supposed to establish its own POM unit. However, when World War II broke out, plans for rebellion were delayed and POM began to demobilize. During the invasion scare of 1940, POM veterans were used to form the cadre for the Palmah. > see also: **World War II**.

Plugat ha-Kotel (פלוגת הכתל, PHK), "The (Western) Wall Company," Betar defense unit in Jerusalem established in the 1920s. PHK was organized to defend Jewish worshipers at the Western Wall; at the time access to the holy site was restricted to an alley behind Arab-owned houses and worshipers were frequently stoned. PHK apparently existed independently of the Irgun Zvai Leumi (although some IZL members may have been recruited from PHK) and continued to operate throughout the *Yishuv*'s history. > see also: **Kotel ha-Ma'aravi**.

Plugot Mahatz (פלוגות מחץ), "Strike Companies," official name for the Hagana's commando units, better known by their acronym, Palmah (פלמ"ח). The Palmah was activated in response to the invasion scare of 1940. At the time, the Hagana had a barely adequate mobile reserve (the Heyl Sadeh, Hish), but feared that the *Yishuv*'s forces were not able to provide significant defense capabilities should the British withdraw more troops or, in the case of an absolute disaster, should they retreat from Egypt and Palestine/*Eretz Israel* altogether. As a result, in 1941, the Palmah was founded as a full-time operational reserve capable of offensive or defensive operations. The Palmah was intially organized into individual companies, a few of which were framed around linguistic specialization (e.g., the German Company). During 1941 and 1942, Palmah units participated in numerous joint operations with the British, including the high point of cooperation during the Allied invasion of Syria. As the Axis threat receded, so did cooperation with the British, but the Palmah remained a crucial part of the *Yishuv*'s defenses. In 1941–1942 the Palmah was organized into six companies with a total force of between five hundred fifty and a thousand personnel, of which almost 20 percent were women. Almost all Palmah members derived from socialist Zionist parties, and nearly half were *Kibbutz* members. After the war, the Palmah was reinforced, rising to 3,100 personnel in six battalions, and was given the additional task of overseeing the reception of *Ma'apilim*. This placed the Palmah into the forefront of the JA and WZO strategy of defiance against the British and made the Palmah the best-known of the underground movements. On the eve of independence, the Palmah was again enlarged, to 6,000 personnel in nine battalions that were organized into three brigades in early 1948. However, the politicized nature of the Palmah and the fact that most senior officers supported ha-Shomer ha-Zair and Ahdut ha-Avoda rather than Mapai made the Palmah's continued existence untenable. The provisional Israeli government desired to create a regular, nonpartisan army and could not accept the continuation of any "private armies." As a result, the Palmah high command was disbanded in 1948 and the brigades were integrated into Zva ha-Hagana le-Israel. Commanders: Yitzhak Sadeh (1941–1945), Yigal Alon (1945–1948). > see also: **World War II**; **Aliya Bet**; **War of Independence**; **Zva ha-Hagana le-Israel**.

Plugot Sadeh (פלוגות שדה, Fosh, פו"ש), national reserve force created by the Hagana in 1937. The Arab Revolt forced the Hagana high command to reevaluate its doctrine and organization. Previously, the Hagana had been committed to an exclusively defensive role and had relied on a loose local organization. Hagana units were, therefore, composed largely of local residents who defended the settlements they lived in. This system was inadequate for the magnitude of attacks during the revolt. At that point it became increasingly clear that local forces would need timely reinforcements or would be overwhelmed. Fosh was created to provide the Hagana with such a reserve. Additionally, Fosh units could operate in the field, in anticipatory self-defense by intercepting Arab bands before they opened an attack on settlements. In 1937–1938, Fosh also oversaw the operations of the joint Anglo-Jewish Special Night Squads. At its height Fosh numbered 2,500 personnel, organized into companies and platoons on an ad hoc basis. In 1939, Fosh was disbanded. Its place as a mobile reserve was then taken over by Heyl Sadeh (Hish) while its offensive potential was explored in the Palmah which was established during World War II. Sole commander: Yitzhak Sadeh. > see also: **Arab Revolt**.

Shai (ש"י), abbreviated name for the Hagana intelligence service, Sherut Yediot. The abbreviated name was more commonly used than the full name but was generally restricted to the Hagana's staff. > see also: **Yishuv, Yishuv Organizations (Underground Organizations, Sherut Yediot)**.

Sherut Yediot (שרות ידיעות), "Intelligence Service," official name for the Hagana's intelligence-gathering apparatus, more popularly known as Shai (ש"י) or Havazelet (חבצלת,

fleur-de-lis). Shai was founded in 1936, when the Hagana's Agaf ha-Aravi (אגף הערבי, the Arab branch) joined with the JA's research department and other secret bodies. Shai continued to develop throughout the Arab revolt and was fully organized in 1940, by which time it had incorporated all the intelligence-gathering sections of the Hagana. For official cover purposes, the JA maintained its research division as part of the Political Department. Shai's operations ran the gamut of information gathering. Additionally, Shai assisted the Mossad le-Aliya Bet, providing information and clandestine communications for the operation to rescue Jews from Nazi Europe. The close connection between Shai and the Mossad became so ingrained in the popular imagination after Israeli independence that most authors writing about Israel's intelligence network assume that the two were actually one organization. Shai's overall operations were undertaken by the General Department (המחלקה הכללית). In addition to Shai's general operations, three discrete branches existed to gain information on groups of special interest: ha-Agaf ha-Aravi (האגף הערבי, the Arab Branch), which was created in 1929 and was actually the first section of Shai established; ha-Mahlaka ha-Komunistit (המחלקה הקומוניסטית, the Communist Section), organized in 1942 and headed by David Arian to monitor Communist and pro-Soviet activities in the *Yishuv*; and ha-Mahlaka ha-Revisionistit (המחלקה הרוויזיוניסטית, the Revisionist Section), founded in 1942 and headed by Ze'ev Sharef to monitor the activities of ha-Zach, Betar, the Irgun Zvai Leumi, and Lohame Herut Israel. The latter section was especially active during the "Hunting Season." Furthermore, Shai was also responsible for counterintelligence and had a separate department for that purpose (מחלקה ריגול נגדי, Counterintelligence Department). Finally, Shai was also responsible for providing bodyguards for JA and WZO leaders. Given the secret nature of Shai's operations, its exact personnel rosters will probably never be known. Albeit,

it can fairly be said that Shai was a sophisticated intelligence apparatus that provided the *Yishuv*'s leaders with an important weapon: information.

Tenuat ha-Meri ha-Ivri (תנועת המרי העברי, TMI), "The (United) Hebrew Resistance Movement," official name for the short-lived coalition between the Hagana, Palmah, Irgun Zvai Leumi (IZL), and Lohame Herut Israel (Lehi) established in October 1945. TMI was formed to coordinate resistance activities after it became clear that the British would not concede on the Zionist demand that 100,000 Jewish Displaced Persons be admitted to Palestine/*Eretz Israel*. The coalition hoped to coordinate activities and thereby avoid clashes between the undergrounds. The very fact of creating TMI implied compromise by both sides: the Hagana and Palmah (and by implication the JAE and the WZO) recognized the legitimacy of IZL and Lehi operations, while the latter, at least in theory, recognized their subbordination to the national institutions. The coalition worked well initially, since the four groups specialized in different aspects of the struggle. However, these tactical differences also spelled TMI's undoing. When the IZL exploded a bomb in the British military headquarters in Jerusalem's King David Hotel, the negative publicity (due to the loss of civilian lives) and the forceful British response led the JAE and WZO to reconsider. Shortly thereafter, TMI split up and the underground movements resumed uncoordinated activities. > see also: **King David Hotel Incident**.

Va'ad ha-Hagana (ועד ההגנה, VH), "The Defense Committee," committee established within the Histadrut in 1920 to provide oversight for the newly founded Hagana. Although many members of the Hagana sought a nonpartisan organization, underground defense operations needed a cover and only the Histadrut could provide it. Still, suspicion remained that the Histadrut sought to control the Hagana for partisan purposes. This suspicion created a tense situation in the early 1930s and led to the creation of a parallel underground organization, the Irgun Zvai Leumi.

Va'ad ha-Keniot (ועד הקניות), "Purchasing Committee," civilian agency founded in January

1948 that oversaw the Hagana's finances and expenditures, mainly by coordinating equipment purchases. Given the ad hoc nature of purchases during the War of Independence, the committee had little impact on events. After the war, however, the committee was incorporated into the newly organized Ministry of Defense and provided manpower for that agency. Sole chairman: Pinhas Lubianker (Sapir).

Va'ad ha-Mathil (*ועד המתחיל*, VM), "Beginning Committee," entity created in January 1920 to coordinate *Yishuv* defense activities, mainly in the Galilee. Eight members — two each from ha-Shomer, the Jewish Legion, Ahdut ha-Avoda, and ha-Poel ha-Zair — met with Joseph Trumpeldor, who served as commander of Tel Hai and was (for all intents and purposes) responsible for defense of the threatened Galilee settlements. VM proposed the creation of an independent self-defense agency to be called the Hagana. This organization was created after the Arab attack on Tel Hai and the tepid British response to violence in Palestine/*Eretz Israel*. VM's proposal, however, was modified. For cover purposes the new Hagana was placed under the authority of the Histadrut, an act that would later spark considerable controversy.

Zva ha-Mahapeha (*צבא המהפכה*), "The Revolutionary Army," semiofficial name for the cadre units that provided reserves for the Irgun Zvai Leumi. These units were more commonly known by their acronym, ZAM (*צ"ם*). > see also: **Yishuv, Yishuv Organizations (Underground Organizations, Irgun Zvai Leumi)**.

Educational and Cultural Organizations

Agudat ha-Sofrim ha-Ivriim be-Eretz Israel (*אגודת הסופרים העבריים בארץ ישראל*), "Association of Hebrew Writers in Eretz Israel," cultural association dedicated to building the *Yishuv* by creating a new Jewish culture, established in Tel Aviv in 1921. The association provided an outlet for the publication of original works of Hebrew literature and sponsored lectures and symposia that displayed the work of *Yishuv* literary figures. The association helped to define the nature of the new culture being developed in the *Yishuv*. Key members included Haim Nahman Bialik and Shaul Tschernikowsky, both of whom served as presidents. Publication: *Moznayim* (monthly, 1931f).

Aliyat Yeladim va-No'ar (*ילדים עליית ונוער*, YA), "Youth Aliya," organization and movement for the immigration of young people, founded as Jüdische Jugendhilfe in 1932. Initially concentrating on German Jewish youth, YA was the brainchild of Recha Freier. In 1933 the YA idea became the central focus of Henrietta Szold and the Hadassah organization. YA's plan was to bring young people to *Eretz Israel*, provide them with vocational training, and thereby permit their permanent settlement. In all, YA was able to rescue some 30,000 Jewish children between 1933 and 1945. Activities continued after the war with displaced Jewish children (and indeed continue up to this day). YA was the only legal immigration permitted by the British during World War II.

Beit ha-Sefarim ha-Leumi veha-Universitai (*בית הספרים הלאומי והאוניברסיטאי*), "National and University Library," premier cultural institution now located on Hebrew University's Givat Ram campus and serving as the national repository for all printed matter of the Jewish people. The library was first founded in Jerusalem in 1892 as part of the local Bn'ai B'rith chapter. Responsibility for the library's functioning was transferred to the WZO in 1920 and was transferred again to Hebrew University in 1930. That same year, the library's first permanent home was built on Har ha-Zofim. The library moved to its current home after Israel's War of Independence.

Bezalel (*בצלאל*), art academy founded in Jerusalem in 1906 by Boris Schatz. Schatz was convinced that the only way to establish a Jewish national home was to revive Jewish culture and the only way to do that was to create an atmosphere conducive to all kinds of artistic endeavors by providing an arts and crafts education to talented students. By 1911, Bezalel had over 450 students and faculty working in studios in Jerusalem and in the Yemenite Quarter of Ben-Shemen. The school was forced to close down during World War I but reopened under WZO auspices in 1919. Financial difficulties forced another closure in 1929, but the school was revived again in 1935. It has been in continuous operation since then.

Brit ha-Hashmonaim (ברית החשמונאים, BHH), "Covenant of the Hashmoneans," religious scouting movement established in the mid-1930s as an auxiliary to Brit Yeshurun. Both movements were founded as front organizations for ha-Zach, which sought to influence religious Zionist youth toward a more activist orientation. Almost from its inception, BHH also served as a recruiting agency for the Irgun Zvai Leumi, a function for which it was particularly well suited.

Brit Yeshurun (ברית ישורון, BY), "Covenant of the Righteous," revisionist Zionist organization active among Orthodox Jewish youth in the *Yishuv*. Organized in the early 1930s as an auxiliary to Betar, it peaked in 1935 with 7,000 members. BY had an associated scouting movement called Brit ha-Hashmonaim, which attempted to instill an activist Zionist orientation in Orthodox youth. Both movements represented a concerted effort by ha-Zohar and ha-Zach to reach out to the religious community. The Revisionists could point to the many attitudes that they held in common with Mizrachi, in particular, relating to maximal territorial demands and to the idea that all Jews should immigrate without regard to their adaptibility to conditions in the *Yishuv*. Nonetheless, the revisionists' efforts came to nought as Mizrachi's leaders preferred to remain in a coalition with Mapai despite some glaring differences with that party on critical Zionist issues. > see also: **Organizations, Revisionist Zionist (International, Brit Trumpeldor); Historic Coalition.**

Daniel Sieff Research Institute (DSRI), scientific research institute established in Rehovot by the Sieff family in 1934. DSRI was directed by Chaim Weizmann and operated (until 1949) as part of the Hebrew University. In 1949 DSRI incorporated the

WZO's Agricultural Research Institute (also located in Rehovot) and became a university in its own right. In 1952 the new school was renamed in honor of Weizmann, henceforth being known as the Weizmann Institute for Science.

El-Al (אל-על), "Heavenward," revisionist Zionist fraternity active among students in the *Yishuv*'s two universities (Hebrew University in Jerusalem and the Technion in Haifa). El-Al paralleled the Yawne we-Yodphat fraternity among revisionist Zionist students in Belgium and may have been founded by graduates of that organization. Both were apparently founded in 1934. El-Al's members were closely associated with Abba Ahimeir and the entire organization may well have been a cover for his activities in Brit ha-Biryonim. > see also: **Yishuv, Yishuv Organizations (Underground Organizations, Brit ha-Biryonim).**

Hevrat Mahzirei Atara le-Yoshna (חברת מחזירי עטרה לישנה, HMAY), "Restorers of Ancient Glory," short-lived quasi-Zionist organization founded in 1870 by Rabbi Akiva Joseph Schlesinger to hasten the Messiah's arrival. Schlesinger believed that the Messiah's arrival could be speeded up if Jews began to work the land and resumed the daily use of Hebrew. To that end, HMAY advocated the creation of modern schools to teach Jewish youth farming techniques and to help revive the Hebrew language. Although Schlesinger was careful to couch his proposals in traditional terms (and his own commitment to Orthodox Judaism was unquestioned), HMAY was bitterly opposed by the leaders of the Ashkenazi community in Jerusalem and ceased to function after a few years.

Palestine Philharmonic Orchestra (PPO), all-Jewish musical ensemble established in Tel Aviv in 1936. Created at the initiative of Bronislaw Huberman, PPO was designed to provide artistic opportunities to Jewish musicians fleeing persecution in Central and Eastern Europe. PPO's first season commenced in December 1936; the first conductor was Arturo Toscanini. Representing a great leap forward in musical culture in the *Yishuv*, PPO was rapidly recognized as one of the finest orchestras in the world. Additionally,

PPO served a critical educational role, training native Israeli musicians to a degree that would otherwise have been impossible in the *Yishuv*. Between founding and 1948, PPO toured widely. In 1948, PPO changed its name to the Israel Philaharmonic Orchestra, but its reputation remains untarnished to this day.

Shivat ha-Heresh ve-ha-Masger (שיבת החרש והמסגר), "Return of the Plough and the Smith," agency founded in 1882 by Bilu members in Jerusalem to offer vocational training to new *olim*. Although Bilu was oriented toward Jewish national rebirth via a mass return to the soil, realities in the *Yishuv* during the First Aliya soon made it obvious that no future development of a Jewish national home could happen unless Jews also acquired the skills needed to support an active economy. As a result Shivat ha-Heresh sought to to obtain apprenticeships with Jewish artisans in Jerusalem for new *olim*.

Social, Service, and Immigrant Organizations

Agudat ha-Tayasim (אגודת הטייסים), "The Pilots Association," friendly society founded in 1939 by the ten licensed Jewish pilots then living in *Eretz Israel*. The association was the culmination of aviation clubs founded as early as 1926 and was dedicated to raising the *Yishuv*'s awareness of aviation related-issues. Officially nonpolitical, the association was in reality a front for the Hagana. It operated as a legal way to obtain flight training for a cadre of young *Yishuv* members who would later form the core of the Hagana's air service. > see also: **Yishuv, Yishuv Organizations (Underground Organizations, Aviron).**

Agudat Poalim (אגודת פועלים, AP), "Workers' Association," friendly society established in Rishon le-Zion in 1887. Created by agricultural workers in the Rothschild-sponsored settlement, AP had two major goals: to provide social and financial aid for needy workers and to provide vocational training to new *olim*. AP participated in the settlers' strike against Rothschild's administrators in 1887–1888,

but disappeared after the strike collapsed.

American Zionist Medical Unit (AZMU), humanitarian aid organization created in 1916 by Hadassah, the Women's Zionist Organization of America. AZMU operated under the joint auspices of Hadassah, the WZO, and the Zionist Organization of America. AZMU was established to help stabilize the medical situation in the *Yishuv* during a period of great stress. Epidemics of cholera and typhus fever were worsened by the fact that much of the trained Jewish medical personnel in the *Yishuv* were deported by the Turks due to their foreign (mainly Russian) citizenship. Because the United States was still neutral, it was hoped that the Turks would permit AZMU to enter *Eretz Israel* and begin work. Indeed, it should be noted that Turkey's allies, Germany and Austria-Hungary, provided AZMU with the passes necessary to ensure safe passage through the North Atlantic. This plan nevertheless proved abortive since the Turks demurred and America entered the war in April 1917. AZMU was therefore unable to begin operating until the British completed their conquest of the country. Officially, AZMU began to function on August 17, 1918. At its height AZMU numbered forty-four American medical personnel augmented by local volunteers. In November 1918, AZMU was incorporated into the Hadassah Medical Organization and ceased to function separately.

Bnai Binyamin (בני בנימין, BB), "Sons of Benjamin," fraternal organization founded in 1921 by descendents of Jews who had settled in *Eretz Israel* during the First and Second Aliyot. BB was named in honor of Baron Edmund de Rothschild, whose Hebrew name was Benjamin and who was the patron of the earliest Zionist settlements. In addition to its social functions, BB operated as a contractor in the agricultural sector, facilitating improvements in infrastructure and building housing for members who moved to new settlements. Among others, BB helped to build Nes Ziona, Even Yehuda, Herzliya, and Netanya. During the 1930s, BB also operated ha-Notaiah, the *Yishuv*'s largest plantation cooperative. BB was crippled by the White Paper of 1939 and shut down completely during World War II.

Ha-Kibbutz ha-Meuhad (הקיבוץ המאוחד, HKHM), "The United Kibbutz (Movement)," federation of collective settlements founded in 1927 to foster growth in the agricultural sector of the *Yishuv*'s economy while also providing coordinated action to absorb new *olim*. HKHM was identified with the parties that eventually merged into Mapai but was always associated with the party's left wing. This translated into a narrower socialist focus and included uncompromising opposition to the revisionist Zionists and emphasis on *Halutzic Aliya*. During the 1940s HKHM openly associated with Mapai's *Siya Bet*; when the latter withdrew from Mapai in 1944, HKHM followed suit. However, since HKHM was designed as a loose federation, individual members and individual *Kibbutzim* were permitted to maintain party affiliations as they saw fit. In January 1948, HKHM was one of the factors that facilitated the merger of Ahdut ha-Avoda, ha-Shomer ha-Zair, and Poale Zion Smol into Mifleget ha-Poalim ha-Meuhad (Mapam). Thereafter, however, a large percentage of HKHM members and *Kibbutzim* withdrew to reaffiliate themselves with Mapai.

Ha-Tnua ha-Meuhedet (התנועה המאוחדת), "The United (Youth) Movement," popular name for the unified socialist Zionist youth movement created in 1945 by the merger of Gordonia and Maccabi ha-Zair. Designed to cater to youths between the ages of ten and eighteen, the movement was involved in a wide range of educational and social activities. Additionally, it provided paramilitary training for older members, many of whom later joined the Palmah. Ideologically, the movement was close to Mapai and the Hever ha-Kvutzot. Membership peaked at 2,775 in 1945 but fluctuated considerably due to repeated schisms and mergers. In March 1947, the movement founded its first *Kibbutz*, at Ma'ayan Baruch near the Lebanese border.

Ha-Va'ad Lema'an ha-Hayal (הועד למען החייל), "The Committee for the Soldier," social service agency founded in 1940 to offer services to *Yishuv* personnel then serving with the British armed forces. The committee was not officially recognized by the Royal Army until 1943, by which time most Jewish units had moved out of the *Yishuv*. Nonetheless, committee volunteers followed these units during their operational trek across North Africa and into Italy and Europe. The committee also served as a liaison between Jewish units, the British authorities, and local Jewish communities (such as they were) attempting to reconstitute themselves after liberation. > see also: **World War II**.

Hever ha-Kvutzot (חבר הקבוצות, HHK), "League of Collective Settlements," union of smaller *Kibbutzim*, associated with the Gordonia youth movement and with Mapai. HHK was founded in 1931 and operated parallel to ha-Kibbutz ha-Meuhad. In the main, it offered assistance to smaller collective settlements (distinguished by the name *Kvutzot*, a distinction that no longer pertains). HHK did not withdraw from Mapai when *Siya Bet* and ha-Kibbutz ha-Meuhad did in 1944.

Histadrut ha-Sefaradim be-Eretz Israel (הסתדרות הספרדים בארץ ישראל, HSBI), "Union of Sephardi Jews in Eretz Israel," friendly society of Sephardi *olim* founded in 1920 to promote greater WZO attention to the needs of Sephardim and to the potential support to be gained for the *Yishuv* among Jews of Spanish descent in Europe and the Middle East. HSBI wanted to play a more prominent role within the Zionist movement and the *Yishuv*. To that end, in 1925, HSBI organized a subsidiary political party (the first ethnic party in the *Yishuv*) that ran for elections to Assefat ha-Nivharim. In the same year, HSBI organized the World Federation of Sephardi Jewry, a diaspora organization linking Sephardim worldwide. Although partly successful in its endeavors, many members felt (with some justification) that the WZO leadership was too preoccupied with European Jewish communities. The large-scale destruction of European Sephardi communities during the Holocaust and the mass *aliya* of Jews from the Middle East after 1948 changed conditions considerably. However, HSBI did not survive the transition, its political wing being absorbed into Mapai during the 1950s.

Hitahdut ha-Ikarim (התאחדות האכרים, HHI), "The Farmers' Federation," union of smallholders and farmers founded in 1926 but tracing its roots back to the First Aliya. HHI represented the *Moshav* population in a way that paralleled the *Kibbutz* movements: acting as a lobbying group to protect the interests of private farmers and as a cooperative providing financial and technical assistance to members in need. Although officially nonpartisan, HHI gravitated toward the center-right on most Zionist issues during the prestate era. This was particularly evident during the conflict between the Histadrut and Betar during the early 1930s over accusations that Betar was providing scab workers and strikebreakers during labor conflicts between the Histadrut and HHI member farms.

Hitachdut Olei Czechoslovakia (התאחדות עולי צ׳כוסלובקיה, HOC, הע״צ), "Association of Czech Immigrants," friendly society founded in 1939. During the war HOC coordinated its activities with the rescue committee of the Jewish Agency. HOC later merged with Hitachdut Olei Germania to form Irgun Olei Merkaz Europa.

Hitachdut Olei Germania (התאחדות עולי גרמניה, HOG, הע״ג), "Association of German Immigrants," friendly society founded in 1932. From 1933 on, HOG operated as an immigrant aid and absorption agency, closely coordinating its activities with the JA and the Va'ad Le'umi. Increasingly politicized after 1935, HOG dovetailed into the unsuccessful Achdut ha-Am party in 1938.

Igud ha-Hayalim ha-Meshuchrarim (איגוד החיילים המשוחררים), "Organization of ex-Servicemen," self-help agency founded by veterans of the Jewish Brigade Group in Italy in February 1944. The Igud's main tasks were to help veterans find housing and jobs to ease their reentry into civilian life after the war. In 1945, the Igud was a founding member of the International Organization of Jewish Soldiers and Veterans. > see also: **World War II.**

Kibbutz Arzi (קיבוץ ארצי, KA), "National Federation of Collective Settlements,"

nationwide federation of *Kibbutzim* associated with ha-Shomer ha-Zair, founded in 1927. KA strongly supported the concept of ideological collectivism then popular with the Zionist left. As a result, all KA affiliated *Kibbutzim* had to accept a few basic premises: collective ownership of all goods in the *Kibbutz*; collective parenting for children; instituting safeguards for the "organic" nature of each settlement by banning any outside labor; and limitations on the number of members permitted to join each *Kibbutz*. In addition, all member *Kibbutzim* were to maintain and foster the organization's positive attitude toward the Soviet Union. Since 1948, KA has been a major source of support for Mifleget ha-Poalim ha-Meuhad (Mapam).

Kupat Holim (קופת חולים, KH), "Sick Fund," Zionist health maintenance and insurance organization established in 1911. Previously, each socialist Zionist party had its own health fund, with these funds merging with KH in 1920. Thereafter, KH operated as a Histadrut subsidiary, with all members automatically enrolled. KH operated on the basis of local health clinics whose staff were also Histadrut employees. Membership was 2,000 in 1920 but rose steadily, to 100,000 in 1941 and an estimated 500,000 in 1948. In 1931 an agreement between KH and the JAE provided automatic KH membership for all new *olim*, thereby guaranteeing their basic health care. KH continues to operate clinics throughout Israel. > see also: **Yishuv, Yishuv Organizations (Political Parties and Organizations, Histadrut).**

Kupat Holim le-Ovdim Leumiim (קופת חולים לעובדים לאומיים, KHOL), "Sick Fund for Nationalist Workers," health insurance organization founded in 1933 to cover all workers who were not Histadrut members. In practice that meant only members of Histadrut ha-Ovdim ha-Leumiim, an arm of the revisionist movement in the *Yishuv*. Unlike the Histadrut's Kupat Holim, KHOL operated purely as a health insurance provider: patients selected their own doctors who were reimbursed for their services by the organization. Despite intense pressure to merge with the central Kupat Holim, KHOL has remained since founding.

Kupat Poale Eretz Israel (קופת פועלי ארץ ישראל, KPEI, קפא"י), "Fund for Workers in the Land of Israel," friendly society founded in 1910 by the World Union of Poale Zion. KPEI functioned to assist members in *aliya* and settlement, mainly by providing them with the financial resources to purchase land, build houses, and obtain necessary supplies. KPEI's most important single accomplishment was building Shchunat Borochov near (now part of) Tel Aviv. In 1925, KPEI transferred all its assets to the Histadrut and ceased to function. > see also: **Yishuv, Yishuv Organizations (Political Parties and Organizations, Histadrut).**

La-Asirenu (לאסירנו), "For Our Prisoners," public service body dedicated to helping members of the *Yishuv* incarcerated in British prisons for security offenses. Founded as a private venture in 1945, the agency received financial sponsorship from the Va'ad Leumi after June 29, 1946 (better known in *Eretz Israel* as "Shabbat ha-Shahor"). La-Asirenu dealt with prisoners' personal needs and eschewed any political involvements. Sole director: Simcha Even-Zohar. > see also: **Shabbat ha-Shahor.**

Legion ha-Avoda (לגיון העבודה), "Workers' Legion," paramilitary group founded by Israel Shohat in 1909 and operating parallel to ha-Shomer. Shohat felt that ha-Shomer's focus on defense matters was too narrow. Instead, he felt that Jewish laborers should conquer both defense and labor simultaneously. Although operating parallel to ha-Shomer, the legion was not really a competitor. The two groups co-operated in founding at least two *Kibbutzim* in 1909 and 1910. > see also: **Yishuv, Yishuv Organizations (Underground Organizations, ha-Shomer).**

Magen David Adom (מגן דוד אדום, MDA), "Red Star of David," emergency health service agency founded in Tel Aviv in 1930. In the aftermath of the Arabs riots of 1929 it was discovered that emergency services in the *Yishuv* were inadequate. MDA hoped to address that situation by equipping ambulances to offer immediate first aid in cases of natural disasters or intercommunal

violence. After the Tel Aviv chapter proved successful, the idea was copied throughout the *Yishuv*, leading to the establishment of a national MDA in 1935. During the Arab Revolt MDA proved its worth, acting as an auxiliary to the Hagana. Authority for MDA was transferred to the civil defense network during World War II but reverted to the Hagana in time for the War of Independence. In 1948, MDA operated sixteen local branches staffed by doctors, nurses, and other medical professionals. After the War of Independence, MDA was transferred back to civilian authority, under whose auspices it still operates today.

Palästine Treuhandstelle (Paltreu), "Palestine Trust and Transfer Company," the agency that oversaw the Ha'avara agreement. > see also: **Ha'avara.**

Pidyon Shevuyim (פדיון שבויים), "Redemption of Captives," fund created in 1938 by the Va'ad Leumi to assist with Aliyat ha-Noar. For technical reasons, the fund was not overwhelmingly successful and was terminated at the outbreak of World War II.

Rural and Urban Settlement Corporation (Rassco), arm of the Keren ha-Yesod created in 1934 to assist in the immigration and absorption of thousands of German Jews. Rassco's principle activity was offering loans, often in conjuction with other agencies, to help new *olim* buy homes or begin new businesses. Rassco continued to operate, under ever changing circumstances, until the early 1950s. > see also: **World Zionist Organization, Subsidiary Agencies (Keren ha-Yesod).**

Tnuat ha-Moshavim (תנועת המושבים, THM), "The Moshav Movement," federation of non-collective farms established in 1931. THM represented the interests of smallholders on agricultural settlements. These individiuals were not socialists but were not inherently opposed to Mapai. THM organized more effectively after its second national conference, held in 1925; thereafter, growth was steady. In addition to representing the settlements before national institutions, THM provided financial and other assistance to its members. Prestate membership peaked in 1946 with 9,000 settlers in fifty-five *Moshavim*, but THM has continued to grow since the establishment of the State of Israel.

Miscellaneous Organizations

Mekorot Water Company (MWC), national corporation founded in 1937 as a co-operative venture of the JA, Keren Kayemet le-Israel, Keren ha-Yesod, and the Histadrut. MWC was tasked with developing, improving, and distributing the *Yishuv*'s water resources as well as conserving those resources for the future. Prior to the establishment of the State of Israel, MWC operated mostly on a local or regional basis. MWC's major projects prior to 1948 were irrigation programs in the Jezreel and Bet Shean valleys (completed, respectively, in 1937 and 1944). After Israeli independence, MWC was tasked with building the National Water Carrier system.

Palestine Airways (PA), airline incorporated in London during December 1934 as a subsidiary of British Imperial Airways. The founders hoped that PA would employ Jewish and British pilots as a way to build an aviation industry in the *Yishuv*. In fact, when PA began to operate (in 1937), only British pilots were employed. Flights were supposed to leave from and arrive at the airport in Lod (Lydda, now the Ben-Gurion International Airport), but the Arab Revolt rendered that location insecure. As a result, most flights originated or ended at the Sde Dov airport in north Tel Aviv. PA aircraft were appropriated in 1940 by the Royal Air Force and Sde Dov was supposed to be closed down. The airport later became the center for Sherut Avir activities. > see also: **Yishuv, Yishuv Orgainzations (Underground Movements, Palavir)**.

Palestine Broadcasting Service (PBS), radio station that began broadcasting from Jerusalem in April 1936. Administered by a British director, PBS was divided into Hebrew, English, and Arabic departments, in addition to a musical section. In 1948, PBS was incorporated into the Israeli Broadcasting Service.

Palestine Electric Corporation (PEC), first public utility in modern Palestine/*Eretz Israel*, established in 1923 at Pinhas Rutenberg's initiative. Electrification of mandatory Palestine/*Eretz Israel* began shortly after PEC's incorporation on March 29, 1923. Initially, one generating plant was set up in Tel Aviv, providing electricity to Tel Aviv and Jaffa. In 1925, two further plants were opened: one in Haifa and one in Tiberias. a final plant, at Mahanayim was built in 1932 and used hydroelectric power drawn from the Yarmuk River. With this plant's opening, the entire *Yishuv* was electrified. The Mahanayim plant was destroyed by the Trans-Jordanian Arab Legion during the War of Independence, but PEC continued to operate, being incorporated into the Israeli government.

Yishuv ha-Aretz [ישוב הארץ, H] "Settling the Land": Traditional Hebrew term for the commandment to settle in *Eretz Israel*. Despite considerable rabbinic debate over the term's precise religious and legal significance, the term's historical import is clear. The concept testifies to the traditional Jewish hope for redemption and restoration during the long years of the diaspora. > see also: **Shivat Zion; Zion.**

Yishuv Oved [ישוב עובד, H] "Working Settlement": Term used during and shortly after World War I for the orientation in the WZO and its affiliated organs after socialist Zionism began to dominate the Zionist movement. In this version of Zionist thought, the WZO's goal was the creation of a labor-oriented community that was settled on the soil and undertook agricultural work as its means of eventually creating a Jewish national home and, after an unspecified era of "organic" growth, a Jewish state. This concept dovetailed nicely into gradualist positions then accepted by the WZO's majority and led to some controversy (most notably with the nascent revisionist Zionist movement) during the 1920s. > see also: **Gradualism; Agricultural Settlement(s); Halutzic Aliya; Constructive Socialism;**

Yom ha-Azma'ut [יום העצמאות, H] "Independence Day": The anniversary of Israel's independence, celebrated on 5 Iyyar (usually late April or early May) as the declaration of Israel's independence took place on that day in the Hebrew year 5708 (equating to May 14, 1948.

Yom ha-Pekuda [יום הפקודה, H] "Command Day": Popular term for the day after the White Paper of 1939 was published, May 18, 1939. The day was supposed to be dedicated to the beginning of Jewish protests against the new British policy but passed quietly. The most important single anti-British act undertaken on that day was a census of all military-age men in the *Yishuv*, the purpose being to prepare for the eventuality of conscription within the *Yishuv* should violent clashes (a revolt being planned for the early autumn) erupt.

Yom ha-Zikaron le-Hallalei Zahal [יום הזכרון לחללי צה"ל, H] "Memorial Day for IDF Fallen": Official memorial day in the State of Israel to commemorate the deaths of all individuals — both before and after 1948 — who gave their lives on behalf of the Jewish State. The day, generally 4 Iyyar (late April or early May), is one day before Yom ha-Azma'ut. Yom ha-Zikaron is commemorated as a solemn day on which all places of entertainment are closed. > see also: **Yom ha-Azmaut**.

Yom Kippur Letter [HT]: popular name for the statement issued to the American Jewish community by President Harry S. Truman in October 1946. Although this was not the first presidential letter to the Jewish community, it came at a time of substantial tension over *Eretz Israel* and the fate of Jewish Displaced Persons (DPs) in Europe and was thus guaranteed considerable prominence. The letter expressed the president's sympathy with the DPs and his hope that they would soon find a secure haven. Mentioning the issue of Palestine/*Eretz Israel*, Truman did not directly support the Zionist position but did not reject it either. Although the letter caused considerable consternation in the Zionist camp, it was particularly disappointing to the British. The Atlee government had hoped to coopt Truman into supporting continued British rule and maintenance of the white paper restrictions on *aliya*. While overstating Truman's commitment to Zionism, the British cabinet viewed the statement as unequivocal. As a result, Foreign Minister Ernest Bevin tried one last gambit, threatening to refer the issue to the United Nations. > see also: **Hershel Ish-Emet; United Nations**.

Zabar [צבר, H] "Sabra": Hebrew term for the prickly pear, a fruit of cactus plants native to the Middle East that is commonly used to identify native-born Israelis. The term serves a dual role of emphasizing the natives' concrete connection with the Land of Israel while also telling about their self-view of their nature. Like the cactus fruit, the Sabra is said to have a rough (and gruff) exterior but a sweet and soft interior. > see also: **Oleh.**

Zeeland Program [GN]: Economic plan for *Yishuv* development formulated in 1920 by Louis D. Brandeis during his return trip from the London conference. The Zeeland Program called for intensive investment in the *Yishuv* by Jewish small businessmen who would be induced to immigrate after their investments began to show a profit. The plan became part of the Brandeis-Weizmann dispute, as it represented a fundamental difference of opinion about how to develop the Jewish national home in both the long and short terms. The Zeeland Program was never implemented; the Weizmann faction that sought intensive and collective agricultural development defeated Brandeis's followers after a bitter struggle. Nevertheless, much industrial development did take place during the Fourth Aliya (1924–1929), which was composed of small businessmen immigrating from Eastern Europe. > see also: **Brandeisists.**

Ze'evim [זאבים, H/PN] "Wolves": Postwar Hagana code term for members of Betar, the revisionist Zionist youth movement. The name derives from Betar's founder, Ze'ev Jabotinsky, and may also be translated "Ze'ev's Followers." The term was apparently not part of general Hagana usage and may have been limited to *Briha* and the Mossad le-Aliya Bet. > See also: **Organizations, Zionist (International, Betar).**

Zevulun [PN]: Hagana and Mossad le-Aliya Bet code name used in 1946–1948 to designate: (1) A radio operator's course conducted during the winter of 1946–1947 for Gid'onim who escorted the Mossad's blockade runners on the journey across the Mediterranean. Held at a Mossad safe house in a suburb of Marseilles, France, the course comprised thirteen trainees who spent three months studying their trade. (2) The same term was used in 1948 for a safe house in Marseilles where volunteers for the Israeli army from North Africa stayed until they could be transferred to Israel. (3) In 1948, a short form of the term, Zevu, was used to designate the radio network operated by former members of the Armée Juive on behalf of the Hagana. The radio network transmitted information to Jewish communities in Algeria, Tunisia, and Morocco. > see also: **Yishuv, Yishuv Organizations (Underground Organizations, Mossad le-Aliya Bet); Aliya Bet; World War II, Jewish Military Units (Armée Juive); Giyus Hutz la-Aretz; Zva ha-Hagana le-Israel.**

Zion [ציון, H]: One of the traditional names for Jerusalem and, more broadly, for *Eretz Israel*. The exact origins are unknown, but its identification with Jerusalem (or with parts thereof) can be traced back to the prophetic era. The term occurs frequently in biblical poetry, for instance, in the citation "Daughter of Zion" (Isaiah 1:8). In some texts Zion is identified with the Solomonic Temple or with the Temple Mount. Regardless of the specificity of the usage, the term is laden with restorationist overtones and its repeated use in Jewish prayers testifies to the longing for a return to *Eretz Israel* during the extended exile. This restorationist overtone is most clearly seen in the term "Zionism," the political movement dedicated to returning Jews to their national home. > see also: **ha-Aretz**; **Shivat-Zion**; **Zionut**.

Zionei Zion [ציוני ציון, H] "Zionists for Zion": Nickname adopted in 1904 by Zionists who opposed the policy endorsed by WZO president Theodor Herzl during the Uganda affair. These Zionists felt that the Jewish nation could only be restored in its ancestral homeland; any other territory accepted by the WZO, even as a "temporary haven," was unacceptable. Spanning the spectrum of Zionist groups, *Zionei Zion* were united in their opposition to the WZO accepting any form of territorialist solution, an issue that became moot when the Jewish Territorialist Association withdrew from the WZO in 1905. > see also: **Uganda Plan**.

Zioniburo [HT]: Cable address for the London offices of the JA, based on condensing the two words Zionist Bureau. The London bureau did not function as an independent agency but acted in close coordination with the JAE in Jerusalem and the JA's consultative office in New York. The bureau was institutionally separate from the English Zionist Federation even though the two shared many common members. > see also: **Sochnut Yehudit**.

Zionist Leadership

1. Scope and Definition

As an organized entity, the Jewish community long predated the modern era. Whether in the context of a *Kehila*, Gemeinde, synagogue, or community, Jewish leadership has always played a primary role in securing Jewish rights, Jewish status, and — in times of dire emergency — Jewish lives. In modern times, as communal bonds weakened, membership in the Jewish community ceased to be mandatory; nevertheless, the community's role, especially the leaders' role, in securing the Jewish future took on even greater significance. In the modern era, however, Jewish leadership has only rarely been unified; throughout the nineteenth and twentieth centuries, no issue proved more divisive than Zionism. The following entry provides a thumbnail sketch of the most significant Zionist leaders of the last century. > see also: **Organizations**; **Yishuv**.

2. Major Zionist Leaders

Aaronson, Aaron (1876–1919): Agronomist and member of a leading pioneer family in *Eretz Israel*. His father, Efraim Fishel Aaronson, was one of the founders of Zichron Ya'akov. During World War I, Aaronson and associates (including his brother and sister) founded the Nili spy ring to assist the British. After the war, Aaronson served as an adviser to the Zionist delegation at the Paris Peace Conference. While returning to England, Aaronson's airplane crashed and he was killed.

Agnon, Shmuel Yosef (Czaczkes, 1888–1970): Israeli novelist. Born in Galicia, Agnon settled in *Eretz Israel* in 1907 and published his first collection of short stories in 1912. It was then that he adopted his pen name. Agnon traveled to Berlin in 1913 and remained there until 1924, when he returned permanently to *Eretz Israel*. Agnon's writings reflected his commitment to Jewish tradition, and were laced with allusions to biblical and rabbinic literature. His major themes were Jewish life in the diaspora (mainly Galicia) and in the old and new *Yishuv*. His works have been widely translated and Agnon won the Nobel Prize for literature in 1966.

Ahad ha-Am (pseud., Asher Ginsburg, 1856–1927): Father of spiritual Zionism. Ginsburg's Zionist orientation derived from Russian populism, a fact reflected in his choice of pseudonyms. His populism led him to emphasize the need for Jewish spiritual, cultural, and intellectual rebirth, rather than for Jewish political sovereignty. In this he differed considerably from the mainstream of Herzlian Zionists of his era. Ahad ha-Am's ideological orientation led him to advocate the creation of a cultural center in *Eretz Israel*, where a select group of *halutzim* would work and become the focal point for the entire Jewish world.

Allon, Yigal (1918–1980): Labor Zionist leader and military commander. Born in Kfar Tabor (lower Galilee), Allon joined the Hagana as a youth and rose rapidly through the ranks. From 1945 to 1948, he commanded the Palmah. Elected to the Knesset in 1954, he later served in a variety of cabinet posts.

Alterman, Nathan (1910–1970): Israeli poet and feuilletonist, best known for satirical poetic commentaries on key political and diplomatic events. Born in Warsaw, he immigrated in 1925 and settled in Tel Aviv. Ideologically close to Mapai, Alterman used "Tor ha-Shvi'i" (the "Seventh Column"), his regular contribution in *Davar*, as a pulpit to comment on events and their meaning.

Amichai, Yehuda (b. 1924): Israeli poet and novelist. Born in Germany, he arrived in *Eretz Israel* via Youth Aliya in 1936. His writings have incorporated the Israeli experience from World War II through the War of Independence.

Amiel, Moshe A. (1883–1946): Rabbi and communal leader. Born in Poland, Amiel served as a rabbi in Antwerp prior to his appointment as chief rabbi of Tel Aviv in 1936. His main contribution as chief rabbi was the creation of a network of modern Orthodox schools in the Tel Aviv area.

Arlosoroff, Haim (1899–1933): Mapai leader and theorist, author of the book, *Das Jüdische Volkssozialismus*, in which he developed a theory of "constructive" (non-Marxist) socialism for *Yishuv* development. From 1929 to 1933, Arlosoroff headed the JA Political Department and was thus responsible for Zionist foreign policy. Arlosoroff was one of the negotiators of the Ha'avara agreement. He was killed by unknown assailants (members of Brit ha-Biryonim being suspected) on June 16, 1933.

Aronson, Solomon (1862–1935): Rabbi and religious Zionist leader. Serving as chief rabbi of Kiev between 1906 and 1921, Aronson was the founding leader of the Mizrachi movement in Ukraine. After the Bolshevik takeover, Aronson briefly led a Zionist underground in the country, but he was forced to flee in 1921, first to Berlin and then to *Eretz Israel*. Between 1922 and 1936 he served as chief rabbi of Tel Aviv and continued his active participation in Mizrachi.

Assaf, Simha (1889–1953): Israeli Talmudist and jurist. Assaf headed a yeshiva in Odessa prior to his *aliya* in 1921. Settling in Jerusalem, Assaf taught at Hebrew University, later becoming rector. He served as a member of the Israeli Supreme Court between 1948 and 1953.

Bambus, Willi (1863–1904): Proto-Zionist organizer and activist. Bambus was one of the founders of the Esra Verein, which assisted the settlements founded by Bilu. However, Bambus opposed Herzl's Political Zionism. After the Esra Verein transferred its activities to the WZO, Bambus cofounded the non-Zionist Hilfsverein der deutschen Juden.

Baratz, Joseph (1890–1968): Labor Zionist leader. Born in Kamenets, Ukraine, Baratz settled in *Eretz Israel* in 1906. He was one of the founders of Degania. Active in ha-Poel ha-Zair and Mapai, he served in a number of capacities in the party and the Histadrut. He headed the first Histadrut delegation to the United States in 1921. From 1940 to 1963, he served as chairman of the Soldiers' Aid Committee.

Bar-Ilan, Meir (1880–1949): Russian born leader of the Mizrachi movement, originally known as Meir Berlin. In 1926 he Hebraized his name, adopting Bar-Ilan. That same year, he settled in Jerusaelm and was elected president of the World Mizrachi Union. A staunch supporter of Mizrachi's efforts to create a Jewish national home based on *Halacha*, Bar-Ilan nonetheless supported the party's coalition with Mapai. Notwithstanding support for this coalition, Bar-Ilan was a maximalist in political terms: he opposed partition and was one of the earliest supporters of statehood.

Barth, Aharon (1890–1957): Israeli banker and religious Zionist leader. Born in Berlin, Barth was active in Mizrachi from youth. A lawyer by training, from 1921 to 1938 he served as WZO attorney. Settled in *Eretz Israel* in 1933; in 1946, he was appointed chairman of the Bet Din ha-Kongress (the WZO court) and in 1947, of the Anglo-Palestine Bank (which changed its name to Bank Leumi in 1951). He remained at that latter position until his death.

Bartov, Hanoch (b. 1926): Israeli novelist. Born in Petah Tikva, Bartov served in the Jewish Brigade Group during the Italian Campaign in World War II. His novels have incorporated the experience of Jews at war and particularly, the pathos of Jewish soldiers from *Eretz Israel* meeting the She'erit ha-Pleta. > see also: **World War II**.

Begin, Menachem (1913–1992): revisionist Zionist leader and sixth prime minister of the State of Israel. Born in Brest-Litovsk, Begin became a leader of Betar in Poland and began a career as a lawyer prior to World War II. Escaping to Soviet territory from Nazi-occupied Warsaw, Begin joined the Polish armed forces in the USSR. He deserted when the force reached Palestine/ *Eretz Israel*. In 1943 he assumed command of the Irgun Zvai Leumi (IZL) and began its revolt against the British in 1944. Strongly opposed to partition, Begin continued to advocate Ze'ev Jabotinsky's idea of a Jewish state on both sides of the Jordan River. Although he opposed the policies of the Israeli provisional government, which he defined as minimalist, Begin agreed to accept its orders in 1948. After the Altalena affair, Begin agreed to disband the IZL, converting the organization into the Herut party. He served in the Knesset from 1949 onward, being

elected prime minister in 1977. In 1979 he signed the historic peace treaty with Egypt.

Bein, Alex (1903–1988): Israeli archivist and historian. Bein was educated in Germany and served on the staff of the German State Archives until 1933. Dismissed from his position by the Nazis, he migrated to *Eretz Israel* where he became the founder and first head of the Central Zionist Archives. He was appointed state archivist of Israel in 1956.

Belkind, Israel (1861–1929): Belorusian Zionist leader and educator. Belkind was one of the founders of Bilu and led the first group that immigrated to *Eretz Israel* in 1882. He eventually settled in Jaffa, founding a Hebrew school there in 1889. In 1903, He founded the Kiryat Sefer Agricultural School in Shefeyam. The school closed in 1906, reopened in 1919, and closed permanently after Belkind's death.

Ben-Avi, Itamar (1882–1943): Journalist and political advocate. Ben-Avi was Eliezer Ben-Yehuda's son, and he inherited his father's passion for the Hebrew language and Jewish nationalism. Leaving *Eretz Israel* temporarily, he studied journalism in Paris and Berlin, returning in 1908. Deported with the majority of the *Yishuv*'s male population during World War I, Ben-Avi settled in the United States, returning after the war. It was at this point that Ben-Avi defined his political orientation more clearly: although not an open supporter of the revisionist Zionist movement, he was a staunch critic of the labor Zionist movement. Ben-Avi was the founding editor of *Doar ha-Yom* and *The Palestine Weekly*.

Ben-Gurion, David (1886–1973): Labor Zionist leader and first prime minister of the State of Israel. Born in Plonsk, Poland, as David Gruen, he immigrated in 1906, settling at *Kvutzat* Sejera. Ben-Gurion was one of the founders of the Bar-Giora and ha-Shomer organizations but was exiled by Turkish authorities in 1915. He joined the Jewish Legion during World War I and returned to *Eretz Israel* after the war. In 1920 he was one of the founding organizers of the Histadrut; he served as general secretary from 1920 to 1934. Ben-Gurion was also one of the instigators of the merger between Ahdut ha-Avoda and ha-Poel ha-Zair, leading the resulting Mapai party

David Ben-Gurion in His
Jewish Legion Uniform, 1918.
Courtesy of the Central Zionist Archives, Jerusalem

through the crucial era of Zionist history. In 1934 he was appointed to the JAE, serving as chairman from 1935 to 1948. In this role he established the *Yishuv*'s general policies and priorities on the entire panoply of Jewish and Zionist issues. It was he who passionately advocated partition during the 1930s as a means to obtain a sovereign Jewish state and rescue European Jewry. During World War II, Ben-Gurion advocated a dual policy of supporting the British in the anti-Nazi war while keeping open the *Yishuv*'s options for actions to subvert the White Paper of 1939. After the war, he oversaw the *Yishuv*'s revolt against the British. In 1948 he was appointed head of the provisional Israeli government and he served as prime minister and minister of defense of the State of Israel from 1948 to 1963.

Ben-Yehuda, Eliezer (1858–1922): Father of modern Hebrew and a major advocate of Jewish cultural rebirth during the Second Aliya. Born in Lithuania, Ben-Yehuda began to advocate a Jewish nationalist orientation in 1879. He began to compile the first modern Hebrew dictionary in 1881 and transferred the project to *Eretz Israel* when he immigrated. In 1890, Ben-Yehuda help to found the Hebrew Language Council to promote the use of Hebrew. Although committed to Jewish national rebirth, Ben-Yehuda became a strident critic of the WZO toward the end of his life.

Ben-Zvi, Rachel Yanait (1886–1979): Labor Zionist leader and educator, wife of Yitzhak Ben-Zvi. Rachel Yanait was born and raised in the Ukraine, beginning her career as a teacher in Kiev. She settled in *Eretz Israel* in 1908. Already active in Zionist politics, she had been among the founders of Poale Zion in Kiev, and of ha-Shomer in the *Yishuv*. She was active in educational affairs and in raising consciousness of women's issues in Zionist forums. Yanait married Ben-Zvi in 1918, but remained active in political affairs. She was elected to both Assefat ha-Nivharim and Va'ad Leumi during the 1930s and 1940s and was selected as a delegate to every Zionist Congress from 1921 to 1946.

Ben-Zvi, Yitzhak (1884–1963): Labor Zionist leader and second president of the State of Israel. Born in the Ukraine, he immigrated in 1907, living in Jerusalem. Ben-Zvi was one of the founders of the Bar-Giora and ha-Shomer organizations. He was exiled by the Turkish authorities in 1915 and joined the Jewish Legion during World War I. A passionate advocate of reformist socialist Zionism, Ben-Zvi was among the founders of Ahdut ha-Avoda and the Histadrut. Ben-Zvi was one of the instigators of the merger between Ahdut ha-Avoda and ha-Poel ha-Zair, and he remained active in the resulting Mapai party. He also researched and wrote about Jewish history, specifically Middle Eastern Jewry. Ben-Zvi was keenly interested in those communities that lay at Jewry's peripheries, including, among others, the Samaritans in *Eretz Israel*. From 1931 to 1948 he served as chairman of the Va'ad Leumi and president of Asefat ha-Nivharim. In 1948, Ben-Zvi joined the Israeli provisional government and served in the Knesset from then until 1952. Ben-Zvi succeeded Chaim Weizmann as Israel's president upon the latter's death in 1952.

Members of Poale Zion Pose With the Ben-Zvis in Jerusalem in 1924.
Yitzhak Ben-Zvi is Seated Center and His Wife, Rachel Yanait Ben-Zvi is Seated to His Left.
Courtesy of the Central Zionist Archives, Jerusalem

Bergmann, Shmuel Hugo (1883–1975): Jewish philosopher and labor Zionist advocate. Born and educated in Prague, Bergmann settled in *Eretz Israel* in 1920. From 1928 he taught at Hebrew University and directed the Jewish National and University Library. Bergmann was an advocate of a humanistic and particularly Jewish form of socialist Zionism. He rejected Marxism as wholly inappropriate for the Jewish national home.

Bergson, Peter H. (pseud. Hillel Kook, b. 1915): Revisionist Zionist leader in *Eretz Israel* and the United States. Bergson organized the *Yishuv*'s anti-Nazi boycott in 1933 and continued to advocate economic warfare against Nazi Germany throughout the 1930s. In 1939 he was appointed a member of the Irgun Zvai Leumi (IZL) delegation in the United States, escorting Ze'ev Jabotinsky during his final visit to that country. Remaining in the United States

after Jabotinsky's death, Bergson founded a number of front organizations that advocated help for European Jewry while also collecting money for the IZL. He created, among others, the Committee for a Jewish Army (CJA), the Emergency Committee to Save the Jewish People of Europe (ECSJPE), and the Hebrew Committee for National Liberation (HCNL). Bergson returned to Israel after independence but shunned political activity.

Bernstein, Fritz (Peretz, 1890–1971): Dutch Zionist leader and Israeli politician. Although born in Germany, Bernstein served in various capacities in the Dutch Zionist federation between 1917 and 1935. He settled in *Eretz Israel* in 1936. A moderate leader in the World Union of General Zionists (WUGZ), Bernstein advocated cooperation with Mapai and Mizrachi in building the *Yishuv*. In 1941, Bernstein was appointed chairman of the WUGZ; he was appointed to the JAE in 1946, with responsibility for commerce and industry. He served in the provisional government and in Ben-Gurion's first cabinet in the same capacity.

Bialik, Chaim Nachman (1873–1934): Poet laureate of the Jewish national rebirth. Best known for his poetry reflecting the alienation and search for roots among Jewish youth at the end of the nineteenth century, of necessity he turned to Zionism as the antidote for alienation and became a passionate advocate of Jewish national rebirth. Although holding no official position in the Zionist movement, Bialik was considered a major cultural figure within the movement. He immigrated in 1924, settling in Tel Aviv. From then until his death he was active in virtually every aspect of the *Yishuv*'s cultural life, acting as author, editor, or facilitator for almost all of the major literary developments of the period.

Blaustein, Rachel (1890–1931): Writer, best known as "Rachel the poetess." Blaustein published her first poem at sixteen and continued to write until her death. Rachel's poetry expressed a deep longing for *Eretz Israel*, a desire to commune with nature, and love for the Halutzim. Under the circumstances, however, most of her poetry was also imbued with a deep sense of sadness and pessimism. She immigrated in 1909, settling in *Kvutzat* Kinneret but remained in *Eretz Israel* only a short period: Blaustein was forced to emigrate to France because of illness. Blaustein spent World War I in Russia and returned to *Eretz Israel* in 1919, settling in Tel Aviv.

Birnbaum, Nathan (1864–1937): Father of the term "Zionism." Born in Vienna, Birnbaum was trained in political philosophy but made his living as a journalist. He is widely credited by historians as having been the first to use the term Zionism in the sense of modern Jewish nationalism. An early supporter of Theodor Herzl and the WZO, Birnbaum soured on Herzl and broke from the WZO in 1899. Thereafter, he advocated forms of diaspora nationalism and Yiddishism until embracing Orthodox Judaism toward the end of his life.

Bodenheimer, Max (1865–1940): German Zionist leader. One of Theodor Herzl's closest assistants, Bodenheimer was active in the WZO from founding and was one of the first directors of the Keren Kayemet le-Israel (KKL). Although receiving an assimilationist education, he joined the Hibbat Zion movement in his youth. An eager Zionist by the time Herzl founded the WZO, Bodenheimer was a delegate to the First Zionist Congress and served on the committee that prepared the text of the Basel Program. In 1898, Bodenheimer was a member of the delegation that accompanied Herzl during his meeting with Kaiser Wilhelm II in *Eretz Israel*. He put the statutes of the KKL into their final form and served as its director from 1907–1914. Bodenheimer supported the policy of strict Zionist neutrality during World War I, surrendering his leadership positions to Zionists with connections in England after the war. He did, however, remain active in Zionist affairs until his death.

Borochov, Ber (Dov) (1881–1917): Labor Zionist leader and foremost theoretician of socialist Zionism. Borochov was born in the Ukraine and became active in Zionist affairs during the Uganda controversy. As a disciple of Menahem M. Ussishkin, Borochov adopted a Palestinocentric orientation and opposed all territorialist schemes for the WZO. The task of socialist Zionism, Borochov maintained, was to prepare *Eretz Israel*, through a pioneering effort, for the concentration of the masses of Jewish migrants. Borochov traveled widely on behalf of the Poale Zion party, which was founded by his followers. However, dichotomies in Borochov's ideology — mainly concerning the relative importance of socialism and nationalism to Zionism — later led to a series of schisms among Borochov's followers.

Brandeis, Louis D. (1856–1941): American Jewish jurist and Zionist leader. Born in Kentucky, Brandeis made his reputation as a labor lawyer during the Progessive era. In 1916, he was appointed to the Supreme Court by President Woodrow Wilson and served as an Associate Justice until retirement in 1939. Brandeis became involved with Jewish causes relatively late in life, but after 1912 he became a fervent convert to Zionism. Brandeis assumed the leadership of the Federation of American Zionists in 1914 and helped to strengthen that organization almost immediately. Brandeis played a pivotal role in obtaining Wilson's support for the Balfour Declaration and hence for laying the foundations of the League of Nations Mandate for Palestine/*Eretz Israel*. In the 1920s Brandeis clashed openly with WZO president Chaim Weizmann, over methods to be used for Zionist work in the short term, and he resigned from Zionist work after 1925. Brandeis resumed his activities on behalf of Jewish causes and the *Yishuv* after the 1930 Passfield White Paper and redoubled his efforts to obtain open *aliya* after the Nazi rise to power. > see also: **Brandeisists; Zeeland Program; Between Washington and Pinsk**.

Brenner, Yosef Haim (1881–1921): Hebrew author. Brenner was born and raised in the Ukraine. In his youth he supported the Bund and advocated diaspora nationalism. Between 1904 and 1907 Brenner resided in London and during this time his ideas about Jewish political life changed radically. He returned briefly to Russia and emigrated to *Eretz Israel* in 1909. However, in light of his earlier adherence to the Bund, Brenner remained on the left of the *Yishuv*'s political spectrum. Supportive of labor Zionist parties, Brenner called upon Jews to conquer the workplace as a first step in rebuilding their homeland. He was killed during Arab riots in Jaffa in 1921.

Brod, Max (1884–1968): Austro-Czech author, musician, and Zionist advocate. Born in Prague, Brod was raised in a Zionist household. When Czechoslovakia was founded, Brod took an active part in creating the Jewish National Council; he also served as chairman of the Czech Zionist federation. He left Prague after the Nazi occupation, being among the few able to get out at that point, and settled in Tel Aviv. Active in immigrant organizations, Brod was also involved in a variety of cultural projects.

Brodetsky, Selig (1888–1954): Anglo-Jewish professor and Zionist leader. Born in the Ukraine, Brodetsky was raised and educated in London. From his earliest youth, Brodetsky was a dedicated Zionist and joined the English Zionist Federation (EZF) when it was founded. Educated in mathematics, Brodetsky taught at the University of Leeds from 1920 to 1949. Active in Zionist politics and Jewish communal affairs, Brodetsky was a major force in the EZF, the JAE's London branch, and the Board of Deputies of British Jews. Between 1939 and 1949, Brodetsky served as president of the latter organization. In 1949, he left England for Hebrew University, which he served as president until retirement in 1952.

Brodie, Israel (1895–1979): Anglo-Jewish clergyman and Zionist advocate. Brodie was born in England and served at rabbinic posts in that country and in Australia. During his tenures, Brodie's commitment to Jewish national rebirth made him the foundation for local Zionist chapters, and he was successful in transmitting his view of Jewish nationalism in many contexts. During World War II he served as chief Jewish chaplain for the Royal Army, and he was elected chief rabbi of the British empire in 1948.

Buber, Martin (1878–1965): German Jewish theologian and philosopher. Born in Vienna, he was active in Zionist affairs from 1898 onward. A disciple of Ahad ha-Am, Buber was a delegate to the Third Zionist Congress, where he emphasized the importance of education over political work. During the interwar years, Buber — with many other German Jewish intellectuals — toiled tirelessly to reverse the assimilationist trend in German Jewry. During the Nazi era, he worked to shore up Jewish morale while also working to obtain emigration facilities for German Jewish youth. Buber himself left Germany in 1938 and settled in Jerusalem; he taught philosophy at Hebrew University until he retired in 1951.

Chajes, Zvi Peretz (1876–1927): Austro-Italian rabbi and communal leader. Chajes was born in Galicia and served in a number of rabbinic and teaching posts in Florence, Trieste, and Vienna. he served as chairman of the WZO Va'ad ha-Poel ha-Mezumzam 1921–1925.

Chazanovitz, Joseph (1844–1919): Lithuanian Jewish physician, bibliophile, and Zionist activist. Chazanovitz practiced medicine in

Russia and Poland for most of his life. A committed Zionist, he was one of the first members of Hovevei Zion and joined the WZO in 1897. Active in promoting cultural developments in the *Yishuv*, Chazanovitz bequeathed his extensive library to the WZO; the collection formed the basis for the Jewish National and University Library located at Hebrew University.

Cohen, Israel (1879–1961): Anglo-Jewish writer and communal activist. Cohen was born in England and was raised in a traditional Jewish home. He was an early and active member of the English Zionist Federation, serving as the organization's secretary from 1922 to 1961. On behalf of the federation, Cohen traveled extensively throughout the Jewish world and collected his impressions in his various publications.

Cowen, Joseph (1868–1932): English Zionist. Cowen was the founder and first leader of the English Zionist Federation. He accompanied Theodor Herzl during the latter's 1902 visit in the Middle East, when Herzl met Sultan Abdul Hamid II for the last time. From 1902 until just after World War I, Cowen also served as chairman of the Jewish Colonial Trust.

Dayan, Shmuel (1891–1968): Zionist pioneer and political leader. Born in the Ukraine, Dayan immigrated to *Eretz Israel* in 1908. He was among the founders of Degania and Nahalal, the latter being the first *Moshav Ovdim* in the *Yishuv*. Dayan achieved prominence in the *Moshav* movement, leading the latter to support Mapai. He served as a Mapai member of Knesset during the 1940s and 1950s.

Dinur, Benzion (Dinaburg, 1884–1973): Israeli historian and educator. Dinur immigrated to *Eretz Israel* in 1921; shortly thereafter he was appointed to a teaching position at the Jerusalem Teachers College. He taught there until 1948, serving for part of that time as the school's rector. In 1948 he was appointed professor of modern Jewish history at Hebrew University while simultaneously serving in the Knesset. Dinur also served as minister of education during the 1950s. Dinur's major contribution to

Zionist historiography was made prior to the establishment of the State of Israel: he argued that Zionism was the most significant of modern Jewish political movements and should thus be accorded a central place in Jewish history.

Dizengoff, Meir (1861–1937): Israeli politician. Born in Bessarabia, Dizengoff was active in Hibbat Zion. He immigrated in 1892 and tried to open a bottle factory with the help of the Rothschild family. When this failed, Dizengoff returned to Europe. He immigrated again in 1905 and settled in Jaffa. Active in the Jewish community's political life, Dizengoff was one of the founders of Tel Aviv; he served as the city's first mayor until his death in 1937.

Dobkin, Eliyahu (1898–1976): Labor Zionist leader. Born in Russia, Dobkin lived in Poland until 1932, when he settled in *Eretz Israel*. While in Poland, he was active in he-Halutz and he served as chairman of the World he-Halutz Union from 1923 to 1932. From 1932 to 1937, Dobkin held posts in the Histadrut dealing with *aliya*, Youth Aliya, and absorption. In 1937 he was appointed a junior member of the JAE and was promoted to full membership in 1945, at which point he took over the JA Immigration Department. In the prewar era he supported the gradualist wing of Mapai, although he abandoned this position after the Holocaust.

Dori, Ya'akov (1899–1973): Israeli military leader. Born in Odessa as Jacob Dostrovsky, Dori's family immigrated to *Eretz Israel* in 1906 and settled in Haifa. Dori served in the Hagana in his youth and rose through the ranks to command the Haifa region in 1931. In September 1939, he was appointed chief of staff of the Hagana. Illness forced him to give up that position for the period between 1945 and 1947, during which time he headed the Hagana's military mission in the United States. Dori resumed command in time for the Israeli War of Independence and served as first chief of staff of Zva ha-Hagana le-Israel. But, his illness cut this career short and he retired in 1949. He later served as president of the Haifa Technion.

Druyanov, Alter (1870–1938): Zionist journalist and writer. Born and raised in Vilna, Druyanov was active in Zionist affairs from his youth. He was a member of Hibbat Zion and served as general secretary of that organization from 1890 to 1905. He immigrated to *Eretz Israel* in 1906 but left in 1909. He returned in 1923 and remained there for the rest of his life. His most important contribution was the publication of an extensive documentary on the Hovevei Zion and the First Aliya. Druyanov also published extensively and edited the WZO newspaper *ha-Olam* during the 1920s.

Eban, Abba (Aubrey, b. 1915): Israeli diplomat. Born in Cape Town, South Africa, Eban was educated in England. During the late 1930s he was a lecturer in Middle Eastern history at Cambridge University. From 1938 onward, he was also an advisor to the London JAE. During World War II he served as a liaison between the JA and the British Special Operations executive. In 1947 and 1948 Eban represented the WZO before the United Nations and became first Israeli ambassador to that institution when the State of Israel achieved independence. Joining Mapai, Eban rose rapidly in politics, ending his career as foreign minister.

Eder, M. David (1865–1936): English psychiatrist and communal activist. Eder was born and educated in London, building a highly successful practice as a child psychiatrist. He was one of the founding members of the English Zionist Federation and served in a number of leadership capacities in the WZO: member of the Zionist Commission, member of the WZO Va'ad ha-Poel, and member of the Zionist Executive. > see also: **World Zionist Organization**.

Einstein, Albert (1879–1955): German Jewish scientist. In addition to his numerous contributions to physics and mathematics, Einstein took a great interest in Jewish communal affairs. An early advocate of Zionism, Einstein was probably introduced to Jewish nationalism while in Prague around the turn of the century. Einstein's concept of Zionism was heavily influenced by German Zionist leaders, notably Kurt Blumenfeld, and was very much a cultural rather than political orientation. Einstein remained actively supportive of the *Yishuv*

and world Jewry throughout his life. When Israel's first president, Chaim Weizmann, died, Einstein was offered the presidency, but he declined.

Elath, Eliyahu (Epstein, b. 1903): Israeli diplomat. Elath was born in Russia and settled in *Eretz Israel* in 1924. He joined the staff of the JA Political Department in the early 1930s. From 1934 to 1945 he headed the Political Department's Middle East section and was widely regarded as the keenest Israeli observer of Arab affairs. Between 1945 and 1948, Elath headed the JA office in Washington, D.C., and he was first ambassador to the United States. He also served in London during the 1950s and was president of Hebrew University.

Eldad, Israel (Scheib, 1910–1996): Jewish underground leader and publicist. Born in Galicia, Eldad joined Betar as a teen and rose to a leadership position prior to World War II. Escaping from Nazi-occupied Europe during the war, Eldad arrived in *Eretz Israel* in 1941. Shortly after arrival, he came into contact with dissident members of the Irgun Zvai Leumi and joined Lohame Herut Israel (Lehi). Widely considered to be Lehi's keenest ideologue, Eldad wrote or edited all of the movement's key statements. In 1944 he was captured by the British and was injured trying to escape. Imprisoned in Latrun, he was transferred to prison in Jerusalem and managed to escape in 1946. After his escape, Eldad joined with Nathan Yellin-Mor and Yitzhak Yezernitzki-Shamir to form the triumvirate that oversaw Lehi operations. Eldad continued his publicistic activities after the State of Israel was established, proving himself to be a staunch critic of the government.

Epstein, Yitzhak (1862–1943): Israeli educator. Born in Belorussia, Epstein settled in *Eretz Israel* in 1886. From 1908 to 1915 he directed the Alliance Israélite Universelle school in Salonika, but he returned to the *Yishuv* after World War I. Actively committed to Hebrew education, Epstein designed the so-called *Ivrit be-Ivrit* (Hebrew-in-Hebrew) method of teaching language through total immersion.

Eshkol, Levi (Skolnik, 1895–1969): Labor Zionist leader and Israel's third prime minister. Born in the Ukraine, Eshkol settled in

Eretz Israel in 1914. After World War I, he was active in organizing *Kibbutz* members in support of Mapai. Eshkol served as party secretary from 1942 to 1945. He was elected to the Knesset in 1949 and succeeded David Ben-Gurion as prime minister in 1963.

Ettinger, Akiva J. (1872–1945): Agronomist and diplomat. Born in Belorussia, Ettinger was in London during the negotiations over the Balfour Declaration and served as an adviser to the Jewish negotiators. He settled in *Eretz Israel* in 1918, serving as director of the Keren Kayemet le-Israel from 1918 to 1924. During the 1920s and 1930s he was active in purchasing land for Jewish settlements and in promoting agriculture in the *Yishuv*.

Farbstein, David Zvi (1868–1953): Swiss lawyer and communal leader. Born in Warsaw, Farbstein settled in Switzerland after studying law at the University of Zurich. From 1919 to 1939, he served in the Swiss parliament. A lifelong Zionist, Farbstein headed the Keren ha-Yesod in Switzerland from inception until his death. In 1948, he recommended adoption of a Swiss-style constitutional system for the new State of Israel.

Farbstein, Joshua Heschel (1870–1948): Polish Jewish communal activist and Zionist leader. Farbstein was born and raised in Warsaw. A lifelong Zionist, he served as president of the Polish Zionist federation from 1915 to 1918 and of the Mizrachi federation from 1918 to 1931. He also headed the Keren ha-Yesod campaign in Poland and served as head of the Warsaw *Kehila* between 1926 and 1931. In 1931 he settled in Jerusalem, continuing his activities on behalf of Mizrachi and the WZO. Farbstein served as Mizrachi representative to the JAE in 1933 and 1934. He was elected chairman of the Jerusalem Community Council in 1938, serving until his retirement in 1945.

Feiwel, Berthold (1875–1937): Austrian Zionist leader and poet. Born in Moravia, Feiwel studied law in Vienna. He was a close associate of Theodor Herzl's and helped to organize the First Zionist Congress. From 1897 to 1902, he edited the WZO organ *Die Welt*. In 1902, however, he clashed with Herzl over the relative merits of diplomatic and educational activity, resigning his position as editor. Thereafter, he joined Martin Buber and Chaim Weizmann to found the Democratic Fraktion within the WZO.

Fishman, Jacob (1878–1946): American Jewish journalist and editor. Born in Russian Poland, Fishman immigrated to the U.S. with his family when he was still a child. He was educated in New York and became a journalist, associating with some of the major Yiddish press organs of the era. He edited, respectively, the *Tagblatt*, the *Varheit*, and the *Yiddisher Morgen Zeitung*. An enthusiastic follower of Theodor Herzl, Fishman helped to organize the Zionist Organization of America.

Fishman-Maimon, Judah L. (1875–1962): Religious Zionist leader and Israeli public figure. In 1900, Fishman-Maimon met Rabbi Isaac Jacob Reines and took part in the founding conference of Mizrachi, which was held in Vilna. Beginning with the Second Zionist Congress, he participated in all subsequent Congresses and for many years was a member of Zionist General Council. Fishman-Maimon settled in *Eretz Israel* in 1913 and was among the founders of the Mizrachi educational network. Together with Rabbi Abraham Isaac Kook, he helped establish the chief rabbinate's constitution and organized its founding ceremony. Fishman-Maimon served as the Mizrachi representative at the JAE from 1935 to 1948. As such, he was uncompromising in his belief that the JAE should adopt a maximalist policy to achieve Zionist goals as quickly as possible. He remained committed to both religious Zionism and the coalition with Mapai throughout his career. Fishman-Maimon served as first minister of religious affairs of the State of Israel and advocated reinstituting a Sanhedrin as a supreme religious authority.

Fleg, Edmund (1874–1963): Swiss-French writer and Zionist activist. Fleg was raised in a nominally Orthodox home but was alienated from Judaism while growing up. The Dreyfus Affair brought him back to Jewry but not to Judaism. He could not see a future in any religion but did accept the premise that Jews form a nation. After attending the Third

World Zionist Congress, he became a passionate advocate of Jewish nationhood. His advocacy of Zionism as an antidote to Jewish apathy and assimilation resonated widely in interwar French Jewry and many saw Fleg as the guiding force behind the postwar renaissance of French Jewry.

Flexner, Bernard (1865–1945): American Jewish jurist and Zionist leader. Born and raised in Kentucky, Flexner served as a labor lawyer in Kentucky, Illinois, and New York. Concerned with issues of social justice, Flexner served as counsel to the Zionist delegation at the Paris Peace Conference in 1919 and headed the Palestine Economic Corporation during the 1920s.

Frankfurter, Felix (1882–1965): American Jewish jurist. Born in Vienna, his family migrated to the United States when he was young. Frankfurter was nominated to the U.S. Supreme Court in 1939 and he served as an Associate Justice until 1962. Throughout his long public career, Frankfurter was involved in numerous Jewish causes and had an especially close relationship with Zionism. In 1919 he had signed an agreement with the Emir Faisal that signaled a first, albeit abortive, effort to obtain Arab concurrence to the building of a Jewish national home.

Freier, Recha (1892–1984): German Jewish communal activist. Living in Berlin, Freier was concerned mainly with issues of Jewish education and youth. In 1932 she originated the idea of Youth Aliya, helping to organize the first groups after the Nazis seized power in 1933. She left Germany for England in 1939, settling in *Eretz Israel* in 1941.

Friedenwald, Aaron (1836–1902): American ophthalmologist and Zionist leader. Born in Baltimore, Friedenwald taught ophthalmology and undertook a wide range of communal activities in that city. He was one of the founders and the first president of the Federation of American Zionists.

Friedenwald, Harry (1864–1950): American ophthalmologist and Zionist leader. The son of Aaron Friedenwald, he was brought up in a home that emphasized deeds on behalf of the community at large. Friedenwald was

president of the Federation of American Zionists between 1904 and 1918, after which the organization was thoroughly reorganized as the Zionist Organization of America. He also undertook a number of medical missions to *Eretz Israel* on behalf of the WZO.

Frug, Shimon S. (1860–1916): Ukrainian Jewish poet. Frug was the first Jewish poet in the Russian empire to deal with specifically Jewish themes in Russian (he also wrote in Yiddish). Many of his poems are suffused with the hope that Jews would be restored to productive agricultural labor in their ancestral homeland.

Galili, Israel (1910–1986): Labor Zionist leader. Born in the Ukraine, Galili immigrated to *Eretz Israel* with his parents in 1914. Active in Ahdut ha-Avoda and Mapai, Galili helped to organize ha-Noar ha-Oved in 1924. In the mid-1920s he joined the Hagana, rising through the ranks to become de facto chief of staff during the late 1930s (technically, Galili was not chief of staff because that position was created only in 1945). During Galili's tenure, the Hagana adopted a more activist military doctrine and created the Mossad le-Aliya Bet: developments that represented the beginning of a shift from a militia to an independent military force. After World War II, Galili resigned his post in the Hagana, becoming an adviser on defense to JAE chairman David Ben-Gurion. In 1948, he was appointed deputy minister of defense by the provisional government.

Gaster, Moses (1856–1939): English rabbi and scholar. Born in Bucharest, Gaster was expelled from Romania in 1885 for protesting officially sanctioned antisemitism. Thereafter, he settled in England, and was appointed Haham (chief rabbi) of the London Sephardi community, a post he held from 1887 until retiring in 1918. A life-long Zionist, Gaster attended every Zionist Congress from 1897 to the 1930s; he served as vice president of the plenary for most of them. One of the co-founders of the English Zionist Federation, Gaster originally supported Theodor Herzl, but Gaster became a staunch critic during the Uganda controversy. Throughout, Gaster retained his commitment to the creation of a Jewish national home in *Eretz Israel* and opposed all forms of territorialism.

Glickson, Moshe J. (1878–1939): Journalist, editor, and public leader. Born in Russia, Glickson was active in Zionist youth movements. He became a journalist and edited a number of short-lived Russian Zionist periodicals. In 1919 he immigrated to *Eretz Israel* and in 1922 he was appointed editor in chief of *ha-Aretz*, a position he held until his death. Ideologically linked to the General Zionist movement, Glickson viewed himself as a centrist on most Zionist issues.

Glueck, Nelson (1900–1971): American archeologist and educator. Born in Ohio, Glueck was educated at the Hebrew Union College and was among the first students to actively promote Zionist causes on campus. Glueck was founder and first director of the American School for Oriental Research and was best known for his discoveries relevant to the early history of Jewish settlement in the Negev.

Gold, Ze'ev (1889–1956): American rabbi and religious Zionist leader. Born in Poland, Gold migrated to the United States in 1907. A prominent leader of Mizrachi, Gold served as president of the organization's American branch from 1932 to 1935. In 1935, he settled in *Eretz Israel* and worked for the JAE. In the early 1950s he headed the Torah Education Department of the JA.

Goldberg, Abraham (1883–1942): American journalist and labor Zionist activist. Goldberg was born in Russia but settled in the United States in 1901. He was co-founder of the Poale Zion party in North America, serving as editor of the party's Yiddish and Hebrew journals. Between 1920 and 1942, he also edited the Hebrew monthly, *ha-Toren*.

Goldberg, Isaac Lieb (1860–1935): Russian Zionist leader and philanthropist. One of the first members of the Hibbat Zion movement, in 1882 he founded the Ahavat Zion society in Vilna. Goldberg was a delegate to the First Zionist Congress and took part in the establishment of the Geulah Company, whose aim was to acquire land in *Eretz Israel*, and the Carmel Company for marketing wine produced by the Jewish settlements in *Eretz Israel*. In 1908 he bought two plots of land in *Eretz Israel*. One, near *Moshav* Hartuv became his home when he immigrated in 1919 and engaged in orange growing. The other plot of land, on Mount Scopus, became the first plot of land donated to the Hebrew University after World War I. He was one of the founders of the *ha-Aretz* daily newspaper which he supported financially.

Goldmann, Nahum (1895–1982): Zionist leader, Jewish communal activist, and Jewish diplomat. Goldmann was born in Lithuania, but was raised in Germany. Active in ha-Poel ha-Zair, Goldmann left the party in the 1920s to help found the Radical Zionists. Simultaneously, he helped to organize the Eshkol Publishing Company in Berlin which sought to publish a comprehensive Jewish encyclopedia. Intimately concerned with the fate of Eastern and Central European Jewry, Goldmann embarked upon a series of diplomatic endeavors after the Nazi rise to power in 1933. Inter alia, he helped to found the World Jewish Congress, of which he became president in 1936, and was active in promoting Jewish causes in London, New York, and Paris before, during, and after World War II. An engaging speaker, Goldmann was a controversial figure who argued frequently and persistently with the other Zionist leaders of his day, notably with WZO president Chaim Weizmann and JAE chairman David Ben-Gurion. Goldmann remained in the U.S. when the State of Israel was established, although he immigrated there when he was elected president of the WZO in 1962.

Goldstein, Alexander (1884–1949): Russian Zionist leader. Born in Belorussia, Goldstein joined the Russian Zionist federation while still a student. A talented writer, he used his skills to promote the Zionist cause in a variety of forums. Goldstein served on the central committee of the Russian Zionist federation until 1918, when he exiled by the Bolsheviks. He served on the Comité des Délégations Juives at the Paris Peace conference, settling in London in 1920. A founder of Keren ha-Yesod, Goldstein dedicated the rest of his life to fundraising for Zionist causes.

Goldstein, Angelo (1890–1947): Czech legislator and Zionist activist. Goldstein practiced law in Prague, where he was born and raised. An active Zionist from youth, Goldstein rose rapidly in the Czech Zionist federation. He served as a general Zionist member on the Zionist General Council from 1931 to 1939. Simultaneously, he was elected to two terms in the Czech parliament, where he established a reputation as a fighter for Jewish rights and an opponent of both Nazism and antisemitism. He fled Czechoslovakia in 1939 on the heels of the Nazi occupation and settled in Tel Aviv, resuming his law practice there. Active in Hitahdut Olei Czechoslovakia, Goldstein undertook a diplomatic mission to Prague in 1946 that guaranteed Czech support for Jewish statehood.

Goldstein, Israel (1896–1986): American Zionist leader and Conservative rabbi. Born in Pennsylvania, Goldstein was rabbi of the B'nai Jeshurun Congregation from 1918 to 1961, when he retired. Active in numerous Jewish causes, Goldstein played a pivotal role in the Zionist Organization of America (ZOA). He served as ZOA's president between 1943 and 1945; he was also president of Young Judea (1930–1933), president of the World Union of General Zionists (1946–1970), and honorary president of the Keren Keyemet le-Israel from 1944 onward. In 1947–1948, Goldstein served on the JAE New York branch and on the WZO political advisory board. An avid consensus builder, Goldstein helped to heal many of the rifts within ZOA that had developed during the 1930s and 1940s. Equally, his emphasis on education served the Zionist movement and the American Jewish community well in an era of dramatic changes. In 1961, Goldstein fulfilled his lifelong dream of settling in Israel, where he lived out his remaining days as a teacher and writer.

Golomb, Eliahu (1893–1945): Zionist underground leader. Born in Belorussia, Golomb settled in *Eretz Israel* while still a child. He was a member of the first graduating class of the Herzliya Hebrew High School in Tel Aviv. Just prior to World War I Golomb became active in ha-Poel ha-Zair and in ha-Shomer. He served in the Jewish Legion from 1918 to 1920. As a result of the Arab riots of 1920, Golomb was tasked with creating a new defense organization for the *Yishuv*: that body became the Hagana, which Golomb commanded for the rest of his life.

Goodman, Paul (1875–1949): Anglo-Zionist writer and historian. Born in Estonia, Goodman was brought to England as a child. He heard Theodor Herzl speak in London in 1896 (Goodman was then secretary to the Spanish-Potuguese congregation) and was immediately mesmerized. Goodman was among the founders of the English Zionist Federation and the World Union of General Zionists. During World War I he served on the Zionist Political Advisory Committee established by Chaim Weizmann. In addition to his political activity, Goodman was a prolific writer and editor. Gradualist in political orientation, Goodman remained a staunch supporter of Weizmann during the stormy period 1939–1949.

Gordon, Aaron David (1856–1922): Spiritual father of the labor Zionist movement and of the Second Aliya. Born in Russia, he immigrated in 1904, settling in Petah Tikva; later he joined *Kvutzat* Degania, where he wrote most of the publications that set out his ideology, which is best known as *Dat ha-Avoda*. Gordon strongly believed that the only way to revive the Jewish nation was to restore the Jews to agricultural labor: all culture derived from the close connection between a people and its homeland. > see also: **Dat ha-Avoda**.

Gordon, Shmuel Leib (Shalag, 1865–1933): Zionist poet and educator. Born in Russia, Gordon published his first Hebrew poetry when he was twenty-five years old. He settled in *Eretz Israel* in 1898, working as a teacher, but left in 1901. He lived in Warsaw from 1901 to 1924, founding and heading one of the first modern Jewish schools there. Considered a pioneer of modern Jewish and Zionist education, Gordon wrote the curriculum for his school and taught Hebrew. He also wrote the first modern textbooks for Jewish school use. Gordon returned to the *Yishuv* in 1924 and continued writing, his major project being a multivolume commentary on the Bible.

Gottheil, Richard J. H. (1862–1936): American Zionist leader. Born in England, Gottheil migrated to the United States with his family in 1873. Educated in New York, he was appointed professor of Semitic languages at Columbia University in 1886. Additionally, he served as head of the Oriental Division of the New York Public Library. An avid Zionist, Gottheil was the first president of the Federation of American Zionists, a position he held from 1898 to 1904. He remained active in the Zionist Organization of America until his death.

Greenberg, Hayim (1889–1953): American labor Zionist leader. Born in Bessarabia, Greenberg was almost completely self-educated. He was a delegate at the Helsingfor's Conference at the age of seventeen and remained active in Zionist affairs throughout his life. Skilled as a writer and speaker, his services were much in demand. Greenberg remained in Russia until after the Bolshevik takeover. In 1921 he left and settled in Berlin. In 1924 he migrated again, to the United States. Closely linked to the Poale Zion party, Greenberg flourished in New York. As editor of the two major labor Zionist organs, *Yiddisher Kempfer* and *Jewish Frontier*, Greenberg was also able to formulate his ideology and he influenced labor Zionists worldwide. He argued that Zionism was not merely Jewish nationalism but was a manifestation of the universal dream for redemption that was inherent in the Jewish tradition. A nationalist movement could achieve its aims by any means, but Zionism could only achieve its aims through a policy of social justice, which Greenberg defined as Mapai-style reformist socialism, in order to ensure that Jews were a "light unto the nations." Greenberg was appointed to the JAE in 1946 and headed its education department until his death.

Greenberg, Ivan M. (1896–1966): Anglo-Jewish journalist and editor. The son of Leopold J. Greenberg, he was raised in an avidly Zionist household. Greenberg joined the staff of the *Jewish Chronicle* in 1925 and inherited the editorship in 1936. During his tenure, however, he brought the newspaper into a more right-wing orientation: he opposed the enlargement of the JA and strongly supported the Irgun Zvai Leumi.

These positions led to his resignation from the *Jewish Chronicle* after World War II. From 1946 to his death, Greenberg was a leader of the revisionist Zionist movement in England.

Greenberg, Leopold J. (1861–1931): Anglo-Jewish journalist and editor. Born and raised in England, Greenberg was an early devotee of Theodor Herzl and the Zionist movement. In 1907, Greenberg led a conglomerate that bought the *Jewish Chronicle* and became its editor. Under his stewardship, the *Jewish Chronicle* became a mouthpiece for advancing the Zionist cause and for advocating Jewish rights throughout the world. Greenberg strongly supported the Jewish Legion and the Balfour Declaration but became critical of the JA's policies toward the end of his life. He began to move the *Jewish Chronicle* to the right, an editorial policy that was further developed when his son, Ivan M. Greenberg, became editor in 1936.

Greenberg, Uri Zvi (1895–1981): Zionist poet and ideologue. Born into a Hasidic household in Galicia, Greenberg served in the Austro-Hungarian army during World War I. Already known as a poet, he settled in Warsaw immediately after the war but migrated to Berlin and then to *Eretz Israel* in 1924. Initially close to the socialist Zionist movement, Greenberg moved to the right during the 1920s. By 1928, his writings were laced with extreme nationalist visions and shortly thereafter he joined the revisionist Zionist movement. He returned to Poland between 1931 and 1935 on a mission for the revisionists but departed in 1936 and settled in the *Yishuv* again. Thereafter, Greenberg became a staunch critic of the JA and of *Havlaga*. As a result, his poetry became required reading for all members of the Irgun Zvai Leumi and Lohame Herut Israel. Greenberg served in the first Knesset as a member of the Herut party.

Grossman, Meir (1888–1964): Revisionist Zionist leader and journalist. Born in Russia, Grossman became involved with Zionist youth groups and combined his Zionism with a journalist's career after 1905. He edited or contributed to a large number of Yiddish and Hebrew journals during World War I, thereby spreading the Zionist message. Grossman returned to Russia briefly after the Bolshevik takeover but left again in 1918. During the brief interlude of Ukrainian independence, Grossman served as a representative at the national assembly. In 1919, Grossman helped to found the Jewish Telegraphic Agency. Closely linked to Ze'ev Jabotinsky, Grossman joined the Union of Zionist Revisionists when it was founded in 1925. However, the increasingly strained nature of intra-Zionist relations — largely but not exclusively over the issue of revisionist secession from the WZO — led Grossman to found the Jewish State Party (JSP) as a faction within the revisionist movement in 1933. When Jabotinsky and the main body of revisionists withdrew from the WZO in 1935, JSP remained as a loyal opposition. Grossman settled in *Eretz Israel* in 1934 but moved to New York in 1939. He returned to Israel in 1948, by which time he had been appointed to the JAE. In 1951 he joined the General Zionist party, with which he remained associated for the rest of his life. > see also: **Revisionist Schism**.

Gruenbaum, Yizhak (1879–1970): Polish communal leader and Zionist advocate. Born in Warsaw, Gruenbaum grew up in Plonsk and became active in the Zionist movement as a teenager. He was one of the guiding spirits behind Helsingfors Conference and formulated the Russian Zionists' commitment to a policy of Gegenwartsarbeit. After World War I, Gruenbaum returned to Warsaw and helped to organize the political life of the Polish Jewish community. Gruenbaum was elected to the Polish Sejm in 1919, holding a seat on the Zionist slate until 1930. A staunch opponent of the Polish government, he based his position almost exclusively on the government's antisemitic proclivities. In 1933 Gruenbaum was appointed to the JAE, heading the Absorption and Labor Departments. During World War II, Gruenbaum headed the JA rescue committee but was widely criticized for the lack of action to save European Jewry. After the war, he remained active in the JAE and served as minister of the interior in the first government.

Ha-Cohen, Mordechai Ben-Hillel (1856–1936): Russian journalist and Zionist advocate. Born in Belorussia, ha-Cohen was active in the Jewish agricultural movement in Russia. A gifted writer, he published his first piece when he was eighteen years old. In 1881 he joined Hibbat Zion, helping to organize fund-raising and other activities on behalf of the settlers. Ha-Cohen migrated to *Eretz Israel* in 1907 and was one of the founders of Tel Aviv. Thereafter, he remained active in the *Yishuv's* cultural life.

Halprin, Rose L. (1896–1978): American Zionist leader. Born and raised in New York, Halprin was among the founders of Hadassah. She served as the organization's president twice: 1932–1934 and 1947–1951. From 1934 to 1939 she lived in *Eretz Israel*, acting as a correspondent for Hadassah's journals. An ardent advocate and supporter of Youth Aliya, Halperin was elected to the JAE in 1947.

Hankin, Yehoshua (1864–1945): Zionist settlement activist. Born in the Ukraine, Hankin immigrated to *Eretz Israel* in 1882. Acting as a private citizen, Hankin purchased a group of plots in the Jezreel Valley in 1897, purchases that were not completed until 1909. Although he acted as an individual in making these purchases, Hankin cooperated with other Zionist land-purchasing organizations and he coordinated his activities with the WZO office in Jaffa. In 1915, Hankin was arrested by the Turkish authorities; unlike other *Yishuv* members who were exiled, however, he was imprisoned in Anatolia. Hankin was freed at the end of World War I, returned to *Eretz Israel*, and resumed his activities. In particular, he continued to purchase plots in the Jezreel Valley, resulting in almost complete Jewish ownership of that land by 1930. In 1932, Hankin was appointed head of the Palestine Land Development Corporation, a position he held until the 1940s.

Hershberg, Abraham S. (1859–1943): Polish writer and Zionist leader. Hershberg was born in Bialystock, making a living as the owner of a textile mill. An avid supporter of Rabbi Shmuel Mohilever and Hovevei Zion, he settled in *Eretz Israel* for eighteen months in 1899. On his return to Poland, he devoted himself to promoting Zionism through cultural and literary activities. He helped to found Bialystock's Hevrat Tora and lectured to the society on topics in Jewish history. Prior to World War I, he edited the *Bialystoker Togblatt*, a Yiddish-language, Zionist daily. World War I disrupted his activities, but he resumed them in independent Poland in the interwar era. A supporter of Mizrachi, Hershberg was murdered by the Nazis in 1943.

Hertz, Joseph Herman (1872–1946): Chief rabbi of the British empire and advocate of Zionism. Hertz was born in Slovakia but was brought to the United States by his parents. Obtaining a rabbinic education, he assumed pulpits in Syracuse, New York, and Johannesburg, South Africa. In 1913, he was elected chief rabbi of the British empire. An advocate of modern Orthodoxy, Hertz was also a passionate defender of Jewish rights throughout the world, as well as an avid supporter of Zionism. He cofounded the South African Zionist Federation during his tenure there. He also supported the English Zionist Federation for his entire life. One of a small circle of Jewish leaders who were consulted in regard to the Balfour Declaration, Hertz was equally at home supporting cabinet action on behalf of the Jews as he was criticizing the anti-Zionist trends in the cabinet during the 1930s. A fervent advocate of rescue at all costs during the Holocaust, Hertz continued to hammer home the twin themes of Jewish national rebirth and justice during the Nazi era.

Herzl, Theodor (1860–1904). Father of modern Zionism. Born in Budapest, Herzl was raised and educated in Vienna. His early career was framed around journalism and attempts at a literary career. Herzl covered the Dreyfus Trial for the *Neue Freie Presse* and witnessed French antisemitism firsthand. In 1896, as a result of his experiences, Herzl wrote *Der Judenstaat*, considered a Zionist classic. In the book he argued that only a Jewish national home could regulate relations between Jews and non-Jews. The impact of the book was immediate: Herzl soon planned to convene a Zionist Congress (the first of which met in 1897) and to launch the World Zionist Organization. As WZO president, Herzl defined the organization in its early years and was its most easily identified spokesman. Nevertheless, Herzl's political vision was limited. He saw Zionist activity exclusively in political, that is, diplomatic terms and belittled efforts at settlement undertaken by Practical Zionists. This inner tension, combined with Herzl's inability to achieve Zionist goals through personal diplomacy, led to the creation of an opposition movement within the WZO and eventually led to the creation of political parties and blocs in the Zionist movement. Then too Herzl saw Zionism in terms of a refuge for Eastern European Jewry. He was willing, therefore, to negotiate settlement schemes outside of *Eretz Israel*. One such scheme, for settlement in East Africa (the so-called Uganda plan) led to Herzl's virtual undoing. The uproar over Uganda that ensued within the WZO led to failing health, and Herzl died of heart failure at the age of forty-four. Nonetheless, Herzl's accomplishments cannot be belittled. He created the modern Jewish nationalist movement and is rightfully considered a father of the State of Israel.

Herzog, Isaac (1888–1959): Rabbi and religious Zionist leader. Born in Poland, Herzog migrated with his family to England when he was a young child. He studied for the rabbinate and obtained pulpits in Belfast and Dublin, where he served as chief rabbi of Ireland. In 1937 Herzog was elected second Ashkenazi chief rabbi of Palestine/*Eretz Israel*, a position he held for the rest of his life (from 1948 to 1959 Herzog served as first Ashkenazi chief rabbi of the State of Israel). An advocate of rescue at all costs during the Holocaust, Herzog continued to advocate mass *aliya* after his visit to Europe in 1946. Herzog supported the JAE and Mizrachi, considering himself to be a moderate on Zionist questions.

Horowitz, David (1899–1979): Israeli economist. Born in Galicia, he immigrated to *Eretz Israel* in 1920. He held a variety of jobs at the JA, from 1935 to 1948, rising to head of the JA Economic Department. In 1948 he was named director general of the Ministry of Finance and in 1954 he founded the Bank of Israel.

Imber, Naftali Herz (1856–1909): Poet and author. Imber is best remembered for "ha-Tikvah" (The Hope), the Zionist and (since 1948) Israeli national anthem. Imber was born in Galicia and he traveled *Eretz Israel* between 1882 and 1888, as secretary to the famous orientalist and Gentile Zionist Laurence Oliphant. This trip inspired Imber to write the poem "Tikvatenu" (our hope), which became "ha-Tikva." Imber continued his many travels throughout the world, but virtually lost contact with the Jewish community in the 1890s.

Jabotinsky, Ze'ev (1880–1940): Zionist writer, activist, and political leader. Jabotinsky was born in Odessa and worked as a journalist in Italy and Switzerland. Apparently he became aware of Zionism during his stay abroad and became an avid supporter of Jewish nationalism. After he returned to Odessa — during a wave of pogroms that began in 1903 — Jabotinsky helped to organize Jewish self-defense. During World War I, he advocated the creation of a Jewish Legion under British command to liberate *Eretz Israel* from the Turks. When the legion was founded, Jabotinsky was commissioned as an officer and served for the duration of the war. After World War I, Jabotinsky served on the Zionist Executive and worked closely with other WZO leaders. In 1920 he again organized self-defense units, this time in Jerusalem, to repel Arab rioters. However, Jabotinsky was arrested by the British for his actions and was briefly imprisoned. During the mid-1920s, Jabotinsky began to grow increasingly uncomfortable with the gradualist stance adopted by other Zionist leaders, notably by WZO president Chaim Weizmann. By this time, Jabotinsky had formulated most of his ideology, of which the most important component was his commitment to establishing a Jewish majority in *Eretz Israel* in order to attain Jewish statehood. It would be fair to say that Jabotinsky was the last of the pure Political Zionists, operating in the Herzlian mode. In 1925 he organized the Hitahdut ha-Zionim ha-Revisionistim (ha-Zohar), the party he led

until 1935. In 1931, Jabotinsky strongly, but unsuccessfully, urged all Zionists to support an "Endziel" declaration and to work toward the creation of a Jewish state, rather than a small Jewish spiritual center. He viewed anti-semitism as "the most significant component" in Nazi ideology and consequently supported the anti-Nazi boycott as well as the evacuation of European Jewry. In 1935, feeling that he was unable to influence the WZO, Jabotinsky withdrew ha-Zohar and formed Histadrut ha-Zionist ha-Hadasha (ha-Zach). He continued to advocate a maximalist position on all Zionist questions, including defense. From 1936, Jabotinsky served as supreme commander of the Irgun Zva'i Leumi, although he did not exercise day-to-day operational command of that organization. Jabotinsky died during a trip to the United States.

Jacobson, Victor (1869–1935): Russian Zionist leader. Born in Crimea, Jacobson was active in the Russian Zionist federation from its inception. In 1899 he was appointed to membership on the Va'ad ha-Poel ha-Gadol and opposed the Uganda scheme in 1903. Jacobson was one of the founders of the *Zionei Zion* faction, that is, those who inalterably opposed Zionist settlement activities anywhere but in *Eretz Israel*. From 1906 to 1908, Jacobson headed the WZO office in Beirut and from 1908 to 1913, he headed the office in Constantinople. Just before World War I, he was appointed to the WZO executive; in this capacity he chaired the WZO's Copenhagen Bureau during World War I. Establishing the WZO policy of neutrality during the war, Jacobson nonetheless warmly welcomed the Balfour Declaration. After the war, Jacobson served as a Zionist delegate to the Paris peace talks. He remained in Europe, acting as WZO representative to the League of Nations. A pacifist and binationalist in orientation, Jacobson was a founder of Brit Shalom.

Jaffe, Leib (1876–1948): Russian writer and Zionist leader. Born in Belorussia, Jaffe was a delegate to the First Zionist Congress and was appointed editor in chief of the Russian Zionist federation's organ. After the Bolsheviks seized power, Jaffe fled to Lithuania, where he was elected president of the Zionist federation. In 1920 he immigrated to *Eretz Israel*, becoming an editor at *ha-Aretz* while also making substantial contributions to the *Yishuv's* literature in Russian, Yiddish, and Hebrew.

Janner, Barnett (1892–1982): British politician and communal leader. Born in Wales, Janner served in Parliament from 1931 to 1970, first as a Liberal and later as member of the Labour Party. A lifelong Zionist, Janner served as a member of the Board of Deputies and as president of the English Zionist Federation during the 1950s.

Kaplan, Eliezer (1891–1952): Labor Zionist leader. Born in Russia, Kaplan was active in Zeirei Zion and Mapai in Russia and *Eretz Israel*. Appointed to the JAE in 1933, Kaplan served as head of the JA Finance Department until 1948. Largely responsible for using the WZO's slender financial resources to the maximum, Kaplan was a close colleague of David Ben-Gurion and Moshe Shertok. He held the Finance Ministry portfolio in the provisional government and in the first cabinet (he also served as deputy premier in the first government).

Kaplansky, Shlomo (1884–1950): Polish labor Zionist leader. Born in Bialystock, Kaplansky lived in Vienna before World War I. During this period he became active in Poale Zion. During World War I, Kaplansky was in London, serving on the Zionist Executive: from 1919 to 1921 as chairman of the Finance Committee and from 1927 to 1929 (by which time the Zionist Executive had moved to Jerusalem) as head of the Settlement Committee. After the JAE "enlargement," Kaplansky returned to London as Mapai's emissary to the British Labour Party. In 1932, he was appointed director of the Haifa Technion, a position he held for the rest of his life.

Katznelson, Berl (1887–1944): Labor Zionist leader and ideologue. Born in Belorussia, Katznelson immigrated in 1909 and settled in *Kvutzat* Ein Ganim. He was one of the founders of Ahdut ha-Avoda, the Histadrut and Mapai. Katznelson remained active in the Histadut and Mapai for his entire life; however, he saw himself primarily as an educator and a promoter of

Berl Katznelson, Mapai Ideologue
and Editor of *Davar*.
Courtesy of the Central Zionist Archives, Jerusalem

ideas. Thus he placed his main emphasis on his most lasting brainchild: the *Davar* daily newspaper, which he edited from its founding to his death. A strident opponent of fragmentation in the Zionist movement, Katznelson unsuccessfully tried to play the role of conciliator during the dispute between Mapai and the revisionists during the 1930s. Katznelson advocated *aliya* at all costs and was one of the first Mapai leaders to call for the party to support *Aliya Bet*. In 1936–1937 Katznelson differed from Chaim Weizmann and David Ben-Gurion in opposing the partition of Palestine/*Eretz Israel* into a Jewish state and an Arab state.

Kellner, Leon (1859–1928): Austrian Zionist leader and scholar. Born in Vienna, Kellner taught English and literature at a number of Austrian universities prior to World War I. During the war, he served as an adviser on English affairs to the Austro-Hungarian government. Kellner joined the WZO when it was founded and he was one of Theodor Herzl's closest advisers. After World War I, Kellner dedicated himself to publishing Herzl's writings. He also published a partial biography of the great Zionist leader.

Kisch, Frederick Hermann (1888–1943): British military engineer and Zionist leader. Born in India to the family of a British officer, Kisch followed in his father's footsteps and chose a military career. Kisch served in Baluchistan during World War I, mainly in staff and intelligence positions. Immediately after the war, he was appointed to the military intelligence branch of the War Office. Kisch also served on the British delegation to the Paris peace talks and it was there that he first became involved with the WZO. He resigned from the army in 1923 and accepted Chaim Weizmann's invitation to become a member of the Zionist Executive in Jerusalem. During his tenure (1923–1929) Kisch headed the JA Political Department, by far the most sensitive of the JAE posts. Despite his close association with Weizmann, Kisch was a maximalist in his Zionist orientation. This led him to resign from the JAE when it was "enlarged" in 1929, since he feared that the addition of non-Zionist representatives would water down the JAE's work. Despite this disagreement, Kisch remained in the *Yishuv* and advised JAE leaders on defense matters. When World War II broke out, Kisch returned to active duty. It was hoped that he would lead the Jewish division that the British government promised to raise, but nothing materialized. In 1942, Kisch was appointed chief engineer for the Eighth Army fighting in North Africa. He was killed in action while overseeing a mine clearing party in Tunisia in early 1943.

Klausner, Joseph G. (1874–1958): Zionist historian and political advocate. Born in Lithuania, Klausner was educated in Odessa and later moved to Warsaw, where he began his teaching career. Klausner settled in *Eretz Israel* in 1919 and was appointed to the faculty of Jewish history at Hebrew University when it opened. Widely published in a variety of fields, Klausner influenced three generations of Israeli students. Some of his books, notably *Jesus of Nazareth*, were very controversial in their day. Part of the controversy derived from Klausner's methods: he sought to uncover a usable past that could be brought to bear in Zionist propaganda. Linked to the right wing of the Zionist movement, Klausner was formally nonpartisan.

Kollek, Theodor (Teddy, b. 1911): Labor Zionist leader and Israeli public figure. Born in Vienna, Kollek immigrated to *Eretz Israel* just after Austrian Fascists took power in 1934, and was a lifelong adherent of Mapai. From 1940 to 1947 he served as an adviser to the JA Political Department. In 1947, Kollek was sent to the U.S. as head of the secret Hagana mission in New York. His assignment was to obtain supplies and volunteers for the fledgling Israeli army. After the State of Israel was established, Kollek served as director of the premier's office and was elected mayor of Jerusalem.

Kook, Abraham Isaac ha-Cohen (1865–1935): Rabbinic authority and thinker. Born in Latvia, Kook studied in *yeshivot* in Lithuania and immigrated to *Eretz Israel* in 1904. Initially, he served as chief rabbi of Jaffa. Committed to religious Zionism, Kook developed a unique view on the role of Zionism in Jewish history. He was convinced that in spite of the decline of religion, humankind was moving toward imminent divine redemption. Therefore, Kook believed that the return to *Eretz Israel* marked the beginning of the process, despite the secular origins of the Zionist movement and the non- (or even anti-) religious attitude of many Zionist leaders. In 1921, Kook was appointed first Ashkenazi chief rabbi of *Eretz Israel*, a post he held for the remainder of his life.

Kovner, Abba (1918–1987): Lithuanian-Israeli poet and underground leader. Born in Sevastopol, Crimea, Kovner was raised and educated in a socialist Zionist milieu in Vilna, the "Jerusalem of Lithuania." During the Holocaust Kovner led the Jewish partisan movement in the Vilna ghetto and commanded the "Nekama" (revenge) battalion in the forests of Lithuania. After the war, Kovner was among the first to realize that Jewish life could not be restored in postwar Eastern Europe and with other surviving partisan leaders he founded the *Briha* movement. Settling in Israel, Kovner built up his well deserved reputation as the poet of Jewish national tragedy and rebirth.

Krementzky, Jonah (1850–1934): Austrian industrialist and Zionist leader. Born in Odessa, he settled in Vienna as an adult. Krementzky made his career as the owner of one of the largest electrical appliance concerns in Austria. An ardent follower of Theodor Herzl's, Kremenetzky served as a member of the WZO Va'ad ha-Poel ha-Gadol and the Zionist executive. In 1920, he built the first major factory in the *Yishuv*, located in Tel Aviv. Krementzky headed the Keren Kayemet le-Israel from 1902 to 1907 and helped to place the organization on a solid financial foundation.

Lavon, Pinhas (Lubianiker, 1904–1976): Labor Zionist leader. Born in Galicia, Lubianiker was an organizer of the Gordonia youth movement in interwar Poland. He left Poland for *Eretz Israel* in 1929 and became active in Mapai. He served as party secretary in 1938 and 1939 and later rose to prominence in the Histadrut. He served at a variety of ministerial posts during the 1950s but became embroiled in a dispute with David Ben-Gurion that culminated in the latter's final retirement from politics in the mid-1960s.

Levi-Bianchini, Angelo (1887–1920): Italian naval officer and Zionist leader. Born in Venice, Levi-Bianchini served in the Italian navy and achieved staff officer rank. He lectured at the Italian Naval Academy prior to World War I. A lifelong Zionist, Levi-Bianchini played the crucial role in obtaining Italian government support for the Balfour Declaration and was a member of Va'ad ha-Zirim (the Zionist Commission). He played a critical role at the San Remo Conference, which approved the League of Nations mandate on Palestine/ *Eretz Israel*, but he died shortly after the conference.

Levin, Shemaryahu (1867–1935): Russian Zionist leader. Born in Belorussia, Levin received a rabbinic education and officiated at pulpits in Grodno and Vilna. Levin was elected to the Russian Duma in 1905. An impassioned Zionist, Levin was the first of the Russian Zionists to express opposition to the Uganda plan, in a speech to the Sixth Zionist Congress. He left Russia prior to

World War I, living for a time in Germany and the United States. He settled in *Eretz Israel* in the late 1920s and helped found the Haifa Technion.

Levinthal, Bernard (1865–1952): American Orthodox rabbi and communal leader. Born and educated in Lithuania, Levinthal migrated to the United States in 1891. Serving as a rabbi in Philadelphia, he helped to organize numerous rabbinic bodies in Pennsylvania and the United States. In particular, Levinthal was one of the founders of Mizrachi in North America.

Levinthal, Israel H. (1888–1978): American Conservative rabbi and communal leader. Born in Philadelphia, the son of Rabbi Bernard Levinthal, he served as spiritual leader of the Brooklyn Jewish Center, the premier institution of the Jewish center movement. A prolific writer and dynamic speaker, Levinthal, like his father and brother, was active in the Zionist Organization of America and in Mizrachi.

Levontin, Zalman D. (1856–1940): Russian banker and Zionist sponsor. Born in Russia, Levontin visited *Eretz Israel* in 1882 and began to sponsor the Bilu movement. His first major accomplishment in the *Yishuv* was purchasing the land on which Rishon le-Zion was built. In 1901 Theodor Herzl requested Levontin's assistance in organizing the Jewish Colonial Trust and the Anglo-Palestine Bank (APB). Levontin agreed to do so, and he served as the president of APB for many years.

Lilienblum, Moses Leib (1843–1910): Hebrew writer and political journalist. One of the leaders of the Russian *Haskalah*, Lilienblum was originally oriented toward assimilation as a solution to the Jewish problem. The pogroms of 1881 and 1882 caused him to assume a nationalist orientation and he became a leader of the Hibbat Zion. In 1897 he joined the WZO and remained a member of that organization for the rest of his life. Lilienblum believed that it was necessary to concentrate the nation as one group in its own territory; he regarded *Eretz Israel* as the only suitable location for Jews, since that was the only place where they would not constitute a foreign body. In his view, the only viable solution to the Jewish problem that was acceptable to Jews was the elimination of the diaspora and the return to Zion; this he felt could be implemented if the nation willed it.

Lipsky, Louis (1876–1963). American Zionist leader, journalist, and author. Born in Rochester, New York, Lipsky was active in promoting the Zionist idea even before the WZO existed. Lipsky made his reputation as a writer and editor, founding, among others, *Shofar* and *The Maccabean,* which, under the title *New Palestine,* served as the official organ of the Zionist Organization of America (ZOA). Lipsky was editor in chief of the *American Hebrew* and also played an active role in many Zionist organizations, serving as president of ZOA between 1922 and 1930. Simultaneously, Lipsky was intimately involved in the founding of such diverse organizations as the American Jewish Congress, Keren ha-Yesod, and the World Jewish Congress. From 1934 to 1945, Lipsky served as chairman of the governing council of the American Jewish Congress. A prolific writer, Lipsky's collected Zionist works included three volumes of essays and one volume of biographical sketches.

Lowenthal, Marvin (1890–1969): American Jewish author and Zionist organizer. Born in Pennsylvania, Lowenthal moved west in the 1920s. He helped to organize Zionist societies in California and to promote Jewish issues in communities that were, until that time, somewhat isolated from the mainstream. From 1924 to 1929 Lowenthal resided in Europe, but he served as a contributing editor to the *Menorah Journal.* Returning to the United States, Lowenthal resumed his active role in Zionist affairs, serving as a member of the Zionist Organization of America's advisory board between 1946 and 1949.

Luz, Kadish (1895–1972): Russian Zionist organizer and activist. Born in Belorussia, Luz served in the Russian army during World War I. In the turmoil that followed the revolutions of 1917, Luz became active in Zionist affairs. He helped organize Jewish self-defense groups and was one of the founders of he-Halutz. He settled in *Eretz Israel* in 1920 but was not active in politics

prior to the State of Israel's establishment. He served in the Knesset as a Mapai member during the 1950s and 1960s.

Magnes, Judah L. (1877–1948): American rabbi, educator, and Zionist activist. Born in San Francisco, Magnes was educated in New York and served as a Reform rabbi in the city. In 1922, he immigrated to *Eretz Israel,* where he helped build the Hebrew University into a first-rate academic institution. He served as chancellor of the university from 1925 to 1935 and as president from 1935 to 1948. Politically, Magnes was a gradualist, but his orientation was even more moderate than the majority of the WZO. He was openly binationalist in orientation and was a founder of both the Ihud and Brit Shalom movements. > see also: **Hebrew University**.

Marks, Simon (1888–1964): Anglo-Jewish industrialist, philanthropist, and communal activist. Born in England to a family of recent immigrants, Marks inherited the small dry-goods store his father had opened in 1884. He parlayed this store into the world famous Marks and Spencer department store chain, attaining considerable wealth in the process. From 1919 onward, Marks used his wealth to promote a variety of Jewish causes; Zionism held a special place in his philanthropic endeavors. Marks served as secretary of the Zionist delegation at the Paris Peace Talks. During the 1920s and 1930s, he served as chairman of Keren ha-Yasod in England and as vice president of the EZF. Marks was knighted in 1944 and was elected to the JAE in 1950. Marks's philanthropic contributions were considerable. Over four decades he and his family donated some 10 million pounds sterling to Jewish and Zionist causes.

Marmorek, Oscar (1863–1909): Austrian architect and Zionist leader. Born in Galicia, Marmorek's family moved to Vienna, where he was educated and worked. He was best known for designing synagogues that were modern, but were designed in a traditional style. In 1896, Marmorek joined the newly created WZO and became a close confidant of Theodor Herzl's. Elected to the WZO executive, he attended the first six Zionist congresses but curtailed his activities after 1904 due to ill health.

Meir, Golda (Meyerson, 1898-1979): Labor Zionist leader and Israeli prime minister. Born in the Ukraine, Meir's migrated to the United States with her family in 1906. Under the influence of family members, Meir joined Po'alai Zion in 1915. In 1921 she and her husband immigrated to *Eretz Israel*, initially settling in *Kibbutz* Merhavia. For a variety of reasons, the Meirs left the *Kibbutz* after a short stay. Even so, Meir remained active in the Histadrut and in Mapai. In 1934, she was invited to join the Histadrut executive committee, mainly in areas dealing with foreign contacts and women's issues. In 1938, for example, Meir attended the Evian Conference on political refugees as part of the *Yishuv*'s delegation. In 1948, the provisional government nominated her to be Israel's first ambassador to the Soviet Union, a post she held for one year. Elected to the Knesset in 1949, Meir continued to rise in the Mapai hierarchy. In 1969, she became the fourth prime minister of the State of Israel.

Meir, Ya'akov (1856–1939): Israeli rabbi and communal leader. Born and educated in Jerusalem, Rabbi Meir was elected haham bashi of the Jewish millet in 1906. He held this post for two years and then accepted a pulpit in Salonika, where he remained until 1919. Returning to *Eretz Israel* in 1920, he helped to organize the chief rabbinate of mandatory Palestine/*Eretz Israel* and was elected first Sephardi chief rabbi in 1921. An avid Zionist, Meir strongly supported the revival of Hebrew as a first step in fulfillment of the Zionist dream.

Mendelssohn, Erich (1887–1953): German-Israeli architect. Born and raised in Germany, Mendelssohn was one of the leaders of the revivalist architectural movement in Europe during the 1920s. He left Germany for England in 1933 but settled in *Eretz Israel* shortly after arrival. Between 1934 and 1939, he designed many prominent buildings in the *Yishuv*, including the Anglo-Palestine Bank's headquarters in Jerusalem and the Hadassah Hospital on Mount Scopus.

Monsky, Henry (1890–1947): American Jewish communal leader. Born in Russia, Monsky grew up in Nebraska. He was an ardent Zionist and was active in the Zionist Organization of America and in B'nai B'rith (BB). He was credited with moving the American branch of BB toward support for Zionist goals during the 1930s and 1940s. During World War II, Monsky came to the conclusion that American Jewry had to assume a position of leadership in the Jewish world. Yet, to do so required a greater degree of interinstitutional cooperation than existed at the time. In light of this need, in 1943, Monsky organized the American Jewish Conference. Although it did not immediately fulfill all its tasks, the conference was active after the war in promoting a united Jewish front on behalf of statehood.

Montefiore, Moses (1784–1885): Anglo-Jewish communal leader. Born in Livorno, Italy, but raised in London, Montefiore became famous as a financier to the British royal house. He was knighted in 1837, the first English Jew so honored. In 1827, after his first visit to *Eretz Israel*, he became an observant Jew. Montefiore used his influence to promote Jewish causes throughout the world. In particular, he helped obtain justice for the Damascus Jews falsely accused of using Christian blood during the blood libel in 1840. Coincidentally, Montefiore was on a pilgrimage to Jerusalem at the time and was shocked to see the squalor in which Jerusalem Jews lived. To rectify this situation, Montefiore donated the money to build the first Jewish neighborhood outside the Old City's walls (now known as Yemin Moshe in his honor) and built a windmill to provide energy for a textile mill that he hoped to build in the city. Although the textile mill was never built, the windmill has become a cherished historical site. Montefiore supported the *Yishuv* for his entire life.

Montor, Henry (1905–1982): American Zionist leader. Born in Canada, Montor was active in the United States and was principally identified with the Zionist Organization of America (ZOA). Between 1926 and 1930, he edited *New Palestine*. From 1930 to 1939, he headed the United Palestine Appeal (UPA), ZOA's fundraising arm. In 1939, when UPA merged with other funds to form the United Jewish Appeal

(UJA), Montor served as executive vice president. Retiring from the UJA in 1950, he served in a variety of posts encouraging Jewish investment in the State of Israel.

Motzkin, Leo (1867–1933): Ukrainian Zionist leader. Born in Kiev, Motzkin studied in Berlin. In Germany, Motzkin became a supporter of Hibbat Zion and helped found its youth organization. However, Motzkin soon became one of the strongest critics of Hovevei Zion's methods. With the appearance of Theodor Herzl, Motzkin immediately joined the newly formed WZO and headed a group of delegates that demanded a clear and decisive wording of the Basel Program. By the Fifth Zionist Congress, Motzkin began to have second thoughts about Herzl and joined the Democratic Fraction. Motzkin strongly opposed settlement in East Africa, even though he did not support the Practical Zionists. During World War I, Motzkin advocated Zionist neutrality. He headed the WZO's Copenhagen Bureau during the war and was a member of the Comité des Délégations Juives at the Paris peace talks. In 1919, Motzkin helped frame the terms for the national minorities treaties that were signed by the League of Nations and the Eastern European successor states. In 1925, Motzkin was appointed chairman of the Va'ad ha-Poel ha-Mezumzam, a post he held until his death.

Namier, Lewis (1888–1960): English historian and Zionist leader. Born in Poland, he migrated to England in 1906. In 1914, Namier volunteered for the British army. After his war service, Namier devoted himself to the Zionist cause. From 1929 to 1931, Namier served as political secretary to the Zionist Executive and was the chief draftsman of the JA enlargement plan of 1929. Closely linked to WZO president Chaim Weizmann, Namier shared Weizmann's belief that gradual development was best for the *Yishuv* and would minimize potential conflicts with the British government.

Neumann, Emanuel (1893–1980): American Zionist leader. Born in Latvia, Neumann immigrated to the United States

with his family. In 1909, Neumann helped found the Young Judea organization, a non-partisan youth movement under Hadassah's auspices. After World War I, Neumann headed the Zionist Organizations of America's (ZOA) Education Department and was chairman of the Keren ha-Yesod in North America (1921–1925). From 1925 to 1928, Neumann was chairman of the United Palestine Appeal executive committee. He served as president of Keren Kayemet le-Israel in the United States from 1928 to 1930. Neumann settled in *Eretz Israel* in 1931 and served as chairman of the JAE from 1931 to 1935. Although a general Zionist, Neumann was an ally of David Ben-Gurion. The two shared a maximalist approach to Zionist issues and both sought the creation of a Jewish state. Neumann continued to serve the JAE in a number of capacities after relinquishing the chairmanship in 1935. Leaving the *Yishuv* in 1941, he was elected president of ZOA in 1947, holding the position until 1948 and again from 1958 to 1968.

Niemirower, Jacob I. (1872–1939): Romanian rabbi and Zionist advocate. Born and educated in Galicia, Niemirower served as rabbi of Iasi. In 1911 he was nominated head of the Sephardi community in Bucharest and later chief rabbi of Romania. He was active in the Zionist movement and strongly opposed Romanian antisemitism. In 1936 Niemirower survived an attempt on his life by Garda de Fier members. He retired in 1939 due to ill health but died a short time later.

Nissenbaum, Yitzhak (1868–1942): Polish rabbi and Zionist leader. Born in Belorussia, Nissenbaum started his career in Minsk. He became involved in Zionist affairs early on and was fervent about the idea of Jews taking a hand in their redemption. He was active in Mizrachi from the beginning, serving on the executive of Mizrachi's Polish branch. In 1900 Nissenbaum settled in Warsaw and continued to preach the Mizrachi message. Remaining in Poland at the start of World War II, he was incarcerated in the Warsaw ghetto. He originated the concept of Kiddush ha-Hayim — spiritual resistance designed to elevate preserving life to the status of a positive *mitzva*. In 1942 he was deported to Treblinka and was murdered there.

Nordau, Max (pseud., Simon Zidfeld, 1849–1923): Hungarian Zionist leader. Born in Budapest, Nordau studied and practiced medicine in Paris. He became a close confidant of Theodor Herzl's and in 1897 helped found the World Zionist Congress and the WZO. Nordau drafted the Basel Program and delivered the keynote address to every Zionist congress from 1897 to 1911. A dedicated Political Zionist, he opposed both Practical and Spiritual Zionism as advocated by Ahad ha-Am. Nordau withdrew from the central position he played in the WZO after 1911 but remained an active Zionist. In 1920 he proposed a massive *aliya* scheme that would have brought 600,000 Jews to *Eretz Israel* in two years. When this scheme was rejected by the WZO leadership as unrealistic (due to underdeveloped conditions in *Eretz Israel*), Nordau severed all further direct relations with the WZO.

Nossig, Alfred (1864–1943): Polish artist and Zionist advocate. Born in Lemberg, Nossig made his reputation as a sculptor. Initially an assimilationist, Nossig converted to Zionism around 1908. He then became involved with organizations seeking colonization in *Eretz Israel*. His contributions to Jewish scholarship included collection of statistics that later served as the basis for the Jewish Statistical and Demographic Institute in Warsaw. Nossig lived in Germany during the 1920s, but returned to Poland in 1933. In 1943 he was sentenced to death by the Jewish underground in Warsaw on suspicion that he was working as an agent for the Gestapo.

Nurock, Mordechai (1879–1962): Russian-Latvian religious Zionist leader. Born in Courland, Nurock was educated in Moscow and obtained rabbinic ordination. He served at a number of pulpits in Latvia. He joined the Russian Zionist federation in 1902 and was elected a delegate to the Sixth Zionist Congress in 1903. Nurock's stand against settlement in Uganda catapulted him into the forefront of Russian Zionism. Late in World War I, Nurock left Latvia (then occupied by the Germans) and settled in Moscow. He was elected vice president of the Moscow Jewish community in its first open election in 1918 and succeeded in uniting disparate elements into a cohesive community. Nurock hoped to organize a Russian Jewish congress, but this came to nought after the Bolshevik takeover. Nurock fled Moscow and returned to Latvia in 1921. Elected to the Latvian parliament on a religious Zionist list, Nurock was asked to form a coalition government in 1926. Although he did indeed establish a stable (but short-lived) coalition, Nurock did not directly serve in the government. Nurock attended every Zionist Congress after the sixth, and he chaired the closing session of most of the congresses. After the Soviets occupied Latvia, Nurock was declared an enemy of the state. He was arrested in early 1941 and imprisoned for some fourteen months. As a result, he was not in Riga when the Nazis occupied the city; his wife and sons were there, however, and were murdered. In 1945 Nurock was permitted to leave the Soviet Union. He settled in the United States and then immigrated to Israel in 1948. He was elected to the first Knesset, one of only a few members to have served in a foreign parliament. He remained in the Knesset for the rest of his life, being elected speaker in the late 1950s.

Pines, Yehiel M. (1843–1913): Russian Zionist leader and journalist. Born in Belorussia, he was an early and ardent opponent of assimilation. Pines played a critical role in some of the early efforts to establish agricultural settlements in *Eretz Israel*. He himself moved to Jerusalem in 1878. Although traditional in outlook, Pines opposed *Haluka* and engaged in a bitter and lengthy dispute with the Ashkenazi rabbinic leadership. > see also: **Haluka**.

Pinsker, Leon J. (1821–1891): Russian physician and Zionist advocate. Born in Poland, Pinsker studied medicine at the University of Odessa. Although he was originally oriented toward assimilation, Pinsker abandoned hope of Jewish emancipation in czarist Russia in the aftermath of the pogroms of 1881–1882. In 1882, Pinsker published *Auto-Emancipation*, a pamphlet in which he called upon Jews to abandon emancipation and assimilation and instead focus on national rebirth through settlement in *Eretz Israel*.

Pinsker voiced many of the same arguments that would later be used by Theodor Herzl, notably regarding the immutability of anti-semitism. Pinsker offered a novel psychological explanation for Jew-hatred: Having no country of their own, Jews were ethereal, a disembodied spirit (in effect, a ghost); however, most humans fear ghosts. Hence antisemitism, according to Pinsker, derived from the unusual circumstances in which Jews lived. In order to rectify this situation, Pinsker advocated the creation of a Jewish national home in *Eretz Israel*. Pinsker's booklet influenced many like-minded Russian Jewish intellectuals who organized the Hibbat Zion movement. Pinsker was elected Hibbat Zion president in 1884 and held the position until his death. However, when Pinsker died, Hibbat Zion collapsed. > see also: **Proto-Zionism; Hibbat Zion**.

Rabinowitz, Samuel J. (1857–1921): Lithuanian rabbi and Zionist leader. Born in Vilna and ordained as a rabbi, Rabinowitz joined Hibbat Zion as a young man. When that organization ceased to function, he joined the WZO and was elected a delegate to the Second Zionist Congress. His forthright position on Zionist issues made a deep impression on other religious Zionist leaders and on Theodor Herzl as well. Rabinowitz served on the Va'ad ha-Poel ha-Gadol for many years. In 1900, He accompanied Rabbi Isaac J. Reines on his mission to Eastern Europe. Hoping to influence Hasidic leaders to support Zionism, they issued a clarion call for Orthodox Jews to take part in the grand national undertaking. Meeting with only limited success, Rabinowitz elected to stay in Poland in an effort to expand Zionist work there. In 1902, he joined with other religious Zionists in founding he Mizrachi movement. He remained active in Mizrachi for the rest of his life.

Rabinowitz, Saul P. (1845–1890): Polish Zionist leader and writer. Better known by his initials, Shepher, Rabinowitz was born and educated in Lithuania. Already as a young man he supported efforts to re-create a Jewish national home and was a vocal supporter of Rabbi Zvi Hirsch Kalischer.

In 1881, he helped to organize efforts to find new homes for Jews fleeing the pogroms. In 1884, Rabinowitz joined Hibbat Zion, serving as secretary of the Warsaw office. In addition to his Zionist work, Rabinowitz found time to contribute to Jewish scholarship, notably by translating Heinrich Graetz's monumental history of the Jews into Hebrew.

Raziel, David (1910–1942): Revisionist Zionist underground leader. Born in Lithuania, Raziel was brought to *Eretz Israel* by his parents. In 1929, Raziel joined the Hagana. He was soon disenchanted with the Hagana's defensive doctrine, however, and in 1931, he joined with dissident members to found the Irgun Zvai Leumi (IZL). In 1937, Raziel assumed command of the IZL and moved the organization further to the right. During his tenure as commander, IZL placed heavy emphasis on *Aliya Bet* and on retaliation for Arab terrorism. Raziel was arrested in 1939, but was released in 1940. Agreeing to a truce with the British for the duration of World War II, Raziel worked with British intelligence in the Middle East. He was killed during an air raid while he was on a joint intelligence mission in Iraq.

Reines, Isaac J. (1839–1915): Lithuanian rabbi and Zionist leader. Reines was born and educated in Vilna. Although he officiated at Orthodox pulpits, Reines was an advocate of secular education in addition to the standard curriculum of Talmudic study current in yeshivot at the end of the nineteenth century. Reines was one of the first rabbis to answer Theodor Herzl's call to convene a Zionist congress to discuss the means to restore Jews to their ancestral homeland. After the Fourth Zionist Congress (1900), Reines undertook a lengthy mission in Eastern Europe attempting to obtain approval from Hasidic and other Orthodox leaders for expanding the role played by Orthodox Jews in the WZO. His mission was not a complete success but did obtain the support of a number of prominent rabbis. In 1902, Reines convoked Orthodox supporters of Zionism into a single movement that adopted the name Mizrachi. Reines led Mizrachi until his death.

Remez, David (Drabkin, 1886–1951): Labor Zionist leader. Born in Russia, Remez settled in Turkey in 1911 and immigrated to *Eretz Israel* after World War I. Active in Poale Zion in Russia, Remez joined the Histadrut when it was founded and was elected secretary-general, a position he held between 1926 and 1936. He undertook a number of diplomatic missions thereafter, being elected chairman of the Va'ad Leumi between 1944 and 1948. He was elected to the Knesset in 1949, serving in ministerial positions in the provisional government and in the first cabinets.

Ringelblum, Emmanuel (1900–1944): Polish Zionist leader, communal activist, historian, and educator. Born in Galicia, Ringelblum was educated in Warsaw and taught high school there. In 1938, he was appointed one of the representatives of the American Jewish Joint Distribution Committee in Warsaw. An active Zionist, Ringelblum was a member of Poale Zion and the Hitahdut. He remained in Warsaw during the Nazi occupation and founded the Oneg Shabbat archive. One of the founders of the Jewish Combat Organization, Ringleblum was removed from the ghetto by sympathetic Poles during the Warsaw Ghetto uprising. Hiding with his family in the Aryan part of the city, he and his family were betrayed and were murdered by the Nazis in 1944.

Rosen, Pinhas (Fritz Rosenblüth, 1887–1978): German Zionist leader. Born in Berlin, Rosen was active in the German Zionist organization, rising to chairmanship between 1920 and 1923. Rosen settled in *Eretz Israel* in 1923 and was one of the founders of the Hitahdut Olei Germania. In 1925, Rosen was appointed to the London JAE and served there until 1931. Returning to the *Yishuv* in 1931, Rosen was active in the General Zionists and in the Aliya Hadasha party. In 1948, he helped to found the Progressive party and served in the provisional government as minister of justice (a position he held until 1961).

Rothschild, Edmond de (1845–1934): Franco-Jewish philanthropist. A scion of the famous banking family, he was born and raised in France. Although originally cool to the idea of Zionist settlement in *Eretz Israel*,

Rothschild felt compelled to help the settlers. Rothschild remained cool to Zionism even after meeting with Theodor Herzl, and he continued to operate independently of the WZO. Over the course of some thirty years, Rothschild or his representatives purchased nearly 125,000 acres of land in *Eretz Israel*. In 1900, due to ill health, Rothschild gave up day-to-day oversight of the settlements, transferring that task to the Palestine Jewish Colonization Association (PICA). However, Rothschild served as president of PICA until his death. Given the critical nature of his support, Rothschild was known throughout the Jewish world as *ha-Nadiv ha-Yadua* (the well-known benefactor). > see also: **Ha-Nadiv ha-Yadua.**

Ruppin, Arthur (1876–1943): Sociologist, economist, and Zionist settlement expert. Born in Poland, Ruppin was educated in Germany. From 1903 to 1907 he directed the Bureau for Jewish Statistics in Berlin, applying basic sociological research to the Jewish people. While undertaking his research, Ruppin joined the Zionist movement. In 1907, Ruppin was

Dr. Arthur Ruppin,
Zionist Settlement Expert and JAE Member.
Courtesy of the Central Zionist Archives, Jerusalem

sent to *Eretz Israel* by the WZO. He headed the Jaffa office and was responsible for both land purchase and settlement building. In this capacity, Ruppin had a major impact on the settlements of the Second Aliya. It was his decision, for instance, to allow recent *olim* to settle at the WZO training facility at Sejera that facilitated the creation of the first *Kvutzot*. This in turn led to the creation of the collective settlement movement that became a hallmark of the *Yishuv*. Ruppin was deported by the Turks in 1916 but returned and resumed his work in 1920. He joined the Zionist Executive in 1926 as director of the Colonization Department, remaining in this position when the "enlarged" JAE was created. A liberal by nature, Ruppin was also binationalist in orientation. Even so, he was entrusted with highly sensitive positions in the JAE during the 1930s, mainly relating to *aliya* and settlement from Central Europe.

Rutenberg, Pinhas (1879–1942): Zionist engineer, businessman, and political leader. Born in the Ukraine, Rutenberg was active in the Russian Social Revolutionary party. He participated in the revolution of October 1905 but was forced to flee the country after the counterrevolution. In 1917, Rutenberg returned to Russia and resumed his work for democratic reforms. He left again, this time permanently, after the Bolshevik takeover. Although active in a general party, Rutenberg always maintained contacts with the Jewish community. When he left the Soviet Union, he settled in *Eretz Israel*. Seeing a need for electrification, Rutenberg founded the Palestine Electric Company (PEC). As head of PEC Rutenberg oversaw the creation of the *Yishuv*'s electrical grid and many other improvements in infrastructure. Elected to the Va'ad Leumi in 1929, Rutenberg considered himself above partisan Zionist politics. In 1934 he made the initial contacts that led to the abortive Ben-Gurion–Jabotinsky agreement.

Sadeh, Yitzhak (Landsberg, 1890–1952): Israeli military leader. Born in Poland, Sadeh served in the Russian army during World War I. He left the Soviet Union after the Bolshevik takeover, settling in *Eretz Israel* in 1920. Sadeh joined the Gdud ha-Avoda and was a trusted adviser of Joseph Trumpeldor. After the Gdud collapsed, Sadeh joined the Hagana, rising through the ranks. In 1941, Sadeh was ordered to create a strike force for the Hagana; what emerged was the Palmah, which he commanded until 1945. The Palmah was heavily influenced by Sadeh's personality, emphasizing bold operations and an egalitarian spirit among the fighters. Most Palmah members belonged to *Kibbutzim* and *Kvutzot* associated with ha-Shomer ha-Zair, an organization that Sadeh was also associated with. Between 1945 and 1948, Sadeh served on the Hagana staff; in 1948, he commanded the Israeli army's only armored brigade. He retired after the war.

Samuel, Herbert L. (1870–1963): Anglo-Zionist leader and statesman. Born in England, Samuel was elected to Parliament as a Liberal in 1902. He served in successive governments, both in Parliament and as privy councillor, postmaster general, and home secretary. He was active in the English Zionist Federation (EZF) almost from its creation and provided a useful contact between Zionist leaders and members of the British government. His April 1915 report on British imperial interests in the postwar Middle East began the process that culminated in the Balfour Declaration. When Britain assumed the League of Nations mandate for Palestine/*Eretz Israel*, Samuel was appointed first High Commissioner. Samuel resumed his parliamentary career in 1931, holding honorary positions in the EZF. During the 1930s, Samuel was in the forefront of those advocating action to rescue German Jewry, presiding over the Council for German Jewry from 1936 to 1939. Samuel was elevated to peerage in 1944, being knighted as Viscount Samuel of Palestine.

Samuel, Maurice (1895–1972): Romanian-American author and Zionist advocate. Born in Romania, Samuel emigrated to England with his family when he was a child. In 1914, he settled in the United States, establishing a reputation as an author and translator. Mainly writing about antisemitism and the Jewish problem, Samuel advocated Zionism as a means of regulating the tension inherent in relations between Jews and their neighbors. His book, *Harvest in the Desert*, helped introduce American Jews to the work of Zionist pioneers in *Eretz Israel* and gained wide support from many Americans — Jews and non-Jews alike — who might not have otherwise supported Zionism.

Sapir, Pinhas (1907–1975): Labor Zionist leader. Born in Poland, Sapir immigrated to *Eretz Israel* in 1924. He initially worked in citrus groves and was active in the Histadrut. During the 1940s he was appointed head of the civil defense network in the Negev, a post he held until after the War of Independence. During the 1950s and 1960s he served in the Knesset as a Mapai member; he held ministerial posts in most governments from 1955 until his death.

Schapira, Hermann Zvi (1840–1898): Lithuanian Zionist. Born and educated in Lithuania, Schapira held a variety of rabbinic posts in Lithuania and Germany during the 1860s and 1870. After the pogroms in Russia in 1881, he became a supporter of Hibbat Zion. In 1897, Schapira served as a delegate at the First Zionist Congress, where he proposed the creation of a Jewish national fund. Although he did not live to see the realization of his idea, Schapira is rightfully considered the father of the Keren Kayemet le-Israel.

Schechter, Solomon (1847–1915): Anglo-American scholar, educator, Conservative rabbi, and Zionist advocate. Schechter was born in Romania and migrated to England as an adult. He began teaching Semitics at Cambridge University in 1890. His most famous scholarly achievement was the discovery of the Cairo Geniza. In 1901, Schechter was appointed chancellor of the Jewish Theological Seminary of America, the premier institution of Conservative Judaism in North America. Schechter was of the opinion that Jews survived because of their spiritual compass. Nevertheless, he became increasingly convinced that Jewry's spirituality could only be preserved if Jews lived in a land that was conducive to their spiritual growth. Schechter, therefore, became a strong supporter of Zionism in the last decade and a half of his life.

Schipper, Ignacy (1884–1943): Polish Zionist leader and Jewish historian. Born in Galicia, Schipper was educated in Warsaw and was an early advocate of Zionism. He served as president of the Polish general Zionist federation from 1922. Between 1922 and 1927, he also served in the Polish Sejm. During the 1930s, Schipper lectured in Jewish history at the Institute for Jewish Studies in Warsaw. Schipper remained in Poland during World War II. He was deported to Treblinka in the aftermath of Warsaw ghetto uprising and perished there.

Schocken, Salman S. (1877–1959): German publisher and Zionist advocate. Born and raised in Germany, Schocken was a collector of rare books and manuscripts. Obtaining financial independence thanks to his Schocken Verlag (publishing house), he donated considerable time and effort to create the Research Institute for Medieval Jewish Poetry. In 1934 he moved, with most of his operations, to Tel Aviv. In the early 1950s he moved to New York and he opened a branch of his publishing house.

Schwarzbart, Ignacy I. (1888–1961): Polish Zionist and communal activist. Born and educated in Galicia, Schwarzbart was among the founders of the World Union of General Zionists in 1929. He was active in finding residences for Jewish refugees from Nazi Germany in 1938 and 1939, a period when he also served in the Sejm. Electing to leave Poland after the Nazi invasion, Schwarzbart served as Jewish affairs adviser in the Polish government in exile.

Shamir, Yitzhak (Yezernitzki, b. 1915): Israeli underground leader and politician. Born in Poland, Shamir immigrated to *Eretz Israel* in 1935. He had been active in Betar and joined the Irgun Zvai Leumi (IZL) shortly after he arrived. Representing the right wing of the IZL, Shamir joined with Abraham Stern in seceding from the IZL to form Lohame Herut Israel (Lehi). Arrested in 1941, Shamir escaped and rebuilt Lehi in 1943. He continued to oversee operations as part of a triumvirate that included Israel Eldad and Nathan Yellin-Mor.

Shamir continued to lead Lehi until 1948, when he was arrested for involvement in the assassination of Count Folke Bernadotte, the Swedish diplomat appointed U.N. mediator in the War of Independence. Shamir's actions between 1948 and 1973 are virtually unknown; he served as a member of the Knesset from 1973 to 1992, however, and was prime minister from 1984 to 1992.

Sharef, Ze'ev (1906–1984): Israeli civil servant and labor Zionist activist. Born in Bukovina, Sharef settled in *Eretz Israel* in 1925. He became active in Mapai and the Histadrut, and was appointed secretary of the provisional government's emergency civil administration agencies. As such, Sharef laid the groundwork for the creation of the Israeli civil service during the 1950s. He remained in the government until retirement in 1977.

Sharett, Moshe (Shertok, 1894–1965): Labor Zionist leader, Israel's first foreign minister and second prime minister. Born in the Ukraine, Sharett immigrated to *Eretz Israel* in 1906. Active in Poale Zion, Sharett became involved with the Histadrut in 1920 and with Mapai a decade later. In 1933, he was selected to replace Haim Arlosoroff as head of the JA Political Department, in effect, the *Yishuv's* foreign minister. He held that position uninterruptedly until 1948. Neither a gradualist nor a maximalist, Sharett's positions were largely based on what he considered possible to achieve and what he considered necessary for the *Yishuv* and the Jewish people. From 1948 to 1953, he served as Israeli foreign minister and from 1953 to 1955 as prime minister. He was appointed chairman of the JA in 1955.

Shazar, Zalman (Schneur Zalman Rubashov, 1889–1974): Labor Zionist leader and third president of Israel. Born in Belorussia, Shazar was raised in a Hasidic household but was educated at a modern yeshiva established in Lithuania by Baron Joseph Gunzburg. Shazar's father was a devotee of the Lubavitch Hasidic sect, Sahazar being named after the Grand Rabbi, Schenur Zalman of Lyady, but he was also a Zionist and a follower of

Theodor Herzl. Shazar grew up an able writer and speaker and a passionate Zionist. Arrested by the czarist authorities, he was exiled in Germany when World War I broke out. Shazar settled in *Eretz Israel* in 1924 and immediately became involved in the Histadrut and Mapai. He worked as a contributor and an editor on *Davar*, as well as in a series of education-related posts in Mapai, the WZO, and the JAE. Shazar served as minister of education and culture in the provisional government and in the first Knesset. Elected third president of Israel in 1963 he retired in 1973.

Sieff, Israel M. (1889–1972): Anglo-Jewish industrialist, philanthropist, and Zionist. Born and raised in England, Sieff was a collaborator in chemical research with Chaim Weizmann. Sieff was introduced to Zionism by Weizmann, who appointed him secretary of the Zionist Commission that visited *Eretz Israel* in 1918. In 1934 the Sieff family donated the funds for a scientific research center (named after their son Daniel) that later became the Weizmann Institute of Science.

Silver, Abba Hillel (1893–1963): American Zionist leader and rabbi. Born in Lithuania, Silver was raised and educated in the United States. In his youth, Silver had created a group in honor of Theodor Herzl, and he remained committed to Zionism for his entire life. In 1933, he strongly supported the anti-Nazi boycott as well as a variety of other measures to help distressed German and Eastern European Jews find a haven. Silver was appointed president of the United Palestine Appeal (UPA) in 1938 and immediately set out to convert it from a minor fund-raising agency to a central clearinghouse for Zionist political work. This same zeal followed Silver to the American Zionist Emergency Council which he cochaired, in the 1940s. An activist by nature, Silver distrusted President Franklin D. Roosevelt and emphatically disagreed with the "behind-the-scenes" approach to Jewish diplomacy advocated by such leaders as Stephen S. Wise. Silver served as president of the Zionist Organization of America and chairman of the JAE American branch. He remained active in Zionist affairs after the State of Israel was established but remained in the United States.

Nahum Sokolow, Seen During His Tenure As President of the WZO.
Courtesy of the Central Zionist Archives, Jerusalem

Smilanski, Moshe (1874–1953): Israeli writer and Zionist activist. Born in the Ukraine, Smilanski immigrated to *Eretz Israel* in 1890, and soon began his own farm in Rehovot. A frequent contributor to the *Yishuv's* press, he also published a number of historical novels that captured the spirit of the First Aliya.

Sneh, Moshe (Kleinbaum, 1909–1972): Labor Zionist politician and leader. Born in Poland as Moshe Kleinbaum, Sneh joined the General Zionist movement in 1935. He fled Poland to *Eretz Israel* when World War II broke out, arriving in 1940. In 1941, Sneh was appointed to the national command of the Hagana. In 1945, he was nominated to the JAE but resigned shortly after his appointment. Simultaneously, Sneh left the General Zionists and joined Mifleget ha-Poalim ha-Meuhad (Mapam), with whom he served in the Knesset. He later left Mapam and joined the Israeli Communist party.

Sokolow, Nahum (1859–1936): Polish Zionist leader and writer. Born in Poland, Sokolow began his career as a journalist. He joined the WZO as a young man and held the post of organization secretary between 1905 and 1909. At the same time, he edited the WZO's organ, *Die Welt*. Sokolow left Berlin for London just prior to World War I. He was thus in an opportune location when negotiations over the Balfour Declaration began. After the war, Sokolow continued his activities, undertaking an important mission to France and serving with the Comité des délégations Juives in Geneva. Sokolow was elected to the WZO executive and served as its chairman between 1921 and 1931. When Chaim Weizmann was removed as president, Sokolow took his place (1931–1935).

Spire, André (1868–1966): French Zionist leader. Born in France, Spiré joined the French government in 1894. He worked at the Ministry of Labor between 1898 and 1902 and at the

Ministry of Agriculture between 1902 and 1926. Active in Alfred Dreyfus's defense, Spiré became an ardent Zionist. In 1919, he represented the French Zionist federation at the Paris peace talks. Spiré fled France for the United States during the Nazi occupation, but he returned and continued to advocate Zionism as a means of fending off Jewish communal apathy for the rest of his life.

Sprinzak, Yosef (1885–1959): Labor Zionist leader. Born in Russia, Sprinzak was one of the founders of Zeirei Zion. Sprinzak immigrated to *Eretz Israel* in 1908. He was active in ha-Shomer before World War I and in the Histadrut and Mapai in the interwar era. Elected to the Knesset in 1949, he later served as speaker of the house.

Stern, Abraham (Yair, 1907–1942): Israeli underground leader. Born in Poland, Stern immigrated to *Eretz Israel* in 1925. He was among the first members of the Irgun Zvai Leumi (IZL) and was appointed to the underground's high command in the mid-1930s. Although considering himself a disciple of Ze'ev Jabotinsky, Stern was not as committed to the liberal democratic tradition as his master. In 1940, he withdrew from the IZL with other members who disagreed with the policy of reaching a truce with the British while fighting the Nazis. Stern advocated continued revolt against the "real" enemy of the Jews, that is, against the nation occupying *Eretz Israel*. Stern and his followers founded the rival Lohamei Herut Israel underground in late 1940. Stern's most controversial act was his attempt to contact the Italians and the Germans with an offer of alliance. He hoped the Axis would support a Jewish revolt against Britain but seemed to have completely misunderstood the nature of Nazi antisemitism. In any case, the Axis powers never responded. Stern himself became the target of an intense police search in 1942. He was discovered and was killed by British police officers in April 1942.

Stricker, Robert (1879–1944): Austrian journalist and Zionist leader. Born and educated in Austria, Stricker was active in the Vienna Jewish community prior to World War I. In 1915, he founded the Jewish War Archives to document the heroism of Jewish soldiers and to refute the antisemitic canard that Jews did not serve in the Austro-Hungarian army. Stricker was a founder of the Jüdische Volkspartei in 1919 and served as party president for most of the 1920s. A close associate and friend of Ze'ev Jabotinsky, Stricker joined ha-Zohar in 1931. However, he disagreed with Jabotinsky's decision to secede from the WZO and joined the Jewish State Party instead. Remaining in Austria when the Nazis occupied the country in 1938, Stricker was incarcerated in concentration camps. Despite efforts to obtain his freedom, he was murdered in 1944.

Sukenik, Eliezer L. (1889–1953): Israeli archeologist. Born in Poland, he settled in Eretz Israel in 1912. Sukenik was involved in some of the most important archeological discoveries in modern Israel. He excavated the walls of Jerusalem, the cities of Bet Alpha and Samaria, and was the first to identify the Dead Sea Scrolls as a major historical source. Sukenik taught at Hebrew University for his entire career.

Syrkin, Marie (1899–1988): American Zionist writer and educator. Born in Switzerland, she was the daughter of Nachman Syrkin. She remained a devoted socialist Zionist all her life and was active in Mapai in the United States. A prolific writer, she spent considerable time in the displaced persons camps in Europe after World War II.

Syrkin, Nachman (1868–1924): Socialist Zionist visionary. Born in Belorussia, Syrkin was a delegate to the First Zionist Congress. After a stay in Berlin he settled in New York in 1907. Although he was a committed Zionist, Syrkin dallied with territorialism during the early years of the twentieth century. Nonconfrontational in his approach to both socialism and Zionism, Syrkin advocated cooperation with nonsocialist Zionists, although he clearly did not accept them as equal partners in regard to the future of the Jewish people. After World War I, Syrkin played an active role in the American Jewish Congress and the Comité des Délégations Juives.

Szold, Henrietta (1860–1945): American Zionist leader, born in Baltimore. Her father, Benjamin Szold, was a prominent rabbi and Zionist activist. Szold served in a variety of communal posts, including as secretary of the Jewish Publication Society. In 1912, she founded Hadassah, the Women's Zionist Organization of America. When Szold was appointed to the Zionist Executive (the first woman so appointed) she was given the health portfolio. As a result Hadassah became involved in improving health care facilities in the *Yishuv*. In 1933, Szold assumed responsibility for Youth Aliya. Although she never married and had no children of her own, she had a strong motherly bond with the youth. Youth Aliya was a crowning achievement for Szold and for the *Yishuv*: it was the only element of the *Yishuv* rescue efforts during the Nazi era that was not terminated by the White Paper of 1939.

Tabenkin, Yitzhak (1899–1971): Labor Zionist leader. Born in Belorussia, Tabenkin was one of the founders of Poale Zion. Settling in *Eretz Israel* in 1912, Tabenkin was a member of ha-Shomer, but he remained in *Eretz Israel* during World War I. After the war, he joined Gdud ha-Avoda and was one of the founding members of Ein Harod. Although he was a founding member of both the Histadrut and Mapai, Tabenkin increasingly identified with the left wing of both organizations. For most of the 1930s he was certainly situated to the left of David Ben-Gurion on most issues, especially on the thorny relations between Mapai and the revisionists. As a result of these open disagreements with the Mapai leadership, Tabenkin's followers emerged as Mapai's *Siya Bet* during the late 1930s. When he left Mapai in 1944, *Siya Bet* followed, organizing into the new Ahdut ha-Avoda party. In 1948, Tabenkin oversaw the merger of this party in Mifleget ha-Poalim ha-Meuhad (Mapam). Elected a delegate to every Zionist congress from 1921 to 1970, Tabenkin served in the Knesset from 1948 to 1959.

Tartakower, Arye (1897–1982): Polish Jewish sociologist and educator, born in Galicia. Tartakower taught at the Institute for Jewish Studies in Warsaw, and was active in the Polish Zionist federation. In 1939, he was sent to the United States on a mission to collect funds for relief work and thus was not in Poland when World War II broke out. In 1946, Tartakower settled in *Eretz Israel*. He taught at Hebrew University and was active in Yad Vashem. He was also active in Mapai and the World Jewish Congress, heading its Israel office between 1948 and 1971.

Treitsch, Davis (1870–1935): German-American Zionist advocate. Born in Germany, he moved to the United States as a young man. He was an expert on Jewish migrations and was elected to the First Zionist Congress. Treitsh advocated Jewish settlement in Cyprus and El Arish, but did not join the territorialists when they withdrew from the WZO in 1906. Treistch continued to advocate schemes for mass *aliya* until the early 1930s. He himself immigrated to *Eretz Israel* in 1932.

Trumpeldor, Joseph (1880–1920): Russian Jewish military hero and Zionist leader. Born in Russia, Trumpeldor volunteered for service in the czarist army and rose to the rank of a subaltern. He lost his left arm, when he was wounded and captured during the Russo-Japanese war. Converted to Zionism during the war, Trumpeldor left for *Eretz Israel* in 1912. Deported to Egypt by the Turks, Trumpeldor was in the forefront of advocates for a Jewish Legion. He commanded units in the Zion Mule Corps and the legion during World War I. After the war, Trumpeldor briefly returned to Russia, where he helped to organize he-Halutz. Trumpeldor returned to *Eretz Israel* in 1919. Finding himself on the left of most Zionist organizations, he decided to create his own independent organization, Gdud ha-Avoda. The Gdud was designed to settle areas and protect them, thus opening new regions for Zionist settlement. Trumpeldor was killed by Arab marauders — ostensibly rebels looking for French soldiers — at Tel Hai in February 1920. > see also: **World War I**; **Tel Hai**.

Tschlenow, Jehiel (1861–1918): Russian Zionist leader, born in the Ukraine and educated as a physician. Active in Hibbat Zion, Tschlenow joined the WZO in 1897. He was a delegate to the First Zionist Congress and most of the subsequent congresses as well. A dedicated Zionist, Tschlenow strongly opposed the Uganda plan and helped organize the *Zionei Zion*. An advocate of wide-ranging Zionist activities, Tschlenow convened the Helsingfors Conference in 1906. He left Russia for Western Europe, spending World War I in Copenhagen and London. He returned to Russia after the first revolution (February 1917) in the hopes of organizing a mass Russian Zionist movement. The Bolshevik takeover and his untimely death put an end to these plans.

Unterman, Isser Yehuda (1886–1976): Russian-Israeli rabbi and religious Zionist leader. Born in Belorussia, Unterman was ordained and served at pulpits in Lithuania and England (where he was a member of the Chief Rabbi's Bet Din) prior to 1946. In 1946, Unterman was elected Ashkenazi chief rabbi of Tel Aviv. A strong supporter of Mizrachi, Unterman was an eloquent speaker known for his ability to turn a phrase. Unterman was elected Ashkenazi chief rabbi of Israel in 1964.

Ussishkin, Menahem Mendel (1863–1941): Russian Zionist leader. Born in Belorussia, Ussishkin was raised in Moscow. He was one of the founders of Bilu and also a founding member of Bnai Zion in Moscow and of Hibbat Zion. In 1897, Ussishkin was elected a delegate to the First Zionist Congress, and he attended every congress until 1939. An ardent Zionist, Ussishkin was a charismatic speaker whose discussions of Zionist policy carried considerable weight. For example, Ussishkin's booklet *Our Program* (1903) was the first attempt to synthesize both Political and Practical Zionism, a policy later adopted by the Democratic Fraction led by Chaim Weizmann. Ussishkin was one of the most vocal opponents of the Uganda plan and, during the 1930s, of partition. Ussishkin settled in *Eretz Israel* in 1903, leaving in 1909 and returning after World War I. During his lengthy public career, he was a member of the Va'ad ha-Poel ha-Zioni (both the larger and smaller comittees), a member of the

JAE, and chairman of the Keren Kayemet le-Israel. He was well respected by members of all political blocs, who saw him as a legendary figure beyond politics.

Uziel, Benzion Meir Hai (1880–1954): Israeli rabbi and communal leader. Born and educated in Jerusalem, he served in pulpits throughout Eretz Israel prior to 1912. In 1912, Uziel was elected Haham Bashi of the Sephardi community of Jaffa. In 1945, he was elected Sephardi chief rabbi (Rishon le-Zion) of *Eretz Israel*. He held this position until his death in 1954.

Viterbo, Carlo A. (1889–1974): Italian Zionist leader. Born and raised in Florence, Viterbo was active in the Italian Zionist federation and was elected its president in 1931. From 1931 to 1938 he edited *Israel*, the official organ of the Italian Zionist federation. Viterbo was arrested by the Fascists in 1943 and was imprisoned in the Sforzacosta internment camp. He was liberated in 1944 and resumed his editorial work, which continued until his death.

Vitkin, Joseph (1876–1917): Labor Zionist leader and ideologue. Born in Belorussia, Vitkin settled in *Eretz Israel* in 1898, working as a farmer and later as a teacher. He was one of the founders of ha-Poel ha-Zair and strongly believed that the Jewish people could be restored to their ancestral homeland only by combining Jewish nationalism with moderate socialism. Vitkin contemplated the implications of his ideology in his influential 1905 pamphlet, *A Call to the Youth of Israel*.

Warburg, Max (1867–1946): German Jewish banker and communal leader. Born in Hamburg, Warburg was active in the German Zionist organization. After World War I, Warburg represented the German Zionists at the Paris peace talks. In 1933, he was one of the Zionist leaders who initiated the *Ha'avara* (transfer) agreement by which German Jews immigrating to *Eretz Israel* could export some of the capital from the Reich. He settled in the United States in 1938.

Warburg, Otto (1859–1938): German Zionist leader and botanist. Born in Hamburg, Warburg was related to the Warburg banking family; Max Warburg was his cousin. He was appointed to a professorship in botany at the University of Berlin in 1892. Warburg joined the WZO in 1897 and was active in the German Zionist organization. At Warburg's initiative, the WZO opened an office in Jaffa in 1898. Although he never sought leadership positions, Warburg was elected president of the WZO in 1911 and served at this post until 1920. In 1921, he settled in *Eretz Israel*, where he headed the WZO Agricultural Research Station in Rehovot and taught at Hebrew University until his death.

Weisgal, Meyer W. (1894–1977): American Zionist leader and writer. Born in Poland, Weisgal moved to the United States with his family when he was eleven. He was active in the Zionist Organization of America, and acted as Chaim Weizmann's representative in the United States during the 1920s and 1930s. During World War II he served as political secretary of the JAE's American section. He settled in Israel in the late 1940s and eventually was appointed president of the Weizmann Institute of Science.

Weizmann, Chaim (1874–1952): Zionist leader and first president of the State of Israel. Born in Pinsk, Weizmann was educated as a chemist and was appointed to a professorship in chemistry at the University of Manchester in 1904. A lifelong Zionist, Weizmann was elected to every Zionist congress from 1901 onward. He was one of the organizers of the Democratic Fraction, the group of younger Zionists who opposed WZO president Theodor Herzl's methods and sought to reform the organization. A vehement opponent of the Uganda plan, Weizmann was a believer in what he termed Synthetic Zionism, that is, a synthesis of the diplomatic methods used by Herzl with the patient, steady building of "facts on the ground" as advocated by the Practical Zionists. Weizmann was one of the participants in the negotiations that led to the Balfour Declaration. Elected to the presidency of the WZO in 1921, Weizmann adopted a gradualist orientation in the hopes of building the *Yishuv*

WZO President Chaim Weizmann in a Conversation With the Last British High Commissioner for Palestine/*Eretz Israel*, Sir Alan Cunningham.
Courtesy of the Central Zionist Archives, Jerusalem

while avoiding too much conflict with the British administration. Although Weizmann was a staunch general Zionist, ironically, most of his steadiest supporters were socialist Zionists. Weizmann was removed from office between 1931 and 1935, although he resumed the WZO presidency after his successor, Nahum Sokolow died. By then, Weizmann's gradualism was no longer an asset and his conflict with David Ben-Gurion over activism versus moderation was a visceral one. Nonetheless, Weizmann was the WZO's most public asset and he could not simply be disposed of. In 1948, Weizmann was elected first president of the State of Israel, a position that was (and remains) largely symbolic.

Wise, Stephen S. (1874–1949): American Rabbi, Zionist leader, and communal activist. Born in Hungary, he migrated to the United States with his family when he was a child. Pursuing a rabbinic career, Wise held pulpits in Oregon and New York City. Wise was active in the Zionist Organization of America (ZOA), and he served as that organization's secretary. He was appointed to the Provisional Committee for Zionist Affairs in 1916, and was elected chairman immediately. The Provisional Committee represented ZOA at the Paris peace talks and in subsequent meetings prior to the adoption of the mandate. Wise was a founder, and the first president, of the American Jewish Congress and the World Jewish Congress. He supported an anti-Nazi boycott during the 1930s and was vocal in calling for rescue action on behalf of threatened European Jewry. However, during World War II, he opposed public protests that would embarrass the Roosevelt administration. From 1939 to 1944, Wise was cochairman of the American Zionist Emergency Council, where he worked with Rabbi Abba Hillel Silver. A gradualist by nature, Wise was a general Zionist all his life.

Wolffsohn, David (1856–1914): German Zionist leader. He was born in Lithuania and moved to Germany as a young adult. Wolffsohn joined the WZO in 1897 and actively participated in many of the early congresses. Wolffsohn was appointed Theodor Herzl's assistant during the fateful trip to meet Kaiser Wilhelm II in Jerusalem in 1898. Wolffsohn was elected president of the WZO after Herzl's death, serving in that capacity from 1905 to 1911. Although he was not as dynamic as Herzl, Wolffsohn played an important role in the WZO's growth. He held the organization together during the difficult era after Herzl's death, an era that saw the territorialists secede from the organization and that represented the nadir of Zionist fortunes.

Yadin, Yigael (1917–1984): Israeli military leader and archeologist. The son of Eliezer L. Sukenik, Yadin was born and raised in *Eretz Israel*. Yadin joined the Hagana as a young man and rose rapidly through the ranks. He served as deputy chief of staff and chief of operations during the War of Independence, rising to chief of staff in 1949. He retired from the military in 1952 and pursued a career as an archeologist, teaching at Hebrew University. Yadin entered politics in 1977.

Yellin, David (1864–1941): Zionist leader. Born and raised in Jerusalem, Yellin was a scholar and educator who taught at a number of seminaries and colleges. He ended his teaching career as a professor of literature at Hebrew University. Yellin was always active in *Yishuv* politics and was a dedicated Zionist. He served on the communal governing board in Jerusalem between 1910 and 1914. Appointed one of the *Yishuv*'s representatives to the Paris peace talks in 1919, Yellin also attended the San Remo Conference. Yellin served as chairman of the Jewish community of Jerusalem from 1919 to 1921, as deputy mayor of Jerusalem between 1920 and 1925 and as chairman of the Va'ad Leumi in 1928 and 1929.

Yosef, Dov (Bernard Joseph, 1899–1980): Canadian-Israeli Zionist leader and bureaucrat. Born in Canada, Yosef joined the Jewish Legion in 1918 and settled in *Eretz Israel* after World War I. In 1936, Yosef was appointed adviser to the JA Political Department, representing the JA in Jerusalem and London over the next ten years. In 1945, Joseph was appointed to full membership on the JAE. During the War of Independence, Yosef served as military governor of Jerusalem. Under the circumstances, he was virtually the sole authority in the city and operated with a wide degree of autonomy from the provisional government. A lifelong member of Mapai, Yosef was elected to the Knesset in 1949. He held a number of cabinet level posts during the 1950s and 1960s.

Zionut [ציונות, H] "Zionism":

1. Scope and Definition

Popular term for the movement and the ideology dedicated to re-creating a Jewish state in Palestine/*Eretz Israel*. The term derives from the Hebrew name *Zion*, a Biblical geographic name often used as a synonym for Jerusalem (e.g. Isaiah 2:3). Although there is some controversy about the first person to use the term in its modern sense, all scholars agree that the term "Zionist movement" came into general use during the last third of the nineteenth century. It certainly predates Theodor Herzl and, although never explicitly used in this form, animated the choice of the name for the Hovevei Zion Movement. > see also: **Hibbat Zion.**

In addition to its geographic derivation, the Hebrew term has messianic and redemptivist overtones in its traditional usage. Even so, the usage of the term "Zionism" in its modern, nationalistic sense was purely secular. This dichotomy may be explained by the rejection of modern nationalism by most of the Eastern European rabbinic leadership and by the rampant secularization of Eastern European Jewish society after the *Haskala*. Even as used by secular nationalists, however, the term was framed specifically as an expression of Jewish hopes for redemption and drew heavily upon historical and religious (or semireligious) roots.

2. Forms of Zionism

General Zionism, the form of Zionism identified with WZO members not otherwise affiliated with political blocs. When Theodor Herzl created the WZO, he did not consider the possibility that parties might emerge within the movement. General Zionists did not consider themselves to be a bloc until they ceased to be the majority of WZO members, after World War I. General Zionists were deeply divided among themselves between gradualists and maximalists and between those who supported an alliance with socialist Zionists and those who opposed it.

Political Zionism, the form of Zionism created by Theodor Herzl and dedicated exclusively to the goal of creating a Jewish state while paying relatively little regard to the internal structure of that state.

Religious Zionism, the form of Zionism associated with the Mizrachi party and dedicated to the creation of a Jewish state living under the terms of traditional Jewish law (*Halacha*), with emendations to permit the operation of a modern state.

Revisionist Zionism, the form of Zionism associated with Ze'ev Jabotinsky and dedicated to the creation of a Jewish state on both sides of the Jordan River. Jabotinsky created his movement in order to force the WZO leadership of his day to enunciate a maximalist position on Zionist demands. In effect, Jabotinsky sought a return to pure Political Zionism and rejected all of what he considered to be hyphenated Zionisms.

Socialist Zionism, the form of Zionism associated with Ber Borochov (and others) and dedicated to the creation of a Jewish workers' community in *Eretz Israel* that would become the central focus for a renewed Jewish world. Socialist Zionist parties generally agreed that Jews needed to return to agricultural labor, but they disagreed on almost all other fundamental issues: whether Zionism's goal was the creation of a sovereign Jewish state or merely a "national home;" whether a Jewish majority was needed to accomplish Zionist goals or not; whether Zionist fulfillment even needed *Eretz Israel* or could be accomplished in some other Jewish entity (such as Birobidzhan); and whether Zionism was the goal and socialism the means or socialism the goal and Zionism the means.

Spiritual Zionism, the form of Zionism associated with Ahad ha-Am (Asher Ginsburg) and dedicated to the creation of a national center in the Land of Israel that would lead to a period of intellectual and spiritual renewal among world Jewry.

Synthetic Zionism, the form of Zionism associated with Chaim Weizmann and dedicated to the creation of a synthesis between Spiritual and Political Zionism. In Weizmann's view, Zionism could not succeed in re-creating the Jewish community or in establishing Jewish sovereignty as two discrete goals. Rather, both had to be accomplished for either to have a chance to succeed.

Zionut Lohemet [ציונות לוחמת, H] "Fighting Zionism": Term associated with David Ben-Gurion and his turn to Zionist militancy after 1938. Ben-Gurion distinguished among a number of different eras in Zionist history, each of which was reflected in its own brand of Zionism. At the time he formulated this idea, Ben-Gurion saw two main forms of Zionism in conflict: "Building Zionism," which he saw as characterizing Chaim Weizmann's less militant approach to relations with the British, and "Fighting Zionism," which he saw as his own form of Zionist militancy. Central to Ben-Gurion's approach was the idea of an *Aliya* War; he preferred to use nonviolent means in the anti-British struggle since violence would alienate the British people while the Jews' struggle was only with the British government. Despite much tough rhetoric, fighting Zionism could not be manifested during World War II. After the war, Ben Gurion returned to this ideology until statehood was achieved. > see also: **Diplomatic Zionism**; **Gradualism**; **Milhemet Ha-Aliya**; **Biltmore Resolution**.

Zipora [צפורה, H] "Bird": Zahal code name for the mobile task force from the 8th (Armored) Brigade that attacked and captured the international airport at Lod on July 11–13, 1948. The term derived from the slang identification of an airplane as a bird, and was also used as a code name for the airport operation, which was part of a larger operation code-named Operation Dani. > see also: **War of Independence**.

Zivoni [צבעוני, H] "Tulip": Nickname for Holland, popular among troops of the Jewish Brigade Group (JBG) in 1946–1947. Immediately after the war, the JBG was assigned to occupation duties in Holland. The country became a center for illegal arms acquisition and *Aliya Bet* undertaken by Hagana officers serving in the JBG. The term derives from Holland's National Flower. > see also **World War II**.

Zva ha-Hagana le-Israel [לישראל צבא ההגנה, H] (ZAHAL, צה"ל) "Israel Defense Forces" (IDF):

1. Scope and Definition

Official term for the unified Israeli army. Zahal was created by order of the provisional government on May 31, 1948. The force thus created was an amalgam of the four undergrounds that operated during the mandatory era: Hagana, Palmah, Irgun Zvai Leumi (IZL), and Lohame Herut Israel (Lehi). The newly created army was immediately subordinated to civilian control, with Prime Minister David Ben-Gurion assuming the defense portfolio (a portfolio he retained throughout his career). Unlike the underground movements it replaced, Zahal was designed from the outset to be a conventional military force. Given prevailing conditions, particularly Zahal's creation during the War of Independence, most operations were ad hoc. Real organizational work began only after the signing of armistice agreements with Israel's neighbors.

Because the Hagana was the premier Zionist underground prior to independence and was (in fact) the *Yishuv's* militia, Hagana organization and doctrine predominated in Zahal. Zahal's creation had not been without controversy, however. Advocates of both the IZL on the political right and the Palmah on the political left initially opposed the unification of all bodies into one army. Relations with the IZL actually came to blows and nearly to a civil war during the so-called Altalena affair in June 1948. In essence, the IZL had agreed to unify all its forces with Zahal except those in Jerusalem. It is not clear whether those forces would have been unified into Zahal as well without military action, since the sailing of an IZL arms ship forced the government's hand and resulted in complete unification. The Palmah represented a different problem for the new Zahal high command. The Palmah served as the Hagana's de facto strike forces, but had always had an independent (and more politicized) command structure. The Palmah also had its own training and supply facilities. Integration of the Palmah command structure into Zahal was seen as a means to reduce the influence of parties opposed to Mapai, which derived their strength from the same *Kibbutzim* that supplied the Palmah's manpower, of any political influence on the new army. Despite the controversies, which still swirl in scholarly circles, Ben-Gurion's move was animated by a sense that a single army under civilian control was a better guarantor of democracy than an army fractured along any political lines, no matter how popular. The experience of other countries (in the Middle East, Europe, Asia, and Latin America) under similar circumstances seems to bear this idea out. Over nearly fifty years and six wars Zahal has remained the guardian of Israel's borders but has played no overt role in Israeli politics. > see also: **Yishuv, Yishuv Organizations (Underground Organizations); Israel, State of; War of Independence; Altalena Affair.**

2. Major Zahal Combat Units in 1948

Alexandroni Brigade, Zahal's third brigade, operating in the Sharon region. Comprising six infantry battalions (numbered 31 through 37) and supporting units, Alexandroni also included a battalion of instructors and advanced trainees from the Hagana's infantry training school. Alexandroni units were responsible for the defense of all Jewish settlements from Ramat Gan to Zichron Ya'akov. Major engagements: Operation Nahshon, Mishmar ha-Emek, Latrun, and the Jezreel Valley. Commanders: Dan Even, Benzion Ziv, Zvi Gorman.

Carmeli Brigade, Zahal's second infantry brigade, operating in Haifa and the western Galilee. Comprising four infantry battalions (numbered 21 through 24) and supporting units. Major engagements: Mishmar ha-Emek, Ramat Yohanan, Haifa, Jordan Valley, Nazareth, and Jenin (an attack that failed). Commanders: Mordechai Makleff, Moshe Carmel, Max Cohen, Zvi Gorman.

Ezioni Brigade, Zahal's sixth infantry brigade, operating in and around Jerusalem. Comprising three infantry battalions (numbered 61 to 63) and supporting units. Operated mainly in Jerusalem and the hills of Judea. Major operations: Operation Nahshon, defense of Gush Etzion, Har-Tuv, Ramat Rachel, Jerusalem. Commanders: Israel Amir, David Shaltiel, Moshe Dayan.

Givati Brigade, Zahal's fourth infantry brigade, formed from Heyl Sadeh (Hish) units in Tel Aviv and the northern Negev. Comprising seven infantry battalions (numbered 51 through 57) and supporting units, including a mounted cavalry unit and a jeep-mounted reconnaissance squadron known as Shualei Shimson (Samson's Foxes). Major operations: Majdal/Bet-Guvrin, Operation Nahshon, Har-Tuv, Operation Yoav. Commander: Shimon Avidan.

Golani Brigade, Zahal's first infantry brigade, operating in the Upper and lower Galilee. Comprising five infantry battalions (numbered 11 through 15) and supporting units. Major engagements: Tirat Zvi, Mishmar ha-Emek, Nazareth, the Negev, and Elat. Commanders: Moshe Man, Michael Shohat (Schechter), Nahum Golan (Speigel).

Ha-Mishuryenet, Zahal's only armored brigade during the War of Independence, founded in 1948 and serially numbered as Zahal's eighth brigade. Comprising supporting units and two battalions, the 82nd and 89th: the former concentrated most of Zahal's motley collection of tanks while the latter was a jeep-mounted "commando" (actually, motorized infantry) unit. Major operations: Operation Dani, Lod/Ramle, Operation Yoav. Commander: Yitzhak Sadeh.

Ha-Negev Brigade, Zahal's twelfth infantry brigade, ha-Negev was a Palmah brigade that was integrated into Zahal in 1948. Comprising three infantry battalions (numbered 7 through 9) and supporting units. Major operations: Operation Yoav, Operation Uvda. Commander: Nahum Sarig.

Harel Brigade, Zahal's tenth infantry brigade. Harel was a Palmah brigade that was integrated into Zahal in 1948. Served mainly in the Jerusalem area. Comprising four battalions and supporting units: three were infantry battalions (numbered 4 through 6) and one (10) was an "armored" (i.e., mechanized) infantry battalion. Major operations: Operation Nahshon, battles for the Jerusalem roadway, Sha'ar ha-Gai, and Gush Etzion. Commanders: Yitzhak Rabin, Yosef Tabenkin.

Kiryati Brigade, Zahal's fourth infantry brigade, operating in Tel Aviv and Jaffa. Comprising three infantry battalions (numbered 42 through 44) plus supporting units. Major engagements: Jaffa (in conjunction with an offensive by the Irgun Zvai Leumi), Lod, Ramle. Commander: Michael Ben-Gal.

Oded Brigade, Zahal's ninth infantry brigade, organized from Palmah units and conscripts after May 1948. Comprising two battalions (numbered 91 and 92) plus supporting units. Raised for the defense of the eastern Galilee. Major operations: Operation Yoav. Commanders: Uri Yaffe, Max Cohen.

Seventh Brigade, Zahal's only unnamed brigade at the time. The Seventh Brigade was established in 1948 mainly of new immigrants, recent conscripts, and foreign volunteers. Comprising three battalions (numbered 71, 72, and 79), two of which were almost entirely composed of foreign volunteers, and supporting units. Major operations: Latrun, western Galilee, Nazareth, Operation Hiram. Commanders: Shlomo Shamir, Haim Laskov, Ben Dunkelman, Yosef Eitan. > see also: **Mitnadvei Hutz la-Aretz**.

Yiftah Brigade, Zahal's eleventh brigade. Yitfah was a Plamah brigade that was integrated into Zahal in 1948. Served mainly in the Galilee and the nortern valleys. Comprising two infantry battalions (numbered 1 and 3) plus support units. Major operations: Tirat Zvi, Mishmar ha-Emek, Safed, Jordan Valley campaign, Lod-Ramle, Operation Yoav. Commanders: Yigal Allon, Mula Cohen.

TABLE Z.1: Zahal Battalions in the War of Independence

Number	Name	Brigade
1	ha-Emek	Yiftah
2	ha-Negev ha-Zfoni	ha-Negev
3	ha-Galil	Yiftah
4	ha-Porzim	Harel
5	Sha'ar ha-Gai	Harel
6	Yerushalayim	Harel
7	Be'er Sheva	ha-Negev
8	ha-Negev ha-Dromi	ha-Negev
9	ha-Peshita	ha-Negev
10	ha-Meshurian	Harel[1]
11	Alon	Golani[2]
12	Barak	Golani
13	Gideon	Golani
14	Dror	Golani
15	Goren	Golani
21	—	Carmeli

[1] The battalion name was unofficial.
[2] Transferred to Oded during June 1948.

22	—	Carmeli
23	—	Carmeli
24	—	Carmeli
31	—	Alexandroni
32	—	Alexandroni
33	—	Alexandroni
34	—	Alexandroni
35	Agaf Hadracha	Alexendroni[3]
37	—	Alexandroni[4]
42	—	Kiryati
43	—	Kiryati
44	—	Kiryati
51	—	Givati
52	—	Givati
53	—	Givati
54	—	Givati
55	—	Givati
57	—	Givati
58	—	Givati
61	Moriah	Ezioni
62	Bet Horon	Ezioni
63	Michmas	Ezioni
71	—	Seventh
72	—	Seventh[5]
79	—	Seventh[6]
82	—	Eighth
89	—	Eighth[7]
91	—	Oded
92	—	Oded
—	Nahshon I[8]	
—	Nahshon II[9]	
—	Nahshon III[10]	

Source: Archion Toldot ha-Hagana (ATH).

[3] Composed of instructors and advanced trainees who were organized into an infantry battalion in the summer of 1948.

[4] In some documents this battalion was referred to as Battalion 35B, implying that it was detached from the 35th Battalion. In fact, the two were completely independent.

[5] Composed almost entirely of Canadian, British, South African, and American volunteers, the 72nd Battalion was commanded by Benjamin Dunkelman. The battalion bore the unofficial nickname of "Anglo-Saxon." > see also: **Mitnadvei Hutz la-Aretz**.

[6] Composed largely of foreign volunteers, the battalion was redesignated 73rd in July.

[7] Redesignated 81st Battalion in July 1948.

[8] Battalion-sized battle group composed of units from the Palmah and from the Alexandroni and Givati Brigades for the duration of Operation Nahshon, April 3–15, 1948.

[9] Battalion-sized battle group composed of units from the Palmah and from the Harel Brigade operational for the duration of Operation Nahshon.

[10] Battalion-sized battle group composed of units from the Palmah and the Givati Brigades operational for the duration of Operation Nahshon.

TABLE Z.2: Zahal Weapons Holdings as of May 28, 1948

Manufacturer/Caliber/Weapon Type	Number Available[1]
Pistols (all types)	5,607
Sten 9 MM Submachine Gun	8,892
Thompson .45 Cal. Submachine Gun	681
Other Submachine Guns	691
Lebel 8 MM Rifle	589
Lee-Enfield .303 Inch Rifle	7,842
Mauser 7.92 MM Kar-98K Rifle	13,124
MG-34 7.92 MM Light/Medium Machine Gun	1,650[2]
RKM Machine Gun	159
Stu Light Machine Gun	527
Besa 7.7 MM Medium Machine Gun	22
Browning .30 Cal. Medium Machime Gun (Air Cooled)	20
Browning .303 Cal. Medium Machine Gun (Water Cooled)	37
Schwarzlose 7.92 MM Meduim Machine Gun	67
Vickers .303 Medium Machine Gun (Water Cooled)	488
Hotchkiss 13.2 MM Heavy Machine Gun	38[3]
Besa 15 MM Tank Machine Gun	12[4]
2 Inch British Mortar	682[5]
3 Inch British Mortar	105[5]
120 MM French Mortar	12
Davidka Mortar	16[6]
Boys Anti-Tank Rifle (0.55 Inch)	27
Projector Infantry, Anti-Tank	48
Hispano-Suiza 20 MM Anti-Aircraft Gun	30
Italian/French 65 MM Light Field Gun	30
French 75 MM Medium Field Gun	10

Source: Archion Toldot ha-Hagana (ATH).

---

[1] Details given where pertinent; when no manufacturer is cited, it is either unknown or not applicable.

[2] Of these, 1,364 had only recently arrived and had not yet been distributed to combat units.

[3] Of these, fifteen arrived in April 1948 and had not yet been distributed to combat units.

[4] According to some sources, these weapons were removed from captured Egyptian Mk VIC light tanks, which were of British manufacture.

[5] Including some versions locally manufactured by Ta'as.

[6] A homemade and home designed weapon of approximately 60 MM caliber. > see also: **Davidka**.

Table Z.3: Zahal Squadrons in the War of Independence

Number	Name[1]	Base/Composition[2]	Operational Region
1	Namer	Sde Dov/Mixed	Entire country[3]
2	Gamal	Nir Am/ Lt. Aircraft	Negev
3	Lavi	Yavniel/Lt. Aircraft	Galilee
4	Reconnaissance	Sde Dov/Auster	Entire country

Table Z.4: Aircraft Holdings of Zahal, October 15, 1948

Manufacturer/Name	Type	Number
Avia S-199	Fighter-Bomber	20[4]
Boeing B-17 Flying Fortress	Heavy Bomber	3
Bristol Beaufighter	Fighter-Bomber	5
Curtiss C-46 Commando	Transport	6
De Haviland Mosquito	Fighter-Bomber	1
Douglas C-47 Skytrain	Transport	5[5]
Lockheed A-29 Hudson	Light Bomber	2
Lockheed Constellation	Transport	3
Noorduyn C-64 Norseman	Liaison	6
North American P-51 Mustang	Fighter	4
Supermarine Spitfire	Fighter	50[6]

Source: Chris Bishop, ed., *The Aerospace Encyclopedia of Air Warfare*, vol. 2 (Westport, Conn: AIRTime Publishers, 1997), pp. 146–147.

Żydzi do Palestini [P] "Jews to Palestine": Second half of an antisemitic political slogan, that was popular in Poland during the interwar era. The full slogan was, "Rzeczypospolita Polska dla Polakow, Żydzi do Palestini" (Republic of Poland for the Poles, Jews to Palestine). The second part of the slogan echoed the ambivalent attitude adopted by the Polish government toward the *Yishuv*. Zionism was not supported by the Poles out of a sense of its merits but only as a means to remove the surplus Jewish population that the Poles sought to evict. Although that meant considerable Polish support for the *Yishuv*, Polish policy-makers also supported Territorialist schemes to remove Jewish population. During the 1930s, Poland sought to create its own Jewish colony on Madagascar. > see also: **Sjonizm albo Eksterminacja**.

---

[1] Squadrons 2 and 3 also had an unofficial name, that was identical with their area of operations.

[2] Composition has been given in only general terms, with the following basic rule of thumb: Mixed = all aircraft types; Lt. Aircraft = transport or liaison aircraft only.

[3] The first squadron operated throughout the country but was primarily tasked with air defense of the Tel Aviv region.

[4] The Avia S-199 was the Czech variant of the World War II Messerschmidt Bf-109.

[5] Some may have been militarized versions of the DC-3 airliner.

[6] Purchased in Czechoslovakia.

FOR FURTHER READING

I. Primary Sources

A. Archives

Archival records and illustrations pertaining to Zionism have been researched in the following collections, although space does not permit the citation of specific record groups and files:

1. Archion Toldot ha-Hagana (Hagana Historical Archive, ATH), Tel Aviv.
2. Ben-Gurion Research Center (BGRC), Kiryat Sde Boker.
3. Central Zionist Archives (CZA), Jerusalem.
4. Histadrut Archive (HIS), Tel Aviv.
5. Jabotinsky Institute Archive (JIA), Tel Aviv.
6. Jewish Division, New York Public Library (NYPL), New York.
7. Leo Baeck Institute (LBI), Jerusalem and New York.
8. United Nations Archive, New York
9. YIVO Institute Archives and Library, New York.

B. Press and Periodicals

American Jewish Archives
Be-Shvilei ha-Tehiya
European Historical Review
Freiland
Gal-Ed
Ha-Zionut
Herzl Yearbook
Israel Affairs
Israel Studies
Israel and Middle East
Iyunim be-Tekumat Israel
Jerusalem Quarterly
Jewish Book Annual
Jewish Chronicle, The
Jewish Political Studies Review
Jewish Social Studies

Journal of Israeli History
Journal of Contemporary History
Journal of Modern History
Kiryat Sefer
Kivunim
Leo Baeck Institute Yearbook
Living Age, The
Proceedings of the American Academy for Jewish Research
Review des Etudes Juives
Shorashim ba-Mizrah
Statistical Abstract of Israel
Studies in Bibliography and Booklore
Studies in Zionism
Studies in Contemporary Jewry
World Review
Yahadut Zemanenu

C. Published Primary Sources and Collections

Adler, Cyrus (ed.). *Voice of America on Kishineff*. Philadephia: Jewish Publication Society, 1904.

Antonius, George. *The Arab Awakening*. New York: G. P. Putnam's Sons, 1946.

Babel, Isaac. *Red Cavlary*. London: Alfred A. Knopf, 1929.

Bechor, David et al. דין וחשבון של ועידת החקירה לחקירת רצח דר. חיים ארלוזורוב (Report of the Commission to Study the Murder of Dr. Chaim Arlosoroff). Jerusalem: Israel Government Printing Office, 1983.

Ben-Avram, Baruch (ed.). מפלגות וזרמים פוליטיים בתקופת הבית הלאומי (Parties and Political Movements during the Mandatory Era), Jerusalem: The Zalman Shazar Institute Press, 1978.

Ben-Gurion, David. *Letters to Paula*. Pittsburgh: University of Pittsburgh Press, 1968.

———. ממעד לעם (From a Class to a Nation). Tel Aviv: Am Oved, 1938.

Bericht des Actions-Comités der Zionistische Organisation an den XI. Zionisten-Kongress, Wien. Vienna: Zionisten Welt-Kongress, 1913.

Bialik, Haim Nachman. שירים (Poems). Tel Aviv: Dvir, 1967.

Blau, Bruno (ed.). *Das Ausenahmerecht für die Juden in deutschland, 1933-1945*. Dusseldorf: Verlag Algemeine Wochen-zeitung der Juden in deutschland, 1965

Blue-White Papers. London: Union of Zionist Revisionists, 1935.

"Colonies for Poland," *World Review*, vol. 2 (1936): 60-61.

A Commitment to Excellence: Kerem Hayesod, United Israel Appeal, 1920-1990. Jerusalem: Information Department of Keren ha-Yesod, 1990.

Druyanow, A. ציונות בפולניה (Zionism in Poland). Tel Aviv: Masada Press, 1932.

Dubnow, Simon. *Nationalism and History: Essays on the Old and New Judaism*. edited by Koppel S. Pinson, Philadelphia: Jewish Publication Society, 1958

Duker, Abraham G. *The Situation of the Jews in Poland*. New York: The American Jewish Congress, 1936.

Ehrmann, Eliezer (ed.). *Readings in Modern Jewish History*. New York: Ktav, 1977.

Ellern, Hermann and Bessi Ellern (comps.). *Herzl, Hechler, the Grand Duke of Baden and the German Emperor, 1896-1904*. Tel Aviv: Ellern's Bank, LTD., 1961.

Feldman, Eliyahu. *Russian Jewry in 1905 Through the Eyes and Camera of a British Diplomat*. Spiegel Lecture in Jewish History #6, Tel Aviv: Tel Aviv University Press, 1986.

Freundlich, Yehoshua (ed.). *Political Documents of the Jewish Agency. Vol. 1. May 1945-December 1946*. Jerusalem: ha-Sifriya ha-Zionit, 1996.

Goodman, Paul. *Great Britain and the Jewish National Home*. London: English Zionist Federation, 1937.

———. *Zionism and the Jewish Diaspora*. London: English Zionist Federation, 1921.

Government of Palestine, Ordinances, 1933, London: His Majesty's Stationary Office, 1934.

Gurevich, David (comp.). *Statistical Handbook of Jewish Palestine*. Jerusalem: Jewish Agency for Palestine, 1947.

Hebrew Education in Eretz Israel. Jerusalem: Keren ha-Yesod, 1930.

Hertzberg, Arthur (ed.) *The Zionist Idea*. New York: Atheneum, 1969.

Herzl, Theodor. *Altneuland*. Haifa: Haifa Publishing Company, 1960.

———. *The Jewish State*. New York: American Zionist Emergency Council, 1946.

———. *Zionist Writings*. 2 volumes. edited by Harry Zohn, New York: Herzl Press, 1973–1975.

Hess, Moses. *Rome and Jerusalem*, New York: Bloch Publishing, 1943.

Heymann, Michael (ed.). *The Minutes of the Zionist General Council: The Uganda Controversy*. 2 volumes. Tel Aviv: Institute for Zionist Research, 1977.

Hirsch, Samson Raphael. *Collected Works*. Elliot Bondi and David Bechhofer, eds., New York: Philipp Feldheim, 1984.

Keeping the Promise: UJA 50 Jubilee, the First Fifty Years of the United Jewish Appeal, 1939-1989. New York: Public Relations Department of the UJA, 1989.

Klieman, Aaron S. and Adrian L. Klieman (eds.). *American Zionism: A Documentary History.* volumes. New York: Garland Publishing, 1990.

Klinger, Stefan. *The Ten Year Plan for Palestine*, London: The New Zionist Organization, 193.

Korn, Yitzhak. *The Centrality of Israel — A National Imperitive.* Tel Aviv: World Labor Zionist Movement, 1974.

Laqueur, Walter (ed.). *The Israel-Arab Reader.* New York: Bantam Books, 1970.

Lazare, Bernard. *Job's Dungheap.* New York: Schocken Books, 1948.

Leikin, Ezekiel (ed.). *The Beilis Transcript.* Northvale, NJ: Jason Aronson, 1993.

Lenin on the National and Colonial Questions: Three Articles. Peking: Foreign Language Press, 1970.

Lev-Ami, Shlomo (ed.). "הפרוטוקולים של מפקדת 'האירגון הצבאי הלאומי', יולי-נובמבר 1944" (Protocols of the IZL High Command, July to November, 1944). הציונות vol. 4 (1975): 391-440.

Levensohn, Lotta. *Hashomer: The First Jewish Watch in Palestine.* New York: Va'ad Bitachon, 1939.

Levine, Samuel H. *Manual on Palestine and Zionism.* New York: Zionist Organization of America, 1920.

Levinthal, Louis E. *The Credo of an American Zionist.* Washington, DC: Zionist Organization of America, 1943.

Lowdermilk, Walter C. *Palestine: Land of Promise.* New York: Harper & Brothers, 1944.

Mack, Julian. "Political Status of the Zionist Movement." *Bulletin of the Zionist Society of Engineers and Agriculturists.* vol. 1 #2 (February, 1920): 19-21.

Merhavia, Chanonch (ed.). קולות קוראים לציון (Voices Calling for Zion). Jerusalem: The Zalman Shazar Center for the Study of Jewish History, 1976.

Nordau, Max. *Zionistische Schriften.* second edition. Berlin: Jüdischer Verlag, 1923.

"The Pact of Glory": The Jewish Agency for Palestine. New York: NP, 1929.

Patai, Raphael (ed.). "Herzl's Sinai Project: A Documentary Record." *Herzl Yearbook*, v. 1 (1958): 107-127.

—— and Harry Zohn (eds.). *The Complete Diaries of Theodor Herzl.* New York: Herzl Press, 1960-?

Protokol des I.Zionistenkongress in Basel, vom 29 bis 31 August 1897. Prague: Executive of the World Zionist Organization, 1911.

Reinharz, Jehuda (ed.). *Dokumente zur Geschichte des deutschen Zionismus, 1882-1933.* Tübingen: J.C.B. Mohr for the Leo Baeck Institute, 1981.

Report of the Executive to the XXI Zionist Congress. Jerusalem: WZO, 1939.

Reports of the Executive of the Zionist Organization to the XII. Zionist Congress. London: National Labour Press, 1921.

Robinson, Jacob. *Palestine and the United Nations: Prelude to a Solution.* Washington, DC: Public Affairs Press, 1947.

Sachar, Howard M. (editor-in-chief). *The Rise of Israel: Selected Documents in Thirty-Nine Volumes.* New York: Garland, 1987.

Shavit, Ya'akov (ed.). *1936-1939 היכוח בישוב היהודי הבלגה או תגובה?* (Self Restraint or Response? The Jewish Debate, 1936-1939). Ramat Gan: Bar-Ilan University Press, 1983.

——. "1919-1920 מאמרי ז'בוטנסקי" (Jabotinsky's Articles, 1919-1920). הציונות. vol. 6 (1981): 323-358.

Schiper, Ignacy et al (eds.). *Żydzi w Polsce Odrodzonej* (Jews in Independent Poland). 2 Vols. Warsaw: NP, 1935.

Simon, Leon (ed.). *Selected Essays of Ahad ha-Am.* New York: Atheneum, 1962.

Stafford, Ronald S. H. *The Tragedy of the Assyrians*. London: Allen and Unwin, 1935.

Stalin, Joseph V. *The National Question and Leninism*. Chicago: Liberator Press, ND.

Stein, Leonard. *Syria*. London: E. Benn, 1926.

Stenographisches Protokol der Verhandlung des 12. Zionistische Kongress. London: Central Office of the World Zionist Organization, 1922.

Stenographisches Protokol der Verhandlungen der 17. Zionistische Kongress. London: Central Office of the World Zionist Organization, 1931.

Stenographisches Protokol der Verhandlung des 18. Zionistische Kongress. London: Central Office of the World Zionist Organization, 1933.

Tavin, Eli and Yonah Alexander (eds.). *Psychological Warfare and Propaganda: Irgun Documentation*. Washington, DC: Scholarly Resources, 1982.

World Jewish Congress Fiftieth Jubilee, 1936-1986. Jerusalem: World Jewish Congress, 1986.

Zangwill, Israel. *A Land of Refuge*. London: ITO, 1907.

——. "Zionism and Territorialism." *The Living Age*. vol. 265 #3,440 (June 11, 1910): 668.

Zimmer, Urie. *Torah-Judaism and the State of Israel*. London: Jewish Post Publications, 1961.

Zweibom, B. (ed). די פארטייען און גרופירונגען אין ציוניזם (Parties and Groupings in Zionism). Warsaw: Zionistische Organizatsye in Warashe, 1934.

D. Diaries, Autobiographies, and Memoirs

Avriel, Ehud. *Open The Gates!* New York: Atheneum, 1970.

Ben-Gurion, David. זכרונות (Memoirs). six vols. Tel Aviv: Am Oved, 1976-1987.

Bodenheimer, Max I. "The Story of the Hindenburg Declaration." *Herzl Yearbook* vol. 2 (1959): 56-77.

Jabotinsky, Ze'ev. אוטוביוגרפיה (Autobiography), Jerusalem: Eri Jabotinsky, 1948.

Kurisky, Leibel."1946-1949, הקואורדינציה הציונית לגאולת ילדים בפולין השנים" (The Zionist Coordinating Committee to Rescue Jewish Youth in Poland, 1946-1949). גל-עד, vol. 7/8 (1985): 253-261.

Landau-Duchan, Leah (ed.). "ועד הצירים היהודים - מיומנו של דר' אלכסנדר זלקינד" (The Comité des Délégations Juives – As Seen From the Diary of Dr. Alexander Zelkind). הציונות, vol. 12 (1987): 371-399.

Mayorek, Yoram (ed.). "יומן פאריס של נחום סוקולוב, ינואר-פברואר 1918" (Nahum Sokolow's Paris Diary, Janury-February 1918). הציונות, vol. 16 (1991): 213-255.

Samuel, Viscount Herbert. *Memoirs*. London: Crescent Press, 1945.

Shazar, Zalman. *Morning Stars*. Philadelphia: Jewish Publication Society, 1967.

II. Secondary Sources

A. Encyclopedias and Guidebooks

Alexander, Yonah et al (comps.). *A Bibliography of Israel*. New York: Herzl Press, 1981.

Amrami, Ya'akov (ed.)., ביבליוגרפיה שימושית: ניל"י, ברית הבריונים, הארגון הצבאי הלאומי, לוחמי חרות ישראל (A Functional Bibliography: NILi, Brit ha-Biryonim, ha-Irgun ha-Zvai Leumi, Lohame Herut Israel). 2 vols. Tel Aviv: Hadar Publishers/Jabotinsky Institute, 1975-1990.

Attal, Robert (comp.). *La Presse Périodique Juive D'Afrique Nord*. (H/F). Tel Aviv: Tel Aviv University Institute for the Study of Jewish Journalism, 1996.

Birnbaum, Philip (tr.). *The Daily Prayerbook*. New York: Hebrew Publishing, 1949.

Carta's Historical Atlas of Israel. Jerusalem: Carta, 1977.

Chamberlain, Wlado et al (comps.). *A Chronology and Fact Book of the United Nations, 1941-1976*. Dobbs Ferry, NY: Oceana Publications, 1976.

Cohn-Sherbok, Dan (comp.). *The Blackwell Dictionary of Judaica*. Oxford: Basil Blackwell, 1992.

Doron, Eliezer and Moshe Schaerf (eds.). ערכים: לכסיקון לציונות וישראל (Entries: A Lexicon on Zionism and Israel). Jerusalem: Reuven Mass, 1983.

Edelheit Abraham J. (ed.). *The Literature of Jewish Public Affairs: A Ten Year Compilation*. New York: The Jewish Book Council, 1996.

——. and Hershel Edelheit (eds.). *The Jewish World in Modern Times: A Selected, Annotated Bibliography*. Boulder, CO: Westview Press, 1988.

Edelheit, Hershel, and Abraham J. Edelheit. *Israel and the Jewish World, 1948-1993: A Chronology*. Westport, CT: Greenwood Press, 1995.

——. *A World in Turmoil: An Integrated Chronology of the Holocaust and World War II*. Westport, CT: Greenwood Press, 1991.

Eisenstein, J. D. אוצר דינים ומנהגים (A Digest of Jewish Laws and Customs). New York: The Author, 1917.

Elazar, Daniel J. and Stuart A. Cohen. *The Jewish Polity*. Bloomington: Indiana University Press, 1985.

Encyclopaedia Judaica. 16 vols. New York/Jerusalem: Macmillan and Keter, 1972.

Federbusch, Simon (ed.). *World Jewry Today*. New York: Thomas Yoseloff, 1959.

Gilbert, Martin. *The Jews of Russia: Their History in Maps and Photographs*. London: National Council for Soviet Jewry, 1976.

Glickson, Paul (comp.). *Preliminary Inventory of the Jewish Daily and Periodical Press Published in the Polish Language, 1823-1983*. English/Hebrew/Polish. Jerusalem: Hebrew University Center for Research on the History and Culture of Polish Jews, 1989.

Goldin, Hyman (comp.). המדריך (The Rabbi's Guide). New York: Hebrew Publishing, 1939.

Gurevich, D. (comp.). *Statistical Handbook of Jewish Palestine*. Jerusalem: The Jewish Agency, 1947.

Ikan, Yael. *The World Zionist Organization, the National Institutions: Structure and Functions*. Jerusalem: Department of Organization and Community Relations, World Zionist Organization, 1997.

Jüdisches Lexicon. 4 vols. Berlin: Jüdischen Verlag, 1927.

Kressel, Getzel (comp.). *Guide to the Hebrew Press*. Zug, Switzerland: Inter Documentation Company, 1979.

Legatus: Guide Jüdischer Institutionen. Zürich: Serenada Vaerlag, 1992.

Lerman, Antony (ed.), *The Jewish Communities of the World: A Contemporary Guide*. 4th ed., New York: Facts on File, 1989.

Naor, Mordechai (editor in chief). "לכסיקון כוח המגן ה'הגנה" (The Hagana Lexicon). Tel Aviv: Ministry of Defense Publications, 1992.

Olitzky, Kerry M. and Ronald H. Isaacs (comps.). *A Glossary of Jewish Life*. Northvale, NJ: Jason Aronson, 1992.

Prager, Leonard (ed.). "A Bibliography of Yiddish Periodicals in Great Britain (1867-1967)." *Studies in Bibliography and Booklore*, vol. 9 #1 (Spring, 1969): 3-32.

Reich, Bernard (ed.). *Historical Dictionary of Israel*. Metuchen, NJ: Scarecrow Press, 1992.

——. *An Historical Encyclopedia of the Arab-Israeli Conflict*. Westport, CT: Greenwood Press, 1996.

Reichler, Perla (ed.). "ספרות, עתונות, עלונים, וכרוזים של יהדות אורוגוואי בשנים 1920-1966 (Jewish Publications and Ephemera in Uruguay, 1920-1966). הציונות, vol. 1 (1970): 484-503.

Rivlin, Gershom and Aliza Rivlin (comps.). זר לא יבין: ספר הכינויים (A Stranger Would Not

Understand: The Book of Code Names). Tel Aviv: Ma'arachot/IDF Press, 1988.

Talmi, Ephraim (comp.). ‏מה ומי בהגנה ובשמירה‎. (Who Was Who In the Hagana and Struggle). Tel Aviv: Sifriyat Davar, 1975.

——. ‏מה ומי בשמירה ובהתגוננות‎ (Who Was Who On Guard and In Self-Defense). Tel Aviv: Sifriyat Davar, 1978.

——. ‏מה ומי: לכסיקון מלחמת העצמאות‎ (Who Was Who: A Lexicon of the War of Independence). Tel Aviv: Sifriyat Davar, 1964.

Teed, Peter (comp.). *Dictionary of 20th Century History*. New York: Oxford University Press, 1992.

Wallach, Jehuda et al (comps). ‏אטלס כרטא לתולדות ההגנה‎ (Carta's Atlas for the Hisotry of the Hagana). Jerusalem: Carta Publishing Hosue. 1991.

B. Journal Articles

Ackerman, Walter A. "Religion in the Schools of Eretz Israel, 1904-1914." *Studies in Zionism*, vol. 6 #1 (spring, 1985): 1-13.

Adler, Elchan N. "Obadia le Prosélyte." *Revue des Etudes Juives*, vol. 69 (1919): 129-134.

Adler (Cohen), Raya. "Mandatory Land Policy and the Wadi al-Hawarith Affair, 1929-1933." *Studies in Zionism*, vol. 7 #2 (Autumn, 1986): 233-257.

Albert Phyllis C. "Israelite and Jew: How Did Nineteenth French Jews Understand Assimilation?" in Jonathan Frankel and Steven J. Zipperstein (eds.), *Assimilation and Community: The Jews in Nineteenth Century Europe*. New York: Cambridge University Press, 1992.

Altshuler, Mordechai. "The Attitude of the Communist Party of Russia to Jewish National Survival." *YIVO Annual*, vol. 14 (1969): 68-86.

Arendt, Hannah. "The Jew as Pariah: A Hidden Tradition." *Jewish Social Studies*, vol. 6 # 2 (1944): 99–122.

Ariel, Yaakov. "An American Initiative for a Jewish State: William Blackstone and the Petition of 1891." *Studies in Zionism*, vol. 10 #2 (Autumn, 1989): 125-137.

Avni, Haim. "‏וההתיישבות הטריטוריאליזם, התיישבות טריטוריאליסטית, הציונית‎" (Territorialism, Territorialist Settlement, and Zionist Settlement), in ‏יהדות זמננו‎, vol. 1 (1983): 69-87.

Ayoun, Richard. "‏ההתאזרחות הקולקטיבית של יהודי אלג'ריה והתתקוממות המוסלמית ב-1871‎" (The Collective Enfranchisement of Algerian Jewry and the Muslim Uprising of 1871). ‏שורשים במזרח‎, vol. 1 (1986): 11-35.

Bacon, Gershon. "Rabbis and Politics, Rabbis in Politics: Different Models Within Interwar Polish Jewry." *YIVO Annual*, vol. 20 (1991): 39-59.

Barad, Shlomo. "‏הפעילות הציונית במצרים, 1917-1952‎" (Zionist Activities in Egypt, 1917-1952). ‏שורשים במזרח‎, vol. 2 (1989):

Baron, Salo W. "The Emancipation Movement and American Jewry." in *Steeled By Adversity: Essays and Addresses on American Jewish Life*. Philadelphia: Jewish Publication Society, 1971. pp. 80-105.

——. "Jews and the Syrian Massacres of 1860." *Proceedings of the American Academy for Jewish Research* vol. 4 (1932/1933): 3-31.

Bat Yeor. "Islam and the Dhimmis." *Jerusalem Quarterly* #42 (Spring, 1987): 83-84.

Bein, Alex. "The Origin of the Term and Concept 'Zionism'." *Herzl Yearbook* vol. 2 (1959): 1-27.

Ben-Anat, Baruch. "‏הרגע הגדול מצא דור קטן - תוכנית נורדאו, 1919-1920‎" (The Great Moment Confronted A Small Generation - The Nordau Plan, 1919-1920), ‏הציונות‎, vol. 19 (1995): 99-103.

Ben-Avner, Yehuda. "‏ציונות ואוטונומיזם באירופה המזרחית בראשות המאה העשרים‎" (Zionism and Autonomism in Eastern Europe at the Beginning of the Twentieth Century).

כיוונים, vol. 16 (August, 1982): 91-101.

Ben-David, Benjamin. "כמה ביטויי ערגה לציון" (How Many Terms of Longing for Zion). כיוונים, vol. 27 (May, 1985): 155-164.

Breuer, Mordechai. "על המושג 'דתי-לאומי' בהיסטוריוגרפיה ובהגות יהודית" (The Concept of Religious Nationalism in Jewish Historiography and Thought). בשבילי התחיה, vol. 3 (1988): 11-24.

Brzoza, Czeslaw. "The Jewish Press in Kraków (1918-1939)." *Polin*, vol. 7 (1992): 133-146.

Cesarani, David. "The Transformation of Communal Authority in Anglo-Jewry, 1914-1940." in *The Making of Modern Anglo-Jewry*, Oxford: Basil Blackwell, 1990, pp. 114-140.

Cohen, David. "הפעילות הציונית בחברה הקולוניאלית של צפון-אפריקה בין שתי מלחמות העולם" (Zionist Activities in the Colonial Societies of North Africa between the Two World Wars). שורשים במזרח, vol. 2 (1989): 211-274.

Cohen, Mitchell. "Between Revolution and Normalcy: Social Class in Zionist Political Thinking." *Modern Judaism*, vol. 12 #3 (October, 1992): 259-276.

Cohen, Naomi W. "The Abrogation of the Russo-American Treaty of 1832." *JSS*, vol. 25 #1 (January, 1963): 3-41.

Cohen, Stuart A. "Same Places, Differnet Faces – A Comparison of Anglo-Jewish Conflicts over Zionism during World War I and World War II." in Stuart A. Cohen and Eliezer Don-Yehiya (eds.), *Conflict and Consensus in Jewish Political Life*, Ramat Gan: Bar-Ilan University Press, 1986, pp. 61-78.

Dawidowicz, Lucy S. "Louis Marshall's Yiddish Newspaper the *Jewish World*: A Study in Contrasts." *Jewish Social Studies*, vol. 25 #2 (April, 1966): 102-132.

Don-Yehiya, Eliezer. "אידיאולגיה ומדיניות בציונות הדתית: הגותו של הרב ריינס ומדיניות 'המזרחי' בהנהגתו" (Ideology and Politics in Religious Zionism: Rabbi Reines' Orientation and Mizrachi Policy Under His Leadership). הציונות, vol. 8 (1983):

———. "תפיסות של הציונות בהגות היהודית האורתודוקסית" (Views on Zionism Within Orthodox Judaism). הציונות, vol. 9 (1984): 55-93.

Dothan, Shmuel. "ראשיתו של קומוניזם לאומי יהודי בארץ-ישראל" (The Origins of Jewish National Bolshevism in Eretz Israel). הציונות, vol. 2 (1971): 208-236.

Druyan, Nitza. "על הציונות בקרב ארצות האיסלם" (On Zionism in the Muslim Countries). כיוונים, vol. 28 (August, 1985):

Edelheim-Muehsam, Margaret T. "The Jewish Press in Germany." *Leo Baeck Institute Yearbook*, vol. 1 (1956): 163-176.

Edelheit, Abraham J. "Jewish Responses to the Nazi Threat, 1933-1939: An Evaluation." *Jewish Political Studies Review*, vol. 6 #1/2 (Spring, 1994): 135-152.

———. "The Soviet Union, the Jews, and the Holocaust." *Holocaust Studies Annual*, vol. 4 (1990): 113–134.

Elath, Eliahu. "Phoenician Zionism in Lebanon." *Jerusalem Quarterly*, #42 (Spring, 1987): 38-56.

Elazar, Daniel J. "Toward a Political History of the Sephardic Diaspora." *Jewish Political Studies Review*, vol. 5 # 3/4 (Fall, 1993): 16-18.

Engel, David. "The Frustrated Alliance: The Revisionist Movement and the Polish Government-in-Exile, 1939-1945." *Studies in Zionism*, vol. 7 #1 (Spring, 1986): 11-35.

Friedman, Isaiah. "Lord Palmerston and the Protection of Jews in Palestine, 1839-1851," *JSS*, vol. 30 #1 (Winter, 1968): 23-41

———. "The McMahon Correspondence and the Question of Palestine," *Journal of Contemporary History*, vol. 5 #2 (1970): 83-122.

Frankel, Jonathan. "Nachman Syrkin: The Populist and Prophetic Strands in Socialist Zionism." *Zionism*, vol. 1 #2 (Autumn, 1980):

Friesel, Evyatar. "New Zionism: Historical Roots and Present Meaning." *Studies in Zionism*, vol. 8 #2 (Fall, 1987): 173-189.

Gal, Allon. "Zionist Foreign Policy and Ben-Gurion's Visit to the United States in 1939." *Studies in Zionism*, vol. 7 #1 (Spring, 1986): 37-50.

Ganin, Zvi. "Activism Versus Moderation: The Conflict Between Abba Hillel Silver and Stephen S. Wise During the 1940s." *Studies in Zionism*, vol. 5 #1 *Spring, 1984): 71-96.

Gelber, Yoav. "The Defense of Palestine in World War II." *Studies in Zionism*, vol. 8 #1 (Spring, 1987): 51-81.

Giladi, Dan. "המשבר הכלכלי בימי העלייה הרביעית 1926-1927" (The Economic Crisis during the Fourth Aliya, 1926-1927). *הציונות*, vol. 2 (1971): 119-147.

Gil-Har, Yitzhak. "הגיבוש והעיצוב הארגוני של הישוב בראשית המאה העשרים" (The Origins and Political Organization of the Yishuv at the Beginning of the Twentieth Century). *הציונות*, vol. 6 (1981): 7-47.

——. "שאלת הפרדת עבר הירדן המזרחי מארץ ישראל - זווית ראיה אחרת" (The Separation of Trans-Jordan from Eretz Israel - Another Angle), *יהדות זמננו*, vol. 1 (1984): 163-177.

Goldstein, Joseph. "The Beginnings of the Zionist Movement in Congress Poland: The Victory of the *Hasidim* over the Zionists?" *Polin*, vol. 5 (1990): 114-130.

Goldstein, Yaacov. "Mapai and the Seventeenth Zionist Congress (1931)." *Studies in Zionism*, vol. 10 #1 (Spring, 1989): 19-30.

Gorny, Yosef. "Zionist Voluntarism in the Political Struggle: 1939-1948." *Jewish Political Studies Review*, vol. 2 #1/2 (Spring, 1990): 67-104

——. "השינויים במבנה החברתי והפוליטי של העלייה השנייה בשנים 1904-1940" (Changes in the Social and Political Structure of the Second Aliya, 1904-1940), *הציונות*, vol. 1 (1970): 204-246.

Govrin, Yosef. "Landmarks in the National Awakening of Romanian Jews, 1870-1900." *Romanian Jewish Studies*, vol. 1 #1 (Spring, 1987): 27-33.

Gruenwald, Max. "About the Reichsvertretung der Duetschen Juden." *Imposed Jewish Governing Bodies Under Nazi Rule*, New York: YIVO Institute for Jewish Research, 1972, pp. 41-47.

Gurevitch, Zali and Gideon Aran. "The Land of Israel: Myth and Phenomenon." *Studies in Contemporary Jewry*, vol. 10 (1994): 195-210.

Halamish, Aviva. "Illegal Immigration: Valus, Myth, and Reality." *Studies in Zionism*, vol. 9, #1 (Spring, 1988): 47-62.

Heymann, Michael. "Max Nordau at the Early Zionist Congresses, 1897-1905." *Journal of Israeli History*, vol. 16 #3 (Autumn, 1995): 245-256.

——. "The Zionist Movement and Schemes for Jewish Settlement in Mesopotamia After the Death of Herzl." *Herzl Yearbook*, vol. 2 (1959): 129-174.

Himmelfarb, Milton. "The Jews: Subject or Object?" *Commentary*, vol. 40 #1 (July, 1965): 54-57.

Hyman, Paula. "The Dynamics of Social History." *Studies in Contemporary Jewry*, vol. 10 (1994): 93-111.

Jochmann, Werner. "The Jews and German Society in the Imperial Era." *Leo Baeck Institute Yearbook*, vol. 20 (1975), 5–11.

Johnpoll, Bernard K. "Why They Left: Russian-Jewish Mass Migration and Repressive Laws, 1881-1917." *American Jewish Archives*, v. 47 #1 (Spring/Summer, 1995): 17-54.

Kabakoff, Jacob. "Some East European Letters on Emigration." *American Jewish Archives*, v. 45 #1 (Spring/Summer, 1993): 77-80.

Kochavi, Arieh J. "The Struggle Against Jewish Immigration to Palestine." *Middle Eastern Studies*. vol. 34 # 3 (July, 1998): 146-167.

Korzec, Pawel."הסכם ממשלת ו' גראבסקי עם הנציגות הפארלאמנטרית היהודית" (The Agreement Between the Government of W. Grabski and the Jewish Parliamentary Delegation). *גל-עד*, vol. 1 (1973): 175-210.

Landau, Jacob M. "הערות על יחסם של התורכים הצעירים לציונות" (Notes on the Young Turks' Attitude Towards Zionism). *הציונית*, vol. 9 (1984): 195-205.

Lederhendler, Eli. "Interpreting Messianic Rhetoric in the Russian Haskalah and Early Zionism." *Studies in Contemporary Jewry*, vol. 7 (1991): 14-33.

Levene, Marc. "Lucien Wolf: Crypto-Zionist, Anti-Zionist, or Opportunist *par Excellence*?" *Studies in Zionism*. vol. 12 #2 (Autumn, 1991): 133-148.

Levi, Ze'ev. "ארץ ישראל במחשבה היהודית בגרמניה מהירש ועד רוזנצווייג" (Eretz Israel in German Jewish Thought from Hirsch to Rosenzweig). *כיוונים*, Vol. 4 (August, 1969): 55-66.

Lipset, Zvi. "השקפות פוליטיות של סטודנטים יהודים בקיוב בשנת 1909" (Political Views of Jewish Students in Kiev in 1909). *הציונות*, vol. 2 (1971): 64-73.

Margalit, Elkana. "Binationalism : An Interpretation of Zionism, 1941-1947. *Studies in Zionism*, #4 (October, 1981): 275-312.

——. "Socialist Zionism in Palestine: Collective and Equalitarian Tradition." *Jerusalem Quarterly*, #28 (Summer, 1983): 95-110.

Marrus, Michael R. "Jewry and the Politics of Assimilation: A Reassessment." *Journal of Modern History*. v. 49 (1977): 89-109

Mctague, John J. "Zionist-British Negotiations Over the Draft Mandate for Palestine, 1920." *Jewish Social Studies* vol. 42 #3/4 (Summer/Fall, 1980): 281-292.

Medina João and Joel Barromi. "The Jewish Colonization Project in Angola." *Studies in Zionism*. vol. 12 #1 (Spring, 1991): 1-16.

Melamed, Abraham. "Isaac Abravanel and Aristotle's *Politics*: A Drama of Errors." *JPSR*, vol. 5 #3/4 (Fall, 1993): 55-75.

Mintz, Matityahu. "Ber Borochov." *Studies in Zionism*, #5 (April, 1982): 33-53.

Mittleman, Alan L. "Some German Jewish Orthodox Attitudes Toward the Land of Israel and the Zionist Movement." *Jewish Political Studies Review*, vol. 6 #3/4 (Fall, 1994): 107-125.

Mosse, Werner E. "Problems and Limits of Assimilation: Hermann and Paul Wallich. 1833–1938," *Leo Baeck Institute Yearbook* vol. 33 (1988), 43–65.

Myers, David. "Dual Loyalty in a Post-Zionist Era." *Judaism*, vol. 38 #3 (Summer, 1989): 333-343.

Myers, Judy E. "The Messianic Idea and Zionist Ideologies." *Studies in Contemporary Jewry*, vol. 7 (1991): 3-13.

Nicosia, Francis R. "Revisionist Zionism in Germany." Pt I: *Leo Baeck Institute Yearbook*, vol. 31 (1986): 209-241; Pt. II: *Leo Baeck Institute Yearbook*, vol. 32 (1987): 231-266.

Parzen, Herbert. "The Enlargement of the Jewish Agency for Palestine: 1923-1929, A Hope Hamstrung." *Jewish Social Studies*, vol. 39 #1/2 (Winter/Spring, 1977): 129-158.

Perlman, Moshe. "Arab-Jewish Diplomacy, 1918-1922." *Jewish Social Studies*, vol. 6 #2 (April, 1944): 123-154.

Persky, Daniel. "חמישים שנות עתונות עברית באמריקה" (Fifity Years of Hebrew Journalism in America). *Jewish Book Annual*, vol. 9 (1950/51): Hebrew Section, pp. 1-8.

Porat, Dina. "The Transnistria Affair and the Rescue Policy of the Zionist Leadership in Palestine, 1942-1943." *Studies in Zionism*, vol. 6 #1 (Spring, 1985): 27-52.

Porath, Yehoshua. "Weizmann, Churchill, and the 'Philby Plan' 1937-1943." *Studies in Zionism*, vol. 5 #2 (Autumn, 1984): 239-272.

Ran, Leyzer. "בין (דבורה) – אירגון צופים סוציאליסטי של נוער לומד ועובד בווילנה ובסביבתה" (Binn (the Bee) – A Socialist Scouting Movement of Students and Working Youth in Vilna and Its Environs). *גל-עד*, vol. 3 (1976): 191-212.

Rinott, Moshe. "Religion and Education: The Cultural Question and the Zionist Movement, 1897-1913." *Studies in Zionism*, vol. 5 #1 (Spring, 1984): 1-17.

Rogel, Nakdimon. "Weizmann's Man in Damascus: Dr. Shlomo Felman's Mission to Faisal's Court, September 1919–July 1920." *Studies in Zionism*, #8 (Autumn, 1983): 237-268.

Rubinstein, Shimon and Shmuel Even-Or. "הקמת ועד העיר ליהודי ירושלים ב1918 והאישים המרכזיים שבו" (The Establishment of the Va'ad ha-Ir of Jerusalem Jewry in 1918 and the Major Personalities Involved). *כיוונים*, #35 (May, 1987): 53-66.

Schweid, Eliezer. "The Rejection of the Diaspora in Zionist Thought: Two Approaches." *Studies in Zionism*, vol. 5 #1 (Spring, 1984): 43-70.

Shapira, Anita. "The Concept of Time in the Partition Controversy of 1937." *Studies in Zionism*, vol. 6 #2 (Autumn, 1985): 211-228.

——. "*Gedud Ha-Avodah*: A Dream That Failed." *Jerusalem Quarterly* #30 (Winter, 1984): 62-76.

——. "The Origins of 'Jewish Labor' Ideology." *Studies in Zionism*, # 5 (April, 1982): 93-113.

——. "Reality and Ethos: Attitudes Towars Power in Zionism." *Herzl Yearbook*, vol. 9 (1989): 68-119.

——. "השמאל בגדוד העבודה והפ.ק.פ. עד 1928" (The Gdud ha-Avoda's Left Wing and the Palestine Communist Party to 1928). *הציונות*, vol. 2 (1971): pp. 148-168.

Sheffer, Gabriel. "Political Considerations in British Policy-Making on Immigration to Palestine." *Studies in Zionism*, #4 (October, 1981): 237-274.

Shimoni, Gideon. "Selig Brodetsky and the Ascendancy of Zionism in Anglo-Jewry." *Jewish Journal of Sociology*, vol. 22 #2 (December, 1980): 125-161.

Shpiro, David H. "The Political Background of the 1942 Biltmore Resolution." *Herzl Yearbook*, vol. 8 (1978): 166-177.

Stein, Joshua B. "Josiah Wedgwood and the Seventh Dominion Scheme." *Studies in Zionism*, vol. 11 #2 (Autumn, 1990): 141-155.

Stone, Lilo. "German Zionists in Palestine before 1933." *Journal of Contemporary History*, vol. 32 #2 (April, 1997): 171-186.

Szajkowski, Zosa. "The German Ordinance of November 1916 on the Organization of Jewish Communities in Poland." *Proceedings of the American Academy for Jewish Research*. vol. 34 (1966): 111-139.

Tcherikower, Elias. "Jewish Martyrology and Jewish Historiography." *YIVO Annual of Jewish Social Science*, vol. 1 (1946): 17-19.

Tomaszewski, Jerzy. "Vladimir Jabotinsky's Talks With Representatives of the Polish Government." *Polin*, vol. 2 (1988): 276-293.

Tyler, W.P.N. "The Beisan Lands Issue in Mandatory Palestine," *Middle Eastern Studies*, vol. 25 #2 (April, 1989): 123-162.

Tzahor, Ze'ev. "Ben-Gurion's Mythopoetics." *Israel Affairs*, vol. 1 #3 (Spring, 1985): 61-84.

Unger, Shabetai. "עברי והעברי: פרק בתולדות תנועת העובדים הציונית בגאליציה" (Ivri and ha-Ivri: A chapter in the History of the Socialist Zionist Movement in Galicia). *גל-עד*, vol. 3 (1976): 83-109.

Urofsky, Melvin I. "Rifts in the Movement: Zionist Fissures, 1942-1945." *Herzl Yearbook*, vol. 8 (1978): 185-211.

Vereté, Meir. "Why Was A British Consulate Established in Jerusalem?" *English Historical Review*, vol. 85 #335 (April, 1970): 316-345.

Wagman-Eshkoli, Hava. "Three Attitudes Toward the Holocaust Within Mapai, 1933-1945." *Studies in Zionism*, vol. 14 #1 (Spring, 1993): 73-94.

Wistrich, Robert S. "Theodor Herzl: Zionist Icon, Myth-Maker, and Social Utopian." *Israel Affairs*, vol. 1 #3 (Spring, 1995): 1-37.

Wynot, Edward D., Jr. "A Necessary Cruelty: The Emergence of Official Antisemitism in Poland, 1936-1939." *American Historical Review*, vol. 76 #4 (October, 1971): 1035-1958.

Yanai, Nathan. "Ben-Gurion's Concept of Mamlahtiut and the Forming Reality of the State of Israel." *Jewish Political Studies Review*. vol. 1 #1/2 (Spring, 1989): 151-177.

Yehoshua, Ben-Zion. "אהבת ציון וציונות אצל יהודי אפגניסתאן" (Love of Zion and Zionism Among the Jews of Afghanistan). *כיוונים*, vol. 7 (May, 1980): 43-57.

Yisraeli, David. "The Struggle for Zionist Military Involvement in the First World War." Pinhas Artzi (ed.). *Bar-Ilan Studies in History*. vol. 1 (1978): 197-213.

Zipperstein, Steven J. "The Politics of Relief: The Transformation of Russian Jewish Communal Life During the First World War." *Studies in Contemporary Jewry*, vol. 4 (1988): 22-40.

C. Anthologies and Collections of Essays

Almog, Shmuel (ed.). *Zionism and the Arabs*. Jerusalem: Zalman Shazar Institue Press, 1983.

Avni, Haim and Gideon Shimoni (eds.). הציונית ומתנגדיה בעם היהודי (Zionism and its Jewish Opponents). Jerusalem: ha-Sifriya ha-Zionit, 1990.

Ben-Avram, Baruch and Henry Near (eds.). עיונים בעלייה השלישית: דימוי ומציאות (Studies in The Third Aliya: Image and Reality). Jerusalem: Yad Yitzhak Ben-Zvi, 1995.

Cohen, Israel (ed.). *The Rebirth of Israel*. London: Goldstein, 1953.

Cohen, M. J. and Martin Kolinsky (eds.). *Britain and the Middle East in the 1930s*. London: MacMillan, 1992.

Don-Yehiya, Eliezer (ed.). *Israel and Diaspora Jewry: Ideological and Political Perspectives*. Ramat Gan: Bar-Ilan University Press, 1991.

Elazar, Daniel J. (ed.). *Kinship and Consent: The Jewish Political Tradition and its Contemporary Uses*. Ramat Gan: Turtledove Publications, 1981.

Eliav, Mordechai (ed.). ספר העלייה הראשונה (The Book of the First Aliya). 2 volumes. Jerusalem: Yad Ben-Zvi and the Israeli Ministry of Defense, 1982.

—— and Yitzhak Raphael (eds.). ספר שרגאי (The S. Z. Shragai Memorial Volume). Jerusalem: Mossad ha-Rav Kook, 1981.

Flinker, David et al (eds.). די ייִדישע פּרעסע וואָס איז געווען (The Jewish Press That Was). Tel Aviv: World Union of Jewish Journalists, 1975.

Frumkin, Jacob et al (eds.). *Russian Jewry, 1860-1917*. New York: Thomas Yoseloff, 1966.

Gerber, David A. (ed.). *Antisemitism in American History*. Urbana: University of Illinois Press, 1986.

Gutman, Israel et al (eds.). *The Jews of Poland Between the Two World Wars*. Hanover, NH: University Press of New England for Brandeis University, 1988.

Halpern, Israel (ed.). ספר הגבורה (The Book of Jewish Heroism). reprint edition. 3 vols. Tel Aviv: Am Oved, 1977.

Kedourie, Elie and Sylvia Haim (eds.). *Zionism and Arabism in Palestine and Israel*. London: Frank Cass, 1982.

Klier, John D. and Shlomo Lambroza (eds.). *Pogroms: Anti-Jewish Violence in Modern Russian History*. New York: Cambridge University Press, 1992.

Levy, Avigdor (ed.). *The Jews of the Ottoman Empire*. Princeton: The Darwin Press, 1994.

Mosse, George L. *Confronting the Nation: Jewish and Western Nationalism*. Hanover, NH: University Press of New England for Brandeis University Press, 1993.

Naor, Mordechai (ed.). *1903-1914,* העלייה השנייה (The Second Aliya). Jerusalem: Yad Yitzhak Ben-Zvi, 1985.

Pinkus, Bejamin and Doris Bensimon (eds.). יהדות צרפת, הציונות, ומדינת ישראל (The Jews of France, Zionism, and the State of Israel). Kiryat Sde Boker: Ben-Gurion Research Center, 1992.

Reinharz, Jehuda (ed.). *Living With Antisemitism: Modern Jewish Responses*. Hanover, NH: University Press of New England, 1987.

—— and Anita Shapira (eds.). *Essential Papers on Zionism*. New York: New York University Press, 1996.

Wallach, Jehuda L. (ed.), *Germany and the Middle East, 1835-1939*, Tel Aviv: Institute for German History / Tel Aviv University Press, 1975.

Weitz, Yehiam (ed.). *בין חזן לרוויזיה: מאה שנות היסטוריוגרפיה ציונית* (Between Vision and Revision: One Hundred Years of Zionist Historiography). Jerusalem: Mercaz Zalman Shazar, 1997.

Wistrich, Robert S. *Between Redemption and Perdition: Modern Antisemitism and Jewish Identity*. London: Routledge, 1990.

Yavnieli, Shmuel (ed.). *ספר הציונות: תקופת חיבת ציון* (The Book of Zionism: The Era of Hibbat Zion). 2 volumes. Jerusalem: ha-Sifriya ha-Zionit, 1961.

Yehoshua, Ben-Zion and Aaron Kedar (eds.), *ציונות אידיאולוגיה ומדינות* (Zionist Ideology and Politics), Jerusalem: The Zalman Shazar Institute Press, 1978.

יהודי ליטא (The Jews of Lithuania). 4 vols. Tel Aviv: Igud Yotzei Lite be-Israel, 1972.

D. Books

Akavia, Avraham. *אורד וינגייט: חייו ופעולו* (Orde Wingate: His Life and Mission). Tel Aviv: IDF Press, 1993.

Alderman, Geoffrey. *Modern British Jewry*. Oxford: Clarendon Press, 1992.

Avihai, Avraham. *Ben-Gurion: State-Builder*. Jerusalem: Israel Universities Press, 1974.

Avineri, Shlomo. *The Making of Modern Zionism*. New York: Basic Books, 1981.

Avizohar, Meir. *בראי סדוק: אידיאלים חברתיים ולאומיים והשתקפותם בעולמה של מפא"י* (National and Social Ideals as Reflected In Mapai). Tel Aviv: Am Oved, 1990.

——. *הציונות הלוחמת* (Fighting Zionism). Kiryat Sde Boker: Ben-Gurion Research Center, 1985.

Avneri, Arieh L. *The Claim of Dispossession: Jewish Land Purchase and the Arabs, 1878-1948*. New Brunswick, NJ: Transaction Books, 1984.

Avneri, Yitzhak L. *מולוס עד טאורוס: עשור ראשון להעפלה* (From Velos to Taurus: The First Decade of Illegal Immigration). Ramat Efal: Yad Yitzhak Tabenkin, 1985.

Avni, Haim. *Argentina and the Jews: A History of Jewish Immigration*. Tuscaloosa: University of Alabama Press, 1991.

Bahat, Dan et al. *רציפות הישוב היהודי בארץ ישראל* (The Continuity of Jewish Settlement in the Land of Israel). Tel Aviv: Ministry of Defense/Chief Training Officer, 1978.

Barad, Shlomo. *לתולדות התנועה הציונית בתוניסיה* (On the History of Zionism in Tunisia). Ramat Efal: Yad Yitzhak Tabenkin, 1980.

Barbarash, Ernest E. *Bnai Zion, 75 Years: A Stellar Role*. New York: Bnai Zion, 1983.

Barkai, Abraham. *Nazi Economics: Ideology, Theory, Policy*. Oxford: Berg Publishers, 1990.

Baron, Salo W. *The Russian Jews Under Tsars and Soviets*. New York: Macmillan, 1976.

Bat Ye'or (pseud.). *The Dhimmi: Jews and Christians under Islam*. Rutherford, NJ: Fairleigh Dickenson University Press, 1985.

——. *Oriental Jewry and the Dhimmi Image in Contemporary Arab Nationalism*. Geneva: World Organization of Jews from Arab Countries, 1979.

Bauer, Yehuda. *From Diplomacy to Resistance*. New York: Atheneum, 1973.

——. *The Jewish Emergence From Powerlessness*. Toronto: University of Toronto Press, 1979.

Be'eri, Eliezer. *ראשית הסכסוך ישראל-ערב* (Origins of the Israel-Arab Conflict). Tel Aviv: Sifriat ha-Poalim, 1985.

Bein. Alex. *The History of Jewish Agricultural Settlement in Palestine*. Jerusalem: Reuven Mass, 1947.

——. *The Jewish Question: Biography of a World Problem*. Rutherofrd, NJ: Fairleigh Dickinson University Press for the Herzl Press, 1990.

——. *Theodor Herzl: A Biography of the Founder of Modern Zionism*, New York: Atheneum, 1970.

——. *תולדות ההיתישבות הציונית מתקופת הרצל ועד ימינו* (A History of Zionist Settlement from

Herzl's Time to Today), 4th edition, Ramat Gan: Masada Press, 1970.

Benjamin, Leo. *Arab-Jewish Brotherhood*. New York: Impress House, 1973.

Benjamini, Eliahu. מדינות ליהודים: אוגנדה, בירוביג'אן ועוד שלשים וארבע תוכניות (States for the Jews: Uganda, Birobidzhan, and Thirty-Four Other Projects). Tel Aviv: Sifriat ha-Poalim, 1990.

Bercuson, David J. *Canada and the Rise of Israel*. Toronto: University of Toronto Press, 1985.

Berk, Stephem M. *Year of Crisis, Year of Hope: Russian Jewry and the Pogroms of 1881-1882*. Westport, CT: Greenwood Press, 1985.

Berkowitz, Michael. *Western Jewry and the Zionist Project, 1914-1933*. New York: Cambridge University Press, 1997.

——. *Zionist Culture and West European Jewry Before the First World War*. New York: Cambridge University Press, 1993.

Best, Gary D. *To Free a People*. Westport, CT: Greenwood Press, 1982.

Bet-Zvi, Shabetai B. הציונות הפוסט-אוגנדית במשבר השואה (Post-Ugandian Zionism in the Crucible of the Holocaust). Tel Aviv: Bronfman's Agency, 1977.

Biale, David. *Power and Powerlessness in Jewish History*. New York: Schocken Books, 1986.

Birnbaum, Ervin. *In the Shadow of the Struggle*. Jerusalem: Gefen Books, 1990.

Black, Ian. *Zionism and the Arabs, 1936-1939*. New York: Garland, 1986.

Blau, Joseph L. *Modern Varieties of Judaism*. New York: Columbia University Press, 1964.

Brenner, Lenni. *Zionism in an Age of Dictators*. New York: Croom Helm, 1983.

Brenner, Michael. *The Renaissance of Jewish Culture in Weimar Germany*. New Haven: Yale University Press, 1996.

Caplan, Neil. *Futile Diplomacy*. London: Frank Cass, 1983.

Cesarani, David. *The Jewish Chronicle and Anglo-Jewry, 1841-1991*. New York: Cambridge University Press, 1994.

Clarke, Thurston. *By Blood and Fire*. New York: Putnam's. 1981.

Cleveland, William L. *A History of the Modern Middle East*. Boulder, CO: Westview Press, 1994.

Cohen, A. *The Teachings of Maimonides*. New edition with a Prolegomenon by Marvin Fox. New York: Ktav, 1968.

Cohen, Israel. *Theodor Herzl: His Life and Times*. London: Jewish Religious Educational Publications, 1959,

Cohen, Michael J. *Palestine and the Great Powers, 1945-1948*. Prinecton, NJ: Princeton University Press, 1982.

Cohen, Naomi E. *Zion's Founding Fathers*. New York: Education Department of Hadassah, N.D.

Cohen, Naomi W. *American Jews and the Zionist Idea*. New York: Ktav, 1975.

Cohen, Stuart A. *English Zionists and British Jews:The Communal Politics of Anglo-Jewry, 1895-1920*. Princeton: Princeton University Press, 1982.

Cohn, Norman. *Warrant for Genocide*. New York: Harper and Row, 1966.

Cohn-Sherbok, Dan. *Israel: The History of an Idea*. London: SPCK, 1992.

Crankshaw, Edward. *The Shadow of the Winter Palace: Russia's Drift to Revolution, 1825-1917*. New York: Viking Press, 1976.

Davies, W. D. *The Territorial Dimension in Judaism*. Berkeley: University of California Press, 1982.

Dothan, Shmuel. פולמוס החלוקה בתקופת המנדט (The Partition Controversy During the Mandatory Era). Jerusalem: Yad Yitzhak Ben-Zvi, 1979.

Drabek, Anna et al. *Das Österreichische Judentum: Voraussetzungen und Geschichte*. Vienna: Jugend und Volk Verlag, 1974.

Edelheit, Abraham J. *The Yishuv in the Shadow of the Holocaust: Zionist Policy and Rescue Aliya, 1933-1939*. Boulder, CO: Westview Press, 1996.

—— and Hershel Edelheit. *History of the Holocaust: A Handbook and Dictionary*. Boulder, CO: Westview Press, 1994.

Elam, Yigal. שנים ראשונות:הסוכנות היהודית (The Jewish Agency: Early Years). Jerusalem: ha-Sifriya ha-Zionit, 1990.

——. הגדודים העבריים במלחמת העולם הראשונה (The Hebrew Battalions in World War I). Tel Aviv: Ma'arachot/The IDF Press, 1973.

Elazar, Daniel J. and Harold M. Waller. *Maintaining Consensus: The Canadian Jewish Polity in the Postwar World*. Lanham, MD: University Press of America, 1990.

—— and Stuart A. Cohen. *The Jewish Polity: Jewish Political Organization from Biblical Times to the Present*. Bloomington: University of Indiana Press, 1985.

Eliav, Mordechai. דוד וולפסון:האיש וזמנו (David Wolffsohn: The Man and His Era). Jerusalem: ha-Sifriya ha-Zionit, 1977.

Eloni, Yehuda. *Zionismus in Deutschland: Von den Anfängen bis 1914*. Stuttgart: Bleicher Verlag for Tel Aviv University, 1987.

Erlich, Avi. *Biblical Zionism: The Biblical Origins of the National Idea*. New York: Free Press, 1995.

Feingold, Henry L. *Zion in America: The Jewish Experience from Colonial Times to the Present*. New York: Hippocrene Books, 1974.

Finkelstein, Norman. *Captain of Innocence: France and the Dreyfus Affair*. New York: Putnam's, 1991.

Fraenkel, Josef. *Theodor Herzl: A Biography*. London: Ararat Publishers, 1946.

Frankel, Jonathan. *Jewish Politics and the Russian Revolution of 1905*. Spiegel Lecture in Jewish History #4. Tel Aviv: Tel Aviv University Press, 1982.

——. *Prophecy and Politics: Socialism, Nationalism, and the Russian Jews, 1862-1917*. Cambridge: Cambridge University Press. 1981.

Friedenreich, Harriet P. *Jewish Politics in Vienna, 1918-1938*. Bloomington: Indiana University Press, 1991.

Friedman, Isaiah. *Germany, Turkey, and Zionism, 1897-1918*. New York: Oxford University Press, 1977.

——. *The Question of Palestine, 1914-1918: British-Jewish-Arab Relations*. London: Routledge and Kegan Paul, 1973.

Gaisbauer, Adolf. *Davidstern und Doppeladler: Zionismus und jüdischer Nationalismus in Österreich, 1882-1918*. Vienna: Böhlau Verlag, 1988.

Galnoor, Yitzhak. *The Partition of Palestine: Decision Crossroads in the Zionist Movement*. Albany: State University of New York Press, 1995.

Gamliel, Shalom. *Aliya To Israel From Yemen*. English/Hebrew. Jerusalem: Shalom Research Center, 1987.

Ganin, Zvi. *Truman, American Jewry, and Israel, 1945-1948*. New York: Holems and Meier, 1979.

Giebers, Ludy. *De Zionistische beweging in Nederland, 1899-1941*. Assen: Van Gorcum, 1975.

Glazer, Nathan. *American Judaism*. Chicago: University of Chicago Press, 1957.

Glick, Edward B. *The Triangular Relationship: America, Israel, and American Jews*. London: Allen and Unwin, 1982.

Goldberg, David J. *To The Promised Land*. London: Penguin Books, 1996.

Goldscheider, Calvin and Alan S. Zuckerman. *The Transformation of the Jews*. Chicago: University of Chicago Press, 1984.

Goldschmidt, Arthur Jr. *A Concise History of the Middle East*. fifth edition. Boulder, CO: Westview Press, 1996.

Goldstein, Ya'akov. ללא פשרות:הסכם בן-גוריון-ז'בוטינסקי וכשלונו (Without Compromise: The Ben-Gurion-Jabotinsky Agreement and its Failure). Tel Aviv: Hadar Publications, 1979.

Gorny, Yosef. *The British Labour Movement and Zionism, 1917-1948*. London: Frank Cass, 1983.

——. *From Rosh Pina and Degania to Demona: A History of Constructive Zionism*. Tel Aviv: MOD Books, 1989.

——. *The State of Israel in Jewish Public Thought: The Quest for Collective Identity*. New York: New York University Press, 1994.

——. *Zionism and the Arabs, 1882-1948: A Study in Ideology*. Oxford: Clarendon Press, 1987.

Gottlieb, Moshe R. *American Anti-Nazi Resistance, 1933-1941: An Historical Analysis*. New York: Ktav, 1982.

Grant, Michael. *The Jews in the Roman World*. New York: Scribner's, 1973.

Greenberg, Louis. *The Jews in Russia: The Struggle for Emancipation*. Two volumes bound as one New York: Schocken Books. 1976.

Gribbon, Walter. *Agents of Empire: Anglo-Zionist Intelligence Operations, 1915-1919*. London: Brassey's, 1995.

Grose, Peter. *Israel in the Mind of America*. New York: Schocken Books, 1983.

Gross, Nahum. *The Economic Policy of the Mandatory Government in Palestine*. Jerusalem: Falk Institute Press, 1982.

Grunblatt, Joseph. *Exile and Redemption: Meditiations on Jewish History*. Hoboken, NJ: Ktav, 1988.

Haim, Sylvia. *Arab Nationalism*. Berkeley: University of California Press, 1964.

Ha-Levi, Nadav. *Banker to an Emerging Nation: The History of Bank Leumi le-Israel*. Haifa: Shikmona Publishing, 1981.

Halpern, Ben. *A Clash of Heroes: Brandeis, Weizmann, and American Zionism*. New York: Oxford University Press, 1987.

Halpern, Samuel. *The Political World of American Zionism*. Detroit: Wayne State University Press, 1961.

Handler, Andrew. *Dori: The Life and Times of Theodor Herzl in Budapest*. University: University of Alabama Press, 1983.

Hartman, David. *Conflicting Vision: Spiritual Possiblities of Modern Israel*. New York: Schocken Books, 1990.

Hattis, Susan L. *The Bi-National Idea in Palestine during Mandatory Times*. Haifa: Shikmona Press, 1970.

Hazan, L. and Y. Peller. דברי ימי הציונות (A History of Zionism). Jerusalem: Kiryat Sefer, 1969.

Hein, Virginia H. *The British Followers of Theodor Herzl: English Zionist Leaders, 1896-1904*. New York: Garland, 1987.

Heller, Celia S. *On the Edge of Destruction*. New York: Schocken Books, 1980.

Heller, Joseph. *The Stern Gang: Ideology, Politics, and Terror, 1940-1949*. London: Frank Cass, 1995.

Hertzberg, Arthur. *The French Enlightenment and the Jews*. New York: Columbia University Press, 1968.

Hillel, Marc. *La Maison du Juif: L'Histoire Extraordinaire de Tel Aviv*. Paris: Librairie Académique Perrin, 1989.

Hochstein, Joseph H. and Murray S. Greenfield. *The Jews' Secret Fleet*. Jerusalem: Gefen Books, 1987.

Hyamson, Albert. *The British Consulate in Jerusaelm in Relation to the Jews of Palestine*. London: His Majesty's Stationary Office, 1939.

Hyman, Paula. *From Dreyfus to Vichy: The Remaking of French Jewry, 1906-1939*. New York: Columbia University Press, 1979.

Janowsky, Oscar I. *The Jews and Minority Rights*. New York: AMS Press, 1966.

The Jews of Czechoslovakia. 2 vols. Philadelphia: Jewish Publication Society, 1968-1971.

Kaddish, Sharman. *Bolsheviks and British Jews*. London: Frank Cass, 1992.

Katz, Jacob. *Out of the Ghetto*. New York: Schocken Books, 1978.

——. *From Prejudice to Destruction, 1700-1933*. Cambridge, MA: Harvard University Press, 1980.

Katz, Samuel. *Fire and Steel: Israel's Seventh Armored Brigade*. New York: Pocket Books, 1996.

Kechales, Haim. קורות יהודי בולגריה (History of the Jews of Bulgaria). 5 vols. Tel Aviv: Davar Publishing House, 1969-1973.

Kedourie, Elie. *The Chatham House Version and Other Middle-Eastern Studies*. New York: Praeger, 1970.

——. *Nationalism*. New York: Praeger, 1960.

Kieval, Hillel J. *The Making of Czech Jewry: National Conflict and Jewish Society, 1870-1918*. New York: Oxford University Press, 1988.

Kimche, Jon. *The Unromantics: The Great Powers and the Declaration*. London: Weidenfeld and Nicolson, 1968.

Kirk, George. *The Middle East in the War, 1939-1946*. Oxford: Royal Institute of International Affairs, 1953.

Klieman, Aharon. הפרד או משול: מדיניות בריטניה וחלוקת ארץ ישראל (Divide or Rule: British Policy and the Partition of Eretz Israel). Jerusalem: Yad Yitzhak Ben-Zvi, 1983.

Klier, John D. *Imperial Russia's Jewish Question, 1855-1881*. New York: Cambridge University Press, 1995.

Kobler, Franz. *Napoleon and the Jews*. New York: Schocken Books, 1976.

Kohn, Hans. *Nationalism: Its Meaning and History*. New York: Van Nostrand Company, 1965.

Kolinsky, Martin. *Law, Order, and Riots in Mandatory Palestine, 1929-1935*. London: St. Martin's Press, 1993.

Kosmin, Barry A. *Majuta: A History of the Jewish Community of Zimbabwe*. Salisbury: Mambo Press, 1981.

Krajzman, Maurice. *La Presse Juive en Belgique et Aux Pays-Bas: Histoire et Analyse Quantitative de Contenu*. 2nd edition. Brussles: Éditions de l'Université de Bruxelles, 1975.

Krämer, Gudrun. *The Jews in Modern Egypt, 1914-1952*. Seattle: University of Washington Press, 1989.

קיצור תולדות ההגנה (Short History of the Hagana). Tel Aviv: Ma'arachot/IDF Press, 1978.

Langer, Michael. *Labor Zionist Ideology Reconsidered*. Tel Aviv: Ichud ha-Bonim, 1978.

Laskier, Michael M. *The Jews of Egypt, 1920-1970*. New York: New York University Press, 1992.

——. *North African Jewry in the Twentieth Century: The Jews of Morocco, Tunisia, and Algeria*. New York: New York University Press, 1994.

Laskov, Shulamit. הביליים (The Biluim). Jerusalem: ha-Sifriya ha-Zionit, 1979.

——. טרומפלדור: סיפור חייו (Yosef Trumpeldor: A Biography). Third Edition. Jerusalem: Keter Publishing, 1995.

Lazar-Litai, Haim. בית"ר בשארית הפליטה (Betar Among the Holocaust Survivors). Tel Aviv: Mahon Jabotinsky be-Israel, 1997.

Lederhendler, Eli. *The Road to Modern Jewish Politics*. New York: Oxford University Press, 1989.

Lev-Ami, Shlomo. במעבק ובמרד (In Struggle and Revolt), Tel Aviv: Ministry of Defense Publications, 1978.

——. העם הציונות נכשלה? (Was Zionism a Failure?). NP: Ami Publications, 1988.

Levin, Nora. *The Jews in the Soviet Union Since 1917: Paradox of Survival*. New York: New York University Press, 1988.

——. *While Messiah Tarried: Jewish Socialist Movements, 1871-1917*. New York: Schocken Books, 1977.

Lewin, Isaac. *The Jewish Community in Poland*. New York: Philosophical Library, 1985.

Lewittes, Mendell. *Religious Foundations of the Jewish State*. Northvale, NJ: Jason Aronson, 1994.

Lipman, V. D. *A History of the Jews in Britain Since 1858*. New York: Holmes and Meier, 1990.

Lorch, Netanel. *One Long War: Arab Versus Jew Since 1920*. Jerusalem: Keter Books, 1976.

Louvish, Misha. *Nineteenth Century Zionist Theories*. Glasgow: University Zionist Federation, 1933.

Luz, Shmuel. *Paralells Meet*. Philadelphia: Jewish Publication Society, 1988.

Mandel, Neville J. *The Arabs and Zionism Before World War I*. Berkeley: University of California Press, 1976.

Maor, Yitzhak. *התנועה הציונית ברוסיה* (The Zionist Movement in Russia). Jerusalem: Ha-Sifriya ha-Zionit, 1973,

Marcus, Jacob R. *The Rise and Destiny of the German Jew*. reprint ed., New York: Ktav, 1973.

Markovitzy, Ya'akov. *בקף הקלע של הנאמנות: בני היישוב בצבא התורכי, 1908-1919* (A Conflict of Loyalties: The Enlistment of Palestinian Jews in the Turkish Army, 1908-1919). Ramat Efal: Yad Yitzhak Tabenkin, 1995.

Mendelsohn, Ezra. *On Modern Jewish Politics*. New York: Oxford University Press, 1993.

——. *Zionism in Poland: The Formative Years, 1915-1926*. New Haven: Yale University Press, 1981.

Merhav, Peretz. *The Israeli Left: History, Problems, Documents*. San Diego: A. S. Barnes, 1980.

Meshel, Miriam. *רמת-גן* (Ramat-Gan: A History). Ramat-Gan: Avivim Press, 1991.

Meyer, Michael A. *Jewish Identity in the Modern World*. Seattle: University of Washington Press, 1990.

——. *The Origins of the Modern Jew*. Detroit: Wayne State University Press, 1979.

——. *Response to Modernity: A History of the Reform Movement in Judaism*. New York: Oxford University Press, 1988.

Milstein, Uri. *History of Israel's War of Independence*. 3 vols. Lanham, MD: University Press of America, 1996-1998.

Mittleman, Alan. *The Politics of Torah*. Albany: State University of New York Press, 1996.

Mosse, George L. *German Jews Beyond Judaism*. Bloomington: Indiana University Press, 1985.

——. *Toward the Final Solution: A History of European Racism*. New York: Harper Colophon Books, 1978.

Mossek, Moshe. *Palestine Immigration Policy under Sir Herbert Samuel*. London: Frank Cass, 1978.

Near, Henry. *The Kibbutz Movement: A History*. 2 vols. Oxford: Littman Library of Jewish Civilization, 1992-1997.

Netanyahu, Benzion. *Don Isaac Abravanel: Statesman and Philosopher*. Philadelphia: Jewish Publication Society, 1972.

Neumann, Emanuel. *The Birth of Jewish Statesmanship: The Story of Theodor Herzl's Life*. New York: Zionist Organization of America, 1940.

Newman, Aubrey. *The United Synagogue, 1870-1970*. London: Routledge and Kegan Paul, 1977.

Nicosia, Francis R. *The Third Reich and the Palestine Question*. Austin: Texas University Press, 1985.

Nini, Yehuda. *תימן וציון: הרקע המדיני, החברתי, והרוחני לעליות הראשונות מתימן* (Yemen and Zion: The Political, Social, and Spiritual Background to Early Yemenite Aliya). Jerusalem: ha-Sifriya ha-Zionit, 1982.

Norman, Theodore. *An Outstretched Arm: A History of the Jewish Colonization Association*. London: Routledge and Kegan Paul, 1985.

Oppenheim, Israel. *The Struggle of Jewish Youth for Productivization: The Zionist Youth Movement in Poland*. Boulder, CO: East European Monographs, 1989.

Pail, Meir. *התפתחות כוח המגן העברי, 1907-1948* (The Emergence of Jewish Defense Forces, 1907-1948). Tel Aviv: Ministry of Defense/Chief Education Officer, 1987.

Parfitt, Tudor. *The Road to Redemption: The Jews of the Yemen, 1900-1950*. Leiden: E. J. Brill, 1996.

Patai, Raphael. *The Jews of Hungary: History, Culture, Psychology*. Detroit: Wayne State University Press, 1996.

Penslar, Derek. *Zionism and Technocracy: The Engineering of Jewish Settlements in Palestine, 1870-1918*. Bloomington: Indiana University Press, 1991.

Peri, Yitzhak. קיצור תולדות היהודים בהונגריה מהימים הקדומים ועד השואה (The Short History of Hungarian Jewry from Ancient Times to the Holocaust). Tel Aviv: The Author in Association with Hitagdut Olei Hungaria, 1994.

Plaut, Joshua E. *Greek Jewry in the Twentieth Century, 1913-1983*. Madison, NJ: Fairleigh Dickinson University Press, 1996.

Poll, Bernhard. *Jüdische Presse im 19. Jahrhundert*. Aachen: Internationalen Zeitungsmuseum, 1967.

Poppel, Steven M. *Zionism in Germany, 1897-1933*. Philadelphia: Jewish Publication Society, 1977.

Porat, Dina. *The Blue and Yellow Stars of David*. Cambridge, MA: Harvard University Press, 1990.

Porath, Yehoshua. *The Palestinian Arab National Movement: From Riots to Rebellion, 1929-1939*. London: Frank Cass, 1977.

Pulzer, Peter J. *The Rise of Politcal Antisemitism in Germany and Austria*. rev. ed., Cambridge, MA: Harvard University Press, 1988.

Rabinowicz, Harry M. *The Legacy of Polish Jewry, 191-1939*. New York: Thomas Yoseloff, 1965.

Reinharz, Jehuda. *Fatherland or Promised Land: The Dilemma of the German Jew, 1893-1914*. Ann Arbor: University of Michigan Press, 1975.

——. *Chaim Weizmann: The Making of a Statesman*. New York: Oxford University Press, 1993.

Rejwan, Nissim. *The Jews of Iraq*. Boulder, CO: Westview Press, 1985.

Rivlin, Gerson. לאש ולמגן: תולדות הנוטרות העברית (In Fire and Defense: History of the Jewish Supernumerary Police). Tel Aviv: Maarachot/IDF Publishing House, 1964,

Rose, Norman A. *The Gentile Zionists: A Study in Anglo-Zionist Diplomacy, 1929-1939*. London: Frank Cass, 1973.

Roth, Cecil. *A History of the Marranos*. New York: Meridian Books, 1959.

——. *The House of Nasi*. Philadelphia: Jewish Publication Society, 1948.

Rubenstein, Sondra M. *The Communist Movement in Palestine and Israel, 1919-1984*. Boulder, CO: Westview Press, 1985.

Rubinstein, Hilary L. and W. D. Rubinstein. *The Jews in Australia: A Thematic History*. 2 vols. Port Melbourne: Heinemann Australia, 1991.

Rubinstein, W. D. *A History of the Jews in the English-Speaking World: Great Britain*. London: Macmillan, 1996.

——. *The Left, The Right, and the Jews*. New York: Universe Books, 1982.

Sachar, Howard M. *The Course of Modern Jewish History*. second edition, New York: Dell, 1977.

——. *The Emergence of the Middle East, 1914-1924*. New York: Knopf, 1969.

——. *A History of Israel: From the Rise of Zionism to Our Time*. New York: Knopf, 1976.

Samuel, Maurice. *Blood Accusation*. New York: Knopf, 1965.

Sanders, Ronald. *The High Walls of Jerusalem: A History of the Balfour Declaration and the Birth of the British Mandate for Palestine*. New York: Holt, Rinehart, and Winston, 1983.

Schaary, David. מ"סתם ציונות" ל"ציונות כללית" (From "Plain Zionism" to "General Zionism). Jerusalem: Reuven Mass, 1990.

Schama, Simon. *Two Rothschilds and the Land of Israel*. New York: Alfred A. Knopf, 1978.

Schapiro, Leonard. *The Russian Revolutions of 1917*. New York: Basic Books, 1984.

Schechtman, Joseph B. *The Life and Times of Vladimir Jabotinsky*. 2 vols. New York: Thomas Yoseloff, 1956-1961.

——. *The United States and the Jewish State Movement: The Crucial Decade*. New York: Thomas Yoseloff, 1966.

——. *Zionism and Zionists in Soviet Russia: Greatness and Drama*. New York: Zionist Organization of America, 1966.

Schenkolewski-Kroll, Silvia. *1935-1948 ,התנועה הציונית ומפלגות הציוניות בארגטינה* (The Zionist Movement and Zionist Parties in Argentina, 1935-1948). Jerusalem: Magnes Press and ha-Sifriya ha-Zionit, 1996.

Schiff, Ze'ev. *A History of the Israeli Army, 1870-1974*. San Fransisco: Straight Arrow Books, 1974.

Schifter-Sikora, Jacobo. *El Mundo Judio en Costa Rica, 1900-1960*. Heredia, Costa Rica: Instituto de Estudios Latinamericas, Univesidad Nacional Press, 1979.

Scholem, Gershom. *Major Trends in Jewish Mysticism*. New York: Schocken Books, 1961.

——. *Shabbetai Sevi: The Mystical Messiah*. Princeton: Princeton University Press, 1973.

Schorsch, Ismar. *Jewish Reactions to German Antisemitism*. New York: Columbia University Press, 1972.

Schweid, Eliezer. *The Land of Israel: National Home or Land of Destiny?*. Rutherford, NJ: Fairleigh Dickinson University Press for the Herzl Press, 1985.

Segel, Benjamin W. *A Lie and a Libel*. Lincoln: University of Nebraska Press, 1995.

Segev, Tom. *The Seventh Million: The Israelis and the Holocaust*. New York: Hill and Wang, 1993.

Seton-Watson, Hugh. *Eastern Europe Between the Wars, 1918-1941*. Hamden, CT: Archon Books, 1962.

——. *Nations and States*. Boulder, CO: Westview Press, 1977.

Shafir, Gershon. *Land, Labor, and the Origins of the Israeli-Palestinian Conflict, 1882-1914*. New York: Cambridge University Press, 1989.

Shaltiel, Eli. *פנחס רוטנברג* (Pinhas Rutenberg: His Life and Times). Tel Aviv: Am Oved, 1990.

Shapira, Anita. *ההליכה על קו האופק* (Visions in Conflict). Tel Aviv: Am Oved, 1988.

——. *Land and Power: The Zionist Resort to Force, 1881-1948*. New York: Oxford University Press, 1992.

Shapiro Robert. *Leadership of the American Zionist Organization, 1899-1930*. Urbana: University of Illinois Press, 1971.

Shapiro Robert M. *The Polish Kehile Elections of 1936: A Revolution Reexamined*. New York: Yeshiva Univesirty Press, 1988.

Shapiro, Yonathan. *The Formative Years of the Israeli Labor Party: The Organization of Power, 1919-1930*. London: Sage Publications, 1976.

Shavit, Ya'akov. *Jabotinsky and the Revisionist Movement, 1925-1948*. London: Frank Cass, 1988.

——. *מרוב למדינה* (From a Majority to Sovereignty: The Revisionist Movement in Zionism). Tel Aviv: Hadar Publications, 1978.

Shimoni, Gideon. *Jews and Zionism: The South African Experience*, Cape Town: Oxford University Press, 1980.

——. *The Zionist Ideology*. Hanover, NH: University Press of New England for Brandeis University, 1995.

שורשי ההגנה העצמית (The Roots of Jewish Self-Defense). Ramat Efal: Yad Yitzhak Tabenkin, 1983.

Shpiro, David H. *From Philanthropy to Activism: The Political Transformation of American Zionism in the Holocaust Years, 1933-1945*, New York: Pergamon Press, 1994.

——. *לעלות בכל הדרכים* (Aliya By Any Means). Tel Aviv: Am Oved for the Institute to Study Aliya Bet of Tel Aviv University, 1994.

Shva, Shlomo. *עיר קמה* (A City Rises). Tel Aviv: Zmora, Bitan, and Modan Publishers, 1989.

Sicker, Martin. *Judaism, Nationalism, and the Land of Israel*. Boulder, CO: Westview Press, 1992.

Silver, Abba Hillel. *A History of Messianic Speculation in Israel*. Boston: Beacon Press, 1959.

Slater, Leonard. *The Pledge*. New York: Simon and Schuster, 1970.

Sloves, Chaim. *ממלכתיות יהודיות בברית המועצות* (Jewish Sovereignty in the Soviet Union). Tel Aviv: Am Oved, 1980.

Stanislawski, Michael. *For Whom Do I Toil? Judah Leib Gordon and the Crisis of Russian Jewry*. New York: Oxford University Press, 1988.

Stein, Leonard. *The Balfour Declaration*. London: Vallentine Mitchell, 1961.

Stern, Eliahu. *1840-1943 ,יהודי דאנציג* (The Jews of Danzig, 1840-1943). Kibbutz Lohame ha-Getaot: Bet Lohame ha-Getaot al Shem Yitzhak Zuckerman, 1983.

Stillman, Norman A. *The Jews of Arab Lands: A History and Sourcebook*. Philadelphia: Jewish Publication Society, 1979.

——. *The Jews of Arab Lands in Modern Times*. Philadelphia: Jewish Publication Society, 1991.

Story of the Jewish Agency for Israel, The. New York: Jewish Agency American Section, 1964.

Sykes, Christopher. *Cross-Roads to Israel*. London: Collins, 1965.

Telushkin, Joseph. *Jewish Wisdom*. New York: William Morrow, 1994.

Teveth, Shabtai. *Ben-Gurion and the Holocaust*. New York: Harcourt, Brace, and Company, 1996.

——. *Ben-Gurion: The Burning Ground*. Boston: Houghton Mifflin Company, 1987.

——. *Ben-Gurion's Spy: The Story of the Political Scandal that Shaped Modern Israel*. New York: Columbia University Press, 1996.

Toury, Jacob. *Die Jüdische Presse im Österreichischen Kaiserreich, 1802-1918*. Tübingen: J. C. B. Mohr for the Leo Baeck Institute, 1983.

Tzahor, Zeev. *בדרך להנהגת הישוב-ההסתדרות בראשיתה* (On the Road to Yishuv Leadership: The Histadrut's Early Years). Jerusalem: Yad Yitzhak Ben-Zvi, 1981.

Urofsky, Melvin I. *American Zionism From Herzl to the Holocaust*. second edition. Lincoln: University of Nebraska Press, 1995.

——. *We Are One! American Jewry and Israel*. New York: Anchor Press, 1978.

Van Praag, H. et al. *Joodse Pers in de Nederlanden en in Duitsland, 1674-1940*. Dutch/German/English. Amsterdam: Hat Nederlansch Persmuseum, 1969.

Vital, David. *The Origins of Zionism*. Oxford: The Clarendon Press, 1975.

——. *Zionism: The Crucial Phase*, New York: Oxford University Press, 1987.

——. *Zionism: The Formative Years*. New York: Oxford University Press, 1982.

Wasserstein, Bernard. *The British in Palestine: The Mandatory Government and the Arab-Jewish Conflict*. 2nd edition. London: Basil Blackwell, 1991.

Weinbaum, Laurence. *A Marriage of Convenience: The New Zionist Organization and the Polish Government, 1936-1939*. Boulder, CO: East European Monographs, 1993.

Weinberg, David H. *Between Tradition and Modernity*. New York: Holmes and Meier, 1996.

——. *Community on Trial: The Jews of Paris in the 1930s*. Chicago: University of Chicago Press, 1977.

Weinryb, Bernard D. *The Jews of Poland*. Philadelphia: Jewish Publication Society, 1972.

Weisbord, Robert G. *African Zion*. Philadelphia: Jewish Publication Society, 1968.

Wischnitzer, Mark. *To Dwell in Freedom*. Philadelphia: Jewish Publication Society, 1948.

Wistrich, Robert S. *The Jews of Vienna in the Age of Franz-Joseph*. Oxford: Oxford University Press, 1990.

——. *Revolutionary Jews From Marx to Trotsky*. London: Harrap, 1976.

Yaffe, A. B. et al. *יהדות רומניה בתקומת ישראל* (Romanian Jewry and the Rise of Israel). 4 vols. Tel Aviv: Shevet Yehudei Romania, 1992.

Yegar, Moshe. *צ'כוסלובקיה, הציונות, וישראל* (Czechoslovakia, Zionism, and Israel). Jerusalem: ha-Sifriya ha-Zionit, 1997.

Zadok, Haim. *יהדות איראן בתקופת השושלת הפהלוית* (Iranian Jewry During the Pahlavi Dynasty). NP (Israel): Mitsag, 1991.

Zeitlin, Solomon. *The Jews: Race, Nation, or Religion?*. Philadelphia: Dropsie College Press, 1936.

——. *The Rise and Fall of the Judean State*. 3 vols., Philadelphia: Jewish Publication Society, 1962-1978.

Zer, Peninah. *לוחמים בלילה: סיפורו של אורד וינגייט* (Night Fighters: The Story of Orde Wingate). Jerusalem: Yad Yitzhak Ben-Zvi, 1992.

E. Doctoral Dissertations

Allswang, Bradley B. Anti-Judaism, Anti-Semitism, Anti-Zionism: A Theoretical and Empirical Analysis of the Anti-Jewish Phenomenon Throughout its History To the Present. Doctoral Dissertation: Loyola University of Chicago, 1986.

Cannon, Ellen S. The Political Culture of Russian Jewry During the Second Half of the Nineteenth Century. Doctoral Dissertation: University of Massachsetts, 1974.

Kadosh, Sandra B. Ideology Vs. Reality: Youth Aliyah and the Rescue of Jewish Children During the Holocaust Era, 1933-1945. Doctoral Dissertation: Columbia University, 1995.

Krinsky, Fred. The Renascent Jewish Nationalism: A Study of its Leading Concepts and Practices. Doctoral Dissertation: University of Pennsylvania, 1951.

Lichtenberg, Naomi A. Hadassah's Founders and Palestine, 1912-1925: A Quest for Meaning in the Creation of Women's Zionism. Doctoral Dissertation: Indiana University, 1996.

Narrowe, Morton H. Zionism in Sweden: Its Beginnings until the End of World War I. DHL Thesis: Jewish Theological Seminary of America, 1990.

Pentland, Pat A. Zionist Military Preparations for Statehood: The Evolution of "Haganah" Organizations, Programs, and Strategies, 1920-1948. Doctoral Dissertation: University of Idaho, 1975.

Raider, Mark A. From the Marigns to the Mainstream: Labor Zionism and American Jews, 1919-1945. Doctoral Dissertation: Brandeis University, 1996.

Rosenbloom, Howard I. A Political History of Revisionist Zionism, 1925-1938. Doctoral Dissertation: Columbia University, 1986

Yehuda, Zvi. 1900-1948 הארגון הציוני במרוקו בשנים (The Zionist Organization in Morocco in the Years 1900-1948). Doctoral Dissertation: Hebrew University, 1

ABOUT THE BOOK AND AUTHORS

This two-part volume combines an accessible overview of the history of Jewish nationalism with a unique dictionary of terms related to the development of the Zionist movement. In attempting to assess Zionist success and failures, Part 1 of the book places the emergence of Zionism into its historical, communal, and ideological context, permitting readers to obtain a better understanding of the process by which the State of Israel came into being. The authors also consider key historiographical and methodological issues related to Zionism.

Part 2 provides a complete dictionary of terms relating to Zionism, Jewish nationalism, and the emergence of an organized Jewish community in Palestine/*Eretz Israel* culled from dozens of primary and secondary sources in a range of languages. Included here is a comprehensive set of tables on Aliya, Aliya Bet, Zionist and non-Zionist organizations, publications, and personalities. Each table is prefaced by a descriptive overview of pertinent issues.

Graphs, photographs, and documents supplement the text, and an extensive bibliography as well as person, place, and subject indexes make this unique work invaluable as a reference tool.

Hershel Edelheit (1926-1995), was founder and director of ERICH (the Edelheit Research Institute for Contemporary History), a private nonprofit research institute dedicated to the study of Jewish history in the twentieth century. His son, **Abraham J. Edelheit** is a visiting professor at Kingsborough Community College in New York and a consultant to the President's Commission on Holocaust Assets. Together they edited seven reference books on the Holocaust and modern history, notably the three-volume *Bibliography on Holocaust Literature* and the companion to this volume, *History of the Holocaust: A Handbook and Dictionary*, published by Westview Press.

NAME INDEX

PLACE INDEX